The Complete
Encyclopedia of Antiques

The Complete Encyclopedia of Antiques

COMPILED BY THE CONNOISSEUR

Editor: L. G. G. Ramsey, F.S.A.

HAWTHORN BOOKS, INC.

Publishers

NEW YORK

CONTENTS

The illustrations of traditional crafts and processes which appear at the end of some sections in the book are reproduced from Diderot's *Encyclopédie* (*Recueil de Planches, sur les sciences et les arts,* 1769) and Jost Amman's *Stände und Handwerker* (1568).

Acknowledgments

The publishers and producers wish to acknowledge that material appearing in this work is adapted from *The Concise Encyclopedia of Antiques* Volumes 1–5 and *The Concise Encyclopedia of American Antiques* Volumes 1–2. The contributors include:

Josephine L. Allen
Edward H. H. Archibald
Amos G. Avery
John Ayres
F. W. Barker
John I. H. Baur
David Bland
John Boardman, M.A.
Alf Bøe, B.Litt.
Handasyde Buchanan
Kathryn C. Buhler
Adrian Bury, Hon. R.W.S.
Ralph E. Carpenter, Jr
R. A. G. Carson, M.A.
John Carter
R. A. Cecil
R. J. Charlestone
Erwin O. Christensen
Helen Comstock
Ruth Bradbury Davidson
Frank Davis
Bernard Denvir
Shirley Spaulding DeVoe
G. Wingfield Digby
M. L. D'Otrange-Mastai
Martha Gandy Fales
Ian Finlay
John Fleming
Peter Floud, C.B.E.
Geoffrey Godden
F. M. Godfrey, Ph.D.
Arthur Grimwade, F.S.A.
Rupert Gunnis
Yvonne Hackenbroch

Reginald G. Haggar
The Hon. Richard Hare
J. F. Hayward
Luke Herrmann, M.A.
G. Heywood Hill
John Hillier
M. T. Hindson, A.I.B.
Hugh Honour
G. Bernard Hughes
Mrs Therle Hughes
Eric de Jonge
E. T. Joy
Henry J. Kauffman
H. H. Knowland
P. Lasko
Frances Lichten
Raymond Lister
Nina Fletcher Little
H. Alan Lloyd, F.S.A., F.B.H.I.
Agnes Lothian
Jeremy Maas, M.A.
Harold McCracken
Lord Mackintosh
Joseph V. McMullan
Francis Maddison
Paul Magriel
Sydney J. Maiden
Jonathan Mayne
Barbara Morris
Howard M. Nixon
Sydney P. Noe
Gregor Norman-Wilcox
Oliver van Oss

Arnold Palmer
Virginia D. Parslow
Josephine H. Peirce
Harold L. Peterson
E. H. Pinto
C. F. Pitman, M.A., F.M.A.
Ada Polak
Tamara Talbot Rice
B. W. Robinson, M.A., F.R.A.S.
F. Gordon Roe, F.S.A.
Elizabeth E. Roth
Marvin D. Schwartz
Carolyn Scoon
Robert Sherlock
Horace Shipp
Harold S. Sniffen
Kenneth Snowman
Frank O. Spinney
Capt. A. V. Sutherland-Graeme, F.S.A. (R.)
Denys Sutton
Patrick Synge-Hutchinson
M. W. Thomas, Jr
James Tudor-Craig, F.S.A.
Malcolm Vaughan
C. Malcolm Watkins
Frank Weitenkampf
Geoffrey Wills
Alice Winchester
Franz Windisch-Graetz
Gordon Winter
Rudolf Wunderlich
John Cook Wyllie

INTRODUCTION

Many attempts have been made to define the connoisseur. He is lauded for his appreciative awareness of beauty, for the unerring taste that selects the masterpiece and rejects the fashionable novelty. Especially he tends to be credited with a flair for detecting works of art and relics of antiquity where lesser mortals look in vain. Few, however, stress the background of serious, prolonged study essential to his development. That such study may be intensely enjoyable is beside the point: usually it is the delight derived that leads him from book to museum, from museum to private collection and thence to the exhilarating experience of filling his own shelves. Still, in the course of his quest, he finds himself seeking ever more exact guidance until he *knows* the piece that is right, and can clear his collection of second-quality workmanship and clever imitation.

It is a matter for no small congratulation today that the very pace of modern existence is prompting more and more intelligent interest in the splendid design, craftsmanship, and materials of much home furnishing preserved from earlier centuries. Not only has the number of collectors increased of late with remarkable rapidity, but also the knowledge regarding the antiques of their choice and the taste to appreciate subtle details of quality and thus display them to greatest advantage.

The home furnished today by the collector of antiques possesses an interest, an atmosphere of lively, intelligent purpose, even when the collection is numerically small and monetarily of little significance; for today the collector adorns his home rather than displays status symbols in locked cabinets. The purposes of yesterday's tools are being remembered, the beauty of old ornaments and wall decorations rediscovered by the simple method of giving them living room.

In the course of his study, however, the collector soon discovers the tremendous difficulties of specialization. Always he finds he needs to read and learn not only more intensively but more widely. He tends to become engrossed in the life of the times that produced the antiques he treasures and from there must question the beginnings of the craft, its spread through different countries, its exciting divergencies in different climates of taste and development. The American especially has the opportunity to study products from all parts of Europe and also their adaptation in his own land.

To find out about America's spectacularly successful pressed glass, for example, or England's world-renowned flint-glass, leads inevitably to a need for knowledge of exquisite Venetian achievement and flamboyant Bohemian work, of the distinctive nineteenth-century French contribution, of Scandinavian manufactures, of deep-cut Irish glass. The purpose of this book is to help the collector in thus taking a wide view of his subject. In some instances the chapters presented offer most of the known facts: in others where the subject is too immense, as in jewellery, the reader is given a clear general survey and suggestions for further specialized reading. It is expected that he will turn especially to the glossaries that end the sections. The collector of silver, for example, is offered concise summaries of the world's leading silversmiths, their countries' characteristics, and the features of particular interest today, whether the silver is American, English, Scottish, Dutch, French, German, Italian, Norwegian, or Russian, but he will turn to the well-illustrated glossary to establish, say, the meaning of "wax-Jack", or "planishing" or "German silver".

Similarly, work in such metals as copper, brass, pewter, and japanned tin plate is surveyed with particular reference to American, British, and Continental sources from andirons to caskets and from keys to cutlery and concludes with twenty-one invaluable pages of glossary and pewter-work definitions, suggesting endless collector-byways, from

Betty-lamps to kettle idle-backs. And that, too, may be regarded as being among the aims of this factual book. Here, it is thought, the casual browser among antiques may find the basic information to start him on some intriguing quest. Despite the upsurge of interest, innumerable opportunities await him. The history of collectable items in America and Europe is long: the criteria only that design, materials, and workmanship shall be good in themselves are probable reasons for an item's long preservation.

Few people are inclined to collect anything solely for its antiquity: rather it must be good to live with, even if no older than the many items of Victoriana whose long-promised revival still waits upon the spread of exact information. In this volume coins are considered from their earliest development in western civilization some 700 years B.C. and pottery inspired by ritual bronzes of the Chinese Han dynasty (20 B.C.–A.D. 220). Also Islamic astrolabes, among the scientific instruments now rising in popularity but not yet expensive, are to be found dating from the ninth century. The collector who delights in medieval pageantry may seek the ancient styles of filigree and granulation jewellery and rejoice in the rich ornament of the Renaissance. Chinese porcelain of the Ming dynasty (1368–1644) may be an enthusiasm financially restricted to the moneyed few, but it is rivalled in interest today by the early majolica wares. These were developed in Italy from the lustred Spanish pottery of Valencia and spread their inspiration across the Alps early in the sixteenth century, acquiring in the Netherlands new qualities of glaze and ornament, and reaching England by the third quarter of the sixteenth century to become the seventeenth and eighteenth centuries' eminently collectable "English delft". Alongside this work the collector may consider the peculiar characteristics of French and German faïence, handled in this volume with similar factual thoroughness.

From the late fifteenth century, too, medals became important and were soon acquired by discriminating collectors, and already by then lace was beginning to speak its universal language of twist and stitch.

More collectors, however, are fired by the brilliant developments of Elizabethan and Stuart days. They will find guidance in the collection of early still-life and flower paintings, for example, and the intriguing *trompe l'œil* pictures that succeeded mural extravaganzas in this mood. Dutch and Flemish work of this period is given due emphasis, including magnificent marine paintings. Early French and German masters too, and the wonders of Italian, Persian, Russian, and Spanish work, find a place in this immensely full section; but since the book is intended to help the inexperienced, due prominence has been given to the dangers of fakes and forgeries.

Other work here considered that is richly associated with this period includes embroidery, bookbindings, iron, brass and pewter, and furniture in massive oak and in the walnut veneers and colourful lacquer that transformed the late seventeenth- and early eighteenth-century home.

With the eighteenth century, however, the possibilities for the collector and connoisseur become great indeed. Every section in this book reflects the inspired design, the wealth of materials, and the splendid craftsmanship that render well-chosen eighteenth-century antiques the most satisfying contributions to modern home-making. Not only earthenwares and stonewares are appraised but also the porcelains of all western Europe, Russia, and China. Flint-glass is shown at its most delicate. Sheffield plate appears, accompanying silver through the grace of later eighteenth-century neo-classicism, and japanned tin plate receives the credit due to ambitious work soundly executed. Eighteenth-century mirrors are seen at their most brilliant, and every kind of furniture through its changing moods – baroque, rococo, neo-classic – always with the opportunity to compare American, English, French, and Italian work.

For his walls the collector may find miniature portraits, American and English, mezzotints, glass pictures, early American prints – historical subjects, college views, and the like – marine paintings, English sporting pictures, and the glory of the early English water-colour painters. Here especially the collector's interest carries him on into the succeeding century, with American folk art and sporting pictures, with prints of many techniques – here clearly differentiated and their terms and "states" explained – and with all that is implied by the art of the French Impressionists. Indeed, this volume draws deserved attention to the many fascinating highways and byways of collecting suggested by the quickening pace of life in the nineteenth century, the railroad prints, the silhouettes, the Japanese treasures "discovered" only in the 1850s.

Nineteenth-century glass includes the "popular art in glass" expressed in America's pioneer work with mould and press; ceramics range from the long-proved redwares, stonewares, creamwares, and lustrous brown Rockingham to the refinements of porcelain and England's world-famous bone china. The survey of furniture covers much new ground regarding successive Victorian moods: and the embroidery section, too, recognizes the interest now reawakening in Victorian stitchcraft. Omissions are inevitable in a book of so many interests, but the collector who does not find some use and, it is hoped, some pleasure in its pages will be already an expert – indeed a connoisseur!

L. G. G. RAMSEY
Editor: The Connoisseur

THE COMPLETE
ENCYCLOPEDIA OF
ANTIQUES

ARMS AND ARMOUR

There still exists among the uninformed a certain prejudice against the collection of arms and armour on the grounds that they represent the least sympathetic aspect of man's evolution. Whatever one's moral judgement of the preoccupation of the nobility in the past with the profession of arms may be, it should not be forgotten that until nearly the end of the eighteenth century a finely ornamented sword performed a decorative function in male costume analogous to that of jewellery in the female costume of the time. The best armours of the fifteenth and sixteenth centuries too have a sculptural quality that gives them a not unimportant place in the history of the plastic arts.

Armour

From the fall of the Roman Empire in the West until the early fourteenth century most armour was made of mail worn over a padded undergarment and accompanied by a plate helmet and a shield. But from as early as the beginning of the thirteenth century there is evidence to show that subsidiary defences of plate were coming into use. The first of these was probably a breastplate concealed under the fabric surcoat that was regularly worn over the armour from the end of the twelfth century onwards. By the late thirteenth century this plate had developed into a complete defence for the trunk formed of large overlapping plates riveted to a fabric lining or cover, now usually called the coat of plates. During the second half of the century also plates of metal or hardened leather (*cuirbouilli*) were attached to the mail at the elbows, knees, and shoulders, while gauntlets constructed in the same manner as the coat of plates were introduced. During the first quarter of the fourteenth century complete plate defences for the limbs were generally adopted, and from *c.* 1330 mail was relegated to a subsidiary role.

The armour for the trunk remained concealed by fabric throughout the fourteenth century, but in the period round about 1420 the coverings were generally discarded. By this date armour had achieved what was virtually its full development, and the majority of subsequent changes were ones of form rather than of basic construction. The complete harness now consisted of breast and back-plate, each formed of a single plate of steel, fauld – from *c.* 1430 equipped with tassets – cuisses, poleyns, greaves, sabatons, pauldrons, vambraces, gauntlets, and helmet.

Armour reached the highest point of its development during the second half of the fifteenth century. Much fine work was produced after this, but from early in the sixteenth century there were indications of the beginning of a decline. For example, a fashion started for elaborately embossed decoration which, though often of superb quality, made the armour quite useless for anything other than parade purposes. From the middle of the sixteenth century the weight of armour began to be increased as a result of improvements in the quality and power of firearms, and in consequence soldiers began to discard the less essential pieces, beginning with the

legs. By the early seventeenth century the defensive equipment of the pikemen, who were now the only infantry to wear armour, had been reduced to a cuirass with large tassets and an open helmet. The heavy cavalry wore three-quarter armours until *c.* 1650, but from the 1620s there was an increasing tendency for the lighter units to use only a cuirass, an open helmet, and an elbow-gauntlet in conjunction with a buff-coat. This equipment became general for all cavalry in the second half of the century. It remained in use until *c.* 1700, after which date armour was gradually discarded.

From the second quarter of the fourteenth century until the seventeenth century special armour was used for the joust and tournament. For the most part this resembled the normal war armour of the period, except that it was fitted with various reinforcing plates.

Arms

Swords

The commonest form of sword throughout the Middle Ages had a straight two-edged blade and a guard formed by a single crossbar (quillons). As early as the fourteenth century, however, an additional guard was occasionally provided in the form of a single loop alongside the base of the blade; this enabled the user to hook his finger over one quillon, so obtaining a better grip on the sword. During the sixteenth century the introduction of the

practice of duelling, as opposed to armoured combat in the lists, and the corresponding development of the science of fencing, led to the adding of more supplementary guards, finally producing the swept-hilt rapier of the second half of the sixteenth century. This remained in vogue until the second quarter of the seventeenth century, when a lighter form of rapier was introduced with a simple shell-guard and a single curved bar over the knuckles, ulti-

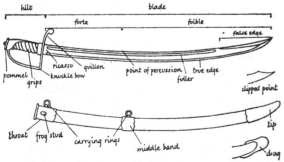

FIG. 1. Terminology of the sword

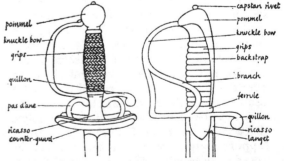

FIG. 2. Terminology of hilt

mately developing into the smallsword. In Southern Italy, and more particularly in Spain, at this period, the swept-hilt was superseded by the cup-hilt, with a guard formed by a circular bowl supplemented by straight quillons and a knuckle-bar, which remained in use until the eighteenth century.

The two-hand sword, which had been used occasionally from the fourteenth century onwards, enjoyed a brief period of popularity in the sixteenth century, picked men being specially trained to its use. The basket-hilted sword, usually with a broad blade, was introduced in the middle of the sixteenth century; it has survived in a modified form until the present time. (*See also* Backsword, Broadsword, Cinquedea, Claymore, Cutlass, Falchion, Hand-and-a-half sword, Hanger, Heading sword, "Pappenheimer" Rapier, Sabre, Schiavona, Smallsword, Swept hilt.)

Daggers

The dagger, the diminutive of the sword designed chiefly for thrusting, was common in a variety of forms from the earliest times. It appeared as an adjunct to the sword in the late thirteenth century, usually being worn on the right hip. During the sixteenth and seventeenth centuries it played an important role in fencing. (*See* Bayonet, Ballock-knife, Cinquedea, Ear-dagger, Left-hand dagger, Quillon dagger, Rondel dagger, Stiletto.)

Staff weapons

This category includes any weapon mounted on a haft. Apart from the club and the spear – the earliest of all weapons – and their derivatives, nearly all forms were derived from agricultural implements. A wide variety of different types exists, only a few of which can be included in the Glossary.

(*See* Lance, Pike, Vouge, Partizan, Mace, Hammer, Halberd, Bill, Guisarme, Glaive.)

Firearms

It now seems quite certain that gunpowder was discovered in the East, but it was apparently used there only for pyrotechnic devices and weapons. Guns, which were almost certainly a Western invention, are first recorded in Europe at the beginning of the second quarter of the fourteenth century. They did not start to become common until after *c.* 1350, but by *c.* 1400 were in general use. The earliest hand-guns, which first appeared in the middle of the fourteenth century, consisted simply of a barrel attached to a wooden or metal pole and were ignited with a piece of smouldering tinder held in the free hand. Early in the fifteenth century the earliest form of match-lock appeared and made possible the development of a gun that could be aimed and fired in much the same way as a modern one. The butts of many of these guns were designed to be held against the cheek, not the shoulder, and an improved version of this form remained common in Germany until the eighteenth century.

Hand firearms did not start to play a major role in warfare until the end of the fifteenth century, but by the second half of the sixteenth century they had become the most important of all military arms. This was partly a result of improvements in their design, but was chiefly because of improvements in the quality of gunpowder. A development of particular importance was the introduction of the wheel-lock in the second decade of the sixteenth century. This, by obviating the inconvenient and tell-tale match, made possible the production of both a practical cavalry firearm, the pistol, and a satisfactory sporting-gun. The result was that firearms began for the first time to be used generally by the upper classes, who demanded finely made and finely decorated guns. Henceforth the gunmaker was assured of the kind of patronage that made it possible for him to improve his products. The sixteenth century, therefore, was a period of experiment, but after the general adoption of the flint-lock in the second quarter of the seventeenth century no major development took place for nearly two hundred years. The invention of the percussion-lock in 1807, however, led to another period of experiment, lasting for the greater part of the nineteenth century, during which most of the different types of firearms in use at the present day were evolved.

Though the majority of firearms in use prior to *c.* 1850 were single-shot muzzleloaders, experiments with breech-loading and repeating mechanisms were made at regular intervals from the early sixteenth century onwards. Apart from some revolvers, all were more or less failures, partly because of the fouling produced by gunpowder, which prevented most breech-mechanisms from functioning after a few shots, and partly because of the problem of obturation, that is the prevention of the backward leak of gases through the breech-mechanism. Only with the adoption of the self-obturating brass cartridge in the third quarter of the nineteenth century did really satisfactory breech-loading and repeating arms, other than revolvers, become possible.

CENTRES OF PRODUCTION

Most of the major European countries had their own armourers and weaponsmiths, but certain centres became especially famous for the making of arms and armour. Little is recorded about such centres in the early Middle Ages, but we know that by the fourteenth century northern Italy, in particular Milan, and southern Germany were supplying large quantities of armour and weapons to the rest of Europe. Of the German centres Augsburg, Nuremberg, Landshut, and Innsbruck were especially noted for armour, and Passau and Solingen for swords. The smiths of Solingen, in fact, supplied a very high proportion of all the blades used in Europe from the late sixteenth to the late eighteenth century, many of which they unashamedly signed with the names of eminent foreign makers. In the sixteenth and seventeenth centuries blades made in Toledo were greatly esteemed, though this city seems never to have become as great a centre of production as Solingen.

During the sixteenth century Milan, Nuremberg, and Augsburg developed an important trade in firearms. Other noted centres were Suhl in Germany and Brescia in northern Italy, the latter being especially noted for arms with elaborately chiselled steel mounts. But from the middle of the seventeenth century until the great Birmingham arms industry started to develop in the late eighteenth century, by far the most important centre of firearms production in Europe was the city of Liége in Belgium.

Glossary

The glossary which follows includes all major technical terms which the beginner collector will encounter in a study of European and American arms and armour. Oriental armour has not been included. Most of these terms have their individual translations in French, Italian, German, and Spanish. These will be learned by the serious student in the course of acquiring knowledge.

Armet. A term used in fifteenth- and early sixteenth-century texts, apparently to denote a close-helmet (*q.v.*). Modern writers generally confine it to the early form of this helmet with hinged cheek-pieces overlapping and fastening at the chin, and usually having at the back a steel disc (rondel) on a short stem (Plate IC, D).

Arquebus. A term derived from the German *Hackenbusch* (hooked gun) applied originally to a hand-gun with a flat lug on the underside of the barrel that could be hooked over a parapet to serve as a recoil stop. In the second half of the sixteenth century it denoted a light musket and in the seventeenth century a heavy carbine. The term is now often applied loosely to any wheel- or match-lock gun.

Back-strap. A metal strap along the outside of back of the grip of a pistol or revolver.

Backsword. A sword having a blade with a back on one side and a single cutting edge on the other (Plate 2A).

Ballock-knife. A form of dagger used from the fourteenth to the seventeenth centuries with a guard formed by two lobate protuberances. It is often called a kidney-dagger by modern writers.

Bands. Loops of metal encircling the barrel and stock of a firearm as a means of fastening these two structures together.

Barbute. A fifteenth-century open helmet of Italian origin. It was tall, at first with a pointed apex, later becoming rounded, and extended over the cheeks, leaving only the eyes, nose, and mouth exposed. Some examples closely resemble the classical Greek Corinthian helmet, on which they may perhaps have been directly based (Plate 1B).

Barrel tang. A metal strap attached to the breech of the barrel of a firearm and projecting towards the butt. It was used to anchor the barrel more firmly in place.

Bascinet. The characteristic light helmet of the fourteenth and early fifteenth centuries. At first rounded, it later became conical in shape and usually had a mail curtain (aventail) laced to its lower edge, protecting the

FIG. 3

throat and neck. In the second half of the fourteenth century it was often worn with an acutely pointed "pig-faced" visor, a form for which the rare medieval term "hounskull" is now generally used. In the fifteenth century the helmet again became rounded, and the aventail was replaced by a plate gorget; in this form it remained in use for fighting on foot in the lists until the beginning of the sixteenth century (Fig. 3).

Bastard sword. *See* Hand-and-half sword.

Battery. *See* Steel.

Bayonet. A dagger, or short sword, fitted to a musket to convert it into a pike. Known early in the seventeenth century, it was not generally adopted for military purposes until the second half of that century. At first simply a dagger with round grip, tapered to fit into the musket muzzle, a form which remained in use until well into the eighteenth century, but this was gradually superseded by the socket-bayonet introduced in the late seventeenth century. This had a tubular hilt fitting over the muzzle, the blade being set to one side so that the musket could be fired with the bayonet fixed. It was superseded in the nineteenth century by the sword-bayonet, attached to a lug on the barrel by a spring-catch and with a hilt like that of a sword.

Besagew. A small plate, usually circular, suspended over the front of each armpit on armours of the fourteenth to the sixteenth century.

Bevor. A chin defence, at first separate but from the early sixteenth century forming part of the close-helmet (*q.v.*).

Bill. A staff-weapon derived from the hedging-bill, which it resembles.

Blade sight. An upright elongated front sight of a firearm.

Bluing. A heat or chemically induced oxidation used to colour iron or steel in shades of blue and black.

Blunderbuss. A short firearm with a large bore flaring at the muzzle. The flared muzzle was designed to facilitate quick reloading by acting as a funnel.

It was particularly popular as ship's arms for repelling boarders and for defending streets and staircases. Apparently introduced into England from the Continent in the middle of the seventeenth century where it was used until well into the nineteenth century. The period of the blunderbuss's greatest popularity in America was the eighteenth century. Although popular myth insists that the Pilgrims were armed with them, very few of these guns were used in this country prior to 1700, and certainly none was used at Plymouth. Many eighteenth-

and early nineteenth-century blunderbusses are equipped with a hinged spring-bayonet, which is thrown forward into the fixed position when a catch is released.

Bootleg pistol. Peculiar form of percussion-cap pistol made largely in Massachusetts, with the hammer underneath the barrel and the grips at a right angle (Fig. 4).

FIG. 4

Bore. The interior of the barrel of a firearm. Also used as a designation of the diameter of the interior of the barrel in terms of the number of spherical lead balls of corresponding diameter in a pound weight. In this connotation it is synonymous with gauge.

Breech. The rear of the barrel of a firearm.

Breech-loader. A firearm receiving its charge at the breech.

Breech plug. A cylindrical plug screwed in at the breech of muzzle-loading firearms to close the bore.

Brigandine. A light, flexible body defence consisting of small, overlapping metal plates riveted to the interior of a canvas or leather jacket. It was usually covered with coloured silk or velvet, the rivet heads on the exterior being gilt to produce a decorative effect. The term first occurs at the end of the fourteenth century, but the majority of surviving examples date from the sixteenth and early seventeenth centuries.

Broadsword. A sword with a straight double-edged blade. The term is applied chiefly to the basket-hilted cavalry sword of the seventeenth and eighteenth centuries. It survived in the Scottish basket-hilted sword, often erroneously called a claymore.

Browning. A process to colour the iron or steel parts of a firearm in shades of brown. Sometimes this was done through artificial oxidation, and sometimes a lacquer was used.

Buff-coat. A coat of thick buff-leather, usually with full skirts and often sleeved. It was thick enough to withstand a sword-cut and became very popular, particularly for cavalry, when armour was falling into disuse in the seventeenth century.

Buffe. The sixteenth- and seventeenth-century term for a chin-defence, more especially the type worn with the burgonet (*q.v.*).

Burgonet. An open helmet, used chiefly by light-horsemen in the sixteenth and early seventeenth centuries. It usually had a peak (fall) over the eyes and hinged cheek-pieces fastening under the chin. It was sometimes worn with a deep chin-piece (buffe) (Fig. 5).

FIG. 5

Butt. The portion of a long arm which fits against the shoulder, or the terminus of the grip of a pistol.

Butt-cap. A metal covering for the butt of a pistol.

Butt-plate. A metal plate used to cover and protect the extreme end of the butt of a shoulder-arm.

Cabasset. *See* Morion.

Caliber or calibre. The diameter of the bore of a firearm expressed in hundredths of an inch.

Caliver. A light musket used in the sixteenth century.

Cap. A small charge of a percussion-igniting compound, usually fulminate of mercury, sealed within a paper or metal container and used to ignite the main charge of a firearm.

Carbine. A short shoulder-arm intended for the use of mounted troops.

Cartridge. A combination of the ball and powder charge for a gun fastened together in a single container. The earliest cartridges were wrapped in paper or cloth. Later metal cartridges were developed which contained their own detonating charges as well (Fig. 6).

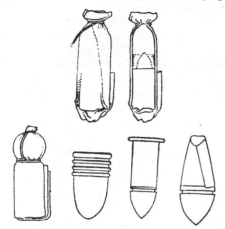

Fig. 6. A series of cartridges: paper cartridge; self-contained; rim fire; combustible.

Chamber. That portion of the bore of a firearm which receives the charge.

Chanfron. The plate defence for a horse's head, introduced early in the fourteenth century and remaining in use until well into the seventeenth.

Cinquedea. An Italian term for a dagger of uncertain form. It is now applied to a type of large dagger or short sword with a flat, triangular blade some five fingers wide near the hilt (the term being thought to derive from the Italian *cinque dei*), and often elaborately etched and gilt. It was essentially a civilian weapon, used chiefly in Italy, in the late fifteenth and early sixteenth centuries.

Claymore. From the Gaelic *claidheam-mor*

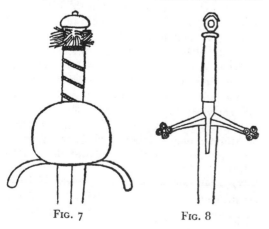

Fig. 7   Fig. 8

(great sword). The Scottish two-hand sword introduced in the sixteenth century. Of very large proportions, it usually had straight quillons inclining at a sharp angle towards the broad, straight blade. In the seventeenth century the quillons became curved and were supplemented by two (sometimes only one) large solid shells bent towards the hilt. Since the eighteenth century the term has been applied erroneously to the basket-hilted Scottish broadsword (Figs. 7 and 8).

Close-helmet. A close-fitting, visored helmet completely enclosing the head. The term is now usually confined to the type of head-piece introduced early in the sixteenth cen-

Fig. 9

tury, with the visor and chin-piece pivoting at the sides, as opposed to the armet (*q.v.*), which has hinged cheek-pieces fastening at the chin (Fig. 9).

Cock. The pivoted arm of a flintlock or snaphance mechanism which holds the flint and snaps forward to bring it in contact with the steel in order to produce the spark necessary to ignite the charge.

Colichemarde. *See* Smallsword.

Counter-guard. Comprises those structures in addition to the quillons which are interposed between the hilt and the blade of a sword. It may take the form of a solid plate or a network of bars.

Couter. An elbow defence.

Crossbow. A bow mounted at right-angles upon a stock, which is grooved for the arrow (bolt), and fitted with a trigger-mechanism so that it can be discharged from the shoulder like a gun. The bow was made variously of wood, steel, or a composition of layers of wood, horn, and sinew glued together; it could be spanned by hand, a stirrup at the end providing purchase for the foot, by a forked lever, or by various forms of windlass. It was known in Europe as early as the fourth century, but did not become popular until the tenth. Its use against Christians was prohibited by the Church in 1139, but despite this it was used extensively in warfare throughout the remainder of the Middle Ages. As a sporting weapon it has remained in use until the present time, especially in Switzerland.

A light version of the crossbow fitted with a sling to fire bullets or stones, and known as a stone-bow, was much used from medieval times onwards for shooting small game. It remained popular, particularly in Lancashire and East Anglia, until well into the nineteenth century. The sixteenth-century term *brodd* is often applied to this sort of bow, though its original meaning is uncertain (Plates 4c and 5A).

Cuirass. The breast and backplate of an armour together.

Cuirassier armour. Armour for the heavy cavalry of the first half of the seventeenth century, consisting of a close-helmet and defences covering the whole of the body down to the knees (Plate 4B).

Cuisse. A thigh defence.

Culet. The seventeenth-century term for the hooped buttock-defence attached to the backplate.

Cup-hilt. A modern term for the type of rapier hilt, introduced in the second quarter of the seventeenth century, in which the main guard is formed like a bowl. It was used chiefly in Spain and Italy.

Cutlass. A term first appearing in the sixteenth century, denoting a short, single-edged sword, usually curved, the successor of the medieval falchion (*q.v.*). In the eighteenth and early nineteenth centuries it was a standard naval weapon.

Cutlass pistol. A type of single-shot percussion-cap pistol with a heavy cutting blade mounted underneath the barrel, patented by

George Elgin in 1837 in the United States (Fig. 10).

Cylinder. The portion of a revolver which holds the chambers for the charges. It revolves around an axis and presents its loads successively to the breech of the barrel.

Dagger. The diminutive of the sword, designed to be used chiefly for thrusting, and common in a variety of forms from the earliest times.

Deringers. One of the foremost U.S. gunsmiths was Henry Deringer of Philadelphia. A fine craftsman, noted for the excellent workmanship on his products, Deringer at first made both rifles and duelling pistols, but shortly after 1825 he began to concentrate on short pocket pistols with large calibres. These little weapons, ranging from $3\frac{3}{4}$ to 9 inches in overall length, had calibres varying from 0.33 to 0.51 inches. Thus considerable power was packed into arms that could be carried easily and inconspicuously almost anywhere. They were always fired with percussion-caps and were almost always rifled. Deringer's pistols quickly became immensely popular, especially in the south and west, and his name became synonymous with the type of pistol he had developed. In fact, often spelled derringer, it was soon applied to any short pocket pistol, even cartridge arms with two or more barrels, and in that connotation it is still in use today. Because of the pistol's popularity, there were many imitators, some of whom put Deringer's name or slight variants such as Beringer on their own products, hoping to fool the unsuspecting. Deringer himself died in 1868, three years after one of his pistols (Plate 13c) had achieved national notoriety in the hands of John Wilkes Booth when he assassinated President Abraham Lincoln.

Dirk. A term applied to: (i) the characteristic long sheath-knife of the Scottish Highlander, which seems to have developed from the early-seventeenth-century form of ballock-knife (*q.v.*); (ii) the light dagger carried by some naval officers, especially midshipmen, in the late eighteenth and nineteenth centuries.

Ear-dagger. A form of fifteenth- and sixteenth-century dagger with the pommel formed by two flattened discs, like ears, set at an

FIG. 10

angle. It was of Eastern origin but was much used in Spain and occasionally elsewhere in Europe.

Elbow-gauntlet. A form of gauntlet, introduced in the late fifteenth century, with a cuff extending to the elbow. In the seventeenth century the armour for the arms was often confined to a gauntlet of this type worn on the bridle-hand, whence it is often called a bridle-gauntlet.

Escutcheon plate. A metal plate set in the wrist of either a pistol or shoulder-arm as a place to engrave the name or monogram of the owner or other similar data.

Falchion. A short, curved, single-edged sword, known as early as the twelfth century. The medieval form had a broad, cleaver-like blade.

False edge. *See* Sabre.

Flint-lock. A term used from the late seventeenth century onwards to denote the snaphance (*q.v.*). Most modern writers confine it to the form of lock with the pan-cover and steel made in one. This first appeared in the late sixteenth century and completely supplanted the earlier form during the second quarter of the seventeenth century everywhere except in Italy. The earliest version of this lock had a horizontal sear working through the lockplate, as on the early snaphance. The fact that the pan-cover and steel were made in one, however, meant that once the gun had been primed the cock had to be kept pulled back. This led to the introduction of a safety device in the form of a small pivoted hook (so-called dog-catch) which engaged in a notch at the rear of the cock and held it in the half-cocked position. In *c.* 1600 a separate half-cock sear appeared, a feature that remained in use in Spain on the miquelet-lock (*q.v.*) until the nineteenth century. Elsewhere what has been termed the true flint-lock came into general use during the second quarter of the seventeenth century. This, which had a vertical sear engaging in one of two notches in an internal tumbler (for half- and full-cock), was probably invented between 1610 and 1615 by Marin le Bourgeoys (d. 1634) of Lisieux, France. It remained in wide use until the second quarter of the nineteenth century.

Foible. The portion of the blade of a sword near the point which is weak from the standpoint of leverage. Usually it comprises from half to two-thirds of the length of the blade.

Fore-stock. The portion of a gunstock in front of the trigger guard.

Forte. The strong portion of the blade of a sword, usually about one-third, nearest the hilt.

Frizzen. *See* Steel.

Frog. A sleeve-like device, normally of leather, used to attach the sword to the belt. Usually the scabbard was thrust through the sleeve and a stud on its throat engaged in a hole in the frog.

Gauge. *See* Bore.

Glaive. A staff-weapon with a large cleaver-like blade. Early writers also applied the term to the lance, and later poets to the sword.

"Gothic" armour. A modern term for the style of plate armour, characterized by slender elegant lines, and decorated with cusped borders and shell-like rippling, developed particularly in Germany in the fifteenth century. The term is extended to cover the fifteenth-century Italian style, which was rounder in form than the German, and usually had smooth, plain surfaces.

Grandguard. A reinforcing piece worn with sixteenth- and early seventeenth-century tilt-armours. It covered the left side of the breastplate and the lower left side of the helmet.

Greave. The plate armour for the lower part of the leg, excluding the foot.

Greenwich armour. Armour made in the only English royal workshop, founded at Greenwich by Henry VIII in 1515. It was staffed largely by foreign workmen, of whom one of the most important was Jacob Halder, master workman, 1576–1607. He was almost certainly responsible for an album of drawings of armours made at Greenwich, now in the Victoria and Albert Museum, which has made possible the identification of a number of surviving suits, several of which are in the Tower of London. The workshop was closed down in about 1637.

Guisarme. A term applied in the later Middle Ages to a long-handled axe. Modern writers use it to denote a form of bill (*q.v.*).

Halberd. A staff-weapon with a flat axe-blade balanced by a fluke and with a long, sharp spike above. Introduced in the fifteenth century, it survived as a parade-weapon, and as the arm of certain non-commissioned officers, until the nineteenth century.

Half-armour. A light armour covering the whole body excepting the legs, and often also excluding the arms (Fig. 11).

FIG. 11

Hammer. In a percussion-cap or cartridge gun the movable arm which strikes the primer and sets it off either directly or through the use of a firing pin. Modern collectors often use the term incorrectly to refer to the cock of a flint arm. In the eighteenth and early nineteenth centuries it was synonymous with steel (*q.v.*).

Hand-gun. The earliest form of hand fire-arm, introduced early in the fourteenth century. It consisted simply of a tubular barrel attached to a long wooden stock designed to be held under the arm, and ignited at the touch-hole by hand.

Hand-and-a-half sword. A large sword with a long grip that could be used with either one or two hands. It appears to have been known as a bastard sword in the fifteenth and sixteenth centuries.

Hanger. (i) A light, single-edged civilian sword used by horsemen, huntsmen, and sailors in the seventeenth and eighteenth centuries; (ii) the triangular buckled sling attached to the belt, in which a rapier was car-

ried in the late sixteenth and early seventeenth centuries (Fig. 12).

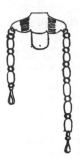

FIG. 12

Haute-piece. One of the upstanding neck-guards found on the pauldrons (*q.v.*) of some armours of the first half of the sixteenth century.

Heading sword. An executioner's sword, usually with a plain cruciform hilt long enough to be used with two hands, and a broad, straight, two-edged blade with a rounded or squared point. It was employed on the Continent, and especially in Germany, from the sixteenth to the early nineteenth century.

Helm. A large headpiece, covering the entire head and face and reaching nearly to the shoulders, introduced at the end of the twelfth century. The top was at first flat, but by the middle of the thirteenth century had become conical, giving an improved glancing surface.

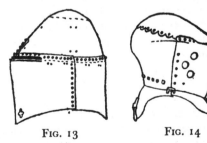

FIG. 13   FIG. 14

During the first half of the fourteenth century the helm was often worn over the bascinet (*q.v.*) in warfare, but was subsequently relegated to the tilt-yard, where it remained in use until well into the sixteenth century. In its later form it was usually bolted down to the breast and back (Figs. 13 and 14).

Hunting sword. A short, light hanger

with a straight or very slightly curved blade and usually no knuckle-bow. Originally designed to be worn while hunting, as its name implies, it was often affected by high-ranking

FIG. 15

officers during the eighteenth century (Fig. 15).

Jack. This was a cheaper form of the brigandine (*q.v.*), its plates, which were often of horn, being held in place by stitching.

"Kentucky" or Pennsylvanian rifle. Developed by the Dutch, German, and Swiss colonists in Pennsylvania. These people had long used rifles in their native lands, and they set out to adapt them to meet the needs of their new environment. They lengthened the barrel, decreased the calibre, and evolved a style of ornamentation that soon set these U.S. rifles completely apart from their European predecessors. The evolution of the U.S. rifle began quite early in the eighteenth century, and its final distinctive form was reached possibly by 1740–5. It was a fine, accurate gun in the hands of a man who knew how to use it, but it was slow to load and had no bayonet, so that it was not well adapted for the formal warfare of the period. The early rifles were simple, with straight lines and thick butts. The lavish inlays and sharply dropping butt did not develop until after 1790.

Kettle-hat. An open helmet, usually with a brim, used from the thirteenth to the early sixteenth centuries, when it was replaced by the morion (*q.v.*). Sometimes referred to as the *chapel-de-fer* or war-hat.

Key. A wedge-shaped device used to fasten the barrel of a firearm to the stock through corresponding slots in the fore-stock and lugs on the underside of the barrel. The term is also now applied sometimes to the spanner for winding a wheel-lock.

Kidney-dagger. *See* Ballock-knife.

Lance. The horseman's spear. From the fourteenth to the early seventeenth centuries it was often equipped with a large metal guard for the hand (vamplate).

Lands. The uncut portions of the original

surface left between the grooves in the bore of a rifled gun.

Left-hand dagger. The dagger used in conjunction with the rapier in sixteenth- and early seventeenth-century fencing. It usually had quillons (often strongly arched to entangle an opponent's sword-blade) and a side-ring, but a special form, with a triangular knuckle-guard, was used in Italy and Spain in conjunction with the cup-hilt rapier (*q.v.*). It remained in use in the latter country until well into the eighteenth century.

"Lobster-tail" helmet. A modern term for a form of burgonet (*q.v.*) worn by cavalry in the seventeenth century. It had a laminat-

FIG. 16

ed tail, hinged cheek-pieces, and a peak (often pivoted), with one or more bars extending from it over the face. The English form with three bars was the characteristic helmet of the Civil War (Fig. 16).

Lock. The mechanism of a firearm used for igniting the explosive.

Lock-plate. The basic iron or steel plate on which the movable parts of a gun lock are mounted.

Long arm. Those small arms designed to be fired from the shoulder. Synonymous with shoulder-arm.

Lucerne Hammer. A staff-weapon with a hammer-head balanced by a fluke and with a long spike above. On late sixteenth- and seventeenth-century examples the hammer is often formed by three claws.

Mace. A horseman's club. From the fourteenth century onwards the head was normally flanged. On examples of the fifteenth century and later the haft was usually of metal like the head.

Magazine. A device for holding a number of cartridges together to facilitate loading for

successive discharges. Also the part of a repeating firearm containing cartridges for successive discharges.

Mail. Armour made of interlinked rings
which, on most European examples, are riveted. It was known in Europe at least as
early as the second century B.C., and was the
normal defence during the early Middle
Ages. It was relegated to a subordinate role
with the general adoption of plate armour in
the fourteenth century, but nevertheless remained in common use until well into the
seventeenth. The extension of the term to
cover all forms of defensive armour and the
word chain-mail are both of comparatively
recent date.

Manifer. A large, often rigid, gauntlet for
the bridle hand worn with jousting armours
from the fourteenth century onwards.

Maingauche dagger. *See* Left-hand dagger.

Match-lock. The earliest form of mechanical ignition for a gun, introduced in the first
quarter of fifteenth century, in which an arm
holding a lighted match (cord made of tow
soaked in a solution of saltpetre) is brought in-

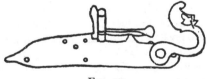

FIG. 17

to contact with priming powder at the touch-
hole by pressure on a trigger. Despite the
invention of the wheel- and flint-locks, it
remained in use for military purposes, on
account of its cheapness, until the end of the
seventeenth century (Fig. 17; Plate 12A).

"Maximilian" armour. A modern term
for the style of fluted armour which came into
use in Italy and, more particularly, in Germany during the reign of the Emperor Maximilian I (1494–1519). It is rarely found after
c. 1540, but examples dating from as late as
c. 1560–70 are occasionally encountered.
Modern writers sometimes use the rare sixteenth-century English term for fluted, crested, to describe this style.

Minié bullet or Minié ball. A cylindro-
conoidal projectile with a cavity in its base
which expanded when the powder charge was
fired and caused the bullet to fit the bore
tightly and thus take the spin imparted by the
rifling. It was named after Captain C. E.
Minié of the French Army, who originally developed the principle on which it functioned.
Because this type of bullet allowed a muzzle-
loading rifle to be loaded as rapidly as a musket, it ended the supremacy of the musket as a
military arm.

Miquelet-lock. A modern term for a form
of flint-lock (*q.v.*) used in Southern Italy and
Spain from the early seventeenth century onwards. It was a development from the early
form of flint-lock with two sears (giving half-
and full-cock respectively) operating through
the lockplate. It went out of use in Italy in the
first half of the eighteenth century, but survived in Spain until well into the nineteenth
century.

Morion. An open helmet much used by
foot-soldiers in the second half of the sixteenth
century. Contemporary texts mention two
forms: (i) the Spanish-morion, called a cabasset by many modern writers, with a pear-
shaped, pointed skull and a narrow, flat brim;
(ii) the comb-morion, with high comb and a

FIG. 18

curved brim peaked before and behind. The
modern term peaked-morion refers to an
intermediate type with a curved brim, and a
pointed apex terminating in a small stalk
(Fig. 18; Plate 4A).

Musket. A military match- or wheel-lock
firearm introduced in the third quarter of the
sixteenth century. It was heavier than any
other hand firearm of the period and had to
be fired from a forked rest. The rest was
discarded in the second quarter of the
seventeenth century, and henceforth the

(A) Sallet, German (Innsbruck), second half of fifteenth century. *Collection of R. T. Gwynn.*

(B) Barbute, Italian (Milanese), second half of fifteenth century. *Collection of R. T. Gwynn.*

(C) Armet, Italian, late fifteenth century. *Collection of R. T. Gwynn.*

(D) Armet, probably English, beginning of fifteenth century. *Formerly Collection of W. R. Hearst.*

PLATE 1

A

(A) Backsword, the hilt damascened with gold. English, early eighteenth century. *Victoria and Albert Museum, London.*

(B) Smallsword, the hilt chiselled and gilt. French, mid-eighteenth century. *Musée des Arts Décoratifs, Paris.*

(C) Sword, Italian, fourteenth century. *Collection of R. T. Gwynn.*

(D) Sword, German, early sixteenth century. *Collection of R. T. Gwynn.*

(E) Sword with swept hilt. Saxon, late sixteenth century. *Collection of R. T. Gwynn.*

(F) Rapier with pierced cup-hilt. English, mid-seventeenth century. *Victoria and Albert Museum, London.*

B   C   D   E   F

PLATE 2

A   B   C   D   E

(A) Rondel dagger. German, second half of fifteenth century. *Kunsthistorisches Museum, Vienna.* (B) Cinquedea, the blade etched and gilt, perhaps by Ercole Roberti. Italian (Ferrara), late fifteenth century.
Collection of E. Oakeshott. (C) Dagger, the hilt gilt. German, late sixteenth century. *C. Blair Collection.* (D)
Dagger, Italian, late sixteenth century. *Victoria and Albert Museum, London.* (E) Stiletto, Italian, mid-seventeenth century. *Victoria and Albert Museum, London.*

(F) Shield, etched and gilt in the "Pisan"
manner. Italian (Milan), late sixteenth
century. *Victoria and Albert Museum,
London.*

PLATE 3

(A) Morion, etched and gilt. Saxon, late sixteenth century. *Collection of R. T. Gwynn.*

(B) Breastplate and tassets painted with vertical panels of trophies. English, first half of seventeenth century. *Victoria and Albert Museum, London.*

(c) Cross-bow winder (Cranequin). German, dated 1716. *Victoria and Albert Museum, London.*

PLATE 4

(A) Cross-bow, the stock inlaid with engraved staghorn. German, early seventeenth century. *Formerly W. R. Hearst Collection.*

(B) Halberd, etched and gilt. German, dated 1570. *Collection of J. F. Hayward.*

(C) Glaive with device of Duke Wilhelm V of Bavaria. German, dated 1580. *Bayrisches National Museum, Munich.*

PLATE 5

(A) 1798 American cavalry sabre
by Nathan Starr. *Collection of
Harry D. Berry, Jr.*

(B) American foot artillery
sword, 1832, made by Ames.

(C) American artillery sabre, 1840,
in use about fifty years.

(D) Heavy cavalry sabre, adopted
in America in 1840 after a French
type.

(E) American infantry non-commissioned officer's sword, 1840.

(F) Naval cutlass; a French type
adopted in America in 1860.

PLATE 6

(A) Mounted officer's sabre; cast brass grips and pommel, c. 1790.

(B) American naval officer's sword with later form of the eagle head pommel, 1815–30.

(C) American officer's sword with Indian head pommel, 1821–50.

(D) American naval officer's sword, 1841.

(E) American staff and field officer's sword, 1850.

(F) American staff and field officer's sword, 1860. This became regulation for almost all officers in 1872.

PLATE 7

(A) Silver-mounted small-sword by Timothy Bontecou, Jr., of New Haven, Connecticut, c. 1750. *Collection of Herman W. Williams.*

(B) Silver-mounted smallsword by Joseph Draper of Wilmington, Delaware, c. 1815. *Collection of Hermann W. Williams.*

(C) Silver-mounted hunting sword by John Bailey of Fishkill, New York, which belonged to George Washington. *U.S. National Museum.*

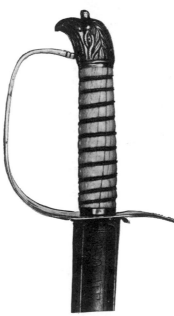

(D) Silver-mounted hunting sword by William Gilbert of New York City, c. 1770.

(E) Silver-mounted sabre by William Ball, Jr., of Baltimore, c. 1790. *Collection of Charles West.*

(F) Silver-mounted sabre by Johnson & Reat of Philadelphia and Richmond, c. 1810. *United States Marine Corps.*

PLATE 8

(A) Congressional presentation sword of the American Revolution. *United States National Museum.*

(B) Congressional naval presentation sword of the Anglo-American War of 1812. *United States Naval Academy Museum.*

(C) New York State presentation sword of the Anglo-American War of 1812. *United States National Museum.*

(D) Presentation sword of the Mexican War. *United States National Museum.*

(E) Presentation sword of the American Civil War. *United States National Museum.*

(F) Presentation sword of 1887. *United States National Museum.*

PLATE 9

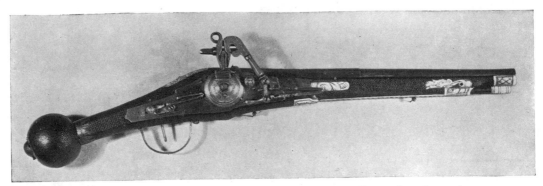

(A) Wheel-lock pistol, the stock inlaid with engraved staghorn. Saxon, late sixteenth century.

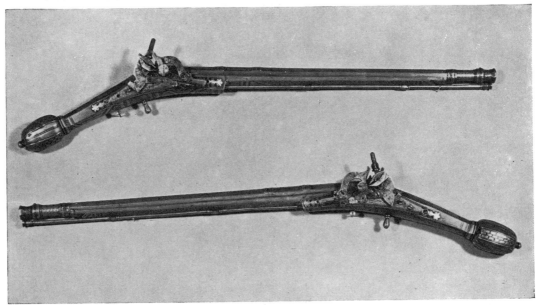

(B) Pair of snaphaunce pistols, the stocks and barrels of engraved and gilt brass. Scottish, dated 1614.

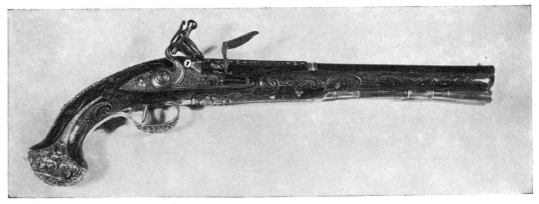

(C) Flint-lock pistol with mount of chased silver, the stock inlaid with silver wire, signed H. HADLEY. English (London), about 1770.

All the above from the Collection of R. T. Gwynn.

PLATE 10

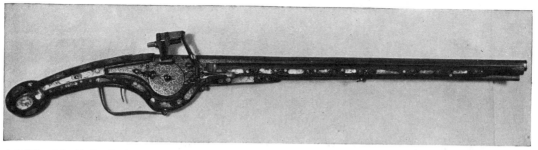

(A) Wheel-lock pistol, the stock inlaid with mother-of-pearl and brass wire. French, early seventeenth century. *Collection of R. T. Gwynn.*

(B) Flint-lock pistol, the barrel signed LAZARINO COMINAZZO, the lock signed GIO BATTA TIANIA. Italian (Brescia), third quarter of seventeenth century. *Collection of R. T. Gwynn.*

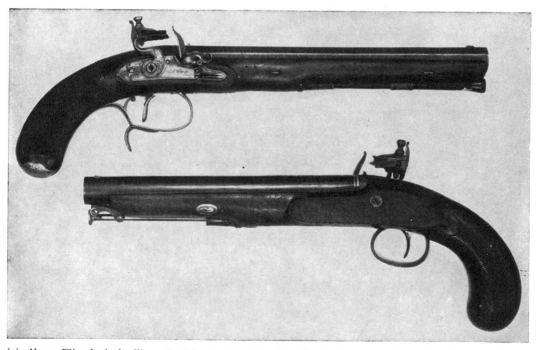

(C) *Above:* Flint-lock duelling pistol by D. Egg. English (London), about 1800. *Below:* Officer's pistol by W. Peacock. English (London), about 1820. *Collection of J. Winsbury.*

PLATE 11

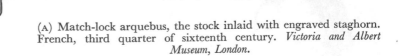

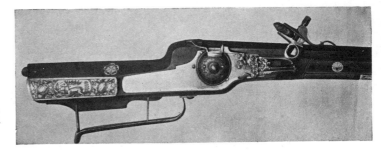

(A) Match-lock arquebus, the stock inlaid with engraved staghorn. French, third quarter of sixteenth century. *Victoria and Albert Museum, London.*

(B) Wheel-lock rifle. German, second quarter of seventeenth century. *Private Collection.*

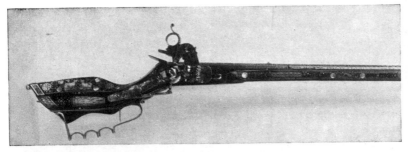

(C) Wheel-lock Tschinke, the stock inlaid with engraved staghorn. German, mid-seventeenth century. *Formerly W. R. Hearst Collection.*

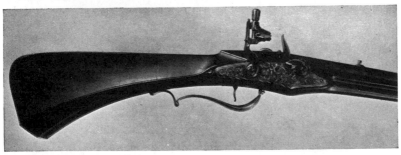

(D) Flint-lock carbine, the lock signed by Felix Werder of Zürich. Swiss, dated 1652. *Kunsthistorisches Museum, Vienna.*

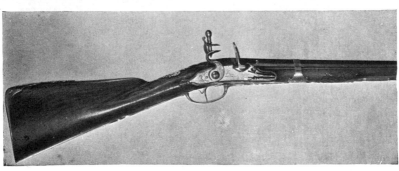

(E) Flint-lock rifle, the mounts of engraved silver, signed TANNER. German (Gotha), dated 1724. *Victoria and Albert Museum, London.*

PLATE 12

(A) Patent model of the Allen pepperbox. *United States National Museum.*

(B) Colt 1860 American Army model revolver. *National Rifle Association.*

(C) Deringer used by John Wilkes Booth to assassinate Abraham Lincoln. *National Park Service.*

(D) American Dragoon third model. Cut for shoulder stock and fully presentation engraved. *National Rifle Association.*

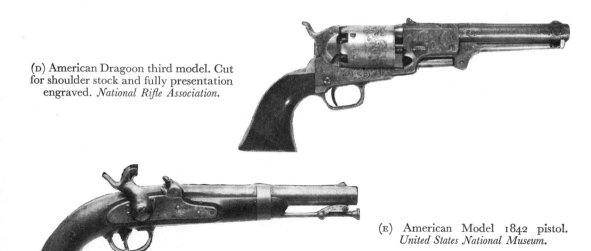

(E) American Model 1842 pistol. *United States National Museum.*

PLATE 13

Pair of American
"Kentucky" pistols,
c. 1775–83. *Collection
of Joe Kindig, Jr.*

PLATE 14

(A) North and Cheney pistol (U.S.A.), 1799. *National Rifle Association.*

(B) Harpers Ferry pistol (U.S.A.), *c.* 1805. *National Rifle Association.*

(C) American Model 1816 pistol by Simeon North. *United States National Museum.*

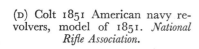

(D) Colt 1851 American navy revolvers, model of 1851. *National Rifle Association.*

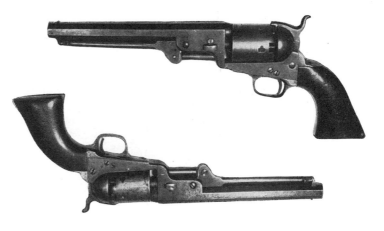

PLATE 15

(A) Model 1817 "common" rifle (U.S.A.). *National Rifle Association.*

(B) Volcanic rifle, 1855. *National Rifle Association.*

(C) Two American Hawken "plains" rifles, *c.* 1800-20. *National Rifle Association.*

(D) American Spencer rifle with breech open and tubular magazine lying below. *National Rifle Association.*

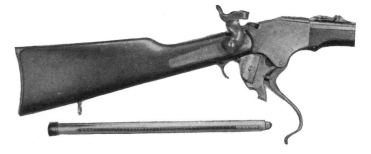

PLATE 16

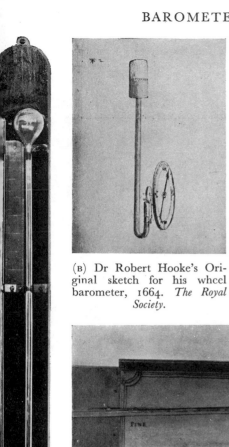

The Torricel-
experiment,
. Science Mu-
m, London.

(B) Dr Robert Hooke's Original sketch for his wheel
barometer, 1664. *The Royal
Society.*

(C) Triple diagonal barometer, by John Boll.
On oak back with later mahogany front, 1666.
John Bell of Aberdeen.

(D) John Boll, 1666.

(E) Portable barometer, by
Daniel Quare, *c.* 1700. Walnut. Height 41 ins. *G. Jetley.*

(F) Base of Quare's baro-
meter showing his patent
screw-plug.

PLATE 17

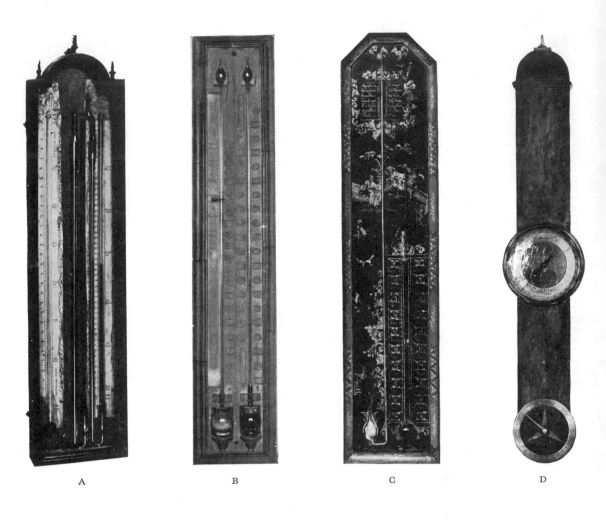

A   B   C   D

(A) Double barometer by Dom Sala, London, with Fahrenheit's standard scale, *c.* 1750. *Pratt & Sons Ltd.*

(B) Hooke's marine barometer, *c.* 1697. *Museum for the History of Science, Oxford.*

(C) Syphon barometer, by Robelau, with Fahrenheit's early thermometer scale, 1719. *Science Museum, London.*

(D) Walnut wheel barometer, by George Hallifax of Doncaster. The days of the month inscribed on the dial (indicating hand for this missing). Comparison dial at bottom, *c.* 1730. *Phillips of Hitchin.*

PLATE 18

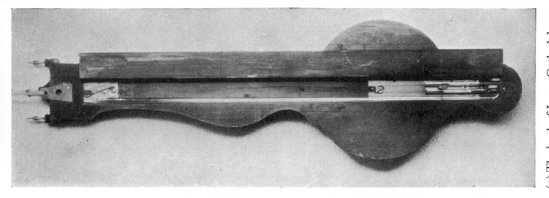

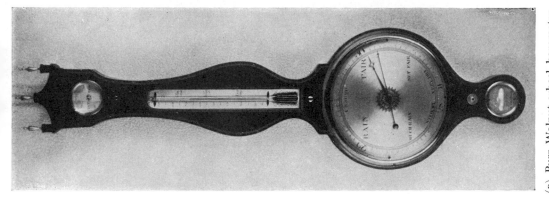

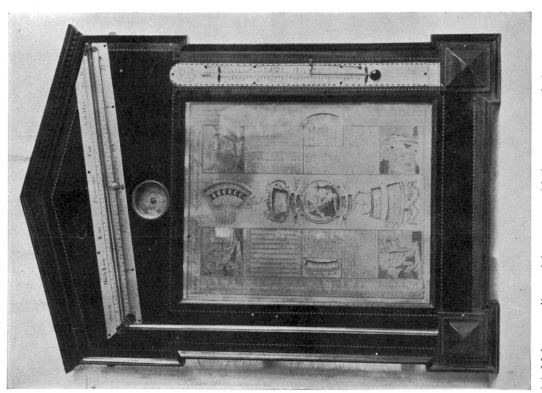

(c) The back of James Gatley's barometer.

(B) Burr Walnut wheel barometer, by James Gatley, High Holborn, London. No. 130, with gut hygrometer, c. 1770. *Frank Sherrard, London.*

(A) Mahogany diagonal barometer with hygrometer and thermometer, 38 × 26 ins, by Watkins & Smith, London. Mid-eighteenth century. Perpetual calendar for the new style, 1753. *Stanley Marling.*

PLATE 19

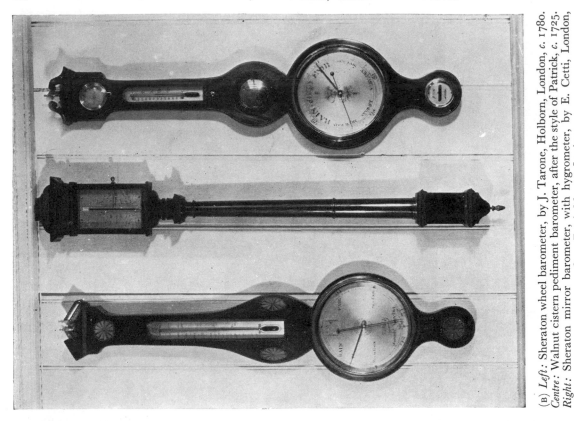

(B) *Left*: Sheraton wheel barometer, by J. Tarone, Holborn, London, *c.* 1780. *Centre*: Walnut cistern pediment barometer, after the style of Patrick, *c.* 1725. *Right*: Sheraton mirror barometer, with hygrometer, by E. Cetti, London, *c.* 1800. *Frank Marson, London.*

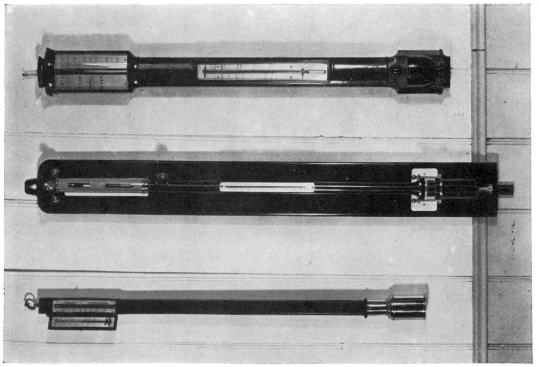

(A) *Left*: Georgian marine barometer, as used in Nelson's time, *c.* 1800. *Centre*: Fortin barometer by Spencer Browning. Invented 1815. Note the ivory tooth seen impinging on the mercury level in the cistern. *Right*: Georgian bow-fronted pediment barometer, by Dolland, *c.* 1810. *Frank Marson, London.*

PLATE 20

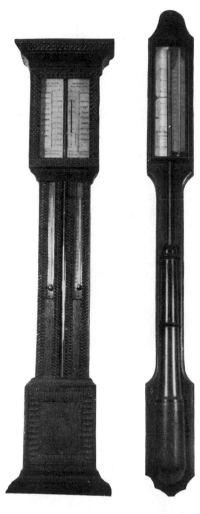

(A) Barometers: H. A. Clum, Rochester, New York. Patented 1860. B. C. Spooner, Boston. Patented 1860. *Collection of B. W. Brandt.*

(B) Watch, marked *J. Sargeant Springfield, Massachusetts,* and probably made by him, *c.* 1795. *Collection of Percy L. Small.*

Photo: R. Coffin.

(C) New York Watch Co., Springfield, Massachusetts, 1870. Keywinding and set from back. *Collection of Hamilton Pease.*

Photo: R. Coffin. *Photo: R. Coffin.* *Photo: R. Coffin.*

(D) E. Howard & Co., Boston, 1859. *Collection of Hamilton Pease.*

(E) American Waltham Watch Co., *c.* 1878. Chronograph. *Collection of Hamilton Pease.*

(F) Benedict & Burnham Co., Waterbury (U.S.A.), 1878. First successful cheap watch; has a revolving train seen through the cut-out dial. *Collection of Hamilton Pease.*

PLATE 21

(A) Three sizes of gothic or steeple clocks, *c.* 1850–60. *Left:* C. Jerome, New Haven. *Others:* Brewster and Ingraham, Bristol (U.S.A.). *Private Collection.*

(B) Beehive clock, Forestville Mfg. Co., Forestville, Connecticut. *Collection of Edward M. Mitchell.*

(C) Shelf clock, New England Clock Co., Bristol (U.S.A.), 1850. *Private Collection.*

(D) Beehive clock, J. C. Brown, Bristol (U.S.A.), 1850. *Collection of Edward M. Mitchell.*

PLATE 22

(A) Eli Terry and Sons, Plymouth, Connecticut, *c.* 1820. Height 35 ins; stencilled posts and splat with well painted tablet; wooden movement. *Private Collection.*

(B) Eli Terry, Jr., Plymouth, Connecticut, *c.* 1830; carved case, 30-hour wooden movement. *Collection of Fraser R. Forgie.*

(C) Chauncey Jerome, Bristol, Connecticut, *c.* 1840. Height 29 ins. 30-hour movement; weights travel inside columns. *Private Collection.*

(D) J. C. Brown, Forestville, Connecticut, *c.* 1840. Ogee, with coloured decalcomania on tablet; 8-day brass movement. *Private Collection.*

PLATE 23

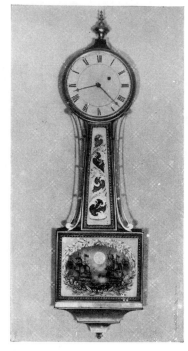

(A) Aaron Willard banjo clock, Boston (U.S.A.), c. 1820. *Owner unknown.*

(B) Aaron Willard, Jr., Boston, c. 1825; Arabic numerals unusual. *Collection of Edwin B. Burt.*

(C) Unknown American maker, c. 1825. Tablet with Constitution and Guerriere. *Private Collection.*

(D) Lyre clock with a striking movement; Abiel Chandler, Concord, New Hampshire, c. 1830. *Collection of Edwin B. Burt.*

(E) "Girandole" wall clock by Lemuel Curtis, Massachusetts, c. 1815. Height 45 ins. *Old Sturbridge Village, Sturbridge, Mass.*

(F) Lyre clock; carved mahogany case; William Grant, Boston, c. 1830. Height 37 ins. *Private Collection.*

D   E   F

PLATE 24

(A) Elnathan Taber, Roxbury (U.S.A.), *c.* 1800. Apprentice of Simon Willard. *Collection of Edwin B. Burt.*

(B) Aaron Willard, Boston, *c.* 1805. Height 93½ ins; mahogany case; rocking ship in arch of dial. *Old Sturbridge Village, Sturbridge, Massachusetts.*

(C) Simon Willard, Roxbury (U.S.A.), *c.* 1810. Height 102 ins. Inlaid mahogany case of "Roxbury" type. *Old Sturbridge Village, Sturbridge, Massachusetts.*

(D) Ellis Chandlee, Nottingham, Maryland, *c.* 1800; walnut case, moon phase in arch. *Collection of Dr Everett P. Barnard.*

PLATE 25

(A) Pillar and scroll clock, escapement in front of dial; 30-hour wooden movement. Eli Terry, Plymouth, Connecticut, c. 1817. *Old Sturbridge Village, Sturbridge, Massachusetts.*

(B) Unusual movement having pendulum hung "off-centre" and a seconds hand. Seth Thomas, Plymouth, Connecticut, c. 1817. *Private Collection.*

(C) Seth Thomas, Plymouth, Connecticut, c. 1820. Height 31 ins. Typical pillar and scroll clock. *Collection of Edwin B. Burt.*

(D) Early Connecticut shelf clock with 8-day brass movement. Heman Clark, Plymouth, c. 1815. Height 20 ins. *Private Collection.*

PLATE 26

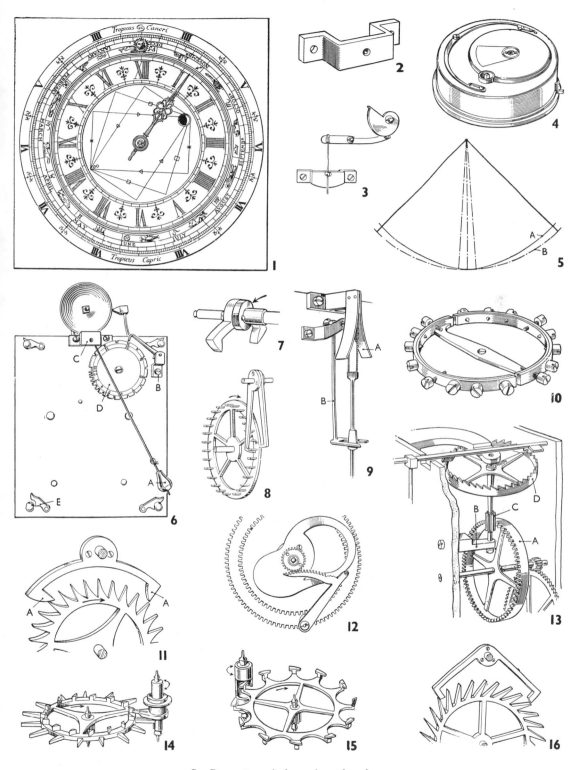

See Barometers, clocks, and watches glossary

PLATE 27

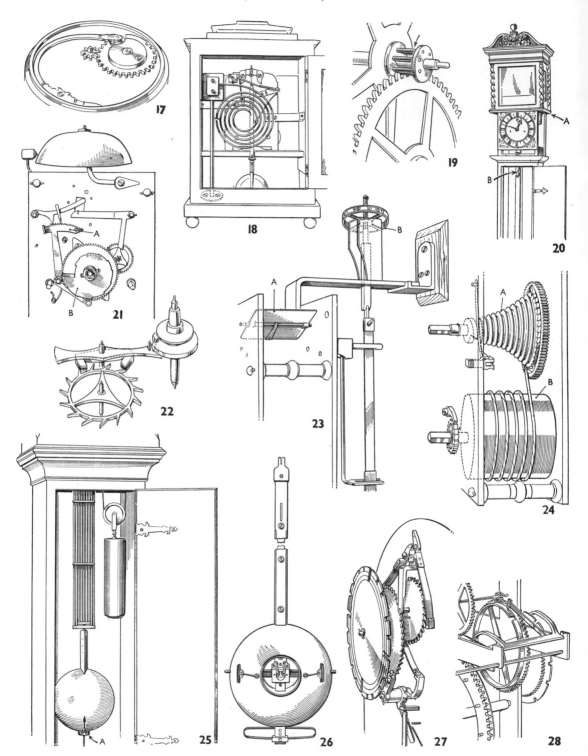

See Barometers, clocks, and watches glossary

PLATE 28

CLOCK DIALS: (A) Dial with bolt-and-shutter maintaining power, c. 1685. (B) Dial to which a third (musical) train has later been added, c. 1695. (C) Dial with universal tidal dial in the arch, c. 1735. (D) Dial with musical dial in the arch, c. 1735. (E) 24-hour dial with shutters showing sun's rising and setting, also its daily course; below, the short hand gives the equation and the long hand the date, c. 1750. (F) Dial with concentric equation hand, c. 1755. (G) Dial with annual calendar disc with the equation engraved upon it, c. 1785. (H) Planetarium. (I) Dial with lunar and tidal dials for a specific port, c. 1810.

PLATE 29

LONG CASE CLOCKS: (A) Architectural clock with lenticle, *c.* 1680. (B) Arched dial clock with calendar dial in the arch, *c.* 1720. (C) Arched dial clock with annual calendar dial in the arch, concentric equation hand and mercury pendulum, *c.* 1730.

PLATE 30

BRACKET CLOCKS: (A) Early iron clock with foliot, *c.* 1550. (B) Table clock, *c.* 1650. (C) Lantern clock, *c.* 1660.

PLATE 31

A   B   C   D

(A) Watch with arrowhead hand; no minute hand; *c.* 1650. (B) Backplate of A, showing early form of cock and tangent and worm regulation. (C) Movement of A, with early tulip pillars and gut fusee drive; verge escapement. (D) Early stop-watch with seconds hand; "pulse watch"; beetle and poker hands, *champlevé* dial; *c.* 1690. (E) Backplate of D, showing later style of cock and pulse "stop piece".

E

F   G   H

(F) and (G) Gold repeater watch with *repoussé* case, *champlevé* dial, hall mark 1724. (H) Movement of watch with cylinder escapement and the late baluster pillars, *c.* 1750.

I   J   K   L

(I) Centre seconds watch with enamel dial, hall mark 1750. (J) Watch in shagreen case, enamelled dial, with hour, seconds, calendar, and "up and down" subsidiary dials, 1774. (K) Landscape watch, *c.* 1800. (L) Watch in studded tortoiseshell case made for the Turkish market, *c.* 1780.

ACKNOWLEDGMENTS: *B. Brooks* for Plate 29D. *T. P. Camerer Cuss* for Plates 32A, B, C, H, K, L. *The Clockmakers' Company* for Plate 32/I. *W. F. Greenwood & Sons* for Plate 29G. *Lord Harris* for Plate 30A. *C. A. Ibert* for Plate 30C. *The late W. J. Iden* for Plates 29A, E. *Mrs A. Murray* for Plate 29B. *The Museum for the History of Science* for Plate 29H. *James Oakes* for Plates 30B and 32F, G, J. *H. Silver* for Plate 31C.

PLATE 32

term was applied to any heavy military long-gun.

Musketoon. A short musket.

Muzzle. The distal or front end of the barrel of a firearm.

Nipple. The small tube at the breech of a percussion-cap firearm on which the cap is placed.

Pan. The receptacle on the outside of the barrel or lock plate of a firearm used to hold the priming powder. Sometimes called the flash pan or priming pan.

"Pappenheimer". A heavy rapier with a form of swept hilt (*q.v.*) incorporating two large perforated shells. It was used during the

FIG. 19

first half of the seventeenth century and was named after the celebrated imperialist general of the Thirty Years' War, Gottfried Heinrich, Count von Pappenheim (d. 1632). Sometimes referred to incorrectly as a Walloon sword (Fig. 19).

Partizan. A staff-weapon with a long head formed like an equilateral triangle, usually with two small pointed lugs at the base. Introduced in the fifteenth century, it survived as a parade weapon until the nineteenth century.

Pasguard. A reinforcing plate worn over the left couter (*q.v.*) on sixteenth- and early seventeenth-century jousting armours.

Patch-box. A receptacle in the side of a

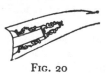

FIG. 20

rifle butt designed to hold greased patches or small pieces of equipment (Fig. 20).

Pauldron. Plate defence for the shoulder.

Pepperbox. Percussion-cap muzzle-loading pistol which achieved great popularity in the United States during the 1830s and '40s. This was by no means a U.S. invention. It had developed gradually for well over a century and a half, but it found a definite market at this period, and Americans were quick to make improvements and alterations in the basic design. Fundamentally, the pepperbox was a series of barrels grouped around a central axis that could be fired one after another by a single hammer. Some were single-action, some double-action. On some the barrels revolved automatically and on others it was necessary to turn them by hand. Normally these pistols had from three to six barrels, but occasionally there were more – eight, ten, twelve, and even eighteen. When first developed, they were the fastest-firing guns of their time, and they were widely carried as personal arms both by civilians and soldiers. The most prolific maker of U.S. pepperboxes (Plate 13A) was Ethan Allen of Grafton and Worcester, Massachusetts, in partnership with Charles Thurber and later with T. P. Wheelock. Second was the firm of Blunt & Syms of New York City, but there were many others. Even in the cartridge era there were pistols that still qualified as pepperboxes, notably those four-barrelled pocket pistols made by Christian Sharps of Philadelphia.

Percussion lock. The latest form of ignition for a firearm, involving the use of a detonating compound. The first patent for a lock of this type was taken out in 1807 by the Rev. Alexander Forsyth (d. 1843). As put on the market, this had a small, flask-shaped magazine which could be rotated on a central spindle, and which contained detonating powder in the lower end and a spring-loaded striker in the upper. By turning the magazine through 180 degrees a small amount of powder was deposited in a recess in the central spindle, connecting through a channel to the touch-hole; when the magazine was returned to the normal position this powder was detonated by the striker, which was itself struck by a hammer-like cock (Fig. 21A).

Improvements made on the Forsyth lock included the pellet- or pill-lock, in which the detonating powder was replaced by a pellet, sometimes enclosed in a paper cap, and the

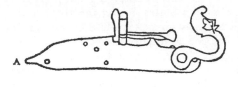

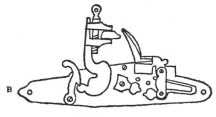

FIG. 21

tube-lock, which used a tubular metal primer held by a spring clip. All types were superseded by the percussion-cap system, apparently invented between 1818 and 1820, in which a thimble-shaped copper cap containing detonating powder was placed on a hollow nipple communicating with the chamber, and fired by the action of the cock. Many flint-lock guns were converted to this system, which remained in use until the second half of the nineteenth century (Fig. 21B).

Petronel. A large pistol, or short arquebus, fitted with match- or wheel-lock and used in the late sixteenth and early seventeenth centuries. It had a curved stock, which was rested against the chest when fired.

Pike. A long infantry spear, usually with a small, leaf-shaped head. During the sixteenth and seventeenth centuries, when the pikeman played a major part in military tactics, it often attained a length of as much as 22 feet.

Pill lock. *See* Percussion lock.

"Pisan" armour. A misleading modern term for a type of late sixteenth-century armour, apparently produced chiefly in Milan. Its chief characteristic consists of bands of coarsely etched decoration of confused design (Plate 3F).

Pistol. The smallest type of firearm, designed to be fired with one hand, introduced

c. 1530. It was fitted at first with a wheel-lock and subsequently snaphance, flint- and percussion-lock, but in Europe with a match-lock. The earliest pistols were used chiefly by the cavalry, being carried in large holsters attached to the saddle, but in the late sixteenth century smaller forms were devised to be carried in the belt, and later in the pocket. Numerous attempts were made to produce a revolving pistol, but none was really successful until the invention of the Colt percussion-revolver (*see* Revolver), patented in 1836 (Plates 10 and 11).

Plackart. A reinforcing breastplate.

Point of percussion. The point which divides the forte (*q.v.*) from the foible (*q.v.*), the theoretical spot at which a blow should be struck to achieve its greatest force.

Pole-axe. A term applied from the fifteenth to the seventeenth centuries to a long-handled axe or hammer for fighting on foot. It is now confined to axes of this type only.

Poleyn. A plate defence for the knee.

Pommel. The shaped terminal of the hilt of a sword or dagger, designed to counterbalance the weight of the blade. The term is also applied to the rounded end of a pistol butt.

Pot. A term used in the seventeenth century apparently to designate any type of open

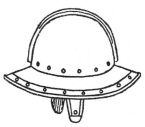

FIG. 22

helmet. Modern writers usually confine it to the large, wide-brimmed variety used by seventeenth-century pikemen (Fig. 22).

Powder-flask. Flask for carrying the black powder used for charging muzzle-loading guns. It was made in a variety of different shapes and materials, and was usually fitted with some kind of measuring device. A smaller flask was often carried for the finer powder used in priming.

Quillon. One of the branches of the cross-guard of a sword.

Quillon dagger. A modern term applied to any dagger with quillons (*q.v.*).

Ramrod. A rod of wood or metal used to force home the charge in a muzzle-loading firearm.

Ramrod pipes or thimbles. The metal tubes on the underside of a muzzle-loading firearm which hold the ramrod.

Rapier. A sword with a long, straight blade, introduced in the sixteenth century. It was at first designed for thrusting and cutting, but as the science of fencing developed emphasis was laid increasingly on the former. It was primarily a civilian weapon, and in the sixteenth and seventeenth centuries was usually used in conjunction with a dagger or a cloak held in the left hand (Plate 2F).

Rerebrace. Plate armour for the shoulder and upper arm. The term was generally replaced by pauldron (*q.v.*) during the first half of the fifteenth century.

Reverse. *See* Obverse.

Revolver. A firearm with a rotatable cylinder containing chambers for the charge that can be brought in turn into the firing position behind a single barrel, or one with a group of rotatable barrels. The term is applied especially to a pistol working on the former system.

Experiments were made with revolving firearms at regular intervals from the second quarter of the sixteenth century onwards. But the first really satisfactory system was that patented in England in 1818 by the American Elisha H. Collier. This was a flint-lock with an automatic priming device and an ingenious mechanism for locking the barrel and the appropriate chamber in the cylinder together at the moment of discharge. Only a small number of Collier's revolvers, both pistols and long-arms, was made, and his invention was not a commercial success. In 1835, however, another American, Samuel Colt, was granted patents in England and France, and in 1836 in the United States, for the percussion revolver that was to be the prototype for all subsequent successful revolvers.

Despite the importance of Colt's invention, he had considerable difficulty in selling it. His first manufacturing plant was established at Paterson, New Jersey, in 1836, and it produced pistols, rifles, carbines, and shotguns, all with revolving cylinders. Orders were slow in coming, however. The venture failed, and the factory was sold. Today the revolvers made at this factory are known as "Colt Patersons" and they are much sought after by collectors.

In 1847 Colt finally succeeded in obtaining a government contract for a thousand of his pistols based on an improved design suggested by Capt. Samuel Walker of the Texas Rangers. With this order Colt was able to resume manufacturing his pistols, and soon his fortunes prospered. The Walker Colts were extremely large guns, $15\frac{1}{2}$ inches long, but poorly made. They saw considerable service in the Army, and those specimens that have survived are considered by modern collectors the most valuable of all standard Colt models.

Following the Walker, the trend was to decrease the size of the revolver and improve its construction. There were three subsequent models for dragoons (Plate 13D) and two pocket pistols before the advent of the so-called 1851 Navy revolver (Plate 15D). This well-balanced .36 calibre arm was the most popular of all Colt percussion-cap military revolvers, and it was widely used by both the Army and Navy as well as by civilians from its first production through the Civil War and as long as percussion-cap revolvers were used. In 1860 Colt also developed a .44 calibre revolver for the Army (Plate 13B) which also was widely used during and after the Civil War. In addition to these principal models, Colt also produced numerous others, both pistols and long guns, to meet almost every possible need. Examples of all models were frequently engraved (Plate 13D) and they had carved grips of bone, ivory, special woods, or even silver, for presentation purposes. Colt himself died in 1862, well before the company he founded reached its greatest peaks of production.

From the late 1840s onwards many revolvers, all more or less based on Colt's invention, were made both in Europe and the United States. Notable among these were the

English Deane-Adams and Webley and the American Remington. *See also* Pepperbox.

Ricasso. A modern term for the oblong, blunt section at the base of some sword and dagger blades.

Rifle. A firearm with a series of spiral grooves down the inside of the barrel designed to make the projectile fly more truly by causing it to rotate on its own axis.

According to an unconfirmed tradition, rifling was invented at the end of the fifteenth century, but it was used rarely, if at all, before the late sixteenth century. From this time onwards many sporting-guns were made with rifled barrels, especially in Germany. During the seventeenth and eighteenth centuries a number of experiments were made with rifled military arms, but the rifle was not widely adopted for service use until well into the nineteenth century.

See also Kentucky rifle.

Rifle-musket. A term used during the nineteenth century to designate a firearm of musket size with a rifled bore.

Rifling. The grooves cut into the sides of the bore of a firearm which impart the spin to the projectile. Also the act of cutting these grooves.

Rondel dagger. A form of dagger used from the fourteenth to the early sixteenth century with a disc-shaped guard. Most examples have a pommel of similar form to the guard.

Sabaton. A laminated plate defence for the foot.

Sabre. A sword with a single edge designed primarily for cutting. Usually there is also a short edge along the back near the point which is termed the false edge. Some sabre blades are sharply curved and some are only slightly curved or absolutely straight. These straight or only slightly curved blades are frequently called cut-and-thrust blades.

Sallet. The characteristic helmet of the fifteenth century, usually worn with a deep chin-piece (bevor). Its form generally followed that of the modern sou'wester, although it comes well down over the face, either having a movable visor, or a vision slit in its forward edge. The German type usually has a long, graceful, pointed tail, often laminated. The

barbute (*q.v.*) is regarded as one of the forms of this helmet (Plate IA).

Schiavona. A basket-hilted sword with a straight, two-edged blade, used during the seventeenth and eighteenth centuries by the

FIG. 23

Dalmatian troops (stradiots) in the employ of Venice. It is often erroneously described as the prototype of the Scottish basket-hilted broadsword (Fig. 23).

Screw plate. An elongated plate opposite the lock of a firearm which acts as a washer for the screws holding the lock in position. Sometimes also called the side plate, key plate, or nail plate.

Shield. Probably the earliest form of defensive arm. Shields have been used from prehistoric times, and made of a variety of materials, including wood, leather, wicker-work, metal, etc. They were usually attached to the left arm by straps (*enarmes*) or, when not in use, hung round the neck on a sling (*guige*). The earliest shields seem to have been mainly circular, oval, or rectangular, but in the eleventh century the tall kite-shape appears, remaining in use until the thirteenth century, when the "flat-iron" (heater) form was introduced. This survived until well into the fifteenth century, when a large variety of shapes appeared, many of which had a notch (*bouche*) cut in the upper edge for the lance. In the sixteenth century the majority of shields were circular, one of the most popular types being the buckler (introduced as early as the thirteenth century), which was held in the left hand by means of a crossbar on the inside. Shields have at all times been the subject of adornment, particularly with the owner's coat-of-arms or personal device after the introduction of heraldry in the twelfth century. Many of those made for parade purposes in the sixteenth century were of metal elaborately embossed or etched and gilt (Plate 3F).

Short arms. A classification name often applied to pistols of all kinds.

Side plate. *See* Screw plate.

Skean Dhu. The small knife worn in the stocking with Highland Scottish dress. It appears to have been first introduced in the early nineteenth century.

Small arms. A military term applying to all arms carried on the person and designed to be fired without a support.

Smallsword. A light civilian sword with a simple hilt, often richly decorated, which succeeded the rapier (*q.v.*) in the third quarter

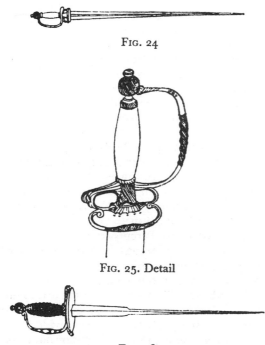

FIG. 24

FIG. 25. Detail

FIG. 26

of the seventeenth century, with the beginnings of fencing as it is known today. The slender blade, although designed principally for thrusting, was at first double-edged, but from *c.* 1700 one of hollow triangular section became almost universal. The eighteenth-century French term colichemarde (Fig. 26)

often used by collectors, designates a blade which is wide near the hilt and narrows suddenly half-way along. The smallsword remained in active use until the end of the eighteenth century, and still survives in the sword worn with modern court dress (Plate 2B).

Smoothbore. Any firearm without rifling.

Snaphance. A type of gun-lock first recorded in the middle of the sixteenth century. It is fitted with a pan (*q.v.*) with a flat steel (*q.v.*) pivoted above it. When the gun is discharged a specially shaped flint, held in the jaws of a spring-operated cock, strikes the steel, throwing it back and at the same time sending a shower of sparks into the priming. On the earliest form of the lock the pan was fitted with a separate cover that had to be opened manually immediately before firing, but this was soon replaced by a cover that opened automatically as the cock fell. The early lock also had a horizontal sear, the tip of which projected through the lock-plate and engaged with a projection on the heel of the cock, holding the latter back until released by the trigger.

Modern writers usually confine the term

FIG. 27

snaphance to the form of lock with a separate steel and pan-cover, and flint-lock (*q.v.*) to the form on which these features are combined. In fact, the first term was applied indiscriminately to both constructions until the second half of the seventeenth century when it went out of use. Other than in certain parts of Italy, where it survived until the early nineteenth century, the snaphance was generally superseded by the flint-lock in the second quarter of the seventeenth century.

Spontoon. A miniature partizan (*q.v.*) carried by infantry officers from the seventeenth to the late eighteenth century.

Spurs. Early spurs were of the prick type,

with a single spike, usually pyramidal or cone-shaped and often mounted on a ball to prevent deep penetration. There is some evidence for the introduction of the rowel spur, with a wheel equipped with points instead of the single spike, in the middle of the thirteenth century, but it did not become common until the second quarter of the fourteenth. In the second half of the fifteenth century spurs had straight necks of great length, while those of the seventeenth had their necks bent down almost at right-angles.

Steel. That portion of a flint-lock or snaphance (*qq.v.*) that serves as a steel for the flint to strike against and so produce sparks. It is sometimes called the battery or frizzen, the latter term being a modern corruption of the dialect word frizzle. During the eighteenth and nineteeth centuries it was also known as the hammer.

Stiletto. A form of quillon dagger (*q.v.*), introduced in the sixteenth century, with a stiff, narrow blade designed for stabbing only. The gunner's stiletto has a scale on the blade for converting weight of gun-shot into diameter of bore.

Stirrup guard. A form of knuckle-bow which resembles half of a stirrup.

Stock. The wood or metal structure of a firearm used to hold the barrel and lock together in proper position and to provide a suitable means of holding the arm.

Swept hilt. A modern term for the type of rapier hilt, introduced in the sixteenth century, in which the guard consists of a complicated series of curved bars (Plate 2E).

Swivel-gun. A heavy military firearm shaped like a normal rifle or musket but de-

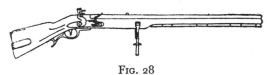

Fig. 28

signed to be fired from a swivel mount. Such guns were popular from the seventeenth through the early nineteenth century (Fig. 28).

Tace. A form of tasset (*q.v.*). Incorrectly used by nineteenth-century writers as a synonym for fauld.

Tang. (i) The narrow portion of the blade which passes into the hilt; (ii) *see* Barrel tang.

Tapul. A rare sixteenth-century term of uncertain meaning connected with armour. Incorrectly used by nineteenth-century writers to denote a projecting central ridge to a breastplate.

Tasset. One of a pair of defences for the upper thighs which hung from the fauld. Tassets appeared in the second quarter of the fifteenth century, when they were usually pointed and made of a single plate. From the beginning of the sixteenth century they were normally rounded or straight at the bottom and made of a number of horizontal lames. From the second quarter of the sixteenth century light-horsemen's armours were sometimes fitted with knee-length tassets in place of cuisses. This form became usual after *c.* 1600.

Three-quarter armour. An armour extending to the knees only.

Touch-hole. A small hole or channel used to convey the sparks from the priming charge outside the barrel of a firearm to the propelling charge inside the barrel.

Trigger. The lever which activates the lock mechanism of a firearm and sets off the discharge.

Tschinke. A light wheel-lock gun, generally rifled, used for bird-shooting in the area of Germanic culture during the seventeenth century. The butt usually takes a sharp downward curve while the lock has an external mainspring (Plate 12C).

Tube-lock. *See* Percussion lock.

Tuile. A nineteenth-century term, no longer used by the enlightened, for the early one-piece pointed tasset (*q.v.*).

Vambrace. Plate armour for the arm from below the shoulder to the wrist, and including the couter (*q.v.*). Modern writers divide it for convenience into the upper cannon and the lower cannon, above and below the couter respectively.

Vamplate. *See* Lance.

Vouge. Probably originally the French equivalent of the English bill (*q.v.*). Used by modern writers to denote a staff-weapon with a cleaver-like pointed blade attached by two rings to the haft.

Walker Colts. *See* Revolver.

War-hammer. A short staff-weapon, used by horsemen, with a hammer head balanced by a pointed fluke.

Wheel-lock. Mechanism for igniting a firearm, in which a piece of pyrites, held in the jaws of a cock, is pressed against the grooved edge of a wheel projecting through the bottom of the pan (*q.v.*). The wheel is made to rotate by a spring, released by the trigger, so striking a shower of sparks from the pyrites and igniting the priming-powder. The lock is usually wound by means of a spanner, but on rare examples this is effected automatically when the cock is drawn back.

The earliest known illustration of a wheel-lock occurs in the *Codex Atlanticus* of Leonardo da Vinci (d. 1519), who has a very strong claim to being regarded as the inventor of the system. It was probably being made in Italy as early as 1510, but the earliest definite record of its existence comes from a German source of 1515. In 1517 and 1518 the Emperor Maximilian banned the use and manufacture of the lock in his territories, which probably accounts for the fact that the vast majority of surviving examples date from after the second decade of the sixteenth century. Wheel-locks are rarely found on military weapons, probably because they were expensive to make, but were much used on sporting and target guns, especially in Germany, until well into the eighteenth century.

Wrist. The slender portion of the butt stock of a firearm immediately behind the lock.

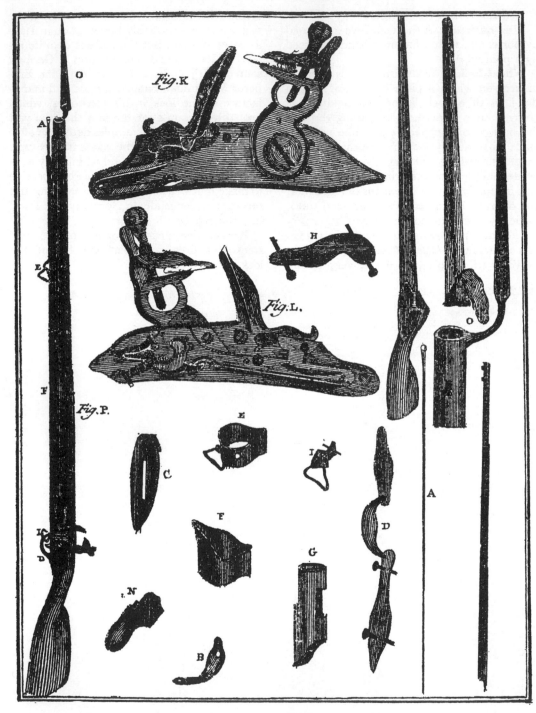

Fabrique des Armes, *Fusil de Munition.*

BAROMETERS, CLOCKS, AND WATCHES

There would seem to be little connexion between barometers, which are dependent for their functioning on a natural phenomenon, and clocks and watches, which are actuated by man-designed mechanical means, but in England the earliest barometers were made by clockmakers.

Italy and France in the mid-seventeenth century saw the inception and proof of the idea that the weight of air varies. When this principle was brought to England, London became the first centre of production for barometers. The names of Tompion, Quare, Graham, Ellicott may be mentioned as well as those of John Patrick and Francis Hawksbee (the inventor of the vacuum pump), who were instrument makers. Later provincial production appeared, mainly anonymous and following current furniture design. Charles Orme of Ashby-de-la-Zouch and John Whitehust of Derby were among the most outstanding in this field. In the United States barometers were mainly imported.

The field of clocks is a much older and wider one, and we have records of weight-driven turret clocks in England at the end of the thirteenth century, as well as on the Continent. We do not know whether the clocks in England were made by an Englishman or by a Continental visitor.

From this period there was steady progress on the Continent, with the invention of the spring drive in the middle of the fifteenth century and the personal clock, or watch, in the last quarter of that century. Production in England reappeared only towards the end of the sixteenth century, and from then onwards it was centred in London. The craft gradually extended over the whole country during the eighteenth century, but relatively few makers achieved renown, and they were not grouped in any locality.

In the United States the chief centres of production were in the Eastern Atlantic states – Connecticut, Massachusetts, New Hampshire, and Rhode Island – but some earlier clocks had come from Philadelphia.

Barometers

The word barometer derives from the Greek root *baros*, meaning weight. Thus, we have an instrument for measuring the weight of the atmosphere.

C*

Scientists in the first half of the nineteenth century had noticed that water could not be raised above about 33 feet with a single-stage suction pump. The French philosopher Réné Descartes (1596–1650) had rejected the idea of the existence of a vacuum, and so had undermined the idea that Nature's abhorrence of a vacuum was the explanation of the action of water-pumps, thus leading the way to the correct explanation – that is, pressure resulting from the weight of the atmosphere. He claimed to have anticipated Torricelli, an Italian, who conceived the idea of experimenting with mercury, because of its much greater density, and in 1643 found that the atmosphere would support a column of about 30 inches of mercury; but he did not appreciate that the height of the column varied with the state of the atmosphere. That the atmosphere has weight was shown by Galileo, who, in his book *Two New Sciences* (1638), estimated that the weight of the air was about one four-hundredth of that of the same volume of water. Torricelli was acquainted with Galileo and succeeded him as Grand Ducal mathematician on Galileo's death in 1642.

Descartes also claimed that in 1647 he had suggested to Blaise Pascal (1623–62) the idea of experimenting with a mercury column at the bottom and top of a tower. This experiment Pascal carried out on the tower of the church of St Jacques in Paris, and established the fact that the height of the mercury column was greater at the bottom of the tower than at the top, thus demonstrating that the weight of the atmosphere varied with height.

On September 19, 1646, under Pascal's direction, his brother-in-law, Florin Perier, carried out the historic full-scale experiment on Puy-de-Dôme in Auvergne.

At a meeting of the Royal Society on December 6, 1677, Dr Robert Hooke (1635–1703), that great seventeenth-century genius, affirmed that he had "for these 15 or 16 years constantly observed the Barascope and that he had always found that in the said instrument the ☿ [☿ is the symbol for mercury] was always very exceeding low and fell to that stacion very suddenly whensoever any considerable Storme of Wind and Raine had happened in that time. . . ." And on December 12, 1695 Dr Hooke read "an account of the several Barometers he had invented. That he was the first that had observed the changes of the height of the Mercury to answer the changes of the Weather." From this we gather that Hooke was actively noting the connexion between the barometer level and the weather since about 1661.

At this date there was no recognized scale, and Hooke probably used a scale of his own contrivance. Fahrenheit was the first to devise a scale with fixed points. His first scale was divided between 90 and −90. An example of this is seen in Plate 18c, where the zero point occurs in the middle of the scale and is designated "Temperate". The earliest date for this scale, as we know it today, is given as 1717.

Plate 17A shows a reproduction of the "Torricellian Experiment" as demonstrated in the Science Museum, London. The tubes are inverted and filled with mercury. A finger is then placed over the open end and removed when this is below the level of the mercury in the cistern. The mercury in the tube then runs out until the column remaining represents the height of mercury that the atmosphere can support at that moment. Torricelli thought that if there were any force due to the vacuum it would be greater in the larger vacuum. But as the two columns are of equal height, it shows the force to be wholly external and equal.

This simple device, by which changes of atmospheric pressure on the surface of the cistern are reflected in the height of the column in the tube, is that adopted by the earliest barometer makers. Later the siphon barometer was invented. In this type the tube for the mercury column turns up at the bottom to form a J, the short end being left open to the atmosphere (*see* Plates 17c and 18c). Both systems were employed side by side for a hundred years or more, the cistern being more common in England and the siphon on the Continent.

On December 30, 1663, the Journal of the Royal Society records that Dr Hooke produced "a little engine to make the ascent and descent of Quicksilver in glasse-canes more discernible. It was ordered to prepare against the next Meeting a tube with Mercury and fit the Instrument to it."

Hooke's original sketch, from the records of the Royal Society, is seen in Plate 17B. A small compensated weight floats on the surface of the mercury in the shorter arm, which is open to the air. To the weight is attached a silken thread carrying at the other end the compensating weight, the silken thread being wound round the arbor, or shaft, of the indicating hand. Thus, any movement of the surface of the mercury is transmitted to the arbor of the indicator and magnified to any desired extent by regulating the length of the indicating hand.

This remained one of the principal types of barometer until the coming of the aneroid barometer towards the middle of the nineteenth century. Early wheel barometers with finely designed cases were made in the latter years of the seventeenth century by Tompion, Quare, and other leading clockmakers of that time. But since these are very rare, and nearly all are already held in royal or museum collections, none is illustrated here.

Plate 19B and C shows a pleasing wheel barometer of the mid-eighteenth century and its construction. At the top is a hygrometer. The small ivory setting knob for the barometer can be withdrawn and used to set the hygrometer, for which gut is now used instead of the beard of a wild oat or the cod of a vetch, as recommended by Hooke in 1666. At the bottom is a spirit-level to check that the barometer hangs truly vertical, and, as is the case with most barometers, a thermometer is provided. For really accurate observations, allowance has to be made for the effects of temperature on the height of the mercury column.

One of the various ways of extending the reading scale of the barometer suggested by Hooke may have been the diagonal barometer, sometimes known as the sign-post or yard-arm type. The maximum variation of the mercury at ground level is about 3 inches, and all the variations in the ordinary vertical tube have to be registered within these limits.

A very interesting and early example of the diagonal barometer is seen in Plate 17 (c and D). The printed back-paper gives John Boll as the maker and the year as 1666. The construc-

tion is quite simple: three siphon barometers are used, each having a vertical tube about 1 inch longer than that preceding and having a rise of about 1 inch in about 20 inches of inclined arm. Thus, these three tubes of 28, 29, and 30 inches in length start recording only when the mercury reaches the height at which their respective bends are situated. The maximum anticipated variation of about 3 inches in this country is spread over 60 inches of tube, thus giving a spread of 1 inch for each twentieth part of an inch variation in the height of the mercury column.

The early barometers were not portable, and an early attempt to remedy this is recorded in the Royal Society's Journal, May 28, 1668, when "Mr Boyle brought in his Travelling or Portable Barascope, devised by himself to compare, by the help thereof the weight of the Atmosphere at the same time, not only in differing parts of the same country, but in differing Regions of the World: which is thus contrived, that the vessel containing both the sustained and stagnant Mercury is all of one piece of glasse of like bigness . . ."

Just what this means is not clear, but it seems to be a siphon in which the return part is of the same diameter as the main tube.

Hooke's wheel barometer was not altogether successful. It is reported that it was liable to be jerky in movement and not easy to adjust. On February 3, 1685, he produced a tube in which a column of lighter spirits of wine was supported by a column of mercury. The tube was so long as to be unwieldy, but the idea developed into the double barometer, which is seen in Plate 18A. The top of the left-hand tube is evacuated as the pressure falls, and the mercury in this tube falls and the spirit in the right-hand tube rises over the extended scale for the oil. Low readings are therefore at the top. In this example, of c. 1750, it will be noticed that the thermometer carries the Fahrenheit scale.

Hooke made a careful study of the relationship between atmospheric pressure and storms and in Vol. II of the Royal Society's Journal on December 6, 1677 he reported that "whenever the said ☿ was observed to fall suddenly very low, it had alwaies been a forerunner of a very great Storme to follow, sometimes within

12 houres and therefore he hoped that his Instrument might be of very good use at sea in
order to the foreshowing of an ensuing
Storme". On January 2, 1677/8, he pursues
the idea, and, after dealing with the difficulties of using a wheel barometer at sea, he
suggests "as a better alternative, a Weather
Glasse made with pure Air and Quicksilver,
which latter is left open to the Pressure of the
Air and so becomes agitated by a double principle of Motion, i.e. by Heat and Air Pressure . . ." To ascertain the changes due to
heat, he provides a sealed thermometer with
spirits of wine and graduates the two together
in an oven. A table of differences is established, so that the resultant differences should be
that due to air pressure.

This idea of Hooke, thrown out in 1667/8,
seems, like so many of his ideas, to have lain
dormant for many years. He returns to the
question of a marine barometer in December
1694. At a meeting on the 5th of that month
he was authorized to spend forty shillings on
an example of his marine barometer. At a
meeting on November 13, 1695, this instrument was presented and was ordered to be
hung in the Meeting Room. What is possibly
this instrument is seen in Plate 18B. The
thermometer with spirits of wine is on the
right and that with mercury on the left.

In principle this idea is the air-thermoscope
or weather-glass, invented at the end of the
sixteenth or the beginning of the seventeenth
century, later forming the basis of the Sym-
piesometer, patented by Adie in 1818. A more
simple type of marine barometer was developed (see Glossary and Plate 20A).

In the meantime, in spite of Robert Boyle's
idea in 1668, barometers were not portable.
The Minute Book of the Royal Society for

January 16, 1694/5, however, records: "Mr
Daniel Quare, Watchmaker, produced his
Barometer so contrived as to be Portable, and
even Inverted without spilling of the Quicksilver, or letting in any Air or excluding the
pressure of the Atmosphere, which the Society
were pleased to Declare, That it was the first
of that sort they had seen. Mr Quare desired
to be excused from Discovering the Secret
thereof."

Quare's secret was the use of a plug at the
end of a screwed thread, which could be used
to seal off the bottom of the tube under the
mercury. An example of such a Quare barometer and its sealing screw is seen in Plate
17E and F.

The first self-recording barograph was
made in 1765 for King George III by Alexander Cumming and is now in Buckingham
Palace. A second, made by Cumming for his
own use in 1766, is now in the possession of
Mr Geoffrey Howard. A pointer is carried
by a ring floating on the surface of the mercury and, rising and falling with this, traces a
continuous line on the outer dial, which is
fitted with a graduated vellum disc and revolves once a year.

By the end of the seventeenth century practically all the problems had been solved.

Once established, the barometer was of
easy construction. After the early years of the
eighteenth century, with the possible exception of Patrick, there are no great names of
barometer makers. One finds good and bad
examples in both London and provincial productions.

*The sketch of Hooke's Wheel Barometer and the
quotations from the Royal Society's Journal and
Minute Books are given by permission of that Society.*

Clocks and Watches

AMERICAN

The production of American timepieces in
any quantity extends back little more than
two hundred years, as compared to more than
three times that in Europe.

CLOCKS

It is now impossible to say positively who was the first clockmaker in America. In 1638 Thomas Nash was one of the early settlers of New Haven, Connecticut. That Nash was a clockmaker is indicated by the inventory of his estate in 1658. Among his tools is listed: "one round plate for making clocks".

It is well established from inventories of their estates that many of the wealthier early colonists had clocks. It may be assumed that most of these had been brought over as original household equipment or had been imported later. In addition, some of the larger towns had one or more public clocks quite early; Boston had a tower clock in 1657. Undoubtedly the oldest American-made tower clock now in existence is one in Guilford, Connecticut, which was installed in the meeting-house there in 1726 by Ebenezer Parmele.

There are other men of whom some scant records exist of clockmaking activities before 1700. But for two or three exceptions, no clocks by these early makers are known to be in existance today.

From about 1715 there were a number of clockmakers to whom existing clocks can certainly be attributed. Benjamin Chandlee, who was the first of a large family of clockmakers, came from Ireland to Philadelphia in 1702 and was apprenticed to Abel Cottey, the first established clockmaker of Philadelphia. Peter Stretch, who was born in England and there learned his trade under English masters, came to Philadelphia in 1702 and became a community leader as well as a prosperous clockmaker. Benjamin Bagnall from England appeared in Boston as a clockmaker about 1710. William Claggett, born in Wales, about 1715. He went later to Newport, Rhode Island. Slightly later than these were Gawen Brown, who came to Boston some time before 1750; and David Blaisdell, one of a family of clockmakers, who was in Amesbury, Massachusetts, by 1740.

By 1750 a number of skilled clockmakers were at work in Philadelphia and surrounding areas. The most famous of the Philadelphia group was David Rittenhouse (at work c. 1750–90), scientist, mathematician, astronomer, and a President (1791) of the American Philosophical Society. A large grandfather clock by Rittenhouse, now in the Drexel Institute of Technology, Philadelphia, is a superb example of the finest in American clocks.

The clocks made by the eighteenth-century clockmakers were mostly of the grandfather type. Each clock was individually made by hand and fitted to the case, which had also been made in the same shop or by a local cabinet-maker. It was not until towards the end of the century that clockmakers were making unordered clocks in quantity. These early tall clocks usually had brass eight-day movements, although a few thirty-hour movements are found. The dials were usually of brass with cast brass spandrels. A few small and simple hang-up, or wag-on-the-wall, clocks were made for the less wealthy customers or by less skilled craftsmen. Members of the Blaisdell family of Massachusetts made a number of such quaint little clocks, examples of which may be rarely found.

From 1750 to 1800 clocks, principally tall or grandfather, were made in increasing numbers. About the middle of the eighteenth century a few clockmakers in Connecticut were making innovations. The most revolutionary of these new ideas was the use of wood in movements to replace brass, which was both expensive and difficult to obtain.

Benjamin Cheney, together with his younger brother Timothy of East Hartford, Connecticut, is usually credited with making, about 1745, the earliest of the existing Connecticut wooden movements.

These early Connecticut wooden clocks were clumsy, thirty-hour grandfather clocks which were wound by pulling down on cords. They usually had brass dials, or brass-covered wood dials and were often in attractive cases. Although crudely made, they were satisfactory timekeepers and were inexpensive. These earliest wooden clocks by the Cheneys, Gideon Roberts, John Rich, and others of Connecticut are now rare and keenly sought by collectors.

The influence of these craftsmen of central Connecticut spread to Massachusetts. Benjamin Willard was born in 1743 in Grafton,

Massachusetts. About 1760 he went to East Hartford as an apprentice of Benjamin Cheney. After completing his apprenticeship he returned to Grafton and opened (c. 1765) a clock-shop at the old family home. His three younger brothers, Simon, Ephraim, and Aaron, also became noted clockmakers. From Grafton the four brothers moved to Roxbury, Lexington, and Boston and independently established profitable clockmaking businesses. From these Willard brothers, there developed an extensive clockmaking industry in eastern Massachusetts, southern New Hampshire, and Rhode Island. Clockmakers of this "Willard" or "Boston" school made clocks of many types of the highest quality. Little attempt was made to produce an inexpensive clock, as was the trend in Connecticut. No wooden movements were produced by any of these men.

Simon Willard is the most famous of the four brothers on account of his patented (1802) timepiece, which is now known as the banjo clock. He worked first at Grafton (1774–80), and from 1780 to 1839 in Roxbury. Among his many apprentices who became prominent clockmakers were Abel and Levi Hutchins, Elnathan Taber (Plate 25A), and Daniel Munroe, besides his sons, Simon, Jr., and Benjamin.

Aaron Willard produced large quantities of clocks and is particularly noted for developing the Massachusetts shelf clock. He opened a shop near Simon's in Roxbury about 1780 and later moved to Boston, where he established a small factory. He was succeeded by his sons, Aaron, Jr., and Henry. Aaron, Jr., is often credited with originating the lyre clock (Plate 24E, F).

Two other clockmakers at work in Connecticut during the last part of the eighteenth century deserve special notice, particularly because of their influence on the beginnings of clockmaking as a great industry. Thomas Harland, a skilled clockmaker from England, settled in Norwich in 1773. Daniel Burnap, the most noted of Harland's apprentices, opened his own shop in East Windsor about 1780, and ultimately surpassed his master as a craftsman. Clocks by either of these makers are rare and choice. Soon after Burnap open-

ed his shop at East Windsor he took as an apprentice Eli Terry, born in 1772. After completing his apprenticeship, Eli Terry opened his own shop in 1793, in Plymouth, Connecticut. The first clocks that Terry made were brass movements for tall clocks. However, he soon turned his attention to producing wooden clocks. About 1803 Terry began to use water power to turn his machines. In 1806 he accepted an order for four thousand clocks. To meet the demands for such numbers he devised standardized or interchangeable parts. He now made large numbers of identical parts which went to an assembly line where the complete clocks were put together, the first application of the modern manufacturing methods to clock production.

These early wooden clocks of Eli Terry were thirty-hour movements intended for grandfather cases. In most instances they were sold without cases and the buyer had a case made to his own specification, or the movement could be used as a wag-on-the-wall. Many others began to copy Terry's methods and by 1815 the making of wooden clocks was an important industry. Clocks of this period with no indication of the maker are not especially valuable.

Eli Terry invented a shelf clock about 1814. He produced some seven or more known models, culminating about 1818 with a design which was made in large numbers by Terry and his sons and was extensively copied (Plate 23A, B) until about 1840, when the introduction of an inexpensive brass movement brought all production of wood movements to an end. Probably in 1817 the first pillar and scroll was produced. Some of these first models are recognized by having the escape wheel and pendulum in front of the dial (Plate 26A). All of these early models are very rare.

Being cheaper and more portable than a tall clock, the new wood-movement shelf clock soon became popular, and the production of tall clock movements ceased about 1825. By 1830 wooden shelf clock cases had been simplified by Chauncey Jerome and others to a much plainer form. To compete with the eight-day brass clocks being made by the Massachusetts clockmakers certain Connecticut makers were producing a few shelf clocks with eight-day brass movements.

In 1838 Noble Jerome, at the suggestion of his brother, Chauncey, devised a simple thirty-hour weight movement of rolled brass. This type of clock almost immediately forced all wooden clocks out of production, for it was cheaper and better in every way. No wood-movement clocks were in commercial production after about 1842. The simple ogee case, which had occasionally been used with wooden movements before 1838, now became the predominant style (Plate 23D). It was now found profitable to export large numbers of these cheap clocks to England and other countries.

Factory-produced inexpensive steel springs first became available in this country soon after 1840. The use of coiled springs for power made it possible to design smaller cases. Small clocks of many types began to appear before 1850 and were produced in increasing numbers (Plate 22A, D). This period of mass production of inexpensive clocks yielded very few items which may now be considered desirable from the collector's standpoint.

Few antique clocks can now be found which do not need some restoration. The restoration of such damage to fine clocks should be entrusted only to qualified craftsmen.

A signed clock usually commands a higher price than a similar one not signed, and one signed by a famous maker even higher. There are many fine unsigned clocks available which in beauty and mechanical quality are equal to any by famous makers, and which may be acquired at much lower prices.

WATCHES

The watch collector must be a true specialist; he must be informed on the complex history of American watchmaking; he must also be familiar with the fine mechanical characteristics of the many types of watches. Within the field of watch collecting an even narrower specialization will probably be made by the serious collector. He may try to collect watches by early makers, watches by extinct companies, or mechanically unusual ones. He will need to examine carefully every old watch to make sure that no important example is over-looked. American-made watches dating before 1800 are practically non-existent, and those before 1850 are rare. All of these old watches are key-winders and are usually of large size.

Many of the early American clockmakers also advertised as watchmakers. The few watches which they produced were entirely hand-made. Most examples of watches made before 1815 and signed with American names are so similar to contemporary English pieces that it is generally assumed that they were English imports or assembled from imported parts (Plate 21B). They are all very rare.

It is impossible to say who made the first complete American watch. In 1809 Luther Goddard opened a small shop in Shrewsbury, Massachusetts, for the production of watches. It is not certain what proportion of the watch was imported and what was locally made. However, Goddard is usually credited with the first manufacture of watches in quantity in America. By 1817, when production ceased, about five hundred watches had been made.

Probably the first manufacture of an all-American watch was begun in Hartford, Connecticut, in 1837 by the brothers, Henry and James Pitkin. The Pitkins had also designed and made the crude machinery with which the watches were manufactured. Owing partly to competition from the lower-priced Swiss watches, the company ceased operations about 1845, when fewer than a thousand watches had been produced.

In 1843 Jacob Custer of Norristown, Pennsylvania, was granted a patent for watches. Custer and other craftsmen, about the middle of the nineteenth century, constructed a few watches of their own design. These watches often have unusual features and are extremely rare.

The modern American methods of watch manufacturing had their origin in the shop of Edward Howard (a clockmaker) and Aaron Dennison of Boston about 1850. From this small beginning grew the great Waltham Watch Company. The first model, an eight-day watch, was produced in 1850 (Plate 21D). For making watch parts, Howard and

Dennison invented machines which, with only minor changes, are used in modern watch factories. In 1885 the company became the American Waltham Watch Co., which produced some of the finest watches ever made (Plate 21E).

In 1864 Don J. Mozart was making, in Providence, Rhode Island, a very unusual watch with what he called a "Chronometer lever escapement". In 1867 with others he formed the New York Watch Co. (Plate 21C), which in 1877 became the Hampden Watch Co., later moving to Canton, Ohio, as the Dueber-Hampden Watch Co. The early watches by Mozart are very rare.

The inexpensive ("Dollar") watch of 1890–1920 had its beginning with the invention in 1877 by D. A. A. Buck in Worcester, Massa-

chusetts, of a watch which could sell for four dollars. These were first manufactured in Connecticut by Benedict & Burnham, which later became The Waterbury Watch Co. Inexpensive watches were also later made by the Ingersoll Co., New Haven Watch Co., and others.

A great many mechanical innovations in watch movements have been designed by American makers. In the design of escapements used there is great variation.

It has been the usual custom for watchmakers and watch companies to sign and number watch movements. From these numbers the age of the watch can be ascertained. *The Book of American Clocks* lists by years the serial numbers used by some of the American watchmakers.

BRITISH

When clocks as we know them today, i.e. a series of wheels and pinions geared together with a weight as a motive force, first came into use is a matter of conjecture. The only early records are monastic manuscripts, and these use the term "horologium" indiscriminately, whether referring to a sundial, a water clock, or a mechanical clock.

A water clock is usually a device whereby the recording of time was effected by the constant inflow or outflow of a regulated stream of water. There has recently come to light an eleventh-century Chinese manuscript describing a clock, which, although actuated by a constant stream of water, caused a step-by-step indication of the time in which may be discerned the germ of the escapement as we know it today.

In Europe there are certain rough guides. Dante describes the motion of a clock in his *Paradiso* of 1321, and we have definite written evidence of a very elaborate astronomical clock being in existence in Strasbourg about 1350. In 1344 Jacopo Dondi of Padua, Italy, constructed a clock of which details are not known, but which was sufficiently outstanding for its time to earn for him the title of Del' Orologio (of the clock), a title still carried by his descendants today. In 1364 his son,

Giovanni, completed his astronomical clock, which showed the movements of the sun, moon, and five planets as well as the nodes. His drawing of this clock is the oldest known depiction of a mechanical clock.[1] If by the middle of the fourteenth century there were men capable of making very complicated astronomical clocks, we can assume that the earliest and simplest mechanical clock, with weight and foliot, was evolved a good deal earlier. A date of 1280–1300 is assumed. At all events, the unknown inventor or inventors of the verge escapement with foliot and the locking-plate striking arrangement, with its fan, or air brake, were geniuses; they had nothing earlier to guide them.

In England there has been discovered lately documentary evidence of three turret clocks being made for King Edward III in the years 1365–70. Unfortunately only the names of the clock-keepers are given and not those of the makers. The oldest surviving mechanical clock in the world is that made for Salisbury Cathedral, and it is now there in its restored state; the second oldest is that which was made for Wells Cathedral, in Somerset in

[1] This clock has been reconstructed and can be seen in the Smithsonian Institution in Washington D.C.

1392; now in the Science Museum, London. From the maker's marks it is thought that both were made by the same hand.

The weight-driven clock is not portable, but the use of a coiled spring as a driving force made this practical. There is a spring-driven clock in the background of the portrait of a Burgundian nobleman of date about 1450, and King Charles VII of France bought a clock *sans contrepois*, that is without weights, in 1459. Spring-driven clocks so small that they could be carried on the person are first heard of in Italy about 1485; there were both time-pieces and striking movements.

The unequal force of an uncoiling spring was corrected by the introduction of the fusee, possibly in Italy or Flanders. This invention has now been ante-dated to about 1445–50; a manuscript has been found, now in the Royal Library in Brussels, which shows several clocks, one of which is a table clock fitted with a fusee. Previously Jacob the Zech was credited with the invention of the fusee on the basis of his clock dated 1525, now with the Society of Antiquaries in London.

The attribution of the invention of the portable timepiece or watch to Peter Henlein of Nuremberg is now seen to be wrong, although there is no doubt he did much to popularize it by producing a great many of them.

The South German method of equalization of power was the stackfreed, and since this is much less efficient and was later universally replaced by the fusee, it seems likely that the two systems were developed independently and more or less concurrently; both localities were the cradles of early clockmaking.

It has heretofore been assumed that the foliot preceded the balance wheel, but Dondi's drawing of his clock, already referred to, shows a balance wheel, so that it is probable that the two progressed simultaneously. Neither has much advantage over the other as regards efficient timekeeping; both are very poor.

For the years between the fourteenth century and the late sixteenth century there are no records of clockmaking in England. Such examples as survive are mainly the work of foreign refugees in London, such as Nicholas Vallin, a Fleming, Nicholas Urseau or Or-

seau, who, possibly, made the Windsor Castle clock. Towards the end of the seventeenth century English and Scottish names, such as David Ramsay, Randolf Bull, Michael Nowen, and Richard Grinkin, appear, and in 1632 the Clockmakers of London were granted their Charter. From this period onwards English clocks and watches took their place in the world's production, and for one hundred and fifty years remained supreme.

One of the original Members of the Court of Assistants, under the Mastership of David Ramsay, was Edward East, who died in 1695 aged ninety-three. His work is distinguished by a great simplicity combined with good proportions. He was Clockmaker to both King Charles I and King Charles II.

In 1657 came the momentous discovery of the pendulum by Christiaan Huygens. Galileo had earlier perceived the principle of the pendulum, but there is no evidence to show that he developed it other than as an accurate recorder of oscillations to be counted by an observer. Huygens's work can be described as independent, and certainly he was the first to apply the pendulum to clocks.

The vastly improved timekeeping of pendulum clocks, even with the verge escapement, over foliot and balance, was due to the fact that the pendulum was the controller of the driving force, whereas formerly the driving force controlled the clock. Most clocks were converted to this new method of timekeeping, and it is very rare today to find a clock with its original foliot or balance.

Only thirteen years later came the revolutionary invention of the anchor escapement by William Clement. This largely abolished circular error and made time-keeping sufficiently accurate for use in astronomical observations.

The brothers Joseph and John Knibb of London and Oxford are noted for their fine productions of both long-case and bracket clocks. Joseph Knibb introduced what is known as "Roman Striking", the blows up to four being struck on one bell and the five, either alone or in conjunction with a one, being indicated by a single stroke on a different-toned bell. Joseph also introduced the skeleton dial, in which the whole of the chapter

ring is cut away except where actually engraved. This was doubly expensive, as it also
involved a matted dial of about twice the
normal area.

In 1675 Christiaan Huygens introduced the
spiral balance spring for watches. This did for
the watch what the pendulum had done for
clocks in the matter of improved time-keeping. Robert Hooke claimed priority, and
there are grounds for his support, but he did
not make any public claim until after Huygens had published his invention, when he
charged him with plagiarism. The truth is
that both men probably worked independently.

We are now entering the age of the "Great
Ones" of English Horology. Thomas Tompion is justly famed as the chief contributor to
England's supremacy in clockmaking at this
time. Tompion's main contribution to clockmaking was his genius in designing complicated movements and the meticulous finish to
all his work. Later George Graham and John
Harrison made further improvements to timekeeping, as opposed to clockmaking, which
kept England in the lead for the whole of the
eighteenth century.

George Graham's deadbeat escapement,
about 1715, held the field for astronomical
observations for over two hundred years.
Graham's mercury pendulum is still in use today, as is John Harrison's gridiron pendulum,
although recent researches tend to show that
this invention should rather be credited to his
younger brother, James. Graham's cylinder
escapement for watches, about 1725, put his
work in the lead for eighty years or so, until
the lever escapement, invented about 1759 by
Thomas Mudge, became more generally adopted in the early part of the nineteenth century.

John Harrison's name is always associated
with the winning of the prize of £20,000 for
the solution of the problem of "the Longitude", i.e. making a timepiece sufficiently accurate to enable mariners to ascertain their
longitude when at sea. Harrison's efforts,
starting with long-case clocks made entirely of
wood (he was a carpenter by trade), progress-
ing through the three trial machines that took
the form of clocks of unique design, and end-

ing with his finally successful piece, in the
form of a large watch, can properly be included in this brief survey. But Harrison's
work was too complicated and expensive for
general use, and it remained for John Arnold
and Thomas Earnshaw to introduce the simplified types of chronometers that are the basis
of those made today.

In 1760 James Cox invented his atmospheric Pressure Clock, which was wound up
either on the rise or fall of the air pressure.
This is the forerunner of the Atmos Clock of
the 1920s which today operates on the change
of temperature.

In 1765 Alexander Cumming made for
King George III the first self-recording barograph. A carrier floating on the surface of a
mercury column held in its upper end a pencil
which rose or fell with the change in atmospheric pressure and recorded its positions by
tracing a line on a graphed paper disc that
was rotated by the clock once every six
months. A second clock by Cumming inspired Luke Howard to make the recordings he
later collated and published as his *Climate of
London*, 1820. On this book is based the whole
of modern meteorology, so that a clockmaker
can be considered instrumental in the founding of this science.

Up to the beginning of the eighteenth century astrology played an important part in
day-to-day life, and clocks embodying the relative aspects of the planets are not infrequent. Clocks indicating the day of the month
and those showing the phases of the moon are
common. From time to time, but more rarely,
we find dials to tell the time of high tide,
at first for London, where the Thames was
the main highway, and later for marine
ports.

In the latter part of the seventeenth century and in the early eighteenth, when clocks
were only to be found in the spacious rooms of
large mansions, we find various systems of
complicated striking, which indicate the time
at more frequent intervals than one hour. Until clocks became sufficiently cheap, handles
were attached so that they could be carried
from room to room. In those made towards
the end of the eighteenth century the handles
were ornamental, in keeping with the decora-

tion of furniture at the time. Movement of bracket clocks from room to room accounts for the retention of the verge escapement in this type for a hundred years or so after the invention of the much superior anchor escapement – the verge does not require the accurate levelling called for by the anchor.

Again, we find repeating clocks in use until about the time of the invention of matches; the repeating watch, being carried on the person, indoors and outdoors, was favoured until a later period.

BRITISH CLOCKMAKERS OF IMPORTANCE
(1600–1830)

All clocks and watches before 1700 are interesting, as are many in the period 1700–35; there are fewer exceptional makers, until in the last thirty or forty years of the eighteenth century and thereafter, the clock or watch that is to be prized for its horological, as opposed to its furnishing or utilitarian value, is the exception rather than the rule.

The dates given are the approximate years between which signed pieces may be expected. For this purpose the first date is when the man is twenty-five or enters the Clockmakers' Company. The last date is the known or estimated date of death.

Antram, George	1707–1723
Arnold, John	1757–1799
Barker (*Wigan*)	2nd half 18th c.
Bradley, Langley	1697–1738
Clement, William	2nd half 17th c.
Colston, Richard	1682–1709
Cole, Ferguson	1818–1880
Cox, James	1740–1788
Delander, Daniel	1702–1733
Duchesne, Claude	1693–1730
Earnshaw, Thomas	1774–1829
East, Edward	1627–1697
Ebsworth, John	1667–1710
Ellicott, John	1731–1772
Emery, Josiah	1750–1797
Finney (*Liverpool*)	
Various members, 1730–1830	

Fromanteel (*London*)	
Various members, 1625–1725	
Garon, Peter	1695–1730
Goode, Charles	1686–1730
Gould, Christopher	1682–1718
Graham, George	1713–1751
Gray, Benjamin	1681–1764
Harrison, John	1715–1776
Hilderson, John	2nd half 17th c.
Hindley, Henry (*York*)	1726–1771
Holmes, John	1787–1815
Jones, Henry	1664–1695
Knibb, John (*Oxford & London*) c. 1650–1710
Knibb, Joseph	c. 1650–1711
Knifton, Thomas	1640–1662
Lister, Thomas (*Halifax*)	1770–1814
McCabe, James	1781–1811
Margetts, George	1779–1810
Markwick, A family	1666–1805
Moore, William	1704–1720
Mudge, Thomas	1740–1794
Norton, Eardley	1750–1795
Pinchbeck, Christopher	1695–1732
Pinchbeck, Christopher, Jr.	1735–1783
Prior, George	1765–1810
Prior, George (Son)	1815–1830
Quare, Daniel	1674–1724
Ramsay, David (*Edinburgh & London*)	
	1590–1655
Recordon, Louis	1778–1824
Reid, Thomas (*Edinburgh*)	1771–1831
Robinson, Francis	1696–1750
Roskell, Robert	1798–1830
Selwood, William	1633–1652
Staunton, Edward	1666–1710
Tomlinson, William	1699–1745
Tompion, Thomas	1671–1713
Vallin, Nicholas	1580–1630
Vulliamy, Benjamin	1775–1820
Vulliamy, Benjamin Lewis	1809–1854
Vulliamy, Justin	1730–1790
Watson, Samuel (*Coventry & London*)	
	1675–1715
Webster, William	1697–1725
Whitehurst, John (*Derby & London*)	
	1738–1788
Williamson, Joseph	1697–1725
Windmills, Joseph	1671–1725

All makers are in London, except where specified.

Glossary

BAROMETERS

Banjo. The type in which the case resembles this instrument.

Barograph. A self-recording barometer actuated by clockwork.

Capacity error. That introduced by the alteration in the level of the cistern or siphon reservoir by the inflow or outflow of mercury from the vertical tube.

Cistern. The type in which the lower open end of the vertical tube is placed below the level of the mercury in open reservoir. The earliest type.

Diagonal (also called Signpost and Yardarm). A type in which the recording part of the tube is at an obtuse angle with the lower upright part, so that the possible variation of the mercury height of about 3 inches may be spread over the inclined length of the tube.

Double. A type in which the mercury column is divided into two approximately equal halves fixed vertically side by side and connected by a tube filled with a lighter fluid substance, such as oil or air.

Fortin. A type in which the level of the cistern is adjusted to a fixed pointer before a reading by difference is taken, thus eliminating capacity error.

Marine. A type in which part of the bore in the vertical tube is constricted in order to minimize a movement of level in the vertical tube by reason of the ship's motion. This type must also be capable of plugging when not in use.

Meniscus. The surface of a liquid in a tube. It is usually curved, owing to surface-tension effects.

Portable. A type in which the cistern or siphon can be entirely enclosed, and in which the mercury can be plugged in the vertical tube.

Siphon. A type in which the reservoir is situated in the return portion of a J-shaped tube.

Wheel. A siphon-type in which the variation of the mercury level is magnified and registered on a circular dial.

CLOCKS AND WATCHES

Acorn clock. A type of Connecticut shelf clock, in shape suggesting an acorn. *c.* 1850. Rare.

Act of Parliament Clock. A misnomer applied to a timepiece, usually weight-driven, with seconds pendulum having a large unglazed dial and a small trunk. According to legend, these clocks were first put into inns and post taverns for use of the general public, many of whom had sold their clocks and watches when Pitt introduced his Act in 1797 levying 5*s* per annum on all clocks and watches. Such distress was caused in the trade that the Act was repealed in the following year.

Alarm. A mechanical attachment which, at a predetermined time, rings a bell or activates some other alarm. Found on many types of portable clocks, but rarely on tall clocks. The time for the release of the alarm is usually determined, or "set", by a brass disk numbered 1–12, or by a third hand.

Arbor. The shaft or axle to which pinions and wheels are attached.

Architectural clock. A clock in which the hood, in long-case, and the top in mantel clocks, is in the style of a classical pediment, with or without supporting columns. Usually a sign of work in the third quarter of the seventeenth century, although these pediment tops were revived for a short period early in the nineteenth century (Plate 30A).

Arch top, plain. A case, usually in bracket clocks, where the arch rises directly from the sides of the case.

Astrological dials. These are embodied in many early clocks and watches and show the relation or aspect of the planets to one another at any time. They are usually shown as related to the moon, whose phases are to be seen through an aperture in the dial for this purpose. The distances in degrees are shown by the Trines $\triangle$ ($120°$), Quartiles $\square$ ($90°$), Sextiles $*$ ($60-$), Conjunction δ ($0°$), and Opposion δ ($180°$) (Plate 27, Fig. 1).

Automatic winding. A pocket watch which is wound up by means of a weight actuated by the motion of the body. A patent was taken out in London in 1780 by Louis Recordon, but prior claim is made for Abraham Louis Perrelet, of Le Locle. The automatic wrist-watch was invented by J. W. Harwood of London, England, in 1914.

Balance or Balance wheel. One of the first forms of oscillating control in a mechanical clock or watch. In 1675 Christiaan Huygens announced his spiral spring fitted to the balance, but Robert Hooke claimed priority. With this spring the watch could keep as good time as a pendulum clock.

Balance staff. The arbor or shaft which carries the balance wheel.

Balloon. A type of waisted clock popular in the late eighteenth and early nineteenth centuries.

Banjo clock. The recent term applied to various wall clocks somewhat resembling a banjo in shape. The earliest American example was the "Improved Timepiece" produced by Simon Willard before 1800 and patented by him in 1802. It became one of the most popular types of clocks. Others copied and modified the original design in so many ways that an almost endless number of varieties resulted.

The banjo, in its best form, is a finely made piece. The movements used, although varying in details, were ordinarily brass, weight-driven eight-day timepieces, with a pendulum about 20–26 inches long. A few striking, as well as **alarm**, movements were also used. A very few Connecticut wall clocks, somewhat resembling the true banjo, were made using the 30-hour wooden movement.

Since 1800 there probably has not been a single decade when banjos have not been manufactured, so popular have they been. The clocks produced by the Willards, their apprentices, and other contemporaries until about 1830 are the most pleasing in design. Later plainer, and not so perfectly made, banjos were sold in large numbers. After about 1845 Edward Howard in Boston, alone and with others under various company names, manufactured large numbers of simple banjos in several sizes.

Because of the popularity of the banjo clock and the rarity of the best examples, a great many reproductions and rebuilt pieces have appeared. It is probably a fact that more deliberate faking has been attempted in "making" old banjos than any other type of clock. Many old banjos have been "improved" by adding the name of a famous maker. Such imitations or fakes are sometimes very difficult to detect. There are no consistent and positive characteristics by which genuine banjos by the Willards or other famous makers can be identified (Plate 24A, B, C).

Banking pins. Two fixed pins which limit the motion of the lever of a lever escapement.

Barrel. A cylindrical box containing the mainspring in both clocks and watches. American clocks before 1900 often have unenclosed springs.

Basket top. A pierced metallic and roughly dome-shaped case top current at the end of the seventeenth and early in the eighteenth centuries.

Basket top, double. Two pierced metallic basket tops superimposed.

Basket top, wooden. Where a smooth wooden dome replaces the metallic bracket.

Beat. The sound made by the action of the escapement – the "tick-tock". A timepiece is "in beat" when the intervals between beats are even.

Beehive clock. A form of small Connecticut shelf clock, also called "flatiron" clock; so named because of the resemblance of the shape to an old-time beehive or flatiron. *c.* 1850–60. Common. (Plate 22B, D).

Bell top. The top of a clock case where the lower portion is shaped like the bell of a turret clock with concave sides.

Bell, inverted. Similar to a Bell top, except that the lower portion has a convex outline.

Bezel. The metallic framing of a clock or watch glass.

Blinking-eye clocks. In which the eyes are connected to the escapement and move in harmony with it. Made in South Germany in the seventeenth and elsewhere in the late eighteenth century, a few were made in the United States in the nineteenth century.

Bob. The weight at the base of a pendulum rod. The earliest were pear-shaped or nearly spherical. Later the general form was lenticular; in some regulators and special clocks cylindrical (Plate 27, Fig. 6 at A).

Bob wire. The wire loop which passes through the bob of many American clocks. One end is threaded for the regulating nut.

Bolt and shutter. A form of maintaining power. The shutters cover the winding squares so that the clock cannot be wound without pushing them aside. This action brings into play a small subsidiary force that keeps the clock going during the period of winding (Plate 27A).

Bow. The loop at the top of the pendant of a watch.

Bracket clock. Many clocks of the seventeenth and eighteenth centuries were provided with their own brackets, usually designed to harmonize with the case. Only rarely have original brackets survived. They frequently contain a drawer to hold the winding key. Portable clocks are known as both mantel and bracket clocks.

Bridge. A shaped metallic support having two terminal plates (Plate 27, Fig. 2).

Broken arch. An arch terminating on either side with a horizontal projection. There are broken arch dials and cases. If a full semicircle, they are known as deep; if less, and this usually applies to the earliest, as shallow arches.

Buhl. Inlay of brass or silver, usually on a base of tortoiseshell. Invented by André Charles Boulle in the latter half of the seventeenth century.

Bun feet. Small, circular, flat, "cheeselike" feet, sometimes found on early long-case and bracket clocks.

Bushing. The filling up of worn pivot holes and their subsequent opening to size.

Calendar clock. Any clock which indicates the day, month, or year. Earliest known is that of Govanni Dondi of Padua, Italy (1364), which showed the length of daylight for every day, and the day of the month through the year. Calendar clocks have been produced throughout the ages in all countries.

Cam. A part so shaped as to turn rotary motion into reciprocal or variable motion (Plate 27, Fig. 3).

Cannon pinion. The pinion to which it is usual to fit the minute hand.

Cap (dust). A movable cap, first used early in the eighteenth century to help keep the movement clean. Only used in watches (Plate 27, Fig. 4).

Cartel clock. A mural clock, usually of somewhat flamboyant design. More often found in France than in England. The English ones are usually of carved wood, whereas the French are usually of cast brass or bronze and gilt.

Cartouche. A decorative panel, sometimes applied, and framing an inscription (Plate 29D and G).

Case. That which contains the clock or watch movement. Any solid material as metal, stone, or wood may be used. The variety of designs, selection of woods, and the quality of cabinet work contribute to the fascination of clocks to the collector.

Case, pair. For a hundred years, beginning about the latter part of the seventeenth century, watches were usually provided with two cases, of which the outer was frequently highly ornate. In some instances a third case was provided to protect the decoration on the second.

Centre seconds. A clock or watch in which the seconds hand is placed on the same arbor as the hour and minute hands (Plate 32I).

Champlevé. The cutting away of the dial of a watch, so that the hour numerals, minute ring, and inter-horary marks remain raised (Plate 32D and F).

Chapter ring. The applied circle, found in earlier clocks, upon which are engraved the hour numerals. Derives its name from the fact that hours are struck on a bell. Originally a clock served to rouse the sexton, who then struck the hour of the chapter, or religious office, on a bell.

Chiming clock. A clock which sounds at the quarters a chime on four or more bells in addition to striking the hour.

Chronograph. A watch, stop-watch, the hands of which can be started, stopped, and returned to zero without stopping its motion (Plate 21E).

Chronometer. An especially accurate portable timepiece, as a marine chronometer.

Chronometer escapement. A special type of escapement used in chronometers, also called a detent escapement.

Circular error. Christiaan Huygens, who invented the pendulum, discovered that the truly isochronous swing of a pendulum was not the true arc of a circle but on a cycloid (Plate 27, Fig. 5A and B). The course of the latter is more U-shaped than the true circle; but for a short distance at the bottom of the swing the two paths coincide. Any lack of time-keeping due to a pendulum swinging beyond this common path is said to be due to circular error.

Clepsydra. A timekeeper motivated by water running either into or out from it. Water clocks are among the earliest forms known; before the discovery of the verge escapement and the weight as a motive power.

Click. The pawl that works against the ratchet wheel of the winding drum; its action causes the clicking when a timepiece is wound.

Cock (Clock). (i) The bracket that supports the pendulum (Plate 27, Fig. 6 at C); (ii) a bridge with only one terminal plate (Fig. 6 at B).

Cock (Watch). The bracket covering and protecting the balance, it also supports the upper end of the balance staff (Plate 32E).

Collet. (i) A dome-shaped washer used to render firm the hands of a clock (Plate 29A); (ii) a flange (Plate 27, Fig. 7).

Compensation balance. A balance that corrects the influence of heat and cold upon its timekeeping. Usually of bimetallic construction (Plate 27, Fig. 10).

Compensation curve. A bimetallic curve in contact with one end of the balance spring. The action of temperature on the curve causes a compensating change in the effective length of the balance spring.

Contrate wheel. A wheel in which the teeth stand perpendicularly to the plane of the wheel. It is used to transmit motion from the arbor of one wheel at right angles to the first (Plate 27, Fig. 13 at A).

Cottage clocks. Name now given to many small Connecticut spring clocks in wood cases. *c.* 1850–1900. Common (Plate 22C).

Crown wheel. The escape wheel of the verge escapement (Plate 27, Fig. 13 at D).

Crutch. That part of the clock mechanism which, fixed to the pallet arbor, transmits the impulse to the independently supported pendulum (Plate 27, Fig. 9 at B).

Curb pins. Two pins astride the outer end of a balance spring. These are moved by the regulating device, and so alter the effective length of the spring.

Cycloidal cheeks. Curves fitted to a pendulum clock to overcome circular error. It was found, however, that the errors they introduced were greater than those they eliminated, so they were soon abandoned. Only found in the very earliest pendulum clocks (Plate 27, Fig. 9 at A).

Cycloidal path. The curve described by a point on the circumference of a circle rolling along a straight line.

Declination. The angular distance of a star north or south of the celestial equator. In clocks the star is usually the sun, whose declination varies between $23\frac{1}{2}°$ north and south of the equator.

Detent. That which detains. The term is applied to the pawl or click that takes into the ratchet wheel.

Dial. The face of a clock or watch on which are marked the hours, minutes, and seconds. The division of the circle into 360 equal parts is believed to have originated with the Sumerians about 4000 B.C. Finding that 10, the number of the fingers, was not easily divisible, they chose a unit of 6, divisible by 3 and 2.

They then adopted a combination of 6 and 10 up to 6 × 10 = 60. This formed the basis for another series up to 10 × 60 = 600. This again formed a basis, but when they reached 6 × 600 = 3,600, they considered that they had reached finality or completeness, which they symbolized as a circle.

Dial, or motion wheels. The wheels that cause the hour hand to turn twelve times slower than the minute hand.

Dominical letter. The 1st of January is allotted the letter A and the six succeeding letters, B–G, assigned to the six succeeding days. The letter thus falling on the first Sunday of the year is the Dominical letter for that year. In leap years two letters are required, one up to February 29 and the next succeeding letter, if necessary recommencing with A, for the rest of the year. Used in connexion with the fixing of Easter Day.

Drum. The spool on to which the cord to the weight is wound.

Dutch striking. The repetition of the hour at the half-hour on a different toned bell.

Ecliptic. The apparent orbit of the sun. Total eclipses of the sun or moon are only possible when the moon is in the plane of the ecliptic. The plane of the orbit of the moon is inclined at an angle of 5° to that of the sun. Where the two intersect is termed the Nodes. They appear on clock dials as ♌.

Epact. The age of the moon on January 1.

Epicycloid. The curve traced by a point on the circumference of a circle as it rolls around another circle. It is a curve used in the cutting of teeth for wheels.

Equation dial. A dial that records both Solar and Mean Time (Plate 29E, F, G).

Equation kidney. A kidney-shaped cam, invented by Christiaan Huygens in 1695, which made possible the transformation of simple forward rotary motion into a backward or forward motion, varying daily, both in direction and amount, necessary to indicate the daily difference between Solar and Mean Time (Plate 27, Fig. 12).

Equation of time. The solar day or time as recorded by a sundial varies each day in length; whereas Mean Time, or time shown by a clock, is exactly twenty-four hours each day. This difference, which varies irregularly daily, is known as the equation of time.

Escape wheel. The wheel that gives impulse to the balance or pendulum.

Escapement. The means by which the motion of a clock or watch is checked and the energy of the motive force, weight, or spring, is transmitted to the controller, pendulum, or balance.

ANCHOR. Invented about 1670 by William Clement. It revolutionized timekeeping. With it the pallets are in the same plane as the escape wheel, instead of being at right angles to it, as in the verge escapement. It largely eliminated circular error and also made practical the use of long pendulums swinging more slowly, and thus with a lesser cumulative error. It is still used today for most domestic clocks, and particularly in long-case clocks with pendulums beating one second. It is also known as the recoil escapement, which recoil is seen in the slight shudder at each beat in the seconds hand of long-case clocks so equipped. The vastly improved timekeeping of this escapement made really practical the use of clocks for astronomical purposes. Flamsteed, the first Astronomer Royal at Greenwich, in 1675, used clocks made by Thomas Tompion, equipped with the anchor escapement and with 13-foot pendulums, beating two seconds, suspended above the clocks which reduced the amplitude to about 1 inch, thus eliminating circular error. This largely accounted for the far greater accuracy of his observations as compared with his contemporaries. From this invention followed, directly or indirectly, practically all the subsequent improvements in timekeeping in clocks (Plate 27, Fig. 11).

CYLINDER. A type for use in watches. A form of this escapement was patented by Tompion, Barlow, and Haughton in 1695, but it was never developed. It remained for Tompion's successor, George Graham, to perfect this escapement about 1725. Graham used it very extensively in his watches, and this greatly helped him to gain the reputation of being the best watchmaker of his day. As with the anchor escapement, the pallets are in the same plane as the escape wheel (Plate 27, Fig. 15). This escapement remained the best for watches until supplanted by the duplex and the lever escapements about the end of the eighteenth century.

DEADBEAT. Invented by George Graham about 1715. Graham was the leading astronomical instrument-maker of his day, and from his close connexion with astronomers was doubtless aware of their demand for still greater accuracy than could be attained with the anchor escapement. The deadbeat escapement is an improvement on the anchor in that it eliminates the recoil, and remains steady at the end of each beat. It held the field for the most accurate escape for astronomical work for nearly two hundred years. It is still used today in high-grade clocks, both long-case and mantel (Plate 27, Fig. 16).

DETENT. In which the escapement is locked by a pin on the detent and the impulse is given every alternate vibration to a pallet on the balance staff by the escape-wheel teeth. A detent escapement goes "tick-tick" and not "tick-tock". *See* p. 87.

DUPLEX. Invention uncertain. Usually attributed to Pierre LeRoy, Paris, about 1750. The escape wheel has two sets of teeth, one long and pointed, the other short and triangular and rising from the plane of the escape wheel. The long teeth escape through a small notch in the balance staff, which also carries a long arm by which the impulse is given through the short triangular teeth (Plate 27, Fig. 14).

LEVER. First invented about 1758 by Thomas Mudge and incorporated in a watch given by King George III to Queen Charlotte. Mudge only made one or two other examples and does not seem to have realized the importance of his invention, which lies in the fact that the balance is free from interference for the greater part of its swing, thus leaving it free to perform its true function as controller. From the beginning of the second quarter of the nineteenth century the lever escapement, in one of its many forms, became the standard escapement for watches, and still is so today. Before that date, despite the appearance of the cylinder, duplex, and lever escapements, the standard watch escapement was the verge (Plate 28, Fig. 22).

PIN-PALLET. Invented by Amant, Paris, about 1740. A type in which the pins stand out from the side of the escape wheel. Not much found in English clocks (Plate 27, Fig. 8).

TIC-TAC. A modified form of the anchor escapement found in some early clocks. The "anchor" embraces only two or three teeth of the escape wheel.

VERGE. This was the original escapement for mechanical clocks. Date of invention unknown, possibly thirteenth century. Although it is an escapement in its worst form, in that it never leaves the pendulum or balance free for an instant, nevertheless it was in its day as revolutionary an invention as was, later, the anchor escapement. It held the field unchallenged for about four hundred years; even thereafter it remained in use for clocks and watches, along with better types, for another one hundred and fifty years (Plate 27, Fig. 13 at D).

Escape wheel. The final wheel of the time train of a clock or watch which gives impulse to the pendulum or balance. Often shortened to 'scape wheel.

Fan, or fly. A rapidly turning vane on the final arbor of the strike train which slows and governs the rate of striking.

Finials. The turned, carved, or moulded ornaments, usually brass or wood, at the top of various types of clocks.

Foliot. With the balance wheel the earliest form of controller in a mechanical clock. Always found with a verge escapement. The balance wheel and, especially later, the pendulum so improved timekeeping that it is very rare to find a clock with its original foliot. Its origin is unknown, but presumably attributable to the inventor of the verge escapement. Consists of a horizontal rod fixed to a pivoted bar carrying the verge pallets. Regulation was by moving the weights carried at each end. The word may be derived from the French *esprit follet*, a goblin associated with Puck and represented by its to-and-fro motion (Plate 31A).

Form watch. A watch made in some form that departs from the standard of the period, e.g. book, cruciform, skull, dog, etc. These are found in the seventeenth century. Later, at the end of the eighteenth, there are lyres, mandolines, baskets of flowers, fruit, etc.

Fly. A rapidly revolving vane, the final component of the striking train, which acts as a governor for the rate of striking. Date of invention unknown, but presumably concurrent with the locking plate (Plate 28, Fig. 23 at A).

Franklin clock. A type of wooden movement shelf clock made (1825–30) by Silas Hoadley of Plymouth, Connecticut, and called by him "Franklin". It is perhaps the earliest instance that a clock was given a specific (model) name by a maker. This movement is characterized by being practically an inverted form of the movement then being made by Terry and others.

Frets. Pierced metallic decorative pieces, originally used to hide the balance in lantern clocks. Later, either in wood or metal, inserted into clock cases to facilitate the elimination of sound (Plate 31C).

Fusee. A conically shaped and spirally grooved pulley which, utilizing the principle of the lever, equalizes the pull of the mainspring of a clock or watch on the train. The inventor about 1460–70 is unknown, but the invention has not been bettered, and is still in use today in high-grade spring-driven clocks. Catgut was originally used to connect the fusee with the main-spring barrel, but from the end of the seventeenth century a chain is usually employed (Plate 28, Fig. 24 at A; also Plate 32C).

Gathering pallet. A pin or finger that revolves when the clock is striking and gathers up, at each revolution, a tooth of the striking rack.

Girandole. A type of wall clock designed by Lemuel Curtis. Considered by many to be the most beautiful American clock. *c.* 1820. Very rare (Plate 24D).

Gong. A piece of hardened, tempered wire wound in a volute, on which the hours are struck, instead of a bell. First used in the last quarter of the eighteenth century (Plate 28, Fig. 18).

Gothic clocks. A term applied generally to all German, Swiss, or Italian clocks of the sixteenth and seventeenth centuries made on gothic lines (Plate 31A). Pointed-topped Connecticut shelf clocks introduced about 1845. The most popular were called "sharp gothic"; now commonly known as steeple clocks. Including round and sharp-topped gothics, variations in style and size of cases, and variations in types of movements, there are probably over a hundred different forms. Most are attractive and deserve the interest of the advanced collector as well as the beginner (Plate 22A).

Grandfather clock. Properly known as a long-case clock. Came into existence directly after the invention of the anchor escapement, 1670. The narrow arc of swing of this escapement made possible the enclosing of the weights and pendulum in a narrow trunk.

Grandmother clock. A small long-case clock, not exceeding 6 feet 6 inches in height.

Grand sonnerie. A system of striking whereby the hour and the quarter are struck at each quarter. The earliest is a clock about 1660 by J. G. Mayer of Munich in the locking-plate system. The next earliest known example is the movement with the silent escapement made by Tompion about 1676–80. This system of striking was rendered much more simple by the invention by Edward Barlow, in 1676, of the rack and snail method of striking.

Gravity escapement. An especially accurate escapement often used in tower clocks or regulators. Impulse is given to the pendulum by two weighted arms which are raised by the clock mechanism.

Gregorian calendar. The old Church calendar (based on the Julians introduced by Julius Caesar) assumed a solar year of exactly $356\frac{1}{4}$ days and that 19 solar years contained exactly 235 lunations. Neither of these is quite accurate. By 1582 the cumulative error amounted to 10 days. Pope Gregory XIII introduced the Gregorian calendar – or New Style – which brought the vernal equinox back to March 21 instead of March 11. This change was not adopted in England till 1752, by which time the error was 11 days. In that year September 2 was followed by September 14. The ignorant populace rioted, saying, "Give us back our eleven days!" This change accounted for the financial year ending on April 5 instead of March 25 in 1753, and it has so remained ever since.

Hairspring. The fine spring which regulates the motion of the balance wheel.

Hands. The pointers of a clock or watch. Originally clocks had no hands – they merely struck one at each hour, later the dial was made to revolve before a fixed pointer. Some time towards the end of the fourteenth century the fixed dial with a single revolving hour hand was introduced. Minute hands did not become general until the introduction of the pendulum made timekeeping sufficiently accurate to warrant their use. The study of the evolution of the design of hands will give a good guide to the date of a clock up to about 1830; after that designs are too numerous to be classified.

Hollow column clocks. Weight-powered shelf clocks with free-standing hollow columns as part of the case decoration within which the weights travel. c. 1830–40. Rare (Plate 23c).

Hood. The upper removable portion of a long-case. In all, except very early cases, it draws forward.

Hood, rising. The earliest form, before the door was introduced in the front, in which the hood slides up on grooves in the back-board and is held in place by a catch, thus allowing access to the dial (Plate 28, Fig. 20 at A). As clocks increased in height, the rising hood became impracticable, and the draw-forward type with door was introduced.

Hoop wheel. A wheel, forming part of the striking train of a clock, to which is affixed a narrow band, having slots and projecting at right angles to the plane of the wheel. This serves as a regulator between each blow of the hammer (Plate 28, Fig. 28).

Hourglass clock. Any of several styles of Connecticut clocks in the general shape of an hourglass. c. 1850. Rare.

Hours, Babylonian. The Babylonians are believed to have divided the day into 24 hours of 60 minutes, each of 60 seconds, starting at sunrise.

Hours, canonical. Time signals were given in ancient Rome at three-hourly intervals, starting at 6 a.m. They were mane, tertia, sextes, nona, and vespera, and were later adopted by the Christian Church. In time other offices were added to the Church day, and the times of these offices or chapters advanced, until nona fell at noon. The original function of a clock was to let off an alarm every hour to warn the sexton to ring the bell for the office.

Hours, Italian. The Italians reckoned the time as 24 hours a day, starting from sunset. In some early Continental clocks dials were marked I to XII twice over and had a movable ring marked 1–24 in Arabic numerals, enabling the clock to be set daily at sunset for the Italian hour.

Hours, Nuremberg. In South Germany, until the early part of the seventeenth century, time was recorded as so many hours of daylight and so many of darkness. These varied from 16 hours of daylight and 8 of darkness in mid-summer to the converse in mid-winter. Public tables told when a hour should be transferred from one section to the other. In the town of Rothenburg this system of time recording was retained up to the early nineteenth century.

Hours, temporal or canonical. The division of the 24 hours into 12 of daylight and 12 of darkness, the length thus varying with the seasons. This system gradually disappeared in Europe with the coming of the mechanical clock, but persisted in Japan till 1873; clocks had to be adjusted every fourteen days.

Indiction. A period of fifteen years arising from Roman taxation laws. Used in ecclesiastical calculations. Dials marked 1–15, with a hand revolving once in fifteen years, are sometimes found on astronomical clocks.

Involute curve. The curve described by a point on a taut line unwound from a cylinder.

Involute gear teeth. Wheels having teeth cut on the principle of the involute curve.

Iron-front clocks. Small Connecticut shelf clocks with fronts of cast iron in many forms, painted and often decorated with shell inlays. c. 1860. Common, but interesting.

Isochronous. Performing the same motion in equal time, i.e. when the balance of a watch or the pendulum of a clock performs each vibration in the same time irrespective of the arc of vibration or swing.

Jewels. When the bearings of pivots are formed of jewels to reduce wear and friction. Jewels were first introduced by Facio de Duillier in 1704; he was a Swiss settled in London.

Rubies and sapphires are usually used. Jewels are sometimes found as pallets in very high-grade regulators.

Labels. Engraved, lithographed, or printed papers are found inside many American clocks but not in European. Cabinet-makers' labels, as well as those of clockmakers, are found in a few tall clock cases made about 1800 or earlier. Clock labels became a usual feature of shelf clocks from their very earliest production (c. 1815). These labels give the maker's name and place of business and usually the directions for setting up, regulating, and caring for the clock. Occasionally some additional useful knowledge may be given, as the equation of time, postal rates, or census figures. Such papers are of the greatest importance in identifying and valuing any clock.

Lancet clock. Design of late eighteenth and early nineteenth centuries, in which a bracket clock has a pointed "gothic" top.

Lantern clock. A typically English design evolved in the early part of the seventeenth century, and persisting, especially in the provinces, until well into the eighteenth century (Plate 31C). Erroneously called a Cromwellian clock. Much copied today. All original lantern clocks are weight-driven and, with the rarest exceptions, never exceed a thirty hour going period.

Lantern clock, wing. A type, popular for about a quarter of a century at the end of the seventeenth century, where the pendulum was placed between the going and striking trains, and took the form of an anchor, the flukes of which appeared each side of the main framework, and were protected by wings.

Lantern pinion. An early type in which the leaves are formed by wires affixed between two circular end plates (Plate 28, Fig. 19).

Latched plates. The retaining plates of the movement where the distance pillars are secured at one end by swivelled catches instead of by pins passing through the head of the pillar (Plate 27, Fig. 6 at E).

Leaf, Pinion. The longitudinal teeth of a pinion are known as leaves.

Lenticle. The glass let into the door of a long-case clock to allow the motion of the pendulum bob to be seen (Plate 30A).

Lighthouse clock. (a) A clock made in small numbers by Simon Willard and suggesting a lighthouse in form. c. 1820. Very rare; (b) any of several later novelty clocks resembling a lighthouse.

Locking plate. A plate with notches set at increasing intervals around its circumference, which allows the striking train to sound the correct number of blows before the locking arm falls into a notch and stops the train. Invention unknown, probably thirteenth century, concurrently with the verge escapement (Plate 27, Fig. 6 at D).

Long-case. The correct horological term for a grandfather or grandmother clock.

Lunar dial. A dial which shows the lunar periods (Plates 29I).

Lunar work. That part of the train which actuates the lunar dial.

Lunation. A period of 29 days 12 hours and 45 minutes, being the time taken by the moon to make a complete revolution round the earth and occupy the same position relative to the sun. Except in very special astronomical clocks, the period is usually taken as $29\frac{1}{2}$ days.

Lyre clock. Wall or shelf clocks with cases in the general shape of a lyre; the original design is attributed to Aaron Willard, Jr. Many variations in detail of cases. All of excellent quality; eight-day movements; mostly by Massachusetts makers, c. 1820–40. Rare (Plate 24E, F).

Mainspring. A coiled strip of steel that provides the motive power for portable clocks. First invented about 1450. To compensate for the loss of power as the spring unwinds it is used in conjunction with a fusee, or else only a limited number of turns are used, before rewinding. Steel springs were not successfully manufactured in America for use in clocks until about 1840. Brass springs are occasionally found in small Connecticut clocks of 1840–55.

Maintaining power. A device used in weight clocks and in clocks and watches fitted with a fusee, whereby a subsidiary force is brought into play to keep the clock going while it is being wound. In early clocks the winding squares were often covered by shutters, which, when pulled aside, brought into operation the maintaining power, thus ensuring its use (Plates 29A and 30A, C).

Main wheel. The first, and largest, wheel of the train; the one which first receives the power from the mainspring or weight. Also called the great wheel.

Mantel clock. Nearly synonymous with shelf or bracket clock, but used mostly in reference to modern clocks.

Massachusetts shelf clock. A type made by the Willards and others, chiefly of Massachusetts. Also called half-clock, box-on-box, or case-on-case. Eight-day brass movements, timepieces or occasionally striking clocks. *c.* 1800–30. Rare.

Matting. A system of rendering dull the surface of the brass dial plate. The art is now lost. Usually confined to the centre of the chapter ring. In some early pendulum clocks the dials are matted all over (Plates 29A and 30A, c).

Metonic cycle. The Greek astronomer Meton discovered that the days of the month on which full moon occur constitute a cycle of 19 years. This was considered so wonderful that the Greeks had it carved on stone in letters of gold. Clocks are to be found with a dial marked 1–19, the hand revolving in 19 years.

Minute wheel. The wheel which is driven by the cannon pinion and of which the pinion drives the hour wheel, to which the hour hand is attached.

Micrometer adjustment. A graduated wheel fixed to the pendulum suspension to give accurate adjustment for regulation (Plate 28, Fig. 23 at B). Early use of this was made by both Wm. Clement and A. Fromanteel, but who had prior claim is uncertain. Later replaced by a subsidiary dial on the clock face, the hand of which actuated a rack and pinion or a cam connected with the pendulum suspension (Plate 29E).

Mirror, or looking-glass clock. Any clock having a mirror as a prominent part of the case. In 1825 Chauncey Jerome (Bristol, Connecticut) invented the "looking-glass" clock to compete with the pillar and scroll case then being made by other manufacturers.

Mock pendulum. A swinging bob attached to the escape arbor, which shows through a slot in the dial plate. Only used in clocks with the verge escapement. Sometimes called a false bob.

Month clock. A clock that goes for a period of one month with one winding. The usual period is 32 days.

Movement. The "works" of a clock or watch.

Mural clock. A clock made to hang on the wall.

Musical clock or watch. One that plays a tune at each hour or other predetermined time, as opposed to a chiming clock (Plate 29D).

New Hampshire mirror clock. As now used refers to a distinct type of rectangular wall clock produced by several makers, mostly of New Hampshire, U.S.A. These usually are about 28–36 inches tall, 14–16 inches wide, and about 4 inches deep. The cases may be plain or with a scroll at top, or top and bottom; sometimes partly gilded; and usually have a square decorated glass over the dial. Weight-powered, eight-day brass movements. *c.* 1820–40. Rare.

Night clock. A clock that shows the time by night, usually by means of a light shining through a pierced dial.

Nuremberg egg. A misnomer applied to early South German watches. Arose from the misreading and mistranslation of "Uhrlein" into "Eierlein" (little clocks into little eggs). These early watches were usually drum shaped.

Off-centre pendulum. A pendulum which is not hung in the centre. Specifically used in America in reference to certain early shelf clocks with wood movements by Eli Terry or Seth Thomas (Plate 26B).

Oil sink. A shallow cup cut in the outside of a clock or watch plate concentric with a pivot hole, to retain oil.

Ogee, or O. G. clock. Technically a moulding with a reverse curve like the letter S. Used to designate the plain rectangular clocks with such an ogee moulding on the front. Probably originated in Connecticut about 1830 and made in great numbers until the first quarter of the twentieth century. The design was simple, inexpensive to make, easy to ship, and attractive. Made in numerous sizes, ranging from less than a foot to over 4 feet in height. Many types of movements, wood or brass eight-day or thirty-hour, weight- or spring-powered, were used in these cases. They were primarily shelf clocks, but could be hung as wall clocks. Probably more O. G. clocks have been produced in Connecticut than any other type. Some are desirable on account of their rare movements or other features.

Pallet. That part of the escapement through which the escape wheel gives impulse to the balance or pendulum (Plate 27, Fig. 11 at A).

Paperweight clocks. Small (4–6-inch) clocks with cases of moulded glass in several shapes, sizes, and colours. c. 1880–1910. Occasional.

Papier mâché clocks. Usually small shelf clocks, the cases of which are moulded of papier mâché; of many forms – some with shell inlays. Connecticut. c. 1860. Occasional.

Parquetry. A type of veneer in which the applied woods are worked into a pattern with straight-sided components – e.g. squares, diamonds, rectangles, etc.

Pendant. The small neck of metal connecting the watch-case to the bow.

Pendulums.

Bob. The earliest form invented by Christiaan Huygens in 1657 and used with the verge escapement. In England the pendulum rod was usually fixed to the end of the escape pallet arbor, but on the Continent suspension was generally from a silk cord, the pendulum being actuated by a crutch (Plate 27, Fig. 9). In England regulation was by means of a fine thread cut on the lower end of the pendulum rod. The hole in the bob had a softwood core which "took up" the threads on the rod (Plate 27, Fig. 6 at A). On the Continent regulation was by means of turning the arbor from which the silk was suspended.

Double bob. A spring-suspended type, appearing towards the latter part of the eighteenth century in which the rod carries two lenticular-shaped bobs.

Half seconds. Length 9·8 inches, beats twice a second. This is the longest pendulum normally found on verge-escapement clocks.

Seconds. This pendulum, 39·14 inches long, and those of greater length were made practical by the invention of the Anchor escapement. The vastly improved timekeeping

resulting from the adoption of the seconds pendulum and the anchor escapement in the early 1670s caused it to be called the Royal pendulum. It is the standard pendulum today for long-case clocks.

One and a quarter seconds. 5 ft. 1 in. When the improved performance of the seconds pendulum and anchor escapement were realized, attempts were made to increase this by using longer pendulums. Wm Clement first made clocks with $1\frac{1}{4}$-second pendulums. The seconds dial of a clock originally so made should have four divisions between each 5-second interval on the seconds dial. Sometimes clocks have their escapements and pendulums altered from 1 second to $1\frac{1}{4}$ seconds in order to enhance their value. These will generally have their old seconds dials with five divisions. The base of a $1\frac{1}{4}$-second clock should have a door to allow access to the bob.

Two seconds. 13 ft. $0\frac{1}{2}$ in. When making the first two clocks for Greenwich Observatory, in 1676, Thomas Tompion introduced 2-second pendulums and year movements, in an attempt to secure the greatest accuracy. These are thought to be the first clocks so designed in England. 2-second pendulums are now only found in some turret clocks.

Compensation. A pendulum which provides for the compensation of the effects of heat and cold.

Conical. A pendulum that rotates in a circle, the point of suspension being the apex of the cone. This was first designed by Jost Bodeker, bishop of Osnabruck in Germany, in 1578. Huygens made experiments, but it is seldom found in practice.

Ellicott. Invented in 1752, utilizing the principle of the difference in the expansion between steel and brass. The heavy bob is carried on two angular hinged supports. As the length of the pendulum rod changes with temperature, the vertical arms of the support are raised or depressed, giving a complementary movement to the horizontal arms carrying the heavy bob. Very expensive to make and not materially better than the gridiron, hence not extensively used (Plate 28, Fig. 26).

Gridiron. Invented about 1725 by John Harrison, a carpenter born in Soulby in Yorks, 1693. Sometimes attributed jointly with his brother James. Harrison discovered that brass and steel have an expansion ratio of 3 : 2. This property is utilized in this pendulum, with its alternate rods of brass and steel. One side only is required, the other rods being put in for balance and symmetry. Still used today in high-grade clocks (Plate 28, Fig. 25).

MERCURY. Invented in 1726 by George Graham, who had previously experimented with brass and steel without conclusive results. The bob of the pendulum consists of a jar containing mercury. As the temperature changes the length of the pendulum rod, the level of the mercury in the jar alters in the inverse sense, thus keeping constant the centre of oscillation of the pendulum. Still in use today in high-grade clocks (Plate 30C).

SIMPLE. A theoretical conception consisting of a weight or mass suspended by a weightless thread.

WOOD. A pendulum rod made of well-seasoned, straight-grained, and varnished wood is little affected by temperature or humidity. It is sometimes used in high-grade clocks and regulators.

Perpetual calendar. A calendar which corrects itself for the short months, and more exceptionally for leap year. Usually consists of a slotted wheel revolving once a year (or four years) with slots of varying length which control the movement of a lever, allowing it to pass one or more teeth of the calendar wheel at a time (Plate 28, Fig. 27).

Pillars. The distance pieces separating the back and front (or top and bottom) plates of a clock or watch. Their style is a guide to the date of the piece (Plate 32C, H).

Pillar and scroll. The modern name given to a style of shelf clock having delicate feet, slender pillars, and a broken arch or double scroll at the top. The design was probably an adaptation from eighteenth-century styles. Sometimes called "Terry-type" clocks, as Eli Terry (c. 1816) was the first to manufacture them in large quantities. Large numbers and several variations were made by Terry, Seth Thomas, Silas Hoadley, and other Connecticut makers until about 1830. Thirty-hour wood movements of several types were usually used, although some fine

examples are found with eight-day weight brass movements. The pillar and scroll clock was the first successfully mass-produced shelf clock in America. Similar clocks are found with labels of makers working (1825–40) in Pennsylvania, Massachusetts, and Nova Scotia. In addition to being so historically important, these are, perhaps, the most pleasing in appearance of all shelf clocks. Rare (Plate 26A, B, C).

Pin drum. The spiked drum of a musical or chiming clock, the spikes of which actuate the hammers as the drum revolves.

Pinion. A small-toothed wheel, in which the ratio of the axial length to diameter is greater than in a wheel. The teeth of pinions are called leaves. In clock and watch movements wheels and pinions alternate in the train (Plate 27, Fig. 13 at C).

Pivot. The reduced end of an arbor, round which it revolves.

Planetarium. A representation of the chief celestial bodies, sun, moon, earth, and planets, which, when put into action, usually by turning a handle (although some are driven by clocks), shows the relative motion of these bodies. More usually called "Orreries", after Richard Boyle, 4th Earl of Orrery, in the mistaken belief that the first of these was made for him. The first was made by Tompion and Graham for Prince Eugene, in about 1705 (Plate 29H).

Plates, back and front and top and bottom. Plates between which are pivoted the trains of a clock or watch. Early back plates in clocks were quite plain, except for the signature; later they began to be decorated, and the decoration became more and more ornate, reaching a peak in the first quarter of the eighteenth century. From this point it declined until the last decade of this century saw the return of the plain back plate. These back plates are a useful guide to the date of a clock.

Plinth. Properly speaking, the base of a clock, but more usually applied to its skirting.

Positional error. The variations in the rate of going of a watch due to change of position; pendant up, pendant down, dial up, dial down, etc.

Potance. The bracket supporting the lower

pivot of the crown wheel arbor in a verge escapement (Plate 27, Fig. 13 at B).

Pump across. In ting-tang quarter-striking clocks the quarters are struck on different-toned bells. Usually there are two hammers, one for each bell, and the striking action is "pumped across" from one hammer to the other.

Quarter clock. A clock striking at the quarters as well as at the hour.

Quoins. Representations of the corner stones of a building. In almost all cases it will be found that the long cases so decorated originate in Lancashire, late eighteenth century.

Rack and snail striking. A system invented in 1676 by Edward Barlow which, except for turret clocks, has practically superseded the locking plate in this country. This type of striking made repeating clocks more practical (Plate 28, Fig. 21).

Rate. The regular amount by which a clock gains or loses in a stated period of time, usually per day.

Rating nut. The nut placed below the bob of the pendulum and used to regulate it. In some early nineteenth-century clocks the rating nut appears above the bob, in these cases movement of the rating nut is inverse (Plate 28, Fig. 25 at A).

Regulator. A high-grade long-case clock with compensation pendulum and possibly other refinements, such as roller bearings and jewelling. The hour is frequently read off a disc revolving behind the dial proper, and showing through an aperture.

Repeater. A clock or watch on which the hours, and generally also the quarters, and in rare cases the five minutes and even the minute, can be made to strike at will by the pulling of a cord, the pressing of a knob, etc. Repeating clocks were common until the end of the first quarter of the nineteenth century, when matches were introduced.

Repeating work. The motion work necessary to make a clock or watch repeat.

Ringing. The practice at the turn of the seventeenth and eighteenth centuries of surrounding the winding square holes, and sometimes the seconds hand arbor, with concentric decoration (Plate 29B, C).

Ripple or piecrust trim. Wavy wood trim occasionally used to decorate the fronts of some small Connecticut, U.S.A., clocks. Occasional (Plate 22B).

Rise and fall. The subsidiary dial of a clock for pendulum regulation purposes (Plate 29E).

Roman strike. A system devised by Joseph Knibb in the latter part of the seventeenth century to reduce the power needed, in spring-driven clocks especially, to drive the striking train. The hours are struck on two different-toned bells, one striking up to III and the other once for V, and twice for X. In clocks so made the IIII is usually marked IV. Sometimes found also in long-case clocks.

Saddle or seatboard. The wooden platform to which the movement of a tall clock is fastened. Also found in certain smaller clocks.

Sandglass or hourglass. An early device for measuring time consisting of two glass globes one over the other, containing fine sand which may pass from one to the other through a small opening. Their origin is unknown, but they are believed to date from the fourteenth century. Supporting frames are of wood or metal, and some from the Renaissance period, when they often appear in sets of four registering the four quarters of the hour, are very decorative. They, together with sundials, were the principal time-measuring device in the Middle Ages and in colonial America. They are usually anonymous and are frequently reproduced, but genuine ones up to the late eighteenth century are always made in two pieces and wrapped and bound round the junction.

Seconds dial. The subsidiary dial on a clock on which the seconds are marked.

Sedan clock. A large-dialled watch some 4–6 inches in diameter, with bow for hanging in a conveyance. Usually has a small watch type of movement behind the much larger dial.

Sheepshead. A lantern clock in which the chapter ring extends appreciably beyond the rectangular frame of the front dial plate.

Shelf clock. A clock, either weight- or spring-powered, designed to be placed on a shelf.

Skeleton dial. One in which the metal is cut away from the applied chapter ring, leaving only the numerals, minutes and inter-horary marks.

Spandrels. Decorative corner-pieces found on clock dials for about a hundred years from 1675–80. Their design is a guide to the date of the clock (Plate 29A, B).

Splat. The decorative panel, painted, veneered, or carved, placed at the top of many clocks.

Spoon. A hinged hook on the inner side of the top of the front of a long-case clock, so that when the door is closed the lower "spoon handled" part of the hook is pressed back and the upper hooked part pressed forward to keep the hood locked until the trunk door be opened again. Only found in early long-case clocks with rising hoods (Plate 28, Fig. 20 at B).

Stackfreed. An early South German device of unknown origin to be found in very early watches, whereby a roller attached to a strong spring bears against a shaped snail or cam, the radius of which decreases. This cam is mounted on an incompletely cut wheel which is driven by a pinion on the mainspring arbor. The rate of uncoiling of the mainspring is checked in a diminishing degree as the roller presses against the diminishing diameter of the cam, until, after the spring has unwound about three turns, the pinion strikes the uncut part of the wheel and the watch has to be re-wound, thus limiting the use of the spring to those turns of most nearly equal force. The principle of the lever underlies this as in the fusee. Both methods are found in the early sixteenth century, but the fusee ultimately supplanted the stackfreed everywhere (Plate 28, Fig. 17).

Stencilled clocks. Name now given to many American shelf clocks which have painted and stencilled columns and splats. Also called "Hitchcock" on account of the similarity of the decoration to that on Hitchcock chairs. Usually with wooden movements. Desirability depends on maker, type of movement, and condition of tablet and stencilling. c. 1825–40. Common (Plate 23A, B).

Stop watch. One in which the seconds hand can be stopped or restarted at will without stopping the whole movement. In the earliest stop watches, c. 1680–90, the stop stopped the whole movement. They were used by doctors and were called "pulse watches" (Plate 32D, E).

Strike-silent. Any mechanism that stops at will the striking or chiming of a clock. The early forms had a pin showing through the dial, attached to a lever, and had the dial marked "N" and "S" (Not and Strike). Later a subsidiary dial appeared for this purpose.

Sundial. Probably the earliest device to show the time of day by the shadow of a gnomon, or standard, on a base. They were the general method of recording time throughout the world until clocks became cheap enough for universal use. Multitudinous forms, both portable and static, have been produced over the ages. They were frequently provided with a compass and were adjustable for latitude. In the eighteenth century some were made to record time to the minute. The better ones in England and Europe were signed, but it is rare to find an American signature.

Sunray clock. A type developed in the late seventeenth century at the time of the cult of the "Roi Soleil", Louis XIV. A central circular dial with carved wooden sun's rays emanating therefrom. Much copied to-day. Original clocks have the rays of hand-carved wood.

Suspension. Refers to the method of supporting the pendulum of a clock, spring, silk, knife-edge.

Table clock. A clock with a horizontal dial, designed to be placed on a table and viewed from above (Plate 31B).

Tablet. The painted or otherwise decorated glass panel found in many American shelf and wall clocks. In clocks made to about 1830–5 the designs were hand-painted on the back of glasses. Scenic designs with gilt or gold-leaf borders were most common, while floral or conventional designs were also used. Most of the scenes appear to have been drawn as synthetic compositions and not from real life. Original tablets in fine condition are scarce and add much to the value of a clock. The restoration and reproduction of these reverse paintings is a specialized art, and few artists are now able to duplicate the appearance of original glasses.

The tablets in clocks since 1840 are usually printed decalcomanias, plain or coloured. Etched glasses or stencilled designs are also found in clocks of this period.

T-bridge. A type of pendulum support particularly used by Simon Willard in his banjo clocks. The suspension spring is pinned to a T-shaped unit which fits into and is held by a support on the clock movement.

Three-tier or three-decker clock. A variety of large weight-driven Connecticut shelf clock, the front of which usually consists of an upper and a lower door with a fixed panel between. *c.* 1828–50. Occasional.

Tidal dial. A dial that indicates daily the time of high tide at any given port. Not found on Continental clocks. The earliest English dials were made for London, and show high tide at new and full moon at 3 o'clock. Since the 24-hour cycle is completed each lunation, by having two circles, one fixed and marked 1–29½ (the days of the lunation) and the other movable, marked 1–12 twice over; if the time of high tide at any port at new moon be known, by placing that hour under 29½, the daily times of high tide for that port will be shown (Plate 29C, 1).

Time, Mean. Time calculated on an average basis of a day of 24 hours exactly. A year contains 365¼ mean days.

Time, Sidereal. Time as calculated by the successive passage of a selected star across the meridian. A sidereal day is 23 hours 56 minutes 4 seconds of mean time. There are 366 sidereal days in a mean year of 365¼ days.

Time, Solar. Time as calculated by the successive passages of the sun across the meridian, as shown on a sundial. This varies daily.

Tin-plate movement. A clock movement the plates of which are of tinned iron. Invented (patented 1859) in an attempt to save brass and reduce the cost of clocks. Small Connecticut clocks. Rare.

Ting-tang. The sounding of the quarters on two different-toned bells.

Torsion pendulum. A pendulum in which the bob rotates by the twisting and untwisting of a long suspension spring. Usually found on clocks designed to run a long time on one winding, as year clocks. A few eight-day, thirty-day, and year clocks with torsion pendulums were produced under one or more patents to Aaron Crane of Newark, New Jersey, and Boston, Massachusetts. *c.* 1840–60. Several styles, all rare.

Tourbillion. A watch in which the escapement is mounted on a revolving carriage, which carries it round. Invented by A. L. Breguet in 1801 to avoid positional error.

Tower or turret clock. A large clock as used in the towers of churches and other public buildings; often with two, three, or four dials. Probably the first clocks made in America were of this sort. Some in New England were made with wood movements.

Train. A series of wheel and pinions geared together, forming the mechanism of a clock or watch. They are going, striking, chiming, musical, astronomical trains, etc.

Tropics. The interval in the celestial sphere between the parallels of latitude demarking the maximum declination of the sun north and south of the ecliptic. The Tropic of Cancer in the north and the Tropic of Capricorn in the south.

Trunk. That part of a long-case clock between the hood and the base.

Up and down. A subsidiary dial in highest-grade watches to indicate the extent to which the spring is rung down (Plate 32J).

Verge. Commonly used to designate the unit including the two pallets of the escapement; it is fixed to an arbor or directly to the crutch.

Visible escapement. An escapement which is visible or directly in front of the dial. Certain experimental models or shelf clocks by Eli Terry are rare examples (Plate 26A).

Wagon-springs. Flat-leaved springs used to power certain Connecticut shelf and wall clocks. Invented by Joseph Ives, also made by Atkins, Birge, and Fuller, and others. *c.* 1825–55. Rare.

Wag-on-the-wall. An American term applied to any wall clock in which the weights and pendulum are not enclosed in a case. Some of the earliest American clocks were of this sort. Many of the Connecticut wooden movements intended for tall clocks (*c.* 1800–25) were sold without cases and often used as wall clocks until a case might be provided. Some used in this way were provided with simple hoods to protect them from dust.

Warning. The partial unlocking of the striking train, which precedes the full release at the precise moment of striking.

Warning-piece. That which arrests the warning-wheel between the warning and the time to strike.

Warning-wheel. A wheel in the striking train which carries a pin and which is arrested and then released by the warning-piece.

Watch bow. The loop at the end of the pendant.

Watch-Paper. In England towards the end of the eighteenth century it was sometimes the practice to place a circular paper engraved with the maker's or repairer's name as a protection to the double case and as an advertisement. In the United States cloth was at first used, and later silk with a design or tender message. After 1800 printed papers appear.

Water clock. A contrivance used in Egyptian, Greek, and Roman times for measuring time by the regular flow of a stream of water changing the level in a container, on the surface of which floated a means of indication on a fixed scale. Water clocks in the seventeenth and eighteenth centuries were drums with internal pierced sloping divisions, causing the water to pass slowly from one to the other, making the drum revolve and its axis roll down a graduated framework. Very few genuine examples exist.

Weights. The masses used to provide motive power in fixed clocks. Usually of lead in early clocks, later cast iron. From the late seventeenth century onwards the best clocks had brass sheeting to the weights. In some primitive and country turret clocks, natural stone is used. Weights of many American grandfather clocks, especially those with wooden movements, were often cylinders of thin sheet iron (tin) filled with scrap iron or any other heavy material. These latter are called "tin-can" weights.

Wheel, Centre. The wheel to which the cannon pinion is attached.

Wheel, Great. That which is attached to the going barrel, fusee, or, in weight-driven clocks, the gut barrel.

Year clock. A clock designed to go for one year with one winding.

Year, Sidereal. The period of one complete revolution of the earth round the sun.

Year, Tropical. The interval between two successive returns of the sun to the same tropic, or equinox.

Yorkshire clock. A broad and ill-proportioned long-case clock made for some years towards the end of the eighteenth century and early nineteenth.

Zodiac. A belt of the heavens outside which the sun, the moon, and the planets do not pass. Divided into twelve signs, each of 30 degrees, termed in astrology Celestial Houses: Aries (The Ram), Taurus (The Bull), Gemini (The Twins), Cancer (The Crab), Leo (The Lion), Virgo (The Virgin), Libra (The Balance), Scorpio (The Scorpion), Sagittarius (The Archer), Capricornus (The Goat), Aquarius (The Water Carrier), and Pisces (The Fishes).

Der Vhrmacher.

BOOKS AND BOOKBINDINGS

Book-collecting is at once the most various, the most sophisticated, and the least income-taxing of all the pursuits discussed in the present volume.

It is true that a Gutenberg Bible or a First Quarto of *The Duchess of Malfi* or a large paper copy of the first edition of *Gulliver's Travels* costs much more than most of us can afford. And the few illustrations to this article have been selected for distinction, not as examples of austerity. But compare, for instance, the *editio princeps* of Homer or *Lycidas* or *Le Rouge et le Noir* with Poussin or Lamerie or Riesener (to look no higher), and it becomes immediately apparent that book-collecting even on a fairly lordly scale is a positively economical indulgence by comparison with most of its competitors for the connoisseur's attention. It is therefore useful for those, not already addicted, who judge it by the occasional newspaper reports of the sale of a First Folio or a set of Audubon's *Birds of America*, to be reminded that an enjoyable and rewarding and significant library can be formed for the price of either of these books by a man of taste and intelligence.

The variety of book-collecting, indeed, is almost infinite; for there are books about every subject under the sun, books of every physical kind, shape, and size, books in a profusion which has steadily increased from the 38,000 or so editions recorded before 1500

– that is, the output of the first forty-five years of printing – to the 18,066 new books and new editions published in Great Britain alone during the single year 1951. Far too many laymen equate bibliography with the accumulation of first editions, and first editions of pure literature at that. One of the most instructive collections within my own acquaintance was of second editions, which (its owner reasonably considered) told us more about their author's effect on the public than the firsts, besides being in many cases much harder to find – an attraction rather than a deterrent to the true believer. It is perhaps twenty years too late to expect to assemble for a song a collection of original editions illustrating the development of the romance of chivalry, of electricity, of the Victorian novel, of African exploration, of Italian opera, or of the detective story. But the history of mountaineering, of art criticism, of nuclear fission; English hymn-writers, the minor Romantic poets, the Edwardian novelists; Renaissance latinity, the Oxford Movement, Mr Wise's forgeries; baroque book-design, the illustrators between Bewick and the sixties, distinguished printing between Kelmscott and Nonesuch; chancery-style italic, eighteenth-century Irish bindings, non-fiction issued in serial parts – it would be easy to fill a couple of pages with inviting and only partially explored fields. The complaint is often heard that the supply of desirable books is drying up, that everything has gone to America, that all the fine things gravitate to public or academic libraries, whence they can never emerge. It is true that even a millionaire would be ill advised today to start collecting Elizabethan drama or the *editiones principes* of the Greek and Latin classics with any serious expectation of achieving completeness. Yet history has shown (so far) that for every section of obvious foreground that becomes hopelessly overrun, at least two enticing vistas open up in the middle distance.

This limitless potentiality for the expansion of interest – for the relating of unconsidered books to some instructive or attractive pattern of collecting – is based upon the threefold nature of bibliography's appeal. For a book may appeal to the eye, by its beauty or singularity of printing, illustration, or binding; it may appeal to the intellect, by the power, influence, or significance of its content; or it may appeal to the imagination, to that sense of the past which is active in some of us, latent in all of us – the emotion evoked as sharply by

the dim, scrubby print of Pascal's *Les Provinciales* or *The Pilgrim's Progress* or *The Communist Manifesto* in their original form as by the elegance of Gray's *Elegy* or *Adonais* in theirs – the feeling that, whether we care about first editions or not, Pope should be read in folio, Gibbon in quarto, and Jane Austen in small octavo. And to whichever aspect of this fundamental variety may attract the collector is added the third quality claimed in the opening sentence of this note: a range of technical connoisseurship as sophisticated, as esoteric, and as minute as could be demanded by the most exacting devotee of prints or silver, china or furniture. If books are not always as prolific of "states" as some prints; if hall-marks can be trickier than colophons; if an imitative porcelain factory can cause as much initial confusion as a piratical publisher; if chairs are more often "restored" than incunabula are "made-up"; nevertheless, books can hold their own with any competitors for an all-round standard of delicate nicety in the sphere of collecting technique.

Bookbindings

AMERICAN

The earliest American bookbinder of whom we have any knowledge is John Sanders, who took the freeman's oath in Boston in 1636 and bought himself a shop there in the following year. In 1663 John Ratcliff was binding some copies of Eliot's Indian Bible and appears to have worked in Boston until 1682. Two of his bindings have been identified by MS. inscriptions and a number of others have been attributed to him on the grounds of his characteristically poor workmanship. His tools seem to have passed into the hands of another Boston binder, Edmund Ranger (active 1671–1705), who was a better craftsman. Ratcliff and Ranger both produced some bindings with simple gold tooling and with pasteboards, but

the typical seventeenth-century Colonial binding is of undecorated sheep or calf over thin wooden boards or "scabboards".

In the eighteenth century the absence of wealthy collectors restricted the production of elaborate bindings in America, and those few that have survived are the work of immigrants and are typical of their native countries rather than their adopted home. There was a strong influx of binders trained in Scotland, and two very typical Scottish bindings, one with a "herring-bone" and the other with a "wheel" pattern, were probably produced in Williamsburg between 1736 and 1744. Later in the century the best-known binder in America was another Scot, Robert Aitkin, who was active in Philadelphia as a printer and publisher as well as a binder, and whose most elaborate efforts include three bindings in the Chinese Chippendale style on the Blair's *Lectures* he published in 1784. Elsewhere in Pennsylvania, the German and Dutch immigrants were producing a very different style of binding, the products of the German monastery at Ephrata and the workshops of the Saur or Sower family in Germantown and Bethlehem, Pa., being almost medieval in character, with heavy wooden boards, blind-tooled leather, and metal bosses and clasps.

The early years of the Republic were marked by an increase in French influence on the designs of both tools and bindings, but the next notable figure in American binding was the native-born John Roulstone, who figures in the Boston directories from 1803 to 1825

and who followed English models. After him interest turns towards the blocked or "stamped bindings" found most frequently on annuals and keepsakes up to the time of the Civil War. Most frequently found on cheaper-grade leathers, this type of block could also be used on cloth, which from 1827 onwards rapidly began to replace leather as the normal covering in which books were issued. Casing replaced binding about 1830, and the remainder of the nineteenth century was marked by the rise of edition binding and its increasing mechanization. Hand-binding was kept alive largely to serve the needs of the new wealthy book-collectors, the most skilful practitioners being immigrants such as William Matthews (1822-96) from Aberdeen, the German Otto Zahn (1856-1928), and the French and English binders who worked for the Club Bindery between 1895 and 1909.

ENGLISH

Collecting bookbindings is generally thought to be a rich man's hobby, and a long purse is certainly needed to form a truly representative collection containing the most beautiful and the most interesting bindings of all periods. Yet by intelligent specialization in a limited field, such as the blind-tooled bindings of the sixteenth century, the less elaborate gold-tooled work of the eighteenth century, early nineteenth-century signed bindings, or the plainer trade bindings of any period, an interesting, attractive, and historically valuable collection can be brought together by the ordinary impoverished British citizen of today.

Condition

As in any form of book collecting, condition is an all-important consideration. The aspiring collector must set himself standards of condition which accord with his bank balance, bearing in mind that he will probably derive more pleasure from the possession of a humble trade binding in mint state, almost as fresh as when it awaited a purchaser in a seventeenth-century bookshop, than from a soiled example from a famous collection, lavishly gold-tooled but so badly worn as to be beyond restoration.

The more ambitious collector will, when possible, avoid acquiring any binding that has been at all extensively repaired, but the leathers used in England, with the exception of the best moroccos, have not lasted very well, and some compromise may often be necessary. The decorated calf bindings which survive from the library of Thomas Wotton, the "English Grolier" (1521-87), seldom retain their original backs; but as long as they have been suitably rebacked in a close imitation of the original style, they need not be excluded from a collection of the first rank – except by the purist who wishes to collect English bindings only and not bindings produced for Englishmen in France. The morocco of Charles II's reign, on the other hand, has usually lasted excellently, and for this period it should not normally be necessary to adopt anything that has undergone more than a little judicious titivating of the caps at head and tail or a very skilful repair of a joint.

Leathers

The leather used for a binding will give the first clue to its date. On a medieval manuscript, sheep or deerskin (either white or pink) is the commonest material, while what is customarily described as calf (but is more probably cowhide) runs a poor third until the last quarter of the fifteenth century. Throughout the sixteenth century this so-called calf was the normal covering of all decorated bindings, whether blocked in blind or tooled in gold. From 1525 onwards, however, limp vellum (or its cheaper form known as forel) became increasingly popular for smaller undecorated books. Morocco (tanned goatskin) was very rarely used before the reign of James I, and in the first half of the seventeenth century it was usually brown or olive green. Red and blue moroccos began to appear after 1650 and were the normal material of the finest bindings of the Restoration, which were often further adorned with thin onlays of different-coloured leathers. Gold-tooled vellum bindings were fashionable in the first half of the seventeenth century, but the material was gradually ousted on the plainer bindings by sheep or calf. In the eighteenth century sheep was relegated to the cheapest work – school books or the chapbooks peddled round the country by itinerant chapmen – and was in turn replaced from 1770 onwards on these books by the earliest form of bookcloth, a rather coarse, brown canvas. Vellum or parchment was found only on the elaborate Edwards of Halifax bindings, which have designs painted on the under-surface of transparent vellum, or on half-bindings such as Newbery's "vellum manner" of the 1770s.

For the better class of book, calf was the most popular material until the introduction, also in the 1770s, of paper-covered boards – a style which was intended to give the book temporary protection until the owner should have it properly bound to his personal taste. The moroccos in use in the first half of the eighteenth century were still generally dyed red or blue, and were often of poorer quality than those tanned in Charles II's reign. About 1760, however, new and more delicate shades of colour were introduced, and about ten years later "straight-grain" moroccos, with an artificial pattern of raised parallel lines, came into fashion. In the 1820s came the rise of edition binding, when the publisher, rather than the bookseller or the purchaser, took over the responsibility for having the book bound. Bookcloth was introduced about 1823 by Archibald Leighton at the instigation of William Pickering, the publisher, and when casing replaced binding for cloth-covered books about 1830 the modern era had arrived.

Blind-tooled bindings

The earliest known English decorated leather bookbinding is that on the Stonyhurst Gospel, which was removed from the tomb of St Cuthbert in 1104 and probably dates from the seventh century. One other binding that may be English is now at Fulda, having belonged to St Boniface, the eighth-century English missionary to Germany. These, however, are fabulous rarities, and hardly more accessible to modern collectors are the small group of "Romanesque" bindings of the twelfth and thirteenth centuries decorated in blind with beautifully engraved tools. London, Oxford, Winchester, and Durham may all have had binders working in this manner, but it is now clear that the great majority of these Romanesque bindings – once all confidently assumed to be English – were produced in Paris. Hardly any decorated leather bindings were produced in England in the fourteenth century, and the earliest examples likely to find their way into the antiquarian book market are the blind-tooled bindings of the second half of the fifteenth century. At first single tools only were used on these "calf" bindings, although one enterprising craftsman, known as the Scales binder, essayed some naïve cut-leather bindings in feeble imitation of the splendid works of art being produced in this technique in German-speaking lands. The first labour-saving decorative device – the panel stamp – was probably introduced into England by William de Machlinia about 1487. It enabled the decoration of the cover of a book to be completed at one operation in the binder's press. These panels are often signed with initials or names, but these are normally those of booksellers rather than binders. Many of them, particularly those decorated with figures of saints and Biblical scenes, are of Continental origin. There is, however, an interesting series of panels decorated with the royal arms and

Tudor rose (used decoratively by booksellers and not as a mark of royal ownership) which are distinctively English (Plate 39A). Panel stamps continued in use until about 1550, and there seems to be a gap of ten years or so before they were replaced by new designs, blocked in gold, which remained a popular form of decoration for smaller books throughout the Tudor and Stuart periods. A second short-cut to decoration was the roll, engraved with a wide band of ornament, which came into use in England about the year 1500. Tooled in blind, it remained in vogue for a long period, being *de rigueur* for the heavier theological tome well into the seventeenth century. One very late example (characteristically produced in Oxford) dates from 1654. From the Restoration onwards, blind-tooling was usually restricted to the delineation with a fillet or a very narrow roll of a rectangular panel on the covers and the back of a calf binding until it was revived in the 1790s for use in conjunction with gold-tooling on bindings of the highest quality.

Gold-tooled bindings

The earliest English gilt binding (now in the Bodleian) was probably bound for Cardinal Wolsey in 1519; it is decorated with what appears to be a wooden block, with panels of St George slaying the dragon and Tudor emblems. A unique example of one of John Reynes' royal arms panels blocked in gold survives in the Paris Bibliothèque Nationale on a book presented to Henry VIII by Thomas Linacre, who died in 1524. The use of small tools impressed in gold by hand, however, does not appear to have been introduced much before 1530. From the next twenty-five years quite a number of bindings have survived bearing the royal arms, which were formerly all ascribed to Thomas Berthelet, the King's printer in Henry VIII's reign. He certainly supplied fine bindings to the King, but there is no evidence that he had his own binder's shop. The bindings undoubtedly came from a number of different shops at present distinguished by names such as King Henry's binder (the earliest, who based his designs on Italian models), the Medallion binder, and King Edward and Queen Mary's binder (whose work

D*

seems the least rare and who copied the French bindings of his day) (Plate 38A).

Queen Elizabeth I showed a marked partiality for embroidered bindings, and this probably retarded the progress of gold-tooling in England. In the 1560s and 1570s some interesting bindings, decorated with small tools of French design, were produced in London for Archbishop Parker, who at one time had binders working for him at Lambeth Palace. Some bindings from the same shop were, however, also executed for Parker's enemy, Robert Dudley, Earl of Leicester, so that it is unlikely that all this group was bound at Lambeth. The most typical Elizabethan fine leather bindings are in the international style known as Lyonese, on which heavy centre- and corner-pieces were blocked in a press, and this style continued in use until about 1642. Some imitations of the French *fanfare* style (Plate 38B) were made in the last few years of the reign of James I, but distinctively English bindings now began to appear. Among these are versions of the centre- and corner-piece style, to which has been added an outer frame decorated with impressions of large tools, often wedge-shaped pieces of conventional foliage. Cambridge produced some characteristic bindings in the twenties and thirties of the seventeenth century which have small tools arranged in a circle in the centre and quarter-circles in the angles. It is at this period that we can begin to identify some of the binders by name, and these bindings are probably the work of Henry Moody and Daniel Boyse.

From Cambridge also came some of the earliest mosaic bindings of the Restoration period – the golden age of English bookbinding – and these can be attributed to John Houlden. He had been preceded in London by the brothers Stephen and Thomas Lewis and by Henry Evans, both of whom produced unexpectedly gay works in the last years of the supposedly gloomy Commonwealth period. Fletcher and Samuel Mearne were prominent in the 1660s, and the latter's shop was probably one of the most important in London until the death of his son Charles Mearne in the 1680s. To Mearne were long attributed all the decorative leather bindings of this period;

it was then asserted that, although he held the office of Royal Binder, he was not a binder himself and only commissioned bindings from others; it is now known that he was apprenticed to a bookbinder and that he had a binder's shop attached to his bookselling business, and a considerable number of bindings from his shop have been tentatively identified. Other binders whose work can be recognized include Samuel Mearne's apprentice, Robert Steele; Richard Balley, who was trained under Suckerman "at Mr Mearne's"; and Roger Bartlett, who retired to Oxford after the Great Fire. There are still, however, some distinctive groups of important bindings which cannot be ascribed to any known craftsman, and can only be attributed to the Queen's binder, the Devotional binder, and the Naval binder (Plate 37). During the reign of Charles II new and distinctive English binding designs were developed, including the Cottage style and the all-over pattern with drawer-handle tools, although some of the decoration was still based on the French *fanfare* style of a hundred years earlier.

The first half of the eighteenth century proved rather dull, exhibiting debased versions of the Cottage style and the rather insipid Harleian bindings. Some rather tasteless examples of mosaic binding came from Oxford in the 1720s. Others were produced in London between 1741 and 1745 on a group of bindings which includes three presentation copies of the illustrated edition of Faerno's *Cent Fables* printed at London in 1743. Andreas Linde perpetrated some Teutonic excesses for the future George III, *c.* 1751, but it was not until the next decade that any really important bindings were executed. The finest of these were designed by Robert Adam and by "Athenian" Stuart for books intended to popularize their architectural styles and theories, and neo-classical decoration of the same type appears on an attractive binding on a book printed by Horace Walpole at Strawberry Hill, which is now in George III's library.

Two interesting eccentrics now enliven the collector's scene – Thomas Hollis, an ardent republican in theory and a dutiful subject of George III in practice, and Jonas Hanway, founder of the Marine Society, opponent of tea-drinking and protagonist of the umbrella. Unfortunately the more elaborate Hollis bindings, the work of Richard Montagu, were only executed for presentation to Harvard, or to Swiss or Italian public libraries, where they still remain. In the 1760s rococo decoration made a tardy appearance; it was probably introduced in London by John Baumgarten, although the best-known bindings in this style are the work of James Scott of Edinburgh, where, as in Dublin, the binders outstripped their London rivals for much of the century. The eighties and nineties were marked by the rise of Roger Payne and by the flourishing school of German immigrants, including Baumgarten, Kalthoeber, Hering, Staggemeier, and Welcher, Benedict and Bohn, who were attracted by the boom in English book-collecting and the passion of the collectors of the period for full morocco. They were responsible for popularizing in England the admirable practice of signing bindings. Generally this was done with an engraved ticket, but not infrequently the binder's name was tooled on the leather or on a fly-leaf. Payne, notorious for alleged insobriety and for his endearingly verbose bills, worked almost single-handed, but in the last decade of the eighteenth century he set new fashions in design with his elaborate "gold-studded" backs These backs were not only copied by his German contemporaries in London but also achieved the unusual distinction of being imitated (not very successfully) in Paris. Egyptian and Pompeian motifs are found on some of the bindings of the Regency period, and soon after 1810 "Cathedral" bindings appeared on a number of the large books on ecclesiastical antiquities popular at the time. Some of the cheaper bindings decorated with the fly-embossing press introduced about 1830 were also decorated in this Cathedral style (Plate 39B). The 1820s, however, saw the introduction of a nearly fatal influence on English binding design – the copying of an historical style such as the "Grolier" or "Cottage". For the next sixty years magnificent workmanship was lavished – and wasted – on the production of dreary pastiches, and it was not until the mid-1880s that the ex-barrister

T. J. Cobden-Sanderson injected new ideas and new enthusiasm into his adopted profession.

The patrons

Some of the finest English bindings were no doubt ordered by collectors like Pepys, who visited Nott in Westminster in 1669 "to bespeak a book to be bound, only that I might have one of his binding". More, however, probably cover Bibles or Prayer Books intended for a church or nobleman's private chapel. A third group – particularly the bindings on the various works of the author of *The Whole Duty of Man* – were evidently bought ready-bound as presents. The most numerous class, however, is that of dedication and presentation copies from the proud author, and the more obscure the author, the more lavish is the binding.

CARE OF BOOKS AND BINDINGS

The main enemies of books are excessive dry heat, which can make both leather and paper brittle; excessive dampness, which can lead to mould growths; sulphur in the atmosphere, which can lead to leather decay; and insect pests. Air conditioning with a temperature of about 60° F. and a relativity humidity between 50 and 60 per cent is the ideal solution. Where this is not possible note that normal English living conditions are about right for books, while the average American home may be rather too warm and too dry; in industrial towns with a polluted atmosphere books are best kept in glass-fronted cases, but in a sulphur-free atmosphere open grilles are preferable, allowing air to circulate and preventing the formation of stagnant pockets of moist air. Many insects which attack books start by eating wooden shelves. Treat these with a suitable insecticide and keep both books and shelves clean. A specially prepared leather dressing is preferable to a commercial saddle soap or furniture cream, which may contain deleterious chemicals.

Glossary

Many of the definitions given here are based, with Mr John Carter's permission, on his invaluable *ABC for Book-Collectors*, published by Rupert Hart-Davis. The prevalence of these abbreviations in booksellers' catalogues varies with the descriptive formula. An elaborate catalogue will have few, but most cataloguers use the familiar ones, and in short-title or clearance lists there may be a good many – sometimes explained at the beginning, more often not. Even the abbreviations in common use are not all wholly standardized, nor does the following list pretend to be exhaustive.

A.d. and **a.d.s.** Autograph document, and autograph document signed, as distinguished from an a.l. or a.l.s., is likely to have relatively less collector's value; thus ship's papers, commissions, and land grants made out to or signed by famous men would be described as a.d. or a.d.s.

Ad. or **adv.** or **advt.** Advertisement or advertisements.

Advertisements. Separately quired advertisements edition-bound into the end of books were once used as bibliographical evidence of priority of issue, but for this purpose they have as little value as dust jackets.

A.l. and **a.l.s.** Autograph letter, and autograph letter signed; these, as opposed to l.s. and t.l.s., mean that the letter, in the one case without, in the other with, a signature, is in the hand of the writer, that the letter is not typed, not a copy (unless the writer's own), and not in the hand of a secretary.

All-over. A style of decoration in which the same motif is repeated at equal intervals all over the covers; particularly used to describe late seventeenth-century bindings with "drawer-handle" tooling (*q.v.*).

Americana. Books, etc., about, connected with, or printed in America, usually, but not exclusively, the United States of North America, e.g. dime novels; or relating to individual Americans: as distinct (properly, though nowadays not invariably) from books by American writers.

A.n. or **a.n.s.** Autograph note or autograph note signed. The expression refers to ms. memoranda, fragments, etc.

Ana. A collective noun meaning a compilation of sayings, table talk, anecdotes, etc. Its most familiar use is, however, the original one (from which the noun was made) in the form of a Latin suffix meaning material related to as distinct from material by, e.g. Boswelliana, Railroadiana, Etoniana.

Anon. Anonymous; i.e. published without the name of the author.

Antiquarian Booksellers' Association. The British trade association (open to foreign membership), founded in 1906. A list of members can be had on application to the ABA's headquarters, 15 Orange Street, London, W.C.2.

Armorial. As an adjective, used of (1) a binding stamped with the coat-of-arms, usually in gilt, of its original or a subsequent owner, and (2) of book-plates based on, or incorporating, the owner's arms. As a noun, used colloquially for an armorially bound book.

Association copy. This term is applied to a copy which once belonged to, or was annotated by, the author; which once belonged to someone connected with the author or someone of interest in his own right; or again, and perhaps most interestingly, belonged to someone peculiarly associated with its contents.

Azured. Descriptive of tools decorated with a series of slanting parallel lines. (From the method of depicting azure in heraldic engraving.)

Backless bindings. A whimsical style of the sixteenth and seventeenth centuries in which the spine of a binding is replaced by a fabric which is covered with gilt paper, so that the book appears to have four gilt edges.

Bands. Horizontal projections on the spine where the leather crosses the cords on which the book is sewn. On a hollow-backed book or one with sewn-in cords the same effect can be obtained with false bands.

Bd. Bound.

Bdg. Binding.

Beau livre. A book provided with original illustrations, initial-letters, or other embellishments executed in the particular graphic medium chosen by the artist himself: that is to say, copper or wood engraving, etching on metal, lino-cutting, or lithography. In other words, each illustration, each embellishment, whether it be an initial-letter, vignette, or tail-piece, is, if not unique, at any rate an original on which, in the case of a copper-engraving, the plate-mark may be said to have set its seal. Necessarily, for technical and economic reasons, "limited", the editions vary from fifty to three hundred copies, occasionally more for lithographed books.

Bevelled edges or **bevelled boards.** A style of binding in which the edges of the boards – usually extra thick boards – have been bevelled, i.e. cut to an oblique or slanting angle, before being covered.

Bibliography. The word has two main meanings, really quite different, despite the fact that they may shade into each other in some cases. One (the more familiar to the general public) is a reading list, a guide for further study, or a list or works which have been consulted by the author; and this will not normally give any detailed description of the books listed. The other, familiar to collectors, is a book about books as physical objects. Bibliography in this sense is the systematic description of books according to subject, class, period, author, country, or district; or of the products of a particular press or publishing house. Bibliography may be enumerative, analytical, or descriptive: ranging in method from a hand-list to a heavily annotated catalogue.

Binder's cloth. Any cloth binding, whether old or new, which is individual to the copy, i.e. not edition-binding.

Binding. Involves the cords or tapes on which the book is sewn being securely fastened into the boards, which are then covered with leather of other suitable binding material. Cf. Casing.

Binding variants. A general term for the variations, whether of colour, fabric, lettering, or decoration, between different copies of the same edition of a book bound (cased) in publisher's cloth. They are usually the result of the publisher's practice of binding up an edition, not all in one operation, but in batches as required; sometimes of his selling copies wholesale in quires for binding to another's order.

Blank leaves, blanks. Where these are an integral part of the book as completed by the printer, the fastidious collector will insist on their presence, though he may make allowances in the case of a very rare book. Blanks sometimes occur at the beginning of the book, sometimes at the end of a clearly marked division, more often at the end of the last gathering. In seventeenth-century or earlier books an initial blank may carry a signature letter. In a leather-bound book it is necessary to distinguish these printer's blanks from any extra leaves which the binder may have used in the front or back – conveniently called binder's blanks.

Blind. When decoration or lettering on a binding is said to be blind or in blind, this means that a plain impression has been made in the leather or cloth by the tool, die-stamp, or roll, without any addition of gold or colour.

Block. A piece of wood or metal, without a handle, being an engraved design for decorating the cover of a book, and intended to be used in a press.

B.M. A reference, generally, to one of the British Museum's printed catalogues of books. "Not in B.M." is a loose expression of American dealers meaning the book is probably English and may also be rare.

Boards. (1) In the widest sense, the wood, paste-board, strawboard, or other base for the sides of any bound or cased book, i.e. any book in hard covers. As commonly used, the term includes the covering of the actual board. (2) Also used in a specialized sense, to mean the *original* boards, backed with paper, in which most books were temporarily encased for distribution between about 1780 and the 1830s, when edition-binding in cloth began to take hold.

Book sizes and formats. The size of a book depends upon the size of the sheet it was printed on and the way the sheet was folded. A book's format, in turn, depends upon how its sheets were folded and then how these sheets were gathered into quires.

Since the two terminologies overlap and are used by the professionals in their variant meanings with precision, it is well for the amateur to understand these matters from the beginning.

For sheet sizes in detail, see Labarre's *Dictionary and Encyclopaedia of Paper and Papermaking*, pp. 251–72; but here are the most common sizes, each of these commonly subdivided into large and small:

Foolscap	$13\frac{1}{2}$ ×	17 inches
Post	15 ×	19 inches
Crown	15 ×	20 inches
Demy	$17\frac{1}{2}$ ×	$22\frac{1}{2}$ inches
Medium	18 ×	23 inches
Royal	20 ×	25 inches
Imperial	22 ×	30 inches

If the printed sheets are each folded once (to make 2 leaves or 4 pages), then the book is a folio. The Hakluyt folios (printed on sheets of about foolscap size) stand about 13 inches high by about 8 inches wide. But it will be noted from the above table that an Imperial folio (such as the Mark Catesbys) would be nearly twice this size. Folios other than chart books are typically gathered into 6 leaves or 3 sheets of 12 pages per quire. Thus, in the bibliographer's annotation, a book described as "fo. A–D⁶" would be made up of four quires (A to D) each made up of 6 leaves or 3 sheets, with A1ʳ: p.1, A1ᵛ: p.2, A6ʳ: p.11, A6ᵛ: p.12. The conjugate pairs of full sheets in the A signature would be A1 and A6, A2 and A5, A3 and A4; and the outer and inner formes would be in the pattern of outer: p.1 and 12, inner: p.2 and 11.

If the printed sheet is folded twice, into 4 leaves of 8 pages, the book is a quarto.

Folded once again, into 8 leaves or 16 pages, the book is an octavo. It should now be clear why a Crown Octavo is $7\frac{1}{2} \times 5$ inches, whereas a Royal Octavo is $10 \times 6\frac{1}{4}$ inches.

There are several ways of imposing 12mos, but the most common is a four-leaf cut-off from the top of the sheet inserted into an eight-leaf fold.

By the time one reaches the 16mo fold, the book is small enough to be uncommon, and the folds so numerous that half-sheet imposition is likely. The quiring in half-sheets of 32mos would be normal.

Publisher's Weekly in recent years has established an arbitrary standard for size-indication in its *Weekly Record of Books Published*, and this, for the most common sizes, is given below in juxtaposition with the measurements that might be taken as normal for the antiquarian book trade. The discrepancy between the two columns arises from *Publisher's Weekly*'s measurement of bindings rather than of sheets, and from *Publisher's Weekly*'s adhering to a theoretical standard for sheets; even though, as a practical matter, printers tend to vary the sheet size inversely with the height of the finished book.

Format	PW	Antiquarian
F°	over 30 cm.	13 inches
4to	30 cm.	9 inches
8vo	25 cm.	8 inches
12mo	20 cm.	5 inches

c. Used indiscriminately to mean copyright or *circa*. When anyone wants to be sure of not being misunderstood, the "c" for "copyright" is raised and "ca" is used for "*circa*".

Calf. Leather made from the hide of a calf: the commonest leather used in bookbinding. It is smooth, with no perceptible grain, and its natural colour is brown.

Calf can be treated in a number of ways, and for books full-bound (as distinct from half-bound) it will often be further described as polished, sprinkled, mottled, stained, tree (a special pattern), marbled, diced, scored, or grained. There are also special styles, such as rough, reversed, divinity, law, and antique.

Cancels. A cancel is any part of a book substituted for what was originally printed. It may be of any size, from a tiny scrap of paper bearing one or two letters, pasted on over those first printed, to several sheets replacing the original ones. "The most common form of cancel is perhaps a single leaf inserted in place of the original leaf" (McKerrow). The original sheet or leaf is called the cancelland (or *cancellandum*). That which is printed to replace it is called the cancel (or *cancellans*). The usual method for indicating to the binder that a certain leaf was to be cancelled was to slit it upwards at the foot. Occasionally a leaf slit in this way, having been overlooked by the binder, will be found bound up in the book (with or without its substitute).

C. & p. Collated and perfect.

Cartouche. A tablet, for inscription (e.g. the titling of maps) or ornament; originally in the form of a scroll, but sometimes used loosely (especially in descriptions of bindings) for round, oval, or decorated labels.

Casing. Involves the preparation in quantity of the boards and covering material (usually cloth) to form ready-made cases. These are attached by gluing a strip of mull to the back of the book, gluing the overlaps of the mull to the case and pasting down the endpapers.

Cat. Catalogue.

Cathedral. Applied to bindings of the period 1810–40, decorated in gold or blind with Gothic architectural motifs, which often include a rose window.

Cent. Century.

Cf. Calf.

Chapbooks. Small pamphlets of popular, sensational, juvenile, moral, or educational character, originally distributed by chapmen or hawkers, not by booksellers. Not in current use since about 1830, except as a conscious archaism.

Chemise. A prolongation of the covering material at the foot of a binding. Existing examples (in leather and velvet) date from the fifteenth or early sixteenth centuries. Cf. Girdle-book.

Chinoiserie. Most English bindings in the Chinese taste date from the 1770s and 1780s, Chinese figures mingling with rococo shell ornaments and C-shaped curves.

Cl. Cloth. Refers to the cloth covering the binder's boards on books.

Col(d). Colour(ed).

Collation. In the sentence, "This copy has been collated with the one in the British

Museum", the cataloguer is using the word in its simpler sense of "to compare"; and the implication is that the two copies are of the same composition. When he pencils on the back endpaper "collated and perfect" (or simply "c. & p."), he is using it in the special sense of "to examine the sheets of a printed book, so as to verify their number and order".

But collation has acquired a further (and to most collectors more familiar) meaning: the bibliographical description of the content of a book, expressed in a standardized formula. Thus, "Collation: A-L⁸ M⁴" means a book of 92 leaves, gathered in eleven quires of 8 and one of 4 leaves: there is no J (or U or W) in the signature alphabet.

Colophon. The finishing stroke (from the Greek work meaning summit): a note at the end of a book (sometimes accompanied by a device or mark) giving all or some of the following particulars: name of work, author, printer, place of printing, date. (See also Imprint.) In very early books most of these particulars may not be found elsewhere, and when inspecting the credentials of an incunable, it follows that one begins by turning to the last page, not the first.

Colour-plate books. A broad category, common in booksellers' catalogues, including any book with plates in colour, whether picturesque, sporting, or satirical, and whether these are wholly printed in colour, aquatinted with hand-coloured detail, or wholly hand-coloured on an engraved or lithographed base. Many books in the two last-named classes were originally issued in alternative states – coloured and uncoloured; and a very sharp eye is sometimes needed to distinguish skilful modern colouring from contemporary work.

Despite the existence of technical and descriptive studies by Burch, Martin Hardie, Strange, Dunthorne, Tooley, and others, the bibliography of colour-plate books is not yet adequate to the specialized complexities of a hybrid form of publishing.

Cottage style (of binding). A style of decoration in which the top and bottom of the rectangular panel (which itself will be filled with smaller ornaments in a variety of rich designs) slope away from a broken centre,

thus producing a sort of gabled effect. The cottage style was popular with binders of the last forty years of the seventeenth century and was still being used on pocket almanacs and prayer-books as late as the 1770s.

Cont. Contemporary. As in Cont. cf., meaning that the leather binding is contemporary with the printing of the book.

Cr. or **Cr. 8vo.** Crown octavo. *See* Book sizes.

Cul-de-tampe (Fr.). Tail-piece.

Curvette (Fr.). Plate-mark.

C.w.o. Cheque or cash with order. Dealers often advertise that they will send books post-free to collectors sending c.w.o. This is the book dealers' inversion of the abbr. c.o.d., which means "cash on delivery".

D.e. Deckle edges.

Dec. Decorated.

Deckle edges. The rough, untrimmed edges of a sheet of hand-made paper (the deckle being the frame or band which confines it in manufacture). Much prized by collectors, especially in books before the age of edition-binding in cloth, as tangible evidence that the leaves are uncut; for the deckle edge normally would be – and indeed was meant to be – trimmed off by the binder.

Dedication copy. It is customary for an author to present an early copy of his book to the person (if any) to whom it is dedicated. This is known as the dedication copy; and it will rank very high, in the estimation of most collectors, among presentation or association copies of the book.

Dentelle. A binder's term (from the French = lace) meaning a border with a lacy pattern on the inner edge, usually gilt. Dentelle decoration may be used on the outside of the covers; but in bindings of the past hundred years or so it has been more often used, in a somewhat emasculated form, on the inside – usually described as inside dentelles.

D.j. *See* D.w.

Doc. Document.

Dos-à-dos. A style of binding used mostly for small devotional works in the sixteenth and seventeenth centuries in which two volumes are bound back-to-back with a common lower board.

Doublure. A binder's term, meaning that

the paste-down (or inside lining of the covers) is not of paper but of leather, usually decorated.

Drawer-handle Tool. An ornament in the shape of an Ionic capital, first used on binding tools in the second half of the seventeenth century.

D.s. *See* A d.s.

12mo (**duodecimo or twelvemo**). *See* Book sizes.

D.w. or **d.j.** The book's printed or unprinted wrapper or "jacket", as it is generally called in America, though the unhyphenated expressions book jacket, dust cover, dust jacket, and dust wrapper are all also widely used.

Ed. Edition, editor, edited.

E.D.L. Edition de luxe.

Endp., e.p. Endpaper.

Endpapers. With rare exceptions, endpapers are not part of the book as printed. They are the double leaves added at front and back by the binder, the outer leaf of each being pasted to the inner surface of the cover (known as the paste-down), the inner leaves (or free endpapers) forming the first and last of the volume when bound or cased. Leather-bound and vellum-bound books of the sixteenth and seventeenth centuries sometimes had no endpapers. For leather and half-leather bindings marbled endpapers have been used since the late seventeenth century. In more elaborate bindings they may be of silk or some other special material, when they are called linings. In really sumptuous bindings the paste-down may be replaced by a doublure of leather.

Engr. Engraved; that is, printed from the indentations in a plate, as opposed to lithographed (from a flat surface) or letterpressed (from a raised surface).

Errata. Mistakes and misprints discovered after the book has been printed; also called corrigenda, and in some early books by the homely name of "faults escaped". If the errors are noticed before the preliminary leaves have been completed (these being customarily printed last), there is sometimes a spare page or part of a page to accommodate them. If not, they may be printed on a slip, or on an extra leaf, to be tipped in when the book is bound. When a book was published in several volumes appearing at intervals, later volumes sometimes contained lists or errata or addenda for the earlier.

Etruscan style. Descriptive of bindings in calf (*c.* 1780–1825) decorated by acid staining with classical decoration.

Evans. A reference to Charles Evans' *American Bibliography*, which lists all books printed before 1800 within the bounds of the present United States. "Not in Evans" means that the work is listed in one of the supplements to Evans.

Ex-lib. Ex-library.

Ex-library. This term is used of a book which has at one time been in a lending library. For cloth books, whether outside labels have been left in place or whether, as often with books of any consequence, they have been removed, their presence or traces are regarded with lively disfavour by most experienced collectors.

Extra-illustrated. In 1769 James Granger published a *Biographical History of England* with blank leaves for the addition of portraits, etc., to the taste of the purchaser. Hence grangerizing, for the practice which he formalized and promoted. Grangerized, or extra-illustrated books as they are now more commonly called, are copies which have had added to them, either by a private owner or professionally, engraved portraits, prints, etc., usually cut out of other books, and sometimes also autograph letters, documents, or drawings.

Frequently plates have to be inlaid in larger paper to suit the size of the book. Occasionally a whole book, originally of smallish format, has its text inlaid throughout, in order that plates of larger format can be inserted without folding.

Facs. Facsimile.

Fakes and forgeries. Most of the well-known bookbinding forgeries purport to be foreign examples. In the British Isles – apart from a brisk production of fore-edge paintings – activity seems to have been limited to the addition of royal arms or ciphers (particularly that of Mary Queen of Scots) to otherwise genuine bindings. Two well-known bindings with the arms of Henry VIII of England in the centre, surmounted by the Virgin and

Child and surrounded by a motley collection of armorial escutcheons, were probably produced in France in the nineteenth century.

Fanfare style. Originated in Paris, *c.* 1565. Copied in England from 1620 onwards. Interlacing ribbons, bounded on one side by a double line and on the other by a single line, outline geometrical compartments of varying shapes which (with the exception of a large central one) are filled with conventional floral ornament. The English imitations often have the interlacing ribbon bounded by a single line on each side.

FC. The file cope of an a.l.s., as opposed to the RC.

Fcap or **fcp.** Foolscap. A size and quality of writing paper which, when folded once, measures about 13 × 8 inches, or a little larger than what would in America be called "legal size"; formerly identified by its watermark of a fool's cap and bells.

Fillet. A wheel tool used for impressing one or several parallel straight lines; applied also to the lines produced by the tool.

Fl. Flourished. When an author's dates of birth and death are unknown, it is common in America to distinguish him from others of the same name by saying that he flourished on the date of the publication of his book or books. Thus the author of *Cytherea*, identified in England as John Smith of Sneton, is in America identified as John Smith, fl. 1677.

Fol., fo., f. Folio. *See* Book sizes.

Fore-edge painting. This term is most commonly used for an English technique originating in the seventeenth century and revived about 1785 by Edwards of Halifax, whereby the fore-edge of the book, very slightly fanned out and then held fast, is decorated with painted views or conversation pieces. The edges are then gilded in the ordinary way, so that the painting remains concealed (and protected) while the book is closed: fan out the edges, and it reappears.

Foxed, foxing. Of paper: discoloured, stained, usually with brownish-yellow spots.

Frontis., Fp., or **front.** Frontispiece.

G. or **Glt.** or **Gt.** Gilt; especially in the combinations g.e. for gilt edges, and g.t. for gilt top.

Gauffered (of the gilt edges of the book).

Decorated with the impression of a heated tool.

G.e. Gilt edges.

Gesamtkatalog. A reference to the *Gesamtkatalog der Wiegendrucke*, an alphabetical listing of incunabula, interrupted at the letter E by the Second World War and never resumed.

Gilt tops or **top edges gilt.** Interchangeable terms meaning that the top edges only have been gilded, and implying that the other edges have been cut smooth or at least trimmed. If they have not, the book is described as *gilt tops, other edges uncut,* or simply *t.e.g., uncut.*

Girdle-book. Some pre-Reformation service books were bound in a chemise (*q.v.*) gathered into a knop or button which could be attached to the owner's girdle. Small folding almanacks were similarly attached with a cord.

G.t. Gilt tops.

Haebler. A reference to one of Konrad Haebler's works on incunabula, most likely his *Typenrepertorium der Wiegendrucke*.

Hain. A reference to L. Hain's *Repertorium Bibliographicum*, a list of incunabula.

Half bound. This normally means that the spine and outer corners are of leather, while the rest of the sides are covered with cloth or paper (often marbled). If there are no leather corners the book is said to be quarter bound; if the leather corners are very wide it is said to be three-quarter bound.

Half-title. The leaf in front of the title-page (and of the frontispiece, if any) which carries on its recto the title (sometimes abbreviated) of the book, possibly a volume number or indication that the book belongs to a series, and occasionally the price. The verso is often blank, but sometimes carries the printer's imprint, or, in modern books, a list of other works by the same author or from the same publisher.

Harleian. In the manner of the eighteenth-century bindings executed for the library of Robert Harley, Earl of Oxford, and his son, Edward. They were usually of red morocco, with a border made up of one or more rolls (or rows of single tools), and often had a large central lozenge made up with small tools.

They were the work of several different binders, including the rival firms of Thomas Elliott and Christopher Chapman.

Harrisse. A reference to Henry Harrisse's *Bibliotheca Americana Vetustissima*, which describes Americana of the period 1492–1551.

Hf. Half; especially in the expressions hf. cf. for half calf, hf. mor. for half morocco, hf. bd. for half bound.

Horæ, or **Books of Hours.** Manuscript or printed collections of prayers, etc., for private devotional use at the canonical offices of the Roman Church. Variations of detail between one diocese and another are indicated by such phrases as "Horæ of the Use of Rouen", or "a Book of Hours of the Sarum Use".

Horn-book. "A leaf of paper containing the alphabet (often, also, the ten digits, some elements of spelling, and the Lord's Prayer) protected by a thin plate of translucent horn, and mounted on a tablet of wood with a handle" (*SOED*). Horn-books were used to teach children their rudiments from the sixteenth to early eighteenth centuries.

Ill., ills. Illustrated, illustrations.

Imp. Imperial. *See* Book sizes.

Impft. Imperfect.

Imprint. A notification to the reader (and to the legal authorities) of the person or persons responsible for the production of a book. Many of the earliest printed books bore no such note; but from about 1465 till late in the sixteenth century the printer's imprint was generally placed at the end of the book (and there properly called the colophon). It normally comprised the place of printing, the name of the printer, and the date.

With the development of the title-page during the sixteenth century the printer's imprint tended to be transferred thither (even if it was repeated at the end of the book); and from the latter half of the sixteenth to the middle of the eighteenth centuries it was often combined with the publisher's imprint, in such forms as *Printed by A.B. for P.Q.*. Later, the lower half of the title-page came generally to be reserved for the publisher's imprint – again normally comprising place, name, and date; the printer's name (and perhaps address) being relegated either to the back of the title or of the half-title or to the end of the

book. Either type of imprint may be accompanied by the printer's or publisher's device or mark.

Incunable, incunabula. The special use of incunabula (Latin for "things in the cradle") to mean books produced in the infancy of printing has for many years been further specialized to mean books printed in the fifteenth century.

Inlaid. (1) Of bindings: the use of coloured leather or leathers stuck, like mosaic, into the main skin; (2) of paper; (*a*) the insertion of a leaf or a plate or a cut, in a larger and usually stouter leaf, to enlarge its margins, and thus its whole size (often in order to range with other larger leaves in a composite volume, when it is usually described as inlaid to size); (*b*) the laying down, or re-margining on all four edges, of a badly damaged leaf.

Inlaid bindings. *See* Mosaic.

Inscr. Inscribed, inscription.

Inscribed copy. Unless specifically qualified, this term means that the copy has been autographed or inscribed by the author. It often implies, further, that the copy has been inscribed *to* somebody or *for* somebody; but it is important to distinguish, where possible, between a presentation copy, which is a spontaneous gift, and a copy inscribed by the author, often some while after publication, in response to an owner's request. The former naturally appeals much more strongly to the sentiment of collectors.

Introd. Introduction.

Issues and states. When alterations, corrections, additions, or excisions are effected in a book during the process of manufacture, so that copies exhibiting variations go on sale on publication day indiscriminately, these variant copies are conveniently classified as belonging to different *states* of the edition. It may or may not be possible to determine priority of manufacture between them, but any priority of publication must be assumed to be accidental. When similar variations can be clearly shown to have originated in some action taken after the book was published, two (or more) *issues* are distinguishable.

Ital. Italic letter.

Juveniles. Children's books. A jargon word but well established; borrowed from the publishing trade. To be distinguished from juvenilia, a writer's youthful productions.

L. or ll. Leaf or leaves; not often used in America because of the prevalence of the typewriter, which fails to distinguish between the letter l and an Arabic numeral one.

Label. (1) Leather labels (or lettering-pieces) have been commonly used by binders since the seventeenth century. They are generally of a different colour from that of the main skin, and almost always of morocco pared very thin (even if the book itself is bound, or half-bound, in calf). When two labels are used, sometimes of different colours, the conventional description is "double lettering-pieces". (2) Paper labels, printed from type or occasionally engraved, began to be used in the second half of the eighteenth century on the paper spines of boarded books. They must have been almost universal during the first quarter of the nineteenth century, on books put up in this form; and they continued as the regular method of titling for boarded books even after this style was generally superseded by publisher's cloth. They were also used on the early cloth books, though with sharply decreasing frequency after 1832, when the process for applying titling and decoration directly on to the cloth was perfected. (3) Library labels: *see* Ex-library.

Large paper copy. One of a (usually small) number of copies printed on a larger size of paper than the main bulk of the edition; either for presentation, or for subscribers, or to be sold at a higher price. The paper will often be of superior quality; and, in the eighteenth century particularly, these were generally called fine or royal or imperial paper copies.

L.C. A reference, generally, to one of the printed bibliographical tools of the Library of Congress based on their printed catalogue cards. "Not in LC" is a phenomenon so common with very rare books as to have little meaning.

Lettrine (Fr.). Initial letter.

Lev. Levant morocco.

Levant. A kind of loose-grained morocco leather, considered during the past hundred years the most elegant of the family. It is usually highly polished.

Lge. Large.

Limited edition. Any edition which is limited to a stated number of copies (books described as limited editions which fail to specify how many copies they are limited to should be regarded with scepticism). In many cases the copies are individually numbered, and perhaps contain the author's and maybe also the illustrator's signatures. Some limited editions are printed for private distribution only, such as those printed by publishers and printers for their friends at Christmas; many are published only for the members of clubs, such as the Roxburghe, Grolier, First Edition, and Limited Editions Clubs; other non-commercial limited editions are books printed experimentally. (*See* Press books.)

L.P. Large paper.

L.s. *See* A.l.s. When the A is omitted the letter is probably in a clerk's hand, with the signature only being the writer's.

Made-up copies. A made-up copy is one whose imperfections – the lack of a single leaf or more – have been made good from another copy of the same edition.

Marbled. "Coloured or stained with variegated patterns like those of marble, 1671", says *SOED*. Marbled paper, used since the latter part of the seventeenth century for the sides of binding and for endpapers, is made by lowering a sheet of paper on to a bath of gum or size, on the surface of which colours have been stirred with a stick or comb into a pattern. Marbled calf, introduced about the same time and also from Holland, is stained to a stylized pattern something like marble. Marbled edges are executed by a modification of the same technique as is used for marbling paper and are common on books bound since 1800.

Masonic bindings. The earliest English bindings decorated with Masonic emblems date from the second half of the eighteenth century. Robert Black and John Lovejoy specialized in their production.

M.e. Marbled edges.

Mint condition. A term borrowed from the numismatists, meaning as good as new and extended to such uses as "mint copy", "dust jacket defective, otherwise mint".

Mor. or **Mco.** Morocco.

Morocco. Originally leather made from the skin of North African or Moroccan goats, morocco today has no geographical significance, for most of it used for binding comes from other parts of the world; and the only common denominator among the numerous varieties of leather which go under the name is that they are all goatskin.

Of the various types of morocco commonly specified in catalogue descriptions, levant, hard-grain, and niger refer to differences of grain, pattern, or texture in the actual skin when tanned and dyed; straight-grain and crushed morocco refer to its treatment before it is put on the book; and morocco extra, super-extra, or elegant (an old-fashioned term) refer to the degree of elaboration and the amount of gilt which have been lavished on it by the "finisher" in the bindery.

Mosaic bindings. Bindings with polychrome decoration, produced by using: (i) paint; (ii) onlays of very thinly pared leather applied on top of the leather of the covers; (iii) genuine inlays of different-coloured leather inserted into the leather of the covers. Onlay is very much more common than inlay.

Ms. or **mss.** Manuscript or manuscripts. The expression is used arbitrarily about most documents other than letters, but may also refer to these. Thus the mss. of an author would include, say, the ms. of one of his novels, besides numerous a.d.s., a.l.s., t.l.s., etc. The ms. abbreviation is peculiarly confusing to autograph collectors having to do with German catalogues, since in German "MS" (for *Maschinenschrift*) is used to indicate that the ms. is not ms., but rather is typewritten. The German refers to the ms. proper as an "HS" (for *Handschrift*) when it is handwritten.

N.d. No date on the title page.

N.p. No place of publication (or perhaps publisher's or printer's name) given on the title page. The abbreviation is also used by professional cataloguers in America to mean a book for which there is no prospect of getting a Library of Congress card.

Ob., obl. Oblong.

8vo or **oct.** (**octavo**). *See* Book sizes.

Offprint. A separate printing of a section of a larger publication (generally of composite authorship) made from the same setting of type.

Offset. The accidental transfer of ink from a printed page or illustration to an adjacent page. This may be caused either from the sheets having been folded, or the book bound, before the ink was properly dry, or from the book being subsequently exposed to damp.

Onlaid bindings. *See* Mosaic.

O.p. Out of print.

Or. or **orig.** Original.

Original state or **original condition.** As used – and very widely used – by cataloguers and collectors, this almost always refers to the book's exterior; and it will be found applied to books in cloth, boards, wrappers, leather, or indeed any other covering for which the quality of originality can be claimed.

That it is claimed more often, especially of leather-bound books, than can in fact be substantiated, is an index of the steadily increasing importance attached to it since the last quarter of the nineteenth century; and indeed it is accepted doctrine with most collectors today that, to a copy in a fine binding or an appropriate binding, must be preferred (other things being equal) a copy in original binding.

P. or **pp.** Page or pages. In America the usage of p. for both singular and plural is superseding the pp.

Pallet. A tool with a short strip of decoration designed primarily for decorating the panels of the back of a binding. Specialized kinds can be used for lettering or signing bindings.

Panel, panelled. A term used in the description of bindings, meaning a rectangle, formed of single, double, or triple fillets (ruled lines), whether gilt or blind (plain), either on the sides or between the bands on the spine of the book.

Panel-stamped. A term used by writers on bookbinding (but not bookbinders) to describe leather bindings of the fifteenth and sixteenth centuries decorated in blind with engraved blocks.

Parts, part-issues. To most collectors parts means first and foremost the best-selling fiction published in this style from *Pickwick*, which started the vogue in 1836–7, to *Daniel Deronda* (1874–6), which was a late example. During this period most novels continued to be published in three volumes and *borrowed* by their readers from the circulating libraries. But a number of books by popular writers were published (usually with illustrations by a popular artist) in paper-covered parts, to be *bought* in instalments – monthly, fortnightly, or weekly – and bound up when complete. These part-issues were mostly of large octavo size and usually sold for a shilling. The final part, which contained the title-page and other preliminaries, would often be a double number, when the complete set is described as "in the original 13/12 parts".

The Victorian novels so issued are mostly not nearly as uncommon as might be supposed from their fragile character and intentionally impermanent coverings. But it is true that they have very seldom survived in fine unrestored condition.

Phillips. A reference, usually, to P. Lee Phillips' *A List of Geographical Atlases in the Library of Congress*, but sometimes instead to the same author's *A List of Maps of America*.

Pict. Pictorial.

Pl. or **plts.** Plates.

PoC. Polygraph copy. Thus, with Jefferson letters dated 1804 or after, of two nearly identical specimens, both would be a.l.s., but one would be a PoC, and the chances are that the PoC would be the FC, the one written by the pen held in the author's hand, the RC.

Pointillé. Used of tools, first introduced in France *c.* 1640, having a dotted and not a solid outline.

Points. A point is any peculiarity in a book whose presence in or absence from a particular copy calls for note. It is most often used of bibliographical peculiarities: the evidence (or alleged evidence) for priority of issue, binding variants, misprints, variant advertisements, cancels, textual changes, etc.

Pol. Polished.

Port. Portrait.

PrC. Press Copy. An offset impression, made under pressure on a damp tissue from the original. The FC of a Jefferson a.l.s., before Jefferson started using PoCs in 1804, is likely to have been a PrC. Letterpress copies were used for file purposes well into the present century.

Prelims or **p.l.** Preliminary leaves.

Pres. Presentation (*sc.* by the author).

Presentation copy. When used without qualification, this may always be taken to mean that the book was the gift of the author. But only a book spontaneously presented properly qualifies for the description; one merely signed in response to an owner's request is called an inscribed copy.

The pre-eminent quality in any presentation copy will always be that of its association – the interest or importance of the recipient, his connexion with the author, or other such special recommendation. This will override most of the niceties distinguishable in the wording of the presentation inscription.

Press books. A jargon term, but a useful one, covering the products of : (*a*) private presses proper, e.g. Kelmscott, Strawberry Hill, Lee Priory, Eragny, Gregynog; (*b*) concerns which, though not printing houses, call themselves "presses" because they specialize in fine book-production, e.g. Vale, Nonesuch, Grabhorn (U.S.); and sometimes (*c*) printers whose work is collected for its own sake, whether it was executed for a commercial publisher, e.g. Bulmer, Chiswick, Curwen, Bruce Rogers, or issued over their own imprint, e.g. Aldus, Estienne, Plantin, Baskerville.

Priv. pr. or **P.P.** Privately printed.

Proctor. A reference to R. Proctor's *Index to the Early Printed Books in the British Museum*.

Provenance. The pedigree of a book's previous ownership. This may be clearly marked by the owner's name, arms, bookplate, or other evidence in the book itself; it may be less clearly indicated by shelfmarks; or it may have to be pieced together from such outside sources as auction records or booksellers' catalogues. Provenance is interesting in proportion to the interest of the previous owners, whether as contemporary with its publication, or as persons of importance in their own right, or because they were book-collectors of note. It may be important, in the appraisal of an outstanding or very rare book, either as identifying it with one of *x* copies known, or for the guarantee of quality bestowed on it by having belonged to a respected connoisseur.

Pseud. Pseudonym; an assumed name, as Mark Twain or O. Henry.

Pt. Part.

Ptd. Printed.

Pub(**d**). Publish(ed).

Publisher's cloth. The use of cloth for edition-binding by the publisher dates from about 1823. For the collector this meant the establishment of a uniform original binding functionally inseparable from the book within it and readily identifiable, if not on sight at least by comparison with other copies of the same edition. And it has become an established convention that no book issued in publisher's cloth should be admitted to the fastidious collector's library in any other dress. Exception would be made for *presentation* or *association* copies, and (by any except fanatics) for books so rare that even a rebound copy may present the only chance of a lifetime. But the exceptions are few.

4to or **Qto** (**quarto**). *See* Book sizes.

RC. Recipients copy of an a.l.s., opposed to the FC.

R.e. Red edges.

Re-backed. This means that the binding of the book has been given a new backstrip or spine. It is mostly used of leather-bound or boarded or wrappered books, for this often necessary but usually unsightly form of repair is seldom resorted to for publisher's cloth. Unless otherwise stated, it is assumed that the new back is of similar material to the old.

Re-cased. A book which, being shaken or loose, has been taken out of its covers and resettled in them more firmly is said to be re-cased.

Rect. or **r°**. Recto.

Recto. The front, or obverse, side of the leaf, i.e. the right-hand page of an open book. Its complement is the verso.

Re-jointed. When the outside joints of a book have deteriorated through the stages of rubbed, tender, and weak, to being more than merely "slightly" defective, its owner may decide to have it re-jointed. If the damage has not gone too far and if the binder is skilful, this can be done so neatly as to be hardly per-

ceptible on the shelf – and occasionally even in the hand.

Re-margined. When one or more of the three outer margins of a leaf has been restored, it is said to be re-margined. If it is the inner margin only, the proper term is extended. If all four margins have had to be renewed the leaf is described as inlaid.

Remarques (Fr.). Separate illustrations containing insets.

Remboîtage. The transference of a book from one binding to another or the result of this nefarious practice.

Re-set. (1) When a leaf or leaves, or a whole section, has come loose from the binding and has been stuck back again, usually with paste or glue, it is said to be re-set; (2) if the whole book is so shaken and loose as to be unserviceable, it may be re-set in its binding (see also Re-cased); (3) a printer resets type for a new edition.

Rev. Revised.

Roan. A thin, soft kind of sheepskin used by binders as a cheap substitute for morocco from about 1790 onwards. Not at all durable, and seldom elegant, even when well preserved.

Rococo bindings. Rococo decoration was surprisingly late in affecting bookbinding design, and most English bindings with the typical asymmetrical ornaments, C-shaped curves, and fantastic shells of the style date from the late 1770s and the 1780s.

Roll. A tool (or the impression of a tool) leaving a continuous or repeated design engraved round the edge of a wheel.

Rom. Roman letter.

Royal bindings. Any binding blocked with the royal arms. Very often these do not denote royal ownership, but are used purely decoratively, e.g. the blind-stamped panels of Henry VIII's reign or the calf bindings, *c.* 1600, with Queen Elizabeth I's crowned falcon badge; both of these groups are trade bindings. Bibles and Prayer Books with the royal arms are very unlikely to have been personal possessions of the sovereign. They may have been part of the chapel furniture issued to all English ambassadors abroad; they may have come from a royal chapel; or they may even come from a parish church. Even books in an elaborate binding with the royal arms and a dedication to the King may never have been in royal possession, for sometimes an author seems to have had identical bindings made for his presentation copies. The dedication copy of Robert Adam's *Ruins of the Palace of the Emperor Diocletian at Spalatro*, 1764, is one of six copies known which bear the royal arms of George III.

Russia leather. Cowhide tanned by a special process, giving it a very rich, smooth effect; and originally scented. It was particularly popular with English binders between about 1780 and 1830, often being decorated with a diced or lozenge pattern in blind. But it is apt to fail at the joints, and it is not much used today.

Sabin. A reference to Joseph Sabin's *Dictionary of Books Relating to America*. "Not in Sabin" generally means that Sabin thought the work of too little American interest to list.

S.a., s.d., s.l., s.n. The abbreviations beginning "snas" or "sine" for no year (anno), date, place (loco or lieu), or name (nomine) are seldom used in America, and then only from snobbishness or affectation. *See* n.d., n.p.

Semis. A repeating pattern of small ornaments "sown" over the covers.

Sgd. Signed.

Sheep. A soft leather, with little grain. Good sheepskin, well handled, can make a not despicable binding. It was a popular trade binding for seventeenth-century poetry and other small books. But it has mostly been used for the commoner and cheaper sort of work; and it is all too liable to loss of surface on the covers, weakness at the joints and tearing off in long strips.

Sig. Signature.

Signatures. The letters (or, in some modern books, numerals) printed in the tail margin of the first leaf (at least) of each gathering or section of a book, as a guide to the binder in assembling them correctly. Signatures normally run from A to Z (omitting, by convention, J and U, which in earlier days were capitalized as I and V, and also W). If the whole alphabet has been run through, they usually proceed to AA, BB, or Aa, Bb, etc.

Signature is also used, by extension, to mean the gathering or section itself, e.g. "last signature stained", or "two signatures missing", or "lacks first leaf of sig. F".

Signed bindings. The binder's name will usually be given in a catalogue description if the binding is of any quality or interest, and if its executant or designer can be identified. Bindings can be positively attributed on several kinds of evidence: (1) By the printed or engraved label, known as a binder's ticket, such as have been in use since the eighteenth century. (2) By the binder's name, letter-stamped in gilt or blind inside the front or back cover; or by French binders of the late eighteenth and early nineteenth centuries, at the foot of the spine; or sometimes in ink at the edge of one of the endpapers. These are known as name-pallets. (3) By a manuscript note of the owner for whom it was bound. (4) Very occasionally, by some external documentary evidence, such as the binder's bill or a reference in correspondence.

Often, however, no such evidence is available; and then the cataloguer must fall back on an inferential attribution, based on stylistic grounds. The degree of credence to be accorded to such an attribution will depend on one's confidence in the person who makes it: confidence first in his knowledge and judgement; secondly, in his integrity.

Sm. Small.

Sombre bindings. Bindings of black leather, tooled in blind and often with black edges. The style (no doubt connected with mourning observances) was much in use on devotional books between 1675 and 1725. They were produced by all the important binders.

Spanish calf. A method, originating in Spain, of decorating the sides of a calf binding by bold dashes, or large flecks, of red and green acid dye.

Spr. Sprinkled.

Sprinkled. Used (1) of calf bindings, and (2) of the edges of leaves, and meaning coloured with small specks or spots. In sprinkled (or speckled) calf these are normally of a darker brown than the natural leather (stained calf is very rarely sprinkled). For edges the commonest colour is a dull red.

Sq. Square.

STC. A reference either to the *Pollard and Redgrave Short-Title Catalogue* (1475–1640) or to *Wing's Short-Title Catalogue* (1641–1700). In either case, the books referred to are English. The date will show which STC is meant, and if the numerical citation is without a preliminary letter, then the reference is to the earlier work. The later one is generally cited as "Wing" or "Wing STC". "Not in STC" or "Not in Wing" generally means that the dealer supposes the work to be of extreme rarity because he has not found how one of the STCs listed it.

Swd. Sewed.

T.e.g. Top edge gilt. This refers to the gilding by the binder of the trimmed top edges of the folded sheets.

Thk. Thick.

Tipped in. Lightly attached, by gum or paste, usually at the inner edge. Plates, errata slips, or a single inserted leaf will sometimes be described as being tipped in, as distinct from being sewn in. But the term is much more frequently used of something originally alien to the book which has been put with it by an earlier owner, e.g. an autograph letter from the author, or some similar associated document.

T.l.s. Typed letter signed. Cf. A.l.s.

T.p. Title-page. Americans eschew the hyphen except in adjectival use: thus, "Ornaments on the title page" and "Title-page ornaments".

Tr. Transcript. Used indiscriminately of manuscript copies without regard to the period of transcription unless specified.

Trade bindings. Executed for a retail or wholesale bookseller prior to the development of publishers' bindings in the nineteenth century. Before 1820 ready-bound books formed only a portion of a bookseller's stock, much of which would be in sheets (or after 1770 in paper-covered boards, uncut ready for binding to the customer's order).

Tree calf. A calf binding (popular in the nineteenth century, less common today), the sides of which have been stained by the interaction of copperas and pearl-ash to a design resembling a tree, and then highly polished.

12mo (twelvemo). *See* Book sizes.

Unb., unbd. Unbound.

Unct. or **unc.** Uncut.

Uncut, cut (of edges). Collectors have always, and rightly, cherished copies with ample margins; for it has been the habit of binders from earliest times to trim off more rather than less of the rough edges of the leaves than was intended by those who designed the printed page; and every time a book is rebound it is liable to lose more. Of books published before the age of edition-binding, therefore, a tall copy is preferable (other things being equal) to a short one.

With the adoption (1825–35) of publisher's cloth as the original and intentionally permanent covering of the majority of books published in England and America, the collector's attitude to their edges is radically changed. For if he is in pursuit, as he usually is, of a copy in its original condition as issued to the public, he will require that its edges (whether uncut, rough-trimmed, or cut smooth) shall conform to a now standardized margin. All that he needs, therefore, in this particular respect, is an assurance that the edges have not been cut down by a re-binder or repairer.

Unopened. This means that the leaves of a book issued entirely untrimmed (and therefore having the folding of its component sections still intact at the top and fore-edges) have not been severed from their neighbours with the paper-knife. It must not be confused with uncut.

Variant. A general-purpose term used to describe a copy or copies of an edition exhibiting some variation, whether of text, title-page, illustrations, paper, or binding, from another copy or copies of the same edition. Its use does not necessarily imply that the copy or copies in question are abnormal; in fact, it is most frequently and properly used when doubts exist as to the priority, or even the precise relationship, between the two or more observed variants, and where in consequence no norm has been established.

V.d., v.p., v.y. Various dates, various places, various years.

Verso. The back, or reverse, side of the leaf, i.e. the left-hand page of an open book.

V.g. Very good (copy).

Vol(s). Volume(s).

Vso. Verso.

W.a.f. With all faults, i.e. the dealer or auction house will not refund the money if there are additional defects not described. Not to be confused with w.f., which means in U.S. "wrong font", or, in England, "wrong fount".

Waste. Spoiled or surplus sheets of printed matter, often used before 1650 by binders for lining the back of a book, making boards of compressed layers of paper, or as endleaves. Bookseller's waste – surplus quires of recent books or discarded fragments of old ones – is of little value in localizing a binding. Printer's waste, however – proofs, trial sheets, over-printings, etc. – is not so likely to travel as sheets from a completed book, and may give a clue to the place of binding.

Watermark. A distinguishing mark, some-times including the maker's initials, name, or device, and occasionally the date, impressed in the pulp during the process of papermak-ing, and visible in the finished product when held against the light. They have been index-ed, and approximately dated, in such works as Briquet's *Les Filigranes* (1282–1600), 1923, and Heawood's *Watermarks mainly of the Seven-teenth and Eighteenth Centuries*, 1950.

Wrappers, wrappered. Paper covers, plain, marbled, or printed. A wrappered book, in antiquarian parlance, is what would ordinarily be called a paper-back, and it has nothing to do with dust-wrappers or dust-jackets.

Wraps. Wrappers.

Y.e. Yellow edges.

CARPETS AND RUGS

The covering of floors is as old as civilization. The first carpet was probably nothing more than a few rushes or straw to form the floor covering, but that at least was something upon the cold stone or earth, and better than nothing. Later the reeds were woven or plaited to make a rush matting; then came patterns and colours and, finally, weaving and embroidery to make durability and softness march with decoration and comfort, not only for floors but also for walls and furniture.

The earliest authenticated records of carpet weaving in its present form are to be found in the Assyrian and Babylonian bas-reliefs *c.* 700 B.C., but there is no doubt that a substantial carpet-making industry had existed from a much earlier period. There are many references in Greek and Roman literature to the magnificence of Eastern rugs, which the opulence and luxury of the Oriental satrap demanded. Wear and tear, combined with the comparative fragility of their constituent silks and wools, have prevented the survival of any of these products of the looms of deep antiquity.

We have, however, many examples of antique carpets and rugs four or five centuries old. These early specimens have never been surpassed in quality of fabric, design, and colour, and although Oriental carpets have kept the traditional patterns and techniques, it is sad to record a history of gradual decline in the art, albeit with many occasional flashes of

brilliance and inspiration, but none, it seems, equalling the oldest pieces. During the late eighteenth and almost the whole of the nineteenth centuries the carpet industry of Asia Minor and Persia became organized for export, and large shipments were sent to Europe and America, very largely to the detriment of the general quality, which, by virtue of the painstaking nature of the hand-knotting, could not be maintained under the increasing pressure of demand. Nevertheless, the discriminating collector may still find excellent pieces of a high quality if he knows what to look for, and it is among this class and age of carpet that there is the great opportunity. Those older pieces of great antiquity are rarer than pearls, although during the period between the two world wars an effort was made to revive the ancient glory of the Persian carpet industry, and many fine rugs were woven.

One of the most remarkable features of Oriental rug-weaving is that the industry is so spontaneous and widespread. From Asia Minor to China; from Caucasia to India, rugs are woven by identical methods, materials, and dyes, but the patterns and colourings differ enormously and reflect the widely differing temperaments of their makers.

PERSIAN

The very finest of all the great carpets and rugs come from Persia. The Persian carpet at its best is worthy to be ranked among the great examples of creative art. Springing naturally from a luxury-loving and refined civilization, and finding at hand an unsurpassed quality of wool from the highlands of Persia, combined with a natural feeling for colour and form in all classes of its people, it is not surprising that many of these lovely pieces are so beautiful. There are secrets of dyeing: the ability to use brilliant colours impervious to strong sunlight and time alike, yet applied without damage to the sometimes delicate fabric. The apogee of Persian craftsmanship seems to have been reached during the reigns of Tashmak (1524–77) and Shah Abbas (1588–1629), and it is in this period that a number of the most famous carpets now existing were woven, usually under royal decree or patronage, and irrespective of cost.

The Persian designs can be classified as Medallion, Hunting, Garden, Vase, and Prayer. These designs are the basic constituents of Persian carpet-weaving, and are the inspiration of much of the Oriental textile designs. (*See* Glossary.)

Persian carpets of certain districts may be identified by the special knot which is used in a certain district and by the materials of which the carpet is woven. These basic materials are cotton, linen, wool, or silk, and often a combination of two or more. The knots are the Sehna and the Ghiordes knots. (*See* Glossary.)

CAUCASIAN

The designs of Caucasian rugs, which come from the Caucasian Mountains between the Caspian and Black Seas, show both Persian and Chinese influence, but retain strong characteristics of their own. The employment of the local highland wool, which is unsurpassed, combined with excellent weaving, has given these rugs lasting quality, and many examples of merit exist.

Among the earliest specimens are the famous Armenian Dragon rugs, woven in the sixteenth century. The main motifs consist of conventional upright dragons, forming panels, flowering trees with birds, and often elephants and camels. A pleasing shade of soft rose relieved by dark blue or black is the predominant colour. The dragon design has influenced many later specimens.

The knotting is almost exclusively Ghiordes.

The most prevalent motif is of jewel shapes, both diamond and octagonal in form, with use of latch hook in white or cream. The detail is generally of conventional small flowers.

TURKISH

Turkish rugs from Anatolia and Asia Minor are probably the most numerous of antique rugs to be found in Europe, largely due to the Venetian and Florentine Levantine trade. Large numbers were imported from the fifteenth century onwards and, owing to their distinctive designs and fine quality, were not used on floors but as wall hangings, and more often as table coverings, a custom which is still in general use in Holland. Many sixteenth- and seventeenth-century painters, notably Holbein, featured these rugs in their pictures, and they have, in fact, influenced textile design throughout Europe. These rugs come from Ladik, Kouba, Ghiordes, and Kir-Shehr, and the main design is usually what is called the Mihrab representation of the Oriental mosque arch, often embellished by a hanging lamp between pillars.

They were, of course, originally intended for and used as prayer rugs, and many, once the property of wealthy Moslems, are of incredible quality and striking beauty. During the fourteenth and fifteenth centuries the Ottoman Turks invaded Persia on several occasions, and they enriched their own carpet and rug industries by importing skilled Persian craftsmen. The influence of these carpet-weavers is most marked and a tradition of design and quality was established. The greatest period was during the reigns of Selim the Great and Suliman the Magnificent, when the Persian carpet weaving was at its zenith. Contemporary specimens bear a marked resemblance to Persian rugs, but the national characteristics are clearly apparent. The flowing lines familiar in the finest products of Tabriz and Ispahan have become bold and angular. The use of stronger colours and realistic flowers are other distinguishing features.

The Persian medallion with matching

corner-pieces can be seen in Ushak carpets. Kufic borders kindred to Caucasian designs were used in many rugs.

TURKOMAN

Most rugs from Turkestan are woven in traditional variations of the same motif, the octagonal "guls" (flowers) known as the "elephant's foot", and generally dyed in deep, glowing Turanian red, with dark blue and black.

CHINESE TURKESTAN

The influence of Chinese Art is clearly defined in these rugs.

The Plate medallion, cloud-bands, and Lotus, Pomegranate, and Peony from the motifs are all distinctly Chinese, but in·subtle manner the rugs show Persian influence.

The knotting generally is not fine; the merit of these rugs is in the extremely varied and unusual colouring — yellows, lacquer red, blues in infinite variety.

The main types are from Khotan and Kashgar, and are often called Samarkand.

٠,١,٢,٣,٤,٥,٦,٧,٨,٩, ai
O, 1, 2, 3, 4, 5, 6, 7, 8, 9, SANA (YEAR)

The Arabic numerals with the English, for identification of dates.

EUROPEAN

When carpets first came to Europe from the Near East in the fifteenth and sixteenth centuries they were used as covers for tables, cupboards, and chests, or were placed before the altar in church or chapel. Only kings and the higher nobility used foot-carpets, and they were a mark of rank. A small number of knotted pile carpets in imitation of Oriental ones were made in Europe. English examples date from the sixteenth and early seventeenth centuries. Some of the patterns follow Turkish models, others are like contemporary English embroideries. It was in France, at the Savonnerie, that a Western style of carpet was created which was taken up by different countries when the use of floor carpets became more general in the eighteenth century. But Oriental carpets were also imitated with the needle, working in tent and cross-stitch on canvas. In the eighteenth century this was developed into a purely European type of needlework carpet, especially in England. Besides these, cheaper forms of carpeting were used in the sixteenth, seventeenth, and increasingly in the eighteenth centuries. Apart from tapestry, woollen cloth with a nap, patterned ply-weaving, and moquette (woven as a velvet or plush) were used, the narrow woven strips being sewn together.

AMERICAN

Embroidered rugs were popular from 1800 to 1835. Rugs, braided or woven on the loom, from rags, were also used, but their exact period remains unknown. Carpets were home-woven about 1820 from multi-coloured woollen yarns and were probably in use until about 1850. Double-woven carpets were being produced by the professional coverlet weavers in the 1820s and 1830s, but all large-sized floor coverings were very expensive, and the average housewife produced smaller rugs from scrap material. It is probable that at first these were scraps of cloth sewn to a fabric base and later were strips hooked through the base.

Yarn sewn rugs are those in the bedrug technique which are sometimes described as embroidered, needle-tufted, or reed-stitched. In this technique a homespun linen or tow ground fabric was used and the pile surface was formed of several strands of two-ply yarn. The yarn was sewn through the ground, taking a short stitch and leaving a loop on the surface. Another stitch was taken close to the first and in a line following the curves of the design. Sometimes the pile is very long and sometimes exceedingly short. Rugs with short loops made of fine yarns may have been intended for use as table rugs. This technique produces a very soft, flexible rug. The colours usually found in yarn sewn rugs are the ones made from natural dyestuffs. Rugs in this technique were probably first made some time in the middle of the eighteenth century and continued until about 1830.

Patched rugs may be constructed in two general ways. The basic fabric may be new or used homespun linen, tow or woollen cloth, or it may be cotton sacking. The scraps of woollen cloth may be sewn to the surface of this ground material in two ways. In the first technique, which has been called button or patchwork, the pile cloth was cut into small square or circular patches from one-half to one inch across. These were folded in fourths and sewn down at the folded point to the ground. When sewn close together the effect is the same as the hooked rugs which have been sheared.

The second way, sometimes called Chenille or caterpillar (Plate 39A), was to cut strips from one-quarter to one and a half inches wide which were shirred and sewn to the ground. Sometimes the wider strips, cut on the bias, were folded through the centre and shirred before being sewn on, and sometimes the strips were shirred through the centre and sewn on with the two edges standing straight up. They were also constructed by cutting the strips very narrow, on the straight of the goods, and sewing them on flat so that they form small cartridge-pleats and look very much like an unclipped hooked rug. Most of the specimens seem to have orginated between 1840 and 1860.

Hooked rugs form the third group in regard to technique. The background material for these rugs was homespun linen, factory woven cotton or burlap. The cloth scraps were cut in strips and a hook was used to draw these up in loops from the back of the ground fabric. Sometimes the loops were cut when made, sometimes not, and in some rugs the loops were varied in length to give a raised or sculptured effect to parts of the design.

The best material for the pile was woollen rags, and the more cotton fabric that is found

in a rug the later in period it may generally be presumed to be. The ones hooked through a linen foundation are usually earlier than the ones with burlap. Burlap was probably not used to any extent before 1850. Almost any colour may be found in a hooked rug. Hooked rugs in general probably date from 1840 to 1900. They come not only from New England but from Pennsylvania and other states, where the hooking is likely to be coarser and much cotton fabric included. The designs used for hooked rugs encompass almost everything known to tradition.

Among the simplest patterns, which were ideal for using up the accumulation of vari-coloured scraps unsuitable for a formal design, are: block and basketweave, which consist of squares or other geometrical forms, filled with stripes running at right angles to the stripes in adjacent forms; wave or zigzag where one colour follows another in undulating rows looking like mosaic work; inch square with multi-coloured squares resembling a simple quilt design from which it may well have come; log cabin which is definitely like the quilt pattern of the same name and shows the same variations of shading; shell or fish scale design which is a very old pattern of overlapping arcs. There are also repeating geometrical forms such as circles, squares, diamonds and medallions which are often filled with stylized flowers.

In the floral designs, the flowers in vase or jar or loose sprays or bands of flowers may occupy almost the entire rug area or may be confined to a central medallion with a scrolled border surrounding it. The flowers became less stylized and more realistic as the Victorian era advanced.

Animal forms in hooked rugs may be early but are more common in the Victorian period. They include dogs, stags, parrots, lions, swans, cats with kittens, and various unnamable species. Landscape designs are also found and these may include buildings or animals. Nautical designs are more common near the seacoast where some of them were probably made by sailors.

Patriotic, fraternal, and symbolic designs are not so common and are, with the exception of the popular eagle of the 1820s, usually of rather late vintage. A common patriotic design celebrated the centennial of the Declaration of Independence in 1876. Along with these Victorian patterns go the rugs with mottoes, such as *God Bless Our Home, Good Luck*, etc. Many of the Victorian designs seem to be derived from the designs for Berlin work which were published in *Godey's Lady's Book* and *Peterson's Magazine*.

Commercial designs were certainly available by 1870 when one Edward Sands Frost, a tin pedlar from Biddeford, Maine, was already selling his designs. These he printed in colours on burlap by means of metal stencils.

Hooked rugs are found in all shapes and sizes. There are half-round threshold or "Welcome" mats and round, oval, square, and rectangular rugs of all sizes from one-and-a-half feet square to large carpets and hall and stair runners.

Floorcloths or oilcloths, made of canvas or linen heavily coated with paint, were fairly common in the eighteenth century. In the first half of the century they were decorated with a design in imitation of marble tiled floors, but later design kept pace with the times, and imitations of Wilton or Brussels carpeting are known. These floor coverings were so perishable that almost none have survived.

THE ORIENTAL "CARPITT" IN COLONIAL AMERICA

Rugs from the Orient have enjoyed distinction in the West from earliest times. Rome, Byzantium, Venice, France, and Flanders have in turn exerted extraordinary efforts to secure them. They came rather late to England, less than a century before the colonists brought with them to America an appreciation of the Oriental rug as an object of luxury.

Knowledge of the appearance of the early examples to reach Europe is gained from paintings. Italian frescoes of the fourteenth century depict almost exclusively simple repeat panels containing either stylized birds or animals. As the fifteenth century progressed animal styles continued, frequently more complex in execution and with such motifs as the dragon and phoenix, an early design migrant from China. At the same time, highly developed abstractions appeared in large numbers, based primarily on tree, shrub, and flower motifs in which geometric drawing becomes evident. This second type soon became predominant.

Strong evidence of rug importations into western Europe is furnished by Van Eyck and Memling, whose paintings show rugs which parallel those depicted by such fifteenth-century Italian masters as Ghirlandajo.

Tudor England

The insular position of England and her distance from sources of supply delayed introduction of these rugs to any extent until the sixteenth century. It was time for a distinguished collector to appear and he was at hand – Henry VIII. His new palace of Hampton Court was not a fortress, but matched in luxury the Fontainebleau of Francis I. Henry VIII had almost certainly seen a sufficient number of rugs on the Continent to excite his interest. He sought the proper connexions and found that Cardinal Wolsey, through Rome and particularly through Venetian traders, could supply the needs of Hampton Court for the prized Oriental weavings.

From Holbein, court painter to the King, much can be learned regarding the colour, design, and scale of the rugs obtained. One of his portraits shows the King in characteristic stance on a Turkish rug with indented repeat medallions of a type now known as a "Star" Ushakh, in a style which persisted into the eighteenth century. In Hans Eworth's portrayal of the royal family the floor is covered with another of Cardinal Wolsey's carpets, a well-known type with a central medallion on a rich red ground. This too is a Turkish rug from the vicinity of Ushakh, a type which has continued in more or less degenerate form almost to our own day.

In Holbein's *Ambassadors* at the National Gallery, London, two envoys stand one on either side of a table covered with a small rug differing in design from the rugs in the royal collection and almost entirely geometric in character. It probably came from an outlying village, not from one of the great weaving centres.

The English nobility were quick to follow the royal example. The Montague family have at least two rugs of the "Star" Ushakh type, one of which has embroidered in the end selvage the date *1580*. These two rugs are in the collection of the present Duke of Buccleuch and have been published many times.

In America

There are no seventeenth-century portraits of colonial owners of Oriental rugs, and not until the following century do these appear. It is therefore necessary to look elsewhere for some indication of their arrival in the colonies. For the time being, inventories provide us with the only information·available, and as they are mentioned in inventory after inventory, it is apparent that the colonists must have valued the Oriental as much as their contemporaries in England.

Contrary to general opinion, a number of colonists were men of some property on arrival, or soon created it through superior enterprise in their new environment. This was particularly true in New England, where ships were built almost at once and ocean trade with the West Indies and Europe began to flourish. Successful merchants managed to acquire the means to supply themselves with "Turkey carpitts" in comparatively short time. Such a one was William Clarke of Salem, the inventory of whose estate, taken after his death in 1647, just twenty-seven years after the landing of the Pilgrims at Plymouth, included the following: "1 Turkey carpitt" valued at £1, and "1 old Turkey carpitt" valued at 8 shillings. These are in contrast to entries of "1 Red Rugg, 1 Greene Rugg", etc., in the same inventory. This early example is the forerunner of many as the century advanced.

It is generally stated that carpets were used as a covering for tables and not on the floor, and it is undoubtedly true that many were so used. However, it seems wrong to argue that they were never used on the floor, in the light of the following announcement from the *Boston Gazette*, 26 March, 1754: "To be sold at public vendu at the dwelling house of the late Ebenezer Holmes in King Street, Boston . . . a large Turkey carpet measuring eleven and a half by eighteen and a half feet. . . ." This could obviously have been used only on the floor and in a room of considerable size.

The acquisition of Oriental carpets could be made at that time, legally, only through England, or beyond the legal pale through smuggling. A successful raid on a Dutch or Spanish merchantman might also have yielded such a prize.

An indication of the esteem in which the Turkey carpet was held is seen in an advertisement in the *Boston News-Letter* 20 February, 1755: "Stolen out of a house in Boston a Turkey carpet of various colors, about a yard and a half in length, and a yard in width fringed at each end. Three dollars reward." In pre-Revolutionary America the dollars were the Spanish milled dollars which were important in the financial dealings of the day, and their value was considerable, so that the reward was actually a high one.

Colonies such as Pennsylvania and Virginia had many families of wealth and culture, but as these colonies had no such stringent laws regarding the inventories of the deceased as existed in New England, more is to be learned from New England, particularly Massachusetts, in this respect.

Up to the present time, no American family has been able to offer one shred of evidence of an existing Oriental carpet which has come down to them from their seventeenth- or eighteenth-century ancestors.

Portraits showing Oriental rugs

The only visual evidence of the types of Oriental rugs known in early America is found in portraits, particularly in four that are very well known. These are:

1. John Smibert's *Portrait of Bishop Berkeley and his Entourage*, done in 1729, during Berkeley's two-year sojourn in America spent chiefly in Newport, Rhode Island. This, which is now in the Yale University Art Gallery, New Haven, Connecticut, shows the group seated at a table covered with an Oriental carpet.

2. Robert Feke's *Portrait of Isaac Royall and*

A John Ratcliff binding, done in Massachusetts about 1680; the volume is Increase Mather's *A Call from Heaven*, 1679. *Mather Collection, University of Virginia Library.*

PLATE 33

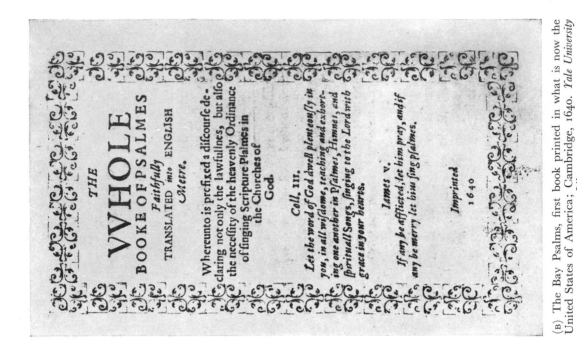

(B) The Bay Psalms, first book printed in what is now the United States of America; Cambridge, 1640. *Yale University Library.*

(A) The first Bible printed in America, the John Eliot Indian Bible, Cambridge, 1663. *McGregor Library, University of Virginia.*

PLATE 34

In CONGRESS, July 4, 1776.

A DECLARATION

By the REPRESENTATIVES of the

UNITED STATES OF AMERICA,

In GENERAL CONGRESS ASSEMBLED.

WHEN in the Course of human Events, it becomes neceſſary for one People to diſſolve the Political Bands which have connected them with another, and to aſſume among the Powers of the Earth, the ſeparate and equal Station to which the Laws of Nature and of Nature's God entitle them, a decent Reſpect to the Opinions of Mankind requires that they ſhould declare the cauſes which impel them to the Separation.

WE hold theſe Truths to be ſelf-evident, that all Men are created equal, that they are endowed by their Creator with certain unalienable Rights, that among theſe are Life, Liberty, and the Purſuit of Happineſs---That to ſecure theſe Rights, Governments are inſtituted among Men, deriving their juſt Powers from the Conſent of the Governed, that whenever any Form of Government becomes deſtructive of theſe Ends, it is the Right of the People to alter or to aboliſh it, and to inſtitute new Government, laying its Foundation on ſuch Principles, and organizing its Powers in ſuch Form, as to them ſhall ſeem moſt likely to effect their Safety and Happineſs. Prudence, indeed, will dictate that Governments long eſtabliſhed ſhould not be changed for light and tranſient Cauſes; and accordingly all Experience hath ſhewn, that Mankind are more diſpoſed to ſuffer, while Evils are ſufferable, than to right themſelves by aboliſhing the Forms to which they are accuſtomed. But when a long Train of Abuſes and Uſurpations, purſuing invariably the ſame Object, evinces a Deſign to reduce them under abſolute Deſpotiſm, it is their Right, it is their Duty, to throw off ſuch Government, and to provide new Guards for their future Security. Such has been the patient Sufferance of theſe Colonies; and ſuch is now the Neceſſity which conſtrains them to alter their former Syſtems of Government. The Hiſtory of the preſent King of Great-Britain is a Hiſtory of repeated Injuries and Uſurpations, all having in direct Object the Eſtabliſhment of an abſolute Tyranny over theſe States. To prove this, let Facts be ſubmitted to a candid World.

He has refuſed his Aſſent to Laws, the moſt wholeſome and neceſſary for the public Good.

He has forbidden his Governors to paſs Laws of immediate and preſſing Importance, unleſs ſuſpended in their Operation till his Aſſent ſhould be obtained; and when ſo ſuſpended, he has utterly neglected to attend to them.

He has refuſed to paſs other Laws for the Accommodation of large Diſtricts of People, unleſs thoſe People would relinquiſh the Right of Repreſentation in the Legiſlature, a Right ineſtimable to them, and formidable to Tyrants only.

He has called together Legiſlative Bodies at Places unuſual, uncomfortable, and diſtant from the Depoſitory of their public Records, for the ſole Purpoſe of fatiguing them into Compliance with his Meaſures.

He has diſſolved Repreſentative Houſes repeatedly, for oppoſing with manly Firmneſs his Invaſions on the Rights of the People.

He has refuſed for a long Time, after ſuch Diſſolutions, to cauſe others to be elected; whereby the Legiſlative Powers, incapable of Annihilation, have returned to the People at large for their exerciſe; the State remaining in the mean time expoſed to all the Dangers of Invaſion from without, and Convulſions within.

He has endeavoured to prevent the Population of theſe States; for that Purpoſe obſtructing the Laws for Naturalization of Foreigners; refuſing to paſs others to encourage their Migrations hither, and raiſing the Conditions of new Appropriations of Lands.

He has obſtructed the Adminiſtration of Juſtice, by refuſing his Aſſent to Laws for eſtabliſhing Judiciary Powers.

He has made Judges dependent on his Will alone, for the Tenure of their Offices, and the Amount and Payment of their Salaries.

He has erected a Multitude of new Offices, and ſent hither Swarms of Officers to harraſs our People, and eat out their Subſtance.

He has kept among us, in Times of Peace, Standing Armies, without the conſent of our Legiſlatures.

He has affected to render the Military independent of and ſuperior to the Civil Power.

He has combined with others to ſubject us to a Juriſdiction foreign to our Conſtitution, and unacknowledged by our Laws; giving his Aſſent to their Acts of pretended Legiſlation:

For quartering large Bodies of Armed Troops among us:

For protecting them, by a mock Trial, from Puniſhment for any Murders which they ſhould commit on the Inhabitants of theſe States:

For cutting off our Trade with all Parts of the World:

For impoſing Taxes on us without our Conſent:

For depriving us, in many Caſes, of the Benefits of Trial by Jury:

For tranſporting us beyond Seas to be tried for pretended Offences:

For aboliſhing the free Syſtem of Engliſh Laws in a neighbouring Province, eſtabliſhing therein an arbitrary Government, and enlarging its Boundaries, ſo as to render it at once an Example and fit Inſtrument for introducing the ſame abſolute Rule into theſe Colonies:

For taking away our Charters, aboliſhing our moſt valuable Laws, and altering fundamentally the Forms of our Governments:

For ſuſpending our own Legiſlatures, and declaring themſelves inveſted with Power to legiſlate for us in all Caſes whatſoever.

He has abdicated Government here, by declaring us out of his Protection and waging War againſt us.

He has plundered our Seas, ravaged our Coaſts, burnt our Towns, and deſtroyed the Lives of our People.

He is, at this Time, tranſporting large Armies of foreign Mercenaries to compleat the Works of Death, Deſolation, and Tyranny, already begun with circumſtances of Cruelty and Perfidy, ſcarcely paralleled in the moſt barbarous Ages, and totally unworthy the Head of a civilized Nation.

He has conſtrained our fellow Citizens taken Captive on the high Seas to bear Arms againſt their Country, to become the Executioners of their Friends and Brethren, or to fall themſelves by their Hands.

He has excited domeſtic Inſurrections amongſt us, and has endeavoured to bring on the Inhabitants of our Frontiers, the mercileſs Indian Savages, whoſe known Rule of Warfare, is an undiſtinguiſhed Deſtruction, of all Ages, Sexes and Conditions.

In every ſtage of theſe Oppreſſions we have Petitioned for Redreſs in the moſt humble Terms: Our repeated Petitions have been anſwered only by repeated Injury. A Prince, whoſe Character is thus marked by every act which may define a Tyrant, is unfit to be the Ruler of a free People.

Nor have we been wanting in Attentions to our Britiſh Brethren. We have warned them from Time to Time of Attempts by their Legiſlature to extend an unwarrantable Juriſdiction over us. We have reminded them of the Circumſtances of our Emigration and Settlement here. We have appealed to their native Juſtice and Magnanimity, and we have conjured them by the Ties of our common Kindred to diſavow theſe Uſurpations, which, would inevitably interrupt our Connections and Correſpondence. They too have been deaf to the Voice of Juſtice and of Conſanguinity. We muſt, therefore, acquieſce in the Neceſſity, which denounces our Separation, and hold them, as we hold the reſt of Mankind, Enemies in War, in Peace, Friends.

WE, therefore, the Repreſentatives of the UNITED STATES OF AMERICA, in GENERAL CONGRESS, Aſſembled, appealing to the Supreme Judge of the World for the Rectitude of our Intentions, do, in the Name, and by Authority of the good People of theſe Colonies, ſolemnly Publiſh and Declare, That theſe United Colonies are, and of Right ought to be, FREE AND INDEPENDENT STATES; that they are abſolved from all Allegiance to the Britiſh Crown, and that all political Connection between them and the State of Great-Britain, is and ought to be totally diſſolved; and that as FREE AND INDEPENDENT STATES, they have full Power to levy War, conclude Peace, contract Alliances, eſtabliſh Commerce, and to do all other Acts and Things which INDEPENDENT STATES may of right do. And for the ſupport of this Declaration, with a firm Reliance on the Protection of divine Providence, we mutually pledge to each other our Lives, our Fortunes, and our ſacred Honor.

Signed by ORDER *and in* BEHALF *of the* CONGRESS,

JOHN HANCOCK, President.

ATTEST.
CHARLES THOMSON, Secretary.

PHILADELPHIA: PRINTED BY JOHN DUNLAP.

The first printing and the only authoritative text of the American Declaration of Independence; printed by John Dunlap, Philadelphia. *Harvard University Library.*

PLATE 35

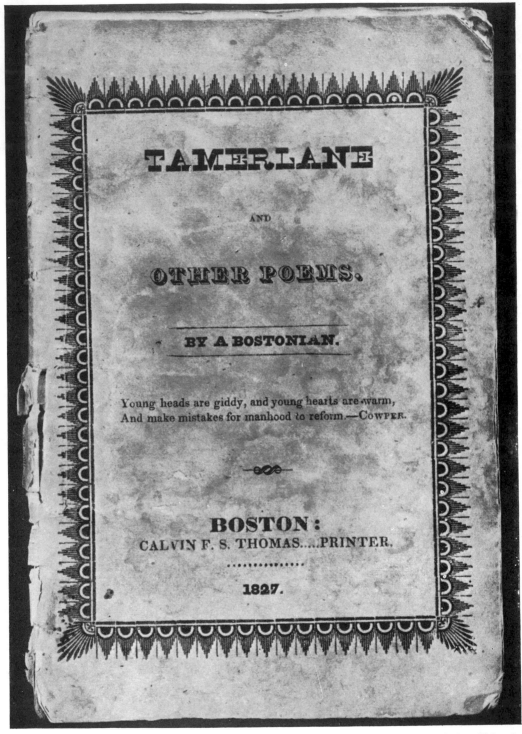

Front cover of Poe's first book of poetry, *Tamerlane*, Boston (U.S.A.), 1827. *Barrett Collection, University of Virginia Library.*

PLATE 36

A binding by the so-called Naval Binder, *c.* 1675. *Abstract of the Accompt of Payments made by the Earle of Darby . . . as Treasurer of His Majesty's Navy . . .* 1671–3. Black morocco, with red and orange onlays, tooled in gold. *British Museum, London.*

PLATE 37

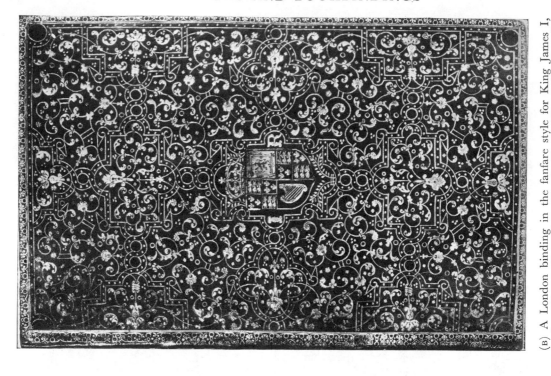

(B) A London binding in the fanfare style for King James I, c. 1620. Thevet. *Pourtraits et Vies des Hommes Illustres.* Paris, 1584. Dark green morocco gold-tooled, with the royal arms inlaid in

(A) A London backless binding for King Edward VI by the so-called King Edward and Queen Mary binder, 1552. Bembo. *Historia Veneta.* Venice, 1551. Brown calf with gold-tooled interlacing strapwork enamelled

PLATE 38

(B) A trade binding, c. 1830, blocked in blind with a cathedral design. *Holy Bible*, 1828. Red morocco. *Chas. J. Sawyer Ltd.*

(A) A trade binding, c. 1530, blocked in blind with the arms of King Henry VIII impaling those of Anne Boleyn. Whitinton. *Grammatical Tracts*, c. 1530. Brown sheep. *British Museum, London.*

PLATE 39

FRENCH BEAU LIVRE: (A) Etching by Beaudin, *Les Bucoliques*, Virgil, Skira 1936. Actual
size 13 cm × 16·5 cm.

FRENCH BEAU LIVRE: (B) Aquatint by Villon, *Œuvres Poétiques*, Ganzo,
Sautier, 1957. Actual size 11·2 cm × 13 cm.

PLATE 40

(A) Yarn sewn American rug. Geometric design in blue, rust, yellow, and green. May have been used as a table carpet. *Nina Fletcher Little, Brookline, Massachusetts.*

(B) Yarn sewn American rug. Floral design – natural colours. *New York State Historical Association, Cooperstown, New York.*

PLATE 41

(A) Shirred strip American rug. "Caterpillar" technique. *New York State Historical Association, Cooperstown, New York.*

(B) Hooked American rug. Floral design with leafy scroll border. Maine, mid-nineteenth century. *Winterthur Museum, Delaware.*

PLATE 42

Pile Carpet by Passavant of Exeter, dated 1757. *Victoria and Albert Museum, London.*

PLATE 43

Pile Carpet. Beauvais or Aubusson, late eighteenth century. *The Vigo Art Galleries*.

PLATE 44

Looped Pile Carpet. Spanish, 1797. *Victoria and Albert Museum, London.*

PLATE 45

(B) Kilim Rug. Rumania (Bessarabia), first half of nineteenth century. *Perez Ltd.*

(A) Kilim Prayer-rug. Yugoslavia, first half of nineteenth century. *The Vigo Art Galleries.*

PLATE 46

Ispahan rug. Exceptionally fine knot and delicate detail.

PLATE 47

Ispahan prayer rug, with tree and garden scene through Mihrab, or archway.

PLATE 48

Tabriz rug, hunting scene type. Note the clear drawing of animal and human figures.

PLATE 49

(B) Anatolian prayer rug, Ghiordes design. *Perez Ltd.*

(A) Tabriz rug. A typical example showing medallion on plain field. *Perez Ltd.*

PLATE 50

(A) Section of Kashan carpet, showing floral and tree motifs in medallion design. *Perez Ltd.*

(B) Section of Caucasian Chichi rug. *Perez Ltd.*

(C) Section of Turkish Ghiordes rug of conventional design. *C. E. Huggett.*

(D) Section of Kasak rug, a typical specimen. *Perez Ltd.*

PLATE 51

A   B   C

D   E   F

G   H   I

Sections of: (A) Kerman rug, Laver quality. (B) Feraghan carpet, Herat design, "Fish and Rosette" design. (C) Sehna rug, with cone design. (D) Caucasian Kouba rug, with conventional floral design. (E) Caucasian Hila rug, with cone and medallion design. (F) Caucasian Shirvan rug, with jewel design. (G) Turkoman Saloros rug, so-called Bokara. (H) Turkoman Bokara rug, Tekke. (I) Anatolian saph, or family prayer rug.

PLATE 52

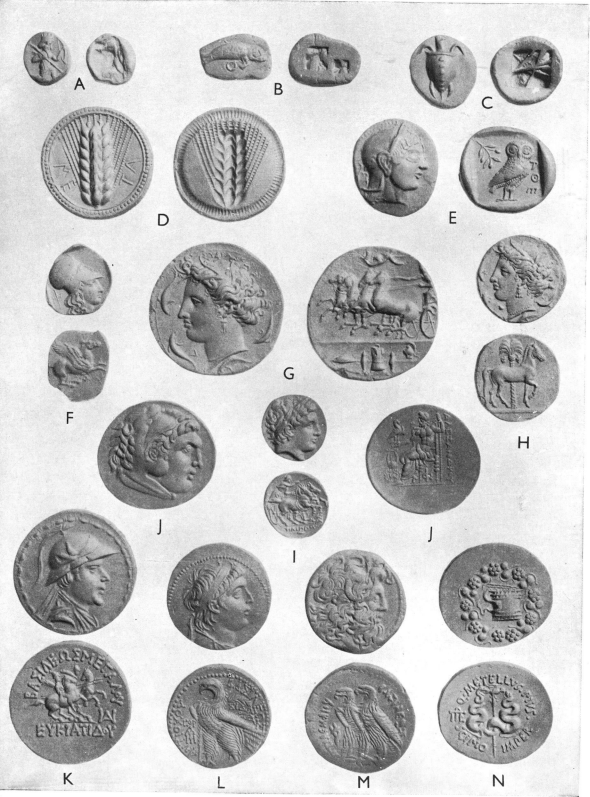

For a description of this plate, see page 157

PLATE 53

For a description of this plate, see page 157

PLATE 54

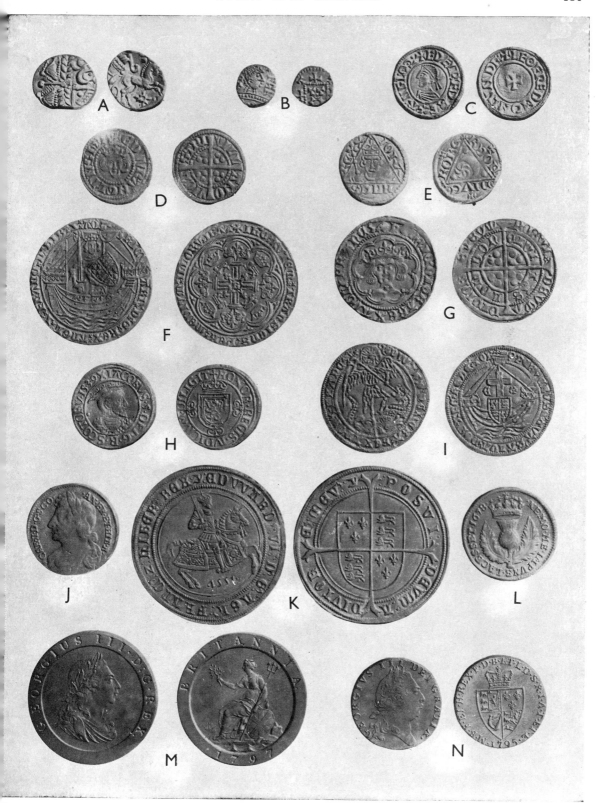

For a description of this plate, see page 157

PLATE 55

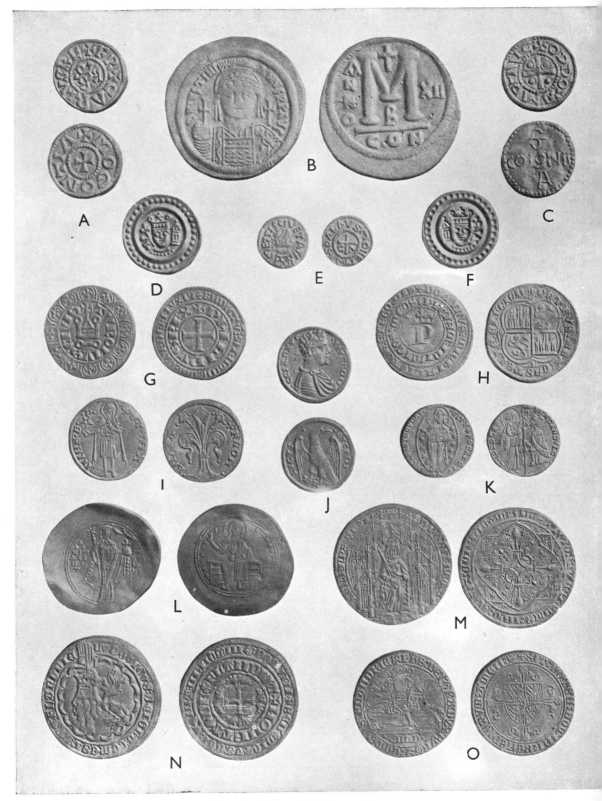

For a description of this plate, see page 157

PLATE 56

For a description of this plate, see page 157

PLATE 57

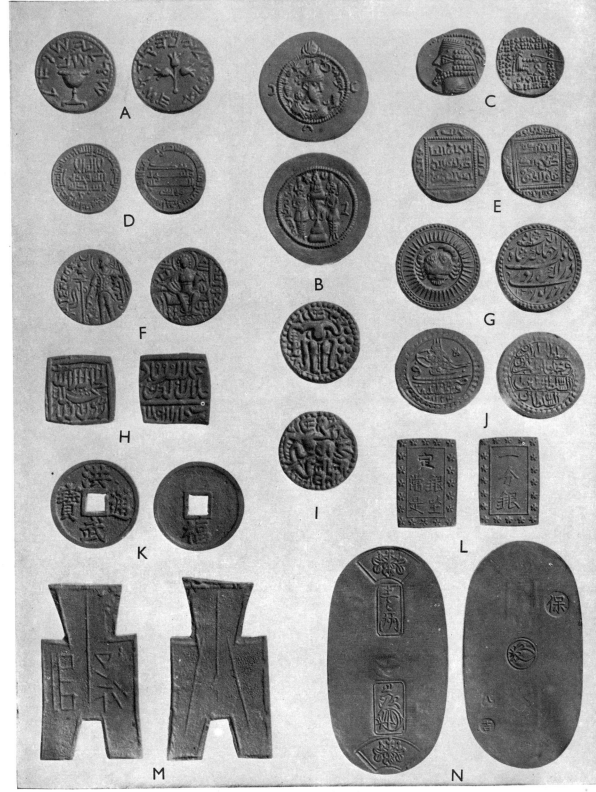

For a description of this plate, see page 157

PLATE 58

A

B

C

D

E

F

For a description of this plate, see page 157

PLATE 59

A

B

C

D

E

For a description of this plate, see page 157

PLATE 60

Description of Plates

American coins: (A) Half dime 1792, (B) reverse; (C) Half dime, 1794, (D) reverse; (E) Chain type cent, 1793, (F) reverse; (G) Half cent, 1793, (H) reverse; (I) Three dollars, gold, 1858, (J) reverse; (K) Bechtler five dollars, gold, (L) reverse; (M) Liberty Cap cent, 1794, (N) reverse; (O) Eagle 1795 type ($10 gold), (P) reverse; (Q) Eagle 1797 type ($10 gold), (R) reverse; (S) Silver dollar, 1795, (T) reverse; (U) Gobrecht silver dollar, 1836, (v) Confederate half dollar, 1861, (w) reverse.

PLATE 62

(A) Washington oval Indian Peace Medal, obverse and reverse.

(C) Saltus Medal, American Numismatic Society, Weinmann.

All illustrations by courtesy of the American Numismatic Society.

(B) Jefferson Indian Peace Medal.

PLATE 63

Italian medals: (A) Pope Innocent XII, anonymous, 1691–1700. *Museo Nazionale, Florence.*
(B) Pope Innocent X by Gaspare Mola, 1644–55. *British Museum, London.*
(C) Reverse of (A) with an allegory of charity. *Museo Nazionale, Florence.*
(D) Pope Innocent XI by Girolamo Lucenti, *c.* 1676–7. *British Museum, London.*
(E) Jubilee medal of Pope Benedict XIII by Ermenigildo Hamerani, 1725. *Museo Nazionale, Florence.*
(F) Reverse of (B) showing the Piazza Navona, Rome. *British Museum, London.*
(G) Reverse of (E) showing Agostino Cornacchini's statue of Charlemagne. *Museo Nazionale, Florence.*

PLATE 64

his Family, painted in 1741, is now owned by the Law School of Harvard University, Cambridge, Massachusetts. Isaac Royall's fine house at Medford is one of the historic New England houses open to the public. A copy of Feke's picture hangs over the mantel where the original once hung. Feke was familiar with Smibert's picture, as he has copied the arrangement, and shows the carpet in a similar way on the table, but the carpet itself is entirely different, which argues for the actuality of the original in Royall's possession. Although of the same type, it is of later date than the rug in the Berkeley portrait.

3. John Singleton Copley's *Portrait of Colonel Jeremiah Lee*, 1768, shows the wealthy Marblehead merchant standing on a Smyrna carpet. This portrait is now in the Wadsworth Atheneum, Hartford, Connecticut.

4. Gilbert Stuart's "Lansdowne" *Washington*, 1796, is not properly of the colonial period. It shows Washington standing on an eighteenth-century medallion "Ushakh", definitely of a late eighteenth-century origin and lacking much of the refinement of the mid-eighteenth-century type.

Terminology

It has become the custom to use the word rug for what our ancestors in England and America called the "Turkey carpitt", and the word carpet is generally reserved today for the machine-made product, acquired in strips and used to cover an entire room. The carpets of the eighteenth century, and earlier, were more frequently used on the table, but as trade made them more common they were used on the floor. The advertisement of 1754 makes it clear that Boston had homes where Oriental rugs were used on the floor in mid-century. After the Revolution, when trade directly with the East and Near East was undertaken, Oriental rugs must have become still more familiar.

While carpets took their place on the floor, the "rugg" remained what it had been, a cover for a bed. What is called today a coverlet was often recorded as a "bed rug". The steamer rug represents a survival of the old use of the term.

Collections

Recognition of the importance of the Oriental rug in colonial and post-colonial decoration has advanced rapidly in recent years. Henry F. du Pont, in furnishing the matchless series of American rooms at the Winterthur Museum, Winterthur, Delaware, was a pioneer. The buildings of the restored colonial capital of Williamsburg, Virginia, show an admirable selection of authentic types in the Governor's Palace, the Wythe house, Brush-Everard house, and elsewhere. The American Wing of the Metropolitan Museum in New York will soon have rugs especially chosen to agree with the period of each room. The houses in Fairmount Park, Philadelphia, under the care of the Philadelphia Museum of Art, the houses at Old Deerfield, Massachusetts, and at the Shelburne Museum, Shelburne, Vermont, as well as interiors in the museums in most of our large cities, show the use of such rugs as were known in early America.

Glossary

Abruzzi. *See* Italy.

Afghan. Afghan rugs are coarser in texture and design, but follow tradition of the other Turkoman types, looking rather like a much coarser Bokhara (*q.v.*).

Alpujarras. *See* Spain.

Aubusson. Knotted pile carpets were made at Aubusson from 1742 and at nearby Felletin from 1786. An upright loom was used as at the Savonnerie, but the carpets were considerably cheaper. Women, who were not allowed to work at the *basse-lisse*, and children, were employed for low wages. Eighteenth-century Aubusson carpets were designed by the Court painters and were of excellent quality. Tapestry or smooth-faced carpets were also made, especially in the nineteenth century. With the Revolution the production of moquette carpets (*q.v.*) was introduced.

Axminster. Thomas Whitty began the weaving of knotted pile carpets, at first inspired by Turkish models and then learning from Parisot at Fulham (*q.v.*) (1750–5). In 1757–9 he won three awards from the Royal Society of Arts, submitting six carpets for the 1759 competition. His prices were more moderate than Moore or Passavant (*q.v.*), and his industry thrived and was continued by his son. The large carpet made for Carlton House (*c.* 1790, at Buckingham Palace) and a fine carpet at Ramsbury Manor, Wiltshire, are surviving examples of his work. A little later Axminster carried out import orders for Brighton Pavilion (1810–20). Parts of these still exist. The Victoria and Albert Museum has a carpet of this period, or slightly later. Before the Axminster workshops closed down in 1835 two important carpets were made for the Goldsmiths' Hall and the Sultan of Turkey. The looms were taken over by Wilton (*q.v.*).

Beauvais. Knotted pile carpets in the Savonnerie manner were made between 1780 and 1792 and again for a few years under Napoleon.

Belouchistan (Turkoman). Early rugs often in prayer designs, the use of blue and lustrous yarn, combining with the coppery red, giving an iridescent effect to otherwise heavy colours.

Bergama (Turkish). Bergama rugs usually have a Mihrab on each end, giving a balanced design. These rugs, woven entirely of very lustrous wool, though not fine in texture, have pleasing colours, the borders bearing a marked affinity to the Caucasian weaves.

Beshire or **Bushire** (Turkoman). Carpets actually made in Bokhara City. They provide a variation in the design strongly reminiscent of the Herat "fish" design, but the colouring is the usual red, often on dark blue; a strong yellow outlines the design.

Bessarabia. *See* Rumania.

Bokhara or **Bokara** (Turkoman). These rugs have long been popular in England, and are, in fact, from three tribes; the Tekke is the most esteemed, the "guls" being well balanced and the side borders following variations of the same motif. The end borders are usually latch hook in diamond formation, and conventional tree of life forms. The yarns are very fine, often knotted 300–400 to the square inch on a weft and warp usually of wool, but sometimes of fine hair (Plate 52H). Woven in prayer rugs and also in fine camel bags.

Brussels carpets. *See* Moquette.

Central Eastern Persian Carpets. These come from Feraghan, Herat, and Khorassan (*q.q.v.*). They are all very similar in design, often with conventional flowers on a dark field, generally blue.

Chichi (Caucasian). These rugs have small jewel effects in the centre panel, with multitudinous borders (Plate 51B).

Djoshagan (Persian). Generally of Palmette or Vase designs, these rugs are simpler in design than those of Ispahan or Tabriz, with blue or deep red predominating. Knot: Ghiordes.

Donegal. Alexander Morton organized the weaving of coarse knotted carpets in Donegal at the request of the Congested Districts Board in 1898. Pile carpets are still woven there.

Ersari (Turkoman). In this type the octagonal "gul" is usually enclosed by bands forming a distinct diamond design.

Exeter. Claude Passavant, a native of Basel, and successful wool merchant and manufacturer at Exeter, started the subsidiary enterprise of making expensive hand-knotted carpets. He bought up Parisot's equipment in 1755 (*q.v.*) and took many of his men to Exeter. In 1758 he was a competitor for the Royal Society of Arts prize and gained an award. A beautifully made and excellently designed carpet by him in the Victoria and Albert Museum is marked "Exon 1757" and may be the prize-winning piece. Another dated 1758 is at Petworth. Giuseppe Baretti, secretary of the Royal Academy, wrote a favourable account of his factory in 1760 and reported on his success; but his carpets, which were more expensive than Thomas

Moore's of Moorfields (*q.v.*), are extremely rare.

Feraghan (Persian). Woven with a Sehna knot, it has enjoyed great popularity in this country, and varies slightly in the treatment of the traditional Herat design; the two most distinctive effects known as Guli Hinnai and Mina Khani. (*See* Plate 52B.) Knot: usually Sehna.

Finland. The Ryijy (pronounced R-üi-y-ü) rugs of Finland are in the old Norse tradition of knotted pile technique, which may go back to the Danish Bronze Age quite independently of Near Eastern influence, as Sirelius states (*see* Bibliography). Although derived from Norway and Sweden, in the sixteenth century Finnish pile-weaving already enjoyed a special reputation. Made primarily for bed-coverings, sleigh-rugs, or horse-cloths, they have a very long knotted pile, but the ground texture of wool or linen is not thick and there are usually ten to twenty shoots of weft between the rows of knots. The knotting technique is also curious and varied. Made on a

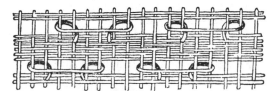

FIG. 1. A variety of Finnish carpet knot. (From U. T. Sirelius, *Handwoven carpets of Finland*, 1925.)

narrow loom, two widths were joined together, but a wide loom was also used. Patterns vary from plain-colour weavings and geometric motifs to simple floral patterns. It was customary for a girl to make a rug for her dowry, and many such pieces are dated, though few after 1860. The making of these exceptionally attractive rugs has been revived in the present century.

Frome. William Jesser, of Frome, entered (unsuccessfully) for the Royal Society of Arts prize for hand-knotted carpets in 1759, but nothing further is known about his manufacture.

Fulham. Peter Parisot, an ex-Capuchin monk from Lorraine, procured the patronage of the Duke of Cumberland for a carpet-knotting factory in Fulham. He is supposed to have employed as many as a hundred workmen, many from the Savonnerie, but owing to extravagances he was forced to sell up within five years (1755). A portrait of the Duke, dated 1755, is probably his work, and pile fire-screens are occasionally found.

Garden carpets. Persian carpet design showing a formal garden with alleys, trees, and pools.

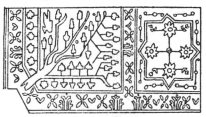

FIG. 2

Ghiordes. These rugs are the finest of the Turkish types and represent the apex of Turkish weaving. The knot is usually Turkish; yarns are very fine, warp and weft often being of silk. The colours are very varied, while the borders usually consist of bold conventional floral designs, beautifully treated (Plates 50B and 51C).

Ghiordes or Turkish knot. Used in most carpets from Turkey and some from Persia.

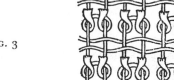

FIG. 3

Guls. *See* Turkoman "guls".

Hamadam (Persian). The marketing centre for Kurdish rugs (*q.v.*) which are often known by this name. Heavy, long pile of great durability, rather coarse in knotting, but well coloured, designs often embellished with animal figures Are often found under the general "Persian" classification.

Herat. These carpets are the aristocrats of the Central Eastern Persian group. The de-

sign most closely associated with this weave is
a close conventionalized all-over effect. With
a recurring leaf or "fish" motif and small
rosettes. This is copied throughout Persia,
ground shade is usually dark blue, and a distinguishing feature of fine specimens is a soft
green border. Knot: Ghiordes or Sehna.

Hila (Caucasian). These rugs often have a
small centre medallion with matching corner-
pieces, the subsidiary design being a clearly
defined cone, as shown in Plate 52E. Ice-
blue is the distinguishing shade of these
rugs.

Hispano-Moresque. *See* Spain.

Hunting Carpets. Persian carpet design
with elaborate hunting scenes, realistically
depicted.

FIG. 4

Ispahan (Persian). The great carpets so
called were probably made in Herat. Medallion and Vase designs were used, and a wide
range of colours, the composition being very
well balanced. Plate 47 is an example of a
fine Ispahan rug and Plate 48 a Prayer rug
of a typical "Tree and Garden" design. Knot:
Sehna.

Italy. Pope Clement XI founded a carpet-
weaving establishment at San Michele, Rome,
in the Savonnerie manner (early eighteenth
century). Peasant weavers in the Abruzzi
highlands and in Sardinia have continued to
weave rugs which are really stout coverings
for beds, marriage coffers, or carts, although
knotted pile pieces and kilims are very occasionally found. Generally they are ply or
double-cloth weaves (called *Karamania*) or
woven with a floated weft pattern. The patterns have a marked geometric tendency, but
derive from traditional Late Medieval and
Renaissance designs, just as the better-known
Perugia linen and cotton fabrics do.

Jacquard loom. *See* Moquette.

Jugoslavia. Kilim or tapestry-woven rugs
were woven in Bosnia, Serbia, and the Banat
throughout the nineteenth century; looped or
knotted pile examples are occasionally found.
Typical Slav geometric patterns of lozenges
and zig-zags are general, with floral and tree
motifs also treated geometrically. Prayer
carpets with a niche are not uncommon.
These rugs have many points of similarity
with Rumanian rugs.

Kabistan. Districts from which the principal rugs of the Caucasus come. The rugs
considered the finest of the type are from the
Baku district, and include the Kouba and
Hila rugs.

Kasak (Caucasian). These rugs bear panelled designs of bold character and in striking
colours. They are deep pile rugs and have a
masculine character entirely their own.
Strong deep red, clear yellow, and blue are
the predominant shades. Woven with extra
weft threads, the pile lies flat and is very
strong (Plate 51D).

Kashan (Persian). Medallion and Prayer
designs predominate, woven in wool or silk;
they are orthodox in conception, and are
notable for the use of ivory as a ground shade;
the most favoured colours are rich tones of
red or blue. The famous Polonaise rugs, remarkable for the use of gold and silver thread
as a base and the unusual colour effects in
pastel greens and browns, were probably
woven in Kashan. It is thought that they were
woven as gifts to foreign monarchs by the
order of Shah Abbas. Plate 51A shows a remarkably fine Kashan carpet combining the
Medallion with the Floral and Tree Motif.
Knot: usually Sehna.

Kerman. This Persian district has produced many rugs of merit, although they are
usually of later manufacture. Medallion and
tree designs are popular, introducing floral
effects in graceful intertwining vines. The
yarn used is rather soft. The colours are
beautifully toned, and are particularly suitable for English furnishings. This is well illustrated by the beautiful Kerman rug in
Plate 52A. Knot: Sehna.

Khorassan (Persian). In these carpets the
yarn is generally softer; the knotting is fine
and the general effect is more splendid than

Feraghan carpets (*q.v.*), but they are not so durable. Knot: usually Sehna.

Kidderminster. Probably the oldest centre of rug production in England, the early pieces were smooth-faced and without a true pile – that is to say, a cheap form of carpeting. Kidderminster carpets were often mentioned in inventories: for example, "4 carpetts of Kidderminster stuff", in the Countess of Leicester's inventory, 1634. Two-ply or double-cloth carpets were made there from 1735, when Pearsall & Brown built their factory. But in 1753 Brussels carpets or moquette (*q.v.*) was introduced by Brown in rivalry with Wilton. A thousand looms were at work in 1807, rising to 2,020 in 1838. Jacquard looms were introduced about 1825, and the use of jute rather earlier.

Kilmarnock. Double-cloth carpeting was made from 1778, and three-ply was perfected in 1824.

Kir Shehr. These rugs show typical Turkish designs. The Mihrab is usually filled with a very angular tree, border and panel are conventional, while the colours are bright and virile, varying reds being a feature of the weave. Warp and weft are usually wool.

Kouba. The design of these rugs consists often of independent flower heads, palmettes, and eight-pointed stars, with well-balanced borders carrying the same motifs. (*See* Plate 52D.) Some early examples show an elongated panel with interlocking tree forms.

Kula. These Turkish rugs are less varied in colour than the Ghiordes rugs (*q.v.*), and the panels of the Mihrab are usually fully patterned. Borders are popular with repeating floral miniature motifs.

Kurdish (Persian). Nomadic tribes wove these rugs. The virile designs are often bold and the colours limited. The yarns employed are generally coarse, but the effects are pleasing and the wearing quality excellent, often found in long runners. One of the outstanding types is the Bidjar, probably the heaviest of all Oriental rugs. Woven on a twofold warp, designs are diversified, but often a bold medallion and corner-pieces on a plain field and borders with Herati influence. Knot: Ghiordes.

Ladik (Turkish). These rugs follow the Ghiordes (*q.v.*) design very closely, though the use of Rhodian lily motifs is a distinguishing feature.

Medallion design. Persian designs common in all Eastern decoration. The Ardebil carpet in the Victoria and Albert Museum is considered the finest example of this type.

FIG. 5

Moorfields. Thomas Moore, of Moorfields, successfully competed for a Royal Society of Arts award in 1757. An account of his workshop, where hand-knotted carpets of the highest quality were produced, was given by Lady Mary Coke in 1768. A carpet was then being woven for Lord Coventry, to cost 140 guineas. Moore was extensively used by the architect Robert Adam, and a number of his carpets have survived in beautiful condition, as well as Adam's designs for them at the Soane Museum. The carpet at Syon House is inscribed "by Thos. Moore 1769". There are two at Osterley, made about 1775 and 1778; and Chippendale recommended him to Sir Edward Knatchbull in 1778, who paid him £57 for a carpet for Mersham le Hatch. Moore's carpets in neo-classical design were sumptuous additions to the houses they furnished.

Moquette. Woven on the principle of velvet, but in coarser wool and linen materials, moquette is allied with plushes and Utrecht velvet as an upholstery or carpeting material. Tournai seems to have been its chief centre in the Middle Ages. It was much used in the sixteenth to eighteenth centuries. Abbeville was the chief centre of production in France from 1667. Antwerp, Amsterdam, Utrecht, and

Leyden and Thuringia, in Germany, were other centres of production. Known as "Brussels carpet" in England, it was made at Norwich and Bradford besides Kidderminster and Wilton in England. The use of the Jacquard loom greatly increased and cheapened production in the early nineteenth century.

Morris, William. His first carpets were made about 1878 at Hammersmith (mark: hammer, river, and letter M); from 1881 at Merton Abbey. The later two- and three-ply carpets were woven for Morris & Co. at Heckmondwike (Yorks).

Needlework carpets. In the sixteenth and early seventeenth centuries Oriental carpets were much copied in Europe in cross- and tent-stitch on canvas. This was quite suitable for use on tables and cupboards, for which they were intended. There is a good collection in the National Museum, Zürich, and some superb English examples in the Victoria and Albert Museum. In the eighteenth century they were again in favour, but the designs were now purely European, with lavish floral patterns for the floor of boudoir or drawing-room. Many of these carpets have survived in England, but they are rarely found in good condition, as they wear easily. Their beauty depends as much on the brilliant dyes used as on the design. The fashion continued into the nineteenth century, but these pieces can be recognized by design and colour. Italian carpets embroidered entirely in silk are occasionally seen.

Norway. Double-cloth rugs for covers and cushions were made in the eighteenth and nineteenth centuries; a looped-pile technique is rarer.

Norwich. Norwich carpets are mentioned in seventeenth-century inventories. Possibly Turkey-work (*q.v.*) was made there as well as cloth carpeting and moquette (*q.v.*).

Poland. Peasant kilim rugs, like those of the Ukraine and Rumania, were woven in the eighteenth to nineteenth centuries. Some knotted-pile rugs of the seventeenth century are also known. They are West European in style and the quality is excellent.

Prayer rugs. Persian design, the central feature of which is the "Mihrab", a design derived from the traditional form of altar of the Mohammedan mosque.

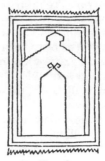

FIG. 6

Rumania. Tapestry-woven rugs were woven in every village as covers and wall-hangings, and many pieces are dated (eighteenth to nineteenth centuries). Lozenge and geometric patterns prevail in Wallachia and Moldavia, floral designs in Oltenia and Bessarabia. The floral patterns tend to be large and sprawling and the field and border are scarcely differentiated. Oltenian rugs are reputed to have the best dyes, and Turkish influence is evident in their more regular and compact designs and their firmer borders. The main tradition of Oltenian designs is supposed to derive from the period of Constantine Brancovan (late seventeenth century). Floral, tree, and bird patterns are common in Bukovina. Although apt to be garish and loud, the best Rumanian weavings are a very attractive form of peasant art. Knotted-pile rugs are occasionally found in Bessarabia.

Salor (Turkoman). These rugs are similar in texture to the Tekke rugs, but the octagonal "gul" is more pronounced and the red is usually slightly brighter (Plate 52G). Woven in prayer rugs and also in fine camel bags.

San Michele. *See* Italy.

Sardinia. *See* Italy.

Saruk (Persian). These carpets follow closely the tradition of the Kashan carpets, often using the Herat motifs and medallion designs. The construction is sturdy, closely knotted deep pile. Knot: Sehna.

Saryk (Turkoman). These rugs are generally not so fine in texture, but bear a similar design.

Sovannerie. Knotted-pile carpets in the Turkish manner were first successfully made in France by Pierre Dupont, whom Henry IV installed in the Louvre in 1606. In 1627 the old soap works on the Quai de Chaillot, called the Savonnerie, were acquired and Dupont's partner, Simon Lourdet, began work there with orphan children as apprentices. The Louvre and Savonnerie workshops flourished, particularly under Louis XIV. Large carpets were made for the Grande Gallerie du Louvre and the Salle d'Apollon (pieces still preserved in the Louvre), while others were given as diplomatic presents, including one to the King of Siam, which was restored at the Gobelins in 1910. A suite of carpet and upholstery for chairs and settees was made for Mazarin. Pierre Dupont died in 1644 (he wrote a treatise on carpet-making, *La Stromatourgie*) and was succeeded by his son, who removed to the Savonnerie in 1672. During the eighteenth century work continued steadily at the Savonnerie, although many of the workmen emigrated. Not till 1768 were Savonnerie carpets available to private individuals, but prices were very high and few pieces sold. Under Napoleon the looms were kept busy. The Savonnerie was amalgamated with the Gobelins in 1825, where some looms

FIG. 7. Savonnerie carpet knotting. Note the gadget for forming the knotted loops, which are subsequently cut. (From *Diderot's Encyclopedie*, 1760–80)

are still at work. It was the Savonnerie which set the standard for European hand-knotted carpets and created a style which was copied far afield. Fig. 7 shows the method of knotting

used for a line of knots of the same colour; the Turkish knot was used.

Scotch carpets. Double-cloth or ply weavings for the floor, also known as Kidderminster or Ingrain.

Sehna or **Sennah** (Persian). The knot, generally described as Persian, is named after this weave. Finely woven in small Herat and cone designs, although lighter in colouring and general effect. These rugs are of real merit and can be distinguished by the very short, upstanding pile. The typical cone design is well shown in Plate 52c.

Sehna or **Persian knot.** Used in carpets from Sehna, Ispahan, Tabriz (also the Ghiordes knot, *q.v.*), Saruk, Serebend, Feraghan, Kerman, Shiraz, and Herat.

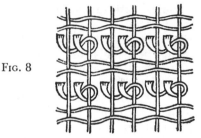

FIG. 8

Serebend (Persian). Cone design usually on red or blue field, the border following Herat influence. Fine examples are known as Mir. Knot: Sehna.

Shiraz (Persian). Designs are of a conventional Moselm character, woven by Kashkai Nomads bearing relation to Caucasian types. Diamond medallions predominate, while cone designs and latch hooks are also used. The term Mecca is often used to describe pieces of outstanding merit. Knot: Ghiordes or Sehna.

Shirvan (Caucasian). These rugs are similar in design but generally coarser in quality and lack the detail of the Hila rugs (*q.v.*). Crude animal forms are often introduced (Plate 52F).

Soumac (Caucasian). These rugs have a smooth-faced weave with conventional designs. Large octagonal and star panels; colourings are mainly a deep copper and blue.

Spain. Hispano-Moresque carpets were

woven in Spain in the early Middle Ages. Unlike Near Eastern carpets, they were generally woven with the single-warp knot. Murcia was still the centre of production in the fifteenth

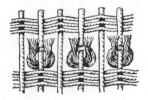

FIG. 9

century, when many carpets were woven with the arms of leading Spanish families. After the defeat of the Moors, the "Mudéjar" style, based largely on Renaissance silk patterns, developed in the sixteenth and seventeenth centuries, with important centres at Cuenca and Alcaraz. There is a fine collection of all these types at the Victoria and Albert Museum. There was a royal factory at Madrid in the eighteenth century.

The looped-pile peasant weavings, chiefly from the Alpujarras Mountains in South Spain, are the best of all European peasant rugs, and until recently were plentiful and cheap. They were made as bed-covers and rugs for out-of-doors use in a great variety of patterns, often in black and white, but also in red and green and mixed colours. Cross-stitch needlework carpets in similar style were also plentifully made. Cloth rugs or covers with floated weft pattern in wool, like the Italian Abruzzi weavings, were also made in Spain.

Sweden. Knotted-pile rugs as in Finland (*q.v.*) were made throughout the eighteenth and nineteenth centuries as well as double-cloth weavings.

Tabriz. The capital of Ancient Persia. Rugs and carpets from here show greater realism of design than those from Spahan, and it is in Tabriz that the greatest of the Hunting carpets were woven; the most famous, considered by many experts to be the greatest, example of Persian weaving, may be seen in Oest. Museum fuer Angewandte Kunst, Vienna. The use of court figures and a wide range of animals and birds appear in the designs (Plate 49), although the Medallion on

a plain ground is common (Plate 50A). No other district has woven such a wide range of designs or used such variety of colour. Silk is sometimes used in fine specimens, either for contrasting effect with wool or sometimes alone. Knot: Ghiordes or Sehna.

Tekke. *See* Bokhara or Bokara.

Turkey work. This was the name generally given to carpets, cushions, and upholstery knotted in the manner of Near Eastern rugs in sixteenth- and seventeenth-century inventories. Apart from larger carpets and rugs, Turkey-work cushions appear to have been made in not inconsiderable numbers in England, though they are now rare. Examples can be dated throughout the seventeenth century, and armorial cushions are noteworthy: for example, a set at Norwich Cathedral (1651); at Pembroke College, Cambridge (1666–7); at Brasenose College, Oxford (1666). In the eighteenth-century cross-stitch embroidery took the place of knotted pile for upholstery.

Turkoman "guls" or flowers

FIG. 10

Saryk	Yarmout	Afghan
Tekke	Beshire	Afghan
Salor	Afghan	Belouchistan
Tekke		Beshire and
		Belouchistan

Ukraine. Tapestry-woven rugs, akin to those of Rumania and Yugoslavia, were made as a peasant craft. The Turkish influence in some is clear; others have the sprawling floral patterns akin to those of Bessarabia. West European influence appears in the middle and latter nineteenth century.

Vase carpets. Persian design, with grace-ful interlocking palmettes and floral designs, developing from a central motif.

FIG. 11

Wilton. Although a charter for clothiers was granted in 1701, it is doubtful whether carpets were then made there. Lord Pembroke introduced Brussels carpet or moquette (*q.v.*) looms in 1740. From that date Wilton was in keen rivalry with Kidderminster. The cutting of the looped velvet pile was probably an early speciality of Wilton, a type of carpeting subsequently called by its name. Wilton carpets, made on velvet or moquette looms in narrow strips with simple geometrical patterns, were certainly much used in eighteenth-century houses, as well as the costlier knotted-pile carpets. The Brighton Pavilion accounts, for example, record orders for both. It is unlikely that knotted-pile carpets were made at Wilton until the acquisition of the Axminster looms in 1835, since when they have continued to work.

Yomud (Turkish). Rugs usually having diamond-shaped motifs, often composed of latch hooks and cloud-band borders.

Der Weber.

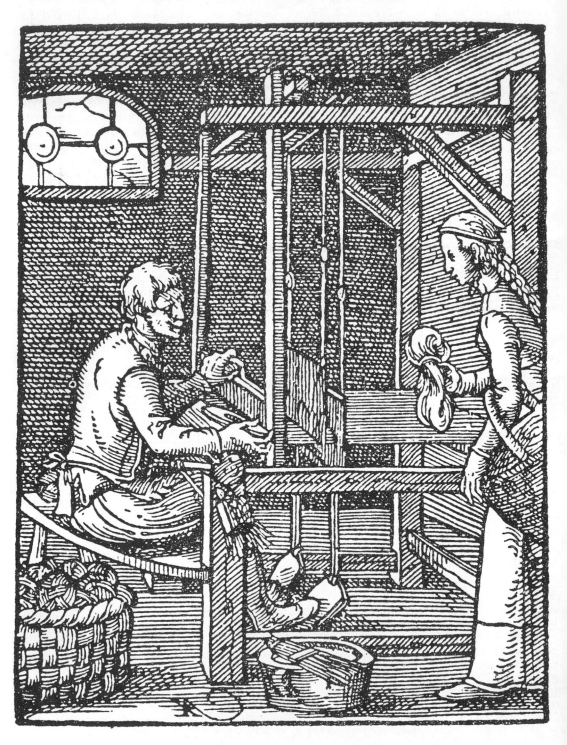

COINS AND MEDALS

Coins

The collecting of coins has almost as long a history as coins themselves, for we are told by Suetonius that the Roman emperor Augustus, if not actually a collector, did at least assemble some ancient pieces, presumably Greek, which he gave as gifts to his friends. The princes of the Renaissance were the first collectors proper of coins, and ever since then collections have been formed by all sorts and conditions of men.

The attractions of coin-collecting are manifold. There is, initially, the fascination of handling objects that have passed through the hands of men in all the civilizations from the seventh century B.C. onwards. Coins were first used in Europe after the destruction of the Mycenean civilization in 1200 B.C. The refugees, who settled in western Asia Minor, traded money with the Greeks, and were making their own coins some 700 years before the beginning of the Christian era. Coins form, moreover, the most complete series of artistic objects that can be assembled from the pristine vigour of classical Greek art, through the formalism of Byzantinism and the strivings of the Middle Ages to the heights of the Renaissance and on to our own day. Again, in

the great sweep of centuries before the invention of printing, coins provide a great, continuous series of historical documents, giving contemporary comment on events and recording the likenesses of history's great men, the details of ancient architecture and the accompaniments of the world's religions. Unlike many other antiquities, where each piece is unique, the special work of a craftsman or artist never exactly repeated, many of the most beautiful coins of all ages were produced in their thousands and exist, even today, in their hundreds; for once the artist had engraved his dies, or made the model for his mould, the limit to the number of pieces which could be produced was the physical limitation of these instruments.

To form a collection of coins is not, even in this present age, the privilege of wealth; but since the field is so vast, complete coverage can be contemplated by, say, only a national collection, formed over centuries, and the private collector will be counselled to select an artistic or historical period which appeals to him. Even within the major periods which are described below, a selected portion – one century or one state – will provide great variety and range.

GREEK

The term Greek coins is loosely used to cover not only the coinage of Greece proper but also of all the places in the Mediterranean basin to which Greek civilization spread, including Egypt, the Near East and the Black Sea. Greek coinage is the earliest coinage of Western civilization, and its development from the seventh century B.C. till the extinction of its last remaining forms in the third century A.D. provides a continuous illustration of that civilization and art from which most subsequent European forms spring.

ARCHAIC (700–480 B.C.)

The earliest coins in the seventh century in Asia Minor were simply pellets of electrum with, on one side, the badge of the city, guaranteeing the piece (Plate 53B). Croesus, King of Lydia, struck similar pieces in the sixth century, but in gold and silver, an example followed by the Persian kings with their silver shekels and gold darics (Plate 53A). In Greece proper the earliest coins, also with a badge on one side and a rough incuse square on the other, were struck at Aegina (Plate 53C). Other states, such as Corinth and Athens, quickly adopted the idea. Probably the earliest coinage with devices on both sides was developed at Athens in the sixth century (Plate 53E). The early coins of Magna Graecia were round and flat, and some cities, such as Metapontum, have a curious fabric with the same device on both sides, in relief on the obverse and incuse on the reverse (Plate 53D). The coinage of this period is somewhat angular and stiff in style, and the human eye, even when shown in profile, is drawn as if seen from the front.

CLASSICAL (480–336 B.C.)

The features of this coinage are the delicate and detailed rendering of the subjects, particularly the human body and the high relief of the experiments in portraiture, including facing heads. In the Asian cities the incuse of the Archaic period remained popular, though later two-sided types appeared. In the fifth and fourth centuries in Greece proper the coinage of Corinth (Plate 53F), with its obverse type of Pegasus, rivalled that of Athens in its circulation. Mid-fourth century, however, saw in Greece the rise of Macedonia under Philip II to political hegemony, of which the symptom and instrument was the rich series of gold staters with head of Apollo and *biga* reverse (Plate 53I). This popular coinage was copied extensively in Europe, successively in the Danube basin, Gaul, and Ancient Britain. In the West a magnificent series of coins issued from the cities of southern Italy and Sicily, particularly from Syracuse after the Athenian defeat (Plate 53G). Of equal quality are the coins of the Phoenician merchant city Carthage (Plate 53H).

HELLENISTIC (336–1 B.C.)

The extension of Macedonian hegemony over most of the Greek world in the East by the conquests of Alexander the Great brought a reduction in independent coinages and the establishment of the first "world" coinage with his series of gold staters and silver tetradrachms (Plate 53J) issued at mints throughout his Empire. The kingdoms into which Alexander's empire split on his death lasted till the establishment of the Roman Empire in the last century of the era. The features of the coinage of these kingdoms is the development of true and expressive portraiture as in Bactria in North-west India (Plate 53K) and the Seleucid kingdom (Plate 53L) and in Egypt under the Ptolemies, though on much copper coinage the gods retained their place (Plate 53M). The silver *cistophoros* with its Bacchic *cista* and snakes types, beginning in the second century B.C., was the standard coinage of western Asia Minor into Roman times (Plate 53N).

IMPERIAL (A.D. 1–296)

Under the Roman Empire, almost the only autonomous coinages of the Greek cities were in bronze. These and the "imperial" issues with emperor portrait from Greek cities and colonies, though of comparatively poor workmanship, provide an interesting record of local cults, ancient works of art and architecture (Plate 54B). A continuous series of tetradrachms with an imperial portrait was issued from Alexandria in Egypt, but by the close of the third century A.D. the tetradrachm, shrunk and debased, is scarcely recognizable as the ultimate descendant of the great Greek series (Plate 54A).

ROMAN

Roman coinage, beginning only in the third century B.C., combines a native Italian bronze coinage with a coinage of silver didrachms in the Greek style. This latter was replaced in the second century by the silver denarius, which, with a modified bronze series and an occasional issue in gold, provided the staple coinage throughout the Republic. The features of early Roman coinage are the absence of portraiture and the prolific variety of types alluding to events in Rome's history and legends and to the family history of the moneying magistrates. The Imperial coinage, instituted by Augustus at the end of the first century B.C., added a consistent gold coinage and a new series of bronzes. Portraiture, begun during the civil wars preceding the establishment of empire, is the prime feature throughout all Imperial coinage, while the reverses provide a commentary on events, actions, and policies. Currency reforms in the third and fourth centuries A.D., though changing denominations, did not alter greatly the shape of the Roman coinage.

ORIENTAL

In the Near and Middle East some series of Oriental coins preserve the characteristics of the Greek and Roman coinages with which they are contemporary. The Jewish coinage, under the Jewish rulers in the last two centuries B.C., under the procurators of the Roman Empire, and during the two revolts against the Romans, normally eschewed portraiture but had types in Greek fashion with inscriptions in Hebrew. The coinage of the Parthians from third century B.C. to third century A.D. was a portrait coinage in the Hellenistic manner but with a distinctive Assyrian flavour. The features of the Sassanian coinage from third to seventh century A.D. are the portrait types with Pehlevi inscription and an invariable fire-altar reverse.

The rise of Islam in the seventh century and the subsequent extension of its power produced in the Near and Middle East, across North Africa and into Spain, and into West and South-west Asia a coinage mainly of gold dinars and silver dirhems, uniform but for the titles of rulers, names of mints, and religious formulae. Portraiture on Mohammedan coinage is rare, and artistic effect lies in the calligraphic designs.

In India, on the other hand, the types of coinage are as numerous as the constituent states. An outstanding medieval series was that of the Gupta kings, a rich succession of gold coins with figure types, showing still some connexion with the Graeco-Bactrian coins of the north-west. In the extensive series of the Mogul emperors, as well as the calligraphic patterns, common to all Mohammedan coins, there was a rich variety of representations on some of the gold coins. In medieval Ceylon the designs on the coinage were a uniquely formal art style, of its own culture (Plate 58I).

Coinage in China is said, traditionally, to date from the second millennium B.C. Early types were small-scale reproductions in bronze of objects exchanged in barter – knives, spades, etc. From about the middle of the first millennium B.C. these pieces were inscribed. Although this type of coinage lasted down to the beginning of the Christian era, round money in bronze, with a square hole in the centre, and inscribed with characters, was in circulation several centuries before this. Apart from varying characters, Chinese coinage retained this form till comparatively recent times. The Japanese coinage is a derivative of the Chinese, which it closely resembles apart from its distinctive characters. In the sixteenth century gold coins in the form of thin, oval plates began to be issued, and there were also small rectangular silver blocks.

BRITISH

The Ancient Britons struck a coinage of gold staters, imitating the types of the stater of Philip II of Macedon, and later, in the first century A.D., produced some silver imitating Roman types. The first Anglo-Saxon coinage was of small silver sceattas with designs elaborated from late Roman coins, but in the eighth century the silver penny, parallel to the Continental denier, began to be struck. This denomination, acquiring in time a royal portrait type, persisted, with variations of design, as the standard coin till the fourteenth century, when the fourpenny piece, or groat, was added, together with a coinage in gold. With the Renaissance and prosperity under the Tudors, larger denominations of greater intricacy of design made their appearance in both gold and silver. The introduction of mechanical means of coin production after the Restoration brought a standardization of coin types and the discarding of unusual denominations, leaving the coinage in much the form which it retains to-day.

MEDIEVAL

Sixth–fifteenth centuries

Following the break-up of the western Roman Empire in the late fifth century, the Visigoths in Spain and the Merovingians in France produced a coinage of small gold, imitating the tremissis of the late Empire. Under the Carolingian Empire, covering a great part of Western Europe, a new coinage of silver deniers, rated at 240 to the pound, was established in the eighth century. This denier, under various names and with varying types, remained the standard coinage throughout Western Europe under the German Empire and in the great number of independent states and kingdoms which emerged through the centuries. In the early fourteenth century larger silver pieces, roughly equivalent to the groat in England, were added, while about the same time increasing trade and prosperity re-introduced coinages in gold.

The eastern Roman Empire, which held precariously together till the mid-fifteenth century, continued the Roman coinage of gold *solidi* and bronze coins but little silver. A new series of bronze coins was introduced in 492, and the dumpy *solidus* became thin and scyphate, and from the eleventh century this, the *nomisma*, became the sole gold coinage. This Byzantine coinage influenced the shape of coinage in the Balkans and Eastern Europe and, till the eighth century, North Africa and much of Italy.

MODERN

The later fifteenth century, when the spread of the Renaissance in art and technique began to make its effect felt, marks the beginning of modern coinage. Increasing prosperity arising from the unification of petty states into sovereign powers and the growth of commerce, making necessary a wider range of coinage, coincided with the discovery of supplies of precious metals in the New World. Larger silver pieces, such as the franc in France, the teston in Italy, and the papal giulio, were introduced, while Spain, with its control of American silver, issued her large "pieces of eight". In Bohemia the silver from the Joachimstal was issued as thalers, a denomination copied in many German states and the antecedent of the American dollar. Coinage in gold in a variety of denominations became more abundant, particularly in mercantile Western Europe. Demand for small change produced a coinage in copper or bronze somewhat later, while in Northern and Eastern Europe readily available supplies produced for a time a full-value copper coinage, not merely tokens. By the seventeenth century mechanical production of coins had effected a standardization of design and denomination, and with the adoption of the decimal system in most of Europe and America in the late eighteenth and early nineteenth centuries, coinage settled down into its modern shape.

AMERICAN

The collector of American coins usually starts by trying to obtain a specimen of one denomination for each year. Once he has done this he will probably specialize in one of the fields to which he finds himself particularly attracted. Forming a cabinet of types is likely to prove much more ambitious than it seems at first. It is hardly possible for a collector of Americana to go far without learning much about his country's history, and coins often bring home the significance of events previously disregarded.

Colonial coinage of Massachusetts

Until 1773 no advantage was taken of the right of coinage granted in the charter of Virginia. No such grant was made in the charter of the Massachusetts Bay Colony. The coinage struck at Boston between 1652 and 1683 is perhaps the most interesting in American history. The shortage of small change was one of the most serious handicaps which the colonists had to face. Petitions to Charles I for a colonial mint had proved fruitless. A like inadequacy of the coinage prevailed in England at this time. Granting the right to coin money was a prerogative of the King. Within a few years after the death of Charles I, whether with or without the consent of the Commonwealth is not known, a mint was set up in Boston. John Hull was placed in charge along with his partner, Robert Sanderson, both silversmiths. The earliest pieces bear merely the initial letters *NE* in script capitals (for New England) on the one side and the value in Roman numerals on the other side. With but one exception, all the subsequent coins bear the date 1652. With the return of Charles II to the throne in 1660, the colonists were in a serious predicament, and the charge of having infringed the royal prerogative was one of those alleged as a cause for the withdrawal of the charter in 1683.

Because the NE pieces had a large part of their field blank, it was realized that this would offer opportunity for clipping, so a design which would fill the field was ordered, namely "a tree". This tree-type has three forms. The first of them, and the crudest, has since been dubbed the *Willow Tree*, to which the design bears but slight resemblance. Many of the *Willow Tree* pieces have been double-struck, with the traces of the first striking interfering with the other. Their crudity must have been one of the reasons why this type is the rarest of the tree forms.

A marked improvement characterizes the succeeding type, called the *Oak Tree*, to which the design does bear some resemblance. In 1662 an oak tree twopence was added to the three previous denominations, and this bears the date of its authorization; it is the only issue with a date other than 1652.

The type known as the *Pine Tree* is the latest of the three. At its initiation it is on the same-sized flan as its predecessors, but about half of the known dies are constricted, from 30 to 25 mm. All of these tree forms were engraved in the die and resemble line drawings rather than modelled reliefs. This is less noticeable in the inscriptions, which are marked by interesting letter forms and variations. The spelling *Masathusets* continues unchanged (with one exception – the H omitted), and this gives that spelling some claim to having been considered official.

Despite long-drawn-out efforts to overcome opposition, it became apparent that the colony's charter was about to be rescinded, and since the coining of money was one of the offences charged, and because any minimizing of the offence was impossible, the production seems to have been increased, for we find more than the usual number of dies being used at the same time. The thinness of these pieces permitted bending, from which one very interesting phenomenon resulted, for they were believed to be a protection from witches and were worn (bent or pierced) on the person for this purpose.

Perhaps the rarest of the Massachusetts issues, and the most ambitious artistically, is the Good Samaritan shilling, with the two figures of that parable on its obverse. It was struck from dies, but in the placing and form of the inscription it differs from all previous forms. The occasion for its production, probably unofficial, has not been discovered.

Maryland, New Jersey, Connecticut

A coinage for Maryland dated 1658 was struck in England by the Proprietor, Cecil Calvert, Lord Baltimore, whose bust occupies the obverse. The reverse bears the family coat-of-arms. There were three silver denominations – the shilling, the six pence, and the groat (four pence) as well as a copper penny, which has a crown with two penants for its reverse type.

In 1682, in order to relieve the shortage of small change, the General Assembly of the Province of New Jersey authorized the circulation of halfpence and farthings, which are believed to have been issued in Dublin and brought to the colony by Mark Newby the preceding year. Because of the type, representing St Patrick in ecclesiastical robes, these pieces are known by both names. The supply must have been fairly considerable, to judge from the number of dies known.

The patent granted to William Wood for making copper tokens for Ireland and the American colonies resulted in two types. Both bore on the obverse the head of George I. The former has for its reverse a beautifully con-

ventionalized rose, and bore the inscription ROSA AMERICANA and UTILE DULCI with the date for all but the first issue. The denominations are twopence, penny, and halfpenny; the dates are 1722, 1723, 1724, 1733 (this last for a pattern twopence only). The issue for Ireland had for its reverse a seated woman with a harp; the dates are 1722–4. When these pieces proved unpopular in Ireland they were sent to America. The denominations were halfpenny and farthing only.

A small group of coppers having a connexion with Connecticut is known as the "Highley Coppers", named after their producer, John Higley, who controlled a small copper mine near Cranby, from which came the metal for these coins. The earliest pieces had for type a stag to left with the inscription *Value of Three Pence*. When refused for this equivalent in circulation a second die was prepared with the words *Value me as you please*. Later there was a second reverse die having a hatchet for its type and for legend *I cut my way through*. This last and another type (a wheel) are undated; the others show the date 1737.

Latin America

The abundance of coined silver in Latin America explains why some collectors have been turning to the coinages of the Spanish mints in the New World. It is from these that much of the silver which circulated here came after the coining in Boston was stopped. It is these Spanish milled dollars, in which payment was promised on the Continental Congress's paper notes which, to a large extent, financed the Revolution. The paper notes of the Continental Congress were printed in large numbers and so soon counterfeited that they quickly depreciated, becoming "not worth a Continental". Besides Mexico City, Santa Fe de Bogota in Columbia and Potosi and Lima, then both in Peru, were the most prolific mints for the "pieces of eight". Some of the gold in circulation came from Brazilian sources, possibly by way of Jamaica. They were known as "Joes" and "half-Joes" because they bore the Latin form of the name of the Portuguese king (Johannes). The New Englanders brought their salted codfish to the West Indies, exchanging it there for other desirables, including hard cash. A little later, when coins in small denominations became very scarce in the West Indies, they resorted to an interesting substitute which has intrigued many collectors. The Spanish mainland coins were cut into segments or lowered in weight by having a portion cut away. Some perversions consist in having cut the "piece of eight" into five "quarters", with the shortage so slight that it would escape the observation of the unwary. Gold pieces were sometimes plugged with added metal to raise them to a standard required by local legislation.

Other pre-Revolutionary coinage

Shortly before the outbreak of the American Revolution Virginia took advantage of permission given in her charter to have an issue of half-pennies struck in England. Although these bear the date 1773 the shipment did not reach its destination until 1774, and since the obverse shows the head of George III, they can scarcely have become popular.

A few specimens of a dollar bearing the date 1776 and the inscription *Continental Currency* are known. There are strikings in pewter and brass as well as in silver, and this seems an indication that it never got beyond the pattern or trial-piece stage. The interval between the signing of the Treaty of Peace in 1783 and the ratification of the Federal Constitution in 1788 found several of the states authorizing the coinage of cents, and one of these issues was by provision of the Continental Congress and bears the dates 1787 and 1788. The design, showing a sun-dial and the word FUGIO, had for reverse a chain of thirteen links – one for each state – a device which had been used for the earlier Continental dollar, which is thought to have been supplied by Franklin.

The devices used on issues authorized to relieve the currency shortage by the several states display wide variety and some ingenuity. One of the first to appear, that of Vermont, came from a state which was not among the first thirteen to ratify. Massachusetts issued a half cent. New York and New Jersey used a latinized form of their names. The coinage for Connecticut was one of the heaviest. There is an unofficial issue (1783–6) bearing the inscription NOVA CONSTELLATIO. Unofficial coinings often bear the head of Washington. The absence of specific laws prohibiting such coins was taken advantage of by several goldsmiths or jewellers, such as Ephraim Brasher in New York, who fathered a very well-designed doubloon (gold) on which he counterstamped his initials EB. In Maryland, I. Chambers of Annapolis struck silver shillings, sixpences, and threepences dated 1783, and in 1790 in Baltimore Standish Barry produced a silver threepence bearing his name. The federal mint did not come into operation until 1792.

Federal mint established

The initial coinings at the mint set up in Philadelphia are an indication of the great need for the smaller denominations. A few pieces were struck in 1792 – the disme and its half (Plate 62A, B) – traditionally believed to have been struck from silver plate supplied by Washington. These were obviously patterns, as were designs for cents prepared by Thomas Birch. By 1793 cents and half cents had been put into circulation, the former in several varieties – chain type (Plate 62E, F), wreath, Liberty head (Plate 62M, N). By 1796 a type with a draped bust had become established. In 1794 dollars as well as half dollars and half dimes (Plate 62C, D) were issued. 1795 saw the striking of gold; the half eagle ($5.00) preceded the eagle (Plate 62O, P). Not until 1796 were quarter eagles minted ($2.50); the quarter dollars of this date were without indication of their value, and further strikings did not occur until 1804. Pieces of these early dates in prime condition are eagerly sought today, but it is impossible to list the many varieties. Sometimes changes are very considerable, such as that in the diameter of the cents in 1857, when the flying eagle type appeared officially. Pieces of this type bearing the date 1856 are considered patterns; only one thousand are believed to have been struck. Other patterns are known to have been considered but never sanctioned. Among these is the gold stella of 1879 and 1880, with a gold value of four dollars, but patterns were also struck in other metals. Three dollar pieces in gold were struck between 1854 and 1889 (Plate 62I, J).

When the mint at New Orleans fell into the hands of the Southerners they found dies there for half-dollars bearing the date 1861. A reverse die with the inscription *Confederate States of America* was cut, and a small number (four?) of specimens was struck (Plate 62v, w). One of the coins and both dies were found in the possession of a citizen of New Orleans in 1879 and later acquired by a New York coin dealer. He obtained five hundred half-dollars of the New Orleans mint for 1861, planed off their reverses and re-struck them from the Confederate die. A die for a cent was ordered but never delivered. It was used later for re-strikes by the dealer who acquired the die.

Territorial gold coins

The private or territorial gold coins constitute a series from which considerable American history may be learned. Prior to the California Gold Rush of 1849 the supply of gold came from two southern states, Georgia and North Carolina. Local assayers were responsible for pieces of honest weight, and these circulated without government prohibition. The first, struck by Templeton Reid, bore the words *Georgia Gold*, his name and the date 1830, along with indication of their value – ten, five, and two and a half dollars. Later (1849) pieces having the value of ten and twenty-five dollars bear his name, but it is accompanied by *California Gold*. He must have gone to the west in the interval.

In Rutherford County of North Carolina a family of German metallurgists named Bechtler coined one, two and a half, and five dollar gold pieces (Plate 62K, L) over a period of twenty-two years. These too were without type or symbol, merely giving name, date, and denomination.

The exigencies of the Gold Rush to California are brought out by the pieces struck there by accredited assayers while that state was still a territory, and both before and after Augustus Humbert had set up as U.S. assayer. The earliest of the fifty-dollar gold slugs coined by him are dated 1851, and the previous issues of smaller size were discredited, with a very inconvenient shortage of small change resulting. Authority for ten- and twenty-dollar coins were finally accorded in Feb-ruary 1852. By 1854 eagles and double eagles were being struck by the San Francisco branch mint. A state assay office provided by law in 1850 seems to have been discontinued as soon as the U.S. assay office was established. Bars and ingots, stamped with their intrinsic value and the name of the assayer, circulated as late as 1860 and are collected by some enthusiasts, although they can scarcely be classed as coins.

Five- and ten-dollar pieces struck by the Oregon Exchange Company have a beaver as type and are dated 1849. The Mormons in Salt Lake City struck pieces in 1849 with the inscription *Holiness to the Lord* and with clasped hands on the reverse. In Colorado several firms, among which that of Clark, Gruber & Company were prominent, struck gold coins dated 1860 and 1861, the largest denomination being twenty dollars. Many of these bars and slugs must have gone into the melting-pot when the stabilized price for gold was less than their pure content.

Tokens

In two periods of our history tokens played a part which entitle them to the attention of collectors. Shortly after 1837, during the presidencies of Jackson and Van Buren, a period of widespread depression, there was a considerable striking of these unofficial coins which are now called "Hard Times Tokens". Many are of a satirical nature and reflect the economic situation. More than a hundred varieties are recorded, chiefly in the large cent size.

A second period of coinage stringency occurred during the war between the states. The mint did not strike cents in sufficient quantity to meet the needs of circulation, and substitutes were put out by commercial firms, redeemable at their establishments, to overcome the shortage. Many have a local interest because they bear the names of issuers no longer in existence. These little tokens were of the size of the small cents introduced in 1857 and were usually in bronze. The varieties run into thousands.

New designs

During the presidency of Theodore Roosevelt, and with his enthusiastic encouragement, an effort was made to improve the artistic standard of the coinage. Augustus Saint Gaudens (and his pupils) were entrusted with the making of new designs. His design for the twenty-dollar gold piece was of great beauty, but by the time the mint officials had modified it to meet the requirements of minting and circulation it had lost much of its initial attractiveness. The half-dollar and the dime were designed by A. A. Weinmann, the quarter by H. A. MacNeil and the five-cent piece (perhaps the most characteristically American of the types) by James E. Fraser. The Lincoln cent was the work of V. D. Brenner. In 1921 a Peace Dollar was authorized; the design, selected from a competition in which eight invited sculptors participated, was by Anthony de Francisci.

Medals

The art of the medal is patently related to that of coins, but it is a special and comparatively modern development of certain features of coin art; for the medal is no older than the Renaissance of the fifteenth century. It is true that certain large Greek coins and, to an even greater extent, the Roman Imperial medallions have a medallic character, but these pieces were primarily monetary, whereas the medal is essentially an artistic commemoration in metal of persons and events.

ITALIAN RENAISSANCE

In Italy, in the growing interest in the civilization and art of the ancient world, one feature in ancient coinage which obviously fascinated was the great series of Roman Imperial portraits, particularly those on the large bronze sesterii. From this and similar inspirations developed the school of Italian Renaissance medallists, of whom the earliest, and possibly the greatest, was Pisanello (*fl.* 1452) (Plate 59A). The qualities of the art of this century are realism of portraiture and naturalism of design, a striking antithesis to medieval art. Of the very numerous artists of this period, mention can be made of only a few such as Matteo de Pasti, Sperandio, and Niccolo Fiorentino.

SIXTEENTH-CENTURY EUROPEAN

Although by the end of the fifteenth century medallic art had spread to most countries in western Europe, examples are rare outside Italy, but the sixteenth century saw the medal firmly established with a great variety of practitioners and styles. Already far removed from the style of Pisanello is the richly ornate English medal by Nicholas Hilliard on the defeat of the Armada in 1588 (Plate 59C). In Italy there was a more continuous development by such artists as Benvenuto Cellini (1500–71), Leone Leoni (1509–90) (Plate 59D), and Jacopo da Trezzo (*fl.* 1589). In France, where the qualities of sculptural art were being blended into the medal, two of the great masters were Germain Pilon (1539–90) and Guillaume Dupré (1574–1647) (Plate 60A). The peculiar quality of the German medal of this century, a certain rough strength, is due to the fact that the original models were carved in wood or stone, not modelled in wax as elsewhere. Prominent artists were Hans Schwarz (1493–1530), Hans Reinhardt (*fl.* 1535–49), and Cristopher Weiditz (1523–37), and a number of medals are regarded as being at least from the designs of Albert Dürer (Plate 59B).

SEVENTEENTH-CENTURY PORTRAIT MEDALS

Much of the pristine freshness and vigour of medallic art disappears in this century with the establishment of a more formal "classical" style. The exponents of this style were principally French, medallists such as Jean Varin (1604–42), Jean Mauger (1648–1722), and his pupil Jean Dassier (1676–1763), the last of whom produced numerous series of medals of famous characters in history. This style became international and varied only according to the quality of the individual artist. A particularly successful portrait modeller was Thomas Simon in England (Plate 59E), though only one of quite a school in this country. An unusual treatment of the portrait is that of the Dutch artist Jerian Pool (*fl.* 1653–67) in his three-quarter facing portrait of Admiral Tromp (Plate 60B).

ITALIAN BAROQUE

Surprisingly little attention has been given either by scholars or collectors to the medals of the seventeenth and eighteenth centuries which are well worth the attention of all lovers of Italian baroque art. With their portraits of crowned popes, birettaed cardinals and heavily bewigged princes, generals and artists, they present one of the fullest portrait galleries of Italian notabilities. On their reverse sides one may find representations of such buildings as the façade of S. Giovanni in Laterano or the Arco S. Gallo at Florence, boldly rendered allegories or views of harbours and ships. Fortunately such medals are valued mainly for their rarity rather than their aesthetic merits, and the discerning collector may therefore find magnificent examples of high artistic quality at a fraction of the price of a bronze statuette of the same date.

In the seventeenth and eighteenth centuries Italian noblemen, and even some visiting grand tourists (Baron Stosch and Sir Richard Molesworth among them), commissioned portrait medals of themselves. Medals were also made of important artists, writers, and mathematicians. The vast majority of the medals of this period are, however, of a more official nature.

Papal medals naturally attract most interest, since they provide a valuable portrait gallery of the popes and often show on their reverse sides the important architectural works they commissioned. A medal produced by Ottone Hamerani for Clement XII in 1732, for instance, was a portrait of the Pope on the obverse and a view of the recently completed façade of S. Giovanni in Laterano on the reverse. A pope normally had a medal struck to mark his election, and Clement XI, who persisted in the *grande rifuto* against the wishes of the conclave for three days, issued one with an image of Christ falling beneath the cross on the reverse. Several thousand brass medals were struck each year for the pope to give to pilgrims, and in the *Anno Santo* or jubilee year (1600, 1625, 1650, etc.) special medals were issued, bearing a portrait of the pope on one side and usually a view of the Holy Year door to the Lateran on the other. Medals were also issued to mark the ceremony of canonization, with images of the newly sanctified on the reverse. From 1610 to 1625 the papal medals were principally the work of Giacomo Antonio de Mori. He was succeeded by Gaspare Mola, who was chief engraver to the *Zecca* until 1640, when he was followed by his nephew, Gaspare Moroni. On Moroni's death in 1669 the post of chief engraver passed to Alberto Hamerani, whose family held it until the end of the eighteenth century.

The official papal medals were not the only ones to be executed in Rome. Apart from the cardinals, many of whom wished to have their likenesses recorded in this way, the Queen of Sweden and, later, the Old and Young Pretenders to the English crown were among the medallists' most frequent patrons. Jacobite medals are numerous, and many of them, by members of the Hamerani family, are of great charm. They also throw some light on an aspect of English history. The earliest of them, struck at the Pope's order in 1689, shows Innocent XI condoling with James II. A later medal, bearing a portrait of Prince Charles Edward with the motto *Hunc saltem everso juvenem*, was seen by Horace Walpole at Hamerani's in 1740 and convinced him that the Stuarts were planning an imminent assault on Britain. This medal had, in fact, no more political significance than the many others commissioned by the exiled family.

Outside Rome, the principal towns where medals were produced in this period were Florence, Naples, and Turin. Some of those produced at Naples in the eighteenth century, bearing portraits of the Bourbon kings, are of good quality. At Turin the Lavy family, who controlled the mint from 1749 until the mid-nineteenth century, engraved some fine medals of a somewhat frenchified appearance. But from the artistic point of view the best Italian baroque medals are probably those designed by Massimiliano Soldani for the Grand Duke of Tuscany. His portrait medals, whether they represent writers like Francesco Redi or commemorate the *déraciné* features of the later Medici Grand Dukes, have a strangely vigorous baroque vitality. When he went to Paris to model a portrait medal of Louis XIV in the 1680s Colbert remarked that France did not possess a medallist of the same ability. Unfortunately, Soldani was unable to cut his own dies, and this work was entrusted to other craftsmen, who were seldom capable of producing work as technically accomplished as that of the Hamerani at Rome, even though the design might be far superior.

Soldani was by no means the only Italian sculptor to provide models for medals. Indeed, even G. L. Bernini has been said to have done such work. It also seems highly probable that the medallists sometimes derived their portraits from carved or painted likenesses rather than from the life. Stylistically, therefore, the Italian medal is closely connected with the history of Italian sculpture. Early in the seventeenth century Italian medals showed both in their portraits and their allegorical devices the influence of Mannerism. By the 1620s, however, the early baroque style is clearly evident in the medals produced in Rome, and a complete series of papal medals reveals the gradual development of the baroque in all its exuberance. Some patrons chose to have themselves represented in a classical manner, with hair cut in the ancient Roman fashion. Before the middle of the eighteenth century the pomps and splendours of the baroque had given way to the elegancies of the rococo, and portrait heads on medals were handled with a greater delicacy and precision. It was not until the last quarter of the century, however, that the neo-classical style began to exert any very strong influence on the official medallists. Neo-classical medals are marked by the late eighteenth-century desire for simplicity and nobility. Generally they are much more deeply cut than the medals of the previous hundred and fifty years and instead of bearing a quarter-length portrait of their subject they show the head alone, sometimes surrounded by a laurel wreath, but more usually on an undecorated ground. Numerous portraits of Napoleon, the various members of his family, and Gioacchino Murat, were executed in this style, with heads treated in a manner strongly reminiscent of Canova's busts.

In the seventeenth and eighteenth centuries most Italian medals, apart from those produced by the engravers to the large mints of Rome, Florence, Naples, and Turin, were cast, though the practice of die engraving became more usual towards the end of the period. It should be remembered that those medallists who signed their works with initials normally added the letter *F* for *fecit* at the end: thus, Filippo Balugani signs F. B. or F. B. F.

EIGHTEENTH AND NINETEENTH CENTURIES

Medallic art in this period underwent a continuous decline in standard, although medals continued to enjoy a great vogue and to be produced by artists in all countries. The best of the medals, however, seldom achieve more than a high level of technical accomplishment, and the decline in standard was possibly hastened by the introduction of the reducing machine, so that the artist no longer worked his original model on the scale of the finished product. It may suffice for this period to cite a few typical medals, such as the extremely popular series struck in England in 1739 in honour of Admiral Vernon by a variety of artists (Plate 60C) or the Nelson medal of 1805 by Conrad Kuchler (Plate 60E). In France towards the end of the eighteenth century the Revolution injected some fresh life into the art, producing pieces such as those by Benjamin du Vivier (Plate 60D).

AMERICAN

Until the U.S. mint was established in 1792 facilities for preparing medals were almost entirely lacking, and it was necessary to rely on English or French artists. The direct cutting of steel dies was arduous, and there were few in the colonies with experience for doing this. Later, hubs, modelled in relief, were used for portrait medals. Not until a reducing machine had been imported well after the mid-nineteenth century were medals produced in any considerable number. There is one outstanding exception to this statement, however: the Indian Peace Medals, which have exceptional antiquarian interest. Intended as marks of favour to prominent chiefs, whose aid, along with that of their tribe, it was desirable to enlist, they had been used with considerable effect by the French in Canada, and later by the English. Possession of one of these medals was a fairly clear indication, and this was sometimes needed, of the side to which the wearer belonged. Indeed, several of the French medals are known with the LUDOVICUS of their inscription erased and GEORGIUS (in one case GORGIUS) substituted to indicate a change of front on the part of the owner. In consequence the Congress was early faced with the necessity for attracting Indians they wished to draw away from their allegiance to the English forces in the north. How could this be done when no equipment for striking medals was available? During Washington's administration the situation was met by presenting large oval plaques of silver with the design engraved (Plate 63A). As these were considerably larger than the struck English medals, they seem to have made a deeper impression and to have been more highly prized. An early recipient was the famous and rightfully distinguished leader, Red Jacket, who received the largest of the three sizes distributed; and it is by his name that these engraved medals are sometimes known. The preparation of an engraved medal was possible much more quickly than would have been the case had dies been made, and their popularity with the red warriors satisfied both parties. Such engraved medals with the dates 1789, 1792, 1793, and 1795 are known and are assumed to indicate that they were awarded during the visit of a formal nature to the capital in those years. The designs are in some instances signed with the initials *JR*, probably to be identified as those of Joseph Richardson of Philadelphia. Another countermark, *JL* or *IL*, is less certain.

A group of three Seasons Medals, 45 mm in diameter, were ordered in England by Rufus King, the American minister. They are dated 1796, and their design was entrusted to the painter John Trumbull, at that time an art student in England. His designs were rather fanciful and intended to persuade the Indians of the advantages of the pursuits of peace, such as cattle raising and agriculture. These medals in silver and copper were not received until 1798. Under Thomas Jefferson and most of the succeeding presidents, struck medals were prepared at the mint; a common reverse displayed clasped hands and the words PEACE AND FRIENDSHIP (Plate 63B). There are three sizes for the medals of Jefferson, just as there had been three grades of the engraved pieces, and there are further variations in size or method of manufacture. A supply of Jefferson medals is known to have been taken by Lewis and Clark on their expedition to the north-west. A supplementary group consists of medals given by the American Fur Company to its Indian trappers. One, in silver, bearing the portrait of John Jacob Astor and PRESIDENT OF THE AMERICAN FUR COMPANY, is to be dated about 1834. The second (in pewter) is that of Pierre Chouteau, Jr. Both bore the customary clasped hands on the reverse; the latter is dated 1843. The privilege of distributing such medals was withdrawn by the Secretary of War in 1843.

An excellent selection of recent medals, of which one is illustrated (Plate 63c), will be found in the Museum of the American Numismatic Society.

Glossary

Aes. The term used for coinages in copper and bronze.

Aes grave. The heavy cast bronze coinage of the Roman Republic in the third century B.C. The unit was the As with its fractional parts.

Aes signatum. The earliest Roman coinage. Large rectangular blocks of bronze, stamped with a design on either side.

Akce. Turkish silver coin issued between fourteenth and seventeenth centuries with inscription types on both sides.

Albertin. Gold coin named after its issuer, Albert, Archduke of Austria, governor of Spanish Netherlands (1598–1621). Types, busts of Albert and wife Elizabeth with reverse cross and date.

Altun. Turkish gold coin introduced by Muhamad II in 1454. Obverse type, Sultan's name and mint and date; reverse, titles.

Ambrosino. (1) Gold coin of Milan of thirteenth century with type of St Ambrosius; (2) silver coin of thirteenth to fifteenth century with types, cross, and St Ambrosius.

Ange d'or. Gold coin instituted by Philip IV of France in 1341 with types of St Michael and the dragon and an elaborate cross with four crowns. Imitated with variations in the Low Countries.

Angel. Gold coin of value 6s 8d, introduced by Edward IV in 1465 with types of St Michael slaying dragon and ship bearing shield with cross above. The angel was struck up to the reign of Charles I (Plate 55I).

Anna. Copper subdivision of the silver rupee in India. Types, badge of East India Company and balance.

Antoninianus. The double denarius, instituted by the emperor Caracalla in A.D. 215. The obverse bears an Imperial portrait wearing a radiate crown. The piece was originally issued in silver, but through successive debasements it became by mid-third century a copper piece with a surface wash of silver, and disappeared in Diocletian's reform of A.D. 296 (Plate 54J).

Aquilino. Silver coin of *gros* class, struck in Tyrol and North Italy in thirteenth century with types of eagle and double cross.

Argenteus. The larger Roman silver coins issued from the reform of 296 throughout the fourth century.

As. The unit of the early Roman Republican bronze coinage with, obverse, head of Janus and, reverse, the prow of a galley and sign of value (Plate 54D). After the reorganization of the coinage by the emperor Augustus in 27 B.C. the *as* was struck as a quarter of the large bronze sestertius. On the Imperial *as*, which continued to be struck till the late third century A.D., the types are, on obverse, the Imperial portrait and titles and, on reverse, a personification or scene (Plate 54K).

Augustalis. Gold coin of Frederick II of Sicily (*c.* 1231), with profile portrait type in Roman manner on obverse and eagle reverse (Plate 56I).

Aureus. The chief Roman gold coin. Little issued in the Republic except by the contenders for power in the civil wars at the end of the first century B.C. Under the emperors the aureus became a regular issue and was struck at varying standards till its replacement by a new piece in A.D. 312 (Plate 54H).

Baiocco. Papal copper coin of eighteenth and early nineteenth centuries. Usual types, papal arms with reverse, word Baiocco.

Bawbee. Billon coin issued in sixteenth and seventeenth centuries in Scotland with types of thistle and cross. Later, royal portrait on obverse (Plate 55J, L).

Bezant. General name given to gold coins of the Byzantine Empire and their imitations.

Bolognino. Silver coin originally issued by Bologna from twelfth century with types, Imperial title and word BONONI. Widely copied throughout Italy.

Bonnet-piece. Scottish gold coin of James V with profile portrait of King wearing bonnet and Scottish arms on reverse (Plate 55H).

Botdrager. Silver coin of double *gros* class in fourteenth century in Brabant and Flanders. Name derived from obverse type of helmeted lion, colloquially termed the "pot-carrier".

Bracteate. Thin silver coins with type in relief on one side and incuse on other, widely issued in Germany and Switzerland from twelfth to fourteenth centuries. Types, facing portraits, buildings, and heraldic devices (Plate 56D, F).

Carlino. Gold and silver coins introduced by Charles II of Naples in 1287 with types of angel greeting the Virgin and shield reverse.

Cash. Generic term for many small Oriental copper coins, particularly Chinese.

Cast. A piece produced by pouring molten metal into a previously modelled mould. The early Roman *aes grave*, many coins of the Greek "imperial" period, and medals of the fifteenth and sixteenth centuries were cast. In most other series the minute roughness of a cast surface is indicative of a forgery.

Cent. Copper coin of the United States, one hundredth part of a dollar. Various types of which the most famous is the Indian head.

Chaise d'or. Large gold coins issued in France in fourteenth century with type of king enthroned.

Ch'ien. Chinese round copper coin, first introduced in twelfth century B.C. Earlier type up to sixth century B.C. has round hole in centre and characters indicating weight and source. Later types up to nineteenth century have square centre hole. Still later, characters indicating value were added (Plate 58K).

Cistophoros. Large silver coin, issued from *c.* 200 B.C. under the kings of Pergamum and in other cities of western Asia Minor and continuing under Roman proconsuls and emperors. Types, mystic Bacchic *cista* and entwined snakes.

Contorniate. Roman bronze pieces with a distinctive flattened edge issued in the fourth century A.D. Types are heroes of mythology, former great emperors, and scenes alluding to sports. These were not coins but a kind of token used in connexion with the public games.

Countermark. A symbol, letter, or group of letters punched into the face of a coin to extend the validity of the coin in time or space. Commonly found on bronze coins of the early Empire.

Crown. (a) Gold coin of value 5s struck in the reigns of Henry VIII and Edward VI with Tudor rose types, and in reigns of Edward VI, James I, and Charles I with various portrait types; (b) large silver coin of same value first struck by Edward VI with equestrian portrait (Plate 55K). Continued in all subsequent reigns, usually with profile portrait.

Daalder. Silver coin of the thaler class in the Low Countries. Most common type is a standing mailed figure holding shield and provincial arms.

Daric. Gold coin of the Persian kings, with type of king shooting with bow – incuse reverse. Name derived from Persian King Darius.

Denarius. The standard silver coin of the Roman Republic and early Empire, first introduced in 187 B.C. Types under the Republic: first, the helmeted head of Roma on obverse with mark of value X (ten *asses*) and Dioscuri on reverse; later, scenes alluding to the family history of the moneying magistrates appeared on the reverse (Plate 54E). In the first century B.C. both obverse and reverse have personal allusions (Plate 54F), but portraiture of living persons is not found till the issue of Julius Caesar in 44 B.C. Throughout the Empire the denarius had on obverse the portrait and title of the Emperor or one of his family and on reverse a personification with well-marked attributes as a pictorial shorthand for various qualities and acts of the Emperor (Plate 54G). The denarius was ousted by the antoninianus in mid-third century.

Denga. Russian silver coin issued from fourteenth century by Dukes of Moscow and Kiev. Often of irregular shape. Common type, figure on horseback.

Denier (denar, denaro, etc.). Silver coin similar to English penny issued from time of Charlemagne (768–814) and copied all over western Europe. Variety of types including the inscription type with monogram of Charlemagne (Plate 56A), ecclesiastical buildings, portraits, mint names (Plate 56C).

Die. The metal punch in which the design for a coin or medal is engraved in intaglio. From the die, placed on a piece of metal and struck, a coin is produced.

Dinar. Islamic gold coin. The earliest dinars in later seventh century were imitations of Byzantine solidi. From beginning of eighth century the dinar has Arabic inscription types on both sides, giving mint, date, and religious formulae. Later, ruler's name was added (Plate 58D).

Dinara. Gold coin of the Kushan kings in North-west India and later in fourth and fifth centuries of the Gupta kings in India. Types, commonly standing figure of the king and, reverse, a seated god with inscriptions in Sanscrit (Plate 58F).

Dirhem. Islamic silver coins with types generally similar to those of dinar (Plate 58E).

Dobra. Gold coin of Portugal of two, four, and eight escudos struck by John V (1706–50). Types, royal portrait and Portuguese arms.

Dollar. Large silver coin of the United States issued from 1785. Name probably derived from thaler. Types, the head of Liberty and American eagle (Plate 57J).

Doubloon. More properly dublone, Spanish gold coin of two escudos. Introduced in later Middle Ages, but struck in quantity from gold of the New World. Types, Spanish arms with value and arms of Leon and Cas-

tille. Multiples of four and eight escudos (Plate 57B).

Drachm. Small silver coin struck by many Greek cities and states. The didrachm, the double, is the commoner. Multiple of four, the tetradrachm, was the standard large silver coin, while the ten piece, the decadrachm, was issued only occasionally. Also the common silver coin of the Parthian and Sassanian kings. Parthian types, bust of king with, reverse, seated figure and inscription in Greek (Plate 58C). Sassanian types, bust of king with head-dress and, reverse, fire-altar (Plate 58B).

Ducat (Venetian). The gold *zecchino* of Venice, struck from late thirteenth century with types of Christ in oval frame and kneeling Doge receiving standard from St Mark. Name derived from part of the Latin inscription (Plate 56K).

Ducat (European). Gold coin continued from Middle Ages. Name applied to many other similar gold coins throughout western Europe with varying types. One of the most important was that of the Netherlands with types, mailed figure and inscription reverse (Plate 57D).

Dupondius. Roman two-as piece in *aes*. In the empire it was in size and types similar to the *as* but was distinguished from it by the radiate crown worn by the emperor.

Edge. On medals of all periods, usually smooth. On coins up to the introduction of mechanical striking in the sixteenth to seventeenth centuries, also smooth; thereafter, milled or ribbed to prevent clipping. Some large coins have an inscription engraved on the edge.

Electrum. Natural mixture of gold and silver found locally in Asia Minor; the metal of the earliest coins.

Escudo. Spanish gold coin originally with types of Spanish arms and cross; latterly from Charles III, royal portrait and Spanish arms. Multiples of two, four, and eight.

Exergue. The portion of a coin or medal below the ground line of the design. Often contains specific information, such as mint-mark or date.

Fabric. The metal from which a coin is made, including the characteristic surface and appearance imparted by production.

Fanam. Small gold coin of southern India, Ceylon, and Malabar coast, struck with great variety of types from tenth to eighteenth centuries. Silver fanams also issued from sixteenth century.

Farthing. Struck in silver commonly from time of Edward III in England and Alexander III in Scotland, with types similar to those of the penny. Farthing tokens in copper issued by James I and Charles I. Types with obverse portrait and Britannia reverse first struck in 1672.

Fels. Islamic copper coin. Earliest were imitations of Byzantine pieces, but from beginning of eighth century have types similar to those of dinar and dirhem.

Field. The flat portion of either side of a coin not occupied by the design.

Florin. The *fiorino d'oro* struck in Florence from 1252, with types of St John the Baptist and reverse the lily, the arms of Florence (Plate 56J). The *fiorino d'argento* of same types also issued. In England gold coin of value 6s struck briefly in 1344 by Edward III with obverse type of king enthroned.

Follis. The large *aes* coin introduced by the reform of Diocletian in A.D. 296 (Plate 54M).

Franc. French silver coin in sixteenth and early seventeenth centuries of testoon class with types, royal portrait, and floreate cross. In 1795 established as the unit of the decimal system, and issued in one-, two-, and five-franc pieces. Types, head of Liberty or royal portrait and reverse, value in laurel wreath.

Fuh. Another name for early Chinese copper cash.

Genovino. Gold coin issued in Genoa from thirteenth century with types of gateway and cross.

Giulio. Papal silver coin of *gros* class, originally issued by Julius II (1503-13) but continued into later centuries. Types, portrait of pope, and reverse figure of saint (Plate 57C).

Groat. Silver coin of value 4d. Issued commonly from Edward III to William IV with types similar to penny and, later, royal portrait and shield (Plate 55G). Scottish groat from time of David II.

Gros (groot, groschen, grosso). Silver multiples of the denier. Issued commonly throughout western Europe from twelfth century on-

wards, with great variety of types. An example is the *gros tournois* of France, with representation of Tours and cross reverse (Plate 56G).

Guiennois. Large gold coin of Edward III and the Black Prince, issued in their French possessions in Guienne. Types, prince in armour and elaborate cross reverse.

Guilder. Silver coin of the United Provinces of the Netherlands in seventeenth and eighteenth centuries, with types, provincial arms, and personification of the Netherlands with hat on spear. Multiples of one-and-a-half, two, and three.

Guinea. Gold coin of varying value, finally settling at 21s. Issued from 1670 to 1813. Types, royal portrait obverse and heraldic design on reverse (Plate 55N). Multiples of five and two guineas and fractions also issued.

Halfpenny. Silver coin with same types as penny, struck occasionally in the Saxon coinage and commonly in later Middle Ages. Copper halfpenny with royal portrait and Britannia reverse first issued in 1672 by Charles II.

Hardi. Gold coin of the Black Prince struck in the French possessions with types, half-length figure of prince and elaborate cross.

Heller. From seventeenth to nineteenth centuries a copper coin of many German states, especially Cologne and Aachen. Multiples of two, four, eight, and twelve, with variety of types (Plate 57G).

Incuse. A design or mark sunk into a coin; the opposite of relief.

Inscription. The words which often accompany a coin design. These usually run circularly round the coin, but can occupy any position.

Koban. Thin, flat, oval gold coin of Japan issued from late sixteenth to early nineteenth century. Plain surfaces except for stamps indicating value, etc. (Plate 58N).

Kopek. In sixteenth century Russian silver coin with type of Tsar on horseback. In eighteenth century a value, not token, copper coin with types Imperial arms and monogram of ruler within wreath. Variety of multiples and divisions (Plate 57H).

Kreuzer. Billon coin of sixteenth and seventeenth centuries and copper in eighteenth century in many German states. Name derived from its cross design. Multiples in silver in later eighteenth century in Austria, Hungary, and German states.

Larin. Thin silver bars in shape of fishhook, sometimes with stamp. Current in coastal districts from Persian Gulf to Ceylon in sixteenth and seventeenth centuries.

Laurel. Gold coin of 20s, issued by James I. So called from obverse portrait crowned, in the Roman manner, with a laurel wreath.

Legend. Another term for inscription.

Lion (or St Andrew). Scottish gold coin issued from Robert III to Mary. Types, arms of Scotland and St Andrew on cross.

Louis. French gold coin introduced by Louis XIV in 1640 with types, royal portrait and elaborate cross with *lis* in angles. Continued, with variations of type, up to the Republic (Plate 57A).

Matapan. Silver coin of Venice issued from late twelfth century onwards with types similar to the ducat.

Maundy money. Silver coins of 4d, 3d, 2d, and 1d given by the English sovereign as alms on Maundy Thursday. In the earlier reigns these were the ordinary current coins, but from George II were special issues with royal portrait obverse and plain figure giving value on reverse.

Medallion. Large pieces of medallic type (in all three metals) issued by the Roman emperors on special occasions. Many issues in gold and silver were, from their weight, intended to be multiples of the standard coins. The larger flan – a disc of metal before stamping – provided opportunity for more elaborate portraiture and types (Plate 54L).

Miliarense. Silver coin equal to one-thousandth of the gold pound; introduced by Constantine the Great in the early fourth century.

Mint-mark. The mark, in the form of a small symbol, letter or series of letters, placed on a coin to indicate the place where it was struck.

Mohur. Gold coin of the Mogul emperors in India, introduced by Akbar in 1563 and issued into nineteenth century. Early examples were square, but remainder round. Types, names of early Caliphs and, reverse,

Emperor's name and titles with date and mint. Jehangir (1605–28) struck some portrait types and designs illustrating the signs of the Zodiac (Plate 58G).

Mouton. Gold coin of France of fourteenth and fifteenth centuries with types of Lamb of God with cross and standard, and floreate cross reverse. Widely copied with variations of design in the Low Countries.

Noble. Large gold coin first issued by Edward III in 1344 of value 6s 8d with obverse, king standing in ship and reverse an ornate cross (Plate 55F). A Scottish noble appeared under David II.

Nomisma. The gold coin of the later Byzantine Empire. Usually scyphate in form with types of the Emperor, Christ, the Virgin, and saints (Plate 56L).

Nummus. Generic term for coin, but commonly applied to the multiple bronze coins of the Byzantine Empire with emperor's portrait and Greek numeral of value (Plate 56B).

Oban. Multiple of ten of the Koban with similar types.

Obol. Generally small silver coin, one-sixth of a drachm. Various multiples also issued.

Obverse. The principal side of a coin ("heads") on which the more important design appears. From Hellenistic times the obverse has usually been reserved for the ruler portrait.

Onza. Spanish gold coin of eight escudos (Plate 57B).

Pagoda. Small gold coin issued in great number of states in south India from seventh to eighteenth century. Great variety of types, often representation of a god.

Pavillon. Gold coin issued by Philip VI of France (1328–50) with obverse type of king seated under canopy. Imitated by the Black Prince in his possessions in France (Plate 56M).

Penny. The standard silver coin from eighth to fourteenth century. In the early Saxon kingdoms the obverse bore the king's name and the reverse that of the moneyer; types, usually, cross motif. An occasional portrait type was used for obverse and became common after the unification of the kingdom when the place of minting also appeared on the reverse (Plate 55c). Types with variations of cross reverse continued under the Normans and Plantagenets (Plate 55D). Similar pennies were struck in Scotland and Ireland (Plate 55E). The familiar types of copper penny were first issued in 1797 (Plate 55M).

Peso. Spanish silver coin of four or eight reales (piece of eight) struck from late fifteenth century. Types, originally Spanish arms with value VIII and arms of Castille and Leon. From Charles III royal portrait on one side. Pillars of Hercules type on peso struck in Latin American mints (Plate 57F).

Pistole. Spanish gold coin, a double escudo, introduced by Philip II. Type and standard copied in most west European states.

Plate money. Large flat squares of copper with mark of value in each corner and centre, issued in Sweden in seventeenth and eighteenth centuries.

Pu. Early Chinese bronze coin of the type imitating, in miniature, original objects of barter, such as knives and spades. In circulation in last half of the first millennium B.C. (Plate 58M).

Punch-marked. Flat, square silver coins of India of the last few centuries B.C. Surfaces covered with small punch marks of natural objects, animals, and symbols, probably the marks of merchants and states guaranteeing the pieces.

Quadrans. Quarter of the Roman *as*. In the Republican *aes grave* types are head of Hercules on obverse and prow on reverse with mark of value ● ● ● . The quadrans is found only occasionally as a small bronze coin in the early Empire.

Quadrigatus. The commonest of the Roman Republican silver didrachms with types, young Janus head on obverse and, on reverse, Jupiter in a four-horse chariot (Plate 54C).

Quinarius. The half-denarius, a rare issue, both in the Roman Republic and Empire. Types usually identical with the denarius. Early quinarii have mark of value V.

Rappen. Small Swiss copper coin of late eighteenth and early nineteenth centuries with types of shield in wreath and value and date (Plate 57E).

Real. Silver coin of *gros* class, issued in Spain from fourteenth century onwards, with types the crowned royal initial and arms of Castille and Leon (Plate 56H).

Relief. The protrusion from the field of the design of a coin.

Reverse. The less important side of a coin ("tails").

Rider (or rijder). Gold coin also called the Phillipus, struck by Philip le Bon for Brabant in 1435 with obverse type of prince on horseback and reverse elaborate cross (Plate 56O).

Rose-noble (or Ryal). Large gold coin of value 10s issued by Edward IV in 1465 to replace the noble. Designs similar to those of noble but with rose on ship's side. This coin with variations in design was struck by the Tudor and Stuart monarchs.

Rouble. Large Russian silver coin of thaler or crown class, issued from time of Peter the Great with types, Imperial portrait and Russian double-headed eagle.

Rupee. Indian silver coin, first commonly issued by Mogul emperor, Akbar (1556–1605) and continued to nineteenth century. Types as for Mohue. Often square in shape (Plate 58H).

Salute. Gold coin of Charles VI of France (1380–1422) and Henry V and VI in the English possessions in France. Types as *carlino*.

Sceatta. Small English silver coin issued in seventh and eighth centuries with developments of types and designs copied from late Roman coins (Plate 55B).

Scudo. Large silver coin in Italy, particularly in papal states from sixteenth century onwards with types of ruler's portrait and various reverses – eagle on globe, shield, etc. Scudo d'oro with similar types.

Semis. The half-*as* piece of the Roman Republican *aes grave* with prow reverse and obverse, laureate head of Saturn with mark of value S. In the late Empire the semis was the half solidus and of similar types.

Sen. Cast copper coin of Japan from eighth to tenth century, similar to Chinese cash. Issue resumed in sixteenth century.

Sequin. Popular name, derived from Venetian zecchino, for Turkish gold altun (Plate 58J).

Sestertius. In early Roman Republic a small silver coin, the quarter of the denarius with identical types. In the Imperial coinage the sestertius was the major bronze piece, equal to four *asses*. The types after the first two emperors are, consistently, an Imperial portrait and titles on the obverse and a personification or scene on the reverse with the letters SC (Plate 54I).

Shekel. Jewish silver coin issued in the two revolts against the Romans in 132 B.C.–A.D. 5 and A.D. 66–70. Types, chalice, screen of Tabernacle, etc. (Plate 58A).

Shilling. Silver coin first issued by Edward VI with types of profile portrait and shield on cross. With minor variations in design this remained a standard denomination.

Shu. Rectangular silver coin of Japan, issued from seventeenth to early nineteenth centuries. Types, normally Japanese characters indicating value (Plate 58L).

Siliqua. Small Roman silver coin of the fourth and early fifth centuries. Types, diademed imperial head on obverse and reverse commonly a seated figure of Roma.

Solidus. The lighter gold piece introduced by Constantine the Great about A.D. 312. Obverse type a diademed Imperial portrait. Reverse types limited to Victory types and a few personifications of Imperial qualities (Plate 54N).

Sovereign. Large gold coin of value 20s introduced by Henry VII in 1489 with types of king enthroned and Tudor rose on shield. Continued under the Tudors with variations of portrait. The modern sovereign with reverse type of St George and the dragon was introduced in 1820.

Stater. Generically a piece of a given weight. Sometimes applied to the principal silver coin of each Greek city, but more commonly denotes a gold or electrum coin. The Ancient Britons of first century B.C. imitated the gold stater of Philip II of Macedon. Of original types of laureate head of Apollo and horse-drawn chariot, little survived after successive copying across Europe except the wreath on obverse and disjointed horse on reverse (Plate 55A).

Struck. The term applied to coins produced from dies. The surface of a struck coin is characteristically smooth.

Tari. Silver coin, principally of Knights of St John in Malta. Multiples of eight, twelve, sixteen, and thirty. Types, bust of Master of the Order with reverse, shield or St John's cross.

Thaler. Large silver coin of crown class. Name derived from original coins struck from silver from Joachimstal in Bohemia in 1518. This quickly became the pattern for large silver coins throughout western Europe and was struck in most countries under variety of names and with many types, latterly with ruler's portrait obverse and armorial shield reverse (Plate 57I).

Thrymsa. Small English gold coin struck in seventh and eighth centuries with types imitating the tremissis of the late Roman Empire, usually obverse portrait and cross motif reverse.

Tical. Silver coin of Siam. Small silver bars bent inwards in bullet shape. Plain, except for punch-mark, usually on inside and outside of bend. Issued from fourteenth to nineteenth century.

Toison. Gold coin of Philip le Beau (1496–1505), issued in Brabant with obverse type crowned shield with, below, insignia of Order of the Golden Fleece. Also a silver piece of similar types.

Tremissis. Small Roman gold coin, the third of the solidus. Widely copied throughout Western Europe from sixth to eighth century, particularly by the Merovingians in France. Favourite types, obverse portrait and cross reverse (Plate 56E).

Triens. Third of the Roman Republican *as*. Obverse type, head of Minerva in crested helmet and mark of value • • • • .

Type. The design, whether in relief or incuse, on either side of a coin or medal.

Unite. Gold coin of value of 20s first struck by James I. So named from the allusion of the inscription to the Union of the Crowns. Types, a profile portrait and an heraldic design. Charles I also issued this denomination together with some triple unites struck at provincial mints during the Civil War.

Victoriate. Early Roman Republican silver coin, normally with head of Jupiter on obverse and Victory crowning a trophy on the reverse.

Der Müntzmeister.

FURNITURE

Sydney Smith, writing in the early nineteenth century, said that there is "no furniture so charming as books". It is not necessary to be in agreement with him to admit that a finely illustrated book on furniture is the next best thing to owning the furniture, although many of us have to be content merely with the books. The aim of the Furniture section in this volume is to acquaint the reader with the basic styles which were prevalent throughout Europe and America from the Renaissance to the late nineteenth century, and also to fit into this complex picture the leading designers and cabinet-makers who were instrumental in the birth of the various styles.

In many ways the study of the history of furniture seems to have been completed, but this is, in fact, far from the truth, and we are only now beginning to understand the complexity of the subject.

It has been the practice for many years to hang furniture styles on convenient pegs in the guise of the names of reigning sovereigns, leading designers, or architectural styles, many of them in fact being complete misnomers. Thus, terms such as George I or Louis XVI, Chippendale or Sheraton, the Baroque or the Neo-classical, are frequently used in books and auction catalogues to denote periods which are in many cases only remotely connected with the literal meaning of these phrases. Recent research has now tended to expose the fallacy of this system and, although the sovereigns' names still give some indication as to the periods, the hitherto accepted *œuvres* of the leading designers and cabinet-makers are now being ruthlessly pruned, in much the same way as the works of the Great Masters are being systematically sifted from that of their pupils and followers. If Chippendale, Hepplewhite, and Sheraton had been instrumental in the production of a quarter of the pieces that have been ascribed to them by enterprising dealer and optimistic collector, then they must have run their businesses on the lines of modern mass production.

Of these three, we can only be certain that Chippendale owned a workshop and ran a cabinet-maker's business and, notwithstanding this, he is primarily remembered by posterity for the publication of his *Gentleman and Cabinet-maker's Director*. Sheraton and Hepplewhite also published highly successful design books, but, as far as we know, neither of them actually made any important furniture. Many of the designs in these books were freely plagiarized from the creations of rivals and were, in their turn, shamelessly copied by cabinet-makers throughout the country. Thus a pierglass, the design for which is in Chippendale's *Director*, may not necessarily have been produced in his workshop, because any of the numerous cabinet-makers who subscribed to the book, or who even borrowed it, could have easily made the glass.

Therefore a piece of furniture can be proved to have been made by a certain cabinet-maker only if its original account, or some contemporary description, is extant. The fact that a similar piece is illustrated in a design book is not evidence enough to as who was the maker, although it is, of course, often a very good pointer. It would, therefore, appear that the essence of the true study of English furniture design is contained in contemporary bills and day-books, and the increased study of these is enabling us to view the subject in a completely fresh light and from a new angle. The collections of the Victoria and Albert Museum include photostat copies of notable accounts, bills, and inventories of household furniture and other objects of art. Additions are constantly being made. A number of these in the charge of the Department of Woodwork, are accessible to students. The names of many cabinet-makers, carvers, and designers are emerging from obscurity and, in years to come, let us hope that we may have a list of British cabinet-makers, together with their histories, which may rival those long and detailed records that the French have published of their *ébénistes*.

In this section of the book the reader is given a highly erudite and comprehensive essay on French furniture, and thus, with Mr Francis Watson's recently published *Louis XVI Furniture*, we may at last start to enjoy the study of this complex subject in his own language.

The analysis or *expertise* of a piece of French furniture almost puts one in the place of a detective, for there is often so much of the false and contradictory in a piece that one needs a very level head and practised eye to separate the spurious from the original.

The importance of Italian furniture has now at last been realized, primarily because the Italians have been so intent on the tracking down of their furniture, which has for five hundred years been poured into the melting pot of Europe, owing to the series of holocausts which swept over Italy during that period. The essay devoted to its history is not solely directed to the creations of the Renais-

sance, as has been the tendency in earlier publications, but covers its entire history to the early nineteenth century, with special reference to Venetian lacquered furniture and Lombard *intarsia* decoration.

After the inclusion of French and Italian furniture the compilers were faced with the decision of what boundaries to set with regard to the other European countries. Spain, Portugal, Austria, Germany, Holland, and the Scandinavian countries, to mention only a few, have all produced important and individual furniture styles. These have to a great extent been moulded by national traits, historical influences, the dictates of climate, local conditions and indigenous woods, and the great general art impulse engendered by the Renaissance. The study of the furniture of the majority of these countries in this language is still in its infancy, and the need for systematic research and scholarship is acute. A comprehensive work on the entire history of Continental furniture is badly needed in this country before the subject can be properly understood and appreciated. All these countries produced national and individual styles during, and following, the Renaissance, which thrived and blossomed until Louis XIV superimposed his artistic autocracy on France and then Europe, and thus extinguished their short-lived careers. The Grand Style which *Le Roi Soleil* created for himself at Versailles, with the help of Le Brun's direction from *Les Gobelins*, completely shattered any vestiges that remained of national styles (with the exception of England), and the princelings of Germany and the grandees of Spain thus vied with one another in the emulation of all that was Gallic. From 1680 onwards the applied arts obeyed the dictates of Versailles and Paris, and the Louis XIV, Régence, Louis XV, Louis XVI, and Empire styles were freely copied and slavishly adopted throughout Europe; thus Swedish and Spanish Empire furniture appear very similar and can be differentiated only after prolonged study. However, long scrutiny is not required to distinguish them from Parisian furniture, as neither kingly neighbour nor country cousin could truly emulate the pure *style français*.

The chapter on American furniture is of

A

(A) Press cupboard of oak, pine and maple; New England, 1660–80. *Metropolitan Museum of Art, New York.*

(B) Arm-chair with Carver type back and rush seat; New York, late seventeenth century. *Metropolitan Museum of Art, New York.*

(C) American wainscot chair, oak, c. 1650. *Brooklyn Museum.*

B

PLATE 65

(A) Carved oak chest of Thomas Dennis type; Ipswich, Massachusetts, 1660–80. *Israel Sack, New York.*

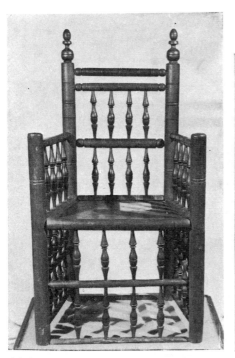

(B) American Brewster-type chair, actually belonged to Governor William Bradford, d. 1657. *Pilgrim Hall, Plymouth, Massachusetts.*

(C) The American "Hartford", "Connecticut" or "Sunflower" chest; late seventeenth century. *Formerly Collection of Luke Vincent Lockwood; courtesy Parke-Bernet Galleries.*

PLATE 66

(A) Painted chest, oak, pine, and maple; graining on body, with panels, red, black, and white; Massachusetts, c. 1700. *Brooklyn Museum.*

(B) American wing chair with rudimentary Spanish foot; c. 1700. *Blair Collection, Metropolitan Museum of Art, New York.*

(c) Walnut double gate-leg table; New England, 1690–1725. *Metropolitan Museum of Art, New York.*

PLATE 67

(B) Leather upholstered side chair of maple and oak; Massachusetts, 1685–1700. *Metropolitan Museum of Art, New York.*

(A) William and Mary American caned maple side chair, *c.* 1700. *Metropolitan Museum of Art, New York.*

(C) William and Mary high chest on rope-twist turned legs; late seventeenth century. *Metropolitan Museum of Art, New York.*

PLATE 68

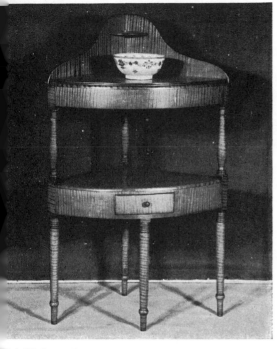

(A) Eighteenth-century American corner washstand in curly maple, a tiger-stripe marking much desired by collectors. *Ginsburg & Levy, New York.*

(B) Finely proportioned Philadelphia Queen Anne armchair, *c.* 1740–50, with "stump" rear feet. *Ginsburg & Levy, New York.*

C

D

E

(c) Butterfly table, a type of table believed to be uniquely American. The butterfly "wings" are pivoted in the stretchers. *John S. Walton, New York.*

(d) Philadelphia Chippendale mahogany Pembroke table, mid-eighteenth century, with Marlborough legs. *Ginsburg & Levy, New York.*

(e) New York Chippendale mahogany card table, *c.* 1760–70, with claw-and-ball feet. *Parke-Bernet Galleries, New York.*

(f) Martha Washington satinwood sewing table by Duncan Phyfe, so named because she is supposed to have had one at Mount Vernon. *Ginsburg & Levy, New York.*

F

PLATE 69

(A) New England Queen Anne wing chair, 1725–50. *Blair Collection; Metropolitan Museum of Art, New York.*

(B) Philadelphia Queen Anne walnut arm-chair, *c* 1730–50. *Former Haskell Collection; courtesy Parke-Bernet*

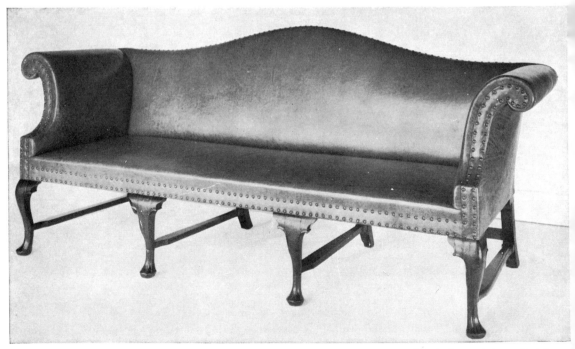

(C) Queen Anne walnut leather-covered sofa, arrow-shape stretchers, carved web feet, and scrolled knee blocks; Philadelphia 1740–50. Downs's *American Furniture, No. 269, Winterthur Museum, Delaware.*

PLATE 70

(A) Chippendale upholstered settee of mahogany and maple; Massachusetts, *c.* 1765–75. *Metropolitan Museum of Art, New York.*

(B) New York mahogany oval drop-leaf dining-table, *c.* 1770. *Metropolitan Museum of Art, New York.*

(C) Philadelphia mahogany pier or side table with top of black and white marble; carved fret on rounded frieze; *c.* 1760–75. *Metropolitan Museum of Art, New York.*

PLATE 71

(B) Tripod tea-table with piecrust edge and birdcage attachment; Philadelphia, 1765–80. *Karolik Collection Museum of Fine Arts, Boston.*

(A) Blockfront mahogany chest-on-chest, Townsend-Goddard, cabinet-makers; Newport, 1765–70. Downs' *American Furniture, No. 183, Winterthur Museum, Delaware.*

(C) Tea-table made by John Goddard, Newport 1763, for Jabez Bowen. Downs' *American Furniture No. 373, Winterthur Museum, Delaware.*

PLATE 72

A

B

C

(A) Philadelphia high chest; the Van Pelt high-boy, formerly in the Reif-snyder collection; *c.* 1765–80. Downs' *American Furniture, No. 195, Winterthur Museum, Delaware.*

(B) One of the six so-called "sample chairs" of Benjamin Randolph; design of back from Chippendale's *Director*, Plate IX, 1762 ed. Downs' *American Furniture, No. 137, Winterthur Museum, Delaware.*

(C) Philadelphia dressing-table or lowboy with fine rococo ornament; made for the Gratz family, 1769; companion to the high chest also at Winterthur. Downs' *American Furniture, No. 33, Winterthur Museum, Delaware.*

PLATE 73

(A) Connecticut blockfront cherry desk signed by Benjamin Burnham of Norwich (U.S.A.); dated 1769. *Metropolitan Museum of Art, New York.*

(B) Chippendale arm-chair with Marlborough leg; Boston (U.S.A.), 1765–70. *Metropolitan Museum of Art, New York.*

(C) Charleston chest-on-chest with fret on frieze; of type attributed to Thomas Elfe, *c.* 1775. *Heyward-Washington House, Charleston Museum.*

A

B

C

PLATE 74

(A) New England Hepplewhite mahogany serpentine-front sideboard, *c.* 1780. American sideboards tend to be more vertically slender than the English, and less ornamented. *Israel Sack, New York.*

(B) New York Sheraton mahogany sofa table, *c.* 1800–15, by Duncan Phyfe, who designed several fine variants of Sheraton's sofa table. *Israel Sack, New York.*

PLATE 75

Baltimore Hepplewhite mahogany and satinwood break-front bookcase with writing section; *c.* 1790.
C. W. Lyon, New York.

PLATE 76

(A) Salem sofa with carving attributed to Samuel McIntire, *c.* 1800. *Metropolitan Museum of Art, New York.*

(B) Baltimore Hepplewhite inlaid mahogany card table, 1790-1800. *Karolik Collection, Museum of Fine Arts, Boston.*

(C) Duncan Phyfe medallion back side chair; reeded stiles are one with the seat rail; *c.* 1800–10. *Ginsburg & Levy, New York.*

PLATE 77

(A) New Lebanon shaker trestle table 20 ft long; four-board pine top 34 ins wide; birch trestles; *c.* 1810.

(B) Sabbathday Lake sewing table has cutting board in drawer to be used also for writing. New Lebanon "Shaker red" stand; swivel sewing stools.

PLATE 78

Armed rocking-chairs with mushroom arms and cushion rails for Shaker eldresses at Hancock; for comfort a shag mat was sometimes hung from top rail. Tape seats were woven in various colour patterns. Cherry and maple table has typical turnings, braces, and long drawer.

PLATE 79

A

B

(A) Mahogany commode with cupboard ends; Duncan Phyfe, *c.* 1810–15. *Ginsburg & Levy, New York.*

(B) Philadelphia Sheraton drapery back arm-chair with inlay on legs; *c.* 1800–10. *Ginsburg & Levy, New York.*

(C) Duncan Phyfe mahogany dressing-table with curule legs; *c.* 1810–15. *Ginsburg & Levy, New York.*

C

PLATE 80

(A) Three of the six basic American Windsor types: low back; comb-back; fan-back. From *The American Windsor* by J. Stogdell Stokes, *Antiques*, April 1926.

(B) Hoop-back; New England arm-chair; loop-back. From *The American Windsor*, J. Stogdell Stokes, *Antiques*, April 1926.

PLATE 81

(B) The hutch table with storage space in the seat was made in America in the seventeenth, eighteenth and nineteenth centuries; this one is pine, painted red; mid-eighteenth century.

(A) New England tavern table, maple with marbleized top; pine bottle chest has grooved and painted decoration; the pipe box is decorated in green and grey.

PLATE 82

A

B

C

(A) Slat back New England chair; three, four and five slats, turned members and finials, rush or splint seats, arms and rockers gave variety to a basic form.

(B) Country Chippendale chair of curly maple. Often made in sets; local cabinet-makers made numerous interpretations for almost a century.

(C) Painted pine New England settle, narrowed to a single seat; settles were made for two centuries.

PLATE 83

Victorian parlour from the Milligan house, Saratoga, New York; mid-nineteenth century. *Brooklyn Museum.*

PLATE 84

(A) American rosewood side chair; neo-gothic back designed by A. J. Davis, *c*. 1830. *Museum of The City of New York.*

(B) Carved walnut side chair inlaid with crotch walnut; by Thomas Brooks, Brooklyn, *c*. 1856–76. *Brooklyn Museum.*

Photo: Metropolitan Museum of Art.

(C) American rosewood table with marble top, inside frame inscription J. H. BELTER AND CO. *Antiques*, September 1848.

PLATE 85

(A) Dresser by John Belter, New York, *c.* 1850.
Brooklyn Museum.

(B) Bed by John Belter, New York, showing laminated construction; *c.* 1850. *Brooklyn Museum.*

PLATE 86

DRAWING-ROOM CHEFFONIER,
executed from a Design by A. W. Blomfield.

A

(A) Design for "drawing-room cheffonier", from East-lake's *Hints on Household Taste*, first American Edition, Boston, 1872.

(B) (C) Cast-iron garden furniture, James and Kirkland, New York, *c.* 1850. (Plate marked Janes, Beebe and Co., 356, Broadway, New York.) *New York Public Library.*

No. 144.

B

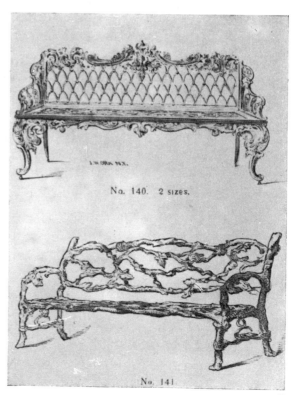

No. 140. 2 SIZES.

No. 141

C

PLATE 87

Oak hutch, demonstrating perforated work of a type in vogue early sixteenth century. *S. W. Wolsey.*

PLATE 88

(A) Oak box-stool, early sixteenth century, showing typical "slab" construction akin to that of the boarded chest. *Mary Bellis.*

(B) Child's table (square joined stool), first half seventeenth century, with unusual dentil ornament. *Private Collection.*

(C) Oak falling-table, with one flap and single gate, early seventeenth century. A type ancestral to the characteristic gate-leg. *Mary Bellis.*

(D) Oak joined stool, first half seventeenth century. *S. W. Wolsey.*

PLATE 89

(A) Windsor-type oak chair of very unusual design. *Mary Bellis.*

(B) Caryatid and Atlanta on oak bedhead, *temp.* James I. *Private Collection.*

(C) Detail of foot of late sixteenth-century half-headed oak bed. *Private Collection.*

(D) Oak chair of so-called "Farthingale" type, early seventeenth century. *S. W. Wolsey.*

PLATE 90

Oak settle, with lozenge or "diamond" carving, seventeenth century. *S. W. Wolsey.*

PLATE 91

(A) "Welsh" oak dresser of fine colour and quality. Deriving from the junction of the seventeenth and eighteenth centuries, the type has features which became traditional (e.g. arched-top, raised-centre panels). *H. W. Keil Ltd.* (B) Welsh tridarn, dated 1705. *Leonard Wyburd Ltd.*

PLATE 92

(A) Table-chair, or chair-table, oak, the top dated 1668. *S. W. Wolsey.*

(B) Child's chair in oak, mid-seventeenth century. *Private Collection.*

(C) Oak box-stool, or "Stoole with a Lock", seventeenth century. *Mary Bellis.*

(D) Oak gate-leg table, with twist-turned ("barley sugar") legs, second half seventeenth century. *Mary Bellis.*

PLATE 93

Cane-chair of so-called "Restoration" type, in oak, carved with Royal Arms and "boys and crowns" and dated 1687–8. *S. W. Wolsey*.

PLATE 94

(A) Long table and set of joined stools in oak, seventeenth century. *Mary Bellis.*

(B) Oak dresser, *temp.* Charles II, showing use of mitred mouldings. *Mary Bellis.*

PLATE 95

Oak trestle-table of *c.* 1660, its traditional type preserving medieval characteristics. *H. W. Keil Ltd.*

PLATE 96

great interest and is a fitting introduction to a difficult subject. The Americans, in their borrowing from English and French styles, have in many ways improved on them, and their furniture has a vigorous and unmistakable national appearance.

In this section the reader will find a useful survey of lacquered furniture, the history of which is traced in detail throughout Europe from the first importation of Oriental lacquer in the sixteenth century. The difference has clearly been shown between the European copies of Eastern lacquer, or the art of japanning as it was called, and the incorporation of Oriental lacquered panels in Occidental furniture.

American

Until recent years so little was known about American antique furniture that it was widely supposed to be provincial English. Thorough study by scholars, some of them English, now tells us it has a character of its own, independent of the English furniture on which it was styled. Some connoisseurs, impartial Continental Europeans, comparing a Philadelphia "Chippendale" highboy, a Rhode Island block-front secretary, a Duncan Phyfe sofa table (unique American types) with their nearest English parallels today, give preference to the American creations. Even when the comparison is between two of a kind, two fairly similar and equally well-made chairs or desks or chests of drawers, the choice often goes to American examples.

From the arrival of the original Pilgrims in 1620 down to the opening of the Revolutionary War in 1775, most of the early settlers in America were British. There were settlements of Dutch, of Germans, Swedes, Spanish, and French, but the vast majority of the people were British, blood and bone. From the first the different conditions in the two lands made for different circumstances in the lives of the peoples, their homes, and their furniture. The two countries lay in isolated hemispheres, separated by three thousand miles of ocean. The climates were different; the requirements for survival of life were different; and the social, moral, intellectual, and economic environments were as opposite as effort and ease.

As to things that the two peoples might build with their hands, such as furniture, one circumstance outweighed all others: the Americans were thrown on their own resources. They might want to model their furniture on English examples or designs, but by necessity they had to do it in their own way. In adapting their product to American use each furniture-maker had to rely for the rendering upon himself. The result was variation – individuality. So marked was this variation, that today not only can we separate English from American antique furniture but we can trace most American examples to the section of the country – northern, middle, or southern – in which they were made; often to the city – Boston, Hartford, New York, Philadelphia, Baltimore, Charleston – and on occasion actually to the shop of the man who made them.

Save in local regions where the settlers were Dutch, German, etc., Americans followed the English furniture styles. Perched along the shore of a vast continent which had to be broken tame to the plough, they had no time in which to work out polite modes of their own. They turned for their fashions to the country from which most of them had come. They were usually ten to twenty years behind the style, but followed in the path. It was hardly possible to follow the fashions, except in an independent way, because of the scarcity of models and the absence of guides. Only the merest scattering of families imported their furniture. Ships were few and small; furniture is bulky; and cargoes were given over to goods that could not be readily produced in the New World. Furthermore, it had been early discovered that imported furniture woefully suffered shrinking and cracking in America's drier air; also, that it offered no resistance to American insects. In short, almost every eventuality tended to make American furniture, though English in style, American in distinctive spirit and characteristics.

Much English antique furniture, when compared with American, appears to have been inspired by the desire for impressive show. No such noble grandeurs occur in American furniture, no broad and spacious sizes, no courtly elegance, no lavish luxury, no sumptuous ornamentation, no massive, monumental plainness. American furniture is unsophisticated, informal, democratically modest. Based on English originals though they be, American examples tend to be more forthright in design, more straightforward in construction, smaller in size, quieter in taste, and more utilitarian in the practicalities.

The spirit of early American furniture-makers was one of buoyant vitality, of energies released by exhilarating opportunity and channelled into handicraft by freedom of choice. Some workmen might be rude in skill, some naïve, some expert, but almost never were they routine. Their spontaneity was as endlessly fresh as life itself in the New World. Added to the spontaneity was the aspect of unassuming skill. To be sure, there was pride. Early American furniture-makers clearly were as proud of their work as artists are of their art, yet none, not even the most adroit, showed overweening self-assurance.

Sobriety, spontaneity, informality, democratic modesty, unassuming skill; there is a common denominator in these qualities of spirit, and the factor can be summed up in one word – simplicity. American antique furniture is simpler than English antique furniture. The tendency holds true not only up to the Declaration of Independence in 1776 but also from 1620 to 1820, and the reason is obvious. In America the environment, the times, and the people were simpler. This simplicity of spirit manifests itself in physical characteristics. The forthright design in American furniture becomes, in the working out, a physical

characteristic. So does straightforward construction, modest approach, spontaneity, and unassuming skill. The excellence of the American handiwork often astonishes Englishmen. Skill that was rough and ready did occur – possibly too much of it – but there are surviving examples which show masterly skill, on occasion as fine, though never as formidable, as any achieved in London.

Several scholars have remarked on the generally smaller size of American furniture, and given as the reason for it the smaller size of the American home. Few, however, have as yet pointed out another physical characteristic equally central: that while English antique furniture tends to be broad and horizontal (perhaps the broader size led naturally towards the horizontal), American furniture tends to be vertical. Slender, lean, thin, tallish, these are the adjectives that generally describe it. The tendency appears in every American furniture style from Queen Anne on through Sheraton, and appears in every type of article – the height of the side-chair in relation to width, of the arm-chair as well, and the wing-chair, the highboy, the secretary, and so on. Even in post-Revolutionary forms, late forms such as the sideboard, the American accent is on vertical line, the English on horizontal. This American tendency to be tall and slender, combined as it is with less carving than the English liked – indeed, less ornament of any sort – makes for a quite distinctive and non-English character.

Comparisons aside, American antique furniture is worthy of praise for its own sake. At its best it has the vigour of direct, of functional design, the merit of harmonious proportions, the grace of slender line and outline, the charm of informal size, the beauty of richly grained wood surfaces, and the force born of lack of elaboration, simplicity.

CHIEF PERIODS AND STYLES

Jacobean. The first furniture made in North America was based on the English Jacobean style. Modelled after characteristic household pieces which the Pilgrims of 1620 and later permanent first settlers brought with them from England to the New World, the earliest examples now surviving probably date between 1650 and 1670. They are of strong, straightforward, simple design and construction, generally bulky, yet often remarkably well proportioned. From the many Jacobean examples which have been gathered into museums, we judge that the woods employed were mostly American oak, pine, and maple. Perhaps most numerous are oak chests, usually with a bottom drawer or two, and all but covered with flat carving. Handsomest are three more forceful forms: (1) Jacobean court cupboards, a kind of buffet, generally oak, adorned with applied and often ebonized wood panellings, mouldings, bosses, spindles, and bulbous or columnar supports; (2) press cupboards, very similar cupboards, in which the lower section is closed with doors or made as a chest of drawers for holding household linens, etc.; and (3) separate chests of drawers, likewise much ornamented with mouldings, bosses, and panellings. Among American Jacobean tables are dining boards on trestles or plain frames and, for other rooms, stout smaller tables on four legs generally connected by sturdy stretchers. Often the legs and stretchers are spiral-twisted for the sake of ornament, or lathe-turned in the shape of balls, knobs, etc. Similar legs and stretchers are generally found on the most popular table in seventeenth-century America, the gate-leg. American chairs in the Jacobean manner may be divided into three groups: three-legged arm-chairs, plain or carved wainscot chairs, and "Dutch" type arm-chairs made of posts and spindles. Americans subdivide the latter kind into Carver chairs, with one row of vertical spindles in the back, and Brewster chairs, with two rows. These are names of Pilgrim Fathers who are said to have brought them over in the *Mayflower*. A later chair, quite the most luxurious made in seventeenth-century America, is the high-back cane chair, boldly turned and scroll-carved, the so-called "Charles the Second" chair. A few day-beds of this luxurious "Carolean" type also have survived.

William and Mary. After Queen Mary and her Dutch husband, William of Orange, came to the throne in 1689, a Dutch-influenced style of furniture gradually began to appear in England. Examples of it reached America just before the beginning of the eighteenth century and started a new fashion there, a number of cabinet-makers being skilled enough to adapt the new style admirably to American use. Americans liked this furniture in the William and Mary style. They found it less ponderously heavy and bulky than the Jacobean, and therefore better suited to their small houses. They liked its decorativeness, its pleasant inlays, its marquetry work. That they also liked the few lacquered pieces which reached them is indicated by several surviving examples of quaintly simulated American lacquering. This lacquering, then called japanning, was practised from about 1712 up to the time of the Revolution, and seems to have been done best by a group of Boston workmen. American furniture based on the William and Mary style is definitely less massive and formal than English pieces, less imposing. It is often fine furniture none the less, the finest made in America up to 1720–5, unless we except "Charles the Second" chairs. Perhaps the most notable single development was the tall chest of drawers, evolved by setting five or six tiers of drawers on a stand high enough for the drawers to be opened without stooping down. The combination is nowadays called a highboy, and when the stand is made as a separate piece of furniture, a sort of dressing-table with drawers, it is called a lowboy. By the addition of other features, highboys and lowboys became unique American designs. Those in the style of William and Mary were mostly of walnut or walnut veneer, the stand on six tall legs with connecting stretchers and ball-shaped feet, making for an attractive silhouette, doubly so because the stretchers were curved and the six legs prettily turned in the shape of inverted cups, trumpets, or balls-and-cones. Among other developments of the William and Mary style perhaps the most widely adopted in America was the cabriole leg.

Queen Anne. The Dutch influence introduced into England by William and Mary transformed English furniture in the reign of her sister and successor, Queen Anne (1702–14). The transformation was from large to smaller furniture and from fairly stiff and formal lines to lovely curves, the happiest change in English furniture in hundreds of years. Furthering this air of grace, a touch of carving, notably the scallop shell, was added. The style of Queen Anne seems not to have reached America until after her death. However, for the next half-century, even up to 1755–60, it was the fashion and standard in good furniture. Expansion was the order of the day in America. The wilderness was being pushed back ever farther from the coast; new villages and towns were being founded; cities were growing larger; trade and agriculture were increasing by leaps and bounds; many new and especially pleasant houses were being built; Queen Anne furniture was ideally suited to dress them; and cabinet-making had reached a new high level of skill. In consequence, a good deal of fine furniture in the Queen Anne style was made in America. Hogarth's "line of beauty", the wavelike, cyma curve, characterized it. Chair legs, chair seats, chair backs, chair splats, all were curved, front view and profile. Spacious wing-chairs, comfortably upholstered, came into use. Also corner chairs, and those stick-and-spindle chairs, open, cool American Windsors. Even sofas in the Queen Anne style were made, though not many. On case pieces as well as on chairs and sofas the rounded Dutch or club foot was much used, its popularity continuing long after the claw-and-ball foot came in. On highboys and lowboys the six turned legs were superseded by four cabriole legs, with hints of the missing two appearing as pendant knobs, centre front. Secretaries and clothes cupboards incorporated Queen Anne style elements, such as doors with the panels arched. A few four-post bedsteads with cabriole legs and Dutch feet have survived. Tables also often had Dutch-type feet and cabriole or at least curved legs, while that most popular American table up to then, the gate-leg, gradually gave way to the drop-leaf table, in which hinged leaves were propped up by swinging arms or legs without gate features. Many drop-leaf tables are squares or rectangles when open; numerous oval and circular ones also occur. A separate word about Queen Anne mirrors should be added, since they were probably the first fine mirrors made in America. Usually the glass is in two parts, quite visibly, no moulding or other covering masking the joint. The upper glass section is shaped to fit the cyma-curved and arched frame in which a cresting is sometimes carved. They continued in favour almost up to the time of the Revolution.

Early Georgian. Since furniture based on the Queen Anne style was popular in America until 1755–60, sundry features and developments readily recognized in England as Early Georgian features are often combined with it. The term Early Georgian is, however, seldom used in describing American-made furniture. In fact, the transition from Queen Anne to Chippendale's style is far more abrupt in America than in England.

Chippendale. In 1754 Thomas Chippendale published in London his now celebrated book of English furniture designs that gathered into one volume the various new tendencies which had been appearing in English furniture since the death of Queen Anne in 1714. Chippendale's designs brought to a head the transitional furniture tendencies of Early Georgian England, a transition which may be briefly described as a turning from the Dutch towards the French style. A few American adaptations of these Early Georgian characteristics had appeared a decade or two before Chippendale's book was published. But the force of the change from Queen Anne lines was not felt in America until about 1760, when the Chippendale style burst forth with all the popular impact of a triumphant fashion. Americans from that day to this have used the term Chippendale to mean Early Georgian furniture with Dutch characteristics (shell-carving, cabriole legs, claw-and-ball feet, the Cupid's bow top rail), and to include the mid-eighteenth-century Georgian Gothic, Chinese, and French Louis XV features which occur in Chippendale's drawings, as well as the flowing rococo carving and embellishment in which he loved to specialize. American furniture based on his designs reached its most elaborate development in Philadelphia between 1760 and 1776, under superb cabinet-makers such as Affleck, Folwell, Randolph, and Savery. However, neither in Philadelphia nor anywhere else were American Chippendale pieces as large, as lordly, or as lavishly ornamented as in England. In fact, tending towards the functional in form, American Chippendale often offers little curvature, considerable restraint in ornament, and crisp rather than flowing forms, a far cry from his rococo flights of fancy. In Puritanical districts such as New England where adornment never had been smiled upon, Chippendale-style furniture was often so simplified as to appear succinct, so straight and strict as to seem prim. To call such furniture by Chippendale's name is out of character, and is so recognized increasingly, though a more satisfactory term has not yet turned up.

But make no mistake, American "Chippendale" did constitute a new style in America, the most elaborate and luxurious up to that time. The style continued till 1785, or thereafter, bringing in the whole series of new developments that had begun about 1750, when Queen Anne chairs with looped top rails and club feet gave way to chairs with the Cupid's bow top rail, and claw-and-ball feet, while the solid vase-shaped or fiddle-back splat gave way to the open carved, interlaced splat, showing Gothic, Chinese, or French motifs. Also the "Marlborough" leg appeared, and chairs with square, straight, footless legs, generally connected by stretchers. In all these chairs the American tendency was towards smaller size, suited to a smaller chair seat than was the rule in England, American taste being modest, and American rooms not as palatially large as in fashionable English houses. Chippendale chair-back settees were made, and a few upholstered Chippendale sofas with open-rolling arms.

In England secretaries and chests of drawers with cabinet tops generally had glass doors. In America the doors were more often of wood, attractively panelled. Cabriole legs were always used on highboys and lowboys, while low-standing cabinet pieces were given either the short cabriole or a bracket foot, the bracket straight or ogee. Both cabriole and square, straight legs were used on tables, and the apron of smallish tables, like the apron of cabinet pieces, was variously treated: plain, curved, or carved with a band of ornament. Tripod tables became quite popular, elaborate examples carrying acanthus carv-

ing on the legs and pedestal. Sometimes the pedestal flaunted a surpassing luxury, a tilting top boldly shaped and carved like the notches in a pie-crust. A bit of carving might also appear on the knees of bedposts with short cabriole legs. Generally, however, before the Revolution American bedpost legs were square and plain, with round, fluted foot posts. The headposts, covered by draperies, were mostly plain, and headboards also tended towards the plain. Always we must remember the freedom with which American furniture craftsmen interpreted the English style, making not only for individual variation on the form but also for differences from the English style.

Adam. The furniture style that superseded Chippendale's in England – the "beautiful spirit of antiquity" which inspired the classical designs of the Adam brothers – had no following in America. The reason is that the designs were never published, and therefore were not available to Americans; that the furniture itself was made for the rich and not for export; and that in 1775, just about the time that Americans might have heard about the Adam style, the Revolutionary War broke out. When relations between the two countries opened up again in 1784 the Adam style was already on the wane in England, giving way in the next few years to the Hepplewhite and Sheraton styles. The result was that in America the style called Chippendale was followed by the styles of Hepplewhite and Sheraton, the two arriving at much the same moment and sharing the honours as to esteem. It is true that some Adamesque mirrors (probably Hepplewhite mirrors with motifs derived from Adam) were made in America; also that there were installed a few mantelpieces in the classical manner. But no American furniture in the Adam style was produced. Fittingly enough for the new republic, a revival of classical architecture, encouraged by Thomas Jefferson himself, arose in the United States immediately after the Revolution. The first Government building constructed, the Bank of the United States, in Philadelphia, was designed as a Romanesque temple in 1795. Both in public and in residential architecture the classical revival swept the country for the next three-quarters of a century, streaming westward three thousand miles across the continent to the Pacific coast, and losing favour only when set aside by untoward circumstances, notably the Civil War of 1860-5. How appropriately these houses in the new republic would have been dressed had they been furnished in an informal American version of Adam's classical style!

Hepplewhite. In American furniture the style of Hepplewhite so often tends towards, or incorporates, features of Sheraton's style, that many articles called Hepplewhite are best described as combination Hepplewhite–Sheraton. This American mixture of two English furniture fashions was natural in the circumstances. The peace treaty ending the war between England and the United States had been signed in the latter part of 1783; trade between the countries had begun again in 1784; and by 1785 the type of furniture then the latest vogue in England, Hepplewhite was being advertised in American newspapers as the latest importations. Another five years were to pass, however, before the economy of the United States had sufficiently recovered from the war for many citizens to buy these importations or to order American-made furniture based on Hepplewhite designs. By that time, 1790, a new type of furniture, the Sheraton, had sprung into being in England, and American cabinet-makers were shortly beginning to adapt it to American use. It was inevitable in these circumstances that elements of the two styles (which already had certain features in common) should often be combined.

The two styles can be differentiated, however, in a great many pieces of American furniture, though the distinction is not easy to sum up in words. American Hepplewhite chairs generally have shield-draped backs (or shield variants, such as the interlaced heart, the oval, etc.) with either openwork splats or banisters in the back. The splats may be touched with carving, such as plumes, wheatears, or leaves. The legs on these chairs are generally square and tapered, often ending in spade feet. Such legs also generally appear on Hepplewhite wing-chairs, sofas, tables, and, that new convenience in the dining-room, the

sideboard. In most late eighteenth-century sideboards the front was designed in a serpentine curve, and it is said that if the ends of the curve are concave the design is Hepplewhite; if convex, Sheraton. All are generally veneered in finely marked mahogany and carry a bit of inlay – satinwood or maple strings bordering the drawers, a few bellflowers dropping down the legs, etc. In the main, American sideboards are so much less ornamented than English as to be easily distinguished.

A word should be added about the new type of drawer-handle introduced about 1780: a bail pull attached to an oval brass plate. Such handles, the plate often stamped with an eagle, acorn, oak leaves, grapes, or some such design, continued to be used until 1820, though small round brass knobs were sometimes used instead. Wall mirrors now began to be made in smaller sizes. These Hepplewhite mirrors seem to have been much influenced by Adam's classical (Pompeiian) mirror designs, and the influence carries over into American Hepplewhite mirrors to the extent that the frames are elegantly thin (Pompeiian), carved, gilded, often bear garlands of leaves and flowers hanging half-way down the sides, and are surmounted by a finial, usually an urn, set in a scrolling ornament as delicate as filigree work.

A major change in the dressing of American rooms was visible by the end of the eighteenth century; for sundry articles of furniture were going out of fashion – lowboys, highboys, tall chests of drawers, etc. – the replacements being chests of drawers of more moderate size, decorative types of tables, and several new furniture forms. The increased use of occasional furniture, such as card, tea, side, Pembroke, pedestal, and sofa tables, alone would have changed the appearance of rooms. Add waist-high chests of drawers (bureaux), modest-size bookcases, tambour desks, china closets, sideboards, etc., and the change becomes pronounced.

Sheraton. As in England, so in America, Sheraton's designs were so much an anthology of other men's ideas – Adam, Hepplewhite, Shearer, not to mention his debt to the French creators of Louis Seize furniture – that the style which bears his name is more eclectic than original. Sheraton's designs incorporate, one way or another, almost every characteristic of Hepplewhite. Nevertheless, the prevailing elements are the straight lines, rectangular forms, and vertical rhythms of classical architecture which Sheraton had got from Adam and French revivers of the classical. Sheraton-style furniture is less forceful than Hepplewhite, more delicate. Where Hepplewhite is masculine, Sheraton is feminine, even, on occasion, dainty. So much refinement charmed Americans. It was in contrast to their rugged environment and might be said to have represented to them the triumph of art over necessity, of grace over Nature. The result was that there was made in America a great deal of beautifully skilful furniture based on Sheraton's designs. Much of it survives; though many pieces nowadays have become so fragile as to be more suited to museum than to home use. Among the many American cabinet-makers who produced fine furniture in the Sheraton taste, the most noted is Duncan Phyfe, of New York. Phyfe's fame has risen so high that many persons today mistakenly describe American Sheraton as "Phyfe style" furniture.

The chair backs, characteristically, are square or squarish with banister backs or open-work splats combined with banisters. Chair legs are straight and tapered; sometimes square, sometimes round. When round they are often reeded. Sofas having now come into widespread use, many were made from 1795 to 1825 in the Sheraton style. Their legs resemble the chair legs. Their backs are often a horizontal D-shape, but usually they have rectangular backs with narrow arms in line with the legs and connected to the legs by columnar supports, often in the form of an elongated vase. Back rail, arms, supports, legs, all are often reeded, but at times the back rail bears, instead, a bit of cameo carving. The distinctive feature of Sheraton dining, card, and Pembroke tables is that the legs are generally round and reeded or, if supporting a pedestal or platform, splay-curved. Chests of drawers (bureaux) may be distinguished by reeded or ringed corner-column supports ending in round, tapering feet. These columns stand out from the body of the bureau, the

top corners of which are cut almost circular in order to cover the columns. Of sideboards (as already pointed out), it is said that when the front ends of the serpentine curve are convex the style is Sheraton. Tambour desks, moderate-size bookcases, china cabinets, and occasional furniture were increasingly in demand. Sheraton himself designed no mirrors. His name, however, is given to the type of mirror that was most favoured during his vogue in the United States (1795–1820). The characteristics are a vertical rectangle with thin columns projecting at the sides and an overhanging cornice ornamented with a row of balls or acorns. The columns often carry delicate reeding. Between the cornice and the glass is generally found a quaint painting or an applied decoration, often of a patriotic nature.

An authority, Lockwood, has pointed out as a special feature of American Sheraton cabinet furniture, that "it is almost devoid of mouldings", the bareness of the straight edges often "being relieved by inlay" or some slight ornament. Inlay became much more used than hitherto, though still far less than in English Sheraton. This tendency towards embellishment was increased by the use of discreet carving such as cameo-cutting on chairs and sofas, reeding, fluting, and the use of applied classical swags, festoons, and rosettes or paterae: also, the painting or stencilling of certain articles such as occasional chairs, and by exceptionally decorative, even fanciful, veneering.

Directory. Early in the nineteenth century (c. 1805–25) American furniture was to a certain extent inspired by the French classical Directoire mode. Whether this influence came direct from France or, indirectly, through England, is not quite clear. In any event, in American furniture the Directory influence is limited mostly to chairs and sofas. It is marked by concave, "sabre-shaped" curves. The stiles of the side chair are sabre curved; the stiles turn forward as seat rails which repeat the concave curves; these curves are repeated again in the sabre-shaped front legs; and again, at least somewhat, in the concave curved rear legs. The back may contain a crossbar or a splat of either lyre or vase form.

Every line and outline of the chair is curved except the seat. Add curving arms to this form and you have the Directory arm-chair, which sometimes, as in a library chair, is partly upholstered. Directory sofas are in the shape of a broad, squat lyre which rests on short, sabre-curved legs, the upper outward curves of the "lyre" transformed into outrolling arms. The wood of these chairs and sofas is mostly mahogany. As to decoration, reeding is sometimes added, or a little carving, such as cameo-cut leaves, wheat-ears, or "sheaves of lightning". The master of the Directory style in America was Duncan Phyfe, whose finely harmonious proportions and curving rhythms have been fully praised. Aronson, for example, said: "There is little in any furniture, American or European, to excel in beauty or technique the grace of these interpretations."

Empire. When the war of 1812 between England and the United States was ended (1814) few Americans were in the mood to follow the classical Regency furniture style then the vogue in England. They turned, instead, to Napoleon's classical style – French Empire – for which they had cared little until then. This style was marked in America, as in France, by largish, bulky furniture in cube or rectangular forms, which gained a showy effect from sumptuous veneers of mahogany or rosewood. As usual, the Americans interpreted the style with much freedom, leaving out most of the Roman and Egyptian motifs so dear to Napoleon. There were no gilded bronze mountings as in France, only a little brass ornamentation, and few, if any, Egyptian sphinxes or Roman allegorical figures and military symbols, such as fasces and laurel wreaths. In brief, the adaptation followed the traditional American tendency to be simple and inornate.

While many of the chairs combine motifs borrowed from other periods – for example, sabre-curved stiles and side rails from the Directory together with reeded or ringed-and-collared straight round front legs from Sheraton – the characteristic American Empire chair has a downward-sloping, loop-like top rail, a vase-shaped splat with a hood fitted between it and the top rail; concave-curved front legs, often with projecting knees, and raked or sabre-curved rear legs. American Empire sofas also show motifs from other periods such as Directory "roll over" arms. But as a rule the whole conception and construction of the sofa is more massive, and the squat-lyre form outline curves tend to become swan-neck or cornucopia curves, a tendency emphasized by carving them to resemble swan-necks or cornucopias. The legs of these sofas are scrolls or, later, winged legs with animal feet (representing the Egyptian griffin). Animal feet, with or without wings, also characteristically, are found on bureaux, wardrobes, sideboards, pier tables, etc. In many American Empire bureaux (chests of drawers) the top drawer overhangs the lower drawers and the overhang is supported by columns, some plain, some variously ornamented with ring turnings, reeding, or carving, such as quilted or "pineapple" designs. The columns and overhang also appear on American Empire desks, secretaries, and sideboards. In some cases, probably late examples, vertically elongated scroll supports are used instead of columns. Another feature often found on American Empire cabinet pieces is the treatment of the top drawer as a broad, convex-curved "torus" moulding. Frequently the sides of such cabinet pieces are panelled. A type of chair and sofa not previously mentioned now made its appearance: the ancient Roman curule seat, formed by joining two half-circles back to back, X-shaped. Other singular forms such as sleigh-shaped beds, and "Grecian" sofas, became popular. A new development in mirror frames also appeared. The columns at the sides became larger and heavier yet were used decoratively rather than structurally. Instead of delicate reeding, they carried broadly carved leafage, spirals, or rings; and sometimes the columns were partly gilded and partly painted black. In brief, they lose their architectural character and, consequently, are no longer wall mirrors but, rather, looking-glasses to hang on a wall.

The handles in the Early Empire period were, characteristically, projecting round brass knobs often stamped with the American eagle, the head of Washington, or some other patriotic motif. The characteristic Late Empire handle was a ring pull hanging from the mouth of a brass lion's head. The tawny gleam of brass was in happy accord with the glowing red mahogany or rosewood in rich "crotch-grained" veneers. Seldom has veneering been used with more brilliant effect. The forms of the furniture grew stiffer, colder, and more austere, but the surfacing grew more resplendent. Despite the fact that the style was in the hands of master cabinet-makers, eminent among them Duncan Phyfe, the taste of the day was deteriorating. By 1830 American Empire had fallen from bad to worse, the forms becoming bulky, the proportions coarse, the rhythms heavy. Phyfe himself called it "butcher furniture". The decline continued until about 1840, when Americans began to turn from it and take up a new furniture style, the early Victorian.

CABINET-MAKERS

Affleck, Thomas. Born in Aberdeen, Scotland, he learned his trade in London where, as a young man in 1763, he was chosen by John Penn, commissioned governor of Pennsylvania, to go with him to Philadelphia as resident cabinet-maker. Affleck died there in 1795, a prominent citizen who counted among his friends eminent persons such as Benjamin Franklin. He is generally reckoned the most skilful cabinet-maker in eighteenth-century Pennsylvania and the leader of the Philadelphia Chippendale school. Evidence indicates that he owned a copy of Chippendale's *Director*; and several of his documented chairs do closely parallel certain plates in the *Director*. Joseph Downs says that Affleck's Philadelphia work "brought an unparalleled urbanity of . . . Chippendale pattern to Philadelphia furniture".

Allison, Michael. New York cabinet-maker who flourished about 1800–20. Some of his furniture is stamp punched; many of his other pieces have been attributed to Duncan Phyfe.

Appleton, Nathaniel. Early nineteenth-century Salem, Mass., cabinet-maker distinguished for his furniture in the Federal styles.

Ash, Gilbert. Much-respected New York joiner and chair-maker (b. 1717, d. 1785). Some of the earliest American Chippendale chairs were from his hand. He often repeated, with attractive variations, the diamond lattice-back chair.

Burling, Thomas. New York cabinet-maker (*fl.* 1772, d. 1800), whose superior skill has been established by five or six examples which still bear his label. He was selected by George Washington in 1795 to make a "writing desk and apparatus" (price 40 guineas) for the first official residence of the President.

Chapin, Eliphalet. Leading member (b. 1741, d. 1807) of a well-known Connecticut family of furniture-makers. Eliphalet practised for a time in Philadelphia, with the result that the Chippendale highboys and secretaries made by the Chapins incorporated Philadelphia features such as elegant pediments with delicately pierced scrolls and a fancy finial. But they are generally in Connecticut cherrywood rather than mahogany, and far simpler than Philadelphia work; indeed, show the spare ornament, narrow proportions, and slender vertical rhythms prevalent in New England.

Claggett, William H. Newport, Rhode Island, master clockmaker (b. 1716, d. 1749?). In youth he had a brief career in Boston, where he may have been trained.

Cogswell, John. One of the most distinguished of Boston cabinet-makers (*fl.* 1769, d. 1818), whose work is more elaborate than was the custom in New England. Perhaps best known for his Chippendale bookcases and bombé chests of drawers; also, together with his son, Junior, for Hepplewhite and Sheraton sideboards and blue-lined tambour desks.

Disbrowe, Nicholas. Earliest known American furniture-maker (b. 1612–13, d. 1683). Born in Walden, Essex, England, the son of a joiner. One of the settlers (before 1639) of Hartford, Conn. A signed chest made by him shows flat-carving of tulips covering the entire front, and might be called the first of the so-called Hadley chests.

Dunlap, Samuel (II). New Hampshire cabinet-maker (b. 1751, d. 1830) known for his maple highboys and secretaries with a distinctively scrolled pediment and interlaced cornice. Leading member of a New Hampshire furniture-making family that included John I, John II, and Samuel I.

Edgerton, Matthew. Leading cabinet-maker of New Brunswick, New Jersey (*fl.* 1742, d. 1787). Several fine examples of his skill have been identified from existing labelled pieces.

Elfe, Thomas. Perhaps the most prominent of the Charleston, South Carolina, cabinet-makers (*fl.* 1751–71). His elaborate Chippendale mahogany case pieces are much prized. He employed a dozen or more Negro slaves, trained craftsmen, whom he owned.

Elliot, John. Philadelphia cabinet-maker (*fl.* 1756, d. 1791) noted for his wall mirrors. After his retirement in 1776 his business was carried on by his son, Junior.

Folwell, John. Philadelphia master cabinet-maker of the Chippendale school (*fl.* 1775), whose works, according to Hornor, "are unsurpassed in historic appeal and artistic significance". Just before the Revolution, Folwell solicited subscriptions for his proposed book of American furniture drawings, titled *The Gentlemen and Cabinet-maker's Assistant*. In consequence, he is sometimes called the Chippendale of America.

Frothingham, Benjamin. Foremost cabinet-maker of Charlestown, Mass. (*fl.* 1756, d. 1809). Several soberly elegant pieces, such as a block-front chest of drawers and a reverse serpentine desk, still bear his label. Son of a Boston cabinet-maker, Benjamin became a major of artillery in the Revolution and counted his commander-in-chief, General Washington, as a friend.

Gaines, John. Gifted cabinet-maker of Ipswich, Mass. (*fl.* 1724, d. 1743), earlier of Portsmouth, N.H. He may have originated the Queen Anne chair variants which combine the solid splat with the earlier caned Flemish and banister-back chairs. His son, George, a major in the Revolution, also became a well-known cabinet-maker.

Gillingham, James. Skilful cabinet-maker of Philadelphia (b. 1735, d. 1791). Several of his Gothic Chippendale chairs, with distinctive, trefoil-pierced slats, have been identified.

Goddard, John. The originator, perhaps together with his brother-in-law, John Townsend, of block-front and shell-carved cabinet furniture. Widely reckoned the foremost Rhode Island furniture-maker of his day (b. 1723/4, d. 1785). Apprenticed to Job Townsend, of Newport, whose daughter he married. His sons, Stephen and Thomas Goddard, became first-class cabinet-makers. (*See* Townsend, John.)

Gostelowe, Jonathan. Outstanding Philadelphia cabinet-maker (b. 1744, d. 1806). His mahogany furniture in late Chippendale patterns is unsurpassed. He designed several patterns of his own, among them "imposing serpentine and fluted-corner chests of drawers".

Harland, Thomas. Sometimes called the ablest Connecticut clockmaker of his day (*fl.* 1773, d. 1807). A number of his workmen became well-known clockmakers on their own, including William Cleveland, grandfather of the twenty-second President of the United States, Grover Cleveland.

Hopkins, Gerrard. Baltimore cabinet-maker (*fl.* 1767–93), trained in Philadelphia. Especially remembered for his furniture in the Chippendale manner. Son of another furniture craftsman, Samuel.

Hosmer, Joseph. Concord, Mass., cabinet-maker (*fl.* 1775). He learned his trade from an American Frenchman, Robert Rosier. He produced skilful and distinctive works often in cherry or other New England woods. In 1775, his house, barn, and shop were burned by the British. Later that year, as a lieutenant of Minute-men, Hosmer became an historical figure. Shouting "Will you let them burn the town down?" he led the attack on Concord bridge, in which the British suffered their first defeat in the American Revolution.

Lannuier, Charles Honoré. New York cabinet-maker (*fl.* 1780–1819). Perhaps trained in France, he produced elegant, often elaborate, furniture, and is especially remembered for his work in the Directory style. His pieces are often attributed to Phyfe.

Lemon, William. Master cabinet-maker of Salem, Mass. (*fl.* 1796). Of peerlessly refined skill, he is noted for his superb furniture in the Hepplewhite manner.

McIntire, Samuel. Famous architect, woodwork designer, and carver of Salem, Mass. (b. 1757, d. 1811). A superior craftsman, he is by some students considered the leading American furniture-carver, especially of Sheraton ornament in the Adam (classical) manner. There has been hot controversy as to whether or not he was a cabinetmaker. There is no documentary proof that he was. His son, Samuel, also did furniture-carving.

Moore, Robert. Brother of Thomas and William, all cabinet-makers of prominence in pre-Revolutionary Baltimore (*fl.* 1769).

Nash, Thomas. Earliest recorded clockmaker in America (*fl.* 1638-58). He was a gunsmith of New Haven, Connecticut.

Phyfe, Duncan. New York master cabinet-maker (b. 1768, d. 1854). Born in Scotland, he went in his early 'teens to Albany, New York, and there became apprenticed to a cabinet-maker. In 1790, aged twenty-one, he arrived in New York City, where shortly he set up a shop and made fine-quality furniture in the Sheraton and Directory styles. Phyfe's work possesses a grace of line, a refinement of proportions, and a delicacy of ornament – reeding, fluting, cameo-carving – which lends it both elegance and a distinctive air. Among his chairs, sofas, and tables he produced so many little masterpieces incorporating the lyre motif that he is now considered its chief American exponent. Phyfe's individuality again stands out in his Empire-style furniture. He was so successful that at one time he employed a hundred workmen; eventually his work suffered from his success. He retired from business in 1847. Fine collections of Phyfe furniture are owned by the Museum of the City of New York; the Metropolitan Museum, New York, the Taft Museum, Cincinnati, Ohio; and Henry Ford's Edison Institute, Dearborn, Michigan.

Pimm, John. One of the ablest Boston cabinet-makers in the Queen Anne style (*fl.* 1735, d. 1773). A handsome japanned highboy, signed by him, survives.

Prince, Samuel. Able and highly prosperous New York cabinet-maker (d. 1778). He is especially identified with furniture in the Chippendale manner. Thomas Burling was apprenticed to him.

Randolph, Benjamin. Shares with Thomas Affleck the reputation of being the leading exponent of the Philadelphia Chippendale school (*fl.* 1762, d. 1792). He owned considerable property and is believed to have had the largest cabinet-making shop in Philadelphia. Of him Nagel says: "No other American cabinet-maker mastered the true spirit of the rococo more completely or came closer to the English tradition than Randolph." A finely carved French Chippendale wing-chair attributed to him has been sold at auction to John D. Rockefeller, Jr, for $33,000.

Rittenhouse, David. Noted American astronomer, surveyor, inventor, and clockmaker of Philadelphia (b. 1732, d. 1796). Of his grandfather clocks, already famous in his day, only a few survive. He is said to have constructed his first clock when he was only seventeen. Thomas Jefferson, third President of the United States, wrote of him: "We have supposed Mr Rittenhouse second to no astronomer; that in genius he must be first because he is self taught." Rittenhouse (from the original Dutch, Rittenhuisjen) was a grandson of the first Mennonite bishop in America. He became Director of the United States Mint, and succeeded Benjamin Franklin as President of the American Philosophical Society. His brother, Benjamin, was also a clockmaker.

Sanderson, Elijah. Able cabinet-maker of Salem, Mass. (b. 1751, d. 1825). Together with his brother Jacob (b. 1757, d. 1810) he employed the finest craftsmen available, including the carver Samuel McIntire. They shipped much of their furniture to Southern states, where it is said to have been sold on the piers. They also shipped furniture to South America.

Savery, William. Renowned cabinet-maker of Philadelphia (b. 1721, d. 1787). At one time reckoned the paramount furniture craftsman in Pennsylvania, he is still considered peerlessly sound. Joseph Downs tells us that his career began in 1742, continued forty-five years, and that his work ranged from simple maple rush-bottom chairs to soberly elegant carved Chippendale mahogany highboys.

Seymour, John. Master cabinet-maker of Boston (*fl.* 1790–1820). His distinctive Federal furniture interprets Hepplewhite, Sheraton, and Directory designs, often combining features of each. He is famous for his masterly satinwood inlays and tambour doors. He had a son in business with him.

Shaw, John. Exceptionally skilful cabinet-maker of Annapolis, Maryland. He flourished in the late eighteenth century. There exist several labelled examples of his work in Hepplewhite and Sheraton styles.

Terry, Eli. Master clockmaker of Connecticut (b. 1772, d. 1852). He developed nine clocks, which he patented, the best known being the so-called "Terry" clock, a then inexpensive shelf or mantel timepeice with wooden works running thirty hours. It is housed in a case with a scrolled-arch top, small round pillars at the sides, and delicately small feet. Early in his career Terry toured the countryside, peddling his clocks from door to door.

Thomas, Seth. Connecticut clockmaker (b. 1785, d. 1859), once a workman for Eli Terry. He bought up the rights to make "Terry" clocks, but seems to have created no clock of his own. Today clocks bearing the name Seth Thomas are still being manufactured.

Townsend, John. Renowned cabinet-maker of Newport, R.I. (b. 1733). He made excellent block-front furniture and is believed to have been associated with his brother-in-law, John Goddard, in originating it. Captured in the Revolution, he was released from a British prison ship in 1777, took up residence in Norwich and, later, Middletown, Conn., where groups of block-front furniture-makers sprang up around him. Outstanding member of a famous furniture-making family, including his father, Job, several brothers, sons, and nephews. Some scholars think the Townsends deserve most of the credit now given to John Goddard for originating block-front furniture.

Tufft, Thomas. Well-known cabinet-maker of the Philadelphia Chippendale school (*fl.* 1765, d. 1793). His identified work is not as elaborate as some, but his chairs and carved highboys and lowboys set "a standard of exquisite detail".

Weaver, Holmes. New port, R.I., cabinet-maker (b. 1769, d. 1848). Produced excellent work in Hepplewhite and Sheraton styles. Was at one time clerk of the supreme court of his county.

Willard, Simon. Widely regarded as America's foremost clockmaker (b. 1753, d. 1848). Member of a famous family of Massachusetts clockmakers, including his father, Benjamin; three brothers (Benjamin, Jr, Ephraim, and Aaron); a son, Simon, Jr; nephews and cousins. His most famous clock – a weight-driven, accurate, eight-day movement, housed in a banjo-shaped case – he patented in 1800, having invented it several years earlier. He also made grandfather clocks of the finest workmanship. His reputation grew so great that other clockmakers are known to have put his name on their clocks.

AMERICAN VICTORIAN FURNITURE

The American Victorian style, in existence from 1840 until about 1910, displays strong English influence, as the name implies. Designs and design books were simultaneously published in London and New York. Basically the Victorian is an eclectic style. Many different sources were used for inspiration, with innovations introduced in construction and proportion. Most of the misunderstanding of this style comes from the fact that its originality is not accepted as anything more than lack of ability at imitating. Actually, the Victorian designers tried to remain close to their models but also wanted to create practical furniture, and they changed the scale and some of the details to suit the rooms for which the furniture was intended.

The style has been referred to by Carol

Meeks as one of "Picturesque Eclecticism". The emphasis is on visual elements. Covering and screening new types of construction with traditional motifs is general.

New designs were always based on previous periods. At times the sources were close at hand in the various eighteenth-century styles, but occasionally the more exotic and distant models, such as Jacobean and Near Eastern, were employed.

Very important to the development of furniture production was the partial industrialization that became typical of the craft in the United States. The large workshop with the bare beginnings of mass-production and specialization, gradually became common in the centre where furniture was made. This was responsible, in part, for some of the changes in what might be considered traditional forms.

By 1840 many manufacturers in American cities were known to employ from forty to one hundred men, most of whom were unskilled workers. Furniture designs were created by the shop owner, and a minimal number of skilled men were required to follow the designs. The larger shops produced inexpensive furniture that could be shipped easily. John of Cincinnati supplied many small Mississippi river towns with stylish furniture. The furniture of Hennesy of Boston was available in many smaller towns along the sea-coast.

We can get some idea of the Victorian conception of styles from the writings of the American architect, A. J. Downing. In *Cottage Residences*, published in New York in 1842, he implies the use of more than one furniture style when he says, "A person of correct architectural taste will . . . confer on each apartment by expression of purpose, a kind of individuality. Thus in a complete cottage-villa, the hall will be grave and simple in character, a few plain seats its principal furniture; the library sober and dignified . . .; the drawing room lively or brilliant, adorned with pictures. . . ."

He continues in the same vein in another book, *The Architecture of Country Houses*, one edition of which was published in 1861 (others earlier); "Furniture in *correct taste* is characterized by its being designed in accordance with certain recognized styles and in-tended to accord with apartments in the same style." Downing goes on to describe the various styles and he includes Grecian (or French) Gothic, Elizabethan, Romanesque, and a version of the Renaissance style. Each has its place. The idea of using the different styles was criticized later by Charles Eastlake, an English architect who was influential in America. In 1872 he said, "In the early part of the present century a fashionable conceit prevailed of fitting up separate apartments in large mansions each after a style of its own. Thus we had Gothic halls, Elizabethan chambers, Louis-Quatorze drawing rooms, etc. . . ."

These various styles of the Victorian period were used at about the same time, but fashion determined when they were replaced and none lasted throughout the period.

The earliest significant style was a continuation of American Empire. This furniture was heavy in proportion and differed from the earlier models only in a few details. The wavy moulding was a border introduced late; medallions and other small details of applied carving in leaf or floral motifs reduced the simplicity and classicism characteristic of earlier furniture. In the Victorian versions drawers rarely have borders of moulding, but rather are flush with the front surface. Marble tops for small tables and bedroom chests are common. Bracket feet are a frequent support for heavy case pieces. On tall legs turning as well as heavy carving was employed. Popular as finer woods were mahogany, black walnut, and rosewood. Simpler, less expensive pieces were made of maple, butternut, or other hard woods, which are often stained quite dark in red or brown. Veneers in prominent grains were used on case pieces as well as on the skirts of sofas and chairs.

In general, there were few new forms developed. Among the new were such peculiarities as the Lazy Susan and the ottoman; however, the wardrobe and the bookcase, which were known only infrequently before, were better known in the Victorian period.

With the factory replacing the craftsman's workshop, techniques requiring less skill developed. Machine sawing and planing were used with hand-fitting and finishing. The lines were planned by someone higher in rank than the man who operated the saw or did the finishing. The larger-scale operations made competition a more important factor than ever before, with price more important than workmanship.

A Baltimore cabinet-maker, John Hall, published a book of furniture designs in 1840. One of the objectives of his book he describes by saying, "Throughout the whole of the designs in this work, particular attention has been bestowed in an economical arrangement to save labour, which being an important point, is presumed will render the collection exceedingly useful to the cabinetmaker." The designs are Grecian, he says in his commentary and ". . . the style of the United States is blended with European taste . . ." This is the style that A. J. Downing refers to as Greek, modern, and French and "the furniture most generally used in private houses". Contemporary cartoons and illustrations confirm his remark by usually including this kind of furniture. A popular woman's magazine of the time, Godey's *Lady's Book*, consistently presented suggestions for furniture in the style from the late 'forties to the 'sixties which was called "cottage furniture".

The Gothic style in Victorian furniture has two aspects. As a variation of the classical, it involves only the use of the pointed arch (Plate 85A) and related motifs in what is basically the classical style. As a more ambitious innovation, it involves the use of Gothic ornament in a more serious attempt to create a special style. The first approach was used by Chippendale, who included Gothic motifs in his rococo suggestions. Later, Sheraton included Gothic arcades in suggestions of designs, primarily neo-classical. This continued in early Victorian furniture in the Greek style. The other aspect was connected with the Gothic revival in architecture, which, although begun in the eighteenth century, had an important effect on home building after 1830. Suitable to houses in the Gothic style was furniture repeating the motifs. Large bookcases, which seem almost like architectural elements, and hall chairs, high-backed side chairs carved elaborately, are often the most spectacular examples of the style.

Some of the finest examples were designed by architects for use in their buildings. Occasionally spiral turned columns, seventeenth century in inspiration, are combined with elements of earlier inspiration. The characteristic feature of the style is the pointed arch of simple or complicated form used with incised or pierced spandrels and bold raised mouldings. The Gothic style is one favoured for hall decoration and used less frequently in the parlour. Sets of bedroom furniture in the style are known. Tables are extremely rare in this style.

When referring to furniture of various kinds Downing says in *The Architecture of Country Houses*, "There is, at the present moment, almost a mania in the cities for expensive French furniture and decorations. The style of royal palaces abroad is imitated in town houses of fifty foot front. . . ." This style was often called Louis XIV, although it is a combination of various French styles from Louis XIV to Louis XVI (Plate 85B, C).

Revival of rococo style had started in France as a reaction to its classicism which was dominant shortly before the Revolution. With the Restoration came a desire for the good old days and a style related to them. Napoleon's Romanism was as distasteful as his political upsets. From France the revival spread to the rest of the Continent, England, and the United States. In the Victorian home, where each room varied in style to suit its proper mood, the French style was most popular in the parlour, although bedroom furniture in the style is known.

The American Victorian pieces were smaller in proportion than the eighteenth-century models. The curving lines of the back stiles are often exaggerated so that the back is balloon-shaped. Cabriole legs are restrained in their curve. Console tables with marble tops come in scallop shapes. Curving fronts are typical for case pieces. Carving in rose, grape, or leaf motifs with elaborate details in high relief is seen on chairs and sofas. On other forms this carving is flatter. Elaborate carving was frequently used on cabriole legs.

The curve becomes all important as a contrast to the straightness of the classical. Small boudoir pieces were made in this style as well as whole matching parlour sets which include a sofa or love seat, gentleman's arm-chair, lady's chair, four side chairs, an ottoman, and centre table (Plate 84). In a drawing-room set there are additional pieces such as an extra sofa, more side chairs, and possibly a matching *étagère*. There seem to be no dining-room pieces in this style. Introduced in America about 1840, it was important until some time in the 1870s. One of the most important cabinet-makers working in this manner was John Belter of New York (Plate 86A, B). Born in Germany, he opened a shop in the city of New York in 1844 and continued in business until his death in 1863. Belter's work was a distinctive variation of the Louis XV style. He invented a laminating process for curing wood that he used in making the sides of case pieces and chair and sofa backs. He destroyed the means of doing this laminating shortly before his death, so that it was never used later. Solid curving pieces are characteristic of Belter's shop, as is elaborate carving in high relief and balloon-shaped chair backs. Belter's parlour sets are best known, but he also made bedroom furniture.

The Louis XVI style was more specifically popular after 1865 when there was some reaction to the exuberance of the rococo revival evident in the Louis XV-inspired examples. The straight line and the fine detail are distinctly opposed to the heavier curving style.

Other revivals of interest occur in the early period, but to no great extent. Downing's suggestions include pieces in what he refers to as the Flemish style, but actually of William and Mary origin.

After 1870 there were several other adaptations of eighteenth-century models. The Adam and Sheraton styles served as inspiration for dining-room and parlour pieces done with greater faithfulness to the model and less of a re-interpretation for modern requirements.

The Renaissance style was introduced at the Crystal Palace exhibitions of 1851 (London) and 1853 (New York). It is a style heavy in proportion and generally straight in line. Decoration is elaborate and frequently in-

spired by architectural rather than furniture design. The pediment is used to top many of the forms, from chairs to large case pieces. Bold mouldings, raised cartouches, raised and shaped panels, incised linear decoration, and applied carving in garlands and medallions are all characteristic. Occasionally, animal heads and sporting trophies appear on dining-room pieces. The style was used primarily for bedroom, library, and dining-room pieces, but there are examples of parlour furniture also. This style continued to be important until about 1880.

Factory production inspired spool-turned furniture, a particular type easy to produce for the lower-priced furniture market. In the main, designs were simple and the sizes were right for easy handling in lower-middle-class interiors. This furniture was decorated by turning on a lathe the legs, arms, and supports and obtaining identical units repeated in any of a variety of motifs that include the bobbin, knob, button, sausage, and vase and ring. The lines are generally rectangular and simple. This furniture did not include every form, but rather emphasized beds and tables.

The first seeds of modernism can be traced from the reactions against bad craftsmanship in the Victorian period. As a period of mass-production and keen competition, the Victorian period saw the development of truly bad design as well as some very good design that has been misunderstood. By attempting to make things cheaply without simplifying the design and method of production, some makers produced surprisingly unsuccessful results.

One of the first important reactions was the book, *Hints on Household Taste*, which had an American edition in 1872. The author was the English architect, Charles Lock Eastlake, who decried bad craftsmanship and the shams it involved. He sought to inspire simple honest work in solid woods. He disliked shoddy veneer and too elaborate work. His argument was: "I recommend the re-adoption of no specific type of ancient furniture which is unsuited, whether in detail or general design, to the habits of modern life. It is the spirit and principles of early manufacture which I desire to see revived and not the absolute forms in which they found embodiment."

Eastlake proposed that craftsmen follow appropriate models that would not be difficult to execute. He disliked the over-ambitious attempts of the 'fifties in which the rococo was used to excess. The resultant style was simple and rectangular (Plate 87A). Most of what he suggested was to be executed in oak, a durable but inexpensive wood. Carving could be simple, and turnings were to play an important role. This style was gradually more and more important on the American scene. Related suggestions follow in ensuing decades, and the oak furniture of the turn of the century by Gustav Stickley is probably basically of the same inspiration.

Attempts to find new and more appropriate sources of design resulted in furniture of exotic inspiration, such as that of the so-called Turkish style, seen in overstuffed pieces for parlour use.

The Victorian period is marked by variety of inspiration, stimulated by the use of different styles to suggest different moods. In the first half of the period the changes from the original to the Victorian interpretation were probably greater. After 1880 there was a more faithful adherence to the lines of the models, although the results always differed from the originals. About the same time attempts to make furniture only vaguely connected with earlier styles were evident, and there was also a search for new sources of inspiration.

In the Victorian age mass production was a key factor in the development of the kind of competition which made bad craftsmanship profitable. This resulted from cutting costs without considering the need for simplification in design. The contrast between good and bad craftsmanship was probably greater after the beginning of factory production.

CAST-IRON FURNITURE

The manufacture of cast-iron furniture in the United States began in the 1840s and continued until the first decade of the twentieth century. The manufacturers were firms making grille work, architectural ornaments, and building fronts. Both indoor and outdoor furniture was produced, although, with few exceptions, the indoor furniture was popular for a much shorter time than the outdoor furniture. Cast-iron furniture for interiors was introduced in the 1850s, a little later than the garden furniture. It was designed as an imitation of wooden furniture in the various Victorian styles and was painted to simulate wood. The exceptions to this characterization were the beds and hatracks in which imaginative forms were developed. These two forms continued to be popular after cast-iron furniture for interiors had become unfashionable.

Garden furniture of cast-iron was used for a longer period, and the designs became standardized. The dominant influence was the romantic garden which had come into fashion at the end of the eighteenth century. It was created to appear wild, as if man had not had a hand in it. The furniture was designed to have a rustic look, to appear to be made of unhewn logs, or boughs of trees, vines, or flowers (Plate 87B, C). The various patterns used seem to have been followed by many manufacturers. The same designs appear in early and late examples. The earliest catalogue known to contain an illustration of cast-iron garden furniture appeared in the 1840s in Philadelphia, but almost every American city of any size produced it some time during the nineteenth century. Often the mould contained the name of the manufacturer, and the piece can be dated by consulting city directories.

English

THE AGE OF OAK

English furniture from the Middle Ages to the Restoration in 1660 was made almost entirely of oak. William Harrison, writing late in the sixteenth century in his *Historical Description of the Island of Britaine*, said that "nothing but oak was any whit regarded".

The oak, which is the most common species of tree in this country, is hard and heavy, the colour varying from white to brown. Evelyn, in 1663, writes that it was "of much esteem in former times till the finer grain's Norway timber came amongst us which is likewise of a whiter colour". Although the oak is a very tough tree, it was discovered at an early date that there was little difficulty in splitting it along the lines of the medullary rays, provided that this were done before the fibres hardened. However, it must always have been necessary to use a saw for wood of a great age, or for wood that had been allowed to harden after felling. These saw-cut logs were immersed in flowing water for a period of up to two years and were then stored for a further ten to twenty years, after they had been converted into planks. The timber, thus seasoned, was thus considered to be ready for use.

CONSTRUCTIONS

Furniture of the oak period is generally rectangular in construction and is very strongly built. Its component parts are put together with mortise and tenon, which in turn are held in position by wooden dowels. Evelyn, describing the furniture of the early seventeenth century, writes "they had cupboards of ancient, useful plate, whole chests of damask for table . . . and the sturdy oaken bedstead and furniture of the house lasted the whole century". Much of this oak furniture has, of course, lasted far longer than a century, and on account of its strength has come down to us in almost pristine condition.

SURFACE DECORATION

Early Gothic furniture, which is extremely rare, was of relatively plain form and relied on colour for its decoration. Its surface was often lime-whitened, and to this ground was added a polychrome scheme of decoration executed in oils or tempera. By the middle of the sixteenth century the surface was frequently left in its natural state, and by the seventeenth century some kind of preservative such as beeswax was rubbed in, which now gives to the oak its deep and rich patination. The use of gilt and gesso, so dear to the Italians during the Renaissance, was seldom if ever used in England during the period under review.

CARVING

The Gothic style of carving and ornamentation, which had grown very flamboyant by the end of the fifteenth century, was gradually superseded during the reigns of the Early Tudors by Renaissance motifs. These were introduced from the Continent by Italian, French, and Flemish craftsmen. The earlier linen-fold panelling was often combined with the new forms of decoration, such as grotesque masks, arabesques, and carved caryatids. During the Elizabethan period every kind of carved motif was employed and we find strapwork, terminal figures, bulbous supports, festoons, swags, geometric and medallion panels, lozenges, arcading, and pilasters.

There was a marked reaction against this flamboyant style by the early seventeenth century, and carving began to give way to applied decoration. Bosses, demi-balusters, and other forms of pendant decoration, often stained black in imitation of ebony, were applied to the plain or panelled surfaces, and moulded geometric panels were a favourite form of ornamentation. The sober spirit of the Commonwealth was reflected in its furniture, which was simple to an almost monotonous degree, as every form of decoration was frowned upon. The Restoration of the Monarchy, which heralded the walnut period, was a complete antithesis to the austerity of the Interregnum, and the exuberance and vivacity of the Court of Charles II were immediately attracted to the International Baroque.

INLAY

The use of an elaborate pictorial marquetry of many exotic woods was a feature of Renaissance decoration and entire rooms were panelled in this extravagant form of ornamentation. It was greatly favoured on the Continent, as the panelled rooms at the Escurial outside Madrid and the Ducal Palace at Urbino bear witness, and it was also popular in the North of England. The finest extant example in this country is the room from Sizergh Castle which has now been reassembled in the Victoria and Albert Museum.

Pieces of Elizabethan and Jacobean oak furniture were often inlaid with a chequered design of marquetry – or parquetry, as a geometric, mosaic, or cube design inlay of woods is called – in boxwood, holly, poplar, and bog oak. The last-named was obtained from portions of trees which were found submerged in peat bogs – hence the black hue. The most elaborate form of marquetry found in oak furniture is in the so-called "Nonsuch Chests". The term is derived from the name of the celebrated palace which was built by Henry VIII at Cheam, and representations of it were inlaid into the front panels of coffers or chests, and occasionally smaller objects. Chests of similar design were made in Scandinavia and southern Germany, and it is probable that chests of this type originated in one of these countries, the design then being copied by craftsmen in England. Burnt poker-work, which is employed in conjunction with floral marquetry, is another form of decoration which is sometimes found in this country. It is usually used on chests which are of a distinctly Italian appearance. However, there is evidence enough to show that some were made

in this country, and the style of dress worn by the figures which are portrayed is definitely of British origin.

Shaped slivers of wood about the thickness of a piece of paper are laid on the ground which is to be inlaid, and the required design is then marked round them. This is in turn cut out from the surface and the prepared pieces of wood are inlaid and glued down. A distinctive style of inlay was evolved during the latter half of the seventeenth century in which pieces of engraved bone and mother of pearl were inset as a form of surface decoration. The Portuguese in India and the Moors in southern Spain both used this form of inlay, and it was probably introduced to this country from one of these two centres.

CHIEF PERIODS AND STYLES

The history of early furniture is in many cases affiliated to the architectural styles. Oak furniture can therefore be readily divided into the Gothic, the Renaissance, and the Jacobean and Commonwealth periods. The Gothic forms of design and ornamentation, although they were firmly established, offered little resistance to the new influences of the Renaissance. The wealth which was suddenly acquired by Henry VIII and his friends from the Dissolution of the Monasteries, the stability of the country at large, and the King's and Wolsey's personal taste for grandiose building schemes were all important factors which helped towards the adoption of the new designs.

During Queen Elizabeth's reign wealth and prosperity were even more abundant, and this new gracious form of living was not reserved for the nobility and gentry alone, as is shown by Harrison's reference to yeomen farmers who were able to "live wealthie, keep good houses, and travell to get riches". They also bought "costlie furniture", and they had learnt to "garnish their cupboards with plate, their joined beds with tapestrie and silk hangings, and their tables with carpets".

By the mid-sixteenth century the High Renaissance style had percolated through to England via Flanders and Northern Europe. It had become rather vulgar and over-elaborate and the true decorative motifs were considerably coarsened. The style was introduced by Continental craftsmen, who were either invited over to carry out special commissions or who were attracted by the general prosperity of the country. Pattern books were also being published in Italy, France, and Germany, and these had a wide influence on the embryonic Elizabethan style.

Many ambitious building schemes were put in train during the early years of the seventeenth century, and of course the necessary furniture and furnishings had to be produced to decorate these new rooms and apartments. "No kingdom in the World spent so much on building as we did in his time," writes a diarist of James I's time. Most of the oak furniture which survives today was made in the early seventeenth century, and it must be borne in mind that much of the extant furniture of Elizabethan design was actually produced in the reigns of James I and Charles II. Craftsmen were conservative to a degree, and new ideas and designs travelled slowly to the provinces.

THE AGE OF WALNUT

There is some doubt about the exact date when the walnut tree was introduced into England, but it is certain that it was being used for furniture in the Tudor period, especially for beds. One of Henry VIII's great beds had a headpiece of walnut, and in 1587 we read of "a bedsteed of wallnuttrye in Ladies chamber". But as the chief wood of fashionable furniture the great period of walnut can be considered to cover the best part of the century beginning at 1660. Two main kinds of walnut were used, the European (*Juglans regia*) and the North American (*Juglans nigra*, the black or Virginia walnut). The former had many good qualities for furniture. Its attractive colouring, with beautiful figure and uniform texture, made it very suitable as a veneer, on a carcase of yellow deal. When properly seasoned (a process which might take seven to ten years) it was a solid and compact wood, hard enough to carve into delicate shapes, and, unlike oak, comparatively free from shrinkage or swelling. The burr and curl woods were particularly beautiful, the former being cut from the burrs or abnormal excrescences which grew at the base of the trunk and produced a finely mottled grain, and the latter from just below a fork in the tree. The timber's one great defect was that it was liable to worm, especially in the sap wood. In this respect the Virginia walnut was much better, as the well-seasoned timber was largely immune from worm.

The *Juglans regia* grew throughout most of Europe and was the chief kind used until about 1720. The English variety was considered to be somewhat coarse and featureless for high-quality work, though at times it produced some good varieties of figure. Italian walnut was rated very highly, for the timber which grew in the mountainous regions had a close-grained texture with dark streaks, ideal for decorative work. French walnut was also greatly esteemed; it was straight-grained with a lighter, quiet grey colour. The Grenoble area produced timber which became a hallmark of distinction in furniture. Spanish walnut was similar to the French, but it was liable to have more faults. The superiority of these foreign timbers over the English led to considerable imports of walnut into England, especially from France. In the three years 1700–2 inclusive, just before the Spanish Succession War (1702–13), imports of "wallnut tree plank" from France amounted to £534 8s, £1,009 4s, and £339 respectively, and just after the outbreak of war, in 1704, walnut worth £1,330 was registered among the prize goods captured from the enemy.

There are indications that English walnut was relatively scarce in the seventeenth century. John Evelyn, in his *Sylva* (first published in 1664), wrote: "In truth, were this timber in greater plenty amongst us, we should have far better utensils of all sorts for our houses, as chairs, stools, bedsteads, tables, wainscot, cabinets, etc., instead of the more vulgar Beech." He praised the black walnut highly: "The timber is much to be preferred, and we might propagate more of them if we were careful to procure them out of Virginia . . . yet those of Grenoble come in the next place and are much prized by our cabinet-makers." Some of the black variety was grown in England in the seventeenth century, but there is little doubt that the shortage of English walnut and the cost of imported walnut had much to do with the great use of veneers. After the Spanish Succession War, during which the severe winter of 1709 had killed off many trees, the French Government prohibited the export of walnut in 1720, with the result that from that date, though supplies continued to come in from Holland and Spain, much more of the North American variety was imported. Virginia walnut was darker and of a more uniform colour than European (it is the only walnut with traces of purple), and its strength and excellent working qualities explain the bolder designs in the solid after the Queen Anne period. But after the first quarter of the eighteenth century walnut was beginning to feel the effects of competition from mahogany, and was entering on its last phase as the fashionable timber. In 1803 Sheraton wrote in his *Cabinet Dictionary* that "the black Virginia was much in use for cabinet work about forty or fifty years since in England, but is now quite laid aside since the introduction of mahogany".

CHIEF PERIODS AND STYLES

In the walnut period the styles take their names from the reigning monarchs – Charles II (1660–85, and including the short reign of James II, 1685–8); William and Mary (1689–1702); Anne (1702–14); and the early Georgian (George I, 1714–27, and George II, 1727–60). The furniture of the whole period reflected the growing standards of wealth and comfort; many new pieces were produced to satisfy social needs, and adapted to conform with improving standards of design. Two factors which helped to make the knowledge and use of good furniture widespread were the increased skill of the craftsmen and the development of London as the chief furniture-making centre of the country. This was the period when the joiner was being replaced by the cabinet-maker as the supreme furniture craftsman. It will be noted that Evelyn, in the passage quoted above, was already referring to cabinet-makers as early as 1664, and he frequently used this term in his various works. The English craftsmen had to learn many new techniques at first from foreigners, but on the whole it can be said that they assimilated them and interpreted them with good sense and balance; and by the end of the seventeenth century they were not only supplying the home market but had also built up a flourishing export trade in furniture to all parts of the world. London's size was meanwhile making it a focal point for the whole kingdom. By 1700 the capital had half a million inhabitants; the next largest towns had no more than 30,000. Though there were other notable furniture centres – Lancaster, for instance – there was no doubt about London's leadership in styles. The social convention of the seasonal migration of the landed gentry to London helped to spread furniture fashions throughout the country, as Defoe noted early in the eighteenth century, and for the first time it was possible to distinguish town and country pieces.

The reign of Charles II was marked by an exuberance and flamboyancy which was reflected in such things as costume and plays, as well as in furniture. The reaction to the Puritanism of Cromwell's regime and the return of Charles and the aristocracy from exile abroad opened the country to a flood of Continental fashions – French, Spanish, Portuguese, Italian, Dutch, and Flemish. Increased trade and colonization brought riches to the upper and middle classes. The Great Fire of 1666 both led to a greater output of furniture and brought it under the influence of architects like Sir Christopher Wren and of craftsmen like Grinling Gibbons. New ideas, or new twists to older ideas, were apparent in the use of glass, cane, turning, veneering, marquetry, gesso, and japanning. The reign of William and Mary saw, in general, a sobering down in furniture styles, due to William and his Dutch background, and the work of his great craftsman Daniel Marot, a Huguenot refugee, who in his furniture for his royal patron interpreted Louis XIV fashions in a quieter Dutch idiom. But there was no decrease in output. The revocation of the Edict of Nantes by Louis in 1685 sent many Huguenot refugees to England, and one result was the flourishing Spitalfields silk industry and improvements in upholstery. There were developments in such things as writing-desk furniture (in which increased letter-writing, due to improved postal services, was a major factor), card- and tea-tables, bookcases, chests of drawers, and cabinets, the last-named due to the upper-class fashion for collecting "rarities" or curiosities of all kinds. It was in the Queen Anne period that walnut furniture reached its best phase. With its emphasis on graceful curves, and a return to veneers to bring out the beauty of figure, compared with the previous Dutch fashion of marquetry, this reign is distinguished by its simple elegance, shown in such details as the hooped-back chair, the cabriole leg, the bracket foot, and a general stress on good design. The earlier Georgian period produced a heavier and more florid baroque style, partly perhaps as a reaction to simpler fashions, but mainly due to the Palladianism of William Kent, the architect (1684–1748), who affected much elaborate gilt ornament with classical motifs, carried out in softwoods or gesso.

OTHER TIMBERS

Though walnut put the seal on fashionable furniture, many other timbers were important during the same period. The great popularity of veneers, inlay, and marquetry led to a demand for a wide range of coloured woods. Among the native timbers used for these purposes, lighter shades, white or yellow, could be obtained from apple, holly, dogwood, boxwood, maple, laburnum, sycamore, and plane, and darker colouring from olive, pear, and yew. Elm and mulberry were also prized for their burr veneers. Timbers imported from the East, South America, and the West Indies included ebony (black), fustic (yellow, turning to a dead brown), and kingwood, lignum vitae, partridge wood, rosewood, and snakewood (all giving various shades of brown and red). For carcase work, and as a ground for veneers, yellow deal was almost always used. But for clock cases wainscot oak was used. Great quantities of deal were imported from Baltic countries in the late seventeenth century. Oak and ash were used for drawer linings.

DECORATION

Gesso. Gesso work came into fashion in England just before 1700 and was a popular form of decoration until about 1740. It was a mixture of whiting and parchment size which was applied coat after coat and allowed to dry. When there was sufficient, a pattern was formed in relief by the background being cut away. The former was burnished and the latter left mat. Furniture was given a brilliant and highly ornate effect when gold leaf was used, but there was also much cheap colouring which tended to fade. Gesso lent itself to the Kent style of decoration, and it had the same appearance as the work on the carved and gilt table in Plate 104. Perhaps the most celebrated exponent of the use of gesso during the early eighteenth century was the Royal cabinet-maker, James Moore.

Japan work. Japanned or lacquered furniture enjoyed a considerable vogue in the walnut period. As early as 1661 Pepys recorded seeing "two very fine chests covered with gold and Indian varnish". Lacquer work was originally imported from the East, and was known variously as Indian, Chinese, or Japanese, but the best kind was made in Japan, and was called "fine" or "right" Japan, to distinguish it from substitutes. Most of the genuine Japanese work was brought to England by the Dutch, but the English East India Company handled Chinese and Indian varieties, which had a ready sale in the home market and went under the general name of "Indian" goods (and were sold in "Indian" shops). So great was the demand for these goods that some English merchants exported patterns and models of all kinds of furniture to be copied and lacquered by native workmen, who could thus manufacture English-style furniture. The completed goods were re-imported and sold at home. But meanwhile an English japan industry had sprung up. In 1688 Stalker and Parker published their *Treatise of Japaning and Varnishing*, and in 1693 a company was formed with the title of "The Patentees for Lacquering after the Manner of Japan". Naturally, the home producers of japan disliked the practice of sending goods abroad to be lacquered, and so did other cabinet-makers, who looked upon it as unfair competition. In 1701 the London cabinet-makers, joiners, and japanners petitioned Parliament to put a stop to it, and an Act was passed imposing heavier duties on all imported lacquer (12 & 13 William III, c. 11). Thus from that date nearly all japan work was home made. It was very popular until about 1740, and much of it was exported. The colours used were bright ones, often scarlet, yellow, etc., and carried out Eastern designs (Fig. 1),

FIG. 1

but English work lacked the high quality of the true Oriental variety. In fact, inferior work was merely varnished. It was usually applied on a background of deal for carcases, or of beech for chairs. Good-class work often had a smooth-grained, veneered surface as a basis. Normally, designs were raised on the surface, but a rare form of lacquer work, known as Bantam work, used incised designs. Cabinets, chairs, bureaux, screens, clock cases, and mirrors were among the more usual pieces for japanning. There was a revival of this fashion in the later eighteenth century.

Mouldings. Mouldings, the contours given to projecting members, were an important part of the decorative treatment of walnut furniture. On tall pieces – cabinets, tallboys, clock cases, etc. – the profiles of the straight cornices, which were popular until the Queen Anne period, were built up in architectural style, usually in layers of cross-grained wood. One characteristic feature of the later seventeenth century was the convex (torus or swell) frieze. The convex was not universal, however, for the concave (cavetto) frieze was used at the same time, and superseded it early in the next century. Mouldings also accentuated the arched curves and the varieties

of broken pediments when these came into fashion. Towards the end of the walnut period dentil mouldings (tooth-like cubes) were often found on straight-line cornices or angular pediments.

Another moulding of convex profile, called the ovolo (or lip), was applied to the top edges of chests of drawers, stands, and tables (Plate 102), and on the upper sections of bureaux (Plate 97). Chests of drawers and bureaux sometimes had plinth mouldings, above ball, bun, or bracket feet (Plates 97 and 98). The general development of drawer furniture produced several kinds of smaller mouldings (sometimes called reeds) around the drawer fronts, to offset the otherwise flat surface. These were normally cross-banded veneers of walnut glued to a back of deal, and applied at first to the carcase, and later to the drawer edge. From 1660 to about 1700 the most usual kind was a convex half-round moulding on the rails between the drawers (Plate 102), but just before the end of the century two smaller half-round mouldings (Plate 98), or sometimes three reeds together, were applied to the rails, and this vogue lasted until about the end of Anne's reign. From 1710 a distinct change in method was beginning; the mouldings were now applied to the edge of the drawer, in ovolo section, and projected sufficiently (about a quarter of an inch) to hide the join between opening and drawer when the latter was shut (Plates 97 and 101A). From about 1730 cock-beading, a half-round bead projecting outwards from the edge of the drawer, was introduced, and became the chief drawer moulding for mahogany furniture. Mouldings also edged the doors on clock cases (Plate 101B) and surrounded mirrors or panels on cabinet doors (Plate 98). On the latter, broader types of moulding were common, in astragal section, semicircular with the addition of a fillet at each side.

Turning. Until about 1700 turning was one of the outstanding features of the legs on chairs, tables, and stands, and of the uprights on chairs. It was carried out on the foot-operated pole lathe which rotated the wood while the turner's chisel cut the required shape. Twist turning, which came to England from the Continent shortly after the Restoration, and replaced the earlier bobbin turning, resulted from a mechanical device which moved the chisel continuously to produce the oblique curves. For this walnut was a much better medium than the more brittle oak. At first the Flemish "single rope" style was used, but this was followed by the English double rope or "barley sugar" twist, finished by hand and sometimes pierced. The design was working itself out on chairs by 1685, but it persisted on tables for some time longer. Another form, baluster turning, was produced by the turner holding the chisel himself and varying the pressure to get a number of diverse shapes. This type is connected with William and Mary furniture. There was an almost bewildering variety of such designs, but among the more popular can be distinguished the Portuguese swell, a bulb-like shape, followed by the mushroom, and, later still, by the inverted cup. Some legs were squared off by hand to octagonal and other patterns. Plate 102 illustrates the inverted cup. *See also* Chairs.

Veneers, marquetry, and parquetry. Veneering was the chief decorative feature of walnut furniture. It originated on the Continent, and gave opportunity for flat decoration, which showed to the full the beauties of the grain. Veneers were thin layers of wood cut by hand-saw, perhaps one-eighth of an inch thick, and glued to a carefully prepared surface, which was nearly always of imported yellow deal, a variety of pine or fir which was better able to take glue than oak. Not only did the veneers preserve and strengthen the wood underneath, but they were found to be the only practical way to use the rare woods like walnut burrs, which would twist if worked in the solid. The chief patterns were the "curl" or "crotch", a plume effect taken from the junction of a side branch with the main trunk (Plate 97), the "oyster", cut from branches to show the rings in the wood and the "burr", an intricate figuring from abnormal growths at the base of the trunk (bureau section of Plate 98). Successive veneers from the same piece of wood, showing duplicated patterns, were often quartered, or glued in sections of four, on suitable surfaces

(Plates 97 and 98). Besides walnut, yew, elm, and mulberry made high-quality veneers, and laburnum and olive produced excellent oyster figures.

Marquetry was an advanced form of veneering, much employed in Holland, which first came into prominence in English furniture in about 1675. With infinite patience and skill veneers of various coloured woods were cut into delicate patterns and fitted together like a jigsaw puzzle. For this process walnut could be changed in colour by dyeing, scorching with hot sand, staining, bleaching, and fading, but, naturally, many other timbers of suitable colour, both native and foreign, were used (as indicated under "Other Timbers" above). At first English marquetry followed the Flemish mode and concentrated on bird, flower, and foliage designs (Fig. 2),

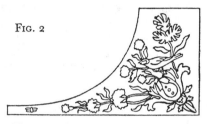

FIG. 2

sometimes with the aid of materials other than wood, such as bone and ivory. The colours tended to tone down to quieter dark or golden shades about 1690. By 1700 arabesques were popular, together with the most intricate form of all, the seaweed or endive marquetry, which was shown to great effect on clock cases (Plate 101B), cabinets, and table tops. Early in the eighteenth century the marquetry phase was running out, and there was a return to the plainer veneering. Parquetry was a form of marquetry which emphasized geometrical patterns, with the same skilful use of contrasting colours. It was used far more widely on the Continent.

Veneered surfaces had two characteristic decorations, cross-banding, or cross-grain, veneered strips bordering other veneers, and herring-bone banding, two smaller rows of tiny strips of veneer applied diagonally, often in contrasting colours. Each could be used singly, or together, on drawer fronts, table tops, bureau flaps, and similar fields.

(Plate 97 illustrates herring-bone banding and cross-banding inlay together.) The popularity of veneering introduced distinct changes in the construction of furniture as well as in its appearance. The panelling technique of oak was unable to provide the flat, smooth surfaces necessary for taking veneers. For angles on carcases and drawers the old method of dovetailing (the through or common dovetail), though the strongest form, had the great disadvantage of showing the

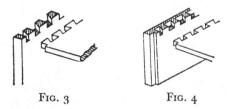

FIG. 3   FIG. 4

end grain on both sides of the angle, and this was unsatisfactory for holding veneers (Fig. 3). Shortly before 1700 it was replaced by the lap or stopped dovetail, which had the end grain on the side only, leaving the front quite clear for veneering (Fig. 4).

Bureaux, cabinets, bookcases, etc.

The bureau was one of the pieces of furniture which met the demands of the new habit of letter-writing in the Restoration period. Early bureaux were mounted on stands and were nearly always of narrow width, with one or two rows of drawers under the sloping writing fall. The stands were gradually discarded and bureaux became wider and more solid. Most were now 3 ft 6 in. wide, though narrower ones (for standing between the windows of a room) continued to be made. The legs of the early stands followed contemporary side-table developments, while the more solid bureau followed the chest of drawers (*see* separate sections below). Plate 97 illustrates the fine proportions and appearance of the Queen Anne bureau. It has bracket feet, slides for the flap, and ovolo lip moulding round the drawers, which also have cross-banding and herring-bone inlay. The veneers are good, and the matching on the flap, and on the drawers (both across and upwards), are worth close attention.

Another piece was the writing cabinet, which developed in two main stages. The first stage was the scrutoire, a box-like structure consisting of an upper part of drawers and pigeon-holes, enclosed by a hinged let-down front which made a large writing surface, and a lower part formed by either a chest of drawers or a stand with legs and stretchers. The disadvantage of having to clear away all papers before the front could be closed led to the second stage, the bureau writing cabinet or the bureau-bookcase as it is now termed. This had a shallow cupboard enclosed by two doors for the upper part and a bureau for the lower. The space in the bureau top for papers made this a more convenient piece than the scrutoire; it was also more elegant. Plate 98 illustrates a Queen Anne bureau-bookcase. Here the cornice balances the arched mouldings, which contain quartered veneers on the doors. The bureau drawer fronts have burr veneers and reeded mouldings. The opened flap displays the neat arrangement of the bureau top. The bureau-bookcase became fashionable in William III's reign and was either veneered with walnut or japanned.

Meanwhile, the cabinet was assuming the forms which had long been known on the Continent, and from the increasing skill required in making it was producing the first English cabinet-makers. It developed from the chest, acquired a number of drawers (many of them "secret"), cupboards, and pigeon-holes, and was mounted on tall stands or chests of drawers. At first the tops were straight, with rather heavy cornices, and two doors enclosed the front. Later the frieze was developed; the swell variety became more common, and a shorter stand was used. One type of cabinet that was mounted on a chest of drawers was copied from Chinese cabinets, and had engraved hinges and lock-plate, and finely figured walnut veneers to vie with japanned pieces. Other cabinets were excellent show pieces for decorating with marquetry and parquetry, applied to the many small drawers as well as to the doors inside and out.

There was, however, from 1600 onwards considerable diversity of decoration and design in these pieces, as the cabinet could be used for various purposes. With glazed front and shelves, it was used as a bookcase or display cabinet. It now seems clear, contrary to former belief, that cabinets were not used to display china but held small curios like medals and miniatures. Other cabinet doors had mirror-plates instead of clear glazing, or no glass at all, relying upon panels of finely figured walnut for effect; mirrors and panels were often enclosed in mouldings which had a graceful curving form at the top. These shapely curves were a predominant feature in the late seventeenth century and in Anne's reign, and were applied to the tops of cabinets in various ways – double, and occasionally, triple arches and broken circular pediments (Figs. 5, 6, and 7). They showed the applica-

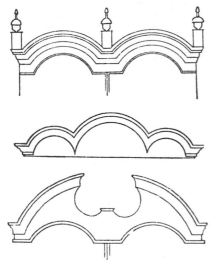

FIGS. 5, 6, and 7

tion of architectural principles to these larger pieces of furniture. But there was still a strong liking for the simple straight cornice, as shown in Plate 98. It is not always certain now for what purpose some cabinets were intended. Many which resemble bureaux-bookcases, with the bureau replaced by a chest of drawers, have survived. They have been used for storing clothes in the bedroom or as a cupboard in the parlour.

For larger bookcases, such as those which Pepys bought from Simpson the joiner in 1666, the doors were glazed in rectangular panes like windows. The growing popularity of glass fronts made glazing bars important.

At first they were usually semicircular, veneered with cross-grained walnut, or astragals, a half-round moulding worked on the edge. In the eighteenth century another form of astragal, with a small fillet at the top of the curve, came into use. These astragals, often larger in shape, framed the mirrors or veneers on doors which did not have clear glazing.

Chairs, day-beds, stools, and settees

Plate 99A illustrates the type of chair that was produced in the Charles II period. These chairs were distinguished for their elaborate carving and turning. Twist turning was at first often applied to the back and front legs and uprights, and carving was the treatment for the top rail between the uprights and for the wide stretcher set half-way up between the front legs. Another novelty, canework, was found on the seat and back, framed in a carved panel, rectangular or oval in shape, separated from the uprights and seat. After the middle of the century carving improved considerably. At first it was heavy looking, emphasizing scrolls, foliage, and crowns; later it became much lighter and pierced, and top rail and stretchers curved upwards, often ending in a crown (Fig. 8) supported by

FIG. 8

amorini. From about 1675 S-shaped scroll designs (the "Flemish" scroll) were popular for front legs, and on arm-chairs this shape was continued in the arms which curved downwards in the centre and formed deep scrolls over the supports. By the end of Charles's reign twist turning was being replaced by baluster turning. Canework was also becoming finer in texture, and many specialist craftsmen were making large numbers of cane chairs for export as well as for home use. The back legs were splayed for steadiness. There was also a fashion for some chairs to be entirely upholstered with overstuffing, carried out in fine materials, damask, velvet, embroidery, or Mortlake tapestry.

The lightness of cane helped to popularize a pre-Restoration piece, the day-bed, or couch. This had a chair back (sometimes one at each end) and a long seat carried on six or more legs joined by richly carved stretchers. It was used in the living-room (which no longer had a bed in it), and had to be easily movable. Some day-beds were ornately japanned.

William and Mary chairs saw distinct changes in design. The flamboyancy of the previous period tended to give way to a simpler style, though there was still much rich carving. Backs (99B) had a tall and narrow appearance, due to the fashion in women's hair styles, and took on a pronounced backward tilt. Chair legs either kept the scroll form or were decoratively turned in one of the many baluster or geometrical shapes. Prominent among these were the Portuguese bulb (Fig. 9), mushroom (Fig. 10), inverted cup and square (Fig. 11). Feet were ball or bun

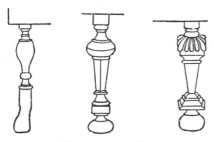

FIGS. 9, 10, and 11

shape, or else carved in the Spanish foot design. Another novelty was the introduction of curved stretchers under the chair, going diagonally from squares just above the feet, and either crossing directly, tied in the centre with a finial, or fixed into a central platform. Front stretchers in the older form still persisted, but the fashion now was to set them back from the front legs and fit them to the side stretchers. The upright aspect of the backs, very characteristic of this time, was accentuated by the arching of the cresting rail above the back uprights. Usually seats were upholstered, with a tasselled fringe, but backs were treated in various ways – pierced carving, canework (in thinner panels), or upholstery.

All these changes were nothing compared to the revolution in chair design in the early eighteenth century (of which Plate 100A repre-

sents a somewhat later development). Straight lines gave way to curves, turned legs and stretchers to cabriole legs without stretchers, and overstuffing to the drop-in seat. The back uprights took a graceful hoop form, and the centre of the back was occupied by a single solid splat, often veneered, showing a variety of smooth curves. For the first time the chair back was shaped for the sitter, giving the aptly named "bended" back. The cabriole leg came from France about 1700. Taking its shape from an animal's leg, it had various endings, a hoof, a pad, or club (Figs. 12 and 13), or the celebrated ball-and-claw

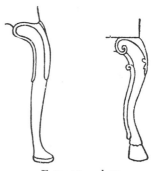

FIGS. 12 and 13

foot, which came in about 1720. These legs, worked from the solid by hand, were strong enough to hold the chair without stretchers. The general emphasis on curves was continued in the frame of the seat. Carved decoration was usually limited to the knees of the cabriole legs, cresting rail, and seat rail, in the form of shell or acanthus designs, or, later, as in Plate 100A, a mask on the rail. A new treatment of chair arms was to set them back in a curve from the front of the chair, to allow room for the wide-hooped dresses of the time.

Another pleasant type of chair which had made its appearance by about 1700 was the upholstered wing variety (see Plate 100B). The wings at the shoulders curved down to wellpadded arms which scrolled outwards. The legs often had cabriole shape, but the size and weight of the chair required stretchers, of the simple turned kind.

Towards the end of the walnut period some of the simple grace of the Queen Anne chairs

was lost. In the early Georgian era they tended to become heavier and more squat in appearance, and carving was more ornate. The
splat was not left plain,
but was carved and
later pierced with
strapwork designs (Fig.
14).

From 1660 stools
closely followed the
prevailing chair de-
signs. They had an im-
portance which today
may be easily over-
looked. In general,
their form was that of

FIG. 14

chairs without backs, except that all four legs
were the same shape. They were often richly
upholstered. A later development was the
settee, which sprang from the fusion of two
arm-chairs, with double backs, outer arms,
and five legs. In their earlier forms – later
seventeenth century – they were often two
cane chairs together.

Chests of drawers and tallboys

The time-honoured chest, long distinguished for its frame construction and carving in
the oak period, became the more useful chest
of drawers after the Restoration. Already in
1661 Pepys bought "a fair chest of drawers"
in London. The chest itself did not disappear
quickly; it persisted well into the next century, made in the traditional oak, then walnut
and, later, mahogany, or japanned, when
that form of decoration was popular. But long
before 1660 its future development was indicated when the bottom drawer was added
to it, to form the mule chest. The chest
of drawers developed along three lines:
the familiar solid type, from the chest; the
chest on stand; and the chest on chest, or tallboy.

The solid type was still being made in oak
in Charles II's reign, but it gradually replaced by walnut and incorporated all the refinements and techniques due to the new
wood. Larger chests of drawers stood up to
3½ feet high, usually with five drawers, three
long ones at the bottom and two smaller ones
at the top. But many fine smaller ones were

also made. They were admirably suited for
veneers (applied to the top and sides of good
pieces, as well as to drawer fronts, with cross-
banding and herring-bone patterns), marquetry and japan. Besides walnut, or used
with it, other woods, particularly yew, fruit
woods, and burr elm, made good veneers.
Laburnum and walnut were used for oyster
veneering. This effect, which resembled a row
of oysters lying side by side, was achieved with
slices of wood cut transversely from small
boughs or saplings, showing a series of irregular concentric circles. To overcome the
straight-line effect of the drawers, various
mouldings, at first on the frame and then on
the drawer edges, were applied to give decorative effect. The tops also had larger ovolo
mouldings jutting out over the edges, and
similar mouldings at the bottom of the carcase, above the feet. The development of the
feet showed a constant search for good design.
At first they were of the turned ball or bun
type, but as this did not harmonize with the
general appearance of the chest, they gave
way to the square bracket feet, flanked by
small curved pieces.

The use of stands for mounting chests of
drawers was common after the Restoration,
and lasted until the early eighteenth century.
The chest of drawers developed on the same
lines as the solid type, and the stand bore very
close relationship to contemporary side tables
(see Tables). At first the stand was low in appearance, on thick turned legs linked by a
succession of arches, but by the 1690s it was
higher, with twist-turned and later baluster-
shaped legs joined together by curling
stretchers. Drawers were added to the stand,
usually a shallower central one and a deeper
one at each side. The apron piece, an important decorative feature, took the form of
smooth-flowing curves, which balanced the
severer lines of the upper work. During the
William and Mary period two other significant characteristics were the inverted cup
legs and the pronounced swell frieze below
the cornice. The drawers in the stand tended
to shorten the legs once more, and they took
cabriole form by Anne's reign. From about
1710 there was a natural transition to the tallboy, in which the stand was replaced by

another chest of drawers. Tallboys reached monumental proportions, and came in for a great deal of architectural treatment. The frieze lost its swell outline and became concave. Plate 101A shows the stage of development which had been reached by about 1730. The drawers throughout are cross-banded and have ovolo mouldings. The corners of the upper section have been canted to take partly fluted and partly reeded pilasters, and the feet have gone from the plain bracket to ogee form, resembling cabrioles. The tallboy had a long vogue in the eighteenth century as a cabinet-maker's show-piece, until the awkward height of its top drawers led to its gradual disuse in England. It persisted longer in America, where some very fine examples were produced.

Clock cases

The long clock case (or grandfather clock) was another new piece of furniture which appeared at the time of the Restoration. Two major factors in its development were Robert Hooke's invention of the anchor escapement (which made the long pendulum possible) about 1670, and the outstanding work of great English clockmakers like Thomas Tompion and Joseph Knibb. From its beginning the case took on the familiar design of a hood for the dial and movement, a long, narrow body for the pendulum, and a pedestal base. The body became wider as the clock dial increased in size, but retained its slender waist appearance until mahogany was extensively used. Naturally, the size of the cases (up to 7 feet in even the earliest examples) and their prominent position in the house brought out all the case-maker's skill, and the large space available was ideal for the best decorative work in veneers, marquetry, and japan. At first – about 1660 – the cornice of the hood was surmounted by a classical pediment, which was followed after 1670 by a carved and pierced cresting. The glass face of the dial was usually flanked by two columns, which were either twist-turned or plain-turned with tiny capitals and bases. Oak was the usual carcase wood, veneered with ebony and walnut and often finely decorated with the various kinds of fashionable marquetry. The door on the body

was edged with half-round moulding in rectangular lines. Many of these features can be seen in Plate 101B, a late William and Mary clock case with a movement made by Samuel Stokes of London about 1699. It is veneered with seaweed marquetry, and there is a narrow fret-carved frieze below the cornice. By 1700 the hood had begun to change its appearance. A flat dome (Fig. 15) was added to

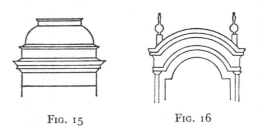

FIG. 15   FIG. 16

the top, which was sometimes ornamented with brass or gilt wood finials at the corners and centre. From about 1715 the clock dial was arched (Fig. 16), and the cornice above it took the same curving shape, as did the moulding over the door in the body. The clock case, in other words, underwent the same treatment of arched curves as cabinets and mirrors. English japanners had a partiality for clock cases, and hundreds were exported during this period; but walnut enjoyed a considerable vogue for cases, and retained its popularity until after 1750.

Mirrors

Mirrors began to play an important part in interior decoration in late Stuart times, and an indication of their growing use is that while in 1660 they were still being imported (particularly Venetian glasses), by 1700 English-made glasses were being sent abroad. Between those two dates progress was largely explained by the establishment of the Duke of Buckingham's famous glass works at Vauxhall in 1665 and the emergence, some twenty years later, of the specialist looking-glass makers. Mirror plate was expensive for some time to come, but wealthy people used it in many ways, for wall mirrors, toilet mirrors, tall ornamental glasses, and on cabinet doors. Until about 1690 wall mirrors were square in shape and the glass, with bevelled edges, was enclosed in frames up to 6 inches in width, topped by a semicircular crest in the Italian manner. They were naturally picked out for fine (especially oyster) veneers and marquetry work. By 1700 taller mirrors were becoming fashionable (of large Vauxhall plates, or smaller mirrors joined together with a moulding to cover the join) and the influence of Wren and Gibbons was shown in architectural features like pediments and pilasters, or in intricately carved lime-wood frames. Colourful decoration was emphasized and took several forms, bright gilding, marquetry, japan, gesso, and even silver. These forms continued into Anne's reign, but there was also a return to simpler styles. Three main trends can be distinguished among the many varieties. One attractive type of wall mirror had a frame narrow at the sides, the glass itself surrounded by a thin gilt gesso moulding, and wide flat crest and base, both carved in graceful flowing curves, veneered with walnut and holding two circular inset pieces with the shell motif. Another kind had an inch-wide frame all the way round following the top of the scalloped glass in simple arched curves. It was this design which was often found on cabinet doors, the mouldings surrounding the mirror plate taking the same curves as the top of the cabinet (similar to Plate 98). A third kind was the pier glass, tall and narrow in shape, usually made in pairs to stand between windows, in elaborately carved and gilded frames, often with another mirror in the arching crest, and with pilasters at the sides. John Gumley, who opened his glass works at Lambeth in 1705, specialized in these. Some of the mirrors that he made for Hampton Court Palace and Chatsworth are still extant and can be seen in the two Palaces. Towards the end of the walnut period gilded mirrors were common, and came under architectural influence. A typical example of this type has the frame enriched with gadrooning, drapery, and foliage; the shell decoration in the base; and the broken pediment with a central cartouche (other finials were a plume, shell, mask, or eagle). There were, however, other examples carried out with burr walnut veneers and gilt gesso ornament.

The early eighteenth century also saw the introduction of the "chimney glass", a wide mirror above a chimney-piece, consisting of three plates, two smaller ones flanking a larger one, and all topped by flowing curves, framed in walnut or following the other decorative fashions. Another development, the toilet mirror, had the same curved top and was mounted on two uprights resting on a miniature chest of drawers (Fig. 17). Some of

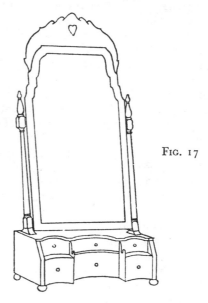

Fig. 17

these, in walnut or japan, were beautifully made and were designed for the slender dressing-tables of the period. When these toilet mirrors were mounted on miniature bureaux they were called "Union Sets".

Tables

The walnut period inherited the gate-leg tables introduced during the preceding oak period, and these continued in use for dining, with modifications due to the new timber. Gate-leg tables retained their popularity for a long time, and in larger houses several were used together, when required. Their legs gradually took on cabriole form. But a new feature from 1660 was the variety of small tables, many of them multi-purpose, the more formal side and occasional tables, and others used for specific requirements such as writing, tea-drinking, dressing, and card-playing. At first solid walnut was usual, but later table tops (and drawer fronts, wherever these were found) were decorated with veneer or marquetry, with cross-banded or herring-bone borders and ovolo-moulded edges. Plates 102–104 show three well-defined stages in small-table design between the Restoration and early Georgian periods.

A side table, with oyster veneers, single drawer, twist-turned legs, and a waved flat stretcher, was very characteristic of the later part of Charles II's reign. The legs ended on ball or bun feet, immediately above which the stretcher terminated in small square platforms. The stretcher was noted for its curves and central shelf. Twist-turning persisted on tables for some time after it had passed out of fashion on chairs. But by the William and Mary period varieties of baluster turning, or the more elaborate scroll form, were coming into use. Plate 102, a side table of about 1690, shows the inverted cup legs and bun feet. The stretcher has become more slender and has a pronounced X-shape. The finial on the shelf is matched by similar finials, inverted, on the apron piece, which has become an important part of late seventeenth-century work. Tables like the one shown on Plate 102, fitted with drawers and a knee-hole, could be used as dressing- or writing-tables. The marked change in design by the early eighteenth century is well illustrated by the Queen Anne card table (Plate 103). The slender cabriole legs and ball-and-claw feet did not require stretchers and gave the table a shapely line. The tops of these card tables unfolded and were supported by swinging out one of the legs; or else in some cases the whole top was pivoted sideways and opened to rest on the frame. The surface was covered with cloth or veneered. To protect it the corners were rounded to hold candlesticks (later small movable trays, hinged to the top, were used for this) and small circular depressions were made for money or counters. The wide ovolo mouldings found at the edges of the earlier table tops were now replaced by flatter, vertical mouldings. Decoration was usually limited to a carved shell or leaf on the outside of the knee and a scroll on the inside, and to a curve on the frieze. These tables emphasized the beautiful figure of walnut. Despite subsequent changes, this simple design was never entirely lost, for small tables were made in walnut, even when mahogany was becoming fashionable. But, by contrast, from about 1725 pier tables (standing between mirrors and windows) and console tables (permanently standing against the wall with bracket-shape legs) had a florid magnificence, in the Kent tradition, as shown in Plate 104. Made of gilded softwoods, or with the addition of gesso, they relied for effect on masks, scrolls, foliage and classical designs, and heavy marble tops.

Small tripod tables also appeared after 1660 for use as candle-stands, in the form of a tray held by a turned pillar standing on jutting-out feet. As can be expected the upright at first was often twist-turned, and the feet had scroll shapes. From about 1685 the feet began to show sharper angles where the various curves met. By the Queen Anne period the feet were beginning to show cabriole form and the ball-and-claw ending. This type of table was to have a long vogue, as candle-stands were in great demand when large plate mirrors came into use and as much light as possible was called for to add brilliance to large rooms.

THE AGE OF MAHOGANY AND SATINWOOD

Mahogany was competing with walnut after the first quarter of the eighteenth century and had supplanted it for the highest-quality work about 1750. From then on its many virtues made it the premier wood in cabinet-making. It had a beautiful patina which improved with age; a metallic strength which led to remarkable advances in carving and outlines; a fine figure which made it equally suitable for veneers; a range of colour from light-reddish to a rich dark shade; and a natural durability which was resistant to decay. It also seasoned readily, and the great size of the trees produced excellent timber for table tops, wardrobe doors, and similar pieces. Altogether, for furniture of every kind, for work in the solid, for carving, inlay, or veneer, it was an excellent medium for the great cabinet-makers of the Georgian era. Two main varieties of mahogany were used. One kind (*Swietenia mahogani*) came from the West Indies, mainly San Domingo, Jamaica, and Cuba. The San Domingo timber (usually known as "Spanish", or sometimes as "Jamaican") was prized more highly at first. It was a dense, hard wood, with little figure, and was used mainly in the solid. Then the Cuban mahogany became more popular, as it had two outstanding qualities: it was easier to work and had a fine figure for veneers. The other species (*Swietenia macrophylla*) came from Central America, particularly from Honduras (whence it obtained its other name of "baywood"). It was lighter and softer than the Cuban, and was often used as carcases to take Cuban veneers. There was considerable overlapping in the periods when these various kinds were most in use, but it can be said that San Domingo mahogany was popular until about 1750, when it was replaced by Cuban for best work, while Honduras was found in later eighteenth-century carcase construction.

Mahogany had been used for shipbuilding since the sixteenth century, and for inlay and panelling since the seventeenth. It was known at first as cedar or cedrala. Evelyn referred to its worm-resisting qualities in his *Sylva* under its French name of *acajou* from "the Western Indies". The date when it came into use for furniture cannot be given exactly. The story of Dr Gibbons of Covent Garden, who is said to have had some mahogany made into furniture by his cabinet-maker Wollaston about 1700, and to have thus popularized this wood, has now become a tradition. Its use was no doubt encouraged by the shortage of European walnut after the Spanish Succession War, though supplies of Virginia walnut were to be had. Probably mahogany advertised itself well enough. An Act of 1721 allowed timber from any British plantation in America to be duty free. Another Act in 1724 mentioned mahogany by name; it had a special rate imposed upon it instead of the declared value by the importer, but if it were from British possessions it was included in the terms of the 1721 Act and allowed in duty free. From the

1720s, therefore, Jamaican mahogany had preferential treatment. This not only assured supplies from British sources but also encouraged timber dealers in the West Indies to send the popular Spanish wood to England via Jamaica and other colonies to avoid the duty. This practice went on throughout the century. In fact, the British Government connived at it, for it allowed, and later legalized, the entrepôt trade with the Spanish settlements. There was thus no lack of mahogany, once trade had got under way, as there had been with European walnut. Mahogany was certainly competing strongly with walnut for fashionable furniture by the 1730s. In 1733 the poet James Bramston, in his *Man of Taste*, written to defend the modes of his day against those who complained of lost hospitality, asked: "Say thou that dost thy father's table praise, Was there Mahogena in former days?" By that time, also, British logwood cutters in Campeche Bay, Central America, were leaving that area to cut the more valuable mahogany in the Belize district of Honduras, thus provoking a long-drawn-out dispute with Spain. The ever-growing demand for mahogany can be judged in the rise of import values from £276 in 1722 to £77,744 in 1800. In the early nineteenth century import duties which had been imposed on mahogany during the French Wars began to affect trade figures, but Crosby's *Pocket Dictionary* of 1810 still described cabinet-makers as "workers in mahogany and other fine woods".

CHIEF PERIODS AND STYLES

The furniture styles of the eighteenth century take their names not from the reigning monarchs but from outstanding designers, both craftsmen and architects. In the case of the craftsmen like Chippendale, Hepplewhite, and Sheraton this distinction must be recognized as doing less than justice to many contemporary cabinet-makers whose work equalled or even in some cases excelled theirs. Indeed, it is not certain that Sheraton had a workshop or produced furniture of his own. Their claim to fame rests on their famous design books, which interpreted prevailing styles with a high degree of skill, and thus their names serve as a very convenient label for particular phases of development. The whole period showed a ceaseless spirit of experiment and a constant demand for novelties from the upper classes, whose needs were supplied by a succession of great cabinet-makers and upholsterers; some of these cabinet-makers' shops, like that of George Seddon (b. 1727, d. 1801), were large-scale businesses. Their products displayed a technical excellence fully equal to the work of the best Continental craftsmen. Their patrons, with wealth from land, trade, and industry, showed, in general, a high standard of taste. Much furniture was designed for the many new town and country houses, and this explains the importance of architects like Robert Adam, whose planning of a house covered every detail, inside and out.

The earlier Georgian period, to the mid-forties, when mahogany was beginning to come in, was dominated by the Palladian revival, largely inspired by Lord Burlington, and interpreted by William Kent (b. 1684, d. 1748) and another contemporary architect, Henry Flitcroft. Kent was the first architect to include furniture in his schemes of work. He used mainly softwoods to take carving and gilding, but some of his pieces were in mahogany parcel (i.e. partly) gilt. His designs, somewhat modified, appeared in one of the earliest design books, *The City and Country Workmen's Treasury* by Batty and Thomas Langley (1739). But it is noteworthy that a prominent contemporary cabinet-maker, Giles Grendey (b. 1693, d. 1780), produced mahogany furniture in a simpler style, reminiscent of the Queen Anne period.

Palladianism went out of fashion in the mid-century, and was replaced by a diversity of styles, the rococo from France (then called the "modern" taste), Chinese, and Gothic. This was the period of Thomas Chippendale (b. 1718, d. 1779), whose *Gentleman and Cabinet Maker's Director* first appeared in 1754. No mention of mahogany appeared in the first edition, and only a passing reference (to six designs for hall chairs) in the third, in 1762. But much first-class furniture was made in this wood by Chippendale himself and the best contemporary craftsmen, such as John Bradburn, William Vile and John Cobb (these two in partnership) and Benjamin Goodison.

Chippendale's great service was to apply the rococo style of decoration to a wide range of furniture and generally to curb its more excessive forms. He is now known to have employed on the *Director*'s plates two artists, Matthias Lock and Henry Copland, who were pioneers of the rococo in England. The taste for Chinese and Gothic furniture, the former largely inspired by the works of Sir William Chambers, and the latter by Horace Walpole, was cultivated by sections of the upper classes. While rococo relied for its effect on the use of flowing lines, Chinese work was seen in the popularity of geometrical fretwork patterns and Oriental figures and designs, and Gothic in the use of the pointed arch.

The neo-classical revival began in the sixties, inspired by Robert Adam. His furniture, beautifully designed and made, was decorated with delicate classical motifs, paterae, pendant husks, urns, fluting, etc. (Figs. 18–20).

FIGS. 18–20

His liking for furniture of a more elegant appearance led to a revival of fine inlaid work, and much use of satinwood and other timbers. But mahogany, used as a veneer by itself, or with other woods, or for carving the classical motifs, was well adapted to the new mode, shown in the work of Chippendale (who worked for Adam) and Cobb in their later periods, John Linnell, William France, and others. In 1788 appeared George Hepplewhite's *Cabinet-makers' and Upholsterers' Guide*, two years after the author's death. The great merit of this work was that it interpreted the new classical styles skilfully for all kinds of furniture. The explanations of the designs in the Guide constantly stress the suitability of mahogany both for small work, like cellarets and knife-boxes, and for larger pieces, like tables and bookcases.

Thomas Sheraton (b. 1751, d. 1806) produced the *Cabinet Makers' and Upholsterers' Drawing Book* between 1791 and 1794 and bridged the gap between the neo-classical and the Regency periods. Sheraton favoured light, delicate furniture, including painted work, and for his finest pieces he recommended satinwood. He also used other tropical woods, popular about 1800, for the best apartments of the house, such as the drawing-room and boudoir. His period is distinguished for the dainty, almost fragile, appearance of some of his furniture. This cannot be said of the final period, the Regency, ending about 1830. There was a renewal of classical forms inspired by the Directoire and Empire styles in France, but these were carried out in a strict and narrow fashion, a "chaste" and literal interpretation of Greek, Roman, and Egyptian examples. The designer Thomas Hope in his *Household Furniture* (1807) heralded this stress on an archaeological approach. Furniture took on a heavier appearance. One result was to re-emphasize dark, lustrous, or heavily figured woods, especially to show brightly gilt mounts in the prevailing mode. This explains the popularity of rosewood after 1800, but there was also a great demand for mahogany because of its suitable colour and grain.

OTHER TIMBERS

The popularity of satinwood from 1770 has already been mentioned, paving the way for a lighter, more delicate, aspect of furniture design. This trend, emphasized by a revival of veneers and fine inlaid work, led the cabinet-makers to experiment with a wide range of exotic timbers, brought to them from all parts of the world, especially from tropical areas, by enterprising merchants. Satinwood itself, from both the East and West Indies, was yellowish in tone; so was fustic, from the West Indies, but this faded to a dead brown and was decried by Sheraton. Other woods, which showed rich shades of brown and red, varying from light to deep, included calamander, snakewood, coromandel, and rosewood from India and Ceylon, thuya from Africa, ebony from the East, kingwood, partridge wood, purple wood, and tulip wood from Central and South America, and amboyna from the West Indies. Camphor from the East Indies was also used for boxes and trunks, and red cedar from North and Central America for drawer linings, trays, and boxes. Native woods were not neglected: holly, pear, maple, and laburnum were used for inlays on first-rate pieces, and there was a demand for sycamore, which was stained a greenish-grey colour, and known as harewood, for veneers. Mahogany was used with these woods, which led to a closer study of its beautiful figure and fine range of colour, and made it appreciated more than ever. Figure and lustre were fashionable qualities after 1800, hence the importance of rosewood, large fresh supplies of which were now available from the opening up of trade with South America (particularly Brazil), calamander, coromandel, snakewood, tulip wood, and zebra wood: the last, as its name implies, having an effective dark stripe. Imported deal continued to be the favourite wood for carcase work during this period, but from 1750 red deal from North America largely replaced the former yellow variety.

DECORATION

Fret work. This form of decorative work was popular in Chippendale's time, particularly to show Chinese patterns. Fret designs could be either open or applied. The open fret was seen on table and cabinet tops and the applied fret was found on the flat surfaces of chairs, tables, cabinets, etc. (Plates 105 and 109A for applied fret, Plate 112 for open fretwork).

Inlay. Robert Adam revived fine inlaid work, which in technique resembled seventeenth-century marquetry (*see* Walnut) but differed from it in the use of classical designs and figures, and of new, lighter-coloured woods. An effective form of inlay much favoured by Sheraton was stringing, or lines of inlay in contrasting woods or brass, some of the work being of extreme delicacy (Plate 115).

Metal mounts. These were made of brass and were fine gilt, which gave them a rich and golden appearance. They were used for work in the rococo style (Plate 108) and decorative effect in the Regency period. The finest quality ormolu mounts were made by Matthew

Boulton in his factory at Soho, outside Birmingham. His best period was 1762–76.

Veneers. Mahogany had a variety of beautiful figures or mottles. Some of the early San Domingo wood had "roe" mottles, dark flakes running with the grain (as on the drawer fronts, Plate 105), giving attractive effects of light and shade, and at their best when the lines of figures were broken, they then varied in appearance according to the angle from which they were viewed. Cuban and Honduras mahogany, however, had a wider range of figures and were in great demand for veneers after 1750. Cuban "curls" (giving the effect shown in Plates 105, 106, 107, and 115) were highly prized. Their feather was obtained by cutting the tree where a large branch joined the trunk. This limited their size, and made them expensive and somewhat brittle ("Cross and unpliable" – Sheraton), unlike most mahogany veneers. The "fiddle-back" came from the outer edge of the trunk and had even streaks running across the grain. The "rain" mottle was similar but had wider and longer streaks. The "stopped" or "broken" mottle had irregular but brilliant flame-like markings. Dark and oval spots in the wood produced the "plum" – or "plum-pudding" – mottle. All these veneers were saw-cut and thick enough by modern standards to be considered more as facings than veneers.

Bureaux, cabinets, desks, bookcases, etc.

Endless varieties of writing, display, and cupboard furniture were produced in the mahogany period, many of them being directly descended from the walnut prototypes. Bureaux followed very much the same development as contemporary chests of drawers. Mahogany was a favourite medium for these until Sheraton's time, as the figure of the wood, especially Cuban curls, made a fine show on the flaps and drawers (Plate 106). A newer development was the desk, which had taken its place in the rich man's library by 1750. This was usually solid in appearance, with side drawers or cupboards of similar proportions to the classical pedestals of early sideboards (*see* Tables). Plate 108 shows a desk of about 1760. Other kinds were serpentine-fronted and often had canted corners with rococo carving like the commode (Plate 110). Mahogany was particularly suitable for all kinds of library furniture, and both Hepplewhite and Sheraton stressed this in their design books. Sheraton, however, gave his bureaux a lighter appearance. Many of them were intended for ladies' use, and he favoured the employment of satinwood. He also preferred the tambour or cylinder front instead of the flap.

But what specially exercised the best Georgian cabinet-makers were the combined pieces – the bureau-bookcase, cabinet, press, and their variations – which demanded the highest skill in design and decoration. Their size encouraged an architectural treatment. Such pieces in the walnut period had been topped by arched curves, but these were replaced in early Georgian times by forms of broken pediments, angular or swan-neck. The open space in the centre was filled with a carved piece, or left free. Kent emphasized his pediments, and used classical pilasters on the corners of the doors, with much gilding. Many cabinet-makers, however, preferred a simple straight cornice, and one effect of the wider use of mahogany was the return to a general lighter style. Pediments were retained but often their only decoration was carved dentil mouldings, also found on the cornice (Plate 105). Towards 1750 mirror plates on cabinet doors were going out of fashion. They gave way either to clear glazing or to panels of carefully chosen mahogany framed in applied mouldings or in stiles (Plate 112) with curved inner edges.

The mid-century Gothic and Chinese fashions affected these pieces in several ways. The glazing bars of glass-fronted cabinets formed geometrical patterns or pointed arches. Carving or fret-work with similar designs was applied to the frieze and bottom edge of the cabinet, and to the frieze and feet of the bureau. A pagoda roof was sometimes added, and the pediment was pierced with fret-cut outlines. Rococo treatment might be found in ornate carving or fine gilt mounts. Some of these designs were used with extravagance, but Plate 105, a mahogany clothes press of about 1760, is an excellent example of balance and restraint. The angular broken pediment has a dentil moulding on one edge, repeated on the cornice and plain central platform. The doors have cross-banded borders and incorporate two fine curl panels within applied astragal mouldings. A fretted frieze in Chinese style and carved paterae at the corners of the doors complete the upper decoration. The drawers have cock beadings and the whole is supported on feet of cabriole shape. Loop handles without back plates were popular in the 1730s.

Plate 106 shows a bureau-bookcase of the late eighteenth century. Below the plain cornice is a "pear-drop" moulding, popular after 1770. There is a delicate key pattern at the central edge of the doors, along the top and bottom edges of the bureau, and on the uprights separating the small drawers within the flap. The curved apron piece and slender outward-pointing feet are characteristic of this particular period. The bureau drawers have notable matched curl veneers. Equally simple, despite its size, is the bookcase illustrated in Plate 107. This is an example of break-front design. The glazing bars show the pointed Gothic arch. The whole piece is finely proportioned and is built to bring out the beauties of the figure on the drawer fronts and cupboard panels. The octagonal handles in Plates 106 and 107 dated from about 1785. In the Regency period a feature of the bookcases, apart from the new forms of decoration, was their low height, to leave the walls above them free for pictures.

Chairs

In the transitional period between walnut and mahogany the graceful Queen Anne hooped-back chair had become more ponderous in appearance, with an emphasis on the carving of ornament. At the same time Kent was designing his elaborate chairs for wealthy clients making use of walnut or mahogany, partly gilt, or of softwoods entirely gilt, for scroll-shaped legs, or versions of the cabriole, and a great deal of flower, fruit, and mask ornament. This vogue was passing about 1745, when mahogany really came into its own in chair design. The general effect was to re-emphasize form and proportion, and to initiate an era in which much ambitious splat-work became the fashion. Chippendale used the rococo, Chinese, and Gothic motifs in a great variety of chair backs. The typical rococo chair consisted of a back framed by two outward-curving side-rails meeting in a Cupid's-bow top (which had made its appearance some little time before Chippendale), usually with scrollwork on the corners, and the splat pierced with interlaced strapwork. The back legs tended to curve away noticeably. The cabriole leg was lighter in treatment than the Queen Anne variety and the ball-and-claw foot, though it was found on many chairs, was sometimes replaced by the French knurl or scroll toes. (The scroll foot can be seen in Plate 109B.) The famous "ribband-back" chairs showed mahogany carving and rococo decoration in perhaps their most dazzling forms, the ribbons and bows forming intricate patterns which in some chairs joined up with the side-rails (Fig. 21). This was an extreme form. In general, Chippendale avoided the excessive ornament of the Continental rococo. In some of his chairs he showed the craftsman's eye for a well-

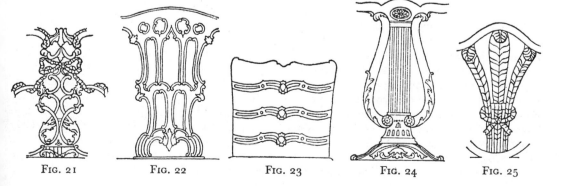

FIG. 21   FIG. 22   FIG. 23   FIG. 24   FIG. 25

balanced design. These had carefully restrained rococo carving in the splat, which tended to be narrower in shape, and straight legs, sometimes fluted, joined by plain stretchers, which were now being reintroduced on chairs of this type. The contrast between straight legs and curved backs and the use of carefully chosen upholstery for the seat (including plain leather) was pleasing. Plate 109A shows a Chinese chair, about 1755. The characteristic features are the pagoda cresting-rail, the splat pierced and carved with geometric patterns, the fretted work in similar designs on the back uprights, legs and feet, the cluster column legs, and the bracket between legs and seat. Other chairs of this type had stretchers which, together with the front legs and brackets, might be pierced and fretted with patterns, or, alternatively, applied ornament might be found on legs, stretchers, and seat front. In the case of Chinese arm-chairs, lattice work also filled the space between arms and seat. Gothic chairs showed interlacing pointed arches in the splats, or covering the whole of the back. Another attractive chair design was the "ladder-back", taken from a traditional country style. At its best it showed undulating curves on the cross- and cresting-rails, which were pierced and carved and often had a small carved emblem in the centre (Figs. 22 and 23 for Gothic and ladder-back).

The interest of the Adam brothers in classical art influenced chair design by introducing a lighter type of chair, emphasizing oval lines in the backs and using straight legs tapering from square knee blocks to feet set upon small plinths. The construction of chair backs changed, as the splat gradually lost its link with the back rail of the seat and became enclosed within the uprights. In this, again, the strength of mahogany was a definite factor. There was a sympathy for delicate fluting and channelling on the back, arms and legs and the addition of classical ornaments on the seat-rail and (especially carved paterae) at the top of the front legs. But another kind of chair which enjoyed a long vogue was the "French Adam" type illustrated in Plate 109B. Dating from about the mid-1770s, it shows the cabriole leg in its final form, ending on scrolled feet. This chair is distinguished by the use of gentle curves, of gadrooning on the edges of the legs, arms, seat, and back, and of beautiful upholstery, all treated with the utmost refinement. Other French-style chairs had straight, tapering legs, usually fluted, and some of the backs were square in shape, with a lyre, including brass strings, for the splat (Fig. 24). The versatility of form cannot be over-stressed. Adam liked both painting and gilding; beech was used if chairs were to be gilded, and satinwood was becoming popular for fragile-looking drawing-room chairs. He also reintroduced cane seats.

As Hepplewhite's chairs are famous, it is worth noting his own directions for making them: "Chairs in general are made of mahogany, with bars and frame sunk in hollow, or rising in a round projection, with a band or list on the inner and outer edges. Many of these designs are enriched with ornaments proper to be carved in mahogany." Plate 109C shows one of his shield backs, his most celebrated form (which he varied with heart or oval shapes). The top rail rises in the centre over a splat consisting of narrow curving bars which terminate in a carved wheat-ear design. The bottom of the shield is just above the back of the seat. The arms add distinction to the chair, with the pronounced backward-sweeping curve from the top of the front legs straightening out at the arm-rests which join the shield about half-way up. The tapering legs and plinth feet, the carefully limited carving on legs and arms, the channelling throughout, the serpentine front to the seat, overstuffed, are all typical of Hepplewhite's work. Other carved ornaments in the back included the Prince of Wales' feathers (Fig. 25), leaves vases, and drapery. He also used satinwood inlay on a mahogany background and, like Adam, designed some lyre-backs.

The refinement in chair design reached its peak with Sheraton, and Plate 109D shows some of his features. He preferred rectangular shapes to emphasize lightness. The wide cresting-rail overrunning the uprights and shaped for the sitter's back is particularly worth noting, as this was a novelty in chairs and was found in wide use after 1800. The back has merely a single rail, and the legs are forward splaying, with little attempt at foot design. Carving is replaced by clear, straight-lined inlay, in a contrasting coloured wood, on the cresting-rail. For upholstery a striped material was popular, in keeping with the general rectangular effect of the rest of the chair. Like other designers, Sheraton did not confine himself to one pattern. On the whole he preferred to leave the back of his chairs as open as possible, and broke away from the vertical splay designs of his predecessors. He brought in a revival of painted chairs (of beech), usually decorated with bright floral devices on a black background and having plain cane seats and turned legs. He did not neglect carving by any means, but he is particularly noted for his employment of string-ing as decoration. Basically, this was the same as the inlay on the cresting-rail in Plate 109D, but he carried it to extreme delicacy by using very thin lines of wood or brass. Chair arms often took a wide sweep upwards immediately above the legs, and another at the back to join the uprights at the cresting-rail.

Sheraton's work already reflected many features of the so-called French Empire style, which blossomed out fully in the Regency period. Painted chairs remained popular, and the sweeping forward of the front legs, balanced by a similar outward curve on the back legs, was accentuated because of its resemblance to the chair figured on classical Greek vases. The cresting-rail, in a variety of shapes, was a prominent feature, and the whole back was often given a very pronounced rake. Much of Sheraton's lightness disappeared with the extended use of lion's-paw designs for legs and arms (Fig. 26), and the addition of gilding and novelties like Egyptian motifs. A throne-like arm-chair, in which the whole sides – front and back legs, uprights and arms – were made in units, into which the back and seat fitted, tended to give this type a somewhat heavy and ornate appearance.

FIG. 26

Chests of drawers, commodes, and tallboys

Until about 1750 chests of drawers were still straight-fronted, with, normally, four or five drawers, bracket or cabriole-shape feet, and ovolo or cock-bead moulding on the drawer edges. Not much change had been made in the Queen Anne design except that the front corners were usually canted and carved, as were the top edges. Classical pilaster designs were popular on the corners. From 1740 chests of drawers began to be designed with their shape serpentine after the French style. Such chests of drawers were called commodes (though these in France had perhaps special reference to drawing-room pieces). A commode made completely in the French taste had pronounced outward-curving front corners, short legs, curved bottom framing, rococo carving or fine gilt mounts on the sides and legs, and often doors on the front to enclose the drawers. Plate 110 shows a more restrained use of French decoration. This serpentine-fronted commode has on each canted corner a carved console and *cabochon* (at the top and bottom respectively) linked by foliage, acanthus leaves on the bracket feet, gadrooning on the top edge (which is squared at the corners), and beading on the bottom rail. Gothic and Chinese motifs might appear in the same parts of other chests of drawers, Chinese fretted ornament, for example, on the corners, or along the top and bottom front edges.

Adam's work expressed itself principally in two ways. Where solid work persisted, the carving naturally became classical in treatment, emphasizing the corner pilasters, and making use of dentil and key patterns on the cornice moulding. On the other hand, fine inlay, in all the fashionable woods, was used eagerly by designers when drawing-room commodes were in great demand and their doors were ideal for showing first-rate work. Great patience was expended in devising ovals and circles to show figures or scenes from classical mythology, surrounded by inlaid designs. This set the taste for a lighter appearance in chests of drawers, in satinwood especially, or for painted decoration. Sheraton is connected with the bow-fronted chest of drawers, which was now used with the serpentine and straight-fronted types. He by no means emphasized the new style, however. He designed in all shapes, including a return to the simple straight lines of early pieces. Two other innovations were the stringing (in wood or brass) on the drawer fronts and the use of an exceptionally deep frieze above the top drawer, which gave the chest of drawers a characteristic tallness. In the Regency period the decline of marquetry decoration gradually led to the replacement of the drawing-room commode by the chiffonier, a low cupboard with shelves, and often with a built-up superstructure above. Bedroom chests of drawers, tall, and either bow- or straight-fronted, had

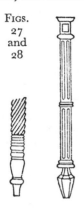

Figs. 27 and 28

turned feet, and a distinctive feature on many were the quarter columns, spiral-shaped or reeded, on the front corners (Figs. 27 and 28). By this time tallboys were going out of fashion, after a long vogue; they followed closely the designs for chest of drawers, and in their final period a few bow-fronted ones were made. These pieces do not require any separate description, therefore, except to stress that their great size led to special care being taken over their proportions and decoration.

Clock cases

Mahogany affected clock-case design somewhat later than other pieces of furniture, for japanning and walnut veneers enjoyed a long vogue; indeed, figured walnut cases continued to be made until late in the eighteenth century. But by about 1760 mahogany was sufficiently in use to begin to give cases a heavier and broader appearance. At first veneering on an oak carcase was normal, followed by solid mahogany carcases for the best work, and carving. Hoods came in for elaborate treatment. As the arched dial was usual, the cornice was also strongly arched and moulded above it, and surmounted by a broken pediment, usually swan-neck, with finials as in the earlier fashion, or a simple plain pedestal in the centre. Naturally, full advantage was taken of the high case front to show the fine figure of the wood, and some very beautiful Cuban curls are found on outstandingly good

work. In the mixture of styles of the Chippendale period detailed decoration was carried out in various ways; Chinese pagoda hoods (Fig. 29) and japanned cases, Gothic arches in the mouldings above the door, ornate rococo motifs; or fretwork in the frieze, across the top of the body below the hood, and around the bottom edge and sides of the base. The classic-

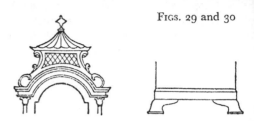

Figs. 29 and 30

ism of the latter part of the century emphasized the proportions of the case, used capitals at the sides of the hood (sometimes two at each side), and showed fluted pilasters worked in the canted front corners of the body, as on chests of drawers. The base was mounted on a solid plinth at first, but later acquired small bracket (Fig. 30) or cabriole-shape feet. Later work also included fine inlay such as satinwood inlays in classical designs on a background of mahogany. By Sheraton's time the tall clock case was going out of fashion. His period produced some fine inlaid and veneered work in many woods, but such pieces were by this period comparatively rare.

Mirrors

Mirrors were no longer a novelty in the eighteenth century. Improved methods of production led to a greater output of glass and to larger plates. Very large mirrors were still expensive, but small wall and toilet mirrors in simple styles were cheap enough for tradesmen's houses. In larger houses mirrors of all kinds adorned the best rooms, from smaller wall mirrors to pier and chimney glasses, often with wall-lights (sconces and girandoles), and their conspicuous position singled them out for highly decorative treatment, especially gilding. For this reason it cannot be said that mahogany played any decisive part in their development. In the Kent period pier glasses, already reaching a height of 6 or 7 feet by the 1730s, were given brightly gilded frames and broken pediment tops, and this design affected wall mirrors in general. The pediments sometimes ended in a graceful acanthus leaf, and there was a prominent central motif in the form of a spread eagle, cartouche, or shell. The gilding was carried out on softwoods. On the other hand, the simpler kind of Queen Anne mirror with carved flowing curves on crest and apron piece continued to be made. These had mahogany frames, sometimes partly gilt, and incorporated a dominating centrepiece in the prevailing fashion.

There was a distinct change after the mid-century, when mirrors provided perhaps the best examples of the almost fantastic limits to which the new styles could go. Several designers, including Lock, Copland, and Johnson, paid particular attention to applying rococo and Chinese ornament to mirrors, and these trends were made fashionable by Chippendale, who employed the first two artists to produce designs for the *Director*. Mirror frames now avoided a symmetrical appearance and were carved and gilded in an intricate pattern of scrolls and foliage in the rococo mode (Fig. 33), and to these were added numerous Chinese designs such as exotic birds, pagodas, mandarins, and bells, or even Gothic elements. Nowhere else were these styles so intimately united. This vogue did not last long, for Adam, and after him Hepplewhite, designed beautiful and delicately proportioned mirrors, oval or rectangular in shape, surrounded by much simpler scrollwork picked out with paterae, husks, and honeysuckle and leading up to a vase or similar classical motif. Adam favoured gilt work, usually on carved

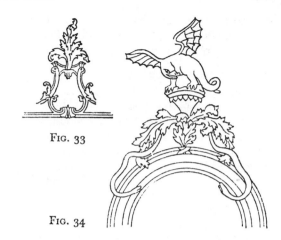

FIG. 33

FIG. 34

pine, and he used the mirror frames to show fluting, the key pattern, and Vitruvian scrolls.

Typical of the Sheraton and Regency periods was the circular gilt convex mirror, 1–3 feet in diameter. The gilt frame usually had an ebonized fillet on the inside edge and a reeded band on the outside; between the two was a pronounced hollow filled with small circular patterns of flowers or plain spheres. Above the frame was foliage, usually the acanthus leaf, supporting an eagle, one of the most popular designs for mirror crests during the whole of this period, or a winged creature (Fig. 34).

Mahogany played a much more important part in the evolution of the toilet mirror. From early in the eighteenth century many dressing-tables were designed with collapsible mirrors which fitted into the tops of the tables, and the latter usually followed the design of chests of drawers, with a knee recess. But there was a great demand for the separate toilet glasses, the rectangular swing mirrors above minute drawers, made in mahogany. They preserved their simple, attractive shapes and avoided excessive decoration. In the Hepplewhite period the mahogany frames followed the design of the shield-back chair (Fig. 31); later still, about 1800, they became flat rectangles. The tiny chests of drawers were often veneered and had serpentine or bow fronts. Sheraton devoted much skill to incorporating mirrors in dressing-tables. He also popularized cheval glasses, known for some time before. These tall glasses stood between two uprights ending in

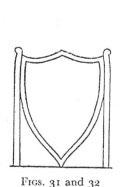

FIGS. 31 and 32

outward-curving feet connected by a stretcher, and had decorative headpieces often painted, inlaid, or fretted (Fig. 32).

Tables and sideboards

Small Tables. As mahogany came into general use and the heavy side-table of the Kent period (Plate 104, Walnut Section) went out of fashion, there was a return to the simpler style of small and occasional table which had been produced in Anne's reign. By the time of the publication of Chippendale's *Director* the constantly changing needs of the upper classes were reflected in endless varieties of tea-, breakfast-, card-, writing-, and dressing-tables, as well as the more formal side- and pier-tables. One very characteristic piece of the mid-century was the Chinese tea-table. This had Chinese patterns on the frieze (usually in applied work), on tiny fretted galleries which ran round the edge of the top, and on the straight legs, which were fretted or perhaps carved in the solid. Some of these tables had fretted stretchers which crossed diagonally between the legs. Breakfast-tables, made for the convenience of fashionable people who rose late and had their first meal in their bedrooms, had the same kind of decoration but a different form; they usually included flaps and drawers and a shelf, which was enclosed on three sides by trellis-work in mahogany or brass wire. A restrained French taste showed itself in slender, curved legs, sometimes with metal mounts, and curved friezes edged with gadrooning. Plates 112 and 113 are examples of two small tables of about 1760. Plate 112, a table cabinet which could be used for writing, has a Chinese fret gallery at the top. The cabinet doors, displaying good figuring, are framed in curved stiles (a fashion which dated back some time before 1750), and are finished off with small foliage carving at the corners. Plate 113 is a tea-table with hinged top, and has traces of Gothic work in the legs, which are fluted in ogee section and have a tiny trefoil arch at the top. The delicate carving on the table edge and at the bottom of the frieze, and the curved bracket, as well as the veneers, show the many admirable uses to which mahogany could be put. The Adam period introduced two distinctly new trends. Besides

rectangular shapes, others were appearing – oval, semicircular, kidney-shaped, and serpentine – with tapering and fluted legs or, as on some contemporary chairs, slender cabriole legs ending on knurl or scroll toes. For the daintier kinds of tables, satinwood and other exotic woods, inlays and gilding, and the choicest figured mahogany were all used, and in some of the best examples the tops were painted by Angelica Kauffmann, Pergolesi, and others. On the other hand, for the large rooms of the new town and country houses were produced many long side-tables in mahogany, as illustrated in Plate 111. In this table straight lines were emphasized. The legs are fluted, and taper to plinth feet. Carved decoration appears on the frieze in the classical moulding and the typical paterae over the legs and on the small central panel, where they are linked by husks. This kind of table represented the midway design between the dining- and side-table, and from it developed the sideboard, as is indicated below, as a separate piece of furniture.

This development of the sideboard seemed to re-direct the designers' attention to small tables. Hepplewhite continued on Adam lines, but Sheraton designed a number of extraordinarily delicate tables, some, like his ladies' work-tables, with an ingenious arrangement of drawers and sliding tops, being specially

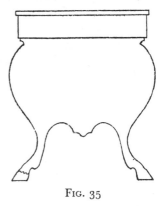

FIG. 35

made for carrying from room to room. Neatness was indeed Sheraton's own word for this kind of work: "These tables should be finished neat, either in satinwood or mahogany." He also popularized the Pembroke table (though it had been known for some time before), with two semicircular flaps hinging on a rectangular centre. Usually the legs on his tables were unmistakable for their long, fragile-looking, tapering forms, but on some he showed a radical change in treatment which was to last through the Regency period. He used two solid end uprights, in the old trestle style (Fig. 35), resting on short, outward-curving legs; or else a lighter version, with a central stretcher joining the ends.

Plate 114A shows another kind of table which was common in the early nineteenth century. This is the drum or capstan kind, with a deep frieze for drawers (sometimes this was left open for books) and a central support in tripod style, the legs having the pronounced curve typical of the period. Some of these tables had a solid three-sided pedestal base or monopodium mounted on claw feet. Rosewood or mahogany was usually the wood; some had light-coloured mahogany veneers and classical designs inlaid on the top and pedestal sides, in a contrasting colour.

Tripod tables. The application of the tripod construction to tables in general, from about 1800, indicates how popular this feature had become during the previous century. The small tripod tables developed from the candle-stands of the walnut period, but by Chippendale's time they were being used for other purposes, as occasional and tea-tables. Mahogany led to a considerable increase in them, as the tops could be made from one piece of wood, and, naturally, they became show-pieces for the various fashionable enrichments. Plate 114B shows one of the celebrated "pie-crust" tables, named after the scalloped and slightly raised edge of the top, which is hinged so that it can stand against the wall when not in use. The legs show cabriole treatment with the ball-and-claw feet, but in this case the ball has been modified to increase stability. The knees are decorated with carved acanthus leaves and the upright has been given contrasting forms of mouldings. Other tripod tables had elaborate carving on the top as a border to the edges. On others, again, a small fretted gallery appeared, like those on contemporary Chinese tables. Feet might be hooves, paws, or dolphins (the

third copied from French tables). Later in the century the tops had often fine inlaid work when this fashion revived under Adam. About 1800 the legs had tended to become very delicate in appearance, with definite concave or convex curves finishing on thin, pointed feet. Sheraton used these on screens as well as tables. But even in Hepplewhite's work the three legs had sometimes been replaced by a solid base, and the extension of this practice, and the many varied leg forms, meant the loss of the original "pillar and claw" principle.

Dining-tables. For the better part of two centuries it has been almost a convention to associate mahogany with good dining-room tables. One of the chief uses to which the early imports of San Domingo mahogany were put was to make the spacious tops of these tables. They had remarkable weight and strength, and yet the mahogany legs were able to support them without stretchers. This gave clean lines to even the biggest tables and led to many developments in flaps and pivoted legs. In the second half of the eighteenth century large dining-tables were made up of two smaller ones which were joined, when necessary, by flaps supported on gate legs. These legs at first either had cabriole form or were turned. The same construction continued in the Adam period, but very effective use was made of the size of the tables to give them figured veneers instead of solid mahogany, straight, tapering legs and the classical ornament typified in Plate 111. The side-table in this illustration in every way resembled the contemporary dining-table, except that the latter had ten legs, four each for the two end-tables and an extra two for the flaps. The tops were of varied shapes – rectangular, semicircular, or D-shaped – but, naturally, the central flaps were rectangular. Cabinet-makers produced, and in some cases patented, many ingenious devices for extending tops, such as the "Imperial" dining-tables made by Gillow of Lancaster. From about 1800 changes in design became marked. The circular table for dining – an enlarged version of the drum table referred to above – and long tables supported on two or three tripods or similar stands were Regency features. Sheraton also designed a "universal table" with the old-fashioned draw-leaf top on four tapering legs. "This," he wrote, "should be made of particularly good and well-seasoned mahogany, as a great deal depends on its not being liable to cast" – a reminder that dining-tables had missed much of the changing fashions in new woods and applied decoration.

Sideboards. The sideboard was a late eighteenth-century development and sprang from the table. It is said to have been originated by Adam, who introduced the custom of standing a classical pedestal mounting an urn at each end of a side table, of the kind in Plate 111. The obvious advantage of having this storage space so close to the table led to pedestals and tables becoming one unit, and later to the replacement of the pedestals by either smaller cupboards or drawers. The cupboards were used for many purposes; some were lined with metal to keep plates warm, or to hold water or wine-bottles. At first the urns which stood on the pedestals contained the cutlery, but this was transferred to a drawer when urns went out of use. Both Hepplewhite and Sheraton designed light and elegant sideboards. The former is credited with serpentine- and bow-fronted shapes and the latter paid special attention to the brass rail which often stood at the back of the table to hold plates. The serpentine-fronted sideboard is a typical example of Hepplewhite's finely proportioned work. This has the usual arrangements of legs, four in front and two at the rear, found on longer sideboards, and of a single central drawer flanked by two others (or in some cases single deep ones) on each side. The central arch (an important feature on these sideboards) has delicate inlay work, like the drawer fronts and apron piece, and there is also line inlay on the legs. The curving front makes a very effective display of figuring. So does the serpentine, break-front example in Plate 115, which is typical of the smaller Sheraton sideboard. It has two side cupboards, a sharper curve to the arch, and stringing decoration. The four legs on this piece are turned and reeded, a style for which Sheraton showed a preference in his later work (and which also appeared on his chairs). In the Regency period there was a return to the pedestal type of the early sideboards. Other versions discarded the side drawers or cupboards altogether and replaced them with two or four legs, often carved in animal forms. The deepening of the table frieze and the elaboration of the brass gallery in classical designs on these pieces deprived them of the graceful symmetry of previous examples.

VICTORIAN FURNITURE

In the history of the decorative arts Victorian furniture occupies a strange position. Although it is probable that fifty per cent of all the furniture ever made in this country was made during the sixty-four years of Victoria's reign, and that even today perhaps twenty per cent of all surviving furniture dates from those years, it is almost a closed field to serious scholarship or collecting. All standard works on the history of furniture stop at 1830, and the same terminal date is recognized, for example, by the Antique Dealers' Fair. In the last few years some dealers and collectors have begun tentatively to edge their way into the 1840s, usually with a limited interest in one line only (e.g. papier mâché), and a few books have skated over the surface. The main course of Victorian furniture remains, however, totally uncharted, with the result that whereas there are thousands who can confidently date a fifteenth-century brass-rubbing to within thirty years, there is no one in this country who can be equally certain about a Victorian sideboard.

The normal justification given for this curious position is that after about 1830 there was such a disastrous deterioration in standards of taste and craftsmanship that Victorian furniture does not merit the attention legitimately bestowed on earlier periods, and that in particular the eclectic enthusiasm of Victorian designers for copying the historic styles of the past deprives their productions of that degree of originality which is essential to serious connoisseurship. These arguments are not convincing. Firstly, the deterioration can be established only if the evidence is studied rather than ignored. Secondly, ugliness in the products of earlier periods has never proved a bar to serious research or enthusiasm on the part of either antiquarians or collectors. Thirdly, the accusation of unoriginal eclecticism can equally be brought against the furniture designers of the eighteenth century, and was indeed used by many nineteenth-century writers to dismiss the works of Chippendale and the Adams brothers, for example, as debased rehashes of Chinese, classical, and renaissance elements. Finally, it is surely absurd to suppose that the vast amount of earnest and informed effort put into the design of furniture by leading architects and others, especially after 1850, could have produced nothing whatever of interest.

The real explanation for the neglect must be sought elsewhere, namely in the totally different research techniques which are required to investigate Victorian furniture by comparison with that of earlier periods. The difference arises mainly from the change in the nature of the documentary evidence available after about 1840. Research into earlier furniture has always taken actual examples as its starting-point, and has, where possible, worked back from the furniture to surviving documents (family records and the like) as supporting evidence for attributions and dating. For these earlier periods the tangible evidence of the furniture itself far outweighs that of the fragmentary documentary references, and even after the appearance of pattern books in the eighteenth century the majority of surviving examples must be assessed without the aid of any contemporary visual or even verbal sources. After about 1845 the development of illustrated periodicals, trade catalogues, and exhibition catalogues rapidly transformed the situation, so that for the Victorian era the bulk of systematic contemporary day-by-day visual evidence far outweighs the quantity of authentic surviving furniture, with the result that research must necessarily take the documents as the starting-point and work from them to the furniture instead of vice versa. This necessarily places collectors at a disadvantage, for it means that those who might hope to pick up interesting Victorian items at country auctions will probably find their time wasted unless they have first spent many tedious hours ploughing through trade periodicals in Shoreditch Public Library.

The clearest proof of the significance of this change in research requirements after about 1840 is that fact that the small amount of systematic research into Victorian furniture that has hitherto been undertaken has appeared in journals such as the *Architectural Review* rather than the *Connoisseur*, and has been the work of experts on twentieth-century taste (who take the bulk of contemporary visual evidence for granted) pushing their researches backwards, rather than of eighteenth-century experts (who are trained in the opposite technique) pushing forwards. It is equally significant that the only substantial collection of Victorian furniture in existence – that of the Victoria and Albert Museum – has been mainly built up as a result of a systematic search for particular pieces, the original existence of which had first been established from a study of contemporary periodicals and catalogues.

It is as well that this watershed which divides pre-1840 from post-1840 research and collecting should be widely recognized as soon as possible, for otherwise there is a serious danger that the established practice of collecting without prior documentation will itself produce a cumulative distortion in the public assessment – even in informed circles – of Victorian design, by fostering a process of "selective survival". For example, in the absence of a study of the contemporary records, there is a general but erroneous belief that Early Victorian furniture (in contrast to mid-Victorian) retained some of the lightness and elegance of the Regency. Once such a stereotype is established, collectors tend to be interested only in pieces whose authenticity seems to be attested by their conformity to it, and dealers will come to prefer such pieces and reject others as atypical, until in the long run the only pieces which survive in quantity are those which fit into the mistaken picture, while the examples whose survival would establish its falsity are weeded out. By that time it will be too late to redress the balance and all the really interesting pieces will have disappeared.

However, even after it is recognized that the prior research into and the subsequent collecting of Victorian furniture is a legitimate, indeed a praiseworthy, pastime, there still remains the problem of the type of furniture to be sought, for so much has survived, and there is documentary evidence of so many parallel levels of taste, that some choice is inevitable. The problem is aggravated by the appearance for the first time after 1850 of two separate streams: namely the *avant garde* (what would today be called the "contemporary") furniture, consciously produced by designers from outside the ranks of the trade – often inspired by a missionary zeal to reform public taste – and appealing to a very small educated clientele; and the enormously larger bulk of trade productions designed anonymously in the studios of the large manufacturers on conservative and traditionalist lines. At first sight these two streams appear to be not only separate but entirely opposed, each contemptuous of the other; the former believed by the latter to be constantly changing in a feverish search after novelty at the whim of each individual designer, the latter believed by the former to be stolidly unchanging and impervious to any progressive influence. Both pictures are distorted, for the evidence shows that a clear logical development can be traced through the apparently unrelated twists and turns of the *avant garde* designs, and that this in its turn, and with a long time-lag, is reflected in a modified form by changes in the trade designs. The length of the time-lag naturally varies between London and the provinces and according to such factors as the price of the furniture and the nature of the firm, so that a comparison of trade catalogues demonstrates at any one time the whole gamut between the most advanced and the most conservative in current production side by side. Any systematic charting of the history of Victorian furniture – at least after 1850 – must therefore take constant account of this overlapping of styles, though necessarily giving prior attention to those pioneer, and indeed often rebel, designers upon whose inspiration the entire development ultimately depends. Collectors have the choice of furniture at every level of taste, though for obvious reasons it is usually only the more "advanced" pieces, in so far as they survive, which can provide the additional interest of exact dating and documentation.

In the absence of an accepted body of doctrine on Victorian furniture, the opinions expressed in the survey which follows are necessarily personal and tentative. Moreover, they are unavoidably based as much on an examination of contemporary documents as of actual surviving furniture. The survey concentrates on cabinet-makers' furniture, and excludes upholstered furniture and those sidelines, such as metal furniture, wicker, cane, and bent-wood furniture, and garden furniture, which require separate study.

Early Victorian furniture: 1837–51

The first fifteen years of Victoria's reign mark the lowest ebb ever reached in the whole history of English furniture design. Indeed, the most severe structures so often applied indiscriminately to Victorian taste as a whole are entirely justified if only directed against the products of this initial period. It would, however, be absurd to suggest that a sudden deterioration set in as soon as the new reign had begun; the most that can be said is that a debasement which was already evident as early as the late 1820s gained steady impetus during the 1830s and 1840s. The Great Exhibition of 1851 is always taken to mark the culmination of this debasement. In a sense this is true; although it is only right to remember that by stimulating competitive ostentation among manufacturers it tended to exaggerate the most vulgar elements in Early Victorian design, while the fact that, for the first time, the various illustrated catalogues of the exhibition provide a permanent record of its horrors, unfairly weighs the evidence against the Early Victorians. Had a similar exhibition been held in 1837 instead of 1851, it would hardly have demonstrated a higher average standard.

As always in such debased periods, it is impossible in retrospect to discern any logical development of design, to distinguish the personal styles and influences of the leading designers and manufacturers, or even to specify any criteria enabling one to date a surviving piece in default of documentary evidence. The pattern books of this period, such as those of R. Bridgens, R. Brown, Thomas King, and Henry Whitaker, throw no light on the matter, for each exhibits the same tepid eclecticism in which a slavish copying of past styles is accompanied by a straining after novelty in trivial details. Judgement is made more difficult by reason of the fact that no surviving examples have so far been precisely related to these patterns, with the exception of a few commonplace pieces designed by Whitaker for Osborne House in about 1845, which are still there.

Two characteristics stand out in the general confusion: an emphasis on rich and elaborate carving, preferably with a narrative or anecdotal interest, and a delight in the numerous new substitute materials which technical progress was making available. Lacking any accepted architectural framework, the shape and outline of such items as cabinets and sideboards were frequently entirely subordinate to an overall covering of carving, often worked not by hand carving but by new methods such as the burning techniques of the Burnwood Carving Company's "Xylopyrography" and Harrison's Wood Carving Company (Pimlico), or the machine stamping of Jordan's Patent Wood Carving, or even produced from materials such as gutta-percha, Jackson's "cartonpierre", Bielefeld's "Patent Siliceous Fibre", White and Parlby's "furniture composition", or Leake's sculptured leather.

Elaborate carving became so established as the hall-mark of fine furniture during this period that the furniture section of Wornum's Report on the Great Exhibition is actually headed "Carving and Modelling", and the only artists known to have been commissioned during the years 1837-51 to design furniture from outside the trade (with the exception of Pugin, to be mentioned below) were not architects as one would expect, but sculptors, such as Sir Francis Chantrey (1781-1841), John Thomas (1813-62), and Baron Marochetti (1805-67). Inevitably the most popular examples of English furniture at the Great Exhibition were the elaborately carved cradle presented to Queen Victoria by W. G. Rogers (1792-1875) – known as the "Victorian Grinling Gibbons"; the monstrous "Kenilworth" buffet (now at Warwick Castle) the *chef d'œuvre* of the Warwick school of wood carvers which flourished throughout the nineteenth century; and Arthur J. Jones' ludicrous patriotic carved furniture in Irish bog-oak.

The only one of the new materials which may be said to have produced something new and attractive was papier mâché, enriched after 1842 with Jennens' and Bettridge's patent jewelled effects. This plastic material, though suitable for trays, caskets, and the like, is, however, basically unsuitable for load-bearing furniture, and has no real place in the development of Victorian furniture. Owing to the natural attraction of the smaller items for collectors, it has, nevertheless, received disproportionate attention, and has helped to spread the myth that Early Victorian furniture is lighter and less clumsy than mid-Victorian. In a few cases, of which the settle illustrated in Plate 116A is a good example, the techniques for decorating papier mâché (e.g. lacquer painting and encrustation with shell and mother-of-pearl) were applied to a normal wooden framework, thus producing a legitimate piece of furniture; but such examples are rare.

Mid-Victorian furniture: 1851–67

The furniture of the period 1851–67 differed very markedly from that of the preceding period. In particular, the wild eclecticism and confusion of styles was rapidly replaced after 1851 by a surprising uniformity, and a single consistent style soon imposed itself on the great bulk of fashionable productions. Victorians themselves gave no name to this style, but usually described examples of it with generalized phrases such as "following the purest taste of the Italian Renaissance". Twentieth-century writers have hitherto ignored its existence, although a careful analysis of, for example, the copious records which have survived from the vast Modern Furniture Court of the 1862 Exhibition makes its existence perfectly clear.

Its main characteristics were the use of solid wood, usually walnut or mahogany, rather than veneers or inlay, a repudiation of baroque or rococo curves in favour of more severe outlines, and a continuing emphasis on carving. The latter, however, was now no longer allowed to sprawl over the whole surface with a profusion of unrelated motifs, as in the 1840s, but was concentrated into carefully disposed and deeply cut masks, swags, and trophies (usually of "appropriate" objects, such as dead game birds on sideboards), and almost invariably incorporated human figures in the form of caryatids or brackets. Indeed, this emphasis on human figures became something of an obsession with designers during this period, so that no fashionable sideboard or cabinet was considered complete without them – as large as possible and preferably free-standing. Equally indispensable was an enormous mirror, backing, and usually dwarfing, the whole piece – a direct consequence of the technical developments in the industrial section of the 1851 Exhibition.

It cannot be doubted that the best examples in this manner – however unacceptable to present-day taste – show a sense of style and consistency that had been completely lost in the 1840s, and certainly justify the enthusiasm with which all writers in the 1860s refer to the great improvement in the stylistic purity of English furniture since the nadir of 1851. The improvement must be mainly attributed to the influx of French designers imported from Paris by all the leading firms after the 1851 Exhibition had so clearly exposed the general superiority of French design. Some, such as Eugène Prignot and Alfred Lormier, who acted as chief designers to Jackson and Graham throughout the 1850s and 1860s, were brought over permanently, while in other cases designs were commissioned from artists in Paris, such as Ernest Vandale and Hugues Protat. In either case, the manufacturers always emphasized that "the piece has been entirely executed by English workers".

Although this dominant style was pervasive enough to influence not only the productions of all the leading London houses (i.e. Gillow, Trollope, Howard, Thomas Fox, and John-stone and Jeanes) but also the cheaper mass-production manufacturers, such as Lucraft, Smee, and Snell, and the leading provincial firms (i.e. Henry Ogden, Henry Lamb, and Bird and Hull in Manchester, John Taylor, Whytocks, and Purdie, Bonnar and Carfrae in Edinburgh, and C. and W. Trapnell in Bristol), some furniture was, of course, produced in other manners. Thus, a few firms (Charles Hindley, William Fry of Dublin, and J. G. Crace) worked in the "Gothic taste" (*see* below); Write and Mansfield produced an entirely atypical series of copies of original Adams designs; and Dyer and Watts had considerable success with cheap, stained bedroom furniture, an example of which was even purchased by the Empress Eugénie from the Paris Exhibition of 1867.

This nameless mid-Victorian style must be regarded as the last style to have originated within the trade. Thereafter all further developments took place under the shadow of the individual reformist artist-designers and architect-designers whose appearance on the scene so decisively changed the whole trend of English furniture design.

The Gothic revival

The first conscious reformers of Victorian furniture design – A. W. N. Pugin (b. 1812, d. 1852) and William Burges (b. 1827, d. 1881) – cannot be said to have had a direct or decisive influence on the general trend of trade design. Nevertheless, the developments of the late 1860s cannot be explained without a reference to their role. Though they both worked within the orbit of the Gothic Revival, their actual designs differed very radically.

The influence of Pugin on English furniture design has usually been overrated. His general influence as a propagandist, his key position in the mid-century transition from a sentimental to a scientific medievalism, and the significance of his teachings on church furnishings have tended to obscure the fact that his own domesitc furniture had little influence and that his following among furniture designers was always small. He himself designed a good deal of furniture in an extremely plain and unromantic Gothic style for the numerous houses which he erected in the 1840s, but as this was never published, it had no effect on the trade.

By contrast, the much more ornate and monumental furniture which he designed for the Houses of Parliament, and in particular the elaborate display piece which he designed for J. G. Crace for the Medieval Court of the 1851 Exhibition, and which was purchased by the Museum of Ornamental Art in 1852 (illustrated in Plate 117A), were much publicized and copied. Consequently the trade furniture of the 1850s which was claimed by its manufacturers to be "in the purest Gothic taste, after recognized authorities", and dismissed by its detractors as "Puginesque", tended to repeat all those faults of over-elaboration with architectural conceits in the way of finials, crockets, and the like, which Pugin himself had so trenchantly attacked in his *Contrasts* and which his own domestic work so skilfully avoided. In fact, this type of architectural Gothic furniture was far too closely associated in the public mind with Pugin's catholicism to have any wide vogue, and soon came to be the exclusive preserve of a number of specialized houses – of which the most prominent were Hardman and Cox – dealing mainly in church fittings, and generally referred to by contemporary writers as the "Wardour Street ecclesiastical upholsterers". It is true that in 1862 the young Norman Shaw (b. 1831, d. 1912) designed an elaborate bookcase in this style, which has often been quoted since, merely by virtue of having been illustrated in the official catalogue of the Exhibition, but it typified no general trend and was produced not by a furniture firm but by James Forsyth, a specialist in stone carving.

The Gothic furniture of William Burges occupies a somewhat different position. The main body of his furniture – designed largely for his own use or as part of the huge schemes of interior rebuilding which he undertook for the Marquis of Bute at Cardiff Castle and Castell Coch – involved a far too personal interpretation of thirteenth-century Gothic to have any wide influence (a typical example is illustrated in Plate 119). Its fanciful – even facetious – adaptation of medieval forms to present-day needs, and its garish polychromatic decoration, made its incorporation into a normal domestic interior quite impractical. However, two particular pieces in a rather more restrained style, which were shown in the Medieval Court – not (significantly) in the Modern Furniture Court – of the 1862 Exhibition, received a great deal of favourable attention and publicity and deserve separate consideration. They were a huge bookcase, admittedly castellated but otherwise severely unelaborated, painted by no fewer than eleven leading artists, and now in the possession of the Ashmolean Museum, Oxford, and a celebrated plain rectangular cabinet painted to Burges' specifications by E. J. Poynter (b. 1836, d. 1919) with scenes representing "the Battle of the Wines and the Beers" (bought for the South Kensington Museum from the Exhibition). The main significance of these pieces is that they are both in the plainest possible shape, entirely unlike the Wardour Street architectural Gothic, and depend entirely for their appeal on the painting of their surfaces. A subsidiary significance lies in the fact that their message to the trade was simultaneously endorsed at the 1862 Medieval Court by the furniture here displayed to the public for the first time by the newly created association of Morris, Marshall, Faulkner and Co.

Morris furniture

Several pieces exhibited by the Morris firm in the 1862 Court have survived (the most attractive example is the "Backgammon Players" cabinet), and all are similar to Burges' exhibits in being solidly constructed, supposedly Gothic, carcases, used as surfaces for painting. They belong by rights to the history of painting rather than of furniture. However, the Morris firm also produced (though it did not exhibit in 1862) several other types of non-Gothic furniture, each of which had an influence on the general trend of furniture design. So many misconceptions are current about Morris furniture that it is necessary to examine these in some detail.

Morris himself (despite frequent statements to the contrary) never designed any furniture, nor do his writings indicate much interest in it. All the furniture produced by the firm was the work of his various collaborators. Four different types were manufactured in these early years. Firstly, Philip Webb (b. 1831, d. 1915), the architect, designed a number of large tables depending for their effect entirely on the use of unstained oak and on the interest of their unconcealed joinery construction, thus marking a conscious revolt against the debasement of mid-Victorian cabinet-making. Though they were exaggeratedly massive and monumental (one of the most interesting is illustrated in Plate 116B), their proportions and their simple chamfered decoration reveal the hand of a sensitive architect. Their importance lies not in any immediate influence on the trade but in their delayed influence on the Arts and Crafts furniture designers of the 1890s, and they can be legitimately regarded as the original prototypes of the whole Cotswold school of joinery.

Secondly, Ford Madox Brown designed a set of cheap bedroom furniture, produced by the Morris firm in large quantities, usually in a green-stained version, of which a few examples have survived. These appealed particularly to those mid-Victorians who felt that the introduction of examples of good plain design into servants' bedrooms could not but help raise the taste, and even the morals, of the lower classes. Their success led to plagiarism by many firms in the 1880s.

Thirdly, the firm produced and sold right up to the 1920s a set of cheap rush-bottomed chairs and settle in turned ebonized wood, including seven alternative shapes, which quickly became immensely popular with middle-class families anxious to escape from the general philistinism of contemporary decoration. These also were copied with minor modifications by numerous other firms. This set was not originally designed by the firm, but was adapted from a traditional-type country chair seen by William Morris in Sussex.

Fourthly, the firm produced with equal success a drawing-room easy-chair with an adjustable bar at the back, which became so popular that in the United States the type is still known as a "Morris" chair (one is illustrated in Plate 118B). Though often spoken of

as designed by Morris himself, it was in fact copied directly from a chair seen in 1866 by Warington Taylor, the young manager of the firm, at the workshop of a Herstmonceux furniture maker named Ephraim Coleman.

Later in the century the firm evolved several entirely different types of furniture, which are referred to below in connexion with the Arts and Crafts movement.

Bruce J. Talbert and C. L. Eastlake

Although neither the architectural Gothic of Pugin nor the painted-plank Gothic of Burges and the Morris firm had much direct influence on trade design, they were nevertheless responsible for providing the point of departure for the development of what ultimately became the most widespread and original of all Victorian styles – a development that was so rapid that in the decade 1868–78 it transformed the whole course of Victorian furniture design. Two stages – or rather two overlapping strands – can be traced in it: the first associated with Bruce J. Talbert (1838–81) and C. L. Eastlake (1836–1906), the second with T. E. Collcutt (1840–1924). Once again the usual Victorian confusion about labels has served to obscure the significance of these changes and the originality of the furniture which developed from them, for contemporary writers gave the style no name and referred to its products as simply Gothic, Early English, Old English, or even Jacobean.

The first stage dates from 1867, when Talbert, a prolific and neglected designer, won a silver medal for Holland and Sons at the Paris Exhibition with a so-called "Gothic dressoir" and several smaller cabinets. The influence of this success was consolidated by the publication in the same year of Talbert's *Gothic Forms, applied to Furniture, Metalwork, etc. for Interior Purposes*, and in 1868 of Eastlake's *Hints on Household Taste*, a book which exerted an enormous influence in sophisticated middle-class circles – especially in America, where it gave rise to a so-called "Eastlake style".

Although Talbert's Paris Exhibition pieces were still in a heavy semi-Gothic style, not so far removed from the "Puginesque", the more unpretentious examples in both his book and in Eastlake's, which were, of course, those which had most influence on trade production, marked a definite step away from the Gothic of both Pugin and Burges towards a style more practical and three-dimensional. Its main characteristics were a rigid avoidance of curves or florid carving, a concentration on straight lines and an elaboration of surface colour and texture (but always in the lowest possible relief) by the use of a great variety of different techniques and materials, including the insertion of painted and stained panels, tiles, stamped leather, embroidery, enamels and chased metal. Talbert produced large quantities of this furniture, not only for Hollands but also for Gillow, and for Marsh, Jones, and Cribb of Leeds. However, only two authenticated examples of his work have so far been traced (both of which have been acquired by the Victoria and Albert Museum). They are both in this modified Gothic style, and demonstrate the particular flavour of rich sobriety which characterized his work. Other examples must certainly survive, along with pieces by Eastlake himself (he designed for Heaton, Butler, and Bayne), and those designers who closely followed this style in the 1870s, such as E. J. Tarver (working for Morant Boyd) and Owen Davis, the eclectic assistant of Sir Matthew Digby Wyatt and author of *Art and Life* (1885) (working for Shoolbred).

Despite the acclaim with which Talbert's book was received and the designs in it copied, he himself quickly abandoned the style, and already in the early 1870s turned towards a dull and unoriginal rehash of Jacobean motifs, with a tedious elaboration of carved strapwork and a generally baronial air. This change can be clearly traced in the designs which he exhibited at the Royal Academy over these years, and in his second book of designs, *Examples of Ancient and Modern Furniture*, published in 1876. Its influence was slight for it merely provided additional models for the large firms of traditionalist decorators, such as Gillow and Trollope, who had in any case always found in late Elizabethan and early seventeenth-century oak carving a ready-made source of inspiration for their more pretentious schemes.

T. E. Collcutt

The second stage in these developments, though it stemmed directly from the first and rapidly followed on its heels, was due neither to Talbert nor Eastlake, but to Thomas Edward Collcutt. Though remembered as the architect of the Imperial Institute, his role as a furniture designer has been entirely forgotten. It opens in 1871, when Collcutt exhibited at the South Kensington International Exhibition a cabinet designed for Collinson and Lock (illustrated in Plate 118c), which was bought by the Commissioners of the Great Exhibition and finally found its way into the South Kensington Museum. The publication in 1872 of a large catalogue of designs by Collinson and Lock (mostly the work of Collcutt, although J. Moyr Smith, the author of *Ornamental Interiors* (1887) later claimed some credit for them) gave the style a wide currency in the trade, so that already by the time of the Paris Exhibition of 1878 firms such as Cooper and Holt, and Bell and Roper of London, and Henry Ogden of Manchester were copying it precisely. By 1880 its influence appears in the catalogues of mass-production firms such as Hewetson and Milner, Smee, and Lucraft.

In Collcutt's hands the style, though following Talbert in the emphasis on straight lines and the use of coved cornices and painted panels, was elaborated in a far more fanciful and light-hearted spirit, which marked a further stage in the evolution away from the medieval. A simultaneous emphasis on both verticals and horizontals, and a proliferation of shelves and divisions, diversifies the façade and provides variety by giving space for the display of knick-knacks. As always, the rapid spread of the style was accompanied by an equally rapid debasement, so that by the early 1880s it was responsible for a mass of elaborate but gimcrack cabinets, what-nots, corner-cupboards (a particular favourite) and the like, with spindly supports, a profusion of small pigeon-holes, often divided off by little railings of turned balusters or embroidered curtains, and panels painted with floral sprays or willowy female figures, usually on a gold ground. A persistent cliché which became almost a trade-mark for the style was a double panel in which an inner oblong or hexagon is joined to an outer frame by ties at the four cardinal points.

At its best, the style must be regarded as the Victorian era's most individual contribution in the whole field of furniture design. Quantities of its cheaper manifestations have survived, particularly in country rectories. Overmantels, usually backed with numerous small mirrors, have tended to survive as being fixtures, and examples of a drawing-room version of the style, decorated in black and gold, can also be found. Authentic pieces from the Collinson and Lock 1872 catalogue are, however, very difficult to come by.

The surprisingly rapid spread of Talbert's original style, and Collcutt's later version of it, can only be explained if account is taken of the way in which Eastlake and the many publicists who followed him supported their influence with arguments which seemed to provide would-be connoisseurs and purchasers with certain easily remembered maxims for judging furniture, and which buttressed their own uncertain taste with apparently authoritative criteria. These all derived ultimately from the teachings of Pugin, Owen Jones, and Ruskin on "honesty in design". The most telling was the proposition that because wood has a straight grain it should always be used in the plank and never debased by being carved or curved into twisted shapes more appropriate to plastic or ductile materials. This argument was strengthened by simultaneous appeal to economic and nationalist considerations, for the carving or curving of wood obviously involves the cutting-to-waste of good timber, while "wanton curves" and "meaningless scrolls" could be condemned as symbolizing the decadent extravagances which had so recently brought the French Second Empire to the ground.

During this period a parallel movement in favour of straight lines, a lighter and more varied colouring and texture, and a shunning of the deep carving of the 1860s can be traced even in the luxury productions of firms such as Jackson and Graham, and Wright and Mansfield. At its best it produced some very handsome pieces, such as the cabinet by Wright and Mansfield illustrated in Plate

117B, which won the highest awards at the Paris Exhibition of 1867 and was purchased for the South Kensington Museum for £800. Judging from contemporary descriptions, the elaborate inlaid furniture produced by Jackson and Graham in the early 1870s for Alfred Morrison's palace at 16, Carlton House Terrace, to the designs of Owen Jones (b. 1809, d. 1874), must have reflected the same trend. The 1870s also saw the production of furniture designed by Norman Shaw for Lascelles and Co. Unfortunately, in the absence of surviving photographs or specimens, the wildly conflicting opinions of contemporary critics provide no clear picture of its style.

The Anglo-Japanese style

Owing to the absence of furniture in the European sense in the traditional Japanese home, the revolutionary influence on Victorian design of the displays of Japanese craftsmanship at the International Exhibitions of 1862 (London) and 1867 (Paris), following the opening-up of Japan by the West, had rather less effect in the field of furniture design than in those, for example, of wallpapers, textiles, or book illustration. Nevertheless, the impact of the new culture – providing, as it did, a heaven-sent stimulus to jaded designers in search of some authentic historical style that had not already been copied *ad nauseam* – was sufficient to inspire a vogue for so-called "Anglo-Japanese" furniture in the 1870s and 1880s.

The first enthusiast was E. W. Godwin (b. 1833, d. 1886), the architect and stage designer and associate of Whistler and Ellen Terry. He is said to have decorated his own house in the Japanese manner as early as 1862, and was certainly designing furniture showing a strong Japanese influence by the late 1860s. An illustrated catalogue issued by William Watt in 1877 contained many examples of his work and did much to familiarize the general public and the trade with his particular style. His best pieces, such as two fine cabinets in the Victoria and Albert Museum (one of which is illustrated in Plate 118A) and a collection of furniture belonging to the Bristol Art Gallery, show a remarkable capacity for translating into European terms, and into the scale of full-size furniture, the asymmetrical elegance, the attenuated supports, and in particular the subtle three-dimensional interplay of void and solid, which are the main characteristics of the Japanese lacquer boxes and cabinets which were then being imported in large quantities. To these he added certain personal mannerisms of his own, such as the use of elbow-like struts, square in section but rounded at the angle, which serve no function but to span the spaces between the component parts of a cabinet or sideboard and thus draw the whole composition together.

Inevitably the trade version of Godwin's style, worked out in the 1880s by hack designers, produced some deplorable furniture, in which the Japanese inspiration was limited to such obvious tricks as imitation bamboo legs, and asymmetrical fretwork panels. However, a few of the better professional designers managed to design some quite pleasing pieces by grafting certain Japanese motifs on to the Talbert–Collcutt style. The most successful of these was H. W. Batley, who designed some very elaborate furniture for James Shoolbred and for Henry Ogden of Manchester. It is possible, also, that some of the "Anglo-Japanese" furniture produced by the short-lived "Art Furnishers' Alliance", founded in 1880 by Christopher Dresser (1834–1904), the indefatigable but eccentric designer and publicist (he was for a time Art Editor of the *Furniture Gazette* in the 1880s), may have been of interest, for Dresser had a real understanding of Japan, which he visited officially in 1876; but the only two surviving examples are too unimportant to justify an opinion.

This Anglo-Japanese vogue was accompanied in the 1880s by a revival of interest in other exotic styles, such as the Indian, Persian, and Moorish, as a result of which such features as "Anglo-Arab lounges" and "Hindoo smoke-rooms" became popular, particularly in clubs and hotels. However, this fashion was largely met by the importation and adaptation of genuine Oriental examples (Egyptian mushrabiya panels, Chinese embroidered screens, Indian mother-of-pearl and ivory tables, and the like) by firms such as Liberty's, rather than by Western manufacturers, and no serious English designers seem to have been influenced by it.

The Arts and Crafts movement

Late Victorian furniture design – indeed, the Late Victorian decorative arts generally – was dominated by the birth of what has come to be known generically as the "Arts and Crafts movement" (i.e. the Century Guild, 1882; the Art Workers' Guild, 1883; the Arts and Crafts Exhibition Society, 1888; the Guild of Handicraft, 1888; the Home Arts and Industries Association, 1889; the Wood Handicraft Society, 1892; and many others). In fact, during the last dozen years or so of the Victorian era no furniture of interest was designed outside its orbit.

In these its initial stages the movement gave rise to a bewildering variety of different styles of furniture, and it would be quite wrong to suppose that its productions were in the main limited to that particular type of austere and undecorated cottage-style joinery which, as we have already seen, had been practised by Philip Webb in the 1860s, and which has come to be associated with the Arts and Crafts movement during the twentieth century and particularly with its important Cotswold offshoot. Indeed, two equally strong tendencies were pulling in exactly contrary directions.

In the first place the movement fostered a revival of interest in the styles and craftsmanship of the eighteenth-century English cabinet-makers, partly no doubt as a natural reaction against the disrepute in which they had been held by the medievalists of the 1860s, partly as a corollary to the renewed interest in eighteenth-century architecture stemming from the Queen Anne revival, and partly in continuation of that general movement towards greater lightness and elegance of detail which we have already noted in the work of both Collcutt and Godwin. In the second place, the move away from austere joinery was stimulated by the natural temptation for furniture designers to put into practice the movement's beliefs about the need for greater co-operation between the various crafts, by calling in workers in pewter, ivory, brass, stained glass, leather, and so on to adorn the efforts of the carpenter and cabinet-maker.

These contrasting tendencies can be seen very clearly in almost all the furniture shown at the various Arts and Crafts Exhibitions (1888, 1889, 1890, 1893, 1896, 1899). They are certainly evident in the Morris furniture, for though almost all designed by George Jack (1855–1932), Philip Webb's closest pupil, it bore little resemblance to the latter's solid-wood joinery. Most of it consisted of florid and very expensive walnut and mahogany pieces, covered all over with elaborate floral marquetry and inlay. Two particular pieces have survived in several versions, namely a free-standing escritoire (illustrated in Place 120C) and a handsome glass-fronted bookcase. The latter, as also an elegant circular mahogany tea-table with shaped legs, are entirely urban pieces and as far removed as possible from any Gothic or medieval influence. The same is true of some curious furniture which the firm produced at this date to the designs of W. A. S. Benson (b. 1854, d. 1924), the metalworker, in which he incorporated elaborate metal panel-frames, locks, handles, and hinges.

Curiously enough, it remained for Ford Madox Brown (b. 1821, d. 1893) – now no longer associated with the Morris firm – to produce the type of furniture which would presumably have accorded better with Morris' philosophical views than did Jack's expensive projects. In 1890 he exhibited a "Cheap Chest of Drawers for a Workman or Cottager" which created a great deal of interest. Judging from a contemporary photograph, the piece was so far in advance of its times that it could easily have passed for an example of utility design in the Second World War – even to the use of sunk finger-holes instead of drawer handles.

The furniture of the short-lived association of architect-designers known as Kenton and Co. (named after a street near its Bloomsbury workshop), which lasted for eighteen months in 1890–1 and exhibited at the Arts and Crafts Exhibition of 1890, throws these contradictory tendencies within the movement into even sharper relief. Reginald Blomfield (b. 1856, d. 1942) and Mervyn Macartney

(b. 1853, d. 1932) used the workshop to produce eclectic walnut and mahogany pieces in adaptations of eighteenth-century styles. (R. S. Lorimer produced some similar designs at the very end of the century.) Ernest Gimson's designs (apart from some turned ash chairs which he made himself by the traditional methods which he had learnt from a Herefordshire chair-turner in 1888, and one or two Windsor-type examples) were entirely original, and clearly adumbrated that combination of angularity and elegance and of austere outlines and elaborate surface decoration which he later developed so successfully in the Cotswolds (one of his Kenton pieces is illustrated in Plate 121C). On the other hand, Sidney Barnsley's solid pieces in unstained oak acknowledge a direct debt to Philip Webb and clearly anticipated the more unsophisticated and rustic side of the Cotswold movement. The same is true of W. R. Letheby's (b. 1857, d. 1931) essays in the use of a coarse type of floral marquetry using unstained woods (an example dating from a few years later than the Kenton experiment is illustrated in Plate 121A), though, as if to emphasize the confusion of styles, Lethaby was simultaneously designing in 1890 some entirely dissimilar rosewood and mahogany drawing-room furniture in a modified Chippendale manner, executed by Marsh, Jones, and Cribb of Leeds.

When we come to consider the furniture designed by other pioneers of the Arts and Crafts movement, the picture is even more complex. On the one hand, each tended to strike out in his own individual direction, uninhibited by the existence of any accepted norms. On the other hand, the very frequency of the Arts and Crafts exhibitions, and in particular the extent to which the illustrated journals immediately published photographs of every interesting piece as it appeared, made it quite impossible to design in isolation. As a result, the years between 1888 and 1901 witnessed a most complicated pooling of ideas and interplay of influence and counter-influence which would require a large volume to unravel. For example, a characteristic square-cut tapering leg with an enlarged foot, first used by Mackmurdo in the 1880s, was taken up and exploited by Voysey in the 1890s; the latter's weakness for fanciful spreading hinges was immediately copied by C. R. Ashbee; Ashbee's use of thonged leather was plagiarized by Baillie Scott and Wickham Jarvis – and so the list could continue. In fact, so interwoven are the various strands that it is difficult to date precisely, and to pin down initial responsibility for, the introduction of even the most emphatic mannerisms of the period, such as the addition of elongated finials to the corners of cupboards and sideboards (probably first used by Walter Cave on a piano exhibited in 1893) or the decoration of chair backs with cut-out heart shapes (almost certainly due to Voysey).

Although a painstaking examination of the huge mass of contemporary periodical literature of these years is an indispensable prerequisite to any definitive unravelling of these developments, the story must equally remain obscure until more of the key-pieces of the period are unearthed. Many have unhappily disappeared for ever, but others undoubtedly survive, as yet unrecognized and awaiting discovery by enterprising collectors. Century Guild furniture, for example, which was designed by A. H. Mackmurdo (b. 1851, d. 1942), is known only by a small group of pieces in the William Morris Gallery at Walthamstow (one of which is illustrated in Plate 120A), and yet much more must surely survive, for a good deal was sold by Wilkinson's of Old Bond Street in the late 1880s. Examples of the work of C. R. Ashbee's (b. 1863, d. 1942) Guild of Handicraft are even scarcer, for only three have so far been traced (one is illustrated in Plate 120B). Contemporary photographs exist, however, of many more examples, and it is inconceivable that they have all disappeared.

C. F. A. Voysey (b. 1857, d. 1941) is rather easier, and a fair amount of his furniture has already been located. It is unlikely that many more of his elaborate – and often eccentric – individual pieces have survived untraced, but many examples of the several styles of chair which he designed for standard production (one of which is illustrated in Plate 121B) must still be in use. Furniture by Charles Rennie Mackintosh (b. 1868, d. 1928) the Glasgow architect, is in a different category, for although considerable quantities of it survive (a typical example is illustrated in Plate 121D), it is almost all concentrated in the hands of the Glasgow School of Art and the Glasgow City Corporation, and therefore unavailable to the private collector. It also differs from all other Victorian furniture in that it has already been fully catalogued and documented.[1] There should be considerable scope for pioneer collecting in the early furniture of M. H. Baillie Scott (b. 1865, d. 1945), for though a number of his Edwardian pieces have survived, notably in Switzerland, nothing of his work in the Isle of Man (1887–1900) has been traced. Minor figures of the movement such as Edgar Wood, Charles Spooner, Wickham Jarvis, and Walter Cave, all of whom designed interesting if not startlingly original furniture in the last years of the century, await the attention of both research workers and collectors. Many photographs of their work exist in contemporary periodicals, but nothing has so far been traced.

If so many different cross-currents are discernible among the furniture of the leading Late Victorian designers, it is not surprising that the changes of fashion in the run-of-the-mill trade furniture produced during the 1890s should be even more difficult to chart. The days when the trade could afford to ignore the existence of the reformers were now long past, and Arts and Crafts developments were recorded as a matter of course – and usually respectfully – in the various trade periodicals. Indeed, in 1893 the firms of Gillow, Howard and Sons, and Collinson and Lock participated in force at the Arts and Crafts Exhibition, though for some reason this experiment was not repeated.

The direct influence of the movement on the trade seems to have operated at two quite different levels. In the first place, a certain number of hack designers simply added to their repertory of styles some of the more obvious mannerisms of the Arts and Crafts designers and evolved from them a bastard concoction which they christened the "Quaint Style". This first appeared in 1891, and be-

[1] See Thomas Howarth: *Charles Rennie Mackintosh and the Modern Movement* (London, 1952).

came more monstrous as the century ended, especially after 1893, when the so easily aped and misunderstood extravagances of Parisian "Art Nouveau" were added to the mixture. This so-called style is too debased and spurious to merit serious attention, though the student of the bizarre can trace its ramifications week by week by simply following the so-called "original" designs by A. Jonquet and H. Pringuet published for the use of manufacturers in the *Furniture Gazette* and the *Cabinet-maker* respectively. Its existence need hardly be drawn to the attention of collectors were it not that in the early stages of collecting, before the field has become familiar, there is always a danger that the most extreme and fantastic specimens will be given undue prominence, both because they are the most easily identifiable and because their very extravagance exercises a certain ludicrous charm. It would, however, be a great pity if, for these reasons, the attention of collectors was diverted from the serious work of the real pioneers of the movement to the entirely derivative corner cupboards and ingle-nooks of the "Quaint Style" with their shoddy stained glass and machine-stamped repoussé tulips.

On an entirely different level was the furniture produced at the very turn of the century by a few firms, such as Heal and Son, the Bath cabinet-makers, J. S. Henry, and Wylie and Lockhead, which had taken the trouble to assimilate the basic principles of the Arts and Crafts movement. Though the full fruits of this most important development fall properly outside the Victorian era, some of the exhibits at the Paris Exhibition of 1900 and the Glasgow Exhibition of 1901 (the most striking of which is illustrated in Plate 122) already herald the change.

SMALLER FURNITURE OF ALL PERIODS

A fairly wide interpretation has been given here to the term "small furniture". It includes, in general, those smaller pieces which are not dealt with elsewhere in this section, but for which entries are to be found in the glossary (e.g. canterbury, cellaret). It has also been assumed that readers will be familiar with the main developments of English furniture

styles, to which smaller furniture, as well as the larger, conformed; with the warning that "country" furniture might continue to be made in a style which had passed out of fashion, perhaps some considerable time previously, in London and the chief provincial towns.

The collection of small pieces of furniture can be a most fascinating pastime, not only for obvious financial reasons but also because they are a constant delight to the eye, and – a point of special weight in these days when living room is not so spacious as in times gone by – because they can be frequently used as their original makers and owners intended.

The study of the evolution of smaller articles of furniture can also be a study of social history; for they portray, as Horace Walpole wrote of the furniture in Hogarth's pictures, "the history of the manners of the age". One can see how they came into use as the rooms of houses began to take on their separate character and as new conventions established themselves in society. Note, for example, how at the end of the seventeenth century the two new fashions of tea-drinking and displaying china produced a whole range of small pieces, among which can be included on the one hand, tea-boards, kettle-stands, and caddies, and, on the other, china-stands, brackets, and shelves. With the coming of home manufacture of mirror glass, the development of special processes of decoration such as Tunbridge ware and straw-work and the introduction of new materials like Clay's papier mâché, many new articles came into production or new forms and modes of decoration were given to older ones. The great diversity of small pieces in Georgian dining-rooms tells its own story of the importance placed by the upper classes in those days on eating and drinking.

With regard to the furniture which is described hereunder, one might be tempted to write, as did Sheraton in his *Cabinet Dictionary*, that "the reader will find some terms which he will probably judge too simple in their nature to justify their insertion". One feels, however, that this apology is unnecessary; the simplest articles are often the most useful, and their names, though no doubt very familiar, do not give what is, after all, the intention of this section, viz. their history and development. It might be added, in conclusion, that Sheraton's own period delighted in small furniture which combined, to a greater degree than at any other time, usefulness with extreme delicacy of appearance.

European Lacquer Furniture

Great cabinets, bureaux, console tables, daybeds, and chairs of green, vermilion, or jetblack lacquer added the final touch of opulent magnificence to many a late seventeenth- or early eighteenth-century salon. "What can be more surprising than to have our chambers overlaid with varnish more glossy and reflecting than polisht marble?" asked Stalker and Parker, the authors of the first English *Treatise of Japaning and Varnishing*, in 1688. "No amorous nymph need entertain a dialogue with her Glass, or Narcissus retire to a fountain to survey his charming countenance when the whole house is one entire speculum." They even went so far as to declare that "the glory of one country, Japan alone, has exceeded in beauty all the pride of the Vatican at this time and the Pantheon heretofore". Lacquer had already been introduced into Europe, and soon there was hardly a great house in England, France, Germany, or Italy that could not boast a few pieces of lacquered furniture, if not whole rooms "overlaid with varnish more glossy and reflecting than polisht marble". Many such works in lacquer have survived to our own day, mellowed but hardly decayed by time, and in their shining surfaces, between the exotic birds and wispy trees, we may still catch a reflection of the brilliant world of which they were created.

Before proceeding to an account of how and when lacquer was used for the embellishment of European furniture a few words must be said about the substance of this brilliant paint or varnish. Although intended to imitate Oriental lacquer, European lacquer was, perforce, made in a different way. Chinese and Japanese craftsmen derived the lac, the basic constituent of the varnish, from the resin of a tree, the *Rhus vernicifera*, and applied it to the wood they wished to decorate in many layers, each of which was allowed to dry before the next was applied. The surface was then highly polished and decorated with designs in gold leaf. As the resin from which true lac was obtained was unavailable in Europe and could not satisfactorily be imported from the East, craftsmen had to resort to other means to achieve the same effect, and they propounded a wide variety of different receipts. Filippo Bonanni, an Italian who wrote a treatise on lacquering in 1720, listed some ten different methods employed by English, French, German, Italian, and Polish craftsmen. Usually the wood was prepared with a mixture of whitening and size and then treated with numerous coats of a varnish composed of gumlac, seed-lac, or shell-lac, different preparations of the resin broken off the twigs of the tree on which it is deposited by an insect, the *coccus lacca*, and dissolved in spirits of wine. The decorations were outlined in gold size, built up with a composition made of gum arabic and sawdust, coloured, polished, and gilt with metal dust. The surface was burnished with a dog's tooth or an agate pebble. Such methods could not, of course, produce a substance as hard and glittering as Oriental lacquer, but as experiment succeeded experiment, European craftsmen gradually improved their technique and were eventually able to produce a varnish of great beauty. Some, indeed, thought they had improved upon their models and Voltaire rhapsodized over

> . . . les cabinets où Martin
> A surpassé l'art de la Chine.

By the irony of chance, time has dealt more

kindly with these European imitations than with Oriental lacquer of the same period, much of which has now faded to a drab and unappetizing hue.

Importations of Oriental lacquer. Although considerable quantities of Oriental porcelain had been brought to Europe before the end of the sixteenth century, importations of Chinese and Japanese lacquer had been on a much more modest scale. Two varnished boxes which were in the collection of the Queen of France in 1524 and a "purple box of Chine" which the Emperor sent from Aachen to Queen Elizabeth in 1602, may have been lacquered, but we cannot be sure. There is no doubt, however, of the attention which Oriental lacquer held for sixteenth-century travellers to the East. "The fayrest workemanshippe thereof cometh from China," wrote Van Linschoten in 1598, in the account of his voyage. And he went on to praise the "Desks, Targets, Tables, Cubbordes, Boxes, and a thousand such like things, that are all covered and wrought with Lac of all colours and fashions". By 1610, indeed, one Jacques l'Hermite had sharpened his taste for lacquer to such a degree that he was able to despise a consignment sent to Holland from Bantam, declaring that it was far inferior to that which came from Japan.

Lacquer was imported into Europe in ever-increasing quantities during the first half of the seventeenth century. An inventory of "goodes and household stuffe" belonging to the Earl of Northampton in 1614 refers to a "China guilt cabinette upon a frame", and in the same year the East India Company's ship *Clove* returned to London, after the first English voyage to Japan, loaded with a cargo of Japanese wares which included "Scritoires, Trunkes, Beoubes (screens), Cupps and Dishes of all sorts and of a most excellent varnish". Lest the market should be flooded, these objects – the first of their kind to reach England in quantity – were sold off slowly to inflate their commercial value. This device had such good effect that "small trunkes or chests of Japan guilded and inlaid with mother of pearle having sundry drawers and boxes" which fetched £4 5s and £5 in 1614 commanded as much as £17 apiece four years later. Lacquer

was also popular in France during this period. By 1649 Mazarin had three Chinese cabinets in his collection of orientalia, besides many pieces of Eastern porcelain and embroidery, and he acquired more lacquer furniture in the next few years.

Mid-seventeenth-century travellers to China, whose *Voyages* were translated into many languages and read throughout Europe, were full of admiration for the lacquer they had seen in Peking and elsewhere. John Nieuhoff, the steward to the abortive Dutch embassy to the Emperor of China in 1655, described the process by which it was made, enlarging on the beauty and utility of lacquer: "There is also in divers places throughout the whole Empire, a certain sort of Lime which they press from the Bark of a Tree, being tough and sticking like Pitch; of this, which I suppose I may call a Gum, they make a certain sort of Paint wherewith they colour all their Ships, Houses, and Household-stuff, which makes them shine like Glass; and this is the reason that the houses in China, and in the Isle of *Japon*, glister and shine so bright, that they dazzle the eyes of such as behold them. For this paint lays a shining colour upon Wood, which is so beautiful and lasting, that they use no Table-cloths at their Meals; for if they spill any grease, or other liquor upon the Table, it is easily rubbed off with a little fair water, without loss or damage of colour."

In addition to the painted lacquer – of the type described by Nieuhoff – incised Coromandel lacquer was extensively imported into Europe in the seventeenth century, mainly from the Dutch trading station at Bantam in the Malay peninsula, whence it derived the name "Bantam work". Cabinets and vast sixfold Coromandel screens were brought to Europe but enjoyed a somewhat wavering fashion, perhaps on account of their gaudy, if not garish, colour schemes, which have only now faded to an attractively subdued tone (fragments of Coromandel lacquer preserved inside cabinets give one an idea of its startling pristine colours). In 1688 Stalker and Parker, who were certainly prejudiced in favour of painted lacquer, declared that Bantam ware was "almost obsolete and out of fashion" in England. "No person is fond of it, or gives it house-room", they scornfully remarked, "except some who have made new Cabinets out of old Skreens. And from that large old piece, by the help of a Joyner, made little ones . . . torn and hacked to joint a new fancie . . . the finest hodgpodg and medly of Men and Trees turned topsie turvie." Without any regard for the figures of the design, strips of Coromandel were used in this way to face the drawers of cabinets or to frame looking-glasses, like that which is still to be seen at Ham House. Nevertheless, Coromandel screens retained their popularity in some circles, and the Duke of Marlborough included one among the furniture he took with him on his campaigns. In Germany and Holland the vogue for Coromandel seems to have been steadier and of longer duration than in England.

The earliest European lacquer. The first attempts to imitate Oriental lacquer in Europe were made in the early seventeenth century. Marie des Médicis is known to have employed a skilful cabinet-maker named Etienne Sager to make "with lacquer gum and gold decoration in the manner of the same country (China), cabinets, chests, boxes, panelling, ornaments for churches, chaplets, and other small articles of Chinese goods". She also established a vendor of Oriental wares in the Louvre, and his shop would, no doubt, have contained articles of European lacquer as well. At about the same time imitations of lacquer were produced in Italy, and when William Smith wrote to Lord Arundell from Rome in 1616 he was able to list among his many accomplishments that he had "been emploied for the Cardinalles and other Princes of these parts, in workes after the China fashion wch. is much affected heere". Imitations were also made in England, as is shown by the inventory of furniture belonging to the 1st Earl of Northampton on his death in 1614. In addition to a few genuine Oriental articles, Lord Northampton owned several examples of "china worke" (i.e. European lacquer). He had, for instance, a "large square China worke table and frame black varnish and gold", a "small table of China worke in gold and colours with flies and wormes upon a table suteable", and a "Field bedstead of China worke blacke and silver

branches with silver with the Armes of the Earl of Northampton upon the head piece". These must have been European and were perhaps of English lacquer. Next year, in 1615, Lady Arundell was matching curtains to her "bedde of Japan" which may also have been of English make. Unfortunately, none of these objects has survived, but a small group of English lacquer pieces dating from the second decade of the seventeenth century may give us some indication of what they were like. These consist of a ballot box dated 1619, in the possession of the Saddlers' Company at London, a cabinet (Plate 126A) and a box of twelve roundels in the Victoria and Albert Museum. All are of oak painted in gold and silver with a curious *mélange* of European and Eastern motifs on a thickly varnished black ground. Similar lacquer work, though of somewhat higher quality, was also produced in Holland (Plate 126C). The fashion for imitation lacquer appeared in Denmark in the 1620s, when a remarkable room in Rosenborg Castle at Copenhagen was decorated with panels of dark green and gold lacquer, set in imitation tortoiseshell frames and painted by Simon Clause with views of fantastic buildings and fragile little junks (Fig. 36).

Fig. 36. Panel of lacquer painted by Simon Clause, in the Rosenborg Castle, Copenhagen

Although European craftsmen had greatly improved the technique of lacquering by the middle of the seventeenth century, they had not yet succeeded in producing wares which could vie with the genuine Oriental articles. Importations of chests and screens from China and Japan continued unabated. But Eastern cabinet-makers did not produce all the objects of furniture deemed necessary for a European house, and merchants therefore sent out designs of various objects to be copied in the East. Here again there was a difficulty; for although Eastern craftsmen excelled in lacquer decoration, their cabinet-making was found to be of surprisingly poor quality. As Captain William Dampier remarked in 1688, "The Joyners of this country (China) may not compare their work with that which the Europeans make; and in laying on the Lack upon good or fine joyned work, they frequently spoil the joynts, edges, or corners of Drawers and Cabinets: Besides, our fashion of Utensils differ mightily from theirs, and for that reason Captain Pool, in his second voyage to the Country, brought an ingenious Joyner with him to make fashionable Commodities to be lackered here, as also Deal boards. . . ." Very few such European carpenters seem to have been taken out to China, but unpainted furniture was occasionally shipped from Europe to the East to be lacquered and returned home for sale. This costly procedure was not practised for long, however, as European lacquerers had attained sufficient skill in their medium to satisfy all but the most fastidious connoisseurs before the end of the seventeenth century.

The great age of European lacquer begins in the late seventeenth century. French, English, Dutch, German, and Italian craftsmen had discovered a means of imitating the fine hard polish of the Oriental substance; they had, moreover, learned to decorate it in a freer style with designs which expressed the European's strange vision of the infinitely remote and exotic lands of the East. At Versailles and in some of the greater English country mansions whole rooms were lined with lacquer panels, of European or Oriental origin, and great Chinese, or Chinese style, cabinets mounted on ponderous gilt baroque

stands became an essential feature in the furnishing of any truly grand house. Towards the end of the century the art of lacquering was also practised by amateurs in France and England, where many a young lady spent her leisure hours "japanning" any piece of furniture – large or small – on which she could lay her hands. Changing in style with the times, lacquer furniture maintained a fluctuating popularity until after the end of the eighteenth century. During this period lacquer was produced in England, France, Germany, Holland, and Italy, and the furniture made in each of these countries must be considered separately.

English lacquer. Great square cabinets were probably the most popular objects of Oriental lacquer to be imported into England in the late seventeenth century and seem to have been the most widely imitated. Such cabinets have two doors, with elaborate metal hinges and lock guards, which open to reveal numerous small drawers and sometimes a central cupboard. Oriental examples can be recognized not only by the style of their gilt decorations but also by their metal work. In China such cabinets stood on the floor or on simple hardwood tables, but in England they were mounted on grandiose frames intended to set off their importance and make them harmonize with the other furniture of the rooms in which they were kept (Plate 127A). The cabinets themselves usually had black or imitation tortoiseshell backgrounds, but red ones were also made, especially for export to Spain and Portugal, where this colour was preferred. England was indeed famous for its red lacquer, which Bonanni, in 1720, declared to be of a colour more beautiful than coral – "si bello che vince il colore di corallo".

The stands for these cabinets were either gilt or, more usually, silvered and varnished so that they appeared to be gilt (it seems probable that most of the surviving silver stands were originally varnished in this manner). In the 1660s and 1670s the stands normally had four legs, sometimes crowned with *putti* or blackamoors, joined by aprons which were richly carved with figures, and swags of fruit and flowers, amid a profusion of swirling baroque scrolls. Towards the end of the century the design changed and stands were often made with three or four legs along the front connected by aprons carved in a lighter style. These stands usually had stretchers which were provided with round plates on which vases of Oriental porcelain might be placed. The top of the cabinet was sometimes enriched with a cresting carved in the same style as the stand, but was more often left free to serve as a table for more Oriental vases. In the second decade of the eighteenth century the heavy baroque stand went out of fashion and was replaced by a lighter and more elegant frame with cabriole legs, but these, alas, were seldom able to support the weight of the cabinets, and relatively few have survived. At about the same time a few craftsmen departed from the traditional shape of the cabinet itself, giving it a shallow domed top.

When John Evelyn visited Mr Bohun in 1682, he noted that his "whole house is a cabinet of all ellegancies, especially Indian; in the hall are contrivances of Japan skreens instead of wainscot. . . . The landskips of these skreens represent the manner of living and Country of the Chinese." Many other such rooms, including those at Burghley House, Hampton Court Palace, and Chatsworth, are mentioned in diaries of the period. One such room has actually survived at Drayton in Northamptonshire. It is a small closet off the State Bedroom which has been lined with ten panels cut from a Chinese Coromandel screen.

Lacquer was at this date used for decorating nearly all articles of household furniture. In 1697 a company of "The Patentees for Lacquering after the manner of Japan" (founded in 1694) was offering for sale "Cabinets, secretaires, tables, stands, looking-glasses, tea-tables and chimney pieces". Other lacquer objects made at the same time included chests of drawers, corner cupboards, clock-cases, day-beds, chairs, and small articles for the dressing- or writing-table. These pieces were usually made of deal, oak, or pear-tree wood on patterns which were identical with those of contemporary walnut furniture. The lacquer grounds were of various colours: black, vermilion, tortoiseshell, dark green (particularly popular for clock-cases), yellow

or blue, and the gilt decorations represented a wide variety of fanciful scenes copied from genuine Oriental objects, taken from Stalker and Parker's treatise or invented by the craftsman. Stalker and Parker claimed to have derived their designs from Oriental cabinets, somewhat ingenuously confessing that they had, perhaps, "helped them a little in their proportions where they were lame or defective, and made them more pleasant, yet altogether as Antick". In the late 1720s chinoiserie decorations suffered a temporary eclipse and were replaced by flowers painted in naturalistic colours on a light ground.

In the late seventeenth century much lacquering, or "japanning" as it was called, was executed by amateurs who applied themselves to the difficult art with a will, and the principal book on the subject, Stalker and Parker's *Treatise of Japaning and Varnishing* (Fig. 37), seems to have been designed mainly for a public of amateurs. By the 1680s the art of lacquering had taken its place among the genteel occupations suitable for young ladies, and in 1689 Edmund Verney permitted his daughter to take this extra subject at school, telling her: "I find you have a desire to learn to Japan, as you call it, and I approve of it; and so I shall of anything that is good and virtuous, therefore learn in God's name all Good Things, and I will willingly be at the charge so far as I am able – though they come from Jappan and from never so farr and Looke of an Indian Hue and colour, for I admire all accomplishments that will render you considerable and Lovely in the sight of God and man. . . ." That the art of lacquering – like water-colour painting in a later age – rendered young ladies lovely in the sight of man is, perhaps, confirmed by Dryden's lines to Clarinda (1687) in which he remarks that:

Sometimes you curious *Landskips* represent
And arch 'em o'er with gilded *Firmament*:
Then in *Japan* some *rural Cottage* paint.

Nothing was sacred to these eager japanners, who seized on any object that could be decorated with Chinese figures. Sometimes they may have applied themselves to specially prepared furniture, but often they were content to lacquer ordinary walnut pieces. Nor was

FIG. 37. A design for a comb-box, from Stalker and Parker's *Treatise of Japaning and Varnishing*, 1688

this pastime reserved for the young. Mrs Pendarves (later Mrs Delany) declared in 1729: "Lady Sun(derland) is very busy about japanning: I will perfect myself in the art against I make you (Mrs Anne Granville) a visit, and bring materials with me." "Everyone is mad about Japan work," she later remarked, "I hope to be a dab at it. . . ." Even the Prime Minister's wife, Lady Walpole, applied herself to the art and it was to her that John Taylor dedicated his book: *The Method of Learning to draw in perspective. . . . Likewise a new and Curious Method of Japanning . . . so as to imitate China and to make black or gilt Japan-ware as Beautiful and Light as any brought from the East Indies* (1732). Horace Walpole preserved an example of his mother's handiwork – a cabinet – at Strawberry Hill.

Amateur japanners, it may be guessed, kept alive the vogue for lacquer furniture which, after a temporary eclipse, returned to fashion in the late 1740s. In 1749 Mrs Montagu – the Queen of the Blues – remarked that "sick of Grecian elegance and symmetry, or Gothic

grandeur and magnificence, we must all seek the barbarous gaudy *gout* of the Chinese. . . . You will wonder I should condemn a taste I have complied with, but in trifles I shall always conform to the fashion." Accordingly, three years later she ordered a suite of japanned furniture, in full conformity with the chinoiserie taste of the moment, from Mr (presumably William) Linnell; some of it is now at Came House, Dorset. This revived fashion for chinoiserie did not, however, escape the attention of critics, who poked merciless fun at the Mandarins and Mandarinesses of England. One of them, an anonymous writer in *The Connoisseur* (1755), gave a graphic description of a fop's dressing-table: "But the toilet most excited my admiration; where I found everything was intended to be agreeable to the Chinese taste. A lookingglass, inclosed in a whimsical frame of Chinese paling, stood upon a Japan table, over which was spread a coverlid of the finest Chints. I could not but observe a number of boxes of different sizes, which were all of them Japan, and lay regularly disposed on the table. I had the curiosity to examine the contents of several: in one I found lip-salve, in another a roll of pig-tail, and in another the ladies black sticking plaister. . . ."

Many of the mid-eighteenth-century examples of English lacquer furniture were wholly designed in the Chinese taste, with fret-work doors and square legs carved with a similar fretted pattern. The cabinet and table made by Linnell for Mrs Montague were in this style. Thomas Chippendale intended many of his designs for chinoiserie furniture (Plate 128B), especially the standing shelves designed for the display of Chinese porcelain, to be embellished with japanned decorations, but furniture in the current "French" style, notably commodes and bureaux, were also decorated with panels of European or Oriental lacquer. A commode in the possession of the Shaftesbury Estates Company (Plate 128A) has a veneer of Chinese lacquer on the front and is painted with English japan on the top and sides. Many smaller articles, like those on the fop's dressing-table, were prettily lacquered with gay Oriental figures. Snuff-boxes and other trifles in lacquer were produced by John Taylor at Birmingham, who seems to have made a fortune out of this trade.

After about 1765 the fashion for lacquer furniture began to decline in England, though the art of japanning remained a popular amusement among amateurs, for whom such books were written as *The Ladies Amusement or the Whole art of Japanning made easy*. This valuable manual, illustrated with numerous plates after Pillement and others, advised its readers of the liberties which might be taken with Indian or Chinese designs, "for in these is often seen a Butterfly supporting an Elephant, or things equally absurd". Among amateur japanners of the late eighteenth century, the King's third daughter, Princess Elizabeth, was surely one of the most passionate and decorated two whole rooms at Frogmore, one with scarlet and gold and the other with black and gold lacquer. Perhaps it was from her that George IV acquired his fondness for chinoiserie which was largely responsible for the third revival in lacquer furniture towards the end of the century.

Although lacquer does not seem to have been used to furnish the famous Chinese drawing-room at Carlton House, it was freely applied to furniture in the Sheraton and Hepplewhite styles during the last decades of the eighteenth century. In 1804 the Prince Regent sent Dr James Grant to collect lacquer and other orientalia in the Far East, and the panels with which he returned were probably among those used to adorn the furniture of the Royal Pavilion at Brighton. Other pieces of furniture at Brighton were painted with English lacquer, which also enjoyed a popular vogue, especially for the decoration of cabinets and bookcases. The design of such furniture conformed with the usual Regency patterns. Amateurs continued their labours for some time, and even as late as 1828 Mrs Arbuthnot, the Duke of Wellington's friend, could be found "making up a japan cabinet I painted last year. . . . The cabinet is really excessively pretty." Lacquer seems finally to have gone out of fashion in the late 1830s, but at the Great Exhibition of 1851 Messrs W. W. Eloure were showing various papier mâché "imitations of japan work. Cabinet doors, and folding fire screens in imitation of India-Japan, ornamented with gold and inlaid with mother of pearl".

Dutch and Flemish lacquer. Of all European countries, Holland was perhaps the most closely connected with the trade in Oriental lacquer during the seventeenth century. Before the middle of the century Dutch merchants had, indeed, established a virtual monopoly in the export of lacquer from Japan. Nevertheless, a need seems to have been felt for a greater supply of lacquer than the trading ships could provide, and early in the century craftsmen set themselves to the imitation of lacquer in Holland. The style of their work, which was of much higher quality than contemporary English work, may be judged from a casket decorated with birds perching among flowering plants, in the Rijksmuseum (Plate 126c). Dutch *Japanish Verlaker* – japanners – attained great skill in the second half of the century and produced some of the closest imitations of Oriental lacquer made in Europe. It has even been suggested, with some probability if no evidence, that Japanese lacquer workers were brought to Europe to school the Dutch craftsmen. Late seventeenth- and early eighteenth-century Dutch lacquer was usually somewhat sparsely decorated with chinoiserie designs in gold on a lustrous black ground. A good though miniature example is provided by the doll's house cupboard in the Rijksmuseum (Plate 126B). Lacquer furniture decorated in colours on a cream or white ground was also popular in Holland. In style, Dutch lacquer furniture was similar to the walnut and marquetry pieces produced at the same time. Cabinets – whether Dutch or Oriental – which were as fashionable here as in England, seem usually to have been mounted on scroll-shaped legs which were also lacquered (Fig. 38) rather than on gilt baroque stands. In the

FIG. 38. Cabinet and stand by Gerard Dagly, *c.* 1700

early eighteenth century lacquer with chinoiserie decorations was most notably applied to large chests of drawers and wardrobes. Good examples are in the collection of Graf van Aldenburg-Bentinck at Schloss Amerongen.

Spa, the watering place near Aix-la-Chapelle which was for centuries the Mecca of European hypochondriacs, was the principal centre for the production of lacquer in Flanders. A lacquer industry grew up here in the late seventeenth century and its products,

known as *bois de Spa*, soon became famous throughout Europe. All manner of large and small objects from snuff-boxes to corner cupboards were produced at Spa in the eighteenth century and purchased by those who came from far and wide to drink the famous medicinal waters or gamble in the scarcely less celebrated gaming-rooms. *Bois de Spa* was usually decorated with gilt chinoiserie motifs on a black ground. Spa was, moreover, the birthplace of one of the foremost masters of European lacquer, Gerard Dagly (*fl.* 1665–1714), who, though he executed most of his work in Germany, may fitly find mention here.

Gerard Dagly was born at Spa some time before 1665 and went at a fairly early age to seek his fortune in Germany. In 1687 he was appointed *Kammerkünstler* to the Kurfürst of Brandenburg and in this capacity was principally employed in producing lacquer work in the Chinese manner. In 1696 he lacquered four black and gold coin cabinets, one of which is at Berlin – a fine piece of work mounted on a stand with twist-turned legs on which small floral motifs are picked out in gold. Another cabinet, formerly in the Hohenzollernmuseum at Berlin, was painted with a lovely prospect of mountains on the outside of the doors and dancing Chinese figures on the inside. He also produced very elegant lacquer furniture decorated in gold on a white ground; a good example of this type of his work is, or was, in the Schloss Monbijou. Other works by Gerard Dagly are to be found in the Royal Palace at Stockholm and the museum at Brunswick. He attained wide renown in Germany, and when the Kurfürstin of Hanover sent her Prussian son-in-law a clock-case she felt bound to remark that "it comes from England but Dagly makes much better ones". On the accession of Frederick William I to the Prussian throne in 1713 Dagly was among the many Court employees who were promptly dismissed. He seems to have returned to Spa. For a full account of Gerard Dagly see *The Connoisseur*, 1934, vol. XCV, pp. 14 ff.

French lacquer. In the earlier seventeenth century Oriental lacquer was imported into France from Portugal and it was to the

Portuguese stalls at the Foire de Saint Germain that Scarron directed the connoisseur's attention for "beaux ouvrages de vernis". After the foundation of the French *Compagnie des Indes* in 1664 importations were considerably increased and the vogue for lacquer furniture reached a new height. The French attitude to lacquer at this date and during much of the eighteenth century was, however, somewhat unusual. Lacquer seems to have been prized more for its rarity and commercial value than for its style of decoration. Louis XIV evidently thought it in no way incongruous to have silver plaques engraved with the Labours of Hercules applied to a Chinese cabinet.

As we have already mentioned, lacquer was made in France early in the seventeenth century, though no examples of it are known to have survived. Nor is much known of the productions of "Les Sieurs Langlois, père et fils", who, in 1691, were making "cabinets et paravents façon de la Chine, d'une beauté singulière" with ormolu mounts which were expressly intended to make them harmonize with other pieces of furniture in the great salons. Like the English, the French occasionally sent furniture out to the East to be lacquered, and it seems probable that Mme de Sévigné's writing-desk in the Musée Carnavalet at Paris, which is of a normal French pattern embellished with Oriental lacquer, is one such piece.

In 1713, or shortly after, the Flemish craftsman Jacques Dagly (b. 1655, d. 1728), brother of Gerard Dagly (see p. 286), settled in France and obtained a licence to "establish . . . a factory to make varnish", but this paint seems to have been primarily intended for application to textiles. Not until some years later did French craftsmen succeed in producing lacquer of conspicuously high quality. Between 1733 and 1740 the Duc de Bourbon was maintaining at Chantilly an atelier where, according to a contemporary, lacquer furniture was produced in such close imitation of Chinese models that even the greatest connoisseurs had been deceived by it. Meanwhile, the brothers Martin – Guillaume (d. 1749), Etienne Simon (d. 1770), Julien (d. 1782), and Robert (*fl.* 1706–65) – had perfect-

ed the lacquer to which they gave their name, *vernis Martin*. Letters patent, issued in 1730 and renewed in 1744, granted them the exclusive monopoly of "toutes sortes d'ouvrages en relief et dans le goût du japon ou de la Chine" for twenty years. They did not, however, confine themselves to decorations in the Chinese style, and many of the best examples of *vernis Martin* are either without any ornament or simply stippled with gold specks – like the sedan chair made for the Montmorency children and now in the Musée de Cluny at Paris. *Vernis Martin* was produced in several colours, of which the green was the most celebrated. Among the larger works undertaken by the Martins were the decorative paintings in several of the *petits appartements* at Versailles. They were also much patronized by Mme de Pompadour.

Lacquer was extensively used for the decoration of furniture in the Louis XV period, but, whether of French or Oriental make, was usually treated in a cavalier fashion. The curling tendrils of rococo mounts were allowed to clamber over it and obscure much of the pattern, while handles were screwed on without any regard for the figures on the design. On a chest of drawers in the Wallace Collection – the so-called Marriage coffer of Marie Antoinette (Plate 129c) – the exquisite panels of Japanese lacquer on the front and those of French lacquer at the sides are half hidden behind bronze fret-work grilles. Here the lacquer seems to have been considered purely as a precious substance which could add the final touch of opulence to a magnificent piece of furniture. The famous *ébéniste B. V. R. B.* (recently identified as Bernard van Risen Burgh) treated lacquer, which he very frequently used, in a much more respectful manner. But he, too, chose to emphasize the beauty of its glossy substance rather than the charm of its gilt decoration (Plate 129A).

With the development of the Louis XVI style this attitude seems to have changed. The greater rigidity of the furniture produced in this period enabled *ébénistes* to show off panels of fine Japanese lacquer much more effectively. Indeed, objects like the secretaire by P. Garnier in the Louvre (Plate 129B) seem to have been conceived mainly as frames for exquisite panels of lacquer. Much of the furniture bought in Paris for George IV and now at Windsor Castle is of this type. French lacquer was applied to various types of furniture, but perhaps most notably to these pieces which could not easily have been veneered with Oriental lacquer. In the Victoria and Albert Museum there is an exceptionally fine harpsichord made by Pascal Taskin in Paris in 1786 and painted on the lid and sides with engaging little gilt Chinamen dancing on a puce ground (Plate 130A).

The taste for lacquer does not seem to have survived the French Revolution. Lacquer furniture clearly had no place amid the Greek and Egyptian style objects of an Empire salon. It may perhaps have been used after the Restoration by those cabinet-makers who reverted to the production of furniture in the Louis XVI style.

German lacquer. As miniature versions of Versailles spring up outside the capitals of nearly every German principality in the late seventeenth and early eighteenth centuries, so the taste of the French court spread throughout Germany. Lacquer consequently became an accepted, indeed an all but essential feature of palatial decoration. Rooms panelled from floor to ceiling in lacquer and provided with whole suites of furniture to match were installed in many a stately *Schloss* and *Residenz*. Small lacquer objects were also produced in Germany before the end of the seventeenth century, and a pattern book of the period gives designs for tobacco boxes and trays to be painted with Chinese scenes from the plates in John Nieuhoff's *Embassy*.

In the last two decades of the seventeenth century the Flemish craftsman Gerard Dagly (see p. 286) was producing exceptionally fine lacquer at Berlin. He attracted several imitators who were probably responsible for some of the pieces of lacquer furniture which are, or were until the war, in the Charlottenburg Palace. These included a table, a writing-table, and a harpsichord decorated with little chinoiserie figures on a white ground – the harpsichord is mounted on a base painted with purely European floral motifs. Among Dagly's named followers was Martin Schnell, who worked with him from 1703 to 1709 and

then returned to his native town of Dresden, where he produced some splendid examples of lacquer work besides providing designs for porcelain during the subsequent three decades. Schnell is best known for his small lacquered trays – the finest of their kind – of which there are good specimens in the Residenzschloss at Dresden. He was also responsible for furniture and decorations in Schloss Pillnitz – the *Japanische Palais* – which contains one of his most notable works, an English style fall-front secretaire.

Lacquer furniture was also made at Augsburg in the first half of the eighteenth century, and a notable example of it is provided by a clock now in the Bayerisches Nationalmuseum at Munich. The clock itself is of a baroque architectural pattern with columns at the corners, and stands on a low table. All the woodwork, including the columns, is decorated with chinoiserie motifs in colours on a white ground, and a painted mandarin squats on the stretcher of the stand. Another centre for the production of lacquer was Hamburg, where a very fine harpsichord was made in 1732 (Plate 130B).

One of the earliest of the several surviving German lacquer rooms was that built for the Kurfürst Lothar Franz von Schönborn in the Neue Residenz at Bamberg in about 1700. It is decorated with a series of panels of black and gold lacquer set amidst a profusion of carved swags, and contains a handsome lacquer cabinet, similar to those popular in England but without doors, set on very short legs to serve as a chest of drawers. Between 1714 and 1722 one Johann Jakob Saenger painted the magnificent lacquer-room in Schloss Ludwigsburg, at Württemburg, with chinoiserie birds and dragons sporting in a garden which is decorated with baroque urns. In the Pagodenburg Pavilion in the Nymphenburg gardens there is a room decorated with red and black lacquer panels of 1718. The Residenz at Munich had a bedroom of about the same date which was adorned with large panels of lacquer each painted with three or four chinoiserie scenes placed inconsequentially one above another. At Schloss Brühl, near Cologne, there is an exceptionally attractive *Indianische Lackkabinet* painted for

A Queen Anne walnut bureau-desk with bracket feet and matched veneers. The drawers and flap have ovolo moulding, crossbanding, and herring-bone borders. *Mallet & Son.*

PLATE 97

A Queen Anne walnut bureau-bookcase, showing burr veneers on the drawer fronts and fine quartered veneers on the doors. The bureau has double half-round mouldings. *Leonard Wyburd.*

PLATE 98

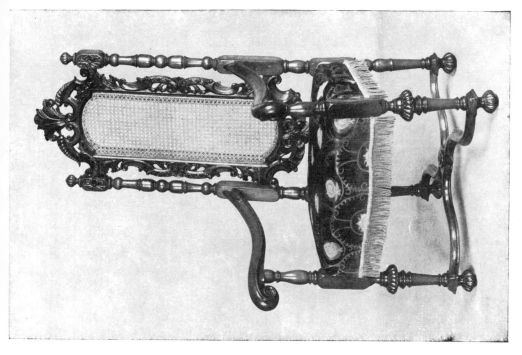

(B) A William and Mary walnut chair. In comparison with (A) note the turned front legs (with mushroom swell), the curved stretchers, and the upward lift of the cresting rail. *Mallet & Son.*

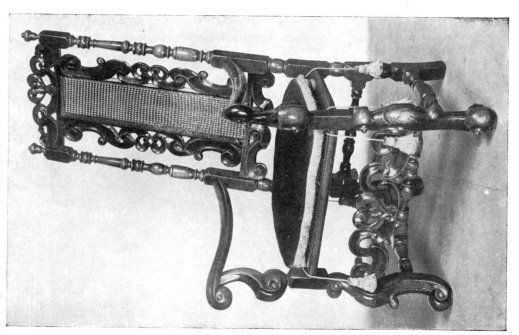

(A) A late Charles II walnut chair. The front legs and arm supports have the scroll design popular after 1675. Other chairs of this type had twist-turned uprights. *Mallet & Son.*

PLATE 99

(B) A Queen Anne upholstered wing chair. The front legs are in cabriole form and have turned stretchers. *Jetley.*

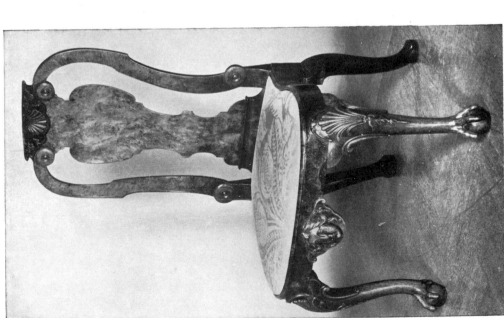

(A) An early eighteenth-century walnut bended-back chair with solid splat, cabriole legs and ball-and-claw feet. *Hotchr.*

PLATE 100

(A) An early Georgian walnut tallboy. Note the canted corners, partly fluted and reeded, the cabriole form of the feet, and the ovolo mouldings on the drawers; *c.* 1730. *Mrs L. G. G. Ramsey Collection.*

(B) A William and Mary walnut clock case with the front veneered in seaweed marquetry; *c.* 1699. *Frank Partridge.*

PLATE 101

A William and Mary walnut side table with inverted cup legs, narrow X-shape stretcher with central finial, and
curved apron piece; *c.* 1690. *Hotspur.*

PLATE 102

A Queen Anne walnut card table with cabriole legs and ball-and-claw feet. *Mallet & Son.*

PLATE 103

A carved and gilt side table in the William Kent style, with marble top. *Jetley.*

PLATE 104

A mahogany clothes press, *c.* 1760, showing effective use of figure and carving. *H. W. Keil.*

PLATE 105

Late eighteenth-century mahogany bureau-bookcase, with Hepplewhite-style feet and apron piece. *Stuart & Turner.*

PLATE 106

Late eighteenth-century mahogany break-front bookcase with fine matched veneers and Gothic glazing bars. *Mallet & Son.*

PLATE 107

A Chippendale period mahogany desk with cock-beaded drawers and carved gilt handles. *Frank Partridge & Sons.*

PLATE 108

(A) A mahogany chair in the Chinese style, *c.* 1755. *Hotspur.*

(B) An Adam period mahogany upholstered armchair in the French style, showing a late version of the cabriole leg, and scroll feet. *M. Harris.*

(C) A shield-back mahogany elbow chair of the Hepplewhite period, with a wheat-ear design. *M. Harris.*

(D) A mahogany Sheraton chair, showing the wide cresting rail and forward-splaying front legs. *M. Harris.*

PLATE 109

A serpentine-fronted mahogany commode of the Chippendale period showing French influence in the carving on the canted

PLATE 110

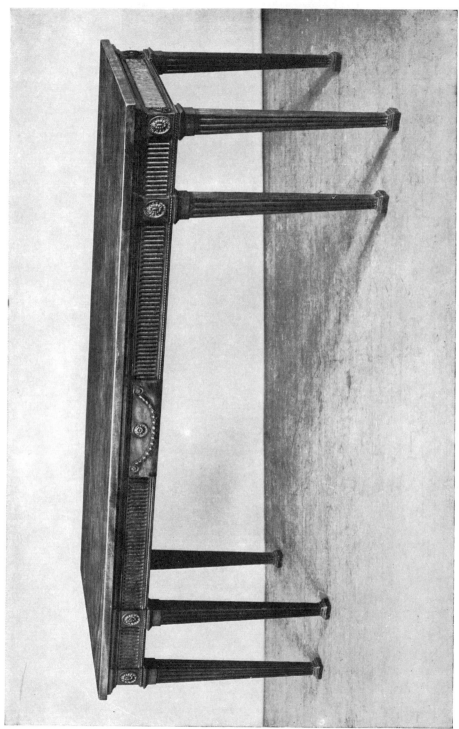

An Adam style mahogany side table with classical treatment. This kind of table with a classical pedestal at each end was the forerunner of the sideboard. *Leonard Knight.*

PLATE 111

A mahogany table cabinet, *c.* 1760, with Chinese fret gallery, curved stiles on the doors, and cock-beaded drawer. *Hotspur.*

PLATE 112

A Chippendale period mahogany tea table. The legs are fluted in ogee section, and the frieze has matched curl veneers. *Stuart & Turner.*

PLATE 113

(A) A mahogany drum table associated with the Sheraton and Regency periods, with characteristic jutting handles. *H. Blairman & Sons, Ltd.*

(B) A Chippendale period mahogany tripod table with hinged "pie-crust" top, cabriole legs, and ball-and-claw feet. *Leonard Knight.*

PLATE 114

An example of the smaller serpentine- and break-front mahogany sideboard of the Sheraton period. The turned and reeded legs are characteristic Sheraton designs. *Frank Partridge & Sons.*

PLATE 115

(A) Wood settle with painted panels and encrusted decoration, *c.* 1845. *Victoria and Albert Museum, London.*

(B) Oak table, designed by Philip Webb, 1859. *Dr D. C. Wren, Kelmscott Manor.*

PLATE 116

(A) Oak cabinet, designed by A. W. N. Pugin, and made by J. G. Crace, 1851. *Victoria and Albert Museum, London.*

(B) Satinwood cabinet inlaid with Wedgwood plaques; Wright and Mansfield, 1867. *Victoria and Albert Museum, London.*

PLATE 117

(A) Ebonized wood cabinet with metal fittings, designed by E. W. Godwin, made by William Watt, *c.* 1877. *Victoria and Albert Museum, London.*

(B) Adjustable chair, made by Morris, Marshall, Faulkner and Co., *c.* 1866. *Mrs Tozer.*

(C) Painted and ebonized mahogany cabinet, designed by T. E. Collcutt, made by Collinson and Lock, 1871. *Victoria and Albert Museum, London.*

PLATE 118

Carved and painted wood washstand with marble and silver fittings,
designed by William Burges, 1880. *Victoria and Albert Museum, London.*

PLATE 119

(A) Satinwood cabinet, designed by A. H. Mackmur-do for the Century Guild, made by E. Goodall and Co., Manchester, 1886. *William Morris Gallery, Walthamstow.*

(B) Painted oak cabinet, designed by C. R. Ashbee, 1889. *Abbotsholme School, Rocester, Staffs.*

(C) Escritoire decorated with sycamore marquetry, designed by George Jack for Morris and Co., 1893. *Victoria and Albert Museum, London.*

PLATE 120

(A) Oak dresser inlaid with ebony and bleached mahogany, designed by W. R. Lethaby, 1900. *Victoria and Albert Museum, London.*

(B) Oak chair, designed by C. F. A. Voysey, made by ...ory and Co., 1899. *...ictoria and Albert Museum, London.*

(C) Cabinet inlaid with ivory, designed by Ernest Gimson for Kenton and Co., 1890.

(D) Oak chair, designed by Charles Rennie Mackintosh, *c.* 1900. *Glasgow School of Art.*

PLATE 121

Oak wardrobe inlaid with pewter and ebony, designed by Ambrose Heal, made by Heal and Son, 1900.
Lt-Col. C. G. Price.

PLATE 122

Kedleston Hall, Derbyshire. The dining-room by Robert Adam, showing candle-stands, sconces, knife-cases, and fire-screen.

PLATE 123

(B) Late eighteenth-century plate-pail with bras
handle, and cellaret of octagonal form. *Mallet & Son*

(A) Mahogany Canterbury music-stand, *c.* 1810.
Hotspur.

(C) Mahogany tripod pole
screen with needlework panel,
c. 1750. *Frank Partridge & Sons.*

(D) Late eighteenth-century mahogany tripod basin-
stand with shelf and drawer and soap receptacle.
Hotspur.

PLATE 124

(A) Late eighteenth-century mahogany night-table with tray top. *Hotspur.*

(B) Late seventeenth-century brass-bound casket on a George II period carved mahogany stand. *Private Collection.*

(C) Walnut bureau or secretaire on turned legs with curved stretchers and finial, *c.* 1690. *The Hart Collection.*

PLATE 125

(A) English lacquer cabinet, *c.* 1620. *Victoria and Albert Museum, London.*

(B) Dutch lacquer doll's house cupboard, *c.* 1700. *Rijksmuseum, Amsterdam.*

(C) Dutch lacquer casket, early seventeenth century. *Rijksmuseum, Amsterdam.*

PLATE 126

(A) English lacquer cabinet on carved gilt stand, c. 1670. *H. Blairman and Sons Ltd.*

(B) English lacquer secretaire, early eighteenth century. *William Rockhill Nelson Gallery of Art, Kansas City.*

(C) English lacquer commode, first half of the eighteenth century. *Collection of Sir James and Lady Horlick.*

PLATE 127

(A) Commode decorated with a veneer of Oriental lacquer on the front and English japan on sides and borders, *c.* 1765. *The Shaftesbury Estates Co.*

(B) English lacquer display cabinet, probably by Thomas Chippendale, *c.* 1750. *Collection of Sir James and Lady Horlick.*

(C) English green lacquer bracket clock by Thomas Windmills, early eighteenth century. *Moniz Galvãos Collection, Lisbon.*

(D) English lacquer cabinet, *c.* 1830. *H. Blairman and Sons Ltd.*

PLATE 128

the Kurfürst Clemens August between 1720 and 1730 with gay, brightly coloured chinoiserie scenes on a cream ground. A later example of a lacquer-room is that in Schloss Nymphenburg, decorated by J. Hörringer in 1764.

Frederick the Great, an admirer of Oriental lacquer (he gave his sister Amelia the Coromandel panels for a room which is still in the Neue Residenz at Bayreuth), also patronized European lacquer workers, acquiring them in much the same way as he gathered literary lions to adorn his court at Potsdam. In 1747 he commissioned Jean Alexandre Martin, the son of Robert Martin, to decorate the *Blumenkammer* – otherwise known as the *Voltaire Zimmer* – at Sanssouci: and some twenty years later he again lured him away from Paris, appointing him *vernisseur du Roy*. In 1765 Frederick commissioned another French lacquer worker, Sebastian Chevalier, to decorate an oval room in the Neuen Palais at Potsdam. He then encouraged Jean Guérin the son-in-law of Johann Heinrich Stobwasser, who had for long been providing lacquered canes for Prussian army officers, to set up a lacquer industry at Berlin. Stobwasser himself remained at Brunswick, where he produced the many exquisite snuff-boxes, canes, etc., which won him European renown. He also developed the art of lacquering on papier mâché in the English manner. As late as the 1790s the Stobwasser workshop at Brunswick was producing little lacquered objects and small pieces of furniture painted in lacquer with classical figures and motifs.

Italian lacquer. Venice was already famous for its lacquer in 1668 when Maximilien Misson remarked that, "La Lacque de Venise est comme on sçait en réputation: il y en a à toute sorte de prix." Unfortunately no examples dating from this early period can be identified, but a few later seventeenth-century pieces show that the Venetian craftsmen produced both black and vermilion lacquer decorated with gold chinoiserie subjects. A notable example of this style of work is the writing-table formerly in the collection of the late Mr Arthur Spender of Venice and exhibited in the 1938 exhibition of Venetian lacquer. As in other parts of Europe, lacquer was applied to furniture of normal design, but the Venetian attempts to imitate the substance of Oriental lacquer were rather more perfunctory. The base of white wood or *cirmolo* (a type of pine from Cadore) was treated with successive layers of gesso, each of which was polished, gold paint was then applied to the raised decorations, which were generally reserved for the main surfaces, and other portions were painted in tempera, the whole piece was then given a coat of transparent varnish. In the early decades of the eighteenth century the Venetians excelled in the production of dark-green lacquer with gold decorations, of which the finest examples are probably those now in the Palazzo Rezzonico at Venice (Plate 131B).

Venetian eighteenth-century lacquer was the work of the guild of *depentori*, which had, in earlier centuries, included all painters, but from which the painters of pictures (*pittori*) had split away in 1691. Iseppo Tosello, who is mentioned in a document of 1729 as a *depentor alla chinese*, was one of many who produced lacquer, but his name has survived only by chance, and we know of none of his productions. It is also possible that some of the great *settecento* painters occasionally worked in lacquer, and a pair of doors in the Palazzo Rezzonico (Plate 132) has tentatively been ascribed to G. B. Tiepolo, though not, it must be admitted, with much confidence. Whether the work of modest *depentori* or of *pittori*, Venetian lacquer of the eighteenth century is distinguished for its gay colours no less than for the accomplishment and frivolity of its decorations. Early in the century chinoiserie figures in gold or colours on a ground of black, green, red, or yellow seem to have been the invariable rule, but a preference was later shown for floral motifs or little landscapes painted in the style of Zais or Zuccarelli. All manner of objects were thus decorated – from great *armadi* and secretaires (known as *bureaux trumeaux*) to little boxes, fans, trays, brushes, and small ornaments in the form of animals. Perhaps the most satisfying of all non-chinoiserie examples of Venetian lacquer is the harpsichord in the Museo Civico at Treviso (Plate 131A), sprinkled with exquisitely painted little bunches of mid-summer flowers on a brown ground. Similar floral decorations were very happily applied to the undulating surfaces of chests of drawers. These pieces, like so many examples of later Italian furniture, show how the craftsmen concentrated their attention on the decoration rather than the structure, and their joinery is often of poor quality.

Venetian lacquer of the type already described seems to have been reserved for the grander palaces and villas. But a cheaper substitute was also made in the eighteenth century and enjoyed a very wide popularity in Venetia. Works of this type were painted all over in a uniform colour, then decorated with cut-out prints produced for this purpose by the Remondini of Bassano and others. The prints were painted or gilded and the whole surface covered with a coat of transparent varnish. Furniture decorated in this manner looks from a distance as if it were lacquered, but can easily be distinguished on close inspection. Despite their somewhat rustic character, the decorations themselves are often attractive. Most of the surviving examples of furniture decorated with this *lacca contrafatta* are *armadi*, chests of drawers, or secretaires.

Although Venetian lacquer was the most famous, lacquer furniture was made in several other Italian towns in the eighteenth century. At Florence lacquer was made for Cosimo III with ingredients brought back from the Far East, and good examples of Genoese and Lucchese lacquer, little inferior to Venetian, are also recorded. During the second quarter of the eighteenth century there was a vogue for rooms wholly panelled with lacquer in Piedmont. The most notable is that designed by the great architect, Filippo Juvarra, in the Palazzo Reale at Turin. Records show that sixty of the panels in this room were bought at Rome in 1732, but the decorative scheme was not completed until 1736, when one Pietro Massia provided further panels in the same style. Painted with birds and flowers in red and gold, the panels are set within elegant gilded rococo scrolls on a vermilion wall and produce a remarkable impression of sumptuous grandeur. A somewhat simpler room executed at about the same time or a little later was in the Villa Vachetti at Gerbido, near Turin, and is now at the Rockhill Nelson Gallery of Art at Kansas City, Missouri. Here the panels are red and gold set against walls of celadon green. The designs used for the panels of both rooms reveal an Italian interpretation of chinoiserie.

The use of lacquer declined in Italy towards the end of the eighteenth century. Much fake eighteenth-century lacquer was, however, produced after the revival of interest in later Italian furniture in the 1920s.

Lacquer made in other countries. Lacquer furniture was produced in several other European countries during the eighteenth century. The Portuguese produced a certain amount, the most notable pieces being secretaire cabinets, usually with gold chinoiserie decorations on a red ground, containing shrines in their upper parts. But both Portugal and Spain imported English lacquer during the first half of the eighteenth century. Giles Grendy, the maker of a red and gold day-bed now in the Victoria and Albert Museum, seems to have specialized in catering for this export trade.

Surprisingly little lacquer seems to have been produced in Austria. A few examples of Viennese lacquer are in the Museum für angewandte Kunst at Vienna. Lacquer was also produced to a limited extent in Denmark and Sweden.

French

FROM 1500 TO THE REVOLUTION

To collectors and connoisseurs in England French furniture, and particularly that of the late seventeenth and eighteenth centuries, presents certain problems. Firstly, the range of materials employed on the embellishment of certain pieces extends far beyond wood; secondly, the wealth and admixture of motifs, veneers, inlays, and the profusion of metal ornament are often alien to English taste; and thirdly, the number of craftsmen to be found in Great Britain who are competent to appreciate and repair French furniture is still so small that valuable pieces are in constant danger of being badly treated with the wrong substances.

From the historical point of view, the various periods and styles have become so bound up with the reigns of the three Kings of France, Louis XIV, XV, and XVI, that it is frequently difficult to realize that these styles and fashions in designing and decorating furniture often began long before, and ended long after, the rather arbitrary dates connected with them.

Nevertheless, the regnal divisions into which the subject has been conventionally split up have their uses in indicating the approximate style and period in which a piece of furniture may have been produced, and they have therefore been retained for the purposes of this study.

THE RENAISSANCE AND SEVENTEENTH CENTURY

In spite of the large amount of furniture which was made in France in the sixteenth century, not very much has come down to us, and what has is almost completely undocumented. We are thus very seldom in a position to say when a given piece of furniture was made, for whom it was made, or by whom. A great deal of research has at one time or another been devoted to distinguishing between the various provincial centres where furniture was produced in the sixteenth century – whether, for instance, at Lyons or in the *Île de France* – but the theories put forward are not very convincing, and it is safer to assume that most of the best furniture was made in Paris and probably for the Court, and that such known provincial pieces are variations on a style existing at the central point.

By far the largest number of such pieces to have survived are made of walnut, usually elaborately carved. The most common piece is the dresser (*q.v.*), but tables, chairs, beds, cabinets, and cupboards are also found. These take various forms and are often covered with carving, the dressers particularly receiving the most elaborate treatment in this respect.

The carving is usually in the Italian style, imported into France by the wars of Francis I, and the engravings of Du Cerceau and others were important in distributing knowledge of the motifs which were employed at Court. The absence of any local inspiration for design meant that the Court style became predominantly Italian in character, as did the architecture of the period also. Often a decorative motif on a piece of French Renaissance furniture is taken direct from a known Italian engraving or plaquette. It is also important to remember that furniture at this date was intended easily to be taken to pieces and moved about (hence the word *mobilier*), and this can almost always be done with the pieces which we are considering.

With the more secure ways of life which came in with the seventeenth century, furniture began to become more stable, and thus the opportunities for decoration more appropriate. But France sadly lacked the craftsmen to carry out the elaborate inlays which were the fashion in Italy and which were favoured

at Court after the arrival of Marie de Médicis
as Queen of Henri IV. Up to the foundation
of the Gobelins factory in 1663, therefore, the
period is one of constant infiltration of foreign
craftsmen, from whom, of course, Frenchmen
in the next generation were to learn much.

The engravings of Adam Bosse, however,
show how sparsely furnished the rooms of the
prosperous members of society were, and do
not show the elaborate cabinets and *bureaux*
which have come down to us, and which must
have been not only rare luxury products but
almost entirely made by foreign craftsmen.
These often incorporate elaborate carving,
marquetry, and also intricate mirror arrangements in the interiors. They are usually designated as French in the absence of knowledge as to who actually made them, but it
seems likely that Italian and Flemish craftsmen must have been largely involved. The
taste for the Italian style was further extended
by the rise to power of Cardinal Mazarin,
himself an Italian, whose personality dominated the French scene through the minority
of Louis XIV.

THE LOUIS XIV PERIOD

Le Roi Soleil came to the throne in 1643 at the
age of five. It can be well imagined therefore
that the artistic characteristics which have become associated with his name did not come
into existence at once. Indeed, the changes of
style in furniture did not begin to appear until
the King's majority and the establishment
under Colbert of that great organization for
the production of objects of art, the *Manufacture Royale des Meubles de la Couronne* at Gobelins in 1662. This foundation, as much an act
of policy as everything else, was intended to
co-ordinate control of all the applied arts in
France to the glorification of the Crown and
the State, and under its brilliant first director,
Charles Le Brun, achieved its aim at least for
a generation. The establishment of the *Manufacture* is, in fact, the cardinal event in the
history of French decoration and furnishing,
for it was under its aegis that all the foreign
and native talent and experience which had
been employed for two generations previously
was incorporated and made to serve as a
foundation for the establishment of new

standards of taste and craftsmanship, this time
wholy French in style and intended to serve a
national aim.

As is well known, the first great task awaiting the *Manufacture* soon after its foundation
was the decoration and furnishing of the new
palace at Versailles, which was to become the
cradle of French decorative taste for the centuries to come, and to demand an output of
lavish expenditure unparalleled in history. It
is only the more unfortunate that almost all
the furniture produced during the first years
of the *Manufacture*'s existence has disappeared,
and even the celebrated silver furnishings of
Versailles were later all melted down to provide bullion to support the various wars of the
later years of the reign.

What remains, then, must be regarded as
only a fraction of what once existed, and by
far the most important series of furnishings
which have come down to us are the productions of the workshop of André Charles Boulle
(1642–1732), the most celebrated cabinet-
maker of the whole period, and the great
exponent of the marquetry which bears
his name. Boulle was trained under foreign
influences, and his achievement lies in his
adaptation of foreign techniques to his own
original ideas, and to the combination of a
new monumentality and elegance of design
with a perfection of craftsmanship in a very
complicated and elaborate technique.

In his early years he almost certainly worked in wood marquetry, following designs similar to those produced in Italy and Flanders,
and to this was sometimes added the use of
small amounts of metal for decorative purposes; but the intricate marquetry of tortoiseshell and brass with which we associate his
name is, to all intents and purposes, an individual creation.

The principal innovations in furniture design during the period were first of all in the
chest of drawers, or *commode*. It can be said to
date from about 1700, though it probably did
not come into general use until rather later.
The other main type to be evolved was that of
the writing-table, or *bureau*. This first begins
to appear before the turn of the century in the
form of a table-top with two sets of drawers
beneath, flanking a knee-hole, and later took

on its more usual form of a flat table with shallow drawers under the top.

The demand for Boulle furniture diminished in the middle years of Louis XV's reign, but returned in full force in the last quarter of the eighteenth century, when the neo-classical style came into its own. Often the same designs, motifs, and techniques were used, and it is sometimes extremely difficult to be certain in which period a piece was made when the quality of marquetry and bronze are the same.

It must be remembered that all furniture at this time, and indeed later, was made in order to harmonize with the rich carving and painted decoration of the setting for which it was intended, and designs which may appear over-elaborate when isolated would often seem at home in their original positions.

THE LOUIS XV PERIOD

When considering the characteristics of anything connected with what has become known as the Louis XV or rococo styles in France, it is important to remember that their evolution was gradual, and indeed began some years before the date when the *Grande Monarque* actually died. The genesis of rococo design can, in fact, be traced back to the last years of the seventeenth century, and the engraved compositions of an artist such as Jean Berain provide ample evidence of the new feeling which finally usurped the classicism, formality, and monumentality exemplified by the creation of Versailles.

It was, however, the removal in 1715 of the central personality in the formal and centralized Court and Government, and the succession of a small boy, with the consequent reign of a pleasure-loving Regent, which provided the circumstances for the change in taste which can be so readily observed in the years which immediately followed. It is, however, a mistake to isolate the style of the Regency with what followed and to try to identify objects as belonging to the *Style Régence* unless they can be proved to have been created within the years 1715–25. It is much more sensible to regard the products of these years as the first-fruits of what was to become the *Style Louis Quinze* proper, and the absence of

documentary evidence providing the necessary dating makes this course more prudent.

The new style inevitably, however, received its first impetus from the Court of the Regent Orléans at the Palais Royal, and almost at once there is a lightness to be observed in interior decoration and furniture. The relaxation of the rigid etiquette of the Louis XIV's Court, caused apartments, and therefore furnishings, to be smaller and less formal, and gave opportunities for lightness, fantasy, and colour impossible twenty years before. Gradually, therefore, the heavy monumental furnishings made for Versailles at the Gobelins gave place to smaller, more elegantly contrived pieces suited to the lighter and more informal atmosphere of the new type of interior decoration.

More and more, furniture was adapted and decorated to harmonize with wall decoration, which, being also almost exclusively of wood, created a harmony of design and craftsmanship never equalled outside France. The Boulle technique passed temporarily out of fashion, though the *atelier* continued to produce furniture throughout the eighteenth century and Boulle himself did not die until 1732. The new taste favoured elaborate wood marquetry overlaid with delicate gilt-bronze (ormolu) mounts, and during the period the combination of these types of decoration reached a perfection of design and execution only surpassed by the subsequent period. The opening up of trade routes with the Far East brought a large number of Oriental goods on to the home market, with the result that a taste for lacquer was created, both applied in the original from China or Japan, or imitated in France and applied locally. The most celebrated imitation of lacquer was produced by the four Martin brothers, who patented their "Vernis Martin" in 1730 and again in 1744. A number of Oriental woods useful for marquetry were also imported, notably kingwood and, later, purple-wood, which was used very widely. Other woods used for veneering and inlaying were tulip-wood, hazelwood, satinwood, casuarina, and sycamore, often mixed in elaborate floral, pictorial, or geometrical designs, framed with fillets of box and holly. The range of design was very wide and soon began to be used with remarkable skill.

Apart from relaxation in formality, the earlier part of the reign did not witness any very startling change in the actual types of furniture used, and the forms prevalent under Louis XIV still lingered on, particularly the wardrobe, or *armoire*, and the chest of drawers. The former, however, while keeping its monumental proportions, was often constructed of plain wood undecorated except for carving; while the latter underwent a number of changes in design. The main tendency was for straight lines and flat surfaces to become curved and *bombé*, and for the functional purposes of the piece to be concealed beneath the general scheme of decoration. The two commodes on Plate 134 show these characteristics well, the divisions between the drawers being invisible beneath the designs of the marquetry and mounts. There is, however, not one straight line to be found on either piece. The extreme rococo tendency towards asymmetry did affect mounts and *bronzes d'ameublement*, though not for very long.

The latter part of the reign, with its increase of luxury expenditure, saw the creation of a large number of new types of furniture, mainly small, and nearly always intended for female use. The *secrétaire à abattant* began to appear in the fifties, also the *bonheur du jour*, the *bureau-toilette*, work-tables and other pieces, while commodes, chairs, sofas, and *bronzes d'ameublement* of all kinds were produced in large quantities. This is the period also of the greatest *ébénistes*, including Oeben, Riesener, Leleu, Dubois, and others, and it is in the sixties that foreign craftsmen, particularly Germans, began to arrive in Paris to seek their fortunes, usually finding them, in the profusion of demands for furniture. Madame de Pompadour played a large part in forming the taste of her time by her constant purchases of objects of all kinds and the *Livre-Journal* of Lazare Duvaux, from whom she bought so much, gives a very clear picture of how much money was spent. She was not responsible for the introduction of the neo-classic Louis XVI style, however, as she died in 1764, and many of the portraits of her, even just before her death, show her surrounded by furniture, particularly in the advanced Louis XV style.

A word should be said here about the actual creation of a piece of eighteenth-century French furniture. First of all a designer, sometimes the *ébéniste* himself, though sometimes equally a decorator, produced a drawing of the piece. This was then made by an *ébéniste* in wood, veneered and inlaid if necessary. Mounts and fittings were then produced by a sculptor and a *fondeur*, and if required were gilded by a *doreur*, thus often involving members of three craft guilds and two artist designers. Occasionally painters were also involved, thus bringing in yet another guild. When one considers the number of different craftsmen employed on a single piece of furniture, the harmony and perfection so often achieved are the more remarkable.

THE LOUIS XVI PERIOD

As is well known, the main characteristic of the Louis XVI style is the return to classical forms and motifs after the exuberance and fantasy of the rococo. This tendency begins to make itself felt at least twenty years before Louis XV died, and it is indeed this particular regnal division which is so misleading. Between 1750 and 1774 a very large amount of furniture was made incorporating classical tendencies, and it is most important to realize this when attempting in any way to date a given piece of furniture from stylistic evidence. The change of taste was very gradual, as the artistic writings of the time show, and, as elsewhere in Europe, was motivated very largely by the discovery of the Roman remains in the old Kingdom at Naples, at Pompeii, and Herculaneum. The subsequent interest in classical subjects aroused by such writers as de Caylus, and the contempt poured on the rococo also played its part. From a purely stylistic point of view it can be said that the Louis XV style proper had worked itself out, and the return to classicism came therefore as a necessary reaction, and antidote. In spite of the enormous expenditure on furniture in the seventies, both by the Court and private patrons, no very striking innovations took place in actual furniture design. The main feature of the reign was, however, the perfecting of processes used hitherto to an unprecedented degree. This is particularly the case with ormolu, which has never attained before or since such refinement as it did at the hands of Gouthière, Thomire, Forestier (*q.v.*), and others. Apart from the elaboration and refinement of marquetry, plain woods, and particularly mahogany, begin to be used as veneers, and the rather controversial embellishment of furniture with porcelain begins to make its appearance. The large number of German *ébénistes* increased, of which Weisweiler and Beneman (*q.v.*) were the most celebrated. The work of Georges Jacob in making chairs also reached its highest peak, and Boulle furniture became fashionable again and was produced in large quantities.

The influence of Queen Marie Antoinette on the taste and craftsmanship of her time, with particular reference to furniture, has often been stressed. It is true that she employed extensively and lavishly the incomparable craftsmen whom she found in Paris on her arrival as Dauphine, but, apart from this expenditure and a liking for beautiful objects, it is doubtful if she possessed any real understanding of the visual arts, and she certainly was no rival of Madame de Pompadour in this respect. It has also been suggested that her nationality attracted many German-born craftsmen to Paris, but, in fact, the influx of foreign workmen had started and become an established fact long before there was any question of her being Queen of France. She undoubtedly did employ Riesner, Weisweiler, and Beneman very extensively, but chiefly because of their qualities as craftsmen, and only then on the advice of the *Garde Meuble*.

CABINET-MAKERS AND CRAFTSMEN

Beneman, Jean Guillaume. German by birth. Came to Paris *c.* 1784, but seems to have been trained prior to this date, when he is first mentioned as being employed by the *Garde Meuble de la Couronne*. In 1785 he became a *maître-ébéniste* but without going through the normal formalities. His employment by the Crown coincides with the disfavour into which Riesner fell owing to his high charges. Beneman made a large amount of furniture for Queen Marie Antoinette and the Court, and

was employed also to repair earlier furniture in the possession of the Crown. He collaborated with all the leading craftsmen of the time, including Boizot and Thomire, but his furniture retains usually a rather heavy Teutonic appearance. He seems to have specialized in making commodes and *meubles d'entre deux*. He was officially employed under the Directoire and Consulate, but his name disappears about 1804. He used the stamp:

G·BENEMAN

Boulle, André Charles. Born in Paris in 1642, the son of a carpenter, and died there in 1732. His training was very varied, and he appears to have worked at different times as a painter, architect, engraver, and bronze worker, as well as an *ébéniste* of importance. He worked as an *artisan libre* from 1664 onwards, but in 1672 he was appointed *ébéniste du Roi* through the intervention of Colbert. From this time he worked continually for the Crown and established a workshop in which he employed about twenty assistants, who were constantly at work providing furniture for the new palace at Versailles.

Boulle did not invent the marquetry which has become associated with his name, the combination of metal and tortoiseshell in the form of an inlay being used since the sixteenth century in Italy and Flanders; but he did evolve a particular type which he adapted to the taste and requirements of the time.

He possessed a large collection of old master drawings from which he may easily have drawn inspiration for his mounts. His ingenuity as a designer was very great, as can be seen from a series of engravings which he published, and from a number of his drawings which still exist. But throughout his career his actual style changed very little. He never signed his work and his authenticated productions are very rare. The only pieces which can be said definitely to be by him are two commodes originally made for the Grand Trianon and now in the palace at Versailles.

Caffiéri, Jacques. Born 1678, son of Philippe Caffiéri, and came from a large family of sculptors. Became one of the chief exponents of the rococo style in France and was employed extensively by the Crown at Versailles, Fontainebleau, and elsewhere. He also occasionally worked as a portrait sculptor. He often signed his bronzes with his surname only, and his chief works are to be found at Versailles, the Louvre, Paris, the Wallace Collection, and elsewhere. Died 1755.

His son, Philippe Caffiéri, was also a sculptor of note, and occasionally collaborated with his father in bronze work.

Carlin, Martin. Very little is known about the life of Carlin. His place and date of birth are unknown. He died in Paris in 1785. He is first mentioned in 1763 and became a *maître-ébéniste* in 1766. He worked for Queen Marie Antoinette and the Royal Family, but it is uncertain whether he received an official appointment with the *Garde Meuble*. He supplied a large amount of furniture through the dealer Darnault.

Carlin was a most refined and delicate craftsman. He worked particularly in lacquer and with plaques of Sèvres porcelain.

Cressent, Charles. Born at Amiens in 1685, the son of François Cressent, a sculptor, and grandson of a cabinet-maker. He was apprenticed to his father, but probably learned cabinet-making from his grandfather. He became a member of the *Académie de Saint Luc* in Paris in 1714, and in 1719 married the daughter of Joseph Poitou, an *ébéniste* working for the Duc d'Orleans, and he also at this time was given commissions by the Regent. After this seems officially to have abandoned sculpture for *ébénisterie*, but he was several times prosecuted by the *Corporations des Fondeurs* and *Doreurs* for casting and gilding his own mounts. In 1723 he was actually forbidden by law to produce mounts not made by a qualified *fondeur*. This type of litigation was repeated from time to time throughout his life.

The Regent died in 1723, but Cressent continued service with his son Louis, Duc d'Orleans, as late as 1743, on the Duc's retirement from public life. He also worked for important private patrons in France, and carried out important commissions for King John V of Portugal and the Elector Karl Albert of Bavaria. With the profits from the sale of his furniture Cressent formed an impressive collection of works of art, which he three times tried unsuccessfully to sell owing to financial difficulties. The first sale in 1748 was, in fact, withdrawn owing to fresh orders received for work. Cressent died in 1768.

His best work is never stamped. Towards the end of his life he did use the stamp: C. CRESSENT, but it never appears on pieces of very great quality, and should always be treated with suspicion in view of his fame in his lifetime and later. The identification of his work therefore depends almost entirely on documents and tradition.

Dubois, Jacques and Réné. Jacques Dubois was born in Paris c. 1693. He became a *maître-ébéniste* in 1742, and was elected a *juré* of the guild in 1752. He specialized in the use of lacquer both Oriental and European, and died in 1763, the same year as Oeben, whose stock he helped to value. He used the stamp:

IDUBOIS

After his death his widow carried on the business with the help of her sons, the most celebrated of which was Réné (born 1757), who always used his father's stamp. He became a *maître* in 1754, was much patronized by Marie Antoinette, both before and after she became Queen, and also by the Court and nobility. He worked mainly in the Louis XVI style and eventually abandoned cabinet-making for selling furniture. He died in 1799.

Forestier, Étienne Jean and Pierre Auguste (1755–1838). Two brothers, the sons of Étienne Forestier (c. 1712–68). All three were *fondeurs-ciseleurs*, and after the father's death his widow carried on the business with her two sons. Their names constantly occur in the Royal accounts, and they are known to have worked at Versailles and Compiègne, and for the Prince de Condé. After the Revolution, Pierre Auguste established a successful workshop, supplying furniture, *bronzes d'ameublement*, etc.

Gaudreau, Antoine Robert. One of the most celebrated of the known *ébénistes* of the Louis XV period. He was born c. 1680, and was in the Royal service from 1726. He became a *syndic* of the *ébénistes* guild in 1744, and worked for the Crown and also later for Madame de Pompadour. Among his most important works are a medal cabinet and a commode, which were made for the King's private apartments at Versailles. On the latter he collaborated with J. Caffiéri, who signed the bronzes. It is now in the Wallace Collection (Plate 134). He died in 1751.

Gouthière, Pierre. The most celebrated of the late eighteenth-century *fondeurs-ciseleurs-doreurs*. Born at Bar-sur-Aube in 1732, the son of a saddler. He is known to have been in Paris by 1758, where he became a *maître-doreur*. He was employed by the Crown between 1769 and 1777, but after the latter date his name disappears from the Royal accounts. He had, however, a large number of private patrons, including the Duc d'Aumont and the Duchesse de Mazarin. He also worked for Madame du Barry at Louveciennes. He was constantly in difficulties financially, and his patrons were almost always behind with their payments. In 1788 he was declared bankrupt, and he never completely recovered, although he lived on until 1813, and died in poverty. Gouthière's signed works are exceedingly rare and can be supplemented by a few which are able to be identified by documents. Almost all bronzes of any quality of the Louis XVI period have been attributed to him, and it is only recently that the increased study of the Royal accounts have revealed the names of other *ciseleurs-doreurs*, who seem to have been his equals in many cases, even though we know little more than their names.

The attributions of bronzes to Gouthière on grounds of style alone should be made with great caution.

Jacob, Georges. Was born in Burgundy in 1739 and died in Paris in 1814. Little is known of his early life, but he was the founder of a long line of makers of furniture who specialized in the production of chairs. He is thus usually thought of as *menuisier*, although he did carry out some works in the *ébéniste*'s technique. He was made a *maître-ébéniste* in 1765 and carried on his business in his own name until 1796, when he sold it to his two sons, Georges II and François Honoré. On the former's death in 1803 the latter took the name of Jacob-Desmalter and joined with his

father until the latter's death in 1814. He then carried on the business himself until 1824, and his son continued it up to 1847. The first Jacob was a craftsman with an extraordinary wealth of invention, and his designs for chairs are of the utmost elegance, but are also pleasantly varied so that they do not often repeat themselves. He also made a number of beds, which show the same qualities. He worked extensively for the Crown and in consequence was denounced at the Revolution, in spite of his friendship with the painter Jacques Louis David. His own work is usually stamped:

G ✦ I A C O B

Leleu, Jean François. Born in Paris in 1729, and died there in 1807. Trained under J. F. Oeben (*q.v.*), after whose death in 1763 he hoped to be chosen to take over the direction of the workshop. Oeben's widow's choice, however, fell on Riesener, whom she married, and Leleu never became reconciled to this. He became a *maître-ébéniste* in 1764, and worked both for the Court and for private patrons. He was also employed by Queen Marie Antoinette, Madame du Barry, and the Prince de Condé. He became successively *juré* and *deputé* of the *ébénistes*' guild, and in 1780 went into partnership with his son-in-law, C. A. Stadler, who succeeded to the business in 1792.

Leleu was a very versatile craftsman and worked in a number of styles; he seems to have been as equally at home in the advanced rococo as with the most severe neo-classic, and he also used Boulle marquetry and Sèvres porcelain to decorate his furniture. He used the stamp:

J·F·LELEU

Oeben, Jean François. Born *c.* 1720, the son of a postmaster at Ebern in Franconia. He married in Paris in 1749, but we do not know the date of his arrival there from Germany. He entered the workshop of C. J. Boulle in 1751, and on the latter's death in 1754 Oeben succeeded him as *ébéniste du Roi* and was granted lodgings at the Gobelins, whence he moved in 1756 to the Arsenal. While working for

Boulle, he was also employed by Madame de Pompadour and others, and after his move to the Gobelins he began in 1760 his most celebrated work – the monumental *Bureau du Roi Louis XV*, which, however, was not completed until after his death. Riesener, who was one of his assistants, succeeding him at the Arsenal, together with Leleu. Oeben also collaborated with Carlin and with P. Caffieri. He died bankrupt in Paris in 1763, when his widow carried on the business until 1767, when she married Riesener, who then carried on the business in his own name.

Oeben only became a *maître-ébéniste* in 1761 under special circumstances, having worked for the Crown for so long. His stamp on furniture is therefore rare, and when found it is more probable that the piece was made by Riesener before he took over the business, as Madame Oeben continued to use her husband's stamp while running the workshop herself.

After Cressent and Gaudreau, Oeben is the most celebrated *ébéniste* of Louis XV's reign. He specialized in elaborately planned pieces, fitted with secret drawers and complicated locking devices, but, owing to the amount of furniture which must necessarily have left his workshop unstamped, his work cannot easily be identified. He made extensive use of elaborate marquetry and parquetry.

Riesener, Jean Henri. The most famous *ébéniste* of the eighteenth century in France. Born at Gladbeck, near Essen, in 1734, but it is not known when he came to Paris. He entered Oeben's workshop at the Gobelins about 1754, and moved with him to the Arsenal. At Oeben's death he was selected by the widow to take over the workshop, and he married her in 1768, the year when he became a *maître-ébéniste*. In 1769 Riesener completed the great *Bureau du Roi Louis XV*, which his predecessor had left unfinished (*see under* Oeben). In 1774 he succeeded Joubert as *ébéniste du Roi*, and for ten years enjoyed the patronage of the Crown to a hitherto unprecedented degree, as expenditure during that decade was higher than it had ever been. His wife died in 1776, and seven years later he remarried, but unhappily.

After 1784 his prosperity began to decline

and he was made drastically to reduce his prices by the Treasury. It was at this time that Beneman to a certain extent succeeded him in the favour of the Court. Queen Marie Antoinette, however, seems to have remained faithful to Riesener throughout, for she continued to order furniture from him right up to the Revolution.

He continued in business during and after the Revolution, but never actually reinstated himself. He seems to have retired in 1801 and died in Paris in 1806.

Riesener's stamp appears frequently on furniture of all kinds in the Louis XVI period, but it is probable that works bearing Oeben's stamp may also be by him, and made while he was working for Madame Oeben before their marriage (*see* Oeben).

J·H·RIESENER

He was the most versatile, and became the most accomplished, *ébéniste* of the time, and certainly deserved the success he obtained. His work covers nearly all types of furniture in use, and he specialized in highly elaborate marquetry, mostly in geometrical designs.

Thomire, Pierre Philippe. Born 1751, the son of a *ciseleur*. Worked under the sculptors Pajou and Houdon. In 1783 entered the service of the Sèvres porcelain factory. From 1784 onwards he was frequently employed by the Crown to make mounts for furniture, and often collaborated with G. Beneman. In 1785 he was commissioned by the City of Paris to make a candelabra celebrating the American Declaration of Independence for presentation to General Lafayette (now in the Louvre).

He built up a large workshop, which is said to have employed as many as eight hundred workmen. He worked extensively under the Empire and received a number of important commissions from the Emperor himself. The firm was known as *Thomire-Dutherne et Cie*, and Thomire himself retired from business in 1823 but did not die until 1843. It by no means always follows that bronzes stamped with the name Thomire are by Pierre Philippe himself. More probably they are products of the workshop.

Roentgen, David. Born near Frankfurt in

1743, the son of the cabinet-maker Abraham Roentgen, whose workshop at Neuwied on the Rhine he took over in 1772 and developed considerably. He first came to Paris in 1774 and received patronage from Queen Marie Antoinette. This established his reputation, which, by the time of his second visit in 1779, had increased considerably, and he established a depot in Paris for selling furniture, as he did also in Berlin and Vienna. He travelled widely and visited Italy, Flanders, and Russia, where he sold a great deal of furniture to the Empress Catherine II.

In 1780 he was compelled to become a *maître-ébéniste* in Paris, using the stamp: DAVID, and in 1791 was made Court furnisher to King Frederick William II at Berlin. He was ruined by the Revolution, and his depot in Paris was confiscated. His workshop at Neuwied was also overrun by Republican troops. He returned there in 1802, however, and died in 1807.

Roentgen specialized in furniture veneered with extremely elaborate pictorial marquetry and fitted with complicated mechanical devices, concealing secret drawers and multiple locks. His furniture was mostly made outside France and is seldom stamped.

Weisweiler, Adam. Born *c.* 1750 at Neuweid and trained in the workshop of Roentgen (*q.v.*). Established in Paris before 1777. Became a *maître-ébéniste* in 1778. He worked for the dealer Daguerre and, through him, supplied a large amount of furniture for the Royal palaces, and particularly for Queen Marie Antoinette at Saint Cloud. He was a good business man, and in consequence survived the Revolution safely, and was employed under the Empire, during which time he executed commissions for Queen Hortense. He was still in business in 1810. He used the stamp:

A·WEISWEILER

Italian

When collectors turn their attention to Italian furniture they must be prepared to look for qualities different from those they see in the work of the great French and English cabinet-makers. At first they may well be disappointed to find that relatively few pieces show the delicacy and lightness or the superb standards of finished craftsmanship of a Riesener or a Chippendale. Charming boudoir pieces were made in northern Italy, and especially in Venice, during the late eighteenth and early nineteenth centuries, but the Italian craftsman's talents were shown less in the creation of such intimate little objects than in furnishing the sumptuous saloons of great palaces in Rome, Naples, Florence, Genoa, and Turin. Richly carved, lavishly gilded, and upholstered in the most opulent Lucchese silks and Genoese cut velvets, the furniture which stands beneath the vast frescoed ceilings of Italian *palazzi* is outstanding for its air of grandiose magnificence and princely splendour.

It must be admitted that Italian furniture does not show the consistently high finish of French or English work. In fact, its construction is sometimes distinctly shoddy. Yet this is not to deny it high quality in other respects. Generally speaking, the Italian cabinet-maker seems to have been more interested in the design and decoration than the finish of his work, and he seldom bestowed much attention on those parts which were not intended to be seen – the backs of cupboards or the insides of drawers, for example. But such slipshod methods did not always, or everywhere, prevail. In the Renaissance period painters gave as much care to the decoration of a *cassone* as to a great fresco, and in the seventeenth and eighteenth centuries several sculptors carved chairs, console tables, and frames with the same accomplished freedom of hand as they lavished on independent statues. Fantastic arm-chairs by Brustolon (Plate 141A), inlaid tables and cabinets by Piffetti (Plate 142B) and lacquer furniture exquisitely painted by a host of anonymous Venetian artists, reveal impeccable standards of craftsmanship in their design and decoration, even if they occasionally appear somewhat rough and ready in their carpentry.

To speak of Italian furniture as we speak of English or French furniture is, however, somewhat rash. The regional differences which are familiar to every student of Italian painting and sculpture are no less marked in the minor arts and crafts. Although Venice is but 90 miles from Bologna and Bologna no more than 60 miles from Florence, radical differences of style distinguish the furniture produced in these three centres until well into the eighteenth century. The Renaissance which was born in Florence did not affect the Venetian painter, let alone the cabinet-maker, for some fifty years. Similarly, the neo-classical style appeared in Venice long after it had been accepted in Rome and Turin. Moreover, different types of wood requiring different treatment were available in the various districts and helped to produce regional styles. In the south olive wood was often used. In Lombardy and Tuscany, where a rich variety of nut and fruit-tree woods were available, much inlaid furniture was made, while at Venice, where the finer types of wood seem to have been difficult to obtain, a considerable proportion of the furniture was lacquered. We also find that much of the furniture made at Lucca and Genoa was designed mainly to show off the magnificent textiles those cities produced. In general, however, walnut was the wood most widely used in all districts from the middle of the sixteenth century until the late eighteenth century. Mahogany never achieved the same popularity in Italy as in England or France, probably for economic reasons

The foreign influences which played an important part in Italian furniture designed after the middle of the seventeenth century were felt more forcibly in some regions than in others. French influence was, of course, exerted throughout the peninsula as in the rest of Europe, but was at its strongest in Liguria and Piedmont. Venice was subject to a limited German and Austrian influence, while the Kingdom of the Two Sicilies produced furniture which owes a certain debt to Spain. After the middle of the eighteenth century the English pattern books of Thomas Chippendale and later of Sheraton and Hepplewhite circulated in Italy and seem to have been copied by cabinet-makers in many districts. With the Napoleonic conquests the Empire style became generally accepted and, for the first time in history, a general pattern was imposed on the furniture production of the whole country.

In view of the considerable local differences in style, it is hardly surprising that no wholly satisfactory comprehensive account of Italian furniture has ever been written. Books have appeared on the furniture of various districts and periods, but Italian furniture as a whole awaits a historian. Bearing local variations of style in mind, it is, however, possible to sketch the broad outlines of this fascinating and neglected subject.

Renaissance furniture. Very few examples of Italian furniture can securely be dated before the beginning of the fifteenth century, the most important exceptions being two thirteenth-century X stools in the Cathedral at Perugia and the Austrian Museum at Vienna. Similar X chairs and some three-legged stools of a type used in the fourteenth century are also known, but as these objects retained their popularity until well into the sixteenth century, it is seldom possible to date them with any precision. A few *cassoni* and *armadi* decorated with somewhat primitive paintings or flamboyant Gothic carving have been preserved, but most of them derive from northern districts, where the Gothic style lingered on after it had given way to the Renaissance in Tuscany. The history of Italian furniture therefore begins with the Renaissance. Yet to study the furniture even of this period we must supplement our knowledge of existing pieces by reference to paintings. The *prie-dieu* at which the Virgin kneels or the desk at which St Jerome studies in *quattrocento* paintings give us a better idea of the furniture of the period than any surviving examples. And it should be pointed out that the furniture which appears in these pictures acquired a sentimental charm which appealed very strongly to late nineteenth-century collectors, for whom unscrupulous craftsmen produced a large number of similar works.

To judge from paintings, the majority of *quattrocento* furniture was very unpretentious and much of it was usually covered with linen or glowing Turkish carpets. It is, perhaps, significant that the most notable pieces of furniture to survive from this period are *cassoni* and *armadi*, which were seldom muffled in drapery and were thus more richly decorated than the simple tables and *credenze*. *Cassoni* were often painted by the leading artists of the time, while *armadi* were treated in an architecturally monumental fashion. Indeed, these magnificent cupboards often have the same harmonious proportions and noble simplicity of decoration as the façades and interiors of early Renaissance palaces and churches. As the early Renaissance developed into the high Renaissance and, finally, the mannerist style, so furniture-makers enriched their designs, making greater use of figurative carving. Mid-sixteenth-century refectory tables have their legs carved with mythological and human figures, and the *armadio* is often provided with a broken pediment and low relief panels on its doors. At about the same time Bolognese craftsmen began to apply brass handles in the form of cherub or satyr heads to their furniture and maintained this style of decoration throughout the first half of the seventeenth century.

Baroque and rococo furniture. Early in the seventeenth century the nervous angular mannerist line broke into the easy baroque flame in painting, sculpture, and architecture. The baroque style also affected the cabinet-maker, who now developed a greater feeling for three-dimensional form. The top line of the *armadio* swells into a ponderous curve and the front occasionally bellies out in the centre. Richness is supplied by the free use of bulging balusters, by inlays of rare woods, or, on the most sumptuously palatial furniture, by panels of semi-precious stones. At the same time chairs began to take on a more grandiose appearance, with carved and gilded backs which sometimes erupted into a profusion of scrolls

at the sides; they were often upholstered in rich velvets or damasks and were made more comfortable. As the century advanced the use of gilding on all articles of furniture increased, and further tones of opulence were added to the palace interior by the introduction of objects of mainly decorative value, such as console tables and *reggivasi*. The consoles were particularly magnificent, with vast slabs of rare and brilliantly coloured marble supported by human figures, mythological creatures, or gigantic seashells. Furniture made in England to the designs of William Kent in the early eighteenth century reveals the influence of these works.

Whereas Italian furniture had influenced the rest of Europe in the sixteenth and, to a less marked degree, the seventeenth centuries, it began to succumb to French influence before the beginning of the eighteenth century. Indeed, French models were so widely copied in Italy that one is tempted to classify Italian furniture in French periods from *Régence* to *Empire*. Eighteenth-century Italian furniture was also affected by a change in the manner of living; for now the daily life of the palace moved from the great saloons on the *piano nobile* to the smaller rooms on the mezzanine floor, which demanded more delicate furnishings, usually derived from French models.

As the rococo style won general acceptance in the second quarter of the eighteenth century, broken *rocaille* decorations took the place of the great sweeping baroque scrolls, and figures vanished from all furniture except the *giridoni* and *reggivasi*. The new patterns which came from France were not slavishly copied, however. Venetian craftsmen, who were surely the most accomplished furniture-makers in early eighteenth-century Italy, indulged their flair for fantasy by exaggerating the French designs, giving *bombé* commodes more absurdly bellying fronts, extending the sofa to an inordinate length and applying a greater profusion of rococo twists and turns to the woodwork. Elsewhere, especially in Rome and Naples, French patterns seem to have been toned down and made more rigid.

Neo-classical and Empire furniture. The neo-classical style which began to influence painters and sculptors in Rome soon after the middle of the eighteenth century hardly affected the cabinet-maker until the 1770s; though some furniture made in the 'sixties reveals a greater simplicity of line and severity of decoration. In Rome classical term figures and winged lions began to reappear as the supports of console tables, but the force of the new style was most strongly felt in Piedmont, where it was employed by G. M. Bonzanigo. Only the Venetians remained obstinately rococo, treating the new patterns from France in a distinctly frivolous fashion. But France was not the only country to influence the Italian cabinet-maker, for in the second half of the eighteenth century English designs were also copied, and the *salone* might include examples of Italian Chippendale and Sheraton furniture jostling Italian Louis XV and Louis XVI pieces.

The greater rigidity of Louis XVI designs paved the way for the acceptance of the Empire style, which spread over Italy almost as fast and inexorably as the advance of Napoleon's armies. In the early 1800s the slender columns, the Egyptian heads, and the elegant ormolu mounts which had over-run the salons of Paris began to appear also in the great Italian *palazzi*. Much of this furniture was imported from France, but many pieces of high quality were made in Florence and Lucca under the guidance of French *ébénistes*. Moreover, the Empire style long outlived the Napoleonic regime in Italy. It was very successfully used by Pelagio Pelagi to decorate the throne room of the Palazzo Reale in Turin in the late 1830s: and, even in the 1840s, one Peters, an English cabinet-maker, was producing somewhat ponderous Empire furniture at Genoa. In Naples palatial furniture of a late Empire character, in what may be termed the Bourbon style, was made to fill the vast apartments of Capodimonte and Caserta in the late 'thirties and early 'forties. The revival of old patterns had, however, begun, and soon cabinet-makers were everywhere busy producing solid *credenze*, *armadi*, and *cassoni* to furnish houses in the "Dantesque" fashion. Italy still rejoices in numerous craftsmen of great ability who work in a tradition which has been handed on from master to *garzone* for generations. The collector should, perhaps, be warned that many of them devote themselves to making furniture on old designs and with old materials.

CABINET-MAKERS

Relatively few pieces of Italian furniture can be attributed to named cabinet-makers or designers. Household accounts of many great palaces record payments to the *intagliatori*, or wood carvers, and the same palaces are filled with furniture. But the task of associating the names of the craftsmen with the works they produced still remains to be done. Indeed, it is not until we reach the last years of the seventeenth century that it becomes possible to ascribe any individual pieces of Italian furniture to known craftsmen. Of these the most notable was probably the Venetian Andrea Brustolon (1662–1732), a highly accomplished sculptor in wood who executed the superbly fantastic chairs, *reggivasi*, and *giridoni* supported by blackamoors, carved out of ebony and box wood, now in the Palazzo Rezzonico at Venice (Pate 141A). Chairs decorated with *putti*, and a grandiose looking-glass frame in the Palazzo Rezzonico have been attributed to Antonio Corradini (1668–1752), a Venetian sculptor who otherwise worked in marble. The notable Genoese wood sculptor Anton Maria Maragliano (1664–1739) may well have been responsible for some of the finely carved console tables supported by mythological creations in the palaces of his native city. Another Genoese sculptor, Domenico Parodi (1668–1740), carved a magnificent looking-glass frame for the Palazzo Balbi, now Reale (Plate 141D), at Genoa and may also have produced console tables. All these artists were, however, *intagliatori* rather than cabinet-makers, and their works are distinguished primarily for the quality of the carving. Moreover, they are all, with the exception of Brustolon, better known for their statues than for their furniture.

Early in the eighteenth century the architect to the court of Savoy, Filippo Juvarra (1676–1736), designed furniture (Plate 142C, Fig. 39) for the great palaces he built in and near Turin (see *The Connoisseur*, November 1957). A little later the same court was served by Pietro Piffetti (*c.* 1700–77), the first Italian to merit the title of *ébéniste*. He was a brilliant craftsman, but his furniture looks fussy and over-elaborate, as he tended to sacrifice the general design to the details, concentrating on the exquisite panels of inlaid ebony, ivory, and mother-of-pearl with which they were

FIG. 39. Design by Filippo Juvarra for a console table for the King of Savoy

embellished (Plate 142B). Francesco Ladatte (1706–87), a notable sculptor in bronze, supplied the fine mounts for some of Piffetti's furniture. In Lombardy Giuseppe Maggiolini (1738–1814) produced furniture in the Louis XVI style, decorated with *intarsia* panels representing portraits, bunches of flowers, and ruins. At about the same time, in Turin, Giuseppe Maria Bonzanigo (1744–1820) was producing a few exceptionally fine works in the same style, notably a secretaire and a firescreen (Plate 143E), which are carved with a delicacy and precision seldom equalled even in France. In 1782 the Lombard architect, Giocondo Albertolli (1742–1839), published the only important Italian pattern book of furniture designs which shows, perhaps, too strict a regard for archaeological accuracy. During the Empire period fine furniture was produced at Lucca under the French *maître-ébéniste*, Youf, and at Florence by the Italian Giovanni Socchi, many of whose works are still in the Palazzo Pitti (Plate 144C).

Glossary

Acanthus. The leaf used in classical and Renaissance architectural design, particularly on Corinthian capitals. Adapted later as a motif in furniture design. Most important in Chippendale furniture as decorative motif on the knees of cabriole legs.

FIG. 40. Acanthus

Acorn clock. American shelf or mantel clock, generally about 2 feet high, with the upper portion shaped somewhat like an acorn. Popular in New England about 1825.

Ambry (aumbry, almery; *Fr.* **armoire).** Enclosed compartment or recess in a wall or in a piece of furniture, the original sense of the term having been usurped by cupboard, which originally had a different connotation. "Cuppbordes wyth ambries" are mentioned

in inventories of Henry VIII's furniture. To-day aumbry, etc., is principally used architecturally and ecclesiastically, as of the doored compartments or recesses for the Reservation of the Blessed Sacrament, this usage perpetuating the original sense. The French form *armoire* is often applied to large presses or press-cupboards.

Apple. A fruitwood much used in America for turnings, also often in case pieces, such as slant-front desks, etc., to show off the rich-coloured pink-brown wood.

Appliques. *See under* Wall-lights.

Apron-work. Prolongation downwards, beyond what is essential to construction, of the lower edge of a member, such as the shaped lower edge of the front of certain boarded chests, or the lower frontal framework, below the drawers, of certain dressers. In such cases an apron is purely ornamental; in others, e.g.

the seating of close-chairs, its purpose is that of concealment.

Ark. Term frequently encountered in medieval inventories, seemingly meaning: (*a*) a chest with a coped or gabled lid; (*b*) perhaps a structure resembling a reliquary (*Fr. chasse*), as exemplified by the sixteenth-century almery in Coity Church, Glamorganshire. That ark was a distinct term is shown by such entries as the following from an inventory of the contents of St Mary's, Warwick, 1464:

"It: in the Vestrye i gret olde arke to put in vestyments etc.

"It: in the Sextry above the Vestrye, i olde arke at the auters ende, i olde coofre irebonde having a long lok of the olde facion, and i lasse new coofre having iii loks called the tresory cofre and certeyn almaries." (Quoted by Philip Mainwaring Johnston, F.R.I.B.A.: *Church Chests of the Twelfth and Thirteenth Centuries in England*; 1908, p. 60.)

Armadio. The French *armoire,* a large cupboard, usually of a somewhat monumental character, which seems first to have been used to supplement the *cassoni* in the furnishing of Italian houses in the late fourteenth century. Early examples are usually about 4 feet in height, and some are decorated with flamboyant Gothic carving in low relief. An early fifteenth-century example (in the Museo Bardini at Florence) is in the form of a long, low cupboard with several very simply decorated doors and a panelled backboard of the same height as the cupboard. In the sixteenth century two-story *armadi* became popular. They were often decorated with two orders of pilasters or pilasters above elongated consoles (there is a good Tuscan example of this type in the museum at Berlin). Sometimes the two stories were separated by a projecting drawer. This pattern was superseded in the seventeenth century by a still more massive type, with pilasters some 6 feet tall at either end, and sometimes with a pair of drawers in the plinth. When a less ponderous effect was desired the cupboard was mounted on turned legs. The tops of seventeenth-century *armadi* are often shaped in baroque curves. In the

eighteenth century the *armadio* was usually made on a lighter and more elegant pattern and was often designed to stand in a corner. But with the introduction of the chest of drawers the *armadio* lost much of its former popularity in the house.

Many of the early surviving *armadi* were intended originally for the sacristies of churches, where they were used for the storage of vestments, and it is often difficult to distinguish these from domestic examples except when they have specifically religious motifs in their decoration. After the sixteenth century such *armadi* were usually built-in furnishings of the sacristy. Sometimes they were richly carved or decorated with *intarsia* panels.

Arming chest. Chest for the housing of armours and weapons. Arming chests might be fitted with compartments of varying size to accommodate breast-plate, etc. (*see* Chest). (In navigation an arming box contains tallow for the "lead".)

Armoires. *See under* Wardrobes.

Artisans libres. The name given to French craftsmen who chose to work outside the guild jurisdiction and who sought refuge in what were known as *lieux privilégiés* in Paris. Being exempt from guild charges and regulations, they were a continual source of irritation to the guilds, particularly as they included a large number of foreign *ébénistes* who came to Paris in the mid-eighteenth century. These included some of the finest craftsmen of the time, a number of whom later became *maître-ébénistes*.

Ash. The American ash, a cream-coloured hardwood with oak-like graining; much used for furniture parts, such as upholstery frames, where strong, but not heavy, wood was desired. In England it was used in eighteenth-century furniture, particularly for the hooped backs of Windsor chairs.

Athénienne. A form of candelabrum consisting of an urn supported on a classical tripod, invented in 1773 by J. H. Eberts, editor of the famous *Monument de Costume*. The name derives from a painting by J. B. Vien entitled "*La Vertueuse Athénienne*", which shows a priestess burning incense at a tripod of this type. They were made of patinated bronze with ormolu mounts or in carved giltwood, but not many survive. They are, however, typical of the classicizing tendencies of the last quarter of the eighteenth century.

Bail. Half-loop metal pull, usually brass, hanging from metal bolts. First used in America about 1700; slowly grew into use for drawers of William and Mary pieces. The reigning fashion from 1720 to 1780 for drawers of Queen Anne and Chippendale pieces.

Ball-and-claw foot. *See* Claw-and-ball foot.

Ball foot. U.S. term for Bun foot (*q.v.*).

Banister-back chair. Probably simplified from the cane chair (*q.v.*) but with vertical split-banisters in the back. Generally maple, often ebonized. Widely used in rural America, 1700–25 until the end of the century (Fig. 41).

FIG. 41

Banjo. Modern name for the American wall clock with a longish pendulum, the whole housed in a case shaped somewhat like a banjo. Invented in the 1790s by Simon Willard, and patented by him about 1800. Decoratively attractive, its popularity spread from 1800 through the next half-century.

Bargueño (or **Vargueño**). Spanish cabinet with fall-front enclosing drawers and often mounted on a stand. Mixed materials are found.

Barley-sugar. *See* Twist-turning.

Baroque. The late Renaissance style of vigorously elaborate furniture with sweeping curves and resplendent ornament. It originated in sixteenth-century Italy, spread through Europe, but was little practised in England, and known in American only in *bombé* case-pieces and in greatly simplified forms of some William and Mary and Queen Anne furniture (*see* Rococo).

Basin-stand. *See* Washing-stand.

Bedstead. So far as practical collecting is concerned, main basic types are the box- (or enclosed) bedstead, wainscot- (including bed-steads panelled at head and foot), post- (with two or four posts supporting the tester), stump- (or low type), and the truckle- or trundle- (with wooden wheels at base of uprights). These are not hard-and-fast definitions; one type may well overlap another (e.g. box and wainscot). Parts of bedsteads have been re-used for other purposes of a decorative nature, such as overmantels. We know little of the shape of Italian beds before the sixteenth century, save from those which appear in such paintings as Carpaccio's *St Ursula* or Ghirlandaio's *Birth of the Virgin*. One of the earliest is that formerly in the Palazzo Davanzati at Florence (Plate 140A), a handsome piece of furniture mounted on a wide plinth. Sixteenth-century examples often have rich carving on head and foot and are without the plinth. In Sicily iron bedsteads with four posts supporting a canopy were popular from the late sixteenth century. The use of four posts was, however, unusual on later Italian beds, which sometimes have stumps at the corners and are covered by canopies supported from the wall. Lucchese examples (Plate 142A) are often richly covered with fabric which is matched on the bedspread.

Beech. A smooth, close-grained wood of light colour less frequently used in America than England. Found in the underframes of New York Chippendale pieces and occasionally in New England Chippendale as well as early turned pieces.

Beer-wagon. *See* Coaster.

Bell flower. Conventionalized hanging ("belle") flower-bud of three, occasionally five, petals carved or, more often, inlaid one below the other in strings dropping down the legs of a table or chair or, sometimes, a chair splat. Seen in American Hepplewhite and Sheraton, notably Maryland furniture (Fig. 42). It is practically the same as the English "husk" motif.

FIG. 42

Bell seat. The rounded, somewhat bell-shaped, seat often found in late Philadelphia

Queen Anne side chairs. Nowadays often called balloon seat. Mostly about 1740–55.

Bench. A long seat, backed or backless, fitted or movable (*see* Form, Settle, Table-bench).

Bible-box. Popular term for a variety of box, generally of small size. That some such boxes were used to hold the family Bible, or average meagre domestic library, is probable, though they doubtless served other purposes. Lace-boxes enter this category.

Bibliothèque-basse. A low cupboard fitted with shelves for books, and doors often of glass but sometimes fitted with grilles.

Bilbao or **"Bilboa".** U.S. wall mirror framed in coloured marbles or marble and wood with a scrollwork headpiece and gilded mouldings. Adam or Hepplewhite followers might have designed them, yet they are believed to have originated in the Spanish seaport Bilbao. Stylish in New England seaport towns 1780–1800.

Bilsted. Word used in colonial New York for sweet-gum wood.

Birch. Hard, close-grained wood. Stained to substitute for mahogany in country furniture. Resembles satinwood in certain cuts. The American variety, *betual lenta*, was exported to England in the second half of the eighteenth century.

Bird's-eye. A marking of small spots, supposed to resemble bird's eyes, often found in the wood of the sugar maple. Used and much prized from the earliest to present times.

Blister. A marking, thought to resemble a blister, found in various woods – cedar, mahogany, poplar, pine, and, especially, maple.

Block front. A whole range of forms – chests of drawers, chests-on-chests, knee-hole dressing-tables, slant-front desks, secretaries, etc. – in which thick boards, usually mahogany, for the fronts of the drawers and cabinets are cut so that the centres recede in a flattened curve while the ends curve outwards in a flattened bulge. At the top of the three curves, one concave and two convex, a shell is often carved or glued on. Should the piece be in two sections, often only the lower section is block-fronted. The origin of block-fronting is unknown; the development is believed to be American, evolved about 1760–80, by John

Goddard of Newport, Rhode Island, perhaps with the aid of his associate, John Townsend. They may have arrived at it by straightening the curves of the Dutch cabinet. The late American authority Wallace Nutting called block fronts "the aristocrats of furniture". The English antique furniture authority, Cescinsky, described them, especially the secretaries, as "the finest examples of American furniture". They are much sought after.

Boat bed. American Empire style bed shaped somewhat like a gondola. A variant of the sleigh bed.

Bombé. Lit. "inflated, blown out", i.e. of convex form generally on more than one axis.

Bonheur-du-jour. A small writing-table usually on tall legs, and sometimes fitted to hold toilet accessories and *bibelots*. It first appeared in France *c.* 1760, but remained in fashion for a comparatively short time.

Bonnet top. When the broken-arch pediment of tall case-furniture covers the entire top from front to back, this hood is called a bonnet top (Fig. 43). It is usually cut in the

FIG. 43

same curves as the arch, but is sometimes left uncut, a solid block of wood behind the arched fronting. 1730–85. Same as "Hood".

Bookcase. In England bookcases, either fitted or, in some cases, contained in other furniture, were known medievally, but the domestic bookcase mainly derives from the period of Charles II (1660–85). In Italy bookcases were less frequently made individually than as part of the built-in decorations of a library. In Venice there is an excellent example of a late seventeenth-century library with cases carved by German craftsmen in the monastry of S. Giorgio Maggiore (now *Fondazione Cini*) and an exquisite small, early eighteenth-century library, with painted cases, in the Ca' Sagredo. Both of these have two tiers of bookcases which fill the walls. In houses that could not afford to give up a whole room to the library the books were probably kept in an ordinary *armadio*. Eighteenth-century bookcases resemble either a section of a complete library or, more usually, an *armadio* with wire grilles in place of panels in the doors. Although a few enormous early bookcases exist, bookcases were seldom made in America as an article of furniture before 1785–90, the average family before then keeping their books in locked chests, cupboards, and the tops of secretaries. Bookcases are generally large and heavy until about 1800 (Plate 76), when the smaller type came in (*see* China cabinet).

Book-rest. A stand used in Georgian libraries to support large books, consisting of a square or rectangular framework with cross bars, the upper bar being supported by a strut which was adjusted on a grooved base. This kind of stand was sometimes fitted into the top of a table.

Book-shelf. *See* Shelves.

Boston rocker. In America the most popular of all rocking chairs. Apparently evolved from the Windsor rocker (*q.v.*). Usually painted, it has curved arms, a tall spindle back, broad top rail generally showing stencilled designs – a kind of ornamental panel – and a "rolling" seat, curved up at the back and down at the front. When standardized and mass produced (after 1840) it is not a true antique.

Boulle marquetry. The name given to the type of inlay evolved for use on furniture in the late seventeenth century by André Charles Boulle (1642–1732) (*see* under French furniture).

The process involves the glueing of one or more thin layers of tortoiseshell to a similar number of brass. The design of the marquetry is set out on paper, and this is pasted on to the surface. The pattern is then cut out by means of a saw. After this, the layers of brass and tortoiseshell are separated and can be made to form two distinct marquetries by combining the materials in opposite ways: either with the design formed by the brass on a ground of shell, known as *première partie* or first part, or the exact opposite, known as *contre-partie*, or counter-part, with the design in shell on a ground of brass. These two types of inlay can then be glued on to a carcase in the form of a veneer. Often the two types are found side by side as part of the same design, in order to give contrast. Again, when pieces are made in pairs one is often veneered with *première partie* and the other with *contre-partie* marquetry.

The brass in the *première partie* marquetry was often engraved naturalistically, frequently very finely, and was sometimes combined with other substances, such as pewter, copper, mother-of-pearl, and stained horn, again usually to give contrasts and naturalistic effects to the design. Additional colour was also given occasionally by veneering the shell over coloured foil, usually red or green.

The carcases on to which Boulle marquetry is veneered are usually found to be of oak or deal, and the parts which are not covered by the inlay are veneered with ebony, coromandel-wood, or purple-wood, in order to tone with the shell of the inlay.

Finally, Boulle furniture is usually lavishly mounted with ormolu, so as to protect the corners and the more vulnerable parts of the inlay, but the mounts are frequently also adapted in a decorative manner to form hinges, lock-plates, and handles. It will be noticed that the ormolu is sometimes fully gilt, which provides a strong decorative contrast with the inlaid brass; equally, the bronze is sometimes left ungilt, and therefore harmonizes with the metal inlay to a greater extent.

Boulle furniture, so much in demand in the reign of Louis XIV, went out of fashion during most of that of his successor, but it did not cease to be made, and the Boulle *atèlier* continued to turn out pieces from time to time. They were therefore ready when, under Louis XVI and the classical revival, the taste for this type of furniture returned, and at this period a very large number of pieces were made, often using the original designs, mounts, and processes as in the former period. It is thus often extremely difficult to tell whether a piece was made in one period or another, and it is better not to be too dogmatic about this, as there are very few distinguishing characteristics. Two may perhaps be mentioned: the engraving of the brass inlay is less common in the Louis XVI period and, when it does appear, of inferior quality;

secondly, the use of other metals than brass and freer designs are slightly more common.

In the earlier period a large number of designs for Boulle marquetry are derived from the engravings of Jean Berain, who was, like Boulle, also employed by the Crown.

Boulle marquetry is sometimes erroneously referred to as Buhl. This is a Teutonic adaptation of Boulle's name for which there is no justification.

Bow back. *See* Windsor chair.

Bow-front. A curving front used on case pieces in New England during the Chippendale period.

Box and casket. Boxes were among the most attractive of the smaller pieces of furniture, and were used from medieval times for a multitude of purposes – personal effects, toilet and writing materials, valuables, documents, etc. Tudor and early Stuart boxes were usually square in shape and made of oak, carved, inlaid, or painted, and occasionally stood upon stands, few of which have survived. In the later seventeenth century walnut was commonly used (sometimes decorated with marquetry or parquetry), but other materials included parchment, tortoise-shell, and stumpwork, the latter particularly on the boxes kept by ladies for their cosmetics, etc. The interiors were often ingeniously fitted with compartments and drawers. In the eighteenth century some beautiful mahogany and satinwood boxes were made, until they were gradually replaced by small work-tables, though boxes on stands, conforming to the prevailing decorative fashions, were to be found. Among other examples were Tunbridge ware (*q.v.*) boxes, and travelling boxes fitted with spaces for writing, working, and toilet requisites. About 1800 work and toilet boxes covered with tooled leather were in vogue (Plate 125B).

Boxwood (*buis*). A very closely grained wood of a yellow colour found frequently in Europe and elsewhere. Extensively used in France for fillets to frame panels of marquetry.

Boys and crowns. Old term for a type of carved ornament on the cresting of late seventeenth- and quite early eighteenth-century chairs, day-beds, etc. (*see* under Restoration). The motif, a crown, usually, though not necessarily, arched, supported by two flying or sprawling naked boys, derives ultimately from the flying *putti* frequently found in renaissance design. In England, the idea was familiar long before it achieved (*temp.* Charles II) a vogue on chair-backs.

Bracket. The detachable wall-bracket, as distinct from the fixed architectural feature, appeared towards the end of the seventeenth century, and seems to have been used at first for displaying china. Its prominent position in the room singled it out for special decorative treatment in carving or gilding. In the early Georgian period the bracket was often used to support a bust or vase, and as a result it tended to become larger in size and more heavily ornamented; but with the return of the fashion for displaying china about 1750 and the growing use of the bracket for supporting lights, it became altogether more delicate in appearance, and was adapted to the various styles of the Chippendale and Adam periods. The wall-bracket supporting a clock was a popular form of decoration in the later eighteenth century.

Bracket foot. A foot supporting a case piece and attached directly to the underframing. It consists of two pieces of wood, joined at the corner. The open side is generally cut out in a simple pattern. The corner end is sometimes straight, at other times curved in an ogee pattern.

Bras de lumière. *See under* Wall-lights.

Brazier. A portable metal container used from Tudor times for burning coal or charcoal; with handle and feet, or sometimes mounted on a stand.

Breakfast table. A small table with hinged side leaves that can be used by one or two people. After the Chippendale period the name Pembroke is often applied to the type.

Brewster chair. A seventeenth-century American arm-chair of turned spindles and posts with rush seat (Plate 66B). The back has two tiers of spindles. There is a tier under the arms and one under the seat. The chair is usually of ash or maple. Named after William Brewster, elder of Plymouth Plantation, whose chair is preserved at Pilgrim Hall, Plymouth, Massachusetts. Similar to the Carver chair.

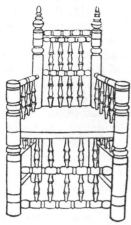

FIG. 44

Broken arch. *See* Scroll top.

Bronzes d'ameublement. A term with no exact English equivalent covering all furniture, practical or decorative, made of bronze, patinated or gilt. It embraces such items as candelabra, candlesticks, wall-lights, chandeliers, fire-dogs, clock-cases, mounts for furniture and porcelain, etc. Their manufacture was the particular province of the *fondeurs*, *ciseleurs*, and *doreurs*.

Buffet. Term variously applied to open, doorless structures, of more than one tier (*see also* Court cupboard, Livery cupboard).

Bull's eye. A popular term for the small round mirror with convex or concave glass and an ornate gilt frame. The type was fashionable 1800–20, and often of English or French manufacture. An alternate meaning is the reference to clear glass with a large centre drop or gather employed as window glass and in cabinets.

Bureau. In America, ever since the eighteenth century, the word bureau means a chest of drawers, with or without a mirror, and regularly used in the bedroom (Fig. 45). Originally, and still in England, a desk. Examples were made in the William and Mary style, dating 1700–10, but the form dropped completely out of use until revived about 1750. They are found in the Chippendale and every style thereafter, the revival probably springing not from the earlier form but from

Chippendale's designs. Many authorities describe bureaux according to the shape of the front – serpentine, reverse serpentine, bow or swell, and straight front – but that is mere grouping, not classification proper. In England the word denotes a writing-desk with a fall, a cylinder, or a tambour front.

FIG. 45

Bureau-plat. A writing-table supported on tall legs with a flat top with drawers beneath. Began to appear in France towards the end of the seventeenth century.

Bureau table. A dressing-table with drawers on short legs and a knee-hole recess.

Bureau-toilette. A piece of furniture for female use combining the functions of a toilet- and writing-table.

Burl. A tree knot or protruding growth which shows beautifully patterned grainings when sliced. Used for inlay or veneer. Found in some late seventeenth- and much eighteenth-century American furniture, and chiefly in walnut and maple burls.

Butler's tray. A tray mounted on legs or on a folding stand, in use throughout the eighteenth century. The X-shaped folding stand was in general use from about 1750, the tray normally being rectangular and fitted with a gallery. Oval trays were sometimes made in the later part of the century.

Butterfly table. A William and Mary style drop-leaf table with solid swinging supports shaped a little like butterfly wings. The

FIG. 46

supports are pivoted on the stretchers joining the legs. Assumption that the type is of American origin is probably incorrect.

Cabinet. The glass fronted cabinet intended for the display of a collection of porcelain or other *objets d'art* is an eighteenth-century invention. Such cabinets were made in Italy in conformity with the rococo and neo-classical styles.

Cabriole leg. The curving tall furniture leg used in American Queen Anne and Chippendale furniture, and almost universally used in the eighteenth century. The adjective is from the French noun, which is a dancing term meaning a goat leap, and is used in the idiom *faire le cabriole* to refer to the agility and grace of a person. The leg is inspired by an animal form, unlike the earlier scroll and turned shapes and is 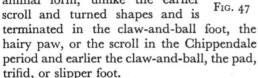 FIG. 47 terminated in the claw-and-ball foot, the hairy paw, or the scroll in the Chippendale period and earlier the claw-and-ball, the pad, trifid, or slipper foot.

Camel back. Colloquial term for a chair or sofa, such as Hepplewhite, with the top curved somewhat like the hump of a dromedary (Fig. 48).

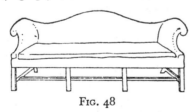

FIG. 48

Canapé. The ordinary French word for a sofa. Evolved in many forms during the Louis XV period.

Candelabrum. A lighting appliance with branches supporting sockets for more than one light. They took many forms, but are usually made of ormolu, sometimes with figures in patinated bronze. They were often made in pairs or sets of four.

Candle-box. A cylindrical or square box, of metal or wood, widely used in the Georgian period for storing candles.

Candle-stand. A portable stand (known also as a lamp-stand, *guéridon*, and *torchère*) for a candlestick, candelabrum, or lamp. After 1660 the fashion arose of having two candlestands flanking a side table with a mirror on the wall above; the stands usually took the form of a baluster or twist-turned shaft, with a circular or octagonal top and a tripod base. At the end of the century more elaborate kinds, copying French stands, became fashionable, with vase-shaped tops and scrolled feet, all carved and gilded. Other examples were of simpler design, but had rich decoration in gesso or marquetry. In the early Georgian period, when gilt stands followed architectural forms, the vase-shaped tops and baluster shafts were larger, and the feet curved outwards, replacing the scrolled French style. About 1750 stands became lighter and more delicate, many of them being enriched with rococo decoration. There was a distinct change in design in the later eighteenth century: the traditional tripod continued, often in mahogany, with turned shaft and a bowl or vase top in the classical taste; but a new type, which was originated by Adam, consisted of three uprights, mounted on feet or a plinth, supporting usually a candelabrum, or with a flat top. Smaller examples of the latter type were made to stand on tables (Plate 123). A much smaller version of candle-stand was also popular after 1750 – with a circular base and top, and sometimes an adjustable shaft.

Candlesticks (*flambeaux*). A portable lighting appliance with one socket for a single light or candle. Large numbers were made almost exclusively of ormolu in the late seventeenth and eighteenth centuries, usually in pairs or sets of four, but sometimes in larger quantities.

Cane chair. First produced in England in Charles II's reign, it was very popular in London because it was cheap, light, and durable. It was used in America first in about 1690, in William and Mary tall-backed chairs (Plate 68A). The type occasionally occurred in Queen Anne, but was revived in the classical style. Duncan Phyfe used it. Caning was introduced from the Orient through the Netherlands.

Canted. Sloping, at an angle.

Canterbury. (1) A small music-stand with partitions for music-books, usually mounted on castors, and sometimes with small drawers, much used in the early nineteenth century (Plate 124A); and (2) a plate and cutlery stand particularly designed for supper parties in the later eighteenth century, with divisions for cutlery and a semicircular end, on four turned legs. "The name 'Canterbury' arose", wrote Sheraton, "because the bishop of that See first gave orders for these pieces."

Carolean. Term of convenience strictly applicable to pieces made in the reign of Charles I (1625–49), those made under Charles II (1660–85) usually being dissociated. Actually the Carolean style is as much an extension of the Jacobean as the latter was of the later Elizabethan.

Cartonnier. A piece of furniture which took various forms. Usually it stood at one end of a writing-table (*bureau-plât*) and was intended to hold papers. It was sometimes surmounted by a clock. Also sometimes called a *serre-papier*.

Cartouche. A fanciful scroll; used in America mostly as a central finial for the tops of Philadelphia Chippendale highboys, clocks, and, occasionally, mirrors.

Carver chair. Modern term for an early seventeenth-century "Dutch" type arm-chair made of turned posts and spindles. It has three rails and three spindles in the back (Fig. 49). Such chairs may be seen in seventeenth-

FIG. 49

century paintings of humbler Dutch interiors, though the source of the American ones was probably an English model. Usually of ash or maple, with rush seats. Named after John Carver, first governor of the Plymouth colony, who is said to have brought one to America with him in the *Mayflower*. Made until the end of the century. Many examples survive, the earliest dating perhaps about 1650. (*See* its variant, Brewster chair.)

Caryatid. Upright carved in semblance of a human figure or, more frequently, a demi-figure on a terminal base. Strictly, Caryatid implies a female, Atlanta or Atlas figure a male figure, though Caryatid is used for either. The term derives from the legend of the women of Carya, enslaved and immured for their betrayal of the Greeks to the Persians. Atlanta refers to the myth of Atlas upholding the heavens (Plate 90B).

Cassapanca. A wooden bench with a built-in chest under the seat. Early *cassapanche*, like that of the fifteenth century in the Ca' D'Oro at Venice or the magnificent sixteenth-century example in the Bargello at Florence, are in the form of a *cassone* with back and arms. After the *cassone* went out of fashion in the early seventeenth century the *cassapanca* survived as a useful piece of entrance-hall furniture. Seventeenth- and eighteenth-century examples often have immensely high backs of thin wood painted with mythological beings or a coat-of-arms amid a profusion of scrolls.

Cassone. The *cassone*, or chest, was clearly one of the most popular pieces of furniture in fifteenth- and sixteenth-century Italy. It was also the most richly decorated, and, for this reason, perhaps, numerous examples have survived. It was used to hold linen or clothes and might also serve as a seat (with or without the upright back which made it into a *cassapanca*). *Cassoni* are frequently referred to as dower chests, and although they were often made to hold the supply of linen which a bride took to her new home, there is no reason to suppose that the majority were intended for this purpose. The *cassone nuziale*, or dower chest, can be recognized as such only if it bears the coats-of-arms of two families between whom a marriage took place.

The earliest *cassoni* were probably very unpretentious affairs, but a few of the early fifteenth-century examples which have survived are decorated with Gothic curvilinear carving or rough paintings of heraldic achievements. In the Renaissance period great ingenuity was expended on their design and adornment. Some were decorated with gesso friezes of *putti* sporting on the front and sides and others were fashioned like antique sarcophagi, but most seem to have been painted on the front (some were also painted inside the lid). Several highly able Florentine *quattrocento* painters, like the famous Master of the Jarves *Cassoni*, seem to have specialized almost exclusively in the decoration of furniture of this type: and some more important artists, like Bartolomeo Montagna (Plate 140B), occasionally turned their hands to this decorative work. In Florence paintings of battles and the triumphs of Roman generals were in particular demand, elsewhere religious and mythological scenes seem to have enjoyed great popularity, but in Venice patterns of ornamental motifs were generally preferred. *Intarsia* views of real or imaginary architecture were also employed to decorate *cassoni*. In the sixteenth century the painted *cassone* seems to have gone out of fashion, and most surviving examples from this period are simply carved with abstract decorations. A few later sixteenth-century *cassoni* are adorned with mannerist term figures at the corners and low reliefs in the same style on the front. The *cassone* survived the sixteenth century only in the form of the *cassapanca* (*q.v.*) or of a simple unembellished utilitarian travelling chest.

Cat. A stand used after about 1750 to warm plates in front of the fire; it had three arms and three feet of turned wood (or three legs of cabriole form). The turning was well ringed to provide sockets for plates of various sizes.

Causeuse. A large chair or small sofa to accommodate two persons. Roughly corresponds to the small English settee. Sometimes referred to colloquially as a love-seat.

Cedar. Handsome pieces of furniture were occasionally made of colourful red cedar wood, though cedar – both the red and the white – was usually set aside for drawers, chests, linings, etc.

Cellaret. The name given generally after 1750 to a case on legs or stand for wine bottles; prior to that date, from the end of the seventeenth century, the same kind of case was called a cellar. In the early eighteenth century cellarets, lined with lead and containing compartments for bottles, stood under side-tables, and they were still made later in the century (Plate 124B) when sideboards, which had drawers fitted up to hold bottles, came into general use. Sheraton classified the cellaret with the wine cistern (*q.v.*) and sarcophagus, and distinguished them from the bottle-case, which was for square bottles only.

Chair. In its old sense chair meant, as like as not, an arm-chair, what is now called a single- or side-chair being a back-stool (stool with a back).[1] To what extent the chair originated from such box-forms as the chest is suggested by early surviving examples of box-like structure. Development from the wainscot chair to the open-framed variety with panelled back belongs in general to the late sixteenth century. Folding or rack-chairs and X-chairs (so called from their shape) have also a long history. Certain sixteenth-century chairs with narrow backs and widely splayed arms are so-called caqueteuse or caquetoire. The so-called farthingale chair (a term freely applied to many pieces, mostly of the earlier seventeenth century) has its back-support raised clear of the seat. Upholstery (not unknown earlier) had arrived, seats and back-pads being covered in velvet or in "Turkey-work". Leather was used, especially on Cromwellian chairs, some of which date from the Interregnum, though the type endured until relatively late in the seventeenth century. Leather or Russia chair are old terms for such items. About the middle of the seventeenth century are found what are often termed "mortuary" chairs, a term of doubtful origin for chairs with a small moustachioed and bearded head (supposedly allusive to King Charles I) in the centre of the shaped and scrolled back-rails. Similar chairs occur without the masks, and the type is a variation of Yorkshire or Derbyshire chair, the geographical distribution of which is undefined.

Cane chairs (*q.v.*) achieved main popularity in the second half of the seventeenth century, their backs and seats being caned. Scrolling, curlicues, boys and crowns, etc., were favoured as carved ornament. Backs lengthen, assuming the form of a narrow panel or centre (often caned or stuffed) flanked by

---

[1] 'Back chaier' occurs (e.g. Unton Inventory, 1620).

uprights. Already had been reached the period of barley-sugar turning (*see* Twist).

Corner-chairs, some of triangular formation, and sundry related types, were already in being. A later variety has the seat disposed diagonally to the low, rounded back. Elbow-chair and roundabout-chair are synonyms in use. An allied type is the circular chair (with circular seat), often Dutch, and known as burgomaster or (again) roundabout-chair, such terms being jargon. Thrown-chairs of various shapes, with much turnery, have been often assigned to the sixteenth century, though many are certainly later. Though scarcely belonging to the Age of Oak, the Windsor chair (*q.v.*) may have owed something to older types. The basic characteristic of Windsors is not the bow- or hoop-back, but the detail that back and under-framing are all mortised into the wooden seat, itself frequently saddle-shaped and "dished", but sometimes circular, etc. The bow-back type (late eighteenth century and later), preceded by the comb- or fan-back (early eighteenth century and later), was itself followed by other formations on more or less "Regency" lines. Types are many with much overlapping; woods are mixed. Scole or Mendlesham chairs are East Anglian types on Windsor lines. Yorkshire and Lancashire Windsors usually show "frilly" splats and developed turnery, but the type was not confined to the North of England. In America Windsors were made from the early eighteenth century, and include some fine types. Lancashire chair is also applied to an extensively made type of bobbin back, much favoured in the eighteenth and early nineteenth centuries, but, here again, as with Yorkshire and Derbyshire chairs in general, the geographical location has been overstressed (*see* Close-chair and -stool; *also* Restoration).

In the Renaissance period those made in France were on the whole very simple, constructed of plain wood, usually walnut, and carved with conventional motifs in the Italian style. Often they are of the ecclesiastical type with high backs carved in relief. Others have carved arms and stretchers. These types continued into the early seventeenth century, usually accompanied by some upholstery.

Such chairs of the Louis XIV period as have come down to us are also almost always of plain wood, carved in the classical manner. The backs are high, often with elaborately carved cornices. The legs are also elaborately carved and are often joined with stretchers. The chairs are upholstered on seats and back, either with embroidery, velvet, or with cane. Tapestry does not appear until later in the eighteenth century.

In the Louis XV period the design of chairs became less formal and the carving soon began to be carried out in the rococo manner. The outlines of the upholstered backs and seats, and the legs, gradually became curved and bowed until there is not a straight line in the whole design. Often chairs of the Louis XV period are of considerable size and of rather a heavy appearance. They are upholstered usually with silk, velvet, or brocade, but sometimes with tapestry, which begins to make its appearance at this time.

In the Louis XVI period chairs, in particular, take up the prevailing neo-classical style, the change being noticeable soon after 1755. Legs gradually become straighter, as do the outlines of backs, seats, and arms, and the motifs employed in the carving derive from classical sources, the most commonly found being the acanthus leaf in various forms, the wave-like band and the Ionic capital, as well as symmetrical garlands of flowers. It was at this time that the carving of chairs, particularly those produced by G. Jacob, reached the very greatest refinement, both of design and detail.

The frames of chairs of the Louis XV and Louis XVI periods are usually made of beech, birch, or walnut, and they are often gilt. It is important to remember, however, that they may not originally have been so. Sometimes the wood forming the frames was left plain and unadorned, more often they were painted white, or white and partly gilt. Equally, a chair may have been originally plain or painted, and then gilt before the end of the eighteenth century. More often gilding or regilding was carried out in the nineteenth century, and often very coarsely. Collectors should bear this in mind when judging both the style and condition of French chairs.

The earliest Italian chairs were probably no more than square stools to which a back and arms had been added, but they do not seem to have been in general use until the fifteenth century. Folding chairs (*sedie pieghe-vole*) were made before the beginning of the fourteenth century, however, and one or two fourteenth-century examples have survived. The most popular form of chair in the fifteenth century seems to have been the so called "Dantesque" or X-chair which might also, if necessary, be folded for travelling. Two thirteenth-century wooden X-chairs are known, but most chairs of this type seem to have been made of metal rods. At first the X-chair was without any form of back but this was added in the sixteenth century, and many examples survive from this period. The so-called Savonarola chair was a development of the simple X-chair with a number of struts following the curve of the design. Chairs of both these types were made throughout Italy in both the fifteenth and sixteenth centuries. Wooden tub chairs seem to have enjoyed a limited popularity in the fourteenth and fifteenth centuries (a good example is in the Horne Museum at Florence). The "Andrea

Fig. 50. Chair with figure
of eight back; Venetian;
mid-eighteenth-century

del Sarto" chair, which has a semicircular seat above which a thin strip of wood supported on balusters serves as both back and arms, was introduced into Tuscany in the early sixteenth century.

In the course of the sixteenth century the upright chair with straight back and arms was developed and ornamented, eventually becoming the standard pattern. Seventeenth-century craftsmen used it as the basis for their richly carved and gilded thrones, such as the one in the Palazzo Rezzonico at Venice (Plate 141B). The easy-chair (*poltrona*) does not appear in Italy until the late seventeenth century. During the eighteenth century Italian chairs differed little from those made elsewhere in Europe (Plate 143D). In Venice, however, chairs with backs in the form of a figure of eight (Fig. 50) enjoyed great popularity.

Chamfer. Bevelled edge, as when the sharp edges of a beam are bevelled off. A dust chamfer (i.e. to throw off dust) is a smooth bevel at the lower edge of framework of a panel, the other edges being moulded, or part moulded and part of rectangular cut. Of stop chamfer there is no better simple definition than Walter Rose's in *The Village Carpenter*: "where slope finishes and square begins" [to arise].

Chandeliers. A branched lighting appliance consisting usually of several lights which can be suspended from a ceiling. Large quantities were made in France in the seventeenth and eighteenth centuries, but not many have survived. They were made of various materials: ormolu, wood, crystal, glass, and occasionally porcelain.

Cherry. A hard, close-grained, reddish or pinkish brown wood, it was used in England for chairs and panels in the seventeenth and eighteenth centuries, though few examples remain. It was often used in America for furniture of the finest design and workmanship. In use as early as 1680. Joseph Downs says cherry was a favourite wood among New York cabinet-makers; was more often used than mahogany in Connecticut, and quite often used in Pennsylvania, Virgina, and Kentucky furniture.

Chest (*see also* Coffer). One primitive form of chest is the dug-out or trunk, its interior gouged in the solid. Some dug-outs are of considerable antiquity; others may be of more recent date than their appearance suggests. In name and rounded lid the travelling trunk, as it is still known, recalls the ancient use of a tree-trunk. Framed chests are also ancient, the earliest surviving medieval examples being formed of great planks so disposed as to present an almost or wholly flush surface at front and back (Fig. 51). Panelled chests were being made in the fifteenth century, later becoming very popular. The earlier "flush" con-

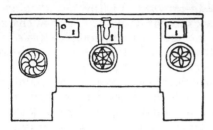

FIG. 51 (*above*). Chest of thirteenth-century construction.

FIG. 52. Nonsuch panel (General characteristics)

struction was, however, to some extent perpetuated until a very late period in the boarded chest, made entirely of boards, including the ends, which also form the uprights (*cf.* Wainscot). Unusually long examples are sometimes, but not necessarily correctly, called rapier chests. The validity of the term is uncertain. Popularly called "non(e)such" chests (Fig. 52), mainly of the latter part of the sixteenth century, are inlaid with formalized architectural designs, thought possibly to represent the Palace of Nonsuch, or Nonesuch, at Ewell, Surrey. Such architectural motifs are, however, exploitations of a Renaissance design favoured on the Continent, though a possible affinity exists between them and the crowded towns in Gothic art. Mule-chest (implying a hybrid) is collectors' jargon of no validity for a chest-*with*-drawers.

Chest of drawers. This derives in name, and to a considerable extent in principle, from the chest, a link being the chest-with-

drawers, with a single range of drawers beneath the box. Such pieces were in being by the latter part of the sixteenth century, a gradual tendency to increase the drawer-space at the expense of the box resulting in the chest-of-drawers. At the same time various structures enclosing a quantity of drawers were also in being, on the Continent and in England, as with the "new cubborde of boxes" made by Lawrence Abelle in 1595 for Stratford-upon-Avon or the "cubborde with drawing boxes" of the Unton Inventory, 1596. "Nests of boxes" is another old term (*see also* Bargueño, Writing-cabinet). The chest of drawers was introduced into Italy, probably from France, in the late seventeenth century. An early example in the Palazzo dei Conservatori at Rome is of a square pattern adorned with pilasters at the corners, but the French *bombé* shape was generally preferred (Plate 143C). In some mid-eighteenth-century Venetian examples the curve of the belly has been ridiculously exaggerated and the top made considerably larger than the base (Fig. 53). In

FIG. 53. Chest of drawers; Venetian; eighteenth century

Rome and Naples rather more reticent designs were adopted. In Venice and Genoa chests of drawers were frequently lacquered or painted, while Lombard examples were often decorated with *intarsia*. Elaborate bronze mounts in the French style are rare on *cassettoni* made outside Piedmont. In the United States it was not common in the Queen Anne period, but was revived, especially in New England, during the Chippendale period. Serpentine, oxbow, and block-front shapes are found on New England Chippendale chests.

Cheval-glass. A larger type of toilet mirror in a frame with four legs; also known as a horse dressing-glass; dating from the end of the eighteenth century. The rectangular mirror either pivoted on screws set in the uprights or moved up and down by means of a weight within the frame ("the same as a sash-window" – Sheraton). Turned uprights and stretchers were often found on these pieces about 1800.

Cheveret. *See* Secretaire.

Chiffonier. A piece of furniture which has given rise to a certain amount of confusion. The French chiffonier was a tall chest of drawers, but the *chiffonière*, a quite different piece, was a small set of drawers on legs. It was the latter which seems to have been copied in England in the later eighteenth century. Another form of chiffonier was popular in the Regency period – a low cupboard with shelves for books. As this was similar to contemporary commodes, it can be taken that the English version of the *chiffonière* was the only true small piece of furniture.

Child's furniture. Mostly small-scale furniture for children's usage, distinct from toy furniture. Some confusion exists between tables and the square joined stool (with unsplayed legs) which certainly existed as such. Chairs follow full-scale design, or are highchair pattern, some of enclosed or wainscot fashion, others elevated on tall legs. A framework on wheels to support a toddler has been given various names, e.g. baby-cage or go-cart.

China cabinet. Seldom, if ever, found in America as a separate piece of furniture before 1790–1800. Even then it is perhaps a "bookcase" (*q.v.*) used for displaying china. In early examples the lower portion is often a shallow cupboard on legs. Most American china cabinets date after 1800 and are in the Sheraton or a later style.

China-stand. An ornamental stand for displaying china or flowers, introduced at the end of the seventeenth century and at first taking the form of a low pedestal on carved and scrolled feet, or of a vase on a plinth. In the early eighteenth century the form was sometimes that of a stool with cabriole legs, in mahogany. More fanciful designs, in the rococo taste, were evident after 1750, as in the "Stands for China Jarrs" presented in Chippendale's *Director*. In the Adam period some attractive stands for flower-bowls resembled the contemporary candle-stands with three uprights. Little four-legged stands with shelves were also made at this time for flower-pots.

Chip-carving. Lightly cut ("chipped") surface ornament, mostly of formal character and including whorls, roundels (*qq.v.*), etc. Such work, known medievally, persisted on items of much later date.

Classical style. Basically any humanistic style emphasizing ancient Greek ideals, and in the arts a style inspired by Greek and Roman art and architecture. In American furniture the style reflected the innovations of Robert Adam, the British architect who was inspired by ancient Roman design. The design books of Hepplewhite and Sheraton helped communicate the style to America, where it has been called after them by dividing the style into two tendencies, the Hepplewhite and Sheraton. This is a difficult distinction to make.

Claw-and-ball foot. An adaptation, probably from the Chinese, of a dragon's claw grasping a pearl. Perhaps first adapted in Europe by the Dutch, it spread to England, from whence it was introduced into America about 1735. Enormously popular as the foot of American cabriole leg furniture in the Queen Anne and Chippendale styles. It remained much in fashion as late as the 1790s. In America a bird's claw was generally used, mostly the eagle's.

Clock-cases. Elaborate clock-cases made their appearance in France in the Louis XIV period and were often treated in the most monumental manner. They became a special product of the Boulle *atelier*, as they did of the workshop of Cressent later. In the Louis XV and Louis XVI periods they took almost any form which appealed to their creators, and a great deal of ingenuity, both of design and craftsmanship, went into their production. Roughly, they divided themselves into five main types: wall or cartel clocks, mantel clocks, pedestal clocks, *régulateurs*, and bracket clocks, the names of which are self-explanatory.

If the movement or make of a clock is known and the date is established the collector should remember that it may have originally been placed in another case. This is not uncommon.

Close-chairs and **close-** or **night-stools.** Were sometimes chair-shaped, sometimes rectangular or drum-shaped boxes (possibly covered and padded), and sometimes rectangular boxes on legs. A type of joined stool with a box-top was so usable, though it does not follow that all stools with this feature were for sanitary usage.

Coaster. A receptacle which came into use before 1750 for moving wine, beer, and food on the dining-table; also variously known as a slider, decanter stand, and beer-wagon. For ease of movement, the coaster was normally fitted either with small wheels or with a baize-covered base, and the materials used in good examples included mahogany, papier mâché, and silver. Beer-wagons were sometimes made with special places for the jug and drinking vessels.

Cock's head. Twin-plate hinge of curvilinear shape, the finials formed (more or less) as a cock's head. Frequently found on woodwork of the late sixteenth and first half of the seventeenth centuries.

Coffer. Term freely confused with chest. In strict definition a coffer was a chest or box covered in leather or some other material and banded with metalwork, but it seems likely that the term was not always precisely used. It may not be wrong to class as coffers various stoutly built and/or heavily ironed strong-chests and -boxes, even though they do not fulfil all the above requirements. Trussing coffers were furnished with lifting rings and shackles or other devices for transportation; but chests and coffers not intended for transport might be chained to the wall for security.

Comb-back. *See* Windsor.

Commode. The normal French word for a chest of drawers, which seems to date from the early eighteenth century.

Concertina action. A device on card and gaming tables for extending the frame to support the table top when it is opened. The back half of the frame is made up of two hinged sec-

tions that fold in to reduce the frame size when the top is closed.

Connecticut chest. So named because chiefly made in seventeenth- and eighteenth-century Connecticut. Decorative chest with or without a bottom drawer or two. Ornamented with applied bosses and split spindles

FIG. 54

which set off three front panels carved, low relief, in conventionalized flowers – centre panel, sunflowers; other panels, tulips (Fig. 54).

Constitution mirror. A term of obscure origin, perhaps a misnomer, widely used in America when referring to a Chippendale-style wall mirror with strings of leaves or flow-

FIG. 55

ers at the sides, a scrolled-arch top, and a fanciful finial, generally a bird. The frame is usually in walnut or mahogany and partly gilded (Fig. 55).

Corner chair. A square or squarish seat supported by two side posts and a back post, the three extending above the seat to a low, strong, semicircular top rail. The fourth support, a leg, is added centre front. Made in America from about 1700 to 1775, it is found in three styles – Dutch–Queen Anne transitional, Queen Anne, and Chippendale. Also called roundabout and writing chair. Some authorities say the American Windsor chair (*q.v.*) may have been evolved from it.

Corner-cupboard. This type of furniture consists of a triangular cupboard containing shelves and closed by a door, which is sometimes curved. It is made to fit into the right-angled corner of a room. *Encoignures* begin to appear in France during the Louis XV period, and are usually made in pairs, often *en suite* with a secretaire or chest of drawers. They continued to be made right up to the Revolution.

Coromandel or **zebra-wood.** A form of ebony with light-coloured striped markings found on the Coromandel coast (*see also under* Ebony).

Couch. A seventeenth- and eighteenth-century term for day-bed; not used as synonym for sofa or settee until recent times.

Counter. Hutch-like structure, sometimes approximating to a table with an under-compartment. The name (surviving in shop-counter, etc.) derives from the top being employed for reckoning accounts with counters or jettons disposed on a marked scale. When not so used the counter was available for a variety of other purposes.

Court cupboard. The earliest fine cupboard in America. A kind of Jacobean buffet (and called a buffet in England), with the upper portion enclosed, the lower open. Sometimes, however, the upper portion is partly open – that is, contains a closed central cupboard with splayed sides. When the bottom portion is also closed, whether with doors or as a chest of drawers, it is in America called a press cupboard (*q.v.*). Early ones are generally of oak, with much sturdy Jacobean ornament, and seldom, if ever, ornamented alike (*c.* 1650–70).

Courting mirror. Small mirror framed with mouldings and a cresting, the crested area often containing a painted picture or design. They were traditionally a courting gift in eighteenth-century New England. Lockwood says their source was a similar mirror made in China for the export trade.

Cradle. The cradle, which had hitherto

been a fairly simple piece of furniture occasionally carved but otherwise of a type that might be found in any other European country, was developed into an object of extravagant fantasy in mid-eighteenth-century Venice. Here cradles were made with rippling rococo rims and lacquered with floral motifs or heavily carved with *putti* and gilded. The most fantastic of all is that formerly in the *Donà dalle Rose* Collection at Venice, in which the cradle itself is swung between two branches of a naturalistically carved tree, with a stork gazing at the occupant from the foot and a chinoiserie parasol suspended over its head.

Credence. Side-table as used ecclesiastically for the Elements prior to Consecration, and for the Cruets, etc., therewith associated. Such tables were sometimes of hutch-like formation, and the term credence has been loosely extended to cover other furniture of more or less similar construction.

Credenza. An Italian sideboard of buffet used as a serving-table on which silver might also be displayed. Fifteenth- and sixteenth-century *credenze* were either simple tables designed to stand by a wall or else long cupboards, sometimes with canted corners, the height of an ordinary dining-table (Fig. 56).

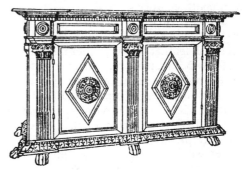

FIG. 56. *Credenza*; Tuscan; sixteenth century

As they were normally covered with linen, they were very simple in design and decoration. A recessed top story containing a cupboard was added to many *credenze* in the sixteenth century, and this was usual in subsequent periods.

Cresting. Shaped and sometimes perforated ornament on the top of a structure, as in the cresting of a chair.

Croft. A small filing cabinet of the late

eighteenth century (named after its inventor), specially designed to be moved about easily in the library; it had many small drawers and a writing-top.

Cromwellian. Term of convenience applied to English furniture of austere character, actually or supposedly made about the time of the Commonwealth or Interregnum (1649–60), but also used loosely of related types.

Cromwellian chair. Spanish-type chair with strips of leather for the seat and back; turned legs and stretchers, occasionally spiral turned. Generally ornamented with brass-headed tacks. A mid-seventeenth-century "Puritan" chair. Very few have been found.

Cross stretcher. X-shaped stretcher in straight or curved lines. Sometimes found on occasional tables, a few chairs, and in America as highboys and lowboys.

Cupboard. Originally cup-board, a species of sideboard for the display and service of plate, etc., and having no essential connection with enclosed and doored structures. When equipped with such features, these might be noted (*see* Ambry). The modern sense of cupboard, as an enclosed structure, is a long-standing usurpation, such items being mostly descended from the press, press-cupboard, etc. Livery cupboard (a much-abused term from Fr. *livrer*, to deliver) was a *doorless* structure, as is clearly stated in the Hengrave Hall contracts, 1537–8. That it was distinguished from the court cupboard is shown by such an entry as "ij court cubbordes, and one liverye cubborde", in Unton Inventory, 1596 ("Liverie table" is also listed). Court cupboard was likewise an open structure, or with a small enclosed compartment in the upper part (*see* R. W. Symonds, "The Evolution of the Cupboard", in *The Connoisseur*, December 1943, and "The Dynyng Parlor and its Furniture", op. cit., January 1944). The tendency to compartment such furniture eventually resulted in enclosed pieces of similar outline being called court cupboard, though press cupboard is preferable. Welsh varieties of the press cupboard are the cwpwrdd deuddarn (two-tiered) and the cwpwrdd tridarn (three-tiered, the top stage often more or less open) (Plate 92B). Dole-cupboard strictly applies to hanging or other structures open-shelved, or doored and railed, used in the charitable dispensation of bread, etc., in churches and other institutions. The term is often wrongly applied to food-cupboard, or, better, food-hutch. Spice-cupboard is a hanging "cupboard", usually of small dimensions, internally fitted with shelves or compartments and drawers, and fronted with a door. Doubtless many were used to hold spices, herbs, and medicaments, though they could have served various purposes. Corner cupboard is a triangular structure, doored or open, independent or fitted, and normally furnished with shelving.

Cupid's bow. A term used to describe the typical top rail of a Chippendale chair back which curves up at the ends and dips slightly in the centre.

Curly. The grainings of some woods – maple, walnut, birch, etc. – sometimes show feather-like, curly or tiger-stripe markings, which are much prized. Not to be confused with other markings, such as bird's-eye, wavy, blister, and quilted.

Cutlery Stand. *See* Canterbury (2).

Cylinder-top desk. A writing-table, incorporating drawers and writing accessories, the functional part of which is closed by means of a curved panel fastened with a lock. It is usually supported on tall legs and differs from a roll-top desk (*q.v.*) in that the curved panel is in one piece and not slatted.

Cypress. Fine furniture was sometimes made of the pale to dark brown (swamp) cypress, especially in South Carolina, Georgia, and other southern American states. More often used for drawers and linings, and for utility-type furniture. It is noted for its resistance to decay.

Daventry. A small chest of drawers with a sloping top for writing; said to be named after a client of the firm of Gillow who claimed to have invented it.

Day-bed. Known in England from the sixteenth century, though authentic examples are mostly of much later date. The original form approximated to a stump-bed with a sloped back at one end. In the period of Charles II, and later, day-beds were caned, their frames often being elaborately carved, quite likely *en suite* with cane chairs.

Decanter stand. *See* Coaster.

Desk. A term of varied meaning, but taken here to refer to two portable pieces. (1) The commonest meaning was that of a box (originating in medieval times) with a sloping top for reading and writing. Early examples in oak in the Tudor and Stuart periods had carving and inlay, and sometimes the owner's initials and date. When bureaux came into use at the end of the seventeenth century these small desks were too useful to discard, and were fitted with drawers and pigeon-holes; many were veneered with walnut, or japanned, and some were mounted on stands. In the Georgian period they became less decorative, and were usually of plain mahogany; few were made after 1800. (2) In the later eighteenth century "desk" was the current term for what would now be called a music-stand (which was also used for reading); it generally took the form of a tripod base supporting a shaft and a sloping, adjustable top.

Desk box. A rectangular box with sloping lid for the storage of books and writing materials; more popularly known in America as a Bible box.

Deuddarn. *See* Cupboard.

Document drawer. A thin narrow drawer in a desk for important papers.

Doreurs, Corporation des. The craft guild responsible for gilding in all its forms in France. The organization was similar to that of the *menuisiers-ébénistes*, except that the apprenticeship lasted five instead of six years. There were three hundred and seventy *maîtres-doreurs* at the end of the eighteenth century (*see also* Ormolu).

Dowel. Headless pin used in construction. Though, architecturally, dowels may be of other materials, wood is understood when speaking of furniture. Trenail (i.e. tree-nail) is another term for a wooden dowel (*see* Nails).

Dowry chest or **dower chest.** Is one made to store the trousseau of a prospective bride. Outstanding among American examples are the Hadley chest (Fig. 61), the Connecticut chest (Plate 66c), and the painted Pennsylvania-German chest.

Drake foot. *See* Duck foot.

Drawer. Box in a framework from which it can be drawn. In some simple or traditional constructions drawers merely rest on the framework, but a typical feature of the late sixteenth to seventeenth century was a groove on each side of a drawer, accommodating projecting runners on the framework. This gave way, in later furniture, to runner-strips at the base of the drawer itself, and the encasing of the interior framing with dustboards.

Dresser. On which food was dressed; a species of sideboard with or without a superimposed "back"; also for service of food, and/or storage of plates, dishes, etc. Some backless dressers are closely allied to the side-table. Dressers are wontedly furnished with storage accommodation (such as ambries, shelving, drawers, etc., or combinations of such). Welsh-dresser is used of local varieties of the tall-back dresser found virtually everywhere (Plate 92A). North Wales and South Wales types are differentiated.

Drop or **tear-drop handle.** The characteristic pull used on furniture with drawers, 1690–1720. Of brass, solid or hollow, this pendant hangs from a brass plate and is attached to the drawer by wire pins. Also called tear drop and pear drop, which picturesquely suggest its shape.

Drop leaf. A table with one or two hinged leaves which can be raised or dropped by bringing swinging legs or supports into use. Many kinds of drop-leaf tables have special names – butterfly, corner, gate-leg, library, Pembroke, sofa, etc.

Drum table. A circular top table on a tripod base with a deep skirt that may contain drawers. The type exists only in the classical style, and American examples appear late.

Duck foot. Colloquial American term for the three-toed club or Dutch foot, mostly found in Delaware River Valley furniture. Also called drake foot and web foot. For some reason the pad foot is often mistakenly called a duck foot.

Dumb-waiter. A dining-room stand, an English invention of the early eighteenth century, with normally three circular trays, increasing in size towards the bottom, on a shaft with tripod base. This established design gave way to more elaborate versions at the end of the century; four-legged supports and rectangular trays were found; and quite different kinds were square or circular tables with special compartments for bottles, plates, etc.

Eagle, American. The Seal of the United States, adopted 1786, emblematizes the American bald eagle with wings outspread (Fig. 57). This emblem promptly became popular as furniture ornament in America –carved (free or engaged), inlaid or painted – replacing the fanciful phoenix which had been used since the mid-eighteenth century.

FIG. 57

Ébéniste. The ordinary French term for a cabinet-maker concerned in making veneered furniture as distinct from a *menuisier* (*q.v.*). The word derived from the ebony (*ébène*) to be found on the earliest veneered furniture in France. It is not found, nor are *ébénistes* associated by name with the *menuisiers'* guild, until 1743, by which time the use of ebony was more or less confined to pieces in the Boulle technique. Although permitted by guild regulations to work in plain wood like the *menuisiers*, an *ébéniste* usually confined his activities to techniques requiring veneer or inlay (*see also under* Menuisiers-Ébénistes).

Ebonize. To stain wood to look like ebony. This was often done in the seventeenth century for the applied ornaments on oak furniture. Also used in William and Mary period when contrasting colours in wood were sought.

Ebony. A hard wood, black and finely grained, sometimes found with brown or purple streaks. Found commonly in tropical climates in Asia, Africa, and America. Extensively used in France for veneering furniture, particularly in combination with Boulle marquetry (*see also under* Coromandel or Zebra-wood and Boulle marquetry). Grandfather and other clock cases were veneered with ebony in England in the seventeenth century.

Egg-and-tongue (egg-and-dart). Repeat ornament of alternated ovolo and dart-like motifs (Fig. 58); as much other ornament of

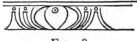

FIG. 58

classical origin, transmitted through Renaissance channels.

Elizabethan. Term of convenience, strictly applicable to furniture, etc., made in the reign of Elizabeth I (1558–1603), though loosely used of pieces of later date displaying Elizabethan characteristics. The reign was long; just as early Elizabethan furniture shows influences from previous reigns, so late Elizabethan merges easily into Jacobean.

En arbelette. An expression used for shapes and forms which have a double curve similar to that of a cross-bow.

Encoignures. *See under* Corner-cupboards.

Espagnolette. A decorative motif popularized by the engravings of Gillot and Watteau and consisting of a female head surrounded by a large stiff collar of a type worn in Spain in the seventeenth century. It was used frequently in the early eighteenth century as a mounted decoration for furniture.

Etagère. A small work-table consisting usually of shelves or trays sets one above the other. The word is of nineteenth-century origin, the ordinary term used earlier being *table à ouvrage*.

Fake or forgery. Furniture (or other objects) made or assembled in simulation of authentic antiquities, with deceptive intent. Fakes are of several kinds, of which a few may be listed: (*a*) the wholly modern fake, though quite possibly made of old wood; (*b*) the fake incorporating old and in themselves authentic parts; (*c*) the "carved-up" fake, as, for instance, a plain chest (itself antique) with modern carving added; (*d*) the "married" piece, of which all, or considerable portions, may be authentic, but which has been "made-up" from more than one source. Difficult of classification are certain items which have been liberally restored (*see* Restoration), each case demanding judgement on its own merits. Though over-restoration is reprehensible, cases occur of pieces reconditioned with innocent intent. An ordinary repair to a genuine antique need not disqualify it. At the same time a watchful eye should be kept for an old faking trick of inserting an obvious "repair" for the sole purpose of making the rest of a spurious piece look older by contrast.

Fan-back. *See* Windsor chair.

Fan pattern. Description of the back of a chair when filled with ribs somewhat resembling the stalks of a half-open fan. Also said of any fan-shaped carving, inlay, or painted decoration. (*See* Rising sun.)

Fancy chair. Almost any variety of decorative occasional chair, generally light in weight, painted, and with a cane seat. The source was probably the late Sheraton occasional chair. Popular in all styles from 1800 to 1850.

Federal style. A term often used in America to describe furniture made in the United States between 1785 and 1830, the early days of the Republic. It includes works showing Hepplewhite, Sheraton, Directoire, and early Empire influence. An inexact, therefore unsatisfactory, term – though at times highly convenient.

Fire-dogs. An appliance, popular in France for use in a fireplace to support the logs of a fire. These were usually made in pairs of iron with bronze ends or finials, sometimes patinated and sometimes gilt. They took various forms during the Louis XV and XVI periods, when the ornamental parts are usually made of ormolu and are often of the finest quality.

Fire-screen. An adjustable screen made from the end of the seventeenth century to give protection from the intense heat of large open fires. Two main kinds were used. (1) Pole screen: with the screen on an upright supported on a tripod base; known as a "screen-stick" in the late seventeenth century; and in very general use in the eighteenth. The screen, often of needlework, was at first rectangular (Plate 124c), but oval and shield shapes were fashionable in the late eighteenth century. In the Regency period the tripod was replaced by a solid base, and the screen was a banner hung from a bar on the upright. (2) Horse or cheval screen – two uprights, each on two legs, enclosing a panel (Plate 123). Elaborate carving and gilding of the crests was often found until the end of the eighteenth century, when lighter and simpler screens were in vogue. Needlework was the popular material for the panel.

Fish-tail. The carving, somewhat resembling a fish tail, on the top rail of a banister-back chair.

Flag seat. Colloquial term sometimes used for a seat woven of rush-like material.

Flambeaux. *See under* Candlesticks.

Flame carving. A cone-like finial carved to represent flames, either straight or spiralling. Used on highboys, secretaries, grandfather clocks, etc.

Flemish scroll. A curving double scroll used on William and Mary style legs; also on the wide stretcher connecting the front legs.

Flower-stand. *See* China-stand.

Fluting. Narrow vertical groovings used in classical architecture on columns and pilasters. In furniture fluting is employed where pilasters or columns are suggested and on straight legs. It is of particular importance in the classical style, but is encountered in earlier work as well.

FIG. 59

Folding table. *See* Gate-leg table.

Fondeurs, Corporation des. The craft guild responsible for casting and chasing metal, either for sculpture, furniture, or *bronzes d'ameublement* in France. It was organized similarly to those of the *menuisiers-ébénistes* and *doreurs*.

Form. Long, backless seat, with any number of supports from two upwards. Of ancient lineage, the form is simply a long stool. "Longe stoole" occurs in old inventories.

Four-poster. Colloquial term widely used for a bedstead with four posts.

Frame. The style of picture frames altered with the style of painting. The earliest to be found in private houses were very simple, of painted or gilt wood. Late sixteenth-century artists seem sometimes to have designed and painted allegorical frames for their own works. Not until the seventeenth century did the richly carved and gilded frame come into its own. Some late seventeenth- and early eighteenth-century frames are, indeed, better and more elaborate works of art than the pictures they enshrine. Later, eighteenth-century frames are usually more discreet and simple.

Gadrooning. A carved ornamental edging of a repeated pattern which, on Chippendale furniture, is often no more than curving, alternating convex and concave sections. Particularly popular in New York and Philadelphia in the Chippendale period.

Garde Meuble de la Couronne. The department which dealt with all matters connected with the furnishing of the royal palaces in France. It was established by Louis XIV in 1663, and survived until the end of the monarchy. Very fortunately, its records survive more or less intact.

The first inventory of furniture belonging to the Crown was completed in 1673 and has been published in full by M. Emile Molinier (*see* Bibliography), but the most important item among the records is the *Journal*, instituted in 1685 and continuing until 1784. In it every piece acquired for the Crown was scrupulously entered and given a number, with dates of delivery, the name of the maker, costs and measurements, its eventual destination in the Royal palaces, and a full description. The numbers often correspond with those painted in the backs of existing pieces (*see* Inventory numbers), and these can be thus identified fairly closely from the descriptions and measurements.

The *Journal* consists in all of eighteen volumes and 3,600 pages, of which only a small proportion are missing, and is preserved in the *Archives Nationales* in Paris. After 1784 a new system of recording was introduced, but the same numbers were preserved, and these, in fact, continued to be used until well into the nineteenth century.

Gate-leg. A form of drop-leaf table with

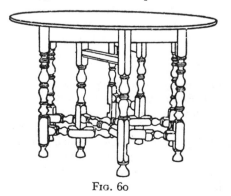

FIG. 60

swinging supports that are legs joined to the main frame of the table by upper and lower stretchers which make a gate. First used in the late seventeenth and early eighteenth centuries.

Gesso. Composition of plaster of Paris or whiting and size for making bas-reliefs and other ornaments. It came into fashion in England just before 1700 and was a popular form of decoration until about 1740.

Giridon. *See* Guéridon.

Glastonbury chair. Is collectors' jargon for a type of chair with X-supports and elbowed arms linking seat and top of back. The name derives from an example at Wells, supposedly associated with the last Abbot of Glastonbury. Examples of like construction have been made or embellished at various, including modern, periods.

Gobelins, Manufacture Royale des. The State-supported organization founded by Letters Patent at Gobelins in 1667 through the inspiration of Colbert, Louis XIV's finance minister. It was designed to provide, apart from tapestry, all products of the luxury arts, including furniture, and its first great task was the equipment of the interior of the Palaces of Versailles. It owed its success and great reputation to the energies of its first director, Charles Le Brun, who made it into the foundation stone of the organized applied arts in France.

Goose neck. *See* Scroll top.

Gothic. A twelfth- to fifteenth-century style revived superficially in the eighteenth century. Chippendale offered designs in the "Gothick Taste", occasionally followed by American craftsmen. These consisted of arcades of pointed arches and quatrefoils on chair backs. In the classical period there are also occasional designs employing Gothic motifs.

Grandfather clock. Long-case floor clock which appeared in England at the time of the Restoration. In America it was in standard use by 1750, though many earlier examples exist. Lockwood mentions one in a Boston inventory of 1652. American grandfather clocks generally follow English models, except when the decorative motives are American – e.g. block-front-and-shell.

Grandmother clock. Modern name for a

smaller floor clock, about half to two-thirds as tall as a grandfather clock.

Guéridon or **guéridon table.** A small piece of furniture, usually circular, intended to support some form of light. In the seventeenth century it sometimes took the form of a Negro figure holding a tray, and the name derives from that of a well-known Moorish galley-slave called Guéridon. Subsequently the term was extended to cover almost any form of small table on which candelabra, etc., might be placed.

Guilloche. Band of curvilinear ornament suggesting entwined ribbons (Fig. 62).

Hadley chest. So called because mostly found in and around Hadley, Massachusetts. A characteristic New England dower chest of 1690–1710. Its distinctive feature is the incised carving of tulips, vines, and leaves which cover the entire front (Fig. 61).

FIG. 61

Handkerchief table. A single-leaf table with leaf and top triangular in shape. Closed, the table fits in a corner, opened, it is a small square.

Hickory. Oak-like American wood often used for furniture parts needing strength without heaviness; also for bent parts; and almost always for spindles of Windsor chairs.

Highboy. Uniquely American tall chest of drawers mounted on a commode or lowboy (*q.v.*) and topped with a broken-arch pediment usually heightened with finials. Characteristically plain in New England; richly carved and ornamented in Philadelphia. It was made in three styles – William and Mary, Queen Anne, and Chippendale. The Philadelphia Chippendale highboy is sometimes thought to be the most remarkable creative

achievement in American antique furniture design. The late authority on English antique furniture, Herbert Cescincky, wrote: ". . . there is little or no kinship between a Philadelphia highboy and anything ever made in England". Much sought today, they bring high prices – up to $43,000 for one; $44,000 for another.

Hitchcock chair. American adaptation of the late Sheraton-style painted and stencilled chair. It has round-turned legs, raked, and an oval-turned "pillow-back" top rail. Almost always painted black with stencillings of fruits and flowers in gold or colours. Named for Lambert Hitchcock, of Hitchcockville, Connecticut, who made them in quantity from 1820 to 1850.

Holly. A hard wood with a fine close grain. White or greenish white in colour. Found commonly in Europe and western Asia. Used extensively for fillets to frame marquetry (*see also* Boxwood).

Hoop-back. *See* Windsor chair.

Hope chest. Colloquial American term, widely used for dowry chest, which itself is a misnomer, since a chest normally serves more purposes across the years than holding a trousseau (*see* Dowry chest).

Horse-glass and horse-screen. *See* Cheval-glass and Fire-screen.

Horseshoe back. *See* Windsor chair.

Hutch. Enclosed structure, often raised on uprights, or an enclosed structure of more than one tier. The name derives from Fr. *huche*, a kneading-trough or meal-tub, but the significance of hutch was much wider. Food-hutch, often confused with dole-cupboard, is a name given to a hutch with perforated panels (Plate 88).

Inlay. Surface ornament formed by insetting separate pieces of differently coloured woods, or bone, ivory, shell, etc., in a recessed ground (Fig. 63).

Inventory numbers. These are often found usually painted or branded on furniture made for the Crown or Royal Family of France. They often refer to the *Journal du Garde Meuble de la Couronne*, which has survived intact for some periods between the late seventeenth century and the Revolution. When accompanied by a palace letter (*q.v.*), the numbers may refer to the inventories made of that particular royal residence which may or may not be still extant. Considering everything, the documents of furniture made for the French Crown have survived in an extraordinary number of cases.

The discovery of an inventory number o any kind on a piece of French furniture of whatever date is always worth the closest investigation, as it may be possible to identify it.

Jacobean. Term of convenience usually applicable to furniture made in the reign of James I (1603–25), and perhaps, though unusually, to that of James II (1685–8). In general, loosely applied to furniture styles in direct descent from the Elizabethan tradition. It is thus employed of certain types of furniture covering virtually the whole of the seventeenth century and even later, though from the time of Charles II it is generally restricted to pieces of unmodish or traditional character. Jacobean is not now favoured as a descriptive label by scholarly writers, except in cases of uncertain dating, preference being given to a more precise system involving such approximations as "*c.* 1620" or "first quarter of the seventeenth century", etc.

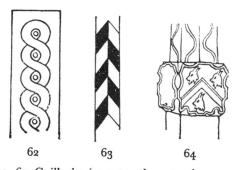

FIG. 62. Guilloche (seventeenth century)
FIG. 63. Herring-bone Inlay
FIG. 64. Knop on bedpost (sixteenth century)

Japanning. European and American version of Oriental lacquering often substituting paint for the layers of varnish on lacquered wares. Raised chinoiserie in plaster is generally the added decoration. The technique became popular in England late in the seventeenth century; a book of instructions, *Treatise of Japaning and Varnishing*, by Stalker and Parker, was published in 1688 in London. In America the technique was practised before 1715 and continued to be used throughout the century.

Jewel. Ornament with raised devices distantly suggestive of gem-stones, often combined with systems of reeding (*q.v.*) (Fig. 83).

Joined. Term used in describing furniture made by a joiner.

Kas. The Dutch word, *kast*, for wardrobe incorrectly spelled. Used to refer to the wardrobes made by Dutch settlers in America. They are generally large, with wide mouldings, heavy cornice, and on ball feet. Their style is of the seventeenth century, but they were made for a great part of the eighteenth.

Kettle-stand (also **urn-** and **teapot-stand**). A special stand which was introduced with tea-drinking in the later seventeenth century, of two main kinds. (1) A small table, tripod or four-legged, with a gallery or raised edge round the top. Slender four-legged tables were common in the later part of the eighteenth century, nearly always with a slide for the teapot. (2) A box-like arrangement set on four legs; the box was usually lined with metal, and had an opening in one side for the kettle spout, as well as a slide for the teapot. Another version of the box type had a three-sided enclosure with a metal-lined drawer. The two main types of kettle-stand persisted until the end of the eighteenth century, when they were superseded by occasional tables.

Kingwood. *See under* Rosewood.

Knife-case. A container for knives (and other cutlery) introduced in the seventeenth century for use in dining-rooms. Two distinct varieties appeared. (1) Until the later eighteenth century the usual shape was a box with a sloping top and convex front (Plate 123); the interior had divisions for the cutlery. Walnut, shagreen (untanned leather with a roughened surface), also made from shark skin, and later mahogany, sometimes inlaid, were the main materials. (2) This was succeeded by the graceful vase-shaped case, the top of which was raised and lowered on a central stem, around which the knife partitions were arranged; this type was designed to stand on a pedestal or at each end of the sideboard. Straight-sided cases were favoured in the early nineteenth century.

Knop. Swelling member on an upright, etc., a knob. Thus a knopped post (Fig. 64).

Knotted pine. Originally a second-best plank of pine with the rough knot showing in the wood and therefore used only when covered with paint. Today the paint is removed, the knot design being liked by enough collectors to make old knotty pine sought after.

Labelled furniture. Mid-eighteenth-century American and British chair- and cabinet-makers often pasted small paper labels, advertising their wares, on furniture leaving their shops. A number of these labels remain to this day on the furniture and, when genuine, help establish characteristics of a particular shop.

Lacche. The word *lacche* is used in Italian to cover all painted decoration applied to furniture, whether or not it has the hard gloss of Oriental lacquer (see p. 321). Painted furniture (*mobilia laccata*) was produced in most districts of Italy in the eighteenth century, but the most celebrated centre for it was Venice. Earlier examples were normally decorated with chinoiseries, but in the middle of the eighteenth century floral motifs were more popular and some *armadi* were painted with landscapes in their panels. Desks were occasionally painted with *trompe l'œil* prints and papers which appear to be pinned to them.

Lacquer. A form of resinous varnish capable of taking a high polish. Its chief application to furniture in France dates from the early eighteenth century, when it was imported for this purpose from China and Japan. The Oriental lacquer was also often imitated in France and then applied to furniture locally (*see also under* Vernis Martin).

Ladder back. A chair back with the vertical centre splat replaced by a series of horizontal bars cut in curving lines. Usually this type of chair has straight legs. It originated in the Chippendale period, but persisted until the end of the eighteenth century.

Lambrequin. A short piece of hanging drapery, often imitated in metal or wood for decorative purposes.

Lantern. A container for a candle or candles; portable, fixed to the wall or hung from the ceiling; especially useful for lighting the draughty parts of the house. Early lanterns (*c.* 1500–1700) were made of wood, iron, latten (a yellow alloy of copper and zinc), and brass, the most common filling being horn (whence the Shakespearean "lanthorn"). After 1700, when glass become more plentiful, lanterns were increasingly fashionable, particularly as they prevented candle-grease from falling about, and their frames, of metal, walnut, and mahogany, followed the main decorative modes of the times. In addition to these more elaborate kinds, simpler lanterns of glass shades, in a variety of forms, were in wide use in the eighteenth century.

Lazy Susan. *See* Dumb waiter.

Library steps. Found in libraries of large houses after about the middle of the eighteenth century, and of two main kinds: (1) the fixed pair of steps, some with hand-rails, and (2) the folding steps, sometimes ingeniously fitted into other pieces of furniture, such as chairs, stools, and tables.

Lighthouse clock. American shelf or mantel clock designed by Simon Willard about 1800 (Fig. 65). The case is judged to have been modelled after the lighthouse on Eddystone Rock in the English Channel. Miller declares that "because of mechanical difficulties . . . very few were made".

FIG. 65

Linenfold. Carved ornament suggested by folded linen, first found late in the fifteenth century, very popular in the first half of the sixteenth, and continuing in diminishing quantity for many years (Fig. 7).

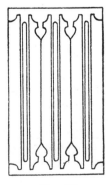

FIG. 66

Attempts to distinguish "true" (realistic) from "mock" (formalized) linenfold need not be taken too seriously. Some of the single-fold types (often cusped and foliated) have been differentiated as parchemin (Fr.), from a supposed resemblance to cut parchment. Apart from its obvious decorativeness, no satisfactory explanation of the origin of linenfold has been adduced. An attractive suggestion is that it was inspired by the Veil of the Chalice, though it could have arisen in other ways.

Linen-press. A frame with a wooden spiral screw for pressing linen between two boards, dating from the seventeenth century.

Lobby chest. Defined by Sheraton as "a kind of half chest of drawers, adapted for the use of a small study, lobby, etc."

Lock-plate (or **scutcheon**). Front-plate of a lock, or the plate protecting a key-hole.

Looking glass. In the sixteenth and seventeenth centuries looking-glass frames were similar to picture frames, though seldom as ornate as the richest examples. During the eighteenth century they were made with delicate mouldings in the wide diversity of shapes which the rococo taste approved and the mirror – unlike the painting – permitted. Large mirrors, or pier glasses, in elaborately carved frames were used in palatial decoration in the early eighteenth century. Small wall mirrors, framed in wood or pottery, and with designs engraved on the glass were popular in the mid-eighteenth century, especially in Venice. They were sometimes designed to serve as *girandoles*. Toilet mirrors with lacquered, gilt, or simple polished wood frames, similar to French and English examples, were made throughout Italy in the eighteenth century.

Loop-back. *See* Windsor chair.

Lowboy. Modern name for an American creation inspired by the English flat-top dressing-table with drawers, yet in its final development closer to the French commode. Attractively plain in New England, much carved and ornamented in Philadelphia. It occurs in three styles – William and Mary, Queen Anne, and Chippendale. Often made as a companion piece to the highboy (*q.v.*). Dressing-table, chamber-table, low chest of drawers were eighteenth-century names for it.

Lunette ornament. Formal carving composed of a horizontal system of semicircles,

FIG. 67

variously filled and embellished, frequently disposed in a repeat-band (Fig. 67).

Lyre. The lyre form as a furniture ornament was introduced to England from France by Adam in the second half of the eighteenth century and reached America after the Revolution and was increasingly used until about 1830 for chair backs and table supports in Hepplewhite, Sheraton, and, notably, Duncan Phyfe furniture

FIG. 68

(Fig. 68). American lyre-form clocks, late Empire style, were popular about 1825–40.

Mahogany. A dense, dark, heavy wood which in the eighteenth century was known in two varieties, the Spanish and the Honduras. The Spanish from Cuba, San Domingo, and Puerto Rico was darker and harder than the variety from Honduras. By 1750 it had supplanted walnut for the highest quality work in England, and at about the same time it became important in America.

Maple. A handsome, pale, satiny hardwood of close grain, plentiful in the northern part of America. Much used for furniture, especially in New England, ever since earliest times. Often it was the inexpensive substitute for walnut or mahogany, also for satinwood inlay, etc. Old maple takes on a rich honey colour. Its regular or plain graining is subject to several very attractive markings – curly (a tiger striping), bird's-eye, blister, and quilted Many pieces of furniture have been established as American because the underframing or secondary wood is maple.

Marlborough leg. Of obscure origin, perhaps originating in England as the trade term for a bed with square or square tapering (pillar) legs and block (plinth) feet. In America, by extension, a whole range of elegant furniture, mostly mid-eighteenth-century Philadelphian, with legs as described, generally with the inside edge chamfered to lighten the appearance. The authority, Horner, says: "A refinement and rival of the cabriole. . . . There were but few pieces of the Chinese-Chippendale ever made in Philadelphia, so that nearly all Pembroke tables and similar articles should be classified as Marlborough. . . ."

Marquetry. The ordinary word for a design formed of substances inlaid on a carcase in the form of a veneer. It can consist of various types of wood, combined with such materials as tortoiseshell, brass, pewter, copper, mother-of-pearl, etc. It first came into prominence in English furniture in about 1675. It is found in Italy, in the sixteenth century and in Flanders in the seventeenth century. It was from these sources that it came to be imported into France mainly by the foreign craftsmen working at the courts of Henri IV and Louis XIII. After the majority of Louis XIV, Boulle marquetry (*q.v.*) came to be used extensively. In the eighteenth century the possibilities of wood marquetry were developed until they reached their ultimate perfection in the works of J. H. Riesener (*q.v.*).

Martha Washington chair. Slender Chippendale – Hepplewhite arm-chair with tapered outlines; a "lady's chair", with upholstered, low, shallow seat and high back, which usually ends in a serpentine curve (Fig. 69). So named because Martha Washington is supposed to have used one at Mount Vernon.

FIG. 69

Martha Washington mirror. Walnut or mahogany wall mirror, Georgian style, with handsome gilded mouldings, strings of leaves, fruits, or flowers down the sides, a scroll top, and a bird finial. The base is cut in a series of bold curves. Made in America from about 1760 to 1800. So named because Martha Washington is supposed to have used one at Mount Vernon. (Same as Constitution mirror.)

Martha Washington sewing-table. Oval box-form sewing-table with rounded ends and hinged top. Fitted with drawers and sewing material compartments. The general style is Sheraton, but the particular type seems to be an American variant. It was so named because Martha Washington is supposed to have used one at Mount Vernon.

Melon-bulb. Jargon and comparatively modern term for the swollen member on legs or posts of furniture (Fig. 70). An exaggeration of the knop, it attained full development in the Elizabethan period, thereafter dwindling away.

FIG. 70

Menuisier. The term corresponds roughly to the English "carpenter" or "joiner". In France, as far as furniture was concerned, the menuisiers were responsible for making chairs, beds, and other furniture made from plain or carved woods, as distinct from veneered pieces, which were the province of the *ébénistes* (*q.v.*). Although permitted by guild regulations to work in both techniques, they seldom did so (*see also* Corporation des Menuisiers-Ébénistes).

Menuisiers-Ébénistes, Corporation des. The craft guild which embraced all craftsmen engaged in making wood furniture in France.

An apprentice began his training with a *maître-ébéniste* or *maître-menuisier* at the age of fourteen, and it lasted for six years, after which he entered on his next stage, known as *compagnonage*. This lasted for three to six years, according to whether the craftsman had served his apprenticeship in Paris or elsewhere. During this time the *compagnon* was paid for the work he did. After his *compagnonage* the craftsman was ready to become a *maître* of the guild, but often the period was extended because of lack of vacancies or because of his inability to pay the fees required. These were fairly large and were devoted to the running expenses of the guild. The number of *maîtres* was limited. In 1723 there were 985, and in 1790 this figure had not increased. The King, moreover, had the right to create *maîtres* on his own authority.

A *compagnon* had to submit a specimen of his work before receiving the *maîtrise*, but once a *maître*, he was permitted to open a shop in his own name, in which he could employ some *compagnons*, and was required to take in one apprentice at least. At his death his widow could continue to direct his business, provided that she had qualified *compagnons* to assist her.

After 1751 a *maître* was also required to stamp the furniture he put on sale (*see* Stamps).

In addition to the apprentices, *compagnons*, and *maîtres*, there were two other types of craftsmen involved in the guild organization. Firstly, the maintenance of standards was in the hands of a *syndic* and six *jurés*, elected once a year from among the *maîtres*, whose duty it was to examine the specimens submitted by aspiring *maîtres* and also to inspect all workshops in Paris four times a year and examine work in hand. All pieces of furniture approved by the *jurés* were stamped with the monogram J.M.E. (*juré, or jurande des menuisiers-ébénistes*) (*see also* Stamps).

Meuble à hauteur d'appui. A term used extensively in France at all periods for any low bookcase or cupboard, usually between 3 and 4 feet high.

Meuble d'entre deux. A term used in France in the eighteenth century for a type of furniture which usually consists of a cupboard or chest of drawers flanked at each side by a set of shelves. Often these are open, but sometimes are enclosed by a curved door forming a small cupboard with shelves.

Mirror-stand. An adjustable mirror mounted on a shaft and tripod base, resembling a pole-screen; popular at the end of the eighteenth century.

Misericord. In ecclesiastical woodwork, bracket on underside of hinged seat of a stall, to support an occupant when nominally standing during certain offices. From a "monastic" usage of L. *misericordia* (pity, compassion), in sense of "an indulgence or relaxation of the rule" (O.E.D.). Miserere is an incorrect alternative.

Mortise and tenon. For joining two pieces of wood. The mortise is a cavity, usually rectangular; the tenon, an end shaped to fill the cavity exactly; characteristic of Philadelphia chairs, where seat rail joins the stiles.

FIG. 71. Mortise and tenon

Mother-of-pearl. Inlay of nacreous shell slices, often used on early nineteenth-century American fancy chairs, tables, etc.

Moulding. Shaped member, such as used to enclose panels; or the shaped edge of a lid, cornice, etc.

Muntin. Upright (other than an outermost upright) connecting the upper and lower stretchers of a framework (Fig. 72). An instance is the bearer between the doors of the lower stage

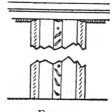

FIG. 72

of a press-cupboard; but the number of muntins depends on the nature of the structure. (*See also* Stile.)

Music-stand. *See* Canterbury (1) and Desk (2).

Nails. A popular notion that iron nails are never found in antique furniture construction is fallacious. In fact, metal nails have been known for centuries, though the use of the wooden dowel (*q.v.*) must not be minimized by implication. Old hand-made nails are very different from the modern, mass-produced variety; but the manufacture of hand-made nails (and screws) has been revived.

Name chests. Colloquial term for chests that bear the decoratively carved or painted name of the original owner.

Neo-Greek. Alternative term for furniture of the brief classical revival in early nineteenth-century America. Mostly said of the late Empire style, 1815–40.

Night-table. A pot cupboard which replaced the close-stool after 1750; sometimes also fitted as a washing-stand (*q.v.*). Among the features commonly found on these pieces may be noted a drawer under the cupboard, a tambour front, and a tray top (Plate 125A).

Some night-tables were given a triangular shape to fit into a corner.

Oak. A hard wood with coarse grain used almost exclusively up to the seventeenth century and as a secondary wood later. Its hardness made it difficult to carve but quite durable.

Occasional table. Any light table easily moved here or there to meet the occasion. Much used in America ever since early eighteenth-century times.

Ormolu. An English word in use from about the middle of the eighteenth century, derived from the French term "*bronze dorée d'or moulu*". Its most accurate equivalents are "*bronze dorée*" or gilt bronze. It was a French speciality, and when found on English furniture it is likely that it was done by French craftsmen. Ormolu is the substance from which all objects covered by the term *bronzes d'ameublement* are made, e.g. lighting fixtures, including candelabra and candlesticks, clockcases, appliances for doors and fireplaces, as well as mounts for furniture. Its manufacture was the function of two craft guilds; the *fondeurs* (*q.v.*) and the *doreurs* (*q.v.*). Its preparation consisted of a model in wood or wax being produced by a sculptor, often of some note; this was then cast in bronze by a *fondeur*, usually by the *cire perdue* method, but sometimes from a mould of clay or sand (*see* article on Bronzes). The casting was then tooled and chased until the required degree of finish had been achieved. This last process (known as *ciselure*) was carried to an extraordinary degree of refinement in France in the eighteenth century, and the tools which the *ciseleurs* used are illustrated in the *Encyclopédie*, showing the precision which could be obtained. The bronzes when finished were often merely dipped in acid and then lacquered, and this often needed to be done more than once, when the surface became dirty.

If they were required to be gilt, this was usually done by the mercury process, of which detailed particulars are also given in the *Encyclopédie*. It consisted of coating the bronze with a paste formed by dissolving gold in heated mercury. The bronze thus coated was then itself heated, and the mercury driven off, when the gold was left adhering to the surface

of the metal. The fumes of the mercury vapour produced at this stage were very dangerous and the heating had to be carried out in a furnace with a strong draught. Finally, when the process was completed the gold was either burnished or given a matt finish, according to requirements, but sometimes both types of finish were used on the same piece for purposes of contrast.

During the Louis XIV period the leaf-gilding of bronzes was sometimes employed, and occasionally bronzes were silvered, although this is rare at any time.

It is important to remember that only the finest bronzes were gilt in the manners described, the remainder being merely dipped and lacquered. The owners of furniture and *bronzes d'ameublement* in the eighteenth century were also not averse from having their ormolu regilt by the mercury process in order to keep it in a bright condition. So far as one can judge from contemporary accounts, ormolu was never allowed to become as dull or dirty as it often is today, and there seems to have been no taste for patina for its own sake.

The craft of making ormolu reached its height towards the middle of Louis XVI's reign, the chief exponents being Pierre Philippe Thomire, E. Forestier, and others. During the Napoleonic period the quality of ormolu declined, mainly owing to the cost of gilding by the mercury process. Later in the nineteenth century, however, with the advent of machinery and mass-production methods, fine ormolu was produced, and although it often lacks the personal perfection which the earlier craftsmen gave it, it is sometimes very difficult to distinguish between a piece produced in 1770 and another made in the same style in 1860. Connoisseurs and collectors should always keep an open mind about this.

Oxbow, oxbow front. The reverse serpentine curve, somewhat resembling the curve of an oxbow. Often employed in the finest eighteenth-century New England, especially Boston case furniture such as chests of drawers, secretaries, etc.

Palace letters. These, with inventory numbers (*q.v.*), are often painted or branded on furniture and occasionally stamped on *bronzes d'ameublement*, made for the French

Crown. On veneered furniture they are usually to be found on the carcase at the back or under marble slabs, but in the case of chairs and *menuiserie* generally, they are often in the under parts and sometimes on the bottom of the upholstered seats. They almost always take the form of the initial letter or letters of the palace concerned beneath a crown. Thus F = Fontainebleau; C.T. = Château de Trianon; W (two Vs) = Versailles; S.C. = Saint Cloud, etc. Like inventory numbers, their existence on furniture of any date is worth careful investigation.

Panel. Compartment usually rectangular, and sunk or raised from the surface of its framework. Panel is the filling of such framework, whereas panelling refers to the framework and its filling (*see* Wainscot).

Papier mâché. Moulded paper pulp used for many small articles and particularly suitable for japanning and polishing; the original process came to England via France from the East as early as the seventeenth century. Considerable stimulus was given to this kind of work in 1772, when Henry Clay of Birmingham, and later London, patented a similar material and began manufacturing various pieces, among which trays, boxes, tea-caddies, and coasters were prominent.

Parquetry. A word connected, as its French equivalent implies, with the laying of floors. It is sometimes used in connexion with furniture inlaid with geometrical cube designs in the manner of a parquet floor. It should be used with caution and is not really applicable to furniture at all.

Patina (and **colour**). Of furniture and woodwork, patina is the undisturbed surface, heightened by centuries of polishing and usage. Contrary to popular belief, some old oak furniture shows clear signs of having been originally varnished; some was also polychromed. Patination and colour pose problems to a faker. To some extent they can be simulated, but, when artificially produced, deteriorate (*see* Fake and Stripping).

Pear drop. *See* Drop handle.

Pedestal table. A table on a round centre support.

Pembroke table. A small table with short drop leaves supported on swinging wooden brackets. The term Pembroke is used in England first in the 1760s. Although Chippendale lists tables of this description as "breakfast tables" in the *Director*, he used the term on bills. Sheraton said this type of table was named after the lady who first ordered it. It was particularly popular in the classical period, and both Hepplewhite and Sheraton suggested designs for it.

Pennsylvania Dutch. The name applied to German settlers in Pennsylvania. Their furniture has many distinctive qualities, since it assimilates English and German peasant styles. Their cabinet-makers worked in soft woods, which they painted and often decorated with floral patterns and other motifs from the vocabulary of peasant design.

Pie-crust table. A round tilt-top tea-table on a tripod base. The top has a scalloped edge finished with a carved moulding which is suggestive of the notched rim of a pie crust; tables in the Chippendale style have pedestals elaborately carved. The tripod consists of three cabriole legs terminating generally in claw-and-ball feet (Plate 72B).

Pier table. A table designed to stand against the pier, the part of the wall between the windows. In America the term is used loosely to refer to a table designed for use against a wall, a side table.

Pilgrim furniture. Term used to describe American seventeenth-century furniture.

Pillar and scroll clock. American shelf or mantel clock by Eli Terry. Its wooden works are housed in a vertical rectangular case with a scrolled-arch top, small, round pillars at the sides, and delicately small feet. Same as the so-called "Terry" clock.

Pine. Often used for panelling rooms in eighteenth-century England. It was also used for the carcases of veneered furniture. From the time of the Pilgrims down to the present, much of the everyday utility furniture in America has been made of pine, especially the soft white pine of New England. Antique examples of it are much prized today for countrified settings. White pine was also much used for the unseen parts of furniture and other secondary purposes, as well as for overlaying with veneer. Its presence often identifies the furniture as American. Short-leaf, yellow, hard pine is often used as the secondary wood in New Jersey, Pennsylvania, and Virginia furniture. The long-leaf, yellow, hard pine, so plentiful in the south, does not made good furniture.

Pin-hinge. Method of hinging, as found on thirteenth-century chests, the lid being pinned through the rear stiles and pendent side-rails of the lid.

Pipe-rack. A stand for clay pipes. Of the various wooden kinds in use in the eighteenth century one can distinguish: (1) the stand of candlestick form with a tiny circular tray on the stem, pierced with holes for holding the pipes, and (2) the wall rack, either an open frame with notched sides so that the pipes could lie across or a board with shelves from which the pipes hung down (cf. spoon-rack). In addition to these, metal pipe-kilns were widely used from the seventeenth century – iron fromes on which the pipes rested, deriving their name from the fact that they could be baked in an oven to clean the pipes.

Pipe-tray. A long and narrow wooden tray with partitions for churchwardens, in use throughout the Georgian period.

Plate-pail. A mahogany container with handle for carrying plates from kitchen to dining-room (often a long journey) in large houses in the eighteenth century; of various shapes, generally circular with one section left open for ease of access (Plate 124B).

Pole-screen. *See* Fire-screen (1).

Poplar. *See* Tulipwood.

Poppy- (popey-) head. Decorative finial of a bench- or desk-end, as in ecclesiastical woodwork. Plant and floral forms are numerous; human heads, figures, birds, beasts, and other devices are found. Derivation of term is uncertain, one suggestion (rejected by some writers) being from Fr. *poupée* (baby doll), or from poppet, puppet.

Porcelain. In the Louis XV and Louis XVI periods there were two important uses of porcelain in connexion with furniture. Firstly, for purely decorative purposes, actual pieces of porcelain were mounted with ormolu, often of very high quality. This is what became known as "mounted porcelain", and the pieces so embellished came not only from the French factories of Vincennes and Sèvres but also from Meissen, and particularly from the Far East, *celadon* and *famille rose* being specially favoured. The ormolu decoration is usually confined to ornamental bases and bands for the necks of vases, but is sometimes extended to form handles, knobs for lids, etc. It is screwed on to the porcelain by means of a hole bored in the latter. The types of porcelain chosen are usually vases of various shapes, shallow bowls, ewers, and particularly the famous bunches of flowers from the Meissen factory, which were imitated at Vincennes. Sometimes groups of *biscuit de Sèvres* were similarly mounted. The demand for all these types was very high and extended right up to the Revolution, the usual changes in style being noticeable.

The other principal use to which porcelain was put did not come into fashion until the latter part of Louis XVI's reign. This consisted of the inlaying of plaques of porcelain into the veneered surfaces of pieces of furniture. This method of decoration, although it sometimes produces an extremely sumptuous effect, is often criticized on the grounds that it lies outside the scope of practical cabinet-making, and it has always been foreign to English taste. The covering of parts of furniture with porcelain does certainly make the pieces much more fragile, and there is evidence to show that a number of the plaques adorning extant pieces are not in fact the originals.

The porcelain so used almost always came from the Sèvres manufactory and often, therefore, has the royal monogram with or without date letters or painters' marks. If a date letter is found and is genuine it may help to date the piece of furniture fairly exactly, but it is always possible that the plaque is not the original, and may have replaced another, in which case the date letter may bear no relation to the year in which the furniture was made.

The porcelain is let into cavities in the carcase and kept in position originally by means of ormolu fillets. Martin Carlin and Adam Weisweiler were two *ébénistes* who appear to have specialized to some extent in making furniture of this kind, and the custom of mounting porcelain of any date on furniture was particularly prevalent in the nineteenth century, during the Restoration and reign of

Louis Philippe. Collectors should always bear in mind that the porcelain on furniture may be a later addition or replacement, and this is particularly to be suspected if there is any lack of harmony between the furniture and the plaques, or any confusion of dating.

Press. Broadly, a tall, enclosed, and doored structure comparable to the modern wardrobe or hanging cupboard. Not to be confused with linen-press, in the sense of a framework with a screw-down smoother. (For press-cupboard *see under* Cupboard.)

Prie-dieu. The earliest surviving examples of the *prie-dieu* in Italy date from the sixteenth century and are simple contrivances with a step for the knees, an upright panel or shallow cupboard, and a shelf on top. Two or three drawers occasionally replaced the cupboard in the seventeenth century and the whole object was treated more decoratively. A magnificent early eighteenth-century example in the Palazzo Pitti at Florence is enriched with swags of fruit in *pietre dure*. Later in the eighteenth century the *prie-dieu* was made in conformity with rococo taste, usually with a single curving column supporting the shelf. Other more substantial examples were made to fold up into chairs.

Puritan. A term applied to simpler seventeenth-century American furniture.

Purple-wood. A wood with an open grain which is fairly hard. It is brown in its natural state, but turns purple on exposure to the air. Found chiefly in Brazil and French Guinea. Very extensively used for marquetry in France in the eighteenth century.

Rail. The horizontal piece in framing or panelling. In a chair back the top member supported on the stiles.

Reeding. Similar to fluting but with the ornament in relief (Fig. 73).

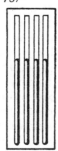

FIG. 73. Combined reeding and fluting

Reggivaso. A vase stand, a purely decorative piece of furniture which enjoyed widespread popularity in Italy in the eighteenth century. *Reggivasi* were made in the form of *putti*, satyrs, chained Negro slaves, or blackamoor page-boys and are often minor works of sculpture of great charm. A superb example by Andrea Brustolon in the Palazzo Rezzonico at Venice is made in the form of a group of river gods holding trays for the porcelain vases.

Renaissance (Fr. for rebirth). Applied to the effects of the revival of learning and embracing the use (often very freely interpreted) of classical as opposed to Gothic motifs. Originating in Italy in the fifteenth century, Renaissance design spread throughout Europe, beginning to make itself felt in England in the early sixteenth century.

Restoration. (1) A proper renewal of a piece by a candid replacement of hopelessly damaged or missing parts; (2) restored is sometimes used to indicate either that a piece has been over-restored or that the extent of its restoration is dubious.

Restoration Furniture. Term applied to certain elaborately carved and scrolled chairs, etc., their backs surmounted by crowns or boys and crowns. It was said that such pieces recorded the restoration of King Charles II (1660), but many so-called Restoration chairs are now known to date from late in his reign when not from a subsequent period. Such chairs may be of mixed woods, and other than oak.

Rising sun. When a fan-shaped ornament is carved half-circle, and the resulting spray of stalks suggests sun rays it is picturesquely called a rising sun (Fig. 74). "Setting sun" is sometimes used. It was so often the only decoration on New England highboys that its presence generally indicates the New England origin of the piece. James (later

FIG. 74

President) Madison recalled that when the Constitution of the United States was finally adopted after much contention, Benjamin Franklin pointed to a decoration of this type painted on the back of the chairman's chair and said he had looked at it many times during the sessions "without being able to tell whether it was rising or setting, but now I . . . know that it is a rising . . . sun".

Rocking chair. A chair of almost any simple type mounted on bends, rockers. An American institution, the rocking chair may also be an American invention. Authentic "slat-back" examples are said to date as early as 1650–1700, though 1800 would seem to be safer. Special types were developed (*see* Boston rocker, Salem rocker, Windsor).

Rococo. An ornate style developed in France from the Chinese forms. It came to England in the Chippendale period. It appeared in its most characteristic forms on sconces, mirror-frames, and console tables, all elaborately carved and gilded by special craftsmen. The American version only barely suggests the exuberance of the Continental rococo style. Ornament rococo in spirit is used on American Chippendale furniture, particularly in Philadelphia, but the lines of the furniture are more conservative.

Roll-top desk. Similar to a cylinder-top desk (*q.v.*), but the writing-table and fittings are enclosed by a curved slatted panel.

Romayne work. Old term for Renaissance carving with heads in roundels, scroll-

Fig. 75. Romayne work with head in roundel

work, vases, etc., some few heads being portraits, but most purely formal (Fig. 75). The taste was widespread in Europe, and traditional traces survived in Brittany until quite a late period. The vogue for romayne work in England was under Henry VIII (1509–47), thereafter dwindling.

Rosette. A round ornament in a floral design.

Rosewood or **kingwood.** A coarse-grained wood, dark purplish brown or black in colour, varying considerably in hardness. Found in India, Brazil, and the West Indies.

Roundabout. *See* Corner chair.

Rounded ends. The top rail of early Chippendale chairs is sometimes made with rounded ends, somewhat in the style of a Queen Anne chair (*see* Cupid's bow).

Roundel. Circular ornament enclosing sundry formal devices on medieval and later woodwork (Fig. 91); also human heads as in romayne work (*see also* Whorl).

Runner. Alternative term for the rocker of a rocking chair.

Rush seat. A seat woven of rushes. Used in America from the earliest times, generally with simple furniture. Still popular for country chairs (*see* Splint seat).

Sabre leg. A term used to describe a sharply curving leg in the classical style which has also been called scroll-shaped and even likened to the shape of a cornucopia. It is generally reeded. This leg is found on small sofas attributed to Duncan Phyfe.

Saddle seat. When the seat of a Windsor chair is cut away from the centre in a downward slope to the sides the shape somewhat resembles the seat of a saddle, and is picturesquely so named.

Salem rocker. Salem, Massachusetts, variant of the Windsor rocker (*q.v.*) and with a lower back than the Boston rocker (*q.v.*), early nineteenth century.

Salem secretary. Salem, Massachusetts, variant of Sheraton's secretary with a china cabinet top; also, by extension, a Salem sideboard with a china cabinet top (*c.* 1800–20).

Salem snowflake. A six-pointed punched decoration resembling a star or a snowflake found as a background in the carved areas of Salem, Massachusetts, furniture.

Sample chairs. A group of six chairs thought to have been made by Benjamin Randolph, a Philadelphia cabinet-maker, as samples of his skill. The group of chairs (one wing and five side chairs) is in the most elegant Philadelphia Chippendale style.

Satinwood. A fairly hard wood, with a very close grain. It is yellow or light brown in colour and has a lustrous surface somewhat like that of satin. It is found in central and southern India, Coromandel, Ceylon, and in the West Indies.

Sawbuck table. A table with an X-shaped frame either plain or scrolled. Frequently found in rural New England and in Pennsylvania German examples.

Sconce. A general name for a wall-light consisting of a back-plate and either a tray or branched candle-holders. Metal seems to have been the chief material from later medieval times until the end of the seventeenth century when looking glass became fashionable for back-plates (and when "girandole" was another name for these pieces). The use of looking glass meant that sconces tended to follow the same decorative trends as contemporary mirrors, but metal back-plates continued to be made, and for a period after 1725 there was a preference for carved and gilt wood and gesso-work, often without looking glass. About 1750 sconces provided some of the freest interpretation of the asymmetrical rococo mode, either with looking glass in a scrolled frame or in carved and gilt wood only; Chinese features were often blended with the rococo. In contrast, the sconces of the Adam period had delicate classical ornament in gilt wood or in composition built up round a wire frame. Cut-glass sconces were in vogue at the end of the century.

Scoop pattern. Popular term for a band or other disposition of fluted ornament, goug-

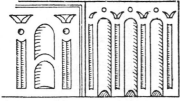

Fig. 76. Double Scoop and Fluting (*left*); Reeding and Fluting (*right*). Seventeenth century

ed in the wood, the flute having a rounded top and, sometimes, base (Fig. 76). A motif of Renaissance origin, its use was widespread (*see* Fluting).

Screen. Although frequently used in the church, screens do not seem to have been introduced into the house until the late seventeenth century. In Italy, as in England, Coromandel screens imported from the East were very popular, but screens, either hung with silk or painted with floral motifs, standing figures, etc., enjoyed a considerable vogue. The fire-screen was more widely used. An excellent example carved by G. M. Bonzanigo, is in the Castello di Stupinigi at Turin. (Plate 143E.)

Scroll top. A curved broken-arch pediment used on case pieces. Also called gooseneck, swan-neck, etc.

Scutcheon. Shield on which are armorial bearings or other devices, and, by extension, sundry shield-shaped ornaments and fitments (*see* Lock-plate).

'Scrutoire, escritoire. Eighteenth-century American term for an enclosed writing-desk, often with a cabinet top. Lockwood differentiates three varieties: fall front, slant top with ball feet, and slant top with turned legs. In England called a bureau or bureau-bookcase.

Secretaire (or **secretary**). The name somewhat loosely applied to different kinds of writing furniture, of which two small varieties call for mention here. (1) At the end of the seventeenth century appeared the small bureau mounted on legs or stand, very similar to the contemporary desk on stand (*q.v.*) (Plate 125c). This kind seems to have been designed for ladies' use, and sometimes had a looking glass at the top. (2) In the late eighteenth century large numbers of light and graceful secretaires were made, one popular kind taking the form of a small table with tapering legs enclosing a drawer and supporting a little stand with drawers and shelf. The stand, which was used as a small bookshelf, was often provided with a handle so that it could be lifted off. This type of table was also known as a cheveret.

Serre-papier. *See under* Cartonnier.

Settee. A low, long seat with upholstered

back and arms, which developed along the same lines as the arm-chair.

Settle. Long, backed seat with boxed base, or on legs, and at each end side-pieces or arms (Plate 91). Fixed or movable, the settle represents a stage preceding the settee, a derivative of the chair. Some quite late settles have one end scrolled like a sofa-head. Some, mostly country-made, settles have a storage press in the back, such being loosely known as bacon-cupboard.

Sewing-tables. *See* Work-table.

Shaker furniture. A whole range of furniture – chairs, tables, chests of drawers – made by early nineteenth-century Shakers, a celibate American sect. This furniture, while provincial, is of such sheer simplicity, so pure in line, so lean and functional in form, so well' proportioned and soundly constructed, that it is much prized today. Usually in pine, maple, walnut, or fruit woods (Plates 78, 79).

Shearer, George. English furniture designer, contemporary of Hepplewhite and Sheraton, whose work first appeared in the 1788 *Cabinet-Maker's London Book of Prices*. The sideboard, as usually made in the classical style, appeared first in his book of designs.

Shearer, Thomas. English furniture designer whose drawings, first published in the *Cabinet-Maker's London Book of Prices*, 1788, influenced many American cabinet-makers from 1790 to 1810, though the credit has to this day gone to his contemporaries, Hepplewhite and Sheraton, both of whom took many a leaf from Shearer's book (*see* Sideboard).

Shelves. Taken here to refer to hanging or standing shelves without doors, for books, plate, and china. Small oak shelves of the Tudor period were square in shape; while arcaded tops appeared in the early seventeenth century. Carving was the chief decoration, and this became more ornate after 1660. It is probable that many walnut shelves were made, but few of these seem to have survived. It was at this time that shelves were used for displaying china; a fashion which continued into the early eighteenth century, but was then replaced by that of keeping china in cabinets and cupboards. Open shelves, however, returned to favour in the Chippendale period, when they were often

decorated in the Chinese taste, and had fretted sides and galleries. Simple, light shelves were generally in vogue in the later eighteenth century (Fig. 77), for books or china;

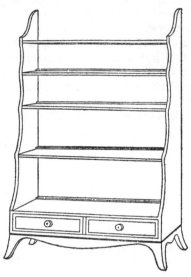

FIG. 77

Sheraton emphasized that shelves should be light enough for ladies to move about and to contain their "books under present reading".

Sideboard. Literally a side-board (as a cupboard was a cup-board); a side-table or other structure convenient for the display and service of plate, foodstuffs, etc., and possibly including storage facilities such as ambries, drawers, etc. A near relative of the dresser, and in some cases indistinguishable from such.

Slant-front desk. A frame or chest of

FIG. 78

drawers with a top section as an enclosed desk for writing, the hinged lid sloping at a 45 degrees angle when closed. Called in England a bureau.

Slat back. A seventeenth-century style chair made of turned posts connected by horizontal slats across the back. Persisted in rural areas to the twentieth century (Fig. 78).

Sleigh bed. American French Empire bed somewhat resembling a sleigh.

Slider. *See* Coaster.

Sofa. The sofa as we know it developed in the Louis XIV period out of the day-bed (or *lit de repos*). It became established more or less in its present form in the Louis XV period as a regular part of a *mobilier de salon*, and was often made to match a set of chairs and *causeuses*, in which case it was upholstered similarly. The sofa was first introduced into Italy in the late seventeenth century. Its stylistic history follows that of the chair: indeed, many Italian sofas resemble a row of chairs joined together. Extraordinarily long sofas with carved wooden backs and, usually, rush seats, were much favoured for the furnishing of eighteenth-century ballrooms (Fig. 79). Padded sofas with outcurving arms were

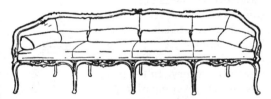

FIG. 79. Venetian sofa; mid-eighteenth century

popular in Venice in the eighteenth century, and some were made in the form of folding beds.

Sofa table. Small, narrow, rectangular table with two front drawers in the apron and hinged leaves at each end; the underframe of two legs at each end, or graceful bracket supports connected by a stretcher. First made in America about 1800 from Sheraton's designs. Duncan Phyfe developed several fine variants (Plate 75B). Popular until the passing of the Empire fashion about 1840. Rare today in America but common in England.

Spanish foot. William and Mary, also early Queen Anne, chair or table foot, with

vertical ribs somewhat like a hand resting on its finger knuckles (Fig. 80). An important detail of elegance in American furniture (*c.* 1700–25).

Spinning wheel. A machine for making yarn or thread, employing foot or hand power. As a piece for the home, it was generally made of turned parts. Used through the nineteenth century in rural areas.

FIG. 80

Splint seat. A seat made of oak or hickory strips interlaced. Used in country furniture through the eighteenth century.

Spool. A turning in the shape of a row of spools which was employed for long, thin members such as legs. Introduced after 1820 and continued through the Victorian period in rural work.

Spoon-back. Colloquially used of a Queen Anne chair with a back, curved like a spoon, conforming to the human back.

Spoon-rack. A stand for hanging spoons, dating from late Tudor times when metal spoons came into general use. The usual form, until the end of the eighteenth century, resembled a miniature dresser – a wooden board with small slotted shelves for spoons, and, attached to it at the bottom, a box for knives and forks.

Stamps. Various names and letters are often found stamped on French furniture made in the eighteenth century or later. The principal and most important of these is the stamp (*estampille*), giving the name and often the initials of the *ébéniste* who made the piece of furniture concerned, which, after 1751, he was compelled by guild regulations to strike on all his work, unless he happened to be a privileged craftsman working for the Crown. Before 1751 *estampilles* are very rarely found.

These stamps are a most important means of identifying the makers of individual pieces of furniture, but it must be borne in mind that sometimes they refer only to the repairer of a piece as distinct from its original maker. Thus some pieces bear more than one *estampille*, and it is often doubtful which *ébéniste* was the actual maker. The importance of the stamps, however, was only rediscovered in 1882, as a result of an exhibition held in Paris under the auspices of the *Union Centrale de Arts Décoratifs*, and as an unfortunate consequence, a number of false signatures have been applied to furniture since that date by unscrupulous dealers. Connoisseurs and collectors should be on their guard against this and also against the attribution of unstamped pieces to individual *ébénistes* on grounds of style alone.

The *estampille* is of roughly uniform size and format, usually incorporating the *ébéniste*'s name and initials, but sometimes the surname only (*see* pp. 327–31). They are usually found in an inconspicuous place on the carcase of the piece, often on the bottom or top rails, front or back, under marble tops, etc. Very occasionally they appear on the surface of the veneer itself, and sometimes panels of marquetry are signed in full by their makers.

Another important stamp to be found on furniture after 1751 is that of the *jurés*. It consists of a monogram incorporating the letters JME (*juré* or *jurande des menuisiers-ébénistes*), and its presence implies that the piece concerned has passed the standard required by the *jurés* of the guild (*see* Menuisiers-Ébénistes, Corporation des).

In addition to the *estampille* and the *juré*'s stamp, furniture made for the Crown sometimes, though by no means always, bears the stamp of the *Garde Meuble de la Couronne* (*q.v.*). Inventory numbers and palace letters (*q.v.*) are usually painted or branded, but seldom stamped, on furniture.

In the eighteenth century *bronzes d'ameublement* are very rarely stamped, but sometimes they do bear signatures. Jacques Caffiéri frequently signed his work with his surname. Inventory numbers and palace letters are even rarer, but they do occasionally occur on bronzes, and where they can be checked with existing documents they are found to be of eighteenth-century origin.

Stars. American ornaments often inlaid or painted on clocks, mirrors, tables, desk tops, etc., usually celebrating the number of states in the Union. The date of the article is sometimes traceable to the number of stars thus employed: the thirteenth state, Rhode Island, being admitted in 1790; the fourteenth, Vermont, in 1791, etc.

Stile. In construction an outermost upright, as a muntin is an inner one.

Stool. Small, backless seat. Apart from rack- or folding stools, the main basic types are trestle and legged. Trestle, with two uprights out from the solid, on the same principle as the ends of a boarded chest, may be included among stools of wainscot. Stools with legs may have three or four supports, and some quite common, and indeed modern, stools of traditional form are of very ancient lineage.

Joined stool (joint is a corruption): is proper to stools made by joinery. The term coffin stool invariably used by beginners is only correct when the use of joined stools as a coffin-bier (as in some old churches) is known. It is incorrect for the domestic article. For close-stool see that section. An old term for a box-top stool was "stool with a lock" (*see English Cottage Furniture*, p. 28).

Folding X stools, with the seat placed on top of the X – and not just above the crossing as in X chairs – were very popular in the fifteenth and sixteenth centuries in Italy. Elegant but very uncomfortable three-legged stools with small octagonal seats and tall, narrow backs, called Strozzi stools (Fig. 81) were made in Tuscany in the fifteenth century. In the sixteenth and seventeenth centuries stools with legs formed out of two carved and shaped planks were usual, but in the eighteenth century the stool was regarded principally as the appendage of a chair or suite of chairs and designed in conformity.

FIG. 81. Strozzi stool; Tuscan; fifteenth century

Strapwork. Of carving, band of ornament more or less suggestive of plaited straps, often

FIG. 82

highly formalized; distinct from guilloche (Figs. 82 and 83).

FIG. 83. Strap and jewel carving. First half of the seventeenth century

Straw-work. A method of decorating furniture, particularly smaller pieces, with tiny strips of bleached and coloured straws to form landscapes, geometrical patterns, etc. This craft came to England from the Continent towards the end of the seventeenth century and

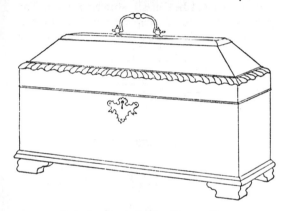

FIG. 84. Rectangular Tea-caddy

was centred at Dunstable. There was a big increase in output during the Napoleonic Wars, when French prisoners, many of whom were craftsmen who had been conscripted into the French Navy, decorated articles in this way during their captivity in England. Among the chief pieces thus decorated were tea-caddies, desks, and boxes.

Stretcher. A horizontal member connecting uprights.

Stripping. Furniture, the old surface of which has been removed and reduced to the wood, is said to have been stripped. Though stripping can be properly used, it should never be lightly indulged, as for a supposedly aesthetic advantage (*see* Patina).

Stump leg. A simple, thick rear leg curved at the corners; used on Queen Anne and Chippendale chairs.

FIG. 85

Stump feet. A plain turned foot – the "stump" of the leg – much used on the back legs of American Queen Anne and Chippendale chairs, etc., with cabriole front supports, particularly in Philadelphia.

Sunburst. English source of the American rising sun ornament (*q.v.*).

Sunflower. From earliest American times the conventionalized sunflower was a popular carved ornament on Connecticut desks and chests (*q.v.*).

Swan-neck. *See* Scroll top.

Sweet gum. Close-grained, silky, red-brown American wood easily stained to look like mahogany and sometimes used as a substitute for it in less-expensive furniture. Miller says that during the Revolution, when mahogany was not obtainable, American sweet gum wood, then called "Bilsted", was often used.

Swing-leg table. A hinged leaf table with a swinging rather than a gate-leg. Handsome examples, some of them cabriole, survive.

Table. Primarily, board forming the top only of such furniture, and by later extension the whole structure. "Table tretteau" (table trestles) in the famous *Epitaphe* of François Villon is thus a precise, as well as a poetic, statement. The trestle table is a very old form (Plate 96), an advantage being in its ease of clearance and storage, but trestle-supports are often ponderous. The other main basic type of table is that supported by a developed framework with a leg at each corner and possibly others along the sides. Of about the early sixteenth century frame-tables constructionally ancestral to later types are in evidence, though authentic examples are all but unprocurable in the market. By the end of the same century tables with a developed under-framing and fixed legs were usual. The term refectory table is popular jargon, better replaced by long table (Plate 95A) or other suitable description. Dining- or parlour-table is used of less extensive items. Drawing- or draw-table had movable extensions of the top, pushed in below it and drawn when needed. Various kinds of side-table include what is now called occasional table. Some small examples are known, correctly or otherwise, as games- or gaming tables. Certain table-constructions are now reclassified as counter. Billiards tables were known in the sixteenth and seventeenth centuries. As apart from the draw-table, the folding, falling (or flap-) table, its top with one or more hinged sections, was in more or less general usage by the early seventeenth century (Plate 89E). Various forms include bow- and bay-front (also found minus flaps). Flaps were supported by a movable bracket or leg. A development of the principle resulted in the gate- or gate-leg table, with oval or circular top, the developed under-framing of legs and stretchers including movable sections or gates. Gate-tables made to fold completely flat are known, but the more usual construction involved a rigid centre-section.

In churches the post-Reformation communion table, replacing the medieval altar, is essentially similar to the domestic long, parlour, or side-table previously mentioned, though some examples have special features.

Table-chair, -bench. Correct term for the absurdly misnamed monk's chair, or -bench. Chair-table is also used. Convertible chair, the back pivoted to form a table-top when dropped across the uprights (Plate 93A). Though the type existed in pre-Reformation times, most surviving examples are so much later in date (say seventeenth century) as to obviate any monastic association in England.

Tarsia. A form of wood inlay or marquetry widely used in Italy but most notably in Lombardy and Tuscany. Tarsia decoration *alla certosina* made up of polygonal tessere of wood, bone, metal, and mother-of-pearl arranged in geometrical patterns was very popular in Lombardy and Venetia in the fifteenth cen-

tury and much used for the decoration of *cassoni*. The art of pictorial *tarsia* was brought to a high level of excellence at Florence in the fifteenth century by a number of craftsmen, of whom Francesco di Giovanni called il Francione was, according to Vasari, the most highly esteemed. In the fifteenth and subsequent centuries *tarsia* was much used for the decoration of both ecclesiastical and domestic furniture. Panels representing views of real or imaginary architecture were popular on *cassoni* in the late fifteenth and sixteenth centuries, but during the seventeenth century abstract designs seem to have been preferred. In the eighteenth century *tarsia* was applied to tables and chests of drawers, usually in patterns of flowers and ribbons. The last great artist in *tarsia* was the Lombard Giuseppe Maggiolini.

Tavern table. Small, sturdy, rectangular table on four legs, usually braced with stretchers. Generally with a drawer or two in the

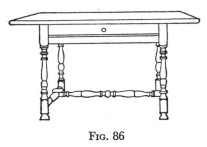

FIG. 86

apron (Fig. 86). Much used in eighteenth-century taverns for serving a customer where he was seated.

Tea-caddy and tea-chest. A small box for storing tea. "Tea-chest" was the common name for this piece from the end of the seventeenth century, when tea-drinking was introduced, until the second half of the eighteenth century, when "caddy", a corruption of "kati", a Malay measure of weight of just over one pound, came into general use. The custom of locking up the family's tea in a box continued long after tea had ceased to be an expensive luxury; caddies, therefore, were invariably provided with locks and were either divided into small compartments or were fitted with canisters (*q.v.*) for the different kinds of tea. A great variety of materials was used in their construction, including woods of all kinds – carved, inlaid, veneered, painted, or decorated with tortoiseshell, ivory, straw-

FIG. 87

work (*q.v.*), Tunbridge ware (*q.v.*), etc. – metal (silver in the best examples) and papier mâché (*q.v.*). There was also considerable diversity in shape, from rectangular (Fig. 84)

FIG. 88

to square and octagonal (Fig. 87); while vase and pear (Fig. 88) forms were introduced after 1750.

Tea-canister. The container for tea in the caddy (if the latter were not already divided into compartments); made of glass, metal, or earthenware; usually bottle-shaped until *c.* 1750, and vase-shaped later.

Teapot-stand. *See* Kettle-stand.

Tear drop. *See* Drop handle.

Toilet mirror (or **dressing-glass**). A small mirror designed to stand on a table or, in early examples, to hang on the wall. This kind of mirror was a luxury in the medieval and Tudor periods, and did not begin to come into wider use until the late seventeenth century. Post-Restoration mirrors were usually square in shape, and frequently had their frames decorated with stump-work; they stood by means of a strut or hung by a ring. By about 1700 oblong mirrors with arched tops, in narrower moulded frames, veneered or japanned, had begun to replace the square shape. In the eighteenth century several changes occurred. Shortly after 1700 appeared the mirror supported by screws in uprights mounted on a box stand; the box was often in the form of a flap or desk above a drawer which contained the many toilet requisites of the time; the mirror had a pronounced arched heading at first, and the front of the box was sometimes serpentine in form. The older type of strut support, without the box stand, continued to be made, however, and occasionally a stand with small trestle feet was found. By 1750 mahogany was in general use for toilet mirrors, though some in the Chinese style were gilt or japanned. Similar designs were introduced in the neo-classical period; mirror frames, in mahogany or satinwood, were often of oval or shield shape, and the uprights were curved to correspond. The stand was also a simpler arrangement, as toilet articles were now placed in the table on which the mirror stood. At the very end of the century and later, a wide oblong mirror was fashionable, and was usually swung on turned uprights. Mahogany and rosewood, often decorated with stringing, were the chief woods for such mirrors at this time.

Torchère. *See* Candle-stand.

Toy furniture. Though toy furniture authentically of the Age of Oak exists, it is rare, and there are many copies or imitations. Toy is here used in its sense of knick-knack.

Some such pieces were children's toys, or dolls' furniture, others were made as models to satisfy the adult love of "miniatures". Yet others are said to have been fashioned as trade samples, or as "prentices' pieces" to demonstrate an apprentice's skill. In practice, it is not always possible to differentiate between these various subdivisions.

Tray. For food, tea-things, plates, etc.; also known as a voider (the medieval term for a tray which was still in use in late Georgian times). Tea-trays (or "tea-boards") were introduced in the late seventeenth century, and most of them were japanned; none, however, seems to have survived. Japanned trays were still popular in the middle of the eighteenth century, though by then ornamental mahogany trays with fretted borders were being made. Later, oval trays decorated with fine inlay were in vogue. About 1800 there was a considerable production of trays in japanned metal and papier mâché.

Trail. Undulating band of formalized leaf, berry, or floral pattern. Thus vine-trail (Fig. 89).

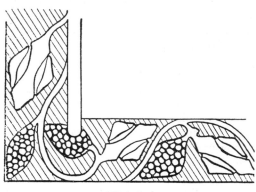

FIG. 89

Treen. Old adjectival form of tree; wooden. Now used of an extensive array of articles, mainly small and of almost any period, such as bowls, Welsh love-spoons, stay-busks, etc., and not excluding furniture.

Trespolo. Elegant three-legged tables known as *trespoli*, usually designed to stand against a wall and to carry a small *objet d'art* or candle-stick, were very popular in the eighteenth century, especially in Venice. Sometimes the supporting column was made in the form of a term figure, but it was more usually carved in a graceful curve (Fig. 90).

FIG. 90. Trespolo; Venetian; mid-eighteenth century

Tricoteuse. A term probably of nineteenth-century origin, applied to a small work-table surrounded by a gallery, part of which can be lowered to contain sewing materials.

Tridarn. *See* Cupboard.

Tuckaway table. A hinged-leaf gate-leg table with cross legs which fold into each other as compactly as if tucked away.

Tudor. The Tudor dynasty reigned from 1485 to 1603; Tudor is loosely used of furniture emerging from the Gothic or not fully developed as characteristic Elizabethan. The periods of Henry VIII (1509–47) and Elizabeth (1558–1603) are usually given their own names.

Tulip-ornament. Formalized ornament of tulip-like form, influenced by the tulip-mania in Holland, when huge sums were paid for rare bulbs. On English furniture the vogue for tulip-ornament continued from about the middle to the end of the seventeenth century.

Tulip wood. A soft, light wood used as a secondary wood and in painted furniture; also called tulip poplar.

Tunbridge ware. A special form of inlay which developed at Tunbridge Wells *c.* 1650, employing minute strips of wood, in a great variety of natural colours, to build up geometrical patterns and, later, floral decoration, landscape scenes, etc.; used for boxes, trays, desks, tea-caddies, etc.

Turtle-back. A type of ornamental boss, shaped somewhat like a turtle's back, often applied to Jacobean-style cupboards, etc.

Twist-turning. Form of turning derived from the twisted columns of Romanesque via Renaissance architecture. In England its main vogue on furniture was in the mid/latter half of the seventeenth century. R. W. Symonds had differentiated the single-roped twist (Dutch-Flemish type) from the English double-roped or barley-sugar twist (*see English Furniture from Charles II to George II*).

Urn-stand. *See* Kettle-stand.

Veneer. Thin sheets of wood applied to surface for decorative effect or to improve appearance of furniture. Though veneering arrives in the second half of the seventeenth century, at the end of the oak period, it is sometimes found as a limited enhancement of pieces which would be classed as oak by collectors.

Vernis Martin. A term applied generically to all varnishes and lacquers used for furniture and interior decoration in France during the eighteenth century. It derives from the brothers Martin, who in 1730 were granted a monopoly to copy Chinese and Japanese lacquer. They also evolved a special kind of coloured varnish, which was applied in a large number of coats and then rubbed down to give it lustre. It was available in a number of colours, including grey, lilac, yellow, and blue, but the most famous was the green, which was often applied to furniture. Vernis Martin was also used to decorate *boiseries*, carriages, fans, and small boxes. The Martin family were much patronized by the Court and by Madame de Pompadour (*see also under* Lacquer).

Wagon seat. An American double seat, generally with a two-chair back of slat-back or Windsor variety, usable both as a farm porch settee and a wagon seat.

Wainscot. Now mainly used of wall-panelling, but anciently of wider significance, its derivation from MLG. *Wagenschot*, perhaps meaning wagon-boarding, referring rather to the planking itself, and thence to a wall-lining as well as to other forms of woodwork. Bed-stead, chair, stool, etc., are frequently listed as being "of wainscot". Though this term in some cases implied that their construction involved a noticeable amount of panelled work, furniture stoutly built of slabs or planks of wood was perhaps "of wainscot", involving various forms of boarded furniture with "slab-ends". As a term, wainscot may have been loosely as well as precisely used (*cf.* definition of coffer).

Wall-lights. A lighting appliance usually of more than one light which can be fixed flat to the surface of a wall. They were very popular in France during the Louis XV and Louis XVI periods, and large numbers were made, usually of ormolu and often in pairs or sets of four to six. The *ciselure* and gilding on many of them are often of very high quality.

Walnut. Finely figured hard wood good for carving, veneering, and turning. Black walnut was used particularly in the William and Mary and Queen Anne periods for elegant furniture, and replaced by mahogany when importations increased. In America it retained popularity in Pennsylvania and the south. White walnut, known better as butternut, grows between New England and Maryland. It is open-grained and light brown, and used mainly in country furniture.

Wardrobes. The wardrobe developed out of the cupboard and the cabinet in the late seventeenth century and was treated monumentally by Boulle and his *atelier*, many being made for the Crown and very sumptuously decorated (*see* Plate 137). From the constructional point of view it consists of a straight, upright cupboard closed by two doors and with one or more shelves on the undecorated interior. It survived into the early Regency, sometimes of plain carved wood, but as rooms became smaller it seems to have disappeared. A number, however, were made in the Boulle technique in the Louis XVI period from earlier designs. Some were also made of plain wood under the Empire.

Washing-stand (or **basin-stand**). Specially adapted for bedroom use after 1750, and of two main kinds. (1) A tripod stand with three uprights, a circular top fitted with a basin, and a central triangular shelf with a drawer (or drawers) and receptacle for soap

(Plate 124D). A four-legged version of this type was also made. (2) A cupboard or chest of drawers on four legs with a basin sunk in the top, the latter covered by a lid or folding flaps.

Water leaf. A carved ornamental motif of narrow leaf with regular horizontal undulations divided by a stem going down the centre. Used in classical style and much favoured by Duncan Phyfe as a leg decoration. In many ways it is the classical style counterpart of the acanthus leaf of the Chippendale period.

Web foot. *See* Duck foot.

What-not. A portable stand with four uprights enclosing shelves, in use after about 1800 for books, ornaments, etc.

Wheat ears. Hepplewhite carved ornament of wheat ears, used in America by McIntire, Phyfe, and others as low-relief decoration on bedposts, chair and sofa backs, etc.

Whorl. Circular ornament on medieval (and later) furniture, the enclosed carving raying from the centre of the circle, or in certain other, including geometrical, dispositions (Fig. 91). The general sense of the term

FIG. 91. Whorl and Roundel

seems to approximate whirl. Whorl is freely used, though in doubtful or obviously inapplicable cases roundel is employable.

Windsor chair. Developed from the buffet chair, made of turned members with a saddle-seat. Until recently the English Windsor chair was made only around High Wycombe, Bucks. Whether the American Windsor chair was evolved from the English Windsor or the English corner chair, or both, is not yet certain. In any event, the American development is unique. In the American Windsor the back has no splat and is formed entirely of spindles socketed into a top rail. There are two main types – comb-back, in which the

top rail is shaped like the head of a comb; and hoop-, or bow, back, the top rail bent like half a hoop (Figs. 92 and 93). Four other

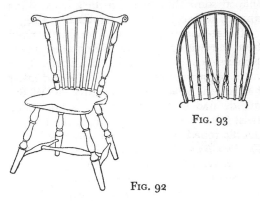

FIG. 93

FIG. 92

types are differentiated – low-back, a semicircular horizontal top rail somewhat like that of a corner chair; New England arm, a simpler form of the hoop-back; fan-back (which some authorities think may have been the side chair to the comb-back arm-chair); and loop- or balloon-back, the top rail loop-shaped. American Windsors have saddle-shaped seats of solid wood or, occasionally, rush seats. The legs, simple turned, are pegged into the seat at a rakish angle, adding a final charm to the stick-and-spindle lines. Windsors were first made in or near Philadelphia about 1725, and were found so comfortable that by 1760 they had become the most popular of all chairs in everyday use. A type fitted with rockers, called the Windsor rocker, is often found.

Wine cistern (or **cooler**). A case for wine bottles, very similar to a cellaret (*q.v.*), but normally larger, without a lid and designed to contain ice or water for cooling the wine. Bowl-shaped wooden cisterns on feet or stand were lined with lead and came into wide use after *c.* 1730; stone and metal (especially silver) cisterns were also found. At the end of the century the tub form, with hoops of brass, was general.

Wing chair. An upholstered chair with high back, stuffed arms, and wing-shaped protectors at head level protruding from the back over the arms (Plate 70A). The chair was known in England during the seventeenth century and was probably introduced in America before 1725.

Winthrop desk. A Chippendale slant-top desk mistakenly named for one of the seventeenth-century governors of Massachusetts.

Work-table. The name usually applied to the special table made in the second half of the eighteenth century for ladies' needlework, etc. In Sheraton's time these tables were of several kinds; some, mounted on four tapered and reeded legs or on trestle feet, might include, in addition to a drawer, such fittings as a pouch for the work materials, an adjustable fire-screen, and a writing-board or slide. Another type, the "French work-table", was a tray on trestle feet with a shelf or shelves below.

Worm-hole. Tunnel bored in woodwork by various types of beetle, collectively and popularly called "the worm". Worm-holes are not *per se* evidence of antiquity, though they *have* been artificially simulated. "Worm" is, however, a condition demanding attention to destroy infection. New worm-holes usually show a light-coloured interior, whereas old ones may be discoloured. A simple, though not final, test for possible activity is to tap the suspected piece and watch for a fall of wood-dust. If the mischief is superficial, furniture may be cured by repeated applications of one of the proprietary fluids sold for this purpose; but more heavily infested articles may need expert attention. In some furniture worm may have been extinct for centuries. When worm-holes are laterally exposed to any noticeable extent, it may be inferred (*a*) that the wood has been recut after infestation; or (*b*) that the surface was formerly painted or otherwise covered with some since-vanished substance which formed a side-wall to the channel. Exposed channels occur on some fakes (*q.v.*), but are not *per se* condemnatory, though, in many cases, suspicious.

Writing-cabinet. Fall-front cabinets, enclosing a system of small drawers, became prominent in the latter part of the sixteenth century, especially in Italy and Spain (*see* Bargueño), some of them serving as writing-cabinets. Such cabinets were sometimes furnished with stands, though others were standless, placed on top of a table or chest as needed. Certain of the latter were supplied with stands at a later period.

Such pieces are ancestral to the fall-front scrutoire, secretary, escritoire (*qq.v.*) (from Fr. *secrétaire*) of later times, the slope-front variety being at least in part a development of the writing-desk.

Writing-table. Many varieties of small writing-tables can be found dating from the end of the seventeenth century, when they were first introduced. Early examples were made with turned baluster legs and folding tops, and were frequently used also as side- and card-tables. Gate-legs were usual and some tables were fitted with a drawer. Decoration with marquetry was often found on them. In the early eighteenth century small knee-hole writing-tables were popular, with tiers of narrow drawers on each side of the central recess. Similar tables, it may be noted, were also used as dressing-tables, and it is not always possible to determine their exact purpose. After the introduction of mahogany, when the fashion arose for larger pedestal tables in libraries, many versions of the convenient lighter table continued to be made. It was at the end of the century that perhaps the most elegant kinds of these smaller tables were seen, frequently of satin-wood. Some closely resembled contemporary secretaires and cheverets; others were fitted with an adjustable board for writing and with a screen.

GLASS

A small goblet still testifies to the fact that Egyptians had mastered the fundamentals of glass-making more than 3,500 years ago. Collectors today, looking back over the intervening centuries, can trace a fascinating story. The Egyptians shaped their hollow vessels round cores of sand and pressed molten glass into open moulds. Some 2,000 years ago came the fundamental discovery that the hot glass could be shaped on a hollow rod by blowing, and Syria and Egypt thus produced great quantities of domestic vessels under the power of Imperial Rome.

From Rome in the first four centuries A.D. glass-makers penetrated to the Roman colonies, and by the time the empire crumbled the craft had gained footholds in the Rhone valley and along the Rhine and the Seine. Little remains from the dark ages that followed the rise and fall of the Roman empire, but in the following pages the story is taken up again with the Venetian triumph of clear "crystal" glass, and the result of this may be observed in the account of Bohemian glass.

England assumed the lead in domestic glassware in the late seventeenth century with Ravenscroft's incomparable flint-glass, and the story of the eighteenth and nineteenth centuries embraces the contrasting purposes and rival techniques of Britain and America, of Scandinavia and France. In particular, the nineteenth century's technical triumphs emphasize that glass-making is still a craft and an art, living, expanding, essential to mankind.

American

"We sent home ample proofs of pitch, tar, glass . . ." wrote Captain John Smith in his *Historie of Virginia*. Whatever the forms given to those 1609 proofs of glass, it is certain they were neither omens of a new national style nor of a New World contribution to glass as an art. And they never expanded into profitable production of this indispensable man-made substance. As to the glass blown and the articles fashioned during the abortive struggles of the four or five subsequent seventeenth-century attempts to root glass-making, they can only be guessed at.

With but few exceptions, all this is true of

the ten or eleven eighteenth-century houses in which hopeful colonial business-men sank their capital. One was sufficiently successful making window glass and blowing bottles and jars to operate for nearly forty years: Wistar's, whose small glass-house community, near Salem in southern Jersey, was called Wistarburg (*c.* 1739–75). Similar utility wares, mainly green glass and inevitably counterparts of European prototypes, were made at the New York and New Windsor (*c.* 1752–67) works of the Glass House Company of New York, and at the Germantown works near Boston (1753–68). Bottles and window glass were to be the financial backbone of glass-making for well over a century.

Only two pre-Revolutionary enterprises (so present evidence indicates) attempted to specialize in tablewares: Henry William Stiegel's second glass-house (1769–74) at Manheim, Pennsylvania, and the · Philadelphia Glass Works at Kensington. But both Stiegel and the proprietors at Kensington produced window glass and bottles also. In fact, these necessities of life were the paying output of Stiegel's Elizabeth Furnace Works (1763) and the principal products of his first at Manheim (1765). However, tableware production was intensive from 1769 into 1774 at Manheim, and from about 1772 into 1777 at Kensington. Each claimed to be the first flint-glass manufacturer in the country, but Stiegel, at least, made non-lead glass as well. Though flint-glass was the popular name for lead glass, it seems likely that in the eighteenth as well as the nineteenth century non-lead-glass tablewares were often called flint because it implied quality.

At Manheim, Continental and English styles met, but apparently did not blend. Actually Continental casually and shallowly engraved glass of the type today called peasant glass was followed so closely that few students consider physical characteristics alone a safe basis for attribution. The same, unfortunately, is true of English pattern-moulded types. The enamelled tumbler, Plate 145 (*right*), having an English inscription is an exception, but not the tumbler, Plate 145 (*left*), with sunken panels below the typical engraved tulips. The perfume bottle, Plate 150A, is pattern-moulded in the diamond-in-hexagon design, one of the

few believed to be a Stiegel original, since, as yet, no exact foreign counterpart is known. Articles listed in Stiegel's account books and his advertisements indicate that the range of articles was wide and followed imports. In 1771 the American Philosophical Society in Philadelphia pronounced the specimens exhibited to its members "equal in beauty and quality to the generality of Flint Glass imported from England". As for Kensington wares, advertisements and owners' nationality indicate they were English. They represented the last effort to make fine glassware until after the Revolution.

In the first forty-two years – from 1783 to 1824 – of the United States as a sovereign nation, about ninety-four glass-houses were built in spite of turbulent, unfavourable economic conditions. The depressed state of trade and commerce following the Revolution could not dampen optimism for various domestic manufactures. Shortly before 1800 westward migrations encouraged the establishment of glass-making in the midwest, where the Pittsburgh Glass Works erected America's first coal-burning furnace (1797) – immediately sealing the doom of many as yet unplanned eastern wood-burning houses and determining the future hub of the glass industry. Optimism ran higher still with President Jefferson's embargo on trade with Britain (1806–7) and the Non-Importation Act (1811). It climbed to greater heights during the war of 1812. With each encouraging event or condition, a graph of glass-houses would rise to ever higher peaks and, between them, their failures drop to greater depths. New houses were built; some old ones were abandoned; others were taken over by new firms. In the whole period at least three times as many firms were formed by an even larger number of glassmen, merchants, brewers, and other business-men. The few houses planned for tableware production either failed, or became green-glass houses, or added its production in order to survive. Not until 1824 did Congress pass a tariff ensuring survival with profit of flint-glass manufacturing as well as window glass and bottles. Fought unsuccessfully by importers and independent glass-cutting shops, the 1828 and 1832 tariffs doubled the insurance.

Among the post-Revolutionary tableware houses important from the collector's viewpoint only one was eighteenth century: the New Bremen Glass-manufactory (1785–95) of John Frederick Amelung & Company, near Frederick, Maryland; an over-ambitious project misreading desires of the fashionable and over-estimating demand for domestic glassware, luxury or ordinary. The New Bremen commercial tablewares presumably followed prevailing fashions, especially some of the finer Continental cut and engraved glass, and were non-lead, as are the authenticated pieces which have been tested for lead content. These latter, among them Plate 146B, are mainly so-called "presentation pieces" or gifts. Their shapes, engraving technique, decoration by individual combinations of mainly Continental motifs and metal are Amelung earmarks. Similarity to their stylistic and physical characteristics has been the basis for attributing other pieces to New Bremen. The decorative techniques practised in addition to engraving were pattern-moulding, applied and tooled decoration, and, to a limited degree, enamelling and gilding.

In the early nineteenth century there were several important houses. Bakewells' (1809–80) was prominent in the Pittsburgh area. This first successful flint-glass manufactory in the country (even so, green glass was added to the output in 1811) was without effective rival among the few other Midwestern houses before John Robinson's Stourbridge Flint Glass Works (1823–45). By then demand and other favourable conditions were sufficient to support several houses. In the east, flint-glass production was rooted firmly by Thomas Cains, to whom the Boston Glass Company gave permission to erect a small flint-glass furnace in its South Boston works. Briefly (c. 1815–22) at Keene, New Hampshire, the Flint Glass Works on Marlboro Street made lead-glass bottles, flasks, and tablewares before becoming just a "bottle" house. At Cambridge, across the Charles River from Boston, the New England Glass Company, for over half a century probably the east's largest producer of fine glasswares (1818–80), took over a post-war casualty, the Boston Porcelain and Glass Company, organized in 1814. In New York, there were the Fisher Brothers' Bloomingdale Flint Glass Works (1822–45) and the Brooklyn Flint Glass Works founded by John L. Gilliland & Company (1823–68, moved to Corning, N.Y.), which won the prize for the best flint-glass metal at the London Crystal Palace, 1851. The Jersey Glass Company (1824–c. 1862), one of the improvers of mechanical pressing, built its works on Paulus Hook, across the Hudson from New York. That all, including the Midwestern, had ready access to water carriage is significant. Their production included pattern-moulded and free-blown wares, new commercial types as they evolved and, naturally, cut and engraved like popular imports. Also, by 1823, export of American glass, particularly to the West Indies and South America, had started.

Vast reaches of country, continual westward expansion, inadequate and slow transportation – by land or water – were among the factors determining locations and quantities of glass-houses. Scattering was logical if the country was to be independent of imports, as its glass-makers so vainly hoped. The increase, checked briefly by the 1830s depression, continued so that at least ninety new works were erected from 1825 to 1850. More than ever before were dedicated to flint-glasswares. For collectors the foremost among them were the Boston and Sandwich Glass Works, Sandwich, Massachusetts (1825–88), the Union Glass Works, Kensington, Philadelphia (1826–?), the Providence Flint Glass Works, Rhode Island (1831–5) (short-lived but leaving marked pressed salts), the Curlings' Fort Pitt Glass Works, Pittsburgh (1826–c. 1900), and the Sweenys' (1831–67) and the Richies' (1829–?) works, Wheeling, West Virginia. However, as always, the majority were bottle and/or window-glass houses. Not all the new houses survived; many old ones drew their fires; the inevitable westward shift accelerated. Most eastern houses, especially in New England and western and northern New York, depended upon wood for fuel. For many exhaustion of wood holdings and prohibitive cost of transporting fuel, even if furnaces were converted to coal, meant extinction. Also canals and improved roads, by enabling some houses to transport materials and wares more efficiently and cheaply, contributed to the failure of less fortunately situated works.

During this period glass-making was ineradicably rooted in the United States. Future pioneering was to be in glass technology and production. Experiments with blowing glass by machine had already begun, and even more immediately fateful to glass-blowing as an art, John P. Bakewell of Pittsburgh obtained a patent on machine pressing in 1825. By the mid-century, the machine had made mass production possible. Experiments in colour and composition bore strange and sometimes lovely fruits, forerunners of the later remarkable art glasses. The conscious effort to create the novel, symptomatic of an industrial society, became habit. Then, too, the term glass-house, with its aura of craftsmanship and the art of glass-blowing, no longer fitted most establishments, but rather factory, with all its twentieth-century connotations.

In all these years neither social, economic, nor psychological conditions were favourable for the emergence of a national style in blown tablewares. Glass-men, manufacturers, merchants, and customers were too fixed in their orientation to Europe's fashions and traditions. The glass-men enticed across the Atlantic brought inherited traditions and techniques practised in European houses. Almost without exception they were Continentals until Stiegel persuaded English blowers and decorators to Manheim. Afterwards the numbers from Britain increased, especially for flint-glass manufacture, familiar far longer and to more British glass-men than to Continentals. If they remained in their crafts, their techniques and traditions were taught to native-born boys. Still, since defection to easier occupations or to the land was constant, thinned ranks had to be refilled from Europe. Thus, unless deliberately diverted, the stream of European traditions in glass-blowing and ornamentation – Continental and British – played continuously upon American-made glass.

The men who started the glass-houses were necessarily more concerned with finances than aesthetics. Many were merchants and importers familiar with the glassware demand, and well aware that competition entailed imitating imports, of which English were considered best. Consequently style and design of commercial glasswares were determined mainly by imports. Nevertheless, along with glass cut or engraved to the "latest London pattern" but within an accepted style, there were inevitable deviations, differing details and features. Though as yet this field of American glass has received limited scrutiny, it seems proved that idiosyncracies and types peculiar to certain houses and areas developed, more Midwestern than eastern. In houses removed geographically and socially from the more European-style-conscious East, conditions were more favourable for the emergence of local features and types. The salt (Plate 147A *centre*) with its combination of broken-swirl ribbing, double-ogee bowl, and ribbed drawn knop, illustrates one such type.

Actually, if flint-glass makers had depended solely upon the carriage trade – and in a free market – few would have survived. Fortunately a sizable pedestrian trade developed and expanded rapidly. Its needs could be met by new commercial wares such as blown-three-mould, early pressed, and lacy glass, and a new type of bottle packaging too – historical, pictorial, and decorative flasks and bottles. These categories contain distinctive United States designs. While they do not represent art in glass, many, especially among the flasks, may be called popular art in glass. The inexpensive blown-three-mould and early pressed wares enjoyed a comparatively brief reign; the flasks, with their blown-moulded designs, such as portraits of presidential candidates, emblems and slogans, monuments and heroes – even George Washington – were popular for nearly three-quarters of a century. They were a national style in packaging potables.

As a type of tableware, blown-three-mould may have originated in the United States shortly after 1812, perhaps at South Boston under Thomas Cains. It was a sort of poor man's cut-glass created by using a full-size mould having its inner surface the size and shape of an article and with an intaglio pattern. The patterns, an earmark, are classified as arch (Plate 152B), baroque, and geometric. Of over 150 examples recorded, the majority are geometric, inspired by and in some instances identical with cut-glass. Also the majority are apparently peculiar to the United States. British production seems to have been limited to a few articles and a few geometric patterns, composed mainly of ribbings and diamond diapering in bands and blocks. The arch and baroque patterns have no known foreign counterparts.

The number of different articles in which each pattern appears and the number of moulds bearing each pattern varies widely. In the most common, McK GII-18 – band of diamond diapering between bands of vertical ribbing – over twenty articles have been recorded, over fifty individual moulds determined. While 400 moulds have been determined by analysis of actual pieces, they were for few articles, principally decanters and tumblers of many sizes and several shapes, castor bottles and inkwells. However, these were used to pattern gathers of glass to be fashioned, partially or entirely, by blowing and manipulation into other articles. For instance, a pitcher would frequently be patterned in a decanter mould, the body form retained but the neck expanded and lipped, and the handle, of course, applied. Bowls and dishes were fashioned free-hand from the gather after it had been patterned in either a tumbler or a decanter mould.

By 1830 the popular demand for blown-three-mould was shrinking and had focused on the early pressed glasses. From 1825, when Bakewell patented mechanical pressing of knobs, the process developed and improved so rapidly that by 1828 creamers could be pressed with handles and bodies in one piece. The invention of mechanical pressing and development of this revolutionary production method has been charged to America. Apsley Pellatt's 1831 specifications (British Patent No. 6091) for his press and mould referred to the "mode" as "lately introduced from America". By 1852, to paraphrase Deming Jarvis, founder of the Boston and Sandwich Glass Works, the American invention had so reduced cost of production, thus lowering retail prices of glasswares, that con-

sumption had increased tenfold. It was undoubtedly a factor also in any successful competition with European glass in the export markets.

By then there had been several phases in pressed-glass design. As in the case of blown-three-mould, the earliest patterns were inspired by cut-glass and adopted its motifs, especially the strawberry and fine-cut diamonds and, for rims, the fan escallop. However, about 1828 lacy glass, which was to be typically American for well over a decade, was evolving. With limitless variety made possible by mechanics, decorative design quickly passed beyond the close confines of contemporary cut-glass, with its simple geometric motifs regimented in stiff bands and into both simple and intricate patterns composed from an infinite variety of motifs on a stippled background. The stippling, tiny relief dots, was a glitter-producing device new in glass-making and the earmark of lacy. The patterned surface of the glass was lustreless; the smooth, through which the innumerable facets and angled planes refracted light, brilliant and sparkling.

Lacy designs reveal a catholicity in taste and free use of many sources in the arts and crafts. They adapted motifs and treatments popularized by the classical and Gothic revivals, from architectural ornament, ceramics; turned to conventionalized and naturalistic flowers and leaves; used local and national emblems, symbols, national heroes' portraits; favoured geometric figures; never completely discarded the various diamond motifs. Many designs were well realized, with motifs in sound balance and accent; many were over-elaborate and poorly composed. Some eastern lacy glass was very similar to some manufactured abroad, and other lacy glass designs have their counterparts in Meissen porcelain forms and decoration. Most designs, however, are exclusive to American lacy glass, and the Midwestern designs are easily distinguishable from their eastern counterparts.

During the depression starting in 1837, apparently another design phase appeared. As lacy moulds with stippling and many-planed patterns were expensive, their cost, as well as general economic conditions, doubtless contributed to the decline of lacy production and the rise of a simpler style. The new designs emphasized form and simple geometric motifs, unquestionably influenced by cut-glass of that period. They were ideal for the pressed-pattern glass, as the table and bar glass popular from around 1840 were called. In many patterns table sets were quite complete, including, as American lacy did not, various types of drinking glasses. The new style found expression also in innumerable lamps, candlesticks, and vases (Plate 147B) produced in all the old and many new tints and tones of greens, blues, amethyst, and yellows, transparent, translucent, and opaque. However, in pressed glass, early or late, good or bad designs, American or derivative, art had passed to the mould-maker.

But even as the machine was dominating commercial glasswares, wherever there were bottle- and window-glass houses the art of glass-blowing was being practised freely and unhampered by fashion or a designer's specifications. So it must always have been in such glass-houses. In the Midwest until about 1835, and in the east into the late nineteenth century, distinctively American glass was fashioned for local custom in the early years and in isolated communities, always for friend and family. Vessels for use in pantry, kitchen, and on the table – they were individual, functional, and honestly sturdy, free-blown from window and bottle-glass, mainly in natural colours. In general, the Midwestern colour range outstripped the eastern in quality of vibrant brilliance, subtle nuances of colour tone, and use of artificial colours. Many were plain or simply ornamented – perhaps a folded rim, threading, or a scalloped foot, the last rare in the east. The Midwestern tended to be thinner walled than the eastern, and in other aspects were quite different, as a comparison of Plates 146A, 147A, and 148 illustrates in part.

Major differences lay largely in shape, proportions, and decorative techniques. In Midwestern houses, shapes evolved which were peculiar to the region; for instance, the sugar-bowl, Plate 147A (left), with its wide galleried rim, high, short, sharply angled shoulder, straight sides sloping abruptly to the base, and the type of double-domed cover. The salt, Plate 147A (centre), and pitcher, Plate 147A (right), are others. Eastern shapes conformed more closely with commercial wares, and more seldom included an eighteenth-century feature or treatment. For bottles and flasks as well as hollow-ware, the preferred Midwestern decorative technique was pattern-moulding, mainly ribbing, fluting, the broken-swirl, and various expanded diamonds. The broken-swirl was tight "popcorn", as on Plate 147A (centre), or widely expanded resembling feathery diamond-on-the-diagonal. Though far from frail in appearance, this Midwestern glass seems to derive lightness and poised strength from its patterned surface and brilliance of metal.

Blowers in New Jersey, New York, and New England bottle- and window-glass houses rarely used the pattern-mould: they practised the centuries-old arts of glass-blowing and decorating, applying glass to itself and tooling it into ornamentation. Of many devices, several of them illustrated in Plates 146A and 148, perhaps the favourites were threading, prunts, quilling, crimping, also swagging, gadrooning, and (nineteenth century) the so-called lily-pads fashioned from a superimposed layer, and embedded loopings. Though the devices were traditional or variations of ancient devices, it is unlikely the blowers, especially in the nineteenth century, realized their vessels' close kinship with Continental "forest glass" and more remote ancestors. In fact, many expressions, the lily-pads in particular, probably were independent inventions. As yet neither true Type II, as on Plate 148 (centre), nor Type III, as on Plate 146A (left), has been identified with any European glass. All these individual pieces, plain and decorated, are called South Jersey type; the first of their kind unquestionably were from Wistar's eighteenth-century glassworks, southern Jersey. They are called folk art in American glass, largely because they are individual within a traditional stream and independent of sophisticated commercial style.

Folk art in American glass is a comparatively new term in the American collectors' glossary, which, as in trades, professions, and other hobbies, contains many words unintelli-

(A) French console table decorated with a panel of Japanese lacquer by Bernard van Risen Burgh, *c.* 1750. *Collection of M. de Cailleux.*

(B) French secretaire decorated with panels of Chinese lacquer by P. Garnier, *c.* 1770. *Louvre, Paris.*

(C) Chest of drawers veneered on oak with panels of Japanese and French lacquer, probably by René Dubois, *c.* 1770–80. *Wallace Collection, London.*

PLATE 129

(A) Lacquer harpsichord case made at Paris by Pascal
Taskin in 1786. *Victoria and Albert Museum, London.*

(B) Lacquer harpsichord case made at Hamburg in 1732. *Kunstindustrimuseet,
Oslo.*

PLATE 130

(A) Venetian lacquer harpsichord case, *c.* 1750. *Museo Civico, Treviso.*

(B) Venetian lacquer commode, *c.* 1750. *Palazzo Rezzonico, Venice.*

PLATE 131

Detail of Venetian lacquer door, *c.* 1760. *Palazzo Rezzonico, Venice.*

PLATE 132

(B) Walnut cabinet, second half of the sixteenth century.
Victoria and Albert Museum, London.

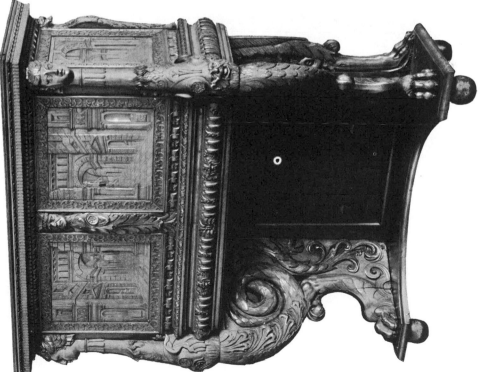

(A) Carved walnut dresser, second half of the sixteenth century.
Victoria and Albert Museum, London.

PLATE 133

(A) Chest of drawers (*commode*), made by A. Gaudreau and J. Caffiéri in 1739, for the bedroom of King Louis XV at Versailles. A perfect example of the Louis XV style on a monumental scale. *Wallace Collection, London.*

(B) Chest of drawers (*commode*), by Charles Cressent. It seems probable that Cressent himself also executed the mounts. *Wallace Collection, London.*

PLATE 134

(A) Writing-table (*bureau-plat*) of deal veneered with ebony and Boulle marquetry of a general type, showing the Louis XIV development of this type of furniture. *Wallace Collection, London.*

(B) Chest of drawers (*commode*), veneered on oak with mahogany, and stamped by J. H. Riesener. *Wallace Collection, London.*

PLATE 135

French toilet mirror of oak veneered with ebony and Boulle marquetry of brass on tortoiseshell. A good example showing marquetry of a design in the manner of Jean Bérain. *Wallace Collection, London.*

PLATE 136

Wardrobe (*armoire*) veneered on oak with ebony and Boulle marquetry of brass and tortoiseshell. Attributed to André Charles Boulle and perhaps made for a member of the Royal Family. A perfect specimen of the monumental style of the Boulle *atelier*. *Wallace Collection, London.*

PLATE 137

(B) Arm-chair of birch carved, gilt, and upholstered with Beauvais tapestry.

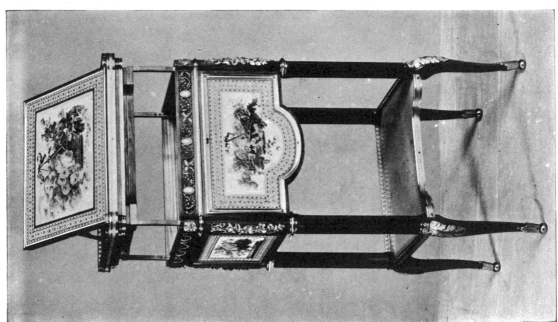

(A) Combined work-, writing- and reading-table veneered on
oak with tulip-wood and mounted with plaques of Sèvres

PLATE 138

French mantel clock of ormolu, perhaps by P. P. Thomire. *Wallace Collection, London.*

PLATE 139

(A) Bedroom, formerly in the Palazzo Davanzati at Florence. All the furniture is Florentine. The bed, chairs and stools date from the fifteenth century, and the *cassapanca* on the left wall from the sixteenth century.

(B) Veronese *cassone* with painted panels attributed to Bartolomeo Montagna, late fifteenth century. *Museo Poldi Pezzoli, Milan.*

PLATE 140

(A) Venetian chair by Andrea Brustolon, late seventeenth century. *Palazzo Rezzonico, Venice.*

(B) Venetian throne, late seventeenth century. *Palazzo Rezzonico, Venice.*

(C) Marchigan bureau decorated with gilt chinoiseries on a grained wood ground, early eighteenth century. *Private Collection, Milan.*

(D) Genoese looking-glass frame, carved by Domenico Parodi, early eighteenth century. *Palazzo Reale, Genoa.*

(E) Console table, in gilt wood, probably Roman, late seventeenth century. *Palazzo Reale, Turin.*

PLATE 141

(A) Lucchese bed, early eighteenth
century. *Palazzo Mansi a S. Pellegrino,
Lucca.*

(B) Bureau, inlaid with ivory and
rare woods, by Pietro Piffetti of
Turin, *c.* 1730. *Palazzo Quirinale,
Rome.*

(C) Gilt wood console table probably executed after a design by Filippo
Juvarra at Turin, *c.* 1730. *Palazzo Reale, Turin.*

PLATE 142

A

B

C

D

E

F

(A) Carved console table probably by Andrea Brustolon, one of a pair, early eighteenth century. *Stoneleigh Abbey, Warwickshire.*

(B) Late eighteenth-century console table made at Turin. *Castello di Stupinigi, Turin.*

(C) Chest of drawers, Roman or Neapolitan, mid-eighteenth century. *Palazzo Quirinale, Rome.*

(D) Genoese arm-chair upholstered in *petit-point* embroidery, late eighteenth century. *Palazzo Reale, Genoa.*

(E) Piedmontese firescreen by Giuseppe Maria Bonzanigo, c. 1770. *Castello di Stupinigi, Turin.*

(F) Sicilian chair decorated with glass over wood painted in imitation of marble, formerly in the Villa Palagonia at Bagheria, late eighteenth century. *Ringling Museum, Sarasota.*

PLATE 143

(A) Gilt bronze table designed by Pelagio Palagi, 1836–40. *Palazzo Reale, Turin.*

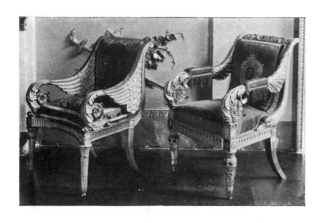

(B) Two chairs, probably Florentine, *c.* 1820. *Palazzo Pitti, Florence.*

(C) Writing-table, probably by Giovanni Socchi of Florence, *c.* 1810. *Palazzo Pitti, Florence.*

PLATE 144

American Stiegel-type tumblers, Continental style; colourless glass. *Left:* Engraved tulips, moulded sunken panels.
Right: Enamelled, probably Stiegel, *c.* 1769. *Corning Museum of Glass, New York.*

PLATE 145

(A) South Jersey type, free-blown, bottle-glass individual pieces, ornamented by glass itself applied and tooled, first half nineteenth century. *George S. McKearin Collection.*

(B) Amelung presentation pieces; colourless glass; engraved decoration characteristic of the New Bremen Glass Manufactory, Maryland. *Left: George S. McKearin Collection. Centre and right: Corning Museum of Glass, New York.*

PLATE 146

(A) Pattern-moulded individual Midwestern pieces, *c.* 1815. *George S. McKearin Collection.*

(B) New England canary candlesticks and vases pressed in two parts, joined by a merese, 1830–50. *George S. McKearin Collection.*

PLATE 147

Individual free-blown bottle-glass pieces (U.S.A.). *Corning Museum of Glass, New York.*

PLATE 148

Bluish-aquamarine American sugar bowl, Redford or Redwood Glass Works, *c.* 1835–50; lily pad decoration, hollow knop stem with coins dated 1829 and 1835 in hollow ball of cover, with chicken finial. Height 11 ins. *Corning Museum of Glass, New York.*

PLATE 149

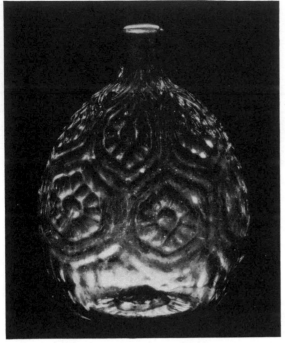

(A) Perfume bottle attributed to Stiegel's Manheim glass-house; the daisy-in-hexagon design has so far not been found in pieces of foreign origin. *Henry Francis du Pont Winterthur Museum, Delaware.*

(B) Amethyst vase, for many years called Stiegel probably Boston & Sandwich Glass Company; n teenth century. Twelve sunken panels around b Height 8¾ ins. *New York Historical Society.*

(C) Amethyst salt; Stiegel-Midwestern type, early nineteenth century; pattern-moulded and expanded in diamond design, petalled foot. Height 3 ins. *New York Historical Society.*

(D) Sapphire-blue salt, possibly Amelung; eighteenth century; pattern-moulded and expande checkered-diamond design. Knop-like stem, circ foot. Height 3 ins. *New York Historical Society.*

PLATE 150

Clear glass goblet, engraved; slight smoky tint, John Frederick Amelung's New Bremen Glass Manufactory. Presented to August Koenig, Baltimore merchant, from whose great-great-granddaughter it was acquired. Height 7¾ ins. *Maryland Historical Society.*

PLATE 151

(A) Cut glass decanter attributed to Dummer's Jersey City Works or Gilliland's Brooklyn Flint Glass Works, *c.* 1845. Height 10¼ ins. *New York Historical Society.*

(B) Clear glass decanter, possibly New England Glass Co., *c.* 1815–30; blown-three-mould in arch pattern. *New York Historical Society.*

PLATE 152

(A) Milk glass covered dish, The Atterbury Company, Pittsburgh, Pennsylvania, 1880s; chicken with eggs design, open edge. Height 7 ins. *New York Historical Society.*

(B) Paper weight, Boston & Sandwich Glass Company, mid-nineteenth century; fuchsia red with blue, green, and yellow stem on *latticinio* background. Diameter $2\frac{7}{8}$ ins. *New York Historical Society.*

PLATE 153

(A) Amberina decanter; New England Glass Co., late nineteenth century; pale amber shading to deep red; pattern-moulded and expanded in ribbing swirled to right. Height 10⅞ ins. *Corning Museum of Glass*.

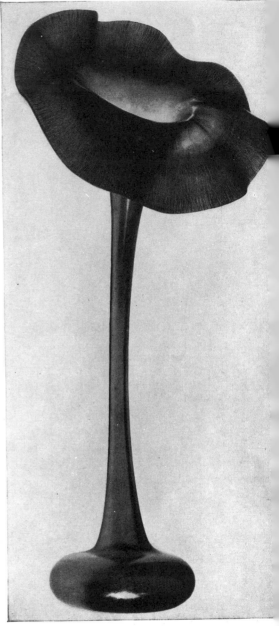

(B) Free blown iridescent glass vase, late nineteenth century; marked on base L. C. TIFFANY. Height 18½ in. *New York Historical Society*.

PLATE 154

American vase, Louis C. Tiffany *favrile* glass, 1875–96; peacock feather design. *Metropolitan Museum of Art, New York.*

PLATE 155

A

B

C

D

E

F

PLATE 156

Opposite (Plate 156)

(A) Champagne glass: flute with compound opaque-twist stem and plain foot. *Victoria and Albert Museum, London.*

(B) Jacobite glass with plain stem engraved with formalized rose and buds and the jay. *Private Collection.*

(C) Jacobite glass with drawn air-twist stem: engraved with Jacobite rose and two buds and the motto FIAT, password of the Cycle Club. *Delomosne & Son Ltd.*

(D) Wine glass with compound opaque-twist stem: bowl engraved with wide border of flowers. *Delomosne & Son Ltd.*

(E) Tazza-shaped champagne glass with ogee bowl fluted at base: collar separating bowl from eight-sided pedestal stem on moulded domed and folded foot. *Private Collection.*

(F) Shouldered decanter with outward-sloping sides. *Delomosne & Son Ltd.*

A   B   C

Decanters cut in deep relief. (A) Cylindrical body. (B) and (C) Prussian-shaped body. From 1790. *Delomosne & Son Ltd.*

PLATE 157

Drinking glasses: (A) Drawn stem containing tear. (B) Multiple air spiral in drawn stem. (C) Compound opaque spiral stem. (D) Facet-cut drawn stem. *Private Collection.*

(E) Drinking glass with incised baluster stem and folded foot. *Victoria and Albert Museum, London.* (F) Sweetmeat glass with ogee bowl and pedestal stem moulded with deep vertical reeds: domed and folded foot. *Mrs William Hopley's Collection.* (G) Toasting glass with slender compound opaque-twist stem on plain foot.

PLATE 158

Three enamelled glasses. (A) Arms of Buckmaster. (B) Inscribed THOS VAUHAN. (C) Arms of Turner of Kirkleatham.

Cecil Higgins Museum, Bedford.

PLATE 159

(A) White opaque vases with chinoiserie decoration. Heights 7¼ ins and 2¾ ins. *National Trust, Fenton House, Hampstead.*

(B) White opaque tea caddy, painted in colours by Michael Edkins. Height 5½ ins. *William Edkins Collection, now in Victoria and Albert Museum, London.*

(C) Goblet, etched with a view of the front elevation of the Phoenix Glass House, Bristol, and the words PEACE AND PLENTY. Height 8 ins. *City Art Gallery, Bristol.*

(D) The trade-card of Ricketts, Evans and Co., *c.* 1800. *City Art Gallery, Bristol.*

PLATE 160

gible to the uninitiated. It is a compilation of the glass-man's obsolete and modern technical terms, English and Anglo-Irish glass terms, and terms coined by American collectors and writers to meet descriptive needs and afford identification of forms, types, and decoration. Many of those in common usage can be found in the glossary.

Bohemian

Bohemian glass is the generic term for the ornamental glass made in and near the mountains covering the borders of Bohemia and Silesia. Glass-houses were established there because the country was rich in natural resources: pine and beech forests provided furnace fuel and potash: pure white sand was plentiful in the hillsides. Forest glass domestic ware, tinged green, yellow, or brown, was made there as early as the fourteenth century. In the sixteenth century a fine soda glass was evolved, faintly tinged topaz yellow; this was decorated with bright enamels. Thus Bohemia became the first country to enter into direct competition with Murano.

During the reign of the Emperor Rudolph II the medieval art of decorating glass with designs cut on the lapidary's wheel was revived by Caspar Lehmann (1570–1622). At the age of eighteen he was appointed lapidary and glass-cutter to the emperor and given a life-patent of monopoly. He was the first of Bohemia's master decorators and operated extensive workshops at Prague, far from the glass-houses. After Lehmann's death the monopoly was granted to his assistant Zacharias Belzer and a scholar George Schwanhard. The latter's sons, George (d. 1676) and Henry (d. 1696) worked on the wheel engraving incavo, and were also skilled with the diamond point. In about 1670 Henry perfected a method of etching glass with fluoric acid, the ground being eaten away and dulled, so that the ornament showed smooth and clear in its original surface against a dull ground. Later in the decade the famous Bohemian ruby glass was perfected by Johann Kunkel, director of glass-houses at Potsdam. This intensely strong colour was obtained by using the recently invented purple of cassius or gold chloride. This ruby glass and the emerald glass, also evolved by Kunkel, rarely come within the reach of the collector.

Then, in 1680, a now forgotten glass-man in northern Bohemia produced a glass of greater clarity by replacing soda with potash and adding chalk. This crystal glass, quickly copied by other Bohemian glass-men, was thicker, heavier, and more resistant to wear than the former ware, and Henry Schwanhard applied to it the methods used for cutting rock crystal. Although cutting produced a hard glitter, this glass did not possess the power of dispersing light as did the English flint-glass. Every kind of picture was cut and engraved, including landscapes, sporting scenes, flowers, animals, coats-of-arms. A stag bounding through the forest was characteristic.

Bohemian glass, engraved, etched, or enamelled by master decorators working to commission in the cities, was for long considered the finest glass in Europe until the 1730s, when tough English flint-glass, produced on a vastly increased scale, superseded it for plain domestic ware. The Bohemian glass when cut lacked prismatic sparkle. Dr Pococke recorded in his *Travels*, Vol. II, that in 1736 he visited the glass-house at Rispen, Bohemia. Their glass, he says, was thick and strong and almost as good as English flint-glass. The blanks were sent to Breslau for engraving, and he saw a glass which was cut at a cost of £20. Some of the large drinking-goblets were so finely cut as to sell for £100 to £150.

Bohemian crystal glass was manufactured on a commercial scale and widely exported, its low price competing successfully against flint-glass. Fine examples by master decorators remained supreme. Then, after the close of the Napoleonic wars in 1815, came a demand for coloured glass, hitherto made only in small quantities. In addition to the celebrated ruby-red, tones of green, blue, and amethyst were perfected. Josef Riedel of Iserberg introduced greenish and yellowish green derived from uranium. Topaz and amber tones were produced from combinations of uranium and antimony.

In the Gratzen district of Bohemia several glass-houses were operated by Count von Buquoy, who specialized in glass coloured sealing-wax red, catalogued as red hydralite. From about 1820 he made jet-black glass in shapes adapted from Wedgwood's black basalts and enriched by painted motifs in gold and silver. At Zechlin black glass had been in production from 1804, also in imitation of Wedgwood ware. Friedrich Egerman, specializing in coloured glass, patented in the late 1830s an almost opaque glass marbled in strong colours which he marketed under the name of lithylin.

Cased or overlay glass began to be made from 1815 in commercial quantities, by a technique nearly two thousand years old. A thick layer of opaque-white enamel was laid over a base of clear glass, and over this were laid films of molten glass in two or three colours, rarely as many as four or five, each applied at a progressively lower temperature. The piece was then cut with facets and geometrical patterns in various colours made by grinding away some of the outer films of colour as re-

quired. Further enrichment might be added in the form of engraving, deep cutting, or acid etching.

Cased glass exported from Bohemia included tall, slim decanters, wine-glasses, wine-glass coolers, finger-bowls, fruit dishes and dessert plates, toilet bottles, powder boxes, and vases.

The much less expensive and not so attractive flashed glass appeared on a similar range of articles at the same period. In this a thin surface layer of coloured glass sufficient to give full colour was applied direct to the clear glass without the enamel underlay. In many instances the wheel was used to cut through the colour into the clear glass. In this way the film of colour was irradiated by the light striking on the cut facets. The Bohemians manufactured stained table glass from the 1830s. Blown-moulded and, later, pressed glass, could be stained. Coloured designs were stained on clear glass with the aid of stencils.

Decorative glass manufactured on a commercial scale encouraged the establishment of more glass-houses. In 1847 Bohemia was operating 160 glass-houses, four times as many as Britain, and exported 21,000 tons of glass, much of it in colour. Twenty-six Bohemian glass-manufacturers exhibited at the Great Exhibition, 1851, and gold medals were awarded to three. The Jury recorded that the Venetian origin of their decorative glass was conspicuous in Eastern forms, reticulated patterns, taper stems, and wide range of colours. The Bohemian exhibits included many millefiori paperweights.

English

English tableware of fine quality was first made in England by Jean Carre (q.v.), who in 1570 established a glass-house in the Crutched Friars, London, for the purpose of producing glass resembling the Venetian. Imported Venetian glass was highly fashionable,

more than fifty families in London being supported by the sale of such glass. After Carré's death in 1572 Giacomo Verzelini (q.v.) acquired the glass-house and commercialized the manufacture of this fragile Anglo-Venetian soda-glass, which was clouded by microscopic air bubbles and discoloured in various hues. He was granted a monopoly to make "Venetian glass". About a dozen of his goblets, elaborately engraved by the diamond-point, are known to remain. Venetian traditions dominated fine glass-making for the next hundred years.

Sir Jerome Bowes (q.v.) acquired the monopoly from Verzelini in 1592. In 1614 James I extended the monopoly to cover all branches of glass-making, and granted it to a group of financiers in return for a payment of £1,000 a year. From 1618 until the King Charles I's death in 1649, when monopolies were ended, the monopoly was under the control of Sir Robert Mansell (q.v.).

Little improvement was made in the quality of Anglo-Venetian glass during the reign of Charles II, and within a decade of George Ravenscroft's (q.v.) introduction of flint-glass in 1674 (see below) its manufacture had virtually ceased. Early flint-glass was, naturally, influenced by Venetian design, and the new metal was blown thinly. By 1682 it was found that by doubling the gather of metal taken from the pot a far more substantial ware was produced without loss of translucency. New forms in tableware now appeared, ponderous and heavy, purely English in character.

Noble goblets, known as tall-boys, with sturdy baluster stems supporting thick-walled, heavy-based bowls of the round funnel or conical type, became fashionable. Other ware was made on similar massive lines. In 1695, when twenty-seven flint-glass houses were operating in England, it was recorded that "the makers of Flint Glasses have long since beaten out all foreigners by making a better glass and underselling them".

Glass collectors must possess a background knowledge of the improvements made in flint-glass manufacture between then and 1820. Each influenced the quality of fine metal, making it possible for specimens to be grouped chronologically, due consideration also being given to form.

Early flint-glass varied considerably in weight and clarity; formulae were not standardized, ingredients were impure, and furnace heat was irregular and could not be raised to a temperature adequate for efficient fusing of the materials. Flint-glass made in these circumstances was highly brittle and its fabric unable to withstand without fracture the stresses caused by sudden changes of atmospheric temperature or slight surface shocks, even though it had been annealed in an oven above the furnace. Improvements in this toughening process were made in about 1740 and again in about 1780. It was found in about 1745 that double annealing produced a stronger and more brilliant glass.

The introduction of the Perrott furnace in about 1734 provided a vastly increased and more uniform temperature than had previously been deemed possible. The capacity of melting pots until now had been little more than that of a large bucket: now they might contain as much as 1,500 lbs of glass. The quality of the glass was itself improved by these means, and by 1740 glass from such furnaces lacked the dark tinge usually associated with early glass and displayed greater clarity and brilliance. The manipulative capabilities were improved, enabling more pieces to be made per pound weight of molten glass. As the eighteenth century progressed the clarity of fine flint-glass was somewhat enhanced.

So prosperous became the glass trade that in 1745, and again in 1777, excise taxes were levied upon glass. Illegal glass-makers working old-style furnaces and not operating a tunnel leer (see Annealing) perforce continued making dark, heavy flint-glass in forms similar to those fashionable early in the century.

Manufacturers of the new metal did not rely upon pure form for ornament, and it rapidly became a field for applied decoration. Toughness resulting from the introduction of the tunnel leer in c. 1740 permitted shallow cutting to be commercialized: the improved leer of 1780 made possible such annealing of the glass that deep-relief cutting could then be carried out on a commercial scale.

Until about 1802 flint-glass was melted in pots "set in a furnace and directly heated", adversely affecting clarity. The new furnace evolved at this time reduced fuel consumption by two-thirds, provided such intense heat that the materials fused in half the time, and produced the more crystalline glass associated with early nineteenth-century deep-relief cutting.

Glass-houses were in existence in the city and port of Bristol in the seventeenth century, and it is recorded that about 1651 "Edward Dagney (or Dagnia), an ingenious Italian, had a glass-house at which the master was John Williams". By the end of the century there were ten glass-works in Bristol, and in 1722 the number had increased to fifteen. Most of them made only window-glass (known as "crown glass") or bottles, for both of which there were good markets locally and overseas.

It was not until the middle years of the eighteenth century that more sophisticated articles of good quality began to be made in quantity, and in pattern similar to the productions of other glass-making centres. The trade-card of the Phoenix Glasshouse of Messrs Ricketts, Evans and Co. (Plate 160D) is engraved with typical pieces that were in fashion at the end of the eighteenth century, and these are no different in appearance from wares that emanated from Stourbridge, Newcastle, or Waterford.

In 1745 the Glass Excise Act laid a duty on glass, which was levied by weight and which seriously hampered the trade. In order to recoup themselves for their lowered turnover from making articles of lighter forms, the manufacturers introduced decoration wherever possible. This took the form of engraving, cutting, gilding, and enamelling, all of which began to flourish shortly after that date. It has been suggested that these same circumstances caused the Bristol makers to produce coloured glass; a material with which their name has been linked inescapably, rightly or wrongly, ever since. In particular, glass of a rich, deep blue colour is termed "Bristol", and the same name is applied to glass in tints of purple, green, and red.

Although coloured window-glass had been made for centuries, particularly for stained-glass windows, it was not until more recent times that colouring was employed in England for domestic articles made of good-quality glass. Certainly, in the case of blue glass there is proof that this was made in Bristol; for pieces are known signed with the name of the maker, Isaac Jacobs, and that

of the city in addition (Plate 161A). The same manufacturer advertised that he made purple glass.

There is less reason for being certain about the west-country origin of glass in colours other than blue and purple. Articles of green glass had been made in England as early as 1700, and by 1751 it was noted by a traveller that Stourbridge was making glass "in all the capital colours". There is no doubt that similar pieces were made by then, or soon afterwards, not only at Bristol but elsewhere.

Of greater artistic importance and more positively identifiable, is the opaque white glass for which Bristol is also famous (Plate 160A). As this is very rare, it is known only to a restricted circle of collectors, students, and dealers, and is generally unrecognized by the devotees of the flamboyant coloured pieces.

White enamel glass was made in several factories on the Continent as well as in England, but that of Bristol was particularly satisfactory and individual. Whereas much eighteenth-century white glass is only just opaque and mostly has a pronounced pink tinge, the Bristol variety is completely opaque, was made very thinly in pleasing shapes, and is of a distinctive creamy colour. It seems probable that it became popular at the time because it was not liable for duty under the Act of 1745. This loophole was, however, closed by the Act of 1777, and it is doubtful if much was made after that date. Unquestionably, it was made also to rival the porcelain then being made, and most of the painting on both glass and china was in parallel styles.

Among the many artists who must have been employed in decorating Bristol white glass, only the name of Michael Edkins is known. At one time both the glass itself and the name of its only recorded painter were forgotten completely; but a century ago, William Edkins, grandson of the painter and a well-known collector of china, made public the fact that he possessed several pieces of this scarce glass, and that these had been painted by his grandfather (Plate 160B).

As further proof of the activities of Michael Edkins, his notebooks have survived and are preserved in the Bristol Museum. These record briefly much of the work he did between

1762 and 1787, and although the majority of it cannot now be identified, there is no doubt that he did paint a quantity of the white glass, as well as gild some of the blue.

A glass-works was opened at Nailsea, a few miles west of Bristol, in 1788 by John Robert Lucas, a Bristol bottle-maker. The factory was taken over during 1810 to 1815 by R. L. Chance, and under various proprietors continued in production until 1873. It has been assumed that J. R. Lucas took advantage of the fact that there was a lower duty on common bottle-glass than on the normal glass used for domestic wares, and decided to make a wide range of articles from the cheaper material.

None of the glass made during the eighty-five years in which the factory was at work bears a mark to indicate its provenance, and for this reason both mystery and argument surround the glass-works itself and the articles that were made there.

A brownish-green glass speckled with splashes of white is said to have been the earliest and most characteristic type made at Nailsea. It is no more than a standard bottle-glass with surface decoration of fragments of opaque white glass scattered on it and melted. A typical piece is shown in Plate 163D. An unusual wine-bottle inscribed *J.S. J.M. Stirling* 1827 is of the same material as the foregoing. However, in view of the fact that it bears a Scottish place name and similar glassware is known to have been made at that date in many places far nearer to Scotland than Nailsea, it is not improbable that this bottle, and many other pieces, came from a more northerly factory.

Other articles ascribed to Nailsea are made with coloured or white stripes in clear glass, and are said to have been made by a group of French workmen introduced by R. L. Chance. It is recorded that a row of cottages named "French Rank" was built in Nailsea, and it was there that this colony of craftsmen resided.

The variety of articles made at Nailsea was probably wide, but certain of them are supposed to have been invented there and to have been a monopoly of the factory. These include such popular "bygones" and "friggers" as inscribed or plain glass rolling-pins, witch-balls, fancy (and usable) glass tobacco pipes, "yards of ale", walking-sticks (solid or filled with coloured sweets), and, more conventionally, cream-jugs and pocket-flasks.

It is agreed generally that the output comprised pleasing, but simple, articles for every-day country use to be sold at country markets and fairs. It is highly probable that much of the production was exported to America by way of Bristol, and that many of the pieces served as models for the glass-manufacturers there. This is especially probable in the case of those in New Jersey, Pennsylvania, and the Middle West, for, as W. B. Honey pointed out: "Much glass preserved in American collections as the work of these makers is indistinguishable from English country-market glasses."

Altogether there has been a tendency to attribute both to the Nailsea and the Bristol glass-works a very large amount of glass that was almost certainly made elsewhere. No doubt in time more thorough research will be carried out and result in the clear definition of just what was made at either place, but in the meantime it is only possible to follow what are thought to be established attributions.

Finally, it should be mentioned that almost all the accepted Bristol and Nailsea types have received careful and ample attention from copyists, and collectors should be on their guard against the numerous reproductions on the market. In particular, Czechoslovakian blue glass is frequently labelled *BRISTOL*, and bought as such by the inexperienced; an occurrence that is the more irritating when the price was possibly that usually paid for an English piece.

French

NINETEENTH CENTURY

In the history of French glass vessels the nineteenth century is *le grand siècle*. During the Middle Ages the French created, in stained glass, an art which has never been surpassed: and from the late seventeenth century they were the leading mirror-makers in Europe. But for vessels glass had been considered a secondary material, well enough suited for the production of utilitarian types like drinking-glasses and bottles, but unworthy of being treated as a serious artistic medium. Apart from the great technical inventor ·Bernard Perrot, who during the seventeenth century received royal privileges, no glass artist was patronized by the Court as were craftsmen working in so many other materials. Charming as is French glass of the sixteenth and seventeenth centuries, it has the character of folk art compared with the English and German glass of the period and with the tasteful and sophisticated French achievements in other branches of the applied arts.

The reasons for the great expansion during the nineteenth century can be at least partly explained. Early in the century the industry grew rapidly, and as firing methods were changed from wood to coal it was reorganized geographically. Many of the factories moved nearer to the big towns and became part of French urban life. As will be seen, several of the factories in and near Paris are among the pioneers in the new French art of glass. During the early part of the century the glass industry was protected from foreign competition by a strict customs-barrier. French art glass between 1830 and 1870 has a definitely experimental character, with technical invention and ingenuity as the main inspiring forces. The long and detailed technical descriptions, which accompany the glass shown at French nineteenth-century exhibitions bear witness to the pride and satisfaction on the part of technicians and directors at difficulties successfully overcome.

The important new feature in nineteenth-century decorative glass is the prevalence of rich and exotic colour. Love of colour is, of course, a general characteristic of the Romantic Age, and can be seen reflected in almost all products of the period, from the canvases of Delacroix to the upholstery of furniture and in ladies' dresses. During the neo-classical period at the end of the eighteenth century the French, like most European glass-makers, had felt the need for more solid material effects than those found in transparent crystal, which had dominated the artistic scene for more than a hundred years. The first expression of this tendency in France was the making of opal-glass, begun some time before 1800. Most coloured glass of the nineteenth century in France is made on a basis of opal-glass (*see* Opaline).

The 1830s seem to have been the time when colour experiments on a large scale began in the French *cristalleries* (*q.v.*) and they were first carried out in imitation of Bohemian and Venetian glass. The new style of cased and flushed glass in bright colours, and with cut and engraved decorations, developed in Bohemian factories during the 1820s and 30s, was just catching the fancy of a wide public everywhere. In 1836 *La Société d'Encouragement pour l'Industrie Française* offered prizes for coloured and decorated glass in the Bohemian style, and directors from French factories visited Bohemian and German glass-works to study their methods. At the same time the highly complicated colour techniques employed by the Venetians during the Renaissance and baroque periods were being revived in Murano on an antiquarian basis, and among glass-makers north of the Alps it became an ambition to re-create latticino and millefiori glass. In France these techniques were the objects of fruitful experiments during the 1830s and 40s.

The history of French nineteenth-century glass can be divided into three main periods: (1) During the first two decades the old eighteenth-century tradition stands more or less unchallenged, with transparent crystal with cut or engraved decoration as the main luxury product. Glass in this genre continued to be made right through the century, and the factory of Baccarat (*q.v.*) was the chief producer of glass in this style. (2) The period from 1830 to 1870 is the exciting time of experiment and discovery in the field of coloured glass, carried on at Baccarat and St Louis, and a group of smaller factories in and near Paris, with Georges Bontemps (*q.v.*) as the central figure. A main product of this time was the paperweight with inlaid colour-patterns. Originating in Venice, but perfected at the St Louis glass-works, it very soon found many imitators, both in that country and elsewhere.

But it is conceded generally that few can vie with the French productions, whether from St Louis or from its contemporaries at Baccarat and Clichy. Not only in the past have these attractive objects suffered the close attention of copyists, but today they are equally carefully imitated. Much of the fine coloured glass of the mid-century received its final shape through moulding. (3) During the latter part of the century the technical achievements in the use of colour are subordinated to the new stylistic development of the time, inspired in its ideas by the Arts and Crafts Movement in Britain and in its forms by the art of Japan. It culminates in the creation of the *Art Nouveau* about 1890, and the art glass of Émile Gallé (*q.v.*) was a characteristic and original expression of the style.

The history of French nineteenth-century glass has not yet been fully investigated. Consequently there are still considerable gaps in our knowledge of it.

Irish

Ireland's earliest flint-glass house was established in Dublin during the early 1690s by Captain Philip Roche. This was known as the Round Glass House, and under various proprietorships continued operating until 1755. Productions by the mid-century, according to an advertisement in *Faulkner's Dublin Journal* quoted by Westropp, included "all sorts of the newest fashioned drinking glasses, water bottles, claret and burgundy bottles, decanters, jugs, water glasses with and without feet and saucers, plain, ribbed, and diamond moulded jelly glasses of all sorts and sizes, sillybub glasses, comfit and sweetmeat glasses for desserts, salvers, glass plates for china dishes, toort covers, pine and orange glasses, hall lanthorns for one to four candles, glass branches, cut and plain barrel lanthorns, glove lamps, etc, all in the most elegant and newest fashioned mounting now used in

London. . . . All sorts of cut and flowered glasses may be had of any kind to any pattern, viz.: wine glasses with a vine border, toasts, or any flourish whatsoever; beer ditto with the same, salts with and without feet, sweetmeat glasses and stands, cruits for silver and other frames all in squares and diamond cut, tea cannisters, jars and beakers of mock china, mustard pots, crests and coats of arms, sweetmeat bowls and covers." It is doubtful if any English glass-house could exceed the scope of productions shown on this list.

The Round House was no doubt a highly flourishing business until the export of glass from Ireland was prohibited under the Excise Act of 1745, which at the same time levied a duty of one penny a pound on English flint-glass. This prohibition was directly responsible for the glass-house closing down ten years later, and from then until 1764 no fine flint-glass appears to have been made in Ireland. Then an already existing bottle-house at Marlborough Green, Dublin, was enlarged to produce flint-glass. By 1770 this glass-house was under the control of Richard Williams & Company, who then announced in the *Limerick Chronicle* that their productions included "all the newest fashioned enamelled, flowered, cut and plain wine, beer and cyder glasses, common wines and drams, rummers, decanters, water-glasses and plates, epergnes and epergne saucers, cruets, casters, cans, jugs, salvers, jellies, sweetmeat glasses, salts, salt linings" in flint-glass. This firm must have operated on a large scale, for in addition to flint-glass and bottles they made and ground looking-glass plates. There is no doubt that Williams made virtually all the flint-glass sold in Ireland during the 1770s.

When in 1780 import restrictions were removed, several well-equipped glass-houses were established in Ireland, notably at Waterford, Belfast, Dublin, and Cork. Orders poured into Ireland from the Continent and America, for prices, and quality, were much lower than English flint-glass. In 1785 Lord Sheffield observes that "nine glass-houses have suddenly arisen in Ireland, and the best drinking glasses are sold at three to four shillings a dozen less than the English".

Although English executives and leading glass-workers and decorators were employed and much of the material obtained from England, it was long before the industry became self-supporting, although still free from paying excise duty. The Dublin Society subsidized several firms: the Williams glass-house, for instance, received £28,145 from this source between 1784 and 1794.

Irish glass of the 1780s and 1790s for the most part displayed a slightly dusky tint. From about 1800 more efficient furnaces were installed by the larger glass-houses and a clearer metal produced. This glass proved ideal for the cutting in deep relief, which now became overwhelmingly popular. Every potful of metal produced two qualities – tale and fine glass. During this period, too, some glass was issued with a faintly blue tint.

The nineteenth century also introduced a new era in blown-moulded glass, new techniques producing a wholly new range of designs, shapes, and decorations at prices lower than formerly. Moulded glass was produced in a fraction of the time possible with handwork. Blown-moulded table-glass was made in shapes and designs approximating to those of free-blown and hand-cut glass. To distinguish it from English pressed work the following three differences should be noted:

(*a*) Mould marks are no more than slightly convex swellings on the surface of the glass in no way resembling the hair lines or threads on pressed glass, which are so sharply defined that they appear to have been applied. The number of mould marks indicates the number of pieces forming the mould. From 1835 blown-moulded glass was finished by fire polishing.

(*b*) The concave–convex relation of inner and outer surfaces of blown-moulded glass increased its refractive properties, thus accounting for its typical brilliance. The inflation of the gather of molten glass within a full-sized mould not only caused the air within the gather to force the glass into the sunk pattern, producing relief ornament on the outer surface, but also made corresponding hollows on the inner surface. A smooth inner surface indicates that the glass has been either free-blown or pressed; a slightly rippled surface proves the glass to have been moulded for pattern only and then expanded.

(*c*) The impression received on the surface of blown-moulded glass differs from that of pressed glass. Decoration motifs of the former appear to merge into each other instead of displaying the sharp, almost photographic definition of pressed glass.

The decline in the Irish flint-glass trade was brought about first by the imposition of an excise duty from 1825, such as had existed in England from 1745, and was hastened from the early 1830s by the introduction in England of glass-pressing machines capable of producing handled hollow-ware at a single operation. Such a machine was first installed by W. Richardson, of Wordsley, who sold pressed glass as intagliated tableware. Other firms quickly followed, but not a single machine is known to have been acquired by an Irish glass-house. Because of vastly lowered prices, the Irish hand-blown trade languished and died soon after removal of the excise duty in 1845.

Even the celebrated Waterford (*q.v.*) firm failed to survive English competition at the Great Exhibition, 1851, and closed immediately afterwards. The only Irish-made exhibit in the glass section at the Dublin Industrial Exhibition, 1853, was some "richly cut flint-glass manufactured by the Dublin Flint Glass Works". At a further exhibition in 1865, Irish flint-glass was not represented.

No Irish glass unless marked or pedigreed, or closely resembling a marked example in metal and in design, can be definitely attributed to any one glass-house. Most designs were copied from the cut-glass men of London and Glasgow.

Scandinavian

The oldest existing glass of Scandinavian make dates from the late seventeenth century and is of Swedish origin. Glass has been made in Sweden ever since. Norway's production of glass began in 1741, and during the latter part of the eighteenth century, when Denmark and Norway were united under one crown, Denmark received all its glassware from Norway. Denmark's own glass production did not start until 1810 with the foundation of *Holmegaards Glasvaerk*, and it is only in comparatively recent times that Danish glass products have become of interest artistically. The same can be said for Finnish glass. The story of Scandinavian glass in the eighteenth century is really the story of Swedish and Norwegian glass.

The earliest preserved Swedish glass was made at *Kungsholm Glasbruk* (*q.v.*) in Stockholm. The early Kungsholm glass has a distinct Venetian flavour. The metal is thin and frequently in a bad state of glass disease, and the shapes are decorated in elaborate furnacework. Picturesque are the goblets where the stems are formed into royal initials (Plate 177B). Royal crowns are frequently used as handles to the covers of goblets, the ornament being a compliment to royalty and an allusion to the factory's name at the same time.

In the early part of the eighteenth century the Kungsholm goblets began to take their cue from Bohemia. The metal becomes more solid, the stem shorter in relation to the bowl, the general effect is solid and sturdy (Plate 177C). Venetian reminiscences are the foot that is folded over from below and the "pressed tomato" member of the stem, which remains a characteristic feature on Kungsholm goblets until about 1750. Otherwise the elaborate furnacework has been discarded and what decoration there is has been carried out on the wheel. Engraving was introduced into Sweden by one Kristoffer Elstermann (*q.v.*) who first appears at Kungsholm in 1698. The engraved patterns are mostly coats-of-arms in a dignified style; a sun and a radiant Northern Star being frequent accompaniments to the royal arms and the monogram of Charles XII. About the middle of the century cutting was occasionally used for stems.

The handsome, but somewhat impersonal baroque style, which was established at Kungsholm early in the eighteenth century, persisted in the products of the factory to the end of its working period, and the engraving continued more or less on the lines laid down by Elstermann, with only the smallest allowances for changes in style and fashion. Rococo and classicism seem both to have by-passed Kungsholm completely. The few more modest products that can be identified as of Kungsholm origin – beakers, decanters, wine-glasses – show the same conservatism in form and decoration.

During the creative period at Kungsholm (*c.* 1700) some types were made which did not survive beyond their period. Most remarkable among them are: a large Römer with a cover and prunts on the stem; a beaker on three feet

with cover (clearly copied after a silver model);
a tall, slim beaker with a high domed cover; a
decanter with conical body, a narrow neck, a
widely turned-out collar, and no stopper. They
are all found with good-quality engraved decoration in the Elstermann style.

Kungsholm was always an aristocratic establishment, situated in the capital and patronized by the King. Sweden's other seventeenth-
century glass foundation had a different social
background, a fact which is clearly reflected
in the products. Skånska Glasbruket (q.v.) began by making purely utilitarian glass, but
in 1715 production of decorative glass was
taken up.

Occasionally efforts were made, not always
successfully, to copy Kungsholm models, but
the majority of the products were of a less
ambitious kind: tumblers, beakers, decanters,
and jugs for the local market, some of them
decorated with engraving. Skånska Glasbruket's engravers sometimes used the same
motifs as their colleagues at Kungsholm, but
their cut was broad and shallow, the motifs
were simplified and the general effect unsophisticated. No great development can be
distinguished in the engraving during the
forty-seven years it was practised at the
factory.

In spite of being simple and unsophisticated, glass from Skånska Glasbruket has its
very distinct character, and in many ways it
has a stronger appeal to the modern collector
than the products from Kungsholm. The
metal is fairly thick and clear and shiny, and
the forms have a pleasant robustness which is
very charming, while the engraving, in spite of
the heraldic motifs of crowned cartouches and
branches of palm and laurel, has almost the
character of folk art (Plate 178D). The royal
monogram is often used as patriotic ornamentation on glass for ordinary customers.

The third of Sweden's old glass factories is
Kosta (q.v.). The products of the eighteenth
and nineteenth centuries were mostly unpretentious things made for daily use by the
people of the districts. Of special interest are
the charming little chandeliers, rustic versions
of Continental types, still to be seen in some
Småland churches. Over the years workers
from Kosta broke away from the mother fac-

tory and founded works of their own in the
neighbourhood. Most of these smaller factories were short-lived, and none of them produced anything but the simplest utilitarian
glass. But this intensive glass-production in
Småland, which has gone on from the middle
of the eighteenth century until today, has
established a solid tradition of craftsmanship
and a general milieu, which in due course has
become the basis for the greater achievements
of modern times. The most famous producers
of modern Swedish art glass, Orrefors and
Strömbergshyttan, are both situated a few
miles from Kosta, which is itself one of the
finest manufactories of modern glass. Småland is, in fact, one of the famous glass districts
of Europe like Lorraine, Bohemia, and Venice. In the "capital" of Småland, the city of
Växjö, is the only museum in northern
Europe devoted entirely to glass.

The Gothenburg factory (1769–1803) is referred to in connexion with the production at
Gjövik in Norway.

The Victoria and Albert Museum possesses
a few pieces of Kungsholm glass, but otherwise old Swedish glass is rarely seen in
England.

The Norwegian glass industry was founded
by royal command and under the personal
patronage of King Christian VI of Denmark
and Norway and his Court in Copenhagen.
Work began in 1741 at Nöstetangen (q.v.) near
Drammen. Experiments were made in all
branches of glass-making, with window-glass,
bottles, table-glass, and decorative pieces. The
glass-blowers came from Thuringia, and the
earliest glasses that can be identified as of
Nöstetangen origin are goblets in a simplified,
German style, large in size, with a royal crown
as handle to the cover, but otherwise without
decoration. Some of them were engraved in
Copenhagen to commemorate royal occasions.
The pair of coronation goblets made for King
Frederik V and his much-beloved English
wife, Queen Louise, can still be seen in the
Rosenborg Collection in Copenhagen. A few
goblets made for the rich bourgeoisie in Nor-
way have also survived from these early days.
Some of them have been engraved by itinerant
German glass-sellers. The production of table-

glass was still on a small scale, and the few existing pieces show little distinctive character.

In 1753 the Norwegian glass-industry was reorganized. The deciding personalities in the undertaking were Count Adam Gottlob Moltke, Frederik V's powerful minister, and Caspar Herman von Storm, a Norwegian officer and landowner and the richest man in Christiania.

The purpose of the reorganization was to make the Norwegian glass industry capable of satisfying the need for glass of all kinds in Denmark and Norway. To this end new factories were built, while the production of tableware and ornamental glass was concentrated at Nöstetangen. The factory was enlarged and modernized, some first-class German glassblowers were engaged; and, most important of all, contact was sought with the English glassmaking industry. By honest and dishonest means Storm managed to gather information about, and get samples of, the much admired English lead crystal and even to lure a Newcastle crystal blower to Nöstetangen. In August 1755 James Keith (q.v.) arrived at the factory, accompanied by an assistant, William Brown, and a few days later Storm reported in a letter: "I have seen the English glassmakers at work. In London itself you would not find them more able."

Another innovation at Nöstetangen was the establishment of a cutters' and engravers' workshop. Head engraver and general artistic manager of the factory was Heinrich Gottlieb Köhler (q.v.). During his Copenhagen years Köhler had engraved many Norwegian goblets, and his signature can be seen, or his style recognized, on many of the great royal goblets now at Rosenborg. Köhler was not only a first-class practitioner of the art of engraving but also an original and imaginative designer, both of patterns for engraving and of glass-shapes. It is probably to a large extent due to him that the German and English styles in glass-making, which converged at Nöstetangen about 1755, were harmoniously merged into a unified style of distinct individual character.

In 1760 the Norwegian glass factories were staffed and fitted out for a large-scale production on modern lines and a royal monopoly for Denmark and Norway was granted. Not until 1803 was it again permitted to import foreign glass into the two countries.

The decade 1760–70 is Nöstetangen's best period, and it is perhaps the most interesting decade in the history of old Scandinavian glass altogether. During this period two different qualities of glass were made: a comparatively cheap soda–lime composition of German type, and a more expensive crystal, which was an adaptation of English lead glass. The soda–lime glass from Nöstetangen is sometimes very rough, light in weight, full of bubbles and imperfections, and with a very distinct pinkish-purple tone. The lead-glass products are usually of a very fine quality, transparent, heavy in weight, and with a deep, ringing tone. All the factory's table-glass models were copied after German and English types. The cheaper glasses for everyday use were mostly based on German models, while the more expensive glasses and decanters were derived from English types. Baluster-stems of Newcastle type and air-twist stems were particularly popular (Plate 178c). For the larger and more elaborate articles, such as chandeliers, épergnes, goblets and the like, the glassblowers at Nöstetangen, developed a style of their own. Its main elements were borrowed from late seventeenth- and early eighteenth-century English glass and can be traced farther back to Venice. These elements are mostly furnace-made surface decorations like trailed threads and chains of glass, prunts, "nipt diamond waies", flammiform fringes, or moulded surface effects (Plates 179B and D), a style that was fashionable in London about the turn of the century; in 1755 it must still have been part of a Newcastle glass-blower's skill. Other elements of the Nöstetangen style were inlaid decoration such as airtwists and "tears". Complicated baluster-stems of Newcastle type were also much used. These decorations were adapted to non-English forms which were popular among Danes and Norwegians from the early part of the eighteenth century. Most famous among them is the goblet, and the royal crown on the handle of the cover, which had been used at Nöstetangen before 1753, was integrated into the Nöstetangen style (Fig. 36).

The new decoration became popular among Nöstetangen's customers, especially the rich merchants in Christiania and the surrounding country, who traded with England and were familiar with English taste and fashions. The Court in Copenhagen was more conservative, and few of the goblets made for royalty after 1753 are in developed Nöstetangen style. After the death of Frederik V in 1766 and the subsequent fall of Count Moltke, royal patronage seems to have been withdrawn from Nöstetangen. The merchants of Bergen also preferred their glass to be in the well-known German style, and for them cut-glass goblets were made at Nöstetangen. These are, however, without originality and of poor quality. Cutting was never practised with much skill at Nöstetangen.

Most famous among the products from Nöstetangen is the set of three chandeliers, made for the church in the town of Kongsberg, where they can still be admired *in situ* (Plate 180). They were made to designs by Köhler between 1759 and 1766. They are in clear glass, with some ornaments in purple and a few in blue. In general style they combine features from Venetian and German chandeliers, but each of the hundreds of standing or hanging ornaments is in rich Nöstetangen style. They must certainly have been made in close collaboration between Köhler and James Keith. Punch-bowls, posset-pots, candlesticks, tobacco-jars, épergnes, salt-cellars, sugar-casters, etc., were also made in Nöstetangen style. But the most typical Nöstetangen product is the goblet with a royal crown on the cover and a stem with many members and fine inlaid or moulded decorations. Many of them are finely engraved by Köhler (Plate 177A).

As an engraver Köhler mastered a dignified allegorical style in the Le Brun tradition, used mainly for royal orders, and a more realistic style based on close observation which he created for his Norwegian customers. Engravings from his hand in this manner give amusing and informative pictures of contemporary life (Plate 178B). Most important among his assistants was Villas Vinter (*q.v.*). Both engravers have left a number of signed works (Plates 177A and 178A), which enable us to distinguish Köhler's quick and fluid hand from Vinter's somewhat stiff, linear manner.

In 1777 Nöstetangen was shut down and the crystal production transferred to Hurdals Verk (*q.v.*). Most of the glass-blowers from Nöstetangen went on to Hurdals Verk, among them James Keith.

While a gay and gracious rococo had been the dominant style at Nöstetangen, a gentle classicism is typical of the products from Hurdals Verk. Enamel twist-stems are used increasingly for wine-glasses, goblets (Plate 178E), and candlesticks, and the shapes become more austere (Fig. 32). The technical quality of the glass is higher than in Nöstetangen products; lead glass is used more extensively. In the cool stylishness of the products from Hurdals Verk one misses the gay exuberance in the glass from Nöstetangen.

As for engraving, Villas Vinter embraces the classical style for his larger compositions from about 1780, but in less ambitious things rococo remains predominant until after 1800. Köhler, the founder of the tradition, was himself exclusively a rococo artist, and even the Nöstetangen style in glass-blowing, with all its baroque elements, has a rococo character, undoubtedly due to Köhler's influence.

A particular kind of cartouche is frequently to be seen on Norwegian drinking-glasses from about 1770 onwards, used as a frame for initials, occasionally with gilt lines. It can be very rich or very simple, and its details can vary quite a lot – a wreath of flowers, some fine trelliswork, an open crown,[1] or a shell can be used to fill in on top or at the sides. But its main line and rhythm remained unchanged for more than a generation (Fig. 3). Most of these "Norwegian cartouches" were made in the workshop of Johan Albrecht Becker (*q.v.*).

A novelty at Hurdals Verk was the wide use made of coloured glass. Cobalt blue and manganese purple had been used at Nöstetangen, but, from about 1780 onwards especially, blue glass was used at Hurdals Verk to an extent unknown at Nöstetangen. The colours were used as artistic effects. The dark

[1] Crowns in Norwegian engraving have not necessarily a noble or royal significance. The royal initials are also used, not only on glass engraved for the royal family but on products for patriotic citizens as well.

deep tones which camouflaged the transparency of the metal suited the austere classical shapes of Hurdals glass very well. The most important type to be made in this "blue style" is the potpourri urn (q.v.). It was first made about 1780. The earliest examples are made in fairly light blue glass and in pleasant rococo shapes. Later the colour becomes deeper and the shape more classical, and about 1800 the urn has a perfect classical shape and is a deep purple blue. Candlesticks, sugar-casters, salt-cellars, and other objects were also made in blue style at Hurdals Verk. Simple engraved ornaments were occasionally added and embellished with gilding.

In 1809 Hurdals Verk closed down, and the production of table-glass and ornamental pieces was transferred to Gjövik Verk (q.v.). The later production at Hurdals Verk and the early products of Gjövik Verk are practically identical with those made in Sweden at the same time. Both Gjövik and Kosta made simple little wine-glasses, identical in shape and decorated with the same simple borders of stylized leaves, check-board patterns, etc. Glass in blue style from Gjövik can hardly be distinguished from that made at Gothenburg about the turn of the century (1796–1803). But since Gjövik Verk worked over a longer period, a greater variety of products can be traced to the Norwegian factory. The origins of the blue style, common to both Norway and Sweden, must be sought on the Continent.

Particularly attractive is the opaque glass in a light-blue shade with white borders, which seems to have been made at Gjövik during the first ten years. The classical style prevailed all through the factory's history, but after about 1830 the genuine classical feeling is lost, and the later Gjövik products are less harmonious and balanced in shape than the earlier ones.

Old Norwegian glass does occasionally appear in Great Britain. The Victoria and Albert Museum possesses two interesting eighteenth-century goblets, one in typical Nöstetangen style, the other lavishly engraved with masonic emblems by Köhler. The Bristol Museum and Art Gallery has a potpourri urn and wineglasses, and decanters often appear in the antique shops.

The technical modernization of the Swedish glass factories began early in the nineteenth century, and in Norway about 1850. With the increasing industrialization of methods and trade, national characteristics were lost and it was not until the period of the First World War that Swedish glass, and to some extent Norwegian glass, became of artistic interest again.

Venetian

The origins of the Venetian glass industry are obscure. In late classical times glass was probably made at Aquilea (mid-way between Venice and Trieste), where so many exquisite specimens of Roman glass have been dug up. Tradition has it that some glass-workers from this town were among the refugees who fled before the Gothic invaders of the fifth and sixth centuries to found the city of Venice on the barren marshy islands of the lagoons. But even if they were, they could hardly have practised their craft in the isolation of the new community. The first Venetian glass-maker to figure in documentary records is one Domenico, who, in 982, was described as a *fiolario*: a maker of phials. Further members of this trade are mentioned in the next two centuries, and by 1255 there were enough glass craftsmen in Venice to form a guild. Indeed, the city authorities became concerned at the risk of fire occasioned by numerous furnaces, and in 1291 gave orders that the glass factories should be transferred to the island of Murano, where they have remained ever since. Early in sixteenth century, the when Sir Richard Guildford passed through

Venice on his way to the Holy Land, he made a visit to Murano to inspect the factories, which were already numbered among the tourists "sights" of the lagoon.

In the fourteenth century the Murano glass factories are known to have been producing enamelled glass, blown glass, and even spectacle-lenses. But very few objects dating from this period have survived. Among fifteenth-century works one of the most notable is a marriage cup of enamelled blue glass (Plate 184A), which has by tradition been associated with a family of glass craftsmen named Barovier mentioned by Filarete in his treatise *De Architetura* (written between 1451 and 1464). Other cups and beakers of the same type are in the Museums of Bologna, Florence, Trento, Berlin, Cologne, the British Museum, and the Victoria and Albert Museum. All are of dark-coloured glass delicately painted with mythological figures, portrait heads, coats-of-arms, or abstract designs of dots and semicircles, in bright enamel. The forms are not unlike those of contemporary silver vessels. At this time the Murano factories seem to have begun the production of looking glasses which soon replaced the polished metal mirrors in use since classical times. They also began to imitate in glass the precious and semi-precious hard stones of which vessels were occasionally wrought by court jewellers throughout Europe in the renaissance period. Most successful of these was the imitation of chalcedony, and a fine ewer in this glass, called *vetro di calcedonia*, is in the Museo Nazionale, Florence.

The golden age of Venetian glass, both commercially and artistically, began in the early sixteenth century, when the art of making clear "crystal" glass was discovered. The factories quickly exploited this new process, and soon Venice was exporting to all parts of Europe, cups, bowls, and dishes of a transparency which was then to be rivalled only by rock crystal. An inventory of 1547 reveals that among the six hundred or more objects in Henry VIII's "Glasse Housse" at Westminster there were numerous goblets, jugs, and ornamental cups of Venetian origin. The fashion for this beautiful substance quickly spread, and in 1577 William Harrison remarked, in his *Description of England*: "It is a world to see in these our days, wherein gold and silver most aboundeth, how that our gentility, as loathing those metals (because of the plenty) do now generally choose rather the Venice glasses, both for our wine and beer, than any of those metals or stone wherein before time we have been accustomed to drink; . . . and such is the estimation of this stuff that many become rich only with their new trade unto Murana (a town near Venice situate on the Adriatic Sea) from whence the very best are daily to be had . . . And as this is seen in the gentility, so in the wealthy communality the like desire of glass is not neglected, whereby the gain gotten by their purchase is yet much more increased to the benefit of the merchant. The poorest also will have glass if they may; but, sith the Venetian is somewhat too dear for them, they content themselves with such as are made at home of fern and burned stone . . ." Not all the glass made in England at this time was the coarse material Harrison describes, however, for one Jacob Verzelini, a Venetian, had begun to manufacture clear glass of the Murano type in London in the 1570s. The secret of crystal or "white" glass had leaked out and Venice had already lost her monopoly.

The vessels of crystal glass made in Venice in the sixteenth century were of elegant form, perfectly adapted to the light weight of their substance and much less dependent on silver patterns than hitherto (Plate 184C). Most of the clear glass – valued on account of its clarity – seems to have been left undecorated, but some examples were engraved either by wheel or with a diamond point. The Venetian factories did not, however, give up the production of coloured opaque glass. They continued to produce glass made in imitation of hard stones and indeed developed a new milky-white glass called *lattimo*, which provided an excellent background for enamel decorations. This white glass seems to have been valued abroad, and there is a mug of it, mounted in silver-gilt in London in 1548, in the British Museum. They also began the production of the *reticello*, *vetro di trina*, or filigree glass, decorated with a pattern of crisscrossing white threads for which Murano has ever since been famous.

The decorations applied to Venetian glass in the sixteenth century reflect the current development from pure Renaissance to Mannerist ornament. Many of them are, indeed, close in style to those found on contemporary maiolica. The forms remained comparatively simple until the end of the century, when a greater sense of fantasy was employed in devising stems for goblets – in the form of dragons, serpents, or sea horses (Plate 181c). In the seventeenth century objects still more fantastic were produced: lamps in the form of horses (Plate 181A), jugs fashioned like ships with reticulated glass rigging, bottles with preposterously attenuated necks; while the greatest ingenuity was applied to varying the stems of cups and reliquaries and the knobs of covered vases. This development may partly be attributed to the exuberance of the baroque spirit. But it was also, perhaps, occasioned by the need to answer foreign competition. Before the end of the seventeenth century crystal glass much clearer than that produced at Murano was being made, often by Venetian craftsmen, in many parts of Europe. Maximilian Misson, when he visited Venice in 1688, remarked: "Formerly the Glass call'd *Venice-Crystal*, was the finest in *Europe*; but at present it does not merit that title. Not that 'tis courser than before, but because they have found the Secret in other places . . . And one of my Friends assured me, that a few Years ago, having carry'd a Vial of the finest crystal of *Murano* to *London*, the workmen were so far from looking upon it as extraordinary or inimitible, that they said they cou'd and sometimes did, make finer Work. The Skill they have acquired in other Countries, and the Manufactures they have erected, have almost ruin'd the Trade of *Murano*." If the Venetians could not make glass as clear as that produced in England, France, and Bohemia, they could, and often did, produce objects of a form far more exuberant and fantastic.

Venetian glass of the eighteenth century is principally distinguished for the bravura of its design and for sparkling gaiety of its painted decorations which reflect the styles of the great masters of the *settecento*, J. G. de Keysler, who visited Venice in the late 1730s, re-

marked: "The *Venetian* glass is very pure and ductile when it is in fusion; on which account it is more easily melted, and answers much better than any others for works of fantasy." He commented with admiration on the mirrors, though, he said, those "of any considerable size are extremely dear, when other looking glasses at present are so cheap", mainly because they were blown and not, like those made in France, cast and ground. The writer also mentions the necklaces and rosaries made of glass beads, sometimes of the form and colour of pearls (*margaritini*). Prominent among the other objects made of glass in Venice at this time are the great chandeliers, often ornamented with opaque glass flowers, bunches of grapes, and other fruit which still decorate many a Venetian salon, where they form an excellent accompaniment to the painted ceilings, from which they hang, and the exuberant rococo furniture.

Having produced so many bizarre splendours in the eighteenth century, Venetian craftsmen seem to have been unable, or unwilling, to keep pace with the change in taste from rococo to neo-classicism. Partly as a result of this, partly on account of the dwindling status of the once Serene Republic (now an Austrian possession), the glass factories of Murano fell on hard times in the early nineteenth century. In about 1820 Lady Morgan commented that the Venetian glass pearl was then "almost all that remains of that superb *arte vitraria* which first rendered Europe independent of the sands of Tyre, and established at Venice a manufacture which, in spite of Nature had supplied the world with one of its most brilliant luxuries. The Venetian shops no longer sparkle with girandoles of seeming diamonds, with flowers more brilliant and frail than the blossoms of a Spring shower, which they imitated; and with mirrors, which first replaced the dimness of metal with the reflecting lustre of crystal." A few years later Lady Blessington was rowed out to Murano and mused on the decadence of the factories. "It is melancholy to see an art, once arrived at perfection, retrograde," she wrote, "as the trifling, though brilliant ornaments shown to us, are the only portion of the trade which now flourishes." But in addition to the beads, which seem to have been their most numerous productions at this period, the factories still appear to have been making ornaments, vases, and goblets of a gay rococo design.

The revival of the Murano glass factories dates from the middle of the nineteenth century, and was largely due to the owner of a glass-works, Pietro Bigaglia. In his factory two craftsmen, Liberale and Angelo Angaro, applied the lessons learned from the study of old glass, which they repaired for Venetian dealers, to the design of new objects. More factories were founded, and soon Murano was once again among the leading centres of glass production in Europe. Many of the objects produced were imitations or adaptations of earlier wares, for which there is a steady market even today. Others, such as the gigantic chandeliers 6 or 7 feet in height, were in a more markedly nineteenth-century style. These nineteenth-century wares are by no means to be despised; for although they are unlikely to win the wholehearted commendation of collectors of old glass, the vases and cups and bowls have many of the merits of seventeenth- and eighteenth-century Venetian products – so much so, indeed, that numerous connoisseurs have been deceived by them. In the present century several factories have begun to produce wares which unite the best qualities of old Venetian glass – its lightness of weight, its gay brilliance of colour, and fantasy of form – with designs which satisfy the most exacting pundits of industrial art. But these objects fall outside the scope of the present chapter.

Glossary

Ale-glass. Long, narrow flute for serving strong ale, a highly alcoholic drink; from 1740 might be engraved with the hop and barley motif (Fig. 1).

FIG. 1

Agata. Mottled finish used chiefly on Amberina glass, in which the article is coated with a metallic stain or mineral colour, then spattered with a quickly evaporating liquid such as alcohol. Made by New England Glass Co., 1886.

Air-twist. Spiral veins of air formed by extension of tears (air bubbles), usually in stems of drinking vessels and shafts of candlesticks; in the United States found occasionally in individual non-commercial pieces of South Jersey Type (Fig. 2).

FIG. 2

Amberina. Made from a gold–ruby compound, an amber glass mixture containing the metal gold; colours shade from yellow-amber to dark red. New England Glass Co., U.S.A., 1883.

Anglo-Venetian glass. Tableware in fine soda-glass made in London from 1570 until about 1680.

Annealing. Toughening flint-glass by raising it to a high temperature and then cooling it gradually. (a) Annealing oven: an oven known as the tower, built above the melting chamber and operated on waste heat from below; (b) annealing tunnel, or leer: a tunnel 5 or 6 yards in length through which newly made glass passes slowly to cool, toughen, and acquire increased brilliance.

Applied decoration, finial, foot, stem. Ornament and parts formed from separate gather of metal and tooled into form. *See* Finials, Foot.

Arabesques. Engraved scrollwork of flowers and foliage on hollow-ware.

Arch patterns. (1) Blown-three-mould patterns classified as arch, having an arch, Gothic or Roman, as a predominating or conspicuous motif from 1823; (2) pressed-glass patterns also.

Art glass. Late-nineteenth-century U.S. glass showing use of new materials and techniques; includes Peachblow, Burmese, Satin, Tiffany, etc.

Aurene. Gold-ruby glass heated to different degrees resulting in iridescent shades of yellow, violet, and pink. Stourbridge Steuben Glass Works, U.S.A.

Aventurine. A dark-brown glass with gold specks, so called from its accidental discovery at Murano, Italy. It was made by mixing copper crystals with the molten vitreous material. In the eighteenth century the Miotti factory specialized in its production.

Baccarat. Together with Cristalleries de Saint-Louis (*q.v.*) the greatest large-scale producer of fine glass in France all through the nineteenth century. It was founded in 1778. The first furnace for lead crystal of the English type was installed in 1819. From 1822 to 1858 it was under the inspiring directorship of Jean Baptiste Toussaint, to whom must go the credit for the very high quality of the products and the progressive technical and artistic style of the colour-glass about the middle of the century. From about 1850 opal-glass was produced in a variety of exquisite colours and elegant shapes, many of them produced by moulding. This production goes on until *c.* 1870. All through the period cut crystal glass in a rich and dignified style remained a main product of the factory (Plate 164A).

Baluster. See Stems.

Baroque patterns. Blown-three-mould patterns classified as baroque, composed of bold motifs in relief; chosen instead of rococo to distinguish typical English and American designs from contemporary French glass re-lated in design but tighter in composition and lower in relief.

Barovier, Angelo. The name of a craftsman or factory-owner, of Murano, Italy, praised by Filarete in his treatise *De Architetura* (1451–64). None of his productions can with certainty be identified, though a marriage goblet in the museum at Murano is traditionally associated with him (Plate 184A).

Batch. Mixture of raw materials ready for melting.

Beads. Called *conterie* of brightly coloured glass imitative of semi-precious and precious stones were made in Venice from a very early period. J. G. de Keysler, who visited Venice in the 1730s, noted that several streets were entirely inhabited by people making and stringing these beads which, he said, "the women of the lower class wear about their necks and arms for ornament. The larger sort are used for making rosaries." They were exported to the East together with *margariti* (*q.v.*) or imitation pearls.

Beakers. Stemless drinking-glasses, or beakers, are among the earliest specimens of Venetian glass. A fine enamelled example is in the Victoria and Albert Museum. They were particularly popular in the eighteenth century, and many of this date are decorated either with engraving or enamelled figures (Plate 184B).

Becker, Johann Albrecht. A Saxon glass-decorator who worked at Nöstetangen, Norway, from 1767 to 1773 and later opened his

FIG. 3

own workshop in Drammen. It was active until 1807, perhaps later, and at times Villas Vinter was attached to it. Most of the engravings, however, seem to have been of an unpretentious nature.

Beilby, William (1740–1819). A celebrated enameller of flint-glass who worked in Newcastle-upon-Tyne from about 1760 to 1776, signing his best work by name and with a lifelike butterfly.

Belfast (Benjamin Edwards). The earliest reference discovered by Westropp was an advertisement dated 1781. The wording suggests that the costly Perrott furnace was in use and "enamelled, cut and plain wine glasses" made as well as cheaper table-glass. From 1783 Edwards was making all kinds of glass-making machinery and hollow-ware moulds, some fluted, which he sold to the newly established Irish glass-houses. By 1805 Edwards was issuing a wide variety of cut table-glass and blown-moulded decanters, as well as lustres and girandoles. The glass-house continued with varying degrees of prosperity until 1829.

Blank. Uncut vessel before it is decorated.

Bloom. An all-over film of opaque dullness occasionally found on the surface of flint-glass, English and Irish alike, although usually associated with Irish. It has been described by Mrs Graydon-Stannus as "rather like the bloom of grapes and if cleaned off it will return". This effect is caused by the use of high-sulphur fuels in the leer. Bands of bloom may be found encircling hollow-ware a little distance below the rim; these are the result of reheating at the furnace mouth. This bloom is not to be confused with the milkiness found inside old decanters.

Blown-mouldings. (a) One-piece moulds were first used in which inexpensive hollow-ware was blown and shaped. Molten flint-glass solidified quickly on the surface in contact with the mould; a quick-setting flint-glass was therefore evolved, not possessing the high brilliancy of metal used for free-blown glass. A gather of this molten metal was taken and blown into a mould smaller than the finished glass vessel; the semi-molten glass was then expanded by further blowing. Such a mould had always to be made slightly greater in diameter at the top than at the base to permit easy withdrawal. Glass shaped by this process may be recognized by its slightly pebbled ap-

pearance caused by contact with the mould. The lower part of the mould interior might be intaglio-cut with a circuit of slender flutes rising vertically from the base. Inflation forced the glass closely against the inner surface, forming a clean impression. The quick-setting glass ensured that the section of the metal remained constant so that the flutes on the outer surface appeared as corresponding depressions within.

(b) The two-piece open-and-shut mould was invented in 1802 by Charles Chubsee of Stourbridge. Glass blown into such a mould was both shaped and decorated with diamond and other motifs in deep relief. Patterns followed those worked on free-blown glass by the wheel-cutters. From 1825 the long-accepted geometrical designs met active competition in the form of baroque scrolls, fan patterns and arch patterns. The gun-metal mould with an intaglio design sunk into the inner surface was the same size as the finished article, which was fully inflated in a single operation.

(c) The three-piece mould, with one fixed and two hinged sections each cut with an intaglio pattern, dates from about 1830. When the glass was inflated within the mould the blowing force caused the joints to open infinitesimally, thus producing slight ridges on the surface of the glass or a slight break in the pattern.

Blown-three-mould glass. Collector's name for a category of inexpensive blown-moulded ware, popular from about 1815 to 1835; blown in full-size piece-moulds for: (1) shape and decoration; (2) decoration and partial shape; (3) for decoration only, thus using the full-size mould as a pattern-mould; transitional between pattern-moulded and fully moulded; characterized by patterns classified in three categories, according to predominating or most conspicuous motifs, arch, baroque, and geometric (the last, the earliest, and simulating cut-glass), concavo-convex surfaces, an identifying characteristic. It was outmoded by pressed glass.

Blowpipe. Long, hollow, iron tube used to hold a gather of molten glass.

Blue glass. The leading Irish glass-houses produced a blue glass resembling the **English**

Bristol blue flint-glass coloured by the addition of smalt. A recipe for such glass was found among the Waterford papers dated 1786. The finer-quality blue glass was prepared in small covered pots, known as piling pots, placed on the ordinary pots. The quality of the glass was improved by keeping the pot in the furnace long after completion of vitrification, thus making it harder and freer from specks and bubbles. In the early nineteenth century a less gorgeous blue was acquired by using less-expensive ultramarine. A wide variety of domestic ware was made. A set of six dark-blue wine-glass coolers has been noted marked "Penrose Waterford".

Bristol blue. Made at most glass-making centres, may be grouped into five basic qualities of glass: (a) 1760–90, intense dark blue with a faintly purplish hue; (b) 1790–1805, harsh dark blue, less intense than (a); (c) 1804–20s as (a) but without the faintly purplish tint; (d) 1821–40s, a costly near-royal blue known as king's blue; (e) as (a) but in decorative forms and not flawed. These may be subdivided into qualities varying with the technical facilities available at individual glass-houses.

Blue tint. The faintly bluish hue present in the texture of some late-Georgian flint-glass. For more than half a century collectors deemed this to be solely a Waterford characteristic, and as such was sold at greatly enhanced prices. This claim for Waterford cannot be substantiated. True, such blue-tinted glass was issued by Waterford, for Mrs Graydon-Stannus exhibited marked examples to the Royal Society of Arts in 1925, but it is found in other Irish glass, as well as among the productions of Stourbridge, Birmingham, Bristol, Scotland, and elsewhere.

This peculiar depth of tone shows the glass to contain lead oxide prepared from Derbyshire mined lead, preferred at many glass-houses because of the superior manipulative properties it gave to the molten metal. Unfortunately the Derbyshire lead contained an impurity which caused this bluish tint, recognized as a defect by the late-Georgian glass-men and which they endeavoured to eliminate.

The Irish glass-houses for the most part used lead oxide made by Wilson Patten, Bank Quay, Warrington, from Derbyshire lead. Not every consignment contained the blue-tingeing impurity, then known to glass-men as Derby blue. There was, therefore, no consistency in the presence of Derby blue in flint-glass during the period concerned, and depth and tone of tint varied.

In 1810 Blair Stephenson, Tipton, Staffordshire, invented a process by which this tint could be eliminated. By 1816 most English and Irish glass-houses were using Stephenson's purified lead oxide, its manufacture proving a profitable monopoly until his manager joined another firm as a competitor. It is doubtful if the Derby blue tint is to be found in Irish glass made later than 1815.

Recent efforts to reproduce the genuine Derby blue tint have failed, but a bogus "Waterford Blue" has been in production for more than thirty years.

Bontemps, Georges (1799–1884). Director of the Choisy-le-Roi (q.v.) factory from 1823 to 1848. The son of an officer, who was descended from one of Louis XIV's valets, he became an enterprising industrialist, an inventive technician, and a learned scholar. He was the real pioneer in France in the discovery and exploitation of coloured glass on a high artistic level. In 1827 he began the production of opal-glass, and in 1839 was making filigree-glass in the Venetian style. In 1844 he made millefiori-glass. He installed a stained-glass workshop at Choisy with an Englishman, Edouard Jones, to direct it, and there also was a painters' studio. The political developments in 1848 forced him to leave the country, and he became attached to the firm of Chance Brothers in Smethwick near Birmingham. His famous handbook on glass-making, *Guide du Verrier* (Paris, 1868), remained a standard work of its kind until quite recent times. By succeeding generations of French glass-makers Bontemps was considered "notre maître à tous" (Appert & Henrivaux).

Bottle glass. *See* Green glass.

Bottles. In the United States, with window-glass, the commercial product of glass-houses of eighteenth and early nineteenth centuries; of dark olive-green or olive-amber metal, blown in full-size two-piece moulds. In

England the use of bottles became widespread in the middle of the seventeenth century. Many were manufactured in Bristol and Nailsea. Shapes and types of English and U.S. bottles are listed below.

Calabash (U.S.A.). Ovoid body tapering into cylindrical neck with collared lip; blown in full-size two-piece mould with intaglio designs falling in the pictorial, decorative, and historical categories; *c.* 1850–70 (Fig. 4).

Carboy (U.S.A.). Large demijohn; usually set in wooden tub; used mainly for corrosive liquids, such as *aqua fortis*.

Carboy (England). A large vessel made of green

FIG. 4

bottle-glass to carry corrosive acids for industrial purposes. They date from the late eighteenth century and were packed originally in wicker containers and more recently in steel frames stuffed with straw.

Chestnut (U.S.A.). Somewhat carelessly free-blown bottles with long neck and fat chestnut-shaped body, frequently full of bubbles and asymmetrical; without uniformity of size, ranging from a few ounces to a gallon or more in capacity; ranging, in natural bottle-glass colours, from ambers through olive-ambers to greens; called also Ludlow because of a tradition of having been made in a Ludlow, Massachusetts,

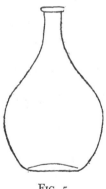

FIG. 5

glasshouse, and junk; made generally, eighteenth–early nineteenth centuries (Fig. 5).

Cylinder (England). Date from the late 1730s, shaped in earthenware moulds. By 1750 one-piece gunmetal moulds had been introduced. These bottles measured 5 inches in diameter, reduced to about 4 inches in the 1770s. In cylindrical bottles until the 1790s a distinct bulge encircled the base of the body.

By the early 1790s bottle-glass could be blown to a thinner section in the mould without loss of strength and diameter and was reduced to 3 inches, with the shoulder higher and less pronounced than formerly. From 1820 shoulders were still further accentuated. Mechanically moulded bottles date from the 1840s.

Demijohn (U.S.A.). Mainly a storage and shipping bottle, often with wicker jacket; free-blown or moulded for symmetrical, globular, or oval form, with long neck and lip usually collared; quart to twenty-gallon sizes. In Britain capacity not less than 3 gallons and not more than 10 gallons.

Nursing (*sucking*) (U.S.A.). Flattened ovoid flask rounded at end, short neck with sheared, sometimes flaring, lip; plain and pattern-moulded in ribs, flutes, and diamonds; eighteenth–early nineteenth centuries (Fig. 6).

Onion (England).

Pocket bottle (U.S.A.). Flask of about half-pint to pint capacity. *See* Flasks.

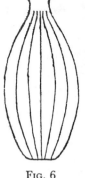

FIG. 6

Shaft and globe (England). Sealed and dated examples show that they developed in four main chronological groups from about 1620 to 1730: (*a*) 1620–60, bulbous body, low kick and long neck encircled half an inch below the smooth, flat-surfaced lip with a thin, sharp-edged string-ring. (*b*) 1650–85, the shoulder angle more pronounced, the sides of the body sloping more steeply inward towards the base, making the kick narrower. The knife-edge was retained on the string-ring. (*c*) 1680–1715, the body was progressively widened and became more squat, with a high kick. The neck, shorter and tapering, joined the body in a smooth curve harmonizing with the more rounded shape of the body. (*d*) 1710–40, the sides of the body became perpendicular or with a slight outward slant, curving into the neck with a shoulder more square and pronounced than formerly. The neck was wide at the shoulder junction and the string rim raised to a position immediately beneath the mouth. These forms were abandoned from the late 1730s in favour of cylindrical bodies.

Stiegel-type pocket or perfume (U.S.A.). Chunky, bulbous form, slightly flattened wide sides; pattern-moulded designs.

Swirl (U.S.A.). A Midwestern type, pattern-moulded in vertical ribs or flutes, swirled usually to right, occasionally to left; wide colour range, from aquamarines to deep greens, olive greens, citron, ambers, and blues; including two distinctive shapes: (*a*) globular, nearly spherical body, slender neck,

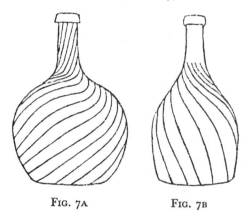

FIG. 7A   FIG. 7B

slightly tapering or straight, collared lip; (*b*) short cylindrical body, sides often tapering slightly, sloping shoulder, short neck, collared lip; proportions, distinguishing features; some forms also with vertical and broken-swirl ribbing or fluting (Figs. 7A and B).

Bowes, Sir Jerome. In 1592 Bowes acquired the "Venetian glass" monopoly in England from Verzelini (*q.v.*), paying Elizabeth I an annual rental of 200 marks (£133 6s 8d) for the privilege.

Bowl forms. (*a*) Bell, 1715–80: a deep, waisted bowl with incurved profile and wide mouth derived from the funnel bowl. The base, until 1740, might be a solid mass of glass and welded to the stem; (*b*) bucket, 1730–70: with sides almost vertical and horizontal base. Some late eighteenth-century bucket bowls are lipped. The waisted bucket and incurved bucket are also found; (*c*) double-ogee, 1700–20: expansive shallow examples of thick section; from 1750, smaller and with thin walls. Ogee and waisted ogee are also found; (*d*) round funnel, characteristic of the seventeenth

century, when rarely with a collar at stem and bowl junction. Until 1690 the bowl was long in proportion to the stem; as the bowl lost depth it became wider at the rim: less massive from 1710; (*e*) straight-funnel or conical; a straight-sided bowl shaped like the frustum of an inverted cone; (*f*) thistle, from 1715: in several profiles in which the lower part is a solid or hollow sphere of glass; (*g*) trumpet: a waisted bowl of incurving profile merging into a drawn stem.

Bowls, drinking-glass. (*a*) Thick-walled type until the 1740s. The stem may be drawn from the base of the bowl, drawn into a short neck to which the stem is attached, or the bowl may be attached to the top moulding of the stem, traces of the weld being visible; (*b*) from 1740, light, thin-walled; (*c*) from 1790, thick-walled with cutting in deep relief.

Briati, Giuseppe (1686–1772). A craftsman who inherited, or founded, a glass-works at Murano, Italy, in the early eighteenth century. He specialized in making glass of Bohemian type and is sometimes said to have worked in Bohemia. In 1739 he transferred his premises to Venice itself, establishing a factory in the parish of S. Angelo Raffaele, where he produced, among other wares, mirrors, picture frames, bizarre table centres, panels for the decoration of furniture, and large chandeliers.

Brocard, Joseph. Enamel painter and decorator of glass, working in a studio in Paris during the latter part of the nineteenth century. His exquisite pastiches of Islamic enamelled glass decoration were highly praised by critics at the Paris Exhibition in 1878. Later he liberated himself somewhat from these models, and used Chinese or naturalistic flowers (Plate 167c) for his designs. He always preserved a stylization of patterns and a coolness of colour, which is reminiscent of Oriental art, and rare and refreshing in the France of the *art nouveau*. In some instances he must have collaborated with the factory which made his glass, as the decorative pattern has been embedded in the glass itself and later picked out in enamels.

Broken-swirl. Pattern-moulded ribbed design obtained by twice moulding a gather in ribbed or fluted dip mould; first impression of vertical ribs, twisted or swirled, gather re-inserted in mould impressing vertical ribs upon the swirled; occurring most frequently in the U.S. on Pitkin bottles, jars and flasks having two-layered body (half-post) and on Midwestern bottles, flasks and hollow-ware blown from single gather (Plate 147A (centre)); ribs varying in closeness.

Brussa, Osvaldo. An eighteenth-century Italian glass painter. In the museum at Murano there is a portrait which shows him holding a beaker on which birds are painted.

Buckets. Either for holy water or for domestic use, these were occasionally made at Murano, Italy, in the sixteenth century and later. Their shapes are derived from silver vessels of the same type.

Burmese glass. See Uranium glass.

Butterfly. A coloured butterfly often occupies the centre of a paperweight. Sometimes the insect is poised over a flower, sometimes above a latticinio, or other filigree, ground. Also an emblem engraved on Jacobite glass, over the signature of William Beilby (q.v.).

Calcedonia. A type of glass which imitates the colour and veining of chalcedony, first produced at Murano, Italy, in the fifteenth century. It appears to have enjoyed great popularity throughout the Renaissance period and again in the eighteenth century. In the nineteenth century made in Bohemia and England.

Cameos. See Sulphides.

Camphor glass. White, cloudy appearance; known in U.S. blown-mould and pressed glass.

Candlesticks. Made at Murano, Italy, in the eighteenth century, usually copied from silver patterns (Plate 181D).

Cane. Familiar name for the rods of coloured glass from which the patterns were formed in many types of paperweights (see Paperweights).

Carré, Jean. In 1570 Jean Carré of Arras established a glass-house in the Crutched Friars, London, bringing over several glass-making families from Lorraine. After his death in 1572 Giacomo Verzelini, his chief assistant, acquired the glass-house.

Case bottles. See Bottles.

Cased glass. Two or more layers of glass differing in colour; called overlay when design is cut through to body colour; popular Bohemian glass technique.

Caster. (1) Bottle form with perforated cap, usually metal; called also shaker; (2) frame for condiment bottles or containers such as casters (shakers), cruets, and mustard-pots.

Caster bottles. Bottles to set in caster or cruet frame – shakers, cruets, mustard-pots.

Chain. U.S. name for applied, tooled de-

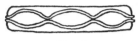

FIG. 8

coration; links formed by drawing together at regular intervals two threads of glass laid-on around a parison or body of partially formed object, called also *guilloche*; in England, trailed circuit or ornament (Fig. 8).

Champagne glasses. English shapes: (a) 1678–1715: tall flute with short stem or button; (b) 1715 to mid-1730s: tazza-shaped bowl, often ogee in form, usually on moulded pedestal stem; (c) 1730–45: drawn flute (Plate 156A); (d) 1745–1830: long-stemmed flute; (e) from 1830: the hemispherical bowl or coupe.

Chance, W. and **R. L.** In 1793 William Chance became a partner in the Nailsea, England, glass-works founded five years earlier by John Robert Lucas (q.v.). Chance's son, Robert Lucas Chance, was manager of the Nailsea factory in 1810, but in 1815 he left the west, sold his share in the glass-house, and went to London. By 1824 he had founded the Spon Lane glass-works in Birmingham, a concern that became exceedingly prosperous and in 1870 bought up the Nailsea firm. The latter was closed three years later, and the Spon Lane glass-works remains in the hands of the descendants of Robert Lucas Chance to this day.

Chandeliers. Of Venetian glass, these seem first to have been made by G. Briati (q.v.), who won praise from Carlo Gozzi for his "magnificent clusters for illuminating the rooms of great Lords, Theatres or the streets on festive occasions". They enjoyed great popularity throughout the eighteenth and nineteenth centuries. Eighteenth-century examples are among the finest objects in Venetian glass, very elaborate and richly decorated with polychrome flowers, but few have survived intact. Good examples may be seen in the museum at Murano, the Ca' Rezzonico Venice, and the Pinacoteca Querini Stampalia (Plate 183A).

Checkered diamond. Decorative motif, large diamond enclosing four small ones: (1) pattern-moulded German diaper design; used in the United States, by Stiegel at Manheim, Pennsylvania (possibly), at the New Bremen Glass-manufactory and in one or more early

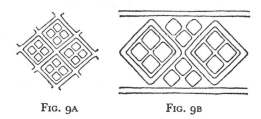

FIG. 9A   FIG. 9B

nineteenth-century Midwestern bottle houses, principally for flasks and salts of type having slender double-ogee bowl and applied circular foot; (2) full-size, piece-moulded, blown-three-mould motif in geometric pattern (McK. GII-29) (Figs. 9A and 9B).

Chestnut bottle. *See* Bottles.

Choisy-le-Roi. Factory in Paris, founded in 1821 by M. Grimbolt and closed down in 1851. Between 1823 and 1848 the factory was under the inspiring directorship of Georges Bontemps (*q.v.*) and became the pioneering establishment in the country in the making of coloured glass and the exploitation of its artistic possibilities (Plates 165E and 167A).

Clichy. Factory founded in 1837 by MM. Rouyer and Maës at Billancourt near Pont de Sèvres in Paris for the production of cheap glass for export. By 1844 the factory had moved to Clichy-la-Garenne and had begun producing coloured glass, a two-layer cased-glass technique with a fine yellow colour being a special achievement. By 1849 the factory's mastery of colour-techniques must have been greatly extended, for by that time it seems to have taken over the role, previously held by Saint-Louis, of the finest producer of paper-

weights. At the Great Exhibition in London in 1851, Clichy was the only French *cristallerie* to be represented. The display consisted of much elaborate colour-glass, cased glass in a great variety of shades, filigree- and millefiori-glass (a fine pair of signed vases are in the Corning Museum of Glass, New York), and coloured and painted opal-glass. At the International Exhibition in London in 1862 an engraved cup from Clichy was acquired by Felix Slade "as one of the best examples of engraving on glass in the Exhibition" (Plate 165A). Slade usually collected only antique glass. In 1868 Bontemps mentions that aventurine glass has been made at Clichy. The high level of craftsmanship and artistry seems to have been kept up until *c.* 1875. About ten years later the factory was absorbed into the Verrerie de Sèvres. Although glass was made at Clichy for almost fifty years, and in spite of the leading position it held among the producers of fashionable glass of its time, very few pieces of the factory's products can today be identified as such.

Collar-rib. Moulded rib simulating round plain collar; mainly on blown-three-mould decanters and toilet bottles.

Collars. U.S. term synonymous with neck-rings. Heavy applied thread or ribbon, plain

FIG. 10

or tooled, laid on around: (1) lips of bottles and flasks; (2) necks of decanters (*a*) plain round, single or double, (*b*) rigaree, single or double, (*c*) triangular, usually single, rarely double, (*d*) triple ring (wide single with medial rib), (*e*) chain, rare; (3) around stem or shaft, also part of composite stem or shaft; vermicular (wavy), rare in American glass (Fig. 10).

Compote. Bowl on standard (stem and foot); also on domed or pedestal foot.

Cordial glasses. During the seventeenth century cordials were taken from miniature wine-glasses measuring 4–6 inches in height (Fig. 11). A distinct type of glass, its bowl shorter, squarer, and of smaller rim diameter than a wine-glass bowl, became fashionable

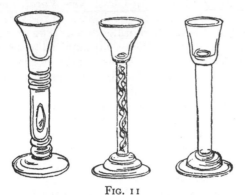

FIG. 11

from about 1720; (a) 1720–40: straight stem of normal length and diameter; (b) from 1735: the stem was lengthened, of extra thick diameter, and might be centrally knopped; (c) from 1740: the bowl was less capacious; (d) 1740–70: the flute cordial, often termed a ratafia glass.

Cords. Slight striae discernible to the fingers on the surface of the glass.

Cork Glass-house, later **Cork Glass-house Company.** Established in Hanover Street, Cork, Ireland, 1793, as makers of plain and cut flint-glass and black bottles. The firm specialized in light-weight *blown-moulded hollow-ware*. Although heavily subsidized by the Dublin Society, such as £1,600 in 1787 and £2,304 in 1793, throughout its existence the Cork Glass-house appears to have laboured under financial instability and ever-changing proprietorship. A newly patented Donaldson furnace was installed under a new proprietorship. This gave to flint-glass a clarity and brilliance never before achieved, and some outstanding hand-cut work was produced. The number of hand-cutters employed was such that they founded the Cork Glass-cutters' Union.

In 1812 the firm, under the proprietorship of William Smith & Company, became the Cork Glass-house Company. Pieces marked "Cork Glass Co." date no earlier than this. In 1817 steam-power was installed in a final effort to survive against competition from the newly established Waterloo Glass-house. A year later, however, the glass-house was closed.

Cork Terrace Glass-house. Established in Cork, Ireland, in 1819 by Edward and Richard Ronayne. Their productive capacity was equal to Waterford, for when the firm closed in 1841 it was announced that they possessed tools and machines for forty glass-cutters. They made all kinds of table-glass as well as lustres and Grecian lamps, and were specialists in cut and engraved dessert services.

Corrugated handle. *See* Handles.

Covers. Made principally for compotes and bowls. (1) Domed: (a) low flattened usually on eighteenth-century set-in type, occasionally individual pieces blown mainly in early nineteenth-century U.S. Midwestern

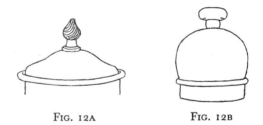

FIG. 12A   FIG. 12B

bottle-glass houses (Fig. 12A); (b) low or high round, flaring rim, plain or folded edge (Plate 148 (*centre*)); (c) low or high conical (sloping), flaring rim, plain or folded edge; (d) double, proportions of upper and lower dome varying, that on Plate 147A (*left*), peculiar to U.S. Midwest; (2) set-in, flanged, with short, straight neck fitting inside bowl's rim so flange rests on bowl's rim (Fig. 12B); (3) set-over, rare type, domed with straight-sided neck fitting over short neck of bowl and resting on moulding applied on bowl (Fig. 12B).

Cresting. Also termed bridge-fluting, c. 1748–1800: an extension of faceting from the stem to bridge the junction of bowl and stem; (a) until about 1760 merely bridging the junction; (b) 1760–80 extending over the bowl base in simple designs; (c) from 1780 might extend half-way up the bowl.

Crimping. Dents or flutes impressed by a tool, usually diagonal, used on the foot or tip of handle.

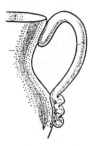

Fig. 13

Cristal – cristallerie. The word *cristal* does not mean only lead glass of the English type (though at times it means that), but describes fine table-glass and decorative glass of all kinds. Correspondingly, *cristallerie* is a factory where any kind of fine and decorative glass is made.

Cristallo. The name given in Italy to clear uncoloured glass, known in England as white glass. Since the earliest times it had been the aim of glass-makers to produce a glass as clear as rock crystal. Clear glass, *cristallo*, produced at Murano in the early sixteenth century – though somewhat grey and cloudy by modern standards – secured the fame of its factories throughout Europe. The decline of the Venetian glass industry dates from the time when factories in other parts of Europe, usually with the aid of Venetian craftsmen, produced a glass as clear, if not clearer.

Crown. Familiar name for a paperweight composed of coloured canes radiating in straight lines from the top.

Crown glass. Early form of window-glass; commercial product with bottles of early glass-houses.

Cruet. (1) Lipped bottle with or without handle; (2) castor bottle.

Cruet frame. *See* Castor (2).

Crystal. Refers to finest colourless or clear flint glass.

Cullet. Cleaned, broken glass used in all new mixtures to promote fusion and improve quality of the metal.

Cup plate. Small plate from about $2\frac{5}{8}$ to $4\frac{5}{8}$ inches in diameter; used as saucer for cup;

also used when beverage was drunk from saucer, a custom among some groups, not sanctioned by fashionable society; found mainly in inexpensive glasswares such as pressed; nineteenth century, mainly second quarter.

Cups and saucers. Made at Murano, Italy, in the eighteenth century, of opaque glass imitating porcelain and usually enamelled with little figures.

Cut-corners. Chamfered; formed by bevelling the corners formed by the meeting of two sides, making eight planes, narrow at corners; term usually applied to square and rectangular bottles shaped in full-size piece moulds (Fig. 14).

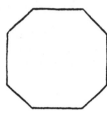

Fig. 14

Cut motifs.

Diamond cutting. (*a*) Relief, convex, deep-cut, and raised are various terms given to diamonds made by deeply incising V-shaped grooves or mitres crossing each other at right angles and at such a distance apart that they produce a series of four-sided pyramids, each with a sharp apex. These were at first shallow-cut in plain bands, but from the 1790s were usually deep, invariably so after about 1805.

(*b*) Cross-cut diamonds were simple relief diamonds with a tiny four-pointed star cut into the apex of each, the star points bisecting each flat surface. Such cutting was difficult to work and is seldom found on large objects.

(*c*) Strawberry diamonds were simple relief diamonds with flat tops produced by cutting the mitred lines farther apart than in (*a*). Upon each flat apex was cut a small relief diamond. In fine-quality work the centre of every tiny diamond rises to a sharp point.

(*d*) Hobnail diamonds were flat-topped diamonds cut with a simple cross or star.

(*e*) Checkered diamonds were large, flat-topped diamonds cut with four minor diamonds.

Fan or escallop shell borders. The rim of the glass was cut into a series of deep arcs, each following the outline of an escallop shell. A fan was then cut with ten, eleven, or twelve flutes radiating to each arc. The extremity of each cut was notched.

Fluting. (*a*) Hollowed or slightly concave is found either above or in association with diamond motifs. The crest might be notched until early in the nineteenth century.

(*b*) Pillared fluting consists of half-sections of cylindrical columns used in broad bands. This was a favourite Irish motif, dating from *c.* 1790 until the early 1800s, although costly to work.

(*c*) Comb-fluting consists of thin hollow flutes closely spaced and encircling the base of a decanter, finger-bowl or other hollow-ware.

Herring-bone or Blaze. Lightly cut upright or slanting lines in graduated lengths forming alternations of crests and troughs.

Notching. An intermittent series of nicks cut into the sharp crests of flutes.

Printies. Circular or oval concavities cut into hollow-ware. These might cover the entire surface; two or three rows encircle the body of a decanter, jug, rummer, or bowl; or a single row might encircle a bowl rim.

Prismatic cutting. Horizontal parallel grooves cut in deep, sharp prisms and requiring metal of thick section for its perfect display. Fashionable 1800–20 and revived during the 1830s. Sometimes termed step-cutting.

Slice or edge-flute. Flat cutting carried out by holding the glass at an incline against a rotating mitred wheel and removing a film of glass.

Split. A small angular groove.

Sprig. Three angular grooves placed to resemble a conventional arrow-head, usually found at the angles of other motifs. Late sprigs were cut more deeply than early examples.

Stars. The early radiating stars were cut with six or eight points: by the nineteenth century, twelve-, sixteen-, or twenty-four-pointed stars were becoming fashionable. The Brunswick star had a considerable vogue on expensive glass: this was based on a sixteen-point radiating star with every seventh point joined. To produce this star twenty-four cuts were required; as many as seventy-two have been noted.

Step-cutting. See Prismatic cutting.

Sunburst. A motif composed of closely spaced cut lines radiating from a printie or other

plain hollow. Associated chiefly with Cork productions.

Vesica. A plain incised oval with pointed ends often containing an eight-pointed star. Where they join, sprigs are cut above and below. The vesica is usually cut, but is also found engraved and the oval filled with trellis-work. Associated chiefly with Cork productions.

Cutting. Depressions ground into the surface of glass by revolving wheels. Three fundamental types of cutting – hollow-, mitre-, and panel-cutting – are capable of producing some fifty variants of design; (*a*) pre-1740: edge-cutting and scalloping; almost-flat cutting in geometric patterns; giant diamonds and triangles in low relief; shallow slices; (*b*) 1740–1805: similar types of cutting with the addition of the sprig motif, fluting, stem faceting, incised zig-zag, sliced motifs, and, from 1750, large diamonds double cut; (*c*) 1790–1830, more especially from 1805: cutting in deep relief (*see below*).

Cutting in deep relief. Some of the more frequent types are: (*a*) checkered diamond – the flat surface of a diamond in relief cut with four small diamonds; (*b*) cross-cut diamonds or hob-nail cutting – large relief diamonds each with a flat point incised with a simple cross; (*c*) herring-bone fringe, or blazes – a row of upright or slanting lines cut in an alternation of crest and trough; (*d*) printies – circular concavities ground into the surface of hollow-ware; (*e*) prismatic- or step-cutting, 1800–20 and 1830–40 – deep, horizontal prisms adapted to curved surfaces; (*f*) splits: formally arranged upright grooves; (*g*) strawberry diamonds from *c.* 1805 – the flattened point of each large relief diamond cut with numerous very fine relief diamonds.

Cyst. A round protuberance in the base of a wine-glass bowl.

Daisy-in-hexagon. Daisy-like flower within hexagon, in pattern-moulded diaper design; believed to be a Stiegel original; found mainly on pocket bottles.

Decanters.

American.

English terminology generally used for shapes, but sugar-loaf synonymous with mallet and semi-barrel instead of Prussian (*see below*). Labelled decanters were made *c.* 1825–50: (*a*) occasionally engraved *wine* or with name of a spirit; (*b*) blown-three-mould with moulded labels in four geometric patterns and one arch. These include WINE, BRANDY, RUM, GIN, H. GIN, CHERRY and WHISKY.

English.

(*a*) 1677–1700: with loop handle and mouth expanded into an almost hemispherical funnel with spout lip and loose stopper; (*b*) 1677–1760 and after 1804: shaft-and-globe, near replica of the long-neck wine-bottle. With a high kick to 1740; (*c*) 1705–30: straight-sided mallet shape; (*d*) 1725–50: quatrefoil body; (*e*) 1740–1800: shouldered decanter in two forms: narrow-shouldered with outward sloping sides (Plate 156F), or broad shoulders narrowing towards the base:

DECANTERS

FIG. 15   FIG. 16   FIG. 17

FIG. 18   FIG. 19   FIG. 20

more slender of body after 1750 (Figs. 15 and 16); (*f*) 1755–80 and 1810–20: labelled with engraved, enamelled, or gilded inscriptions on the body (Figs. 15 and 16); (*g*) 1765–80: tapered body (Fig. 17); (*h*) 1755–1800: barrel-shaped body with shoulder and base of equal diameter, cut with vertical lines to represent staves and incised rings to suggest hoops: sometimes termed Indian club or oviform (Fig. 18); (*i*) 1775–1830: Prussian type, often mistermed barrel: a broad-shouldered type, sides having a greater inward slope than formerly, the lower portion encircled with narrow flutes extending half-way up the body (Fig. 19). Diamond-cut in relief from about 1790 (Plate 157B and c and Fig. 20); (*j*) 1790–1830s: cylindrical body, cut in deep relief (Plate 157A). Decanters of dark-blue glass were made at Bristol, and some of them have survived. These survivors are remarkable for the fact that each of them is decorated in gold with a simulated wine-label suspended from its neck, and some are signed with the name of the maker: Isaac Jacobs (*q.v.*). The decanters are of a slender form and the stoppers lozenge-shaped, which leads many people to attribute to Bristol (and to the Jacobs manufactory in particular) other decanters that are unsigned but of a comparably pleasing outline. This is understandable and convenient, but it is most probable that this style of decanter was copied in other parts of the country as soon as it became popular. Apart from the signed ones, it is extremely difficult to allocate coloured glass decanters to specific makers or even to specific localities.

Irish

The majority of Irish decanters were blown-moulded, the usual size being a quart. In light-weight metal a dozen might cost as little as nine shillings, but those of average thickness with neck-rings were much more costly. The features on some marked examples are as follows:

Collins, Dublin. Have bases on which radiate carefully moulded V-shaped flutes extending to the edge. The vertical sides are encircled with narrow flutes extending half-way up the body, and the punty mark is larger than noted on other marked decanters.

Cork Glass-house Company. Prussian-shaped and mallet-shaped decanters were made by pure blowing and cut with all fashionable motifs of the period. Blown-moulded types were also made. Probably because of its bottle-making activities, decanters are characterized by their long, slender necks. Neck-rings were mainly of the double-feather type, although plain triple rings, square-cut rings, and facet-cut rings were made. Stoppers of the shallow mushroom type pinched with radial gadroons were in the majority, but pinched target stoppers and a conical type encircled with several ridges are found.

Blown-moulded decanters have sides only slightly off-vertical. The flutes start a little above the lower rim and extend about two-thirds up the body. The shoulder is often decorated with vesica pattern.

Benjamin Edwards, Belfast. Pyriform blown-moulded decanters, bearing the name of this firm encircling the punty mark, have basal corrugations radiating to the rim, a pair of triangular neck rings, mouth slightly everted, and finished with a narrow, flat rim. The pinched stoppers are vertical, flat-sided, and impressed with trellis-work, or target type cut with a six-pointed star. Engraving encircling the shoulders consists of scrolls, swags, and stars, carefully executed. The shoulder from the lower neck ring might be encircled with wide-cut flutes.

Waterford. Those by Penrose are usually of squat Prussian shape, with three neck-rings, a wide, flat mouth rim, and a mushroom stopper pinched with radial fluting and a knop below raising it above the lip. The mark is more neatly moulded than on other decanters.

Waterloo Glass-house Company. Decanter shapes and decorations closely followed those of contemporary Waterford. The majority of marked specimens are perceptibly wider at the shoulder than the base. Flutes are longer than those of the Cork Glass-house Company. The vesica pattern was frequent: an engraved band of stars between two pairs of feathered lines; ribbon scroll engraving rows of hollow encircling the shoulders. It is thought that engraved circles and loops encircling the body are a characteristic feature. Neck-rings usu-

ally consist of three of the plain triple variety. Stoppers were low-domed mushroom-shape pinched with radial gadrooning, often with a ball knop immediately below. Pinched target stoppers were also used.

Scandinavian.

A very usual type of Swedish and Norwegian glass in the 1830s and 1840s is the rectangular decanter with a short, inset neck (Plate 179C). This was the popular brandy decanter in a period of drinking unequalled in intensity before or since in either country. Another type of Norwegian decanter is the *Zirat Fladske*, an ornamental decanter made at Gjövik in the 1830s, in three different shapes: (*a*) simple bulb-shape (Plate 178F); (*b*) rectangular, with cut corners and a long neck; (*c*) waisted. All three models are decorated with trailing prunts and flammiform fringes in naïve profusion. The waisted type has parallels in Sweden (Plate 179A) and the bulb-shaped one in England, but the origins and dates of the English versions are obscure and the connexion cannot be traced.

Decanter stoppers. Rarely ground until 1745. Afterwards ground as a routine process.

Diamond. (1) Diamond diaper, blown-three-mould motif, used either in square or in band; (2) expanded diamond, pattern-moulded and expanded in process of fashioning an unformed but patterned gather into an object; in the United States three principal varieties: (*a*) diamond diaper (units varying in size and number in different moulds); (*b*) rows of diamonds above flutes. *See also* Checkered diamond; (*c*) strawberry diamond (cross-hatched relief diamond), pressed, and cut-glass motif.

Diamond-daisy. U.S. design: daisy-like flower within square-diamond, in pattern-moulded diaper design; believed to be a Stiegel original; found mainly on pocket or "perfume" bottles.

Dip-mould. One-piece open-top fluted or ribbed mould, varying sizes and depths.

Dishes. In Ireland date from early in the nineteenth century, and might be circular, oval, or octagonal. Early dishes were cut with shallow patterns in relief and later with deep diamonds. Sections are usually variable;

sometimes one edge will be considerably thicker than the other.

Double-ogee bowl. In U.S., bowls with sides rising in distorted S, varying widely in proportions and lengths of curves; Plate 147A (*centre*), like Haynes' pan-topped, others like his cup-topped (*Glass Through the Ages*); in so-called Stiegel-type salts, often an attenuated S.

Dram glasses. Known also as nips, joeys, ginettes, and gin-glasses (Fig. 21); (*a*) seventeenth century: small tumbler with four tiny feet; (*b*) 1675–1750: cup-shaped bowl with short, heavy knop or moulded baluster; (*c*) 1690–1710: straight-sided bowl of thick sec-

FIG. 21

tion on flattened spherical knop; (*d*) 1710–50: short, plain stem on foot attached directly to bowl; (*e*) 1720–1850: short, drawn-stemmed, trumpet-bowled: some early examples have folded feet.

Drinking glasses. Westropp found the following named in the Waterford papers in his possession: "Regents, Nelsons, Masons, Rummers, Hobnobs, Flutes, Draws, Thumbs, and Dandies." To these may be added Rodneys, Coburgs, and Thistles. These names used also in England and Scotland.

Dublin – Chebsy and Company. An Irish company which made fine table-glass, at a glass-house known as Venice, from 1784 to 1798. Between 1787 and 1793 they sold glass to the value of £37,849, receiving meanwhile premiums from the Dublin Society (Westropp). They made the magnificent lustres for Dublin Castle in 1789.

Eagle, American. Like or derived from (1) seal of the United States; (2) U.S. coins; most common historical motif in pressed lacy glass and historical flasks, occasionally engraved on blown glass.

Edkins, Michael. Michael Edkins was a painter of pottery and of white and coloured glass. He received the freedom of the city of

Bristol on February 21, 1756, but prior to that time is said to have served an apprenticeship in Birmingham. In 1755 he married Elizabeth, daughter of William James, a glass-maker, and it is not unexpected that he should have turned his hand to decorating that ware. He would seem to have started to paint glass soon after 1760, and to have continued at least until 1787.

Edkins' business ledger, now in the Bristol Museum, records that he was employed by the following firms, no doubt in the capacity of a "free-lance" worker:

1763–7	Little and Longman
1767–87	Longman and Vigor, and successors
1765	William Dunbar and Co.
1775–87	Vigor and Stephens
1785–7	Lazarus Jacobs

In the same volume are noted the low payments he received for his work, of which these examples are typical:

1762	Jan. 19	To 1 Sett of Jars and Beakers 5 in a Sett	2.6.
	July 26	To 1 Pint Blue can ornamented with Gold and Letters	0.8.
1764	Oct. 1	To 4 Enamell Cannisters	1.0.
1770	Nov. 6	To 12 Hyacinth glasses blue gilded	2.0.

Michael Edkins was said by his son, William Edkins, senior, to have been "a very good musician and charming counter-tenor singer", and to have performed on the stage both in Bristol and in London. He had a family of thirty-three children, and died about the year 1813. His grandson, also named William, formed a fine collection of pottery and porcelain, which was sold by auction in London in 1874.

The glass decorated by Michael Edkins is unsigned, and much that is claimed as his is the subject of dispute. W. A. Thorpe wrote (*English Glass*, 1949, p. 206) that "Edkins is known for his characteristic perched birds and his intense curly flower-bunches". A tea-caddy in the Victoria and Albert Museum was once owned by William Edkins, junior, and is stated to have been painted by his grandfather. One of a set of Bristol Delft plates, from the same source, also in the Victoria and Albert Museum, is initialled on the back M^EB (for Michael and Betty Edkins) and dated 1760.

Elstermann, Kristoffer. Of German origin, Elstermann introduced engraving into Sweden. He first appears at Kungsholm in 1698 and is mentioned in the factory records up to 1715. He died in 1721.

Enamelling. In England, white, 1720–1800; coloured, 1760–1820: (a) advertised as "white japanned flint-glass" in late 1720s: a thinly applied wash enamel in white; (b) from c. 1750, a dense, full enamel thickly applied (Plate 159) (see Beilby, William).

End-of-day glass. Misnomer for marble glass (q.v.).

Engraving. This seems first to have been used for the decoration of glass in the sixteenth century (first recorded 1530–50). Two methods were used (a) diamond-point: patterns hand inscribed, using the point of a diamond or graver. In England armorial work during 1720s; arabesques and scroll patterns 1725–40; spontaneous efforts of amateurs throughout eighteenth century; early Victorian revival with sporting and coaching scenes. Rare usage in the United States. (b) Wheel-engraving: patterns cut into the glass surface by pressing it against the edge of a thin rapidly revolving wheel. Early wheel engraving was left matt; from 1740 it might be partially polished, the tendency to polish increasing as the eighteenth century progressed. Wheel-engraved rim borders popular from late 1730s to the end of the century: at first simple designs of intertwined scrollwork and leaf arabesques; from 1740 wider borders of flowers and foliage (Plate 156D), daisies predominating and, from 1750, individual motifs sometimes extending the full length of the border.

Etched glass. Glass decorated by biting out designs or motifs by means of acid applied to unprotected surfaces.

Ewers. These, and jugs, of Venetian glass were first made in the fifteenth century and a few survive from this period. Sixteenth-century examples are often very elaborate. A delightful ewer in the form of a ship is in the museum at Murano. Polychrome glass flowers were occasionally applied to them in the eighteenth century. Made in English flint-glass from the late 1670s.

Excise Duty. The duties levied on British glass during the eighteenth century caused much concern to the glass trade, and are supposed to have driven the makers to ornament their wares with engraving, cutting, gilding, and painting to compensate for the use of less glass in the making of any one article. A further result was the widespread introduction of the coloured glass, with which the names of Bristol and Nailsea are linked.

The Act of 1745 laid down that from March 25, 1746, flint-glass should pay a duty of 9s 4d per hundredweight (112 lbs), and bottle glass 2s 4d per hundredweight. Ireland was excluded from this, but more devastatingly the export of glass from Ireland was prohibited. In 1780, when the American War of Independence was harassing the British Government, Ireland asserted herself and was granted free trade: all export restrictions were abolished. Within five years glass-houses were established at Dublin, Belfast, Waterford, Cork, and Newry, all operating on a large scale and underselling English flint-glass tableware, upon which excise duty had been doubled in 1777. In England, as from July 5, 1777, ". . . upon the material or metal of all Plate or Flint Glass, and of all Enamel Stained or Paste Glass 18/8d. for every hundredweight". From May 10, 1787, the rate was raised to 21s 5½d, but bottle glass paid about a fifth of this: 4s ¼d per hundredweight.

Irish glass-making continued as a prosperous industry for forty-five years. Then in 1825, under pressure from English competitors labouring under a heavy excise duty of 10½d a pound, the Government laid the impost on Irish glass too. Each furnace in a glass-house was also required to be licensed at an annual cost of £20.

The duty was reduced in 1835, and finally repealed in 1845. The Irish glass trade had meanwhile rapidly declined, competing unavailingly with the glass presses installed by the English glass-men from the mid-1830s.

Eye-and-scale. Cut, blown-moulded, and pressed U.S. motif having round or oval disc or boss, plain or ornamental, at top of relief scales in vertical or swirled line, usually form-

FIG. 22

ing band; called horn-of-plenty in blown-three-mould glass (Fig. 22).

Favrile glass. Name meaning "hand-wrought" used for U.S. Art glass made by Louis Comfort Tiffany (1848–1933). *See* Tiffany glass.

Figures. Of Venetian glass, usually intended for table decorations and resembling *verre de Nevers*, were made in the eighteenth and nineteenth centuries. Those of religious subjects were probably intended for private chapels (Plate 183D).

Filigree glass. Described as *filiganati* or *a retorti*: an improved and elaborated version of *reticello* (*q.v.*), is decorated with interweaved spirals of white, coloured, and gold threads (Plate 182A). Glass of this type was first produced in Murano, Italy, in the sixteenth century, and seems to have remained popular ever since.

Finger-bowls. In England from *c.* 1760: known variously as wash-hand glasses, finger-cups, finger-glasses until 1840. Not to be confused with wine-glass coolers. In Ireland large numbers of blown-moulded finger-bowls and two-lipped wine-glass coolers were made. They are usually in clear flint-glass, English examples are found in blue, purple, amethyst, red, and green. The finest were in heavy cut-glass.

Finials. (1) Cover knob, drawn or applied, usually with short stem: (*a*) ball (Plate 147A (*left*)); (*b*) ball and button

(Fig. 23A); (*c*) button; (*d*) mushroom, (*e*) pointed globular (spire), plain and ribbed. (2) Decorative finish of plain cover knob, including (*a*) chicken, nineteenth-century hen-like bird into which the eighteenth-century "swan" degenerated, used on nineteenth-century pieces of U.S. South Jersey Type (Plate 148 (*centre*)); (*b*) swan, unswan-like in having crest, in the United States similar to Continental forms, found occasionally on late eighteenth- and early nineteenth-century glass (Fig. 23B); (*c*) turned with or without ornamental fins (wings) (Fig. 23C).

FIG. 23A

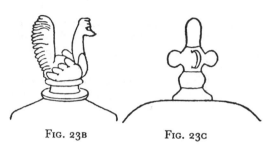

FIG. 23B   FIG. 23C

Fire polishing. A method of processing blown-moulded ware to obliterate tool marks and produce a smooth, even surface. This gave to moulded diamonds, flutes, scrolls, arches, and other motifs smoothly defined edges easily mistaken for cut-glass.

Firing-glasses, also known as hammering glasses. Used for thumping the table as form of acclamation. Stumpy glass with drawn bowl on thick stem and heavy, flat foot.

Flashed glass. Thin coating of coloured glass over clear glass; a ruby stain in imitation of Bohemian glass, the most popular.

Flasks.

American

(1) *Chestnut.* Free-blown and pattern-moulded, rarely blown-three-mould, of the timeless and universal shape resembling a slender chestnut; without uniformity of size, ranging from a few ounces to over a quart capacity, majority of pocket-bottle size;

mainly late eighteenth, early nineteenth century (Figs. 24A end view, 24B side view).

(2) *Decorative*. Blown in full-size two-piece

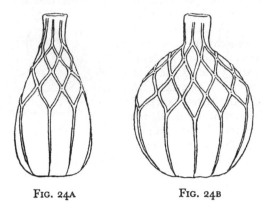

FIG. 24A   FIG. 24B

moulds bearing intaglio devices such as the sunburst, urn of fruit, and cornucopia; mainly half-pint and pint sizes; *c.* 1815–40 (Figs. 25A, B, and C).

(3) *Grandfather*. Midwestern chestnut flask of quart or more capacity; pattern-moulded in ribbed designs.

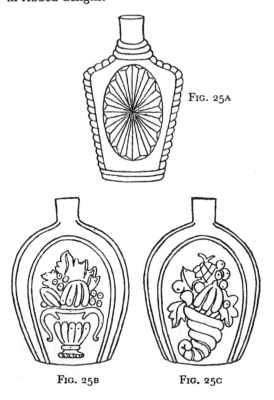

FIG. 25A

FIG. 25B   FIG. 25C

(4) *Historical*. Moulded like (2); designs of historical import; commemorative of events and public figures, emblems, slogans, candidates in presidential campaigns; emblems and designs related to economic life; also national and other symbolical emblems; *c.* 1815–late nineteenth century, majority before 1870 (Fig. 26).

FIG. 26

(5) *Masonic*. Moulded like (2); designs with (*a*) Masonic emblems each side, (*b*) Masonic emblems one side; reverse, different design, American Eagle most common; *c.* 1815–30.

(6) *Pictorial*. Moulded like (2); designs de-

FIG. 27A   FIG. 27B

picting people and/or flora and fauna; *c.* 1815–70 (Figs. 27A and B).

(7) *Pitkin*. Generic term for pocket bottles or flasks, blown by German half-post method and pattern-moulded in ribbed designs – vertical, swirled, and broken-swirl; eighteenth–early nineteenth century; first identified by tradition with the Pitkins' glass-works, East

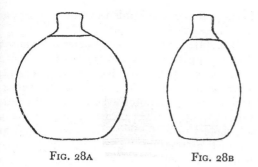

FIG. 28A   FIG. 28B

Hartford, Connecticut, *c.* 1790–1830 (Figs. 28A and B).

English

In flattened baluster or pear-shape of white or coloured glass ornamented with loopings or quillings, these date from early in the nineteenth century and were made at Nailsea, Birmingham, Stonebridge, and elsewhere. Most of them were sold as vessels for toilet waters. The twin flasks with two spouts pointing in opposite directions, known as a gimmel flask, was made in flint-glass throughout the eighteenth century and used as a holster flask. It was made in colour from about 1820, and in some a circular crimped or petal foot was added. Flasks were also made in the shape of hand bellows.

Venetian

In the form of pilgrim bottles, copied from silver patterns, flasks were made in the sixteenth century occasionally of *lattimo* glass decorated with enamelling.

Flint-glass. Now termed lead crystal, developed by George Ravenscroft (1618–81), in England, who was granted a seven-year patent (No. 176) in May 1674 to make a glass in which the silica was derived from calcined flints. In 1675 he first used lead oxide as a flux in place of vegetable potash. This produced a glass denser, heavier, softer, and with greater refractive brilliance than anything previously made. Hollow-ware, if flicked with thumb and finger, emits a resonant tone. After improvements to the process had been made during the 1680s, world glass trade became an English monopoly for more than a century and a half. In the United States a trade name for fine glassware, after 1864, including lime glass of William Leighton, Hobbs, Brockunier & Co., Wheeling, West Virginia.

Flip or **flip glass.** U.S. collector's term for tumblers, usually of pint or more capacity; something of a misnomer, as it was probably rarely used to serve the beverage called flip.

Flowered glasses (1740–80s). Trade name for tableware engraved with naturalistic flowers on the bowl; (*a*) 1740, a single flower ornamented one side of the bowl; (*b*) from early 1750s reverse side of bowl might also be engraved with a bird, butterfly, moth, bee, or other insect.

Flute. A drinking-glass with a tall, deep conical bowl. Also a vertical groove cut into a stem or bowl.

Fluting. Used when wider unit of ridged design is concave; fan-fluting, short tapering flutes or panels, blown-three-mould motif.

Folded Rim. *See* Rims.

Folk art in American glass. *See* South Jersey type (Plates 146A and 148).

Foot

American

On blown and blown-moulded glass. (1) Applied: occasionally square; mainly circular (*a*) short-stemmed, eighteenth-century type (Fig. 29A); (*b*) flat (Plate 146A (*left*)); (*c*) slop-

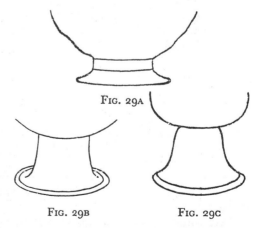

FIG. 29A

FIG. 29B   FIG. 29C

ing (Plate 146A (*centre*)); (*d*) petalled (scalloped) (Plate 147A (*centre*)); (*e*) domed, high and hollow, conical (sloping) or round with flaring

plain or folded rim, eighteenth–early nineteenth century (Plate 146B (*left*)); (*f*) pedestal,
high and hollow, cylindrical (eighteenth-century type) or truncated cone flaring at rim
(late eighteenth and nineteenth centuries)
(Figs. 29B and C); (*g*) flaring (low pedestal),
found also pressed. (2) Drawn: drawn from
the bottom of vessel's body and fashioned by
tooling.

English

(*a*) Folded, to about 1750: the rim was
folded underneath while hot, forming a selvage, giving extra strength to a part most likely
to become chipped in use (Plate 158E, F, and
156E). Pre-1690 the fold was very narrow: (*b*)
domed, to about 1800: with hemispherical,
sloping, or square instep, often surface-mould-
ed from about 1705. Expansive with folded
rim until 1750, then smaller and plain-edged,
except on sweetmeat and allied glasses. Domed and terraced: the foot tooled in concentric
circles rising one above the other; (*c*) plain,
conical foot tapering up towards stem junction, to about 1780: rare in seventeenth century and infrequent until about 1740. Early
examples almost flat beneath; by 1735 concave beneath, resting upon extreme rim. From
1750 instep height gradually decreased, until
by 1780 had become almost flat beneath with
punty mark ground away; (*d*) solid square,
1770 to end of period: might be stepped,
terrace-domed, or domed.

Free-blown. Glass formed by blowing and
manipulation with hand tools, without aid of
moulds; called also handblown and off-hand-
blown.

Friggers. A colloquialism used to describe
the innumerable minor articles made of glass,
of which the principal purposes were to delight and surprise the recipient and beholder,
and to exhibit the prowess of the maker. Into
this category fall such objects as hand bells,
flasks, rolling-pins, walking-sticks, tobacco
pipes, swords, sceptres, crowns, and hats,
which are dealt with under the appropriate
headings.

Less common than the above are model
ships with rigging and crew, birds on perches,
fox-hunts with hounds in full cry, and similar
tours de force (Plate 162A and B). The latter were
perhaps made as suitable table decorations at
hunt breakfasts.

It is stated that the glass-makers of Nailsea
had poleheads of glass in place of the more
usual ones of polished brass. These poleheads
were used by the village clubs of Somerset,
and are fairly common when made of brass,
rare in wood, and very scarce indeed in glass.

Friggers were made both at Bristol and at
Nailsea, as they were at all the other glass-
works in England. Unless such pieces bear a
signature or other mark of identification, there
is seldom any way by which the productions
of one place can be distinguished from those
of another. Nor is it usually possible to tell the
difference between factory-made articles of
these types and those that were made by apprentices to test their skill, or those made by
trained craftsmen in their spare time either
for their own amusement or for sale on their
own behalf.

Frit. A flux of low-temperature melting
silicates used in the manufacture of glass before the invention of the high-temperature
furnace in 1734. The ingredients forming the
frit were fused together, ground to powder
when cold, and added to the pot with the remaining ingredients before final melting.

Frosted glass or *vetro a ghiaccio.* Imitating
the texture of ice more nearly than its modern
name-sake, was produced in Murano, Italy,
in the sixteenth century. A handsome bucket
of this substance is in the museum at Murano.

Fruit. Of opaque coloured glass, this was
made in the Murano, Italy, factories in the
eighteenth century and has frequently been
copied.

Full-size mould. Mould composed of two
or more hinged pieces (leaves), having inner
surface with or without decorative design, and
the size and form of an article; glass thus
moulded characterized by concavo-convex
surfaces.

Furniture. Occasionally decorated with
panels of coloured glass in the eighteenth
century. In 1777 Lady Anna Riggs Miller
noted at Murano, Italy, a suite of furniture inlaid with pieces of blue glass and
looking glass, commissioned by the Sultan of
Turkey for his seraglio. Glass imitating marble
for inlaying in furniture was patented in the

1840s by G. Newberry, London: the furniture was made by George Shove, Deptford, London. At the Great Exhibition, 1851, Zebedee Jones, Clifton, near Bristol, displayed furniture inlaid with a new style of ornamental glass known as "vitrilapis". Stools made entirely of flint-glass from gas-fired furnaces were made in the 1860s, and some still exist.

Gadroon or gadrooning. Heavy rounded ribs or flutes: (1) tooled on layer of glass formed from a pearl (round gather of metal) attached to end of parison and pulled up over it (Plate 148 (*right*)); (2) dip-moulded on cup-like layer (Plate 148 (*left*)); (3) full-size moulded convex ribs, high relief, tapering from rounded end, forming band.

Gallé, Émile (1846–1904). The most famous producer of art glass of the nineteenth century. During the 1870s he took over the table-glass-works owned by his father in Nancy and turned it into an art-glass factory. His early products were free variations of historic styles of Europe and the Orient, mostly in transparent glass decorated with engraving or enamel-painting (Plate 165B). At the Paris Exhibition of 1889 his representation showed the powerful impact of Japanese art. The shapes were simple in outline, and much of the glass was massive and coloured throughout. The cased-glass technique was employed with great mastery, and the decorative patterns showed naturalistic pictures of flowers and insects (Plate 166C). Soon after, he must have developed that style of cased glass, which more than anything gave him fame: vases made of differently coloured glass in many layers, cut away into varying thicknesses to naturalistic pictures of flowers and insects. The shapes are often irregular and suggestive of natural forms such as trees and branches, and the flowers cling to the forms in curving lines. The general impression is one of gentle lyricism. Sometimes lines from famous French poets are found written on the vases in ornamental lettering, having allegedly inspired Gallé to the particular piece. His own name and "Nancy", also in ornamental lettering, are frequently integrated into the composition. Glasses in this style were instrumental in the development of the *art nouveau*, and the

mature examples are among the most typical of the style's manifestations.

Because of their beauty, their novelty and modernity, and to some extent because of Gallé's great talent for publicity (displayed with real genius at the Paris Exhibition in 1900), Gallé's *verreries parlantes* became fashionable all over the world. In order to answer the enormous new demands for his glasses, he enlarged the factory and engaged a numerous staff of decorators who worked under his supervision. From the 1890s it was really a "mass-production of individual glasses" that was carried on. Gallé's later years were spent in a constant search for new designs and new technical tricks. The glasses from this period are sometimes very beautiful, though sometimes forced and affected. When he died in 1904 the factory carried on until 1914 in Gallé's spirit and at a respectable level of quality under the artistic leadership of his old friend and associate, the painter Victor Prouvé. The products of this period are signed with Gallé's name preceded by a star. After the First World War the production was carried on at Épinay. In 1921 it changed hands, and later products were rather debased.

Great quantities of Gallé's glass still exist. Public collections all over Europe tried to acquire examples of his art at the exhibitions in Paris in 1889 and 1900, and private international patrons also acquired his products. No proper survey of this vast material has yet been carried out, but the individual pieces certainly vary greatly in artistic quality. The early pieces have a genuine charm and exuberance, and the products from about 1890 are particularly fine, original, and of great beauty. The glasses of the last period are sometimes of a staggering technical complexity, but frequently lacking in balance and taste. Cased glass vases with purple flowers on a grey background must have been made over a fairly long period to satisfy numerous customers everywhere. They exist in great numbers and vary little, though no two pieces are exactly alike. The type may appropriately be labelled "standard Gallé" (Plate 167C).

Much research is still needed on Gallé's complex personality and varied activities.

Apart from being a glass-maker he had a factory for decorated faïence and one for luxury furniture. He was a learned horticulturalist and botanist, a theorist and writer on art, and an enthusiastic champion for the new styles of the day. The uncritical attitude of his contemporaries is apt to obscure our view of him. He was certainly a great and original glass-maker and an influential personality in the cultural milieu of the 1890s. Through the great fame he gained for his creations he laid the foundation for the modern conception of glass as a serious artistic medium.

His glass was widely imitated, in France and elsewhere. But as his habit of signing his works was emulated as eagerly as his lyrical flower decorations, problems of identification are comparatively simple. The only factory working in his style, whose glass could compete with the real Gallé pieces in beauty of texture and design, was Daum in Nancy.

Galleried Rim. *See* Rims.

Gather. Uninflated and unformed blob of metal taken from the pot on end of blow-pipe.

Gauffered Rim. *See* Rims.

Geometric patterns. (1) Category of blown-three-mould patterns composed of motifs such as ribs, flutes, diamonds, sunbursts, circles, ovals; (2) cut-glass patterns composed of ribs, diamonds, and fans on thick blown-moulded glass, called "imitation cut-glass"; (3) cut-glass motifs, strawberry diamond in particular, on mechanically pressed glass.

Gilding. Traces are visible on existing Elizabethan Anglo-Venetian drinking-glasses; fashionable as rim decoration 1715–90, the finest bowl ornament in this medium 1760–90; (a) early eighteenth-century gilding fixed beneath a film of flint-glass by a process akin to enamelling; (b) 1715–60: japanned gilding, burnished; (c) 1755–65; honey gilding: the rich brilliance of the gold was destroyed and could not be burnished; (d) 1760–1820: amber-varnish gilding, burnished; (e) 1780 onward: mercury gilding; (f) from 1850: liquid gold of sparkling brilliance.

Little Irish glass is known to have been gilded. That such glass was so decorated is shown by the fact that in 1786 the Dublin Society paid John Grahl thirty-five guineas for disclosing glass-gilding secrets, which were then placed at the disposal of the industry. Such gilding appears to have been impermanent, however, and has worn away, leaving the surface beneath pitted and rough. Careful examination of a lavishly cut piece will sometimes reveal traces of gilding.

Gjövik Verk (1809–47). Norwegian glass-manufactory, started when Hurdals Verk (*q.v.*) closed down. Gjövik was a much smaller and less ambitious establishment, but some of the glass-blowers from Hurdal came on and the tradition was continued.

Goblet. A drinking-glass with the bowl large in relation to stem height and holding a gill or more of liquor. Since the fifteenth century they have been among the most popular products of the Venetian factories. The earliest are based on silver patterns. Those of the earlier sixteenth century are of clear glass with simple baluster stems and usually very shallow bowls, like those held by the banquetters in Paolo Veronese's *Feast in the House of Levi* (Accademia, Venice). Later in the century deeper conic bowls became popular and were often supported on elaborately wrought stems. (Plate 184c.)

Green glass. Glass in its natural colour, neither rendered colourless nor artificially coloured; generally made from coarser and less pure materials than those used for fine wares; soda, potash, or lime the principal alkaline base; many bottles and window-glass made from this glass.

Guilloche. *See* Chain.

Half-post. Second gather forming two-layered body, giving added strength through double wall and terminating below neck of vessel; the post (first gather) given a half-post (second gather) by redipping in pot of metal; in the United States associated with Continental and American case bottles and Pitkin flasks and bottles.

Hand bells. Coloured glass hand bells were made between 1820 and 1860 at Bristol, Newcastle, Warrington, Stourbridge, and by John Davenport, Longport, Staffordshire. Authentic bells measure from 9 to 18 inches in height and have clappers of fine flint-glass. Colour combinations are: blue-tinted bell, spirally ribbed handle in pale yellow with opalescent triple-knopped finial; bell with pink strands on an opaque white ground, with moulded opaque-white hand as a handle; bell with white stripes on a translucent red ground, opalescent blue handle; red bell with colour-twist spiral handle; green bell with opaque-white twist handle; opaque-white throughout and may be ribbed; translucent bell with clear handle; red throughout. Glass bells are still in production.

FIG. 30

Hand-blown. Free-blown; used in contradistinction to machine-blown.

Handles. On blown glass, applied: (1) Either round in section or strap (flattened), hollow or solid, ending in (a) turned-back tip, (b) curled tip, (c) crimped end with a or b, (d) leaf (tooled diagonal lines) with a or b, probably after 1825: 1, hollow strap, d; 1, round hollow, c. (2) Principal shapes: (a) "D", rarely found on nineteenth-century glass (Fig. 31A), (b) loop (Plate 146A (*left*)),

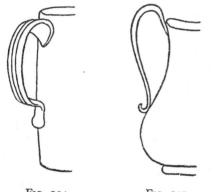

FIG. 31A   FIG. 31B

(c) semi-ear-shaped (Plate 147A (*right*)), (d) swan: long and arching above rim (Fig. 31B). Commonest, b and c. (3) Principal decoration: (a) medial rib: a centre rib, often on round, occasionally on strap, the English *trailed*; (b) corrugated, ridged, or ribbed strap; (c) double; paralleled contiguous sections, occasionally round, usually strap; (d) ribbed: hollow handle formed from

ribbed or fluted (pattern-moulded) gather, drawn out into a tube, English incised and reeded.

Historical glass. Glass bearing decoration associated with national or local events, heroes, public figures; emblems of agriculture, trade, commerce, transportation, etc.; engraved, rare; in the United States mainly moulded in flasks and pressed in lacy glass.

Horn-of-plenty. (1) Cornucopia of fruit or produce; common motif on decorative flasks; occasionally in lacy glass; (2) in pressed pattern ware, stylized cornucopia-shaped motif with waffled disc at top, "horn" with round bosses or vice-versa; similar to the peacock eye in lacy glass. *See* Eye-and-scale.

Hurdals Verk. Norwegian glass-manufactory. When, in 1777, Nöstetangen was shut down, the crystal production and most of the

FIG. 32

glass-blowers were moved to Hurdals Verk, farther up in the country, where wood for fuel was more plentiful. In 1809 Hurdals Verk closed down.

Jacobite glasses. Propaganda glasses bearing emblems and mottoes of a cryptic character associated with the Jacobite cause (Plates 156F and C). Most common is the six-petalled Jacobite rose with one or two buds (Plate 156C): the rose represents the House of Stuart, the small bud the Old Pretender, the large bud on the right being added later, either in honour of Prince Charles Edward's arrival in Scotland or after James' proposal to "abdicate" in favour of his son. Other Jacobite emblems include a stricken and burgeoning oak, oak leaf, bee, butterfly, jay (Plate 156B), Jacob's ladder foliage, carnation, daffodil, fritillary, triple ostrich plumes, and thistle.

Jacobs, Lazarus and Isaac. Lazarus Jacobs was in business as a glass-cutter in Bristol in 1771, and died in 1796. His son, Isaac, styled himself "Glass Manufacturer to His Majesty" (George III). Specimens of

FIG. 33

dark-blue glass with gilt decoration are recorded with the written mark in gold shown in Fig. 33.

Among other pieces, Isaac Jacobs made

distinctive blue glass decanters (q.v.) (Fig. 34). Michael Edkins was employed by the Jacobs between 1785 and 1787, and it is not improbable that he did work for them like the gilding on these decanters.

An advertisement of 1806 referred to: ". . . Specimens of the Dessert set, which I. Jacobs had the honour of sending to her Majesty in burnished Gold, upon Royal purple colored Glass to be seen at his Manufactory, where several Dessert sets of the same kind are now completed from Fifteen Guineas per set to any amount."

FIG. 34

Jean, A. Originally a potter, but during the 1880s a glass-maker in Paris. A small group of audacious and highly original individual pieces are known from his hand (Plate 165D).

Jugs. In Ireland were made in large numbers in the nineteenth century. At first they were tall and narrow on a hollow foot, or, more usually, short and wide, thus giving a more shapely field for cutting in diamonds,

flutes, leaf designs, prisms, and so on. These at first had the base ground flat; from about 1820 a flanged foot extending outwards was usual. Some jugs were free-blown and engraved. In the United States the term is not used synonymously with pitcher.

Keith, James. Newcastle crystal blower who was lured to Nöstetangen, Norway (q.v.) in August 1755. When Nöstetangen was shut down he went on to Hurdals Verk (q.v.), where he was pensioned off in 1787. He left a numerous family, and the name of Keith (Kith, Keth, and other variations) appears in the records of Norwegian and Swedish glass-factories right up to the end of the nineteenth century.

Kewblas. Coloured glass over milk glass with coat of clear on top. Union Glass Works, Somerville, Massachusetts, U.S.A., 1890s.

Kick. The conical indentation to be found in the base of an early bottle or decanter. This was essential for proper annealing when glassmakers had only limited means of toughening their vessels. Continued in small glass-houses to about 1790.

Knob. *See* Finial.

Knop. A protuberance, other than a baluster, either solid or hollow, breaking the line of a drinking-glass or other stem. (*a*) acorn: a tooled motif in the form of an acorn, sometimes inverted; used also as a lid finial; (*a*) angular: a rounded-edge, flattened knop, placed horizontally; (*c*) annulated: a flattened knop sandwiched between two, four, or six thinner flattened knops, each pair progressively less in size; (*d*) ball: a large, spherical motif often found immediately above a shouldered stem; (*e*) bladed: a thin, sharp-edged, flattened knop placed horizontally; (*f*) bullet: a small, spherical knop, sometimes termed the olive button; (*g*) collar: *see* merese; (*h*) cushion: a large, spherical knop flattened top and bottom; (*i*) cylinder: a knop in the form of a cylinder, often containing a tear; (*j*) drop: resembling in shape the frustum of an inverted cone, and usually placed half an inch to an inch above the foot; (*k*) merese: a sharp-edged, flattened glass button connecting bowl and stem, or between foot and stem of a stemmed vessel; (*l*) multiple: knops of a single shape repeated in a stem; (*m*) mushroom:

usually associated with incurved and funnel bowls; (n) quatrefoil: a short knop pressed into four wings by vertical depressions, the metal being drawn out with pincers. The wings may be upright or twisted; (o) swelling: a slight stem protuberance containing an air tear.

Köhler, Heinrich Gottlieb. German head engraver and general artistic manager of Nöstetangen, Norway. To judge from his style Köhler had been trained in the Silesian tradition. He came to Copenhagen in 1746, where he became court engraver. He settled at Nöstetangen from 1756–57 to 1770, after which he worked as a freelance in Christiania for a time and returned to Copenhagen about 1780, where he seems to have died soon after.

Kosta. Swedish glass-manufactory, founded in 1742 and still in operation. Kosta lies in the district of Småland, and was founded by a member of the local nobility.

Kungsholm Glasbruk (1676–1815). Swedish glass-manufactory founded by an Italian, Giacomo Bernadini Scapitta, in Stockholm. In 1678, however, Scapitta was exposed as an imposter and fled to England, and the factory was carried on under the administration of Swedish noblemen and leading civil servants.

Lacy glass. Type of U.S. pressed glass made c. 1828–40; intricate relief designs on finely stippled, lace-like background; characteristically brilliant and sparkling; mainly cup plates and salts with some dishes and plates, and more rarely, bases of lamps and candlesticks.

Lamps. Hanging oil-lamps of a tubular shape with a knopped base were made in Venice in the fifteenth century if not earlier. They were occasionally decorated with enamel. Table-lamps, some of fantastic form (Plates 181A and 183C), others based on metal prototypes, were made throughout the sixteenth, seventeenth, and eighteenth centuries.

In England and America open-flame float-wick lamps were used for centuries under the name of mortars. These were small bowls of poor-quality glass, measuring 2 or 3 inches in height. Late in the seventeenth century the vessel was usually of flint-glass and raised on a short stem and circular foot. From the mid-1780s it might have a thick square plinth beneath the foot.

Open-flame lamps with fixed central wicks date from the 1690s, the bowl being a small, open-topped container covered by a metal disc through which passed a short tube containing wick. These, like mortars, continued in use until the introduction of paraffin in the 1860s. Central-wick lamps were made in numerous forms, including the wine-glass lamp, peg lamp, handled lamps with stems, chamber lamps, and the lamp with a vase-shaped body from which extended three or four hollow branches. After 1820 they might be pattern moulded.

Latticinio. Familiar name for the filigree glass of Venetian origin, composed of crossing and interlacing strips of opaque and clear glass.

Lattimo. The name given to the milky white glass made with lead, first produced at Murano, Italy, in the early sixteenth century (Plate 181B).

Lava glass. Type of glass made in imitation of mosaic lava-ware pottery. Mount Washington Glass Works, South Boston, Massachusetts, U.S.A., 1878.

Lazy-susan caster. Footed caster, usually metal, with shaft terminating in handle and, at top of foot, movable circular frame with rings in which to suspend condiment containers; probably after 1830.

Lazy-susan shape. Caster (cruet) bottle formed with shoulder projecting beyond sides to rest on ring of lazy-susan caster or cruet frame.

Lead glass. Glass containing lead oxide as a flux; called "flint-glass" (q.v.).

Leveillé, E. Continued the production of art-glass in Eugène Rousseau's (q.v.) establishment in Paris from 1885 until some time after 1900. He produced massive glass, frequently crackled, with inlaid colour streaks in Rousseau tradition and a few cased glass pieces with cut-away decoration (Plate 166B). Leveillé's glass was eagerly bought by public collections in many countries at the Paris Exhibition in 1900 and is more frequently seen today than the real Rousseau pieces. Many of them are of fine quality and in good taste, but they lack the magnificence of

Rousseau's own products. Sculptural effects such as dents, incised spirals, and twisted knots seem to have been Leveillé's personal contribution to the style.

Lily-pad. Decoration formed from a super-imposed layer of glass, that is, a rounded gather (pearl) attached to the bottom of a parison, pulled up over it, and tooled into the so-called lily-pad; three principal types: (1) slender stem, beadlike pad (Plate 146A (*right*)); (2) wider and more valleyed stem, blobbly or small flattened pad (Plate 148 (*centre*)); (3) long, curving stem, flattened ovoid pad, probably type giving rise to the term (Plate 146A (*left*)).

Lime glass. Glass containing lime; first produced by William Leighton, Birmingham, in 1864; the metal is as clear as lead glass and cheaper, but not so resonant or heavy.

Looking glasses. Documents reveal that looking glasses were made at Murano and silvered in Venice during the sixteenth century, but no examples from this period are known to survive. The earliest survivors date from the eighteenth century, when the Venetians had been surpassed by the French in the art of making such wares. Eighteenth-century mirrors were often decorated with engraved figures and set in elaborate frames of clear and coloured looking-glass. Sometimes candle holders were attached to their bases (Plate 182D).

In England mirror plates were made by the cylinder process at Sir Robert Mansell's London glass-house in 1625 and by the Duke of Buckingham at Vauxhall from 1663. Cast mirror plate was invented in 1688, and most early examples are wheel engraved. From 1773 finer and larger mirror plates were in production at Ravenhead, St Helens.

Loopings or draggings. Decorative device achieved by applying threads of contrasting  colours to body or parison, which are then dragged upward by a tool and rolled on marver to embed in body; used since ancient times; used at Nailsea, Birmingham, and elsewhere and in American glass on pieces of South Jersey type.

FIG. 35. Looping

Lucas, John Robert. John Robert Lucas was a partner in a Bristol bottle-making glass-works. In 1788 he removed to Nailsea, and there founded a factory where it is said he made articles for everyday use from common bottle-glass. In 1793 Lucas acquired three partners: William Coathupe, Edward Homer, and William Chance. The latter's son, Robert Lucas Chance, founded the Spon Lane, Birmingham, glass-works, which became sufficiently prosperous to buy up the Nailsea works in 1870.

Mansell, Sir Robert. Gained control of the English glass monopoly in 1618. He reorganized the industry on a rational basis with more than four thousand workers under his authority. Charles I demanded £1,500 a year from Mansell and his associates, this being paid until the King's death in 1649, when monopolies were ended.

Marble glass. Pressed glass in variegated tints of purple and milk white made during the mid-Victorian period under the name of vitro-porcelain and now known to collectors as purple slag or marble glass. The makers were J. G. Sowerby, Gateshead, and the Kilner firm of Thornhill Lees, Wakefield. The waste or slag floating on the top of molten steel was normally tapped off into moulds and, when cold, was broken into chunks and thrown on to slag heaps. The first slag to be tapped resembled purple marbled glass. This was acquired by the two glass-houses – and probably others – suitably tempered with flint-glass and pressed into ornamental ware. The Kilner firm impressed their productions with the mark of a griffin from the early 1860s. Challinor, Taylor & Co., Tarentum, Pennsylvania, U.S.A., made purple slag during the 1870s and 1880s (Plate 167B).

Margariti. Imitation pearls, sometimes of prodigious size (called *paternostri*), have been made at Venice since the thirteenth century. They were exported in the fourteenth and fifteenth centuries, and when Vasco da Gama reached Calicut in 1497 he found them in use as currency there.

Marks. A considerable amount of Irish blown-moulded hollow-ware – decanters, finger-bowls, jugs – bears the name of the glass-house in raised letters on a flat ring encircling the punty mark. Such marks are unknown on English glass. Nine such marks are known: Penrose Waterford; Cork Glass Co; Waterloo C° Cork; B. Edwards Belfast; Francis Collins Dublin; Mary Carter & Son Dublin; Armstrong Ormond Quay; C M C° (Charles Mulvany & Co., Dublin); J. D. Ayckbowm, Dublin. The last five were wholesale glass-sellers whose sales were sufficient to warrant the manufacture of special moulds.

Marriage cups. Venetian glass cups, made to commemorate marriages, and decorated with portraits of the bride and groom, seem to have been produced only in the fifteenth and early sixteenth centuries. The most celebrated example is the so-called Barovier cup at Murano, Italy (Plate 184A).

Marver. Polished marble slab supported by frame on which gather of metal is rolled.

Masonic flasks. *See* Flasks.

Merese. Glass wafer or button joining bowl and stem of a vessel or connecting parts of stem or shaft.

Metal. Glass either in the molten or hardened state.

Midwestern. Collector's term for U.S. glass made from about 1790 in glass-houses between the Allegheny Mountains and the Mississippi, principally the Pittsburgh–Monongehela area, Pennsylvania, Ohio, and the Wellsburg–Wheeling area, West Virginia.

Milk glass or **milk-white glass.** Opaque white glass made in imitation of Chinese porcelain, produced by mixing oxide of tin with clear glass; free blown or, in late nineteenth century, pressed in a variety of objects (Plate 153A).

Millefiori. The first millefiori (Italian: thousand flowers) paperweights were made in Venice. St Louis made them in 1845. In the next year they were made at Baccarat, and before long they were produced at Clichy. Also made in England at Birmingham, Stourbridge, and London.

Monteith. (1) A bowl with a scalloped rim to allow ten or twelve drinking-glasses to hang by the foot into iced water for chilling. Late seventeenth century to 1790s. (2) Individual wine-glass coolers resembling finger-bowls, but with one or two lips in the rim. Cata-logued in early nineteenth century as "montiffs", 1760s to 1860s.

Mother of pearl or **satin glass.** This was perfected in 1880 by Thomas Webb of Stourbridge. This purely ornamental glass was produced by blowing a core of white opaque glass in a pattern mould. While the glass was still hot the outer surface was dipped into transparent coloured pot metal. A transparent crystal glazing was applied over this. After annealing, the piece was placed in a tank, where acid vapour acted on the surface and produced a satin-like finish. Several colour combinations might be applied on a single piece. Made from 1885 by the Phoenix Glass Company, Pittsburgh, Pennsylvania, U.S.A.

Mould-blown. *See* Blown-moulding.

Moulded glass. Glass ornamented and/or given partial or final body shape by use of a mould; applicable to pressed glass, but reserved generally for blown-moulded.

Murrini. Otherwise called mosaic glass or millefiori. *Vetri Murrini* are decorated with brightly coloured discs within the glass, composed of sections of the *canna vitrea*. This process of decoration used by the Romans was rediscovered at Murano, Italy, in the sixteenth century.

Mushroom. A paperweight in which the canes are bunched together and raised in a sheaf from the bottom. Usually surrounded by a ring of lacework at the foot.

Neck-rings on decanters. Seven types are found: plain round, plain double, plain triple, feathered, triangular, square, and diamond-cut. The feathered ring is a double ring impressed with transverse lines. Occasionally the rings – there are usually three – do not match. Neck-rings were applied by rotating the red-hot decanter and dropping a thread of hot glass around the neck. This became welded by contact, and the surplus was tapered and torn suddenly away. The whole was reheated and a tool pressed upon the ring, giving it shape and width. Joints are always faulty, and visible as hair-lines having the appearance of flaws.

Newry Flint-glass Manufactory. A small glass-house was established in the early 1780s advertising both cut and plain flint-glass, and closed 1801. A new glass-house was opened in 1824, closing in 1847.

Nöstetangen. Norwegian glass-manufactory situated near Drammen. Nöstetangen was founded by royal command and under the personal patronage of King Christian VI of Denmark and Norway in 1741. When the Norwegian glass industry was reorganized in 1753 the production of tableware and ornamental glass was concentrated at Nöstetangen and German and English glass-blowers were engaged. In 1777 the factory was shut down.

FIG. 36. Nöstetangen

Nursing bottles. *See* Bottles.
Off-hand-blown. Free-blown.
Ogival. U.S. design expanded diamond, pattern-moulded diaper in diamond-like formation reminiscent of English nipt-diamond-waies formed by tooling applied threads; usually loosely formed diamonds above flutes (Plate 147A (*right*)).
Opalescent dewdrop (later called Hobnail). Pressed in full-size moulds; tips of nodules made of opalescent glass; made in various colours. Hobbs, Brockunier & Company, Wheeling, West Virginia, 1886.
Opaline. A word created by modern French collectors and connoisseurs to describe fine colour-glass, made during the nineteenth century mainly on a basis of opal-glass. The French glass-makers of the period called the glass *opale* or *en couleurs opale*.
Open-top mould. *See* Dip mould.

Orrefors. Modern Swedish art glass manufactory situated in Småland.
Overlay. *See* Cased glass.
Painted decorations. On Venetian glass these were usually carried out in enamel. For a brief period in the mid-sixteenth century, however, paintings similar to those on contemporary maiolica were applied to the backs of large plates in oil colours. Such plates must have been made solely for decorative use, since the paint was not resistant to water as it was not muffle-fired. Two methods of painting were used in England: oil or japan colours hardened by heat but not burnt in, and enamels muffle-fired and permanent. The japanned decoration is rare and pre-dates 1760, naturalistic bird, flower, and vine motifs being usual. Enamelling was at first in two styles of white: a thinly applied wash enamel and a dense full white thickly applied. Motifs between 1750 and 1780 include sporting subjects, conventional scenes, and chinoiseries. Armorial work in vivid colours was fashionable until the 1820s. Colours in a wider range than formerly were used from the 1830s, and included figures, ornaments, flowers, birds, landscapes, and marine views.
Panelling. Moulded contiguous round- or oval-topped arches with: (1) narrow flattened upright in bold relief, mainly eighteenth century (Plate 145 (*left*)); (2) thread-like upright and arch top, often tapering at bottom, like Haynes' "moulded wide fluting", late eighteenth–early nineteenth century. Both often called sunken panel.
Pantin. A factory in north-east Paris, founded at La Villette in 1851 by E. S. Monot, and moved to Pantin in 1855. From the first the factory concentrated on elaborate coloured and decorated glass, and, especially between 1865 and 1900, much fine glass in a magnificent and expensive style was produced there. In 1868 Bontemps (*q.v.*) mentions that fine copies of Venetian aventurine glass was being made at Pantin. In 1878 Monot *fils* and a certain M. Stumpf joined E. S. Monot as directors of the factory, and in 1889 they seem to have taken over. By 1900 the owners were Stumpf, Touvier, Viollet & Cie.
Paperweights. The processes involved in making glass paperweights call for great skill.

The final correct placing of the pattern within the clear glass calls for a high degree of craftsmanship. This is even more apparent when it is realized that the operations are performed with the glass in a molten, or near molten, state. Only a general description of the complicated manufacturing process is given here; details vary with the different types of paperweights, and no doubt each factory had its secrets.

The canes to make the pattern are formed by several methods. In one, lengths of coloured glass are heated until they adhere together and form a solid mass. Alternatively, a rod of a chosen colour is dipped repeatedly in molten glass of other colours until a pattern is completed. In both cases, while still hot, the newly made vari-coloured rod is drawn out until the section of it is of the required diameter.

The necessary canes are selected and sufficient thin slices cut from them and polished. The pattern is arranged on a piece of thin glass, a mould is placed over this, and molten glass is poured in. The half-formed paperweight is picked up on a pontil, dipped into molten glass, and shaped to the form of the finished article. Fruit and other subjects are made of coloured glass, but the process followed for making the paperweight is similar.

Great care is needed to maintain the temperature of the components throughout the manufacture, or cracking will result. The final operation is annealing: a slow cooling. When it is cold the mark of the pontil is removed by grinding.

In America the successful sale of French paperweights imported into the United States induced manufacturers there to imitate them with some success. Notably the factories of Deeming Jarves at Sandwich, Cape Cod, opened in 1825, and at East Cambridge and South Boston, in Massachusetts, opened in 1818 and in 1837. Not only were the French designs copied but original models were evolved.

French paperweights were copied widely in England, but it is doubtful whether any were made until quite a few years after the first appearance of the French ones. The glass-making centres of Stourbridge in Worcester and Bristol in Somerset both attempted to produce imitations of the imported article. The Whitefriars Glass-works in London and George Bacchus and Sons in Birmingham also made paperweights in the style of those from Baccarat and elsewhere.

The shapes of the English glass paperweights are usually different from the French ones, and the colour of the glass and of the canes embedded in it is seldom comparable.

The encrusted cameos (sulphides) made by Apsley Pellatt (1791–1863) are, however, a notable exception, and are difficult to distinguish in many cases from the French.

Three glass-works in France were concerned in the production of glass paperweights. They were the *Compagnie des Cristalleries de Baccarat* and the *Compagnie des Verreries et Cristalleries de St Louis*, both situated in the Vosges to the south-east of Paris; and the Clichy glass-works, which stood in the suburb of Clichy in Paris itself.

All three manufactories produced similar work. But there is enough evidence from specimens presented by the manufacturers to the French museums on which to base identifications, in most cases, as to exactly which factory was responsible for certain noticeable differences. Dated paperweights from the Baccarat factory are known for the years 1846–9. The St Louis weights start a year earlier, and also continue until 1849. The dates are often on millefiori weights, are not usually noticeable, and are never set centrally. Any paperweight in which the date is in the dead centre should be regarded with great suspicion.

Parison. Inflated, unformed gather of metal.

Part-size mould. Small two-piece hinged mould; long handle usually attached to each piece to open and close mould; used to impress design on gather.

Pattern-moulded. Term designating glass moulded for decorative pattern or design only, in dip and part-size moulds and expanded; coined to differentiate glass so patterned from that blown in full-size moulds.

Peach glass or **peachblow.** Peach-like tints shading from cream to rose, red to yellow, or blue to pink, made in imitation of a Chinese porcelain. Made by the New England Glass Company, U.S.A., in 1885, but became very popular when Hobbs, Brockunier & Company of Wheeling brought out a copy of the Mary J. Morgan collection Chinese porcelain vase which brought $18,000 at auction in 1886. Their product was a cased glass with milk-white lining, whereas the Peachblow made by the New England Glass Company and by the Mount Washington Glass Works was the same composition throughout.

Peacock eye. Pressed lacy glass motif similar to stylized horn-of-plenty in pressed pattern-ware (*see* Horn-of-plenty); "eye" usu-

FIG. 37

ally a large circular dot within beaded ring and "horn" either stippled or fine-diamonded; called also peacock feather (Fig. 37).

Peasant glass. *See* Stiegel type (2).

Pedestal foot. *See* Foot (U.S. 1, *f*).

Petalled foot. *See* Foot (U.S., 1, *d*), (Plate 147A (*centre*)).

Picot. Tooled decorative device, usually forming crest of wavy decoration or swagging,

FIG. 38

found mainly on U.S. South Jersey Type glass; sometimes called aborted or vestigial lily-pad (Fig. 38).

Piece mould. Part-size and full-size moulds composed of two or more pieces (leaves); necessary for motifs and designs with crossed lines, such as diamond diapering. *See* Part-size and Full-size.

Pillar moulding. A variant of the blown-moulded process by which ornamental domestic ware could be made cheaply was patented in 1835, by Thomas Green, who gave it the

name of Roman pillar moulding. The exterior was corrugated vertically or swirled, while the interior remained smooth. This patent was licensed to others, and a price list issued by Apsley Pellatt illustrates several examples. This was made in colour, too.

Pillar moulding in the United States is associated mainly with a Midwestern commercial glass from the Pittsburgh and Wheeling areas and has widely spaced pillars.

Pillar rib. (1) Pronounced relief, pillar moulded, rib; (2) wide, short, heavy ribs forming band in a geometric pattern.

Pinched trailing. English term; *see* Quilling.

Pitkin. *See* Flasks (7).

Pocket bottle. *See* Bottles.

Pomona glass. Stippled body achieved with acid combined with unstippled portion stained a straw colour; frequently decorated with an applied garland of flowers; New England Glass Company, U.S.A., 1884.

Pontil. *See* Punty.

Pontil mark. *See* Punty mark.

Portrait flasks. Group of historical flasks bearing portraits of public figures and heroes. None of those which have been identified seem to be earlier than the 1830s, and many of them fall in the third quarter of the century.

Potpourri urn. A speciality of Gjövik Verk, Norway, in the early nineteenth century.

FIG. 39A. *c.* 1810   FIG. 39B. *c.* 1825

Their development can be followed in the diagrams. They were mostly made in cobalt

FIG. 39C. c. 1840

blue, the shades of which differ from an ink-green tinge to a soft deep blue. Many of them have borders in white. They were also made in opaque white glass made from bone-ash, with dark borders.

Pressed glass. Glass pressed manually or mechanically in moulds; molten glass is dropped into a patterned mould, a plunger is rammed into the mould, forcing glass into all parts of the mould and impressing the pattern on it; plunger or core has a smooth surface so that inside of piece being pressed is smooth in contrast to blown moulded or blown three-mould glass. Method said to have originated in the United States. It is wrongly called "Sandwich Glass" from the famous factory at Sandwich, Massachusetts, where it was first produced on a large commercial scale. By 1829 at least six eastern and four Midwestern glass-houses were producing pressed glass. In England mechanical presses for making hollow-ware by a single process were installed in glass-houses from 1833. Specialized workers known as "pinchers" used hand-operated presses for making square feet in a piece with a pedestal or double stem. Target and mushroom decanter stoppers were also made in this way.

Pressed pattern ware. Pressed glass sets

for table, bar, etc.; articles matching in pattern; earliest, about 1840.

Prunts. Applied blobs of glass tooled or moulded into various forms.

FIG. 40

Punties. Concave shaping cut on the surfaces of a paperweight. Overlay paperweights are often cut with punties.

Punty mark or pontil mark. A scar left on blown glass when the punty is broken off. Generally found on the base of a glass. Ground and polished into a smooth depression, usually from about 1750, and invariably so on fine glass from about 1780. Seemingly less frequently ground off and polished on early U.S. ordinary wares than on British.

Punty or pontil. A long iron rod attached to one end of blown glass during the finishing processes after removal from the blowpipe.

Purled ornament. All-over diaper moulding with small round or oval compartments.

Purple slag. *See* Marble glass.

Quilling. Ribbon of glass applied and pinched into pleats. U.S. term, synonymous with English pinched trailing.

FIG. 41

Ravenscroft, George (1618–81). Was granted a patent for manufacturing flint-glass (No. 176, 16 May, 1674), the entire output of which the Glass-sellers' Company undertook to market, provided he worked to their standard designs. Ravenscroft introduced lead oxide to his glass in the autumn of 1675.

Reliquaries. In Venetian glass sometimes in the form of covered cups, but more usually simple cylindrical vessels on knopped baluster stems, made of clear glass in the sixteenth century and later periods (Plate 182B). Also made by Apsley Pellatt, London, during second quarter of the nineteenth century.

Reticello (literally net-work). The name usually given to glass decorated with a mesh of opaque white threads beneath its surface, otherwise called *vetro di trina* or lace glass (Plate 181B). It was first made in Venice in the fifteenth century and in 1547 Henry VIII's "Glasse Housse" boasted a specimen of it. Although the process was soon developed to produce many-coloured filigree glass (*q.v.*), *reticello* has held its popularity into the present century.

Reticulated. A moulded pattern in diamond-like formation; also called expanded diamond.

Ribbing. Used when ridged design's wider unit is convex; gadroon ribbing. *See* Gadroon (3).

Rib or diamond-moulding. Straight or twisted lines forming diamonds or other patterns impressed upon the surface of a bowl.

Ricketts glass-works. Wine-bottles with seals are sometimes found bearing the mark

FIG. 42

shown in Fig. 42, that is to say in raised letters round the base. The name seal bearing

the words *Sam!. Archer*, illustrated in Fig. 43, is from a bottle made in the first quarter of the nineteenth century.

The Ricketts family were prominent in the

FIG. 43. Name Seal

business life of the city of Bristol between 1750 and 1850, and one or another of them was connected with such varied occupations as porter-brewing, tobacco, banking, and the manufacture of glass. Jacob Wilcox Ricketts and his brother, Richard Ricketts, were partners with John Wadham and David Evans, successively, in the Phoenix Glass-house, Temple Gate, which was renowned for good-quality cut glass comparable with that made in London and Stourbridge.

FIG. 44. Armorial Seal

In 1811 Jacob Wilcox Ricketts and his third son, Henry, together with two partners, purchased a glass-works known as the Soap-boilers' Glass-house, in Cheese Lane, St Philip's, Bristol. They continued to make cut glass at the Phoenix factory, and made bottles in their newly acquired premises, both trading under the name of Henry Ricketts and

Co. After various changes in the structure of the business it was closed finally in 1923.

Rigaree marks. Applied bands of glass tooled in parallel vertical lines to form tiny contiguous ribs; produced by the edge of a small metal wheel.

Rims. (1) Folded: edge finish of foot or bowl-top, sheared edge folded back forming double wall; called also welted (Plate 146A (*right*)); (2) galleried, nineteenth-century bowl-top finish; flaring rim having short, straight-side and flattened plane at right angles to body, thus forming cover support (Plate 147A (*left*)); (3) gauffered, on vases and occasionally pitchers; flaring with wide-scallop edge; called also ruffled; mainly nineteenth century (Plate 147B (*left centre*)); (4) sheared or plain, excess glass cut away evenly and edge smoothed by reheating (Plate 146A (*centre*).

Rolling-pins. Were originally made as salt containers during the Napoleonic wars when the salt tax was thirty times greater than the cost of the salt itself, which was sold by the bottle. The first of these rollers, produced in about 1800, were of thick bottle-glass, the

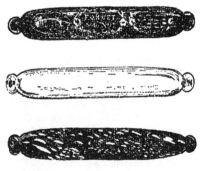

FIG. 45

open end being tightly stoppered. Each end was provided with a solid knob so that it could be safely hung in a dry place. By 1820 salt bottles were being made of coloured glass, purple, blue, mottled, and striped. The cold glass tube weighted with salt proved an excellent rolling-pin for pastry. Hanging conspicuously on the kitchen wall, the rolling-pin became a field for homely decoration, such as a text painted on a background of opaque white glass, and during the 1820s it tended to

lose its purely utilitarian purpose and became regarded as a lucky mascot, its filling chosen to suit the occasion. Gilded, painted, and enamelled, they were inscribed with mottoes and good wishes, Biblical quotations, name of the recipient, and a date; others were decorated with sea-faring subjects. Some were ornamented with the sharpened end of a specially hardened steel tool, the design being portrayed by means of small, closely spaced dots. Decorations included hounds chasing a hare, ploughing, and paddle steamers.

They were made at the glass-making centres of Bristol, Birmingham, Sunderland, and Stourbridge: reproductions have been made in
tens of thousands since 1910.

Romer, 1675–1825. A
drinking-vessel usually of
pale-green glass, consisting
of a bowl more or less spherical with a slice taken off the
top. The bowl opened into
a hollow, cylindrical stem
studded with prunts and
supported by a hollow, conical foot (Fig. 46).

FIG. 46. Romer

Rousseau, Eugène. The greatest French glass artist of the nineteenth century. He began as a dealer in decorative ceramics and appears to have devoted himself to glass from *c.* 1875. His ideas were realized by Appert Frères, one of the most progressive and well-equipped factories in Paris at the time.

Rousseau's glasses are usually made of a heavy transparent metal, tinted into a light champagne colour. Decoration is achieved through cutting, engraving, or enamel-painting, and cased and flushed glass, with cutaway patterns, can also be found. The shapes are borrowed from historical sources, German (Plate 164B) or Italian Renaissance pottery or French Baroque ornament. The Japanese fashion seems to have made a great impression on Rousseau. He reproduced Japanese ornaments and imitated the ceramic technique of running glazes, and seems even to have absorbed the subtler sides of the Japanese message, the preference for simple outlines, and the dislike of rigid symmetry and hard precision. His most famous creation is massive, sometimes crackled glass with streaks of colours, preferably purples and reds, embedded between transparent casings (Plate 164B). The effect is obtained by the use of metal oxides. The grandeur of the execution, the boldness of the colour, and the originality and taste in the decor place Rousseau's glass in a class apart among contemporary art glass.

His works were sold in his shop at 74, Boulevard Haussmann. A few are signed on the base with his name and address. At the Paris Exhibitions in 1878 and 1884 Rousseau's glass was highly admired, and his techniques were imitated, more or less successfully, in France and in other countries. In 1885 he handed over his establishment to E. Leveillé (*q.v.*), who carried on his work.

Rummer, 1760–1850. Short-stemmed drinking-glass with capacious thinly blown ovoid bowl and small foot. From 1790 a series of thicker section and on heavy feet for holding hot toddy (Fig. 47).

FIG. 47

Saint-Louis, Cristalleries de. Together with Baccarat the greatest large-scale producer of fine glass in France all through the period. Founded in 1767 as Verrerie Royale de Saint-Louis. In 1781 the first French production of lead crystal of the English type was started there, and from 1782 it was carried on on a commercial basis. The archives of the factory were to a large extent destroyed during the Second World War, and its history until 1834 is obscure. From 1839 the factory is known to have made excellent coloured glass, the earliest dated examples being from 1844. The colour-products of the middle of the century are distinguished by the brightness of their colour and the simplicity and grace of the shapes. Fresh and unpompous and astoundingly modern in appearance,

they are among the finest examples of glass made anywhere at the time (Plates 165C, 166B, and 167A).

All through the nineteenth century Cristalleries de Saint-Louis were the main producer of fine table-glass in France.

Salts with feet. Small vessel with double ogee bowls, flattened knops, and applied circular feet usually slightly sloping and sometimes scalloped. 1790s to 1850s in English flint-glass.

FIG. 48

Scalloped foot. *See* Foot (U.S.).

Scalloping. A rim outline formed by a series of semicircles with edges ground sharply until about 1750. Castellated rims date from about 1770.

Scent bottles. In England scent bottles made of coloured and of opaque white glass are not uncommon. Some of the latter can be attributed to Bristol manufactories because of their creamy colour and their complete opacity, and because the painting on them is related to that on more important specimens of white glass. Of coloured glass scent bottles, it is not possible to say more than that they were probably made at Bristol. Many of the surviving examples resemble closely in their decoration the work to be seen on watch-cases and other articles known to have been made in London. As it is known that glass "smelling bottles" were being made there as early as 1752, perhaps a London origin was common to them all (Plate 161C). Scent bottles continued to be made in the prevailing types of glass until the 1830s, when, for half a century, they were made in huge numbers and every conceivable shape and colour.

Sealed glasses. Early English flint-glass tableware to which were applied small glass discs impressed with the maker's mark: raven's head, George Ravenscroft, September 1675–1681; the King's arms, Henry Holden, glass-maker to the King from 1683; lion and coronet, Duke of Buckingham.

Seals. The circular glass seals were almost certainly impressed with an original intaglio made of brass. This was made either by a professional engraver working on his own behalf or, in the case of a glass-works specializing in sealed bottles, by one on the staff of the manufactory. No name of any craftsman connected with this particular branch of the art of die-sinking has been recorded, and the makers of these seals, as most of the makers of more elaborate desk seals, have remained anonymous.

Glass bottle seals fall into three categories, whether they bear dates or not, and may be conveniently classified as: armorial, name or initial, and "others", the last including merchant's marks, Masonic signs, and the names of houses.

Seeds. Minute air bubbles in the metal, indication that the glass-house could not raise furnace temperature high enough to eliminate all air bubbles trapped among the raw materials.

Set-in and set-over covers. *See* Covers.

Shaft. Usually applied to section between socket or font and base of candlestick or lamp; in blown glass, applied forms similar to stems; in early pressed glass, in two sections – one with base and one with socket, joined by a merese (Plate 147B); in later pressed glass, in one with socket and base.

Shakers. Term usually preceded by salt or pepper; casters.

Sheared lip. Plain; *see* Rims (4).

Skånska Glasbruket, 1691–1762. Swedish glass-manufactory situated in Northern Scania. Skånska Glasbruket was founded by a certain Göran Adlersten, an enterprising civil servant of the locality. The factory began by making purely utilitarian glass, but in 1715 production of decorative glass was taken up. It lasted until 1762, when the works were destroyed by fire.

South Jersey tradition. Tradition of glass-blowing and decorating presumed to have had its American beginnings in Wistar's and other South Jersey houses; *see* South Jersey type.

South Jersey types. Generic term for individual pieces blown from bottle- and window-glass in natural colours, occasionally artificial, fashioned by free-blowing and manipulation, plain and decorated by glass applied to itself and tooled, very rarely pattern-moulded; first associated with the Wistar's eighteenth-century glass-works, southern Jersey, U.S.A.; then later houses in the area; now known to have been blown in most Eastern bottle- and window-glass houses into the late nineteenth century; called folk art in American glass, largely because of individual rendering and centuries-old traditional techniques in blowing and decorating; types of decoration include the lily pad, prunts, quilling, swagging, picots, bird finials, threading, and crimping.

Spangled glass. Molten glass rolled over flakes of mica or metal particles which fused when heated. Made by Hobbs, Brockunier & Company, Wheeling, West Virginia, U.S.A., 1883; called "Vasa Murrhina"; blue flecked with silver and gold and other combinations are known. Made also in England and Bohemia.

Stems.

Dates apply to English glass.

Air-twist, 1740–65. (*a*) Single-twist air spirals in a drawn stem formed by the extension of air bubbles: multiple spirals throughout the period (Plate 158B), from 1745 two or four corkscrews; not until about 1750 were threads of uniform thickness and spaced regularly; (*b*) single-twist in a three-piece glass: 1740–65 the shank cut from long lengths made by extension of air bubbles; from 1750 spirals made by a mould process, filaments finely drawn and coiled with precision in some thirty variations; (*c*) compound-twist in three-piece glass: 1760–5 in a dozen variations.

Baluster, 1685–1760. Stem consisting of a pure baluster form which might be inverted: also a baluster associated with various knopped motifs; (*a*) 1685–1725: heavy inverted baluster with solid bowl-base and interior bowl depth almost invariably less than stem length; (*b*) 1700–25: simple knop such as angular, annulated, cushioned, or drop knop, with or without a baluster; from 1710 acorn, cylinder, or mushroom knops; from 1715 true baluster alone or with various knops and a pair of balusters placed head to head between a pair of knops; (c) 1725–65: light balusters, true or inverted, supporting bowls with thin bases; illustrated on trade cards of the 1760s. Between 1725 and 1740 the stem and collar baluster in which a merese separated bowl from stem.

Colour-twist, 1755–75. Spirals of glass, opaque or transparent, singly or in combination: commonly in blue, green, or ruby, less frequently in red, yellow, sapphire, black, and greyish blue.

Composite. Built up of two or more parts welded together; found on U.S. drinking vessels, compotes, candlesticks, occasionally on covered sweetmeat dishes, sugar-bowls, pitchers.

Compound-twist, 1760–1800. A pair of air or enamel spiral formations, one within the other: a central spiral or (in enamel) a closely knotted central cable with another formation spiralling around it. In straight stems only (Plates 158C and G, 156A and D, 159A and C).

Drawn, from 1682. A plain knopped or baluster stem drawn directly from a gathering of metal at the base of the bowl (Plate 158A); (a) to 1725 in large, heavy forms; (b) 1720–45 with waisted thick-based bowl; (c) from 1735 the standard pattern was a straw shank drawn from a trumpet-shaped bowl; by 1770 had degenerated into a thin-stemmed tavern glass.

Facet-cut, c. 1748–1800. Almost invariably drawn stems (Plate 158D); (a) elongated diamond facets, two or three times longer than width with angles of 120 degrees and 60 degrees: found throughout the period; (b) 1755–80, elongated hexagonal facets; (c) 1760–80, shouldered and centrally knopped stems; (d) 1760–75, scale facets; (e) 1770–1800, facets cut deeper than formerly; (f) 1790–1800, stems shorter than formerly.

Hollow, early 1760s to late 1780s. Stem in the form of a hollow cylinder, sometimes, though rarely, knopped.

Incised, 1678–1780. Alternating ridges and grooves spiralling around the stem surface; (a) 1678–1720, incised balusters (Plate 158E);

(b) 1740–60, closely spaced medium to coarse spirals with almost imperceptible reduction of stem diameter at centre; (c) 1660–1780, finer, more uniform, incisions on stem of unvarying diameter.

Knopped, 1700–55. Stem composed of four to six knops, none sufficiently large to dominate its fellows; (a) to 1740 heavy knops, well-modelled until 1735; (b) from 1740 light knops.

Mercury-twist, 1745–65. Air-twists of exceptionally large diameter spiralling down the centre of a stem in close coils, or a pair of corkscrew threads.

Mixed-twist, 1750–70. A combination of air-twist and opaque-white twist in a single stem.

Moulded pedestal, 1705–85. Known also as Silesian and shouldered stem; on good-quality ware until about 1730; (a) 1705–20, four-sided moulded stem, never collared at the base; by 1710 the shoulders were being shaped in the form of four arches; (b) 1720–40, sides moulded with deep, vertical reeds (Plate 158F); (c) 1727–35, six-sided pedestal; (d) 1730–50, eight-sided pedestal lacking precision and definition (Plate 156E); (e) 1750–80, thin, coarse-ribbed versions of the earlier types; (f) 1765–85, well-designed pedestal stem with four or six sides enriched with cutting.

Opaque-twist, mid-1740s to end of eighteenth century. Spirals of dense-textured white enamel, varying from fine hairs to broad solid tapes; single or compound in more than a hundred variations; (a) straight stem with single twist (Plate 161E); (b) with shoulder or central knop and single twist, usually multiple spiral; (c) straight stem with compound-twist – the most common type – from 1760 (Plates 158C, G, and 161A); (d) with knops in various positions, shoulder, central, base, or any two or all three, with compound-twist, from 1760.

Rib-twist. See Incised.

Silesian. See Moulded Pedestal.

Single-twist, late 1740s to early 1800s. One formation of air, enamel, or coloured threads spiralling around a clear glass centre, or a pair of reciprocal spirals.

Straight, plain, 1725 to nineteenth century. On three-piece glasses; after 1748 tended to be thinner than formerly.

Stuck shank. A stem made from a separate gather of metal welded to the base of the bowl.

Vertical flute-cutting, mid-1780s–1800. (*a*) To 1790, stem fluted above and below a central diamond-cut knop; (*b*) 1790–1800, long, straight flutes from foot to bowl, either notched on alternate angles, horizontally grooved, or sliced.

Wormed. See Air-twist.

Wrythen. See Incised.

Step. A flattened glass button connecting the stem of a rummer with its foot.

Stiegel tradition. Tradition of glass blowing and decorating by use of pattern-moulds, presumed to have had its American beginnings in Stiegel's second Manheim glassworks (1769–74). *See* Stiegel type (3).

Stiegel type. Term applied to main types of ware produced in Stiegel's Manheim, U.S.A., glass-houses, *c.* 1765–74. (1) Engraved (shallow copper-wheel) and (2) enamelled glass like common Continental commercial wares of mid-eighteenth–early nineteenth century, today called peasant glass in Europe (Plate 145). (3) Pattern-moulded glass, usually flint-glass, like the British ware produced in the early nineteenth century; coloured (mainly blues, greens, and amethysts) and colourless. *See also* Diamond-daisy and Daisy-in-hexagon.

Stiegel-type salt. *See* Salts with feet.

Stippling. Minute raised dots forming the background in lacy glass, glitter-producing device never used in glass-making until made possible by mechanical pressing; an earmark of lacy glass (*q.v.*).

Stones. Red and black specks within the fabric of early flint-glass, the result of imperfect fusion between oxide of lead and silica.

Strap handle. *See* Handles.

Straw shank. *See* Stems, drawn.

Striae. Apparent undulating markings within the metal, perfectly vitrified and transparent, show the metal to be of uneven composition because insufficiently molten before working.

String-course or string-rim. The raised band near the top of the neck of a bottle, which provided a grip under which the string for securing a cork or other cover might be fastened. In seventeenth-century bottles this took the form of a single band of glass about a quarter of an inch below the orifice, and it remains a feature of subsequent bottles.

Strömbergshyttan. Modern Swedish art-glass manufactory situated in Småland.

Stuck shank. *See* Stems.

Sugar-basins. Have a boldly concave outline and a flat base, and are for the most part boldly cut with diamond patterns or moulded with thick gadroons.

Sulphides. Known contemporaneously as *crystallo ceramie* and by some collectors as sulphides or glass-encrusted cameos. The process was patented (No. 4424, 1819) by Apsley Pellatt, London. A pressed bas relief of unglazed white stoneware was embedded in flawless flint-glass, assuming the glowing loveliness of silver. Many of these reliefs were embedded in paperweights, but others enriched tableware and jewellery. Most commonly the sulphide was a profile portrait of a contemporary celebrity: profile portraits were also made to the commission of sitters now unknown.

Earlier crude examples, greyish in tint, had been made in Bohemia and France: later the French glass-houses at Baccarat, St Louis, and Clichy copied Pellatt's invention with success.

Sunken panel. *See* Panelling.

Superimposed decoration. Any decoration or device fashioned by tooling layer of glass formed from a pearl. *See* Lily-pad.

Swagging. Superimposed layer tooled into wavy formation, usually crested by a picot.

Swirl. Familiar name for a paperweight composed of coloured canes radiating spirally from the top.

Swirled ribbing. Pattern-moulded design formed by twisting vertical ribs impressed in a gather inserted in ribbed or fluted dip mould; English, wrythen ornamentation.

Swords, sceptres, crowns, and hats. In England examples of these articles made from glass are occasionally seen. Their original purpose is made clear by the following paragraph from the *Daily Post*, November 14, 1738: "Bristol, Nov. 11. – Yesterday the Prince and Princess of Wales paid their promised visit to this City. . . . The Companies of the City

made a magnificent appearance in their formalities, marching two by two, preceding the
Corporation and the Royal Guests. The Company of Glassmen went first dressed in white
Holland shorts, on horseback, some with
swords, others with crowns and sceptres in
their hands, made of glass." It should be
pointed out, however, that few (if any) of the
surviving examples of these friggers are of
such an early date as 1738, as these items continued to be made and used for a long time
afterwards.

Glass hats were made for similar purposes
to the above; it is said that they were very
uncomfortable to wear.

Table-centres. These usually consisted of
numerous glass figures, and were made in the
eighteenth century. An unusually large, and
very fine example, in the museum at Murano,
Italy, is in the form of a model garden with
balustrades, urns, hedges, and a central fountain, all made of glass (Plate 183C). Birmingham glass-men during the mid-nineteenth
century made large numbers of lavishly designed table centres, particularly George
Bacchus & Sons.

Tale-glass. A second-quality metal taken
from the top of the pot, and sold more cheaply
than the lower, finer metal.

Tears. Bubbles of air enclosed within the
metal for decorative purposes: first appeared
in stems (Plate 158A); from 1715 to about 1760
clusters of spherical or comma-shaped tears
appeared in bowl-base, knop, and finial.

Thread circuit. A thin trail of applied
glass encircling a bowl rim or decorating the
neck of a vessel.

FIG. 49

Three-piece glasses. Bowl, stem, and foot
made separately and welded together.

Tiffany glass. A type of U.S. art glass;
made by Louis Comfort Tiffany (1848-1933)

in New York in the late 1890s; many pieces
marked *Favrile*. Process fused various colours
by heat, then exposed the piece to fumes of
vaporized metals; pieces were hand blown in
fanciful forms; spinning and twisting during
blowing process produced wavy lines suggestive of leaves, waves, or peacock feathers;
bluish-green and gold, light mother-of-pearl,
red, and other more unusual colours; is characteristically iridescent with a satiny finish in
imitation of ancient glass (Plates 154B, 155).

Tint. A residual colour tinge inherent in the
ingredients from which the metal is composed.

Toasting glass. A flute of fine metal with
tall stem drawn to a diameter of one-eighth
to one-quarter of an inch (Plate 158G).

Toastmaster's glass. A thick bowl designed to magnify its capacity, on a tall stem.
Short, deceptive glasses, known as sham
drams, were used by tavern-keepers, 1775-
1850.

Tobacco pipes. Were made at all the glass
centres in England, at first with small bowls
and solid stems of transparent colour often
enriched with spiralling threads of coloured or
opaque white enamel. They lack the affluent
air of the later pipes blown from high-quality
glass. From the mid-1840s their bowls follow-

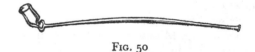

FIG. 50

ed the designs of the new pipe bowls of porcelain with long, slender mouth-pieces. Others
may be found imitating early Victorian briar
pipes. Measurements range from 10 to 25
inches overall with occasional giants more
than a yard long. They were in considerable
demand as wall decorations for small homes.

The most common form has a large bowl
with a flared and welted rim, the mouth-piece
with its curved stem widening as it approaches
the bowl, but reduced to a very narrow tube
at the bowl junction. These are to be found in
all combinations of colour, latticinio work in
milk-white and pink being common. Red
glass was popular and is found in qualities
varying from brilliant unflawed ruby with
opaque horizontal lines on bowl and bobbin

stem to poor-quality colour with striations and other flaws in the glass.

Toddy-lifter. A pipette with bulbous or decanter-shaped body for lifting hot toddy from bowl to drinking-glass, *c.* 1800–40.

Tortoise shell. Pale brownish-amber glass with darker splotches; another glass made in imitation of other ware which was popular in the late nineteenth century; attributed to the Sandwich Glass Company, U.S.A.

Trailed ornament. Looped threads of glass applied to the surface of a bowl or foot.

Trailing, pinched. Applied bands of glass pinched into wavy formation.

Tumblers. Were exported from Murano in fine glass and made in most European countries in poor quality throughout the seventeenth century. By the end of the century they were made in flint-glass with vertical sides and a slightly rounded base with a medium kick. From about 1710 they might be lightly touched with shallow cut diamond-facets or large diamonds and triangles. Pint, half-pint, and quarter-pint tumblers were advertised.

Not until the early 1740s were glass tumblers designed with outward-sloping sides and a height about double the base diameter. The heavy-based waisted tumbler had come into use. From the late 1750s they were made without a kick, and all-over shallow cutting became slightly deeper and a wider variety of motifs used. Finger fluting encircling the lower half of tumblers dates from the same period, at first flat and broad, little more than the surface of the glass being removed. As the century progressed flutes were cut deeper and in varying widths, and between 1790 and 1820 the crests might be notched. Deep relief cutting is found on heavy tumblers from 1790, some fifty varieties and combinations being found after 1805.

Twisted ribbing. Swirled ribs or flutes; on solid canes, used as stems, sometimes handles; English, incised or reeded, *see* Stems.

Two-piece glasses. Stem drawn in a piece from the bowl and a foot added.

Uranium glass. First produced, from the metallic element uranium, in 1857 by Lloyd and Summerfield, Birmingham, using the first gas-regenerating furnace to be built. Early uranium glass was green; it was later made in shades ranging from rose-pink to pale yellow and known as Burmese glass. It can have a dull or glossy finish.

Venetian glass. Thinly blown soda-glass, worked at a low temperature, cooling quickly, and requiring great speed of manipulation. Lacks the brilliance and toughness of flint-glass.

Vermicular collar. A wavy trail of glass encircling a stem or decanter neck.

Verzelini, Giacomo. Verzelini (1522–1606) acquired the Crutched Friars Glass-house, London, on the death of Jean Carré, whose chief assistant he was. In 1575 he was appointed glass-maker to Elizabeth I and granted a monopoly to make "Venetian glass".

Vinter, Villas. Danish or Norwegian born glass-engraver at Nöstetangen, Norway. He was assistant to Köhler, who appears to have taught him the craft. He worked as a freelance after 1777, and signed engravings from his hand are known from as late as 1797 (Plate 178A).

Walking sticks. Glass walking sticks were made in England during the nineteenth century, and some of these no doubt came from the glass-works at Bristol and Nailsea. They were of various types, and were made solid or hollow. The former were occasionally made with lengths of twisted coloured glass within the clear glass stick. The hollow ones were often filled with coloured sweets and are sometimes to be found with their contents intact.

Waterford. The earliest record of flint-glass making at Waterford was discovered by Westropp in *The Dublin Journal*, 1729: "a glasshouse near Waterford now producing all sorts of flint-glass, double and single . . . sold at reasonable rates by Joseph Harris at Waterford, merchant". This glass-house was at Gurteens, three miles from the city, and operated until 1739, producing a negligible quantity of glass.

The now celebrated Waterford glass-house started production in 1784, financed with a capital of £10,000 by George and William Penrose, merchants. The Irish Parliament, however, granted the Penroses a subsidy to cover the expense of building and equipping their glass-house. As works manager they employed

John Hill, member of a family operating the important Coalbournhill Glass-house near Stourbridge. In evidence given before a committee examining commercial relations between Great Britain and Ireland in 1785, John Blades, a leading cut-glass manufacturer in London, stated that, "Mr Hill, a great manufacturer of Stourbridge, has lately gone to Waterford, and has taken the best set of Workmen he could get in the County of Worcester." There is no doubt that the Penroses installed a furnace of the Perrott type costing more than £3,000, such as were already in use at Stourbridge. The Penroses sold flint-glass on a ready-money basis only.

The Penrose glass-house was bought in 1799 by Ramsay, Gatchell, and Barcroft, who built a new factory in Old Tan Yard, advertising the old premises to be let. It is to be assumed that the most modern innovations were included in the new furnace, and that cutting was carried out by means of annealed cast-iron tools, harder and longer wearing than anything formerly available. With these were produced the lavishly decorated cut-glass now inevitably associated with Waterford. Not until 1817 was a steam-driven cutting machine installed.

Gatchell had become sole proprietor by 1811, and with successive partners the firm remained in the family. At an exhibition in Dublin, 1850, George Gatchell displayed table-glass "all of opaque blue, and white or crystal". At the Great Exhibition, 1851, he exhibited a magnificent "etagere or ornamental centre for a banqueting table, consisting of forty pieces of cut-glass, so fitted to each other as to require no connecting sockets of other material; quart and pint decanters cut in hollow prisms. Centre vase or bowl on detached tripod stand. Vases and covers. Designed and executed at the Waterford Glass Works." This was Gatchell's swan-song; his final effort to compete with England was a failure, and he closed the glass-house later in the same year.

Few collectors realize that Waterford imported glass from England for merchanting purposes; Belfast and Cork were also supplied with Waterford glass.

Waterford blue. *See* Blue tint.

Waterloo Glass-house Company, Cork. Established in 1815 by Daniel Foley, a glass and china seller of Hanover Street, who set up as a specialist in extensive table-services in cut-glass for military messes, particularly for regiments occupying France. By the end of 1816 he employed about a hundred men and women, many experienced workers deserting from the Cork Glass-house Company under the lure of higher wages. On Christmas Eve, 1816, an editorial in the *Cork Overseer* recorded that "Foley's workmen are well selected, from whose superior skill the most beautiful glass will shortly make its appearance to dazzle the eyes of the public, and to outshine those of any other competitor. He is to treat his men at Christmas with a whole roasted ox and everything adequate. They have a new band of music with glass instruments with bassoon serpents, horns, trumpets, etc, and they have a glass pleasure boat, a cot and a glass set which when seen will astonish the world." Glass trumpets were made for sale. A steam engine was installed to operate the cutting wheels and other machinery, thus drastically reducing costs.

Geoffrey O'Connell was taken into partnership during 1825, the firm operating as Foley and O'Connell, Waterloo Glass Works Company. They advertised that they had introduced a new annealing process which enabled them to guarantee their flint-glass to withstand hot water without breaking. The excise duty was too heavy a burden, and in mid-1830 the firm ceased operating. Fifteen months or so later it was reopened by O'Connell, who introduced up-to-date methods of blown-moulding and advertised that he had "restored one hundred families to employment". An advertisement in the *Cork Comet* four months later announced that the Waterloo Glass Works continued to enjoy military patronage.

The venture could not compete with English prices, however, and in 1835 he was made bankrupt owing to his failure to pay excise duties. The *Cork Constitution* contained an auctioneer's advertisement regarding the sale of plant and stock "of splendid cut and plain glass at the Waterloo Glass Works until the entire splendid stock is disposed of, consisting of rich decanters, jugs, salad bowls, celery and pickle glasses, dessert plates and dishes, tumblers and wine-glasses of every description, hall and staircase globes, side lights, water crafts and tumblers".

Welted rim. *See* Rims.

Whimsey. U.S. term used for odd or unusual pieces, such as hats, slippers, buttonhooks, made by individual workmen for themselves or their families; or the adaptation of a conventional form to some odd or unusual shape or use.

Wine-glass coolers, 1750s–1860s. *See* Monteiths.

FIG. 51

Witch balls and **reflecting globes.** From late in the seventeenth century glass-makers blew short-necked spherical bottles of clear flint-glass or thick, dark bottle-glass. Their shape was inspired by reflecting globes, but they were intended as containers for holy water. Such a bottle was hung in the living-room or elsewhere as protection against the malign influence of witches. Eventually it became an emblem of good luck.

Late in the eighteenth century spherical bottles of green and blue glass were made for this purpose, sometimes inscribed with scriptural texts in gold. Early in the nineteenth century Nailsea made coloured balls in a variety of tints, such as green, crimson, gold, and deep blue. Soon these were enlivened with various forms of decoration: some are spotted; some show either opaque white or air-thread spirals in the thickness of the glass. Another type has four or more loops of coloured glass festooning the surface of the ball. From about 1830 transfer pictures might be applied to the interior surface. As a background to these the interior was coated white, marbled with various vivid colours. Many were made without any opening and intended as jug covers. These colourful balls were made from about 1780 until 1865.

Glass spheres, lustred to resemble shining silver and capable of mirroring a whole room in miniature, were originally Continental products of fragile soda-glass, but from about 1690 English glass-men made them in flint-glass. Their interior surfaces were silvered with a preparation composed of two parts bismuth, one part lead, one part tin, and four parts mercury. The lead, tin, and bismuth were melted together and the mercury added when the mixture was almost cold. It was then poured into the sphere by means of a paper funnel reaching almost to the bottom. By slowly rotating the ball, the liquid amalgam was spread in a thin film over the glass, to which it adhered.

In these early balls there was considerable distortion in the reflection. In 1843 a method was discovered of coating the interior surface with real silver. Reflecting globes have a slightly yellow tint. An improved method was patented in 1848 and "so great was their power of reflection that the entire details of a large apartment are caught upon them with surprising minuteness and clearness of definition and in amusing perspective". Such glass balls were made in a wide range of metallic hues and in sizes varying from 3 to 30 inches. Originally termed watch balls, this name became corrupted to witch balls.

Writhing. Surface twisting or swirled ribbing or fluting on bowl or stem.

Yard-of-ale. A yard-of-ale is a drinking-glass measuring some 3 feet or so in length. There is a record of one dating from as early as the year 1685, when John Evelyn noted in his Diary on February 10: "Being sent to by the Sheriff of the County to appeare, and assist in proclayming the King [James II], I went the next day to Bromely [Bromley, Kent], where I met the Sheriff and the Commander of the Kentish Troop, with an appearance, I suppose, of above 500 horse, and innumerable people, two of his Majesty's trumpets and a Serjeant with other officers, who having drawn up the horse in a large field neere the towne, march'd thence, with swords drawne, to the market-place, where making a ring, after sound of trumpets

FIG. 52

and silence made, the High Sheriff read the proclaiming titles to his bailiffe, who repeated them aloud, and then after many shouts of the people, his Majesty's health being drunk in a flint glasse of a yard long, by the Sheriff, Commander, Officers and cheife Gentlemen, they all dispers'd, and I return'd." From which it would appear that, at any rate during the late seventeenth century, such feats of glass-making and of drinking were reserved for special public occasions.

Considering their fragile nature, it is not surprising that surviving yards-of-ale are seldom above a century old. The greater number of such survivors are not straightforward drinking-vessels, but trick glasses. In them the flared mouth tapers at length to a bulb at the foot, which ensures that the drinker cannot rest the vessel, and once started the glass must be drained completely or the contents will be spilled. The trick about these glasses is that when the liquid has been nearly all consumed and the glass is raised above the horizontal to finish the remainder, the air trapped in the bulb by the action of lifting the glass forces the residuum violently into the face of the unlucky victim.

Quite a number of the glasses must have been produced in the glass-houses of Bristol and Nailsea, but here again it is not possible to distinguish them from others that were made elsewhere.

Zirat Fladske. *See* Decanters, Scandinavian.

JEWELLERY

Medieval jewellery is less well known than classical Greek and Roman work, since the custom of burying valuables with their owner was discontinued in the Christian era. Few jewels survived the ravages of time. Their very nature made them easily convertible into ready cash at moments of financial stress, when precious stones were broken out of settings consigned to the melting-pot. Literary descriptions and pictorial records, such as illuminations and monumental effigies, help at times to show how jewellery was applied to contemporary costume. Fortunately, much medieval goldwork survived in the sanctuary of church treasures, forming part of liturgical objects. There are reliquaries, portable altars, and altar crosses studded with jewels, statues of saints and of the Virgin wearing jewelled crowns and pectoral ornaments.

Some techniques, known from antiquity, continued in use throughout the Middle Ages. Among these were filigree and granulation work, consisting of small pellets of gold surrounding stones in high box settings, often antique gems: cameos and intaglios. Stones were rarely cut in medieval times, but usually left in their natural *cabochon* shape, which is oval; they were always polished and backed with metal foil to intensify and reflect colour. Among the personal jewellery of this early period are rings, ear-rings, brooches, necklaces, and pendants, often invested with symbolic, magic, protective, or religious significance. The wearing of images of patron saints was particularly popular.

During the Renaissance, pagan and Christian art begin to harmonize, and therewith the history of religious jewellery comes to an end. The magic aspect, however, was not forgotten, and the belief in specific virtues of precious stones remained as strong as ever. Hence the custom of mounting toad-stones or dragons' teeth in rings, serpents' tongues and fragments of narwhal horn in pendants. Great importance was attributed to their inherent prophylactic qualities, which legends supported. Gradually, during the early sixteenth century the jeweller emerged from the goldsmiths' guild, an organization which had previously directed his efforts to the service of the Church. This emancipation coincided with the development of a prosperous *bourgeoisie* and the raising of the respectable matron and housewife to a socially important figure, who extended her patronage to the goldsmith. Henceforth jewellery becomes an integral part of costume, dependent upon changing fashions, which, in turn, reflect the taste and aspirations of a splendour-loving society. Painter-engravers began to design pattern books for jewellers, and it is well to remember that many Renaissance painters were sons or pupils of goldsmiths, Verrocchio, Holbein, and Dürer among them. For the first time in the history of jewel-making the influence of individual artists was felt.

Hans Holbein the Younger was foremost among those who determined the new pictorial style of Renaissance jewellery. In his drawings and engravings for the goldsmith, and in portraits of ladies and gentlemen, richly attired with rings, necklaces, and pendants of latest design, Holbein contributed much towards the creation of a new type of jewellery, centred around the human figure. Scrollwork cartouches supersede the once ubiquitous Gothic thistle leaf, tracery, and pinnacle, while the sparkle of precious stones rivals with bright enamel colours and opalescent pearls.

The hat badge or *enseigne*, as it was then called, is among the most original creations of the period. Contemporary portraits by Bartolomeo Veneto of Italy, François Clouet of France, and Hans Holbein of Germany and England illustrate how men of fashion wore these badges in their berets. Originally derived from the medieval pilgrim sign, the hat badge revealed the wearer's personality in the choice of subject-matter. Humanist interests, based upon classical education, account for the noticeable preference for antique cameos, mounted in contemporary setting, with loops provided for attachment to the hat. Mythological themes, with incidents from the happy lives and adventures of Greek gods on earth, abound. Religious subjects become rare, they usually include the figure of a patron saint, to confirm the bond between wearer and protector. Some hat badges have frames of black-and-white *champlevé* enamel arabesques of a kind believed to have been first introduced in Venice by Oriental goldsmiths.

Finger rings of the Renaissance period show great variety. The signet ring, related to the hat badge inasmuch as it also defines the owner's personality, often contains an antique or contemporary intaglio, a personal cipher, device, or initials, which served as seal. Purely ornamental rings are richly enamelled, the centre stone flat or table cut, supported by caryatid figures extending to either side of the band. Some rings are provided with secret compartments, to serve specific purposes, such as the possible concealing of poison, a practice

always exaggerated in novels. *Memento mori*, or mourning rings, reveal a white-enamelled skeleton beneath the hinged cover of a black-enamelled coffin, and are usually inscribed with the name and date of the deceased. Other types include the fede ring, also used for weddings, made of a band terminating in joined hands, which often hold a heart or a precious stone. Religious rings, engraved with a crucifix or the instruments of the Passion of Christ, are never quite absent, but they are at times outnumbered by those invoking magic through cabalistic signs, or those set with a toad-stone, actually the tooth of a fossil, worn as a charm against evil. Towards the end of the century, especially in England, rings and pendants containing a portrait miniature gained great popularity.

The Renaissance pendant, in all its magnificence, is the most representative jewel of the period. Goldsmith and painter-engraver combine efforts as never before to lend pictorial qualities to the jewel and to introduce new story-telling elements of individual interest. Human figures, enamelled in white, form the centre of elaborate architectural and ornamental stage settings, composed of several layers of pierced and enamelled goldwork, held together by diminutive bolts and nuts. The reverse of the pendants is usually decorated with arabesques and grotesques in translucent or opaque enamel, following the designs of well-known engravers, such as Androuet Ducerceau, Daniel Mignot, Etienne Delaune, and Theodore de Bry. Favourite mythological themes were Diana with her hounds, Venus and Cupid, the Judgement of Paris, and Jupiter pursuing amorous adventures. Symbolic figures include Charity, Faith and Fortitude, and the Pelican in her Piety, while the most popular religious subjects were the Virgin Mary or St George. Baroque pearls form the bodies of birds and animals, or of more fantastic creatures: dragons, hippocamps, mermen and mermaids, tritons and nereids. Other pendants, from the region of the Adriatic Sea, are shaped as ships with full sails, outlined by strings of tiny seed-pearls; these last continued to be made until the nineteenth century. Yet another kind, worn on a heavy chain, incorporated coins, medals, or a badge, their weighty character in keeping with the dignity of office.

Pendants combining the useful with the ornamental were worn at the end of long belts. They include small prayer-books in jewelled bindings (girdle books), and pomanders, or containers for spices and scent, opening into compartments like the sections of an orange. Occasionally toothpicks were worn suspended around the neck as jewels, as were also various charms.

Renaissance necklaces are of extravagant length, encircling the neck repeatedly and reaching down to the waist. Composed of pierced and enamelled links with precious stones, frequently interspersed with pearls, these chains form an integral part of costume, and are, more often than not, matched by ear-rings, bracelets, belts, and buttons. A central pendant, attached to necklace and dress, stresses the contrast between the static qualities of a pictorial jewel and the flexibility of chain links. Their basic design is formed by conventional scrollwork, which continues in countless variations until floral motifs take their place during the seventeenth century. The dainty enamelled chains, found at Cheapside in London, exhibited at the British and the London Museums, give an excellent example of this new style, composed as they are of daisies and other soft-petalled blossoms. Their lightness of touch and texture brings to mind the garden poems of Robert Herrick, whose father was court jeweller to Queen Elizabeth.

With the invention of the rose diamond cut in Holland shortly after 1640 the whole character of jewellery begins to change. The interest shifts from the pictorial to a display of precious stones in settings designed to complement them. Preceded by the table cut, which gave the diamond a mirror-like surface, and, more rarely, by the sharply pointed stone which could serve for engraving and incising, the rose-cut allowed the all-over faceting of diamonds, a method by which their fire and sparkle increased through additional reflection of light. From then on the value of most jewels becomes dependent upon the quality of diamonds and precious stones rather than the finer points of enamel and

goldsmiths' work, which tradition connected only too readily with the name of the most representative goldsmith of the Renaissance, Benvenuto Cellini.

Jewels of the seventeenth century reveal a growing taste for precious stones rather than for elaborate goldwork, with special emphasis upon the diamond. Opaque enamel painted on white ground begins to supersede the translucent kind on gold, characteristic of earlier pieces. Such painted enamel is found on all types of jewellers' work, including watch and miniature cases and mounts for vessels carved of semi-precious stones. Jewels of this period are now exceedingly rare, and fine seventeenth-century enamelling is most likely to be found on watch-cases and lockets; outstanding are those painted by the Toutin family at Blois and the Huet family of Geneva, both active during the second half of the seventeenth century. If one turns over one of these enamelled jewels to examine the back it will probably reveal a miniature-like application of enamel on white ground, forming floral patterns in natural colours, especially tulips and fritillaries, a fashion originating in Holland.

The most characteristic jewels of the late seventeenth and early eighteenth centuries were two types of brooch, worn at the centre of the bodice; they are to be seen in countless portraits of the period, in particular those of the Dutch school. The first was of girandole design, with a large centre stone around which smaller stones were grouped, and with three large pendant pearls. The second type consisted of a large openwork "Sévigné" bow, from which hung a cross usually with one or more intervening links between. Settings, of silver or gold, were finely carved to resemble foliage. The diamond became increasingly fashionable and was soon set almost exclusively in silver, gold being reserved for coloured stones, particularly the emerald, which Spanish jewellers incorporated so attractively in brooches, pendants, and pendant crosses of openwork design. Silver was greatly favoured for the setting of diamonds; being colourless, it was less obtrusive than the brighter gold. Finally, with the introduction of the brilliant-cut early in the eighteenth century, the effectiveness of the stone could be exploited to fullest advantage. The rose diamond, with its twenty-four or, at the most, thirty-six facets, seemed subdued and dull in comparison with the brilliant, which has fifty-eight facets. Today rose-diamond jewellery in original eighteenth-century settings, however, outnumbers by far any similar ornaments enriched by brilliants. The reason is that rose diamonds were no longer considered worth resetting, whereas brilliants have been transferred to jewels of later design.

Floral designs remained popular throughout the century, at first set in diamonds and of rather heavy and dignified character. About the middle of the century coloured stones returned to favour, composed as flower sprays, in which the settings are almost invisible. Until then each stone had its individual place within the composition, but now smaller stones, grouped together, formed the design, while the metal setting was concealed as completely as possible. Rococo decoration, though most successfully applied to snuffboxes, étuis, and all the favourite toys of the lady of fashion, had little effect upon jewellery design beyond lending impetus to the already apparent trend towards lighter designs.

Flower sprays composed entirely of diamonds continued to be made, with little variation of design, during the nineteenth century. However, the setting of precious stones underwent certain changes. Until about the close of the eighteenth century all stones were enclosed in collets or boxes, foiled at the back to intensify their colour. During the nineteenth century settings were left open at the back and the stone held in position by means of claws. Thus more light could surround the stone, though excluding at once all possibilities of improving their colour artificially. Therefore it would be true to state that most stones now used are of finer quality. During the nineteenth century the back of the open silver setting of diamonds was lined with a thin layer of gold. These open settings were adopted for all except "peasant" jewellery, and their presence or absence is a fairly decisive indication of date.

Standards of workmanship remained high until the end of the eighteenth century; though the decoration of the reverse of jewels with engraving or enamelling was discontinued. Cheap jewellery was not by any means unknown; glass pastes were used instead of stones, crystal or marcasite instead of diamonds. Porcelain, Wedgwood ware, and cut-steel all enjoyed periods of popularity as inexpensive substitutes for precious stones. But about the end of the eighteenth century production of jewellery by mechanical means began, with the inevitable consequence of a decline in standards of execution and design. Cheap fancy stones were set in mounts of thin stamped gold and wire filigree. The results are flashy, but owing to the thinness of the metal used the jewels are extremely flimsy. This same criticism may be made of much of the jewellery of the nineteenth century, of which vast quantities survive. Such was the enthusiasm of the manufacturers for experiment and variety that it is difficult to define its character succinctly. The eclecticism which is so marked a feature of Victorian art is just as strongly manifested in its jewellery. There are borrowings from all the expected historical sources and from many less likely ones as well; to the Romanesque, Gothic, and Renaissance style which formed the main sources of Victorian art we may add Indian and North African designs, copied from objects shown at the international exhibitions, and Egyptian, Assyrian, Etruscan, and Scythian designs derived from objects discovered in the course of nineteenth-century excavations. Outstanding among nineteenth-century jewellers was a small group of Italian craftsmen who produced work of the highest quality and technical perfection, though strongly leaning upon ancient designs. These include Castellani, a Roman jeweller who rediscovered the Etruscan secret of applying minute grains of gold to a gold base; Carlo Giuliano, who emigrated from Naples to London; and his two sons, who carried on the business in London towards the end of the century. Even as late as the nineteenth century some of the traditional forms of jewellery were still being made in Europe: and it is these which will probably appeal most to the collector.

GLOSSARY

Aigrette. Jewel supporting a feather or imitating it in form, worn in hair or cap since the end of the sixteenth century.

Cabachon. Stones of rounded, natural form, polished but not cut.

Chatelaine. Useful ornament of silver, pinchbeck, or gilt metal, supporting watches, watch-keys, seals, thimble-cases, and other étuis, worn hanging from a belt.

Diamond-cutting. During the Renaissance diamonds were either cut to a fine point like a pyramid, or given a flat surface, called table- or mirror-cut. The rose-cut, invented in Holland about 1640, gives the stone up to twenty-four facets all over its surface, whereas the brilliant-cut, introduced later during that century, is applied to deeper stones, ending in points at front and back and provided with up to fifty-eight facets, visible in open-claw settings.

Enamel. Powdered glass, fused on to a metal base by heat, applied in opaque or translucent colours in various technical processes. During the Renaissance *champlevé* enamel was popular, consisting of a metal (gold) base, hollowed out to receive the enamel, which formed the design. Enamel *en ronde bosse* covers figures modelled in the round, usually in white. Painted enamel, as the name indicates, is enamel painted upon enamelled ground (copper), much like a miniature, usually with "counter enamel", a thin coating of enamel at the back of the metal recipient, to prevent excessive expanding and shrinkage after the firing process.

Filigree. Gold wire or pellets, applied to a gold base in ornamental pattern.

Gems. Cut or engraved stones. Intaglios, for sealing, are usually cut with the design in reverse, to be seen in the impression. Cameos are cut in relief, the varied strata of stone or shell forming part of the design. Subjects, in great part derived from the antique, include ideal portraits and mythological scenes, the stones preferred for gem cutting include semi-precious stones, agates and carnelians for preference, and a variety of shells.

Girandole. Clasp of alternating ribbon and bow design in openwork, set with stones.

Hair jewellery. Memorial jewels, containing plaited hair in lockets, clasps, or rings, usually together with the initials and dates of the defunct, in black and white enamel.

Marcasite. Iron pyrites, faceted in the manner of precious stones, made by mechanical process.

Paste. Coloured glass, used to reproduce precious stones since Roman times, usually with coloured foil placed beneath in order to enhance their appearance. Colourless paste is practically a modern invention, worn as a substitute rather than an imitation of precious stones.

Pinchbeck. Alloy of copper and zinc, sometimes washed with gold, named after the inventor Christopher Pinchbeck, a well-known watchmaker, active in London about the middle of the eighteenth century.

Sévigné bow. Graduated bow brooch, worn in front of the bodice.

Strass. Paste called after the inventor, Joseph Strass, a Viennese, who came to Paris as a jeweller in the middle of the eighteenth century. It contains a high percentage of lead, hence more closely resembling a natural diamond when faceted.

Tassies. Replicas of intaglios or glass paste impressions, named after James Tassie, who settled in London in 1766, where he became famous for these cast gems.

Engraved Gems of the Eighteenth Century

Greek and Roman engraved gems, originally intended for use as seals but later as objects of jewellery, began to attract the attention of connoisseurs in the Renaissance period. Pope Paul II was among the first collectors to acquire them, and appears to have been the first martyr to their fashion, for he is said to have died from a chill caught by exposing too many cold gems on his fingers. The taste for gems grew, however, and early in the sixteenth century the art of engraving precious and semi-precious stones was revived by numerous Italian craftsmen, many of whom produced work which is difficult to distinguish from the antique. These craftsmen also carved cameo portraits which won great popularity. By the early eighteenth century the fashion for both antique and modern gems had become a rage, and no collection of virtu was considered complete without its cabinet of them.

Two main types of gem were produced in the first half of the eighteenth century: more or less fraudulent copies after antique specimens, and frankly modern works which included both portraits and historical scenes. With the growth of the neo-classical movement in the 1750s, gem engravers began to imitate the style of antique specimens without basing their designs on particular prototypes. This occasioned a revival in the art of gem engraving, led by Edward Burch and Nathaniel Marchant in England, and by the Pichler family at Rome. Students of Greek and Roman art tend to regard the gems produced by these artists in the antique style as fakes. This is misguided, for they are no more fraudulent than the sculptures of Canova and the paintings of Mengs and J. L. David, who, like the engravers, sought to revive the true classical taste. Indeed, at the end of the cen-

tury engravers were copying the statues of Canova even as their Greek forerunners had represented the works of Pheidias and Praxiteles. As evidence of their good faith, the most notable engravers usually signed their work, inscribing their names, however barbaric, in Greek letters to avoid introducing a jarring note.

The practice of faking antique gems persisted throughout the century, however, and if their creators inscribed them, they naturally did so with fictitious Greek signatures. These works were generally copies of genuine antiques with slight, but revealing, variations. The vast number that survive provides some indication of the extent of the fashion for gems in the eighteenth century. Many of them were by artists who also produced original work. J. L. Natter, for example, blandly remarked: "I am not ashamed to own that I continue to make copies (with Greek inscriptions and masters' names) at all times when I receive orders: but I defy the whole world to prove that I have ever sold one for antique." Dealers were less scrupulous than Natter claimed to be, and employed engravers to produce fakes. According to Nollekens, the notorious Thomas Jenkins, an English art dealer in Rome, "followed the trade of supplying the foreign visitors with intaglios and cameos made by his own people, that he kept in a part of the ruins of the Coliseum, fitted up for 'em to work in slyly by themselves. I saw 'em at work though, and Jenkins gave a whole handful of 'em to me to say nothing about the matter to anybody else but myself. Bless your heart! he sold 'em as fast as they made 'em." Many and various were the devices employed for imparting an ageless patina to modern gems. The smooth surfaces of intaglios were carefully scratched and their edges chipped.

Cameos were stuffed down the necks of turkey fowls to acquire, in their gizzards, the dull, chalky appearance characteristic of antiques.

The majority of eighteenth-century gems are engraved with classical subjects. But portrait cameos and intaglios were also popular throughout the century, while a few engravers, notably Jacques Guay, carved modern historical, allegorical, and sentimental subjects. These gems follow the stylistic development from late Baroque to Rococo and finally neoclassicism. The best are those carved in the second half of the century showing their subjects in antique guise.

Technical terms and materials

There are two types of engraved gem: the intaglio, on which the design is sunk into the stone, and the cameo, on which it is shown in relief. The intaglio may be used as a seal, though it was not necessarily intended for that purpose. The material normally used for gems of both types was a semi-precious stone, sardonyx, cornelian, agate, or onyx. Sometimes precious stones were used, including emeralds, amethysts, and even diamonds, though these were, of course, much more difficult to work. Normally the method of engraving was by a wheel, or minute copper disc, driven in the manner of a lathe moistened with olive oil mixed with emery and diamond dust. A diamond point engraver, such as was used in classical times, was employed by a few artists.

Shell cameos were carved from the shells of various exotic crustaceans. The shells normally used were those of the *Cassis Rufa* found in East Indian seas, the *Cassis Cornuta* found off Madagascar, and the *Cassis Tuberca* and *Strombus gigas* of the West Indies. The subjects carved are similar to those on hard-stone cameos, but the workmanship is rarely as fine. Shell cameos are hardly ever signed.

Reproductions

Two methods were used in the eighteenth century for reproducing antique and modern gems. Most numerous are the casts or impressions of intaglios known as sulphurs, made from a composition of sulphur and wax, and showing the engraving in reverse. Many such sulphurs were taken from antique gems, but towards the end of the century engravers began to sell casts of their own work. Nathaniel Marchant, for instance, published a catalogue to accompany a collection of casts from his gems. Sulphurs were often arranged in boxes in the shape of books or gem cabinets. The other type of reproduction was made of a vitreous substance and known as a paste. Unlike the sulphur, the paste reproduced the shape of the original gem and was, in fact, taken from a cast. Most famous of these pastes, which were made according to various receipts, are those produced by James and William Tassie (see biographical notes below). Readers of Keats' letters will recall the poet's several references to Tassie's gems, which he used as seals and gave to his sister Fanny. To provide cameo portraits of celebrities the Tassies sometimes took their pastes from wax models instead of engraved gems.

SOME NOTABLE GEM ENGRAVERS OF THE EIGHTEENTH CENTURY

Amastini, Angelo (1754–1815). Born at Fossombrone and went to Rome before 1778. A fine agate cameo by him is in a private collection in Rome (Plate 188E). His son, Nicolo Amastini (1780–1851), was also a gem engraver and is represented by a cameo in the Metropolitan Museum, New York.

Barier, François-Jules (1680–1746). Born at Laval in France and became the official gem engraver to Louis XV. His works, which included portraits of the Marchese Rangoni and Fontenelle, agate vases, and minute figures in cornelian, won the praise of Voltaire.

Becker, Philipp Christoph (1674–1743). Born at Coblenz and worked in Vienna as a medallist and gem engraver. According to Mariette, he was the best engraver of gems in Germany. His works include a portrait of Charles VI (c. 1711) and numerous seals cut for German princes.

Berini, Antonio (c. 1770–1830). Born at Rome and studied under Giovanni Pichler. In about 1802 he appears to have moved to Milan, where he cut several gems, including a

notorious cameo of Napoleon (by an unhappy
chance a red vein in the stone encircled the
Emperor's neck, and Berini was consequently
imprisoned as a suspected assassin). Most of
his gems are of classical subjects, but at
Windsor Castle there is an intaglio of St
George and the dragon signed by him.

Burch, Edward (1730–1814). One of the
most famous English gem engravers, began
his career as a wherryman. In 1796 he entered the Royal Academy Schools, became an
A.R.A. in 1770 and an R.A. in 1771. In 1788
he was appointed medal engraver to the King
and Duke of York. He engraved numerous
gems and also worked as a wax modeller
(Plate 188G).

Cades, Alessandro (1734–1809). A Roman gem engraver who worked in a style
similar to that of Giovanni Pichler. He is
mentioned in Goethe's biography of Hackert.
His gems are signed with his full name, sometimes in Greek characters (Plate 188c).

Calandrelli, Giovanni (1784–1852). A
Roman who moved in 1832 to Berlin. He executed some gems of religious subjects but was
notorious as a faker. Many of his works were
bought, as antiques, by the Berlin Museum.

Costanzi, Giovanni (1674–1754). A gem
engraver who worked in Rome and Naples.
Two of his sons followed his craft: Tommaso
(1700–47) and Carlo (1703–81). Carlo became famous for his work on precious stones,
especially diamonds. He carved a diamond
intaglio of Leda for the King of Portugal, a
sapphire cameo of Maria Theresa, and an
emerald cameo of Benedict XIV, which took
him two and a half years. In less precious and
hard materials he executed portrait cameos
of several grand tourists, including Sir John
Frederick, J. Hamilton, and Lord Duncannon.
Most of his works were, however, of antique
subjects.

Dorsch, Johann Christoph (1676–1732).
Said to have inundated Germany with cameo
and intaglio portraits of Popes, Emperors,
Kings of France, etc., and unfaithful copies
of famous antique gems. His daughter, Suzan,
was also a gem engraver and carved a copy
of "Solon's" head of Medusa, now in the
British Museum.

Ghinghi or **Ginghaio, Francesco** (1689–

1766). Born at Florence and became gem engraver first to Gian Gastone dei Medici and
then Francesco III of Lorraine. In 1737 he
moved to Naples. Many of his works are in
the Uffizi, Florence, including a cameo of
Gian Gastone dei Medici.

Girometti, Giuseppe (1780–1851). Began his career as a sculptor and a pupil of
Vincenzo Pacetti, under whom he executed
stuccoes for the cathedral of Foligno. He was
also a medallist. His cameos include reproductions of antique gems, portraits of famous
men (including Leonardo da Vinci, George
Washington, and Napoleon), and neo-classical
subjects based either on his own designs or
the statues of Tenerani and Canova. He is
represented in the British Museum by a fine
cameo of Diomede with the Palladium (Plate
188K).

Guay, Jacques (1711–93). The most exquisite of French gem engravers, was born at
Marseilles. He studied painting in Paris under
Boucher, through whom he probably met
Pierre Crozat, who persuaded him to take up
gem engraving. In 1712 he set off on a tour
of Italy, and after studying the antique gems
in the Grand Ducal collection at Florence
passed to Rome, where he executed some
copies after the antique. After his return to
Paris he came to the notice of Mme de Pompadour, who became both his patron and
pupil. She also secured for him apartments
at Versailles. In 1745 he succeeded Barier as
official gem engraver to the King, carving a
cornelian intaglio of the Victory of Fontenoy
after Bouchardon (now lost) on taking office.
He carved many historical scenes in cameo
and intaglio, some allegorical subjects – Mme
de Pompadour protecting the art of gem engraving, for example – and such characteristically rococo subjects as "Cupid as a Gardener" and "Cupid as a Musician". His best
works were his portrait cameos of Louis XV,
Mme de Pompadour, Louis XVI, Marie
Antoinette, Cardinal de Rohan, etc. C. W.
King, author of the British Museum catalogue
of gems, thought his imitations of the Greek
style "perfect", but they do not seem to have
satisfied neo-classical taste. In 1784 the director of the French Academy in Rome suggested
that his place as court engraver might be given

(A) Blue glass finger-bowl, with gilt decoration, signed I. JACOBS BRISTOL. Height 3⅞ ins. *Victoria and Albert Museum, London.*

(B) Silvered-glass witch-ball. Diameter 15 ins. *Private Collection.*

(c) *Left to right:* Scent-bottle of blue glass with painted and gilt decoration. Height 3 ins. Bodkin-case of blue glass with gilt decoration. Height 3⅞ ins. Opaque white glass scent-bottle with painted decoration. Height 2½ ins. Amethyst-coloured glass scent-bottle with gilt decoration. Height 3¼ ins. *Victoria and Albert Museum, London.*

PLATE 161

(A) Three-masted sailing-ship, complete with rigging, made of glass. Length 8 ins. *Victoria and Albert Museum, London.*

(B) Glass model of a playing fountain ornamented with coloured birds. Height 17 ins. *Victoria and Albert Museum, London.*

PLATE 162

(A) Nailsea blue and white glass "Lovers' bottle". Length 7½ ins. *Private Collection.*

(B) Nailsea red, white, and blue glass flask with pewter screwed cap. Length 8 ins. *Private Collection.*

(C) Nailsea green and white glass jug. Height 5 ins. *Victoria and Albert Museum, London.*

(D) Nailsea jug, of greenish-brown glass with splashes of white. Height 6½ ins. *Victoria and Albert Museum, London.*

PLATE 163

(B) Jug of heavy champagne-coloured glass with cracklings, purple streaks, and moulded cut profiles by Eugène Rousseau, Paris, c. 1880. *Meyric R. Rogers Collection, Chicago.*

(A) Vase of transparent cut glass with bronze mounts, Baccarat, 1810–20. *Kunstindustrimuseet, Oslo.*

PLATE 164

(A) Cup with engraved decoration, Clichy, *c.* 1860.
British Museum, London.

(B) Vase of champagne-coloured glass with
enamelled decoration in black, white, and
gold, *c.* 1885. Signed EMILE GALLÉ À NANCY.
The Royal Scottish Museum, Edinburgh.

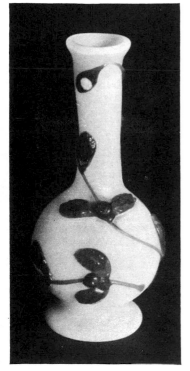

(C) Vase of opal glass with a cling-
ing green wreath, Cristalleries de
Saint-Louis, *c.* 1850. *Conservatoire
National des Arts et Métiers, Paris.*

(D) Vase of red glass with enamelled and trailed decoration
by A. Jean, Paris, *c.* 1880.
*Conservatoire National des Arts
et Métiers, Paris.*

(E) Vase of opal glass with blue
decoration, Choisy-le-Roi, *c.* 1845.
*Conservatoire National des Arts et
Métiers, Paris.*

PLATE 165

(A) Jug in filigree glass with a blue rim, Cristalleries de Saint-Louis, *c.* 1850. *Conservatoire National des Arts et Métiers, Paris.*

(B) Vase of crackled glass with oriental scene cut out of a lacquer red casing by Leveillé, Paris, *c.* 1889. *Conservatoire National des Arts et Métiers, Paris.*

(C) Tazza with enamelled pattern underneath the bowl. Signed BROCARD, 23 R. BERTRAN PARIS. *The Royal Scottish Museum, Edinburgh.*

(D) Vase with white lining and a brown corroded surface with Japanese pattern, *c.* 1890. Signed E. GALLÉ, NANCY. *Ada Polak Collection, London.*

PLATE 166

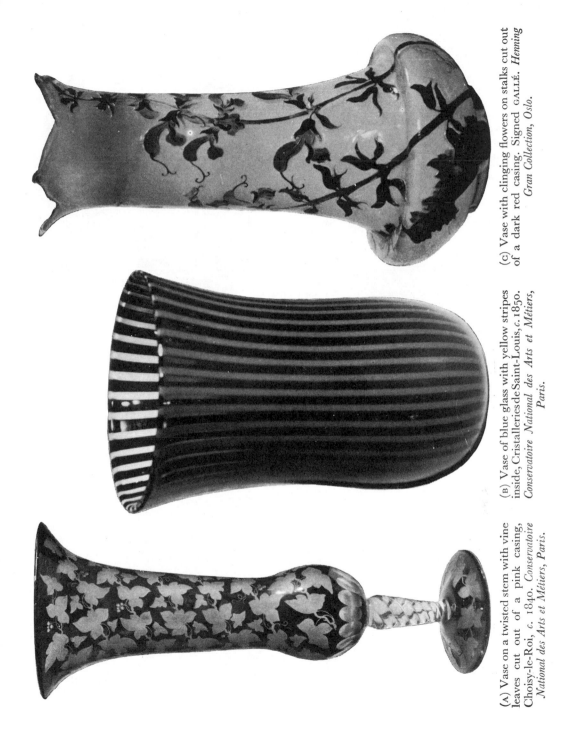

(c) Vase with clinging flowers on stalks cut out of a dark red casing. Signed GALLÉ. *Henning Gran Collection, Oslo.*

(B) Vase of blue glass with yellow stripes inside, Cristalleries de Saint-Louis, c. 1850. *Conservatoire National des Arts et Métiers, Paris.*

(A) Vase on a twisted stem with vine leaves cut out of a pink casing, Choisy-le-Roi, c. 1840. *Conservatoire National des Arts et Métiers, Paris.*

PLATE 167

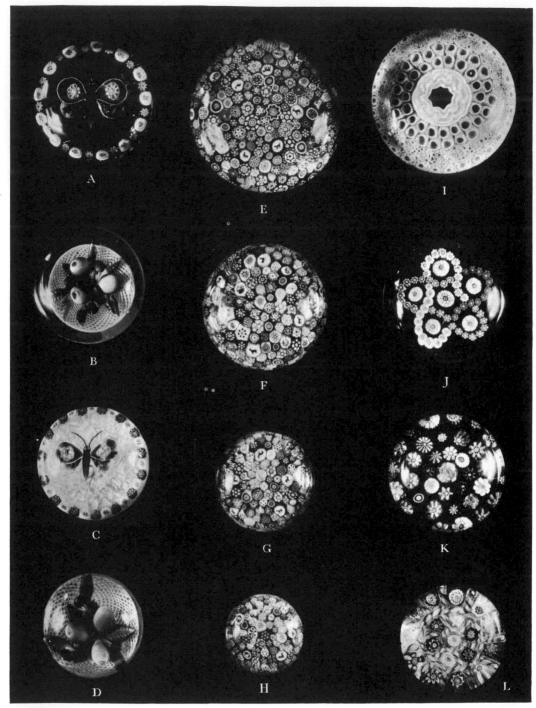

(A) **Baccarat** "butterfly". (B) **Clichy** "fruit" on *latticinio* ground. (C) **Baccarat** "butterfly" on muslin ground. (D) **Clichy** "fruit" on *latticinio* ground. (E) to (H) A set of four **Baccarat** *millefiore* with animal silhouettes. Marked B and dated 1848. (I) English, George Bacchus and Sons, Birmingham. (J) **Clichy** garlanded *millefiore*. (K) **Clichy** – note the centrally-placed typical rose. (L) **Clichy**. *Lories Ltd, London.*

PLATE 168

Part of an Irish table-service of 95 pieces with bands of strawberry diamonds as the main motif, *c.* 1810. *Delomosne & Son Ltd.*

PLATE 169

(A) Pair of blown-moulded decanters with three feathered neck-rings, engraved with the vesica pattern, and impressed on base CORK GLASS CO, early nineteenth century. *Delomosne & Son Ltd.*

(B) A pair of blown-moulded decanters engraved with pendant crescents and stars, marked beneath WATERLOO CO CORK in raised letters, and a blown-moulded jug marked CORK GLASS CO. *Delomosne & Son Ltd.*

PLATE 170

A) Irish finger-bowl cut with deep
concave flutes with notched crests,
band of diamonds, and scalloped
rim, George IV. *Corning Museum of
Glass, New York.*

(B) George IV moulded pickle jar,
flat lid cut with circular prisms,
foot radially cut beneath.

(c) Kettle-drum shape fruit bowl of
Irish glass with knopped stem and
round foot, early nineteenth century. *Corning Museum of Glass, New
York.*

D) Blown-moulded decanter encircled by the vesica pattern
associated with Cork; feathered
neck rings; target stopper, early
nineteenth century. *Corning Museum of Glass, New York.*

(E) Sweetmeat glass with ogee bowl,
facet-cut knopped stem and rims of foot
and bowl edged with scalloping, *c.* 1780.
Corning Museum of Glass, New York.

(F) Sweetmeat glass with band of
large relief diamonds, wide fluting,
and deeply scalloped rim, early nineteenth century. *Corning Museum of
Glass, New York.*

PLATE 171

Wine fountain of Irish glass, with shallow-cut flutes, silver tap, late eighteenth century. *Corning Museum of Glass, New York*.

PLATE 172

Pair of two-light Irish candelabra with deep blue canopies, *c.* 1785. *Corning Museum of Glass, New York.*

PLATE 173

(B) Toddy rummer with engraved bowl. Its metal displays a faintly blue tint known contemporaneously as Derby blue, early nineteenth century.
O. T. Norris' Collection.

(A) Wine glass with drawn trumpet bowl, tear in stem, and engraved with portrait of Dean Swift; dated 1745. *Formerly in the Collection of the Earl of Cork and Orrery.*

PLATE 174

(B) Butter dish or cooler with horizontal and vertical prismatic cutting. Regency period. *Corning Museum of Glass, New York.*

(D) Bowl cut with alternating eight-pointed stars and single diamonds cut with small diamonds. *Corning Museum of Glass, New York.*

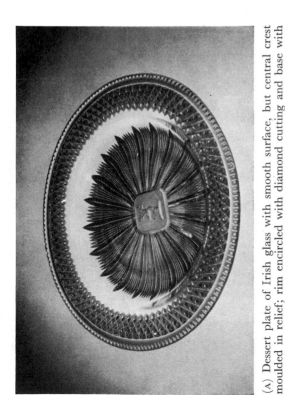

(A) Dessert plate of Irish glass with smooth surface, but central crest moulded in relief; rim encircled with diamond cutting and base with narrow and wide flutes, c. 1830. *Corning Museum of Glass, New York.*

(C) Fruit bowl with canoe-shaped body cut with large diamonds, a trefoil scalloped rim, and moulded foot, early nineteenth century. *Corning Museum of Glass, New York.*

PLATE 175

(A) Stemmed sugar bowl with two bands of cross-cut diamonds and shell border to rim, on knopped stem and round foot. *John Bell Collection.*

(B) A lemon holder with shallow-cut body and round convex foot, *c.* 1780. *Corning Museum of Glass, New York.*

(c) Water jug, body cut with large relief diamonds, shoulder with concave flutes, neck with prisms, and notched rim. *Corning Museum of Glass, New York.*

(d) A Regency cream jug, body deep-cut with diamonds; shoulder with concave flutes; rim and handle notched.

(E) Bowl cut with strawberry diamonds and engraved with a crowned harp and Irish inscription with a wreath of shamrock. *Howard Phillips.*

PLATE 176

(A) *Left:* Goblet, Nöstetangen, engraved by H. G. Köhler, 1764. *Johan Collet, Oslo.*

(B) *Top right:* Seventeenth-century goblet from Kungsholm Glasbruk. *National Museum, Stockholm.*

(C) *Bottom right:* Eighteenth-century goblet from Kungsholm Glasbruk. *National Museum, Stockholm.*

PLATE 177

A B C

D E F

(A) Goblet with the English and Danish coats-of-arms, made for the wedding between Christian VII of Denmark and George III's sister, Caroline Mathilde, in 1767. Engraved by Villas Vinter. *Ragnar Moltzau, Oslo.* (B) Engraved picture of a glass furnace by H. G. Köhler, 1771. *Oslo Kunstindustrimuseet.* (C) Wine glass of Newcastle type, Nöstetangen, *c.* 1760. *Dr Ada Polak.* (D) Decanter from Skånska Glasbruket, 1761. *Nordiska Museet, Stockholm* (E) Goblet with enamel twist stem. Hurdals Verk, *c.* 1780. *Oslo Kunstindustrimuseet.* (F) Decanter, "Zirat-fladke" with SHS 1832 trailed. Gjövik Verk. *Ragnar Börsum, Oslo.*

PLATE 178

(A) Decanter, waisted, with trailed decoration, Swedish, first half of nineteenth century. *Nordiska Museet, Stockholm.*

(B) Jar with lid. Nöstetangen, 1760–70. *Oslo Kunstindustrimuseet.*

(C) Decanter with the monogram of Gustaf IV Adolph (1792–1808). *Göteborgs Museum.*

(D) Ewer, Nöstetangen, 1760–70. *Oslo Kunstindustrimuseet.*

PLATE 179

Central chandelier from Kongsberg Church, Nöstetangen, 1759–66.

PLATE 180

A

B

C

(A) Table-lamp in the form of a horse, late sixteenth or early seventeenth century. *Museo Vetrario, Murano.*

(B) Vase of reticulated glass with swans in *lattimo*, mid-nineteenth century. *Museo Vetrario, Murano.*

(C) Covered cup with dragon stem, late sixteenth century. *Corning Museum of Glass, New York.*

(D) Madonna and Child with two saints, in coloured glass, mid-eighteenth century. *Museo Vetrario, Murano.*

D

PLATE 181

(A) Plate with filigree decorations, mid-seventeenth century. *Museo Vetrario, Murano.*
(B) Reliquary in the form of a cross, second half of the eighteenth century. *Museo Vetrario, Murano.*
(C) Decanter of Bohemian type with decorations in gold, mid-eighteenth century. *Museo Vetrario, Murano.*
(D) Looking glass, engraved by wheel, mid-eighteenth century. *Museo Vetrario, Murano.*

PLATE 182

A) Chandelier with polychrome glass flowers, mid-eighteenth century. Height nearly six feet. *Museo Vetrario, Murano.*

B) Oil and vinegar bottle stand with receptacles for salt, decorated in gilt, mid-eighteenth century. *Museo Vetrario, Murano.*

C) Table-centre in the form of a combined lamp and *épergne*, possibly made by the Briati factory, *c.* 1740–75. *Museo Vetrario, Murano.*

PLATE 183

(A) Marriage cup of dark blue glass with enamel decorations, traditionally ascribed to the Barovier factory, late fifteenth century. *Museo Vetrario, Murano.*

(B) Beaker of turquoise blue glass with gilt and enamelled decorations, *c.* 1480. *British Museum, London.*

(C) Goblet of *cristallo* glass, first half of sixteenth century. *Museo Vetrario, Murano.*

PLATE 184

Pendant with Orpheus and Eurydice, enamelled gold set with precious stones and pearls. Augsburg (?), second half of the sixteenth century. *"A La Vieille Russie"*, *New York*.

PLATE 185

A

B

C

D

E

F

G

H

I

PLATE 186

Opposite (Plate 186)

(A) Pendant with cameo of Emperor Claudius as Jupiter. The cameo, Roman, first century B.C.; the pendant of enamelled gold set with pearls. Italian, sixteenth century.

(B) Pendant, enamelled gold and pearls, St Michael vanquishing the devil. German or French, late sixteenth century.

(C) Pendant with Mars and Venus. Bloodstone plaque with applied relief in enamelled gold, the bodies of the figures formed of baroque pearls. Gold and enamel frame. German or Italian, second half of sixteenth century.

(D) Pendant, gold set with table-cut diamonds. Italian, second half of sixteenth century. *Rosenberg & Stiebel Inc., New York.*

(E) Pendant formed as a pelican, the body a large baroque pearl, mounted in gold enamelled white, set with table-cut rubies. French, mid-sixteenth century.

(F) Pendant in the form of a ship, enamelled gold set with rubies. Italian or Spanish, late sixteenth century.

(G) Pendant, gold and table-cut stones. German, early seventeenth century. *A. & R. Ball, New York.*

(H) Miniature frame, enamelled gold. English or Dutch, first half of seventeenth century.

(I) Pendant in the form of an eagle, the body a large baroque pearl. Hungarian, eighteenth century. *A. & R. Ball, New York.*

Except for (D), (G), and (I), all the above are from the Melvin Gutman Collection, New York.

(A) Aigrette, silver set with brilliants. French, late eighteenth century. *S. J. Phillips.* (B) Suite consisting of necklace, bracelets, earrings, and cross pendant. Gold set with pink topaz and seed pearls. English, first half of nineteenth century. *S. J. Phillips.*

PLATE 187

PLATE 188

Opposite (Plate 188)

(A) Minerva, onyx cameo by Giovanni Pichler. *British Museum, London.*

(B) The Birth of the Duke of Burgundy, sardonyx cameo by Jacques Guay, 1751. *Bibliothèque Nationale, Paris.*

(C) Cupid and Psyche, onyx cameo by Alessandro or Tommaso Cades. *British Museum, London.*

(D) Cupid and Psyche, banded chalcedony intaglio by a member of the Pichler family. *British Museum, London.*

(E) Bacchus, agate cameo by Angelo Amastini. *Private Collection, Rome.*

(F) Apollo, sardonyx intaglio by Luigi Pichler. *British Museum, London.*

(G) Head of a girl, sardonyx intaglio by Edward Burch. *British Museum, London.*

(H) A nereid, beryl intaglio by Filippo Rega. *British Museum, London.*

(I) Hercules, onyx cameo by G. A. Santarelli. *British Museum, London.*

(J) Bacchus and a nymph, sardonyx intaglio by Nathaniel Marchant. *British Museum, London.*

(K) Head of a boy, onyx cameo by Giuseppe Girometti. *British Museum, London.*

A   B   C

D   E

(A) Louis XV, sardonyx cameo by Jacques Guay, 1753. *Bibliothèque Nationale, Paris.*

(B) Napoleon, agate cameo probably by Filippo Rega. *British Museum, London.*

(C) Robert Raikes, paste cameo by William Tassie. *National Portrait Gallery, London.*

(D) Joseph Black, paste cameo by James Tassie, 1788. *National Portrait Gallery, London.*

(E) Adam Smith, paste cameo by James Tassie, 1787. *National Portrait Gallery, London.*

PLATE 189

Low relief in pietre dure of Cosimo II by Orazio Mochi (1619–20) to a design by Giovanni Bilivert. Lapis lazuli, porphyry, cornelian and other hard stones, gold, and diamonds. *Museo degli Argenti, Florence.*

PLATE 190

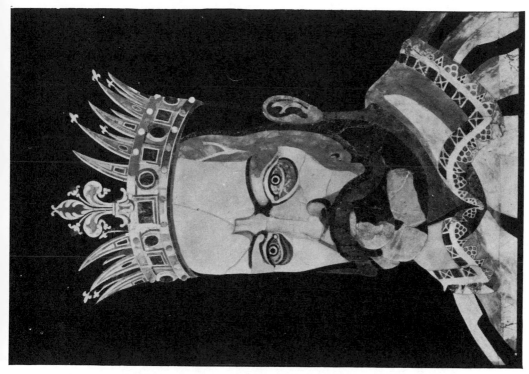

(B) Portrait of Cosimo I by Francesco Ferrucci after a painting by Domenico Cresti, 1598. *Museo dell' Opificio delle Pietre Dure, Florence.*

(A) Bust of Vittoria della Rovere in Black Flanders Marble, chalcedony and agates by Giuseppe Antonio Torricelli (1662–1719). *Museo dell' Opificio delle Pietre Dure, Florence.*

PLATE 191

(A) Florentine Mosaic panel designed by Giuseppe Zocchi, mid-eighteenth century. *Museo dell' Opificio delle Pietre Dure, Florence.*

(B) Table top of porphyry inlaid with pietre dure, early nineteenth century. *Palazzo Pitti, Florence.*

PLATE 192

to the Englishman Nathaniel Marchant. The best collection of his works is in the Bibliothèque Nationale, Paris (Plates 188B, 189A).

Jouffroy, Romain-Vincent (1749–1826). Born in Rouen, went to Naples in 1770 and settled at Paris in 1780. From 1790 to 1805 he worked for Prince Lubomirsky at Warsaw. In 1777 he engraved an amethyst head of Medusa after the Renaissance "Solon" cameo. He executed a large number of antique style cameos and intaglios, three of which are in the Bibliothèque Nationale. He also carved a number of portraits, including those of Napoleon (1801) and Maria Cosway in cameo, and the architect Charles de Wailly in intaglio.

Marchant, Nathaniel (1739–1816). One of the artists principally responsible for the neo-classical revival in the art of gem engraving. He was born in Sussex, studied under Burch, became a member of the Incorporated Society of Artists in 1766, went to Italy in 1772, and worked in Rome for the next sixteen years. He was elected an A.R.A. in 1781 and an R.A. in 1809, and was official gem engraver to the Prince Regent. Marchant's gems, which were highly prized in their day, and of which he published a catalogue to accompany a selection of casts, were all carved in intaglio. Most of them were of classical subjects, but he also carved numerous portraits, including those of William Pitt, Garrick, Prince Lubomirsky, Lord and Lady Lucan, Sir William Molesworth, Major Pearson, Mrs Hartley the actress, Lord Mulgrave, and Pius VI. He was much patronized by the Duke of Marlborough, who sent gems out to be carved by him in Rome. Writing of his intaglio of the death of General Wolfe, then in the collection of Sir Richard Worsley, the notable Roman antiquarian H. Q. Visconti remarked that Marchant was without rival in his profession. Modern connoisseurs have, however, generally found his work too exquisitely fine and finicky (Plate 188J).

Natter, Johann Lorenz (1705–63). Probably the most celebrated German gem engraver of the eighteenth century. He was originally trained as a goldsmith, but in 1732 he visited Italy to study gem engraving in Venice and Florence. In 1735 he went to Rome, where he won immediate fame by his portrait of Cardinal Albani. He went to England in 1740, but three years later left for Denmark, where he was patronized by the King, for whom he engraved gems and medals. After a visit to Sweden and St Petersburg he returned to London in 1751 and published there his *Traité de la méthode antique de graver en pierres fines, comparée avec la méthode moderne . . .* in 1754. Three years later he was appointed engraver to the mint at Utrecht, but went back to London in 1761 and secured a post as assistant engraver to the Royal Mint. Next year he was off again, travelling by way of Copenhagen to St Petersburg, where he died. He produced numerous copies after the antique, sometimes with fake inscriptions, and also carved portraits, including those of George I, George II, Lord and Lady Duncannon, Dr Mead, Baron Stosch, and the Marquess of Rockingham. His charge for engraving a portrait varied between 10 and 25 guineas.

Pazzaglia, Antonio (c. 1736–1815). A lieutenant in the Papal Guard who became a gem engraver. He was adept at imitating antique gems, which he sometimes signed with his name in Greek characters.

Pichler, Johann Anton. Usually known as Antonio (1697–1779), the founder of a very important family of gem engravers who worked at Rome. He was born at Bressanone and began his career by working for a rich uncle who was a merchant at Nice. In the 1730s he visited Italy, took employment at Naples with a goldsmith, and finally settled at Rome in 1743. He excelled in the imitation of antique subjects, but also carved intaglios and cameos from his own designs – and on one occasion at least from a drawing by Mengs – signing them with adaptations of his name, written in Greek characters. Three of his sons, Giovanni (1734–91), Giuseppe (1770–1819), and Luigi (1773–1854), became notable gem engravers. Giovanni Pichler was perhaps the most distinguished. He was trained under his father and the painter Domenico Corvi and became a prominent member of the circle of neo-classical artists in Rome. His gems were highly esteemed, and many stories were told of those that had been passed off as antiques to collectors who brought them unknowingly to their creator and asked him to copy them. Such was his reputation that his own signature was forged by contemporaries. He excelled in the representation of female figures, which he usually endowed with a slightly sentimental look characteristic of the time. His trade card shows that in 1783 he was charging 40 zecchini (about £20) for a portrait, the same for a cameo figure, and 20 for a head in cameo or intaglio. He made paste reproductions of 220 of his works. His son, Gian Giacomo (1778–1829), became a gem engraver and worked principally in Milan. Luigi Pichler (Plate 188F), who succeeded to Giovanni's workshop in 1791, secured for himself a European reputation, became a member of the Florentine, Milanese, and Venetian academies, and was knighted by Gregory XIV. The Empress Josephine commissioned him to carve a gem of an "Offering to the God Terminus" which she gave to Napoleon. He executed gems of antique subjects and also gems representing the statues of Canova. Among his portraits, for which he was celebrated, were those of Canova, the Cardinal de Bernis, Raphael Morgan, and Metternich.

Pompadour, Jeanne-Antoinette Poisson, Marquise de (1721–64). Said to have been an apt pupil of Jacques Guay, under whose tuition and with whose help she engraved several cameos and intaglios. Her work is represented in the Bibliothèque Nationale, Paris.

Rega, Filippo (1761–1833). Born at Chieti. His family moved to Naples in 1767 and later to Rome, where, from 1776 to 1787, the young Rega studied under Antonio and Giovanni Pichler. In 1787 he returned to Naples, where he worked for the rest of his career. He was patronized by the British ambassador, Sir William Hamilton, for whom he cut a portrait of the notorious Emma. Replicas of this work were ordered from him by Lord Bristol (the Earl-Bishop) and Nelson. Among his other portraits were those of Sir William Hamilton himself, the King and Queen of Naples, Joseph Bonaparte, and Gioacchino Murat. His numerous intaglios after the antique, signed with his name in Greek charac-

ters, are more lively and less precise than those of his principal contemporary rival, N. Marchant (Plate 188H).

Santarelli, Giovanni Antonio (1758–1826). Born at Manoppelle in the Abruzzi, and in 1785 went to Rome, where he worked under the Pichlers. In 1797 he moved to Florence, where he spent the rest of his life. Together with Cades and Odelli he carved numerous gems for Prince Poniatowski (Plate 188I).

Siries, Louis (c. 1686–1757). Appears to have been born at Florence, where he was living in 1709, he went to Paris and in 1726 was appointed goldsmith to Louis XV. After six years he returned to Florence, and in 1732 went to Rome. In 1740 he was appointed director of the Opificio delle Pietre Dure at Florence. He published in 1757 a catalogue of 168 gems he had engraved. Many of his cameos were bought by Maria Theresa. He specialized in work on a microscopic scale, and according to Mariette his talent lay in achieving supposed impossibilities, dreading being thought an imitator of the ancients. Some of his works were reproduced by Tassie. He was also a medallist.

Sirletti, Flavio (1683–1737). Born in Rome. At the suggestion of Baron Stosch he revived the ancient practice of working with a diamond point. He excelled in portraits, the best of which is said to be a cameo of Carlo Maratta. He also reproduced the most notable antique statues and busts on gems. But much of his time was devoted to reworking ancient gems, to many of which he applied bogus Greek inscriptions. Some of his works were reproduced by Tassie. His son, Francesco (1713–88), was also a gem engraver.

Tassie, James (1735–99). Together with Henry Quinn, a physician and amateur of gems, Tassie invented in 1763 a vitreous paste suitable for reproducing gems. This material, the secret of which was jealously kept, was an easily fusible glass which could be made to imitate the varied layers of a chalcedony cameo. In 1766 he settled in London, and three years later was supplying casts of gems to Wedgwood. He published in 1775 *A Catalogue of Impressions in Sulphur of Antique and Modern Gems*. Pastes were made from these sulphur casts and sold in great quantity – intaglios costing from 1s 6d to 2s 6d, while he asked from half a guinea to two guineas for cameos. In 1791 Rudolph Eric Raspe, the creator of Baron Munchausen, issued a further catalogue of Tassie's collection of casts, which now numbered 15,800. His original works, all of which are portraits, were derived from waxes and not gems. James Tassie was succeeded in 1799 by his nephew William (1777–1860), who added to the collection of reproductions, of which he issued three catalogues. The last (1830) accounts for 20,000 antique and modern gems (Plate 189C, D, and E).

Torricelli, Giuseppe Antonio (1639–1719). Mainly famous for his large works in pietre dure, also engraved gems. In 1714 he wrote a treatise on jewels and semi-precious stones. His son Gaetano (c. 1691–1752) studied drawing under Tommaso Redi and sculpture under G. B. Foggini and also became a gem engraver, specializing in classical subjects. He is represented in the Kunsthistorisches Museum, Vienna, by a chalcedony head of Laocoon. The family tradition was carried on by his son Giuseppe who worked at Florence and Vienna.

PIETRE DURE

Surprising as it may seem to present-day collectors and connoisseurs, the Grand Duke of Tuscany's *Opificio delle Pietre Dure*, or workshop of semi-precious stones, was once thought to be among the major artistic attractions of Italy. Throughout the seventeenth and eighteenth centuries sophisticated and elegant Grand Tourists vied with each other in praising its products – those smooth, glittering panels and inlaid table-tops of "Florentine Mosaic" as it was then called, choice examples of which still adorn many English country houses. Only the severest and most classically minded of *virtuosi* could resist the charms of pietre dure. During the nineteenth century, however, it fell into disrepute, and since then has found few admirers, even among confirmed addicts of Italian art. The charms of pietre dure are, it must be confessed, of the same gaudy, extravagant, and, to some eyes, rather meretricious variety as captivated the millionaire patrons of Fabergé. Indeed, it is of the great Russian jeweller's more ingenious confections that one is instantly reminded on entering the Pietre Dure Museum at Florence. As Sir Osbert Sitwell remarked, Florentine mosaic will have little appeal for the lover of old oak. But though modern aesthetes may scorn and art-historians neglect them, these strange manifestations of princely taste will continue to fascinate the discerning collector who values high quality in craftsmanship, and is not too squeamishly puritan to acknowledge the attraction of jewels and precious stones. The designs employed by the artists of the Grand Duke's *Opificio* were by no means unworthy of the rare materials and laborious craftsmanship lavished upon them; but it is, of course, the pure and brilliant colours of the stones themselves – of lapis lazuli, onyx, jasper, sardonyx, chalcedony, coral, agate, rock crystal, and many others – which lend these *objets de luxe* so strange and unique a beauty.

The rise and fall of the reputation of pietre dure provides an interesting sidelight on the history of taste, and the comments of one or two of its more eminent admirers and detractors may not be out of place even in so brief a chapter as this one. John Evelyn, for example, after visiting the Uffizi Gallery, Florence, in 1644, declared himself to have been much impressed by "divers incomparable tables of Pietra Commessa, which is a marble ground inlayd with severall sorts of marbles and stones of divers colours, in the shapes of flowers, trees, beasts, birds & landskips like the natural". Especially wonderful, he thought, was a pietre dure tabernacle, intended for the Cappella dei Principi in S. Lorenzo, to which an entire room of the Uffizi was given up. He wrote that it was "certainly one of the most curious and rare things in the world". And as for the sumptuous Cappella dei Principi itself, whose walls were encrusted with vast areas of rare marbles and semi-precious stones, his admiration knew no bounds. It was "the third heaven if any be on Earth". Six very large columns of rock crystal were eagerly noted down by Evelyn in his diary, together with "8 figures of precious stones of several colours, inlay'd in natural figures, not inferior to ye best paintings, amongst which are many pearls, diamonds, amethysts, topazes, sumptuous and sparkling beyond description". So taken was he with these flamboyant displays of technical virtuosity that, like many later visitors to Florence, he purchased nineteen panels of *commesso di pietre dure* and, on his return to England, had them made up into a cabinet which is still at Wotton, his country-house in Surrey.

But the taste for pietre dure reached its height during the next century when few English travellers could resist the fascination of its ingenious craftsmanship and the startlingly realistic *trompe l'œil* effects obtained in so difficult a medium. John, 5th Earl of Cork and Orrery, who was in Florence in 1754, remarked, in words that may easily be paralleled in many another Grand Tour correspondence or diary, that the Florentine mosaic tables in the Uffizi "consist of jasper, topazes, agates, and all kinds of coloured marble so nicely put together, as to form the most beautiful figures and the most natural representations of towns, woods, rocks, rivers, cattle, and people; not to mention a certain pearl necklace the beads of which my daughter tried in vain to take up in her hand".

It is interesting to compare such comments with those of a later visitor to Florence, the poet Walter Savage Landor. Writing in 1851, the year of the Great Exhibition in London, Landor dubbed the *Opificio delle Pietre Dure* a mere school for fashioning "piebald mineralogical specimens into a greater or less resemblance of fruits, flowers and landscapes"; and he deplored the decline in taste, as he thought it, which had "dared at last to rear, by the very side of the tombs of Giuliano and Lorenzo, the so-named (and well-named) Chapel of the Princes". This masterpiece of the *Opificio*, so much admired by Evelyn, was in Landor's opinion, the product of "Chinese industry and Turkish taste". As for the *objet d'art* which had been sent to represent the birthplace of Michelangelo at the 1851 Exhi-

bition, this, Landor remarked, was "neither more nor less than a table in pietre dure that had cost a hundred thousand francesconi, or, in other words, a day's work of four hundred thousand Tuscans". He considered it "stolid impertinence" to send such an object to London instead of some sublime painting or sculpture which would have shown how "genius and sentiment can convert all stone to precious stone; while the obscure diligence of years, uninformed by art, makes but a monument of laborious idleness". So much for the esteem in which Florentine mosaic was held by an eminent Victorian.

History of the Opificio delle Pietre Dure

Pietre dure, or semi-precious stones, had been employed in the manufacture of *objets de luxe* long before the Medici founded their *Opificio* at Florence in the late sixteenth century. Indeed, an exhaustive account of pietre dure and its various uses would take us back into classical antiquity. Suffice it here to mention the lavish use made of porphyry by Roman architects and sculptors, and the popularity of other more exotic and brilliantly coloured stones among the anonymous artists of Byzantium. Wherever early records of Italian churches or palaces have survived they generally include several vessels in pietre dure, such as those of agate and jasper mentioned in the great inventory of the Papal Treasury made by Boniface VIII in 1295, or the early chalices and incense-boats which are still preserved in the Treasury of St Mark's, Venice.

During the fourteenth and fifteenth centuries the manufacture of such costly wares gradually spread throughout the artistic centres of Italy, but by the mid-sixteenth century the Milanese school of artists in pietre dure had established their pre-eminence and Milanese craftsmen could be found all over Europe – in Madrid, Prague, and Vienna, as well as in most Italian cities, including Florence. Among the Milanese craftsmen in Florence were the Carrioni and Giovanni Antonio Miseroni, who were taken into the service of the Grand Duke Francesco I de' Medici in the 1570s. At about this date also a native Florentine school of pietre dure artists began to emerge, at first under the tutelage of these imported Milanese craftsmen. The earliest recorded Florentine craftsmen are Francesco del Tadda, who died in 1576, and his son Romolo, who was active until 1620. Francesco del Tadda worked mainly in porphyry, executing many portrait medallions and a few figures in the round, such as that symbolizing Justice which surmounts the columns in the Piazza di S. Trinità at Florence.

The Florentine *Opificio* may be said to date from about 1580, when the Grand Duke Francesco I established a special workshop in his palace, the Casino di S. Marco, for the Milanese and local Tuscan craftsmen in semi-precious stones. Some twenty years later, in 1599, Francesco's brother and successor the Grand Duke Ferdinando I de' Medici issued a decree establishing the *Opificio* as part of the Grand Ducal Gallery of Works and transferring it to the first floor of the Uffizi. There the *Opificio* remained until 1769, when the Grand Duke Pietro Leopoldo of Habsburg-Lorraine, which family had succeeded the extinct house of Medici, separated the *Opificio* from the rest of the Gallery of Works, and since that date it has remained an autonomous institution, depending directly from the State. The *Opificio* continued to reside in the Uffizi for several more years, however, and it was not until 1796 that it moved to its present location in the former Convent of S. Nicolo in the Via degli Alfani, Florence.

The *Opificio* was founded in order to provide the Medici family and its court with a steady supply of vases, jewellery, ornaments, and mosaic panels in semi-precious stones. But, although the output of the factory was restricted to the Tuscan Court, examples soon found their way abroad in the form of Grand Ducal presents to foreign potentates. A table with an inlaid top of pietre dure, for example, was sent to England in the late sixteenth century, presumably as a gift to Queen Elizabeth I. Unfortunately this table cannot now be traced in the English Royal Collections. Before the end of the sixteenth century, however, a new and infinitely greater task was entrusted to the craftsmen of the *Opificio* – the decoration of the vast mausoleum of the Medici princes with mosaic wall decoration,

an immense altar, gargantuan sarcophagi, and heroic-scale statues of the Grand Dukes, all in pietre dure and the rarest marbles.

The Cappella dei Principi in S. Lorenzo, which contains nearly an acre of wall-space entirely encrusted with semi-precious stones, provides ample testimony to the skill of the *Opificio* craftsmen no less than to the wealth and grandeur of the Medici. This fantastic project – the erection of a mausoleum more grandiose than any other in the whole of Europe to a family whose fortunes were already in decline – seems to have been initiated in about 1597. In that year the Grand Duke Ferdinando I brought back from Rome some three hundred and fifty porphyry fragments of antique sculpture which were to form the basis of the decorative scheme (one of them being the figure of a wolf, now in the Uffizi, which happily escaped destruction).

Work on the chapel began in 1604, under Matteo Nigetti to a design by Giovanni de' Medici, a natural son of Cosimo I, and proceeded by fits and starts over the next two hundred years. It was not, of course, possible to carry out the entire decorative scheme in pietre dure, as originally intended. Yet much wall-space was eventually covered with mosaic panels, the finest of which depict the coats-of-arms of the principal cities of the Grand Duchy in lapis lazuli, coral, mother of pearl, jasper, cornelian, and other brilliant stones. Six great sarcophagi were hewn out of porphyry and a start was made on the altar, though gilt bronze had to be substituted for pietre dure in certain parts, notably for the statues.

During the first few decades of the seventeenth century the *Opificio* was mainly occupied with this chapel, but as the Medici wealth dwindled away work came gradually to a halt and the craftsmen turned their hands to smaller and more profitable work. Various unsuccessful attempts were later made to finish the chapel on more modest lines than those intended by Ferdinando I, but even in its uncompleted state the vast, glittering chamber of princely tombs was sufficiently sumptuous to strike the fancy of most Grand Tourists. They regarded it as one of the principal wonders of modern Italy if not –

like John Evelyn – as "the third heaven if any be on earth".

When the Medici finances began to falter the *Opificio* was slowly converted from an extravagant drain into a source of profit. The Grand Dukes, who had never been too proud to sell the produce from their estates, even at the palace door, set up a brisk trade in pietre dure aimed expressly at the grandest of "Grand Tourists". Cunningly, they displayed in the Uffizi Gallery the exquisite panels and figures intended for the great Cappella dei Principi altar, together with other works made specially for the purpose. These gaudy panels attracted as much attention as the masterpieces of Renaissance painting and sculpture with which they were surrounded.

After the middle of the seventeenth century the *Opificio* seems to have been mainly occupied in catering for this tourist trade. The Habsburg–Lorraine Grand Dukes who succeeded the Medici in 1737 continued this businesslike policy towards the workshop, save for an occasional commission for the decoration of their palaces in Austria. In the mid-nineteenth century the trade was further developed and the *Museo dell' Opificio delle Pietre Dure* was opened in the Via degli Alfani, Florence, as a shop-window for the workshop. Behind the museum the courtyard still resounds with the noise of cutting and grinding as the craftsmen shape and fit together mosaic panels of semi-precious stones, working in much the same way as their predecessors of three hundred and fifty years ago. Only the designs have changed. Now they reproduce in pietre dure the more popular pictures in the Florentine galleries or – with rather greater facility – abstract paintings in the manner of Mondrian.

Table tops

Of all the various categories of work produced by the *Opificio delle Pietre Dure* the table tops are probably the most numerous and successful. The best of these were made in *commesso di pietre dure* or true Florentine Mosaic, a species of *opus sectile* similar to wood *intarsia*. The thin *laminae* of the different stones were cut to take their places in a design which might be either geometrical, arabesque, or pictorial. Perhaps the most notable example of this type of work is the great octagonal table which once stood in the Tribune of the Uffizi and is now in the museum of the *Opificio* (Plate 192B). Ordered in 1633 by the Grand Duke Ferdinando II, this table took sixteen years to complete and is entirely composed of agates, jaspers, lapis lazuli, and chalcedonies inlaid on a background of black Flanders marble. Numerous craftsmen were needed to produce so grandiose a performance. They included Giovanni Merlini, Giovanni Giachetti, Giovanni Francesco and Lorenzo Bottini, Giovanni Bianchi the younger, Cosimo Chermer, Giovanni Giorgi, Carlo Centelli, Pietro Chiarai, and Andrea Merlini, who worked under the direction of Jacopo Autelli, called "il Monnicca". The design for the central motif was provided by Bernardino Poccetti, while Jacopo Ligozzi was responsible for the surround. Like many other works of its period, this design was largely symbolic, incorporating Florentine lilies, the oak leaves of the Della Rovere family, dragons for the Grand Duke, shells with pearls in them for the Grand Duchess, and, in the centre, the shield of the Medici family.

Later seventeenth- and early eighteenth-century tables, of which there are several fine specimens in the Palazzo Pitti at Florence, are rather more simply decorated with arabesques and occasional *trompe l'œil* devices such as the broken necklaces so much admired by the Earl of Cork and Orrery. Pictorial designs used in the seventeenth century frequently included a view of the harbour at Leghorn. In the mid-eighteenth century similar, though rather more elegant, pictorial designs became increasingly popular and held their appeal until the 1790s. The Empire style, however, demanded table tops of a different type. These were less closely ornamented and relied for their decorative effect on a simple still-life group on a background of porphyry or black marble (Plate 192B). Many such tables were ornamented with groups of sea shells, but groups of blue-and-white Chinese porcelain vessels, "Etruscan" or Greek vases, and musical instruments were also popular. The simplest were decorated with no more than a wreath of laurel leaves executed with *trompe l'œil* precision, even to the shadows cast on the background. In the later nineteenth century floral motifs, sometimes combined with shells, returned to favour. In the museum of the *Opificio* there is a particularly fine black table top decorated with a chaplet of white magnolias, made by Edoardo Marchionni in 1881.

Table tops in Florentine mosaic were always an expensive luxury, and it was not long before a cheap and convenient substitute was devised by means of *scagliola*. This material, composed mainly of coloured plaster, had long been used for an imitation marble. But during the early eighteenth century several enterprising craftsmen, notably the Anglo-Florentine Enrico Hugford, adapted it as a medium for painting. Two techniques were developed. The first consisted in painting with scagliola plaster of the required colours on a wet gesso ground and firing when dry so that the finished panel could be given a high polish. The second technique involved the inlay of different coloured sections of plaster into cavities prepared in the gesso ground. Landscapes, still-life, and figure subjects could be depicted by these techniques with an astonishing degree of realism. Indeed, effects of greater delicacy and subtlety could be attained in scagliola than in Florentine mosaic, especially by such skilled craftsmen as Enrico Hugford and his pupil Lamberto Gori. Not unnaturally, scagliola table tops were much in demand among visiting milords; and Sir Horace Mann, the British Resident at Florence for most of the eighteenth century, was frequently asked by English friends to obtain such articles for them.

Pietre dure pictures

Closely connected with table tops were the pictures in pietre dure – portraits, landscapes, and architectural views for the most part – which were also produced in large quantities by the *Opificio* during the seventeenth and eighteenth centuries. The first masterpiece in this genre is the portrait (Plate 191B) of Cosimo I de' Medici executed by Francesco Ferrucci in 1598 after a painting by Domenico Cresti called *Il Passignano*. Although less realistic than the painting, this mosaic derives from the hardness and brilliance of its

medium a magnificent hierarchical effect. The most notable of all pictures in pietre dure are, however, those made between 1737 and 1765 for the Grand Duke Francis of Lorraine to line a room in the Hofburg at Vienna. These fifty pictures represent such subjects as *The Five Moments in the Day of a Lady*, *The Five Senses*, *The Five Seasons*, *Views of Leghorn*, *Scenes from Military Life*, the *Four Quarters of the Globe*, and the *Six Ages of Man*. This series is closely connected with another entitled the *Four Liberal Arts*, which is preserved in the Museum of the *Opificio* at Florence (Plate 192A).

The fifty paintings for the Pietradura-Zimmer in the Hofburg at Vienna were all executed after designs by Giuseppe Zocchi the landscape painter, who is best known for his engraved views of Florentine villas, and who may perhaps be called the Canaletto of Florence. The panels reproduce his paintings with remarkable fidelity and are indeed most skilfully made to simulate the gentle gradations of tone in an oil painting. In 1794 the director of the *Opificio*, Luigi Siries, began work on a series of mosaic pictures with which it was intended to decorate a room in the Palazzo Pitti in emulation of the Pietradura-Zimmer in the Hofburg. Only five panels of views of Roman ruins after paintings by Ferdinando Partini were, however, completed. In these works variations in the colour of the semi-precious stones were cunningly employed to suggest the effect of weathering on the marble of the ancient monuments depicted.

Small pietre dure pictures, intended for insertion in altars or cabinets, were, of course, made in greater quantities than the elaborate series described above. The earliest of these were made for the decoration of the great altar intended for the Cappella dei Principi, and several of them are now in the Museum of the *Opificio*. They represent such Old Testament subjects as *Jonah and the Whale*, *Samson and the Lion*, the *Dream of Jacob*, and *Abraham and the Angels*. Ludovico Cigoli and Giovanni Bilivert, two of the more notable painters working in Florence at the end of the sixteenth century, were among the artists who provided the designs for these panels. Two landscape panels, intended for the same altar, were made by Maestro Fabian, a German, and two others by Maestro Battista of Milan. Panels designed for other altars, dating from the seventeenth century, represented subjects from the New Testament, angels, and flowers. Many other small panels – such as those bought by John Evelyn – were intended to be mounted in cabinets and were usually decorated with floral motifs or groups of birds whose gay plumage might well defy the ornithologist. In the eighteenth century landscape panels became more popular. A good example of this type is the group of panels made by Baccio Cappelli at Florence in 1709 and later incorporated into a cabinet designed by Robert Adam for the Duchess of Manchester in the 1770s.

To avoid the laborious process of cutting numerous small stones into intricate shapes to make a pietre dure picture the *Opificio* craftsmen devised an ingenious though seldom very satisfactory compromise between pietre dure painting and oil painting. This method consisted of painting, in oil colours, on panels inlaid with a few large pieces of pietre dure, much of which could be left to represent the background. Lapis lazuli, for example, was used in this way to represent water or sky in a landscape panel, while the detail of trees, figures, buildings, etc., were added in oil colours, as in the painting of *Latona and the Shepherds* in the *Opificio* Museum. A streaky stone found in the Arno valley (called *lineato dell'Arno*) was also used as a basis for such paintings. The markings of this stone could be used to suggest the waves of the sea or the undulations of a sandy shore, as in the charming painting of *The Vision of St Augustine* (Museum of the *Opificio*), where the figures are over-painted in oil colours.

Sculpture in pietre dure

This section of the *Opificio*'s output was naturally the most limited, and very few examples of it have survived. The most remarkable is a portrait bust (Plate 191A) of the Grand Duchess Vittoria della Rovere, the wife of Ferdinando II de' Medici, which was executed by Giuseppe Antonio Torricelli (1662–1719), the author of an important treatise on pietre dure. By the most skilful use

of black Flanders marble, chalcedony, and various agates, Torricelli achieved an extraordinarily realistic and powerful representation of this imposing Grand Duchess dressed in the habit of the Montalvan Order. It is both a technical *tour-de-force* and a convincing work of art which would deserve a place in any history of Italian sculpture. Hardly less accomplished than this bust is a low-relief portrait (Plate 190) of Cosimo II de' Medici, now in the Museo degli Argenti (Palazzo Pitti) at Florence. This exotic creation, executed by Orazio Mocchi in 1619 after designs by Giovanni Bilivert, is composed of both pietre dure and jewels.

At this period also pietre dure ornaments, carved in high relief or in the round, were produced for the decoration of furniture as, for example, on the gorgeous *prie-Dieu* in the Palazzo Pitti, Florence. Similar ornaments, slightly more restrained in style, were later exported to France for use on furniture. German *ébénistes* working in Paris during the latter part of Louis XVI's reign were particularly fond of pietre dure, and there are splendid examples of its use on a lavish scale by Weisweiler and others in the English Royal Collections.

Statuettes in pietre dure were sometimes made by the *Opificio*, but the finest examples of this category of their output were made for the tabernacle of the altar in the Cappella dei Principi in S. Lorenzo. Similar statuettes were produced for the decoration of reliquaries, notably that of S. Stanislas in the Treasury of S. Lorenzo. This difficult art was revived in the late nineteenth century, when statuettes of Cimabue and Dante were carved by Paolo Ricco.

GLOSSARY

Commesso di pietre dure. This may be translated, literally, as "placing together of hard stones" and is the Italian term for the process known in English as Florentine mosaic. This unique form of mosaic intarsia is distinguished by its use of semi-precious stones (jasper, agate, amethyst, chalcedony, cornelian, blood-stone, lapis lazuli, rock crystal, etc.). The process corresponds in technique to that of wood intarsia, thin *laminae* of different-coloured stones being cut to appropriate shapes and then affixed to panels in ornamental patterns or arranged pictorially so as to form landscape or figure subjects.

Mosaic. This term is usually applied to the decoration of a wall or panel with a design made up of small fragments of stones or coloured glass fixed to the surface with cement or special adhesive. The best-known form of mosaic, usually called Roman or Byzantine mosaic, is formed of small cubes or *tesserae* of coloured stone and glass. The Romans also developed a second technique of mosaic, using, instead of cubes, various-sized segments cut into shapes so as to form a design or picture when joined together. This technique may be regarded as the forerunner of Florentine mosaic.

Pietre dure. This is the Italian term for those stones (literally "hard stones") which are roughly classed as semi-precious in English, i.e. such stones as are composed mainly of silicates in contrasts to "soft" stones, such as limestone and most marbles, which have a large proportion of calcium in their composition.

Scagliola. A technique used for the imitation of marble and especially of Florentine mosaic. The term scagliola derives from the name of the special plaster or gesso, made of pulverized selenite, which is of extremely fine quality, and takes a very high polish. Two processes were developed for the imitation of Florentine mosaic. The first consisted in painting on the wet gesso ground, fixing the colours by heat, and then polishing the surface until it resembled a mosaic of pietre dure. The second consisted in inlaying coloured plasters in the surface of the scagliola panel. This latter process was first developed in Northern Italy during the sixteenth century, and reaches its apogee at Florence in the mid-eighteenth century.

Stone intarsia. A mosaic technique similar to *commesso di pietre dure*, the required design being cut out of the stone surface and pieces of coloured stone, cut into the appropriate shapes, being fitted into the cavities. It differs from Florentine mosaic both in the quality of the stones used and in the less refined methods of applying the stones and joining them together.

Der Steinschneider.

METALWORK

Only from fragments of metal can many details be elucidated concerning the pre-history existence of mankind, and within recorded ages bronze, iron, copper, tin enriched the ancient civilizations, Asiatic, Phoenician, Greek, Roman. Copper and tin, often found together, were probably first combined accidentally – perhaps 2,000 years B.C. – to produce the splendid alloy bronze; and at least as early as 1,000 years B.C. iron was smelted in Central Europe and Assyria. Tin and lead brought fame and Phoenician trade to pre-Roman Britain, and iron smelting had reached this country before Julius Caesar came to Britain.

In medieval Britain as elsewhere the copper alloys were essential for armour and cannon; from Flanders came the fashion for the church effigy brasses invaluable to later historians, and from Germany the encourage-ment of copper mining and brass manufacture.

Collectors must possess a clear understanding of the metals involved, the natural elements, such as iron, copper, tin, lead, and the amalgamations into alloys. Wrought iron at its finest is almost a hundred per cent true iron. By antique bronze is implied a combination of copper and tin. Antique brass consists of the cast alloy of copper and calamine, not to be confused with latten, which is the old term for hammered brass plate. Pewter, in decreasing quality, consisted of tin and copper, tin and antimony, tin and lead. Such analysis, however, suggests nothing of the fascination of these inadequately named base metals. It may be difficult today even to envisage, say, the itinerant bell founder ranging the countryside, but a trace of the ancient magic still clings to the iron horseshoe hung above the door.

American

THE METALS

A study of American tin, copper, and brass should be prefaced with some information about the physical qualities of these metals, for knowledge of their properties will assist the reader in understanding why different metals were selected for different objects. Because tin was cheap, it was used to make inexpensive "pieced ware" such as coffee-pots; the malleability of copper rendered it suitable for making hand-hammered tea-kettles; and brass, the only metal of the three that can be cast satisfactorily, was used for such objects as cast jelly kettles. Each metal has unique qualities. Tin is silvery-white, malleable, and easily fused, and closely resembles pewter, for pewter is 80–90 per cent tin. Tin was used in ancient times, but the production of tin-plate had to be deferred until a way to produce a thin sheet of iron was invented.

In the seventeenth century a small ingot of iron was hammered into a sheet by a man called a "beater", but in the eighteenth century a machine was invented that rolled thin, uniform sheets. These sheets were cleaned and dipped into a vat of molten tin, so that a thin coating of tin rust-proofed the iron. This procedure produced a sheet that had the qualities of iron and some of the qualities of tin. Like iron, it was strong and rigid, and yet could be bent into many useful shapes. Like tin it was rust-proof, white, and ˙easily joined with solder. This useful and inexpensive medium was very popular with colonial craftsmen, and was equally useful when the machine took over the production of stamped tin-ware.

Copper was widely used in both Europe and America in the seventeenth, eighteenth, and nineteenth centuries. Its principal assets are its resistance to rust, efficient conduction of heat, excellent malleability, and attractive red-orange colour. It was particularly well adapted to making such articles as warming-pans and saucepans, where all of its qualities could be used to the satisfaction of the craftsman and his customer. The major objection to using copper for the making of cooking utensils was the disagreeable taste (perhaps poisonous effect) which foods acquired from it. Because of this reason the inside of copper culinary vessels was covered with a thin protective coating of tin. The tinning was preceded by a thorough scraping and cleaning, then sal ammoniac was applied to prevent oxidation during the application of the tin. When the tin coating was worn away in spots the entire vessel had to be retinned.

An alloy is a metal compounded of two or more metals to secure properties which one alone cannot provide. Such an alloy is brass, made of copper and zinc, the most frequent ratio being two parts of copper to one part of zinc. In early times brass was made by combining granules of copper with calcined calamine (impure zinc) in a crucible. The zinc, reduced to a metallic state by intense heat, combined with the copper and formed a lump in the bottom of the crucible. Several of these lumps were combined into a small ingot and sold to the craftsman or merchant. In 1781 James Emerson patented the process of directly fusing copper with zinc to make brass. The two-to-one ratio produces bright gold-coloured metal that is soft to the hammer but hardens quickly and must be frequently annealed or softened. It also produces (with some small changes in its contents) a metal which is free-flowing when molten and can be cast in thin sections, required in the making of furniture brasses, or intricate shapes such as candlesticks. Brass is one of the most valuable alloys known to man and has a number of desirable qualities. It is harder than copper; it is ductile and malleable; it takes a high polish; it is easily joined; and it does not disintegrate rapidly when exposed to the atmosphere. These qualities made it an attractive metal to the colonial artisans, who used it extensively for objects of utility and beauty.

THE CRAFTSMEN

Evidence of overlapping on the trades of the different metal-workers can be found in the newspaper advertisement of E. Brotherton of Lancaster, Pennsylvania, obviously a manufacturer of objects made of sheet-tin, copper, and brass:

> "E. Brotherton, Coppersmith, Brazier, and Tin-plate Worker, Lately from England, Begs leave to inform the public . . ."

Probably the most obscure craftsman involved in this study is the brass-founder.

In order to follow his craft, the brass-founder had to have a melting furnace, a large supply of dampened sand, and a pattern of the object which he planned to reproduce. Sand was rammed around the pattern in a box called a flask, which could be opened for the removal of the pattern without disturbing the sand. After several flasks were prepared the molten metal was dipped from a crucible or a furnace and poured into the cavity in the sand. The casting of heavy objects like bells and cannons was done below ground level so that the molten metal could run directly from the furnace into the mould. Many objects were cast in bronze in essentially the same manner.

Perhaps the most specialized skill connected with the brass industry was metal spinning. The procedure is to rotate a disc of brass on a lathe between a previously formed die on the headstock and a rotating device on the tailstock. A tool is pressed against the rotating disc until the disc conforms to the shape of the die. A large number of concentric circles is the usual evidence that an object has been spun.

PLAIN TINWARE

Decorated and plain tinware were the two types made by American craftsmen. That a larger proportion of the decorated has survived may be due to the fact that the paint gave added protection, and being largely ornamental, it was less used and better cared for.

The question as to what forms of plain tinware were made is answered by early newspaper advertisements and business catalogues. It did not cater only for city trade, for most of the advertisements mentioned that country merchants could be supplied on short notice and on good terms for cash. An interesting listing is that of Thomas Passmore, who had a wholesale and retail tin manufactory in Philadelphia. His advertisement appearing in the *Federal Gazette* on November 30, 1793, lists seventy-six specific items which he manufactured, and concludes by saying that there were other items too numerous to mention.

These objects were usually round, square, or rectangular in form, with wire inserted in the edges to make them strong and rigid. There were large articles such as tin ovens and bathing machines, and small objects such as nursing bottles and funnels. In the early period large objects were often made of several pieces of tin-plate, for pieces of sufficient size were not easily obtainable. Unless an early piece was unusually well cared for, it should show some sign of disintegration, such as rust. Distortion and poor soldering, however, are not necessarily evidences of great age.

Because tin-plate was a cheap and flexible medium there was rapid change of style, and the variety of shapes and joints indicates that the craftsmen were quick to grasp new ideas. Early pieces do not have factory-made spouts and handles like those of the 1850s and 1860s. Because he produced a custom-made object involving machine-made parts, the tinsmith stayed in business a long time. Many tin shops were still operating at the beginning of the twentieth century, and even today a few can be found in rural areas.

It is obvious that a great many of the objects made of tin-plate were used in the home, more specifically in the kitchen. One of the most interesting accessories was the tin oven or roaster (Plate 193A), which stood before the fireplace with a large roast mounted on a spit.

The making of candles was an important project for the pioneer family, and candle-moulds made of tin-plate facilitated the operation. That they must have been very widely used is attested by the fact that there were few attics on the eastern seaboard which could not boast of a few even in the late nineteenth century. Passmore made them in the eighteenth century, and the tin merchants, Hall & Carpenter of Philadelphia, sold machinery to make them as late as 1886. They were made in a variety of heights and unit combinations from two to fifty, units of two, four, six, eight, and twelve being the most common.

The candle box (Plate 193C) was also made of tin-plate and hung in the kitchen to provide a small supply of candles within easy reach. The boxes were 12–14 inches long and usually about 4 inches in diameter; though a few have punched designs in stars and other motifs, the functional use of wire and beading is all that decorates some of them.

Some of the early tinsmiths also made ginger-bread cutters. To the indigenous designs of birds, tulips, hearts, etc., were added eagles, log cabins, Uncle Sams, and Indians. The popularity of the cooky cutter continued late in the nineteenth century. The animal shapes retained the primitive feeling of the earlier designs, but the geometric patterns are uninteresting.

Museums such as Old Sturbridge Village,

Sturbridge, Massachusetts, and the Landis Valley Museum near Lancaster, Pennsylvania, have displays of tinware used on the farms and in small villages during the nineteenth century. Regarded by many people today as a metal of little value, tin-plate was a commodity precious to our ancestors.

SHEET-BRASS AND COPPER

The survival of many objects made of sheet-brass and copper can be attributed to a number of reasons. The inherent quality and beauty of the metals influenced craftsmen to use them for the making of objects of importance. These items served a long time; they were well cared for, and did not disintegrate rapidly when they were discarded for a later and more fashionable object. Generally speaking, the malleability, the colour, and the permanence of sheet-brass and copper gave them a favoured position over tin. Silver was the only superior metal available to make comparable objects.

The copper weathervane of early date, of great interest to collectors, combines functionalism and good design (Plate 194A). This is an object in which the malleability and permanence of copper are important. After years of exposure the copper turns a fine verdigris-green. The earliest vanes were made of two convex pieces of copper, soldered together at the edges, forming a figure in low relief. The early ones, like Shem Drowne's *Indian*, belonging to the Massachusetts Historical Society, were probably knocked out with a mallet on a plank or a piece of lead. In the middle of the nineteenth century, however, such vanes were made by shaping a piece of sheet-copper in a mould of cast-iron, the mould having been cast from a pattern of wood which had been carved in full detail. The later vanes were in higher relief and more detailed than the earlier type. A variety of forms were produced, such as cocks, horses, ships, fish, grasshoppers, and horse-drawn sulkies.

The copper tea-kettle deserves some consideration, for despite a long European tradition in the making of utensils, the copper-smiths of Pennsylvania and New York produced a flaring goose-neck type with a swing-ing handle that is peculiar to the area (Plate 194B). Many of them can be identified because the makers stamped them with an intaglio stamp.

Another significant item produced in quantity was the liquor still, for which there was a brisk demand throughout the grain-growing areas of Pennsylvania. It was easier and more lucrative to carry liquor to the Philadelphia market than cumbersome bags of grain. If the farmers were too poor to own a still for their individual use a number pooled their resources and bought one for a community. Most of the stills show evidence of fine workmanship in the riveting and planished surfaces.

The most common article made of sheet brass was undoubtedly the spun brass kettle from Connecticut, produced in large quantities from 1851 and sold by pedlars on the eastern seaboard. Other objects besides kettles were spun, for in the collection of Old Sturbridge Village at Sturbridge, Massachusetts, can be found a basin that has the typical concentric circles, and on the bottom the stamp usually found on spun kettles. A hammered brass kettle bears the name of William Heyser, a coppersmith from Chambersburg, Pennsylvania.

Many other objects such as braziers, coal-hods, oil-lamp fillers, measures, funnels, fish kettles, chocolate pots, frying pans, house-pouting, butter churns, footwarmers, and many specialized objects for the hatting and dyeing trades were made of sheet brass and copper. There were objects for marine use, and a number of copper dry measures were used by official sealers of weights and measures.

CAST BRASS

It is doubtful if any product of the American craftsman is more difficult to identify as to origin than the object of cast brass. Despite the fact that many skilled men were engaged in the craft, the names of only a few are known, and extremely few of their products can be identified, an obscurity difficult to understand, yet existing.

Early costumes and contemporary newspaper advertisements indicate that brass buttons and buckles were in wide use in the eighteenth century.

Caspar Wistar (who came to Philadelphia in 1717) was one of the first craftsmen known to have engaged in the business of brass casting, and he seems to have made just buttons. His son, Richard, continued the manufacture of brass buttons.

Most plentiful among objects of cast brass, are furniture mounts, whose places of origin are almost impossible to identify. The many English trade catalogues indicate a brisk exporting business, but there is proof that these pieces were made in America also. In 1795 Bolton & Grew of Boston advertised *Cabinet Brass Foundry Goods* and enumerated articles such as pulls, hinges, pendants, etc.

Early cast brass andirons of American manufacture are quite rare, but in recent years a number of these have been found bearing names of American craftsmen. Andirons of iron, from which the name obviously originates were enhanced by adding a finial and plate of brass as interiors of houses became richer. Into this category fall the attractive knife-blade andirons with penny feet and brass urn finials. Late in the eighteenth century andirons of cast brass were popular and are appropriately used in a Georgian setting with Chippendale furniture. These have tall, intricately patterned columns terminating in a variety of finials, such as the urn, ball, steeple, lemon, and double-lemon pattern. They have a modified cabriole leg with a simple ball, snake, or ball-and-claw foot. The most extravagant style had a twisted baluster and diamond-and-flame finial; a pair signed by Paul Revere is now in the Metropolitan Museum, New York.

Another important product of the brass-founder was the brass door-knocker. Popular in the eighteenth century was the modified S-type, while the urn and eagle patterns were popular in the early nineteenth century. Newspaper advertisements indicate they were made in America, but a signed one has not appeared.

A number of brass-founders made mathematical or surveying instruments, lancets, and the famous clockmaking Chandlees of Nottingham, Maryland, made a sundial that is signed. A few cast brass (or bronze) skillets are known to have been made in America. The origins of the many cast kettles, and the button and bullet moulds, remains a mystery.

Objects of cast brass can be easily reproduced, and it is difficult for a novice to tell the old from the new. The absence of makers' marks and of other identifying evidence, such as patina on pewter, forces the buyer to depend chiefly on the integrity of the dealer.

British and Continental

The number of small objects made of metal and used about the house that were treated in a sufficiently attractive or imaginative way to interest the collector is enormous. With the exception of such "big game" as medieval aquamaniles or Limoges enamels, out of reach of the average collector, all the articles referred to are to be found, if not in the more modest antique shops, at least in those specializing in the base metals.

The term "base metal" is an unfortunate one, since it inevitably suggests a certain inferiority of quality. In fact, many of these articles were treated with no less exquisiteness of detail and delicacy of touch than the precious metals. Most suitable for the rendering of delicate ornament is steel, which, by reason of its hardness, could be sawn, filed, or chiselled to a lacelike fineness, such as can be found in the snuff-boxes, étuis, scissors, and chains made at Brescia in the seventeenth century or in England in the eighteenth century. By reason of the enormous labour involved, steel was not used where high relief was required. In this case bronze was the most suitable material, cast, chased, and finally gilt. The reddish colour of the bronze provided a particularly well-suited base for gilding, and a very rich effect was obtained. Among the finest work achieved in this medium are the caskets and clock-cases produced in South Germany in the second half of the sixteenth century. But more remarkable still are the furniture mounts and ornamental articles made by the Parisian ciseleurs-doreurs in the second half of the eighteenth century. The quality of the finish on the finest Louis XVI mounts is unsurpassed in the whole history of metal-working. On the Continent these mounts have long been collected for their own sake, but in England it is only recently that even the excellent work in ormolu produced at Matthew Boulton's Birmingham factory in the late eighteenth century has been recognized.

Not only did the workers in the base metals achieve an excellence of quality which rivalled that of the contemporary goldsmiths, they frequently made use of the precious metals in order to enrich their own productions. The various techniques of inlaying and encrusting the surface of base metal with gold, silver, or another base metal were extensively used by the metal craftsmen throughout the history of the craft. The most ambitious and imaginative use of damascening was made by Italian craftsmen in the sixteenth century, probably inspired by the examples they saw from the Near East. The most elaborate damascened ornament was applied to armour and weapons, but the same craftsmen who decorated Milanese armour also executed the damascened enrichment on caskets and furniture mounts, and these latter can be obtained at a price far below that commanded by armour. The Milanese technique of enriching iron with gold and silver was paralleled by the Venetian technique of damascening brass with precious metal. Their manner was strongly influenced by the Orient, and the earlier brass vessels decorated in Venice are not easily distinguishable from those of Near Eastern origin.

Here we are concerned only with those pieces which have some pretensions to artistic merit. But alongside them, in the limitless field of folk art, innumerable unassuming objects, well designed for their simple domestic function, await the collector.

ANDIRONS

The iron fire-dog or andiron dates back to Roman times, but the earliest known examples date from the fifteenth century. As long as the fireplace occupied the central position in the hall, the fire-dog was of purely utilitarian design, but when the former was transferred to a side wall, becoming an important decorative feature, the fire-dog also received ornamental treatment. The earliest surviving fire-dogs conform to a standard type, whether of English, French, German, or Flemish origin, namely an arched base en-

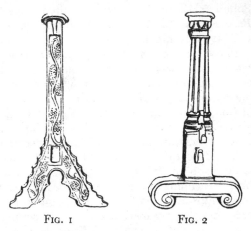

FIG. 1   FIG. 2

riched with Gothic cusping, supporting a pilaster, the front of which is decorated with running scrolls (Fig. 1). Sixteenth- and seventeenth-century fire-dogs were made to the same design but with Renaissance instead of Gothic ornament (Fig. 2). Fire-dogs of this type were made of cast iron, the English ones being produced by the Sussex iron-masters. There seems from an early date to have been a distinction between andirons and fire-dogs. The former term was used for the large dogs, standing 3 feet or more high, which were intended to decorate the fire-place. Though these andirons could also be put to use, they were usually accompanied by a smaller pair of fire-dogs proper, which stood closer into the hearth and supported the burning logs.

The earlier andirons were of wrought iron, but as early as the sixteenth century they were garnished with silver. In the seventeenth century andirons entirely of silver were produced, and there was a fashion for them in England after the Restoration. Numbers have survived from this date not only in the royal palaces but also in many country houses, and are not out of reach of the wealthy collector. The Restoration andiron had a particularly handsome baroque form, consisting of a pedestal on volute or claw feet supporting either a flaming vase or a figure. The finest

FIG. 3

examples, in silver, are of great magnificence and weight. Similar designs were also produced for the less wealthy in gilt brass (Fig. 3). The introduction of the grate in the eighteenth century rendered the fire-dog superfluous.

In contrast to those used in drawing-room and parlour, the various implements for tending the cottage fire remained unchanged and simple. Of purely functional character, they usually bore little in the way of ornamentation. As coal came into use, the poker and the shovel replaced the fire-fork.

Of the Continental andirons by far the most handsome type are the North Italian ones of the sixteenth and seventeenth centuries. These were cast in bronze and take the form of an elaborately worked pedestal supporting a figure of a warrior or a goddess.

AQUAMANILE

This term is used to describe the bronze ewers used in the Middle Ages for pouring water over the hands of guests after each course of a meal. As forks were not normally employed for conveying food to the mouth, frequent washing of the hands was necessary. The term is now confined to a particular type of medieval ewer of naturalistic form, the most popular being a lion on whose back crouched a dragon, serving as a handle. Other forms include a monster, a knight on horseback wearing a great helm, etc. Medieval aquamaniles of this type were cast by the *cire-perdu* process, and no two were exactly alike; many reproductions have, however, been cast from moulds in recent times. The earliest examples date from the thirteenth century, but they continued in use until the sixteenth century, when they were replaced by the more convenient ewer of helmet shape. They are now objects of extreme rarity, and few authentic examples are to be found in private ownership.

BRASS CANDLESTICKS

European candlesticks as early as the twelfth century are known but are not likely to be seen outside museums or cathedral treasuries. The earliest examples obtainable by the collector are the pricket candlesticks of enamelled copper made at Limoges in the thirteenth century. These are exceedingly rare and are pieces of high price. The only medieval candlesticks within the reach of the ordinary collector are the various fifteenth-century types produced in the Low Countries in one or other of the towns in the valley of the Meuse.

The earliest form of candlestick was the pricket, in which the candle was stuck on a metal, usually iron, spike projecting from the wax-pan. The socket type, in which the candle was held in a cup or socket, did not come into common use until the fourteenth century, though it was certainly known much earlier.

The Mosan candlesticks were, until 1466, mostly produced in the town of Dinant, and from there they were exported all over western Europe. Though the brass-workers became dispersed during the latter part of the fifteenth century, they continued to work in just the same style that they had developed at

Dinant. This is indicated by the remarkable uniformity of design of sixteenth-century, and earlier, candlesticks found in different European countries. From the thirteenth century onwards a large range of types were made, beginning with the rare figures of animals or monsters supporting a pricket, continuing with the fourteenth-century tripod prickets decorated with octagonal mouldings, and evolving in the fifteenth century into two main types: firstly, the pricket with tall, domed base, moulded stem, and large grease-pan immediately below the pricket. The second type, which probably reached western Europe from the Near East, has a tall base of trumpet form, to the top of which is attached a wide rim or flange serving as a grease-pan. The stem is decorated with len-ticular mouldings and the socket is provided with a vertical opening resembling in shape a Gothic window, through which a spike could be inserted to eject the candle stub. As the sixteenth century advances the mouldings applied to the stem became more numerous, some four or five in number.

In the course of the late sixteenth and early seventeenth centuries the grease-pan, instead of being formed from the upper surface of the base, became independent and was set on the stem just above the base. About the middle of the century it moved up farther, reaching a position about half-way up the stem, as in the typical English candlesticks of this epoch. They are very simply constructed of a hollow tube of trumpet form decorated with a series of grooves running horizontally around the stem at regular intervals. The contemporary Continental candlestick is usually of more sophisticated form with finely proportioned baluster stem. Towards the end of the seventeenth century the grease-pan completed its upwards move and reached a position just under the socket. Finally, at the end of the century the lip of the socket was turned over to give a small grease-pan, the grease-pan proper abandoned, and instead a depression cut in the top of the base.

The eighteenth-century candlestick went through the variations of style familiar in the evolution of silver, that is, octagonal baluster in the first quarter, shell-base and vase-shaped baluster in the middle of the century, and, finally, the square-base and section of the neo-classical style in the latter years of the century.

Some idea of date can often be gained from the method of construction of brass candlesticks. Until the late seventeenth century the stem and socket were cast solid in one piece and attached to the base by means of a screw thread or a tenon which projected through a hole in the centre of the base and was then burred over to hold it in place. About 1670 a new method was introduced by which stem and socket were hollow cast in two pieces and then brazed together, thus saving much metal. In the nineteenth century there was a return to solid casting in one piece.

BRASS CHANDELIERS

Chandeliers were made in three main materials. There are those of wood and glass, which by reason of their delicacy are most suitable for reception rooms, and there are the ones of brass with which we are here concerned.

It used to be thought that all the brass chandeliers which are found in England were made in the Netherlands. Documentary and other evidence shows conclusively that this is not so and that many were made in England.

Chandeliers of English manufacture

In England there was no difference necessarily between secular chandeliers and ecclesiastical ones. The examples in the House of Commons and in the House of Lords were of brass, and so were those in the Livery Halls of some London Companies. It might be thought that the ones intended for public buildings are never available for collection. This is not so, because many were taken down when gas-lighting was introduced in the nineteenth century and those that escaped the furnace were often rehung in private houses.

The earliest chandelier of those thought to have been made in England is in the church at Sonning, Berkshire. It is dated 1675. The form of construction which it and the one at Langley Marish, Buckinghamshire, and that in the nave of St Helen, Abingdon, Berkshire, exemplify was the typical one until c. 1740. The various parts are normally cast,

The candle-sockets are screwed to the ends of the branches; the grease-pans are wedged between; the body incorporates trays pierced with holes into which are hooked the branches; at the bottom it ends in a globe and pendant, and at the top is an ornamental finial and a suspension-ring. The globe and the parts between it and the finial, exclusive of the trays, are hollow, and the whole of the body is held together by an iron rod with the pendant at one end and a hole to receive a pin at the other. The only departures from this form of construction are caused by different methods of attaching the branches. In some examples they hook into bosses which project from a plain vertical band (Plate 199A). In others there are castings that have a top surface which is pierced and serves the function of a tray.

The branches of most early examples are of circular section; they consist simply of two opposed curves with perhaps a moulding where they join. The inner end is an open spiral, and the outer end is everted so that the screw of the candle-socket passes through it at right angles. They droop heavily. After *c.* 1710, branches become more elaborate: they are often of hexagonal or octagonal section and the inner end consists of multiple scrolls while the outer end is no longer everted but thickened instead.

If there are wide spaces between the branches, these are filled by ornaments fitting

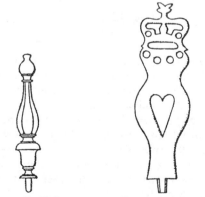

FIG. 4. St Helen,
Abingdon, Berkshire

FIG. 5. Wickwar,
Gloucestershire

into holes or dovetailing into slots. The ornaments take various forms (Figs. 4 and 5). They

may be pins, or they may be branches, each ending in a bud or a flower, or a silhouette representation of three tulips, as at Whitchurch, Shropshire. At Aston Hall, Birmingham, there are cherubs which formerly held objects aloft, and there is the rose and thistle badge of Queen Anne at Tiverton, Devon, and Stratton Strawless, Norfolk. Similar ornaments to

FIG. 6. St Martin-at-
Palace, Norwich

FIG. 7. Llanasa,
Flint

these may occur between the tiers of branches, in which case special trays are provided for them (Figs. 6 and 7). Usually, they consist of S-scrolls, but sometimes there are branches, which at Deane, Lancashire, end in flying cherubs with roses and crowns, and at Llanasa, Fling, and Upholland, Lancashire, in silhouette patterns.

The purpose of the globe is to reflect the candlelight and, by its weight, to prevent the tendency to swing. It is usually spherical. When it is polygonal the candle-sockets and remainder of the body are partly polygonal also. The main development that takes place in the globe is that it acquires a central collar *c.* 1715 and becomes flattened after 1725.

The finial is a feature of most chandeliers (Figs. 8 and 9). The form which was at first most

FIG. 8. Harlow,
Essex

FIG. 9. Langley Marish,
Buckinghamshire

popular on account of its being a symbol of immortality was the cherub-head, but after *c.* 1700 it took second place to the dove, whose justification for use was that it is the symbol of the Holy Spirit. The dove, represented with an olive-spray in its beak, became by far the commonest form of finial. The only other regularly used was the bishop's mitre.

The construction of chandeliers underwent a noticeable change *c.* 1745 (Plate 199B). Now, the branches, instead of hooking into trays, are attached to the globe, and, for this to be possible, the halves of the globe and the collar are three separate castings and the branches are bolted to the collar. The change was not immediate, and there was a period of transition when the branches fitted by means of tenons or hooks into eyes forming a continuation of the collar. The new construction meant that there had to be as many globes as there were tiers of branches, and the result was that all details assume heavier proportions, and mouldings are correspondingly bolder. The body often incorporates sections of gadrooning; so does the pendant, which consists of several parts instead of just one. It may end in a floral motif or in a handle or ring, which is primarily an ornament but was also useful at the lowering and raising of a chandelier whenever the provision of pulley and counterweight made this possible. Branches now are of circular section and droop only slightly. The curves are ornamented with scrolls, where they join is a moulding lozenge-shaped or hexagonal in plan, and the inner end is a closed spiral. The candle-sockets now have separate nozzles. Such nozzles at first are closed at the bottom. Every form of finial is virtually abandoned in favour of the flame. It is, like the cherub-head, a symbol of immortality and has the merit of hiding the device for suspension.

Heavy chandeliers with flame finials continued to be made until *c.* 1770, when a reaction set in. The use of the dove as a finial was resumed, and proportions become more graceful again. The example at Eynsham, Oxfordshire, is typical of what was being designed (Plate 198A). The flame still appears as a finial, and it frequently issues from an urn. Candle-sockets of the latest chandeliers are characteristically urn-shaped, and the place of the moulding where the curves of the branches join may be taken by a pair of acanthus leaves. There were no further changes before 1830, and then the introduction of gas-lighting was bringing the manufacture of

chandeliers almost to an end. After this, only country-dwellers and antiquarians still had a use for them.

This typological study is based almost entirely on the evidence of the chandeliers made in London. The London makers were more progressive than those in the provinces. They were responsible for most of the chandeliers made in England and were the only ones until the nineteenth century to distribute their products throughout the country. There are no obvious characteristics of London work. It has to be recognized by its high quality and by the use of certain castings. Finials are the most significant because they recur with greatest frequency, and one which does so particularly is a dove which appears in 1704 and which survived as a copy into the nineteenth century (Fig. 9). Any chandelier that has this dove as its finial is likely to have been made in London.

The chandeliers made at the various provincial centres have each their own characteristics. The finial is the part to look at first. Early chandeliers made in Bristol have a dove finial, made distinct by its shape and the absence of feathering on the body (Fig. 10).

Fig. 10. Marshfield, Gloucestershire

Late ones have a crown of leaf-like flames. Thomas Bayley and his successors at Bridgwater used a biconical flame finial. At Chester the finial was normally a dove: with tilted tail and prominent rump, if it is early; with fan-tail, if late (Plate 198B). The Cocks's of Birmingham preferred a finial consisting of separate flames of sheet metal, but they shared this preference with some London makers, and their work is best identified by the form of the branches.

Chandeliers of Dutch manufacture

It is in the Netherlands that the brass chandelier has its traditional home. There, they were used for private houses as well as for public buildings. The *tableaux de modes* suggest that in the seventeenth century they were an established part of the domestic scene.

The Netherlands is probably where most, if not all, of the earliest chandeliers were made. These are the medieval ecclesiastical ones. Their central feature is the figure of a saint, which shows that they were looked on as receptacles for candles to be burnt as symbols of devotion rather than as a means of lighting. In view of the purpose which they served, most of these chandeliers were destroyed at the Reformation. If the few that survive are typical, generally the branches were ornamented with vine-leaves, and an animal head with a ring through its mouth was the form of pendant terminal.

After the Reformation Dutch chandeliers were constructed in the same way as the earliest ones of English make. The former may be recognized because designs – at least in the seventeenth century – are normally more intricate and heavier and there is often a double-headed eagle finial. Branches sometimes have a foliage motif or a fish-head where the curves join and a human head at the inner end. Ornaments between branches are more elaborate than those on English chandeliers. There are trumpeters and cherub-heads at Cirencester, Gloucestershire, and scrolls to which are screwed finials at Sherborne, Dorset, and Woodbridge, Suffolk. The form of chandelier normal in England after 1745 does not seem to have been made in the Netherlands. There the tendency during the eighteenth century was towards plainness. Finials and other ornaments are entirely dispensed with. Branches are simply scrolled and the fish-heads which they may incorporate are vestigial. They are usually provided with tenons instead of hooks. These fit into holes in the edges of hollow trays and are held in position by pins that pass through them and through the tops and bottoms of the trays. This method of attaching the branches was never adopted by English makers.

There are other chandeliers besides the ones made in England and the Netherlands. But the collector who studies their products alone will not want further evidence to convince him that chandeliers are among the finest and most spectacular achievements of the brass-founder's craft.

CASKETS

The earliest caskets likely to come the way of the collector are those made in Sicily during the thirteenth and fourteenth centuries. They are constructed of ivory with brass mounts, and are believed to have been the work of Arabic craftsmen. The Near Eastern element in them can be seen, not in any constructional detail but in the painted ornament with which the finer examples were enriched. This ornament often introduces Cufic characters or amorphous scrollwork of Saracenic origin. Caskets or small coffers of the fifteenth cen-

FIG. 11. French casket, blued iron damascened with grotesques in gold

tury are far less rare than the earlier examples; there were two main types, those constructed entirely of iron and those of wood, sometimes covered with leather and always furnished with more or less elaborate bands of iron. Such caskets were made in France (Plate 195A and B), the Low Countries, Germany (Plate 195C), and Spain, and it is often difficult to be certain of the country of origin, especially of the earlier types (Plate 195A). Subsequently, recognized national types emerge. One French type is entirely of iron with arched lid. The earlier examples have applied Gothic tracery ornamentation, the later ones have a plain surface with either etched or damascened ornament (Fig. 11). The Spanish type is of almost rectangular section with only slightly curved walls. It is of wood covered with one or more layers of tinned sheet iron, pierced with reticulated ornament. This type is provided with stout bands and an elaborate lock decorated with Gothic pinnacles.

The most common German type dates from the second half of the sixteenth century and shows no trace of the Gothic ornament which persisted so long into the sixteenth cen-

FIG. 12. South German casket, iron with mounts of gilt brass; late sixteenth century

tury in the locksmiths' workshops. It is rectangular in plan and is constructed of iron sheet sometimes enriched with mounts of gilt brass. The whole of the exterior surface is etched with floral scrolls or with hunting or allegorical subjects. The lock, which is accommodated on the underside of the lid, is of great elaboration, shooting as many as a dozen bolts. These coffers were made in Nürnberg and Augsburg, but are never signed (Fig. 12 and Plate 195D). On the other hand,

FIG. 13. Miniature casket, South German, c. 1600

the miniature caskets of gilt brass, sometimes enriched with silver and even enamel, and engraved instead of etched, are usually known as Michael Mann boxes because so many of them bear the signature of a Nürnberg locksmith of that name (Fig. 13).

Fine coffers of English manufacture do not appear before the second half of the seventeenth century, when we find the very rare but incomparable works of the Bickfords (e.g. the jewel casket of Queen Mary II in the Victoria and Albert Museum) and the fairly common but extremely attractive caskets with fall fronts veneered with oyster marquetry and furnished with elaborate gilt brass hinge-work.

CHISELLED AND CUT STEEL

The art of steel chiselling is a by-product oi the locksmith's and gunsmith's trade. Small articles have been chiselled from iron or steel since the Middle Ages, but from the collector's point of view, four main groups can be recognized. Firstly, the articles made in the northern Italian city of Brescia in the seventeenth and eighteenth centuries. These include snuff-boxes, scissors, tweezers, and thimbles, usually chiselled and pierced with floral scrollwork interspersed with monsters, similar in design to the ornament familiar on

14   15

FIG. 14. Snuff-box, Brescian; late seventeenth century
FIG. 15. Snuff-box, Brescian; dated 1694

Brescian-made firearms (Fig. 14). The most distinguished Brescian artist, who usually signed his works, was Matteo Acqua Fresca (Fig. 15). The second group was produced in Paris by the same chisellers who decorated sword and gun furniture of the period of Louis XIV and Louis XV. Characteristic of their work are the chatelaines, étuis, shuttles, and, more rarely, snuff-boxes, usually chiselled with classical figure subjects against a gilt stippled ground. Similar but somewhat coarser work was also produced in Germany (Plate 195F). The third group was produced by the artists of the Imperial Russian small arms factory at Tula. The factory was founded by Peter the Great, and their work dates from the eighteenth century. The artisans mastered not only the art of chiselling iron but also of encrusting it with various softer metals and of faceting it (cut-steel). Besides smaller objects, such as candlesticks and caskets, the Tula factory also turned out large pieces of furniture and even mantelpieces entirely constructed of cut and faceted steel. The last group is English and flourished at first about the middle of the eighteenth century in Woodstock in Oxfordshire and subsequently at Birmingham in the Soho works set up by Matthew Boulton. The Woodstock cottage industry produced both chiselled and faceted steel, but the Birmingham factory, which eventually put Woodstock out of business, concentrated on cut steel. They made sword hilts, buttons, chatelaines, buckles, and cheap jewellery. Cut steel was used as a more durable alternative to marcasite in the late eighteenth and early nineteenth century.

COPPER-WORK

Owing to the difficulty of working copper in its pure form, it has not been extensively used by the metal-worker. In the sixteenth and early seventeenth centuries caskets, clockcases, and scientific instruments were frequently made of copper, which was subsequently engraved and gilt (Plate 195D). Those parts of the case or instrument which were cast were, however, made of brass or bronze. Owing to its suitability for engraving, it was much used for flat surfaces which were to be decorated in this way. The only other significant European use of copper was by the Italian coppersmiths, who made ewers, basins, and other vessels. The earlier examples were decorated with fine engraving, and in the seventeenth century embossed with bold floral ornament of baroque character, but vessels in this last group do not as a rule rise above the level of peasant art.

CUTLERY

The history of eating-knives goes back to remote antiquity, but for the collector it may be said to commence in the fifteenth century. Knives dating from the Romano-British period have been excavated in considerable numbers, but the condition of these is usually such that they are more likely to attract the archaeologist than the collector. Until well into the sixteenth century the history of cutlery is that of the knife only. Forks were known in the Middle Ages, but were normally used only

for carving the joint of meat. An extremely rare type of fork was also used in noble households for eating certain kinds of fruit, the juice of which might stain the fingers.

The ordinary eating-knife of the fifteenth century was of too simple a character to be considered worth preserving, and the only examples which have come to light have been discovered in the course of excavations. On the other hand, knives with handles of precious materials, either hardstone, gold, or silver, have been valued on account of their beauty, and a few have survived through the ages (Figs. 16 and 17). The most beautiful medieval knives are those made for members of the Burgundian Court; a number of these exist, all in museums. Their handles are of

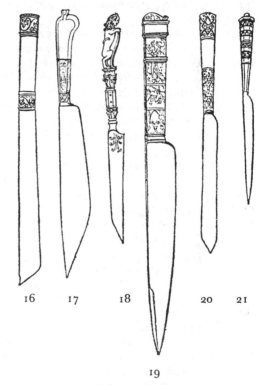

Fig. 16. Carving-knife, ivory handle with silver-gilt mounts; fourteenth century

Fig. 17. Carving-knife, ivory handle with enamelled silver shoulder; Italian; late fifteenth century

Fig. 18. French; sixteenth century

Fig. 19. Italian; late fifteenth century

Figs. 20 and 21. London-made knives of the early seventeenth century silver-gilt enriched with the heraldic bearings of the original owner in translucent enamel.

The inventories of the property of the Tudor monarchs show that they possessed many sets of fine cutlery contained in cases of leather or wood, and mounted in handles of hardstone or ivory. None of these pieces can now be identified, if indeed they still exist, but there are a number of sixteenth-century types of cutlery that may still be found. These include the Flemish type with handle of brass or latten furnished with wooden scales. The finials of the handles are often formed as horses' hooves, and the rivets holding the scales as horse-bells, but the finest examples are engraved with minute religious subjects. These Flemish knives were exported to England in quantity, and many have been dug up in London.

The French sixteenth-century type has a handle of gilt iron, the finial chiselled in the form of an animal or monster, the scales being of ivory or mother-of-pearl (Fig. 18). The most beautiful is undoubtedly the Italian form, which has a flat, pilaster-like handle of silver, sometimes enriched with niello, surmounted by a gilt bronze finial in the form of a capital (Fig. 19).

Although forks had not yet entered into general use in northern Europe, a single fork is usually found along with a set of knives by the latter part of the sixteenth century. It was probably intended for carving and for serving. The true serving knife, sometimes known as a Présentoir, which appears in the fifteenth century, has a thin, broad blade, with the edges either parallel or widening slightly towards the point, which was either cut off square or slightly rounded.

Little is known of English knives made before the seventeenth century, and it is difficult to distinguish them from imported Flemish knives. No sixteenth-century English knives of fine quality are known to exist. By the early seventeenth century, however, the English cutlers were making cutlery as fine as that of any other country. The work of the London cutlers can be recognized by the dagger-mark which was struck on all blades made by members of the Cutlers' Company, in addition to the maker's mark. A characteristic feature of London knives of the first half of the seventeenth century was the decorative treatment of the shoulders, which were either damascened with gold or encrusted with silver (Figs. 20 and 21).

The main source of knife blades in western Europe was the German town of Solingen,

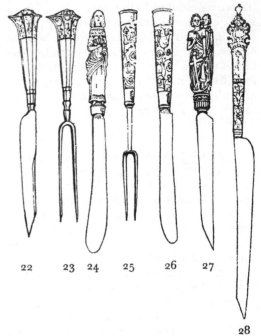

FIG. 22. Ivory handles, gilt brass terminals; German; early seventeenth century

FIG. 23. Carved ivory handle; English, c. 1680

FIG. 24. Ivory handles, piqué with silver; English, c. 1690

FIG. 25. Carved ivory; Dutch; end of seventeenth century

FIG. 26. Dutch; first half of the seventeenth century

FIG. 27. Handle of Venetian millefiore glass; late seventeenth century

FIG. 28. Handle of bow porcelain; mid-eighteenth century

whence blades were exported all over Europe, being fitted with handles in the locality to which they had been sent. A Solingen stamp on a blade does not necessarily signify that the handle was also made there.

In the seventeenth century the usual materials for handles were ivory, silver, and various kinds of hardstone, especially agate.

Of the great variety of types of handle made, the most attractive are the Dutch wedding knives, made in pairs with handles entirely of silver finely engraved with Biblical subjects and grotesques, often after the designs of the Liége-born engraver Johann Theodor de Bry (Fig. 26).

In the eighteenth century ivory and agate gave way to porcelain or stoneware as a fashionable material for handles (Figs. 29, 30), but silver remained usual for all except the cheaper grades made of horn or wood. The characteristic eighteenth-century knife has a handle of pistol shape in which is mounted a curved blade of so-called "scimitar" form. Since the late seventeenth century the fork had become a normal feature of the dining-table in northern as well as southern Europe. Though forks had been familiar objects since early in the seventeenth century, they were long used by pre-ference for holding the meat

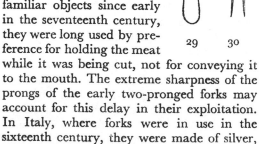

29   30

while it was being cut, not for conveying it to the mouth. The extreme sharpness of the prongs of the early two-pronged forks may account for this delay in their exploitation. In Italy, where forks were in use in the sixteenth century, they were made of silver, which did not take so sharp a point.

Cutlery ceases to be of interest to the collec-tor by the early nineteenth century. The last sets of cutlery worthy of notice are the travel-ling sets composed of knife, fork, spoon, beaker, etc., which were still produced until well into the nineteenth century, and were often mounted in gold or silver.

DAMASCENING

The art of encrusting the surface of iron, steel, brass, or copper with gold or/and silver has been known and practised since anti-quity, especially in the Near East, but at no time in Europe has it flourished more than in Milan during the middle and second half of the sixteenth century, where it was a by-product of the thriving armourers' trade. Thin iron sheets were embossed, often in a rather summary manner, with subjects from Roman history or mythology against land-scape backgrounds and damascened with gold and silver. The Milanese damascening of this period is of fine quality and bears com-parison with the best Saracenic work. Damas-cened plaques were made in quantity to more or less standard shapes and were sold to cabi-net-makers, who mounted them on ebony caskets, chest of drawers, and even large pieces such as tables and mirrors. Though the majority of the damascened ironwork en-countered by the collector is likely to be of Milanese origin, there were highly competent damasceners at work elsewhere in Europe, in Augsburg and Nürnberg, in Paris, and in other Italian cities. In the seventeenth cen-tury some fine damascening was done on Eng-lish sword and knife handles, probably by immigrant Italian artists. The detailed orna-ment that could be achieved by damascening was not appreciated in the age of baroque, when a rather more vigorous spirit was ad-mired, and the art did not survive the six-teenth century in Italy (Plate 195E).

DINANDERIE

Small brassware made in or around the Flem-ish town of Dinant, near Liége. Whereas else-where bronze was mostly employed for the manufacture of domestic vessels, the pre-sence of zinc deposits around Liége led the founders of the valley of the Meuse to adopt brass in preference. The town of Dinant be-came by the late Middle Ages so famous for its brassware that the name Dinanderie was used to describe the production of the whole region. Typical articles made were aqua-maniles, basins, jugs, cooking vessels, and candlesticks, many of them quite simple ob-jects for domestic purposes. Among the more splendid achievements of the Mosan crafts-men may be mentioned lecterns and fonts. In 1466 the town of Dinant was sacked by Philippe le Bon, and as a result the brass-founders emigrated, partly to other towns in the valley of the Meuse, but partly to France and England.

ENAMELLED BRASSWARE

Copper was used for preference rather than brass for enamelling in the Middle Ages, and apart from a few harness ornaments and the Garter stall-plates preserved in St George's Chapel, Windsor Castle, medieval enamelled brassware does not exist. During the seventeenth century a cheap form of enamelling was introduced in England and on the Continent, in which brass was used as a base. The enamel was of the *champlevé* type, but instead of the depressions for the enamel being cut out by hand, they were cast in one with the object. Such a method was unsuited for the production of small or fine objects, but it was applied to quite a variety of brassware, including andirons, candlesticks, stirrups and horse harness, and sword hilts.

Enamelled brass objects of particularly crude quality were produced in Russia until comparatively recent times; coarsely enamelled brass ikons, mostly dating from the nineteenth century, survive in such large numbers that one suspects they must have been made for export. The colour range of all this enamelled brass is restricted: blue, red, green, yellow, and white are most usual.

ETCHED METALWORK

The art of etching is believed to have originated in the process of ornamenting armour with acid etching first introduced in the second half of the fifteenth century. In the sixteenth century small objects of iron, brass, copper, and even silver were commonly decorated with etched ornament. This technique of ornament was particularly popular in Germany in the second half of the sixteenth century, and was applied to a great variety of objects. In the case of small articles, such as cutlery, tools, watch-cases, locks, and scientific instruments, panels of mauresque ornament (Plate 195D) were used, the larger surfaces available on caskets or clock-cases were decorated with figure subjects. The finest etched ornament is to be found on the various tools, instruments, and articles of military equipment made for the Saxon Court. Whether these were produced in Dresden or obtained from Nürnberg or Augsburg

is uncertain. The etched ironwork of Nürnberg and Augsburg had an importance comparable with that of the damascened panels made in Milan. Etched ornament is also found on French and Italian locksmiths' work, but it does not approach the quality achieved by the German craftsmen (Plate 196D).

GEMELLION

This term describes a basin provided with a spout at the base and used for the liturgical washing of the hands at the Mass. Though the ornament found on them is in most cases of secular character, their use seems to have been mainly ecclesiastical. The spout at the side indicates that they were intended to serve as ewers for pouring water rather than as basins for receiving it. The gemellion was one of the standard productions of the enamelling shops at Limoges, and the majority of those known are decorated with Limoges enamel. They date from the thirteenth and fourteenth centuries.

HORSE BRASSES

Horse brasses in gleaming, glowing tones ranging from orange to madder, lemon, and amber are now collected to ornament the fireside or hang upon the wall. Although they have a two-thousand-year-old history in England, it was not until the 1840s that it became customary to enrich the harness of a driven horse with more than a single brass known as a face piece. For the most part Georgian horse brasses were in the design known as the sun flash, with a highly burnished dome radiating beams of sunlight with the horse's every movement.

Collectors now delight in ascribing their introduction to a belief in their power of quelling the evil eye, but there is no evidence to show that they were intended to serve more than an ornamental purpose.

In the saddlers', brass-founders', and other pattern books of the early nineteenth century no reference is made to horse brasses. By the 1860s, however, full ranges of cart-horse harness brasses were illustrated, more than 330 different pieces composing the enrichment for a single set of harness. Fifteen or twenty of these were pendant horse brasses: there was a face piece for the forehead; a pair of ear-brasses for hanging behind the ears; three for hanging on each side of the runners at the shoulders, and as many as ten hanging from the martingale.

The early and mid-Victorian makers of brass horse furniture devised many horse brasses that would have some personal association with the purchaser's trade or district. The Staffordshire knot obviously was at home in Staffordshire; the wool merchant's symbol was always stocked by saddlers in the sheep-rearing districts; the windmill was for the Lincolnshire millers; the dolphin sold well in Wiltshire. Towards the end of the nineteenth century this aspect of horse-brass salesmanship was virtually abandoned in favour of motifs in no way associated with the driven horses of specific trades or regions.

Horse brasses may be collated into nine chronological groups based on manufacturing processes.

1. 1750s to about 1800

Hand-worked from hard-textured latten, chiefly used for Georgian sun flashes. Very rare.

2. Until about 1860

Cast in brass containing calamine. This polishes with far less radiance than latten or later brasses. Its surface is flawed with shallow pitting caused by the impossibility of removing all air bubbles from the molten metal. Rare.

3. Early 1800s to 1850

Hard-worked from rolled calamine brass, soft-textured and dull in appearance, and marred with a few surface pittings. From this metal were made sun flashes – the dome burnished to brilliance – and a crescent design with incurved horns and a rectangular strap loop, a pair of wings extending outward from the loop-plate junction. Uncommon.

4. Late 1830s to 1860

Cast in fine brass alloy of the pinchbeck type, composed of about equal weights of finest quality copper and zinc. This metal,

much more costly than ordinary brass, could be cast in sharper relief. Horse brasses in this metal were chased, then tinged to a beautiful reddish golden hue by heat-and-acid processes. The high lights were then burnished. From this metal were made heraldic brasses which might be gilded. Rare.

5. Late 1830s and 1860

Cast from a copper–spelter metal, known as Emerson's brass, smooth surfaced and brilliant gold in colour. It is easily distinguished from the pinchbeck metal although coloured by the same process. Uncommon.

6. 1860 to early 1900s

Obsolete brass-casting methods had by now been abandoned, and various alloys of commercial copper and zinc were used. The Walsall trade evolved a special alloy displaying a high brilliance when polished. The rough casting was file-finished, pierced by drilling, its relief work carefully modelled, then smoothed and polished. At the back of each brass, when it left the mould, were a pair of small projections known as "gets". In early examples of this period, and in all former cast brasses, these were carefully removed, every sign of their presence being made invisible. Later "gets" were crudely removed with the file, distinct rings remaining as evidence of their presence. In some brasses the "gets" were on the upper edge of the strap loop: sometimes these were removed by grinding. "Gets" on all souvenirs (group 8) noted remain as ugly blemishes which would not have been tolerated by any saddler.

7. 1866 to 1900s

Stamped from malleable rolled spelter brass and made almost exclusively at Walsall and Birmingham. The backs of early examples were filled with lead, and they are now very rare. Stamped brasses weighed no more than 2 oz., less than half the weight of their cast equivalents, and were cheaper to produce in long runs. The metal is smooth on both sides, the relief pattern showing in reverse at the back. Stamped horse brasses may be perforated, and designs bear a close resemblance to earlier cast examples. Surrounds are usually flat, but the inner edge may be raised to form a rim in low relief. Rims and perforations were carefully finished by filing until the 1890s.

8. From about 1920

Souvenirs made from contemporary designs. These are not reproductions of earlier horse brasses, but were and are made for purposes of interior decoration. The collector avoids these. They are usually sold exactly as they leave the foundry, where the removal of sand and smoothing of the surface is carried out by tumbling in an iron barrel. Some dealers hand-finish them, and so treat them that they superficially resemble genuine horse brasses, perhaps unaware that the patterns are new and the metal displays little resemblance to the Walsall alloy.

9. From the early 1920s

This is the period when many fakes were made; that is to say exact copies of genuine horse brasses, intended to deceive the serious collector and abounding in great numbers. Hand-made horse brasses from rolled sheet brass are still being marketed. The metal is of a quality easily distinguishable from the early alloy. Fakes are usually cast, however, and even though handwork and acids may give them an old appearance, close inspection of inner corners of the strap loop will demonstrate the presence of the faker's hand which fails to simulate exactly the effect of surfaces smoothed with years of wear by rubbing against leather. These fakes omit, too, the rubbing and consequent wear which occurred on the back of the lower edge of the brass, making it appreciably thinner. Much hand polishing in the course of years resulted in a silky texture: no amount of mechanical polishing will produce precisely this effect. Otherwise, when given a well-worn appearance it is difficult to distinguish a fake from a genuine example if the alloy has been carefully selected, which is seldom.

When a collector becomes familiar with the appearance, feel, and patterns of undoubtedly genuine horse brasses little difficulty will be experienced in distinguishing between each of the nine groups.

KEYS

The key collector can hope to include not only medieval but even Roman keys in his collection, for these have survived, though almost invariably in excavated state, in considerable numbers. With a very few exceptions that are hardly likely to come within the reach of the collector, the medieval key was devoid of ornament. It had, nevertheless, qualities beyond those of mere function, since

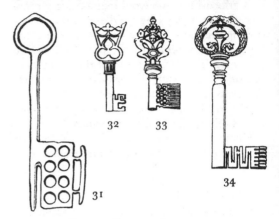

FIG. 31. Fourteenth century
FIG. 32. French; fifteenth century
FIG. 33. French; sixteenth century
FIG. 34. French; second half of the sixteenth century
FIG. 35. French "masterpiece" key; seventeenth century

the form of the bow and the proportion between bow, shank, and bit shows the sense of design that is natural to the craftsman. The bow usually took some simple Gothic form, such as a trefoil or quatrefoil, the shank was plain and the bit was thin with parallel sides. Gothic keys showing great elaboration of ornament should be regarded with suspicion (Figs. 31, 32).

It was not till the mid-sixteenth century that keys became the object of elaborate decorative treatment. The hundred years from about 1550 to 1650 were dominated by the French locksmiths, and in no other country

was the beauty of their fine steelwork even approached. The finest French keys of the Renaissance were elaborate creations; the bow was composed of addorsed winged figures supported by an Ionic or Corinthian capital (Figs. 33, 34). The shank was hollow and of complex section, triangular with incurved sides, square-, heart-, or cloverleaf-shaped. Instead of the thin bit of the fifteenth century, the bit was stoutly built, splaying outwards from the shank. These finely wrought French Renaissance keys were much sought after by collectors during the latter years of the nineteenth century, and numbers of them were faked to meet this demand.

With the French masterpiece lock went a characteristic form of key with a very large bow of pyramidal design. The sides of the pyramid were filled with pierced tracery, and it was supported by a ring, the axis of which was at right angles to the axis of the shank. The ring was filled with tracery of Gothic design. Keys of this type continued to be made according to the regulations of the French locksmiths' guilds right up till the Revolution (Fig. 35).

At the same time as English locks began to achieve a high standard, so also did English

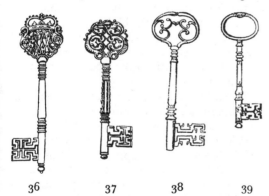

36   37   38   39

FIG. 36. English; crowned cipher of William III
FIG. 37. English, c. 1700
FIG. 38. English; early eighteenth century
FIG. 39. English; early nineteenth century

keys. Among the most attractive English keys are those with the bows pierced with the royal cipher or with the arms of some noble family (Figs. 36–38). Characteristic of the eighteenth century, both in England and on

the Continent, are the Chamberlains' keys, made of gilt brass and worn attached to a silk rosette as a badge of office. Numbers of these survive, especially those of the smaller German princedoms. Neither German nor Italian keys achieved great artistic quality; the latter conformed to one type with a circular bow filled with roughly executed debased Gothic tracery.

LOCKS

Ancient Britons living on the coast of Cornwall nearly three thousand years ago were intrigued by the pin-locks in hard wood introduced to them as objects of barter by the Phoenician merchants. The Britons were soon copying them in fine oak, creating a craft that continued unceasingly until early Victorian times, when precisely similar locks (Plate 205B) were in everyday use in Cornwall, Devon, and Scotland.

The first metal locks are attributed to English locksmiths in the reign of King Alfred: the craft had become well established in London by the twelfth century. The two principles of bolt action then in use remained unaltered until late in the eighteenth century. The majority were of warded construction: others included a tumbler in the mechanism.

Plate locks secured doors until late in the fifteenth century: their manufacture continued uninterrupted until early Victorian days. Plate locks let into rectangular blocks of oak were known as stock locks.

Rim locks, in which the mechanism was entirely enclosed with a metal case and fixed on the inner face of the door stile, became an important feature in the English home from late in the fifteenth century.

Constructional details and the decoration of English locks progressively improved between the fourteenth century and 1660, but the wearing quality of the steel was poor. Complex mechanism was the rule in fine locks, but the majority of rim locks were plainly practical and remarkably secure. By the fifteenth century locks were being made to harmonize with the character of the room into which they were fitted.

Masterpieces of ornamental locks were made by monastic locksmiths, to whom time and cost were of little consequence, cases being raised from silver plate and embossed. Lay locksmiths meanwhile were displaying fine craftsmanship in wrought-iron mouldings, quatrefoils, and floreations. In some instances the lock decoration told the story of the house and its founder. These early locks of iron and steel were enriched with gilding and brightly hued paints.

There was an early Victorian vogue for locks in this style sold under the names of Gothic and Elizabethan. Collectors distinguished these by the punch-and-bed decoration, a purely mechanical process displaying none of the infinite variety of pattern obtained by hand-worked saw-piercing. The concealed movement is also different. Medieval plate locks were also reproduced, the mechanism riveted to rolled or cast-iron plates.

Fine locks until early Georgian days were costly: the *City and County Purchaser*, 1703, quoted prices ranging from £50 to £100. They counted as works of art and were treated as tenants' fixtures to be taken away upon their removal. The quarrel between Queen Anne and the Duchess of Marlborough was intensified when it was discovered that the duchess, upon removal from her "grace and favour" residence in St James's Palace, took with her the brass door locks made by Joseph Key, a celebrated locksmith whose name is found on some of the magnificent locks made between 1700 and 1720. Some of these are still in use. He made the finest locks at Hampton Court at a cost of £800 and retained the royal appointment of locksmith until 1720.

Solid mahogany doors of imposing dimensions and about 2 inches in thickness came into use early in the eighteenth century. This resulted in the introduction of the mortice lock.

The majority of locks were made by master men working in tiny workshops adjoining their homes. The *London Tradesman*, 1747, described such a locksmith as requiring "no Education but Writing and Reading. He earns at his first setting out of his Time, perhaps, Nine Shillings a Week, and as he increases in Strength and Experience, he arrives at Fourteen or Fifteen Shillings a Week, and is pretty constantly employed. . . . This is a species of the Smith Trade; abundantly ingenious; the Keys, Wards, Springs, and the Plates he makes himself; and he employs the Founder to cast his Cases, if in Brass. The nicest branch of this Art is tempering Springs; which almost every different Master performs in a way peculiar to himself."

Locks with brass cases date from late in the sixteenth century, their movements being of steel. Improvements in brass-making technique in the early Georgian period enabled locksmiths to make lock cases from rolled plates of unflawed metal. This was smooth on both sides, of unvarying thickness, and softer than the outmoded latten. These qualities enabled the engraver to work more speedily. At about the same time cases for rim locks began to be produced by the brass founders and were issued with plain square or moulded edges. Towards the end of the eighteenth century Birmingham brassmen were shaping their rimlock cases in a single piece by means of drop-hammers.

Until the end of the eighteenth century emphasis on security was dependent upon wards, which had become more and more intricate as generation followed generation of locksmiths. The weakness of such movements lay in the fact that removal of much of the centre of the key-bit allowed the key to pass the wards and throw back the bolt. The skeleton key reduced the security of warded locks, and the complicated box of wards become less and less in demand as the lever lock was improved from about 1800.

Expensive locks of intricate mechanism, accompanied by keys of comparable strength, continued to be made during the first half of the nineteenth century. The Jury of the Great Exhibition voiced the opinion that this was a serious defect in English locks, "notwithstanding their ingenuity and security that keys should be so ponderous and bulky as to require for themselves special places for deposit and safekeeping".

ORMOLU

The term "ormolu" (from the French *or moulu*) is used to describe decorative objects and furniture mounts of the eighteenth and nineteenth centuries, cast in bronze or brass and gilt. Though cast and gilt bronze was by no means an innovation in the eighteenth century, it was used in France to an extent that could not be paralleled in previous epochs. Ormolu was not by any means an exclusively French production, similar work was done in Germany, England, and elsewhere, but the fineness of design and perfection of finish of the French artists was never equalled. While the main volume of production was of furniture mounts, vases, candlesticks, chandeliers, and-irons, ink-stands, and clock-cases were also made.

These objects were cast, chiselled, and finally fire-gilt. True ormolu should be distinguished from cheaper objects cast in the same moulds and from the same metal, which were roughly finished and lacquered instead of being chiselled and fire-gilt. Ormolu of the Régence and Louis XV periods was never so finely finished as that of the Louis XVI and Empire periods (Plate 196B). During the first half of the century French furniture was very lavishly decorated with ormolu, and the effect was achieved by mass of ornament rather than by detail. Later, when marquetry and parquetry were going out of fashion, we find less florid mounts against a background of figured mahogany, a setting which showed them off to the maximum advantage. In the Empire period the ormolu mounts played, if possible, an even more important role, and furniture was constructed as a vehicle for the display of fine ormolu. Such was the detail of the chiselling put into good work that it was hardly less expensive than similar articles made of silver-gilt.

After the Restoration in France we find a deterioration in standards of production, and the large-scale reproduction of earlier styles, but throughout the nineteenth century there were still craftsmen who could turn out very fine work in this medium, and it is extremely difficult to distinguish between eighteenth-century ormolu and the best of the nineteenth-century reproductions.

In England the Birmingham firm of Boulton & Fothergill produced ormolu vases, candlesticks, and perfume-burners during the 1760s and '70s. The finish was never up to the highest French standards, but the designs, furnished by the Adam Brothers, were of great elegance and fitness for purpose (Plate 196A). Many houses of the second half of the eighteenth century still retain their ormolu door furniture made by Boulton after Adam designs.

PAKTONG

An alloy of copper, nickel, and zinc, of whitish colour, resembling silver when polished. Grates, candlesticks, and other domestic appliances were made of this metal in the last third of the eighteenth century. The name is derived from the Chinese, who used the metal for hinges and furniture mounts. It is also known as Tutenag, which, properly speaking, is zinc without admixture of other metals.

PILGRIMS' SIGNS

Cast from lead, these badges were distributed at the shrines of medieval Europe to pilgrims, and were worn in the hat or on the person as evidence that the pilgrimage had been completed. These little objects, worthless in themselves, usually bore some allusion to the saint at whose shrine they were received. The best-known pilgrims' sign is the shell of St John of Compostella in Spain. The most popular English shrine was that of St Thomas at Canterbury. Pilgrims' signs, being made of lead, bear a superficial resemblance to the notorious class of fake lead medallions and amulets of the Middle Ages, made in London about the end of the nineteenth century, and commonly known after their inventors as "Billies and Charlies". The lettering of any inscription on a putative pilgrims' sign should therefore be examined with care, as it is in this feature that the fakers betrayed themselves.

VENETIAN–SARACENIC BRASSWARE

Among the numerous craftsmen from the Near East who settled in Venice during the later Middle Ages were metal-workers and damasceners. The earlier productions of the Arabic craftsmen in Venice are hardly to be distinguished from those they had made in their native countries, but towards the end of the fifteenth century and in the sixteenth century European elements became more apparent. The brasswares made by these immigrant Saracenic smiths included ewers, dishes, bowls, candlesticks, and perfume-burners or hand-warmers. The earliest examples were engraved with pure, that is completely abstract, arabesques, and damascened with gold and silver, but their Western origin is often shown by the presence of an Italian coat-of-arms introduced into the ornament. By the mid-sixteenth century Italian-born craftsmen using Renaissance ornament had replaced the Saracenic smiths. On these later pieces not only is the ornament derived from contemporary pattern books but it introduces figure subjects. At the same time the damascening, which on the earlier pieces had been of exquisite quality and refinement, was restricted to a few summary details. The craft survived the sixteenth century only in a degenerate form.

Japanned Tin Plate

AMERICAN

There were several tin centres in New England by the end of the eighteenth century which depended on England for their supply of tinplate. The Revolution halted the supply, but at the close of hostilities imports were again available.

The tin shops at first had no machinery. The utensils were made by hammering the metal over a hardwood mould with mallets. They were polished with wood ashes to brighten the plain tin. The shiny new pans and pails appealed to the housewife because they were light in weight. Iron was heavy and hard to clean and brass was expensive.

The size of the tin sheets naturally limited the size of the articles. The cutter had to measure accordingly and use the scrap for pepper and pill boxes or other small items. The octagonal or "coffin" trays seem to have been the only trays made as long as sheet tin remained small. They were made in three sizes; half sheet, one sheet, and two sheets. The latter was made with a centre seam which was a clever way of producing a larger tray. The narrow gallery was a continuation of the floor of the tray and turned up five-eighths to one inch. Other articles were sugar boxes and sugar bowls, trinket and deed boxes, cylindrical and oval tea-caddies, bread trays, pap warmers, tea- and coffee-pots, the popular American apple dish, knitting-needle cases, banks and miniature domestic utensils for toys, and many other objects.

Japanning was introduced into America about the end of the eighteenth century, which furthered the development of the industry. The articles were coated with asphaltum varnish, heat dried, then decorated. After reaching a peak in popularity about 1850, production waned, and japanners wishing to remain in the craft turned to decorating sewing machines, carpet sweepers, typewriters, and other household items.

The tin centres employed pedlars who at first travelled on foot, then on horseback. Baskets for holding the tin were fastened to the saddle. Cash was scarce, so the barter and trade system was used. Many tinsmiths became prosperous through the clever bartering of their pedlars.

Of the many tin establishments, the best known are those of the Pattisons, Stevens, Filleys, and Butlers.

The Pattisons are said to have started the American industry in 1740. They came from Ireland and settled in the Connecticut River Valley in what is now the town of Berlin. Edward and his brother William were English-trained tinsmiths who, when their business prospered, trained local men in the craft. In time these men established their own shops, some in other communities, and Connecticut became the largest producer of tinware in America.

(A) Tin oven; the handle at right was for rotating roast, late eighteenth or early nineteenth century. *Metropolitan Museum of Art, New York.*

B) Tin weathervane in the form of a rooster, nineteenth century. *New York State Historical Association, Cooperstown, New York.*

(c) Tin candle box with hangers reinforced with wire. *Essex Institute, Salem.*

PLATE 193

(A) Copper weathervane, well executed, nineteenth century. *Florene Maine, Ridgefield, Connecticut.*

(B) Rare signed and dated copper tea kettle by William Heyser, Chambersburg, Pennsylvania, 1825. Knob is replacement. *Heyser Collection.*

PLATE 194

(A) Casket, wood, covered with cuir-bouilli, brass mounts. French, fifteenth century. *Collection of Mrs I. G. Wolsey.*

(B) Casket, leather bound with iron straps. French, sixteenth century. *Private Collection.*

(C) Painted wood casket with iron mounts. German, first half of sixteenth century. *Collection of Mrs I. G. Wolsey.*

(D) Casket, etched copper with mounts of gilt brass. South German, late sixteenth century. *Victoria and Albert Museum, London.*

) Casket, iron damascened with gold and ver. Milanese, second half of the sixteenth century. *Victoria and Albert Museum, London.*

(F) Casket, chiselled steel. German or Austrian, early eighteenth century. *Victoria and Albert Museum, London.*

PLATE 195

(A) Perfume-burner, ormolu. English (Birmingham), *c.* 1770. *Victoria and Albert Museum, London.*

(B) Candelabrum. Ormolu with marble base, prob-ably executed by Gouthière. French, *c.* 1770–80. *Victoria and Albert Museum, London.*

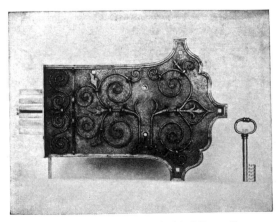

(C) Lock, the lock-plate etched with foliage. German, dated 1610. *Victoria and Albert Museum, London.*

PLATE 196

(A) Central hearth with double-ended andirons.
Penshurst Place, Kent.

(B) Fire-back of floral design, cobirons, and basket-grate.
Penshurst Place, Kent.

(c) Fire-back with mythological scene, and basket-grate supported by cast-iron andirons. *Sutton Place, Guildford.*

(D) Cast-iron fire-back and andirons; the former dated 1706.

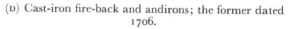

PLATE 197

(B) Brass chandeliers presented to St Hilary's, Denbigh, in 1753. Now at St Marcella's in the same town.

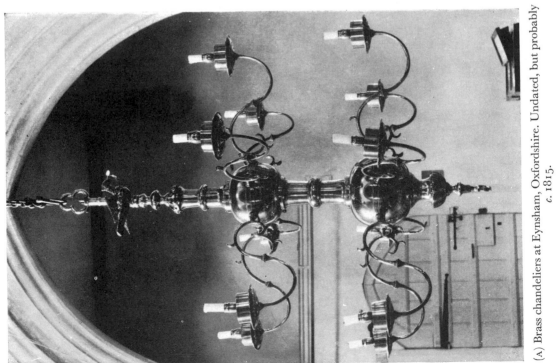

(A) Brass chandeliers at Eynsham, Oxfordshire. Undated, but probably *c.* 1815.

PLATE 198

(B) Brass chandeliers acquired by the church of Northfleet, Kent, in 1752.

(A) One of a pair of brass chandeliers at Somerton, Somerset, presented in 1782. A revival of an obsolete style.

PLATE 199

The fireplace in the kitchen of the Royal Pavilion, Brighton.

PLATE 200

(A) Cast face plates: *Left*: A sun-flash brass with highly polished domed centre and pierced sun rays; *Right*: A flaming heart, symbol of charity. *Bull Hotel, Denbigh.*

(B) Collection of patterned horse brasses: no. 3 is from a head terret; no. 4 the diamond from a playing card set; no. 5 Edward VII coronation souvenir; no. 11 a viscount's coronet and monogram; no. 18 conjoined crescents within a crescent. *Dorset Arms, Withyham.*

PLATE 201

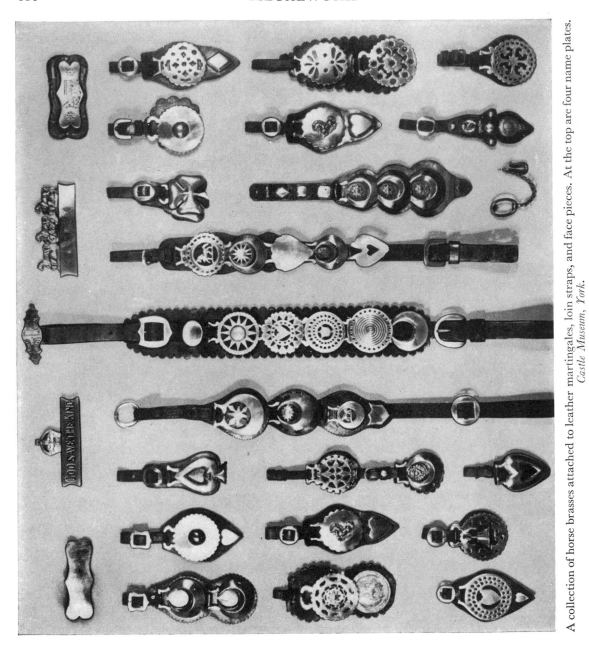

A collection of horse brasses attached to leather martingales, loin straps, and face pieces. At the top are four name plates.

Castle Museum, York.

PLATE 202

(A) Rim lock with key and pair of matching hinges, in pierced and engraved latten over blue steel plates. The lock is signed JOHANNES WILKES DE BIRMINGHAM FECIT. Lock $4\frac{1}{2}$ ins, hinges $10\frac{1}{4}$ ins, early eighteenth century. *Victoria and Albert Museum, London.*

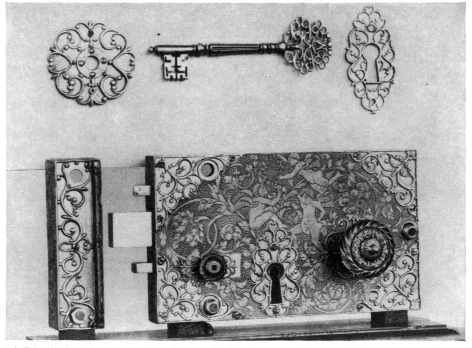

(B) Rim lock with striking plate in punched and engraved latten with corner spandrels in steel. Inscribed PHILIP HARRIS LONDONI FECIT. Length $7\frac{1}{4}$ ins, *c.* 1700. *Victoria and Albert Museum, London.*

PLATE 203

(A) Brass lock inscribed JOHANNES WILKES DE BIRMINGHAM FECIT, a typical Caroline design, $7\frac{3}{4}$ ins $\times$ $4\frac{3}{4}$ ins. *Stoneleigh Abbey, Warwickshire.*

(B) The Beddington lock showing case covered with hand-pierced and cast iron decorative panels. The central panel displays the coat-of-arms and supporters as borne by Henry VII and Henry VIII. Enriched with gilding, late fifteenth or early sixteenth century. *Victoria and Albert Museum, London.*

PLATE 204

(A) Detector lock signed JOHANNES WILKES DE BIRMINGHAM, *c.* 1700. *Victoria and Albert Museum, London.*

(B) Pin locks of oak showing bolt, loose pins, and key: this type lock, Egyptian in origin, was introduced to Britain by the Phoenician traders nearly three thousand years ago. *Science Museum, London.*

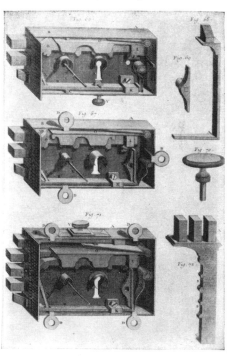

(c) Interior of eighteenth century rim locks illustrating the mechanism: (Fig. 66) bolt and slide latch; (Fig. 67) bolts and handle latch; (Fig. 68) bolts with slide and handle latches.

PLATE 205

(A) Stencilled examples from Berlin, Connecticut; the bank, blue on white; molasses pitcher, green on black; cuspidor, white smoked ground with blue border under stencil, red stripes. *Private Collection.*

(B) New England pieces decorated in bright green, red, yellow on the usual black. The white band as a background is thought to be a Connecticut characteristic. *Old Sturbridge Village, Sturbridge, Massachusetts.*

PLATE 206

A) Oval teapot with straight spout in a form found in silver of the 1780s and 1790s. Chocolate japan ground with a border of fringed festoons in silver, tinged gold by the varnish. On each side is a view of Raglan Castle, Usk. *National Museum of Wales, Cardiff.*

(B) Oblong teapot on rectangular foot. Crimson japan decorated with bands of fine gilded ornament. Usk. *National Museum of Wales, Cardiff.*

C) Chestnut urn with cover, in Pontypool japanned ware, two gilt handles with acanthus moulding. Black japan with flower spray, flowering shrubs with bowl in red and silver with a golden tinge from the varnish. *National Museum of Wales, Cardiff.*

(D) Coffee-pot with tortoise-shell ground with crimson varnish strewn with small sprigs, birds, and insects in silver, to which varnish has given a golden tinge. Pontypool. *National Museum of Wales, Cardiff.*

PLATE 207

(A) *Left*: Levno coffee urn with oval body, heated with a charcoal brazier in the perforated box below. Black japan decorated with Chinese scenes in gold, Pontypool. (B) *Centre*: Coffee urn with oval body in Pontypool japanned ware, with opening for charcoal brazier at rear and tap in front. Decorated with bands of gilded ornament and a rustic landscape with figures and sheep, by Thomas Barker. *National Museum of Wales, Cardiff.* (c) *Right*: Coffee urn with cylindrical body and square box with perforated sides for containing the charcoal brazier. Decorated in shaded gold and

PLATE 208

(A) Porringers: *front row, left:* John A. Brunstrom, Philadelphia, 1783–93; *right:* Thomas Melville, Newport, 1793–6; *centre:* Richard Lee, New England, 1770–1823; *top row, left:* unidentified; *right:* T. D. Boardman, New York, 1805–50. *Brooklyn Museum.*

(B) *Left:* porringer, William Billings, Providence, 1791–1806; *centre:* lidless tankard, Benjamin Day, Newport, 1706–57; *right:* porringer, Samuel Hamlin, Hartford and Providence, 1767–1801. *Brooklyn Museum.*

(C) Pewter teapot by William Kirby, New York, 1760–93. *Metropolitan Museum of Art, New York.*

PLATE 209

(A) *Top:* deep dish by Thomas Danforth III, Stepney, 1777–1818; *below, left to right:* plate by Thomas Badger, Boston, 1737–1815; pitcher by Boardman & Hart, New York, 1827–31; porringer by Samuel Hamlin, Hartford and Providence, 1767–1801. *Old Sturbridge Village, Sturbridge, Massachusetts.*

(B) Pitcher by Parks Boyd, Philadelphia, 1795–1819. *Brooklyn Museum.*

PLATE 210

A B C D E

F G H I J

L M N O P Q

(A–E) A group of church flagons. (F–J) A group of measures. (K) Triple-reed plates with, in the centre, a narrow rim plate, by various seventeenth-century makers. All the lidded measures (L–Q) are stamped with the devices of the taverns to which they belonged.

PLATE 211

A   B   C

D   E   F

Candlesticks: (A) 7½ ins high. Maker J.B., *c.* 1670. (B) 7 ins high. Maker unknown, *c.* 1690. (C) 7 ins high. Touch indecipherable, *c.* 1680.

Three tavern pots: (D) 6¼ ins high. Inscribed THOMAS HUTTON AT YE FRENCH ARMES IN DRURY LANE. Maker John Clarke, *c.* 1670. (E) 5 ins high. Inscribed ARNOLD SWINGSCOE ATT YE GREYHOUND ATT WORDON. Maker John Thomas, *c.* 1702. (F) 6½ ins high. Maker James Donne, *c.* 1685.

PLATE 212

A   B   C   D

E   F   G   H   I   J   K   L

(A) Candlestick, $7\frac{1}{8}$ ins high, unmarked, *c.* 1690. (B) Unusual reeded plate, 10 ins diameter, by J. Taudin, *c.* 1685. (C) Circular bulbous salt-cellar, unmarked, *c.* 1700. (D) Tankard, $5\frac{1}{2}$ ins, with flat lid, lovebird thumbpiece, and drum decorated with wriggle-work. Maker Jonathan Ingles, *c.* 1670.

A group of early spoons: *left to right*, Apostle (St John), *c.* 1680; three maidenheads, *c.* 1500; alderman (unique), *c.* 1550; apostle (St Peter), *c.* 1600; unidentified figure (unique), *c.* 1500; horned headdress, *c.* 1460.

PLATE 213

A   , B   C   D

(A) Tulip tankard, 7 ins high, with dome lid and chair-back thumbpiece. Makers, Bush & Perkins, Bristol, *c*. 1780. (B) Broad rim charger, 18 ins diameter. Mark corroded, *c*. 1690. (C) Guild flagon, the tapering drum engraved with arms and names of officers. With dome lid, embryo ramshorn thumbpiece and rare second thumb purchase on the handle. Maker, W. Charlesley, *c*. 1745. (D) Straight-sided domed tankard with embryo ramshorn thumbpiece. Mark worn, *c*. 1740.

PLATE 214

(A) A decorative side hinge, probably of Pennsylvania-German origin.   (B) A simple Suffolk latch.

PLATE 215

(A) An American baker's peel with a pleasingly
terminated handle.

(B) Two signed and dated pieces by
Peter Derr of Berks County, Pennsylvania. The grease lamp has a
brass chain for the pick and a cup of
brass with a copper bottom. The
rest is iron. The dough scraper,
which is privately owned, has a brass
handle. All the other objects are on
display in the *Henry Ford Museum,
Dearborn, Michigan.*

PLATE 216

(A) Pepperrell family mirror
c. 1700. *Winterthur Museum,
Delaware.*

(c) Bleeker family mirror, c. 1730–40. *Winterthur
Museum, Delaware.*

(B) New York mirror, 1725–35.
Winterthur Museum, Delaware.

PLATE 217

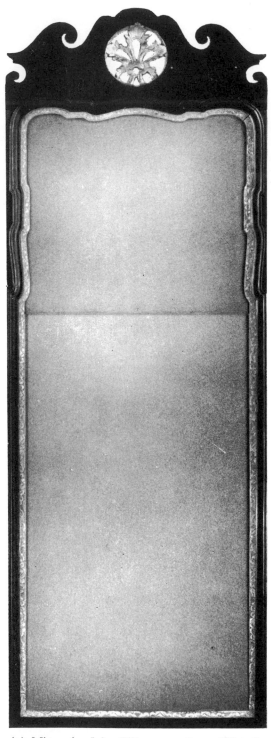

(A) Mirror by John Elliott, *c.* 1762–7. *Winterthur Museum, Delaware.*

(B) Mirror by William Wilmerding, 1794. *Ginsburg & Levy, New York.*

(C) William Wilmerding label-detail. *John S. Walton.*

PLATE 218

(A) Cadwalader family mirror, *c.* 1768–76.
Winterthur Museum, Delaware.

Photo: *The Philadelphia Museum of Art.*

(B) Dressing glass by Jonathan Gostelowe, 1789.
Mabel Brady Garvan Collection, Yale University Art Gallery.

PLATE 219

(A) Dressing glass probably carved by Samuel McIntire; *c.* 1800. *Museum of Fine Arts, Boston.*

(B) Derby family mirror. *Mabel Brady Garvan Collection, Yale University Art Gallery.*

(C) Classical mirror, *c.* 1800. *Winterthur Museum, Delaware.*

(D) Mirror by Peter Grinnell & Son; *c.* 1800. *Israel Sack, New York.*

PLATE 220

(A) Carved limewood frame attributed to Grinling Gibbons, *c.* 1700. *Victoria and Albert Museum, London.*

(B) Mirror in "cushion" frame, the borders and cresting japanned and decorated with Oriental designs, and inset with panels of rolled-paper work, *c.* 1700. *Victoria and Albert Museum, London.*

(C) Three-panel "landscape" overmantel mirror in narrow gilt frame with borders of *verre églomisé*, *c.* 1695. *Mallett & Son.*

PLATE 221

(A) Pier-glass with carved gilt cresting and *verre églomisé* borders, *c.* 1695. *Victoria and Albert Museum, London.*

(B) Mirror in frame with decoration of gilt gesso, *c.* 1720. *Mallett & Son.*

(C) Walnut-veneered frame with shaped cresting and base, moulded border and gilt-metal candle-holders, *c.* 1720. *Mallett & Son.*

(D) Mirror in frame veneered with walnut, with gilt enrichments, *c.* 1745. *Private Collection.*

PLATE 222

(A) Gilt frame carved in the "Chinese Chippendale" style with exotic birds in the cresting, figure of *Pu-Tai* in the base, and rococo ornament, *c.* 1755. *Private Collection.*

(B) Oval giltwood frame carved with rococo ornament. About 1755. *Private Collection.*

(C) Carved and giltwood overmantel mirror, the cresting formed as Ganymede and the Eagle. After a design by Thomas Johnson published in 1758. *Victoria and Albert Museum, London.*

PLATE 223

(A) Gilt-framed mirror designed by Robert Adam, *c.* 1770. At Osterley Park.

(B) Oval mirror with border of alternate blue and white glass facets. Irish, *c.* 1780. *Cecil Davis.*

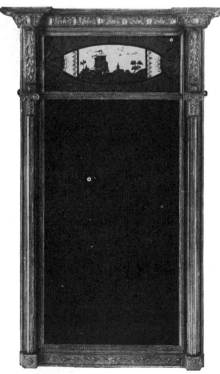

(C) Pier-glass with gilt frame and back-painted top panel, *c.* 1810. *Mallett & Son.*

(D) Convex mirror in gilt frame surmounted by an eagle. About 1810. *Private Collection.*

PLATE 224

The Berlin pieces (1825–50) most easily recognized are stencilled (Plate 206A). A privately owned collection of stencils has established the identity of apple dishes, coffin trays, large and small flat-top boxes, and banks. Backgrounds for such items were often transparent red, blue, green, and asphaltum. The bright tin under the transparent varnish made a rich translucent background. Opaque brown, yellow, green, white, and red were used as well. Berlin workers liked a vermilion stripe as a change from the commonplace yellow.

Not as easily recognized are the Berlin painted designs, with the exception of those attributed to Oliver Buckley. He is identified by the use of a central round spot of colour, usually chrome orange, with smaller satellite spots encircling the centre one. Brush strokes are superimposed on each spot, with heart-shaped leaves and beautiful brush strokes growing out of the centre; they fill and soften the area between spots. The complete design retains an overall circular pattern. Also attributed to Connecticut are running borders in red, green, and black on bands of white (Plate 206B).

Zachariah Stevens abandoned the paternal blacksmith craft and became a tinsmith. His shop was in Stevens Plains, near Portland, Maine, until it was destroyed by fire in 1842.

While the Connecticut influence can be seen in some Maine work, the Stevens designs were more realistic in form and softer in colour, the result of adding white to the colours and more top detail on the flowers. Two overlapping large vermilion cherries were a speciality of Stevens Plains. The borders were original and full where space permitted, otherwise rickrack and cable borders were used. Many of the finer articles had yellow and cream white backgrounds.

Zachariah's great-great-granddaughter, Esther Stevens Brazer, 1898–1945, successfully revived the old methods of japanning and decorating. By her teaching, research, and collections of patterns and tinware, others are now able to continue further research and to perpetuate the craft.

Oliver Filley had been a pedlar when he started what was eventually to be an extensive business. In 1800 he began the manufacture and sale of tinware, selling mostly in Vermont until 1809. Subsequently he had a branch in Philadelphia and one in Lansingburgh, New York. It was a family affair with a brother in the former and a cousin in the latter. Workers and painters were exchanged between the three shops as the need arose.

The Butler family settled in East Greenville, New York, after they moved from Connecticut. A son, Aaron, was sent back to Berlin to learn the tin trade. Upon finishing his apprenticeship, he returned to Greenville and opened a shop. His oldest daughter, Ann, learned to paint tin, using a rather individual style and signature. Ann taught her two younger sisters Minerva and Marilla. Ann's work is tight, crowded, and covers most of the surface area. She liked dots as fillers and to sign her work with her name or initials, framed by heart-shaped borders.

Another firm was the Litchfield Manufacturing Company, 1850–4, makers of papier-mâché. Japanners were brought from Wolverhampton and Oxfordshire to ornament daguerreotype cases, boxes, and furniture. Clock cases became their chief product. All were decorated with paint, pearl-shell, and metal-leaf in the English style of the mid-Victorian period. Trays were not produced.

Hull & Stafford of Clinton, Connecticut, 1850–70, were producing japanned toys.

From about 1820 English-trained stencillers were putting the finest decoration by that method on pianos and Empire furniture. As stencilling became more popular the fashion spread to the tin industry.

The American tin painters developed a forthright style that required little time for execution. It is marked by facile brush strokes and primary colours of pigment and varnish. Quick, shaded effects were cleverly done on fruits, flowers, and leaves by applying light strokes on one half and dark on the other half of a motif. The base-motif was often a round, oval, or scalloped form put on with vermilion or yellow. They left to the English-trained japanner the use of gold-leaf and work demanding high technical skill.

American japanned ware was almost entirely painted by girls. Some were daughters or relatives of the tinsmith or japanner. The designs in all the communities were similar in their unsophisticated quality. The colour was fresh, bright, and lasting, as has been proven by time. The homespun look of the articles and their use in rural areas has caused them to be called "country tin".

BRITISH

Japanned ware's beauty was combined with intriguing inventiveness to serve a host of household needs and customs throughout the reigns of the four Georges and well into Victorian days. The craft of japanning was first practised in England during the reign of Charles II (1660–85), when the ever-increasing demand for Oriental lacquer-ware stimulated efforts at imitation, at first on wood, then on metal. In Bilston, Staffordshire, japanners on metal were working in the late 1690s, specialists in making and decorating snuff-boxes with pull-off lids.

The trade spread to nearby Wolverhampton, where a japanner of ironwork is known to have been operating in 1720, ten years before Edward Allgood founded his celebrated japan workshops at Pontypool, Monmouthshire. Little is known of Allgood productions until 1756, when Bishop Pocock visited the Allgood workshops and wrote in his diary: "Of a thicker kind of plate they make salvers and candlesticks and many other things which they japan. I am told the light parts in this imitation tortoiseshell is done with silver leaf. They adorn them with Chinese landscapes and figures in gold only, and not with colouring as at Birmingham. This ware is very much better than the Birmingham, but it is dear, there being only two brothers and their children who make it and keep it as a secret. They will also japan copper boxes, or anything made in copper which they cannot work well in iron."

The secret of the exquisite lustre, silky smooth to the touch and granite-hard, peculiar to Pontypool work, lay in the use of tin-plate and repeated stoving at a low temperature. A single firing might be continued for as long as three weeks, and each coating of japan was smoothed down by hand. This treatment gave the japan a unique durability and made it resistant to heat. Undecorated Pontypool japanned work could be placed in the heart of a charcoal fire and later removed with a pair of tongs without visible signs of injury. This was a notable achievement for ware largely developed for the manufacture of tea and coffee urns, kettle and charcoal brazier sets, smokers' charcoal burners, candlesticks, snuffers, and their dishes.

Allgood's success was assured by his use of iron plates rolled into smooth, thin sheets of even thickness and tinned. Such tin-plates became possible in 1728, when John Cooke of the Pontypool Ironworks patented an improved rolling machine, adding compressing springs to the upper part of the heavy revolving cylinders. The ductile iron associated with the Forest of Dean was flattened gradually into sheets with both surfaces free from undulations. These small plates measuring about $13\frac{3}{4}$ inches by 10 inches, and not more than $16\frac{3}{4}$ inches by $12\frac{1}{2}$ inches, were tinned by dipping them into molten tin. This penetrated completely into the iron, giving it a white colour throughout its texture. These tin-soaked plates were fabricated into domestic equipment, japanned, and decorated. Such methods, in which unlimited time was an important factor, earned for Pontypool a reputation for fine and costly japanning that has endured to this day.

The quality of Allgood's japanned ware was such that when the Corporation of Cardiff wished "to present the Hon. William Pitt and the Hon. Henry Bilson Legge, Esqre., with the Freedom of that Town" in 1757, the parchments were enclosed in "two Pont-y-Pool Boxes, with the Arms of the Town neatly engraved thereon" (*London Chronicle*, May 10, 1757).

Japanning on tinned plate had been a London craft before Allgood established his workshops. Gumley and Turing in 1728 sent George II an account for "Japanning four fine large tin (tinned) plate receivers in Red with neat drawing in silver". By the mid-eighteenth century there were numerous metal japanners in London; for in 1757 Daniel Mills, Vine Street, near Hatton Garden, advertised in the *London Chronicle* that he not only "Japanned upon all Sorts of Goods made of Copper, Brass, Tin, Lead", but that he sold all sorts of materials for japanners.

Edward Allgood made a competence and retired in 1760, making over the business to his three sons. They failed to agree on matters of policy, however, and the partnerships were dissolved a year later. Thomas, the eldest, retained the Pontypool business, his brothers establishing themselves in opposition at Usk, seven miles away. Each factory developed individual characteristics, Pontypool continuing its reputation for the limited production of superb-quality japanning for the nobility and gentry. Under William Allgood, who succeeded Thomas in 1776, the business was expanded. In 1781 the Hon. John Byng wrote in his diary, "Chepstow, I bought a Pontypool snuff-box, a beautiful and dear ware, and much to be admired."

Archdeacon Coxe in 1799 reported that the Pontypool japanning works was a flourishing concern, but when William Allgood died in 1813 it was described as "declining", and by 1820 had closed. One member of the family, Ann Allgood, moved to Birmingham and founded a japanning business in Lower Hospital Street.

The Allgood factory at Usk, it is assumed, continued the Pontypool processes. The favourite ground colours were deep chocolate brightened with a hard, golden-hued varnish, and crimson applied directly to the tin-plate, giving a translucent appearance. The factory passed out of the family early in the nineteenth century. The new proprietors, observing the decline of Pontypool, introduced Staffordshire processes and materials, including tin iron, and a new japan maturing with less stoving. The factory closed in 1860.

The japanners of Birmingham, Wolverhampton, Bilston, London, and elsewhere produced less costly decorated ware which they eventually named "Pontypool", none of which is known to have been comparable with genuine Pontypool ware. England's first large japanning factories were set up in Birmingham during the 1730s by John Taylor, a journeyman cabinet-maker, and Obadiah Ryton, already established as japanners at Tinshop Yard, Wolverhampton. They eventually named their factory the Old Hall Works.

This factory for more than three-quarters of a century was the centre of the japan and papier mâché trade in Wolverhampton. When Obadiah Ryton died in 1810 his brother was joined by Benjamin Walton and more efficient methods were introduced, affecting the entire japan trade. Between 1820 and the late 1830s continual employment was given to more than 800 people. In 1847 Walton died and was succeeded by his son Frederick, who traded as Frederick Walton and Co.

An industrial dispute at the Ryton establishment in 1800 prompted several of the more skilled operatives and decorators to establish themselves as master japanners. Without exception all prospered, and by 1820 Birmingham, Wolverhampton, and Bilston formed the world centre of the japanning trade. The directory for 1839 entered 57 master japanners in Birmingham, 15 in Wolverhampton, and 11 in Bilston. By 1851 the numbers had increased; Birmingham 72, Wolverhampton 19, and Bilston 22.

The range of japanned ware now of interest to collectors includes equipment for the tea-table, such as tea trays and waiters, tea-canisters, tea and coffee urns, bread and cake baskets, cheese cradles, plate-warming cabinets, smokers' charcoal brazier sets, toilet-table boxes, snuff-boxes, knife cases, candlesticks, snuffers, and dishes. In style they range through mid-eighteenth-century rococo and Chinese fantasy, the chaste classicism of the Adams' day, the solemn pomp of the Regency, and the inexpensive forms of the 1830s and 1840s. These were followed by masses of so-called Elizabethan and classical forms and ornament which did much to destroy the trade when confronted with the clear-cut designs in electro-plate.

American Pewter

Compared with the centuries-old history of pewter in all parts of the world, the history of pewter in America is a rather short one of only about two hundred years.

The record of Richard Graves, who opened a pewterer's shop in Salem, Massachusetts, in 1635, is the earliest reference to a pewterer in the American colonies. Fewer than ten pewterers plied their trade in the colonies before 1700, so far as is known today. For many years no tangible evidence of the handiwork of the early colonial pewterers was found. Excavations at Jamestown, Virginia, eventually brought forth the remnants of a pewter spoon that not only bore a name in its maker's touch but also, by an unbelievable stroke of luck, the locality where he worked. The pewterer, Joseph Copeland, worked during the years 1675–91 in Chuckatuck as well as in Jamestown, both in Virginia. This artifact (now in the museum at Jamestown) is still the only definitely ascertainable pewter specimen of seventeenth-century America. The first definitely attributable pieces may be assigned to about 1725.

The average colonist owned only the most necessary pewterware. Being well aware of the vast, unsettled territory which was open to him, he brought only the things which could be carried easily. Instead of the breakable crockery, the hardier pewter, in the shapes of plates, bowls, beakers, spoons, was selected.

It could not have taken over-long before many of the plates and bowls were battered, or, being left too close to the open hearth, damaged beyond restoration by their owners. The need for trained pewterers became apparent the more pewter utensils suffered by careless handling. Before long English pewterers became aware of the opportunities to themselves which the colonies offered, ownership of land and house and the free exercise of their craft. Free from any restrictive super-vision, they could ingeniously use their few moulds for any purpose to which they could be adapted. With the moulds they had, they fashioned pewter objects for which their English or Continental contemporaries would have required still others. Since they could not compete with the multitude of forms and the variations of styles imported from England, the colonial pewterers concentrated on a few forms. Against the many different rim types of the English plates and the still more numerous rim types of other European countries, they offered only two types, the earlier smooth rim plate and the later single reed plate.

Another compelling reason for the limitation of forms and production was the fact that the colonies, in spite of great natural resources, were entirely lacking in the most important item of the pewterer's trade, tin ore.

Under pressure exerted by the highly organized English pewterers' guilds, and in anticipation of additional revenue, the English authorities soon imposed an *ad valorem* custom duty of 5 per cent upon imported raw tin bars, leaving the finished pewterware duty free. The disadvantages of this arbitrary rule were impossible to overcome.

The American craftsmen were forced largely to rework and recast the old pewter that was taken in trade or brought to them by merchants who dealt in new pewter.

In the reworking of old pewter the pewterer proved himself to be very often an able craftsman. His wares were generally of good quality, and while the quality or workmanship does not compare in general with the product of English or Continental pewterers, many American specimens disclose excellent workmanship and the capabilities and ingenuity of their makers.

The larger towns being centres of trade, the majority of pewterers gravitated towards them, while rural areas depended upon an occasional pewterer working there for a limited time, and on the hawkers and pedlars who in later years were able to supply the needs for pewterware from the larger towns. With incomes curtailed by the restrictions, most pewterers were compelled to apply their skill to other trades as well. Only a few were able to devote their entire time to their craft, and still fewer were comparatively well-to-do.

But the American pewterer was independent. He could work as he pleased; there were no dictates as to form or design, nor any objections to the number of apprentices or journeymen he engaged. If his pewter were of inferior quality, or his workmanship poor, only his customers could object. In spite of, or perhaps because of, this freedom from supervision and restrictions, the American pewterer generally lived up to the best traditions of the craft. He did not need to be afraid to mark his products with his touch, and when we find American pewter unmarked, but definitely identifiable as American, it compares favourable in quality and workmanship with similar European pieces. It may be stated at this point that there is no truth in the belief that unmarked pewter can always be classified as American. If this were the case, the production of our colonial pewterers would have been so large that their need to work at other trades would have been unnecessary.

EUROPEAN INFLUENCES

The early impact of English-trained pewterers and the monopoly of English-made pewterware were largely responsible for the adoption of English styles and forms, modified by the limitations in moulds and material. These limitations were frequently responsible for the clean and unpretentious lines of American pewter which the collector today appreciates. So dominant was English influence that American pewterers who trained in other European countries gradually submitted to it. The pewter of the transitional period, in which the Continental and English characteristics were united, is of great interest to the student and collector.

There are evidences in a pewterer's technique which indicate his probable origin,

lacking other biographical data. If no other information had been found, the hammermarks on Simon Edgell's pewter would point him out as an English-trained "hammerman". The practice of strengthening pewter by light hammerblows, producing the innumerable small indentations which give light to the surface with brilliant effect, had reached such heights in England that hammermen were considered the aristocracy of the craft. Examples of American work by pewterers not trained in England show us, by comparison, the proficiency of the English in this art. The all-over hammered plates and dishes of Edgell, the hammered tankard by Benjamin Day of Newport, are outstanding examples of the tradition. Also excellent, if to a slightly less degree, are the hammered booges on the flatware of the Bassetts, Wills, Danforths, and others, representations of excellent craftsmanship which they in turn taught their apprentices. The art of the hammerman dwindled in the Federal period, so it would seem this time-consuming art was sacrificed to speedier production.

While the New England and southern colonies were settled predominantly by the English, other colonies attracted settlers from Central Europe. In continuing their Old World customs these groups influenced later generations. Central European trained pewterers were able to furnish their compatriots in the new country with pewterware that perhaps was not identical to, but approximated, familiar forms and designs. The accustomed forms prevailed until about the beginning of the nineteenth century. The steady anglicization of the population, the ascendancy of English pewter, and finally the gradual decline of pewter-making extinguished the last traces of Continental influences on American pewter.

Nevertheless, the influence of the past was long discernible. The Dutch settlers of New Netherland retrained the ingrained habits and customs of their original homeland. Traces of this are found for many generations in the working methods and ideas of New York artisans. The evidence of Dutch influence as to style prevailed long after New Amsterdam became New York. The roundness of the bowls of spoons, the sturdiness of hollowware, and solidity of workmanship in general were not greatly changed by English influence.

FUSION OF STYLES

Thomas Paschall, an English-trained pewterer, opened his shop in Philadelphia in 1682; he was followed by other, also English-trained, pewterers; among them was the excellent hammerman, Simon Edgell. Their pewter, in the English manner, suited well the demands of their fellow citizens, most of them of English origin. With the increasing arrival of Continental immigrants a change of taste took place. While the English type of pewter probably never wanted for buyers, Continental immigrants were able to supply their customers with pewterware adhering to other European forms. This resulted in the creation of so many varieties of shapes, designs, and special features that the study of Pennsylvania pewter is often bewildering. There is the highly desirable English style of Cornelius Bradford and Simon Edgell; the transitional features of the pewter of Andrew Brunstrom and Parks Boyd (Plate 210B); the astonishing versatility of Heyne, showing German–Swedish influences; the highly individual work of William Will; not to forget the mysterious maker whose pieces are marked *Love*.

TYPES

The American pewterer offered a wide range of styles in the different vessels and utensils demanded of him, although he could not match European pewter in variety. As far as the colonial pewterer was concerned, the rococo period never existed. Accepted established forms of the early eighteenth century persisted, often long after they went out of fashion in other countries.

The popularity of the porringer (Plate 209B), a small, multi-purpose vessel that apparently made its way from New York to all parts of colonial America, increased steadily and endured far into the nineteenth century, after it had ceased to be a favourite in England and Continental Europe. Whatever ambition to decorate the American pewterer had was apparently lavished on the execution of the porringer handle. With the shape of the body remaining fairly constant, the handle was fashioned in two distinct types, the pierced or open work, and the solid or tab handle. The

FIG. 40. Porringer handles

former was derived from English prototypes; the latter bore definite Continental characteristics. In the ornamental features of the handles great variety of treatment was exhibited, limited only by the great expense of new moulds. Generally a pewterer made porringers according to the preferences of his customers, one exception being the pewterers of Rhode Island, who, probably because of additional trade outlets, cast both types. Another exception was Thomas Danforth III of Connecticut, who, understandably, gave up his English-type porringer for the tab-handled upon setting up shop in Philadelphia.

THE TOUCH

The English or Continental pewterer was free to choose his own design for his trademark or touch. He followed certain patterns, dependent upon the style of the period, on national preferences, and on ordinances issued by governing authorities. Frequently his touch had to contain the numerals of the year in which he was admitted to mastership, or a design denoting the quality of his pewter. The American pewterer was not bound by these rules. While it was important to advertise his work, he was not compelled to strike his touch nor any quality mark, although the legend *London* was frequently struck to show that his pewter compared with the best of England's products or to let the unwary buyer accept the native pewterware as English made. Outside of the American colonies only a master pewterer was permitted a registered touch, a precious possession that he would include in the necessities which he brought to the colonies. Once in a land where no questions of his status were asked and where no proofs of official qualifications were demanded, he could use his touch or change it as he saw fit. The use of a touch was equally free to anyone else turning to pewtering. There is every indication that many a journeyman pewterer set himself up in business and marked his products as if he had qualified before his peers. Many of them became outstanding makers of American pewter.

In the choice of their touches the pewterers evidently followed the traditional patterns of their native countries. We find that the pre-Revolutionary touches closely resemble English and Continental devices, such as the rose and crown (Fig. 41); the lamb and dove motif; the golden fleece. There are lions in circles and ovals, in or out of columns (Fig. 42); shields, urns, hallmarks, plain initials (Fig. 43), and many other symbols. John

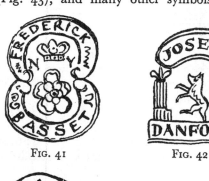

FIG. 41   FIG. 42

Pre-Revolutionary touches

FIG. 43

Will's angel touch, signifying first-quality pewter, was apparently identical to his touch as a master pewterer of his native Germany, except that now his die was American-made,

since his German touch must have shown his given name *Johannes* instead of the anglicized *John*. After the Revolution the designs of the American touches lost their interesting individuality. Apparently, it was found patriotic as well as opportune to employ a device emphasizing the newly won freedom. The eagle of the Great Seal of the United States became

FIG. 44   FIG. 45

Post-Revolutionary touches

a popular motif (Figs. 44 and 45). Dies changed upon the admission of a new state, the number of stars or dots in the frame surrounding the eagle signifying that another state had ratified the Constitution. This aids in the dating of pewter except where the stars form a continuous circle surrounding the eagle, as they were then meant for decoration only.

Not long after the turn of the nineteenth century another drastic change in the type of touch took place. The symbolic and heraldic motifs were completely cast aside to be replaced by the simple initials or name of the

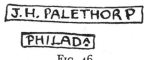

FIG. 46

Nineteenth-century touches   FIG. 47

pewterer, at times surrounded by circular or rectangular frames (Figs. 46 and 47). The age of mass production had arrived, permitting no frills.

BRITANNIA METAL

A steady increase in the amount of ceramics, glass, and tinware, produced at reasonable prices in great quantities, had begun for a long time to affect pewterers everywhere. To meet this competition, pewterers intensified their search for methods to increase their output at competitive prices. Early in the eighteenth century English pewterers developed a pewter composition of tin, antimony, and copper that proved to be exceptionally durable and workable; it was generally advertised as "hard metal". Further experiments created an alloy that could be cast and rolled into thin sheets without cracking. When it was subsequently discovered that this metal could be cold formed over wooden moulds on a spinning lathe, costly bronze moulds and expensive hand-finishing were eliminated,

and semi-skilled labourers could be employed for the simple operations of mass fabrication. When in 1825 Hiram Yale of Wallingford, Connecticut, engaged English workmen to come to America, the spinning method succeeded here also. For a while the new process stemmed the decline in the sale of pewterware, or Britannia metal, as it was now called. But a new era had arrived, a time when almost every designer and artisan aspired to devise new and exaggerated forms and decorative features. Neither pewter nor the new "hard metal" could be successfully adapted to these shapes, and for the present-day collector pewter made after 1850 is not of interest.

British Pewter

Pewter is an alloy, the principal component of which is tin, with minor additions of brass, lead, and antimony. History records so many varieties, however, that it is impossible to dogmatize.

Pewter has been used in Britain for centuries, beginning with the Roman occupation. But for practical purposes the mid-fourteenth century may be taken as a starting-point; for it was during this period that the London Guild promulgated its first ordinances for the control of the Craft. The Pewterers' Company of London had a right to a certain proportion of the Cornish tin, and farmed it out to its members and to provincial Guilds. Pewter succeeded treen (wood), leather, and horn, with, naturally, some overlapping; but at first it was within the reach of only the well-to-do. Inventories of the goods of nobles, knights, and bishops give long lists of vessels, mostly employed in the kitchens of their vast establishments. As time passed its use spread, until by the mid-seventeenth century there was scarcely an article in the plenishing of house or tavern that could not be obtained in pewter. The Church, too, particularly after the Reformation, enlisted the services of the pewterer to supply its needs in regard to alms-dishes, alms-plates, and sacramental vessels:

especially flagons, which were required in order to implement the Jacobean Canon Law concerning the service of wine to the Communion table. The craft of the pewterer, rigidly controlled by the Guilds, was at its zenith in the seventeenth and early eighteenth centuries, and the workshops turned out a profusion of dishes, plates, flagons, tankards, spoons (in which category, incidentally, are found the earliest surviving specimens of pewter), salt-cellars, candle-sticks, basins, bowls, beakers, measures, inkstands, and (later) shoe-buckles, mantel ornaments, and snuff-boxes; a formidable catalogue. Such was the reputation of British pewter, gained not by decoration but by good proportion and functional fitness, that a very large export trade was established.

MARKS

Among the ordinances of the London Guild was one which made it obligatory for a new master-pewterer to invent for himself a mark, or "Touch", as it was called; to register it by striking it upon a Touch-plate at Pewterers' Hall; and thereafter to strike it upon his wares. The Great Fire of 1666 destroyed Pewterers' Hall, and with it the touch-plates. But the system was revived in 1668, when all pewterers were required to restrike upon a new plate, and it continued into the beginning of the nineteenth century, by which time nearly 1,100 touches had been struck upon five plates. In Scotland the Edinburgh Hammermen's Guild also had touch-plates. These cover the period c. 1580–1760, and contain 143 touches.

It is with the aid of these touches, together with other material in the Archives of the Pewterers' Company, that the periods, and often the names, of London pewterers from about 1640 can be ascertained. In many cases

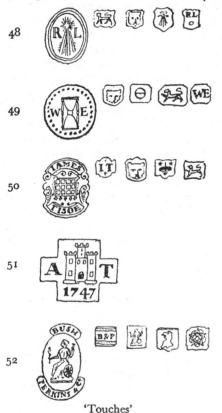

48

49

50

51

52

'Touches'

FIG. 48. Robert Lucas, London, c. 1640
FIG. 49. William Eden, London, 1690
FIG. 50. James Tisoe, London, 1734
FIG. 51. Adam Tait, Edinburgh, 1747
FIG. 52. Bush & Perkins, Bristol, c. 1775

dates appear in touches; these dates, however, represent the year of registration and not the year of manufacture. As the pewterers did not use the date-letter either, the actual year in which any article was made cannot be determined, as it can in the case of silver; but it will

lie between the date of registration and the date, where known, of the pewterer's death, or within a reasonable span of working life.

Other marks were also applied to pewter, including quality marks, excise marks, deacons' marks (in Scotland), and marks erroneously called "hall-marks". The latter were small punches, usually four in number, resembling those used on silver plate; one of them usually contained the maker's initials. These latter marks had no authority whatever, either in law or craft regulation, and indeed at one time, following a complaint by the Goldsmiths' Company, their use was prohibited by the Pewterers' Company. Pewterers, nevertheless, continued to apply them, and as they are often helpful in deciphering a partially obliterated touch, we may be grateful for this disobedience. Examples of touches and "hall-marks" are illustrated here.

. . .

Enormous quantities of pewter articles were remelted as scrap, a fact which has naturally stimulated interest in what remains. These "period" pieces occupy an honoured position in the world of antiques today. In the third quarter of the eighteenth century the competition from cheaper materials began to make inroads on the trade, and soon the demand was too small to make it profitable. The tendency to ignore regulations, and the abolition of the Company's right of search for "false wares", foreshadowed the end; and although pewterware was still made and a few fresh outlets were devised, the Craft was, by 1800, a shadow of its former self. From that date antiquarian interest disappears.

The illustrations have been selected to show some of the principal articles made in pewter from c. 1610 to c. 1775. They will give some idea of the beauty of pieces which are mainly functional in design and owe little to applied decoration.

Acknowledgments are made to R. W. Cooper, Esq., F.S.A., F.R.I.B.A., for permission to illustrate the fine pieces in Plates 211 (top and bottom photographs) and 212 (upper photograph), and to the authorities of the Castle Museum, Norwich, in respect of the flagon in Plate 214 (C). The pieces shown in Plate 213 (upper and lower), Plate 214 (A, B, and D) and Plate 212 (D and F) are in a private collection. The remainder were formerly in various collections now dispersed.

American Wrought Iron

The fabrication of American wrought iron can be said to have begun in 1607 when James Read, a blacksmith, went ashore at Jamestown, Virginia, with the first group of English settlers. But these first American pieces, as with all wrought iron for years to come, must have been American in name only, for certainly the early smiths who emigrated to the colonies in Virginia and New England must have continued to fashion objects in exactly the same manner as they had learned in their native England.

An American style of work cannot be discerned with any degree of clarity until about the beginning of the eighteenth century. Add the fact that wrought iron is seldom dated and almost never signed and it becomes apparent that the would-be collector of early American hardware is faced with a considerable problem in authentication at the very outset. Yet, in spite of these difficulties, there is a great deal of wrought iron which shows characteristics which have come to be regarded as typically American. Its characteristics are simplicity, lack of ostentatious ornamentation, and an appearance of utility. The whorls, scrolls, and other purely decorative effects so often found on ironwork of the old world are conspicuous by their absence on most American pieces. Even the objects made by the Pennsylvania-German smiths, probably the most intricate American ironwork, show a certain restraint that marks them as being of the new world. Nowhere is this tendency towards simplicity better exemplified than at Williamsburg, Virginia, the pre-Revolutionary capital of Britain's wealthiest and most aristocratic colony. The most sophisticated articles in the whole of the enormous collection are a few pairs of shutter hinges from the "Palace" of the Royal Governors. These have been decorated very modestly by a suggestion of foliation on the ends. The remainder of the iron house-hardware of that very imposing

building is quite plain and hardly to be distinguished from the hardware used on the houses of some of the humbler residents of the town.

It is hard to explain this characteristic simplicity of American wrought iron. The collector can only note that differences exist and make use of them as an aid in identification.

The foregoing is not meant to imply that American iron is without aesthetic appeal. The well-designed hinges (Plate 215A), latches (Plate 215B), and shutter fasteners used on early American houses supplement the architecture beautifully. A Suffolk door latch from Connecticut which has had its cusps shaped into the outline of a pine tree by a few cuts with a file and cold chisel exhibits a charm of its own, as does a Pennsylvania latch bearing the simple outline of a heart or tulip. Even the perfectly plain H and HL hinges of Virginia express the dignity and durability of the houses to which they are attached.

Though the colonist often complained about the high cost of ironwork, this complaint was caused by the high cost of blacksmith's labour rather than by a scarcity of material. All of the iron used in the first few years of the struggling new colonies in Virginia and Massachusetts had to be imported from the mother country, but the early settlers were quick to set about finding a means of supplying themselves. Small test furnaces were built at Jamestown in the early years of that settlement, and it is known that a full-fledged ironworks was being constructed at Falling Creek, Virginia, in 1621. This enterprise was, unfortunately, wiped out during the Indian massacre of 1622. This setback delayed iron production in Virginia for many years, but early in the eighteenth century furnaces were again in operation, and by 1750 Virginia was exporting iron bars in considerable quantities to England, in addition to supplying her own smiths. In the North the industry was successfully established in the seventeenth century. A furnace was built in 1685 at Saugus Center, Massachusetts, and was successfully operated for many years. By 1750 New England furnaces, as well as those of Pennsylvania and Virginia, were exporting great quantities of iron bars which were sometimes made into finished articles in England and shipped back to the country of origin for sale.

Practically all American hand-forged iron was made in the material known as wrought iron until about the middle of the nineteenth century, when various grades of mild steel began to be widely used for blacksmith work. These mild steels, particularly the variety known as hot rolled, are generally used today by the few remaining blacksmiths for their everyday work and, on occasion, reproductions of antique pieces. The use of this material often furnishes the collector with a clue as to the age of a piece of ironwork, particularly if it is rusty. A typical object made of wrought iron rusts to a "grainy" appearance with the grain generally running in the direction in which the piece was formed or "drawn" by the smith. Mild steel rusts to an evenly pitted, "orange peel" surface with no indication of grain. The collector should apply this test with caution, however, since it is not infallible. Some genuine old iron exhibits the surface appearance of steel, and some genuine wrought iron is still available from Sweden and is being worked today. It should be noted that a limited amount of fine steel was available to the colonists and was used primarily in tools and weapons, and that cast iron has existed since the first furnace was built, but both of these topics are beyond the scope of this discussion.

Some of the finest American wrought iron is combined with, or embellished by, other materials, such as wood, copper, and brass. Candle-stands frequently have brass finials and drip pans, and lamps (Plate 216B) of various types are often equipped with brass or copper reservoirs. Fireplace implements, too, are commonly decorated with brass finials which add greatly to their appeal. Among the articles esteemed by many collectors are the

countless variety of kitchen ladles, skimmers, spoons, and forks which combine iron, brass, or copper in their make up. Some of these pieces even have the contrasting metal cleverly inlaid in their handles, and it is among this group of highly individual utensils that the signed and dated piece is most often found.

The would-be collector of American wrought iron should acquaint himself with the various types of material which are likely to be encountered and which are worthy of acquiring. It is often found that a single category offers sufficient variety and interest to occupy the antiquarian for a lifetime, and some fine collections have been assembled in this manner. Others have collected in a wholesale manner and, although expensive, this has resulted in several major museum displays. Still others have known deep satisfaction in collecting pieces of all categories to fit their private homes, disposing of individual pieces as better ones were found. Whatever method is adopted it will be found that iron can be grouped in the following general classifications:

Tools and implements

This category includes the tools of artisans and farmers as well as some of the implements of the soldier, except swords and firearms. Many tools are made of a combination of wood, wrought iron, and steel, so that the tool collector often confines himself to this one group of objects and is not thought of as a collector of wrought iron.

Fireplace and kitchen equipment

This group is probably one of the largest and certainly the most diverse type of American iron. It includes such things as andirons, trivets and toasters, spits, hooks, pokers, and trammels, etc. A great deal of individuality is displayed by pieces of this type, since they were often made to order to fit a given fireplace or cooking necessity. It should be noted that most iron pieces which were signed or dated will be found in this group.

Builders' hardware

Hinges (Plate 215A), hasps, shutter fasteners, foot scrapers, and the like constitute this group, and it is here that regional characteristics most often come to light, partly because of the fact that many of these pieces are still attached to the houses for which they were made, and peculiarities of different parts of the country can be noted by the astute collector. Nails, too, were an important product of the early smith, and they offer an interesting small study by themselves.

Cabinet hardware

This group consists mostly of hinges and catches from chests, boxes, and furniture. Though a small group, it often includes some exquisitely fashioned articles.

Vehicular hardware

Structural and decorative parts of coaches, carriages and wagons are included in this group, to which little attention has been paid by the collector as yet. Tool boxes from Conestoga wagons have been avidly sought for, however, and are often fitted with ironwork of unusual decorative interest.

Ornamental iron

Fences, gates, railings, weathervanes, and other similar pieces. As might be expected, this group of rather expensive, custom-made objects often exhibits the ultimate in the iron-worker's skill. There are few collectors who specialize in these things, largely because of the difficulties in housing and displaying such bulky objects, as well as the fact that they are usually an integral part of the structure for which they were designed and are not apt to be available unless a house is demolished. It should be noted that many of the beau-

tiful iron railings and grill works in Charleston and New Orleans are not wrought pieces. They are cast and, as such, are examples of the founder's art rather than that of the blacksmith.

Lighting devices

Many types of lighting devices were made, wholly or in part, of wrought iron. These range from simple grease lamps (Plate 216B) to more elegant candlestands and even, on occasion, to brackets or stands for gas and kerosene lights. Collections of wrought-iron lighting devices are not generally made as such, however, but are included with more comprehensive collections dealing with lighting.

For the student of American wrought iron there are many excellent museum collections on display. All of the larger "outdoor" museums, such as the ones at Shelburne, Vermont; Old Deerfield, Massachusetts; Old Sturbridge, Massachusetts; Williamsburg, Virginia, and Greenfield Village at Dearborn, Michigan, have major collections of iron of all types. The period rooms in the larger art museums and most historic house museums as well as local historical societies have a certain amount of blacksmith work represented in their displays. At the Museum of the Bucks County Historical Society at Doylestown, Pennsylvania, and at Landis Valley, near Lancaster, Pennsylvania, there are truly enormous collections of wrought iron of all types. Farther west, there is an extensive collection of implements in the Museum of the Ohio Historical Society at Columbus, Ohio, and a very large and comprehensive collection of wrought iron in the Henry Ford Museum at Dearborn, Michigan.

Glossary

Agricultural motifs (horse brasses). Stock patterns appealing to country carters included the wheatsheaf; cart horse and wagon between the horns of a crescent or set in a star; shepherd and windmill; wagoner carrying a whip; plough; the nine elms; sickle; and, of course, many variants of the horse.

Alloy. A composition of two or more metals intimately mixed by fusion.

Animals (horse brasses). Horses are most frequent. Sporting subjects include greyhounds and other dogs, stags, foxes and fox masks, and hares. Lesser-known motifs are elephants, sometimes inscribed Jumbo and Alice, and elephant and castle; lions and lion masks; bear and staff, camel, boar, squirrel, and cat.

Antimony. A metallic element used for hardening of alloys.

Astronomical (horse brasses). Outlines of horse brasses from the beginning appear to have been mainly in astronomic forms. The sun was usually represented as a sun flash, sometimes as a disc with rays and often enclosed within a serrated edge frame. The crescent moon, emblem of Diana, was extremely popular. Less frequent was the man-in-the-moon, cast full-face and with rays. Stars with eight points were considered to have some mystic influence regarding horses, and with five points were believed to make any driven horse safe against the dangers of the road.

Barker of Bath. An artist in sporting scenes, Benjamin Barker was engaged by William Allgood as foreman decorator in the late 1770s. He was the father of the celebrated artists, Thomas and Benjamin Barker of Bath, both of whom were born at Pontypool and decorated trays for Allgood. Thomas specialized in rustic groups and figures of shepherds and woodsmen (Plate 208B); Benjamin was celebrated for his landscapes.

Barrel (horse brasses). This was the obvious motif for brasses worn by brewers' dray horses. In the majority of designs the barrel was set vertically in an elongated crescent to which it was attached by struts. The crescent was later extended to form a circular ring into which the cast barrel might be brazed. These rings might be smooth, pierced, with or without serrated rim. Alternatively, the cast barrel with hoops in relief remained unframed and hung as a pendant either vertically or horizontally with the bung to the front, a strap loop being cast on the upper edge. A group of three tuns or barrels, arms of the Brewers' Company, was frequent. Some breweries hung as the lower brass on a martingale a flat shield engraved with the firm's name, address, and date.

Beddington Lock (Plate 204B). Typical gilded wrought-iron rim lock of fine quality. Case and striking plate are enriched with panels fret-cut from cold annealed steel and riveted in two layers to the cover plate. Each pair of pierced panels is separated by cast-iron columns, and slender lengths of twisted wrought iron conceal joints between the various units. The central panel, displaying the arms of Henry VII and VIII, moves to reveal the keyhole.

Bell (horse brasses). The lower brass or brasses on a martingale might contain a small swinging bell cast from bell metal. In some of these the brass itself might follow the silhouette of a bell, with a tiny loose bell set in a bell-shaped perforation. In others a lavishly patterned brass contained a loose bell in the centre.

A set of bells might rise vertically above the horse's collar. In the eighteenth century these were of latten, and those of rolled brass in the nineteenth century were further toughened by hammering. The bells were hung in three or four rows, each row ringing its own chord. Each set hung within a shallow rectangular cover of leather-lined brass, the leather preventing the bells striking a discord upon the metal hood. Four-row sets were most unusual: in these the lowest row, containing five bells, was known as the lead; the next, of four bells, the lash; the third and fourth rows, each containing three bells, were termed body and trill. A single bell might hang in the terret.

Bellows. Contrivances for making a draught artificially, dating from very early times. Mention is made of bellows in wills from 1500 onwards, but as they suffered hard usage, survivors are seldom earlier than the seventeenth century; and any of that date are a great rarity. They received their due share of attention and were decorated in many styles. Carved and inlaid wood, wood overlaid with leather or silver, and even finely stitched needlework were used to ornament them. Lacquered examples were made in the first quarter of the eighteenth century. Apart from the small hand-bellows, which were often decorative rather than useful, more businesslike machines were made; doubtless for the use of those servants on whom the warmth of the house depended. These standing-bellows were in heavy wooden frames, and rested on the ground firmly, to be worked by means of a lever. Another type, lighter in weight, was operated by turning a wheel which was linked to the mechanism by a cord. This last type dates from the early nineteenth century.

The construction of the bellows has not changed in the course of the centuries. It comprises two shaped boards with a spring to keep them apart, held together by a loose leather hinge. One of the boards is pierced in the centre and fitted with a flap of leather on the inside, which acts as a valve, letting air enter, but not allowing it to escape except by way of the nozzle.

Betty lamp. A simple grease lamp, usually made of wrought iron, and consisting of a shallow cup with a vertical handle and an indentation in which a wick was placed. Those made of two cups, one below the other, are generally called Phoebe lamps.

Bird, Edward, R.A. Painted japanned trays with historical scenes during and after his apprenticeship with the Ryton firm in Wolverhampton from about 1786 to the mid-1790s. He became Historical Painter to Princess Charlotte of Wales before his death in 1819.

Birds (horse brasses). A bird motif was usually brazed within a narrow plain or perforated ring having a serrated edge. The bird is usually more carefully finished than the frame and often in a different alloy, suggesting that they were acquired from specialists. The birds include the pelican in her piety, that is, feeding her young with blood drawn from her breast, and symbolic of maternal solicitude. This was used in some districts as a face piece on a brood mare. The peacock, considered sacred to Hera, a goddess of fertility, is seen either full face with a fanned tail, walking, or side view with trailing tail. Other birds include the old English game cock, eagle, and phoenix, the latter dating from 1870. Souvenir pieces are also found.

Bismuth. A metal added to harden pewter. Also called tinglass.

Blowing-tube. Forerunner of, and contemporary with, the bellows was a long metal tube widening from a mouthpiece and with a short projection at the base to raise it from

FIG. 53

the ground. The tube was placed where the draught was needed, and the user simply blew down the mouthpiece.

Blue Steel. Lock plates in this metal date from late in the seventeenth century and formed contrasting backgrounds for pierced latten enrichment riveted over them and polished. The steel plates were blued by heating on sand (Plate 203A).

Bolt. The securing unit of a lock which shoots out of the lock case into a socket or staple in the door frame. A dead bolt is one capable of being moved both inward and outward by the key.

Borders. Usually in imitation of inlaid gold or silver. The most common ranged from the simple star – used also as an all-over pattern – stripes, and intersecting loop patterns to elaborate combinations of scrolls and flowers, rosettes and tendrils. From about 1820 until 1845 the tray rim and the margin of the panel might be decorated with a single pattern, usually gilded or bronzed, leaving the centre plain.

Bramah lock. The first lock to be operated by a small conveniently carried key, invented by Joseph Bramah in 1784. The key did not act directly upon the sliding bolt, but through the medium of the rotating barrel, thus anticipating Yale's cylindrical lock of 1848. Insertion of the key pushed back a number of sliding plates until notches at different positions came into line, allowing the barrel to be turned and the bolt withdrawn.

Brander. A pierced metal plate, with a half-hoop handle by which it was suspended

FIG. 54

from a pot-hook. It was used principally in Scotland for the making of brander bannocks – oatmeal cakes.

Brass. Late in the sixteenth century lock cases began to be made from latten plates. A simple lock case might be raised from the plate, but more frequently it was constructed by brazing suitable plates into a box. This was covered by a removable plate. Keyholes might be strengthened by an applied plate cut from latten and brazed in position. Other brass lock cases were enriched with corner spandrels: at first these were for strengthening purposes only; later they were decorated with punched and engraved work; towards the late seventeenth century spandrels were ornamentally pierced.

Locksmiths found English latten to be of poor quality, pitted with flaws and inclined to split during manipulation. Dutch latten was preferred as softer to work, smoother of surface, capable of taking on a higher polish, and easier to engrave. English latten was of necessity used during periods when the importation of brass and latten was prohibited to protect English brassmen. Fine lock cased in this flawed metal may be dated between 1660 and about 1680.

Brazier. In place of, and in addition to, a fireplace, heating was sometimes provided by a portable iron brazier which burned coke. At a later date the fuel was charcoal. A brazier was at Trinity College, Cambridge, in 1866, and had been in use there "for upwards of 160 years".

Braziers, charcoal. Smokers' braziers for table use were in great demand before the days of friction matches. These were low-footed bowls standing upon trays to prevent scorching the table top, and held small ember tongs used to lift the glowing, smokeless court charcoal to the smoker's clay pipe. In some instances the brazier was fitted with an almost horizontal handle. The brazier for heating a japanned kettle was placed in a low cylindrical vessel, from the rim of which rose four brackets to hold the kettle, and mounted on four ball or bracket feet. It was decorated to match the accompanying kettle.

Britannia metal. A hard form of pewter containing antimony and copper and dating from about 1800 onwards. Japanners shaped hollow-ware by spinning this metal in a lathe. In about 1820 this was superseded by a special copper alloy evolved for spinning.

Bullet. A projection or some other formation in a keyhole to suit a corresponding groove cut into the bit of the key.

Butler. Family of tinsmiths from Connecticut who established the business in East Greenville, New York. Aaron Butler was born about 1799 and died 1860. Associated with him were his daughters Ann, Minerva, and Marilla.

Carron. The Carron Ironworks, Falkirk, Scotland, opened in 1759 and was responsible for the making of much fireside equipment. Small andirons (or rests for fire-irons) of early nineteenth-century pattern are found with the name of the firm cast on the fronts. Many of these have been re-cast from the original moulds, in the present century, but in these instances the name "Carron" appears at the back of each piece.

Case. The exterior box of a lock containing the mechanism and action.

Cast iron. A form of iron containing a relatively high percentage of carbon (approximately 4 per cent) and characterized by hardness and brittleness. Cast iron cannot be worked in a forge but is shaped by being poured into moulds while in a molten state.

Catch plate. A device on a rim night latch which holds the bolt in or out.

Cauldron (kettle). One of the oldest of all cooking utensils and recorded from the earliest times. They were first made of sheets of bronze, hammered to shape and riveted together; later they were of cast bronze. From the sixteenth century they were made of cast iron, and formed an important item in the equipment of the "down hearth". Small-sized cauldrons were known in some regions as "crocks".

CHANDELIER-MAKERS (ENGLISH)

Addison, Richard. Made chandelier for Canterbury Cathedral, 1685. Freeman of Founders' Company. Died 1690/1.

Dickinson, Richard. "Mr Dickinson the

Brasier" was to make three chandeliers for St Lawrence Jewry, London, 1678. Buried at St Lawrence Jewry, June 30, 1681.

Giles, John. Signed chandelier at Framlingham, Suffolk, 1742. Admitted to Founders' Company, 1716. Master 1740–1. Died September 1743.

Giles, William. Signed chandelier at St Nicholas-at-Wade, Kent, 1757. Admitted to Pewterers' Company, 1737. Master 1769. Admitted as Love-Brother to Founders' Company, 1758. Died January 1771.

Hawes, Patrick. "Mr Hawes" supplied chandeliers for Barbers' Hall, 1744. Admitted to Founders' Company, 1721. Master 1753–4. Died 1769/70.

Marshall, Robert. Signed chandelier at Leatherhead, Surrey, 1763 (*Marshall Fecit*). Admitted to Founders' Company, 1738. Died insolvent 1771.

Meakins, Richard. "Mr Meakings ye founder" probably supplied chandelier for St Michael, Crooked Lane, London, 1690/1. Was to have preference for making chandeliers for St Margaret Lothbury, 1690–1. Freeman of Founders' Company. Master 1686–7. Died 1705.

Mist, Mary. Signed chandelier at Wollaston, Northamptonshire, 1777 (*Mist Long Acre Fecit*). Widow of Thomas Mist who died 1766/7. Had son in partnership, 1771; succeeded by Henry Mist, 1788.

Peter, Charles. Signed chandelier at Wymondham, Norfolk, 1712. Admitted to Founders' Company, 1709. Died 1766/7.

Shrimpton, Russel & Co. Probably supplied the chandeliers for Society of Antiquaries, London, 1781.

Sutton, Jacob. Supplied chandelier for St Mary Woolnoth, London, 1727; made lecterns for Salisbury Cathedral and St Paul's Cathedral, 1714 and 1720.

Taylor, Thomas. Supplied chandeliers for St Stephen Walbrook, London, 1679. Died 1679.

Townsend, John. Made chandeliers for Allhallows, Lombard Street, London, 1764/5. Admitted to Pewterers' Company, 1748. Master 1784. Died 1801 (?).

Makers in the Provinces include the following:

Birmingham

Haywood, James. Signed chandelier at St Harmon, Radnor, 1771. Appears in Birmingham rate-books 1751–75.

Thomas Cocks & Son. Signed chandeliers (*Cocks & Son*) at Yardley Hastings, Northamptonshire, 1808, and Wrenbury, Cheshire, 1839 (?). Called Cocks & Taylor, 1801 and before.

Cocks, John. Signed chandelier in nave at Prestbury, Cheshire, 1814. Succeeded Thomas Cocks & Son, 1808. Not in business, 1815.

Bridgwater, Somerset

Bayley, John. Signed chandeliers at Stogursey, Somerset, 1732, and Lympsham, Somerset, 1744.

FIG. 55. Stogumber, Somerset

Bayley, Thomas. Signed chandeliers at Mark, 1758, Ilminster, 1762, Old Cleeve, 1770, Burnham, 1773, Kingston, 1773, and Stogumber (Fig. 55), all in Somerset.

Street & Pyke. Signed chandeliers at St Sidwell, Exeter, 1774, and Over Stowey, Somerset, 1775.

Pyke, Thomas. Signed chandelier at Guildhall, Exeter, 1789.

Bristol

Rennells, Richard. Signed chandelier at Yeovil, Somerset, 1724. Died 1730 (?).

Bill, Francis. Signed chandelier at Dunster, Somerset, 1740. Died 1754.

Rice, Roger. Signed chandeliers at Pilton, Somerset, 1749, and Axminster, Devon, 1750. Admitted Burgess of Bristol, 1740. Of Clifton, 1754.

Wansborough, —. "Mr Wansborough" made chandelier for Evercreech, Somerset, 1761.

Wasbrough, Hale & Co. Signed chandelier at Hatherleigh, Devon (undated).

Chester

Brock,—. "Mr Brock" supplied chandeliers for Malpas, Cheshire, 1726, and Gresford, Denbigh, 1747. Probably was Thomas Brock, admitted Freeman of Chester, October 14, 1697, buried at St Peter, Chester, May 7, 1755.

Thomas, John. Signed chandelier at St Marcella, Denbigh, 1753 (Plate 198B). Apprentice of Thomas Brock; admitted Freeman of Chester, May 26, 1752.

Chester or *Manchester* (?)

Davenport, William. Signed chandelier in chancel at Prestbury, Cheshire, 1712.

Wigan, Lancashire

Brown, —. "Mr Brown" supplied chandeliers for Kirkham, Lancashire, 1725 and 1733.

Tarlington, George. Supplied chandelier for Deane, Lancashire, 1737/8.

Cheap locks. Cases and parts for mass-produced locks were first made in 1796 by Isaac Mason, Willenhall. These were punched and bolstered from sheet iron by the flypress.

Chestnut servers. These urn-shaped containers might be oval or round, their bodies raised from copper in two halves and vertically joined. From about 1800 to 1820 they were spun from Britannia metal; from about 1820 they were spun from a special copper alloy. The vessel was supported on a spreading foot, round or square, and a short, slender stem. It usually had lion mask and ring handles of cast lead gilded and with a domed cover surmounted by a gilt acorn or other simple finial.

Chestnut servers were handed with coffee and contained Spanish chestnuts, boiled and then roasted. They were served hot, and were lifted from the server with a fork; their husks were removed at table and they were eaten with salt (Plate 207C).

Chimney-crane. Known in Scotland as a "Swey", this was a bracket of wrought-iron from which a cauldron or tea-kettle was suspended. Cranes were of many types: large and small, simple and complicated. In the case of the latter the pot could be raised or lowered and swung to any position over the fire.

Coal-containers (coal-box, hod, purdonium, scuttle). It can be well understood that owing to the hard usage they received, the life of these was short. There appear to be no examples surviving from before about 1800, and most of them have been reproduced in quantity in this century.

Scuttles made of sheet copper are described as being of "bucket" or "helmet" shape; the latter modelled on the fifteenth-century helment, the salade, inverted, and with a moulded base and swing handle.

Covered boxes of mid-nineteenth-century date were of japanned metal with gilt decoration, and the hinged lids were often fitted with a panel of shaped glass with "back-painting" of flowers or landscapes. The handles of these boxes and their accompanying shovels were often of white china.

Coal vases. Replaced coal scuttles in wealthy homes from 1840 when the Nasmyth hammer was introduced into japanning factories. They were intended to remain decorating the fireside and be filled from buckets, unlike scuttles, which were carried into the cellar. The coal for the first time was concealed beneath an ornamental cover. Fearncombe of Wolverhampton displayed at the Great Exhibition a coal vase in the shape of a nautilus shell resting on coral, the cover handle representing a seahorse. Others were in the shape of miniature Gothic fonts and great tureens.

Cobirons. These are similar to andirons, but are usually quite plain in design and have rows of hooks on the standards on which spits could be placed. Some examples of cobirons have basket-like tops, and it has been suggested that they are "cressets" for holding a light. Alternatively they may have been intended for containing a cup used in basting meat.

Cock's-head hinge. A form of H-hinge in which each termination

Fig. 56.

Cock's-head hinge

is formed into the silhouette of a cock's head (Fig. 56).

Coffee-pots. Made in the shapes and sizes associated with silver, usually in baluster curves or cylindrical with inward-sloping sides, and with wicker-covered handles. Such a vessel was ornamented in the fashionable styles current at the time of manufacture, often with a scene on each side. It stood upon a tripod, also japanned, containing a charcoal brazier.

Cover. A plate screwed over the lock case covering the mechanism and holding the working parts in place.

Cran. An iron trivet fitted over the fire for supporting a kettle, girdle-plate, etc.

Creepers. These, in pairs, were small irons of similar shape to andirons, between which they were placed in the hearth. Creepers were of very simple design, and they came into use when andirons grew elaborate and costly.

Cresset. Generally an iron basket affixed to a rod and designed to hold wood or other fuel for lighting purposes.

Cross garnet hinge. A type of strap hinge one leaf of which is a horizontal strap and the other a vertical strap; when in position like a letter T lying on its side.

Crystallized decoration. Patented in 1816 by Edward Thomason, Birmingham, and marketed as *moiré* metal. The patent took advantage of the fact that when tinned iron plate is held obliquely to the light it reveals figured patterns. After processing it was silvery in appearance, and covered with stars and other well-composed geometrical figures: it was varnished at once to preserve its brilliancy. In the 1830s Ryton and Walton discovered that splendid effects could be obtained by staining the tin green, lake, yellow, and other colours. This was coated several times with japanner's varnish. Pictures were painted over this ground with outstanding effect by flower painters from the Potteries. Under the name of crystallized ware many japanners issued a variety of domestic goods such as trays and waiters, tea-chests, work boxes, tobacco boxes, and lamps.

Curfew (*couvre-feu*). To enable the fire to be kept alive during the night or when left unattended, a metal cover was placed over it.

This cover, known as a "Curfew", was roughly in the shape of a quarter-sphere and had a

FIG. 57

handle affixed to it. Old specimens are very rare, and existing ones are of brass or copper with embossed ornament.

Dangle-spit. A non-mechanical type of spit which operated in the manner implied by its name. It hung downwards, twisting one way and another on a rope as the latter wound and unwound itself, clockwise and anti-clockwise, sometimes with the aid of two weighted arms.

Decoration. Ornament on early brass lock cases consisted of designs composed of arches, points, and lines applied by means of steel punches cut with a wide range of simple motifs. Stock pattern repeats were drawn

FIG. 58

on parchment and the outlines picked out in closely spaced pinholes. The parchment was laid upon the surface of the unpolished latten and sprinkled with fine charcoal or chalk. This was rubbed through the pinholes, leaving an outline design to guide the craftsmen.

Cover plates by the end of the seventeenth century might be cast throughout in princes metal with all-over decoration in relief and chased and engraved. Delicate filigree work was associated with exquisite reticulated perforations: these might be laid over plates of blue steel. The brass cover plate and the keyhole escutcheon might have applied steel ornaments cut in delicate, lace-like patterns.

Door furniture. Includes locks, knobs, keyhole escutcheons, finger-plates, door closers, hinges, catch plates, and so on, all made to match until early Victorian days,

Dovetail hinge. A butterfly hinge, the leaves of which resemble two dovetails joined at the narrow part.

Down-hearth. A slab of stone or metal raised slightly above the level of the floor of the room, forming the earliest and most simple type of fireplace. The first versions were centrally placed in a room, and smoke rose to escape through a louvre in the roof. The down-hearth built in one side of the room with a flue communicating with the outside has remained in use in cottages to this day.

Dutch metal. Alloy of copper and zinc used in place of gold-leaf in decoration.

Dutch-oven. An open-fronted oven, usually raised on legs, placed before the fire and used for cooking. Dutch-ovens were made of sheet-iron, brass, and even of pottery.

Engraving. Introduced from Italy in the early seventeenth century. By the time of Charles I groups of highly skilled lock-case engravers were established in London and Wolverhampton. All-over designs were incised with gravers, chisels, and flatters forged from Venice steel – probably of Damascus origin. Steel cases were softened before engraving, and after rehardening were fire-gilded to prevent rust.

Some of the most superb brass rim locks were made during the period 1660–1790. The covers were ornamented with elaborate all-over engraving, and sometimes further enriched by the addition of a high relief motif cast in princes metal or pinchbeck extending across the latch end of the cover to which it was riveted. Fashionably such decoration depicted the coat-of-arms or monogram of the owner, but a great variety of designs is found.

Escutcheon. A plate surrounding the keyhole or swinging over the keyhole.

Escutcheon-lift latch. A trick latch resembling the common Norfolk type which is operated by lifting a sliding escutcheon plate rather than the more usual system of pressing a thumb plate.

Face piece (horse brasses).

Fig. 59. Escutcheon-lift latch

A brass suspended on the forehead of the horse. A merchant's catalogue of the 1890s captioned such a brass, "cart-horse face piece". It is often stated that Queen Victoria's portrait on horse brasses in the early years of her reign was responsible for the name face piece as a generic term.

Fire-back. This slab of cast iron, sometimes referred to as a "Reredos", stood at the back of the fireplace, protected the wall, and reflected the heat of the burning fuel. Fire-backs were made by the simple means of pouring the molten metal on to a prepared bed of sand in which a pattern had been impressed. The patterns were carved in wood, and were either of a full-sized design or in the form of single ornaments which were composed into a whole to suit the taste of the maker or his client.

The iron fire-backs of Sussex are the best known; others were made in Yorkshire, Derbyshire, and in the Forest of Dean. Many were imported from Holland late in the seventeenth century and onwards. It is often difficult to determine the origin of one from another; the fire-backs with scenes from the Bible or mythological subjects are usually said to have been of Dutch make, but these were copied in England, and there is no certainty on the point. In Holland the castings were made thinner than in England, but this feature also was adopted here. The earliest English fire-backs were of a wide, low shape, but by the mid-seventeenth century tall ones, of "Tombstone" style, were introduced.

There are fire-backs recorded which bear the coats-of-arms and initials of English sovereigns from Henry VII to James II; others commemorate the defeat of the Spanish Armada (1588), Charles II and the Boscobel Oak (1651), and similar personages and events of widespread contemporary interest.

Fire-board (fire-screen). A decorative panel used to conceal the fireplace cavity when no fire was burning. In the Victoria and Albert Museum is one of wood painted with a vase of flowers, and at Osterley is another covered with tapestry to match the hangings of the room in which it stands.

Nineteenth-century examples in the French

Louis XV style were of gilt metal, chased and pierced, in the form of a fan which folded up when not in use.

Firedog. Andiron, especially one of the lower and simpler sort.

Fire-fork. An instrument made of wrought-iron, some 4 feet or more in length in order that the user would be away from the heat when moving burning logs in the hearth. Usually it had two stout prongs, but some examples have a spike at one side about three-quarters of the way down from the

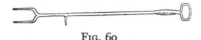

FIG. 60

handle. The fire-fork was the forerunner of the poker, and it went out of general use when coal replaced wood as a fuel.

Fire-irons. In the days of wood fuel these comprised tongs, brush, and fire-fork. For coal, the principal addition was a shove, and the poker was substituted for the fire-fork. The shovel was often pierced so that the coal might be sifted, and the smaller pieces chosen for starting the fire. Late in the eighteenth century the pierced designs were still current, but their retention had become no more than a decorative feature.

The implements were variously ornamented, and although the working parts were of steel or wrought iron, this did not preclude the craftsman from making the handles of more costly metals. The sets of fire-irons enriched with silver, at Ham House, have been described and illustrated frequently since they were seen and commented upon by John Evelyn when he was there in 1678.

Steel fire-irons of eighteenth-century pattern have been much reproduced in the present century.

Flatware. General term for plates, platters, dishes, etc.

Footman. The name given to a four-legged trivet made to stand in front of the fire in the sitting-room or parlour. They were made of wrought iron or brass, or partly of each, and commonly had front legs of cabriole design. The top was often pierced with a central hole so that it could be carried. The footman

dates from the second half of the eighteenth century onwards.

FIG. 61

French tôle peinte (painted sheet iron). Has the same origin as English japan work. The Oriental influence was strongly felt. There is a similarity to the English work in the shape and designs of some pieces thought to be French. This leads to the belief that plain and decorated English products were exported to France. It is known that japanners and painters travelled between the two countries, which confirms the belief and adds to the difficulty of identifying the work. The terms *tôle*, or toleware, have come into rather general use in the United States, however, for all wares of this class regardless of place of production. Japanned tin-plate, or japanned tinware can be used more appropriately.

Girdle-plate. A flat iron sheet on which oat-cakes were baked in Scotland. They were of two types: those with a half-hoop handle which were attached to the pot-hook and the cakes cooked while suspended; and those with a small handle projecting at one end for manipulation. The latter type was placed on a cran.

Grid-iron. This was placed over the centre of the fire for cooking, and comprised a number of parallel bars on which meat, etc., rested

FIG. 62

during the process. Early grid-irons were of simple pattern and made of wrought iron. Later ones sometimes had the bars channelled and leading to a trough at the front, which had a spout for pouring out the gravy and fat collected in it (*see* Fig. 62).

Grisset. An elongated, cup-like, iron basin, generally with a handle, for holding grease so that rushes can be drawn through it to prepare rushlights. These devices are fairly rare.

Ground colours. In Birmingham and Wolverhampton, according to the specification of John Baskerville's patent of 1742, japanned grounds might be of "fine glowing Mahogany colour, Black in no way inferior to the most perfect India Goods, or in imitation of *Tortoiseshell*". Against these might be painted flowers and foliage in colours. At this time Pontypool grounds were black, chocolate, crimson, and tortoiseshell. By the late 1770s Pontypool had introduced new colours, the range including dark green, puce, tomato red, orange, canary, grey, and ultramarine blue. These were coated with varnish displaying an attractive golden tinge.

There is no evidence to show that the basic methods of japanning either in the Midlands or in London differed from those of Pontypool, but tinned rather than tin-plates were used, methods of application were less costly and finish less rich although possessing a lustrous surface. Brilliant colours were soon competing with those of Pontypool. The *Dictionary of Arts & Sciences* (1763) described these as yellow, vermilion, red, lake, blue bice, indigo, green, brown, purple, and flesh white.

In the 1820s a fine green japan was developed, an ideal ground for the fashionable Oriental themes in gold. This costly colour was used only on the finest work, and is frequently found in a remarkably successful series decorated with exotic birds, such as peacocks, parrots, cockatoos, flowers, and foliage, sometimes with a playing fountain.

Guard. A fixed unit within a lock preventing fake keys from turning, or to prevent a lock-picking instrument from reaching the bolt or levers.

Hasp. A hinged strap generally used with a pin or lock to secure a door or chest.

FIG. 63A and B.
Hasp

Heart. These horse brasses appear to have ornamented the check rein. One series of hearts was stamped in silhouette, sometimes in bold relief, perhaps more frequently with a flat surface. Plain hearts were cast within circular perforated frames, rayed piercing sometimes encircling closely spaced circular perforations: variations are numerous. A series of designs in which the heart is cast in the round has a secondary heart rising in relief from the centre. Rare is the heart within a heart, that is, a heart in relief with its centre pierced by a smaller heart. Three or six small hearts arranged into the shape of a larger heart proved an acceptable design during the 1890s, the surface of each heart highly burnished (Plate 201A).

Heraldic (horse brasses). Owners of private stables and country estates considered it a pleasant conceit to use face pieces displaying their coats-of-arms or crests. These appear to have been introduced by Daniel Moriarty of Oxford, who supplied them to order in gilded silver: hall-marks show them to date from the late 1830s. Moriarty also made heraldic face pieces in German silver, and these might be gilded or silver plated. The majority, however, were cast from a pinchbeck alloy – usually prince's metal – and gilded. Robert Hughes of Finsbury specialized in heraldic face pieces from the 1840s until the mid-1860s, supplying them to the commission of saddlers throughout the country.

Estate brasses in the form of a cipher, with or without a coronet, have been noted, the cipher being in a ring or crescent with or without a serrated rim. In later examples of cheap-quality brass the frame was drilled with closely spaced perforations. Engraved crests and ciphers have been noted on early Victorian sun flash brasses (Plate 201A).

H-hinge. A common type of early hinge the leaves of which are formed of vertical straps and affixed to each other by short horizontal straps in the centre so as to resemble the letter H. The HL hinge has an extra horizontal strap extending from one extremity of the H.

Hollowware. A general term for vessels designed to hold liquids.

Horse motifs (in brasses). The most

popular appear to have been the prancing horse of Kent and the horse combatant. Horses carrying sprays of oak leaves in their mouths are associated with the various estates of the Duke of Norfolk. Models include also winged horses, steeplechasers, and racehorses, cart-horses, generally facing to the right, horses' heads in profile and full face. These are given various mountings, from plain crescents and wide rings to the complicated geometric perforated patterns of the 1890s and later. A horse's full face usually looks out from a quatrefoil opening, the mount having a circular outline which may be scalloped. Casting and the quality of the metal are generally poor, thus discounting Walsall as a source of origin. A series of cart-horses were stamped in relief on plain discs with serrated rims. Horse are to be found framed by horse-shoes, pierced or moulded with nail holes, and in almost closed crescents – usually pierced. An interesting though late series are those brasses in which a tiny horse is displayed within a wide pierced inner border enclosing a wide outer border with a serrated edge. The fully harnessed horse cast in the round with a pendant loop rising from the saddle should be classed as a souvenir. It has proved possible to assemble a collection amounting to about eighty brasses bearing horse motifs, without any duplicates.

Horse-shoes (horse brasses). In this symbol of good luck the opening, in most instances, hangs downward. Those noted have been cast, and many contain a profile portrait of a horse's head looking to the left. This might be cast separately and brazed into a stamped horse-shoe. In others a driven horse is shown facing to the right. A stamped or cast horse-shoe with nail-holes may contain a trotting horse on a slender bar joining the horns of the shoe. Others display horses apparently copied or adapted from heraldic crests.

Iron and steel. The English iron industry, to which the fireside owes so much of its equipment, was centred on those places where there was assurance of ample supplies of wood – the essential fuel for melting the ore and for causing chemical changes in it. Iron is divisible into two distinct types: with little carbon content it becomes malleable and is steel or wrought iron, and with more than the minimum of carbon remaining in its composition it is cast iron. All three forms of the metal had their place and purpose at the fireside.

From the fourteenth century until about 1800 the wooded areas of Sussex were the seat of great activity, and the foundries established there grew famous for their products. While the ore had been worked from as early as the time of the Roman occupation, it was in the fourteenth century that a great expansion took place and new methods were brought into use. Today there remain traces of slag ("cinder") from the long-dormant workings, sited near streams which once provided power for the needed draught.

In the sixteenth century Buxted was noted for the making of cannon of cast iron, which were first produced in 1543, together with the ammunition. No less well known were the Sussex fire-backs, and a number of these have been identified with certainty as having been made in that area. One, inscribed "Richard Lenard Founder at Bred Fournis" (*Bred:* Brede) is dated 1636, and another depicts the burning at the stake of an earlier ironmaster, Richard Woodman, and his wife; a couple who suffered that fate in the religious persecutions of Queen Mary in 1557.

Japan. Black asphaltum varnish for coating metal in imitation of lacquer.

Japanner. One who coats the surface with asphaltum varnish. Later it was used in a broader sense in regard to both decoration and manufacture.

Japanning. Was defined by eighteenth-century technical writers as "the covering of wood or metals by grounds of opaque colours in varnish which when varnished and dried may afterwards be decorated with painted ornament, in gold and colours, or left plain".

The secret of the surface lustre which characterized the finer work was to cover the opaque coloured grounds with several coats of clear japan varnish. Each application was followed by stoving at 280° F. in a cupboard-shaped iron oven. This firmly fused the surface, made it extremely hard, and prevented the peeling and cracking that spoilt Continental japanning. This surface was excellent for painting and gilding.

Kettle-tilter ("Idle-back", "Lazy-back", "Handy-maid"). A simple device of wrought iron for tilting the kettle when water was wanted from it. Not only was there no need to soil the hand by touching a smoke-blackened kettle, but the handle of the tilter projected outside the fireplace, was cool, and there would be no risk from scalding steam or water. The kettle was suspended over the fire in the tilter, which in turn hung from a pot-hook or crane.

Knocker latch. A combination door

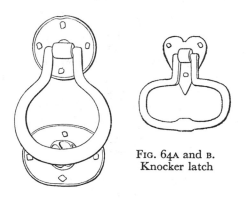

FIG. 64A and B.
Knocker latch

knocker and latch. Turning the knocker opened the latch.

Latch. A lock having a bevelled spring bolt which is self-acting when closing a door. The bolt is then withdrawn with a handle. No key.

Latten. Plate made from brass ingots and composed of copper and calamine and beaten into sheets with heavy horse- or water-powered battery hammers. Horse brasses made from latten are rare. Originally they displayed hammer marks on the back and front: years of polishing may have removed all traces of these from the front of a horse brass, but they remain visible at the back. It must be emphasized that latten was not an alternative name for brass, but was a term distinguishing hammered sheets from brass made by other processes.

Leather. Collectors of horse brasses tend to display them on martingales or other leather straps taken from harness. Until early in the present century such leather was almost invariably horse-hide tanned with oak bark and notable for its lightness and strength. Cow-hides, appreciably heavier, were sometimes used in the nineteenth century. Years of rubbing against the horse and cleaning with wax polish have made it more pliant than modern leather.

Lever lock. The earliest was patented in 1778 by Robert Barron, its mechanism a system of fixed wards in combination with two pivoting or lifting tumblers which he termed levers, held in position by a steel spring. Attached to the tumblers were stumps or studs which retained the bolt in its locked position. Only its own individually made key, cut in steps of different radii, corresponded with the varying lifts of the two tumblers, so that the latter were raised to the exact height to bring the studs into line with the slot in the bolt, and thus allow the top step of the key to act upon the stump and unlock it. Any attempt to pick the lock was frustrated by a number of upper transverse notches in the bolt. This rendered it impossible to tell when the tumblers had been lifted correctly; from this developed, in the early 1800s, the ordinary lever lock. The lever itself is a piece of flat, shaped metal of which one or more must be lifted simultaneously but differently by the various strips in the key to block the bolt either in the open or a locked position. All levers swing on the same pivot. By about 1850 the stump was attached to the bolt.

Lock plate. The background to which all the pins and stumps are riveted and over which the cover is fixed.

Locomotive (horse brasses). Special horse brasses displaying locomotives were issued by more than twenty railway companies for their dray horses, each picturing its favourite type of engine, some including a driver. They were used in association with a brass bearing the monogram or initials of the company pierced into flat plate: later the full title was engraved. A series of saddlers' stock locomotives, intended for martingales, consisted of a set of six locomotives illustrating development from Stephenson's Rocket until the time when these brasses were made, in 1880. Complete sets have been built up from single acquisitions. A rare brass of the mid-Victorian period is a plain crescent engraved with the Rocket.

Martingale. A broad band of leather or series of straps, extending from the nose-band or reins to the girth. By keeping the horse's head down this band prevents the animal from rearing or throwing back its head. From the early 1850s the martingale was hung with brasses as standard equipment. Saddlers usually attached brasses selected at random, but included types most favoured in the district. The topmost brass might be cast in the form of the emblem used by the saddler as his trademark; the lowest brass was often a lunar crescent punched with the saddler's name and address above the engraved inscription "Saddlery and Harness" and the date recording the year in which the harness was made. Rare indeed are special name and date brasses, such as the plain heart, hand-cut from rolled plate brass and engraved with the horse's name and the date of its birth.

Mechanism of locks. Consists of fixed obstructions – wards, guards, and bullets – and movable detainers such as tumblers and levers.

Measure. A vessel of standard liquid capacity.

Meat-fork. Used at the fireside when cooking. It usually had two prongs and was very little (if at all) different from a toasting-fork.

Mortice lock. Concealed from view by inserting it into a hole cut into the door edge. In most early mortice locks only the brass knob remained visible, the keyhole masked by a swinging escutcheon. Decoration might be added in the form of an ornamental end-piece matching the adjoining striking plate: these might be engraved, pierced, or cast and chased, often displaying the owner's coat-of-arms or cipher.

A new style of lock furniture associated with mortice locks was introduced during the mid-1760s. This set consisted of an expansive back-plate of chased and gilt cast brass, in scrollwork designs symmetrically arranged with festoons of husks centring on the door knob and flanked with a keyhole escutcheon

and a matching dummy escutcheon. The centre rosette and the escutcheon harmonized with the knob. In some instances the dummy was replaced by a small knob operating a night latch.

Mug. A handled drinking vessel without cover.

FIG. 65

Norfolk latch. A type consisting of a handle affixed to a large, one-piece escutcheon plate.

Oak leaf and acorn. Motifs favoured during the 1890s and later. A single well-modelled acorn might be enclosed within a wide frame pierced with holes in the form of concentric circles. Others were pierced in complicated patterns. Oak leaves and acorns cast as a single spray are usually within a lunar crescent; in others the crescent is stamped and a spray, cast and chased, is set within held by brazing. The acorn points upward when alone, downward in a spray of foliage (Plate 201B).

Night latch. A spring bolt lock operated by a key from outside and a knob from inside.

Patterns, casting (horse brasses). Fine brasses such as heraldic crests were cast from master patterns skilfully carved in hard mahogany. These remained the property of the purchaser, and so were used only for limited editions, never commercially. More usually master patterns were carved from pear wood, and from these a number of casting patterns were prepared, usually in a tin–lead alloy. These produced clear-cut relief work. Some of these pewter casting patterns have been mistaken for actual horse brasses, and as such are sometimes included in collections.

Pear shape. A term used in identifying a

curved or pyriform shape in hollowware (Plate 209c).

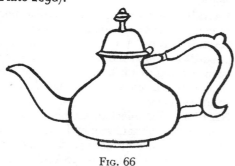

FIG. 66

Perforated ornament. Fashionable on silver and ceramics from the 1770s was also introduced to japanned ware. Most perforations were hand-sawn and finished by filing: a few, such as vertical pales, were die-punched. Perforated borders are notably found on waiters and on the "hand tea-tables" used for setting out the porcelain or Queen's ware tea service. Although such ornament is usually associated with Pontypool, it was also applied to the japanned ware of Birmingham, Wolverhampton, Bilston, and London.

Pewter. An alloy, chiefly of tin, with varying proportions of copper, lead, antimony, or bismuth.

Pin locks. These were usually in oak, the flat bolt passing completely through the locks, one end expanded to engage in the jamb socket, the other shaped to form a handle. Three recesses were sunk into the top edge, into which loose pins fell from above when the key was removed, thus holding the pin immovable. Pin-locks were opened by inserting a wooden key into an aperture immediately above the bolt handle, and lifting it slightly. Projections on its upper surface raised the locking pins so that the bolt might be withdrawn from its socket. (*See* Plate 205B.)

Pintle. A pivot pin for a hinge.

Pipe-kiln. A tubular wrought-iron frame

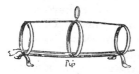

FIG. 67

with a handle at the top and feet at each end. Clay "churchwarden" pipes were placed in the kiln in order to clean them when they had become foul, and the pipe-kiln and its contents were then put into an oven. It is said that in country districts the local baker performed this task.

Plate lock. In these the working parts were exposed, being riveted to a heavy hatchet-shaped plate of wrought iron fixed flat against the door. The iron bolt worked in slides and engaged in a striking plate fitted to the door jamb. The visible working parts might display some decoration. By utilizing only the minimum number of parts, at a time when iron and steel were highly expensive, plate locks were made at comparatively low cost. Ansique plate locks are of iron made close-textured by hammering: the Victorian type have cast or rolled iron plates.

Plate-warmer. This stood before the fire in kitchen, living-room, or dining-room, to heat the plates preparatory to the serving of

FIG. 68

a meal. Several types of plate-warmer have been recorded; all date from the eighteenth and nineteenth centuries, and the surviving examples are not numerous. One variety is in the form of a wrought-iron revolving stand on a tripod base with upright bars to hold the plates in position. Another kind is similar to a Dutch-oven, and has a handle so that the whole apparatus, complete with warmed plates, might be brought from the fireside to the table. A third type is the cat: an ingenious arrangement of three turned wood or metal rods, arranged cross-wise to form a double-ended tripod that could stand either way up.

Pontipool. The industrial japanners of Birmingham and South Staffordshire found it convenient to market their japanned metal under the name of "Fancy Pontipool Ware", the spelling serving to distinguish it from the Allgood japanned ware.

Pontypool. The name given to japanned ware made by the Allgood family at Pontypool, Monmouthshire. Their many agents sold Allgood productions as "Pontypool Japan", and their London agent Edward Binyon, Fenchurch Street, London, advertised in 1783 that his was "The Original Warehouse for the Real Ponty-Pool Japann'd Ware". The terms "Pontypool" and "Pontipool" distinguished japanning on metal from japanned wood and Clay's japanned paper ware dating from 1772.

Porringer. A small, handled bowl or basin used for liquid or semi-liquid food, ranging in size from 2½ to 6 inches (Plate 209A, B).

Portraits (horse brasses). In addition to royal personages a few late Victorian and early Edwardian celebrities were commemorated on horse brasses. The politicians were Gladstone, Lord Randolph Churchill, Joseph Chamberlain, Disraeli, and Lloyd George from 1908. Disraeli's portrait is usually enclosed in a border of primroses or primroses encircled with a narrow pierced rim. Baden-Powell, Lord Roberts, and Kitchener decorated driven horses at the time of the Boer War, and Nelson during the Trafalgar centenary year of 1905.

Pot-hook (Cottrall, Jib-crook, Hanger, Tramelle, Hake). A wrought-iron device that was in use from medieval times for suspending a pot over the fire. By means of a ratchet it could be adjusted for height. In Scotland the same means was attained by using a chain and hook, known as a "Jumping Rope".

Princes metal. A brass alloy evolved in the 1670s and tinged to the colour of gold. The metal was heated until slightly red and laid to pickle in a diluted spirit of vitriol. After removing dirt and scale by washing, it was immersed for a moment in aquafortis, dried, and burnished with a bloodstone.

FIG. 69

Punch. A die for striking the maker's touch or other identification or decorative marks into metal.

Rattail. The tapering extension of a spoon handle unto the underside of the bowl.

Rattail hinge. A type usually found on cupboards in which there is a downward extension, serving as a brace, of the pintle. This extension is curved and terminated with a decorative device.

Rim lock. The mechanism is entirely closed within a rectangular metal case and attached to the inner surface of a door. In addition to the locking bolt, such a lock might have an independent smaller knob operating a spring catch to prevent the lock from being opened from the outside. Both of these entered the striking plate screwed upon the jamb.

Royal (horse brasses). Portraits of Queen Victoria are to be found in four types. Bun portraits taken from the coinage were issued early in her reign, and crowned "young heads" from 1850. "Widows" with three-quarter veiled bust and small crown date from the jubilee year of 1887, while less rare is the full profile designed by Thomas Brock and first issued on the coinage of 1893. This portrait appears on diamond jubilee brasses, many of which are inscribed with the date, but the difference in the portrait anyhow distinguishes the 1887 from the 1897 issue. The diamond jubilee was responsible too for horse brasses in the shape of a Victoria Cross surmounted by a royal crown and inscribed "1837 Diamond Jubilee 1897". Others were in the form of openwork Maltese crosses. *Heart-shaped* brasses with the front in bold relief and burnished might be engraved "Victoria Jubilee 1887".

Prince of Wales feathers were made in several varieties. At first they were mounted in plain circular frames; then came a series with the three feathers stamped and set in a cast ring; and finally, they were in shaped outlines. Edward VII is found full face and in profile, both as Prince of Wales and as king. A dozen variations have been noted, each cast in a single piece. The coronation horse brasses were inscribed "God Save the King 1902" (Plate 201B).

Salamander. A bar of wrought iron with a thick round or oblong piece at one end;

somewhat like a long-handled shovel in appearance. The larger end was heated until it

FIG. 70

became red-hot, and then held near bread, cake, etc., in order to brown it.

Saw piercing. The design was pounced upon the plate, which, if of iron or steel, was softened by annealing. It was then drilled so that the saw-piercer could pass his delicate bow saw through holes and remove surplus metal. After finishing with a file the surface was engraved. The metal was then hardened.

Scallop shells (horse brasses). Single examples cast and burnished date from the 1880s. Sets in graduated sizes were stamped from about 1890, and these are not uncommon.

Sheet tin or tin-plate. Thinly rolled iron coated with tin.

Side hinge. A hinge consisting of only one leaf, usually placed in a vertical position, acting on a pintle (Plate 215A).

Single reed. A single moulding around the edge of a plate rim as compared to multi-reeded rims, where two or more mouldings form the edge.

Skewer. Small iron pin for holding meat on a spit.

Skillet (Posnet, Pipkin). Medieval skillets were shaped like cauldrons, and it was not until the sixteenth century that this ancestor of the modern saucepan became recognizable. These later skillets had no feet, but were made with the sides sloping outwards so that the circumference of the top was greater than that of the base. The handle was popularly used for advertising the name of the maker or for the spreading of texts such as "Ye Wages of Sin is Death". They were made of bronze.

Smooth rim. A flat, unadorned plate rim, where the reinforcing moulding appears on the underside of the rim.

Souvenirs (horse brasses). The motifs used are innumerable and include portraits of George V, Queen Alexandra, George VI, Queen Mary, the rare Edward VIII, Queen Elizabeth II, Sir Winston Churchill, Field-Marshal Viscount Montgomery. Souvenir birds include duck, eagle, emu, lyre bird, magpie, ostrich, raven, and swan. The range of souvenir horse brasses designs extends to many hundreds.

Spider. A three-legged skillet, or sometimes a long-handled skillet.

Spinning. A process by which a thin metal sheet is pressed against a wooden core in a spinning lathe to be forced into shape.

Spit. A metal bar with which meat was pierced and placed on cobirons before the fire for roasting; as the bar was rotated all sides of the meat received the heat equally. The spit had prongs in the centre, and a grooved pulley at one end to connect by chain or rope to some sort of motive power: human, animal, or mechanical. This motive power, if human or animal, was termed a "turnspit", and if mechanical a "Jack". Illustrations in early manuscripts show that boys were employed as turnspits, and by the sixteenth century spit-jacks were in use. These latter were made of brass and iron, and were driven by large weights of stone or metal, which descended slowly into pits dug for the purpose to increase the length of fall. Like the weights of a clock, once they had completely run down they were wound up again. Another mechanical method of turning the spit was by a fan fitted in the mouth of the chimney, which was operated by the rising draught. A further method was the employment of dogs, specially trained for the purpose, which were confined in a small treadmill fixed to the wall of the kitchen. At the end of the eighteenth century spring-driven jacks were in use, and culminated in the neat bottle-jack, brass-cased and driven by clockwork.

FIG. 71

When not in use the spits were kept in the spit-rack: a row of hooks at either end of the space above the fireplace.

Spun hollow-ware. Bodies of urn vases were sometimes spun in Britannia metal from about 1800 and in copper from about 1820 when a special copper was evolved suitable for spinning in the lathe. Spinning was profitable only if orders were substantial.

Steel. Early locksmiths used Venice steel for their finest work, but otherwise a long-wearing steel capable of taking a good heat at the forge was difficult to obtain. Quality was variable and continued so until after the mid-eighteenth century. English steel made in the Forest of Dean had become the locksmith's first choice. Springs were made from gad steel imported from Germany. Less costly goods were made from Yorkshire or Sussex steel.

Stock lock. A plate lock let into a rectangular block of oak and thereby attached to the door by bolts or rivets, later by screws. The mechanism in some stock locks was covered with an iron plate decorated with pierced designs, usually trefoil or cinque foil, with a matching plate covering the wooden block. From the mid-eighteenth century the mechanism was almost invariably covered with a solid iron plate.

Strap hinge. A simple hinge consisting of two horizontally placed iron straps.

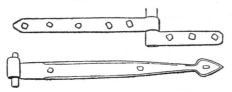

FIG. 72A and B. Strap hinge

Striking plate. The metal plate fixed to a door frame into which the bolt of a lock is shot by the key. The plate is provided with a lip on which the bolt strikes.

Stump. A circular pin within the case of a lock to guide the different working parts. In lever locks it works in the gating, that is, a slot cut in the lever.

Suffolk latch. A type of latch consisting of a handle terminating in large decorative cusps but lacking an escutcheon plate (Plate 215B).

Suites. In large houses rim locks from the 1660s might be made in matching suites, a different key for each lock and a master key capable of opening the entire series. Such a suite of Queen Anne locks was fitted to doors in the apartments of Marlborough House, London, where they still function silently.

Sun flash (horse brass). A face piece, extremely popular in Kent, was originally a disc of latten with its centre hand-raised into a high dome or boss and encircled with a wide, flat rim. This extended almost across the horse's face and weighed about six ounces. In rolled brass the outer rim might be serrated. In some examples of the 1850s–80s the flat rim was pierced with twelve triangular rays extending outward to the rim which, from the early 1870s, might be encircled with drilled perforations. The entire brass, including dome and perforations, might be stamped from 1880. Sometimes the dome might be surrounded by a series of concentric circles in relief, number and width varying. A splash of colour might be given from the mid-1890s by fitting into the raised centre a boss of coloured glass or enamelled china: colours noted include yellow, green, dark blue, red, ringed red, white, blue. A series of uncommon rectangular sun flashes had incurved clipped corners and a central dome against a plain ground: others were shield-shape. Some late cast examples display the sun flash against a wide and elaborately patterned rim (Plate 201A).

Terret (horse brasses). These, more correctly termed fly terrets, are also known as swingers and flyers. The terret is a vertical ring set between the horse's ears and in which swings a horse brass with both faces finished and polished. Such brasses are smaller in diameter than the ordinary horse brass, and instead of a strap loop a solid eye was placed at right angles, fitting into a pair of lugs at the top of the ring. This was held in position by a screw-pin which permitted free swinging. Frequently the full figure of a horse, cast in the round and chased, hung within the ring, or a horse's head, or an heraldic crest. Tradesmen might display a motif associated with their work, such as a hooped barrel shaped in the round. The terret might be surmounted by a tall cylindrical brush, often with dyed bristles, blue and red being common. In other instances there was a tiny bell (Plate 201B).

Tin iron. Midland japanners from 1784 used fine-quality plate rolled from a special iron containing charcoal instead of coke. This was evolved specially for japanners by a Wolverhampton ironmaster and sold under the name of tin iron. The majority of japanned ware was hand-shaped or spun until the introduction of the drop hammer between 1815 and 1820. A heavy stamp head wound up by a winch was allowed to fall on a sheet of iron laid over a sunk die. Repeated blows forced the metal into the required shape much more speedily than had been possible previously, and larger work could be handled. Patrick Nasmyth's first steam hammer was bought by the Walton firm in 1840 making them first in the field to produce finely shaped, heavy work at prices hitherto impossible.

It was the Midland japanners' use of improved qualities of tin iron, together with the introduction of more efficient japanning stoves, japans, and varnishes during the 1790s that brought about the eventual decline of Pontypool.

Tin-plate. Rolled iron soaked in molten tin which penetrated its entire texture and gave the whole a silvery white colour. The tin used was pure-grain tin made in the form of shot.

Tinned plate. Iron sheet, tin iron from 1784, the surface only being coated with tin.

Toaster. These were either in the form of standing toasters or the familiar fork, and were used for the toasting of both bread and

FIG. 73

meat. The fork needs little mention beyond pointing out that it almost always has three prongs. A variation of it is the toast-holder, which has two short upcurved arms at the end of a long handle.

Standing toasters are rare and vary much in design. Four in the Victoria and Albert Museum are worthy of description. Two of them have simple tripod bases and central pillars with turned finials. On each pillar is a bell-shaped fitting with three prongs for holding the food to be toasted, and these are adjustable for height. Another is in the form of a circular trivet with a three-pronged fork, also adjustable up and down. The fourth type stands on the ground and is like a table toast-rack for only one slice of bread, and it has a long handle projecting at the back. The latter

type was for use at a down-hearth, and all four were of wrought-iron.

Tortoiseshell decoration. Fashionable throughout the second half of the eighteenth century.

Tortoiseshell japan was laid over silver leaf or on a white ground. The rich glowing crimson type required gold or silver leaf to be laid over a white ground. This was clouded and stained with yellow or reddish yellow varnish to resemble tortoiseshell. Then followed numerous coats of clear varnish, each being stoved.

Trammel. An adjustable device used for hanging a pot from a crane or the lug pole of a fireplace. Many lighting devices are also equipped with a trammel so that they may be raised or lowered.

Trays. The principal articles of japanners' manufacture were trays and waiters made from tinned sheet iron of thickness varying from 24 to 30 gauge. Trays are rectangular, square or oval, and measure 12–21 inches across: waiters are circular. The corners of early trays were folded and riveted: by 1780 they were cut and welded. Narrow hand-holds might be cut in the rim or D-shaped handles of gilded brass riveted to the sides. Oval trays with plain turn-up rims appeared about 1800 and a few years later came scalloped and gadrooned rims. From about 1820 trays were shaped under the drop hammer, thus greatly reducing the cost. By 1839 there were seventeen factories in Wolverhampton and ten in Birmingham devoted to the production of tray blanks in iron.

Japanned trays might be sold in sets of three, four, or six in graduated sizes with matching decoration, but papier mâché sets of trays had outmoded the metal by the mid-1840s. Each japanner carried some 2,000 different patterns. The weekly output in Wolverhampton in 1840 was estimated to be more than 50,000 trays including about 2,000 sets.

Trivet (Brandis(e)). Strictly a three-legged stand on which utensils might rest before the fire, but the word is used to cover many types of stand. The trivets of the seventeenth and eighteenth centuries were usually circular and of wrought iron; sometimes they had a projecting handle. Later versions, also on three legs, were of an oblong shape with one end curved and fitted with a handle, while the far

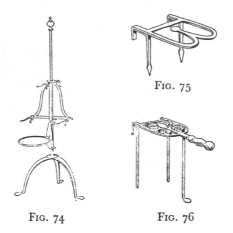

FIG. 75

FIG. 74   FIG. 76

end had curved projections to fit over the fire-bar of a grate. Others dispensed with legs, and were made to hang on the front of a stove; of this last type many were made in the nineteenth century of cast iron with pierced brass tops.

Tumblers. Units in the mechanism to retain the bolt of a lock. These are immovable to any but the right key, which lifts them to pre-determined heights and shoots the bolt.

Urns, tea and coffee. From the late 1780s until the 1820s japanners made urns heated by charcoal-burning braziers. In its simplest form the body of a japanned urn was cylindrical, the lower third perforated to contain the brazier. The Levno urn, dating from about 1800, had a cylindrical body containing a central tube for conveying heat through the urn from a brazier burning in a perforated cube-shaped box below, often raised on four lion-paw feet of gilded brass.

The vase-shaped urn until the 1820s was hand-shaped in copper and heavily tinned within. It was usually mounted upon three cabriole legs with feet of ivory, ebony, boxwood, or other insulating material so that the urn might stand upon a rectangular tray decorated to match. This held the spirit lamp within a low cylindrical box with perforated sides (Plate 208A, B, C).

Usk. A break-away factory established by two of the Allgood brothers in 1761, seven

miles from Pontypool and operated by them until early in the nineteenth century. Maintaining that they were the original makers of Pontypool japan, they marketed their ware under that name.

Varnishing. Painted decoration was varnished to preserve it from the ravages of wear and in the case of trays and waiters from disfigurement by scalding liquids. Such varnish needed to possess a glaze both durable and transparent so that the glow of the colours beneath should not be diminished. Fat varnishes were eventually discovered to possess these qualities. The standard formula called for two parts copal, one part linseed oil, two parts essence of turpentine. This was applied with a large flat brush manipulated with a single backward-and-forward motion, the result being an absolutely smooth surface. Considerable skill was essential in this, for undulations and ridges disfigured the uniform reflection of light over the picture.

Waiters. Japanners listed their circular trays as waiters, sizes ranging from 6 to 20 inches with occasional nineteenth-century giants measuring as much as 30 inches. They were fashionable by the mid-eighteenth century, usually decorated in the tortoiseshell style. They were hammered up from thinly rolled iron plates. Tin-plate was used at Pontypool and in London; tinned in Birmingham and Wolverhampton. Early examples have rather deep galleries slightly flaring and perforated. These, by the late 1780s, were superseded by solid rims enriched with gilded lines. A full-sized circular japanned waiter became a fashionable background to the tea equipage with its hissing urn.

Walsall. The centre of the English saddlery and coach furniture trade in the nineteenth century. Specialist firms were engaged in the manufacture of brass enrichments for leather harness, a trade highly flourishing by 1851, when White's Walsall Directory listed no fewer than twenty-seven harness furniture manufacturers who were also brass founders. The horse-brass trade as an industry rather than a hand-craft dates from the 1840s. The Walsall harness furniture men evolved a special brass alloy of close texture, golden hue, and capable of burnishing to a high, flawless brilliancy.

Ward. A fixed projection in a lock to prevent a key from entering or turning unless correctly shaped.

Wheatsheaf (horse brasses). Known in heraldry as a garb, the wheatsheaf was highly popular in northern counties. Luxuriant sheaves might be inserted between the upward-pointing horns of a plain crescent which might have a serrated outer edge; or they might be framed within a star or a perforated ring; or cast in bold relief on the surface of a plain shield. The majority are one-piece castings, but a stamped series will be found, the wheatsheaf within a plain crescent.

Wilkes, John. A well-known locksmith of Birmingham responsible for a series of signed locks, most of them in latten, some in blue steel serving as a background to applied brasswork, or in engraved steel. Wilkes became celebrated for his detector lock, of which many examples exist *in situ* in England and on the Continent. This lock (Plate 205A) is ornamented with the figure of a late Caroline soldier in relief. The left leg is extended by pushing a secret catch, and this reveals the keyhole. The toe-cap of the boot then points to a number on the dial, by which the number of times the door has been opened is registered, as each turn of the key causes the number to change. The lock bolt is released by pushing back the hat.

Wolverhampton. The finest English locks have been made here from early in the seventeenth century. In 1660 Wolverhampton paid a hearth tax on eighty-four locksmiths' hearths and there were ninety-seven in nearby Willenhall. The Georgian locksmiths of Wolverhampton maintained a high reputation.

Wrought iron. Literally iron which has been worked or formed by a blacksmith. The term has also come to mean a type of iron which contains practically no carbon but a considerable amount of slag, which often gives it a grainy appearance. Wrought iron is readily worked and welded in the forge, and is characterized by great toughness and ductility. Wrought iron cannot be hardened by heating and sudden cooling as steel can be; consequently it is unsuitable for the cutting edges of tools.

TERMS USED IN PEWTERWORK

(A) SADWARE

The pewterer's terms for plates, dishes, and chargers.

Plate. Up to 12 inches diameter.
Dish. 12–18 inches diameter.
Charger. Over 18 inches diameter.

Types of Sadware

Broad rim. Having a rim proportionately wider than the normal.
Cardinal's hat. A deep dish with broad rim.
Marriage plate. One item of a garnish (*q.v.*) decorated with engraved symbols as a souvenir of marriage.
Narrow rim. Having a rim formed solely of multiple mouldings (Plate 211K centre).
Octagonal rim. Self-explanatory.
Paten. A broad rim plate, or a tazza (*q.v.*) used in the administration of Holy Communion.

Plain rim. Self-explanatory.
Sexagonal rim. Self-explanatory.
Single reed. Having one moulding around the edge of the rim.
Tazza. A name commonly (but erroneously) given to a plate supported upon a spreading foot.
Triple reed. Having a rim with multiple mouldings around the edge (Plate 211K).
Wavy rim. Having a rim of alternate convex and concave curves.

(B) HOLLOW-WARE

The pewterers' term for flagons, tankards, measures, pots, mugs, beakers, etc.

Types of Hollow-ware

Beaker. A drinking-vessel, resembling the modern tumbler.
Bleeding bowl. A porringer (*q.v.*) marked internally with lines of liquid capacities.
Flagon. A large vessel from which other vessels are filled.

Loving cup. A drinking-vessel with two handles, originally used for toasting. General term for twin-handled cups.

Measure. A vessel of a standard liquid capacity, used in taverns for serving into drinking-vessels.

Porringer. A shallow vessel with flat, horizontal handle(s), for semi-liquid foods.

Pot (mug). A tavern drinking vessel.

Quaich (Gaelic). A Scottish form of porringer, having two lugs (*q.v.*) and, in its smaller sizes, used for spirits.

Tankard. A drinking-vessel, usually domestic.

(*Note.*—The terms caudle cup, cupping bowl, and posset cup are sometimes applied, without much authority, to some vessels of the cup or porringer class.)

Names used in connexion with hollow-ware

Baluster. A tavern measure, bulging below, concave above (Plate 211H, L–Q).

Beefeater. A flagon having a lid somewhat resembling the head-dress of the Yeomen of the Tower of London (Plate 211E).

Bun lid. Self-explanatory. Many flagons of this type have finials rising from the bun.

Dome lid. Self-explanatory.

Flat lid. Self-explanatory, seventeenth century.

Guernsey. A baluster-shaped measure, encircled by two broad bands, and having a heart-shaped lid and twin acorn thumbpiece; peculiar to Guernsey, C.I.

Haystack. More properly Haycock, which it resembles. An Irish tavern measure, made chiefly in Cork.

Jersey. A plain baluster-shaped measure, with lid and thumbpiece as in Guernsey; peculiar to Jersey, C.I. (Plate 211F).

Moulded base. Self-explanatory. The hollow formed is external (Plate 211A).

Ovolo base. Having a base formed by a plain projecting quarter-curve. The hollow formed is external (Plate 211C).

Pot belly. A Scottish tavern measure with broad belly and narrowing neck (Plate 211J).

Skirt base. Having a wide, spreading base, the hollow formed being internal (Plate 211E).

Tappit hen. A Scottish measure, i.e. a "hen with a top to it" (fanciful) (Plate 211G). The true tappit hen holds 1 pint Scots (equals 3 pints English), but the term is usually applied to all capacities.

Tulip (pear). A tankard or mug with body shaped as described (Plate 214A).

West Country. A tavern measure with bulging body tapering to a narrow spouted neck. Of West Country origin; more numerous in copper.

York acorn. A flagon of acorn shape, peculiar to Yorkshire, having a dome lid with acorn-shaped finial.

York straight-side. A flagon with tapering body, the base without projection but defined by multiple concentric mouldings. Of North Country origin.

Thumbpieces by which a lid is raised

Billet, purchase. Alternative names for thumbpiece.

Bar-and-heart. A plain, wide thumbpiece, pierced by a heart and surmounted by a thick bar (Plate 211B).

Bud. Two ovoids rising from a common stalk and resembling bursting buds (Plate 211N and O).

Chairback (either solid or pierced). Self-explanatory.

Erect. A tall, solid block found on early seventeenth-century flagons (Plate 211C). A lighter, curving form is found on certain Scottish measures, notably tappit hens.

Hammer-head. Self-explanatory.

Love bird. Twin birds, their beaks jointed, surmounted by a volute (Plate 213D).

Ram's horn (full or embryo). Self-explanatory.

Shell (full or embryo). A thumbpiece formed of a ribbed or plain escallop shell.

Sprayed leaf. A thin, wide, fan-shaped thumbpiece with deeply-gouged lines radiating from the foot in a leaf pattern (Plate 211D).

Twin acorn. Two acorns rising from a wedge attached to the lid (Plate 211F).

Twin cusped. Two semi-spheres rising from a broad base (Plate 211A).

Volute. Twin spiral scrolls, chief feature of the Ionic capital, rising from the lid attachment (Plate 211H, Q).

Wedge. A thumbpiece formed by the extension of the lid attachment upwards to a point.

(c) SPOONS

Spoons. Spoons are known by their stem terminals (knops or finials). Some, being unique, have no common name; other names are self-explanatory. The following have general acceptance; descriptions are given where necessary.

Acorn.

Apostle (Plate 213).

Ball (Globe).

Baluster. A small bulge topped by a button.

Diamond. Multi-sided, tapering to a point.

Hexagon. Six-sided and of melon shape.

Horned head-dress. A female bust surmounted by the lofty, mitre-like head-dress worn in the early fifteenth century (Plate 213L).

Horse-hoof.

Lion (rampant or sejant).

Maidenhead. A female bust understood to represent the Virgin Mary. Similar silver spoons are described in a fifteenth-century inventory as "Cum ymaginibus Beatae Mariae in fine corundum" (Plate 213).

Pied de biche (hind's hoof). Post-Commonwealth, with flat stem and broad, flat terminal, twice notched at the top. Some are decorated with cast busts of William and Mary or Anne.

Pumpkin. A ball vertically gadrooned.

Puritan. A Commonwealth spoon with flat stem and no terminal.

Seal. A Baluster, but topped by a flat disc.

Slipped in the stalk. The commonest pre-Commonwealth spoon with plain stem cut off on the slant.

Split end. As Pied de biche.

Stump. Pre-Commonwealth, with plain stem cut off square.

Wavy. As Pied de biche but without notches.

Writhen. A ball diagonally gadrooned.

Rat-tail. A tapering extension of the stem down the back of the bowl.

(d) GENERAL

Booge. The curved portion of a plate, etc., joining rim to bottom.

Box inkstand. A rectangular inkstand with one or two wells, drawers beneath.

Bulbous salt. A globular salt-cellar with shallow circular depression (Plate 213C).

Capstan salt. A salt-cellar shaped like a ship's capstan.

Drip-shield. A wide, circular or multi-sided collar between the base and stem of a candlestick to prevent grease from falling upon the hand.

Drum. The body of a flagon, tankard, etc.

Entasis. A slight bulge between base and lip of a flagon, tankard, etc.

Finial. An erect terminal sometimes added to the lid of a flagon, or the terminal of a spoon.

Gadroon. A geometrical design of small cast ribs, usually radiating from a centre.

Garnish. A household set of plates and dishes.

"Hall-marks". Small punches used by pewterers in imitation of those used by silversmiths.

Hammered. Showing the marks of the pewterer's hammer all over. A strengthening device used on dishes, plates, etc. Normally found on the booge (q.v.) only.

Knop. *See* Finial.

Loggerhead. A circular inkstand with a wide flat base, still used in banks.

Lug. An ear (Scots); the handle of a quaich (q.v.).

Sand-dredger. A box with perforated top, for containing sand, which was used before blotting-paper was introduced.

Spool salt. A salt-cellar resembling a flattened hour-glass.

Standish. An inkstand formed by a rectangular flat plate standing upon four feet, and having a curved edge. Upon the plate stand ink-well, dredger, etc., and there is usually a drawer beneath for quills.

Touch. The pewterer's trade mark (*see* Introduction).

Touch-plate. A flat sheet of soft pewter for recording touches.

Treasury inkstand. A four-footed oblong box, with double lid centrally hinged, containing four compartments for the accessories. So called from an example in the Government Department of that name.

Trencher salt. A low, oblong octagonal salt-cellar, with oval bowl.

Wriggle-work. A form of decoration made by rocking a gouge from side to side in its progress.

MIRRORS

British Wall Mirrors

Before the fifteenth century, in spite of the fact that the process of silvering glass was understood, it would seem to have been little used, and mirrors were made of highly polished plates of metal. Glass had not then the clarity it later attained, and a carefully burnished piece of gold, silver, steel, or other metal was likely to provide a more accurate reflecting surface. Limited in size, it is doubtful whether such mirrors were hung on a wall or merely stood on a convenient piece of furniture. For a considerable period, along with other comparable luxuries, their ownership was confined to the wealthy.

Glass mirror-plates became a monopoly of the republic of Venice, where Murano was the centre of the glass-making industry on the continent of Europe and whence knowledge of the process had come from Germany some time about the year 1500. There is no evidence that they were made in England until early in the seventeenth century, when John Aubrey, the antiquarian, noted in his *Brief Lives* that a man named Robson had commenced their manufacture. In 1618 Robson's enterprise was taken over by Sir Robert Mansell, who by 1623 employed some five hundred

men in the "making, grinding, and foyling of looking glasses".

Half a century later a glass-works was started at Vauxhall by the Duke of Buckingham, and in due course became famous.

Mirror-plate was first made by what was termed the "broad" process. In this, briefly, the liquid glass was taken up from the furnace on a blowing-tube and blown into the form of a large bubble. Two opposite surfaces of the bubble were cut off; the tube remaining was then slit along one side and the whole flattened. The sheet of glass was cooled, ground, and polished until it was as flat and smooth as possible. In spite of the care it received in the two last treatments, the resulting plate was not always satisfactory. Principally it was found that however skilfully the craftsmen blew the glass, it was extremely difficult to ensure that it was of an even thickness over the entire surface; in addition, there was understandably a limit to the size that could be made in this manner.

Late in the seventeenth century, French glass-makers introduced the process of glass casting. The molten glass was poured on to a bed of metal, was swiftly spread evenly over it and rolled flat while it was still hot. Much larger and truer plates could be made by this method, which was also quicker in spite of the fact that the plates had still to be slowly cooled, and then ground and polished. The casting process was used for a short while in England about 1690, but it did not find favour and for some reason was given up. In 1773 "The British Cast Plate-Glass Company" was incorporated, and factories were opened at Southwark and at St Helen's, Lancashire. The venture succeeded in producing glass to supplant the imported French plates, and the company remained in being until the outset of the present century.

The actual "silvering" of the glass is misnamed, as the precious metal is not among the constituents that were used. A sheet of tin-foil and a quantity of mercury were the principal ingredients, and by their use the English and Continental craftsmen of the past produced the mirror-plates of which so many have survived the wear and tear of the centuries to bear witness to their skill. The tin-and-mercury amalgam remained in general use until about 1840, when it was replaced by a process that does merit the name of "silvering", for by a discovery of the German chemist J. von Liebig, a coat of the metal is deposited chemically on the glass.

The framing of mirrors during the seventeenth and eighteenth centuries took many forms, and was the subject of careful study from men of artistic talent ranging from Grinling Gibbons and William Kent to Thomas Chippendale and Robert Adam. At the beginning of the period the pieces of glass were of small size and the frames were usually contrastingly large. Elaborate settings of carved wood, of embroidered stumpwork, coloured beads, ebony, and tortoiseshell, or of chased plaques of silver, were among the many that surrounded comparatively insignificant pieces of mirror-glass, and were the workmanship of the most skilled craftsmen of their time. No material, save gold itself, was so costly that it is not found to have been formed into a surrounding for the glass that reflected the features of Caroline beauties.

By 1675 the framing had grown less varied and the well-known "cushion" type was coming into use (Plate 221B.) Following the customary rectangular form, it was usually veneered with walnut, often in the form of "oysters" of selected grain. More decorative versions were heavily inlaid with marquetry, rare examples were of incised Chinese lacquer, and others, rarer still, overlaid with embossed silver may be seen still at Windsor Castle and at Knole.

As it became possible to manufacture glass in sheets of larger size, it was found that not only the frame but also the mirror within it had decorative possibilities, and also that a nearly square shape was not necessarily the most suitable. Perhaps inspired by the *Galerie des Glaces* at Versailles, completed by Le Brun for Louis XIV in 1682, and by the success of the French in casting large plates, English houses began to be ornamented with mirrors in profusion. These mirrors were for the decoration of the rooms in which they were placed, and not primarily for personal admiration as had been earlier examples.

The increase in the size of the glass was countered by a shrinkage in the size of the frame. To such a degree did this change sweep into fashion that for a while, about the years 1690–1700, the frame almost vanished altogether, and was replaced by a surround of strips of glass decorated with cutting or with patterns in *verre églomisé* (Plate 221C). The French may well have inspired the larger mirror, but undoubtedly the Venetians were responsible for this mode of bordering it.

Following the "frameless" era came the introduction of the gilt frame; in turn following the new taste for gilt furnishings. Whereas polished cabinet-work returned shortly to favour, the mirror frame remained gilt. Few, if any, were in any other finish after 1750, and before that date the exceptions were in a minority. These last comprise the walnut-veneered mirror-frames of small size assigned popularly to Queen Anne's reign, much reproduced in recent years, but, if genuine, dating more probably from the time of George I (Plate 222C); and the larger mirrors of George II date with gilt enrichments on a ground of polished Virginia ("red") walnut.

The placing of mirrors in a room began to assume a regularity that has remained little changed. Above the fireplace was the most popular position, and there the framing sometimes formed an integral part of that most important feature. Some of these overmantel mirrors incorporated within their extensive frames an oil-painting, and examples of the type, dating from about 1740–60, are found usually with landscape or floral pictures. A simpler variation of the large overmantel mirror, the "landscape" mirror (Plate 221C), came into vogue early in the eighteenth century, gradually grew squarer in shape as the years wore on, and in the succeeding century exchanged width for height (Plate 224C). Upright mirrors were placed on the narrow walls (piers) between windows, and pier-glasses, as they were called, were widely employed from their first introduction about 1700. Further, in those great mansions that boasted suites of state rooms, mirrors were hung at their far ends to reflect one into another and artificially increase their length.

As with the design of furnishings in general, the design of mirror-frames varied almost from year to year and month to month, but they may be grouped conveniently under a number of headings. This is the case with many of the smaller and simpler gilt gesso mirrors (Plate 222B), which are assigned to the period of Queen Anne (1702–14), although most are rather later in date. The larger, more heavily designed mirrors with pediments of classical type, are attributed to one of the foremost architects of his day, William Kent.

Following the vogue of the so-called "Kent" or "architectural" frame came the first signs of the combination of French, Gothic, and Chinese styles that culminated in the well-known Chinese Chippendale. From a few years prior to 1754, when Thomas Chippendale's volume of designs was published, mirror-frames were modelled elaborately with exotic birds, Chinamen, goats, sheep, sea-shells, and flowers (among much else), and the carver was able to give full rein to his agile chisel. Many of these frames were from the designs of Linnell, Johnson, Lock and Copland, and others, but all are assigned popularly to Chippendale, whose book conveniently summarized the styles of his time for posterity (Plate 223A, B, C).

The various motifs figured by Chippendale, combined or singly, remained in vogue until the introduction of classical themes by Robert and James Adam. In common with the furniture which became fashionable in the 1770s, the mirror-frame was ornamented with urns, honeysuckle, husks and paterae (Plate 224A). The delicacy of the work proved often to be beyond the resources of the wood-carver, and many of the detailed and flimsy ornaments were of composition on a wire core or were cast in lead.

By the second half of the eighteenth century the pier-glass had reached very large proportions. Sheets of mirror-glass supplied to the Earl of Mansfield in 1769, and still at Kenwood, London, measure 74 inches in height, and a plate measuring 91 inches by $57\frac{1}{2}$ inches was supplied by Chippendale's firm in 1773.

Oval mirrors were made in the 1730s and remained popular throughout the century, during which their framing followed the prevailing patterns in each decade. Distinctive and rare were the Irish mirrors of the last years of the eighteenth century. These were of oval shape, and framed with one or more rows of clear or coloured glass facets (Plate 224B).

Finally, there is the familiar convex mirror (Plate 224D). This was introduced from France, and the majority of surviving examples date from 1800 and later. They had been made several centuries earlier, and one is depicted in Van Eyck's picture in the National Gallery, London, painted in 1434. Van Eyck's mirror is in a simple gilt frame; its more modern counterpart usually bears a carved eagle above the deeply turned gilt border in which are placed small gilt balls. Usually a ball is suspended from the beak of the eagle, and in some examples the frame is flanked by arms for candles; the arms of gilt brass fitted with cut-glass drops. Rare convex mirrors are more elaborately and individually carved, and are known with the frames surmounted by an ornament in the form of the crest of the owner, or with the side supports in the shape of dolphins.

American Mirrors

The early records

Instructing farmers about to settle in frontier areas of the United States in 1789, Benjamin Rush pointed out, "There are several expensive parts of household furniture that he should leave behind him for which he will have no use in the woods, such as a large looking glass. . . ." This advice suggests the reason for the paucity of information about mirrors in America in the early seventeenth century. That they were in use by 1644 is substantiated, however, by the inventory of the estate of Joanna Cummings, of Salem, Massachusetts, which lists a mirror valued at three shillings.

A study of the published probate records of Essex County, Massachusetts, discloses that between 1644 and 1681 at least ninety-four mirrors were owned in that area.

These records reveal that usually the mirrors were placed in the hall or the parlour, the main gathering room in the early homes. Less frequently, they were used in the chamber or bedroom. One of the earliest records of one person's owning more than one mirror occurs in 1661 in the estate of Robert Gray, of Salem: "In the parlor . . . one large lookinge glass . . . In the litle Chamber . . . a lookinge glass and 3 pictures."

By the eighteenth century their usage became less limited, and the following advertisement appeared in *The Boston News-Letter* of April 25/May 2, 1715: "Looking-Glasses of all sorts, Glass Sconces, Cabbinetts, Writing Desks, Bookcases with Desks, old Glasses new Silvered, and all sorts of Japan-work, Done and sold by William Randle at the Sign of the Cabinnett, a Looking-Glass Shop in Queen-Street . . ."

A manuscript book containing inventories taken in New York City between 1742 and 1768 indicates that out of twenty-one colonists of varied circumstances, nineteen possessed at

least one mirror. Notable among these are the three owned by Joseph Leddell, pewterer, in 1754: one listed simply as a "looking glass", one "with black frame", and one "with japanned frame". William Wright, chandler, possessed one old mirror and a "Small looking glass and sconces, old", in 1757. Rice Williams in 1758 had one small mirror and an overmantel mirror.

At this time overmantel mirrors placed above the fireplace on the chimney breast, were frequently found in American houses where they are known as chimney glasses.

Another type of mirror was the pier glass, intended for use on the wall between two windows. "All sorts of peer glasses" were advertised as early as 1732 in the *South Carolina Gazette*.

Benjamin Franklin's inventory taken in 1790 reveals a variety of mirrors. In one chamber there was a dressing-table glass valued at £2 and in Mr Franklin's chamber, a pier glass worth £2 and a mirror. There was a mirror in the parlour, two mirrors valued at £12 in the dining-room, and one in the Blue Room. This indicates the wider use and the variety of mirrors in America by the end of the eighteenth century.

That these were no longer simply utilitarian objects but also an important part of the decorative scheme is indicated by Abigail Adams' letter to her sister on June 9, 1790, in which she asks that her large mirror be sent from her house in Braintree to Richmond Hill. "This House", she explains, "is much better calculated for the Glasses, having all the Rooms Eleven foot high." A similar reference is found in the diary of the Reverend William Bentley, of Salem, Massachusetts, in October 1801, when he speaks of a Mr West's house: "The Mirrors were large and gave full view of every one who passed, and were intended for the house in town but were exchanged as those for this Seat were too large."

This is the earliest known use of the term *mirror* in American writings, *looking glass* being the proper term prior to that time.

By 1840 mirrors had become commonplace items in American homes. Two paintings by Henry Sargent, done in the early nineteenth century, provide one of the first visual records of the use of mirrors in American interiors. *The Tea Party* shows the use of horizontal, rectangular mirrors above the fireplace in each of two parlours and a vertical, rectangular pier glass between the two windows of one parlour. *The Dinner Party* shows a similar, though simpler, pier glass between the windows in the dining-room.

American-made mirrors

How early mirrors were made in America is uncertain. From the beginning, plate glass had to be brought from the old country. William Wood in his *New Englands Prospect* in 1634 suggested to future colonists, "Glasse ought not to be forgotten of any that desire to benefit themselves, or the Country: if it be well leaded, and carefully pack't up, I know no commodity better for portage or sayle . . ." Certainly from an early date there was some reframing of old mirrors. This practice of utilizing the glass in a new-fashioned mirror continued well after the Revolutionary War, as indicated by the advertisements of Samuel Kneeland, one of which appeared in the Hartford, Connecticut, *American Mercury* on November 12, 1787, "N.B. Old Looking Glasses repaired, fram'd and gilt in the neatest manner, so as to look equal to new ones."

Styles and types

The earliest mirrors probably were framed in simple cove-moulded rectangular frames made of oak and pine, perhaps painted or, towards the end of the seventeenth century, veneered with walnut. In the last quarter of the seventeenth century a crest was added at the top, in a separate piece which is often missing today. Because the crest was cut from a thin piece of wood, it frequently warped and curved backward in spite of braces put on the back to correct this tendency. Often the crest was pierced in an elaborate pattern similar to the carved cresting rails on William and Mary

chairs. The mirror illustrated (Plate 217A) is one of the earliest surviving examples made in this country. The frame is made of white pine, native to New England, and is painted to give a tortoiseshell appearance. This mirror belonged originally to the Pepperell family of Kittery, Maine.

Another variety of mirror with a crested design was that called today in America a courting mirror. These mirrors were set in wide moulded frames with stepped crests. Set in between the mouldings were pieces of simply painted glass decorated with bright-coloured leaves and flowers. Many of these mirrors, though their origins are uncertain, are found today in New England along with the wooden cases in which they were carried.

In the early eighteenth century the moulding of the frame around the mirror became more elaborate (Plate 217C), being rounded at the upper corners. By 1720 this moulding had changed from the cove moulding to a channelled moulding. The most popular type of cresting on mirrors of the first half of the eighteenth century was a solid, scrolled cresting. At this time a scrolled skirt was often added at the base of the mirror as well. Often the bevelled glass was set into the frame in two pieces since many of these mirrors were as much as 5 feet high, and glass was precious, especially in large sheets. Because the upper section could not easily be used to reflect a particular image, the glass in that area was sometimes engraved with a floral pattern or a heraldic device. This was particularly true of mirrors made between 1725 and 1750.

Towards the middle of the eighteenth century, japanning became a favourite method of decorating mirror frames. The largest known American example with japanned decoration (Plate 217C) was probably made in New York between 1729 and 1740 and was owned by Jon Johannes Bleeker. Made of soft pine, it is decorated on a black ground with raised Oriental and European designs in gilt. It was in New York at this time, too, that Gerardus Duyckinck advertised in the *Weekly Journal* in 1736, "Looking-glasses new Silvered and the Frames plaine, japand or Flowered . . . made and sold, all manner of painting done."

A simpler version (Plate 217B), originally used on the Luyster farm in Middletown, New York, and made between 1725 and 1735, has exotic gilt decoration on a cerulean-blue ground. Many frames were made of walnut in these same designs and were not painted. One of the most popular designs of all, this style continued to be made throughout the eighteenth century and well into the nineteenth century. Such mirrors can be dated only by their diminished crests, the use of later classical motifs, or the type of moulding surrounding the glass itself.

By the middle decades of the eighteenth century the moulding of frames became further elaborated by having an inner border which was carved and gilded. Especially in Philadelphia and also elsewhere, the cresting of these mirrors was often decorated in the centre with a gilded shell, at first a solid, symmetrical shell which, with the advent of the rococo taste, became pierced and asymmetrical. By this time mahogany was the favoured primary wood. A fine example of this particular type of mirror (Plate 218A) was made between 1762 and 1767 and labelled by John Elliott, Sr, of Philadelphia. This same John Elliott with Isaac Gray owned the Philadelphia Glass Works about 1773–7, a natural association for a cabinet-maker who made numerous mirrors. The first label Elliott used, while at his shop on Chestnut Street from 1756 to 1761, was printed in English and German. From 1762 to 1767 he was working on Walnut Street at the Sign of the Bell and Looking Glass, where he advertised in 1763 that he also "quicksilvers and frames old glasses, and supplies people with new glasses to their own frames; and will undertake to cure any English looking glass that shows the face either too long or too broad or any other way distorted".

Concurrently popular in the mid-eighteenth century was the architectural type of mirror (Plate 218B) surmounted by a broken-arch pediment and a phoenix or eagle finial. This type of frame usually had pendent swags of leaves and flowers on each side, and often had the architectural outlines emphasized by gilt and carved egg-and-dart or leaf mouldings. Bearing a close relationship to the architectural patterns of British designers like James Gibbs or Abraham Swan, these frames were quite suitable for filling wall panels similarly derived from the designs of these men. Crosseted corners in the upper section of the frame, more elaborate scrolling below the base of the glass, and rosettes with streamers in the volutes of the pediment are features which enhanced these designs.

Generally the glass in the architectural examples was in one section, as is the case in the one illustrated (Plate 218B). This mirror is documented by a bill of sale dated "New York, Augst. 25th 1794 Mr Jacob Everson Bo^{t}. of William Wilmerding 1 Looking Glass – £8 – ." The beaded oval decoration and delicate gilt branches in the pediment verify the date of 1794, although the rest of the frame reflects a style at its height in the third quarter of the century. William Wilmerding advertised in New York City between 1789 and 1794. After 1798 he was listed in New York directories as a merchant. Wilmerding's label (Plate 218C), which appears on a mirror owned by John S. Walton, New York, is most interesting, as it shows a portable dressing-box, a cheval mirror with a pedimented crest, a dressing-stand with an oval-shaped mirror, a mirror with a widely pitched pediment and eagle finial, and another surmounted by an urn filled with ears of wheat, a new style introduced in the last decade of the eighteenth century.

As the rococo taste became firmly established, frames became more elaborately scalloped, gilt ornament increased, the inner mouldings became undulating and even pierced with rocaille details. Cartouches as well as gadrooned vases filled with three-dimensional flowers and occasionally papier-mâché figures filled the pediment.

One of the most beautiful examples of mirrors in the rococo taste (Plate 219A) is the lightly carved white-and-gold frame which belonged to the Cadwalader family in Philadelphia. The delicate C-scrolls, fanciful columns, and pendent leaves and flowers are the very essence of the rococo style. A strikingly similar mirror, undoubtedly from the same hand, was made for Richard Edwards, proprietor of the Taunton Furnace in Burlington

County, New Jersey, by John Elliott, of Philadelphia, and bears the label which he used between 1768 and 1776. A third frame of this type is in the Metropolitan Museum of Art and is distinguished by having glass behind the open areas between the inner moulding and the outer scrolls.

A contemporary of Elliott, James Reynolds, advertised in Philadelphia "carved and white, carved and gold, carved mahogany pier, sconce, pediment, mock pediment, ornamented, or raffle frames, box, swinging, or dressing glasses ...." Thomas Jefferson in 1792 recorded in his account book that he "gave James Reynolds ord[er]. on bank of U.S. for [$]141.33 in full for looking glasses", and again in 1793 he paid him $99.53 for framing mirrors.

Shortly after the War of Independence the new classical style began to penetrate mirror designs. One of the earliest intrusions of this new taste was in the oval-shaped mirror set into the older-style frame. A happy combination showing this transition is the dressing-table (Plate 219B) made by Jonathan Gostelowe, a Philadelphia cabinet-maker noted for his serpentine chest of drawers. This mirror along with a chest of drawers was made in 1789 for Gostelowe's bride, Elizabeth H. Towers.

Federal period

With a similar oval-shaped face, but showing the subsequent assimilation of the classical style, is the bedroom mirror (Plate 220A), the carving of which is attributed to Samuel McIntire, of Salem, Massachusetts, about 1800. Delicate string inlay, veneers of flame wood, carved laurel swags, beading, and cornucopias all betray the Federal period of design.

Another inlaid mirror of this type, with French feet, was labelled by Stephen Badlam, Jr (1751–1815), a cabinet- and mirror-maker in Dorchester, Massachusetts. Probably these mirrors in the new style were similar to those advertised in 1784 by Willing, Morris, and Swanwick as having been stolen from their Philadelphia counting house, "Two oval Swinging Glasses with Mahogany frames and black and white string edges – one marked on the back 52s, 6, the other 35s."

In the early nineteenth century these bedroom glasses followed furniture styles in the use of plain dark mahogany surfaces. Often they were supported on brass ball feet. At the same time the chest of drawers with an attached mirror supported by a large scrolled frame became a more common furniture form, especially in the Boston and Salem area. This general type of furniture had been made in New York City during the Chippendale period in the form of a chest of drawers, the top drawer of which contained a collapsible mirror and many compartments for organizing the accoutrements of dressing.

Ordinary mirrors, now frequently made in pairs, similarly took up the new decoration, so that the frames for glasses made between 1790 and 1810 were frequently oval (Plate 220C), surmounted by fragile classical urns, banded with beading or flat water leaves carved around the base. From these urns sprang wired and gilded gesso ornaments of ears of wheat, rosettes, thin classical scrolls, laurel swags, and acanthus leaves. At the base of the oval frames were more leaves, a patera, and often the favoured feather motif of the Prince of Wales. Usually the innermost moulding immediately surrounding the glass was an edge of beading.

This type of frame was readily developed into the more heavily ornamented frame of the early nineteenth century (Plate 220B). One example made for Elias Hasket Derby, of Salem, Massachusetts, has a naturalistic, carved eagle above the three-feathers motif, coarsely carved leaves, and entwined dolphins at the base. The moulding immediately around the glass is reeded with a twisted-rope design in the centre instead of beading. This is an enormous mirror, slightly over 6 feet high, which Abigail Adams undoubtedly would have preferred to see in a room where the walls were at least 11 feet high. Another large, oval-shaped mirror, now in the Museum of Fine Arts, Boston, and owned originally by Elizabeth Derby, is attributed to John Doggett, a well-known picture-framer and mirror-maker in Roxbury, Massachusetts, whose trade label is itself inscribed within a frame which is surmounted by an eagle on three feathers and which has entwined dolphins at the base.

The final development in this type of mirror was effected when the glass became round and convex, in the style of the French mirrors to which Sheraton referred in his *Dictionary*. Having large eagles at the top, which could be associated with the Great Seal of the United States, and outlined by heavy ball carving, an exaggeration of the classical beaded moulding, these mirrors are often mistakenly cherished above others as American made, although they were largely imported from England and France during this Greek Revival period. When candle arms are added they are popularly called *girandoles*, a somewhat loose application of a term belonging to lighting devices.

At the same time, the architectural type of frame continued in the classical period, with a flat cornice gradually replacing the earlier broken-arch pediment. The term tabernacle has sometimes been applied to the flat cornice type. Classical columns flanked the glass, and the upper section was usually filled with painting. Detail on these frames became less refined after 1810, beading being replaced by heavy ball ornament, twisted-rope mouldings, and surfaces left smooth and undecorated. A chaste example of an architectural-type mirror made in 1810 (Plate 220D) is particularly interesting in that not only does it bear the label of Peter Grinnell & Son, of Providence,

Rhode Island, but also its painted glass or *églomisé* panel at the top is signed by the painter, "B. Crehore, Aug. 27, 1810". The painted wall-of-Troy border around the rustic scene gives ample evidence that this frame belongs to the period of the Greek Revival.

An alternative method of decorating the upper section of these frames was to substitute gilded plaster decoration for the *églomisé* panel. A labelled example of this sort made by John Doggett is in the Metropolitan Museum of Art, and has the figure of *Fame* above a floral festoon upheld by two trophies of the Prince of Wales feathers and a bow-knot. John McElwee advertised in the *Pennsylvania Packet* on May 7, 1800, that he had "Also for sale on a liberal credit, a quantity of Composition Ornaments, and Moulds of every pattern necessary for the Looking Glass business".

During this final period in the first half of the nineteenth century, there were many well-known names among mirror makers. Barnard Cermenati worked at No. 10, State Street in Boston and Newburyport, Massachusetts, and in Portsmouth, New Hampshire. Stillman Lathrop, when he moved to Boston in 1806, continued his old business in Salem through an agent, George Dean. Wayne & Biddle succeeded James Stokes in Philadelphia and produced many architectural mirrors with landscapes and seascapes in the *églomisé* panels.

Glossary

Adam, Robert (1728–92). The eminent architect who, in common with his predecessor, William Kent, paid much attention to the interior decoration of his buildings. Adam designed mirrors, principally pier-glasses, and many of them remain in the houses for which they were made. A great number of Robert Adam's original designs are in Sir John Soane's Museum, Lincoln's Inn Fields, London.

Bevelling. The angular shaping of the surface at the edges of a mirror-plate was performed by grinding and then polishing the glass. A patent for a method of doing this with the aid of water-power was granted in 1678. Much glass for mirrors had the edges bevelled, but the finish was not always employed for large plates after the middle years of the eighteenth century.

Bilbao mirror. Name given to type of

mirror in frames veneered with sheets of pink marble imported from Europe to America at the end of the eighteenth century and in the early nineteenth century.

Chimney glass. American term for mirrors designed to fit the chimney breast above the fireplace in a room.

Chippendale, Thomas (1718–79). Cabinet-maker and designer. Two large mirrors at Kenwood, London, were designed by Robert Adam and supplied by Thomas Chippendale in 1769.

Constitution mirror. American term for a rectangular mirror in an architectural frame with a broken arch pediment and shaped apron; reason for use of this term not known.

Courting mirror. American term for mirror of unknown origin, held in moulded, step-crested frames set with panels of glass painted with multi-coloured leaves and flowers, usually accompanied by crude wooden boxes in which they were carried.

Dressing-glass. American term for mirror attached to dressing-table.

Gibbons, Grinling (1648–1720). Carver and designer of Dutch birth and English domicile. He was "discovered" by the diarist John Evelyn. Gibbons' distinctive and realistic carving exists in the form of mirror-frames, but much of the work assigned to him is by his contemporaries, and much is of considerably later date.

Gilding. The process of applying gold, beaten into the thinnest of foils, to a surface. It is divided into two types according to the nature of the mordant by which the gold is made to adhere to the article.

Oil-gilding used a preparation of solidified linseed-oil, and the resulting finish was the more durable and least expensive of the two, as it could be employed directly on to the surface of the woodwork. Oil-gilding would not burnish.

Water-gilding required the woodwork to be painted with several layers of a preparation somewhat like plaster, known as gesso. Gesso was made with a base of glue prepared by boiling scraps of parchment or glover's leather in water. To this was added *bole armoniac*, or *Armenian bole* (a fine clay, now known as gilder's red clay), and some tallow, suet, or beeswax. The coats of gesso were smoothed to as perfect a surface as possible, and then wetted piecemeal to moisten the glue and cause the gold leaf to adhere as it was applied. After allowing time for drying, the gold was burnished where required with the aid of a dog's tooth or a piece of polished agate.

Water-gilding was the method principally employed for woodwork, but it was sometimes used in conjunction with the oil process; the latter on flat surfaces that did not need to be burnished.

About 1720 the gesso surface was often ornamented by being stamped with a tool that covered it with tiny circles. Shortly after that date a granulated finish was in use; this was obtained by sprinkling sand on the wet gesso before applying the gold leaf.

Girandole. Wall-light, sconce, and girandole are recognized generally as being vague and interchangeable terms. In England a girandole is usually a branched support for candles, generally with a mirror backing; used in America to describe the type of convex, circular mirror surmounted by an eagle, with or without candle branches, which is called, in England, a convex mirror.

Gumley, John. Glass-maker and furnisher, living in London in the eighteenth century. A mirror with the name *Gumley* carved on a small gilt plaque is at Hampton Court Palace, and another with John Gumley 1703 is at Chatsworth.

Japan and Lacquer. Lacquer was not only embellished with painting on the surface, but was also incised with designs; this latter being known as "Bantam" or "Coromandel" lacquer. Both types of lacquer work were used in the framing of mirrors. Mostly the lacquering was done in England, but examples are known that were made from Oriental panels, cut to the required size and fitted on a framework.

Jensen, Gerreit (known also as Garrett or Gerrrard Johnson). Cabinet-maker and "glasse-seller", who supplied much furniture to the Royal Household from 1680. A tall mirror at Hampton Court tallies with the description on his bill rendered in 1699, and it is assumed that Jensen had the monopoly of supplying overmantel mirrors and pier-glasses to the royal palaces during the reign of William and Mary.

Johnson, Thomas. Designer and wood-carver of London. He published a volume entitled *Twelve Girandoles* in 1755, and a more ambitious work, *One Hundred and Fifty New Designs*, between 1756 and 1758. Johnson's designs are very fanciful, and appear to be almost incapable of realization, however, he boasted that they "may all be performed by a master of his art". A mirror at the Victoria and Albert Museum (Plate 223c) corresponds with one of his designs, as do a pair of mirrors at Corsham Court, Wiltshire. It is assumed that he worked to his own patterns, but it cannot be taken for granted that anything coinciding with his designs was necessarily from his own hand.

Kent, William (1686–1748). An architect who also planned the landscaping of gardens, painted pictures, and was one of the first of his profession to lavish as much care on the interior of a house as he did on the building of it. He was an exponent of the Palladian style, and his name has been given to the mirrors with frames of "architectural" type that were fashionable in the years 1730–40.

Linnell, John. Cabinet-maker and carver, many of whose designs for mirrors and other furnishings have been preserved and are in the Victoria and Albert Museum. He worked in the period 1760–90, and his designs are mainly in the prevailing "Chippendale" style. He executed work at several of the country mansions that were then building or being refurnished, including Shardeloes, Bramshill, and Castle Howard.

Makers and designers. It is difficult after the lapse of two centuries or more to differentiate between designers, dealers, and actual makers of mirrors and mirror-frames. There would seem to have been much intermingling of these three functions, and it is generally not possible to state who did make any particular specimen. This is particularly the case where a designer and carver published his patterns. which were then available for anyone to copy,

In some instances original bills have been preserved, in others the designs of frames have been traced to their originators, and in a very

few instances the name of the maker (or supplier?) is found on the piece. (*See* Chippendale, Gibbons, Gumley, Ince and Mayhew, Jensen, Johnson, Kent, Linnell, and Moore.)

Mansell, Sir Robert. A financier who organized the English glass industry in the first half of the seventeenth century, and who eventually controlled glass-houses all over the country. He imported skilled workers from Murano, and successfully made mirror-glass.

Moore, James (? 1670–1726). Cabinet-maker, in partnership with John Gumley from 1714. Moore is known to have made much furniture decorated with gilt gesso, on some of which his name is incised. He was concerned in the furnishing of Blenheim, and it is assumed that some gilt pier-glasses and tables there were made and supplied by him.

Stumpwork. A type of fine needlework of which much is in relief; figures, etc., being made to stand out by a stuffing of wool or cotton-wool. Caskets were covered with this type of work, and small mirrors were set within panels of it laid down on a wood framework.

Tabernacle mirror. Generally applied to the Sheraton mirror with flat cornice under which is a row of gilt balls above a scene painted on glass; columns at sides.

Vauxhall. A manufactory of plate-glass was commenced here about 1665 by George Villiers, second Duke of Buckingham. John Bellingham approached the Duke with a secret process for making mirrors, and as a result the Vauxhall factory was started and Bellingham was given the post of manager. Glasshouses continued to operate in Vauxhall until the end of the eighteenth century, and old mirror-plates are often referred to today as "Vauxhall".

Verre églomisé. Glass decorated at the back with designs in colour and gold and silver foils. It is a method that has been practised for many hundreds of years, but for some reason is named after an art-collector, J. B. Glomy, who died in France in 1786. Borders of *verre églomisé* in arabesque patterns and with coats-of-arms were used to frame mirrors *c.* 1695 (Plate 221c).

NEEDLEWORK AND EMBROIDERY

Lace

Lace is fabric at its most exquisite: it is ornament with a cultured sophistication requiring neither colour nor gloss. Not until the splendid days of the late fifteenth century did it develop in Europe, and then it was art-conscious, craft-proud Italy that first rejoiced in such an ultimate in embroidery technique as the stitching of patterns "in the air".

To the collector today old lace is an endless, absorbing passion, but to the beginner its very complexity may prove daunting, with its many sources and techniques, even its terms complicated by four centuries of peasant craftsmanship in Italy, Flanders, France, England, and elsewhere. This survey can distinguish only among the more renowned laces, and any serious collector is well advised to study museum collections, such as the selection, for example, at the Victoria and Albert Museum.

As a first essential the collector must recognize that two basically different kinds of lace were made, quite apart from the application of the term to various cords and gimps. These are here distinguished by their most usual names of needlepoint and pillow lace. The use of the term point alone is merely confusing.

European needlepoints were first made in Italy; pillow lace may have originated in Italy, or in Flanders, where it certainly preceded Flemish needlepoints. Needlepoints developed from cut and drawn thread embroidery; pillow lace from knotted fringes and the network generally known as *lacis*. But by the seventeenth and eighteenth centuries, when man, woman, and child wore lace as the sine qua non of elegance and taste, the differing techniques produced results superficially similar. Even the needlepoints tended to lose their early exquisite characteristic of *bride* and *picot* in favour of the less imaginative grounded laces made in short lengths and joined, until these in their turn were debased by the invention of lace-making by machinery pioneered by John Heathcoat in 1809.

The basic difference between needlepoint and pillow lace is summed up in the fact that needlepoint lace was made with a single thread and a needle using embroidery stitches dominated by buttonhole stitch, and pillow lace was made with a multitude of threads wound, for convenience, upon bobbins, so that the lace could be created in a range of twists and plaits combining various numbers of threads. The difference is fundamental and soon becomes recognizable at a glance, although the collector may still be puzzled by a minority of mixed laces and the lace effects developed with machine-made net.

England's own contribution to this craft has been unspectacular, but for this the lace factors may be blamed rather than the women and children who created it, for the English thread was poor – a characteristic too of much modern handmade reproduction lace. Eng-lish spun flax was never of superb quality, and thread imported from Flanders in the eighteenth century might cost £90 a pound.

In the abbreviated glossary below it has not been possible to include all the synonymous terms used by Europe's lace makers, but it has seemed most useful to adopt the most familiar rather than to adhere rigidly to the English, which, indeed, long ago absorbed many of the more charming Continental words and phrases.

TERMS USED IN LACE-MAKING

À Jours. *See* Fillings.

Alençon. Needlepoint, established 1665. The early Venetian influence soon became less important than lighter, fine-threaded Flemish pillow-lace notions, but like Argentan lace, it was regarded as a heavy winter lace. By 1700 or 1720 the famous grounded *point d'Alençon* was evolved with rich fillings and a stiff *cordonnet* and *picots* sometimes including horse-hair. This was mainly a narrow lace for borders and caps and was reintroduced in the nineteenth century, more flimsy and often on a spotted ground. A softly looped hexagonal mesh was made first and the pattern put in, worked in close buttonhole stitch. *See* Point de France.

Antwerp. Pillow lace, strong and heavy looking, the patterns outlined in a *cordonnet* of thick untwisted thread and made at the same time as the *fond chant* ground. The style of pattern has given this the name of pot lace or potten kant, from the substantial two-handled vase usually prominent in it. This motif was fantastically popular in the eighteenth-century embroideries. It appeared also in Normandy laces.

Argentan. Needlepoint, established 1665. Resembled Alençon lace made ten miles away until they developed meshed grounds. The so-called Argentan lace was made also at Alençon, the work tending to be larger and more perfect than so-called Alençon, with bold patterns and a hexagonal ground, sometimes *picotée*, worked over in tiny buttonhole stitches. *See* Point de France.

Argentella. Needlepoint, variant of point d'Alençon, with a large dotted mesh. *See* Œil de perdrix.

Arras. Pillow lace, sometimes spelt orris in old records. Usually associated with a coarser version of Lille, but with scalloped edges. George I had 354 yards of it for his coronation. *See* Point de France; Blonde.

Ave Maria lace. Pillow lace in long strips with a plaited lozenge ground made at Dieppe until the mid-nineteenth century.

Binche. Pillow lace made with very fine thread and such a close texture that the pattern was almost lost. Gradually it became more open and eventually lost its delicacy. It had much in common with early Valenciennes and some suggestion of Brussels point d'Angleterre.

Blonde. Pillow lace, silk, made in the Arras, Lille, and Chantilly regions from the 1740s, first in unbleached Chinese silk but soon in white and black. Had a ground of the Lille type, loosely twisted.

Bobbin lace. Alternative term for pillow lace, but distinguished from bone lace in early inventories as being coarser, of thicker thread requiring large bobbins.

Bobbins. Spools wound with thread for pillow laces, a separate bobbin for each thread. English bobbins are distinctively ornamental, light and dainty for Honiton and Buckinghamshire lace, but often weighted with spangles, or beads, for the coarser laces.

Bone lace. A term sometimes specifically applied to gold and silver lace, but more often also to all good quality pillow lace, as distinct from needlepoints. It has been variously argued that the name referred to the sheep's trotter bones sometimes used as early bobbins and to the bone pins used in place of metal pins to shape the pattern – fish bones on occasion. Metal pins were priced in 1543 at as much as 6s 8d a thousand. The term has been applied also to the ivory effects of Venetian raised point. It was the accepted term until the early eighteenth century for much pillow lace, and there are many records of its cost: such as 1s 4d a yard for narrow bone lace edging in 1594, and 2s 4d a yard in 1685.

Brides. French term usually preferred to the English bars or ties, used to connect and support the pattern where there was no net ground. Found mainly in needlepoints and mixed laces.

Brussels. Needlepoints and pillow laces. Needlepoint was made from 1720, but took second place to the pillow laces. The ground was a plain looped mesh, and late in the century there was a tendency to restrict the slower needlepoint work to the pattern and introduce a pillow lace ground. Pillow laces include *bride*-linked tape lace of the seventeenth century succeeded by grounded laces, the ground worked after the pattern, its hexagonal mesh consisting of two sides with four threads plaited four times and four sides of two threads twisted. Patterns in the mid-eighteenth century included many rococo-Oriental extravagancies. The Brussels *point plat appliqué* was a pillow lace of the late eighteenth century with a net ground supporting small sprigs worked separately.

Bucks point. Pillow lace, mainly showing the influence of Lille and with much use of Lille's ground (*fond clair*) although often in company with *fond chant* and the soft Mechlin mesh. The patterns were lightened with attractive fillings and outlined with gimp wide and flat. There was some direct copying of Mechlin.

Caen. Pillow lace imitating the silk blondes of Chantilly from the mid-eighteenth century (Plate 238B).

Carrickmacross appliqué. Not a real lace, as the pattern was cut from cambric, applied to net, and given needlepoint fillings.

Carrickmacross guipure. As above but with needlepoint *brides* instead of net.

Chantilly. Pillow lace, silk with *fond chant* ground and some use of *fond clair*. See Blonde

Cinq trous. Ground found in some Flemish lace in which the threads crossing to form the mesh left five small holes.

Clothwork. *See* Toilé.

Collar lace. Early seventeenth-century term for imported Venetian point laces, simple and largely geometrical in vandyke outlines. A few designs are considered identifiable as English.

Coralline point. Needlepoint, variant of Venetian flat point with confused patterns and very many *brides picotées*.

Cordonnet. French term usually preferred to the English gimp or trolly thread for the more substantial outline often given to the solid pattern motif. It might be composed of several threads whipped or buttonholed together, as in Venetian raised point; or be one thread whipped or buttonholed, as in Alençon; or be a different coarser thread as in Mechlin.

Cutwork. Suggested by drawn work, but lighter and more conspicuously ornamental, as part of the fabric was cut away and the holes filled with geometrical patterns worked with needle and thread, and at its most advanced consisting of buttonhole stitch, double loop, darning and knotting stitch. It was important in Elizabethan England.

Devonia lace. Honiton product of the 1870s with flower petals raised in relief by tension on the threads.

Dieppe. Pillow lace suggesting simplified Valenciennes. *See* Antwerp; Ave Maria lace.

Drawn work. Forerunner of real lace. Made from linen with some threads drawn out and the remainder variously grouped and whipped over to form geometrical patterns.

Dresden "lace". Drawn work on muslin.

Dutch. Pillow laces made from the 1660s, tightly woven and solid looking, often with closely grouped scrolls suggesting heavy flower heads. The grounds included the *cinq trous*. Huguenot refugees brought to Dutch lace something of the old Valenciennes style.

English lace centres. Established in Honiton and other parts of Devonshire; Olney, Newport Pagnell, Stony Stratford, and

Aylesbury, Buckinghamshire; Bedford and Woburn, Bedfordshire; Northamptonshire; Wiltshire; Dorset; Suffolk. *See* Bucks point; Devonia; Honiton; Midlands.

Essex. First region in England to develop tambour "lace".

Fillings. Syn. with the French *à jours* or modes for the fancy open stitches introduced in the pattern spaces in both needlepoints and pillow laces.

Fine drawings. Syn. with French *point de raccroc*, the delicate work of joining lengths of lace net.

Fond chant. A six-pointed star ground found in so-called *point de Paris*: English Midlands laces and trolly lace; Chantilly lace, etc.

Fond clair. Syn. with *fond simple* for the mesh ground found in Lille lace, with four sides formed of two twisted threads and two sides of crossed threads. This sometimes suggests diamond rather than hexagonal meshes, depending on the tightness of the work.

Footing. Upper edge of a piece of lace.

Genoa. A centre for gold and silver plaited gimps, and hence developed pillow lace. Alternatively, some consider pillow lace began in Flanders.

Gold and silver. Plaited border laces of gold and silver wire, exported from Genoa as early as the sixteenth century.

"Greek" lace. A name given to drawn and cut-work embroidery, often combined with geometrical needlepoint or pillow lace. When the British occupied the Ionian Isles they brought home great quantities, but probably most of it was imported from Italy while the Isles belonged to Venice.

Ground. Syn. with the French *fond* or *réseau* and basically meaning any background to a lace pattern, but usually restricted to a mesh or net so that grounded laces are contrasted with those where *brides* support the pattern. Some grounds are best known by their French names. *See* Fond chant; Fond clair.

Grounded laces. Laces with meshed backgrounds to their patterns, allowing more freedom of design than the alternative linking of *brides* found in early needlepoints. The mesh might be made along with the pattern, as in, for example, Valenciennes; it might be work-

ed around the pattern afterwards as in *Brussels point d'Angleterre*; or worked first and the pattern put in to it as in Alençon; or worked separately with completed pattern units attached to it as in *Brussels point plat appliqué*. The grounds are considerable aids in identifying old laces, since in pillow laces the tiny hexagons or lozenges are composed of different numbers of threads variously twisted and plaited.

Guipure. Term used confusingly for needlepoint or pillow lace without grounds supported by *brides* (Plate 239B).

Hampshire, Isle of Wight. "Lace" made in running stitch on machine-made net.

Hollie point. Sometimes holy point. Needlepoint in which the pattern was created by leaving spaces or holes in the close *toilé* which was built up with rows of a kind of twisted buttonhole stitch. A dainty lace used in the eighteenth century for babies' caps, shirts, etc.

Honiton. Pillow lace, the best and the first made in England, described as bone lace in about 1620 in Westcote's *View of Devonshire*, and continuing until about 1725. Suggestive of *point d'Angleterre* with the ground worked round the pattern, but with less attractive pattern-shapes. Honiton net, made from costly Antwerp thread, and of excellent quality, was an important product in the eighteenth century. Honiton appliqué lace was made with motifs of pillow lace applied to this net ground, but the net was soon machine-made, with the flower motifs reduced to meaningless ugly shapes. Late in the nineteenth century Honiton made a tape pillow lace with *brides*, sometimes in needlepoint, instead of a mesh ground, and also Devonia lace (Plate 240C).

Ireland. Records show that lace was made in quantity, 1650–1780, but the earliest known dates from the nineteenth century. *See* Carrickmacross; Limerick; Youghal.

Kat stitch. Really *fond chant*, but frequently found in Bedfordshire lace (*see* Midlands lace) and given legendary association with Katherine of Aragon.

Knotted lace. Made in sixteenth-century Italy with short lengths of thread or thin cord. When longer threads were introduced bobbins were developed to carry them, first of lead then of wood or bone, and the threads were twisted and plaited instead of knotted.

Lacis. French term for darned patterns on netting in vogue in sixteenth-century Italy, a direct preliminary to pillow lace.

Lille. Pillow lace, sometimes black, very popular in late eighteenth-century England, but never as a dress lace. Its somewhat meagre patterns were heavily outlined in flat glossy trolly thread and set in a plain *fond clair* mesh.

Limerick. Tambour "lace" introduced from England in the nineteenth century.

Machine-made lace. Can be identified by the meticulous evenness of the work, exactly repeated patterns and smoothly woven *toilé*. The edges tend to be weak and the whole lace light. Stitches are mostly woven or twisted, with no buttonholing and little plaiting.

Maltese lace. Pillow lace made from 1833, the designs including "wheat grains" grouped in fours to make Maltese crosses.

Mechlin. Pillow lace, much imported to England, although it must be remembered that all Flemish laces until the seventeenth century were called Mechlin in England. Queen Anne, who prohibited French lace, allowed imports from the Low Countries. The earliest that can be identified, however, dates only to the 1720s. It developed handsome rococo patterns outlined in a separate, heavier flat thread, the pattern and ground being made together in one operation. The ground was the familiar hexagonal mesh in which four sides were of two threads twisted and two sides were of four threads plaited three times. Structurally this was nearly the same as the Brussels ground, but the effect was altogether less stiff and angular. Other grounds were sometimes used such as the *œil de perdrix*. The spotted patterns of the 1770s onwards consisted of rows of small sprays and the mesh was also variously spotted, the whole effect being subdued in the soft muslin manner of its day, but dull. Some lace in Mechlin style was made in Denmark in the eighteenth and early nineteenth centuries.

Midlands. Pillow lace made in Buckinghamshire, Bedfordshire, Northamptonshire. This appears unlikely to have more than legendary association with Katherine of Aragon. It may have been introduced by Flemish and French refugees from Mechlin and Lille. With local variants the style was mainly similar to Bucks point. Baby lace was made in great quantity, often little more than dotted work on a clear Lille ground. Maltese lace was made in the later nineteenth century, but usually without the tiny Maltese crosses. Black and white blonde laces were made 1860–70 and there was some woollen lace. *See* Bucks point.

Milan. Pillow lace. James I specifically prohibited "all lace of Millan and of Millan fashion". In the later work identified today the pattern was worked first and the ground put round it at all angles.

Mixed lace. Associated with Genoa and Naples, the pillow lace tape patterns supported by needlepoint *brides* or a coarse ground.

Modes. *See* Fillings.

Needlepoint lace. The ultimate development from cut work with threads tacked on to a parchment pattern as the basis for stitches worked with a needle and a single thread. An outline was drawn on parchment stitched to two thicknesses of linen and this outline covered with threads exactly tack-stitched in position about every quarter of an inch. This outline was buttonholed over closely to form the *cordonnet*, and on this the lace was created, the solid areas of pattern – *toilé* – in close rows of buttonhole stitch and these linked and supported by connecting buttonholed *brides* or a regular mesh ground of buttonholed or looped stitches. It must be emphasized that a single thread on a needle was used throughout so that there could be no plaiting or weaving effects such as characterized pillow lace. The lace was released from the parchment by cutting between the layers of linen (Plates 237A, B, 240B).

Œil de perdrix. Syn. with *réseau rosacé* and *fond de neige* or snowflake ground – the most effective of the grounds used in Argentella needlepoint and the pillow laces of Valenciennes and some Binche and early Mechlin. Each of the irregular spidery meshes had a dot in it.

Orris lace. *See* Arras.

Patterns. Followed the same trends irrespective of methods. Briefly, the earliest were geometrical, followed in the sixteenth and early seventeenth centuries by flower and scroll forms leading to the full floral grace of Renaissance work. There was some pictorial work around the mid-seventeenth century. The 1720s to 1770s were dominated by rococo inconsequence and rigid, angular flower bouquets, followed by the late eighteenth-century muslin effects spotted and dotted with small bouquets, bees, and so on.

Picot. French for the purl or tiny loop ornamenting *bride* or *cordonnet*.

Pictorial lace. Made in the mid-seventeenth century and resembling the raised embroidery now known as stump work and with similar use of raised canopies, loose hangings, beads, seed pearls, and disproportionate details to fill in the background.

Pillow lace. The most usual name for laces made with bobbins as distinct from needlepoints, although those too were worked on cushions. Padded boards were used at first (Plate 240A).

Point d'Angleterre. Pillow lace of Brussels, not English. English dealers so named it in 1662 when Flemish lace was prohibited in England and France. It is the loveliest of Brussels laces, distinguished by the raised rib of plaited threads outlining leaves, etc., in a pattern which was loosely woven and edged elsewhere with rows of open stitches. The ground was worked after the pattern and was the Brussels hexagonal mesh, sometimes accompanied by the snowflake ground associated with Valenciennes.

Point d'Angleterre à brides. Pillow lace, variant of above, the meshed ground supplemented by *brides picotées*.

Points d'esprit. Small square dots scattered over the mesh ground, as in Lille pillow lace.

Point de France. Needlepoint. Some collectors limit the term to French raised *bride*-lined laces in contrast to grounded needlepoints made in the eighteenth century. Designs were more flowing than in the raised Venetian needlepoints. The term is more usually accepted in its original usage for the lace made at a number of towns where the craft was established in 1665 with State support, under Venetian tutelage, including especially Alençon.

Point de Paris. Pillow lace believed to be the first made in France, but there is no proof that this had any association with a coarse type of lace now sold by that name.

Point Lace. All French laces, including pillow laces, so that it is impossible to reserve the term for needlepoints.

Pot lace. *See* Antwerp.

Punto in aria. Italian term, stitch in the air, for the beginnings of lace, the cut work fabric reduced to a strip supporting the needlepoint work. The transformation was complete when the line of fabric was replaced by threads laid over the pattern drawn on parchment. The earliest work consisted of simple little vandykes worked wholly in buttonhole stitch.

Réseau. *See* Ground.

Spanish. The name Spanish point was variously applied to loosely woven gold and silver lace, much imported from Italy; to a raised needlepoint resembling the Venetian, similarly imported, and to silk laces mainly from Chantilly and Bayeux until Spain made her own.

Suffolk. Pillow lace, simple and less expert than the Midlands lace and with similar indications of Lille inspiration. Coloured worsted lace was also made.

Tambour "lace". First made in Essex. Imitation lace worked with a tambour hook on machine-made net.

Toilé. French term usually applied in preference to the English clothwork or mat for the solid part of the pattern. In needlepoint it was composed of rows of stitches, buttonhole or loop. In pillow lace the multiple threads achieved an effect of weaving.

Trolly. Pillow lace, coarse, made especially in the eighteenth century in Devonshire, with heavily outlined patterns in a *fond chant* ground.

Trolly thread. Gimp outlining the pattern in Lille lace.

Valenciennes. Pillow lace. True Valenciennes is reputed to have been made in the town and false Valenciennes in the region around, the countrywomen continuing the older style of ground when the townswomen developed a new one early in the eighteenth century, although both were "true" in that they were worked pattern and ground in one operation. False Valenciennes included lace with mixed grounds while true Valenciennes had a clear open diamond mesh worked with four – later three – plaited threads. Patterns were mostly the old Flemish scrolls and conventional flowers without a *cordonnet* and worked with such exactitude that it became important, and rare, for one worker to complete a whole piece. Around the mid-eighteenth century the four pieces for a lady's cap and lappets might cost £45 and represent two or three years' work. Since the early nineteenth century this lace has been made largely in Belgium.

Venetian flat point. Needlepoint with a solid *toilé*, the fillings few and simple and the *brides* numerous and decked with *picots*.

Venetian grounded point. Needlepoint meshed lace introduced to follow the eighteenth-century French fashion and much resembling Alençon. The patterns were in the rococo mood of their time and somewhat florid.

Venetian pillow lace. A minor product dating to the early days of pillow lace and much resembling early needlepoint.

Venetian raised point. Needlepoint. This had a distinctively thick multi-thread *cordonnet* and no mesh ground. It was used on the ends of men's cravats in the seventeenth and early eighteenth centuries and had a sumptuous effect of carved ivory.

Venetian rose point. Needlepoint, lighter than raised point. The *cordonnet* might have two or three rows of *picots* and more *picots* were introduced on the many *brides* which were dotted with tiny roses suggesting a powdering of snowflakes – hence its alternative name *point de neige*. Popular in England in the seventeenth and early eighteenth centuries for men's falling collars, ruffles, etc. (Plate 238A).

Wiltshire. Pillow lace, a coarse simple version of the Midlands laces.

Youghal. Needlepoint, reproducing the Venetian flat point and rose point. This lovely lace was developed in Co. Cork in the late 1840s, but later was largely replaced by crochets (Plate 239A).

American

NEEDLEWORK

In America the professional embroiderer has always been the exception. The great bulk of the needlework for which an American origin can be claimed was produced by amateurs – women who employed this age-old craft to beautify their homes and clothing or, in a later period, young ladies demonstrating the genteel accomplishments acquired at school. This accounts for the difficulty of giving exact dates to many of the oldest and most interesting examples that have survived. Embroidresses in remote parts of the country probably continued, as they do today, to work in styles long since abandoned elsewhere, whether for lack of newer models or simply because they liked the old ways best; they evidently copied nature as well as the transmitted pattern and drew on imagination as needleworkers have always done.

Names and dates in the embroidery are not always a certain means of identification. Leaving aside the possibility that such "signatures" and dates may have been added recently, we can easily imagine how an especially ambitious project, begun by one worker, could have been carried on by her daughters, or even her granddaughters, who would work into it the name of their ancestress and some significant date of her life as a sort of domestic memorial. Not only is it impossible to trace the makers of many "signed" pieces, but the towns, buildings, and human figures depicted in needlework are only rarely to be identified with real places or people. And, it need hardly be pointed out, family histories not bolstered by other evidence are as unreliable here as in the case of other types of antiques.

It is difficult even to say when the story of American needlework properly begins. An early regulation in the Massachusetts Bay Colony forbade the wearing of "cuttworke, embroidered or needle worke capps, bands, & rayles", indicating that at least some of the community were exposed to this temptation, but the objectionable finery may have been obtained from abroad. Inventories of the late 1600s, which indicate a rising standard of comfort, frequently list "wrought", "needle-worked", or "Turkey" chairs, cushions, carpets, cupboard cloths, and hangings. Though many of these embroideries, like other furnishings of the colonists' homes, undoubtedly came from the mother country, there is just as much reason to think that some were made in America.

The Turkey work chairs, cushions, and carpets mentioned in early wills and inventories represent a type of needlework that had come into fashion in England in the late sixteenth century. Simulating the colourful rugs imported from the Near East for the homes of wealthy Europeans, Turkey work was made by pulling heavy wool through canvas or coarse linen, knotting it, and cutting the ends to form a pile. Turkey work carpets were used for table covers, just as Oriental rugs were at this time. In an inventory of 1676 twelve Turkey work chairs are valued at 960 pounds of tobacco, twice the amount estimated for the same number of leather-covered chairs. Among the very few pieces of American furniture that have survived with their original Turkey work upholstery are two chairs, now in the Metropolitan Museum of Art, that date from about this time.

A set of embroidered bed hangings, also in the Metropolitan Museum, is probably typical of many that added warmth and cheerful colour to the American homes of the late seventeenth century (Plate 225A). According to tradition, these hangings were made by the three successive wives of Dr. Gilson Clapp, an Englishman who went to America about

1666 and settled near Westchester, New York. The story, like others that have come down the years with cherished pieces of embroidery, cannot be corroborated, but the work itself represents a type that came into style in England in the late 1500s and remained popular for nearly a century with women of the middle-class provincial society from which most of the American colonists came. Embroidered with red wool in outline, blanket, and seed stitches, the panels have narrow scalloped borders enclosing a ground on which dots, birds, squirrels, and stags pierced with arrows alternate with floral sprays in a close, all-over pattern. Motifs of this sort were originally copied from manuscripts and early printed books on natural history, herbals, and, in the case of the deer pierced with an arrow, books of emblems and devices; they were later redrawn for the use of embroiderers and published in such works as Shorleyker's *Schole House for the Needle* (1624) and the engravings of Peter Stent and John Overton, among others.

The painted and resist-dyed Indian chintzes imported into Europe from 1630 on opened up a rich source of design to the needle-worker. Before the middle of the century, small repeating patterns like that on the Metropolitan Museum hangings had been superseded by typical motifs from the chintzes – the great flowing tree that rises out of a low mound or hillock, with all sorts of exotic birds and butterflies in its scrolling branches and human figures standing on the schematized earth at its base, and the detached, naturalistic flower sprays scattered irregularly over the ground. Embroideries in this style are probably what most people think of first as crewel work, though the name is just as properly applied to those described above.

The word crewel actually designates the loosely twisted, worsted yarns with which the design was worked. Early newspaper advertisements of crewels, "cruells", etc., indicate that imported yarns were available in the major cities, but evidently much of the early needlework produced here was worked with materials spun, woven, and dyed at home. Crewels were supplied commercially in several grades, from coarse to fine; home-made yarns were bound to vary widely in weight and texture. The ground is usually linen or twilled cotton; homespun linen is most common in American examples. One invariable characteristic of crewel work is that the ground material is never entirely obscured by the embroidery, though this may cover more or less of the space. It is generally held that in American work the motifs are smaller and sparser, more of the ground is left showing, and the whole effect is more "open" than in English crewelwork. The patterns inspired by the Indian chintzes demanded a more naturalistic treatment than those in the preceding style, and were accordingly worked in yarns of various rather than a single hue. An exceptional example in shades of blue is illustrated (Plate 225c). At first rather sombre, with many dark blues and greens relieved only by dull tan or mustard yellow, the colour schemes lightened in the course of the following century. Early crewel work was carried out in a variety of stitches, outline or stem stitch (often spoken of as crewel stitch), Oriental, and long and short stitch being the most usual. Chain stitch gained favour in the 1700s.

Besides bed hangings, coverlets, and curtains, cushions, chair covers, and many smaller objects were decorated with crewel work. A notice in the *Boston Gazette* of 1749 calls attention to the loss by theft of a "Woman's Fustian Petticoat, with a large work'd Embroidered Border, being Deer, Sheep, Houses, Forrests, &c." Several petticoat bands preserved in museums today have patterns that might be described in the same words (Plate 225D).

Before the 1700s were well advanced, life in most parts of the American colonies had become relatively safe and easy. In the large cities accumulating wealth brought leisure and the desire for agreeable surroundings in its train. Houses were built and furnished with primary consideration for the comfort and aesthetic enjoyment of their occupants. Among the new forms that served this requirement, easy chairs, sofas, card-tables, and firescreens in particular were well designed for the display of fine needlework, and the lady of the house, free of the heavier duties of earlier homemakers and able to call on the professional services of a tailor or mantua maker for the family's clothing, willingly took up the task of embellishing them. Contemporary newspaper advertisements offering instruction in various kinds of embroidery among other handicrafts speak for the popularity of this occupation. As early as 1719, an insertion in the *Boston News-Letter* announced that at the house of Mr George Brownell young gentlewomen and children would be taught "all sorts of fine Work . . . embroidery in a new way, Turkey work for Handkerchiefs two ways, fine new Fashion Purses, flourishing and plain work . . . Brocaded work for Handkerchiefs and Short aprons upon Muslin", as well as dancing. Among the "Curious works" taught in New York in 1731 by Martha Gazley, "late of Great Britain", were "Nun's-Work", and "Philligree and Pencil Work upon Muslin", all probably types of embroidery, though this teacher also offered artificial fruit and flower making, wax work, and "Raising of Paste". "Flowering", "flourishing", "Dresden flowering on catgut (canvas)", and "shading with silk or worsted, on Cambrick, lawn, or Holland" may take in all the colourful floral embroidery found on women's gowns, petticoats, aprons, pockets, and other accessories of the period, as well as the fine work in silk on satin and velvet "wedding" waistcoats for men.

Tent stitch and cross stitch are frequently mentioned. The first, known today as petit point, is worked on a firm but not too closely woven ground material in rows of short, slanting stitches, each stitch crossing diagonally an intersection of the threads of the ground. Imitating as it did the effect of woven tapestry and offering comparable strength and durability, this kind of work was much appreciated in the eighteenth century, as it is today, for the coverings of chairs and sofas, and it lent itself well to all-over patterns of small, naturalistic flowers and leaves that suited the light, graceful forms of Queen Anne and Chippendale furniture. Cross stitch scarcely requires description; worked in woollen yarns, it was an alternative to tent stitch for upholstery in the 1700s.

A third type of needlework that was

frequently used for upholstery and other purposes in this period was called flame stitch or Hungarian stitch. Its rainbow-like effects were created by making horizontal bands of short, parallel stitches from one side of the work to the other. All the stitches in one row are the same length, but the rows themselves may rise and fall in zigzag patterns of great complexity. Wool or silk yarns were used for flame stitch, depending on the purpose of the work.

Most of the newspaper advertisers who offered instruction in needlework also had materials and patterns to sell. A notice inserted in the *Boston News-Letter* in 1738 by a Mrs Condy reads significantly, "All sorts of beautiful Figures on Canvas, for Tent Stick [*sic*]; the Patterns from London, but drawn by her much cheaper than English drawing." David Mason, "Japanner", was also ready to provide "Coats of Arms, Drawings on Sattin or Canvis for Embroidering". Mrs Condy supplied "Silk Shades, Slacks, Floss, Cruells of all Sorts, the best White Chapple Needles, and everything for all Sorts of Work". "Shaded crewells" and "worsted Slacks in Shades" were also advertised.

Outside the cities and in the more modest urban homes, women continued to decorate their curtains, chair covers, bed furniture, and clothing with colourful crewels up to the end of the century and even later. Among fashionable city folk, however, this useful work had gone out of style. For one thing, the new Hepplewhite and Sheraton furniture that came in during the last quarter of the 1700s required more delicate coverings. Pattern-woven silks and satins were used on chairs and sofas in preference to needlework, and the needlewoman, relieved of this last duty, turned to decoration pure and simple, spending her new leisure on needlework pictures and similar "fancy work".

Pictorial subjects had, of course, been a frequent choice for furniture covers, fire screens, and other objects worked with woollen yarns in tent stitch and cross stitch earlier in the century. A group of thirty-six embroidered panels from New England, presumably the work of young ladies at a Boston finishing school in the mid-1700s, is widely known as the *Fishing Lady* series because of the name given to the central figure in the pastoral scene depicted. Considerable research has been devoted to tracing the source of this design, evidently one or more English prints.

The embroidered pictures of the late 1700s and early 1800s, however, differ from these last examples in their general spirit and intention as well as by the materials and techniques employed in their making. The designs, including landscapes, pastoral scenes, views of architecture and ships, maps, portraits, biblical and mythological subjects, memorials, flower pieces, and allegorical compositions, were worked mainly in floss or twisted silk in a variety of stitches. Large areas like sky or background, as well as faces and other details, were often painted in. The ground material might be fine linen, canvas, silk, or satin. Such pictures were customarily framed like paintings, with a broad margin of black glass setting off the rather delicate colours of the embroidery. Perhaps the most typical of this group are the "mourning pictures", depicting an urn or monument, often inscribed with a name or epitaph, a willow, symbol of sorrow, and one or more figures that may be meant to represent survivors of the deceased. Numbers of these are dedicated to the memory of George Washington. That the drawing of the figures is ordinarily competent points to the use of prepared designs, kept in stock by the vendors of other materials for needlework and traced or "pounced" (by rubbing coloured powder through a pricked paper pattern) on the ground material desired. Many of the most elaborate embroidered pictures are the work of schoolgirls, and testify to the young needlewomen's completion of a course of formal instruction. The school conducted by the Sisters of Bethlehem, a Moravian religious order, in Pennsylvania was famous for the fine needlework developed and taught there in the eighteenth century.

In America as elsewhere, girls and young women had long made samplers to demonstrate their mastery of useful and decorative stitches and to record motifs and patterns for future use. Very few American samplers survive from the seventeenth century; the oldest, preserved in Pilgrim Hall in Plymouth, Massachusetts, was worked by Lora Standish, daughter of Captain Myles Standish, 1653. These early samplers, truly exemplars or patterns, as the name indicates, are long, narrow linen panels, on which the needlework is disposed in horizontal bands. Borders and small separate designs in various stitches, cut work (*reticello*), drawn thread work, and needle lace (*punto in aria*) are found on them. An alphabet or inscription or both is usual, and the maker's name and the date of the completion of the work were almost invariably added. In the course of the 1770s the inscription, which might be a motto, a verse or verses from scripture, or a selection from some such volume as Isaac Watts's *Divine Songs for Children*, occupied an increasingly prominent place, until the sampler became virtually a vehicle for the lettering and numbers. By this time, the shape had changed as well, tending to be square or oblong with the length little greater than the width. A border, which might be either a slender, running vine or a wide band of flowers, framed the embroidered text, and any remaining space was filled in with such motifs as flowers, fruit and leaves, birds, animals, and human figures, all more or less crudely drawn and worked most often in cross stitch or tent stitch. Bright, gay colours were the rule. After the 1830s, both design and workmanship deteriorated. The wide availability of patterns and materials for the popular Berlin wool work of the mid-nineteenth century seems to have put an end to all more individual expressions in embroidery.

An effort has been made in this account to introduce the chief varieties of American needlework in some historical sequence, but it should not be forgotten that their periods of popularity overlapped and coincided with those of other techniques. Concurrently with the vogue for embroidered silk pictures there was a great fashion for tambour work, so-called from the shape of the two hoops between which the foundation material was stretched while being embroidered. A tambour needle, with a hooked end, was used, and the thread was drawn up through the material to form a chain stitch on the right side. Sheer muslin and crêpe were worked in tambour for ladies' caps. The same method, used on machine-made cotton or silk net, produced a lace-like effect that was much used for wedding veils, shawls, fichus, and edgings (tambour lace). "Darned net", embroidered with a needle of the usual sort, was used for the same purposes. Satin stitch was worked in white thread, most often silk or linen, on the gossamer white linen, cotton, and silk dress materials of the 1830s. Large handkerchiefs of the finest white linen were embellished with drawn-thread work and incredibly fine satin-stitch embroidery in white. Mull, a cobwebby silk muslin brought from India, was embroidered in silk with motifs copied from Indian shawls or chintzes.

The fashion for white on white extended to needlework in coarser materials that give a very different effect. Heavy white cotton bedcovers were embroidered with long strands of candlewicking, the typical design of a basket of flowers or a patriotic motif framed by a flowering vine being worked in small running stitches that stand out on the surface of the material and are sometimes looped and cut to make protruding tufts.

Among other types of American needlework that interest collectors are the towel covers made by Pennsylvania-German housewives in the late eighteenth and early nineteenth centuries to hang over and conceal the common towel on its rack in the kitchen. These are long strips of linen, often made up of two or more small towels sewn together, decorated with simple cross-stitch motifs representing birds, hearts, flowers, and human figures. Many are finished off with bands of lace or knotted fringe.

The rare wool-on-wool coverlets, of which a notable example comes from Old Deerfield Village, Mass., apparently represent another regional speciality. Practically all of the small group so far recorded are thought to come from the Connecticut River Valley. Their bold, all-over designs, carried out in woollen yarns on a ground of heavy woollen fabric, seem to acknowledge the same exotic source as the crewel embroideries on linen. Most of the known examples are dated, the earliest 1748, the latest 1826.

An interesting survival of European customs may be seen in the early embroidered hatchments still preserved in some museums today. A hatchment was a coat-of-arms on a lozenge, meant to be carried in the funeral and displayed on the outside of the house of a person who had recently died. It consisted ordinarily of a diamond-shape wooden panel (or canvas stretched on a wooden frame of the same shape), painted black with the arms of the deceased on a shield in colour. In New England, at least, hatchments were copied in embroidery as memorials; the designs were carried out in coloured silks and gold and silver threads, which were couched or worked in long and short stitch and sometimes covered the entire surface of the panel.

QUILTS AND COVERLETS

Quilts and coverlets are primarily bed coverings created for warmth; while counterpanes and bedspreads are decorative covers for the bed produced with no thought of contributing to the comfort of the user. The quilts and coverlets of the nineteenth century, which were primarily utilitarian in their purpose, are the kinds most available to the collector today. They were produced in great quantity, and a remarkable number have survived in good condition. Many of them are very attractive in colour and pattern. The discriminating collector can make good use of them in the decoration of the home. Some knowledge as to their period, however, is desirable if they are to be fitted into their most appropriate setting. An understanding of the techniques involved in their production will make them more interesting and appreciated.

Most eighteenth-century quilts and counterpanes are very large, often 9–12 feet square, as they were used on the high beds of the period and often covered the stacked featherbeds and pillows which were placed on the main bed during the day to be spread on floor and settle for sleeping at night. These early covers were usually made of simple homespun or of imported English, French, or India printed or painted cottons and were often not quilted at all but used only as counterpanes.

As a rule the design of the textile will give a clue as to its approximate age. During the seventeenth and eighteenth centuries the designs of bed-covers tend to develop from a base and to flow outward and upward as in the typical Tree-of-Life design. They may be symmetrical horizontally but not vertically, and there are rarely borders. In the nineteenth century this gradually gave way to more formalized patterns. At first the central design remained free and was surrounded by symmetrical borders; but later, that too disappeared and the whole design became balanced. After 1825 the designs tend to become geometrical in repeating units. Naturally there was a great carry-over of these designs and much copying of older pieces so that a typical eighteenth-century design may well appear as late as 1860. In this case the materials used may date the piece. Fortunately many women were very proud of their work and both signed and dated their more elaborate productions.

Crewel embroidered bedspreads, or counterpanes, were produced in the eighteenth century. Often a complete set of bed furniture was embroidered, including canopy or tester, curtains, and sometimes a skirt. The design was produced in the traditional English way with coloured wools worked in various stitches on a homespun linen ground. The well-known Tree-of-Life design was most popular, but often scattered motifs are found. These usually have the same Eastern feeling, although the subject-matter may be the original idea of the maker.

Among the most interesting of the bedcovers, though they are rare, are the wool-on-wool covers or bedrugs which have large scrolling or Tree-of-Life motifs worked in woollen yarn on a background of natural coloured woollen blanketing. While the technique is often mistaken for hooking, it is usually a product of the needle. Several strands of single-ply woollen yarn were stitched through the ground in a running stitch taking short stitches through the fabric and leaving loops of yarn on the surface. The entire surface is usually covered with a deep pile which is uncut. These textiles often resemble in appearance the woven pile bedrugs of Scandinavia which are called *Rya*. Some have pile in various shades of blue with natural coloured woollen; while others combine these with shades of yellow, brown, and green. The designs appear to stem directly from the early crewel work. Sometimes the woollen sheeting or blanket used for the background is pieced together from fabric in several different weaves, suggesting that it may have been a secondary use of partly worn material. These bedrugs are usually 7 or 8 feet square. Most of them are found in the New England area, particularly in the Connecticut River Valley from Vermont, Massachusetts, and Connecticut. Many are dated, the earliest 1724, and latest in the early nineteenth century.

When cotton cloth became available from the factory soon after 1815 it was used for counterpanes, just as had the earlier chintz, but it needed to be decorated by hand. It was sometimes printed at home by means of carved wooden blocks or stencils. These block-printed or stencilled counterpanes were occasionally made into quilts, and it is in this condition that they are most often found today. The designs are simple and resemble to great degree the appliquéd quilts of the period. The colours usually used were red, green, and yellow.

After 1800 many bedspreads were made of cotton cloth, the earliest hand-woven, embroidered in various stitches with cotton roving or candlewicking. These are all-white counterpanes, with sometimes simple, sometimes elaborate, designs and are often signed and dated. There is usually fringe applied to three sides. The designs become geometric after 1825, and there is often tufting combined with the embroidery stitches.

Closely resembling these embroidered spreads are the all-white woven counterpanes, made on the loom (Plate 228). A cotton roving was raised in loops over a wire to form the pattern on a background of plain cotton. Some of these were produced at home and some by professional weavers. The home-woven ones are usually seamed, while the

others were woven full width and often numbered and dated. These woven tufted spreads can be distinguished from the embroidered variety by the heavy roving, which is continuous across the width, forming a heavy rib where it is not looped on the surface for the design. Stars often form a part of the design with swag borders. These were made from about 1800 to 1820.

QUILTS

There were at this period also all-white quilts made to serve as counterpanes. The interlining of cotton wadding is very thin and the quilting stitches very fine. The pattern may be very elaborate, and often extra padding was introduced from the back after the quilting was completed, in order to accent certain parts of the design. This usually consists of a large central medallion, urn, cornucopia, or basket of fruit or flowers with a series of surrounding borders. Companion pieces, such as bureau covers, were often made as well as separate pieces to cover the pillows. These white quilts may usually be assigned to the first quarter of the nineteenth century.

The technique of quilting developed because three layers of cloth are warmer than one, and has been employed for centuries. Clothing has been made for both warmth and protection, as in the quilted cotton garments of China and the quilted padding worn under medieval armour. Counterpanes have probably been quilted in every century from the fourteenth to the twentieth. In the seventeenth and eighteenth centuries bedhangings and tablecovers were also among the household articles quilted. Clothing also came in for its share of this technique, and articles included petticoats or underskirts, waistcoats, slippers, jackets, and dresses. Petticoats are the most usual surviving articles in this group, and their patterns are inclined to follow rather closely the bedcoverings of the period.

In American bed quilts this technique of quilting is often combined with designs, pieced or patched (appliquéd), of coloured fabrics in order to furnish a colourful, as well as warm, article of bed clothing. The important era of American quilt-making extended from about 1750 to 1860. Quite naturally, many more examples have survived from the nineteenth than from the eighteenth century.

The quilted woollen bedcovers, which are often called Linsey-woolseys, are not often made of that staple household fabric. Rather, they are composed of a top layer of woollen or glazed worsted fabric dyed dark blue, green, or brown, with a bottom layer of a coarser woollen material, either natural or a shade of yellow or buff. The filling is a soft layer of carded wool, and the three layers are held together with quilting done with homespun linen thread. While some of these may date from the eighteenth century, many were made during the first half of the nineteenth. The design of the quilting is often a simple one composed of interlocking circles or crossed diagonal lines giving a diamond pattern. The earlier woollen quilts are thinner and the designs tend to be finer and more elaborate. The size of these quilts may also be a clue to their age, as in the nineteenth century they tend to be blanket size, while in the eighteenth they are likely to be large bedcovers, occasionally with cutout corners for the bedposts.

While the eighteenth-century cotton counterpanes were made of whole cloth, usually imported, and therefore confined to the households of the well-to-do, the ordinary housewife soon came to realize that the expensive patterned chintzes would go much farther if they were first cut up into design units and applied to a linen or cotton ground (Plate 226). The central part of the design of the chintz appliqué counterpane was often the Tree, cut from the chintz generally in one piece and applied to the plain fabric ground with the birds and insects found in these designs applied separately. Borders were then cut from smaller-figured chintz and sewn on all four, or sometimes only three, sides. There were often two or three of these bands, of varying patterns and colours, separated by bands of plain fabric. At a later period a back was added and a thin layer of carded cotton or wool placed between to be stitched in place by the finest of hand sewing. This was almost always a simple running stitch in America; while in England and on the Continent a back-stitch was more generally used.

The quilting often followed the outlines of the appliqué in the central design, which set it off in a raised manner. The plain ground was often simply quilted in closely spaced diagonal rows.

In the later part of the eighteenth century came the first of the pieced quilts. The central design was often a large Rising Sun motif or Star of Bethlehem covering almost the entire bed with the familiar chintz floral patterns cut out and appliquéd to the square and triangular blocks of plain white fabric which filled in the star corners. A chintz border was usually added to complete the quilt top. This star pattern, which continued to be popular for a century or more, was composed of diamond-shaped pieces of small-patterned chintz and calico which were carefully arranged so that the colours radiated from the centre to the points. After 1800 the appliqué filling the corners gave way to pieced blocks arranged in a smaller star pattern. The sewing of these pieced patterns had to be most carefully done, as the seams had to be perfectly regular if the finished design was to lie flat and even.

The earliest coloured quilts made of remnant patches must have been just that, with the odd-shaped pieces sewn down to a fabric backing; but by 1800 women began to use the more convenient method of making the quilt top in units of blocks and setting these together, either in parallel rows or diagonally, with strips of lattice-work or with alternate white blocks. These smaller units could be pieced or appliquéd very conveniently and then assembled and quilted in simple or elaborate designs. If plain white blocks were used in setting the pattern blocks together these were often quilted elaborately; while the quilting in the pieced or appliquéd blocks followed rather closely the construction lines of the block.

The patterns for quilting were often marked on the fabric by snapping a chalk line for the diagonal lines or chalking around a cardboard pattern for the more elaborate designs. Household objects, such as cups, saucers, and plates, were often used as patterns for simple quilting. Pencil, chalk, charcoal, and soap were used for the marking. Background designs included: the Horizontal, the Cross Bar,

Diagonal, Diamond, and Double and Triple Cross-Bars and Diamonds. Running designs for borders and lattice strips included: Running Vine, Princess Feather, Rope, Ocean Wave, and Serpentine. Designs for the plain blocks were: Feather Wreath, Clam Shell, Wheel of Fortune, Spider Web, Pineapple, Bouquet, Weeping Willow, Star Crescent, Heart, American Eagle, Fan, Star and Crown, Oak Leaf, Bellflower, Acanthus, Swirl, and Dove of Peace. Many designs were based on the always adaptable feather motif.

Pieced quilts are generally geometric in design, as it is much easier to seam two small pieces of fabric together if the seams are straight and not curved. There are thousands of designs for these quilts, and many have fanciful names. The same pattern was known by different names in various sections of the country, and often the same name would be used for several totally unrelated patterns. There are Star patterns named for every state in the Union. A few of the more interesting names are:

Cross and Crown	Puss-in-the-Corner
Goose Tracks	Bourgoyne Surrounded
Hen and Chickens	Pine Tree
Bear's Track	Flying Dutchman
Peony	Feather Star
Flying Geese	Drunkard's Path
Lincoln's Platform	Robbing Peter to Pay Paul
Stepping Stones	Dutchman's Puzzle
Morning Star	Wheel of Fortune
King David's Crown	Cats and Mice
Joseph's Coat	Hearts and Gizzards
Jacob's Ladder	Grandmother's Fan
Sunflower	Dresden Plate
Delectable Mountains	Winding Warp
Log Cabin	Turkey Tracks
Rose of Sharon	Irish Chain

These pieced or appliquéd quilts of the nineteenth century were usually made of plain coloured or printed cotton fabrics combined with white. Many were made of random bits of carefully hoarded fabric, and in this case some of the fabrics may be much earlier than the actual date of the making of the quilt. Often the quilt which is best preserved, because carefully kept for use on special occasions, is the one made of two or three colours of fabric which were especially purchased for its construction. Many quilts of this type were made during the 1830s and 1840s of turkey red and green cottons appliquéd on white grounds. It is probable that many of them were brides' quilts, as even though the customary dozen quilts were made of scraps, it would have been that final masterpiece for which new materials would most likely have been purchased. These quilts were often made of identical blocks in a basket or flower design and set together with white blocks on which were lavished the most elaborate quilting. Often each block is quilted in a different design.

The technique of making the quilt top in separate blocks led to a special type of quilt during the 1840s and 1850s. This was known variously as a Signature, Autograph, Friendship, Bride, Presentation, or Album quilt (Plate 227). These quilts were made for a special person. Friends or well-wishers each supplied a pieced or appliquéd block of her own chosen pattern which she usually signed in Indian ink. These friends gathered for an afternoon and assembled and quilted the quilt, which was then presented to the honoured guest. They were often made for a favourite minister or a minister's wife. These are among the most interesting of the nineteenth-century quilts and, if the colours are compatible and the various blocks well chosen and arranged, they may be very lovely as well.

During the late Victorian era the patched covers of the seventeenth and eighteenth centuries were revived but in a more elaborate form. These were the Crazy Quilts made of scraps of silk, satin, and velvet. Like their earlier counterparts, they were made of small irregular-shaped pieces appliquéd to a base fabric, but now the seams were often covered with embroidery stitches and sometimes the patch itself had a design painted or embroidered upon it. These were often most unattractive in colour and design, but occasionally a good example is found. They were impractical as bedcoverings, owing to the material from which they were made, so they were made up into smaller sizes for use as couch throws, piano covers, and other parlour ornamentation of the period.

COVERLETS

Unlike quilts, which were made of already woven fabric, coverlets are woven into patterns on the loom. They may be either the product of the housewife and her family or of the professional weaver. During the early years of the settlement of America not much patterned weaving could have been done. It was all the housewife could do to supply her large family with the everyday clothing and household fabrics which were necessary. The materials for their manufacture were scarce. Sheep were not raised in great numbers and flax was a time-consuming crop. Cotton was obtainable only in limited quantities and at a high price. The housewife spun the flax which she had raised into linen yarn and wove materials for sheets and shirts, underclothing, and towelling. The refuse tow from its processing she converted into sacking and coarse tow cloth. She spun the wool from her sheep into yarn and wove it into heavy material for the clothing of the men and boys and outer garments for the whole family, as well as blankets for the bed. Only when the hardships of the first years had decreased and more time and material were available could she turn her hand to producing the patterned textiles which would adorn her home as well as keep her family warm and protected.

The patterns of these fabrics were not invented by her but were based on a long-continuing tradition. Perhaps she had brought with her some family textiles or perhaps only the written formula for their weaving. These weaving drafts were freely interchanged and travelled through all the colonies. It is likely that the first really intricately patterned fabrics were produced by professional weavers who emigrated to America from the various countries of Europe, bringing with them the old patterns of their homeland. It is certain that the early eighteenth-century pattern books printed in Germany were brought to America and used. The weavers of England and Scotland who came were well trained if they had successfully completed their apprenticeship. They certainly brought with them the patterns which they had been taught to weave. This was true of all the migrant weavers, for German, French, Dutch, Scandinavian, Scottish, and English all contributed their traditional textile designs and techniques to America.

In the category of woven coverlets must be included those woollen blankets also produced on the loom but decorated with embroidery so that they fullfilled both the purpose of warmth and decoration. Rose Blankets are among these. They were woven of soft white wool in the simplest weave of the home loom. It is probable that the ones with a raised nap were woven at a slightly later date than the others either at home or in a factory. After weaving and finishing they were decorated with embroidery in coloured woollen yarns. The pattern used was a stylized wheel design of loose stitches. This decoration was often in two corners and sometimes in all four. The colours used were those readily dyed at home with the natural dyestuffs generally available. Rose, green, yellow, tan, brown, black, and sometimes blue are found. Rose blankets were being produced in the period from 1810 to 1840 in both New York and Pennsylvania and probably throughout New England. They were among the items of domestic manufacture which were being encouraged by the prizes awarded by agricultural societies of this period.

Material was also woven especially for making embroidered bedspreads. These often resemble plaid blankets in design. White or natural coloured cotton was used with blue woollen yarn and woven in a twill weave. Then, after the strips were assembled, a design was embroidered in coloured woollen yarns in the spaces of the plaid. A fringe was often added to finish the edge.

The coverlets produced in their entirety on the loom include several types and techniques. In the order of their complexity, they are: overshot, also known as float weave; summer-and-winter weave; block or double-weave geometric; and the two types of flowered coverlets which are in the so-called Jacquard weave.

Due to the width of the home loom, coverlets were woven in two or more strips, each $2\frac{1}{2}$–3 yards long and seamed together when finished. They were usually about 84 inches wide if in two strips. Sometimes a separate woven fringe was sewn on the sides while the ends of the warp threads formed the fringe at the bottom.

Coverlets are found in shades of blue, blue and red, brown, brown and tan, black, madder rose or rust, yellow, green with rose or yellow, and more rarely in scarlet. The dyes used in producing these colours were the ones most readily available and the ones considered to be most permanent. The most satisfactory dyestuff available was indigo. This had to be purchased from a shop or from the pedlar in the country, but it was widely available from the earliest days. Much was grown in the south during the later half of the eighteenth century, but a large amount was always imported. Indigo produces a fast blue colour on all fibres, and this may be varied considerably in shade. It was also used to produce shades of green by dyeing with it either before or after a yellow dye was applied. The process of dyeing with indigo was an unpleasant one because of the smell of the fermenting indigo vat, which demanded particular care, as the vat had to be maintained at a constant warm heat to keep the fermentation from stopping. Other dyes were easier to apply. The brilliant scarlet was obtained from cochineal, an insect raised under cultivation in Mexico, by boiling the dried and powdered insects with a solution of tin dissolved in acid. As this dyestuff was probably the most expensive of all, it was not often used for home-woven coverlets. The common shades of red were obtained from madder root, which could be purchased as a ground powder or could be raised in the garden. Dyeing with this material followed a standard procedure used for many natural dyestuffs. First the woollen yarn was boiled in a solution of alum or of alum and cream of tartar, and then in a bath with the madder root. Shades from rose to deep lacquer red and rust were obtained. This was the second most popular dye for coverlets, as it was almost as fast to light and washing as indigo blue.

Yellow was obtained from goldenrod and sumac, tan from alder bark and butternut hulls and roots, dark brown from hickory or black walnut hulls and roots, and black by dyeing first with walnut and then with indigo. Other herbs, barks, roots, and berries were used with the alum process for dyeing various shades. Most of these were rather dull in tone due to the natural impurities in the dyestuffs, and most of them faded to some degree in time. Imported dyewoods from South and Central America generally available during the eighteenth and nineteenth centuries included logwood, Brazilwood, and fustic, but the domestic weaver was inclined to trust to the familiar dyestuffs.

The simplest type of coverlet to produce was in the overshot weave, which could be woven on the limited four-harness loom which was to be found in almost every home. It was made of linen warp and woollen weft in the eighteenth century and of cotton warp and woollen weft in the nineteenth. These coverlets are confined, by the limitations of the loom used, to simple geometric patterns, but there are literally thousands of patterns, as the combinations of four blocks in different order and proportions are infinite. Like the names of quilt patterns, the names of coverlet patterns were often very fanciful, reflected the historical events of their day, or were based on the resemblance, either real or fancied, to some familiar object. The fact that these names show late American historical connexions does not mean that they were created at that time. The same old pattern with its origin in Europe was renamed by the weaver to modernize it. Geographic and historical names include:

England Beauty	Downfall of Paris
Monmouth	London Beauty
Governor's Garden	King's Flower
Southern Beauty	Queen's Delight
Tennessee Flower	Western Beauty
Indian Trouble	Jackson's Purchase
Federal Knot	Federal City
Indian Wars	Whig Rose

Those bearing resemblance to familiar objects or merely fanciful include:

Double Bow Knot	Snail Trail and Cat
Church Windows	Tracks
Rose in the Bush	True Love's Vine
Snowball	Irish Chain
Blooming Leaf	Wheel of Fortune
Ladies' Delight	Snow Drop

Ladies' Fancy
Free Mason and
  Felicity
Cards and Wheels
Nine Snowballs
Chariot Wheel
Blazing Star
Pine Bloom

Bachelor's Button
Fox Trail
Young Man's Delight
Bachelor Among the
  Girls
Forsaken Lover
Gentleman's Fancy

The overshot weave is a three-thread construction. There is one warp, usually a two-ply linen or cotton; a binder weft, usually the same material as the warp, but often a single ply and slightly smaller in grist; and the pattern weft, which is a coloured woollen yarn. This may be either single or two-ply, and is always larger than either the warp or the binder weft. The pattern of the overshot is three-tone: dark, light, and half-tone. The dark spots or blocks which form the real design are composed of several pattern wefts where they overlie the basic cotton or linen ground. These are called "floats", "skips", or "overshots". The light spots are the basic ground fabric where the pattern threads lie below it, and the half-tones are formed between the dark and light spots where the pattern weft is bound closely into the ground. Most frequently this type of coverlet is in a four-block pattern. The rectangular blocks may vary in size and proportion, but all the blocks in a horizontal row are the same height, and all the blocks in a vertical row are the same width in any single piece of weaving. This weave was used in all of the Colonies, and travelled westward with the settlers into the new states. Many of these coverlets are still in existence, but most of those surviving were woven in the first half of the nineteenth century.

Coverlets were sometimes woven in the summer-and-winter weave, but this weave did not have as wide a distribution geographically as the overshot weave. These are found most often in New York and Pennsylvania. The opinion of many is that this weave was either brought to America by German immigrants of the early eighteenth century or was developed by them after arrival. A weave closely resembling it and in identical patterns was common in the Schleswig-Holstein area in the seventeenth and eighteenth centuries, where it was used for bed curtains.

Summer-and-winter weave produces a fabric which is two-toned and reversible. On the side where the coloured woollen pattern weft predominates it is dark and on the reverse side, where the light warp and binder weft predominate, it is light. From this it receives its name. It is in fact a small overshot weave in blocks which may be of any size and proportion and may overlap or combine. The pattern is still geometric, but it may be more intricate than the overshot. The fabric is extremely flexible, and the threads being so intimately bound together, it is structurally more sound and wears better than the overshot weave.

The same colours are found in this weave as in the others, since they were the ones commonly available. Indigo blue is the most common, followed by madder rust and rose. More than one colour of pattern weft is never used in summer-and-winter weave. This weave requires a loom slightly more elaborate than the overshot weave, and therefore was used only by the more experienced home weaver. It is doubtful that it was often the product of the professional. These coverlets were probably produced during the first twenty-five or thirty years of the nineteenth century.

Another weave sometimes encountered in Pennsylvania resembles summer-and-winter and can be woven with the same patterns. The blocks, however, show a pattern of bird's-eye weave. It is probable that this technique is an interpretation of the linen patterns found in the German weaving books.

Block or double woven geometric coverlets are among the most beautiful preserved today. These were undoubtedly most frequently the work of the professional craftsman, as few homes would have contained the elaborate loom required for their manufacture. According to the account books of these professionals, they were producing block coverlets during the period from 1820 to 1840. At this same period the same men were weaving the even more elaborately-patterned flowered coverlets. These professional weavers were usually Scotsmen who immigrated to America after having already learned their trade. It is reasonable to assume that such weaves were in use in Scotland, but the patterns are identical with the ones used by the Germans for summer-and-winter weave and are to be found in the German weaving books of the eighteenth century as well as the Scottish weaving books of the early nineteenth century. In both of these published sources they seem to have been intended as patterns for linens.

In colour they follow the style of the day, most often in deep indigo-blue woollen yarn which was usually supplied by the housewife, combined with a natural coloured cotton yarn which was factory spun and supplied by the weaver. Sometimes red and blue were used in the same coverlet, giving a red, white, and blue colouring.

This technique produces a fabric which is really a combination of two fabrics in one. One is a plain-woven coloured woollen, while the other is a plain-woven natural-coloured cotton. Rarely is the second of linen. Two warps are required on the loom, and these are woven together in such a way that the design is produced by the interchanging of the two basic fabrics. It is completely reversible, a block on the one side of coloured woollen fabric being backed on the reverse by a block in natural cotton. Like the summer-and-winter weave, these blocks may overlap and combine, but the pattern is always geometric. Block coverlets, like summer-and-winter and overshot, were woven on the narrow loom; so that two strips were always necessary to produce a full-width coverlet.

The fancy flowered coverlets, now usually called Jacquard coverlets, were always the work of the professional weaver who often referred to them as carpet coverlets. Many of these were woven by Scottish weavers who were already weavers of carpets in the same double-weave and with similar patterns. The German weavers of Pennsylvania also produced many of them. They were being woven as early as 1818 in New York State, but the earliest dated one to come to light so far is marked 1821. They were probably first woven in New York and Pennsylvania and later in Kentucky, Ohio, Indiana, and Illinois. In the opinion of some students the coverlets woven during the most active period, the 1830s and 1840s, were woven on the draw-loom; while later ones were woven on hand-operated looms with the help of the Jacquard attachment. It was not too difficult to install the Jacquard attachment on the old draw-loom, but there was a patent carpet loom used in Scotland which was earlier than the Jacquard and might very well have been in use in America in the 1830s. Many of these flowered coverlets were certainly woven by power in full width on looms with Jacquard attachments in the 1860s and 1870s. These later coverlets have one-piece patterns, usually with a large central medallion surrounded with elaborate borders. The designs are finer and less clear cut than the earlier coverlets. In this late period appear the scarlet-red coverlets which are suitable for rooms decorated in the Victorian manner.

The earliest of these flowered coverlets are always in the double-weave, but instead of being confined to geometric patterns, the weaver could use naturalistic designs. While many weavers used the same repeating medallion designs for the central portion of the coverlet, making one wonder if there were not a published pattern book now unknown, the borders were often most individual in treatment. These might contain designs of eagles, scrolls, festoons, flowers, birds, trees, buildings, portraits, or mottoes, and the weaver could include the name of the person for whom the coverlet was woven, the date, the place, and his own signature. The earliest ones are likely to be more restrained in design and more pleasing to the eye.

Many of these coverlets produced in Pennsylvania and westward in Kentucky, Ohio, and Indiana during the 1830s and 1840s are not in double-weave but in a single or damask weave. These are often in two or more colours of woollen yarn. Damask table linens in cotton and linen and cotton and wool were produced by some New York weavers in the identical designs of their double-woven coverlets.

British

NEEDLEWORK AND EMBROIDERY

The intimate and personal quality of embroidery and needlework has a wide appeal to the average collector, and examples of ancestral skill, handed down from generation to generation, often form the basis of a collection. Embroidered pictures, small screens, and samplers, which can adorn the walls of a home, are naturally more popular than less exhibitable objects. Complete quilts and coverlets are usually more expensive, and do not so readily come within the range of the small private collector. Yet even fragmentary examples of old embroidery have their interest, and almost all types of embroidery can be put to decorative uses.

A study of the embroidery and needlework of all countries and periods shows that while each group has its own special characteristics, certain designs, colouring, and stitchery are common to many of them, even in the case of widely separated countries. Tracing the possible sources of pattern and the interpenetration of influences can be a fascinating and rewarding study.

The type of stitch employed is generally regulated by the type of design. For example, geometric patterns are usually worked in cross or tent stitch on canvas or on a loosely woven material in which the warp and weft threads can be counted to facilitate the accurate working of the pattern. The bewildering number of stitches listed in any encyclopaedia of embroidery is somewhat misleading. The variety of stitches is, in fact, not so great as it would at first appear. The vast majority are nothing more than slight variations of a comparatively few basic stitches or the combination of two simple stitches. Some of the most effective embroidery is worked only in one simple stitch and, generally speaking, great variety of both stitches and colour do not give satisfactory results. A study of fine examples

of embroidery will generally reveal that where a great variety of stitches is used only one colour is employed, as in English white-work. Alternatively, where many colours are employed only one stitch is used, as in the fine chain-stitch embroidery of the Dutch East Indies.

Embroidery is one of the oldest of the applied arts, but the average collector is little concerned with the embroidery of antiquity, or even of the Middle Ages. In England there is a flourishing tradition of domestic embroidery from the sixteenth century onwards.

Elizabethan embroidery is essentially English in character, and most of the designs are based on typically English flowers – roses, carnations, pansies, honeysuckle, and many others, interspersed with butterflies and insects. Embroidery was widely used to decorate bodices, coifs, night-caps, and other items of costume and for domestic articles such as hangings, pillow-cases, and cushion-covers. Another class of Elizabethan embroidery consisted of table and floor carpets embroidered in tent stitch on canvas, but, unlike the smaller articles, many of these were the work of professional embroiderers.

The chief feature of Stuart embroidery is the bed curtains and hangings worked in crewel wools on a linen and cotton twill. The "Tree of Life", based on Indian models, was the favourite pattern. Stump-work was widely used during this period to decorate caskets and mirror-frames and for embroidered pictures. Quilting reached a high standard during the late seventeenth and early eighteenth centuries, and was widely used for household articles and for dress. A great variety of embroidery is found throughout the eighteenth century, both for costume and furnishing. Silk generally replaced wool as the most popular medium, with a consequent refinement

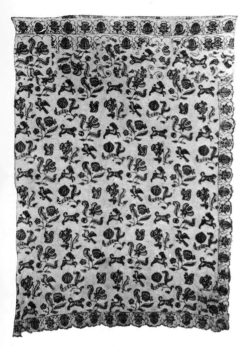

(A) Detail from late seventeenth-century American bed hangings embroidered in red wool. *Metropolitan Museum of Art, New York.*

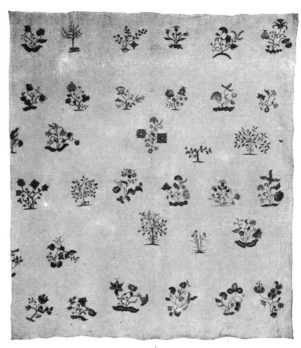

(B) Crewel-embroidered linen bedcover, probably mid-eighteenth century. *Old Deerfield.*

(C) Crewel in shades of blue; CER 1749 PTB worked in lower edge; by Catherine, wife of Peter Ten Broeck. *Ginsburg & Levy, New York.*

(D) Detail, crewel embroidered petticoat band. *Museum of Fine Arts, Boston.*

PLATE 225

Chintz appliqué American counterpane. Motifs from chintz and printed cottons with embroidered details, dated 1782. *Winterthur Museum, Delaware.*

PLATE 226

Friendship or album quilt. Pieced and appliquéd; Yonkers, dated 1847. *The New York Historical Society, New York.*

PLATE 227

Woven counterpane. Loop weave, all white cotton, probably by professional weaver, *c.* 1820. *Smithsonian Institution, Washington, D.C.*

PLATE 228

Photo: Frank Partridge.

(A) Needlework picture. Tent-stitch on canvas. English, early eighteenth century. *Collection of Mrs Geoffrey Hart.*

(B) Embroidered book-binding. English, about 1646. *Victoria and Albert Museum, London.*

(C) Tent-stitch panels. English, late sixteenth century. *Formerly in possession of Arditti & Majorcas.*

PLATE 229

(A) Crewel-work curtain. English, late seventeenth
century. *Arditti & Majorcas.*

(B) Crewel-work curtain and valance. English, late
seventeenth century. *Arditti & Majorcas.*

PLATE 230

Embroidered cover bearing the arms of Morosini of Venice. Silver-gilt thread and silk on linen; chain stitch and couched work. Italian, seventeenth century. *Victoria and Albert Museum, London.*

PLATE 231

Casket embroidered with stumpwork and petit point. English, dated 1668. In possession of C. Rover. Photo: Victoria and Albert Museum.

PLATE 232

(A) Chair back (unmounted) in Berlin wools, cross-stitch on canvas, *c.* 1850. *Victoria and Albert Museum, London.*

(B) Screen, with panel embroidered in cross-stitch in Berlin wools, *c.* 1840. *Victoria and Albert Museum, London.*

(C) Panel embroidered in Berlin wools in cross-stitch on white flannel ground, *c.* 1850. *Victoria and Albert Museum, London.*

PLATE 233

(A) Panel, silk, wool, and gold thread on serge. Designed by William Morris (1834–96) for his own home, Red House, 1860. *Collection of George Howard.* (B) "The Entrance": panel from a screen, embroidered in silk and gold thread. Designed and executed by Phoebe Traquair (1852–1936), signed PAT and dated 1895. *National Gallery of Scotland, Edinburgh.*

(C) Wall-hanging worked in shades of brown in crewel wools. Designed by Sir Edward Burne-Jones (1833–98) and William Morris (1834–96) for the Royal School of Art Needlework, *c.* 1875. *Victoria and Albert Museum, London.*

PLATE 234

(A) Coverlet in shades of blue and yellow silks on dark blue ground. Designed by William Morris and worked by Mrs Catherine Holiday, *c.* 1876. *Collection of Christian Stirling.*

(B) The Pigeon Portière: designed by J. H. Dearle (1860–1932) for Morris and Co., *c.* 1898, worked in floss silks on Morris "Oak silk damask" by Mrs Battye. *Collection of The Misses Battye.*

PLATE 235

(A) Screen with three panels, embroidered in floss silks, designed by May Morris (1862–1938) and executed in the Morris workshops under her direction, c. 1890. *Victoria and Albert Museum, London.*

(B) Screen panel, embroidered in silk and gold thread on satin. Worked by Miss E. D. Bradby (1861–1927) and dated 1899. The inscription is from Psalm xciv, verse 14. *Victoria and Albert Museum, London.*

PLATE 236

(B) Pictorial lace panel, needlepoint, comparable with contemporaneous raised embroidery, first half of the seventeenth century. *Victoria and Albert Museum, London.*

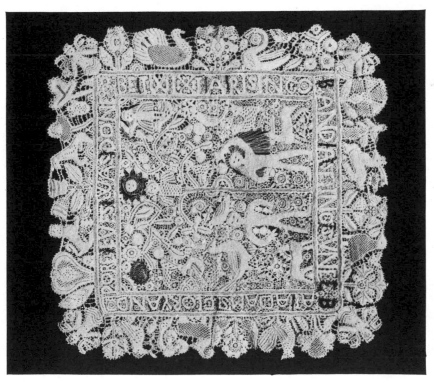

(A) Needlepoint lace fashioned into a pictorial panel – the temptation of Adam and Eve in the Garden of Eden, early seventeenth century. *Victoria and Albert Museum, London.*

PLATE 237

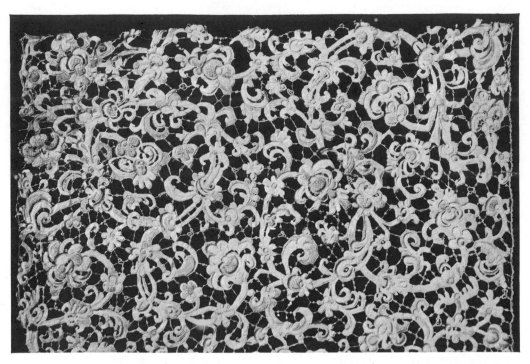

(A) Venetian rose point, an exquisite needlepoint, the conventional flowers and scrolls linked by *brides picotées*.

(B) Silk blonde pillow lace made at Caen, the pattern of a different silk from the ground, *c.* mid-nineteenth century. *Victoria and Albert Museum, London.*

PLATE 238

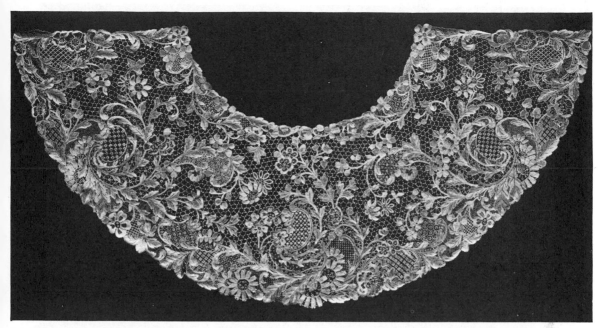

(A) Fan mount in Youghal lace, beautiful needlepoint, reproducing Venetian work, initiated in County Cork in the 1840s. This specimen dates to *c.* 1888. *Victoria and Albert Museum, London.*

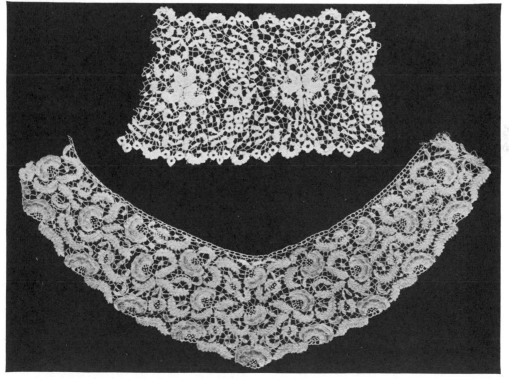

(B) Devonshire pillow lace, sometimes known as guipure as it lacks the meshed ground, *c.* middle of the nineteenth century. *Victoria and Albert Museum, London.*

PLATE 239

(A) English pillow lace: the upper example shows the pattern worked in with the meshed ground and associated with Honiton before the introduction of applied sprigs, the design being a crude version of the acorn and butterfly, found, for example, in old Brussels lace. *Victoria and Albert Museum, London.*

(B) *Top:* border of needlepoint incorporating motifs familiar in English Elizabethan embroideries, thought to be contemporaneous. *Below:* border of needlepoint in geometrical and formal flower pattern, early seventeenth century. *Victoria and Albert Museum, London.*

(C) Two borders of pillow lace, attributed to Honiton. *Victoria and Albert Museum, London.*

PLATE 240

A work, attributed to Ioni, the twentieth-century forger, in which various elements have been combined to give the impression of an early fifteenth-century triptych. Two obvious failures are the fact that the figures standing on either side of the Madonna are quite incongruous in a painting of this kind, and that a subject such as the Annunciation would never have been depicted on the wings of a triptych. *Courtauld Institute of Art, London.*

PLATE 241

(A) Autumn, *c.* 1767. Back painting of engraving after J. Williams by J. MacArdell. *John Beazor, Cambridge.* (B) Chinese mirror painting, *c.* 1780. 1 ft 11 ins × 2 ft 9 ins. *H. Blairman & Sons Ltd.*

(C) Partridge shooting by J. B. Walker. Back painting published 1801. *Hilton Gallery, Cambridge.*

PLATE 242

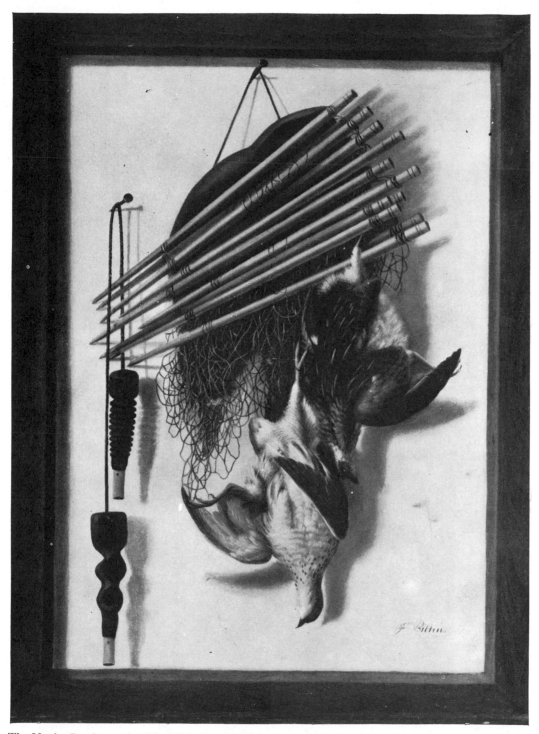

The Net by Jacob van der Bilt (Biltius), painted on canvas, 26⅜ × 18¾ ins, signed and dated: J. BILTIUS FECIT 1671. *William Hallsborough Gallery, London.*

PLATE 243

(B) George III in Windsor uniform by William Hamlet of Bath, *c.* 1800. Painted on the underside of the flat glass and backed with card. 8½ × 7 ins. *Collection of John Woodiwis.*

(A) Chamberlain Worcester vase with contemporary silhouette portrait of George III. Height 8½ ins. *R. M. Waylett.*

PLATE 244

VENUS DONNANT DU NECTAR A L'AMOUR.

Engraving after Boucher: French school, under broken glass, painted in oil on canvas, $12\frac{3}{8} \times 15\frac{1}{2}$ ins. *Collection of Martin Battersby.*

PLATE 245

(A) De Peyster Boy with Deer, 1720–30. Unknown New York artist. *New York Historical Society*.

(B) James Badger by Joseph Badger, 1760. *Metro-tan Museum of Art, New York*.

(C) Isaac Winslow by Robert Feke. *Museum of Fine Arts, Boston*.

(D) Mrs William Walton by John Wollaston. *York Historical Society*.

PLATE 246

(A) The Judith Round-up at Sage Creek by Charles M. Russell. *M. Knoedler & Co.*

(B) The Attack on the Supply Train by Frederic Remington.

PLATE 247

(A) Mrs John Melville (Deborah Scollay) by J. S. Copley. *Worcester Art Museum.*

(B) Mrs John Pintard (Elizabeth Brasher) by John Ramage. *New York Historical Society.*

(C) Mrs John Williamson (Elizabeth Ann Timothée) by Henry Benbridge. *Metropolitan Museum of Art, New York.*

(D) Miss Ross by James Peale. *Metropolitan Museum of Art, New York.*

(E) Mrs Charles Bulfinch (Hannah Apthorp) by Joseph Dunkerley. *Museum of Fine Arts, Boston.*

(F) Major-General Nathanael Greene by C. W. Peale. *Metropolitan Museum of Art, New York.*

PLATE 248

(A) Mrs James Lowndes (Catherine Osborn) by E. G. Malbone. *Metropolitan Museum of Art, New York.*

(B) Sarah Louisa Jenkins by R. Field. *Metropolitan Museum of Art, New York.*

(C) Benjamin Kintzing by Benjamin Trott. *Metropolitan Museum of Art, New York.*

(D) Edward Livingston by Anson Dickinson. *Metropolitan Museum of Art, New York.*

(E) Mrs Manigault Heyward (Susan Hayne Simmons) by Robert Fulton. *Metropolitan Museum of Art, New York.*

(F) Joel Roberts Poinsett by E. G. Malbone. *Metropolitan Museum of Art, New York.*

PLATE 249

(A) William Fuller. Engraved by A. B. Durand after C. C. Ingham, *c.* 1828. *Private Collection.*

(B) The Lower Lake, Central Park by J. M. Culverhouse, 1865. *Museum of the City of New York.*

(C) Croquet Scene by Winslow Homer (1836–1910). *Art Institute of Chicago.*

PLATE 250

(A) Striped Bass Fishing by A. F. Tait (1819–1905). *Collection of Harry T. Peters, Jr.*

(B) Max Schmitt in a Single-scull by Thomas Eakins (1844–1916). *Metropolitan Museum of Art, New York.*

PLATE 251

(A) Music and Literature by W. M. Harnett (1848–92). *Albright Art Gallery.*

(B) The Writing Master by Thomas Eakins (1844–1916). *Metropolitan Museum of Art, New York.*

PLATE 252

Winter Coast by Winslow Homer (1836–1910). *J. G. Johnson Collection, Philadelphia Museum of Art.*

PLATE 253

(A) Dr Smith, Mount Vernon, New Hampshire. Signed E. WOOLSON, PINXT., MAY 1842. *Old Sturbridge Village, Sturbridge, Massachusetts.*

(B) Mrs J. B. Sheldon, Unionville, Ohio. Artist unknown, *c.* 1825. *Garbisch Collection, National Gallery of Art, Washington, D.C.*

(C) Truman Holmes, Jr, New Orleans, Louisiana. Signed BAHIN, 1864. *Abby Aldrich Rockefeller Folk Art Collection, Williamsburg, Virginia.*

(D) Washington and Liberty. Artist unknown, *c.* 1810. *New York State Historical Association, Cooperstown, New York.*

PLATE 254

(A) Nathan Hawley and Family, Albany, New York. Dated November 3, 1801. Artist unknown. *Albany Institute of History and Art, Albany, New York.*

(B) Fishing with Waterfall. Artist unknown, *c.* 1845. *American Heritage Collection, Colby College, Waterville, Maine.*

PLATE 255

(A) Caernavon Castle by J. M. W. Turner. *Matthiesen Gallery*.

(B) Othello and Desdemona by Richard Bonington. *Leger Galleries*.

PLATE 256

of both design and execution. Elaborately embroidered quilts and pillow-cases, often made in sets, are especially characteristic. In the first half of the century embroidered aprons were extremely popular, and throughout the century embroidery was widely used to decorate waistcoats.

In France the general development of embroidery was similar to that in England, but there were certain marked differences in style and technique. For example, in the sixteenth century more use was made of applied work, and in the eighteenth century "chinoiserie" and "rococo" styles had a greater influence on embroidery than in England. Towards the end of the eighteenth century chenille embroidery and tambour work had a considerable vogue in France.

A great variety of embroidery was produced in Italy. In the sixteenth century embroidered linen bands (*see* Assisi work) and various kinds of cutwork are characteristic. Another type of embroidery was worked in floss silks on a net ground. Applied work reached a high standard in Italy, particularly for pilaster hangings. In the seventeenth century altar frontals, chalice veils, and vestments were produced in large numbers, usually with elaborate floral designs in silk and gold thread. The widespread use of laid work is also characteristic of Italian embroidery.

Spanish embroidery has much in common with Italian work, but the general tendency was to use brighter colours, and Moorish influences are often apparent. The use of painting on the satin to obtain effects of shading and a greater variety of colours is a feature of Spanish applied work. A type of embroidery produced both in Spain and Portugal during the sixteenth and seventeenth centuries was worked in closely twisted cord or string, which was usually brown or white. The cord was often plaited or knotted or woven in basketlike effects to give greater variety of texture. The designs were geometrical or floral.

The most notable German embroideries date from the fourteenth and fifteenth centuries. These are, of course, very rare and cannot readily be collected. They consist mainly of church furnishings and are executed in undyed linen thread on a linen ground. The subjects are mostly religious. Other embroideries in coloured silks imitated the well-known Cologne orphreys, which were woven in silk and gold thread.

Both the Near and Far East have produced a wealth of notable embroidery, and most of the main groups are dealt with under separate countries. There is, in fact, no country in the world where embroidery has not flourished at one time or another either as a simple peasant art or on a more sophisticated level. The field of embroidery and needlework is so vast that it has only been possible briefly to touch upon some of the main points. But even such a brief survey gives a hint of the amazing variety of work that can be collected.

Glossary

Algerian embroidery. The most characteristic feature is the colour scheme, which is in subdued mauves and purple. The motifs of palmettes, flowers, and scrolls recall the Turkish work of Asia Minor. Large hangings for the doorways opening on to the inner courtyard of the house were made in three long panels joined together by coloured silk ribbons. Similar patterns decorated towel-scarves, used by Algerian women to dry their hair, and hooded head-scarves. The finest embroideries date from the eighteenth or early nineteenth centuries. Satin, brick, and double-running stitches are most frequently

FIG. 1. Palmette

found, often with the addition of eyelet holes.

American patchwork. American patchwork quilts of the eighteenth and nineteenth centuries show an amazing variety of patterns of much greater elaboration than English examples. There are over three hundred named designs, many of them with a religious origin. One of the most striking and commonest traditional patterns is the "Star of Bethlehem", an eight-pointed star worked either as a single central motif surrounded by smaller stars or as a number of small stars of equal size regularly arranged on a white ground. Other quilts were made with applied coloured patches on white grounds elaborately quilted with geometrical, feather, or floral designs.

Applied work. The sewing of patches on to the surface of a material so that they form a pattern. The edges of the pattern are usually outlined by embroidery. In the Middle Ages applied work was used as a cheaper substitute for tapestry, and during the Renaissance the figured brocades and velvets were initated by this method. In the sixteenth and seventeenth centuries applied work was widely used for altar-frontals and vestments, for hangings, chair-covers, and horse-trappings. Outstanding were the pilaster hangings, usually of plain velvet with appliqué of satin outlined by couching, which were made in Italy and Spain. In England during the sixteenth and seventeenth centuries motifs of animals, floral sprigs, and insects were worked in tent stitch on canvas and then cut out and applied to cushion-covers and hangings. Needlepoint lace motifs, in silk and metal thread, were similarly applied to work-boxes and embroidered pictures.

FIG. 2. Detail of applied work

Aprons. Embroidered aprons were introduced in France as part of fashionable attire during the last quarter of the seventeenth century, and were popular in England during the first half of the eighteenth. The aprons are usually of cream or yellow silk with scalloped edges, embroidered in coloured silks and metal thread, chiefly with floral designs. Muslin and white-work aprons are also found.

Assisi work. A type of embroidery (so called from the modern embroidery made in Assisi) in which the ground is covered in long-armed cross-stitch, leaving the pattern reserved in plain linen. It is usually found in borders or strips, and the earliest examples date from the sixteenth century. The patterns include formal designs in typical Renaissance style, figure subjects, including hunting scenes, and stylized birds and animals. Red silk is most commonly used, but green and brown are also found. A similar type of embroidery comes from Azemmour in Morocco, but the designs are more geometric, often of birds, and somewhat bolder in style.

Bead-work. The earliest surviving English bead-work dates from the seventeenth century. Particularly interesting are the shallow baskets, almost tray-shaped, with a flat bottom and sloping sides, decorated entirely with small coloured glass beads sewn on linen canvas. Pictorial subjects, similar to those of the contemporary embroidered pictures, are most common. Caskets were also decorated in this manner, and some have miniature gardens inside the lid with free-standing flowers made of glass beads mounted on wire. Bead-work purses are also found during the seventeenth, eighteenth, and early nineteenth centuries. Bead-work was commonly used to decorate garters.

Bed valances. Valances or pelmets for four-poster beds are usually found in sets of three, the average length being about 6 ft 6 ins, the depth 1 ft 8 in. Elizabethan bed valances often depict religious or mythological subjects, worked in tent stitch on canvas. In the second half of the seventeenth century valances were embroidered in crewel wools to match the bed curtains.

Berlin wool-work. A type of embroidery in coloured worsteds on canvas in which designs printed on squared paper were copied by counting the squares of the canvas. The designs were published in Berlin and were first imported into England about 1810, but did not reach the country in large numbers until after 1830, the fashion reaching its height about the middle of the century. The first designs were often worked in silk or glass beads, but the garishly coloured worsteds imported from Berlin (which gave the work its name) became the general medium, and tent or cross stitch the usual method of execution. The designs were usually of flowers, depicted with great naturalism, but pictorial subjects, frequently Biblical, were also popular. Samplers on long strips of canvas showing various patterns worked in Berlin wools are also found.

Black-work. The name given to a type of Elizabethan embroidery worked in black silk on linen. It was used widely for both household articles and costume, particularly on long pillow-covers, bodices, coifs, and nightcaps. Gold thread is often found in conjunction with black-work, and coiling-stem designs were most frequently used. Elaborate diaper filling patterns, worked in back stitch, are a feature of this work, and the effect is often similar to the wood-block-printed lining papers of the period. Black-work is also found in Spain.

FIG. 3. Black-work diaper filling

FIG. 4. Bokhara floral motif

"Bokhara-work." The term generally applied to the bright-coloured embroideries of western Turkestan. Large floral sprays or a diapered ground filled with flowers are the most common patterns, and diagonally laid Oriental stitch and chain stitch are most frequently used. Large coverlets and divan covers are most common, and the finest specimens date from the eighteenth century, although nineteenth-century examples are more numerous.

Book bindings. Embroidered book bindings were produced in England and Europe as early as the sixteenth century, but most surviving examples date from the seventeenth. The finest examples are usually of French or English origin, but Dutch and Flemish bindings also reached a high standard, and elaborate examples were produced in Italy. Early seventeenth-century bindings in England were often of petit-point embroidery in coloured silks on a silver-thread ground. Later examples were usually on white satin embroidered in silks and gold thread and enriched with sequins and pearls. A common scheme of decoration was an oval portrait medallion surrounded by floral sprigs, birds, and insects, the spine divided into four or five compartments with a flower, insect, or animal in each. The books are set either with silver clasps, or single or double ties of ribbon of plaited silk. In England the fashion for embroidered bindings died out at the end of the seventeenth century, but in France it continued until about 1810.

Broderie anglaise. A type of white-work (known also as Ayrshire, Eyelet, Madeira, or Swiss-work) in which open spaces are cut or punched with a stiletto. The edges of the holes are then overcast. The finest specimens of this type of work, which was used chiefly for sleeve frills, baby clothes, and underwear, were produced in the late eighteenth or early nineteenth centuries.

Caskets. Embroidered caskets were more common in England during the seventeenth century than on the Continent, and were produced to hold toilet articles, jewels, writing materials, and as work-boxes. Stump-work, bead-work, and petit-point were most generally employed, and the subjects are similar to those of the embroidered pictures of the period. In France, Germany, Spain, and Italy embroidered caskets decorated with pearls are also found.

Chinese embroidery. Although embroidery has flourished in China for centuries, most of the existing specimens date from the eighteenth or nineteenth centuries. Embroidery plays an important part in Chinese costume. The most magnificent are the Imperial Court Robes of the Manchu Dynasty (1759–

1912). The Emperor's Dragon Robes were usually yellow with four front-facing dragons on the upper part and five profile dragons on the lower, and in addition the Twelve Symbols, five-coloured clouds, and the eight Buddhist symbols. Only the Emperor was allowed to wear all twelve symbols – the Sun, Constellation, Moon, Mountain, Dragon, Flowery Bird, Temple Cups Water Weed, Millet, Fire, Axe, and the Symbol of Distinction. The Heir Apparent had a similar robe but without the twelve symbols, and princes of the first to fourth degrees wore similar robes to the Heir Apparent. An interesting type of summer robe was embroidered on gauze in the Chinese equivalents of tent and Florentine stitches, which gave the effect of a woven fabric. In addition to the robes worn by the princes, the eighteen high-ranking officials of the Court had special insignia on their robes, usually known as Mandarin squares. The nine civil officials had birds on their squares and were designated, in descending order, by a white crane, golden pheasant, peacock, wild goose, silver pheasant, Eastern egret, Mandarin duck, quail, and Paradise fly-catcher. The nine military insignia were animals – a unicorn, leopard, panther, tiger, black bear, mottled bear, tiger cat, seal, and rhinoceros. Many other embroidered robes are found – the informal Court robes, theatrical and priest robes. Ladies' robes were often embroidered with butterflies, the emblems of happiness. It is not possible to go into the symbolism of many of the motifs found in Chinese embroidery, but the symbols most frequently found are the Buddhist "Eight Emblems of Happy Augury" and the Taoist "Attributes of the Eight Immortals". The former are the Parasol, the Fish of Gold, the Vase, the Lotus, the Sea Shell, the Mystic Diagram, the Standard, and the Wheel. The latter are the Fan, the Sword, the Gourd, the Castanets, the Flower Basket, the Bamboo Tube and Rods, the Flute, and the Lotus. The dragon and the phoenix, the mythical bird of China, are among the most popular decorative motifs. Flowers of all kinds are found, the commonest being the magnolia, prunus blossom, orchid, chrysanthemum, peony, narcissus, and lotus. A variety of stitches is found in Chinese embroidery, including French knots (often known as Peking stitch), satin stitch, and a special kind of couching, which consists of twisting two silk threads together, which gives the effect of a fine knobbly cord. Appliqué is also found, particularly on fan-cases, cushions, and purses. The separate motifs are sometimes worked on stiffened gauze or tough paper and then applied to the ground. Sleeve bands, long narrow strips of silk or satin about $3\frac{1}{2}$ inches wide, show a remarkable variety of pattern. Landscape scenes, figure subjects, and floral designs are embroidered in coloured silks or sometimes only in couched gold thread. Canton embroidery is remarkable for its naturalism and is worked in brightly coloured floss silks, mainly in satin and split stitches. A type of embroidery in black or dark blue silk or cotton on linen comes from Yunnan Province.

Coif. A close-fitting cap formed of one piece of embroidery seamed along the top of the head. These are often found unpicked or not made up, and are therefore difficult to recognize. The Elizabethan coifs were embroidered in coloured silks and metal thread, or in black silk, in patterns of coiling stems or less frequently with diaper patterns.

FIG. 5. Coif (not made up)

Colfichet. The name given to small embroidered pictures, originating in Italy in the late eighteenth century, worked in floss silks on paper so that each side was alike. They were used either as book-markers or placed between two sheets of glass.

Cretan embroidery. Most surviving Cretan embroidery is of the eighteenth century. Embroidered skirts are the most characteristic feature, the embroidery consisting of a deep frieze worked round the lower edge in brightly coloured floss silks. The patterns are a mixture of floral motifs, conventional vases of flowers, human figures, and animals. There is a combination of Italian and Turkish influences. The carnation is the most popular flower, and the siren, prevalent in the folklore and art of Italy, appears frequently. Originally, in the earliest Cretan embroideries, the siren had two fishlike tails which curled upwards and were grasped one in each hand, but with frequent copying the tails often became carnations, and the siren a human being with legs and feet. Covers and pillow-cases with similar designs are also found, sometimes with a pair of human figures in the centre surrounded by a floral border. A great variety of stitches, including Cretan feather, herring-bone, satin, stem and chain stitch were employed. The designs are mostly worked in many bright colours, but monochrome schemes, usually in red or dark blue, are also found.

FIG. 6. Siren motif in Cretan embroidery

FIG. 7. Crewel work: asparagus pattern

Crewel work. Crewel work is embroidery in thin worsteds, and is the term usually applied to the curtains and bed hangings of linen and cotton twill embroidered in coloured wools during the second half of the seventeenth century.* The design were based on the printed cotton "palampores" (chintz hangings) which were imported into England at that time. The "Tree of Life", with waving stems of acanthus-like foliage rising from a hillocked ground, was the most popular pattern. The embroidery was either polychrome or worked entirely in shades of green which

* This type of work is often called Jacobean embroidery.

has often faded to a dull indigo. Coiling stems and an asparagus pattern are also found.

Dutch East Indian embroidery. Embroidered coverlets were produced in the Dutch East Indies in the late seventeenth and early eighteenth centuries. The designs copied the painted chintzes of the period, and the embroidery, worked entirely in chain stitch in coloured silks, is so fine that at a first glance it appears like a printed cotton. Dresses and skirts made of similarly embroidered material are also found.

Embroidered pictures. A great variety of embroidered pictures is found in England from the mid-seventeenth century onwards. Pictorial compositions as part of the decoration of a cushion or valance are not uncommon earlier, but it was not until about 1940 that the fashion for working purely decorative pictures as an end in itself was evolved. Subjects from the Old Testament were most popular, also allegorical figures of the Virtues, Vices or the Senses, or a king and a queen. Stump-work was the most popular medium for pictures during the second half of the seventeenth century, but bead-work was also employed.

The pictures of the early eighteenth century are generally worked in tent stitch on canvas, and pastoral or "chinoiserie" subjects are most common. During the second half of the eighteenth century subjects were mostly taken from popular paintings or engravings. The designs were either printed or drawn on the material. Portions of the background and the faces and hands of the figures were painted in water-colours and the rest of the design worked in coloured silks. Other pictures were worked in black silk, or even hair, in fine stitches, to simulate etchings. Simple landscape subjects or portraits of eminent people are most common.

During the third quarter of the eighteenth century copies of oil-paintings in coloured wools were made by industrious needlewomen, the most famous being Miss Linwood. The introduction of Berlin woolwork gave rise to embroidered pictures on squared canvas, and by about 1830 these had virtually eclipsed all other types.

Greek Islands embroidery. *See also* Cretan embroidery.

The embroidery of the Greek Islands may be classed as peasant embroidery inasmuch as it was made by the women for their own use and not intended for sale. Although each island, or group of islands, had its own individual characteristic patterns, inter-marriage brought a pattern from one island to another, and varieties of the same pattern are found in different places. Most existing specimens date from the eighteenth or early nineteenth centuries. The group can best be subdivided as follows.

IONIAN ISLANDS. This group consists mainly of bedspreads, bolsters, and pillow-cases worked in fine cross stitch and drawn work. The designs consist of stylized birds, particularly peacocks, and deer, together with floral and purely decorative motifs. Red, blue, green, and yellow are the dominant colours, and the designs show a marked Italian influence. Another group of bed-furnishings are worked in fine split and darning stitches, with rich floral patterns intermingled with human figures, double eagles, parrots, cocks, and sometimes ships. These show a Turkish influence, and are somewhat similar to the work produced at Skyros (*see below*).

FIG. 8. "Queen Pattern" (*Cyclades*)   FIG. 9. "King Pattern" (*Cyclades*)

EPIRUS. The embroideries produced in the Epirus, particularly at Yannina, the principal town, are characterized by floral motifs, mostly variations of the Turkish rose spray, worked mainly in herring-bone stitch.

THE CYCLADES. Most characteristic are the bed-curtains, valances, and pillow-cases. The main patterns are variations of two basic motifs known as the "Queen Pattern" and "King Pattern". These patterns are common throughout the Cyclades, but certain islands have distinctive features. Melos is characterized by the use of the Queen Pattern, worked entirely in red silk, while at Amorgos the King Pattern is dominant. Naxos is charac-

FIG. 10. The Glastra (*Dodecanese*)   FIG. 11. Skyros figure (*N. Greek Islands*)

terized by the use of a leaf-and-star diaper, derived from the King Pattern, worked chiefly in red silk.

DODECANESE. The embroidery of Rhodes, the chief island, is worked in thick red and green floss silks in cross stitch. The stitch is not pulled tight on the right side of the work, which gives the embroidery a slightly raised appearance. Embroidered bed-tents are the main feature of Kos, where the chief motif is the Glastra, combined with Maltese crosses and stars. The Glastra is also found at Rhodes. Patmos employs a version of the Cycladic King pattern.

NORTH GREEK ISLANDS (The Northern Sporades). The best-known embroidery of this group comes from Skyros. Bedspreads and pillow-cases are embroidered with lively designs of human figures, animals and birds, particularly cocks and peacocks, and floral motifs. The designs have a distinct Oriental flavour and recall the patterns of later Turkish faïence.

Hollie-work. A type of white-work embroidery popular during the Georgian period, particularly for babies' clothes and bonnets. It was worked on fine linen lawn or cambric in white thread. Delicate openwork patterns, worked without any foundation in the manner of needlepoint lace, were inserted into holes cut in the material, which were previously edged with buttonhole stitch. Alternatively, the threads of the ground material were drawn out one way only and the pattern worked on the remaining threads.

Indian embroidery. The finest existing Indian embroideries date from the Mughal period, and show a marked Persian influence, but the drawing and colouring of the floral motifs is usually bolder. The group comprises articles of costume, prayer-mats, and wall-hangings. In the late seventeenth and early eighteenth centuries embroidered coverlets and hangings were produced for export in large numbers. The flowering-tree motif was the most popular, but many of the designs were adapted to suit European tastes and were worked from patterns sent out by the English. French, and Dutch trading companies. Quilted bedspreads, with designs showing strong Persian influence, were also made. In the early nineteenth century elaborately embroidered shawls were made in Kashmir in imitation of the more costly hand-woven variety. Most other types of Indian embroidery fall into the category of peasant art, being indigenous to local regions. A common feature of Sind, Cutch, and Kathiawar embroidery is the use of small circular insets of mirror glass. The Cutch embroideries are worked mainly in chain stitch with a needle like a crochet-hook, and an interlaced stitch is also used. Articles of costume, trappings for cattle, and wall-hangings are decorated with sprigged patterns and floral diapers, and a peacock motif is often incorporated into the design of skirt borders. The "toran", a kind of pelmet with a series of tabs at the lower edge, is characteristic of Kathiawar, and a special feature is the almost universal habit of leaving a small corner of the work unfinished. A specialized type of work comes from Chamba. Elaborate pictorial designs, derived from the contemporary schools of hill-painting, were embroidered on fine muslin in satin stitch in bright-coloured silks. A kind of whitework, known as Chikan, comes mainly from Uttar Pradesh in the Ganges Valley. Floral motifs, and patterns representing grains such as rice and millet, are worked on muslin in white cotton.

Jacobean embroidery. *See* Crewel-work.

Japanese embroidery. The art of embroidery was practised in Japan from the sixth century onwards, and reached a high standard of excellence, but most surviving examples must be assigned to the nineteenth century. The finest embroidery was used on the "kimono", the loose, wide-sleeved robe worn by both sexes; the "obi", the broad sash worn round the waist; and the "fukasa", the embroidered squares which covered the lacquered boxes in which ceremonial presents were offered. The most characteristic stitches are satin, long and short (used particularly for realistic feather effects), couching, and knotted-stitch (French knots). Appliqué is also used, and gold thread, consisting of strips of gilt paper twisted round a cotton or silk core, is used in conjunction with coloured silks or on its own. Painting is also combined with embroidery, and some materials are printed with a resist, or tie-dyed before being embroidered. Cranes, landscape, and floral subjects, particularly the chrysanthemum, are popular designs.

Long pillow-covers. Long pillow-covers, or "pillow beres", to give them their contemporary name, unlike the cushion-covers, were always worked on linen and were used in the bedroom. The most usual size for Elizabethan examples was about 35 by 20 inches, and the back of the cover, which was left plain, has rarely survived. All-over patterns of the coiling-stem type were most popular, and "blackwork" was frequently employed. In the late seventeenth and early eighteenth centuries pillow-covers embroidered entirely in yellow silk are often found; also examples quilted in white linen thread or cotton.

Moroccan embroidery. In the eighteenth and nineteenth centuries practically every city in Morocco had its own characteristic type of embroidery. From Rabat come bolster- and pillow-cases embroidered in floss silks, mostly dark blue, purple, and yellow. The designs are of highly conventionalized flowers very solidly worked in herring-bone, satin, and buttonhole stitches. The Tetuan embroideries, usually curtains, are worked in patterns which recall the Artichoke or Pomegranate motifs of Asia Minor. As in Algiers, mauve is the dominant colour. The embroideries of Fez, Meknez, and Sale have certain common features. The embroideries are reversible and are worked in double and quadruple running stitch, cross stitch, and basket stitch. The designs are geometrical, and are worked by counting the threads of the material. The group comprises mainly pillow- and bolster-cases and samplers. Another group, worked in long-armed cross and back stitches, comes from Azemmour, and the designs show a marked similarity to the Italian and Spanish embroidered borders of the sixteenth century. The work of Chechaoen shows a marked Hispano-Moresque influence, and tile-like geometric patterns are worked on divan covers in stem, herring-bone, and cross stitches.

Opus Anglicanum. The name given to English ecclesiastical embroidery of the thirteenth and fourteenth centuries. The art of embroidery had flourished in England from Saxon times, but it reached its highest peak of excellence in the thirteenth century, and was known all over Europe as "opus anglicanum". The figures and other details are mostly worked in fine split-stitch with backgrounds of couched-work. A great deal of "opus anglicanum" was exported to the Continent, where some of it still remains. Towards the middle of the fourteenth century the standard of both design and execution began to decline.

Patchwork quilts. *See also* American patchwork and Resht-work.

In England patchwork quilts did not originate until the eighteenth century, and most surviving examples date from the end of the eighteenth or the early nineteenth centuries. Most patchwork patterns were geometrical or formal, such as the "Honeycomb", which was composed entirely of hexagons, and was the most popular design. Other patterns, such as the "Shell" and various "Feather" patterns, were taken from traditional quilting designs. True patchwork consists of a mosaic of fragments of materials sewn edge to edge, but some so-called "patchwork" quilts are, in fact, applied work, as, for example, are those quilts where floral motifs are cut out from chintzes and applied to the ground of the quilt.

Persian embroidery. *See also* Resht- and Bokhara-work.

No Persian embroidery of a date earlier than the sixteenth century has survived, and most existing specimens date from the seventeenth to the nineteenth centuries. The embroideries may be divided into three main classes: (1) Covers from north-west Persia embroidered in coloured silks, mainly in double-darning-stitch on cotton. The embroidery covers the whole ground, and the patterns of hooked and angular arabesques and medallions recall the designs of Caucasian rugs. Other covers, worked in the same technique, have patterns of figures, animals, and flowers of similar design to the contemporary "hunting" carpets, brocades, and tile-work. (2) Nakshe (women's trousering). These rectangular panels are of cotton, embroidered in coloured silks in diagonal parallel bands of floral patterns. Woven Nakshe are also found, and the embroidered type followed the designs of the more expensive brocade. (3) Prayer-mats and bath-mats worked in coloured silks, with crimson and green predominating, on a white ground, which is usually quilted. The patterns are floral, and a common design is a central medallion surrounded by a network of flowering plants, the whole enclosed in a running floral border.

Pin-cushions. Rectangular embroidered pin-cushions, about 10 by 6 inches, were popular in England from about 1600 to 1700. They were mostly of linen, embroidered in silk and metal thread in tent stitch or in silk in rococo stitch, with designs of floral sprigs. Those which are studded with pins on the reverse side, arranged in a pattern and often with the date, were probably used as christening presents. Smaller pin-cushions are often found in the work-boxes of the period.

Purses. English embroidered purses of the sixteenth and seventeenth centuries are usually flat and about 5 inches square, fastened by a double draw-string at the top. The ground is canvas, usually embroidered in tent or cross stitches in coloured silks and metal thread. Coiling tendrils with typical English flowers are the commonest patterns. Embroidered leather purses of this date are much rarer. Bead-work purses are also found in the seventeenth century. Mottoes are common on French purses, but are rare on English examples. In the eighteenth century purses became more commonplace, and with the introduction of the knitted or crocheted stocking purse embroidered purses died out.

Quilts. *See also* Patchwork.

A quilt is a coverlet with a layer of wool, flock, or down between two pieces of material with lines of stitching, usually back stitch passing through the three layers. In England quilting is a traditional craft, and it reached the height of popularity and excellence in the seventeenth and eighteenth centuries. During the first half of the seventeenth century quilted doublets and breeches were worn, and during the eighteenth century quilted satin petticoats were fashionable. Quilted bed coverlets were made in great numbers from the late seventeenth century onwards. In addition to the pattern formed by

FIG. 12. Corded quilting   FIG. 13. Detail of Resht patchwork

the quilting stitch, which was sometimes purely geometrical, sometimes of elaborate floral arabesques, the quilts were often further ornamented by embroidery in coloured silks. In the late seventeenth and early eighteenth centuries coverlets and pillow-cases were often quilted entirely in yellow silk. Others had a small quilted diaper background with floral

or "chinoiserie" motifs embroidered in coloured silks.

Another type is "corded" quilting (often known as Italian quilting, although there is no evidence to support an Italian origin). This type of quilting, employed for decorative rather than utilitarian purposes, was extremely popular in England during the eighteenth century. Two layers of material, usually fine white linen, were sewn together in an elaborate design, often of scrolling arabesques worked by means of two parallel rows of stitching about a quarter of an inch apart. A cord was then inserted between the two rows of stitching through small holes cut in the back of the material. Quilting was also practised in most European countries, notably Sicily and Portugal, and in Oriental countries, particularly India and Persia.

"Resht-work." A type of mosaic patchwork produced at Resht, Persia, during the eighteenth and nineteenth centuries for covers and prayer-rugs. The designs are inlaid in coloured felts with outlines and details worked in coloured silks in chain stitch and couched work. Inferior examples are often not true patchwork, as the small pieces are applied to the ground and not inlaid. A similar type of work was produced in Ispahan.

Ribbon-work. Embroidery in fine, narrow silk ribbons often combined with chenille thread and aerophane, a kind of muslin gauze. This type of work originated in the third quarter of the eighteenth century and was popular in both England and France, particularly for dress trimmings, bags, handscreens, and other small articles.

Sampler. An embroidered panel originally intended as a reference sheet of stitches and patterns and later as an exercise for a beginner.

ENGLISH SAMPLERS. The earliest surviving English samplers date from the first half of the seventeenth century. These are worked on loosely woven linen in coloured silks and metal thread, and are generally shorter than those of the second half of the century. Tent, rococo, and plaited-braid stitches are common on these samplers, and the patterns are arranged in a haphazard way. Animals, birds, and floral motifs, similar to those found in contemporary bestiaries and herbals, are mixed with geometrical designs.

In the second half of the seventeenth century the samplers are long and narrow on a finer linen, with the patterns formally arranged in horizontal rows. They are worked mainly in pale-coloured silks, chiefly in double-running, cross, and satin stitches with floral and geometrical borders showing a marked Italian influence. Another common type is the white-work sampler of cut and open-work with designs taken from Italian "reticella" (a kind of needlepoint lace).

FIG. 14. "Reticella" motif

Many late-seventeenth-century samplers are a mixture of these two types.

By the eighteenth century the sampler had become a child's exercise. They are generally squarer in shape and are usually signed and dated. The introduction of the alphabet, religious texts, and mottoes or verses is common, and the colours are generally brighter. A more specialized type is the *Darning Sampler*, which was introduced into England from Holland about the middle of the century. These samplers are worked in darning stitches in ornamental patterns in coloured silks, mostly in squares, but sometimes in floral motifs. Another popular type from about 1770 until 1840 was the *Map Sampler*, that is an embroidered map worked in outline, usually in stem stitch in black silk, sometimes enclosed in a floral border.

GERMAN SAMPLERS. Samplers worked in horizontal bands, similar to English examples but often coarser in execution, are found in the latter half of the seventeenth century. Many of the designs, even in eighteenth- and nineteenth-century samplers, are taken from the pattern books of Hans Sibmacher, of Nuremberg, which were published in 1591 and 1604. An interesting variety with elaborate motifs worked in fine cross stitch in black

cotton was produced in the Vierlande, near Hamburg, during the first half of the nineteenth century. The motifs included conventional flowers in pots and geometrical devices packed closely all over the sampler.

DUTCH SAMPLERS. Most of the surviving samplers are of the eighteenth century, and are generally broad and square. Cross stitch is most frequently used, and the motifs, which are detached, include human figures, animals, buildings, and elaborate alphabets.

SPANISH SAMPLERS. Seventeenth- and eighteenth-century Spanish samplers are usually large, either square or rectangular and worked in a series of conventional floral or geometrical borders. In the square samplers the borders are worked round all four sides and the centre is filled with sacred emblems, the Hapsburg eagle or a monogram. In the rectangular samplers the borders are worked in horizontal rows. Drawn-work bands are often included both in white-work and in coloured silks. Vivid colours are characteristic of Spanish samplers, but in many cases the silks have faded to pastel colours. Samplers similar to the English cross-stitch variety of the nineteenth century are also found in Spain.

MEXICAN SAMPLERS. These show similar designs to the Spanish, but they are generally smaller, and dated examples are usually of the nineteenth century. White-work samplers, with flowers, animals, and initials, are also found in Mexico.

MOROCCAN SAMPLERS. *See* Moroccan embroidery.

Stomacher. The breast-piece of fifteenth- to eighteenth-century European female dress which was usually embroidered or jewelled. In some cases the stomacher formed part of the corset, when laced at the back, but when the corset was laced at the front the stomacher was made as a separate piece and pinned over the corset lacing. Few stomachers earlier than the eighteenth century have survived. The basic V-shape of the stomacher, tapering to a point at the bottom, varied with successive changes in fashion until it died out with the introduction of the Empire style of dress. Continental examples are often elaborately shaped at the lower end, and French examples are usually more ornate than those of English origin.

Stump work (or Raised work). Raised embroidery, in which portions of the design were padded to give a three-dimensional effect, was widely used in England from about 1625 to the end of the century to decorate caskets, mirror-frames, and book-bindings, and for embroidered pictures. The type of work originated from the raised ecclesiastical embroideries of the fifteenth and sixteenth centuries in Italy and Germany, and was used earlier for church work in England. Scenes from the Old Testament, the Judgment of Paris, and other mythological subjects, or representations of a king and a queen were most popular. The interspaces of the designs were filled with quaint beasts, birds, and sprigs of flowers.

Tambour work. A form of chain stitch, worked with a steel hook, popular in England and France during the late eighteenth and early nineteenth centuries. The name originated from the way the fabric to be embroidered was stretched over a round frame in the manner of a drum-skin.

Turkey work. This type of work, in knotted wool on linen, though strictly speaking carpet-knotting, is usually classified as embroidery. It was popular in England during the seventeenth century, chiefly for chair-backs and seats and loose cushions. The designs are usually of floral sprigs somewhat geometrically treated. Turkey work was dealt with in detail by R. W. Symonds in *The Connoisseur*, April 1934.

Turkish embroidery. Turkish embroidery may be divided into two main classes. The older type comprises curtains worked in darning stitch or couched-work. The patterns

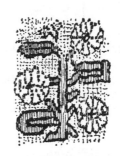 

FIG. 15. Turkey work: floral spray   FIG. 16. Turkish rose spray

consist of repeating designs of an ogival type with pomegranate or artichoke motifs, or vertical waving stems bearing conventionalized leaves and flowers. Red and blue are the predominant colours, and the darning stitches are usually worked diagonally to imitate the twill weave of the more costly silks. The second group consists of towels, kerchiefs, sashes, and bedspreads worked in coloured silks, gold and silver-gilt thread. The towel borders show an amazing variety of patterns, including the rose spray, vases of flowers, and various designs of mosques and cypresses. The earlier embroideries were worked mainly in double running stitch, but by the early nineteenth century other stitches were also used.

VICTORIAN EMBROIDERY

BERLIN WOOL-WORK

In the field of embroidery the first thirty years of the Victorian era were dominated by the fashion for Berlin wool-work, which virtually ousted all other types of decorative needlework. The vogue was indeed so widespread that Mrs Henry Owen opens her preface to the *Illuminated Book of Needlework* (1847) with the words "Embroidery, or as it is more often called Berlin wool-work . . .".

The designs used for the work were hand-coloured on squared paper and were copied stitch by stitch on to square-meshed canvas, each square of the design representing one stitch of embroidery. Its immense popularity no doubt lies in the fact that it required almost no skill in execution other than that of threading the needle and an ability to count. The first Berlin patterns were published in 1804; and although a few patterns reached England almost immediately, their use did not become widespread until 1831. In that year a Mr Wilks of Regent Street, London, began importing both the designs and the wools for working them direct from Berlin, including many designs which were prepared specially for the English market. According to the Countess of Wilton (*The Art of Needlework*, 1840), no fewer than 14,000 different patterns had been published in Berlin between 1804 and 1840.

Before Mr Wilks began importing the wools, which were manufactured in Gotha and dyed in Berlin, the patterns had been worked mainly in silks, but by 1840 the use of wool had become general.

Floral themes formed a high proportion of the patterns, particularly of those intended for upholstery. In the early 1840s wreaths and bunches of flowers were set against a light background. But by 1850 black backgrounds were more common and served to emphasize the harsh, brilliant colours of the wools (Plate 233A). Oversize blooms – cabbage roses, huge bell-like flowers, arum and Victoria lilies – were drawn with great naturalism. The height of achievement was when, by means of elaborate shading, the flowers appeared to stand out in relief from the background. In most surviving examples, the full brilliance is now lost through fading, as the dyes used were fugitive.

Exotic birds, particularly gaily coloured parrots and macaws, were often introduced into the designs. A favourite combination, used for screen panels, was a life-size parrot, together with an ornate vase of mixed flowers drawn with the detail of a Dutch flower-painting, and a basket of luscious fruit. The screen on Plate 233B, formerly in the possession of Queen Mary and now in the Victoria and Albert Museum, is a good example of this type of design.

When used for upholstery there was little attempt to relate the design of the Berlin wool-work to the style of the furniture. In a few cases gothic ornamental detail was introduced to harmonize with a "Gothic" chair, but, generally speaking, furniture in the prevailing styles of "Louis Quatorze", "Elizabethan", or "Francois Ier", to mention only three, were adorned with the same type of

naturalistic floral pattern. For upholstery the whole of the canvas was usually covered with stitchery, but many chairs, as well as screens, pictures, and piano-fronts are found in which the Berlin wool-work appears to have been worked direct on a plain woollen ground (Plate 233C). This effect was in fact achieved by tacking the canvas to a piece of plain material and taking the embroidery stitches through both canvas and material. When the design had been worked, by the usual method of counting the squares, the threads of the loosely woven canvas were withdrawn one by one, leaving the design on the plain material.

Although floral themes were most general for upholstery, engravings of popular contemporary paintings were widely used as subjects for the Berlin patterns and were used for embroidered pictures or fire-screens. Landseer's paintings, particularly such subjects as *Dignity and Impudence* (1840) or the *Monarch of the Glen* (1851), made impressive wool pictures, but more modest subjects, of a single pet dog or cat reposing on a tasselled cushion (Plate 233C), were even more popular. Many versions have survived, either as framed pictures or on the tops of footstools. Biblical subjects, particularly from the Old Testament, or famous historical paintings and romantic landscapes were among the most favoured designs. The Royal Family also received considerable attention from the Berlin pattern-makers. The Prince of Wales (later King Edward VII) appeared in various guises. A panel, originally in the possession of Queen Mary, shows him in Highland dress, and the same picture was used for a printed cotton in 1847. Mrs Merryfield, an early critic of Berlin wool-work, writing in the *Art Journal* of 1855, deplores the use of "the young Prince of Wales as a sailor depicted on a footstool so that on the stool he was lying on his back . . . and subjected to the indignity of being trodden underfoot. In the good old days," she continues, "the greatest honour held forth to a conqueror was that he should set his foot upon the necks of princes . . . and his enemies should be his footstool . . al-though we may acquit the English ladies of such disloyal thoughts and intentions."

Berlin wool-work was mostly worked in

cross or tent stitch, but other types of canvas stitches were employed, particularly after 1850. One of the most popular, known at the time as "Leviathan" or "railway stitch", because it covered the ground so quickly, was in fact no more than a double cross stitch worked on four squares of the canvas instead of one. A stitch known as "perspective stitch" consisted of straight stitches of graduating lengths worked in different colours to form cubes, which appeared to project from the canvas (Fig. 17).

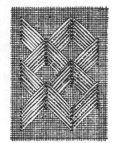

FIG. 17

A popular variation, which combined the use of beads, silk, and chenille with the Berlin wools, was known as German embroidery. Raised Berlin wool-work, introduced in the 1840s, was another common variant. Parts of the design, either individual flowers, a bird, animal, or other details, were worked in plush stitch in a series of loops which were afterwards cut to give the effect of a thick pile carpet. A large picture of *Joseph presenting his Father to Pharaoh* (in the Victoria and Albert Museum) has the collars of the robes worked in this way to imitate thick fur.

The fashion for Berlin wool-work persisted well into the 1870s, but by the 1860s the critics and reformers had at least brought about a change in the type of patterns and in the colouring. Geometric designs, ornamental scrolls, and formalized acanthus and vine leaves, with only a flower here and there, replaced the sprawling, naturalistic blooms. The colours were more subdued, with shades of brown and softer greens predominating. Some details of the design were often worked in beads or silk. For small articles, such as tea-cosies or hand-screens, the flowers were often worked entirely in beads on a wool background. Whereas with the wool flowers the colours were naturalistic, the bead flowers were often worked in white, crystal, and grey beads only. A panel commemorating the death of Prince Albert, worked in the early 1860s, is typical of this type of work.

From the 1860s onwards, Berlin wool-work was less generally used for upholstery, except for small footstools or music-stools, or for loose cushions for chairs and sofas. The printed patterns were also put to other uses. In the 1860s there was a brief fashion for antimacassars, made of coarse net, darned in colours from the Berlin patterns.

Revival of embroidery

Although Berlin wool-work was not finally ousted until after 1875, even in the 1840s critics were protesting at its deadening effect in debasing the art of embroidery. The earliest attacks came from ecclesiastical quarters. In the 1840s both the Anglican and Roman Catholic churches took a particular interest in embroidery. Many new churches were being built which needed altar-furnishings and vestments. In the Catholic church the main instigator of the revival of church embroidery, based on medieval models, was A. W. N Pugin (1812–52), the leading Gothic revivalist of the nineteenth century. In the Church of England the Oxford Movement played an important part in the revival, and the most prominent individual was the architect G. E. Street (1824–81), who, together with his sister and his friends the Blencowes, founded the Ladies Ecclesiastical Embroidery Society with the aim of producing church needlework of a high standard. By the 1850s there was a manifest improvement in the standard of ecclesiastical embroidery, but, although by this time the art periodicals had joined in the campaign against Berlin wool-work, there was little sign of a comparable advance on the domestic front. It was not until the 1870s, largely through the influence of William Morris (1834–96), that secular embroidery showed the same improvement.

"Morris" embroideries

William Morris' first experiments in embroidery were made in 1855 when he was working in G. E. Street's office. He had an embroidery frame made and worsteds dyed to his specification and set about the task with his own hands. This experimental piece, a repeating pattern of flowering trees and birds with a scroll above bearing the words "If I can" now hangs at Kelmscott Manor,

Oxfordshire. Morris' wife, in a note (British Museum Add. MSS 45341) to Mackail, his first biographer, tells how he initiated her into the art soon after their marriage in 1859: "He taught me the first principles of laying the stitches together closely so as to cover the ground smoothly and radiating them properly. Afterwards we studied old pieces and by unpicking etc. we learnt much." Their first joint efforts consisted of a series of embroidered decorations for Red House, built for them by Philip Webb. The bedroom walls were hung with indigo-dyed serge, with flowers designed by Morris simply worked in crewel wools. For the dining-room a more elaborate scheme of figure embroideries, designed to imitate tapestry, was attempted. This scheme consisted of twelve female figures, based on Chaucer's *Illustrious Women*, with trees between them and a running band of flowers at their feet, united by a background of coiling floral stems on a blue-serge ground. Only seven of the figures were completed, three of which survive made up into a screen for Lady Carlisle after they were removed from Red House (Plate 234A). The figures were worked separately on a coarse linen mainly in crewel wools, but with some silk and gold thread, and cut out and applied to the woollen ground. Two unfinished panels, one of a nude female figure and one of a tree, are now in the possession of Mr Halcrow Verstage. Two of the original designs are in the Victoria and Albert Museum: and were it not for the fact that the corresponding finished panel for one of them survives, it might well be thought that they were cartoons for stained glass rather than embroidery.

The embroideries exhibited by the newly established Morris firm at the 1862 International Exhibition were of the same medieval inspiration and were described by the *Ecclesiologist* as "some most antique looking tapestry hangings". It seems clear that most of the early Morris embroideries were intended primarily as a substitute for tapestry, and they were even described as such by the American novelist Henry James when he visited the Morris workshops in Queen Square in 1869. One of the most ambitious was an embroidered frieze, designed by Morris and Burne-Jones for the huge dining-room of Rounton Grange, Northallerton, in 1872. This embroidery now hangs at the William Morris Gallery, Walthamstow. Apart from this frieze and the Red House panels, little of Morris' early embroidery work has survived, and his influence and achievements in the field of embroidery have too often been assessed by the embroideries produced by the firm after about 1875, many of which were not designed by Morris himself.

The characteristic "Morris" embroideries, worked chiefly in darning stitches in floss silks, do not appear until the late 1870s: and most of the surviving examples, in fact, belong to the 1880s or even later. It was the work of Catherine Holiday, wife of Henry Holiday the stained-glass and mosaic designer, which probably first inspired Morris to produce designs for portières, coverlets, and cushions to be sold by the firm. She was a skilled embroideress, and Morris was so impressed by her work that he commissioned a vast quantity of work from her. The letters between Morris and Mrs Holiday, published by Philip Henderson in his *Letters of William Morris to his Family and Friends*, provide a fascinating picture of the close co-operation between designer and executant. Morris was so satisfied with Mrs Holiday's work that he entrusted the technique and colouring to her, and had the silks specially dyed to her specifications by Thomas Wardle at Leek. The coverlet illustrated in Plate 235A was almost certainly worked by Mrs Holiday. Several other examples of her work survive in the possession of her family, and this coverlet shows the same characteristically fine stitchery and delicate colouring. The effect of Morris' embroidery designs depended very much on the skill of the executant and in the choice of materials. For example, the Victoria and Albert Museum possesses two versions of a coverlet designed by Morris in 1880. One is worked in crewel wools, with elaborate shading in the manner of seventeenth-century crewel work: the other is worked in silk almost in outline, and the effect is so different that it is hard to realize that they were both worked from the same design. Since the Morris firm sold not only finished work, executed in their own workshops, but also ready-traced goods and patterns to be worked by the customers themselves, different versions of the same design are often found. The embroideries worked by Morris' daughter May and her assistants, after she took charge of this section about 1880, have, however, a uniform appearance, being worked in floss silks chiefly in darning stitches.

Until about 1880 all the embroidery designs were from Morris' own hand. But thereafter, although Morris' designs continued to be worked, most of the new designs were from the hand of May Morris, or J. H. Dearle. It is not difficult to distinguish May Morris' designs from those of her father. They are stiffer and less flowing, with a broader, simpler treatment. The screen shown in Plate 236A is typical of her work. It is more difficult to distinguish the work of J. H. Dearle from that of Morris himself. Dearle joined the Morris firm as an apprentice at the age of eighteen in 1878 and became Morris' chief assistant. He absorbed Morris' personal style so thoroughly that it is often almost impossible, in the absence of documentary evidence, to tell a design of his from one of his master. The Pigeon (Plate 235B) Portière, designed by Dearle soon after Morris' death, is almost indistinguishable from a design by Morris, and shows the same characteristic treatment of the swirling acanthus leaves that typify so many of Morris' own designs.

The Royal School of Art Needlework

The interest aroused in embroidery by William Morris led to the foundation of several organizations for the promotion of the Art. The first, and the most important, was the Royal School of Art Needlework founded in 1872 under the Presidency of H.R.H. the Princess Christian of Schleswig-Holstein with the twofold aim, according to the prospectus, "of restoring Ornamental Needlework, for secular purposes, to the high place it once held among decorative arts, and to supply suitable employment for poor gentlewomen". The organizing committee of distinguished ladies, most of whom were themselves skilled embroideresses (including Lady Marian Alford, author of *Needlework as Art*, 1886), had

by 1875 assembled a staff of over 100 workers who executed finished work and also undertook the repair of historic embroidery. Designs were commissioned from leading architects and designers of the day, including William Morris, Sir Edward Burne-Jones (Plate 234c), Water Crane, Selwyn Image, G. F. Bodley, and Alexander Fisher. Designs adapted from historic embroideries were also prepared by the staff.

Permanent exhibitions of the work of the School were held in the premises at Exhibition Road, South Kensington. An impressive exhibit, including a series of wall-hangings designed by Walter Crane and a number of works designed by William Morris, was sent by the School to the Philadelphia Centennial Exhibition of 1876. One of the Morris pieces, a large portière with peacocks and vines, is now in a collection at Cincinnati. The most important surviving group of embroideries by the school, however, are those made in the 1880s for 93, Park Lane, the house now occupied by Alfred Pemberton & Sons, the advertising agents. The decorations consisted of an exact copy of the Pomona tapestry (woven at Merton Abbey in 1885), worked entirely in floss silks which cover the whole ground of the fabric. The figure of "Pomona" was designed by Burne-Jones, and the background and inscription by William Morris. On the staircase are a series of figure panels designed by Burne-Jones to follow the curve of the stairs, and in the entrance hall a large panel entitled Music, also designed by Burne-Jones.

Among upwards of fifteen other organizations of varying size designed to promote the sale and improve the standard of embroidery were the Ladies Work Society (founded about 1875) and the Decorative Needlework Society (1880). A rather more specialized body for the promotion of embroidery was the Leek Embroidery Society, founded in 1879 by the wife of Thomas Wardle, of Leek, the silk printer and dyer and lifelong friend and associate of William Morris. The designs issued by the Society, which were usually repeating patterns, were printed by wood-block on tussore silk. The coloured silks for working these designs were specially dyed at Wardle's factory in Leek, and the gold thread was imported direct from the manufacturers in China. Many specimens of Leek embroidery, as it was called at the time, were worked on a block-printed silk which was originally produced as a furnishing fabric, the lines of the pattern being completely covered by embroidery. Some of the designs were made by Thomas Wardle himself, who adapted a number of patterns from Indian art, including one called the "Ajunta", taken from the famous cave frescoes. Other designs were

FIG. 18

commissioned from leading architects and designers such as R. Norman Shaw and J. D. Sedding (Fig. 18). All types of domestic work were produced, but the Leek Embroidery achieved its fame primarily in the ecclesiastical field, and during the 1880s and 1890s many churches commissioned embroidery from the Society.

The basic principle adhered to by all these organizations was that a true revival of embroidery as an art could come about only through a knowledge and study of old embroidery. This attitude of mind is well summed up by Lewis E. Day (1845–1910) in *Art in Needlework* (1900): "Design was once upon a time traditional, but the chain of tradition has snapped and now conscious design must be eclectic – that is to say one must study old work to see what has been done, and how it has been done, and then do one's own in one's own way." It was this point of view which led, during the 1870s, for the first time, to a serious study of old embroidery. Loan exhibitions of both old and modern work were held throughout England, the most important

being that held at the South Kensington Museum (now the Victoria and Albert Museum) in 1873, another held at the Liverpool Art Club (1875), and one which took place at the Edinburgh Museum of Science and Art (1877).

Once it had begun, the revival of embroidery, initiated by societies such as those mentioned above, was swift, and the ideas spread rapidly to the general public.

Art needlework

By the mid-1870s Art Needlework was firmly established, and by 1880 the craze was as widespread as the Berlin wool-work which it had supplanted. But it exhibited more varieties. The *Dictionary of Needlework* (Caulfeild and Saward, 1882) defines art needlework as "a name recently introduced as a general term for all descriptions of needlework that spring from the application of a knowledge of design and colouring, with skill in fitting and executing. It is either executed by the worker from his or her designs or the patterns are drawn by a skilled artist." By no means all of the work classified under this rather pretentious term deserved the name. Elizabeth Glaister, author of several books on embroidery, sums up the fashion thus: "Many people think that no more is needed than to work in crewels on crash instead of as formerly in Berlin wool on canvas. Others think that if the work be in 'dowdy' colours it may pass under the sacred name of Art. Others again show a blind and touching faith in South Kensington (i.e. The Royal School of Art Needlework) and maintain that 'Art Needlework' is only to be had there; while a more enterprising friend replies that most of the shops have it now, though you cannot get it at the 'Stores', and she buys hers at 'Whiteleys'. All would say that it is a modern invention, much in fashion just now, and therefore they must by no means neglect it" (*Needlework*, Art at Home Series, 1880).

The chief characteristic of "art needlework", whatever the technique, was the use of rather sombre colours, no doubt as a reaction against the harsh and gaudy colours of the Berlin wools, and in contemporary periodicals the embroidery shops advertised their silks and crewels as being in "quaint and artistic colours"

The most popular form of "art needlework" was crewel work, usually worked in crewel wools, but also in silks, and mostly worked on crash, linen, Bolton sheeting, or, for heavy curtains and portières, on serge, diagonal woollen cloth, or velvet. The chief stitch employed in the work was crewel stitch (Fig. 19), which was nothing more than an irregularly worked stem stitch. In the United States, where the craze was as widespread as in England, it was known as South Kensington stitch. The direction of the stitch followed the

FIG. 19

shape of the leaf or flower or other motif. Other simple stitches, including long and short stitch, satin stitch, chain stitch, and French knots, were frequently employed. The name was derived from the "crewel work" curtains of the late seventeenth century, and a number of the designs issued were based on the historic models.

Although no elaborate stitchery was required, the work needed some considerable skill in execution and interpretation. The ideal was considered to be for the needlewoman to make her own design, yet many patterns for crewel work were issued. These

FIG. 20

were simply outline drawings (Fig. 20), and the direction of stitch, choice of colours, and shading was left to the worker.

As with almost all types of embroidery, floral themes remained the most popular, but stiff garden flowers, conventionally treated, replaced the naturalistic roses and exotic blooms of Berlin wool-work. Sunflowers, madonna lilies, irises, daffodils, and narcissi were among the most popular. If roses are found, they are wild roses, formally treated. Berries, sprays of bramble or cherry, or strawberry plants were favourite subjects. The screen panel illustrated (Plate 236B) although a late example of "art needlework", is typical in both the choice and treatment of the flowers.

Birds were a popular subject. But instead of the gaudy parrots of Berlin wool-work, waterfowl, cranes and herons, peacocks, swallows, or even the humble sparrow were most favoured. Both the types of bird and the treatment were derived from Japanese art. This Japanese influence, which to some extent affected all the decorative arts in the 'seventies and 'eighties, is apparent in a wall-hanging, designed by the architect and designer Thomas Jekyll (1827–81) for an ironwork pavilion at the Philadelphia Exhibition of 1876. It was worked on a heavy cotton sheeting in crewel wools and silk by a group of Norfolk women.

The larger birds, such as the peacock or heron, were considered particularly suitable for screen-panels. Jananese arrangements, with water-plants and ducks at the bottom, and flying birds and a suggestion of a cloud or spray of blossom above, are also found on many screens.

"Art needlework", unlike Berlin wool-work, was not really suitable for upholstery, but it ran riot elsewhere. The crochet, lace, and silk antimacassars of the early part of the reign were replaced by tidies of linen, embroidered in crewels, and laid on the backs and arms of chairs and sofas. Elizabeth Glaister (*Needlework*, 1880) recalls that "when art brought crewels into fashion, and crewels made swifter progress than art, many rooms were filled with pieces of linen, hung over the furniture in such quantity as to recall a washing day, each decorated with a spray of brightly coloured flowers". Embroidered cloths disported themselves on the tops of sideboards and occasional tables, and in the bedroom, behind the washstand, and on the chest of drawers.

Curtains and *portières* provided ample scope for decoration. For winter use curtains and portières were made of serge, diagonal woollen cloth, or velvet. The ground was usually dark: brown, deep red, olive green, or indigo. A contrasting dado at the bottom was a common form of decoration, and appliqué embroidery was employed for this type of scheme. Typical of this type of work were the curtains designed by Princess Louise for the state rooms of the new Town Hall at Manchester in 1877. The curtains have a dado of darker velvet on a deep-red cloth ground with a bold pattern of applied sunflower and leaves with several threads of crewel sewn round each leaf and flower. A wide border of dark blue, decorated with applied circles of yellow-brown cloth, surrounds the whole. Somewhat similar were the curtains worked for Queen Victoria by the Royal School of Needlework, and designed by the Hon. Mrs Percy Wyndham. These curtains still hang in the private apartments at Windsor, and also have a bold design of sunflowers enriched by the use of gold thread. "Powderings" of sprigs of flowers was another favoured type of curtain ornamentation, also simple repeating patterns worked in outline in crewel wools.

Decorative wall hangings, worked in outline in crewel wools, usually almost in monochrome, were also popular during the 1870s. The panel designed by Burne-Jones and Morris (Plate 234C) is a typical surviving example, and a series of similar panels hangs at Ammerdown, Radstock, Somerset. Figure panels of this type, for use either as wall-hangings or screens, were also designed by Water Crane and Selwyn Image.

For counterpanes and coverlets Persian tile patterns were much favoured, or single flowers set in an all-over diamond diaper. Mantel borders and piano-fronts were generally considered to need rather formal types of design, and the art of the Italian Renaissance provided the inspiration in many cases.

Formal pots of flowers, scrolls, dolphins, or grotesque beasts were combined with floral ornament to make symmetrically arranged, long, horizontal panels.

Italian Renaissance embroidery designs were revived as borders for "chair-tidies". The Cretan skirt borders (acquired by the South Kensington Museum in 1876) were also recommended by Elizabeth Glaister as suitable models for tidies.

So widespread had the fashion for "art needlework" become that almost every piece of household linen, from bath-mats to dessert doyleys, was given some sort of embroidered decoration: and patterns suitable for the embellishment of almost any article could be readily bought.

While the great mass of art needlework was composed from patterns prepared by others, the period produced a number of skilled embroideresses (as well as those connected with the Royal School of Art Needlework) who were artists in their own right. Outstanding among them was Phoebe Traquair (1852–1936), who was a mural painter, enameller, and illuminator as well as an extremely gifted needlewoman. The panel illustrated (Plate 234B) was one of four of her panels, each of which took several years to complete. The panels depict an allegorical representation of four stages in the spiritual life of man, inspired by Walter Pater's account of Denys d'Auxerrois in his *Imaginary Portraits*. Almost equally skilled was Mary J. Newell (1860–1947), who was originally trained as a painter at the Birmingham School of Art. After two years' study in Paris she returned to the School to teach embroidery from 1882 to 1919. Her figure panels, which were usually of medieval subjects, show a marked influence of the work of Burne-Jones. Both Phoebe Traquair and Mary Newill were members of the Arts and Crafts Exhibition Society, founded in 1888, and embroidery featured prominently in all the Society's exhibitions.

The fashion for art needlework continued until the end of the century. There was little change, however, in the type of designs favoured or in methods of execution. There is in fact little essential difference between either the basic principles or the designs in

Lockwood and Glaister's *Art Embroidery* (1878) and Lewis F. Day's *Art in Needlework* (1900).

It is true, however, that towards the end of the period an entirely new approach to embroidery was evolved at the Glasgow School of Art in 1894 under the direction of Jessie R. Newbery (1864–1948), the wife of the Principal, and Ann Macbeth (1875–1948). The tendency was towards simple, flat designs with broad areas of appliqué, and patterns that arose directly out of the stitches themselves. The work of the Glasgow School, the influence of which soon spread throughout England, does not, however, belong to the Victorian era in spirit, but was a pioneering effort which laid the foundation for the embroidery of our own time.

The following types of embroidery, not mentioned in the general survey, are peculiar to the Victorian period:

Arrasene embroidery. A variation of chenille embroidery used mainly for curtain borders, mantel borders, and screens, where the pile of the arrasene (a fine wool or silk chenille thread) was not injured by friction. It was worked on canvas, silk, velvet, or serge, in tent stitch, stem or crewel stitch, and couching.

Braiding. Embroidery executed by means of couched braid chiefly in designs of arabesques or continuous scrolls.

Breton work. A type of embroidery derived from Breton peasant costume worked in coloured silks and gold thread, mainly in chain and satin stitch and used for the borders of garments, necktie ends, and small articles such as book-markers (Fig. 21).

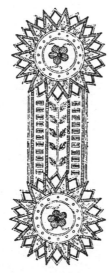

FIG. 21

Broderie anglaise. A type of white-work, first introduced during the 1820s, which remained popular for costume embroidery throughout the Victorian era. The de-

FIG. 22

signs, which were either purely geometric or of conventionalized flowers and leaves, consisted of a series of cut holes, worked round in button-hole stitch (Fig. 22).

Cretonne appliqué (called also Broderie perse). Was composed of groups of flowers, leaves, birds, etc., cut out from printed cotton and applied to a plain ground, usually black. The edges of the motifs were worked round in buttonhole or overcast stitches. Details, such as the veining of the leaves or the centres of flowers, were picked out with embroidery in coloured silks.

Guipure d'Art. A type of embroidery worked in white thread on a netted foundation in the manner of sixteenth-century *lacis* and often classified as lace.

Mount Mellick embroidery. A type of white-work, first introduced about 1830 at Mountmellick in Queen's County, Ireland, and revived as a local industry in the 1880s by a Mrs Millner. It was worked on a stout

FIG. 23

white satin jean in white knitting cotton, which gave a raised effect to the work. The designs were naturalistic, passion-flowers, blackberry sprays, oak-leaves, and acorns being the most favoured patterns. Many designs for this type of work were issued by Weldons and other publishers in the late 1880s and 1890s (Fig. 23).

Der Seydenfticker.

PAINTING

The collecting of paintings has long been regarded as one of the privileges of the rich. It is only recently that there has been more than a grain of truth in this assertion: the world's supply of paintings by the Old Masters is diminishing day by day, and is only partly explained by the fact that more and more paintings are being absorbed by the growing demands of public art galleries and museums. Increasing world population and the spread of education stimulates demand, but does not create a supply, except of course from living artists. Conversely, it is wrong to suppose that those of modest means must confine their interest to prints and drawings. A really discerning collector will accumulate paintings, drawings, and prints, because they all form part of man's comment on the physical world.

The best collector will specialize in one particular school of painting, yet he will have sufficient sophistication to respond to every school. Every school of painting from American primitives to French Impressionists has something valuable to offer, whether on nationalist, topographical, historical, or aesthetic grounds. The greatest collectors of all have always been the ones who have sought quality with single-minded fervour, and allowed fashion to govern the buying of those who regard pictures, which are expressions of man's genius, as status symbols.

FAKES AND FAKING

It has recently been asserted that "at the present time the market is glutted with forged paintings, drawings, and prints", and there can be little doubt that the nefarious skill of the forger is in greater demand today than at any other time in the history of art. Picture prices are reaching unprecedented heights, and the fluctuations of taste attribute an abnormal importance to the personality of certain artists. In an age of anonymous art, the forger was virtually unknown, and indeed the question of authorship troubled neither artist nor patron. Then, too, the political upheavals of the last twenty years have created an atmosphere of instability among the great art collections of the world (Note A). Works of art have been dispersed through the mishaps of war; collectors have been forced to sell for reasons other than economic ones; certain public galleries have been destroyed; others are inaccessible.

VARIETIES OF MISREPRESENTATION

The misrepresentation of a work of art is

therefore today one of the greatest dangers to be faced by any collector, and in this context the phrase "fakes and faking" embraces any transaction in which a work of art assumed to be the work of X, and sold as such, is not in actual fact the work of X. One must also assume therefore, not only that the intentions of the vendor may be honest but that there may have been nothing sinister in the intentions of the creator of the work of art which has assumed a false identity.

HONEST "FAKES"

In the case of artists who worked before the beginning of the nineteenth century, the problem is complicated by the studio methods of the time. Not only did most artists employ apprentices who would assist them in their works, painting in backgrounds, curtains, drapery, and the like, but most of them employed other artists who specialized in some special aspect of their work. There were figure painters, drapery painters, landscape painters, and others, so that when one thinks of an artist like Rubens or Van Dyck, one must always be prepared to acknowledge the fact that even the most authenticated work need not be entirely from the brush of the master to whom it is attributed. Peter Lely, for instance, counted among his assistants John Baptist Gaspars (who also worked for Riley and Kneller), P. H. Lankrink, Joseph Buckshorn, and Nicholas de Largillière. The system employed by popular artists of the seventeenth and eighteenth centuries had, indeed, many affinities with the assembly-line technique of modern industry.

This system persisted for a long time, and its last vestiges are to be found in the nineteenth century, when, for instance, Millais completed several works which Landseer had left unfinished at his death.

In a world in which artists had no exaggerated notion of the importance of their actual individual contribution to the creation of a work of art, other complications could arise. A master, for instance, would sign with his own name the work of a brilliant pupil, and there are known instances of this taking place in the case of Boucher. The farther back one goes in history, the more complicated

does the question of individual authenticity become. In the recently published (1955) catalogue of French paintings in the Metropolitan Museum, New York, M. Charles Sterling of the Louvre, its compiler, draws attention to the important difference between "studio works" and "works by the followers" of an artist.

"Studio" works are those done by assistants or at the direction of the artist concerned. Sometimes these consisted of additions to works, most of which were the productions of the master's brush, but often, and the possibilities of confusion here are clearly endless, an assistant would produce an actual replica to satisfy another patron. A typical example of this process is the portrait of Cardinal Fleury in the National Gallery (No. 903) from the studio of Hyacinthe Rigaud (1659–1743). In the artist's account book there is mention of ten copies made in 1728, one in 1729, one in 1734, and two in 1735.

It is to be presumed that the "studio" work is not only close to the master's work in style and execution but also in intention completely honest. Neither of these suppositions can, however, be relied upon in the case of a follower or imitator. It was for long considered quite natural, in an age which had no strong sense of copyright or of creative "property", that if an artist had been successful, others who were not, should try to capture his market by imitations of his work. The extent to which William Marlow in the early stages of his career followed Wilson, Giacomo Guardi, or Canaletto can often cause confusion, while the possibilities of error are clearly aggravated by the disparity in the prices reached by two such groups of artists. Even when a follower has signed a painting with his own name, subsequent owners may well remove it and substitute his master's.

In many cases, of course, the original intention was not an honest one, and as early as the sixteenth century there were numerous imitators of Dürer who were clearly producing works which they hoped would pass as original works by that artist. On the whole, however, it may be assumed that when a follower or an imitator produces his work within half a century of the death of the artist to whose style he is addicted his intentions must be given the benefit of the doubt.

Other "honest" misattributions of authorship may be described under the following headings.

Instructional copies

The copying of old masters was for long considered one of the main methods of art training. There are numerous authenticated copies of the works of earlier artists by Delacroix, Renoir, Van Gogh, and others. Often enough these are "variations on a theme" rather than literal copies, and in any case no attempt is made to simulate the media used by the original artist.

Traditional errors

Old inscriptions, either on the painting or on the frame, can often lead to an erroneous attribution. A sixteenth-century French work in the National Gallery has written on the back "Leonar de Vincy", though it clearly has no possible connexion with that distinguished Florentine artist. When such attributions are maintained it is clearly a case of the wish being father to the thought.

Original errors

These can be of many kinds. One of the most unusual was the case of a drawing signed by Augustus John which was in the possession of the Fitzwilliam Museum at Cambridge. The Director was startled to receive a letter from an artist claiming that the work was his and not Mr John's. Apparently the owner of the drawing had asked Mr John to sign a drawing which the artist assumed to be a work of his youth, about which he had forgotten, and so complied (Note B).

DISHONEST ATTRIBUTIONS

These are many and various, and the motivation complex. Although in nearly every case money comes into the matter, it is not always the predominant factor. Lack of recognition (and it must be granted that many forgers are men of outstanding artistic ability), spite, the desire to do somebody a good turn, a feeling that "the whole thing's a racket anyway", the delight in sheer virtuosity, or mere impishness

are all possible causes for embarking on the career of a faker. It must be remembered, too, that people often want to be deceived. For reasons of personal, national, or spiritual prestige the owner or possible purchaser of a painting is reluctant to admit errors of judgment (Note C). In execution, in effectiveness, and in conspiratorial purpose, fakes vary extensively. These, however, are the major categories.

Inaccurate or reckless attributions

It is impossible in this category to determine at what point the consciousness of deception appears. Dealers, private collectors, even public art gallery curators are all tempted to attribute a work by a minor artist to a major master. The temptation is understandable, and as long as the attribution is not questioned, no harm, presumably, is done to the purchaser. There is, however, an unfortunate tendency for such "optimistic" attributions to be supported by the testimony of "experts". The whole problem is, of course, an involved one and until every owner of a painting is prepared to have it subjected to exhaustive stylistic and scientific examination it is largely insoluble.

Alteration of signatures

This is the simplest and most naïve form of positive forgery. Most authoritative books on an artist reproduce his signature and its various transformations, but even apart from this, handwriting experts can easily detect a forged signature (Note D).

Alteration of a genuine work to increase its market value or for other reasons

Tampering with works of art by other artists has a long, and in some respects a reputable, history. To protect the susceptibilities of a prudish age alterations were often made which are only now coming to light. Foliage was added, portions of the anatomy were painted over, and changes of one kind or another made. Works of art have often been "improved" by subsequent generations. The *Paumgartner Altar-piece* by Dürer in Munich was completely altered in 1614 by the Bavarian painter Johann Georg Fischer, who added landscapes, modernized the dress, and completely altered the artist's original intentions. Reynolds repainted a work by Velasquez now in the Wallace Collection, and often the owners of paintings had them altered to suit their changed tastes. From this artistic malpractice to ethical dishonesty was not a great step. Under the all-embracing cloak of "restoration", paintings were often completely altered. Torn canvas, broken panel, missing paint all offer the opportunity for making a work of art "more interesting". It is clearly impossible to restore something which is not there, but there have always been restorers who are prepared to do so. As restorers are often painters themselves, they are frequently tempted to improve a work in the process of restoring it, and this of course adds yet more to the element of falsity. Even to change the dating of a painting may add to its market value – e.g. a Cubist Picasso of, say, 1902 would be immensely valuable (Note E), but the more usual thing is to alter the subject. When Sir Henry Raeburn was appointed the King's Limner for Scotland he had not painted a portrait of the King, and indeed never did. A few weeks after the event, however, a print of such a portrait was selling on the streets of Edinburgh. The engraver had substituted the King's head for that of the original sitter in an engraving of Raeburn's portrait of a Scottish doctor.

Alteration of authorship

This is the form of direct forgery which, after alteration of the signature, requires the least exercise of skill on the part of the forger. In the Walker Art Centre, Minneapolis, U.S.A., there is a painting by Gerbrandt Baen, signed and dated 1651, in which the process can be seen actually happening. When the picture was cleaned in 1945 it was discovered that though apparently a portrait of Henry VIII by a member of the school of Holbein, the work was actually a portrait of an unknown Dutch burgher of the seventeenth century. The museum authorities did not proceed with the cleaning, but left the painting half-Henry VIII, half Dutch burgher, as an object lesson in dishonest ingenuity. Countless works by minor artists are adjusted

to suit the style of one more famous. Hack paintings of Venice are converted into Canalettos, works by unknown portrait painters are converted into Gainsboroughs, and some idea of the scale of the industry can be derived from the fact that although Van Dyck died in his early forties, there are several thousand paintings attributed to him.

Another advantage of this method from the forger's point of view is that it requires no special treatment of the canvas, as it is to be assumed that the forged work is roughly contemporaneous with the artist which it emulates.

The creation of a new work of art

This, of course, is the most fascinating and the most difficult species of faking. It is resorted to only in cases where the eventual price of the painting will be large enough to recompense the "craftsman" for the pains he has taken, and it is, as a consequence, the rarest type of faking. It is obvious that the creation of contemporary fakes is a good deal easier than the creation of old masters. No elaborate doctoring of media is necessary, and the stylistic imitation of a contemporary presents less difficulties than does the copying of the mannerisms of a painter dead some centuries ago.

The simplest kind of fake is a mere copy of a painting already in existence (Note F). This presupposes that it should be done without the knowledge of the artist or of his heirs, and this may indeed happen more frequently than one would expect. Although it is unusual for a modern artist to produce replicas of his works, the original painting may be inaccessible, in a private collection, in another country, or destroyed. The task of the forger, too, is sometimes made easier by complications connected with the artist's life. This is especially true in the case, for instance, of Utrillo, forgeries of whose works proliferate. Bound by contract to a firm of dealers, more works of his appear on the market than have been sold by that firm. The usual explanation offered is that to make money "on the side" the artist painted and sold works directly to other contacts. A slightly more elaborate version of this technique of copying already existing works is to transpose work in one medium into another. A drawing or water-colour may be converted into an oil-painting, or vice versa, and as different media often play an important part in the creation of a work of art, the appearance of the fake does not arouse undue astonishment. A forgery of this kind whereby a drawing of Braque's in gouache was transposed into an oil-painting was recently on view at an exhibition in Paris.

Next to replicas the easiest form of creating a new work of art purporting to have been done by an artist of recent date is to rearrange elements from other works by that artist in such a way as to create a new, yet vaguely convincing, picture. Even the mere reversal of a pose is enough to suggest the appearance of a new work, and this method of amalgamating existing works not only reduces the amount of actual creation involved but also predisposes a potential buyer '– often anxious to prove his connoisseurship – in favour of the work. The Brooklyn Museum in New York possesses a Picasso *Absinthe Drinker* based very closely on the original work which goes by that name and superficially most convincing. The forger, however, has slipped in two quite elementary details, which would be apparent to the veriest novice. The signature is clearly a forgery. In the original work the line beneath the name has been drawn from right to left; in the forgery from left to right; in the one the inclination is towards the top right-hand corner of the picture; in the other towards the bottom left-hand corner. Secondly, the painting of the hand and arm is entirely unconvincing.

The fundamental consolation for any collector or connoisseur is that it is absolutely impossible to produce a finally convincing fake. Some of the reasons for this become apparent when we come to consider the question of fakes of living or recently dead artists. A work of art is the creation of a human being, and every brush-stroke reveals the history of that human being as clearly and convincingly as a thumb-print identifies an individual. No outsider can either recapture an artist's feelings as he is painting a picture or reproduce the actual technique which he used – a forger may come close to imitating the superficial appearance of the work of another painter, but he cannot know, for instance, the exact amount of pressure used on the brush, the sequence of the strokes, nor the planning of the entire creation.

In the 'twenties Otto Wacker (his real name was Olindo Lowael), a dancer, produced in Berlin some thirty paintings by Van Gogh. These created a sensation, though close examination showed that, as a result of not knowing *how* Van Gogh produced his effects, the forger imitated ridges of paint without imitating the way in which the artist had built those ridges up.

Close identification with an artist and a meticulous imitation of his technique (paying especial attention to the use of the same media) can produce convincing imitations of a work by another man. But there will never be an absolute identity, and in any case fakers are usually either careless or overconfident. Always one must remember, however, that anyone who is told that X is X will, under normal psychological conditions, retain a bias towards that belief.

THE FORGERY OF OLD MASTERS

The successful forger of old masters needs to be a scientist, an art historian, and a psychologist, as well as an artist of unusual skill and dexterity. That many fakes succeed is not due to the fact that there are many people with these qualifications, but to the intentional or innocent *naïveté* of dealers and would-be purchasers. The tendency of the times, however, is to impel fakers to greater degrees of specialization. In the late nineteenth century a large collection of old masters was offered for sale at a famous London sale-room. After the first day they were withdrawn. Every one was a forgery, the work of Charles Augustus Howell, an intimate of the Pre-Raphaelites and of Whistler, who once passed off a drawing of Brompton Oratory by the latter artist as a preliminary design by Michelangelo for St Peter's, Rome. Brazen attempts of this kind would stand no chance of success today.

In the first place the forger has to pick on an appropriate subject, making sure that the historical accessories are correct. This may be done, as with modern works, by a judicious blending of other works by the artist whose name is to be so invoked. Even then, however, an error of judgment may spell ruin. In 1925 the Burlington Fine Arts Club showed a painting of two women in profile attributed to a fifteenth-century Italian artist (Note G). It had been concocted by combining two individual portraits by Botticelli and Domenico Veneziano, but the whole conception of this kind of double portrait, and especially the way in which it was done, is entirely alien to the age to which it was supposed to belong.

The right choice of materials did not greatly trouble the very early forgers, but the development of scientific methods of examination has made it a most important item in the counterfeiter's essential equipment. The Curator of the Royal Botanical Gardens at Kew, for instance, was able to prove to the authorities of the National Gallery that a painting attributed to a sixteenth-century artist was painted on a pine board. This wood was not used till much later, and so the work was proved a forgery. The easiest way, of course, to obtain the correct canvas or panel is to buy a work of the right period and either paint over it or remove the original work and substitute the forgery. As under-painting can always be detected, the latter method is preferable.

The elaborate technical ingenuity of the forger may best be exemplified by reference to one of the most publicized cases of modern times, the productions of the fake Vermeers by Han van Meegeren (1889–1947). Van Meegeren was rightly proud of his skill, and he described his technique at great length. After four years of experimentation he obtained virtually the same pigments used by Vermeer, by making them out of the chemicals used in the seventeenth century, and by grinding these by hand, so that the irregularities which distinguish these old colours from the machine-ground ones of today should be apparent. In the eighteenth century Hogarth had been aware that forgers baked and "smoked" paintings to get an appearance of age, and to give the medium the hard, compact feeling usually procured by the passage of time. But he did not point out, what Meegeren discovered, that baking a painting tends to produce blisters and to dim the brilliance of the colours. He therefore built an electric oven the temperature of which could be controlled with great accuracy, and used as a medium a resin of phenol–formaldehyde dissolved in liquid, and rendered viscous by the addition of oil of lilacs. This does not blister so easily. To produce the "crackle" of age he rolled the finished paintings around a cylinder with a diameter of about 2 feet, having previously varnished them, and covered the surface with black ink. This seeped through into the cracks, and the accumulation of small particles left by the ink when dry gave the impression of accumulated dust. The ink was then removed and another coat of varnish applied.

To produce a convincing fake stimulates a certain kind of person to perform miracles of misapplied ingenuity, but though, in the long run, even the most elaborate technical deceptions can be discovered, the final weakness of every forger is the strength of his own personality, which keeps breaking through any false identity which he may assume.

THE DETECTION OF FORGERY

It is certain that no forger has yet evolved a technique which can avoid detection. During the last quarter of a century physics and chemistry have dealt a series of deadly blows to the production of fakes. On the other hand, the ordinary collector is not in a position to apply to a prospective purchase those exhaustive scientific tests which can be utilized by great national galleries. Over and above all the various methods of detecting a forgery is the fundamental test of judgment by instinct. Most people who have seen and "handled" works of art on an extensive scale develop an instinct which tells them whether or not a work of art is "right" or not. Dealers must in many cases rely on such instinct, for they cannot possibly have the time to become intimately acquainted with all the different schools with which they may have to deal. Though this instinct can never be finally relied upon, its warnings should never be disregarded.

Provenance and documentation

Before even seeing a work of art, it is possible to discover something about its authenticity. Important works of art are often discovered after being lost for centuries, but there must nearly always be some reference to them in books, literature, or periodicals at some point in their career, and such a reference can nearly always be checked. Very often the artist himself kept some kind of record. Claude and Turner, for instance, kept a "*liber veritatis*", in the form of books of sketches. Other artists kept account books, notebooks, or records of appointments. The account books of agents, of framers, and even of transport agents, and the diaries of critics or of connoisseurs may also throw light on the authenticity of a work of art. Scholarly monographs by modern writers are important, and help may also be obtained by reference to collections of prints or of photographs, such, for instance, as the Witt Collection at the Courtauld Institute.

Of all the documentary sources of evidence mere "certificates" are the least satisfactory. These are statements by some expert that "in my opinion so and so is a fine example of a work by X dating from his best period". Even apart from the fact that an expert's judgment may be warped by the consideration of factors other than artistic ones, human error is an incalculable element, and no redress can be obtained from the supplier of the certificate. The Van Meegeren *Disciples at Emmaus* was published in a scholarly article by Dr A. Bredius, an outstanding expert in the history of Dutch art. The faked murals at the Marienkirche in Lübeck were discussed at great length by several distinguished scholars. An art historian absorbed in the study of style and relevant characteristic can hardly be expected to assume that a work of art may be a forgery before he sets off on his exploratory investigations.

Superficial observation

A close visual examination of a work of art may very often reveal a good deal about its authenticity. The use of a magnifying glass will show all the surface characteristics, cracks, *pentimenti*, unsure brush work, erasures or corrections, mended canvas, suggestions of mechanical reproduction, water-marks, alteration, or forgery of signatures. The back of the canvas and the stretcher may also reveal facts of significance.

The analysis of style, the most authoritative check on authenticity, is also a matter for the naked eye. Stylistic analysis depends on the application to a work of art of those methods of investigation first formulated in the nineteenth century by Morelli, who pointed out that an artist's distinguishing characteristics are to be found rather in the details of his work than in the overall impression. An examination of the details of an authentic work will reveal the technical idiosyncracies of an artist – how he paints eyes or fingernails; how he paints leaves or blades of grass; how he distributes his light and shadow. The nearer one approaches to the minutiae of his execution, the closer one gets to the so-called "scientific" analysis of an artist's style. A Rubens, for instance, is generally recognizable by the particular kind of face which he gave his models, suggesting over-activity of the thyroid gland. To give an overall impression of such a face, however, is easy enough. It is only when one comes to examine how the lights are put into the eyes, which way the hair of the eyebrows grows, the amount of red in the canthus, and other small characteristics that one approaches the kind of criterion which enables one to differentiate between an original work and an imitation. It has been suggested that this method can be systematized by a simple totting up of points in which a work resembles an authentic masterpiece and then subtracting points of dissimilarity.

Close observation, too, should be given to the subject of a work of art. In the case of a portrait, others of the same subject should be consulted. In the case of a landscape, reference should be made to contemporary accounts whenever possible. Often buildings have been constructed, roads made, field boundaries altered, and other topographical changes taken place since the artist's death. Costume, too, changing rapidly with fluctuations of taste, can be a most reliable test. Every incident or detail in a painting should be tested by reference to history. Works by the so-called Spanish forger, who worked in the late nineteenth century, have been detected by his inaccurate rendering of medieval musical instruments. The fundamental stylistic weakness of a forger, however, lies in the fact that he sees the world through the eyes of his own age and personality, and in copying the work of another artist he will emphasize those characteristics which appeal to him. That is why a forgery is often more easy to detect in another age than in the age in which it was executed. Many Victorian forgeries, for instance, reveal a sugary sentimentality which the taste of that century demanded.

Scientific examination

This can reveal those secrets which the forger hopes are known only to himself. It is known that faked Corots abound. In twenty years more than 103,000 works purporting to be by that artist passed through the New York Customs, and even allowing for superhuman energy, when one adds to that figure the number of Corots already in Europe, one must assume that there is something fishy somewhere. A great number of these fakes, however, can easily be detected in that they have been painted in a kind of gouache, whereas it is known that Corot used only oils and water-colours.

Pigments can nowadays be analysed with the greatest of ease and without doing any damage to the picture. Microchemical and spectroscopic examination can provide details of the age and composition of the medium used. The advantages of this are obvious. Some thirty years ago a painting attributed to Franz Hals was proved to contain artificial ultramarine and zinc white, both modern additions to the artist's palette. A painting acquired by the Brooklyn Museum of Art as being by Hobbema and catalogued as such in the authoritative work on that artist was proved, in 1942, to contain Prussian blue, a pigment introduced only in the nineteenth century.

The application of water and ethyl alcohol, and of strong alkalis and acids, can also help to determine the composition of a pigment, and part of the case against Van Meegeren was that the paints on his "Vermeers" did not resist these agents, and so could not have contained fatty substances.

X-ray photographs can not only reveal the condition of the canvas and the manner in which the artist has applied his paint, but because lead-impregnated pigments are more impervious to the effect of the rays than others, they can also reveal the composition of these pigments. Ultra-violet and infra-red rays can also be used to reveal characteristics of the forger's art not visible to the naked eye. Under an ultra-violet light parts which have been repainted show up by differences in fluorescence.

The age and chemical composition of ink and paper, the existence of finger-prints, and countless other small loopholes enable the scientific investigator to worm his way into the shadowy mind of the counterfeiter, who today would need a huge laboratory to be able to produce expert-proof fakes.

NOTES

A. The case of the Vermeers forged by Van Meegeren came to light only because their perpetrator was accused of treason. Heindrich Joerdens, a Bremen dealer, bought large quantities of forgeries from the Lübeck forger Malskat because, he is reported to have said at the trial, "he believed that the paintings might have come from East Germany, or might be Jewish property".

B. In the exhibition *Chefs-d'-Œuvre de l'Art Français*, held in Paris in 1937, there was a painting by Emile Bernard which was, to the publicly confessed annoyance of that artist, attributed to Gauguin.

C. The position of the dealer who effects the sale of a forgery is a complicated one. It must be admitted that there are certain dealers who are prepared to sell works of art without too close an investigation of their authenticity, and the Malskat case proved how deeply involved they may be. On the other hand, most dealers belong to some reputable trade organization which takes a very severe view of such transactions, and in any case their careers are ruined if they are once detected in passing off, honestly or dishonestly, a forged work. In England the legal position is complicated by the fact that a work of art being a "document" it does not come under the Forgery Act of 1913, and can only be dealt with under certain minor Civil or Common Law heads.

D. Millet's son used a stencil employed by his father to copy signatures on works faked by an accomplice.

E. Incredible though it may seem, artists occasionally "forge" their own works. Rubens did, and recently de Chirico has imitated his own early work for polemical reasons.

F. In the nineteenth century F. W. Rohrich produced no less than thirty copies of a portrait of Sophie and Johann Friedrich von Sachsen attributed to Lucas Cranach. It must be remembered, of course, that before the discovery of colour reproductions, rich amateurs often commissioned artists to produce replicas of famous paintings for them.

G. The catalogue of this exhibition, which was devoted to fakes and faking, is invaluable for the study of this subject.

THE COLLECTING OF MINOR MASTERS

The collector faced with the enviable task of forming a cabinet of pictures at the present time might well be forgiven for believing that his task is almost impossible. The view is far too prevalent that works of art are both so expensive and rare that the chance of forming a worthwhile collection is out of the question. The opportunities of discovering works of exceptional importance are obviously restricted, though far more attractive pictures are available than may be suspected, especially if the collector is prepared to venture outside the strict boundaries of fashion.

Works of art, like any other commodities, are governed by the laws of supply and demand. It stands to reason that a potential collector wishing to acquire highly fashionable paintings must be prepared to pay the price. But the price of a work of art is not necessarily an indication of its artistic quality, let alone of its historical importance. At any period different interpretations of the artistic merit of painters and schools exist. The history of taste and collecting reveals that few painters have been so generally appreciated as neither to pass out of fashion nor to fall in value. A large margin exists, which is constantly being adjusted, between the over- or the under-estimation of certain painters. These adjustments are dictated sometimes by the failure to appreciate such artists' real merit, but also because a neglected school does not command an international market. The decline in favour of the English narrative painters of the nineteenth century may be due as much to lack of international support as to their style displeasing the succeeding generation. Our own time may reveal a more just approach to Victorian art, especially to its landscape painters. The present day may well secure a revival of interest in a "classical" master such as Raphael, or in such "eclectic" painters as the Carracci, whose paintings were easily to be found in London only a few years ago.

The last hundred years alone reveal a series of quite remarkable changes in taste. During this period the Italian masters of the seventeenth century, who won such high praise in the 1800s, surrendered to the early Italian masters who had generally been despised. The collector wise enough to anticipate taste was able to secure first-rate examples of thirteenth- or fourteenth-century Italian painting in the 1800s, just as the enlightened connoisseur in our day could acquire splendid Italian seventeenth-century paintings which had fallen from grace. Each generation would tend to consider the underestimated artists to be inferior in quality.

Obviously, the collector's attitude to painting is directed by his personal taste. The ordinary amateur may be intrigued by the aesthetic appeal of pictures only, while the historian may be primarily interested by the way in which a painting, irrespective of its aesthetic quality, fits into an historical development. Their views as to a major or a minor painting will greatly differ from those of a practising artist; he will appreciate those pictures which assist the solution of the artistic problems that puzzle him.

One may put the problem round another way and say that the market value of a picture is dictated by such elements as size or fashion, which have no relation to the intrinsic quality. A collector with sufficient space at his disposal may be able to discover large pictures of quite exceptional quality or importance which are less expensive than those smaller works that more easily accord with the demands of a domestic interior. The art market is complicated by the existence of such extraneous factors, to such an extent that an absolute decision as to the relative importance of artists and schools is highly difficult. It has, if anything, been rendered more confused by the recent trend of investment in paintings as a safeguard against the devaluation of currencies and as a means of preserving wealth in a portable form. The possession of paintings has proved of great assistance, as in Italy at the close of the eighteenth century, when the noble families, hard pressed by Napoleon, met their fiscal obligations by realizing their collections. Yet investment should never be the over-riding consideration behind the acquisition of a work of art; it is the artistic and historical appeal of a picture that should direct the buyer; for fashion can change as radically with paintings as it does with clothes.

If the problem of deciding the importance of many painters must remain a vexed question, at the same time certain artists eminently qualify for the position of minor masters or "petits maîtres" as the French call them; they achieve this place because they never go outside the cultivation of a limited area of artistic experience. The principles of artistic hierarchy are no longer popular, but the painter's ability to secure a deeper emotional expression surely comes when his theme is more closely connected with the major considerations of intellectual or spiritual life, whether seen in terms of classical mythology or the Christian story, or in the expression of a human personality, as conveyed by an artist of the magnitude of Rembrandt or Velazquez. This does not mean that a painter, who willingly limits his horizon to the visual world in its most ordinary sense, is unable to achieve the highest flights; Vermeer's little room is alive with infinite possibilities, and aesthetically satisfactory. Yet the degree of satisfaction is entirely different from that aroused by the

Sistine chapel; it is certainly more tranquil in effect, but it does not achieve an understanding of the human drama at its most poignant. The artist's refusal to embark on more adventurous schemes permits him, by this willing limitation, to achieve a just revelation of his calibre. He does not feel the necessity to deal with those emotional or spiritual problems, of which he may be perfectly well aware but which he realizes cannot be adequately conveyed in his own painting.

The demands of interior decoration largely control the taste of any epoch. The substitution of light-coloured for dark-coloured walls is one of the reasons which have contributed to the fall from favour of those sombre resonant paintings which appealed to the general collector in the late nineteenth century. The solidly painted composition, with its rich browns and heavy greens, surrounded by a solid gold frame, matched the ordered sequence of life and corresponded to a formal manner of behaviour. The tendency of the twentieth century to react against shrouded interiors and to permit light to flood into the room has altered taste in a remarkable fashion. The widespread interest in the mind and its realm has been equally effective, not only in the contemporary painter's attitude to art but also in determining the nature of the work collected. Even those collectors who might protest at being associated, in any way, with psychological analysis will find that their taste has inevitably been influenced by the general climate of ideas.

In the end, of course, the collector must become the eclectic virtuoso who can withstand the appeal of fashion (not that fashion may not fasten upon what is extremely good); he must overcome his prejudices in order to discover the secrets of those artists whose attitude seems so opposed to those of his own time. There is no point in attempting to ask that a neo-classical painter of the late eighteenth century should provide us with the same exhilaration as a landscape artist of the same period. The one may be a better painter than the other; he may appeal more directly to our sensibilities; but he is equally worthy of consideration. He may, in fact, delight those temperaments which are inspired by the same sentiments as motivated his patrons or admirers at the time when his work was fashionable. The collector, in a sense, is constantly invited to build his own museum and to form that collection which corresponds to his own ideal of the nature of art.

STILL LIFE AND FLOWER PIECES

Today we take for granted the artist's right to paint any subject, since the matter of a painting exists not for its own sake but as a chosen field for the virtuosity of the painter. Design, figurative or abstract; quality of pigment and brushwork; plastic relationships; experiments in chiaroscuro: these are the concern of the contemporary art world, and it is almost irrelevant whether they are being exercised on a face, a figure, a landscape, a dead fish or some apples, or upon forms that never were on sea or land. The art which is suspect is that which "represents": the art which has an immediately recognizable subject.

Any understanding, therefore, of the art of still life as it flourished in its apogee, the seventeenth century and the beginning of the eighteenth, demands a conscious attitude of mind, for then the subject in itself certainly was important. The old days when a picture had a purpose in leading the mind by its symbolism beyond itself to some spiritual significance had practically gone, at least in northern Europe. The new days of self-conscious art for art's sake under which we now suffer were not yet born. Representation of the world and all that was in it was the accepted keystone of the whole activity of painting. Rembrandt alone, Titan that he was, had traffic with the spiritual. The rest was a logical culmination of Renaissance humanism which saw the whole world as the province of mankind, with all things subservient to his pleasure and purpose. Like an heir entering into his vast possession, mankind was taking note of all that surrounded him; and the art of still life was an inventory of his possessions.

Paradoxically, as we now recognize, the primary elements of our contemporary art for art's sake were implicit in it. The artist, arbitrarily arranging the things to hand for the sake of his design, his colour, his tone and lighting effect, was asserting his domination over chance natural appearances. But the tension between natural appearances and an aesthetic purpose which organized these was only there in embryo. Three hundred years were to pass before the pull of the artists snapped the cord.

If we thus look forward we may well look back from the period to recognize that this factor of still life was inherent in much which went before. In the final stages of classical art it had thriven as pure decoration. Lost throughout the Dark Ages, it returned slowly in Gothic Christian art as an element, part symbolic, part decorative. One has but to think of the lily in a vase which became an oft-recurring feature in pictures of the Annunciation. It served several purposes: the symbolic one of emphasizing the purity of the Virgin as the vessel of gold betokened her perfection; the practical one of filling an awkward space between the Virgin and the Angel; the purely aesthetic one of emphasizing by its reiteration the swaying curves of the figures. Isolate it, however, and there is a perfect still life. It had to wait for the seventeenth century for that isolation and presentation as a thing-in-itself. Or, take the fruit on the background ledges in Van Eyck's Arnolfini Portrait in the National Gallery. That, too, may be symbolic: the pomegranate, symbol of fertility, in what is clearly a betrothal picture. Or it may be there as decoration to meet the need of a flick of light and colour in that otherwise rather dull part of the work. Or, more nearly to our purpose, it may be included for its own sake, because oranges were a strange new thing in western Europe, as Van Eyck, who had recently travelled to Portugal, and Arnofini, his merchant patron, were excitedly aware. In the painting of the North the fascination of things for their own sake is present from the beginning, and, as it derives from the book art of miniature, they are depicted in loving detail. St Joseph is not only a hierarchic figure but a carpenter who makes an excellent mousetrap, and puts one he has made out on the window-sill for sale. That mousetrap stands in its own right and interest, as it might have done in any seventeenth-century work.

The decorative motive gave excuse for still-life additions long after they had ceased to function symbolically. In an extreme instance we can cite Crivelli's fruit. How delightfully irrelevant are all those oranges and gourds lying about on steps beneath the feet of the saints and angels, or festooned inconsequently around thrones. Not only fruit, but flowers, leaves, insects. Quite obviously he enjoys painting the things for their own sakes, and arranging them in the interests of the picturesque. That is the true spirit of still life which was to burgeon so nobly two centuries after Crivelli was thus naïvely moved by it.

Outside art itself, the evolving life of mankind in Europe made a place for it. The decline of church and then of court patronage; the birth of the scientific spirit; the growing wealth and security of the rising banker and merchant class: everything prepared the way. In Holland especially, when the reaction against both church and court was fanned into a passionate hatred of everything ecclesiastical or aristocratic by the Spanish oppression and war, there remained a vacuum which had to be filled. In fact, it was filled by the artists turning to the depiction of all things Dutch, for new themes and subjects: the landscape, the people, and their own magnificent possessions. Just at that moment trade was diverted to the markets of Amsterdam and Antwerp. There was a bound forward in exotic imports as the sea-ways opened from the East and the New World. Science began the perfection of its instruments, so that the eyes of mankind were given new powers to see the nature and structure of things. Man moved into a new dimension of luxurious living, purse-proud and mentally free to enjoy the sensuous world which he was so busily exploiting. The new patron called upon the artist to depict these things he loved; and as the artist himself shared the passion, there was a ready response. That was the *Zeitgeist*, the inevitable logic of the triumphant Renaissance which had been moving in European thought with

gathering momentum for nearly half a millennium.

That it expressed itself most strongly in Holland and by reflection back in Flanders was, as we have seen, largely the result of history and the Spanish war, but the spirit was universal. In Spain itself it was manifest, and the *bodegones*, the kitchen pieces, flourished. In Italy, where art was more idealized and held in the older humanistic trammels, that pioneering spirit Caravaggio was "obliged to paint fruit and flowers" to earn a sparse livelihood when first he went to Rome. Evidently there was already an encouraging popular patronage for such things. Caravaggio's tremendous influence on the art came through his revolutionary practice of realism of treatment, and theatrical lighting. This opened the door to humble themes and subjects, and influenced the art of all Europe. He sounded the death knell of the grand manner and so helped to create the condition of vacuum which still life was destined partly to fill. Italian art, however, is almost inevitably conceived in the grand manner, since the wall-painting and altar-painting tradition assumed that the spectator stood well back from the work. The art of northern Europe, on the other hand, derived from the manuscript page which was held in the hand, and therefore encouraged small-scale detail.

One of the first steps in still life was the deliberate decoration of the margins of the page with flowers or other objects as decorations. There is one Flemish *Book of Hours* in the Bodleian Library of about 1500 where, around scriptural pictures or pictures and text, an illusory representation of wooden shelves has not only glass vases of flowers in some compartments but also individual vases, dishes of fruit, or dishes placed vertically for decorative effect. All this is quite clearly born of that love of things for their own sake, as well as for their value as organized picturesque. At this stage, of course, the artist was unselfconscious in his cultivation of a new idea in art. He was simply patterning a framework round his actual subject, as Crivelli himself does.

Who can claim to be the actual pioneers? Jacopo di Barbari of Venice (1450–1515), who worked in Nürnberg and the Netherlands, created – perhaps by chance and merely as an essay in texture – the *trompe l'œil Hunting Piece* now in the Pinakothek, Munich: and to this has usually been accredited the honour of being the earliest absolute still life we know, dating as it does from 1504. Happily it is signed and dated on an illusionary card apparently pinned to the wooden background.

Barbari had, of course, innumerable followers. The development of still life and flower painting itself is traced in the various articles devoted to the achievements of individual nations and painters.

GLASS PICTURES

Probably the earliest of all glass pictures were gold-glass engravings, used as early as Roman times for the decoration of glass vessels. The addition of colour to such decorations may have been suggested later by medieval stained-glass windows. Such a combination of ideas could certainly have given rise to the production of glass devotional pictures of the type that became common in the fourteenth century, a type itself which was later to develop into realistic pictures painted on the underside of glass.

In Switzerland from the sixteenth century onwards the art of glass-window painting in fired enamel colours developed a kind of glass picture in its own right. Such were the tiny windows (without lead lines), often measuring only a few inches each way, and painted with an almost unbelievable richness and elaboration, that are often seen in that country. The idea of the art of back-painting probably emanated from a desire to imitate under-glass painting, but so little is known of its origins that one can only guess.

Back-painting

The art of mounting prints on to the back of glass, making them transparent, and colouring them in from behind. This art, which probably originated in England, dates back to the second half of the seventeenth century. It is not known how it originated.

The print itself was first soaked in water for four or five hours to remove the size from the paper. A sheet of fine Bristol glass was then covered with an adhesive (usually Venice turpentine) and the print, when dry, laid face down upon it. When it had set the back of the print was again damped, and the paper rubbed away with a sponge or the finger-tips, leaving only a thin tissue with the impression of the print adhering to the glass. After it had again dried out it was coloured in.

The earlier and more beautiful back-paintings owe their brilliant limpidity to the fact that only the smallest quantity of paper was allowed to remain on the print. Later examples made by amateurs or less-skilled professionals have a much more opaque and stodgy appearance, owing to a greater thickness of paper being allowed to remain, the required transparency being partially produced by a white varnish. Back-painting was an anonymous art, although in its earliest days it is almost certain that the engraver of the print himself produced them.

Under-painting

This art is much older than that of back-painting. Examples are, in fact, known that belong to the fourth century A.D. In these older examples the technique by which they were produced consisted of engraving the picture on the back of a piece of glass (usually a goblet or some similar container) through a layer of gold leaf which had previously been attached to it. Sometimes colour was added from behind. Usually a second piece of glass was used to seal this engraving from behind, although this was more often omitted in later work intended purely as pictures, and not as incidental decorations for glass vessels. Many such pictures were made in Italy in the fourteenth century. The method is known as *gold-glass engraving*.

From this method was developed that known as *agglomizzato*, or *verre églomisé*, so called after Jean Baptiste Glomi (*fl.* 1760), an artist who used it, probably between two and three hundred years after its invention.

The technique of *verre églomisé* consisted of painting the picture in reverse directly on to the underside of a piece of glass and then backing the whole of the glass with either metal foil, wax, or some other such coloured pigment. This method was used widely in Europe in the sixteenth century for painting devotional pictures, many of which were very crude.

From this to ordinary under-glass painting was but another step, and instead of the foil or pigment, realistic or decorative backgrounds could be painted in or, on the other hand, especially in the case of silhouettes produced by this method, the unpainted portion of the glass could be left perfectly clear.

Another method of under-painting was mirror-painting. This was similar to the gold-glass engraving process, excepting that an amalgam of tin and mercury, to make it into a mirror, was first applied to the glass. The parts to be painted were then scraped away and painted in as required. Such paintings were often made in China, where the technique is thought to have been introduced from Europe by Jesuit missionaries. Vauxhall bevelled plate glass was actually exported to China for this purpose in the eighteenth century.

TROMPE L'ŒIL

Trompe l'œil is art which deceives the eye by its illusion of reality. It is arguable – indeed, it has often been argued – that practically all Western art of classical times and from the beginning of the Renaissance until subjectivism intervened in the early years of our own century comes into that definition, since the concern of painting and sculpture has been the imitation of the object represented. With the mastery of perspective by Uccello, Piero della Francesca, the theorist Luca di Pacioli, and their fellows; the invention of oil-painting in the Netherlands; and the conquest of chiaroscuro: all the elements for naturalistic realism were in the hands of the artist. From the thirteenth century until the sixteenth at least this was accepted as the fundamental task of the artist. Almost every painter pursued it, and many of them, such as Leonardo, deliberately added new scientific knowledge for the purpose of its fulfilment. The seventeenth-century Dutch, in their unqualified acceptance of the delight of the sensuous world as the basic matter of art, and the Spaniards in court painting of unassailable naturalism and a religious art which consecrated realism to the service of the church, applied this accumulated knowledge. So did the whole art of portraiture.

All this systematic search for realistic representation in paint of the appearances of nature gave the basis for what we have called *trompe l'œil*: and some of the Dutch still-life pictures came very near to, or even achieved it. For the absolute thing, however, we demand definite intention, an intensity of the power to make the two-dimensional surface look so like the thing depicted that the eye is truly deceived. At this stage the aesthetic pleasure arises from the deception itself, from the artist's virtuosity. It is art for art's sake; and by a paradox it attracts both the most unsophisticated and the most highly sophisticated mind: the gazer at a waxwork figure, and the modern collector of the precious and bizarre.

In this same diversity it is a society primitive or simple, and one with a flavour of decadence to which *trompe l'œil* will appeal. In its vogue as architectural trickery at the peak of the Renaissance we find such a highly cultured mind as that of Federigo da Montefeltro having the flat walls of his study deliberately made to represent cupboards with open fretted doors, the shelves inside apparently crowded with the treasures and curios which he actually possessed elsewhere. One or two of these laid on benches outside brought the illusion into actuality in a third dimension indistinguishable optically from the painted mural. This is real *trompe l'œil*: the elaborate deception by all the artist's devices of drawing, colour, perspective, and the casting of shadows – the link, in fact, with the actual points of the joke, as it were, and the emphasis of that deception.

In a widespread use of *trompe l'œil* for mural painting during the period of the Renaissance, the Italians showed a literally renaissance spirit, for in later classical times it had been usual enough. Perhaps it was in use not only in the falsification of architecture of the Graeco-Roman villas, but in Greek painting of an earlier time. There is the legend of Zeuxis and his rival Parrhasius, who flourished *c.* 424–380 B.C. and produced illusionist still-life panels so realistic that the birds came to peck the painted fruit. There is Pliny's record that Apollodorus of Athens (*c.* 408 B.C.) was "the first to paint objects as they really appeared". But we do not really know what Greek painting was like. Pliny's detailed account of its technique in the 35th Book of his *Historia Naturalis* indicates that it was very modern even to the glazing. Given their desire to imitate natural appearances therefore they may well have created real *trompe l'œil* pictures. Certainly in interior decoration in fresco and mosaic at the time Pliny was writing artists were doing so, and their subjects were largely those which the art pursued in the seventeenth century: dead fish and birds, baskets of flowers, manuscripts, and so forth.

The most famous example – possibly "flagrant" is the better word – is the *Unswept Floor* mosaic now in the Lateran Museum at Rome. There is represented with startling realism the débris of a feast: chicken bones, pieces of cake, fruit rinds, and such like, which would be found thrown down after a Roman banquet. Each has its careful shadow so that the whole floor is one extraordinary example of *trompe l'œil* of Graeco-Roman times. In architecture the Roman villas were sometimes given false painted perspectives and niches to make the rooms look larger and more ornate. This was functional deception, though there would have been aesthetic virtuosity accompanying it.

With the return of humanism in Italy in the thirteenth century began the slow upward climb to rediscover the lost arts of illusionistic painting. One has but to look at the famous frescoes painted by Giotto in 1306 on the walls and vaults of the Arena Chapel at Padua to see that the falsification of architecture by the creation of simulated architecture is alive again in European art, a century before the rules of perspective were established. By the fifteenth century this art of faked architecture was at the flood alike in churches and in palaces. An outstanding example is the apparently long choir chapel in the little church of S. Satiro in Milan rebuilt by Bramante; for this deep choir with its pillars, vaulting, altar, and other features is a *trompe l'œil* painted into the 4-foot thickness of the wall. Uccello's discoveries in perspective enabled him to imitate sculpture so that his painted image of Sir John Hawkswood at Florence, by its foreshortening and cast shadows, appears to be a real statue standing aloft on the walls of the church.

The idea, with its enormous possibilities of the grandiose and its demonstration of the power of the artist over material and the human mind, appealed to the men of the Renaissance. It combined art and science. Let Mantegna's work for Duke Gonzaga stand as an extravagant example, the flat ceiling being painted to counterfeit a balconied dome open at the top to the sky and with people looking over the balustrade of the balcony. The foreshortening and chiaroscuro needed to achieve such an effect convincingly is a triumph of *trompe l'œil*.

By the sixteenth century the art was overreaching itself. Walls and ceilings were painted entirely away to give realistic pictures of the countryside or landscapes filled with classical ruins. In the churches the insides of the domes were converted into skies with clouds and angelic forms, and the painted balcony device was often repeated. There are, too, such conceits as that by Veronese at the villa near Maser, where adjacent to a real door is a painted half-open one round the edge of which a girl peers. Such things are evidence of a delight in deception, and the confounding of the real and the feigned became a fashion. In the newly rising art of the theatre it was justified practically. The forced perspective among the receding streets on the stage of Palladio's theatre at Vicenza is the superb example; and stage scenery notoriously had recourse to apparent extensions of stage-space and other deceptions from that time onwards. The Bibbienas and Piranese created baroque fantasies of grandiose architecture, part solid, part painted, and governed in both aspects by illusion.

One final reference to this period may be made: that to the Jesuit Fra Andrea Pozzo, who became architect and painter to the Order and created, among other things, that "*trompe l'œil* colossal" *The Entry of St Ignatius into Heaven* on the ceiling of their church in Rome. The heavens themselves, and not only the ceiling, appear to open in this supreme example of the baroque with its multitudinous action and vast staffage of persons terrestrial and celestial.

If easel pictures seem humble after such staggering effects of architectural painting, it is in this sphere that *trompe l'œil* was to accomplish its purest effects by sheer insistence upon itself: and it is in this aspect that we tend to think of it today. The technical tricks of illusion which can be played depend upon perfection of perspective, the imitation of surfaces, the meticulous drawing of all the details, and a chiaroscuro of cast shadows: all this is devoted to making the painted image virtually indistinguishable from its prototype in the real world. It is, of course, at its best when the scale in the picture is exactly that of the thing itself.

If this can be achieved with the aid of distance in architecture and the theatre, the demand for virtuosity is greater when we are concerned with a picture immediately to hand. The pleasure of the sheer trickery is greater to that extent. There is always an element of participation in the artist's skill in any aesthetic pleasure; and in the enjoyment of *trompe l'œil* this plays an enormous part. At the worst it is the main source of fascination. Yet there is no reason why a painter of this kind should not combine with his prowess the normal values of composition, colour harmony, tonal subtlety, and the rest. Throughout the centuries, indeed, this is what has happened.

There is even the possibility that the *trompe l'œil* effect may be accidental to good naturalistic painting, as it frequently was in the Netherlandish art of the seventeenth century. One has but to remember those brilliantly contrived dewdrops and insects in Dutch flower-pieces to realise how fine the line is between *trompe l'œil* and pure naturalism. The painted tables, shelves, and niches of these were also verging on this art of illusion. So also were the crumpled screws of paper containing tobacco, the glowing fuses and charcoal, the overturned goblets, and much else in the still life. Always we must remember, however, the difference in intention. In Dutch and Flemish painting the aim was the subjection of art to nature. In *trompe l'œil* proper it is art for art's sake. The degree of artifice is everything.

One trick in this art of trickery is the apparent projection of some object in the picture forward from the picture plane by contriving a heavily cast shadow to be thrown on to that plane itself. The third dimension is thus continued in the direction of the spectator. As we have seen, this was done when the doors of cabinets were painted or created in *intarsia* on the flat wall with an appearance of opening out into the room. In early easel pictures it is most often achieved by painting a niche to fill the whole picture space and projecting some image across the painted base with its shadow emphatically cast thereon, as, for example, in the *Skull in a Niche* by Mabuse in the Louvre, and the violin on the sill in Mieris' *Violinist* in the National Gallery. Mabuse was always hovering on the verge of *trompe l'œil*, as was his friend Jacopo di Barbari, who went to Italy with him to record the things which intrigued their patron, Philip of Burgundy. A fine example of *trompe l'œil* is *The Net* painted in 1671 by Jacob van der Bilt, who called himself Biltius (Plate 243). These early examples introduce two departments in which the art was to flourish: the Vanitas, in which realistic skulls, piles of books, guttering candles, and other *memento mori* were painted to remind man of the transience of life; and the dead game and animals to gratify the huntsmen. J. B. Oudry (1686–1755), the court painter to Louis XV, created wonderful examples in the latter vein, and delighted in all kinds of *trompe l'œil*, as in his superb *White Duck* in the Marchioness of Cholmondeley's Collection. One of the most famous Dead Game pictures is in the Brussels Gallery, *The Dead Cock* by Hondecoeter (1636–95). It represents the bird hanging from a most realistically drawn nail driven in to a wooden wall on which every marking of the grain of the wood is perfectly shown, while the skilfully observed shadows give the stereoscopic effect usual in *trompe l'œil*.

The painting of the grain of wood as background plays a large part in that other subject, the Letter-Rack. In these, tapes are depicted pinned across the boards, and letters and other likely articles are stuck into them, leaning forward with every ingenuity of illusionary realism. If Wallerant Vaillant (1623–77) provides the outstanding example in his picture in the Dresden Gallery, Edvaert Colyer, who worked in Holland at that time but, it is thought, was of English origin, has left us others of quality. This Letter-Rack theme in the *trompe l'œil* convention has been exploited from the seventeenth century both in Europe and America.

Before we leave this Dutch painting of the seventeenth century, in which the methods if not the spirit of the art were so often manifested, we might recall the deliberate optical experiments of that strange genius Samuel van Hoogstraaten (1627–78), who made the fascinating *Peepshow* in the National Gallery at London. Looking through the peephole of this, one is convinced that the interior consists of a number of apartments with elaborate furniture and staffage; but, of course, it is actually deliberate deception painted on a flat surface. This is the absolute spirit of the art, though the means taken to achieve it are, perhaps, too self-conscious.

From the end of the seventeenth century the cultivation of the curious for a long period overcame the spirit of genuine aesthetics. In one way this is all to the good: we are no longer confused by ambiguity or ambivalence. The trickery is for its own sake: the more outrageous the better. In England, France, Germany, and elsewhere in Europe the art established itself firmly during the eighteenth and early nineteenth centuries. Banknotes, newspapers, paintings of engravings, and collections of objects in what we would now call Surrealist juxtaposition were rendered in heightened realism. One amazing idea was to paint what appeared to be a sheet of broken and cracked glass covering the subject. Unreal frames had been part of the

vogue from early times, but who would imagine that any artist would wish brilliantly to paint an engraving after Boucher under broken glass? (Plate 245). This is the perfect thing, the passion for virtuosity in deceptive painting fulfilling itself. A great number of the examples from the eighteenth and nineteenth centuries are anonymous, though names such as Laurent Dabos (1761–1835) occur. Evidently the mode was relegated to a sphere of entertainment values rather than those of art. If it was thus not taken very seriously at the time, the specimens which have survived are now valued as collector's pieces. In the nineteenth century it spread to America (at that date aesthetically unsophisticated) and has consistently remained a vogue there.

In our own time there has been a conspicuous revival as though in counterblast to the subjectivism and growing abstraction of l'École de Paris and its followers. The Surrealists exploited it in creating their dream images; and artists as diverse as Chirico and Salvador Dali (who often uses *trompe l'œil* contrivances in every aspect of his work) challenged reason with the apparent reality of their painted objects.

In Britain, apart from all such extreme theories, a host of names suggest themselves. Edward Wadsworth, Martin Battersby (who was commissioned to paint the mural *trompe l'œil* of the vases in niches in the hall of Mompesson House, Salisbury), Eliot Hodgkin, Tristram Hillier, Roy Hobdell, Richard Chopping, Robin Ironside are foremost among them. Close on their heels come painters – Royal Academy exhibitors sometimes – whose naturalism is so pronounced, so stereoscopic, that it stands on the verge of this art of deception. The line, fine though it is, may be drawn between those who simply pursue representational painting to the utmost degree – Annigoni in certain of his moods, for example – and those who clearly take delight in deception for its own sake. Even so, one wonders where to place such an artist as Eliot Hodgkin with his tiny studies of flowers, fruit, and seed; or Edward Wadsworth's marine still lifes set out on such convincingly grained planks of painted wood, and painted with such objectivity in egg tempera.

Such things are in the exact spirit of *trompe l'œil* as surely as the paintings more confessedly so and more artificial by such an artist as Martin Battersby, whose joy in the creation of the illusion is evidently the *raison d'être* of his work. That is the ultimate test alike of the art, of the artist, and of the connoisseurship of the spectator. So, whether in Pompeii, in Renaissance Italy, in the Netherlands during the seventeenth century, in eighteenth-century France, or nineteenth-century America, or among the artists of today in contemporary picture galleries the enthusiastic recognition and acceptance of the actual deception of the eye is at once the test and the triumph of this fascinating byway of art.

American

EARLY PORTRAIT PAINTING

Not only has it been difficult to discover the names of the first American portrait painters, but it is also in many cases difficult to differentiate between the work done in the colonies and in Europe. The portraits brought over among family possessions, or of colonials who had their portraits painted on a visit to Europe, as did Increase Mather in London in 1688, tend to form a homogeneous group with subjects painted in America.

While the English style dominated early portrait painting, Dutch influence was strong, not only as a distant echo in seventeenth-century English painting, but because of the actual presence of a large Dutch element in the population. In the Hudson River Valley a number of anonymous Dutch-descended painters have left portraits of the wealthy Dutch families, the de Peysters (Plate 246A), Van Cortlandts, Van Rensselaers, and others of the patroons. The Duyckinck family of artists came from Holland (Evert I arrived in 1638), and Pieter Vandelyn (1687–1778), the outstanding painter of the Colonial Dutch School in America, who worked chiefly in Kingston, New York, was born in Holland.

Nathaniel Emmons, the first painter of recorded American birth, worked in Boston in the first quarter of the eighteenth century. His somewhat stiff portraits in the manner of engravings were contemporary with the work of John Watson (born in Edinburgh) in New Jersey and New York, almost equally stiff and lifeless but of historical importance. The work of the German Justus Englehardt Kühn (1708) and the Swedish Gustavus Hesselius (1712) in Maryland, in portraits of the Calvert and Darnall children showing them in elaborate architectural settings and rich costumes, brings the baroque style to America.

Most influential of the English-born painters was John Smibert, who had already made a modest reputation in London before he accompanied Bishop Berkeley to America. He was not without force in his characterizations, and there is an earnestness in his work which made him an admirable recorder of Boston worthies. His work falls between 1730 and 1747, when he ceased to be active. Smibert was studied with great profit by Robert Feke when the latter was in Boston about 1741.

Charles Bridges was one of the more important visitors from England to Virginia, arriving in 1735 and introducing there the style of Kneller about the same time that Smibert was working in Boston. He had more grace than Smibert, and he was not bound to tradition. He introduced suggestions of the new environment, as seen in the cardinal bird, with its red plumage, in his delightful portrait of Evelyn Byrd now in the Governor's Palace in Williamsburg. His portrait of her father, William Byrd of Westover, has a dashing air well suited to please Virginian aristocrats. By contrast with Bridges, the Swiss Jeremiah

Theüs in Charleston in 1739 painted an unflattering, stiff presentation of Gabriel Manigault and his wife, now in the Metropolitan Museum. Theüs remained in South Carolina for over thirty years and painted in most of the leading families.

Robert Feke (*c.* 1705–*c.* 1748) is considered a native of the American continent, although his origin has never been proved. Whether born on Long Island, in the West Indies, or elsewhere, it is reasonably sure that he did not come from England, and it is apparently certain that he was self-taught in that he did not have any formal instruction. He painted a self-portrait at an early age which shows that he must have known Smibert's self-portrait in the Berkeley family group, and this same group has obviously influenced his own group portrait of the family of Isaac Royall. His portrait of the Loyalist, Isaac Winslow (Plate 246c), is one of his best. The pose is traditional in English portrait painting, but the manner has something new, a kind of hard, plastic quality, firm, uncompromising, and possessing a lively vigour.

Local styles were to some extent harmonized and brought into the English pattern by John Wollaston (Plate 246D), a mediocre English painter whose treatment of costumes suggests that he was probably a drapery painter in England. But he had the initiative (well rewarded) to travel extensively along the Atlantic coast before returning to England. He worked in America for a little more than fifteen years, starting in New York about 1751, Philadelphia, 1754; Maryland, 1754–5; Annapolis, 1755; then to Virginia, where he painted in many Tidewater families. Finally, in the 1760s, he went to Charleston. His almond-eyed ladies in gleaming satins represent members of the leading families of North and South. A similar success was enjoyed by Joseph Blackburn in New England: he introduced even more artificial poses in portraits of ladies with shepherds' crooks. His series of portraits from Boston and Portsmouth, New Hampshire, ended in 1763, when he disappeared from view.

In his American period, John Singleton Copley carried portrait painting to a height it had never reached before and he possibly deserves to be considered the greatest American portrait painter ever. Although one sees in his style the conventions of Wollaston and Blackburn, he completely transformed them, while in his delineation of character he has given us a vivid, living impression of the wealthy merchants and their wives of Boston, New York, and Philadelphia just prior to the Revolution.

Charles Willson Peale arrived in Benjamin West's studio in London in 1767 when the latter was thirty and the pupil twenty-seven. Peale remained for two and a half years, supporting himself to some extent with portrait commissions. Such work may have prevented him from absorbing as much of the English atmosphere as Gilbert Stuart did a few years later, or it may have been the result of his own temperament. Peale remained an American painter and his work continued in the direction marked out by Feke and Copley. He was a man of many interests, tried his hand at many crafts including metal-work, engraving, silversmithing, and was deeply interested in natural science. There remains something of the self-taught artist throughout his work, but because of his excellent drawing, firm modelling, and his unaffected simplicity his portraits frequently rise to the level of Copley's, although they do not have the latter's elegance.

The self-taught artist is well represented by John Durand, who left Connecticut in order to play the role of an itinerant portrait painter in New York and Virginia (1767–82). He has a feeling for pattern, for strong outlines and flat masses of colour, all attributes that distinguished the self-trained, gifted provincial painter who appears so often in American art. He is mentioned here as representative of a class which included Winthrop Chandler, Reuben Moulthrop, Richard Jennys, and others.

Gilbert Stuart (1755–1828), on the other hand, represents the American artist who formed himself on the European pattern. After remaining in West's studio for five years, during which time he acted as West's assistant, he finally set up his own studio in London. He married an Englishwoman, and had he been more prudent in his finances would probably have remained in England. But his many debts caused him to make a painting trip to Ireland, in which he was so successful that he remained there until 1792. He returned to America far more of an English painter than any of his compatriots, and he remained one, as is evident in the later portraits in New York, Philadelphia, Washington, and Boston. However, he was no lifeless imitator of Gainsborough and Reynolds, but vied with them in urbane grace and technical skill. His portraits of George Washington have undoubtedly impressed themselves on the national consciousness as no others have done, although Washington himself is said to have preferred his portrait by Joseph Wright. Stuart's portraits of Jefferson, Jay, Hamilton, Knox, and many others of the day show him to have been a great draughtsman, a master of the brush, able to portray the character of his sitter vividly against a severely empty background, with none of the accessories on which the earlier painters depended for effect. The most sophisticated American portrait painter, he was also the most direct.

After Stuart, it is natural to think of another portrait painter who remained long enough in London to have made a place for himself there, Ralph Earl (1751–1801) of Connecticut. He, too, had worked as a portrait painter, just as Stuart had done, before going to London, but he had shown more originality in presenting his sitters in the background in which they lived, as in his portrait of Roger Sherman at the Yale University Art Gallery. In London, where he was studying with West in 1779, he, like Stuart, absorbed much from the art he saw practised around him, as two portraits of his English period now at the Worcester Art Museum prove. He exhibited at the Royal Academy in 1783 and remained in England until 1785. Just why he discarded his acquired accomplishments on his return, when he was painting portraits in Connecticut families, would be difficult to say. He again became a "primitive", but naturally so, without affectation, and allowed his feeling for design and colour full rein. His figures tend to be wooden and expressionless, but as he paints his subjects on country estates or in their best parlours, with a view of a distant landscape from the window, the results satisfy us. Here are portrayals, not of character, but of a period in American life. In Earl the native style comes further into expression. With his death in 1801 the early period comes to a close, and other fields of expression, notably landscape, also still life and genre, absorb the attention of the painter.

THE AMERICAN OLD WEST

From the days of the earliest European explorers until the last Indian war-whoop was permanently silenced, the sprawling territory that stretches westward from the Mississippi River to the Pacific has provided history with one of its most dramatic and colourful epochs. It produced a number of clear-cut types strictly indigenous to the land and the period which created them – the *conquistadores, coureurs de bois*, frontier scout, mountain man, squawman, cowboy, Indian warrior, cattleman, and "tenderfoot". A documentation of the characteristics of these types in their contemporary environment is the broad subject of the artists of the Old West. The value of their work depends on its objectivity. Sometimes there is a happy union with purely artistic virtues.

The West of the early part of the nineteenth century offered the adventurous artist everything he could desire in the way of inspiration and incentive. Here was history in the making, against a backdrop of rolling prairies, arid deserts, giant forests, and mountain grandeur. Millions of shaggy buffalo roamed the plains, and there were scores of Indian tribes distinguished by their own picturesque styles of dress. Here could be seen Indians on the warpath and in the scalp dance; the pageantry of migration; and the recklessness of unexcelled bareback horsemanship in warfare and pursuit of dangerous game.

Among the earliest artists, if not the first, afforded the opportunity of documenting this era as an eye-witness was Samuel Seymour, who accompanied the official U.S. Government expedition of 1819–20 under the direction of Major Stephen H. Long, U.S. Engineers. They travelled up the Missouri River to the Yellowstone, then swung southward along the edge of the Rocky Mountains. Seymour painted one hundred and fifty landscapes and other pictures, eight of which were reproduced in an atlas to accompany the published journal of the expedition in 1823. His *View of the Rocky Mountains* was the first authentic portrayal of its kind.

Following closely after Seymour came Peter Rindisbacher. As a fifteen-year-old Swiss immigrant he came to America with his parents in 1821, in a party of 157 settlers recruited to join Lord Selkirk's doomed Red River colony in the vicinity of Fort Douglas, near the present site of Winnipeg, Manitoba. They were brought by ship into icy Hudson's Bay, from whence they had to make a six-hundred-mile overland journey through the wilderness. The youthful Peter Rindisbacher made an exceptional series of water-colour paintings of the whole journey, and they were supplemented with numerous other scenes of the country in which the family settled. These are the earliest known genre works of any artist in the interior of North America. Forty of this artist's early portrayals of the Red River colony, the Indians, buffalo hunts, and other subjects are today in the Public Archives of Canada.

In 1826, after a disastrous experience, the Rindisbacher family and other settlers abandoned Red River and migrated into the United States. Peter went to St Louis in 1829, where he set up a studio and worked successfully as an artist until his death in August 1834, at the early age of twenty-eight. Ten of his pictures appeared in the *American Turf and Sporting Magazine*. A portfolio of six others, entitled *Views in Hudson's Bay*, was issued in London before his death. Another of his pictures, *War Dance of the Sauks and Foxes*, was selected to be the frontispiece of Volume I of McKenney and Hall's *Indian Tribes of North America* (1836–44).

A third artist who enjoyed an unusual opportunity to become one of the early artists of the West was James Otto Lewis. During the years 1825–8 he was commissioned by the U.S. Indian Department to attend the different Indian councils, for the purpose of making portraits of the distinguished chiefs and depicting the various events surrounding those historic conclaves during which treaties were made and the U.S. Government negotiated the purchase of millions of acres of rich agricultural land. The Indians who gathered for these big council meetings provided a colourful spectacle. Lewis also wrote the text which accompanied his extensive *Aboriginal Portfolio*, published in 1839. This set a pattern for the future, by which artists were sent along with most of the Government expeditions to document the Indian council meetings, explorations, and surveys. Here the school of western American art had a serious beginning.

The first artist of real stature to go into the West for the express purpose of making a documentary record of all the Indian tribes was George Catlin (1796–1872). He covered more territory and visited more tribes, while they were still in their unspoiled primitive state, than any other artist. Furthermore, he accompanied his pictures with comprehensive text in his great opus, *Illustrations of the Manners, Customs and Conditions of the North American Indians* (1841).

Catlin began his career in 1830–1, when he attended several of the important council

FIG. 1. Catlin sketchbook, 1852
Newberry Library, Chicago

meetings with the tribes along the Mississippi River, the eastern margin of the wilderness. In 1832 he made a two-thousand-mile journey up the Missouri River to remote Fort Union, where he began his real work among the northern Plains Indians. He made numerous trips by canoe, up and down the rivers and overland to the homes of the various tribesmen. He usually travelled alone and had remarkable success in gaining the friendship even of the scalp-hunters. His hundreds of sketches and paintings were supplemented by voluminous notes on everything he saw and learned. This pattern of work was carried on year after year, and eventually took this remarkable pioneer across the vast wilderness from north to south and to the Pacific coast. Probably no other artist in history has ever made a greater contribution to the pictorial record of a human race. He even extended his work to South America. Many of his paintings and sketches are preserved today in the Smithsonian Institution, Washington, D.C., and in the Museum of Natural History, New York.

The artists who followed the inspiration of George Catlin are numerous. Many of them were accomplished craftsmen and sincere in their devotion to realism. Among the more noteworthy of these men is Seth Eastman (1808–75). One of the self-taught artists, he produced some highly creditable canvases. A graduate of West Point, Eastman spent most of his life in the West as a military man. He was stationed at Fort Crawford on the upper Mississippi River as early as 1829, and from 1830 at the big military supply base at Fort Snelling, near the present city of Minneapolis. Not only did he make an extensive series of pictures of frontier and Indian life executed during the seven years he was stationed there, but he also painted a series of military fortifications throughout the West which today hangs in the Capitol in Washington, D.C. His unusually accomplished wife, Mary Henderson Eastman, was the author of several books, which contained reproductions of her husband's paintings. Her *Dakotah: Life and Legends of the Sioux* and the accompanying plates was a principal source of inspiration and information for Longfellow's poem *The Song of Hiawatha*.

Alfred Jacob Miller (1816–74) of Baltimore came into rather sudden prominence about a decade ago. He accompanied the Scottish explorer, Sir William Drummond Stewart, in 1837–8 as official artist, when the latter made a trip to the Far West. Miller's pictures of the fur-trading posts and rendezvous of the Rocky Mountain trappers show the influence of his European training and do not have the vigour of the work of Catlin. Much of his work is in the possession of the Walters Art Gallery in Baltimore.

Among those who deserve greater recognition than students have so far bestowed is John Mix Stanley (1814–72). He began his extensive travels in 1842 for the express purpose of delineating the Indian tribes and council meetings of the eastern Great Plains region. In 1846 he accompanied the famous Magoffin expedition over the Santa Fe Trail to the south-west. Later, he went on to California with Colonel H. W. Emory, who was head of a U.S. exploring expedition. The famous Kit Carson was official guide. In 1853 he was the artist on the government expedition sent out to explore and survey the first route for a railroad across the north-west to the Pacific coast. The paintings by John Mix Stanley of the numerous Indian tribes and historic events throughout the West place him well in the forefront of the western artists of America.

The decades before and after the middle of the nineteenth century saw a number of artists devoting their talents and efforts to a serious documentation of the Old West. Among the most important were the Canadian Paul Kane (1810–71); the eccentric Academician Charles Deas (1818–67); Charles Wimar (1828–62), who painted *The Buffalo Dance*; the Swiss Frederick Kurz (active 1851); the Californian Ernest Narjot (active 1865); the German Baldouin Möllhausen (active 1824–57); William Ranney (1813–72); and the illustrator F. O. C. Darley (1822–88).

The Gold Rush to California, which began in 1849, developed into one of the most potent influences upon the course of American history and provided a tremendous impetus to western art. The experiences of the men and women in the covered wagon trains that moved across the Great Plains and Rocky Mountains, as well as the fortune-crazy life at the end of the journey, which was richly spiced with melodrama, completely captured public imagination. The demands of the market led to the production of a great number of lithographs by Currier & Ives in New York, Britten & Rey, Nagel & Weingartner and others in San Francisco.

As the West became settled and the vast wilderness was transformed, it attracted an ever-increasing number of artists. Some of these drifted away from the realism of documentation, adding a strong romantic flavour to their work, as seen in the paintings of the Rocky Mountains by Albert Bierstadt (1830–1902) and Thomas Moran (1837–1926); later by George de Forest Brush (1855–1941).

As the Old West faded into the limbo of things forgotten, there were a few delineators who became intensely interested in perpetuating its final aspect. Two of these stand preeminently above the rest. Both were self-taught; both went west in 1880; and both devoted their whole careers to the subject of the frontier. They were Frederic Remington (1861–1909) and Charles M. Russell (1864–1926). They contributed more to western art than any of the others with the possible exception of George Catlin. In addition to being accomplished painters, they were equally proficient as sculptors and writers.

Charles M. Russell, who was raised in a prosperous St Louis home, went west to Montana Territory and became a rough-riding cowboy when still in his 'teens. He led a rough and rather vagabond life, becoming known as "the cowboy artist" around the cattle round-up camps long before he gained recognition of any consequence. After about fifteen years as a *bona fide* cowboy he married and settled down to the serious profession of an artist, in a log studio. He became eminently successful during a colourful lifetime, and the scope of his work was almost entirely restricted to cowboy and Indian life of Montana (Plate 247A). He never quite ceased to be a cowboy at heart and in temperament.

Frederic Remington was raised in a prosperous family of Ogdensburg, New York. H attended private school and was a football star at Yale. He too went west at an early age in search of adventure and fortune. After four years of wandering from Canada to Mexico, riding horseback over hundreds of miles of wild trails, working as a cowboy, prospector, rancher, and saloon proprietor, he gradually turned to the career of a documentary artist. Returning to New York, he rose to fame as an illustrator in a remarkably brief time and later as a painter and sculptor. He maintained an elaborate studio and country estate, although he continued to spend a considerable part of practically every year in some part of the West. The scope of Remington's work covered the whole story of the West, both geographically and historically – the most comprehensive of any artist. Also a prolific writer, one of his books, *John Ermine of the Yellowstone*, was produced as a play on Broadway. Well over a hundred of his western paintings were reproduced as colour prints, and thousands of these were widely distributed. These are still popular, more than fifty years after his death at the untimely age of only forty-eight, while his original sketches and paintings (Plate 247B) find increasing appreciation among collectors. A memorial gallery of his works is in his native Ogdensburg.

AMERICAN MINIATURE PAINTING

Miniature painting in America followed fairly closely the English and European pattern, allowing for a certain time lag for ideas and fashions to cross the Atlantic. The men and women portrayed, however, have a recognizably American appearance, due probably to their more rugged life and more simple society, especially where Puritans and Quakers held sway. Little is known of any miniatures done in the first half of the eighteenth century, but the earliest painter usually listed is John Watson of East Jersey. Charleston was the home of Jeremiah Theüs, the first painter who worked in full colour on ivory. His paint is neat and opaque, a reduced formula of his life-sized oil portraits. In Philadelphia James Claypoole and Matthew Pratt were working similarly in techniques adapted from oil portraits, if the identification of their miniatures is correct. Benjamin West's self-portrait at eighteen is a sallow work, but more in the manner of true miniatures.

The first real flowering of the art of miniature painting came in Boston with Copley, Pelham, and Dunkerley, in Philadelphia with the Peale family, and in New York with Ramage and Fulton. Copley's miniatures are done on ivory, copper, or wood and show with great clarity and simplicity the essential traits of his subjects. This can be seen in his portraits of Mrs John Melville (Plate 248A) and Samuel Carey and his wife. Copley taught his younger half-brother Henry Pelham what he knew of miniature painting. The few American examples identified as works of Pelham are forceful, showing a decided stipple. Other New England artists were Joseph Dunkerley and Nathaniel Hancock. Dunkerley's little elongated ovals are finely drawn and pale (Plate 248E). Hancock, with less skill but in similar vein, gave his sitters a thin, wispy look. In Connecticut a vigorous painter, John Trumbull, was working out large historical paintings of the Declaration of Independence and various American battles. The series was begun in London under the guidance of Benjamin West. In the process Trumbull painted some remarkably fine portraits in oils of officers and individuals whose heads he needed to use in the large compositions.

Returning to Philadelphia, we find Charles Willson Peale in the 1760s painting portraits in oil and in miniature. His miniatures are on small oval slices of ivory in which the heads fill most of the space. His colours are bright and pleasing, and his sitters are shown with sweet, gentle expressions (Plate 248F). Peale established a museum in Philadelphia for which he collected natural specimens and painted portraits of distinguished personalities. During the war he was able to take his miniature kit along and painted as many as forty portraits of such officers as George Washington, Nathanial Greene, and Arthur St Clair. Having the support of his large

family much on his mind, Peale taught most of them to paint in one form or another, and in 1786 he left the field of miniature painting in Philadelphia to his younger brother James, who came to surpass him in this field.

James Peale's miniatures (Plate 248D) are better composed than his brother's, showing more of the sitter's figure. The size is larger, 2½–3 inches compared with Charles Willson's 1½ inches. His brush work in clear, harmonious colour combines little lines and stipple. His earlier miniatures may be confused with his brother's, but from 1788 on James signed his work with an elongated IP and the date.

After doing his share of the chores around the Peale Museum, such as mounting exhibits and copying portraits, Raphaelle Peale, son of Charles Willson, started to paint miniatures in his turn. His work is somewhat similar to James' but a bit larger and more open in manner.

A native of Philadelphia, Henry Benbridge (Plate 248c) had five years' training in Rome under Mengs and Batoni, and in London, where he was befriended by Benjamin West. His oil portraits and miniatures, smoothly painted in rich colour, are occasionally mistaken for Copleys. Much of his work is found in Charleston.

Another Pennsylvania artist, Robert Fulton (Plate 249E), may have been a pupil of James Peale, his early works showing Peale's influence. At twenty-one, however, he went to England and stayed twenty years, taking on more English mannerisms than any other native-born American who studied abroad. On his return his miniatures of New York ladies have the appearance of fancy portraits with flying locks and pseudo-Greek costume in the Angelica Kauffman manner, though a good deal more vigorous. His time, however, was soon taken up with researches on the steamboat.

The colonies and young republic attracted a number of excellent foreign artists. The earliest of these was an Irishman named John Ramage (Plate 248B), who started to work in Boston just before the Revolution. In 1776 he went with other British loyalists to Halifax. As a result of marital troubles he soon left

Nova Scotia for New York, where he settled down to a flourishing business painting the best families of New York, such as the Pintards, the Ludlows, and the Van Cortlandts. His miniatures are small and exquisite. The women have delicate features and masses of dark hair; the men, wearing elegant clothes, are smoothly painted. Ramage was a goldsmith as well as a painter and made his own frames. Some are lozenge-shaped and others oval; the frames have narrow engraved rims, and in most a scalloped gold border lies inside the frame under the crystal.

Two Scots, Archibald and Alexander Robertson, settled in New York in the 1790s. They opened a school called the Columbian Academy of Painting, at which they were fairly successful. A portrait of Washington painted by Archibald on a slab of marble is in the collection of the New York Historical Society. Another artist of the same name but not related to the first two, Walter Robertson, came from Ireland on the same boat that brought Gilbert Stuart back to America in 1793. Robertson painted General Washington, in uniform, and Mrs Washington. There are only a few of his elegant and sophisticated miniatures in America. He left for India a few years later. William Birch arrived from England in 1794 and set himself up in Philadelphia as an enamel painter, remaining there the rest of his life. He made original portraits of Lafayette and Washington, and also copied Stuart's Washington about sixty times. The portrait of his daughter Priscilla, looking coyly through a lace veil, is especially charming. Birch is the only enameller of note in America.

The most distinguished visitor from England in the last decade of the eighteenth century was Robert Field. His beautiful, luminous miniatures celebrated the beaux and belles from Boston to Washington during the fourteen years of his stay in America (Plate 249B). While visiting in Georgetown, Field painted seven copies of Stuart's portrait of Washington for Mrs Washington and friends of the President. They have been considered the best copies ever painted.

Good as were the products of English painters in America, the works of the native-born American, Edward Greene Malbone,

surpassed them in beauty, charm, and delicacy. He made full use of the luminosity of his ivory and blended and varied his colour to suit each sitter, enhancing the loveliness of the women and showing the strength and character of the men. His portrait of Mrs James Lowndes is a good example of a sweet, assured Charleston beauty (Plate 249A and F). Unfortunately, Malbone's life was tragically short. He taught himself to paint by copying engravings and helping a scene painter in the local theatre. At seventeen he went to Providence to make his living as a miniature painter. An early work now in the Providence Athenaeum shows that he had mastered the skill of producing a likeness. In two years he moved on to Boston, where he had a wider field. Like many other painters, Malbone made the circuit of Boston, New York, Philadelphia, and Charleston, finding patrons everywhere. In 1801 he went to England with Allston for a few months and was especially impressed by the portraits of Lawrence, and the miniatures of Cosway and Shelley. He must have learned a good deal from the last two, for his work most nearly resembled theirs. After a few more years of work in America he died of tuberculosis, not quite thirty years old.

Another fine painter, Charles Fraser, who was a contemporary and friend of Malbone, spent most of a long life in Charleston. He had been prepared for the law and practised until he was thirty-five, but his natural bent for art was early stimulated by a boyhood friendship with Thomas Sully and the visits in Charleston of Malbone and Allston, who encouraged him to spend his whole time in painting. His perception of character shows in each miniature, accurately and sympathetically put down in well-blended colour against grey stippled backgrounds. In 1825, when General Lafayette paid a visit to Charleston, Fraser was commissioned by the City Council to paint a portrait of the great man to commemorate his visit, and a second portrait of Francis Kinloch Huger as a gift to Lafayette. Huger had taken part in an attempt to free the General from imprisonment in an Austrian fortress thirty years earlier and had himself been caught and imprisoned. This miniature is now in the Metropolitan Museum.

Thomas Sully was brought to Charleston from England as a boy of nine. His family were actors and rather hoped that he would succeed in a business career. However, Thomas had a decided leaning towards painting and, although he disagreed violently with his first teacher, he persisted and at eighteen decided to go into the business of miniature painting, together with his older brother Lawrence in Norfolk. Lawrence was not able to teach him a great deal, being an indifferent painter himself, and Thomas moved on to New York and Boston, where he received help from Jarvis and Stuart, and eventually went on to London. He finally settled in Philadelphia. The greater part of his work is in oil portraits, which have a smooth loveliness reminiscent of Thomas Lawrence.

Benjamin Trott comes to mind as making a third fine artist with Malbone and Fraser. His miniatures were neither as fine nor as consistently good as theirs, but he did paint some remarkably fresh and lovely portraits (Plate 249c). He turned out many a romantic young man with wind-tossed locks in the Byronic manner, painted on a lightly washed or almost bare ivory background. He worked in both New York and Philadelphia, made frequent trips to the South, and spent one year in a horseback journey to the West.

Although New York had played host to a number of travelling artists, it was not until the beginning of the nineteenth century that she had a resident group of her own. John Wesley Jarvis was brought by his father from England to Philadelphia at the age of five. He was apprenticed to Edward Savage, an engraver, and at the end of his time in 1802 he went to New York to set up as an engraver. Not long after he joined with a young man from upstate New York, Joseph Wood, to open a studio. From all accounts they were a gay and boisterous pair. Wood's miniatures are delicate with subdued colour and an olive tone in the backgrounds. Jarvis, who also painted in oils, had a stronger, more juicy, brush stroke, especially vigorous in portraits of men. When he portrayed women his colour is more gentle and charming. After

he broke his partnership, Jarvis made several trips to the South during the winters, going as far as New Orleans. With him went a young apprentice, Henry Inman, who later became the most important portrait painter in New York. Joseph Wood stayed on in New York, taking on Nathaniel Rogers as apprentice. In 1813 Wood left for Philadelphia, while Rogers became a fashionable miniature painter in New York. His best work is smooth with well-blended colour; early examples are faulty in drawing.

Henry Inman settled down to marriage at twenty-one and serious work in New York after his wanderings with Jarvis. He took on Thomas Seir Cummings as a pupil, though there was only three years' difference in their ages. Both became prominent in the social and intellectual life of New York and held offices in the newly founded National Academy of Design. Inman's portraits are clearly seen and solidly painted; the character of the sitters is always skilfully presented. His miniatures are rather cool in colour and delicately painted. His portrait of Mrs Alexander Hamilton at the age of sixty-eight is a beautifully sympathetic rendering of an ageing gentlewoman. About 1827 Inman gave up miniature painting to concentrate on his oil portraits, and Cummings continued this side of the business. Cummings' miniatures are warmer in colour and more lively in expression. The Metropolitan Museum has two family mementoes: a portrait of his young wife dressed in a golden-brown frock and a charming necklace of portraits in graduated sizes of his nine children. Two English artists continued after Cummings in painting lovely women with grace and beauty: Richard M. Staigg worked in Boston and finally settled in Newport, and George L. Saunders visited America twice and painted largely in Baltimore, but worked also in Boston and Philadelphia.

As the art of miniature painting approached its deadline in the invention of the daguerreotype, portraits became more and more realistic. Their main attraction was in the smooth, bright colours, and the meticulously painted details of hair and dress. Sarah Goodridge stands out among these artists. She had instruction from Gilbert Stuart and made her way in Boston under his patronage. Her self-portrait shows her strong character in unflattering terms. Collections of European miniatures are most frequently made even in America, but portraits of American forebears are equally rewarding and well worth searching for. Many miniatures have remained in the families for whom they were painted. Identification of the author can often be made by reference to the location of the sitter. Whereas certain artists were known to have moved up and down the Atlantic seaboard, others kept to established centres. The patrons were more apt to have the leisure for sittings when at home.

AMERICAN SPORTING PICTURES

Colonial America was not a sporting country. The Puritans who came to Massachusetts and the other colonies of the new England brought with them firm convictions.

Sports were prohibited because of the Calvinist temper prevailing in the colonies at this time: such pastimes were also made difficult by the economic circumstances of the people. But with developing economic security there came a pronounced need for recreation, and the inherent and traditional English love of sports and games reasserted itself. Hunting and fishing became the chief diversions, with games of skill such as quoits, skittles, and bowls, and ball games of various types also being played.

In the South particularly, hunting on horseback became a favourite sport. The plantation owners were ardent riders and huntsmen, who chose their horses with discernment and knowledge, their fowling pieces, their hounds, and their riding accessories with taste and pride. One of the earliest and certainly one of the most interesting representations of this sporting activity is the painting titled *The End of the Fox Hunt*, painted in 1780. It was in all probability painted for a southern gentleman and depicts the traditional hunt with its numerous hounds and the properly costumed gentlemen riders in pursuit of the elusive fox. The naïve charm and primitive freshness of this over-mantel painting are unmatched in American sporting iconography.

The sport that drew the most spectators was horse-racing, and in some communities in the North and many in the South, racing meets were held which were attended by large throngs of enthusiastic partisans, come to cheer their favourites. Some first-class native horses were bred, though the best were still brought over from England. The largest single group of paintings dealing with sport were those depicting horses.

Edward Troye, working in the tradition of the English artists Wootton, Stubbs and Ben Marshall, painted with extraordinary skill a great gallery of portraits of the equine racers of his time. Most of them were commissioned, for fees of under a hundred dollars, by the horse breeders of Charleston, New Orleans, Baltimore, Richmond, and those of Kentucky. Most of the paintings are faithful individual renderings of the animals – sometimes in solitary calm, as in that of the beautifully proportioned grey mare *Reel* in her stall, more often in the fields, grooms and jockey attending. Edward Troye loved horses, and painted himself in his buggy, drawn by a white horse, observing another one of his beloved racers – a revealing self-portrait of a painter who devoted his entire artistic life to this subject.

The thoroughbred horse was also a subject of interest to other painters. Alvan Fisher painted many of the southern pedigreed stock, and in 1824 also produced a painting of the renowned *American Eclipse*.

Horse-racing was the most popular sport with spectators, but it was hunting, shooting, and fishing at which most men spent their leisure. America was rich in all kinds of game – deer, bear, rabbits, and numerous varieties of fowl. Hunting in the early days was both a business and a pastime, and almost every American man and boy owned a gun.

Shooting matches were very popular in many parts of the country. Usually held on

Saturdays, they were well attended by the local people who came to see their townsmen vie for both a monetary prize and the important title of "best shot". A number of paintings were done of these shooting matches which graphically illustrate their flavour, in both its seriousness and humour. One of the most striking and charming of them is *The Turkey Shoot*, by Charles Deas.

Born in Philadelphia, Deas spent some time at the Pennsylvania Academy and then moved to the Hudson River Valley, where he spent as much time hunting and fishing as he did in sketching. *The Turkey Shoot* was painted in 1836 when he was only eighteen years old. Shown at the Metropolitan Museum of Art in the 1939 *Life in America* exhibition, this work by Deas aroused great interest in this little-known American artist who gave us one of the most individual examples of American sporting art.

The best-known and most interesting of the paintings in this genre is *Shooting for the Beef* by George Caleb Bingham, which was painted in 1850. It illustrates a typical scene of the period – the log cabin at the cross-roads, the eager intense marksmen in frontier attire, and the fat ox, which is to be the winner's prize, chained at the side. The painting shows Bingham's great skill in the placing of the figures and in the masterly ordering of light and shade.

Subjects relating to the hunt and other out-of-door sports were naturally of interest to many American artists. For them, such subjects provided a point of departure from the more formal art of portraiture and historical painting, and enabled them to focus on the leisure-time pursuits and interests of the average American. Though the average man could not afford to own original works by these anecdotal painters, he could have reproductions of them, and often his home had more than one such reminder of the pleasures of life in the open with gun, rod, and reel.

Arthur Fitzwilliam Tait was thirty-one when he went to the United States from England. He saw the new American scene with a fresh eye, and he began to turn out a large number of extremely popular sporting pictures. His original works were eagerly sought

after, but also he contracted with the enterprising printing firm of Currier & Ives to publish his work, so that reproductions of his most popular pictures were seen literally everywhere. It was the first time in American history that a mass market for "works of art" came into existence.

Numerous mid-nineteenth-century paintings dealt with familiar and pleasurable aspects of the American scene as Tait's did. William Sidney Mount's *Eel Spearing at Setauket*, which he painted in 1845 in his native Long Island, is a work of high quality, without the cloying sentimentality of so many genre pictures. Mount's simple, natural style makes his anecdotal subject moving and lucid. There is no sentimentality in Bingham's *Fishing in the Mississippi* either – it is a superior example of American sporting painting done in 1851 when Bingham was at the peak of his talent. Among others which rank among the best as documentary representations of rural sports as well as interesting pictures are *Shooting Flamingoes*, by George Catlin; *Night Fishing*, by Albert Bierstadt; *The Fishing Hole*, by E. L. Henry; and Thomas Doughty's *The Fisherman*. Others which illustrate American leisure-time pursuits are the series of paintings of rail shooting by Thomas Eakins, and the superb group of water-colours and paintings by Winslow Homer. Taken as a whole, this group of paintings of hunting and fishing, pastimes which have been perennial favourites in this country for more than two centuries, constitutes an unsurpassed artistic record of American sporting heritage.

Curiously enough, the games played with a ball, such as golf, cricket, croquet, lacrosse, bowls, and tennis, as well as baseball and football, did not seem to be of special interest to American artists. There are, of course, a small number of paintings that deal with them. Charles Deas painted a violent and exciting picture of Indians playing lacrosse, a subject that was also vividly presented by Seth Eastman in his *Lacrosse playing among the Indians*. Alfred Jacob Miller and George Catlin, admirable reporters of the Western scene, have also given us graphic illustrations of Indians playing this vigorous game.

Croquet was more than a game, it was a

social activity, providing an opportunity for both sexes to indulge in the mildest of physical exercise. It was played a great deal by the fashionable set in the East, where it was at one time so popular that manufacturers made sets with candle-sockets for play at night. The lovely canvas by George Inness titled *Croquet, Conway, New Hampshire* is an ideal evocation of this tranquil game. Homer, who loved so many sports, has also given us two beautiful paintings of this subject (Plate 250c).

Baseball and football, now the most popular spectator sports, were just being developed in the mid-nineteenth century. The iconography depicting them is meagre. Homer executed some drawings for *Harper's* in 1857 which included one of a football match. Of the game of baseball Eakins made a water-colour, *Baseball Players Practising*. Before the turn of the century A. B. Frost became the chronicler of American sports, and his production included drawings of the games of golf and tennis.

As for water sports, the poetic figure pieces of William Morris Hunt and Thomas Eakins depict the joys of swimming, and the pleasures of the beach were also amusingly rendered in the painting *Bathing Beauties*, by James O'Brien Inman. James Buttersworth's paintings of yachts are as faithful as Troye's of thoroughbred horses. And Eakins also produced a great group of oils and water-colours of sculling, unmatched in American art for their rendering of the sport which this painter so dearly loved (Plate 251b).

The pleasures of boyhood were handsomely depicted in Henry Inman's *Mumble the Peg*, and in Winslow Homer's *Snap the Whip* we have a superb example of American genre painting. A water-colour by Homer, *Skating in Central Park, New York*, and an admirable oil by Thomas Birch titled *Skating*, also rank with our most interesting examples of the sporting scene. Another nostalgic vision of this delightful winter pastime is Johann Culverhouse's painting *Skating on the Wissahickon* (Plate 250b).

Though prize fighting was outlawed in America, notices of boxing matches appeared in the Press in the eighteenth century, and as early as 1810 the American Negro Tom Molineaux challenged and fought the great British champion Tom Cribb. The sporting bloods of America went to extraordinary lengths to arrange illegal boxing matches. One of the earliest graphic evidences that the prize ring was in existence was a painting done of William Fuller, who settled here in 1820. Executed in the manner of the formal studied British boxing pose by Charles Cromwell Ingham in 1828, it was shortly afterwards made into an engraving by Asher B. Durand (Plate 250a). It is an excellent portrait study, and the forebear of a whole series of prints depicting individual fighters and matches which became standard features of bar-room decoration.

The gallery of sport by American artists is thus numerous and, taken as a whole, this work is unique. In it the customs, pastimes, and pleasurable pursuits of the people are reflected more fully and vividly than in any other form of artistic expression. In the works of such artists as Winslow Homer and Thomas Eakins, Thomas Birch, William Sidney Mount, and others, we have a sporting art which represents an important and vital aspect of American culture.

AMERICAN NINETEENTH-CENTURY PAINTING

Romantic realism; the early portrait tradition and the Hudson River School

At the opening of the nineteenth century portrait painting was still the major branch of art in the United States, as it had been since the arrival of the first settlers. By 1800 the dominant trend was clearly that established by Gilbert Stuart in the late eighteenth century and carried by him well into the nineteenth. His blend of romantic handling with a generally realistic approach had an immense and persistent influence on American portrait painters up to the time of the Civil War. In many personal variations it was the style of Thomas Sully, Samuel F. B.

Morse, Henry Inman, John Neagle, and a host of lesser figures through two generations.

A somewhat similar fusion of realism and romanticism marked the work of the Hudson River School, America's first widespread landscape painting movement. Earlier artists had largely neglected the subject, but by the 1820s a new appreciation of the country's wild and picturesque beauties began to spread through all levels of society. Under the leadership of Thomas Cole, the men of the Hudson River School broke away from the topographical handling of the eighteenth century and approached nature with a more romantic eye. Many of them had studied abroad – generally in Düsseldorf, Rome, or Paris – and they drew freely on both contemporary European work and on old masters like Salvator Rosa and Claude Lorrain. From these sources came, in large part, the romantic paraphernalia of blasted trees, crags, boulders, precipices, and panoramic views which appear so often in their work.

Yet, much as they owed to Europe, the American wilderness presented new problems for which there was no precedent and aroused feelings that were deeper than any they had experienced abroad. By the middle of the century landscape painting had surpassed all other kinds in popular favour.

It has long been apparent that there was a close link between the work of the whole group and the extensive nature poetry of the day. A strong religious current ran through both, a belief that God's presence is manifest in mountain, lake, and waterfall and that the artist's chief function is its revelation. It was logical, then, to argue – as many did – that the painter should romanticize nature only to the extent of heightening its God-given aspects. This moral conviction was probably the principal force in determining the degree of romanticism permitted within a generally realist approach. The degree varied somewhat with individual artists, being considerable in the case of Cole and his pupil Frederick E. Church, much less with men like Worthington Whittredge and John F. Kensett.

The tonalists

For many years the fame of the Hudson River School obscured the work of a smaller group of contemporary landscape painters who worked in a more precisely realist vein, avoiding the obviously romantic or picturesque and seeking, in general, a serene and poetic interpretation of nature through subtle gradations of tone and light. The tentative beginnings of the movement can be seen in the work of two English born and trained artists, Robert Salmon and George Harvey. Indeed, the latter was so greatly impressed by the unique quality of American light that he projected a series of water-colours called "Atmospheric Landscapes of North America".

The movement culminated about the middle of the century in the work of two men, Martin J. Heade and Fitz Hugh Lane, both of whom were virtually forgotten until their re-discovery a few years ago. While there is no indication that they knew each other, their painting is similar in many respects, just as it is also related to the style of several other still obscure artists like Joseph Rusling Meeker and George Tirrel. Using a tightly descriptive realism, Heade and Lane sought to capture with mirror-like clarity effects of sunlight and atmosphere that the Hudson River School had almost totally ignored. Heade even did a series of haystack views under changing conditions of mist and rain and sunshine, much as Monet was to do later. Thus, in a sense, these men forecast the impressionism of Homer and others at the end of the century. There was, of course, no hint of impressionist technique in their enamelled surfaces, but their lyrical feeling for American light with all its brilliance and sudden changes was an important discovery for those who came after.

Quite apart from their atmospheric studies, they are also notable for transforming realism into a poetic instrument that depends relatively little on the usual expressive elements of design and colour. This quality in their work is difficult to define. It is a kind of intensity of feeling which is imparted to the spectator by the equal intensity of the artist's observation, the infinite care with which every aspect of his scene has been analysed and affectionately

Genre painting

At about the same time that American artists were discovering their native landscape, another group, led by William Sidney Mount, were beginning to paint the daily life of the young democracy. There had been earlier attempts at scattered intervals, like the charming scenes of social gatherings by Henry Sargent, but such pictures had little influence on the school which followed, being more closely related to the formal elegance of the portrait painters. Mount, on the other hand, distrusted "ideality and the grand style" and professed that his aim was "to copy nature . . . with truth and soberness". For this purpose he developed a rather hard, meticulously realistic style, somewhat akin to that of the tonalists, particularly in his many outdoor scenes. With it he told rural anecdotes and recorded the humorous events of country life around his home on Long Island, preferring to overlook its harsher aspects or the industrial life of the nearby city, which was already beginning to make his farm subjects seem like nostalgic memories of an older and happier way of life. Yet in his earthiness, his high spirits, and canny regard for popular taste, Mount reflected accurately the bustling optimism of Jacksonian democracy. Much the same qualities are found in the work of Richard Caton Woodville, Thomas Le Clear, and the host of Eastern genre painters who followed him, creating by mid-century a whole school of anecdotal art in realist vein.

Still-life painting

Like genre and the landscapes of the tonalists, still-life painting followed a predominantly realist vein throughout the century, although it seems to have been more strongly influenced at the beginning by European conventions, particularly those of Dutch art. Raphaelle Peale, who emerges as the most interesting of our early specialists in the field, used many Dutch devices. Nevertheless, he departed from tradition in the extreme simplicity of his designs and in his preference for humble objects. The quality of Peale's work is not to be found so much in his subjects or designs, however, as it is in that same intensity of vision which the best of the tonalists and a few of the genre painters also possessed. Peale had an advantage over both groups in that he was working with small, inanimate objects on which he could focus with a microscopic concentration impossible in landscape or genre. His leaves curl through space with the utmost exactitude; every texture and form is completely stated; even air, light, and shadow seem palpable. In some mysterious way this kind of realism gives the simplest things a heightened significance beyond that of common association. They are miracles of being, sensed for the first time.

For many years the tradition established by Raphaelle and his uncle James Peale continued to dominate American still-life painting. In the last quarter of the century, however, a somewhat different school emerged, led by William M. Harnett (Plate 252A). Working in a style of *trompe l'œil* realism, Harnett and his circle delighted even more than Peale in the exact imitation of the look and feel of things. A burnt match, a piece of string hanging down over the frame, appear so real that the spectator is irresistibly moved to pick them off the surface. Harnett, himself, was also a master of subdued colour and intricately balanced design. His mugs and pipes and musical instruments glow with soft hues, and their apparently casual arrangement is, in fact, a carefully wrought structure with every object playing its part. The beauty of his pictures, to modern eyes, is almost abstract.

Late portrait and figure painters

While genre painting continued to flourish throughout the century, it became more artificial and sentimental with the passage of time. The freshness and vigour, as well as the naïveté, of the early men yielded to J. G. Brown's coy bootblacks, E. L. Henry's nostalgic costume pieces, and eventually to much worse levels of bathos. The true inheritors of the mid-century school were several figure painters who scarcely formed a homogeneous group but who recorded with a sober and more sophisticated realism the much-changed aspects of American life.

In the work of Thomas Eakins the American realist tradition reached its culmination and perhaps its fullest expression (Plate 252B). Eakins' rowing, sailing, and hunting scenes, his old men playing chess or zithers, his family gatherings around the piano grew out of the earlier genre school and are an even more faithful record of middle-class life, now in an urban and Victorian setting. But his paintings are conceived in an analytical spirit, with a passionate concern for accuracy of anatomy and perspective, above all with a seriousness of purpose which removes them far from anecdote and sentiment. In his later life the artist painted portraits almost exclusively. To the literal description of form and action he now added that most difficult quality, the penetrating analysis of character. Never flattering, his likenesses tend to be awkward and graceless in a conventional sense, but they reveal the bare humanity of his subjects with warmth, with insight, and often with sadness. They are memorable images of men and women who have worked and suffered.

By the time of the Civil War the old, remarkably persistent portrait tradition of Gilbert Stuart had finally vanished and for a time the daguerreotype's mounting influence threatened to turn this branch of art into a drably unselective rendering of features. It was rescued, not only by Eakins, but also by several other painters, such as William Page and William Morris Hunt, who succeeded in preserving the realist approach without becoming photographic and who resisted, at the opposite extreme, a growing trend towards the facile brushwork of John Singer Sargent and the fashionable society painters.

Painters of the inner eye

While realism, though sometimes tinged with romantic feeling, was the dominant trend in nineteenth-century American painting, individual artists throughout the period explored other directions and added the leaven of mysticism, fantasy, and satire to the more sober work of their contemporaries. They established no schools and were unrelated to each other except in their general attitude. A few – notably Washington Allston and Robert L. Newman – were deeply influenced by European art, but the majority did not study abroad and developed their individual styles in relative isolation. With one or two exceptions, they were unsuccessful during their own lives, paying a high price of neglect and hostile criticism for their nonconformity to the aesthetic standards of the age.

Allston was probably the first true romantic in American art history. His style was formed, conventionally enough, by long study of the Venetian masters of the Renaissance, but his sensitive imagination dwelt often on supernatural themes from the Bible. These he translated to canvas, sometimes a little theatrically, but at best with grandeur, originality, and a compelling romantic sweep. Allston's kind of mysticism vanished from American art with his death. It was followed in the mid-century by the earlier romanticism of John Quidor and David Blythe, who were, however, quite different in other respects. Quidor's inventive brush embroidered subjects drawn from the tales of Irving and Cooper with a wealth of fantastic detail, his figures contorted in baroque exuberance but never quite slipping into caricature. Blythe's distortions, on the other hand, were frankly satirical, sometimes good-humoured, more often sharp and bitter.

Then, at the end of the century, during one of America's most materialistic ages, mysticism of various kinds became once more the refuge of the non-conformists. With Newman, as with Allston, it was religious or at least Biblical in inspiration. With Ralph Blakelock it was night and the moods of primitive nature, recalled from a youthful trip to the West, that fired his imagination. Over and over until his final insanity he painted visionary glades and Indians engulfed in moonlit landscapes. With Albert Ryder, the greatest of them all, it was a deeper and more ample mysticism, embracing everything miraculous in nature and in myth, both divine and demonic. Living the life of a hermit in his New York studio, he drew on childhood memories of the sea to paint his nocturnal marines with their strange arabesques of cloud shapes and their lonely boats. Even such events as the suicide of a waiter, who had lost his money on a horse-race, haunted his mind until he had given it form and supernatural meaning in *The Race Track*. But, above all, it was poetry and legend that moved him, the stories of Jonah and the Flying Dutchman, of Siegfried, Macbeth, and the dead Christ's reappearance on earth. Under his hesitant brush, beset by endless doubts and changes, these grew slowly into the majestic patterns that evoke so fully the mystery of each theme.

Visual realism; the beginnings of Impressionism

The Civil War was scarcely over in 1865, when a new trend appeared in American art. This was a movement away from the tightly descriptive realism of the mid-century towards a purely visual realism that rendered objects as the eye alone perceived them, greatly modified by light, shadow, and atmosphere. With it came a freer handling of paint, a livelier surface, often a delight in brushwork for its own spontaneous effects. Contours were deliberately broken, form suggested rather than analysed, detail blurred by strong sunlight or lost in shade. Tone rather than design became the prevalent means of unifying a picture.

This was, of course, a common trend in Europe also, from the early work of the Barbizon men through that of the Impressionists, and many of its American forms are traceable to European influence. James Hamilton studied Turner's work in England, as Monet was to do later. William Morris Hunt painted with Millet at Barbizon, W. Allan Gay with Troyon, while George Inness, more than either, adapted the atmospheric style of the Barbizon School to American landscape. At about the same time a quite different kind of impressionism was discovered by Frank Duveneck in Munich, where the influence of Courbet and of old masters like Frans Hals had united to produce a movement of dark tonality, slashing brushwork and rapid, *alla prima* technique. Under Duveneck's leadership a whole generation of American art students went to Germany or absorbed the new approach from Munich-trained teachers like William M. Chase. Still another kind of impressionism, modified by Oriental design, reached this country with the paintings of James McNeill Whistler, who had lived for some time in Paris before settling as a permanent expatriate in England. And Whistler's shadowy *Nocturnes*, with their novel range of twilight and night effects, attracted many followers in America at the century's end.

While one must not underestimate the great effect which these European trends had on American art, it is still apparent that the new way of seeing and the freer way of painting were appearing spontaneously everywhere and would probably have done so there regardless of developments abroad. Indeed, one of the most vigorous forms of American impressionism was purely native in origin, growing logically out of the landscape of the mid-century tonalists and culminating in the broad naturalism of Winslow Homer (Plate 253). The transition from the enamelled surfaces of the earlier men to Homer's style can be traced in the work of several artists. A clear instance is Eastman Johnson, who was trained in the meticulous realism of the Düsseldorf School and whose early canvases are tightly descriptive. Yet soon after the Civil War Johnson's brushwork began to grow freer, his effects of outdoor light richer and crisper until, by the mid-seventies, he was painting his Maine and Nantucket genre scenes with a broad touch which suggests, though still a little timidly, the palpable radiance of sun on beach and meadow.

Homer, himself, went through an exactly parallel development in the same years, but he carried native impressionism much farther than Johnson or any of the other transitional figures. Virtually unaffected by his two brief trips to Europe, he developed in his isolated studio on the Maine coast an art that miraculously preserved the big forms and structure of nature at the same time that it captured the full brilliance of American light and its elusive changes at different seasons or times of day. Unlike the French Impressionists, Homer never permitted atmosphere and light to consume form. His feeling for the solid reality of nature was too deeply rooted in the long tradition of American landscape painting. Rather, his great accomplishment was wedding that tradition to the new vision in a way that seemed, like all good art, inevitable. More fully than any predecessor, he realized the nineteenth century's long dream of revealing, through perfectly appropriate means, the rugged beauty of his native land.

AMERICAN FOLK PAINTING

Confusion regarding terminology has arisen over the years with reference to American folk painting, "popular", "primitive", "pioneer", and "provincial" being among the many designations in current use. Each has its merits, but the term folk art more nearly approximates the dictionary definition of the art "of, or pertaining to, the folk, or used among the common people". In America personal initiative was inherent in the new environment, traditional forms took on added individuality, and the word *folk* assumed a new connotation.

The work of two groups, professional and amateur, is included in the United States under the generic title of folk art. Although their training and technique differed widely, these people possessed in common a fresh and spontaneous approach which rendered their best efforts dynamic, even when lacking in technical proficiency.

Most of the professionals were men who earned at least a part of their living through the painting trade. In the early nineteenth century citizens of the average country town engaged in various seasonal occupations. Some of them taught school in the winter and painted in the summer, when it was feasible to travel from place to place. Many boys began their careers by apprenticeship to master craftsmen who taught them coach, sign, and ship painting, along with gilding, lettering, and general decorating. A few worked for short lengths of time in the studios of recognized artists and eventually achieved distinction as landscape or "face-painters", but the majority remained artisans rather than artists.

Few small communities could provide year-round support for a limner, but many remote families were potential patrons if he could present himself at their doors.

The itinerant painter usually travelled on foot or, if he was sufficiently affluent, with a hand-cart or wagon in which to carry his canvases and equipment. Some of these men covered long distances annually, travelling through the South or penetrating into upper New York State and out into the Western Reserve. Most of them counted on receiving board and lodging in the homes of their clients. Such accommodation might stretch out for a number of weeks if many commissions were secured in one family or neighbourhood. Other artists hired a room in a town where they had been previously successful or believed the prospects to be good, and announced their presence by means of posted handbills or notices inserted in the local Press. Still others were entertained by the landlord of the nearby tavern in return for decorating the ballroom or other apartments with stencilled or scenic designs.

Prices charged for portraits frequently varied from three to twenty-five dollars according to the locality and the reputation of the artist. Profiles and small pictures of children were advertised from twenty cents to one dollar.

Portraits in oil, painted on canvas or wood, formed the larger part of the output of professional folk artists. In their pictures they frequently included accessories to denote the characteristics or occupations of their sitters. Dr Smith of Mount Vernon, New Hampshire, is portrayed (Plate 254A) with the vials and scalpels of his profession spread out on the table beside him. His house and doctor's buggy may be seen through an adjacent window. Mrs J. B. Sheldon of Unionville, Ohio, painted by an unknown artist about 1825, holds her ear trumpet without visible embarrassment (Plate 254B). Here one recognizes the realistic approach of folk art in contrast to the conventional poses employed by the academicians.

It has often been said that the majority of travelling artists carried with them previously painted stock figures to which they subsequently added the heads of their respective sitters. Although this may occasionally have been done, pictures of headless torsos have never come to light to support the contention that it was a general practice. Moreover, the care required to transport partially completed likenesses would have presented far greater problems to the itinerant than the carrying of unused canvases. Occasional duplication of poses, costumes, and accessories by individual painters indicates that repetition of familiar details was the easiest solution for the artist of limited experience.

Landscapes, real or imaginery, were painted to special order. A view of the home of Joshua Winsor, a prominent merchant of Duxbury, Massachusetts, was executed by Dr Rufus Hatheway towards the end of the eighteenth century. Hatheway began his career as a travelling artist, but exchanged the uncertainties of limning for the more stable profession of medicine after his marriage to Judith Winsor in 1795. In the right foreground, Mr Winsor may be be seen with keys in hand, making his way towards the wharves and warehouses which were the centre of his prosperous fishing business. A man (entirely out of proportion) stands on the forward deck of the two-masted vessel at right centre. He is firing a double-barrelled shotgun with results observable in the flight of ducks above.

Perspective was never of paramount importance to the folk artist and this element has been happily disregarded in Alexandr [sic] Boudrou's view of A. Dickson entering Bristol, Pennsylvania, in 1819. Here the subject, astride his white horse, has been featured in the centre of the scene. Far below, however, viewed by the artist from a different vantage point, several small buildings and a group of trade symbols have been painted in the manner of a pasteboard collage.

Genre, or scenes of everyday life, are not prevalent, but when the folk artist looked about him his pictorial observations were usually noteworthy. Apart from aesthetic considerations, folk pictures may be desirable for their documentary content, and domestic scenes are eagerly sought and carefully studied. The representation of the Nathan Hawley family painted in their Albany home on November 3, 1801, records a wealth of detail invaluable both to the antiquarian and the social historian. The combined elements of costumes, furniture, pictures, floor-covering, and window treatment make this interior worthy of special note (Plate 255A).

In addition to portraits and subject pieces some itinerants specialized in ornamental interior painting. Before the Revolution architectural trim painted to simulate marble or handsomely grained woods was fashionable, following European custom. Panelled chimney-breasts embellished with decorative landscapes were to be seen in many houses in New England and the South between 1750 and 1800. After the turn of the century plaster walls, decorated with stencilled and freehand patterns or scenic panoramas, were encountered also in upper New York, Kentucky, Ohio, and as far west as Indiana. At a period when wallpaper was scarce and expensive the travelling decorator was able to offer painted substitutes which provided a variety of patterns applied at minimum expense.

Wall designs were usually repeat-patterns utilizing geometric and floral motifs, or scenes chosen for their decorative quality. However, artists occasionally elected to use a topical subject of local interest, such as the unusual event illustrated in a partially ruined house in Deansboro, Oneida County, New York, and now preserved in the Shelburne (Vermont) Museum. This shows a man leaping over a waterfall, and is believed to represent Sam Patch, who travelled in New York State, making exhibition jumps, in the 1820s.

Amateur folk artists were motivated by social and educational requirements rather than by a desire for financial recompense. Included among the amateurs were men, women, and children, but the majority who painted for pleasure were young ladies who learned the rudiments of art as a requisite of a genteel education. Lessons in drawing and painting were given in academies and independent drawing schools, as well as through the medium of individual instruction books, of which many were available for home use.

During the second half of the eighteenth century decorative embroidered pictures, worked from patterns based on European engravings, were executed by young girls at home or in school. Towards the end of the century water-colour was combined with needlework, and ultimately painting superseded embroidery as a pictorial medium. Water-colour on paper or fabric (such as silk, satin, or velvet) characterized ladies' work, although pastel and oil on canvas were also used. Small portraits were done at home for family or friends. Landscapes were often charmingly unrealistic views of picturesque scenery. Episodes from the popular romantic novel, *Paul et Virginie*, served as inspiration for many schoolgirl pictures (Plate 255B). A carry-over of the influence of needlework technique may be recognized in many of these "fancy" pieces where the foliage is cleverly painted to simulate different types of embroidery stitches.

Still-life compositions – vases of flowers, baskets of fruit, and handsome arrangements which combined the two – were typical of the amateur repertoire. White cotton velvet was a favourite medium for this type of picture during the years from 1810–40. The textured surface imparted a rich background for brilliant colours which were specifically designated in the instruction books for the painting of fruit and flowers.

Religious scenes inspired by illustrations in family Bibles were considered particularly suitable subjects for young amateurs, and included such popular favourites as the *Prodigal Son*, the *Good Samaritan*, *Jephtha's Return*, and *Moses in the Bulrushes*. Two scenes have been found picturing different incidents in the story of Ruth and Naomi. These were apparently often painted in pairs, as several examples by different artists have been found.

Akin to these subjects were the mourning pictures which suggested the preoccupation with death which was widespread in the nineteenth century. Family mortuary pieces reflecting these sentiments followed an ac-cepted pattern and were painted by countless young girls during the first half of the century. The tombs, the river, the weeping willows, churches, and mourners were not intended to be literal representations. They were conventional symbols expressing the universality of death while suggesting a belief in immortality which triumphs beyond the grave. Names of parents, grandparents, and other deceased relatives were placed on these memorials, or they were occasionally left blank according to the fancy of the artist. Glass painting was popular with the professional and the amateur. By the nineteenth century such painting was being done freehand without mechanical aid, and many decorative designs appeared for clock panels, mirror tops and other utilitarian purposes.

While some folk artists were able to paint creatively, many others derived their inspiration from basic sources of design. Copying well-known works of art was an accepted method of instruction at a time when originality was not stressed as it is today. One of the most comprehensive collections of pictorial source material was to be found in the many illustrated art instruction books which were imported from England in the late eighteenth century. Numerous American editions followed which contained illustrations based on English originals. This accounts for the appearance of rustic cottages and picturesque castles, in early schoolgirl art, which are hardly indigenous to the American scene. The lithographs of Currier and Ives, pictures in *Gleason's Pictorial* and *Godey's Lady's Book*, and illustrations such as the Bartlett views in Willis' *American Scenery*, all provided good copy material. If the resulting reproduction was a free and imaginative adaptation, a significant example of folk painting might ensue despite its basic lack of originality.

Folk art has appeared at different periods in many parts of the United States, but the two territories which have produced the most regionally diversified material are New England and Pennsylvania. In New England the professional artists were predominantly of English stock, and American portraits of the seventeenth century reflect the style of provincial English painting of the sixteenth and seventeenth centuries. During the mid-eighteenth century numerous English mezzotints were imported into this country and provided models for aspiring colonial painters whose skill was unable to match the exacting requirements of their aristocratic subjects. Poses and costumes were copied with painstaking fidelity, but backgrounds and accessories were simplified according to fancy, and the faces were the only personal insertions. At this period there was little demand for the genuine but unflattering likenesses of the folk artist, and it was not until immediately after the Revolution that face-painting from life, free from artificiality, became generally acceptable to the average citizen.

As fresh territory was opened up towards the West many New Englanders travelled out to settle on the newly expanding frontier. A few carried their family portraits with them, but the majority were happy to patronize the travelling artists who followed in the wake of the pioneers. Folk painters from New England also journeyed through the South, but they encountered competition from the foreign-born artists who emigrated to Philadelphia, Baltimore, Charleston, and New Orleans. This circumstance, with the factors of climate, exigencies of war, and an economy based on slave labour, accounts in part for the apparent scarcity of southern folk painting.

Differing entirely from the pictorial folk art of the north-eastern states were certain traditional forms brought from the Rhineland by Protestant refugees. These people, encouraged by William Penn and his agents, began their migration to the counties of south-eastern Pennsylvania in the late seventeenth century and continued to settle until the American Revolution. Illuminated family documents – birth and baptismal certificates, religious texts, and rewards of merit – are known as *Fraktur* because of a similarity of lettering to the sixteenth-century type-face of that name. Gay water-colour borders, frequently incorporating stylized birds, angels, animals, or flowers, surrounded the hand-lettered texts. Most of these documents were executed by local ministers, school-masters, or itinerant penmen.

The decline of folk art in America commenced about the middle of the nineteenth century. Mechanical inventions made multiple reproductions possible, and thereby obviated the need for the individual craftsman. Inexpensive lithographs were widely distributed for home consumption, and these gradually replaced the work of the schoolgirls and the hand-lettered texts of the *Frakturschriften*. The invention of the daguerreotype in 1839 was a decisive step towards modern photography, whose speed and accuracy were destined eventually to supplant the traditional methods of the folk painter.

British

As with most countries, the painting of medieval England consisted almost entirely of mural paintings (e.g. those at Canterbury, Eton, and many small country churches such as Pickering, Yorks.) and illuminated manuscripts. The miniature paintings adorning manuscripts are often of great beauty and interest, remarkable for their keen observation of natural phenomena. A few painted boxes, lids, and cupboards exist, but are usually in a bad state of repair. By the time of the early Tudors (c. 1490) panel portraits began to appear. Portraiture was always to be one of the strong points of British art, and for the next two centuries it was its dominant mode of expression. Most sixteenth- and seventeenth-century portraits bear either the subject's coat-of-arms, motto, name, age, or various combinations of all four. In the Tudor and early Stuart period a great number of panel portraits were painted in England. The most important foreign artist to come to England was Holbein, and though only a few local artists attached themselves to him, his imitators have been legion, and the "style of Holbein" covers a multitude of sins. In the Jacobean period, although great attention is still paid to details of dress and accessories, and though as much as possible is done to indicate the subject's social standing, there is a greater freedom of composition and handling apparent. A good deal of the new delicacy of technique seems to have come from the native school of miniaturists. Although inscriptions are sometimes to be found at the base of these pictures, coats-of-arms begin to disappear, their place being taken by distant vistas of parkland or views of houses. All the paintings of this period are marked by a very smooth surface, and since most of them have had a very rough and tumble country-house existence with extremes of heat and cold, dryness and humidity, their physical condition is usually unsatisfying. The collector anxious to familiarize himself with Elizabethan and early Stuart portraiture would do well to examine the portraits to be found in many of the Oxford College halls.

Charles I was largely responsible for the birth of post-medieval English painting. By patronage, and by the importation of artists of such international repute as Rubens and Van Dyck, he liberated English painting from its northern provincialism, and introduced the vital elements of the baroque Renaissance. Rubens had little influence in England at this time, but Van Dyck provided a formula for country-house portraiture which was to outlast the century, engender the "cavalier" type, and provide a wealth of confusion for all subsequent amateurs of art. His influence was to reach as far as Lawrence in the nineteenth century. The Civil War seriously disrupted these encouraging beginnings and Van Dyck's most promising pupil, William Dobson (1610–46), died young. His output was limited, but there was a new spaciousness in his painting, and a sophistication lacking in the work of earlier artists. What Dobson was to the Royalists, Robert Walker (c. 1600–60) was to the Parliamentarians, and there are numerous versions of his portrait of Cromwell. More austere in his conception, he

owed a good deal to the older Flemish tradition.

Peter van der Faes (1618–80), usually known as Lely, arrived in England at the age of twenty-three with another version of Van Dyck's formula more easily reproducible, and perfectly fitted for the modest demands of English patronage between 1650 and 1750. The new sense of informality of which he was master is indicated by the fact that his sitters are in their informal clothes, and the heraldic-like stiffness of the early portrait style survived only among small provincial painters.

Those anxious to analyse Lely's style and methods of execution should study the unfinished *Prince Rupert* in the National Portrait Gallery. He was an assured draughtsman and a fine colourist. But it is estimated that hardly one-fifth of the pictures which bear his name are actually by him, while only a small proportion of those show his real power. He was England's first successful society portrait painter. Of those who worked with Lely the most interesting are John Riley (1646–91) and John Greenhill (1644–76). Godfrey Kneller, the source of the next bout of foreign inspiration (1646–1723), is reputed to have been a pupil of Rembrandt. He laid the foundations on which the portraitists of the eighteenth century were to build. His fine, fluent brushwork is seen at its best in the portraits of the members of the Kit Kat Club. Kneller sketched in his subjects in a few simple tones on a background of grey, and then filled in with brush-point strokes.

By the eighteenth century English painting was beginning to accommodate itself to the larger European developments. Collectors became more active, and threw open their collections to students and England began to escape from the tyranny of the portrait. Landscapes became popular; so, too, did that typical English compromise between landscape, genre, and portraiture, the conversation piece.

The blending of these influences is first seen in the work of Sir James Thornhill (1675–1734), who did a good deal of decorative work, especially at Greenwich. He is chiefly remembered, however, as the father-in-law of William Hogarth (1697–1764). Perhaps the main factor responsible for Hogarth's fame was the fact that many of his moral paintings were extensively engraved, and in that form are still to be found in abundance everywhere. His earliest works are small portraits and conversation pieces, not basically different from those of Gawen Hamilton (1697–1737). All his works are marked by a robust rich handling of paint and by lively colour. They are mostly in a good state of preservation, though some are cracked. Signing is not consistent: sometimes it is *W. Hogarth Pinxit*, or *Hogarth Pinxit*, or sometimes they are not signed at all. His favourite colours, and the most distinctive, were harmonies of rose colour, old gold, and warm green. Though by virtue of the prints he influenced many provincial artists, Hogarth found no disciples, and the only one of his contemporaries whose art approximated to his own was Joseph Highmore (1692–1780).

Meanwhile, the conversation piece was developing in the hands of such artists as Arthur Devis (*c.* 1710–87); Marcellus Laroon (1679–1722); William Hoare of Bath (*c.*1706–92 and George Beare of Salisbury (*c.* 1740). The style of the conversation piece had by now become standardized: a group of figures well to the fore, surrounded, as if it were on a stage, by evidence of domestic or landed wealth.

The growing predominance of landscape in such paintings is indicative of the popularity of the genre. Occasional excursions, usually in wash or opaque water-colour are to be found as far back as the early sixteenth century. By about 1630 Thomas Wyck was painting views of London in the Dutch tradition, and there were several local artists, such as Thomas Ross, who painted views of Herefordshire. George Lambert (1710–65) specialized in views of country houses and produced for the East India Company a series of views of their settlements in collaboration with Samuel Scott (1702–72). Commencing his career in the Dutch "brown" style, but later revealing a rare gift for open-air interpretation, he added a good deal to the tradition of the Dutch maritime artists, who clearly influenced him. He lived at various times in London, Ludlow, and Bath, and his work is distinguishable from that of his many imitators by his strong, well-drawn detail and successful atmospheric effects. Richard Wilson (1714–82) is one of the most admired eighteenth-century landscape painters. Identification is complicated by the fact that he did several versions of one subject. Some of his works bear the monogram RW, the R being in reverse. Topographical accuracy is not always a guide to the authenticity of his works, for he usually made rough drawings on the spot, and then filled in often imaginative details. Although stylistically there are no wide variations in his work, the subject matter ranges from classical views in the Italian style to local paintings, mostly of London and North Wales. He paid little attention to detail, and used thick, fat paint, which often appears in circular pats on his paintings.

Part of Thomas Gainsborough's (1727–88) greatness lies in the fact that he combined landscape with portraiture, and in excelling at both satisfied a most basic English need. A good deal of his life was spent in the provinces, and he lived and worked at various times in Sudbury, Ipswich, Bath, and London. He painted landscape portraits and subject pictures, but did not sign them; and the portraits of the Ipswich period are usually smaller in size than those of other periods. His style is immediately recognizable, and few painters suffer more from the overvarnishing which nineteenth-century taste imposed on them. A supreme master of paint, he used oils rather like water-colour, laying on a fawn-coloured priming one stroke beside another or letting them overlap. This gives his work an extraordinary brilliance and luminosity. His composition is always remarkably full and complete, the portrait fitting in perfectly with the background, the analysis of character sensitive and penetrating.

The half-century of British art between, say, 1760 and 1810, is a golden age, most richly rewarding to collector and critic. Apart from the great names, there are countless lesser artists whose *œuvre* is now being more thoroughly investigated and appraised. Typical of these is Allan Ramsay (1713–84), who was trained in Italy, but who lived and worked in London. His work was uneven, but at its best showed a remarkable technical perfection, smooth in finish and excelling in the vivid meticulous description of textures, and producing some fine portraits of women. Francis Cotes (1725–70) achieved fame in his lifetime mainly as a pastellist; but from this medium he brought into his oil-paintings a vivacity and freshness which are outstanding. Nathaniel Dance (1735–1811), a specialist in the conversation piece, reflected the dominance of the Italian style, closely painted and brown in tonality.

Though the reputation of Sir Joshua Reynolds (1923–92) does not stand so high now as it did a century ago, he will always be acknowledged to be one of the most versatile and competent artists of the eighteenth century. Born in Devon, and travelling in France and Italy, he lived most of his life in London, where he rapidly became the official head of his profession. He relied a great deal on assistants and apprentices, but with a certain amount of trouble it is possible to verify most of his works by reference to his personal papers, some of which have been published, while others are still in manuscript. Some of his paintings are signed in the formula *J. Reynolds pinxit*, with the date of the year. Although greatly concerned with the problems of technique, many of his paintings are in a very bad condition because he used varnish as a medium and because of his injudicious use of bitumen. Many copies of his more popular works exist. His later works are nearly all heads and busts, the larger paintings belonging to his early and middle periods. It is almost impossible to distinguish all Reynolds' disciples and followers from his imitators. But the more outstanding in his circle are James Northcote (1746–1831), Thomas Beach (1728–1806); Daniel Gardner (c. 1750–1805), and Matthew William Peters (1724–1814). Many of the paintings attributed to Reynolds may well have been the work of one of these artists.

George Romney (1734–1802) was born in Lancashire and worked there till 1762, when he moved to London. He never exhibited at the Royal Academy, and is known chiefly as a portrait painter. His works are generally unsigned, and they show a marked deterioration towards the end of his life. Many exist in replica, especially his portraits of Emma, Lady Hamilton, of which there are some fifty versions. Joseph Wright of Derby (1734–94) excelled in dramatic *tenebrosi* paintings, which show strong light and shade.

More and more attention was now being paid to various aspects of social life. The conversation piece reached its apotheosis in the work of John Zoffany (1734–1810), who also specialized in theatrical paintings. His work often possesses a hard mechanical quality with a rather metallic finish. Interest now, however, was turning to more rural subjects, and the market was flooded with those hunting, sporting, and country-life subjects still exemplified in thousands of country-house paintings, most of them well worth the attention of both established collector and amateur. George Morland (1763–1804) produced rather sentimental pictures of country life, marked eventually by a fatal facility. They are mostly signed *G. Morland*. He favoured mahogany panels, and his brushwork is characterized by a scribble-like effect, the paint thick and creamy. Closely allied to Morland in outlook was Francis Wheatley (1747–1801), who had the same facile gifts of sentimentalization. The prints of his "Cries of London" are the most popular and widely disseminated of his works.

Landscape painting meanwhile was going from strength to strength, largely through the influence of the water-colourists and the new interest in topography. There are a few known oil-paintings by Alexander Cozens (c. 1720–86), but his son, John Robert (c. 1752–97), was praised by Constable as "the greatest genius that ever touched landscape". John Crome (1768–1821) lived and died in Norwich, and his landscape paintings, of great amplitude and technical virtuosity, fecundated the art of his native town and bridged the gap between the eighteenth and nineteenth centuries: he linked Wilson to Constable.

Joseph Mallord William Turner (1775–1851) is generally considered the greatest individual English painter: and he is probably the most prolific. His known works run into many thousands, and for the most part are landscapes in which the influence of the earlier water-colourists can be detected. Classical subjects (*Dido Building Carthage*); English landscape (*Crossing the Brook*); Italian and European landscapes (*Venice, The Bridge of Sighs*); sea paintings (*Calais Pier, an English Packet Arriving*); and symbolic paintings (*Rain, Steam, and Speed*) are the main varieties of subject to which he applied himself. He painted on canvas and millboard, and the authenticity of most of his major paintings can be verified by reference to his *Liber Veritatis*, an illustrated catalogue drawn up by himself. His paintings are unsigned, but their amazing virtuosity clearly differentiates them from the work of imitators and disciples. The effects are extremely complex, passages of densely opaque colour alternate with transparent ones. Sometimes the palette knife is used, even in conjunction with expanses of finely brushed colour. John Constable (1776–1837) was more personal. In facing nature as it was, he liberated nineteenth-century art from the dominance of the academy and the studio and founded the modern attitude to landscape. His paintings of East Suffolk, London, Brighton, Salisbury, Weymouth, and a few other places are unique in the history of art. The high price of his works has fostered an assiduous school of copyists and imitators whose productions were appearing in his own lifetime. Several versions also exist of many of his subjects. Great attention is now paid to his sketches, which have an almost miraculous freshness of conception and understanding. Occasionally he signed his earlier paintings *J. Constable f.* Richard Bonington (1802–28) came nearest to Constable in actual inspiration, his translucent landscapes reflected once again the primacy of water-colour, and greatly influenced the French romantics. He signs RPB, *R. P. Bonington.*

A new and grandiose conception of portraiture was growing and was revealed in the work of Henry Raeburn (1756–1823), who introduced a new realism of observation and movement. Thomas Lawrence (1769–1830) was a prodigy throughout his life, the courtier-painter *par excellence*. The restrained rhetoric of his portraits sometimes blinds us to their real painterly qualities. His paintings (unsigned) are usually large, in size as well as conception. His success engendered a whole school of followers, his main contemporary rivals being Sir Martin Archer Shee (1769–1850), William Beechey (1753–1839), and John Hoppner (1758–1810).

The apocalyptic feelings which were current early in the century seemed to foster a growth of strangely eccentric artists, including the Michelangelesque James Barry (1741–1806), the curiously rhetorical Swiss Henry Fuseli (1741–1825), and the most impressive and important of them all, William Blake (1757–1826), many of whose works (apart from the water-colours) are in a state of considerable disrepair because of his experiments in media. Connected with Blake were Samuel Palmer (1805–81), whose reputation is booming, and Edward Calvert (1803–33).

Constable marks the apogee of English painting, and, though the taste for nineteenth century British art is strengthening, its aesthetic basis has not yet been completely vindicated. A prolific master of the nude, William Etty (1787–1849) produced works which were almost Venetian in their coloured abundance. He was more fortunate in his worldly career than Benjamin Robert Haydon (1786–1846), who sought to reinstate "history painting" in its proper place, but succeeded only in creating the prototype of that anecdotal painting to be popular for the rest of the century. His gifts were at least as considerable as those of David Wilkie (1785–1841), who added a rather cloying sentimental gloss to a technically competent pastiche of the Dutch genre painters.

BRITISH WATER-COLOUR PAINTING

Water-colour painting is a branch of aesthetic expression in which the English, as a nation, excel: so much so that water-colour has been called the English art. It is true that other nations have practised it. Individual geniuses, like Dürer, Van Dyck, certain

French artists, and that fine American painter Winslow Homer, have achieved remarkable works in this medium. The Orientals were great exponents, but most water-colour painting of real merit during the last two hundred years has been done by practitioners in the United Kingdom.

The subject is a vast one, but the amateur need not be discouraged by its complexities, as these can be reduced to a logical whole. It is important to remember that the finest work in water-colour was achieved between 1770 and 1830. During those sixty years most of the great masters were born and had their working lives. There were, of course, a few excellent water-colourists prior to 1770 and after 1830. But the collector is reminded that any water-colour bearing a date towards the end of the eighteenth century or in the first three decades of the nineteenth is of good vintage period; though that does not mean that it is necessarily a good or important work. The chances are, however, that it will be interesting. The most important water-colourists who came to maturity during that time were:

JOHN ROBERT COZENS	1752–1797
THOMAS GIRTIN	1775–1802
J. M. W. TURNER	1775–1851
JOHN VARLEY	1778–1842
WILLIAM HAVELL	1782–1857
JOHN SELL COTMAN	1782–1842
DAVID COX	1783–1859
SAMUEL PROUT	1783–1852
PETER DE WINT	1784–1849
A. V. COPLEY FIELDING	1787–1855

Hunting water-colours is a delightful game. To be able to identify styles is but a matter of practice. Reduced to its simplest, the task is like recognizing handwriting; for water-colour painting is, after all, an intricate form of calligraphy.

As to handwriting, a warning is added about signatures. They can be and often are important, but the connoisseur never trusts them entirely. Many great artists did not habitually sign their works; and it is good policy to look at the water-colour first and the signature last. A signature is the easiest work that an artist does, and the easiest thing for

the unscrupulous to forge. Be on guard against the ostentatious inscription, obviously so placed and sometimes enlarged, to attract the eye. Nor are artists' signatures consistent. They vary like the styles of their works. In his youth, for instance, John Varley signed with block letters. Later, he wrote his signatures. Some artists used monograms. Others signed on the backs of their water-colours.

Help can sometimes be gained by studying watermarks of the paper that the artist used, if there is a date on it. Plausible "old masters" that might be taken seriously would appear to have painted after they were dead. Collectors have come across not unattractive works purporting to be by this or that famous man, only to discover that the watermarks are later than the death year of the artists in question.

The amateur should be careful when remounting or reframing an old water-colour to retain or to make a note of any documentation that may be on front or back – name of artist, time painted, description of subject, previous ownership. Pencil wording that the artist might have made to remind him of the colours needed to finish an incomplete work should be studied as useful in comparing such handwriting with the authentic signature.

A word of advice as to preserving old water-colours. Never hang them on walls that hold the sun for any length of time, as they are apt to fade. A few favourites can be exhibited in a quiet light, but it is as well to change them from time to time and keep the collection, generally, in cabinets or portfolios.

For the purpose of studying the subject, the Print Rooms at the British Museum and the Victoria and Albert Museum, as well as the provincial galleries, provide innumerable examples of the school. Much also can be learned from the auction rooms and dealers' galleries; and it is a good idea to keep a water-colour notebook as a help to memorize important examples that come up for sale from time to time. All reproductions of water-colours, and catalogues, should be retained for reference.

A fact to remember is that works by famous artists are constantly available, and sensational finds are not impossible. Within recent years the *Vauxhall Gardens*, by Thomas Rowlandson, a long-lost but very fine work, was bought in a village shop for a pound and subsequently sold at Christie's for £2,730. This is the luck of a lifetime, and very exceptional luck at that. But quite good water-colours can be acquired in the sale-rooms for from five to fifteen pounds.

Beyond such places, and the reputable dealers' galleries, there are bookshops, second-hand-furniture dealers, and stalls that display portfolios of water-colours where interesting old sketches can be acquired at a few shillings each. Following such a plan, a collection can be built up gradually for a moderate outlay.

As in every other department of collecting, the amateur must learn by experience to know what he wants, and though it is always satisfying to one's vanity to get bargains, the true delight of connoisseurship is in making oneself an expert on a matter worthy of one's intelligence.

The reader must be prepared for a slight change in approach as we turn to living artists – men and women who, if ageing, have the best part of a life's work to speak for them and, if young, may exceed or never fulfil the predictions of the critics. Comparison and discrimination become out of place and stupid when dealing with contemporaries.

The two largest of the annual exhibitions of water-colours are those held by the Royal Institute (R.I.) and in the Royal Academy (South Room). The Royal Society of Painters in Water Colours (R.W.S.), founded in 1804, is the oldest water-colour society in our island, if not in the world, and it has never lost the prestige of its seniority. With its forty members and twenty-five or thirty associates, it holds two shows, in spring and autumn, and since works by outside artists are not admitted, the exhibitions are of convenient size; they possess, too, other characteristics worthy of note. Election, eagerly sought and hard to gain, comes only to men and women sufficiently accomplished to satisfy the critical standards of the members; one of the most famous of its senators applied seven times before being admitted. At the Society's gallery in Conduit Street there is always to be had a true indication of the state of the British school, of the endless varieties which may be played on a traditional theme.

The Royal Institute of Painters in Water Colours (R.I.) is only some twenty-five years younger than the R.W.S., but there are notable differences between the two. Besides having a larger membership, the R.I., like the Royal Academy, admits pictures from non-members. In its large exhibitions, therefore, one may see the work not only of the members but also of sundry promising young artists who cannot yet put magical initials after their names. One may see, too, the uncommissioned paintings of some of the leaders of commercial or industrial art, of men like the President, Norman Wilkinson, whose posters one looks for when changing trains at junctions, or Rowland Hilder, whose botanical plates are often the most beautiful and delightful of all the features of the best magazines (Plate 261B). There was a time when such references, to such people and such artists, would have been thought out of place in a serious estimate of the water-colour. Today there are many good judges who believe that if Posterity decides, as well it may, that we are in, or beginning, a minor renaissance, it will pay close attention to the influence of men like Wilkinson and Hilder, of Ravilious, Ronald Searle, John Ward, and others who have sallied out and sought the adversary, and won him over. Indeed, among the famous names of the past, there are more precedents for the industrial artist than is commonly supposed, and anyone starting to make a collection today might take a novel and profitable line by acquiring the spontaneous work of the best designers of posters and advertisements.

Two more happy hunting grounds for the collector must not be overlooked – the New English Art Club, where the water-colour section, if small, is invariably choice, and (in some ways the most important, since it is the best attended of all) the Royal Academy, which, at its summer exhibitions, offers the second largest of the annual displays of water-colours. Ten years ago it was persuaded, by Sir William Russell Flint, to open not merely its doors but also its membership to artists who confine themselves to water-colour.

Unlike their elders, few of the younger

water-colourists have studied abroad, in Paris or elsewhere, or been able to travel so frequently. So, if landscape still predominates in the pictures we hunt in vain for sunsets in the Pyrenees, storms in the Alps, or eruptions in Sicily; instead, we find smaller heights and more restrained weather, a wet afternoon on the Quantocks or, at the most, snow on the Grampians. The gorgeous palaces, the solemn temples have fared worse still, being largely supplanted by the flower-piece, the nature study, the interior, and the unidentified portrait. There is no cause for regret, we may even rejoice that our artists, more than any preceding generation of artists, have taught us to find beauty in our everyday homes and surroundings.

The experienced collector will have decided where his tastes lie and who are the men whose pictures he means to pursue. As for the diffident beginner, his first object should be to train and educate his eye, to form his own tastes. This he can do only by continual searching, and it is for that reason that we have stressed the local arrangements of the art, its principal foci outside the dealers. Though his instinctive preferences will quickly announce themselves, he should be slow to trust them or to assume from the start that painters whose work does not immediately appeal to him are necessarily men of sensitiveness inferior to his own.

Yet when all is said and done, pictures are like faces; other people may be right, one's own opinion may be wrong, but one has to come back to it, to a personal reaction independent of glamour and publicity, to something impossible to pin down. To buy as an investment is unwise, to buy as an investment on the strength of someone else's views is particularly unwise, however instructed and honest they may be. On the other hand, anyone who, having taken pains to form and formulate tastes of his own, chooses a picture as he chooses a friend will be warmed and ennobled by an act of sympathy, cheered by congenial company, and just possibly rewarded, some years later, by the discovery that he has carried off a prize. The chance is slight, but it is the best available.

BRITISH PORTRAIT MINIATURES

When, during the last ten years of his life, Holbein painted a series of small circular portraits in opaque water-colour on vellum, he was not so much inventing a new art-form as giving authority to one which had been in the process of evolution for some time. But it was not until Holbein brought his consummate genius to the problem that the tradition can be said to have been firmly established. In a space of a few years Holbein brought to perfection the experiments of his immediate predecessors and set a standard for all those who came after him.

Holbein's miniatures – or "limnings", as they were called – all belong to his second visit to England: that is, to the period between 1532 and his death in 1543. According to the most recent authorities, not more than a dozen of the limnings sometimes attributed to him can be accepted as authentic; of these the two most readily accessible to the visitor (the *Anne of Cleves* and the *Mrs Pemberton* in the Victoria and Albert Museum) are of superlative quality. The characteristics of Holbein's vision and technique were a minute sensitivity of draughtsmanship, an intense and glowing colour, and a completely unflattering psychological penetration into the personality of his sitter. This detailed concentration he combined with a largeness of conception and design which gives a paradoxical monumentality to portraits which average little more than an inch in diameter.

After Holbein's death there was a short period during which it may have seemed that his challenging example was not to be taken up. But with the maturity of Nicholas Hilliard (1547–1619), any doubts for the future of the art were triumphantly laid to rest. For just as Holbein, in his miniatures and his other portraits, had preserved for all time the outward appearance of the court of Henry VIII, so Hilliard's miniatures became the perfect visual counterpart of the age of Elizabeth I.

(A) Portraits of Mr and Mrs Wilson of Hull, Yorks, with Huntsmen and Hounds by George Stubbs. *Leger Galleries.*

(B) A Groom holding "Tristram Shandy" in a Landscape by George Stubbs. *Leger Galleries.*

PLATE 257

Salisbury Cathedral, Interior, North Transept by J. M. W. Turner. *Collection of Vice-Admiral Sir William Agnew*, K.C.V.O.

PLATE 258

(A) Chiswick from the River by John Varley. *Collection of John Braithwaite.*

(B) Eton College by John Sell Cotman. *British Museum, London.*

PLATE 259

(A) Caen by Samuel Prout. *Fine Art Society.*

(B) Seascape by A. V. Copley Fielding. *Collection of A. Holman.*

PLATE 260

(A) Landscape Study at Hungerford by Paul Nash. *Collection of Dudley Tooth.*

(B) The Medway above Rochester by Rowland Hilder. *Artist's Collection.*

PLATE 261

(B) Loch Earn by Sir D. Y. Cameron. *Collection of Ian MacNicol.*

(A) Stillingfleet All Saints by John Piper. *Collection of Mrs Hughes.*

PLATE 262

(A) The River, Ironbridge by P. Wilson Steer. *Tate Gallery, London.*

(B) Harvest at Fairlight by P. H. Jowett. *Private Collection.*

PLATE 263

(A) Mrs Robert Pemberton by Hans Holbein. *Victoria and Albert Museum, London.*

(B) Queen Elizabeth by Nicholas Hilliard. *Collection of Lord Derby.*

(C) A man, wrongly called "Thomas Howard, 2nd Earl of Arundel", by Isaac Oliver. *Collection of Duke of Portland.*

(D) Lady Catherine Howard by John Hoskins. *Victoria and Albert Museum, London.*

PLATE 264

A

B

C

D

(A) Edward Montagu, 1st Earl of Sandwich, by Samuel Cooper. Signed, and dated 1659. *Victoria and Albert Museum, London.*

(B) Self portrait by Thomas Flatman. *Victoria and Albert Museum, London.*

(C) Colonel Kellet by Bernard Lens. *Victoria and Albert Museum, London.*

(D) An unknown lady by Samuel Cotes. Signed, and dated 1773. *Victoria and Albert Museum, London.*

PLATE 265

(A) An unknown lady by George Engleheart. *H. E. Backer.*
(B) An unknown lady by Andrew Plimer. *H. E. Backer.*
(C) Self-portrait by Sir W. C. Ross. *Victoria and Albert Museum, London.*
(D) The Duchess of Bredalbane by Andrew Robertson. Signed, and dated 1810. *H. E. Backer.*

PLATE 266

An English third rate running in a light breeze by Charles Brooking (1723–59). Signed C. BROOKING.
Canvas 27 × 17 ins. *National Maritime Museum, Greenwich.*

PLATE 267

Lord Hood's action with de Grasse in Frigate Bay, St Kitts, on January 20th, 1778, by Nicholas Pocock (1741–1821). Signed and dated N. POCOCK 1788. Canvas 47½ × 85 ins. *National Maritime Museum, Greenwich.*

PLATE 268

(A) Finish of the Derby, 1846, by Henry T. Alken. *Leggatt Brothers, London.*

(B) Coursers taking the field at Hatfield Park by James Pollard. $40\frac{1}{2} \times 56\frac{1}{2}$ ins. *F. Ambrose Clark Collection, U.S.A.*

PLATE 269

(A) Thomas Smith, Senior, Huntsman of the Brocklesby Hounds and his son Tom, Whipper-in by George Stubbs. *The Earl of Yarborough Collection.*

(B) Gimcrack by George Stubbs. *The Jockey Club, Newmarket.*

PLATE 270

(A) The Smugglers by T. S. Good, *c.* 1840. *Private Collection.*

(B) A Village Choir by Thomas Webster, 1847. *Victoria and Albert Museum, London.*

PLATE 271

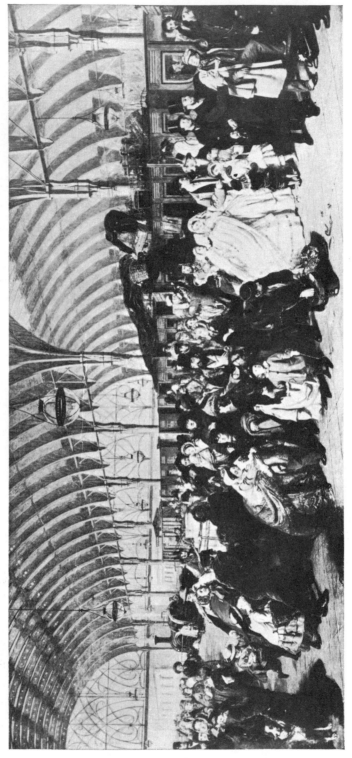

Paddington Station by W. P. Frith, 1862. *The Royal Holloway College, Egham.*

PLATE 272

(B) The Letter of Introduction by David Wilkie, 1813. *National Gallery of Scotland, Edinburgh.*

(A) The Sonnet by William Mulready, 1838. *Victoria and Albert Museum, London.*

PLATE 273

(B) Interior of an Inn by Adriaen van Ostade. *Matthiesen Gallery.*

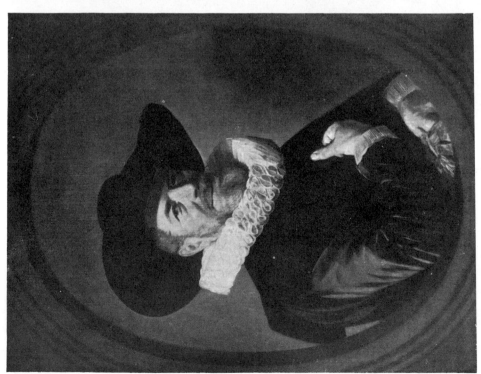

(A) Portrait of a Gentleman by Frans Hals. *Duke of Bedford's Collection. Woburn Abbey.*

PLATE 274

A Girl at a House Door by Rembrandt. *Duke of Bedford's Collection, Woburn Abbey.*

PLATE 275

Still Life by Pieter van Anraadt. *Formerly Duits Ltd.*

PLATE 276

(A) Ruins with Figures by Charles de Hooch. *T. Agnew.*

(B) Landscape by Nicolaes (Claes) Hals. *Harold Vos.*

PLATE 277

(A) The Adoration of the Kings by Peter Bruegel the Elder. *National Gallery, London.*

(B) Venus at her Toilet by Rubens. *Collection of Prince Liechtenstein.*

(C) Portrait of Gailer von Kaisersberg by Cranach. *Munich, Pinakothek.*

(D) Self-portrait by Van Dyck. *Munich, Pinakothek.*

PLATE 278

The Royal Sovereign 100 of 1701 wearing the standard of King William III, by Willem van de Welde the Younger (1633–1707). Signed and dated W. VAN VELDE J. 1704. Canvas 70 by 57 ins. *National Maritime Museum, Greenwich.*

PLATE 279

Shipping off the English coast about 1645 by Simon de Vlieger (*c.* 1600–53). Signed s. DE VLIEGER. Panel 24 × 32 ins. *The National Maritime Museum, Greenwich.*

PLATE 280

The Embarkation of Spanish Troops about 1652 by Andries van Ertvelt (1590–1652). Signed A. V. ERTVELT. Panel 29½ × 48 ins.
National Maritime Museum, Greenwich.

PLATE 281

Portrait of a Young Boy by De Largillière. *Norbert Fischman Gallery.*

PLATE 282

(A) Le Savetier by Jean-Baptiste Pater. *Matthiesen Gallery.*

(B) Perette by Boucher. *Frank T. Sabin.*

(C) Portrait of Madame Seriziat with her Son by David. *Louvre, Paris.*

PLATE 283

Au Concert by Pierre Auguste Renoir, dated 1880. Oil on canvas 38¾ × 32 ins. *Sterling and Francine Clark Art Institute, Williamstown, Masssachusetts.*

PLATE 284

Le Garçon au Gilet Rouge by Paul Cézanne, painted 1890–5. Oil on canvas $31\frac{1}{2} \times 25$ ins. *American Private Collection.*

PLATE 285

Danseuse sur la Scène by Edgar Degas, drawn *c.* 1881. Pastel 25 × 19½ ins. *Parke-Bernet Galleries, New York.*

PLATE 286

(A) Le Pont de Courbevoie by Georges Seurat, painted in 1886. Oil on canvas 18 × 21½ ins. *Courtauld Institute of Art, London.*

(B) Le Pont Neuf, Après-Midi, Soleil by Camille Pissarro, dated 1901. Oil on canvas 28¾ × 36¼ ins. *Parke-Bernet Galleries, New York.*

PLATE 287

(A) Jardin Public à Arles by Vincent van Gogh, painted in 1888. Oil on canvas 28¾ × 36¼ ins. *Rosenberg & Stiebel, New York.*

(B) I await the letter by Paul Gauguin, dated 1899. Oil on canvas 29 × 37½ ins. *Rosenberg & Stiebel, New York.*

PLATE 288

Hilliard was the son of an Exeter goldsmith, and though his work naturally reflects the influence of Holbein and, to a lesser degree, that of other Continental artists, it remained essentially English. While sharing Holbein's absorption in the character of his sitter, Hilliard shared with the leading spirits of his age that curious quality which can best be described as a kind of half-frivolous melancholy – the quality which is most familiar from some of Shakespeare's sonnets. Though it is more evident at some times than at others, this complicated and characteristic sentiment is never far to seek in his miniatures. Hilliard is perhaps best known as the portraitist *par excellence* of Queen Elizabeth, and from 1584 he was granted the monopoly of the Queen's portraits "in little". Although he lived far into the reign of James I, his best work belongs to the Elizabethan period.

Hilliard's pupil Isaac Oliver (d. 1617) is often spoken of as his rival; in a purely worldly sense he probably was so. But we can now see that the personalities and the achievements of the two artists were quite dissimilar. Though his earlier works may often be confused with those of his master, from about 1590 onwards Oliver developed a vision new to British art. The dramatic lighting which he increasingly brought to bear upon his subjects was, in fact, a reflection of the type of lighting adopted by his Flemish contemporaries in oils, and the naturalism of his modelling can be traced to the same source. Nevertheless, Oliver was a perfectly integrated artist, and external influences never disfigure his works in their crude state. Just as Hilliard found his ideal *milieu* in the Elizabethan court, so Oliver found in the court of James I a field of expression for which his talents were by nature adapted. A Huguenot by birth and cosmopolitan by temperament, he also proved an excellent filter through which Continental influences could reach this country.

Both Hilliard and Oliver had sons who practised their fathers' art. The next important miniaturist to be considered, however, is neither Peter Oliver nor Laurence Hilliard but John Hoskins, an artist who was roughly their contemporary. Hoskins was born in the

1590s, and his earliest signed works, which belong to the 1620s, show a natural and attractive development from the art of Hilliard rather than of Oliver. But from the 1630s, when Van Dyck settled in England, a change is seen to come over his work, and Hoskins' great historical importance consists no less in his becoming, as it were, a diminishing-glass for Van Dyck's large-scale innovations in English portraiture, than in his carrying on the classic tradition of his predecessor. For a short time the influence of Van Dyck seems to have unsettled Hoskins' style, but gradually he absorbed and digested it, and the miniatures of his maturity – that is, from about 1635 until his death in 1665 – show an entirely satisfactory fusion of his natural English vision with the baroque qualities of Van Dyck.

Hoskins had two nephews who were brought up under his "care and discipline". These were Samuel and Alexander Cooper, the first of whom was to become the greatest English miniaturist, if not the greatest English portrait-painter on any scale, of his century. He was born in 1609 and died in 1672. It seems almost certain that his uncle was his teacher as well as his guardian, and it may be that some of his earlier works have become confused with those of the older man. There are, however, a few miniatures by Cooper which can be assigned to the 1630s, and from 1642 until his death there is a coherent body of signed work on which to base our estimate of his achievement. In technique Cooper brought a new freedom of brushwork into miniature-painting. He also introduced a new system of lighting, whereby a single source of lighting threw the modelling of his subject into striking relief. But such technical devices were developed not so much on their own account as in order to assist what seems to have been Cooper's major preoccupation – the expression of character. In this he was pre-eminently successful; his portraits of Oliver Cromwell, Catherine of Braganza, and the young Duke of Monmouth, which cover the range from severity to youthful grace, are among the great European portraits of the century. During the last ten years of his life Cooper was limner to Charles II, and his high reputation extended far abroad. His elder brother, Alexander, was also a miniaturist. His career is less well documented than that of Samuel, but he is known to have worked much on the Continent, in Holland, and at the court of the King of Bohemia, and he is said to have died in Stockholm in 1660. His works are rare but excellent, though he does not seem to have developed along the fully baroque lines of his brother.

Of those who followed the lead of Samuel Cooper the most distinguished artist was Thomas Flatman (1635–88), who was also a barrister and a poet of some repute. His earlier miniatures, belonging to the 1660s, are very much dependent on Cooper. But during the last twenty years of his life a personal brilliance comes into his work, along with a further loosening of brushwork, which enable us to see in him a genuinely original artist. The miniaturists R. and D. Gibson, who may perhaps have been father and son, also reflect many of the same influences and are to be included among those who take their cue from Cooper. This is not so, however, of Nicholas Dixon, who was appointed Court Limner after Cooper's death. Neither his date of birth nor of death is recorded, but his earliest works belong to the 1660s, and he is known to have been still living in 1708. In style Dixon shows little or no dependence upon Cooper, springing, it seems, directly from Hoskins. In vision, however, he came strongly under the influence of Lely's mannerisms, and this may perhaps help to account for a gradual deterioration in his work.

The miniaturist Lawrence Crosse (d. 1724) was roughly the contemporary of Kneller. He may perhaps have been the son of an earlier miniaturist, P. Cross, who was the first in England to introduce the technical device of occasional stippling, instead of drawing throughout with fine continuous brushstrokes. Lawrence carried this technique even further, and as a result his miniatures have a characteristically powdery appearance which is most attractive. At his best he was very good indeed, and his work forms a fitting conclusion to the first great period of miniature-portraiture in England.

At the beginning of the eighteenth century portraiture seemed to be suffering a decline, and the art of the miniaturist, no less than that of the full-scale oil-painter, reflected this. The fact that the moment coincided with the introduction of a radically new technique can hardly be said to have simplified the miniaturist's problem. Up to this point miniatures had continued to be painted in essentially the same way: that is, in more or less opaque water-colour on vellum. But about 1700 the use of ivory was introduced as a base. The aesthetic advantage of ivory over vellum is that it gives superior luminosity. But in order to exploit this to the full, transparent pigment would have to be used throughout; and during the first part of the century this fact was not realized. Thus, when we look at them from the standpoint of history, the miniatures of Bernard Lens (1682–1740) and of his sons, Andrew Benjamin (1713?–after 1779?) and Peter Paul (1714?–50?), may perhaps seem unsatisfactory in their somewhat uninventive use of their new medium. Nevertheless, miniatures of the Lens school have a certain stolid charm, and their literalness of vision, which might easily become pompous if enlarged to the full scale of oil-paintings, has made them attractive tokens of the somewhat stolid society which they mirrored. Contemporary with Bernard Lens was the enamellist C. F. Zincke (1683?–1767), who continued with enormous success the craft which had been perfected in the previous century by Jean Petitot (1607–91).

About the middle of the eighteenth century the primness of style which we have remarked in Bernard Lens began noticeably to relax, and we find a group of miniaturists at work whose qualities have for too long been underrated. The main characteristics of the miniatures of this period are a smallness of size and an understatement of effect. Such artists as Gervase Spence (d. 1763), Luke Sullivan (1705–71), Nathaniel Hone, R.A. (1718–84), and Samuel Cotes (1734–1818) all worked mainly within this idiom during the period in question. Although none of them achieved the lightness of touch and the rococo brilliance which was to result from the looser draughtsmanship of their followers, they were capable of a delicacy and a naturalness beyond the scope of their immediate predecessors.

The last thirty years of the eighteenth century produced the climax of excellence in the miniature painted on ivory. That this period coincided approximately with the great epoch of English portraiture in oils can be held only partly responsible for the efflorescence.

The first miniature-painter in England to embody the later eighteenth-century virtues was Jeremiah Meyer, R.A. (1735–89), a German who came to England in 1749. He received some instruction in enamel from the elderly Zincke, and began to exhibit in the 1760s. From the early 1770s he was painting in perfectly transparent water-colours on ivory, and in this medium he developed a linear delicacy and brilliance which had previously been impossible. His works are seldom signed, but they may be recognized both for his personal calligraphy of draughtsmanship and for his predilection for pale lavender tints.

Richard Crosse (1742–1810) might appear to represent a transitional stage of development between the innovations of Meyer and the fulfilment and later degeneration of the school, if it were not that his works normally achieve a realization of intention which is complete. Like Meyer, he painted in enamel as well as in water-colour, and, like Meyer, he was master of a calligraphic style of great delicacy. Perhaps the most evident feature of his practice is the greenish-blue colouring which usually pervades his portraits. Crosse exhibited with success from 1760, but during the last twenty years of his life his output steadily declined in quantity.

There follow the three best-known miniaturists of the late eighteenth and early nineteenth century. Richard Cosway, R.A. (1742?–1821), John Smart (1741?–1811) and George Engleheart (1750–1829) were all of the same generation, and, although their styles were quite distinct, they are normally considered together to form the dominating influence in the late Georgian miniature. The early works of each of these artists already reveal minor mutual divergences, and from about 1780 their personal characteristics were fully formed. Cosway, the best known of the three, ob-

tained the patronage of the Prince of Wales, and the delicate *bravura* of his manner can be readily associated with the temperament of a fashionable portrait-miniaturist such as he rapidly became. Cosway's mature miniatures show a striking economy of colour and a sensitive dash of draughtsmanship that tempted many indifferent imitators. The works of his finest period, however (roughly 1785–1805), were, in fact, inimitable and stand among the most excellent of the century. Cosway virtually never signed his miniatures on the front, though he often wrote an elaborate Latin inscription on a piece of paper at the back. Thus, miniatures purporting to be by Cosway which have initials or a signature on the front are in the highest degree suspicious.

John Smart, who was Cosway's approximate contemporary, was master of a very different style. The subtle, meticulous manner which he developed in his earlier works remained his medium of expression for the rest of his life. Smart's miniatures are nearly all signed on the front with his initials, and dated; and those miniatures which he painted during his ten years' sojourn in India, between 1785 and 1795, are distinguished by the addition of the letter "I". His miniatures have a striking charm when one first approaches them – a charm of colour, finesse, and elegance – but their hardly varied smoothness and relative lack of characterization reflect a certain prosaic and generalizing quality of vision. Nevertheless, his exceptional technical accomplishment and his never less than charming gifts entitle him to his place near the head of his profession.

George Engleheart was a few years younger than Cosway and Smart. In his youth he worked for a time in Reynolds' studio, and his earlier miniatures retain something of the vision of his master, as well as many of the technical characteristics of the "Modest School". During the 1780s, however, he arrived at the distinct and personal style of his middle period, a style which was typified by a brittle and crimped manner of drawing hair and drapery, no less than by the emphatic concentration of the eyes and the effective illusion of a third dimension. Many of Engleheart's best works belong to this period. Before the end of the century, however, he had developed his third and final manner. The size of his ivory and the scale of his forms increased, and, although his technical excellence remained with him until he died, there is noticeably less distinction of imagination in these later works.

It was a time in which patronage of this art reached its highest intensity, calling forth a multiplicity of minor artists whose individual styles are often difficult to disentangle. Of these, one should first mention Ozias Humphry, R.A. (1742–1810), who was on occasion capable of reaching the highest contemporary standards; of roughly the same generation, and often met with, are Samuel Shelley (1750?–1808) and Edward Miles (1752–1828). The brothers Andrew (1763–1837) and Nathaniel (d. 1822?) Plimer had considerable reputations in their day, and are still highly esteemed by some collectors. The enamel tradition of Zincke was carried on to the end of the century by Henry Spicer (c. 1743–1804), among others.

During the first thirty years of the nineteenth century some fine miniaturists emerged; but one can also detect in their work the beginnings of a rapid decline in the art. Contemporary taste called for ever larger miniatures and a new solidity of manner "founded upon the Great Masters' works", by which was unfortunately meant the great masters of oil-painting. Works satisfying these conditions were supplied in increasing quantities by the artists who succeeded Cosway and Engleheart. Such artists as Andrew Robertson (1777–1845) and Sir W. C. Ross, R.A. (1794–1860) were able to retain some of the essential linear quality which can be seen at the basis of the art of all our great miniaturists, but gradually the art began to succumb to a surfeit of rich colours, gummed shadows, and inappropriate forcefulness. It needed only the invention of photography to deal the final blow.

BRITISH MARINE PAINTERS
eighteenth and early nineteenth centuries

It seems that the fortunes of sea power and marine painting go hand in hand. If this premise is correct, then the England of the early years of the eighteenth century was a very rich and ready soil indeed. Of the other two maritime nations, the French Navy was destroyed and the Dutch was subordinate. A lusty commerce, therefore, fed on war and victory, grew and grew, and in the arts literature and architecture flourished.

The first generation of English marine painters was alive and was learning from the Dutch, who were their teachers and their inspiration. Before they grow up, however, it would be only fair to consider what, if anything, had been produced by the generations of their fathers and their grandfathers.

At the National Maritime Museum, Greenwich, is a curious panel which depicts the defeat of the Spanish Armada in 1588. This is believed to be a design for a tapestry, but it is in itself a most artistic, highly stylized, piece of heraldic painting, almost certainly by a Freeman of the Painter Stainers Company.

It has absolutely nothing to do with the Netherlands school, yet at the same time its style was not one that had any future outside of design and heraldry.

First evidence of a serious native marine painter is in Vertue's notebooks when he wrote of an Isaac Sailmaker (1633?–1721) who worked in George Geldorp's studio as a pupil. Sailmaker is always talked of as being the father of the English school: and since he lived and worked in England for over seventy years, the English can probably claim him for their own. Yet he was, it seems, originally a Dutch boy who came early to England.

The mystery about Sailmaker is that though it is believed that he laboured hard all these years, not one signed or authenticated work exists, which would enable us to point to it and say, "That is a Sailmaker." There are, however, a number of paintings which, though based on the Dutch school, are different from it, and which have a rather crude vigour. These we believe to be by him. There are also at Greenwich two large paintings. One was painted in the early 1670s and is signed *H. Vale*, and the other is painted about 1710 and signed *R. Vale*; so there is evidence of a practising English family. But we know no more of them than their signed works.

Now to return to the young painters who were growing up in the shadow of the Dutch masters, the Van de Veldes, who exerted such an overpowering example and influence. The last of these Van de Veldes was Cornelis, and he was probably the master of the best of them. The two outstanding artists of the school of Van de Velde were Peter Monamy (*c.* 1686–1749) and Samuel Scott (1701/2–72).

Monamy was said to have been born in Jersey and came over as a coach painter. He had considerable success as a pure copyist of Van de Velde's paintings. His own style developed, and he adopted a new palette which was much more colourful than the Dutch palette. He was, in fact, a finished artist who could turn out works of sensibility and atmosphere and who had a thorough knowledge of his subject and his paints. Certainly, any painter who could produce such a painting as *An English flagship and other vessels becalmed at sundown* deserved a good reputation.

Samuel Scott, who was also a pioneer of the English school, was a much more versatile artist, and one who was fortunate to have the enthusiastic support of that powerful arbiter of taste and the arts, Horace Walpole. The best-known works of Scott are the views of the Thames in London; he is often referred to as the English Canaletto. Better than these, however, are his dockside scenes, which are very fine. His pure marine paintings are most competent and individual in style and palette, and he had the principal practice in historical marine painting until the Seven Years' War.

Other English painters were working in the first forty years of the eighteenth century, but we know little or nothing about them.

It is in the 1740s that the school really began to find its feet and to produce original and creative artists. Of this second generation of the English marine school, the finest painter was Charles Brooking (1723–59). He was not only the finest of his own generation but also of the generations before and of those to come. It is sad that his work had to cease when he was thirty-six. Brooking was a seaman who understood his subject perfectly. It appears that he was not strong and that rapacious dealers used to pay him so little for his work that he was forced to work much harder than his strength could stand. This aggravated the consumption which brought about his death. The sadness of his life and death have given posterity one benefit in that he had to work so hard that a great quantity of his paintings still survive. There is a fine collection of them at Greenwich. Among them is the splendid little canvas seen in Plate 267, one of his golden grey paintings.

A late pupil of Brooking, and, perhaps because he lived much longer, rather better known, was Dominic Serres (1722–93), a Frenchman who went to sea and became the master of a merchant vessel which was captured by the English in 1758 and brought to England. Instead of returning to the sea and his native France, he settled in London and became a professional marine painter. He had a large practice with naval officers and ship owners for historical paintings of actions and for ship portraits, backgrounds for portraits, and harbour scenes. Although he was a Frenchman, he learnt his trade in England, and must therefore be considered as a member of the English school. As such, he ranks as the most prolific and the most successful. He was also a founder member of the Royal Academy and marine painter to George III. He had two sons who painted marine subjects: Dominic, who exhibited at the Royal Academy from 1783 to 1804; and his much better known elder brother, John Thomas (1759–1825), whose works are still numerous. His painting is fresh, with a bright clean palette, though the execution is sometimes a trifle raw. He nevertheless succeeded his father as marine painter to the King. He was unfortunate, however, in the choice of a wife who was also a painter and who claimed to be a natural daughter of the Duke of Cumberland, a son of George III. Styling herself Princess, she finally ruined her husband by her extravagance and her debts, and he died in King's Bench prison.

Among other painters of the mid-eighteenth

century, the Clevely family made a large contribution. The father, John, is thought to have died in 1792. He was particularly a painter of the docks and of the shipbuilding yards. He also painted seascapes, but not apparently action subjects. His work is very careful and finished, without rising to the greatest heights. Also known are three sons, all of whom were taught to draw and paint: young John (1747–86) and Robert, who both became professional marine painters, and James. The latter went to sea, and, when boatswain of the *Resolution* on Cook's last voyage, made drawings which, on his return, his brother John made into water-colours for a successful set of coloured aquatints.

Another of the Brooking generation of marine painters was Richard Paton (1717–91). He is unusual in this school in that he painted in a variety of styles during his career. If it were not for the existence of prints of his work, it would be difficult to believe that they all came from the same hand. At best he was very vigorous and fresh, but he can also appear mechanical and dull.

The third phase of the English marine school loosely covers the War of American Independence and the French Revolutionary Wars.

Of the older generation, Dominic Serres was still producing large numbers of canvases throughout the American War and into the peace. So, too, was Paton, but the younger generation was taking over. All the best of them worked in London, and with the exception of the Norwich school, continued to do so until well into the nineteenth century.

The best painter of this third phase, and second only to Brooking over all, was Pocock (1741–1821). He was a professional merchant seaman who took up marine painting as a profession rather late in life, since he was still at sea in commands in the early seventies. Some of his captain's logs survive, and these are illustrated each day with a delightful ink and wash drawing showing the condition of the ship and the weather, or any incident that might have occurred. He did not entirely give up the sea even after his practice was established, as he was present at Lord Howe's victory of the First of June, 1794, as a Master.

With the death of Serres, Pocock emerged as the doyen of the school, and deservedly so. His work is most characteristic. In his water-colours he is a colourist; on the other hand, his oils are not generally colourful, as he preferred a tonal effect working from a brown-gold palette with dark olive greens and pale blue. The effect is much more successful than it may sound, and, put on in careful glazes, gives a highly finished appearance. He is an artist who, once known, can never be mistaken again (Plate 268).

One wishes that a similar quality could have been found in his contemporaries, but this was not so. Their work, however, has become widely known through its quantity and the numerous prints from it. Two of them were most prolific artists whose work was much alike. They painted the same subjects in rather the same manner and over the same period, though Thomas Luny (1756–1837) was like Paton in that his style underwent marked changes during his career. He could paint extremely well, particularly when he tried to paint like Pocock, but he had a more colourful palette and the river scenes in his native Teignmouth are delightful, especially when he introduces figures, which he did well. At other times he painted broadly with too wide a tonal range which makes those canvases appear rather crude. There are also late paintings with a cool palette and brittle finish which are not unpleasing.

Thomas Whitcombe (*c.* 1760–1827) was more stable in his style, which once understood is always easily recognized. He tended towards a rather warm palette based on brown. That he was an excellent draughtsman is proved by a large and beautifully finished dock scene at Greenwich, painted in his twenties. It would appear, however, that success and overwork dulled his senses.

Another painter in the upper flight of the times was William Anderson (1757–1837), who is at his best in small, careful, harbour views, painted from a grey palette. He was a Scottish artist who felt obliged to seek his fortune in London, though it is known that he also stayed at Hull, where he strongly influenced the young local painter, John Ward (1798–1849). Ward copied and adopted some of Anderson's compositions, and he then settled down to be one of the better nineteenth-century ship portraitists.

A second Scotsman, though of foreign extraction, was John Schetky (1778–1874), who exhibited paintings at the Royal Academy Exhibitions for nearly seventy years (1805–72). He was a well-known figure in naval circles, as he taught generations of cadets at the Royal Naval College at Portsmouth. His attractive personality brought him success: more, perhaps, than his skill deserved. Once seen he is one of the easiest to recognize again, with his characteristic light-tan palette and his rather flat drawing and high finish. It must be added, though, that his productions are often most effective, and they are executed with spirit and a knowledge and love of his subject. In marine painting this must always please. He became Marine Painter to King William IV and later to Queen Victoria.

Since most of the better-known painters of the third generation of English marine painting lived well into the nineteenth century, it would be as well to look at the trends that appeared in the fourth generation, which aptly take the form of a trident, with the main shaft from the Van de Veldes continuing with its rather mannered, though by now somewhat hackneyed, conventions, in the work of Schetky and J. T. Serres, already mentioned, and more particularly in the Huggins family.

This central prong was now blunted, but the right-hand prong found new strength in a renewed effort to achieve a convincing naturalism, which included a much more interesting and colourful palette than had been used previously. Finally, the left-hand prong consisted of the dangerous barb of impressionism and romanticism under the heady influence and leadership of Turner.

Among the traditionalists, W. J. Huggins (1781–1846) was immensely popular in his day with seamen customers and knew his ships, but he was the model for the soulless portraits of a ship in a sea which, for fifty years after his death, were going to flood the world. He was assisted in his work by a son, J. M. Huggins, whose work is almost identical.

The earliest and most important figure of the naturalist school is Clarkson Stanfield (1793–1867). Though his influence was the greatest, he was not the best of his generation, for George Chambers painted better. He had, however, the great advantage of a good beginning and a large and generous personality. His talent was also considerable. His canvases were very finished and luminous, reflecting the confidence of the hand that painted them. He was a friend of Dickens and painted a number of sets for the theatre, to which he was well used, as his father had been a successful impressario. He deserved his success, as did George Chambers (1803–40), whose beginnings were so unpropitious that it is surprising he was ever heard of at all. It took a very considerable talent and determination, in addition to the kindly patronage of a Wapping publican, to bring him to the notice of the world. Chambers was a sailor who, in his early days, used to delight his shipmates with his drawings. It was on their advice that he took drawing lessons, which had extremely happy results. By the 1830s he was painting most beautifully, and, considering his early death, prolifically. Many of his best works may be seen at the National Maritime Museum.

Yet another painter, Robert Salmon, was painting in England, and later in America, from the beginning of the nineteenth century until the forties. His work is plentiful and deservedly popular. His rather strict stylization is strongly marked and must have been constricting. Nevertheless, his paintings have a brilliant clarity which is always arresting.

Though one would not expect much talent to remain in the provinces, it is rather surprising that flourishing ports, such as Bristol and Liverpool, should be so bereft as they were. Bristol was the best served with the work of Joseph Walter (1783–1856), a native of that town, who painted extremely well with a grey palette in a manner that is somewhere between the traditionalists and the naturalists.

Liverpool had a family bearing a very similar name: Walters. Samuel (1811–83) was the father, and George was the son. They painted competent ship portraits and shipping scenes. These, however, are more valuable as recordings of the vessels than as works of art.

There was another school, artistically of far

more importance: the Norwich School. The Norwich painters were, however, more landscape artists, who painted seascapes, than shipping painters. One must also look elsewhere for the work of J. M. W. Turner and the romantics he inspired. For if Huggins and his admirers sacrificed art to the subject, Turner sacrificed the subject to art.

BRITISH SPORTING PICTURES
eighteenth and nineteenth centuries

One of the most characteristic aspects of British art is that devoted to sporting painting. During the 300 years since Francis Barlow (c. 1626–1704) drew and painted birds, horses, and hounds, the tradition has held, and the last great artist of sporting pictures, Sir Alfred Munnings, fits perfectly into it with, of course, modifications of technique. As in landscape and portrait art, the pioneers of British sporting pictures were to some extent influenced by foreign artists, but whatever they learned from abroad, they soon emerged as personalities in their own right.

Where Francis Barlow, father of English sporting pictures, studied is not known, but he probably took hints and ideas from Dutch and Flemish artists, and his industry is proved by the large number of etchings made either by Barlow himself or by other craftsmen from his originals.

No doubt John Wootton (1682–1764) encountered Barlow's work, at least in print form, but here we have an artist known to have studied with a master who can be identified. He was John Wyck of Haarlem, who worked in England during the second half of the seventeenth century and died at Mortlake in 1702. But early in the eighteenth century Wootton is believed to have been sent to study in Italy by the Duke of Beaufort. On his return he made such rapid progress that he was constantly busy painting sporting pictures for George I and George II, the Duke of Beaufort, the 3rd Duke of Marlborough (Spencer), the Earls of Oxford (Harley of Welbeck), and the Dukes of Devonshire and Richmond, among other members of the nobility. There is a large number of sporting pictures by Wootton in the Duke of Portland Collection, and he is represented at Windsor, Badminton, Goodwood, and Longleat. The artist worked a good deal at Newmarket, and the painting

Warren Hill at the Jockey Club there, showing a string of horses, is a key picture among early racing subjects.

Wootton's animal and human figures are enhanced by his talent for landscape painting, and in this respect some of his work is influenced by Gaspar Poussin and Claude. Such pictures as *The Beaufort Hunt* (Ackermann Gallery, London), *Hunting Scene* (the Duke of Buccleuch Collection), and *Henry* and *Benjamin Hoare* (Stourhead House, Wiltshire), prove his skill in placing equestrians in attractive country settings. He painted many portraits of celebrated racehorses, and his efforts in this respect are very uneven. The *Darley Arabian* is one of his best.

Contemporary with Wootton was Pieter Tillemans, born in Antwerp about 1680. Coming to England in 1708, he soon attracted attention and patrons, and for much of his life Newmarket and East Anglia were the main centres for his activities. His many pictures of Newmarket Heath and its personalities and thoroughbreds are of rare historical as well as aesthetic interest. He died in 1734 at the house of his patron, Dr Marco, Little Haugh Hall, Norton.

James Seymour (1702–52) was born and reared in an atmosphere of culture, his father being a banker who delighted in art, and who was a good amateur performer. He clearly enjoyed painting, for his racing and hunting subjects are contrived with intense thoroughness and *joie de vivre*. *A Match at Newmarket* in the Captain A. S. Willis Collection is a laborious effort, every detail of the horses and jockeys being rendered with care and fidelity to fact. Nevertheless, the picture has a quaintly primitive vision. Yet by all accounts Seymour's racehorses were good likenesses, and he could tackle such a difficult hunting subject as *Going to Cover*, full of horsemen and hounds. It has been suggested that Seymour, Tillemans, and Wootton worked to some collaborative arrangement.

In trying to assess the genius of George Stubbs (1724–1806), greatest of all painters of sport, certain salient facts arise. Son of a prosperous currier and leather-dresser, Stubbs was brought up among horse-flesh and bones, and an insatiable curiosity as to the structure of animals stimulated his intellect. An equally important fact is that, except for a few lessons, he was self-taught, seeking truth with his own eyes and struggling to express it with his own fastidiously won technique. Thirdly, he must needs seek below the surface of things, delve and probe, and disentangle the physical facts in order that he might reassemble them for art purposes. There is something profoundly moving in the story of this remote genius, aided by his devoted, life-long friend, Mary Spencer, dissecting dead horses in the lonely farmhouse at Horkstow, Lincolnshire, the better to understand their being. Considering the life and works of Stubbs as a whole it is difficult to determine whether science or art was his principal passion. But there is no doubt that he could never have been the supreme master of animal and human form had his art not been based on comprehensive scientific knowledge.

It was at Horkstow that Stubbs confirmed the foundation of his own artistic ambitions by making the drawings for his book, *The Anatomy of the Horse*, and set the whole course of horse painting on a broader and deeper basis. Only during the present century has Stubbs' genius been fully resuscitated. London had, in fact, to wait until 1956 to see it in all its grandeur when the Whitechapel Art Gallery held an exhibition that was among the most memorable occasions in art history (Plate 270A, B). He was made an Associate of the Royal Academy in 1780 and was acknowledged a full member in 1805.

Born at Scaleby Castle, near Carlisle, Sawrey Gilpin (1733–1807) came from a long line of not undistinguished ancestors. His father was a soldier and amateur artist, and Gilpin was apprenticed to Samuel Scott. It was in the neighbourhood of Covent Garden, where he studied, that he developed his in-terest for animal form and colour. William Augustus Duke of Cumberland employed him, and other patrons were Colonel Thomas Thornton and Samuel Whitbread. For Thornton he painted his most memorable picture, *Death of a Fox*, remarkable for movement and strong and original handling. Gilpin frequently collaborated with other artists, and an admirable picture, *Hawking*, was the joint work of Gilpin and George Barret. Gilpin was made an Associate of the Royal Academy in 1795 and a full member in 1797. He died in 1807.

By the third quarter of the eighteenth century, thanks to the collective efforts of the early artists, the sporting art tradition was well established, and many animal painters rose to comparative fame during the long life-time of Stubbs. There was Philip Reinagle (1749–1833), pupil of portrait painter Allan Ramsay, and student at the Royal Academy Schools. Discontented with fashionable face-painting, Reinagle concentrated on birds and animals in relation to sport. He collaborated with other artists, including Sawrey Gilpin and George C. Morland. Reinagle's *Grouse Shooting, with Lord Middleton and his Keepers* and *Ptarmigan Shooting* are two of his best works. Richard Ramsay Reinagle, R.A. (1775–1862), his son, was also a prolific painter of sporting subjects.

With Dean Wolstenholme, Senior (1757–1837), we are back in the primitive rhythm of Seymour, but not in Seymour's somewhat rigid manner. As he did not begin to compete for money until middle age, one can appreciate the tremendous resolution that produced many difficult hunting and coursing pictures. His hard-won knowledge of human and animal form is happily supported by a genuine poetic feeling for landscape. His son, variously known as C.D. or Dean, followed his father's style and subjects.

An artist who, but for continuous frustrations, might have become one of the greatest painters of sport was Charles Towne (1763–1840). Born at Wigan, his early and painful wanderings in search of employment are sympathetically recorded in Walter Shaw Sparrow's *Book of Sporting Painters*. Towne's career begins to clarify somewhat when he exhibited at the Society for promoting the Arts in Liverpool. In early life he came temporarily under the influence of Stubbs, both as regards horse and landscape, as may be seen in the picture of *John Yates, of Burton, and The Dun Racehorse, Ninety Three,* painted in Manchester in 1794.

Towne became a founder-member of the Liverpool Academy and was its vice-president in 1812–13. Lack of work, anxiety, and a certain recklessness involved him in debt difficulties; and his wandering career is associated with Essex, Oxfordshire, Cambridgeshire, other parts of Britain, and the Continent. He died in Liverpool in 1840.

In Ben Marshall (1767–1835) we are in the presence of a great artist, and it is not impertinent to couple his name with that of Stubbs. As early as the 1790s he received royal patronage, and by the end of the eighteenth century was an important artist. Marshall built a studio in Newmarket in 1812 and had a house over the Suffolk border. Like Stubbs he was an admirable portrait painter, and such full-length studies as *James Belcher, Gentleman Jackson,* and those in *The Weston Family* are classics.

Marshall wandered about England painting hunt meets and racing subjects, and among his well-known portraits of thoroughbreds are *Haji Baba, Mameluke, Priam,* and *Phantom.* In 1819, on his way to Rockingham Castle to work for Lord Sondes, the coach was overturned and the artist sustained injuries that greatly impaired his health. He painted and wrote alternately until the end of his life, and his articles under various pseudonyms in the *Sporting Magazine* from 1821 to 1833 are written with as much verve as his sporting pictures are painted. Marshall died in London, July 24, 1835.

Few artists had a longer span of life than James Ward (1769–1859). He started as an engraver, and in 1794 was appointed Painter and Engraver in Mezzotinto to the Prince of Wales. As time went on, Ward's original force was obvious, and as a painter of animals he stands very high in the English School.

Possibly Ward's best picture in sporting art is the one of *Ralph John Lambton, Esq., his Horse "Undertaker" and Hounds* (now in the Duke of Northumberland Collection). This was exhibited at the Royal Academy in 1820. Among hundreds of drawings and paintings of animals of all kinds, Ward did many celebrated racehorses and chargers. Ward was made an associate of the Royal Academy in 1807 and a full member in 1811. He continued to work until the end of his long life, and a picture showing no diminution of talent is *The Council of Horses* (Tate Gallery), painted when the artist was eighty. He died November 16, 1859.

When one looks at John Ferneley, Senior's, self-portrait, surrounded by his sons and daughters, one feels that this artist enjoyed his days, his art, and the domestic felicities to the full. His life was well ordered, centred upon the village of Thrussington, where he was born in 1782. Son of a wheelwright, Ferneley served his apprenticeship to this craft and painted pictures in his spare time: and to such good effect that the Duke of Rutland bought *The Great Billesdon Coplow Run,* painted when Ferneley was eighteen. The Duke commissioned other pictures, and the artist was soon tackling immense hunting subjects. It is likely that Ferneley had some tuition from Ben Marshall, since he wrote to Marshall in 1806 asking advice, Marshall replying in a friendly, practical way. Ferneley executed many pictures of hunt meets and racers during the first half of the nineteenth century. These were not with the profundity of Stubbs nor with the ingenious sense of scene and character of Ben Marshall but with undoubted integrity. John Ferneley, Senior, died at Melton Mowbray, June 3, 1860, and was buried at Thrussington. He had four sons by his first wife and one by his second. Two of them, John and Claude Loraine, were sporting artists.

In the annals of sporting art no name is more conspicuous than Alken. The Alken generations were in the saddle, as it were, from the early part of the eighteenth century until the last decade of the nineteenth. The only one who can concern us here is the greatest, Henry Thomas Alken (1785–1851). Known as "Old Alken" or "Alken Senior", his paintings, drawings, water-colours, and etchings are to be numbered in many hundreds. Pupil of Thomas Barber, Alken began by exhibiting miniatures in 1801/2. We know that he married at Ipswich in 1809, but his life is somewhat mysterious until, in 1816, he confessed that he was the anonymous "Ben Tally Ho!", pseudonym of an artist whose work had won admirers in Leicestershire, where he had ridden to hounds and been accepted by the exclusive Meltonians as one of them.

In 1811 "Ben Tally Ho!" had issued seven hunting illustrations relating to Melton, and four hunting and four shooting subjects appeared in 1813. He may have visited the field of Waterloo soon after the battle, as several military pictures and three equestrian portraits, *Wellington, Lord Anglesea*, and *Blücher*, are connected with 1815. *Beauties and Defects in the Figure of the Horse* appeared in 1816, by which year Alken had gained a position in art and sport. In the 1820s he was in high favour, not only with the wealthy devotees of sport who liked to see their antics in paint and pring but also with the critics. Henry Thomas Alken with his pencil and water-colour dexterity did more to popularize field sports than any other artist. The speed at which he worked, his phenomenal output of small drawings and water-colours that could be quickly translated into prints, either by himself or such a great engraver as Thomas Sutherland, helped to spread the cult for sport far and wide.

In 1837 the sixteen plates of *Jorrock's Jaunts and Jollities* and the nineteen of the *Life and Death of John Mytton* were published. A celebrated set is *The Night Riders of Nacton*, illustrating a moonlight steeplechase eccentricity, published in 1839. *The Finish of the Derby* (Plate 269A) is typical of Alken's feeling for speed. It is signed and dated 1846. "Old Alken" declined into poverty during his last few years, but he had done more than enough to hold his name in veneration whenever field sports in art are discussed. He died at Highgate on April 7, 1851.

For versatility of expression James Pollard (1792–1867) may be compared with Henry Alken. He enjoyed painting large assemblies of sportsmen such as *Coursers taking the Field at Hatfield Park* (Plate 269B): and the even more crowded one, *Epsom Races*, beautifully aquatinted by Pollard in 1818 and 1824 respec-

tively. There was also *The Goodwood Cup*, 1832, aquatinted by R. G. Reeve in 1836, and the celebrated *King George III Returning from Hunting*. Best known for the prints after his oil paintings, especially the Coaching series, an irresistibly interesting record of travel in England during Regency times and immediately before the advent of the railway, Pollard has a unique place in the sporting art tradition. His subtle sense of movement and colour, and human and horse character, won him many admirers in his day, and ever since. Like Alken, he outlived his vogue and died a poor man at Chelsea, on October 5, 1867.

John Frederick Herring, Senior (1795–1865), had no such early luck as "Old Alken". Instead of cutting a dash with the Meltonians he had perforce to be a coachee, and for many years in early manhood drove the "York and London Highflyer". A man of rare talent, he painted in his spare time, and through the kind influence of friends found his way into Abraham Cooper's studio. Herring painted no fewer than eighteen Derby and thirty-three St Leger winners. He was a frequent exhibitor at the Royal Academy, the British Institution, and the Society of Artists, and was a member of the latter. Patronage from George IV, Queen Victoria, and the Duke of Orleans put Herring in the forefront of animal painters. The artist comes into the category of Victorian painters, and, as such, thanks to the vagaries of fashion, was temporarily deposed for a time. In recent years he has rightly returned to favour. He died in 1865, and was succeeded by his three sons John Frederick, Charles, and Benjamin, who painted to a greater or lesser degree in the same manner as their father.

Sir Edwin Landseer (1802–73) must also come into this chapter, but rather as a great painter of animals than an illustrator of sport, although he did many pictures with a sporting interest. An Associate of the Royal Academy in 1826, he was made a full member in 1830. He was knighted in 1850, and although elected President of the Royal Academy in 1866, he declined the honour. Landseer died on October 1, 1873, and was buried in St Paul's Cathedral. He amassed a huge fortune, leaving approximately £200,000. One of his most interesting paintings from the point of view of the art student is *Queen Victoria and the Duke of Wellington reviewing the Life Guards at Windsor Castle*, now in an English private collection. It is on less well-known pictures of this kind that the new appreciation of Landseer as a great British painter is based.

One of the most successful painters of sport was Sir Francis Grant (1803–78), the fourth son of the Laird of Kilgraston. Intended for the legal profession, Grant's enthusiasm for art determined a professional career as a painter. Educated at Harrow, his leisure hours were shared between sport and sketching. He acquired technique by copying old masters and drawing from nature. Grant was, however, helped by Ferneley in youth, and their friendship lasted until Ferneley's death.

Grant's first public success was *The Melton Hung Breakfast* exhibited at the Royal Academy in 1834, and widely known from the engraving. The picture that made his name was *H.M. Staghounds on Ascot Heath*, exhibited at the Academy in 1837. It contained a large number of portraits, including the Duke of Beaufort, Earl Errol, the Earl of Chesterfield, and Count D'Orsai. Grant became an Associate of the Royal Academy in 1842 and a full member in 1851. On Sir Charles Eastlake's death in 1866 he took the presidential chair, Landseer having declined the honour. He died October 5, 1878.

This account of British sporting art must, of course, include Sir Alfred Munnings, President of the Royal Academy (1878–1959). Son of a miller, Alfred James Munnings began by drawing horses on his father's property at Mendham, Suffolk. He was later apprenticed in a lithographic studio. Escaping from the drudgery of commercial art, Munnings bought horses and organized his own "caravan", as he called it, in the neighbourhood of Norwich, where he gathered round him a motley company of picturesque characters. Several celebrated pictures relate to that period, especially *The Coming Storm* and *The Ford*. In 1913 Munnings was in Cornwall, and a masterpiece that had its origin in that year is *The Grey Horse*. In the First World War Munnings was attached to the Canadian Cavalry Brigade as a war artist and painted many spirited war records. In the 1920s he was continuously busy with commissioned work, and one of the great pictures that emerged from that period is *The King and Queen Returning from Ascot* (Tate Gallery), of which there are several versions. All sporting painters from Wootton to the present day have spent much time depicting celebrated race winners, and the number that Munnings recorded is remarkable. A comparatively late work is *Saddling Paddock, March Meeting, Cheltenham*: "the one painting I always wanted to paint". Munnings was enrolled an Associate of the Royal Academy in 1919, a Royal Academician in 1925, and became President in 1944. His retrospective exhibition in the Royal Academy Diploma Gallery in 1956 was one of the most inspiring collections of sporting art ever shown in London. He died in 1959.

BRITISH GENRE PICTURES
nineteenth century

Now that the Victorian age has acquired a lamp-lit warmth and an aspect of luxurious velvet-upholstered comfort, pictures which record this snug, homely world of our great-grandfathers in the minutest detail are returning to favour. Indeed, these very pictures may largely be responsible for the rosy modern vision of the Victorian epoch. They present the age as it wished to see itself: prosperous, godly, and content.

Nineteenth-century genre pictures were painted to attract the vast new body of middle-class buyers who crowded each year to the Royal Academy and not to present a documentary record of the times. Life at the extremes of the social scale is excluded: we are shown neither the dingy unsanitary slums of Dickens' London nor the opulent grandeur of Trollope's Omnium Castle. The poor, when they appear, are nearly always rustics jovially content with their lot. The well-to-do are never uncomfortably opulent unless they are intended to show the vanity of excess riches. Some paintings depict the problems of life, but seldom without the suggestion of a happy ending. The girl in Holman Hunt's *Awakened Conscience* will surely return to her loving family or enter an Anglican convent. Abraham Solomon's *Waiting for the Verdict*, which scored such a popular success when it was shown in the 1857 Academy, was followed two years later, by the inevitable sequel, *Not Guilty*. These pictures had, moreover, a theatrical appearance – the passions are strongly marked, the significant details are too carefully emphasized – which endeared them to audiences who sobbed through the several acts of tragi-comedies at the Lyceum.

The majority of nineteenth-century genre scenes reveal a happier world. Throughout the century rustic scenes enjoyed a special popularity. The village church (Plate 273B), the village wedding, the village school provided artists with picturesque subjects which were often touching but never tragic. Such works reveal a wistful longing for the quiet contented pastoral England which was thought to have vanished in the course of the Industrial Revolution and which had really never existed. More realistic are those paintings which introduce us into the middle-class home with its Nottingham lace curtains, chenille table-cloths, what-nots, and bric-a-brac. Here we see the cycle of Victorian life – the baby's first steps, the boyish romps, the young betrothed gazing at each other during a musical evening, the young wife reading her absent husband's letter to a circle of chubby well-scrubbed children, and, the last scene of all, the reading of the will. Fashions change, the crinoline gives way to the bustle, Japanese fans and vases appear upon the mantelpiece, but the subjects remain essentially the same.

The demand for genre pictures made itself felt in the eighteenth century at about the time when the middle-class patron appeared on the scene. Painters, of whom Gainsborough is the most notable, began to produce pictures of rustic life then called "fancy pieces", which secured immediate popularity. The fancy piece was seldom intended, however, as an end in itself. For as Hogarth discovered, before the middle of the century, the artist could make a greater profit from the sale of engraved copies of his work than by the painting. Artists therefore began to work for the engravers and modified their style accordingly. Thus many late eighteenth- and nineteenth-century genre pictures have bold simple compositions which can easily be translated into another medium and reveal scant regard for the niceties of painting which would be lost in an engraved copy. The subject matter was also adapted to suit the taste of the numerous middle-class buyers who acquired the engravings. These pictures made an appeal to that cult of sensibility which is so notable a feature in the fiction of the time.

Early in the nineteenth century a young gawky lad from Cults, David Wilkie (1785–1841), arrived in London and applied himself to painting genre subjects which won him immediate success. Basing himself on the eighteenth-century tradition for subject matter and deriving his style from the Dutch genre painters of the seventeenth century – then enjoying a wave of great popularity – he painted various scenes of village junketings which won him the title of "The Scottish Teniers". He also painted at this time *The Letter of Introduction* which presents a charming picture of an early nineteenth-century upper-middle-class interior (Plate 271B). Wilkie showed greater understanding of his medium than any British genre painter since Gainsborough, but his works were admired for their anecdotic content rather than any artistic qualities. When, therefore, he abandoned the subjects which had made him famous and began to paint in a broader, freer style, inspired partly by a visit to Spain and Italy, he immediately lost his popularity. His numerous imitators prudently clung to the earlier style, which continued to exercise some influence in genre painting, especially in Scotland, until the last decades of the century.

Among Wilkie's contemporaries, William Mulready (1786–1863) stands out as an artist of considerable ability and quiet distinction. He specialized in rural scenes, painted in muted colours, which have a poetic autumnal atmosphere (Plate 271A). The other genre painters of the time tended to emphasize the sentimental qualities in Wilkie's work by painting with ever greater precision and detail. A love of telling detail in works of art has always marked British taste. But this development was also influenced by the new process of electrotype steel engraving which, as A. P. Oppé remarked, "favoured elaborate nicety of execution and helped to turn the painter from broad effects of light and dark to refinements of detail and minute accidents".

A change came over British genre painting soon after 1850 when the Pre-Raphaelite Brotherhood began to make its presence felt. Although they are best known for their medieval scenes, two of the three founder members, Holman Hunt (1827–1910) and Millais (1829–96), painted modern genre subjects. They were, however, genre pieces with a difference, for they were full not merely of anecdotic but of moral content. The idea of painting a genre subject in order to point a moral was by no means new. This type of picture had, indeed, derived its name from the *Tableaux de Genre* which Greuze painted. But the Pre-Raphaelites, not content to tell simple stories, wished to examine the burning questions of the day, especially prostitution, and they drove the moral home remorselessly by giving every detail significance. As Ruskin pointed out in a letter to *The Times*, every detail of the interior in Hunt's *Awakened Conscience* contributes to the story: the painfully new furniture, the books with uncut leaves which showed them to be unread, the discarded glove on the floor, the title of the music "Oft in the stilly Night" on the piano, and the cat torturing a bird beneath the table. But like Ford Maddox Brown's *Work*, this picture should perhaps be regarded as an allegory rather than a genre scene. Millais made drawings for several moral genre scenes (and painted a few), but seems to have realized that his true talent, and the taste of the British public, lay elsewhere. An artist of extraordinary ability, he produced one of the most beautiful and genuinely moving of all Victorian paintings – *The Blind Girl* – but was ruined by the enormous success that greeted

such purely sentimental works as *My First Sermon* (a well-dressed little girl sitting up in her pew) and *My Second Sermon* (the same little girl asleep in her pew).

The Pre-Raphaelites soon acquired several followers, of whom Arthur Hughes (1832–1915) and John Brett (1830–1902) are probably the most important among the genre painters. Both artists abandoned the old academic rules, painted from nature with painful care, and eschewed trivial subject matter, though neither indulged in work of such high seriousness as Holman Hunt. *The Awakened Conscience* had, however, an embarrassingly large offspring in the "problem pictures" painted to cause a sensation at the Royal Academy each year during the last decades of the nineteenth century. If it is possible to ignore the problems posed by these usually rather too large pictures they may be enjoyed as illustrations of the late Victorian scene though unfortunately their artistic merits are seldom great.

By the 1860s the critics had begun to look for a moral in every genre piece, and when Frith's *Ramsgate Sands* was shown at the second International Exhibition they criticized it because it depicted no grateful mother nursing a convalescent child. But the large public who continued to buy genre pictures, and the engravings after them, was little affected by this censorious attitude. Paintings of children at play and domestic scenes, with a touch of pathos but no uncomfortable moral, continued to appear on the Academy walls and to attract purchasers. Indeed, at the end of the century, when the influence of French impressionism was tardily crossing the Channel, the British public was still clamouring for anecdotes in paint.

Nineteenth-century English genre pictures provide a very promising field for the modern collector. Although few of them can be ranked among the great works even of the English school, a very large number have painterly qualities in addition to their fascinating period charm. Most of the leading nineteenth-century artists painted genre subjects at some stage in their career and many minor painters, whose names are barely recorded in the biographical dictionaries, produced attractive and accomplished pictures of this type. To sort out the works of interesting minor artists is a task to beguile the leisure of a generation of collectors.

Dutch and Flemish

DUTCH

Holland, a small republic, enjoyed for a period of about a century great commercial prosperity, untrammelled by either a powerful church or a dominant aristocracy. During this period she produced four outstanding masters, and a host of smaller ones whose works have maintained a high level of popularity in every country of the civilized world and have come to be regarded by most people as typical "old masters". From the very beginning the Dutch were aware of the economic possibilities of the art trade: Amsterdam became one of its centres, and, as Evelyn remarked, every farmhouse had its paintings, every market its selection of canvases. Their popularity was considerable in England too: and the greatest array of Dutch painting outside Holland is to be found in that country. The first great name was that of Pieter Brueghel (1525–69), an Antwerp artist who reflected the agony of his time. His works, still medieval in spirit, are on wood, and are usually signed BRUEGEL, with the date in Roman figures. He was the founder of a dynasty. Jan the Elder, or "Velvet" Brueghel (1568–1625), and his son, Jan the Younger (1601–67), both reflected the growing dominance of Italian influence, and a new sophistication of outlook. Copper and canvas now become popular media, and, with artists like Gerard Honthorst (1590–1656), it is almost impossible to distinguish their work from that of contemporary Italians. Much of this influence came through the medium of Adam Elsheimer (1578–1610), who, though he was a German born in Frankfurt, is remarkable mainly for the effect which he exercised over Dutch painters and collectors. One of his pupils was Pieter Lastman (1583–1633), who was the teacher of Rembrandt van Ryn

(1606–69), the most famous of all Dutch artists. A genuine Rembrandt is for the established collector the equivalent of the gold standard. What is even more encouraging is the fact that his output was very great: about eight hundred paintings, three hundred etchings, and some two thousand drawings. Some seventy pictures and fifteen hundred drawings have been lost track of. The situation is complicated by the fact that, apart from imitators and forgers, Rembrandt had about seventy pupils, many of whom actually worked at his paintings. Biblical and Jewish scenes, portraits, landscapes, and group paintings comprise his *œuvre*, and the main difference between early and late works is in a growing looseness and freedom of handling. Nearly all are marked by a rich brown tonality, and by a sometimes exaggerated contrast of light and shade. Paint is applied thickly; variations of signature are *Rembrandt,* date; *Rembrandt f.*; *Rembrandt fecit*. He uses light as other artists use line and space.

Frans Hals (1580–1666) was really a forerunner of the Impressionists. He painted quickly, vigorously, intent on catching the mood before it passed, and saw his sitters casually in a characteristic pose or movement. In many ways he is the greatest European portraitist, inviting comparison with Velazquez. His works are usually on canvas, sometimes on panel, and only occasionally signed with the monogram FH.

Landscape painting, too, developed with vigour. One of the earliest practitioners was Jan van Goyen (1596–1656), whose precisely observed work indicates very clearly the pattern to be followed by his successors in the genre. What distinguishes the work of the

Dutch landscape painters from that of the French or Italians, and what commended them to the English, is their sense of involvement with what they are painting. Their reaction to landscape is an emotional one, and it is immediately apparent in their work. The key practitioners were Hercules Seghers (1589–c. 1638), who greatly influenced Rembrandt; Jan van Goyen (1596–1656); Philips de Koninck (1616–88); Jacob Ruisdael (1628–82); Aelbert Cuyp (1620–91); and Meindert Hobbema (1638–1709). It is noticeable that most Dutch landscapes contain figures and buildings. The human element is always marked, and this explains the other main activity of the school, the painting of scenes of rural or urban life, and of the things connected with them.

More human achievement is to be recorded in the work of artists such as Philips Wouverman (1619–88);· Adriaen Brouwer (1605/6–1638); Jan Steen (1626–79); and Gerard Terboch (1617–81). All these artists present lively records of the life of their time. Another group of artists concentrated on architectural scenes and interiors. Among them were Pieter de Hooch (1629–83) and Samuel van Hoogstraten (1627–78). Of the interior painters the greatest was Vermeer (1632–75), who also painted portraits and street scenes. When so many experts have come to grief on the authenticity of Vermeers, it would seem otiose to give the collector any helpful advice. Some of his works are signed *I. V. Meer*, and many are painted on canvases of approximately the same size (20 ins by 18 ins).

MINOR MASTERS

Dutch painters of the seventeenth century, springing from a middle-class society, confirmed the existence in life of those surroundings and endeavours which are enjoyed by a large majority of their fellows. They could admirably suggest the subtle atmosphere of repose that resides in a small kitchen, or which is suggested by a pattern of colours on a red brick wall. They understood how to combine soft shadings of blues and pinks and yet give their themes a poetical transposition. The serious nature of the Dutch seventeenth-cen-

tury painter enabled him to paint those fragile and puritanical still lifes; by rejecting any connexion with religious or literary motives, they have become, for our generation, the very essence of a pure aesthetic conception. For the Dutch painter the wine-glass and the loaf of bread, the group of clay pipes and the earthen jug, which we find in Pieter van Anraadt's gentle, miraculous *Still Life* (Plate 276), may have been no more than an exercise in painting; but to our romantic, modern eyes it becomes the quintessence of the silent life of forms. So infectious was the artistic atmosphere of Holland at this period, that a delicate talent such as Claes Hals rendered the sweep of a landscape (Plate 277B) with the breadth of eye and justness of atmosphere more usually associated with Hercules Seghers. Dutch paintings of this period, moreover, are admirably suited for ordinary houses, as was quickly realized in eighteenth-century France. When the large-scale drawing-rooms were replaced by smaller and more intimate salons, in which the wall space was broken up by mirrors, small "cabinet" pictures became highly prized by collectors.

Not the least interesting aspect of Roman life in the early seventeenth century was the emergence of a group of painters mainly of Dutch extraction who found their subject matter in the popular life of the city and surrounding countryside. Painters such as Breenbergh, Poelenburgh, Pynas, or Paul Bril settled in the Vicolo del Pavone and, scouring the *campagna*, found idyllic and Arcadian themes, which they treated with a sweetness and softness that still delights us. Their small and intimate studies are painted for their own pleasure, revealing an immediate reaction to the natural background which is in no way disturbed by the introduction of classical figures (Plate 277A). Inspired by the antique ruins that lay on every side, in Rome, like Charles de Hooch (Plate 277A), they lead on to the landscapes of Claude and later to those of Wilson and Pannini. For the collector these unpretentious little paintings have the same intimacy which we find in the still life; their decorative possibilities have made them appeal in recent years to a group of connoisseurs in many countries. The early generation of foreign expatriates in Rome was particularly attracted by the classical echoes which had appealed also to Marten van Heemskerk, whose enchanting self-portrait in the Fitzwilliam Museum at Cambridge reveals the enthusiasm of the northerner brought into touch with the tradition of antiquity. The second generation was fascinated by the ordinary life of the Roman people; these "birds of a flock", as they were called, settled in the Via Margutta or the Via del Babuino, which then, as now, was the artist's quarter in Rome. It needed perhaps foreign painters to understand and to capture the poetical life of the *campagna* or to give the contradictions and the charms of the crowded Roman streets, with their fruit barrows and street vendors. One can feel the same excitement as they did in looking at the innumerable fountains which Bernini and other artists of the Baroque constructed in Rome. Their painting may well have been one which offended Bellori or Salvator Rosa, but it has a sense of immediacy that is absent in more formal paintings.

Many examples of the popular painting in Rome around 1600–50 may seem like picture postcards, as records of a foreign tour. Yet certain artists, such as Sweets, were to give their works a poetical touch revealing a strain of melancholy and of sympathy for the ordinary way of life.

STILL LIFE AND FLOWER-PIECES
seventeenth and eighteenth centuries

No individual artist can be cited as the man who deliberately and consistently created either the flower-piece or the still life. The actual term was not in use until the Dutch spoke thus of such works in about the middle of the seventeenth century. At first the flower-piece was called by names like "A flower-bottle", "A flower-glass" or "A flower-pot"; while still life was either referred to as "standing" or "lying". Still life was equally prosaically and inadequately referred to by its subject, or, if it were one of those built around food and wine and their accessories, it became "a breakfast". The lack of language, however, did not indicate the lack of the thing itself. And not only the prolific artist and the picture-loving public but the art dealer, the investor, and the inheritance assurer were part of this pattern of living. Happily so, for we today have their wonderful legacy of thousands of Netherlandish paintings from those exciting years.

If we cannot name with certainty the actual pioneer of the independent flower-piece we can consider Jan Brueghel as being among the most powerful of the early influences. Ludger Tom Ring the Younger has two definite flower-pieces in the Landes-museum, Munster: one of irises, the other of lilies and irises, each stiffly arranged in heavy pots. They may have been studies for some religious work, but by their appearance one imagines not. So we can give much of the honour to Jan Brueghel; for surely nobody ever painted more flowers at any period in the history of the art.

Jan ("Velvet") Brueghel was an infant when his father, the great Pieter Brueghel, died. His mother was the daughter of Pieter Coeck and of Marie de Bessemers, a fine miniaturist, and it was from this maternal grandmother that the child learned the art of exact flower-drawing and painting. Jan's life history is a success story. He made a tour to Italy, returned to Antwerp, was appointed Court painter to the Regent Albert and his consort Isabella, married, bought the freedom of the city and went into the palatial studio of Rubens as an assistant. There he mainly provided meticulously drawn flowers as borders for the classical and religious works of that master. It was a curious fashion of the time: another phase of the passion for the science of horticulture which was sweeping the Netherlands. In one picture alone Jan executed ten thousand plants and flowers, each drawn with exactness. There are a host of these works by him at the Prado. There must certainly have been periods when he took off the fine velvet coat which earned him his sobriquet.

When he turned to the creation of his own individual flower-pieces this proliferation and exactness yield an effect tremendously rich. He sets the vast bouquets against a dark background, throws a few stray blossoms on the table beside the vase or pot, and depicts it all with a miniaturist's care and a nature-lover's exuberance. Yet, perhaps he is really at his happiest when he works on a larger scale, choosing half a dozen major flowers and spraying daintier, smaller blossoms around these. In all these flower-pieces throughout the whole period we have to remember that, in fact, they were *arrangements*. The moment we examine them we realize that these species never blossomed together. Spring, summer, and autumn have been put into juxtaposition; each spray or blossom exquisitely drawn and coloured, either balanced against another or organized into careful asymmetry. Probably not a single flower in the piece we most enjoy was copied straight from nature. The artists relied upon their own individual studies for each one, or on the horticultural plates being printed so marvellously by Plantin. It was not for them to worry about plants that changed with the hours or faded with the days. They got to know these forms and colours as a Chinese artist knew those of birds or plants, and from their repertoire could create innumerable arrangements.

Tulips naturally figured largely. The plant had been introduced from Turkey in 1573. Their cultivation in Holland became a rage. New tulip bulbs changed hands at enormous prices, and the leading growers issued "Tulip Books" illustrated in water-colours to show their novelties. The easel artists, catering for this enthusiasm and themselves caught up in it, turned naturally to the creation of works of art showing these things. Growers bribed them to include their house specialities, as our contemporary music publishers arrange with popular band leaders to "plug" their latest tunes. So the aesthetic enthusiasm and miniaturist genius and staggering industry of Jan Brueghel was not the only source of this lovely art. Jan himself, though he never abandoned the flower-piece and was exquisitely inventive in its use (sometimes laying a wreath on the table beside the case, for example), turned to a host of other things: genre landscape, fanciful ideas of the garden of Eden, and all else that gave rein to his quantitative genius.

Hundreds of other men devoted themselves almost entirely to the flower-piece. Not least among them was Daniel Seghers (1590–1661), Velvet Brueghel's pupil. He, too, worked for Rubens, contributing borders and garlands to embellish the work; but later he turned monk and made his much-sought-after pictures for churches and monasteries, using the popular method of depicting a niche containing the Virgin and festooned with flowers. There is a freshness about the flowers, especially the roses of Seghers, which leads us to suppose that he grew them himself, for love in his monastery garden. Others in the group round Jan Brueghel were Roelant Savery (1576–1639) and Ambrosius Bosschaert (1565–1621), who often comes very near to Brueghel's own prodigality. It is likely that the flight of Bosschaert into the Dutch provinces from the religious persecutions in Flanders did much to establish this art of flower painting there.

One other early painter who must be considered is Balthasar van der Ast (1590–1656). He has a curiously scattered form of composition at times, depending on a long horizontal along which were distributed flowers, fruits in a fretted silver basket, shells, insects, or whatever else interested him. He had the scientific curious mind. It was in the seventeenth century that the method of making lenses was perfected and the microscope was invented. Man had penetrated farther than ever before into the infinitely little. Balthasar van der Ast clearly enjoyed it. The new toy enabled the artist to see the exact form of a dewdrop on a leaf or an insect poising on the table edge. They added these things to their repertoire, and their patrons shared their enthusiasm.

For more than a hundred and fifty years, right into the middle of the eighteenth century, this art of flower painting flourished. Truly it has never ceased, but these were the days of the masters and the days when subject matter and the artist's concern with it were perfectly in accord. The de Heems, David, and his son the greater Jan Davidsz de Heem, for example, were both creating flower-pieces of surpassing loveliness. The father delighted in simplicity; the son, encouraged by a very wealthy clientele, chose profusion. Yet he handled it marvellously, with a wonderful eye for the glass and crystal bowls in which flowers were set. One of his pupils was that brilliant illusionist, Abraham

Mignon (1639–97), who came from Frankfort. He affected a chance naturalistic mode. Sometimes he introduced a cat which had knocked over the flower vase, for he was a genius with the showing of water drops, and these were one of the conventions of the mode.

It becomes almost invidious to name individual workers, so many were there and so good. Sometimes there is a particular sign, as with Nicholas van Verendael, who would add still life adjuncts such as a magnificent watch which was doubtless a prized possession of a patron. Sometimes the vase of flowers will be set on the broad sill of an open window with landscape beyond. Jan Fyt (1611–61) was given to this, or even to setting the pot against a background of almost impressionistically painted rock.

Three names of outstanding importance carry us well into the eighteenth century. One is that unbalanced artist, Simon Verelst. Born in Antwerp in 1637, he came to England in 1666. He was an immediate success, being paid high prices for flower-pieces and portraits alike, and he tremendously flattered his sitters. He died in London in 1710, but the art of flower painting did not naturalize itself there, and anyway his achievement was overshadowed by that real "God of Flowers" Jan van Huysum of Amsterdam (1682–1749), who, throughout the first half of the eighteenth century, dominated the field and has never lost his prestige. Like de Heem, he created enormous mixed bunches, but he preferred neo-classical terra-cotta vases and added remarkably unstable birds' nests to the compositions. As he became fashionable – and since the idea of panels of flowers as a form of decoration became a mode – he gained great popularity. The growers competed to induce him to add their novelties to his works. When, under French influence throughout northern Europe, decoration became lighter in tone, Van Huysum trimmed his sails most ably to the wind and began the light-toned brilliant pieces we associate chiefly with him. He was an excellent draughtsman, as his rare drawings reveal, and he infused all his works with a lavish hand.

Rachel Ruysch (1664–1750), daughter of an Amsterdam professor, married a rather dreary portraitist, Jurian Pool, and went with him to the Court of the Elector of the Palatinate. There the Elector saw the beauty of Rachel's painting. When he died the young couple moved back to Amsterdam. Jurian wisely took to commerce, and Rachel combined the bringing up of ten children and her duties as housewife with the slow and careful creation of some of the world's loveliest flower-pieces. She might take seven years to complete one, but when finished, it was perfection. So we may leave this art of the flower-piece in her capable hands, and accept the fact that when she died at the age of eighty-six the art had died too, or awaited resurrection in more modern manners.

The influence of Caravaggio was widespread in the Low Countries in its turn towards realism, and there was hardly an artist who was not affected, even though indirectly, by the new spirit. The "lamplight" pictures of the time show the influence of his theatrical lighting. They also reveal how much the artists were concerning themselves with pictorial method. As art was released from the subject dictation of the older patronage, the painter became more and more concerned with the "how" and "why" of his art, and less and less with the subject, so long only as it gave an opportunity for his virtuosity.

From these roots sprang not only the flower-pieces but also the still life, with just "things" for subject and the freedom of the artist's arrangement and manner for aesthetic impulse.

In the Netherlands, with the wealth of the world coming to the newly rich merchant class, their splendid possessions provided the material of still life: silver and pewter and gold plates and dishes, crystal and glass cups and goblets with wine, precious watches, musical instruments, books. Soon it was realized that the rich, rare foods which they enjoyed so thoroughly were themselves artistic delights of form and colour. The lemons, part peeled and with the long spiral of the rind hanging over the table edge, offered lovely pictorial possibilities and became a convention. Oysters, the insides of the shells iridescent with colours, harmonizing with some exquisite silver plate; rare roemers of wine; ultimately in the luscious work of such men as Van Beijeren and Willem Kalf, magnificent specimens of the goldsmith's art in richest profusion on a table displaying fruit, meats, and fish (the lobsters made brilliant splashes of colour and reflected in the glass and metal): the "breakfast-piece" became at once a triumph for the artist and a demonstration that the patron was, to use a modern idiom, "in the money".

As a curious kind of minority report upon this arose the strange cult of the "vanitas". It may have arisen from the subconscious recognition that all this good life was transient. Puritanism and Protestantism at the Reformation created assemblies of the things which symbolize the fleetingness of human life. It was not always quite conscious moralizing, probably, but became a fashion of the time. Skulls, guttering candles, books, empty shells, and musical instruments were pressed into service to convey the lesson. Herman Steenwijk of Leiden (1612–56) has a perfect example of the vanitas still life, with a skull, empty shell, sheathed sword, pilgrim's water-bottle, extinguished lamp, watch, and books in the National Gallery. The whole genre was almost certainly the retort of Puritanism and religion upon the too-materialistic world of the Netherlandish good-timers.

One other subject which came strongly into still life was that of tobacco. It had come fairly recently into Europe from America, and in Holland certainly held tremendous sway over the people's minds. It became a vice as well as a pleasure. It was also a luxury, and the pipe, the twisted paper of tobacco, the charcoal table-brazier, figure often among the subject matter. There is, for example, a beautiful arrangement by Hubertus van Ravesteyn, in which, with the Delft bowl of walnuts which he loved to depict, he has put a pipe and a packet of tobacco labelled "Oriental Verginis Taback". The smouldering pipe-lighter glowing red at the tip, and expensive charcoal containers often appear.

In the main, however, the theme was that of food and its accoutrements. It may be an exquisitely simple arrangement of a half-filled roemer, a plate with lemon, and a spray of vine leaves with grapes, by that rare artist Jan Jansz van de Velde, whose work in the National Gallery is even more simplified, or it may be one of those cornucopian affairs of Abraham Hendricksz van Beijeren wherein every richness of the table builds up to a massive silver-gilt cup. The art gave a splendid opportunity for painting textures. An almost invariable accompaniment was the table-cloth: sometimes just linen folds, in other examples some treasure from the looms of Turkey glowing with reds and blues. Among the best still-life artists were Willem Klaesz Heda (1594–1678); David de Heem the Elder (1570–1632), father of the brilliant flower painter Jan Davidsz de Heem; and Pieter Claesz, who has often been confused with Heda. David de Heem, the pioneer among these, was an excellent painter. He worked on a dark background against which his carefully chosen, finely arranged few articles stood out in lovely colour. But when he wanted a strong, high light he would underpaint in near white. Heda continued the tradition. He was probably of some affluence, as he became a magistrate, and out of his apparent wealth the sumptuous *Breakfast-Piece* and *Dessert* arose. There is every indication that he saw the value of brilliant colour (in a crab or a lobster) reflected in the surfaces of the noble metal objects of the table; although, in fact, exploitation of such interchange of colour came with Chardin nearly a century later. Heda remains the poet of the silver-grey, and is perhaps most distinguishable from Pieter Claesz, in that Claesz was more luminously silver in his tones. Both knew the supreme value of simplicity and arrangement. If we choose one more name from among the multitude it may well be that of Willem Kalf (1630–93), who followed Van Beijeren in the sumptuous style, though he was not so quantitative. None knew better than he the texture of things. He loved to introduce some splendid Turkish carpet on which to stand the gold and silver, the rare ceramics, the gold watches, and the many other collector's pieces of which he was so conscious.

FLEMISH

Painting in fifteenth-century Flanders follows in the wake of two principal masters, the one reflecting the coloured variety of the visible world, the other the devotional fervour of Christian mysticism. Besides the resplendent illusionism of material things in the work of Van Eyck (c.1385–1441), we find the stern compassionate Christian epic of Van der Weyden's religious calligraphy. Whether or not these two artists stand in any connexion of master and follower, their work proves that in spirit and form they differed so profoundly as to become the protagonists of two schools. The spiritual line of Roger, his sculptural approach to form, found an immediate following in the art of Dirck Bouts, Hans Memling, Quentin Metsys, while the painterly and empirical view of the world was not seen again until the seventeenth century.

For it was Jan van Eyck's vocation to make visible the glow, the splendour, the very fibre and substance of material objects. In his pictures of Madonnas and saints his real interest was in the illusionism of matter, the gold thread of hair, the fall of brocaded robes, the sheen of metal, the Persian rug that covers the steps to the Virgin's throne, or the wrinkled skin and protruding veins on the face of his Canon van der Paele. He had a marvellous conception of individual character and a scientific accuracy of observation by which he captured the secret life from the countenance of his sitters. In his portraits he aimed at a three-dimensional impersonation, a realism of outward form in the surrounding atmosphere. Earlier artists had been satisfied with the linear pattern of the human profile. He painted the air and the light and the space which enveloped the human face. In him was the true Renaissance sense for the discovery of the world and of man. The laws of linear and aerial perspective of rolling country and winding river, the behaviour of coloured matter in light and in shadow, the glow of gems, the nicety of an interior, they all formed part of his pictorial vision.

In portraiture he neither disguised nor embellished. And yet his noble sitters, whether knight or cardinal or royal merchant, are transformed into a homely type of Flemish manhood. Apart from the anatomic minutiae of stubbled chin and wrinkled eye, as in the *Man with the Pinks*, Jan never loses sight of the structural form of a face and never infringes upon personal character, whether he conveys grossness or subtlety, aggressiveness or quiet content. Roger, on the other hand, portrayed the grace, the dignity, the passions of the Burgundian nobility. One need only compare the ascetic seriousness, the taut lines and contours that distinguish a Roger portrait with the fleshy modulations, the material veracity of Van Eyck's sitters, in order to grasp the contrast of their two worlds. If Van Eyck is the painter of the comfortable bourgeoisie of Flanders, we owe to Roger those precise, impeccable, impetuous portraits of the Burgundian aristocracy. His London *Portrait of a Lady*, drawn with an exquisite tracery of line, illustrates the fastidious taste and high breeding of Roger's sitters. The transparent tones of veil and hennin in contrast to the opaqueness of the shadowless face, the utmost purity of the design, give to this princely nun her impassive and saddened beauty. Yet Roger's *chef-d'œuvre* is a work of devotional painting, perhaps the principal monument of Christian worship in all northern art, the *Descent from the Cross*, painted in 1435 for Louvain Cathedral. The *Descent* attains to an emotional and dramatic pitch which is equalled only by its concentration of plastic volumes and emotive gesture. The poise and elegance of the principal mourners, the rhythmical flow, the "veiled symmetry", and secret correspondence of form, are like point and counterpoint of a solemn Passion music. Besides his tragic Pietas and Crucifixions, Roger determined the form of the Flemish Madonna which Memling after him endowed with comeliness and grace, and Bouts with the glowing richness of translucent colour.

Dirck Bouts remains, besides Roger, the foremost medievalist of the Flemish School. Yet this painter from Haarlem, who humbly recalls the Passion story in the idiom of his master, had his own contribution to make in his lyrical sentiment of nature and in his saturated intensity of colour. Bouts has broken down the rigid wall that confined Roger's Passion players to one plane; his saintly figures, walking with angular stiffness on the banks of a river, or crossing the limpid stream, like the Munich St Christopher, come between the intense blueness of the water and the radiant glow of the evening sky, where the rocky ranges dissolve into an infinity of space.

Memling is Roger's heir in the whole realm of religious narrative, but he translates the strident pathos of his master into the language of his own serene and unruffled Christian sentiment. Appealing tenderness and charm combine with an Italianate sense of beauty, especially in his portraits, which are of gentle ardour and lyrical refinement. In his altarpieces for the domestic devotion, his idealized icons of the Madonna and their celestial companions, he attains to a chastity and beatitude of facial expression which has never been equalled. In this he was helped by the evenness, the luminous transparency of his paint, material expression of the peace, and tranquillity of his soul.

Memling's contemporary, Hugo van der Goes (c. 1435–c. 1482), is a much more powerful artist. His was altogether a new vision, told in a monumental language of form. He was a profound interpreter of the human soul. His saints and apostles were "experienced fighters of the faith", brooding, tormented by doubt and by sin even to the brink of madness. What Hugo shares with Roger is his pitch of emotion. But he confides his spiritual experience to an entirely novel type. In his shepherds of the Adoration he revealed a strong human sympathy for the lowly, the menial, painting the wonderfully expressive faces of simple folk with a naturalist's grasp for structural form. As a composer of life-size figures in the three-dimensional space, by their exalted earnestness and physical presence, he is the most revolutionary of fifteenth-century Flemings.

To come from Hugo van der Goes to Gerard David (c. 1464–1523) in the museum at Bruges, from the agonized apostles in the *Death of the Virgin* to the *Baptism of Christ*, is like breathing the air of Paradise after the pangs of Purgatory. Never before was the rippling water painted so blue, moved by the gentle breeze as it circles around the human form of Christ as He stands in the roundness and fullness of body, in the air and the light of an eternal summer. The smooth lofty tree-trunks in the middle distance rise like pillars in the temple of Nature, where, in the shadow of solid rocks, disciples move under the leafy boughs. David was the decisive influence upon Patinir, the first painter of pure landscape in the Flemish School, who conjured up fantastic rock creations and cosmological panoramas in radiant tints of white and of blue.

In the sixteenth century the emphasis shifts from the sustained medieval devotion of the Bruges artists to the florid sentimentalists of the Antwerp School. But Quentin Metsys, though he painted Madonnas of great suavity and feminine languor with soft, suffused outlines, in his masterpiece of the *Lamentation* emulates Roger van der Weyden's rhythmic unity of phrasing. In the melodious flow of figures skilfully interwoven, the wavelike movement of mourners, balanced by the craggy rock of Golgotha, Metsys displays a fastidious sense of form, where courtly grace and asceticism linger side by side.

In the work of the Antwerp Mannerists the archaic solemnity and stillness of the earlier masters is lost in an international style, where architectural forms, culled from Italy, and an elegant, though affected, type of female beauty prevail. Jan Gossaert Mabuse is the virtuoso of an externalized dexterity which excels in a grandiloquent religious pageantry, in crowded compositions where every nook is filled with preciously attired people in the guise of the Three Kings, bringing their ornamental gifts of chiselled gold to the lofty Renaissance manger. As a portraitist Gossaert is "a man of harder temper" whose sharp, incisive contours portray a rather grim and possessive race of man, while in his pagan mythologies, such as the *Danae* at Munich, he displays a brilliantly lustrous conception of the nude.

But the most remarkable painter of the Flemish scene in the sixteenth century, heir of the "ghoulish imagery" of Bosch and begetter of a local school of peasant-genre from Brouwer to Teniers, and even to the Rubens of the *Kermesse Flamande*, is Peter Bruegel the Elder. He represented a complete break with the past, and in his crowded pictures of *Children's Games* and *Proverbs* and peasant merry-making he is above all, an illustrator of Flemish lore, a shrewd observer and humorist with a genius for significant movement and revealing gesture. Bruegel is a draughtsman of line, of coloured planes and silhouettes. Not the individual interests him but the race, the Flemish peasant, the rude and hardly humanized tillers of the soil, romping upon the village green under the high horizon. In his tragic mood he will paint the *Carrying of the Cross* as a festive outing of the Brussels populace upon a vast prospect of rising hills and meadows, or the *Massacre of the Innocents*, with Spanish horsemen descending upon a snow-bound Flemish hamlet, there to perform their task with unrelenting cruelty. A strong sense of the macabre, a bitter taste of the scourge under which mankind is labouring, is expressed in such subjects as the *Cripples* or the *Blind*, whom he shows tumbling like humanity into the inexorable abyss.

But this tragedian-moralist was also a painter of pure landscape. In his youth he had made his way through France to Italy, and the memories of the grandiose scenery of the Alps, the radiant Mediterranean Sea, the towering rocks that line the mountain rivers, have left their mark upon the great series of paintings representing the *Seasons*. These he saw in unison with the labours of the year, with hunter and harvester and herdsman, in a setting of golden corn or of barren trees under the cold blanket of snow in the desolate northern winter.

The consummate painter of Low Life in the seventeenth century who, a pupil of Hals and applauded by Rubens, revealed the less innocent aspects of the human animal, endowing his squat and sinister revellers with an almost Venetian fusion of tones and fluent impasto, was Adrian Brouwer. These habitual inn-dwellers to whom jug and pipe, fist and knife were the principal means of self-expression, served this rabid genius to perfect his alchemy of suffused colour, his experiments in painting the musty air, the transparent chiaroscuro in which his crude and grimacing peasant types live and have their being. If Bruegel's action was built upon swift-moving line, Brouwer softens the shapes of his violent figures by a painterly use of broken tones and atmospheric colour.

Wherever we chance upon the fullness of life and of movement, the richest, the most radiant colours, vigorous and audacious design, a surging wealth of images, Christian and Antique, we are almost certain to be in the presence of Rubens. The change from the hard contours and local colours of the early Flemings to the tempestuous brushwork, the soft interior modelling, the large sweeping movement of Rubens, is not far short of a miracle. It is the painterly expression of the south European Baroque, an architectural style which replaced the classical symmetry by unified phrasing and rhythmical coherence of the picture-whole. Or it may be accounted for by the remarkable kinship which Rubens felt with the great Venetians, especially Titian, of whom, even in his maturity, he copied twenty-five works in the Escorial. Then it was the harmony of golden flesh-tints, the contrast of soft, vibrant rose and blues of Venus, Danae, and Diana, which helped to form the ripest, the most composite style of Rubens. What Rubens saw during his nine years' apprenticeship in Italy and in Spain, the heroic nudes of Michelangelo, the turbulent floating figures of Tintoretto, the orgiastic colour-schemes of Titian, he absorbed it all into his own sovereign self, thus to become the most universally acknowledged painter of the north.

Like Titian's, his work became an apotheosis of the female nude, like him he sought inspiration from classical mythology or from the ecstatic imagery of the neo-catholic emotion which he translated into his native idiom of the Flemish Baroque. For whether he paints the idyllic pastoral of the *Judgment of Paris* or the violent drama of the *Rape of the Sabines*, the sumptuous elegance of the *Garden of Love*, or the domestic intimacy of Helen, his second wife, holding her naked child upon her lap, it is always the nacreous sheen of the flesh, the striking contrast of iridescent nudes with the warm brown tints of the earth and the whole gamut of transitory tones which are a feast to the eye and to the touch. These qualities he brings equally to his epic landscapes, with their glorious sunsets, their impressionist colour-complexity with which the writhing trees, the baroque folds of the land, the primeval forests vibrate.

So vast a genius as Rubens had a far-reaching influence upon the painters of Europe. But in his own time and country his legacy seemed to divide between the elegancies, the refined courtship of Anthony van Dyck and the earthiness, the Flemish sensuality of Jordaens. In his family-feastings and frolics under mythological guise with satyrs and the heavy ripeness of the flesh, Flemish art becomes provincial once more. Van Dyck,

on the other hand, who as a youth was the most brilliant assistant of the Rubens' workshop, and who aspired in all genres to his master's excellence, remained "his best substitute", whose work, especially in portraiture, combined a sensitive spirituality with dash and verve, so flattering to his noble sitters. In Genoa and at the court of Charles I he painted princes and scholars and noble lords in representative poise, full length or on prancing steeds before a decorative background of marble columns and trees and curtains. His self-portrait reveals a handsome man of noble lassitude with fine effeminate hands, an epitome of artistic intelligence, high breeding, and exquisite taste with which the epic of seventeenth-century painting in Flanders sings itself out.

DUTCH AND FLEMISH MARINE PAINTERS

Early in the sixteenth century the Reformation came to certain parts of Europe and destroyed the traditional hold which the Church had exercised on the arts for centuries, particularly in the choice and treatment of the extremely circumscribed range of subjects that were permitted.

Such a place was the Netherlands, where a school of painting already flourished and inevitably the artists began to find new inspiration in the world around them for its own sake, and not merely as a backcloth for figure painting.

Thus it was that a Flemish artist called Joachim Patinir (c. 1485–1524) and his school became the innovators of the landscape in painting, and of the seascape, in a country which was just beginning to feel its power on the sea, and was shortly to become the greatest maritime nation in the world. It was during this period of prosperity, the first half of the seventeenth century, that the Flemish school flourished, and the Dutch school was born and became important. As a school of marine painting, the best examples that still exist are incomparably superior to anything that has been painted since.

Very little is known of the earlier sixteenth-century painters, but that marine paintings

of a very high standard were being produced can be seen from the quality of the *Portuguese Carracks* painted about 1530, which is attributed to a pupil of Patinir's, Cornelis Anthoniszoon (c. 1499–1553).

It convincingly captures the grandeur and the awe that these lofty ships must have inspired as they set forth into the great unknown, or hardly known, packed with soldiers, priests, adventurers, horses, and cattle; all in considerable discomfort, squalor, and danger.

Towards the end of the sixteenth century marine painting in the Netherlands had become well organized, with the Flemish painters still predominating but with the Dutch on the increase. The dominant personality and influence was Hendrik Cornelisz Vroom (1566–1640), a Dutchman from Haarlem who, because he learnt the Flemish way, painted with the bright blues and greens of the Flemish palette.

It should be borne in mind how close to each other are the Netherlands' seaports, and that in such a flat country communications were easy; so that both the Dutch and the Flemings painted in each other's towns in their own way. Indeed, all of them must have known each other or, at least, of each other.

A result of this propinquity on a generation

of artists who were in a state of evolution was the radical changes of approach and technique which may be observed in the life's work of some painters. This was a very healthy sign, and it is a general tendency in the best artists. For the student, however, it is bewildering. Vroom himself did not change radically from his Flemish style. Even after he went to Haarlem he was continuing to turn out Flemish "primitives" when his own pupils were already firmly on the road to naturalism.

This swing towards naturalism is the principal difference between the Flemish and Dutch schools. The Flemish masters continued to paint in the mannered style and with the bright palette of the Brueghels, whereas the Dutch, looking for something more real for a basic colour, chose the most natural and prevalent thing around them, the pearl-grey skies of Holland.

Vroom travelled widely in Europe, going to Spain and Portugal, and in Rome he became a friend of Paul Bril, the landscape painter. On a visit to England he was commissioned by the Earl of Nottingham, the Lord Admiral, to make designs for a series of tapestries of the defeat of the Spanish Armada. These tapestries were made, but unfortunately they were destroyed by fire with the Houses of Parliament in 1834. There is, however, a good set of engravings of them. His finest surviving canvas is the large painting at Haarlam: *The Prince Royal's arrival at Flushing with Princess Elizabeth and Frederick Prince Palatine in 1613*.

Another, much less well-known, large canvas is the *Arrival in England of Prince Charles and the Duke of Buckingham from Spain in 1623*. This painting, which recently came to the National Maritime Museum, Greenwich, is second only in importance to the Haarlem painting, which is a finer composition, but the more formal manner of the Greenwich picture is much more what we expect from him. The allegory, *Trading in the East*, is slightly earlier than either of the paintings mentioned and belongs to a comparatively naturalistic period of Vroom's work, though this is mitigated by the allegorical and, at that time, improbable choice of subject, "peaceful trade between the great nations in the East".

Since Vroom was the father of the Dutch school, it is necessary to set out a brief family tree of his principal pupils at this stage.

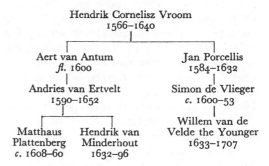

The pupil closest to his master was Aert van Antum, who continued the Flemish tradition which will be examined first. His work changed over the years, but only in its manner, not in its palette. His most typical and best known work has a bright, hard look which, if sometimes a trifle shiny, is nevertheless fresh and vigorous. He is also important as being the master of one of the greatest of Dutch or Flemish painters of any school: Andries van Ertvelt. Ertvelt was a painter with a technique that was brilliantly original in its approach to his subjects, and he possessed that rare gift of aesthetic sense which, in combination, produced pictures with the touch of magic that is genius. Unlike his master, his style changed radically over the years until he went to Italy, where he jettisoned reality and painted impressionistic pictures in which the subject was sacrificed to the artistic effect, which pleased the Italians.

The picture seen in Plate 281 is in a fairly early style; a night scene painted in luminous glazes with *chiaroscuro* effects popular at the time. This, from the figures, must be not earlier than 1625, though the rest of the work suggests an earlier date.

Van Minderhout painted in his master's early style, though he must have known Ertvelt's later paintings as he entered the studio towards the end of Ertvelt's life. For Minderhout, too, artistry was the more important aspect of sea-painting. However, he painted with such charm that he usually gets away with it, particularly if his ships are tied up to a quay. Certainly he must nearly always be forgiven because of his beautiful sense of colour.

He had a palette that included a range of glittering silver white and greys which were all his own and which have nothing at all to do with the greys of the Dutch school. His paintings are all highly romantic, but he was working against the run of taste. With his death in 1696 his style died with him in marine painting, though he strongly influenced Huysman and his school of landscape artists.

Of the two other known pupils of Ertvelt, Gaspar van Eyck copied his master and helped him in his studio, but Matthaus Plattenberg took his master's middle period style with him to Italy and had considerable success with his coastal storm scenes. It was through his friendship with Pieter Mulier the Elder (1615–70) that he came to influence the latter's son, Pieter Mulier II (1637–1701), called Tempesta because he nearly always painted storms.

One of the best known and most entertaining of the Flemish masters was Bonaventura Peeters (1614–52). His work is most carefully finished, the ships are carefully drawn, but the scenes are often in a setting of a fairy tale and are highly romantic.

Perhaps the most delightful of them all was Adam Willaerts (1577–1664). He was a marine painter who was really more interested in the figures he introduced into his compositions, which in many cases quite dominate them. It is this humanity in his approach to his subject, plus a gay and splendid colour sense, that make his paintings so sought after. He had also a pleasing, slightly stiff, yet entirely individual, stylization.

Before 1620 he retired to Utrecht, which is far from the sea, and there he continued to paint marines from memory; though years later, in deference to Dutch taste, his seas went from green to grey. He was assisted in his later years by his sons Isaac Willaerts (1620–93) and Abraham Willaerts (1603–69). The latter was the superior performer, and his work can be mistaken for the father's, particularly if they were working simultaneously.

The painting of English Indiamen was painted after his move to Utrecht, but he still retains his pure Flemish style with green sea and bright blue sky, and he recalls the scenes he had witnessed when he had watched the Indiamen leave on their long, uncertain journeys. There is a moneylender, who would buy a sailor's wages for the trip so that his wife might not starve while he was away. If he didn't come back the moneylender lost, so the premium was high.

Turn now to the Dutch school and the other great pupil of Vroom's, Jan Porcellis. Discarding the colourful and mannered Flemish approach to painting, he arrived at naturalism and worked to a very narrow tonal range based on grey. If the results appear sometimes rather gloomy, they also had a spectacular finish and strength. This rightly brought him to the very forefront of the Dutch marine school, of which, in its classic form, he was to a large extent the inspirer.

He had a son, Julius Porcellis (c. 1609–c. 1664) who was also his pupil, and who combined his father's talents with a rare aesthetic sense. This places the few paintings of his that are known to exist among the first of the very finest paintings that came out of Holland. His *Ships in a gale about 1650*, is one of the most successful storm scenes ever painted; and it was the storm rather than the calm that was the challenge to the Dutch artists of the time, and was the subject that they strove to perfect.

Of the pupils of Jan Porcellis, by far the most important was Simon de Vlieger. It is probable that he was an assistant in Porcellis' studio, though he also appears to have been associated with Leonard Bramer (1596–1674) the history painter, after the latter's return to Delft in 1625.

De Vlieger is probably best known as the master of the younger Van de Velde. He was, however, much more than that; for if Vroom was the father of the Dutch marine school, de Vlieger was its universal uncle. It was not that his influence sprang from a continued excellence in one style, since he was subject to outside influence and he could change his style if he found something he admired in another. Hence the period when he was painting like Van Goyen in his best known and more ethereal moments. Much more typical of him were the later, stronger, paintings with an iron grey, or, ultimately, brown palette. Here his sombre realism, which in a lesser artist could have been dull and uninteresting, became in his hands convincing and inspired with that touch of mystery that is so essential to great painting.

The illustration of his work (Plate 280) shows one of his late paintings with a somewhat brown sea. It is particularly interesting since it proves that he must have visited England: otherwise where would he have seen the chalk caves? It was a careful perfection of this style that the young Van de Velde took back to his father's studio.

De Vlieger must have been a good teacher, because apart from Van de Velde he was also the master of that wizard of atmospheric marine painting, Jan van de Capelle (*c.* 1624–1697). His paintings of very calm calms with masses of limp canvas and splendid skies, have always been the most popular Dutch marine paintings in the art world at large. Indeed, nobody commands so high a price as he.

The other widely known name in Dutch marine painting is that of the Van de Veldes, who, as a family, are historically and artistically the most interesting of their school, whose influence greatly inspired the English school.

Willem van de Velde the Elder (1611–93) started his work in an age dominated by the Porcelis's and by de Vlieger. Whereas, however, de Vlieger was a painter of seascapes with ships, Van de Velde, who was principally a ship draughtsman, painted ships with a seascape, in which the ship, often easily identifiable by name, was dominant to the rest of the subject.

The motive behind this trend, apart from Van de Velde's interest in ships, was the desire of Dutch merchants and naval officers to possess accurate pictures of their ships. Out of this sprang the fashion for large pen and ink drawings on prepared panels or canvases. This fashion flourished in the 'forties, 'fifties and 'sixties of the seventeenth century and continued into the eighteenth century. They are called *grisailles*.

The originator of this type of work appears to have been Herman Witmont (*c.* 1605–83) of Delft, whose drawings, which were mostly in sepia, were very finished, but they lacked a sense of composition.

It was when Van de Velde took up his pen in the 'thirties that the really important *grisailles* were done. Over the next twenty years he turned out large numbers of these exquisite drawings both large and small, usually with a beach in the foreground and with figures. Nobody else ever drew *grisailles* half so well again, so that when he abandoned them for oil painting, the standard of *grisaille* work sank sharply.

To see the largest and best of Van de Velde's *grisailles* is to realize how much time and patience such a picture demanded, and this was one of the reasons why he gave up painting them. He continued, however, to make enormous quantities of drawings, but these were in pencil and were of ships and scenes which he and his son and his assistants could use for paintings in oil, a much more profitable undertaking.

Van de Velde perfected a system of perspective drawing for the placing of his ships. This system he may well have originated, since many previous marine artists show such a weakness in their placing of the ships in the sea as to make them look incorrect at the distance they are set.

When young Willem van de Velde left de Vlieger to work with his father there was formed the most famous partnership in the history of marine painting. The younger man, however, developed a more rapid broader brushwork and distinctive palette. The Van de Veldes were also the only marine painters who troubled to obtain first-hand information on the great battles between the Dutch and the English at sea.

After the battle of Scheveningen in 1653 the Elder Van de Velde made a report on the battle to the Dutch Government and he describes himself therein as "Draughtsman to the Fleet". He was again present in a vessel at the actions of the Second Dutch War, and he did a particularly fine series of the Four Days Fight in 1666.

By the time the Third Dutch War began, however, Holland was in a most precarious state, being pressed by the French on land and by the French and the English on the sea.

Thus the uncertainties of life in their own country and the fact that there was a growing market for their paintings in England, seem to have decided the Van de Veldes to move to that country. They arrived at Harwich in the first year of the war (1672–3), and in the summer of 1673 they made drawings of the last actions of the war from an English vessel.

Both King Charles and the Duke of York showed the Van de Veldes great favour and patronage, and this decided old Willem to bring his wife and family from Holland to stay in England, where many splendid examples of their work can be seen. Although the younger Willem lived in England for over thirty years, it does not seem that either he or his father managed to glean much of the English language. This would have made it difficult for them to work with English assistants. They therefore appear to have kept to themselves, though in the later years J. van de Hagen worked in the younger Willem's studio, where he assiduously copied his master's style. His productions, though inferior, are easily deceiving to the unwary: not that he was faking his master's work, as he always signed his pictures. His daughter married Cornelis van de Velde, a son of the younger Willem's, and a rather mysterious artist who is mentioned with respect as a marine painter of the foremost rank long after his father's death in 1707.

It is not easy to select one picture to represent this brilliant, hard-working family but we have chosen a very late and splendid painting of Willem the Younger (Plate 279), which served as a model for so many copies to come. The majestic first-rate, the finest ship in the world when she was painted, seems to embody all the heroic beauty which had held the Van de Veldes captive for two-thirds of a century, and which they here present in paint, through the hand of the son, as only they could.

Ertvelt, de Vlieger, and the older Peeters died in the early 1650s, and the Willaerts and Julius Porcelis in the early sixties. From this time there is a noticeable change in Dutch taste; a more sophisticated, smoother approach to marine painting was favoured.

The person most qualified to mirror the times was a convivial German from Emden, who went to Amsterdam at eighteen, and who was called Ludolf Bakhuizen (1631–1708). Bakhuizen learnt marine painting under Hendrik Dubbels, who lived and died in Amsterdam (1620–76) and who was the doyen of the guild in 1650. It seems certain that Bakhuizen worked afterwards in the Van de Veldes' studio, as there are drawings and paintings of his in the 'sixties which have a very strong connexion with works of the Van de Veldes at that time. His work had always a brilliant finish, being built up in warm and cool toned glazes. In his younger days he retained also a freshness and spontaneity which is not easy to preserve with so painstaking an execution. He was tremendously admired in his lifetime and after his death, and he was preferred by many to the Van de Veldes. He was an artist who did not change much, but whose early work is the best. *Shipping off the Dutch coast in a fresh breeze* is in his finest vein.

Like the Van de Veldes, Bakhuizen liked big canvases, and this often presents the beholder with a spectacle of brilliant grandeur. He was to be the ideal and the model for several generations of Dutch marine painters.

The other painter of similar talents who, indeed, kept up a rather higher standard of artistry in his late years, was Abraham Storck (c. 1635–c. 1710). This makes him almost exactly contemporary with Bakhuizen, who appears to have had a strong influence on his work. He was not given, however, to the flights of imaginative fancy which characterizes some of Bakhuizen's paintings. Storck just painted what he saw. Or if he was commissioned to paint a scene he had not witnessed, such as perhaps a battle, then he used what he had seen and what within the bounds of a strict probability, his imagination suggested. Thus his best works are those done from sketches of the busy harbour of his native Amsterdam with a beautiful sense of colour and the charming figures with which he liked to fill his canvases.

Where can the student go to see the Dutch marine school? The easiest way to see quite a number is to go to Greenwich. The National Maritime Museum there has the largest collection in the world, and it is particularly complete in the Van de Veldes. Otherwise, there are two good private collections in England: that of Sir Bruce Ingram, and that belonging to Captain Eric Palmer. The latter's collection is particularly interesting from the student's point of view, because it was collected to tell the story of the school, and, as such, it is the only collection of its kind in the world (see *The Connoisseur*, June 1960). There are also many important works scattered among the great houses, and in the collection of Her Majesty the Queen. The Dutch and the Flemish galleries also have a large number, but much less than one would expect. The outstanding canvases there are the great Vroom at Haarlem, already mentioned, and the splendid Van de Velde the younger of the *Gouden Leeuw at Amsterdam*, painted for Cornelis van Tromp, and a pair to the equally splendid *Battle of the Texel* at Greenwich.

French

The most clearly recognizable, and yet the most indefinable, qualities of French painting are lightness, wit, and clarity of observation. For the most part French painting has been centred in Paris, and many of its characteristics are due to the concentration of artistic life there. Its earliest manifestations were in the South of France, where the advent of the Papacy to Avignon made that town the crossroads of Europe, and introduced the works of such artists as Simone Martini. By the latter half of the fourteenth century clearly defined artistic centres had been established at Paris and in Burgundy, where the court of the dukes provided a focus for a highly sophisticated culture. The influence of Flemish art made itself clearly felt; a Chancellor of Burgundy commissioned the Louvre's Van Eyck, and the subsequent history of French painting until the middle of the nineteenth century was to be patterned on the alternating influence of the Netherlands and Italy. Early names which have survived are those of Charenton, Fouquet (*c.* 1415–*c.* 1481), and the Master of Moulins (*c.* 1490).

The political ambitions of Francis I brought Leonardo to France and produced a minor renaissance centred around Fontainebleau, which gave its name to a school of painting under the aegis of two Italians, Rosso and Primaticcio. The works of this school are characterized by a highly stylized formula for the nude in mythological attitudes, the most revealing prototypes being Bronzino's *Venus, Cupid and Time* in the National Gallery, and the *Landscape with Figures* by Niccolo dell'Abbate.

The pattern of French artistic life, with its marked dependence on royal patronage, was now clearly set, and under Louis XIV it was erected into a permanent structure, with the establishment of the French School at Rome, endowed with lavish scholarships and an elaborate series of commissions, pensions, and free apartments in the Louvre.

France had its equivalent of Holbein in the productions of the Clouet group of artists. The personalities of the various members of this coterie, whose portraits are informed by poetic realism and considerable psychological penetration, are confused; though at Hampton Court there is a *Portrait of a Man with a Volume of Petrarch* which may be taken as fairly representative of its highest achievement. It is attributed to Jean Clouet (1486–1540). Another member of the group was Corneille de Lyon (*c.* 1510–74), to whom are attributed several works in the National Gallery. Up to the end of the sixteenth century French paintings are on panel; either mahogany, oak, or limewood.

The rather simple style of the sixteenth century changed rapidly under the stimulus of decorative painting in churches and palaces. Simon Vouet (1590–1649) was the first French artist to undertake large works on an impressive scale. His output was large, and he is known mostly for his Italianized church paintings. Eustache Le Sueur (1616–55) showed more individuality and a more marked Gallic personality, represented at its happiest by the Louvre's *Mass of St Martin of Tours*. The Le Nain brothers (Antoine, 1588–1648; Louis, 1593–1648; Mathieu, 1607–77) represent a curious chapter in French painting. Their work is intensely realistic, slightly dramatic. They deal almost exclusively with plebeian themes: peasants in fields, farm-houses, and the like. It is extremely difficult to disentangle their individualities; but there are two distinct groups of their works, one painted on copper, the other on canvas. They are sometimes signed *Lenain fecit*. Georges Dumesnil de la Tour (*c.* 1590–1652) was an exponent of the style of the *tenebrosi*, whose work occasionally bears a superficial resemblance to that of the Le Nains.

Meanwhile, portraits were beginning to multiply. Many of them survive and keep turning up in the sale-rooms, though it is usually impossible to attribute them more precisely than to "French School, seventeenth-century". The outstanding individual was Philippe de Champaigne (1602–74), whose work is marked by a spiritualized austerity and dedicated realism.

Claude Gellée, Le Lorrain (1600–82) lived and worked in Rome. His works were extremely popular in England in the eighteenth and nineteenth centuries. He was essentially a landscape painter using either classical themes or Italian scenes for his subjects. He kept rough drawings of two hundred of his paintings in a *Liber Veritatis*. This is a valuable guide to the authenticity of any painting attributed to him. He always signed his paintings, usually in the form CLAVDIO G.I.V. ROMAE, date. Roughly the contemporary of Claude, Nicolas Poussin (1594–1665) was also preoccupied with classical themes, though in his work figure painting played a more important and a more integral part, and his almost mathematical composition and regularity have made him the modern father of "classic", as opposed to "romantic" painting. He painted mythological and religious subjects, historical subjects and landscapes with architecture and figures. They are often overlaid with thick coats of varnish, but are distinguishable by a subdued and subtle colour range which at times has a rather metallic quality. He rarely signed his works: when he did, the formula was POVSSIN FACIEBAT, or FECIT, with date. The faces usually have a mask-like quality, and he concentrates on structure and situation at the expense of light and transient effects. Poussin gave rise to an entire school of disciples and imitators, while the historical style, to which he had given added dignity, combined, with the influence of Rubens, to create pompous rhetorical painters of the type of Charles Le Brun (1619–90). Court painters, too, began a flourishing trade, and the most outstanding of the late seventeenth century were Hyacinthe Rigaud (1659–1743); and Nicolas de Largillière (1656–1746; Plate 282).

But the greatest French artist of the eighteenth century was Antoine Watteau (1648–1721). He chose for his subject a semi-pastoral, semi-theatrical world, and inclined rather to the influence of Rubens than to that of the Italians. His works are painted on panel and canvas, and an excess of oil often causes wrinkling. They are unsigned, and the best guide to authenticity is by reference to the complete engraved edition of them in the *Receuil Jullienne*, Paris, 1735. He attracted the early attention of imitators and disciples, the two most famous of the latter being Nicolas Lancret (1690–1743) and J-B. Pater (1696–1736; Plate 283A).

The main stream of eighteenth-century French art, however, moved away from the style of Watteau to a more luscious, sensuous manner typified by the works of François Boucher (1703–70; Plate 283B). A prolific artist, the first to produce drawings specifically for collectors, his canvases usually have a light-grey priming, avoid the use of black and brown, and towards the end of his career have a rather faded appearance. His works are signed *f. Boucher*, date. His most famous pupil was Jean-Honoré Fragonard (1732–1806), almost equally prolific, and with a new feeling for poetic landscape. Fragonard relied on sentiment rather than on sensuality. He devoted a good deal of his talent to glamourizing contemporary life, and after about 1740 there appears a flood of genre pictures dealing with the life of the boudoir and the streets. Many of his subjects are repeated, and his studio props which appear in many of his pictures are often a guide to dating and authenticity. Louis-Léopold Boilly (1761–1845) is typical of the minor contemporaries of Fragonard, with a rather superficial but technically persuasive style. Quite different was Jean-Baptiste-Siméon Chardin (1699–1779), who took scenes of domestic life and kitchen objects and made them into masterpieces of fine painting, warm, imaginative. Probably the greatest European master of the still life, Chardin gave a new meaning to tonal value and explored as none other had done the infinite variations of local colour. Usually signed his name "*chardin*" and repeated subjects a good deal. Popularized to an extent which no other paintings had ever been before by the activities of the engravers, the style of French eighteenth-century genre painters spread widely and rapidly. Artists like Jean-Baptiste Greuze (1725–1805) achieved great fame for their half-maudlin, half-erotic paintings, which maintained their popularity throughout the next century and inspired countless academic paintings.

The career of Mme Vigée-Le Brun (1755–1842) bridged the *ancien régime* and the Napoleonic period. She was mostly a portrait painter who devoted her attention to such celebrities as Marie Antoinette and Lady Hamilton. The discovery of the Revolution was Jacques-Louis David (1748–1825, Plate 383c) a painter of portraits and historical subjects who made himself art dictator of France. His rather dry, metallic manner and predilection for classical subjects show an allegiance to Poussin. Many of his works are signed "*L. David*", date. A more attractive character was Baron Gros (1771–1835), who was attached to Napoleon's staff, painted battle scenes, and greatly influenced the younger generation which grew up reacting against David. Typical of these was Théodore Géricault (1791–1824), whose *Raft of the Medusa*, now in the Louvre, is generally recognized as the first masterpiece of the "romantic" age. The old tradition of craftsmanship was broken, artists were now "gentlemen" and more emphasis was given to freedom of handling and individuality of treatment than to technical traditionalism. Géricault visited England, was impressed by the British attitude to the arts and by the work of British artists. So, too, was Eugène Delacroix (1798–1863), who was the greatest of the "romantics", using that word in its narrower connotation. His output was large, and covered almost every genre of painting. He signed his paintings variously (e.g. EUGE DELACROIX). His technique is marked by the use of broken colour and a freshness and spontaneity which cannot be explained merely by his affection for the works of Constable and Bonington. He painted many subjects from English literature, and in his penchant for Oriental subjects forecast a craze which was to persist throughout the century. If Delacroix relied on colour, Ingres (1780–1867) can be said to rely on line, though the antithesis is not quite as simple as that. Clearly in the tradition of Poussin and David, Ingres' paintings are marked by smooth, unatmospheric colour, fine draughtsmanship, and superficial classical pretensions. The subsequent history of French painting, whether academic or experimental, was to alternate between the two poles of expression and feeling typified by these two artists.

In the 1900s the paintings of the Barbizon School received the same adulation as the Impressionists do now: they were to fall into disgrace when the contribution of the Impressionists themselves was more generally recognized. The painters whose home was the Forest of Fontainebleau had, however, temperaments that should accord well with our own day. The artists of Barbizon were essentially innocents, who withdrew to the secrets of the forest and to the freshness of the sea. The greatest of them, Théodore Rousseau and Corot, were among the most considerable artists of the nineteenth century. If their paintings tend to appear repetitive, it is because we are accustomed to their vocabulary and because the success they won towards the end of their life led them to over-production – a faut not uncommon to the Impressionists. The Barbizon painters were at their best in their most unusual works, as in Diaz's stormy landscape, which has a touch of Expressionist energy, or in Jules Dupré's freshly observant landscape study to nature which is curiously close to some of the Piedmontese landscape artists of the same period.

The modern collector can even find admirable paintings among the late nineteenth- and early twentieth-century schools, which are usually so expensive – for instance, painters such as Emile Bernard and the other members of the Pont Aven circle.

THE IMPRESSIONISTS

On April 15, 1874, there opened in Paris an exhibition of 165 works by thirty artists, seven of whom – Cézanne, Degas, Monet, Berthe Morisot, Pissarro, Renoir, and Sisley – have gone down in history as the originators and chief exponents of the Impressionist Movement. Ten days after the opening the critic of the *Charivari* published a most derisive article under the title "Exhibition of the Impressionists", in which he was especially abusive about one of the five paintings shown by Monet, entitled *Impression, Sunrise*. In his derision this critic summed up the feelings of the general public and of the established artists of the day; in his choice of title he launched the name which quickly came to be used for the major art movement of the nineteenth century, despite its unpopularity with some of the artists principally concerned.

In nineteenth-century France spontaneity and originality in painting had very largely given way to dullness and traditionalism. Obviously there were exceptions to this widespread *malaise*, but it was left to the Impressionists to create a really strong reaction, out of which grew modern painting. A return to nature for inspiration and a lively rendering of light and colour lay at the centre of the Impressionists' revolutionary methods. Stiff classical compositions and dark and often murky colours were replaced by scintillating movement, spontaneity, and brightness. In their early years the Impressionists were ridiculed and unappreciated, but they could not be ignored; today their work has been accepted as forming one of the greatest epochs in the history of painting.

The exhibition of 1874 – the first of eight Impressionist exhibitions in Paris – was the outcome of some ten years of struggle for recognition by this small group of artists who had rebelled against the prevailing traditional and classical fashions of their time. There had been signs of such a movement for many years before this. J. B. C. Corot (1796–1875) and Gustave Courbet (1819–77) were both artists of considerable stature who were painting largely outside the *Salon* tradition, and were both to exert a strong influence on the young Impressionists. Corot's *Le Blanchisserie de Chaville*, which dates from the early 1850s, is an example of the sort of poetic and atmospheric painting which made his work one of the early inspirations of the Impressionists.

The principal link, however, between the traditional and Impressionism was Edouard Manet (1832–83), who is today commonly numbered among the Impressionists, but who, both by his actions and by his inclinations, must be said to stand apart from the central group. Manet drew much of his inspiration from the old masters, and particularly from Spain. His painting technique, however, was a revolutionary and highly individual one, combining great broadness and freshness with strength and firmness. Manet had already made his mark when the future Impressionists were beginning to gather in Paris. At the *Salon* of 1861 he won acclaim and official recognition with his *Spanish Guitar Player*. Two years later, at the notorious *Salon des Refusés*, where Pissarro, Cézanne, and Guillaumin were also represented, *Le Déjeuner sur l'Herbe* (now in the Louvre) was received with violent criticism and ridicule. From his own freedom of treatment it was not a large step for Manet to move towards the even greater freedom of the Impressionists, and this he did in the 1870s. *La Promenade*, which was painted in 1879, is an example of Manet in his Impressionist vein. Yet he never showed at any of the group exhibitions, and maintained to the last his struggle for official recognition. In 1882, the year before his death at the age of fifty-one, he was nominated *Chevalier de la Légion d'Honneur*. As a painter Manet achieved greatness both in the academic tradition and as an Impressionist. As a man he belonged very largely to the former.

From a totally different background and very definitely at the centre of the Impressionist movement was Claude Monet (1840–1926), the son of a Paris grocer. Monet's early life was spent in Le Havre, where he met Eugène Boudin – an important predecessor of the Impressionists in his beautiful seascapes and shore scenes – who persuaded him to take up landscape painting and to work from nature. In 1859 Monet settled in Paris. He studied under Charles Jacque, and also at the Académie Suisse, where he met Pissarro. In 1862 he enrolled at the Académie Gleyre, where Bazille, Renoir, and Sisley were also students, and which, by bringing these artists together, may be considered a starting-point of Impressionism. Monet, who once defined art as "a transposition of nature at once forceful and sensitive", was immensely devoted to his ideals and was really the early driving force of the Impressionist group. For many years he was abused and almost entirely unappreciated, and he suffered from appalling poverty. By the end of his long life, however, he had achieved world-wide fame and success.

Monet was at his greatest as a landscape, or at any rate as an outdoor, painter. *La Grenouillère*, which he painted in 1869, is a fine example of his ability to grasp the elements of his subjects, and to achieve a completely natural composition. Nothing is posed or stiff. In later years Monet developed his ideas in the painting of a number of great series, such as the "Haystacks", the "Water-lilies" and the studies of Rouen Cathedral. In these series – especially in the "Water-lilies" which he studied in his garden at Giverny – Monet's technique became increasingly free and fluid. Outline and form were almost entirely sacrificed and he concentrated on colour and tone. In this way Monet remained a true Impressionist to the end of his days, and in his work lies the very essence of the movement.

The oldest and most consistent of the Impressionists was Camille Pissarro (1830–1903), who was born in the West Indies and came to Paris in 1855. Here he met and was strongly influenced by Corot, and until 1870 he showed regularly at the *Salon*. Pissarro was largely a landscape painter – equally happy to choose his subjects in town or country and often incorporating figures on a small scale. His approach was always direct and natural, and his compositions tend to be rather broad and open. He was not a painter of detail, but rather of the general scene observed from a distance. In *Le Boulevard des Fossés, Pontoise*, dated 1872, one can still clearly see the influence of Corot, while in *Le Pont Neuf, Après-Midi, Soleil* (Plate 287B), painted nearly thirty years later in 1901, Pissarro has obviously assimilated the many facets of the Impressionist movement, including that of pointillism, though he still remains remarkably close to his original concepts.

Pissarro was probably the least temperamental of the Impressionists, and was certainly a steadying influence among his fellow artists. He was the only one to show at all eight group exhibitions between 1874 and 1886, and, as the oldest among them and a family man, he was something of a father figure to the others. Cézanne, Seurat, Gauguin, Van Gogh, and many others were befriended and influenced by him. Four of Camille's sons became painters, most notably Lucien, who settled in England and who did his best work in the pointillist style of Seurat and Signac, which his father had also adopted for a period from 1885. Camille Pissarro was an able draughtsman, and numerous drawings and water-colours by him have survived. He was also a skilled etcher and lithographer, often working in co-operation with Lucien, who founded the Eragny Press in England.

Pierre Auguste Renoir (1841–1919) started his working life as a decorator in a porcelain factory. He joined Gleyre's Académie in 1862, and became very friendly with Monet and Bazille. Renoir was perhaps the most French of the Impressionists. At the Louvre he studied the work of Watteau, Boucher, and Fragonard, and he was also strongly influenced by Courbet. His painting is carefree and sensuous. His choice of subject was wide and varied – landscapes, portraits, nudes, still lifes, and genre scenes – in all he displayed his immense energy and his great mastery of paint. His palette was the richest of any of the Impressionists', and thus many of his paintings retain today wide popular appeal, even though the original brightness of some of his colours has disappeared with the years, because certain of the pigments he used were not permanent ones. Together with richness of colour went a strong flowing line, and these two characteristics culminated in the striking and powerful nudes of his later years, painted after he had settled in Cagnes in 1906. But Renoir also possessed great subtlety and delicacy, as is shown by *Au Concert* (Plate 284), which was painted in 1880 when the artist was at the height of his Impressionist period.

In the following year Renoir visited Algeria and Italy, and on his return to France he began to move away from Impressionism. But in many ways Renoir remained loyal to his beginnings; though he did develop a highly individual style, in which he again drew inspiration from the old masters, especially Rubens. In the last years of his life, when he also turned to sculpture, Renoir was largely crippled by rheumatism, and in the end he painted with the brush attached to his wrist. Even in his early days Renoir had won a certain amount of recognition and patronage, particularly by his portrait painting. During the last twenty-five years of his long life he was famous and successful.

Unlike Renoir, Alfred Sisley (1839–99) was faithful to Impressionism throughout his life. Except at the beginning of his career, he confined himself almost entirely to the painting of landscape, in which he achieved the most perfect sensibility and harmony. In 1882 he settled at Moret, near Paris, and he found the majority of his subjects in the valley of the Seine. Sisley, who was of English descent, was the least ambitious and most modest of the Impressionists, and it was only after his death that his work was acclaimed. *Neige à Louveciennes*, a work painted in 1872, is typical of Sisley's pure Impressionist landscapes. Like the surface of water, that of snow gave the Impressionists ample scope to practise their theories of light and colour. Monet, in particular, painted a number of most effective snow scenes.

In contrast to Sisley, Edgar Degas (1834–1917) was essentially a painter of people and of animals. The son of a banker and a man of means he grew up with a deep admiration for the work of Ingres, and like him he was a masterly draughtsman. In the late 1850s he made several trips to Italy, where he did much drawing after the old masters. The Italian influences further contributed to his classicism at this period.

While most of his fellow-Impressionists, whom he met through Manet, concentrated on factors of colour and light, Degas was far more intent on composition. In moving away from his classical beginnings he worked on a series of subjects in which his essential aim was to capture the spontaneity of movement – the action of a moment. Scenes of the racecourse, the theatre, music halls, cafés, circuses, and from 1868 studies of ballet, gave him a variety of subjects in which he could achieve this aim. The delightful pastel illustrated here, *Danseuse sur la Scène* (Plate 286), is an example of the numerous ballet subjects drawn and painted by Degas, who, like many of his fellow-Impressionists, found pastels a sympathetic medium, particularly in his later days. Degas, however, differed from the other artists in that he rarely painted on the spot, but preferred to work in his studio from his notes and his memory. Though anxious to achieve reality, he did not work spontaneously, but rather composed his pictures in keeping with the classical tradition in which he had developed. But Degas' method had one great disadvantage; he was rarely satisfied with a painting and continually went on "improving" it. Never really close to his fellow-artists, Degas became a lonely figure in the final years of his life, when he worked increasingly on his marvellous sculptures of horses and ballet dancers, which he modelled in wax. He had, however, shown at all but one of the group exhibitions, and he had made a vital contribution to the Impressionist movement.

A recent dictionary of artists has called Paul Cézanne (1839–1906) "probably the greatest painter of the last 100 years", and it it is a claim which many would support. He was certainly the greatest of the Impressionists in that he made of Impressionism something that could be developed. As Manet was the essential link between the Impressionists and their immediate forebears, he was the vital link between the Impressionists and their successors.

Cézanne was born at Aix-en-Provence, the son of a wealthy banker, and was destined for the law. As a student he developed a great friendship with Émile Zola, who was to become one of the few art critics of the time to appreciate the Impressionists. In 1861 Cézanne abandoned his study of law, and went to Paris, where he met Pissarro at the Académie Suisse. After a brief period in his father's bank he settled in Paris in 1862 and devoted himself to painting. At first he painted a series of dramatic and often erotic pictures, reminiscent of Delacroix. But by the early 1870s he had turned to landscape painting, largely under the influence of Pissarro, from whose work Cézanne's canvases of these years are often indistinguishable. At the first Impressionist exhibition of 1874 he showed three paintings, two of them landscapes. He showed with the group only once more – at the third exhibition in 1877 – when his sixteen paintings won high praise from one critic, Rivière. Otherwise, however, Cézanne met largely with ridicule and discouragement, and being essentially a shy man, he withdrew increasingly into himself, so that in the years of his greatest development he was very much on his own. From 1882 on he lived and worked largely in Provence, settling in Aix on the death of his father in 1886, which left him a rich man.

In his early painting Cézanne worked rapidly and freely, making frequent use of the palette knife. Under the influence of Pissarro he adopted the small brush strokes and the colour theories of the Impressionists. In the early 1880s he moved towards his own essential style, based on an even subtler application of colour and tone and on the severe disciplining of his form and composition. He worked more slowly and deliberately. "Treat nature by the cylinder, the sphere, the cone, everything in proper perspective so that each side of an object or plane is directed towards a central point." Here was a development beyond Impressionism – a development of vast influence, in which the basic ideas of Cubism can be detected. Cézanne's greatest working

years lay between 1885 and 1895, and it was in the second half of this period that he painted the four versions of *Le Garçon au Gilet Rouge*, of which one is illustrated here (Plate 285). In this the forceful economy of his style is well illustrated, as is the careful juxtaposition of the various planes and the subtle harmony of the tones. It was in these years also that he painted the many Provençal landscapes – both in oil and in water-colour – which are, perhaps, his most famous works. A shy, patient, and painstaking man, Cézanne was essentially an artist, and as he himself would have wished, he collapsed while walking home from a day of painting and died on the same day.

In the work of Cézanne we have seen a vital development beyond Impressionism based on a new approach to the factors of colour, tone, and form, and the relationship between them. At the same time Georges Seurat (1859–91) was approaching the same problems from an entirely different angle, and, though not at first closely in touch with any of the Impressionists, was trying to put the new methods of painting on a scientific basis. Seurat studied at the École des Beaux Arts, and was particularly interested in the work of Ingres and Delacroix. Like the latter, he was fascinated by Chevreul, and on the basis of these and others he evolved a highly disciplined technique of painting, which he called "divisionism", but which has also been called "pointillism" and "Neo-Impressionism". The Impressionists used pure colours, but they mixed these on the palette and applied them, usually in small brush strokes, according to the instinct and inspiration of the moment. Seurat and his followers used the same pure colours, but applied them as such in small divided brush strokes so placed that an optical mixing of the colours could take place. This technique was methodical and scientific and demanded careful forethought and planning. Compared with the spontaneous paintings of the Impressionists, those of Seurat appear somewhat stiff and formal, though in their harmony of colour, tone, and composition they are in themselves great masterpieces.

In 1882 and 1883 Seurat devoted much of his time to drawing and in his highly individual black-and-white drawings he developed his theories of form and light. In 1883 he felt able to tackle the addition of colour and he painted his first great masterpiece, *Une Baignade*, which is now in the Tate Gallery. This was rejected at the *Salon*, but was shown at the first exhibition of the "Société des Indépendents", which he helped to form. In 1885 through the introduction of his most important follower, Paul Signac (1863–1935), Seurat met Pissarro, who not only adopted the divisionist method for a considerable period, but also insisted that Seurat and Signac should be admitted to what proved to be the final Impressionist exhibition in 1886. Renoir was among those who refused to participate as a result. Seurat showed six paintings and three drawings, including the famous *Grande Jatte* which caused something of a scandal. *Le Pont de Courbevoie* (Plate 287A) was painted in this year, and is a notable example of the carefully planned composition and harmony of Seurat's work. Each of his large paintings was preceded by a considerable number of small oil studies painted on the spot, and then used in the studio in the formulation of the final composition. Seurat was only forty-two when he died, but his theories were kept alive by Signac, himself a considerable artist, painting very largely marine and harbour scenes, and also to be noted for his water-colours.

In marked contrast to Neo-Impressionist, the term "Post-Impressionist" is rather vague and is impossible to define. It is, however, a useful classification for a number of artists who were strongly influenced by, and often acquainted with, the Impressionists, but who were not part of the movement during its relatively brief early homogeneous period. The artists that remain to be discussed here might all be termed Post-Impressionists.

Paul Gauguin (1848–1903), who was then a successful stockbroker, started to buy pictures by the Impressionists in about 1876 and met Pissarro in the following year. Shortly after his marriage in 1873 he had begun to draw and paint, and, as was to be expected, his work was strongly influenced by the example of the artists whose work he collected. He showed at the last four Impressionist ex-

hibitions, and made rapid progress in his painting, largely under the influence of Pissarro. In 1883 he gave up his work as a stockbroker in order to devote himself entirely to art. In this move he met with strong opposition from his Danish-born wife, and his financial resources were quickly exhausted, so that he had to start selling his collection of paintings. But Gauguin persevered, and in 1886 he paid his first visit to Brittany, where he began to draw away from Impressionism and to develop his own powerful style with its clear-cut forms, strong lines, and striking colour contrasts. In 1887 he spent some months in Martinique, and in the following year a stormy period with Van Gogh at Arles. In 1891 he went to live in Tahiti, where, after returning to France in 1893, he settled again in 1895. First in Brittany, then in Martinique, and finally in Tahiti, Gauguin sought a simple and natural environment, based on ancient custom and tradition, in which he could find the stimulus he needed to combat the over-civilization and falseness which he felt to be overwhelming the art of his time.

Gauguin was determined to escape from the domination of nature and to create an art which gave full scope to idealism, symbolism, and imagination. In the native art of many lands and in the medieval art of Europe he found the basis of his own work, which was not confined only to painting, but included sculpture, engraving, and pottery. Thus his painting became more and more non-naturalistic, both in its form and in its colours. The painting illustrated here, which is dated 1899, is one of the masterpeices which Gauguin painted in this development. Entitled *I await the letter* (Plate 288B), it is extremely strong in colour and in composition and provides a wealth of material to stimulate the imagination and feelings of the spectator. The new and vital approach of Gauguin was immensely influential on other artists. Too much has been written about his romantic and tragic life. He was first and foremost an artist, and it is by his art that he should be remembered.

The life of Vincent Van Gogh (1853–90) has been even more popularized than that of Gauguin, but at the same time his painting is certainly more widely known than that of any other artist of this period. The son of a Dutch pastor, Van Gogh was an unstable and nervous man, whose life was dominated by failure. He worked in turn for picture dealers, for a bookseller, as a teacher, and finally as a missionary in the coal-mining district of the Borinage in Belgium. After his dismissal from the mission in 1880 he developed the desire to draw and paint. He worked in Brussels, in The Hague, at his parents' home in Neunen, and in Antwerp, largely teaching himself and relentlessly determined to succeed as an artist. His early work was much influenced by Rembrandt and other Dutch artists, and by Millet. He painted and drew sombre scenes of peasants at work and at rest, of which the *Potato Eaters* of 1885 is the acknowledged masterpiece. In the following year he joined his faithful brother Theo in Paris, and eagerly absorbed the immense stimulus of that great artistic centre.

Here he came face to face with the work of the Impressionists. His palette quickly lightened and he adopted the small brush strokes of Pissarro and the Neo-Impressionists. He painted landscapes in Montmartre, still lifes of flowers, and portraits, and his work began to show that vibrant vitality and sincerity which make him such a great artist. In February of 1888 Van Gogh, feeling the strain of life in Paris, went to Arles, where he was intoxicated by the colour and light of the south. Now began just under two and a half years of feverish and prolific painting, interrupted only by occasional periods of complete insanity, which closed when he took his own life in 1890. In October 1888 Gauguin joined Van Gogh at Arles; the visit ended in disaster when Vincent heralded his first fit of insanity by cutting off his own ear. From then on he was to work entirely on his own, supported only by the encouragement of Theo, and, in his last months, by the friendship of Dr Gachet.

The painting reproduced here, *Jardin Public à Arles* (Plate 288A), was painted in 1888 shortly before Gauguin's visit. Indeed, it is possible that this is one of the four pictures which Van Gogh painted to decorate Gauguin's room. Though he did not seek to do so as positively as Gauguin, Van Gogh also achieved great directness and simplicity in his work. With thickly loaded and tremendously vigorous brush strokes he captured the essentials of his subject, be it portrait, interior, or landscape, and painted canvases radiating with colour, light, and feeling. Gauguin showed future artists the road to non-naturalistic painting; Van Gogh gave them a supreme example of how to capture the very essence of nature with brush and paint on canvas.

Henri de Toulouse-Lautrec (1864–1901) already belongs to the generation after the original Impressionists, but he worked very much in their tradition, being especially influenced by Degas. Crippled as the result of an accident in his youth, Toulouse-Lautrec came to Paris in 1882, and spent nearly all the rest of his life there. His approach to painting was one of extreme directness, and he particularly loathed posed models. Thus he found his favourite subjects in the dance-halls, cafés, cabarets, theatres, and circuses, whose personalities and scenes he painted with great candour and feeling, often choosing the crueller and more macabre side of the characters he was portraying. Like Degas, Toulouse-Lautrec was a superb draughtsman, and he could convey the whole character of his subject, and the atmosphere and movement of a scene, with just a few lines. La Goulue, Jane Avril, Yvette Guilbert, and many other dancers and actresses of the Paris of his day have won immortality through being portrayed by Toulouse-Lautrec, and we also owe largely to him the graphic picture which we still have today of the Montmartre of the 'eighties and 'nineties. A master of form and movement, Toulouse-Lautrec worked feverishly without close contact with any of his fellow artists, and he has made a very personal and individual contribution to French nineteenth-century painting.

Pierre Bonnard (1867–1947) and Edouard Vuillard (1868–1940) were two further leading figures among the Post-Impressionists of Toulouse-Lautrec's generation. They were close friends and strongly influenced each other, becoming central figures of a group of artists known as *The Nabis*, which had formed round Gauguin before he went to Tahiti. Among these were also Sérusier, Maurice

Denis, Roussel, and Vallotton. Both Bonnard and Vuillard excelled in their paintings of interiors with figures, in which they combined great simplicity of composition and outline with subtle delicacy of colour and tone. They developed an intimate and lyrical manner of their own, in which shape and form were often sacrificed in order to achieve atmosphere and harmony. Both artists also painted portraits, and Bonnard frequently painted landscapes.

Today paintings by some of the Impressionists and Post-Impressionists – notably Manet, Cézanne, Van Gogh, and Gauguin – are among the most valuable in the world, and they are well beyond the means of all but the richest collectors. But many great collections of Impressionist paintings have been, and still are being, built up, especially in America, where a number of museums have received rich gifts of the work of the Impressionists. In Britain there have also been some notable collectors, chief among them the late Samuel Courtauld, who not only assembled the marvellous collection now to be seen at the Courtauld Institute of Art in Woburn Square,

London, but also provided the money with which some of the greatest Impressionist treasures in the Tate Gallery were acquired. The National Museum of Wales in Cardiff owes its fine group of Impressionist paintings to the foresight and generosity of the late Miss Gwendoline E. Davies and her sister. Paris, the birthplace and centre of the Impressionist movement, can justly claim to have the most important collection of Impressionist painting in the world, which has been built up very largely by the generosity of private donors. Forming part of the Louvre, most of these works are beautifully hung in the recently rebuilt *Jeu de Paume*.

A visit to this museum brings home the immense hope and vitality which marked the developments of Impressionism. Today its influence is undeniable and widespread. Ignored and ridiculed when they were creating their greatest masterpieces, the Impressionist painters can never again be forgotten and neglected, and several of them must rank among the greatest artists that the Western world has known.

German

The Cologne altar of the *Three Kings* by Stephan Lochner is the work by which German art, Gothic and medieval, emerged into the light of the courtly international style, with notable elements of a native sweetness and loveliness, especially in the coy and impeccable beauty of the Madonna. Lochner still paints upon gold-ground, but his figures stand in stately dignity upon the earth, clothed in brocaded stuffs and velvets which mould their forms in heavy rhythmical folds. But there is no special depth, no landscape background in the pictorial build-up of the processional altar. Only the light varies the rhythmic flow, endowing the worldly throng in their gay Burgundian dresses with a wave-like movement and animation.

If the delicate and dreamlike beauty of

Stephan Lochner can be likened to that of Fra Angelico, the next generation brings forth a German Giotto in the powerful realism of Konrad Witz. In his physical force, his strong sense of mass and of volume, of bodies, however stunted and ungainly, this painter from northern Switzerland is a real innovator. With a northern contempt of beauty and of linear melody, he boldly placed his rather wooden figures into the architectural space with their powerful conglomeration of folds which is truly monumental. His apostle Bartholomew, at Basle, anticipates Dürer's famous panels at Munich by the sculptural form and expressiveness of his contours. But this virile and rabid realist, as gauche and sturdy as Bouts or peasant-Bruegel, also had a new naturalist vision of landscape.

Apart from Witz, with his thorough Teutonic attack upon form, the fifteenth century is dominated by the Flemish model, by Roger van der Weyden above all, who held sway over the great master of the Rhenish south, Martin Schongauer. Schongauer, as Dürer later, was a fine engraver, the abstract calligraphy of line being so much more akin to the intellectual German bend than the sensual illusionism of colour and light. Yet Schongauer has left one great painting, the Kolmar *Madonna in the Rose-arbour*, a life-size figure of the Virgin and Child, reminiscent of Roger in her facial expression and tapering fingers and in the hard, monumental folds of her mantle. In these and in the delicate filigree of the crown, the exuberant drawing of leaf and bough, of bird and flower upon the background of gold, the detailed delineation of arabesque forms, an effectual foil to the large, simple shape of the Virgin.

One artist only before Dürer – and he came from the Tyrolese outpost of Germany – took his inspiration from Italy, from Mantegna's sculptural concept of bodies in the space: Michael Pacher, the "solitary summit" of German art in the fifteenth century. Pacher conceived large rocklike figures of real weight and volume, elongated bodies of saints and holy bishops (St Wolfgang), towering up on the edge of the picture, or angels, powerfully foreshortened, swooping down from the sky. These he placed in the architectural envelope of space, before a deep perspective; their action concentrated in their gestures and balanced by the geometrical planes and sharp-edged verticals of buildings. In Pacher sculptural form attains to a vehemence, a spatial realization and clarity, unique in the whole realm of German pictorial art.

Between Pacher and Dürer there is hardly a link. Dürer is in the Schongauer tradition of draughtsmanship. Painting is only a second string to his bow. The fierce and savage imagery of his *Apocalypse*, the tragic emotionalism of his Passion scenes are a northern, a Faustian antithesis to the classical beauty of the south. Twice Dürer journeyed to Italy to study the works of Mantegna and of Bellini. But the impact of the Venetian School – he went neither to Florence nor to Milan – is

slight. Notwithstanding his phenomenal gift for observation of natural form, his immense curiosity, his visual concept was graphic and intellectual, allergic to the values of atmospheric colour and light. He went to Italy in search of a classical norm of the human body, of which his *Adam and Eve* (Madrid) is the eloquent and academic result. He was a scholar, a humanist, a thinker, who could talk on equal terms with Erasmus. His science overlaid his artistry. He had a marked consciousness of self and wrote his autobiography in his portraits. At the age of thirteen he drew himself before the mirror with an astonishing grasp of fact and a haunted expression in the eye. The self-portraits of his manhood establish a canon of virile beauty and spirituality. In his famous portrait of Oswald Krell (Munich), Dürer's habit of imposing his own analytical temper upon his sitters is clearly manifest. The principal aim of his subtle calligraphy was the exploration of character.

Only after his second Italian journey (1506) he strove after a more unified pictorial form, by means of subsuming the infinite detail and delineation to the larger planes of a face and to sculptural volume. The world-famous portrait of St Jerome of 1521 is a case in point. Here the laborious minutiae of wrinkled skin and silvery beard do not hinder the monumental impression of patriarchal serenity and melancholy wisdom.

The great religious altar-pieces are few and far between. One of the earliest is the Paumgärtner altar of the *Nativity* (1500), poetic, fanciful, huddled, and angular, with the portraits of the donors as saints in contemporary dress upon the side panels; or the more Italianate *Adoration* in Prague of 1605, where the Madonna and Child in the centre are seen crowning Pope and Emperor with wreaths of roses, while a throng of attendants – all portraits of German merchant princes – fill the space of the symmetrical composition. Finally, the *Four Apostles* at Munich, of 1526: Dürer's last will and testament, his great confessional as a man and fighter of the Reformation. The towering apostles stand in groups of two before the dark background, filling the picture space almost to the outer edge. Their powerful, starkly individualized heads, their hardly sustained inward fire, their rocklike strength, are memorably conveyed. It was Dürer's ripest achievement in the study of character and pictorial form.

Contemporary with Dürer is Matthias Grünewald. The fact is of interest, since he stands at the opposite pole in the German endeavour to create graphic beauty and form by a pondered theory of art. Grünewald was a Gothic visionary, a man possessed, a solitary genius, with his roots in the Teutonic past, an ecstatic monomaniac whose *chef d'œuvre*, the Isenheim Altar-piece, is the greatest single achievement in pre-Reformation Germany. Unlike his contemporaries, Grünewald was a painter born. His element was colour, colour used with a ghostly, an unearthly effect, to enhance the cruel vision of Christ's suffering or the celestial glory of His Resurrection. Torrents of light gush out of the bluish night, purple shadows flicker upon the white robes of the angelic host, a vicious green depicts the decaying flesh of the Crucified, whose distorted feet and hands are conveyed with an unspeakable realism. The giant Baptist on His right points a triumphant finger to the victimized Christ, while St John, slender and distraught, holds the broken Virgin, a white nunlike figure, in his arms. The painter who could invest Golgotha with such poignancy, gave to the "Resurrection" the transcending splendour of great spirals of light, in which the luminous body of Christ is wafted to the sky. By contrast he painted the hard reality of the tomb, the tumbling soldiers, with a sculptural vehemence and rigidity of limb which is almost Mantegnesque. In the *Temptation of St Anthony* the Gothic imagery, the sense for the horrific, leaves the spiky monsters of Bosch far behind. In the evolution of German art Grünewald represents an extreme. He bridges the gap between the barbarous Gothicism and Rembrandt or El Greco by the intensity of his religious emotion, his magic effects of light, disregard of proportion, and quite modern use of broken tones and chiaroscuro.

Yet another facet of the German mind is illustrated by Altdorfer and by Cranach. Both painters were actuated by a romantic impulse. They painted fairy-tales, and wove playful romance around the stories of Holy Script. Altdorfer was really a landscapist. When he painted *St George and the Dragon* he conceived an enchanted German wood, a shapely thicket of rustling trees, where the white horse and rider are lost in the foreground. His *Rest on the Flight* takes place by the side of a Renaissance fountain before a vast prospect of lake and hills. Here St Joseph bring cherries to the Child whom a German Virgin holds over the well, so that he might play with the angel-putti who fly around the basin. His masterpiece is the *Battle of Alexander*, where legions of minute horsemen in detailed delineation fill the foreground-plain, which extends to the distant hills and the sea under a cloudy sky, stained by the blood-red sun. Once he painted the *Birth of the Virgin* in a Gothic church interior, with a wide wreath of angels encircling the lofty pillars.

Cranach started in the romantic Altdorfer vein. His *Rest on the Flight* shows one of the loveliest groupings and colour-harmonies of red and blue and green. Resting by the edge of the forest under the feathery trees, by the sheltering rocks, Joseph stands wistfully behind the youthful Madonna, who offers the Child to His winged companions. His early *Crucifixion* in the Munich Museum, set in an alpine landscape of crystalline beauty, represents a complete break with tradition. The Crosses are moved to the outer edge of the picture, while in the centre, large and contained, are the two solitary figures of the Virgin and St John, wringing their hands in silent despair.

By 1504 Cranach had moved to Wittenberg, the centre of the Reformation, and for the remainder of his long life he became the court painter of the Elector of Saxony. Here he painted the portraits of the Reformers – Luther, Melanchton, and others – and here he supplied the new Renaissance demand for pagan subjects, such as Venus, Diana, Judith, and Lucretia. But his treatment of the nude lacks southern volume and grandeur. These stylized German ladies are too angular and affected to be ranked as convincing studies from life.

Hans Holbein the Younger's principal gift was the evenness, the unfailing certainty of accomplishment. Holbein appears almost un-German in the sustained perfection and ease with which he arrives at classical form. He comes as an antidote to the romantic Dürer, the mystical Grünewald. His is the one German contribution to the great southern inheritance of portraiture besides Velazquez and Titian. But other than they he arrives at his immaculate rendering of character and of mood by linear and not pictorial means. He did not paint from nature. The foundation of all his portraits is the silver-point sketch. He is essentially a draughtsman. But his miraculous eye and grasp of form did not stop at the material likeness. He was not a cold, disinterested observer, a scientific recorder of outward fact, but a passionate artist who possessed himself with such power of bodily and spiritual form that he conveyed the essential character, not the passing mood of his sitter. Besides, his portraits are historical documents, since he selects the pose, the accessories best suited to depict the time, the race, and social distinction of the individual. The merchants of the German Steelyard are shown surrounded by the marvellous still life of their office. The wintry form of Archbishop Warham is balanced by his jewelled crozier; that of Erasmus, his hands on his book, by a Renaissance pilaster; the Ambassadors stand amidst the lutes and instruments of their humanist passion; the virile profile of the King's falconer is matched by that of the fierce bird in his hand, and the militant face of the Sieur de Morette is enhanced by his firm grasp of dagger and glove. Costume, poise, and accessories are always fully integrated in the pictorial whole, and the individualization of Holbein's sitters is inalienable and incisive.

Before coming to England in 1526 Holbein's first essays in portraiture had been made at Basle, where he painted the friends of Erasmus, Froben, and Amerbach, and the great prince of scholars himself. In England it was the humanist circle around More,

Collet, and Fisher who became his first patrons. Only during his second stay, when Protestant iconoclasm at Basle had driven him once more from the continent of Europe, did Holbein become the court-painter of Henry VIII and of his Queens. Among these, Henry's "Flemish mare", the impeccable *Anne of Cleves* in the Louvre, with the shadowless face, the bold geometry of brow, the inscrutable direct gaze, is the most mysterious. By the side of her sumptuous red velvet and gold brocade, it is the contrast of sable black and the rosy transparency of the flesh which moves us in the full length of *Christina of Denmark* in London.

Only once did Holbein portray the personal poignancy of human fate, in the family picture of his own wife and children, painted in the deep melodious tones of Venetian colour, revealing the sorrow and disillusion of the ageing matron rather than the wife of the wayward and independent artist. Unlike Dürer and Rembrandt, Holbein rarely recorded his own countenance. The dark, dreamless eye and tightly compressed lips of the minature copy in the Wallace Collection, the wrought marble forehead, the reddish beard, the impetuous temper, are all that remains of Holbein's exterior form. He had no religious message, no Teutonic yearning for the Infinite. He was an artist for art's sake, presenting form, beauty, character, in combination with fine enamel-like colour.

With Holbein the classical age of German painting reached the last of its summits. Its contribution to the south European Baroque lay in sculpture, in music, and architecture, rather than in painting, but for the solitary genius of Adam Elsheimer, who stands in the romantic lineage of Altdorfer. In his small landscapes with figures, mythological and religious, mostly painted on copper, his great-hearted tree-silhouettes and magical night-scapes, this Italianate poet-painter, exiled to the Roman Campagna, anticipates the heroic landscapes of Claude and of Rembrandt.

Italian

Italian painting of the Renaissance, more than any other national school of art in Europe, presents to the budding collector a rather puzzling picture.

The regional division of the country means that a Florentine painter of the Renaissance has hardly anything in common with a Sienese master who lived less than fifty miles away, and differs vitally from an artist of the Venetian school or from a Ferrarese or a Paduan or any other of the great provincial centres.

Writers on the history of painting in Italy have for this reason divided their subject into regional schools such as North Italian, Central Italian, Florentine, and Venetian, though there are numerous contacts among the principal groups. Florence under the Medicean patronage drew the best of Italian talent to herself, and some of her leading masters, such as Verrocchio and Ghirlandajo, kept busy workshops, where men greater than themselves, like Leonardo and Michelangelo, learnt the elements of their craft. Raphael, whose Florentine Madonnas or Roman portraits are known the world over, came from the small provincial town of Urbino, while Leonardo, a native of Tuscany, emigrated to Lombardy and impressed his spirit upon the painters of Milan, such as Luini, Boltraffio, and Ambrogio da Predis.

Rome and Naples were not favoured with many artists of their own, and had to rely upon imports from Tuscany and elsewhere. Florentine painters of all periods eagerly followed the call of successive Popes, and their works adorn the walls of the Vatican and the Sistine Chapel. These murals or frescoes, such as Raphael's *Stanza della Segnatura*, are painted upon wet plaster and lend themselves to great decorative designs. But here we are only concerned with easel pictures on wood or canvas, of portable size, for domestic devotion or secular enjoyment.

Besides Florence, Mantua could claim one great artist for her own, Andrea Mantegna, while Signorelli and Piero della Francesca, though born in Umbria, belong to the Florentine school. Parma brought forth Correggio; but Venice, the munificent Queen of the Adriatic, with her far-flung connexions in the East, could challenge the predominance of the Florentine bankers and wool-merchants in artistic patronage.

At Venice the Bellini workshop, father and sons, established their rule over half a century, bequeathing their legacy to Giorgione and Titian and a host of others. It was an event of the greatest consequence for the development of painting in Italy that a Sicilian, Antonello da Messina, who had learnt how to purify oils and varnishes from a Flemish artist, arrived at Venice in 1475, and caused the abandonment of the old flat tempera method of colours mixed with yolk of egg and water. This was the origin of the painterly style of Venice, of glowing and composite colours and of modelling in the round, as opposed to the incisive linear style of Florence, where colour was superimposed upon drawing. Linear, sculptural, and painterly are the three principal trends of painting. The latter was capable of the greatest achievement in the figurative arts from Masaccio to Michelangelo and Titian. Thus the principal city-states of Italy developed their individual styles of painting, owing to local character, social condition, and available talent, though in the evolution of art the impact of genius is always the most formative influence.

The growth of Florentine painting can be likened to a mighty tree whose roots are in Giotto; Masaccio is its trunk; Michelangelo its crown. Giotto (1270–1337) was the first to free the figure arts from the fetters of formal composition and to endow the human form with the power of life and of movement and physical probability, which all subsequent painters were to develop by means of their increased knowledge of anatomy and perspective. Giotto's presentation of Biblical story, so vitalizing by its native strength and simplicity, is based upon the statuary and the dramatic, upon solid form and emotional gesture. Weight is imparted to bodies, and robes reveal the living limbs beneath. His landscapes of formal rocks are made subservient to the movement of his patriarchal or pastoral figures. In all respects relating to mass and to volume Giotto is the precursor. But he remained without following until the coming of Masaccio.

For nearly a century the art of Florence was eclipsed by the painters of Siena, who reverted to the medieval tradition of telling the Gospel story in a Gothic style of highly wrought surfaces with a profusion of gold and an elegant suppleness of line. The background of gold-leaf precluded any recession in depth, and the flat treatment of robes and bodies retarded the development towards the sculptural ideal. The fame of the School of Siena from Simone Martini to Stefano di Giovanni rests upon suavity of line and spirit, poetic symbolism, and decorative splendour. Sacred personages are endowed with an archaic majesty, while the atmosphere remains one of a static and decorative art, reminiscent of the work of the goldsmith or miniaturist. The Sienese interlude does not lead to the dynamic vitality of Masaccio, but rather to the unearthly beauty, innocence, and saintliness of Angelico, who learned from the younger man how to give mass and substance to his figures. Angelico was by temperament a medieval monk, and a mystic, but he shared the Renaissance enjoyment of beautiful raiment and celestial tints. We see in him a Gothic visionary, whose Virgins and Saints soar on the wings of ecstasy. As an artist he combined a delicate symbolism of facial expression and gesture with a new concept of space and volume. He was the first to paint an idealized picture of the Tuscan countryside. His processional figures under the Cross are as silent actors in a mystery play.

Masaccio was less restrained by medieval tradition. He burst open the confines of space and gave to the human form a heroic mould, a monumental dignity, and power. His apostles in the Carmine Church at Florence are passionate beings, imperious and solid, like the towering rocks behind them. The same feeling for rounded shapes informs his powerful nudes, modelled in planes of light and of shade, breathing the enveloping atmosphere. Nor are Masaccio's three-dimensional forms and receding distances the result of mathematical science, such as created the battle-pieces and mountain backgrounds of Paolo Uccello, gaily coloured patterns of stereometrical bodies in linear perspective, where the knights of the joust or the huntsmen and hounds are arrayed in converging interior lines.

So vital was the interest in artistic science among the painters of Florence and her satellites, that Piero della Francesca (1416?–92) surpassed Uccello not only in his aerial distances and in his architectural settings conformed with mathematical nicety to the laws of the Golden Section, but also in the impassive grandeur of his more than human figures, in the high dignity and seriousness which lends them a statuesque quality. The spirit of antiquity is on no occasion more closely approached in the art of the Renaissance than in Piero's monumental angels in the London *Baptism*. Immutable archaic shapes, they stand motionless in the white fleeting light of summer. As a creator of heroic shapes on a transcending scale, within the confines of marble column and entablature, or of princely portraits before the panoramic vastness of tree-dotted hills and meadows, Piero has no equal in Occidental art.

But the general run of Florentine picture-making in the second half of the fifteenth century was far remote from Piero's strangely exalted and uncompromising otherness. There were flourishing workshops in Florence like Verrocchio's and Ghirlandajo's, where the talented youth was trained, not only for painting but also for sculpture and the goldsmith's art. These masters turned out the commissioned article for the royal merchants of Florence, pageant-pictures upon the walls of their private chapels and panel-paintings for the domestic devotion. Fra Filippo Lippi (1457–1504), a renegade monk, was the inventor of this winsome type of Florentine Madonna, delicately outlined against a river-valley of fantastic rocks, conforming to a new ideal of girlish beauty with high forehead, a transparent kerchief daintily poised upon the gold thread of her hair. Sometimes he prefers a type more robust, more worldly, and his children are always peasant types of the Tuscan countryside, full of roguish laughter and gaiety. As a colourist Fra Filippo surpasses even Angelico by his sensual delight in composite tints of rare blues and purples. His son Filippino is an even finer colourist; but his Madonnas and Angels are more florid, more languid, displaying a "consumptive delicacy" and elegance.

Verrocchio was, above all, a sculptor, but he nursed in his *bottega* the boy Leonardo, whose paintings ascribed to his school, such as the London *Virgin and Child with Angels*, the *Raphael and Tobias*, display the grace and the elegance, the metallic contours and the southern brightness of colouring which we associate with the masters of Florence. This supple linear style reaches its apogee in Botticelli, the pupil of Fra Filippo, from whom he took the rhythmic beauty, the abstract purity of design. But Botticelli was possessed by a more ardent spirit, a penitential sadness which he imparted to his long line of Madonnas as much as to his Goddess of Love. His art is no longer representational, but the blossoming forth of pure poetic fancy. In it he created the unmistakable archetypes of his dream, the chaste, elongated body of Venus, her long tresses yielding to the wind, the small, ovoid head of the Madonna with the "dolorous" glance, the rustic boy-angels, golden-haired and entranced. Beside him Ghirlandajo, who, like Gozzoli before him, covered the walls of Florentine churches with his gorgeous figure art, interspersed with the stately portraits of the Medici princes, appears robust and worldly. He bridges the gap between the passionate Gothicism of Botticelli and the grandezza of the Roman Raphael.

Contemporary with these protagonists of the Florentine genius was Leonardo da Vinci. His intermittent paintings give a true measure of the magnitude, the complexity of his spirit and of his science. His genius for swift notation of human and animal shapes, for swirling movement and architectural form, the profundity of expression, the wisdom of age, the beauty of youth, are reflected in countless drawings. Later he developed his uncanny gift for the interior modelling of the human face in soft chiaroscuro, his supple rendering of curling hair, of writhing plant, of gushing water, and the mysterious atmosphere which filled his stalactitic caves. In the *Last Supper* he brought to fruition his genius for grandiloquent dramatic action and the classic simplicity for centralized composition.

Nothing is more delicate and supple than the soft and fluctuating changes from lighted flesh-tints to deep grey shadows which modulate Ginevra dei Benci's face and her slender neck. For Leonardo attained the alluring sweetness of his female types by an aura of carefully laid shadows (*sfumato*) and magical lights and by the vaunted smile of the "Gioconda" which plays around her lips as much as in her eyes, her dimples, and the corners of her mouth. Nor is this the mark only of Mona Lisa; the angel in the *Madonna of the Rocks*, St Anne in the Louvre, and the youthful Baptist bear the same disquieting and unfathomable smile which became the hall-mark of the Lombard School.

In the concept of Florentine art Leonardo and Michelangelo stand at opposite poles: infinitely supple, effeminate, and sophisticated the one: brooding, heroic, grandiose the other. Michelangelo remained a sculptor even when he painted easel pictures in low relief. His *Holy Family* in the Uffizi is, indeed, a "painted sculpture" by dint of the marmoreal roundness of modelling, the sharply defined contours, and the cool, superimposed colours of the unified group. Michelangelo's main preoccupation was with the human nude in action. It is from Signorelli and his Dantesque vision of the *Last Judgment* that Michelangelo derived great inspiration for the handling of the human body in violent movement, though in power and mass and dignity he is Masaccio's heir. Michelangelo was for ever hankering after the colossal. From the statue of the youthful David to the bulky giants of the Sistine Chapel he strove after the realization in paint of heroic manhood, godlike in character and bursting the very confines of space.

In the mighty triad of the High Renaissance Raphael (1483–1520) is the fulfilment. He had come from Umbria, where he had learnt from Perugino the sweet serenity of devotional painting, how to construct firm, rounded figures, gracefully poised in front of the aerial distances under the intense blueness of a southern sky. Coming to Florence in 1540, he at once absorbed the greater vitality and depth of figure-composition, the impressive rhetoric, the largeness of Fra Bartolommeo. In Rome since 1508 he studied the massive expressionism of Michelangelo's ceiling. His friend Sebastiano del Piombo transmitted to him the Venetian splendour of colouring. Thus equipped, Raphael set out to cover the walls of the Vatican with his grandiose space constructions, where saints and patriarchs and philosophers of old move in majestic poses, now in the Heavenly sphere, now upon the vastness of an antique temple. With his complete command of pictorial means he painted the portraits of Popes and Cardinals and the great Roman ladies in a rich monumental style where body and soul blend in luxuriant unison. In the memory of man Raphael lives above all as the painter of youthful Madonnas. Here he combined his innate gentleness, his Christian humanism with his painterly skill in creating an infinite variety of affectionate Madonnas with playful children in a Florentine landscape of utter loveliness, representing the last authentic icons of religious significance in European painting.

Exception must always be made for Antonio Allegri di Correggio (1494–1534), who, soaring genius, spent most of his active life in the artistic backwater of Parma, where in his vaulted ceilings he vied with Michelangelo, and in his devotional paintings surpassed even Raphael in fair shapes and the unbridled intensity of feeling. Never has feminine grace been endowed with greater sweetness, born of secular, wholly pagan enjoyment of soft-flowing forms and luscious flesh and smiling delight. Though the actors be Virgin and Child and youthful saint, the ecstasy is of quite human affection and life's exuberance. Correggio lived only at the beginning of the Cinquecento, but in his flurried figure-art, his rapturous movement, his iridescence of colour and light, he anticipates the rococo style of the eighteenth century. In his landscape backgrounds he explored the poetic potential of forest murmur and mystery, and in mythological subjects he placed his sensuous antiquity beside the more robust and primeval creations of Titian.

Correggio became the inspiration of the Mannerist School, where his comeliness, his verve, his substance, were dissipated in a new canon of prettiness and of elegance. Religious ardour and earnestness are transformed in Parmigiano's secular and vivacious Madonnas and angels, breathing the air of refined classicism. Other artists sought to emulate the heroic gait and the noble drama of the High Renaissance, in a style of classical revival such as the Caracci brothers and Guido Reni evolved in the late Cinquecento. Finally, Caravaggio reacted against the false pathos and sentimentality of the eclectics by his savage venture into the realm of naturalism, employing ignoble human types and a massive contrast of stage-light and darkness to enhance the vulgar drama of life. These were still great masters of form and daring experimentalists of movement, foreshadowing the dynamic Baroque, but they came at the end of a great age when the spiritual resources were wearing thin.

But it is with the Venetian School that painting in the Renaissance attains to perfection. From Bellini to Titian and Tintoretto religious and classical imagery will gain its emotional force from a new illusionism of the third dimension, due to a colouristic approach to the visual world, a space-creating and light-absorbing concept of colour, bringing in its wake a new solidity and glowing richness.

Giovanni Bellini (1428?–1509), the greatest master of fifteenth-century Venice, can be likened to Raphael in that he, too, created authentic pictures for religious devotion and a long line of Madonnas whom he endowed with the suavity, affectionate earnestness, and hieratic solemnity of his own ardent soul. Bellini arrived at his wonderful synthesis of colour and light and surrounding space only in his maturity. In his youth he laboured under the magisterial influence of Mantegna, the leading master of classical and of sculptural form. The work of this great craftsman and archaeologist presents an impasse in the growth of Italian painting. With his sense for Roman strength and corporality, he should have been a sculptor. For though he was capable of deep religious feeling, his romantic enthusiasm for the antique, fostered by the Paduan humanists, and his own admiration for Donatello, led him to build his painting upon a marvellous precision of line, a cold, relief-like grandeur of form, with which he invested his giant martyrs, and saints, as well as the towering rocks and ruins of his crystalline landscape backgrounds.

Mantegna had been trained in the workshop of Squarcione, a second-rate painter but inspired teacher and antiquarian, who also left his trace upon Carlo Crivelli, the Venetian-born master in whom a medieval Gothicism combined with Renaissance splendour and a Byzantine sense for loaded and gilded ornament.

Bellini's figures attract by a far greater sweetness and gentleness, a spiritual exaltation which overflows into nature, enveloping hills and fields and buildings with warm, diffused light and a unifying radiance of light and colour. Bellini's art was strengthened in solidity and expressiveness by the impact of Antonello's new oil technique, which he imparted to him around 1475. For a time he adopts the massive plasticity of rounded form from Antonello, while his own colour is increased in intensity by a deep inward glow. His great altar-pieces at Venice maintain the same compositional scheme of the Virgin and Child enthroned in a vaulted niche of resplendent ecclesiastical architecture, her hand raised in blessing to the full-length saints below, or offering the Child to the world with maternal warmth and solemnity. In portraiture, too. Bellini enlarges upon the astounding physical presence of Antonello's sitters by his larger humanity, his sensitive eye for psychological variation, endowing the scholar, the poet, the statesman, the warrior even, with the power of spiritual individualization. Foremost among the pupils of Giovanni Bellini, and almost his equal in the favoured Vene-

tian style of the Virgin and Child in a landscape are Cima da Conegliano and Bartolomeo Montagna.

Between Bellini and Titian there occurs an interlude of great consequence, when Venetian painting comes to fruition in the work of Giorgione. Wherever we come upon the Giorgionesque in the art of the Renaissance, whether in sacred or in pastoral subjects, whether we meet it in the nobility of a male portrait or in an arcadian landscape with figures, we are touched by a sense of mystery and by a quality which, for want of definition, men have called poetic. For once pictorial art became the vehicle of an elysian reality, for once a youth living in the first decade of the sixteenth century was able to paint, without earthly slack or residue, a pure image of the beautiful world around him.

Whether we look at the *Madonna di Castelfranco* (1505), enthroned before a rapturous landscape of fragrant hills and the sea, where St Liberale, in shining armour, a paragon of strength and of sweetness, mounts vigil by the side of St Francis, or at his late *Tempesta*, where another vigilant youth looks across to a nursing mother, in front of the most magical landscape in painting, we meet with the same dream-perfection of pastoral fantasy. For Giorgione the figures are wholly integrated in the landscape, form part of the natural mood, where an azure sky with long streaks of rose, parallel to the lie of the land, closes upon an enchanted landscape of changing hills and dainty tree silhouettes, their foliage flecked with light. Such "poesie", as of Apollo pursuing the nymph Daphne or Damon's unrequited love for Amaryllis, he and his followers painted upon small panels or boxes, a distant echo of Virgilian rusticity and bliss.

As the young Raphael painted in the idiom of his master Perugino, so Titian continued for a while after the death of Giorgione (1510) to weave the spell of his master's magic. A number of great Venetian paintings, such as the *Concert* in the Palazzo Pitti at Florence, the twin Venuses of the Borghese Gallery, and the *Noli Me Tangere* of the National Gallery, breathe the spirit of Giorgione; though they show the substance, the power, the breadth of Titian. For Titian was a more elemental painter, more sensuous and dramatic than Giorgione, being propelled not by learned humanism but by an antique life-force, which now appears as celestial ecstasy in the *Assumption of the Virgin*, wafted upon clouds of exuberant boy-angels, now in the feasts of Venus or of Bacchus, where a dionysiac energy creates an abundance of human form and symphonic colour. For colour with Titian is not superimposed upon form: the glowing scarlets and ultra-marines of his youth, the half-lights and broken tones of his old age are carved out of the rich composite pigment; they do not represent, they are the appearances. Like Rembrandt, he painted "more with his fingers than with his brush", slashing the grainy canvas with bold strokes and blotches, so that his great mythologies, *Danae and Europa, Diana and Callisto*, or *Venus and Adonis*, must be seen from a distance.

In his landscape backgrounds, his azure seas and skies, the mountain ridges and plateaux filled with mist, where primeval shepherds graze their flocks, Titian conveys a cosmic solemnity and power. His portraits are instinct with noble reserve, with inscrutable dignity of station or the melancholy marks of Fate. In his religious canvases, the *Crowning with Thorns* or the Venice *Pietà*, a tragic sense for the inexorable suffering, inflicted upon the heroic Christ of the Counter Reformation, assumes a truly monumental form.

But this was not the swansong of sixteenth-century Venice. The grand finale was played by two decorative artists who, between them, covered a vast area of wall space with religious allegory and drama, twin genii of the Serenissima; though as complementary to one another as day is to night. Tintoretto is essentially a tragedian, a Faustian temperament, a restless inquirer and experimentalist, who transmuted the firmness, the earthliness of Titian into his mobile, fantastic vision of Biblical story. His is not so much a synthesis of Titian's colour and Michelangelo's drawing, but a ghostly baroque anticipation of Rembrandt's massed shadows and dazzling lights. Endowed with a seething poetical imagination, he gave to the Counter Reformation its moving theatricals of colossal figures floating upon billowing clouds in a landscape of magical beauty. Veronese, on the other hand, was no mystic, no innovator. His religious banquets are solemn occasions of civic pride and representation, where his genius for spacious design and silvery colour, his sense of largeness and opulence for noble buildings and stately personages have full sway. In Veronese's pillared and arcaded halls, as in his human allegories, we have the epitome of aristocratic life in sixteenth-century Venice, just as in Bassano's Nativities and Adorations reflecting the pastoral life of the Venetian hinterland, we possess the first legitimate paintings of domestic genre upon which he lavished his prodigious colour harmonies.

But so strong was the hold of the Adriatic dream-city upon its painters, that even the eighteenth century, so barren in the rest of Italy, brought forth artists of universal fame like Guardi and Canaletto in the topographical genre and Tiepolo in the realm of decorative arabesque. For it is owing to Canaletto's dexterity as a draughtsman, to his feeling for space and for light, his rococo sense for graceful architectural form, the wide sweep of crowded waterways or city squares, shrouded in misty splendour, and to Guardi's more sketchy, more painterly impressions, that Venice has kept its cherished and permanent place in the visual memory of man.

Persian

Until recent times Persian painting, as we know it, was an art of book-illustration. Literary sources mention early murals, but only a few insignificant fragments survive. Persian painting grew from a fusion of the late classical style derived from Byzantium, of Far

Eastern elements from China, and of an un-
determined, but probably small, volume of
native tradition surviving from Sasanian
times (226–652). The favourite subjects of
illustration were taken from the *Shāhnāma*
("Book of Kings"), completed about 1000 by
the poet Firdawsī. This monumental work of
some 50,000 couplets contains the traditional
history of Persia down to the Arab conquest of
636–52. Its earlier (mythical) portions are
much concerned with Rustam, the national
hero, whose tiger-skin coat is frequently seen
in Persian miniatures. Second only to the
Shāhnāma in popularity was the *Khamsa*
("Quintet"), a set of five romantic poems
written by Niẓāmī between 1175 and 1200.
The second, fourth, and fifth of these are concerned with monarchs who also figure in the
Shāhnāma: Khusraw, Bahrām Gūr, and
Iskandar or Alexander the Great. The first
poem of the quintet consists of moral dis-
courses illustrated by anecdotes, and the third
relates the melancholy Arabian love-story of
Laylā and Majnūn. Sa'dī, Ḥāfiẓ, and Jāmī
(especially his poem of the loves of Yūsuf
and Zulaykhā or Joseph and Potiphar's wife),
as well as a number of other Persian poets and
historians, also provide frequent subjects of
illustration.

The style is conventional. Western rules of
perspective, anatomy, and proportion are unknown, and there is no shading or modelling.
The beholder can thus enjoy the rich patterns
of carpets and tilework undistorted and un-
shadowed, and appreciate the delicate beauty
of the enlarged flowers and plants which
would have escaped him had they been depicted in strict proportion to the human
figures in the same composition. The Persian
painter's purpose was simply to illustrate his
story and to please his patron; his work
must therefore be straightforward and easily
apprehended, on the one hand, and, on
the other, as visually beautiful in line and
colour and as technically perfect as he could
make it. These are the criteria by which
Persian painting must always be judged,
and the simpler our approach to it the
better.

The history of Persian painting falls into
five periods.

The Abbasid Caliphate (up to 1258)

Owing to the thirteenth-century Mongol
devastations, surviving examples are few.
Works illustrated were mainly scientific treatises and books of stories, such as *Kalīla wa
Dimna* ("the Fables of Bidpai") and the
Maqāmāt ("Assemblies") of Ḥarīrī. The style
owed much to Byzantine influence.

The Mongol Period (1258–c. 1380)

The Mongol conquests, stretching from
China to Poland, facilitated intercourse between East and West, resulting in the incorporation of many Chinese features into
Persian painting. Historical works and the
Shāhnāma were the favourite subjects of illustration.

Works of these two periods will probably
never again appear on the market. In that unlikely event, however, they would be offered
privately to museums, libraries, or a few collectors with ample means. They can be
studied in the British Museum, Edinburgh
University Library, the Bibliothèque Nationale, Paris, and elsewhere, as well as in the
text-books. With the next period, however,
we begin to deal with Persian paintings,
which one may still encounter in dealer's
shops and the auction rooms, and, wherever
possible, the illustrations are from examples
so obtained.

The Timurid Period (c. 1380–1499)

The conquests of Timur (Tamerlane) destroyed the remnants of Mongol domination,
but after his death (1405) his empire was split
up among members of his family. The court
style of the early Timurid princes (c. 1390–
1415) (Plate 296B) was derived from that
developed under the Jalairids of Baghdad,
where, about the second quarter of the fourteenth century, the painter Aḥmad Mūsā successfully fused the recently imported Chinese
elements with the relics of the Abbasid style
and with some additional ideas from Europe,
thus laying the foundations of a true national
style. By about 1420 a rift in this normal court
style had begun to appear. The best painters
in the academic tradition were concentrated
at Herat in the north-east under the patron-

age of Prince Bāysunghur, a grandson of Tīmūr, while at the court of his brother, Ibrāhīm Sulṭān at Shiraz in the south-west, an altogether rougher but at the same time bolder and more vigorous style arose. By 1440 Bāysunghur and Ibrāhīm Sulṭān were dead, and the styles of painting they had patronized had both begun to decline. Mid-fifteenth-century Herat work is somewhat dry and academic, and the Shiraz painters lost their earlier boldness and contracted the scale of their compositions (Plate 296A).

Meanwhile the Timurid empire was breaking up as the Turkmans advanced in the west, and, by 1468, when Sulṭān Husayn Mīrzā succeeded to the throne of Herat, the north-eastern province of Khurasan, of which that city was the capital, was all that remained of it. To his earliest years of sovereignty probably belongs the splendid *Kalīla wa Dimna* in the Gulistan Museum, Teheran, though it has usually been dated near the beginning of the fifteenth century. As a patron he equalled his earlier kinsman Bāysunghur, and towards the end of his long reign the greatest of all Persian painters, Bihzād, lived at his court. Bihzād's work began to appear about 1480, and he soon infused new life into the petrifying style of Herat. Figures and landscapes became more naturalistic, though losing none of the delicate and other-worldly charm that emanates from Persian miniatures of all periods. His best authenticated work is in the *Būstān* of 1488 in the Egyptian Library, Cairo, but fine examples of his style can be seen at the British Museum and at Oxford (Plate 297A).

With the Turkman rule in western Persia, and particularly at Shiraz (which the Turkmans took about 1455), appeared a style of simple and rather archaic character which enjoyed a vogue of half a century, after which it merged imperceptibly into the Safawid style of Shiraz. It may be appropriately termed the Turkman style, and it is found in all illustrated Persian manuscripts of the later fifteenth century, apart from those executed at Herat under Sulṭān Ḥusayn Mīrzā and a handful of provincial works. Its simple character and the comparatively small scale of most of its compositions made it ideal for the illustration of manuscripts for patrons of less than princely rank and fortune (Plate 296D).

The Safawid Period (1499–1722)

The Safawid dynasty was founded as the result of a nationalist revival led by Shāh Ismaʿīl (d. 1524) which swept away the last Timurids and Turkmans. Persia was unified, and provincial styles of painting tended to die out, except at Shiraz. Subjects were generally the same as in the previous periods, though late fifteenth- and sixteenth-century poets like Jāmī and Hilālī were added to the repertoire. Shāh Ismaʿīl Ṣafawī established his capital at Tabriz, and took Bihzād under his patronage in 1510. Early Safawid court painting was thus a direct continuation of the late Timurid style of Herat, the only difference at first being the appearance of the "baton" turban, the distinguishing crest of the Safawid family and their supporters (Plate 297B). But under Ismaʿīl's son and successor, Ṭahmāsp, the style became larger and more sumptuous. Bihzād died about 1535, and a new generation of masters, of whom the greatest were Sulṭān Muhammad, Mirak, Mīr Sayyid ʿAlī, and Mīrzā ʿAli, was ready to carry out the King's commissions. The Rothschild *Shāhnāma* of 1537, containing over 200 miniatures, and the British Museum Niẓāmī of 1539–43 are among the most magnificent and sumptuous manuscripts ever produced, and the Jāmī of 1556–65 in the Freer Gallery, Washington, is not much inferior.

By the time this latter manuscript was produced the capital had been moved to Qazwin, and the court style was undergoing certain modifications. Figures were becoming slimmer and more attenuated, with longer necks and rounder faces, and there was a growing emphasis on graceful, sinuous lines. The greatest exponent of this modified style was Muhammadī, son of Sulṭān Muhammad (Plate 297D), and in his native Khurasan a simplified version of it is found in which the drawing is usually crisp and firm, but detail and decoration are reduced to a minimum (Plate 297C).

Shiraz painting under the Safawids was at first a continuation of the Turkman style

(Plate 298c), Gradually, however, the drawing became more rhythmical in imitation of the metropolitan style, though Shiraz painters retained their individuality up to the beginning of the seventeenth century (Plate 298D). Compared with Tabriz and Qazwin work, their tone tends to be lighter, and the general effect is a little flat and provincial.

In 1507 and 1535 Herat was captured by the Uzbeks of Bukhara, who carried off with them, as well as much loot, a number of the Persian painters whom they found working there. Thus, throughout the sixteenth century a considerable mass of painting was produced for the Uzbek rulers of Bukhara in a style at first very close to that of Bihzād, but soon stagnating and deteriorating after about 1560, by which time the imported Persian artists were doubtless either dead or in retirement. Attempts are sometimes made to pass off Bukhara miniatures as Herat work of the late fifteenth century.

Shāh 'Abbās the Great moved the capital to Isfahan, in the very heart of Persia, in 1598, and at the same time another change was coming over Persian painting, initiated by the artist Āqā Riżā, and developed by his prolific successor Riżā-i 'Abbāsī. The drawing became more mannered and calligraphic, while the pure colours of the earlier work began to yield to an increasing use of purples, browns, and yellows. Attitudes became languid and affected, even in illustrations of the *Shāhnāma*. Single-figure portraits and tinted drawings appeared in increasing numbers (Plate 298A). Shiraz lost its individuality as a centre of painting, and by about 1625 work produced there was indistinguishable from the metropolitan style of Isfahan. By the middle of the seventeenth century the foremost artists were Muhammad Qāsim, Mu'īn (pupil of Riżā-i 'Abbāsī), Muḥammad Yūsuf, and Afzal al-Ḥusaynī, all of whom worked in a style closely modelled on that of Riżā-i 'Abbāsī (Plate 298B). 'Abbās II (d. 1666) sent the painter Muhammad Zamān to study in Italy, and on his return he introduced a completely Europeanized style, adding several Italianizing miniatures to the Nizāmī of Shāh Ṭahmāsp and the *Shāhnāma* of Shāh 'Abbās the Great. But the long-lived Mu'īn and a few others still clung to the earlier style, as can be seen in a *Shāhnāma* in the Metropolitan Museum with miniatures dated 1693, where his work appears alongside that of other artists who had adopted the fashionable European manner.

The Post-Safawid Period (from 1722)

The Safawid dynasty was overthrown by the Afghans; the Afghans were expelled by Nādir Shāh; and Nādir Shāh's empire was disputed by the Zands at Shiraz and the Qājārs in the north. The latter family finally (1794) emerged victorious, and retained the Persian crown till 1926. Illustrated manuscripts of eighteenth-century date are rare and of poor quality. A few fine mirror-cases, pen-boxes, and bird-and-flower paintings have survived from this period, but the majority of these belong to Qājār times. The recently imported European style was being gradually digested.

By the reign of Fatḥ 'Alī Shāh (1798–1834), the second monarch of the Qājār dynasty, a definite national style had emerged from this uneasy process. Oils on canvas and watercolours on paper replaced the enamel-like pigments of the Timurid and Safawid miniatures, and European perspective, shading, and landscape were attempted. But the basic character of the work remained unquestionably Persian; indeed, the large oil-paintings of the period, with their bejewelled, hieratic figures, recall the Achaemenid and Sasanian bas-reliefs, and Mihr 'Alī's magnificent life-size painting of Fatḥ 'Alī Shāh (Plate 299) is a worthy successor of the rock-hewn portraits of Darius the Great at Behistun and of Shapur at Naqshi-i-Rustam. Other notable artists patronized by Fatḥ 'Alī Shāh were Mīrzā Bābā, the *naqqāsh-bāshī*, or painter-in-chief in the early part of his reign (large oil portrait of the King in the Commonwealth Relations Office and a miniature one in the Royal Library, Windsor Castle), 'Abdallāh Khān (oil portrait of the King in the Victoria and Albert Museum), Muḥammad Ḥasan Khān (several portraits of princes in the Julian Amery Collection), and Abū'l-Qāsim (pictures of girl-musicians and a dancer in the Amery Collection). But it must be admitted that much Qājār painting, both oils and miniatures, is of very poor quality.

After the death of Fatḥ 'Ali Shāh the general standard of painting declined still further. During the reign of Naṣr al-Dīn (1848–96) sterile imitations of earlier styles appeared, which after a while took on the character of deliberate forgeries.

A final word of warning is necessary. Persian manuscripts and miniatures that have been in Indian and Turkish collections have often been subjected to ill-advised "restorations" at the hands of more or less incompetent painters of those countries. Indians, particularly, delighted to go through a whole set of miniatures daubing over the original delicate Persian faces and repainting them with the coarse and hideous features found in provincial Indian paintings of the eighteenth and nineteenth centuries. The novice should avoid like the plague any miniature that looks "somehow not quite right", however early or splendid it may appear on the surface.

Russian

ICONS

The iconographic tradition is a fairly complex one, tending to puzzle anybody looking at an icon for the first time. Yet once the convention has been understood, the eye quickly learns to assess the artistic merits of a painting, and to distinguish between the archaic style of a backward area and the advanced style of a vigorous centre, even when the latter predates the former by many years.

Icons first appeared in Byzantium in early Christian times, and so quickly gained a foothold there that they soon became an integral and generally accepted feature of the Byzantine church, penetrating to the Balkans and to Russia as Christianity spread into those lands from Byzantium.

Icons were developed from the tomb portraits of the Egyptians, and though the earliest took the form of presentations of single figures, especially Christ and the Virgin, pictorial illustrations to the Gospels also became important. The Byzantine church was quick to recognize their educational value. Artists were, in consequence, encouraged to record as wide a range of Biblical scenes as possible and, almost unconsciously, icons became the repositories of the richly varied and detailed Bible story as it was recounted by the early church. The cycle of scenes appearing on icons thus often includes incidents which, though unfamiliar to Protestant laymen, are well known to the average Orthodox.

Icons are painted on wooden panels, the thickness and size of which varies from district to district and age to age. The dimensions also depend on the purpose for which the icon was intended. The majority were designed to occupy a specific, permanent position in the church, either on the iconostasis or in a side chapel. Certain large icons, however, were made for carrying in processions, the earlier panels of this type being generally painted on both sides of the board. Other icons were used in houses, where it was customary to hang one above each bed as well as in the far, right-hand corner of each room, this spot being called in Russian the *Krasniy Ugol* or "Fair Corner". In Russia, in later times, small bronze, single icons, and also diptychs and triptychs, were likewise current and, occasionally, very small, folding, multiple painted icons, forming miniature iconostasis, were produced for the special use of travellers. At much the same date it also became customary to adorn a painted icon with a halo or cover made in precious material, such as silver, gold, or enamel, often studded with jewels and semi-precious stones.

The panel selected for the painted icon had, as a first step in its preparation, to be smoothed and, if necessary, strengthened with wedges inserted into slats made on the reverse of the board, and, in Russia, it was often finished off with a bevelled edge giving the effect of a frame. After this the face of the panel was covered with a coating of gesso under which a layer of canvas was often glued. The surface of the gesso was then polished to form a smooth, glossy ground on which the outlines of the picture were sketched in. Red paint was generally used in Russia for the purpose. Next the background was filled in, gold leaf being the most usual choice. Only then did the artist begin the picture, painting it in colours diluted in yolk of egg. The intensity and opaqueness of these colours was maintained by the final application of a coat of varnish.

The Byzantine preference for gold backgrounds was probably dictated by the precious nature and intrinsic value of the material, since these characteristics rendered the medium especially suitable for association with the holiest personages in the Gospels and for acting as a fit symbol of the celestial sphere to which these sacred figures belonged. In Russia, however, probably originally because of economic considerations, silver was sometimes used instead, and the innovation gradually developed a new aesthetic approach, with the result that, even in its hey-day, Novgorod showed a marked preference for white grounds, Pskov for green ones, and other regions for red. In Greece blue and green were also used.

Icons were originally intended to instruct the illiterate and to assist the unimaginative in investing the personages of the Gospels with reality by providing each one with a particular, readily recognizable appearance. Christ himself, together with the Virgin and St John the Baptist, were the most common subjects. To begin with they were presented singly, each on a separate panel, but later they were often depicted side by side on a single painting, the group coming to be known as the Deesis or "prayer" for, in it, the Virgin and St John intercede for the sins of the world (Plate 300c). Almost simultaneously, however, many other holy figures, notably the prophets and fathers of the church, were represented on icons, and they were in their turn quickly followed by a whole galaxy of saints and hermits. These personages were sometimes shown in groups, but it was more usual for them to appear singly, when the likeness was often surrounded by a number of small scenes illustrating notable incidents in the life and martyrdom of the selected saint. Both types of representation quickly became widespread throughout the Orthodox world, though certain worthy hermits and divines of purely local significance were apt to be in demand mainly in or near their place of origin.

With the years the role of the icon underwent a change. Its instructional purpose tended to be overlooked as new, mainly intercessionary, characteristics came to be associated with it. Inevitably, the worshippers then began to address their prayers to the icon itself, rather than to the abstract conception of which it was but the emblem, in the hope that the panel, which had now assumed the attributes of a holy patron, might inter-

FIG. 2. Model from a Podlinik

cede on their behalf with the Almighty. This belief resulted in some confusion, for the mediatory character of the icon at times inspired such intense veneration than it seemed to verge almost on idolatry. In the ninth century in Byzantium these fears led to the banning of icons for over a hundred years (727–843).

The symbolism inherent in icons dictated the appearance of the pictorial representations. The style which evolved constituted a blend of realism with unreality. Realism was essential if the paintings were to prove intelligible to the masses, while the unreality was absolutely necessary if the pictures were to evoke a vivid conception of Heaven alike among the illiterate and the most highly educated in the land. The established convention had to be strictly adhered to lest any deviation should distract from the spiritual content of the icon. In Russia the iconographic traditions of the established church were collected into manuals called *Podliniki* (Figs. 2, 3, and 4) – that is to say "Authorized Versions" – which were designed to serve as guides to the

ance in Moscow of some illustrations to the Bible, drawn in the naturalistic manner current in western Europe, induced certain of the capital's leading painters to experiment along the lines suggested by the imported etchings. The paintings which resulted raised a storm of violent opposition in the capital, obliging the authorities to hold an ecclesiastical inquiry into the matter. The traditional-

СН. Іоанна Предотеча.

Fig. 4. Model from a Podlinik

Fig. 3. Model from a Podlinik

painters. The rules laid down in these manuals were followed unquestioned till well into the sixteenth century, when foreign influence and, more particularly, the appear-

ists won the day and the innovators were sharply reprimanded, the offending panels being destroyed. At the same time icon painters were instructed to study their Podliniki anew and to purge their minds of heresy. The painters of Moscow received special rebuke, and the most admired works of an earlier age were brought to Moscow from the provinces to serve as a pure source of inspiration. Henceforth, but for the icons produced for the sect of Old Believers, who adhered to their own conventions, no Russian icon painter ever again tried to deviate from the recognized iconographic tradition. It is this acceptance throughout the centuries of a static formula that, at first, proves so puzzling to Western eyes. But although the formula is static, the style is rich in variations, and it is the degree of skill with which great artists infused the old forms with new and intense meaning that determines the artistic merit of an icon. Icon painters were taught and firmly believed that the highest degree of spirituality was to be attained only by those artists who followed the blameless and devout life enjoined by the Scriptures. As a result, many of the painters became monks. Others learnt their calling from their fathers and taught it to their sons, so that the occupation was often a hereditary one: all strove alike to preserve the anonymity which was advocated for those who worked for God's glory rather than their own.

Though none of these early icons has come down to us, several panels of only slightly later date survive to support this view. The finest of them is the famous icon of the Virgin of Vladimir the Great, Prince of Kiev (Plate 300A), which dates from about 1130. With examples of such calibre before them, it is not surprising to find the Russian artists gaining rapid mastery in the new art. It is all the more unfortunate that the majority of their early works perished in the ruthless Mongol invasion of the country in 1240 and the subsequent occupation of practically the whole of Russia until 1480.

The earliest appearance of the Russian style is to be sought in Kiev, in the surviving mural paintings, since no icons of this early date have as yet been discovered. Though their style is still basically Byzantine, already certain markedly Russian features are to be observed. Most notable is the pervading gentleness and the deeper humanism of the Russian imagery. The faces in these paintings show a certain lack of modelling and the figures are flatter, though the drapery reveals a tendency towards an Impressionistic handling of paint, more particularly in the use of white flecks to indicate highlights and folds. The brighter tones and more varied palette of the Russians likewise breaks through here and there, and reds bordering on vermilion, much white, and a bright yet deep green appear beside the more restrained, grander colours favoured by the Byzantines. A groping after an arresting outline, an innate feeling for rhythm and balance, and a deep interest in

colour are also to be discerned, heralding the birth of a new school of painting.

Kiev was the first city of importance to fall to the Mongols, and it was there that the most effective sacking and destruction took place. It is fortunate that there already existed by this time other centres in which the arts flourished. Novgorod was destined to become the most important of these, largely because it was able to preserve its independence and to establish a prosperous trade with the Western world. Art flourished freely in this congenial setting, and it was there that the trends which were evolving in the rest of the country were finally shaped and fused into a truly national style. First, however, the small principality of Vladimir-Suzdal was to produce some of the most beautiful and distinctive icons of an early date that survive.

Among the finest of this group of icons is a rectangular panel of the twelfth century representing the Deesis (Plate 300c). On it Christ is shown as a beardless youth, while two angels, taking the place of the customary figures of the Virgin and St John, stand on either side of Him. The sophisticated, yet devout, spirit which is concentrated in this remarkably poetic painting is characteristic of the court of Vladimir. Its spontaneous refinement does not in any way detract from the intensity of its feeling. Indeed, the patrician serenity and resolution of the youthful Saviour acquire an added poignancy from the graciousness of His features as well as from the contrast presented by His untroubled eyes and the compassionate gaze of the two angels.

The spirit of this elegant, aristocratic court animates another superb twelfth-century icon of the same school, namely the panel representing St Demetrius of Salonica, a saint who was widely venerated in pre-Mongol Russia (Plate 301A). He is seated on a splendid throne, wearing the magnificent robes of a nobleman and holding the mighty sword of a warrior in both hands. Here again the saint's patrician features express the same ready, yet sad, acceptance of suffering which only those who have a foreknowledge of pain are able to acquire.

Other centres resembled the district of Vladimir-Suzdal in their ability to produce works of great artistic quality, even though the Mongol hold on the areas rendered it difficult for major schools of art to establish themselves there. Nevertheless, cities such as Yaroslavl, Tver, Uglich, Smolensk, and more especially Pskov, to name but some of them, all brought important contributions to the development of Russian painting. Yaroslavl, for instance, had an innate feeling for pictorial composition. It was already fully apparent in the twelfth century, when it expressed itself in particularly noble lines and fine colours (Plate 300B). By the early seventeenth century, Yaroslavl had evolved a particularly decorative style showing a strong preference for genre scenes set in idyllic landscapes.

Though very small, Pskov was no less individualistic in its taste and outlook. Its people were fond of a deep, rather intense shade of green, which they often used for the backgrounds of their icons, combining it with a liking for sombre colours. They were a downright community, and their forthrightness is reflected in their art, though it is tempered there by a deep compassion. This poignancy heightens the emotional appeal of their paintings and tempers any excessive severity arising from the austerity of their colour schemes (Plate 301B).

The earliest examples of Novgorodian painting that survive date from the twelfth century and still bear testimony to the city's link with Byzantium, but even these works already display many purely indigenous features. Some of these are apparent in the fine twelfth-century painting of St George (Plate 301C), where, side by side with the monumental presentation of the figure, the grand, restrained colour scheme, the stylized handling of hair, and the almond-shaped eyes, all of which are typically Constantinopolitan, a more natural oval of the face and a straight nose, with its outlines characteristically extended to form the pronounced arch of the eyebrows, are essentially Russian elements. The saint's features are stamped with a truly native, gentle directness of expression which was to become general by the fourteenth century, though the thirteenth was more concerned in delineating the Russian countenance than in determining its frame of mind.

A mid-thirteenth-century icon of St Nicholas (Plate 301D) is an excellent example of this attitude, with the national type so clearly to the fore that it would be difficult to mistake this panel for the work of a Greek painter. Indeed, by this time Russian artists had become emancipated, and throughout the next three centuries they were to produce a succession of icons in which the splendid Novgorodian idiom is to be seen clearly crystallized.

By the fourteenth century the basic elements of the Novgorodian style had been fully worked out, leaving the artist free to concentrate on attaining a more powerful spirituality. This was achieved by resorting to the elongation of the figures, the new proportions seeming to shorten the gap which separates Earth from Heaven. More glowing colours helped to intensify the spirituality. They were, therefore, retained in the fifteenth century, when the figures underwent even greater elongation (Plate 303A), but they were further refined upon, and their range and luminosity developed until the daring juxtaposition of colours produced a glowing magnificence which invested the ethereal, flowing figures of the saints with a most compelling forcefulness.

Throughout the fourteenth and fifteenth centuries artists flocked to Novgorod. Among them were three painters of quite exceptional talent; they were to win such renown in their own day that their names escaped oblivion to survive to modern times. The earliest of the three artists, Theophanes, was an emigrant from Byzantium. Like El Greco, he was a Greek, and like El Greco, he too retained the pseudonym of "the Greek". Primarily a mural artist, he nevertheless painted many icons as well as some secular pictures, though none of the latter has survived. In Russia he settled at Novgorod, where he quickly became famous. Some authorities ascribe the miraculous icon of the Virgin of the Don, which dates from before 1380, to his hand, but exact information is scarce. Little more is known than that he worked in Moscow in 1395, and that he died there. His style is both sophisticated and vigorous, his brushwork more emotional, his colours more Impressionistic, and his figures even more elongated than was customary at the time.

Most important too was the influence of Theophanes on the Russian-born Andrew Rublev, since the younger man assisted the Greek, or rather worked at his side, when they were both engaged on the mural decorations of Moscow's first Cathedral of the Annunciation. Andrew Rublev may almost be termed the Fra Angelico of Russian painting. He was born in Pskov in about 1370 and was employed in his youth on the mural decorations carried out in the Cathedral of the Annunciation in Vladimir. Later he became a monk of the Spas Andronievsky Monastery in Moscow and spent the rest of his life working in that city. His contacts with Theophanes must have done much to broaden his outlook and stimulate his imagination. The icon of the Old Testament Trinity is perhaps his best-known work, but all Rublev's paintings bear the imprint of his genius (Plate 303B). His style was always clear cut and deeply sincere, and his influence on his contemporaries was very considerable.

The third great artist of this group, Dionysius, presents a complete contrast to Rublev. Dionysius was basically an intellectual, a man much preoccupied with the technical side of his profession, and he was thus more concerned with problems of composition than of sentiment. He was probably born in the 1440s, for thirty years later, when at work on the mural decorations of the Parfuntiev Monastery at Borovsk, some sixty miles to the south-west of Moscow, his sons were there to assist him. He died in 1505. Although his colours are more subdued and his figures even more elongated than those of the Novgorodians, his draperies are handled with a classic feeling, and his backgrounds are enlivened with more realistic architectural features and with hills of a more purely decorative nature.

From as early as the fourteenth century work of great distinction had been produced in Moscow. Much of it – as, for example, the beautiful icon of SS Boris and Gleb (Plate 303C) – retains something of the delicacy and forcefulness of the earlier Vladimir–Suzdalian panels. But in the fifteenth century, when Moscow became the capital of a freed and united country, the outlook of the city altered. The change is reflected in the icons; for although the old way of life persisted and the customary veneration for religion survived, a more pleasing, gayer, less compelling type of beauty was called for, and more sinuous outlines were required (Plate 302B). The old fervour was superseded by a conscious search after the decorative, and, simultaneously, there developed a greater interest in naturalism, a hankering after the discouraged art of portraiture, and an awareness of the problems and the importance of perspective. The foremost artists of the capital were at this time employed on work for the Court, having been installed by the Tsar in special workshops established in the Palace of Arms, which lies within the Kremlin walls. Grouped together there, artists of every type discussed and examined the foreign works available in Moscow, but they continued to produce the traditional icons, allaying their restlessness by evolving complex compositions and including numerous subsidiary scenes, which they grouped round the central subject and also distributed on the margins of the panels. They emphasized the naturalistic elements in the architectural backgrounds, whenever possible trying to transform their settings into stylized landscapes. In a manner not altogether dissimilar from that of the English pre-Raphaelites, they studded their panels with minute flowers and animals. They gave their personages the round heads of the Muscovites and used blood-reds, browns, and yellows, with shadows laid on in black, for their predominating colour tone.

Simon Ushakov stands out among the artists of his day. Though he fretted greatly at the restraint imposed upon him by the old tradition, he nevertheless produced icons which are still convincing works of art (Plate 303D). Yet his style clearly foreshadows a coming change. The new outlook is very apparent in his painting of the Tsar's family tree (Plate 302A), which, with a medallion of the Virgin of Vladimir somewhat incongruously poised high in its branches, includes, in the lower register, likenesses of the Tsar with his wife and sons, while the Metropolitan Peter and John Kalita, the founder of the

Muscovite Empire, dead these three hundred years, stand at the base of the tree.

Yet late in the sixteenth century the art was to provide a final flowering before succumbing to the naturalistic style of seventeenth-century Europe. The incentive was provided by two nephews of the founder of the almost princely merchant family of Stroganov, who were living in the family mansion at Solvichegodsk in the district of Perm. Both greatly admired the paintings of the Novgorodian school; they determined to stem the decline in the art by establishing a centre of icon painting in their village, where artists were to seek inspiration in the masterpieces of an earlier age. Many who gathered there did in fact succeed in producing works of art, and they created a style, now known as the Stroganov in memory of their patrons, which rapidly won the widespread admiration of their contemporaries (Plate 302c). The Tsar's attention was quickly drawn to their works, and eventually some of the leading artists were summoned to Moscow. Procopius Chirin and the brothers Nicephorus and Nazarius Savin are now numbered among the finest painters established in the Palace of Arms workshops, but they retained the Stroganov imprint on their work. Their style had been formed by the exacting taste of connoisseurs and, in the manner of Persian miniatures or book illuminations of Western origin, it showed great finish and paid deep attention to minute detail. Miniature-sized, extremely elaborate icons requiring the utmost technical skill became the vogue, while large icons so studded with exquisite, delicate minutiae as to seem encrusted with jewels were much admired. Both types satisfied the same sort of taste as that which took pleasure, three centuries later, in the works of Fabergé. Each foreshadowed the end of an era.

Spanish

The art of a passionately religious nation, Spanish painting has nearly always been marked by a certain emotional intensity, directed mainly to religion but occasionally, as with Goya, dealing with political and historical subjects. This is reflected both in the general darkness of palette, a penchant for dramatic and theatrical lighting, and a tendency to ornament even secular paintings with religious symbols often of a rather morbid nature. After religious paintings, portraits take pride of place, and the Spanish character is so clearly marked that it is often easy without any other kind of documentation to recognize the nationality of these dark-jowled men, with their deep-set burning eyes, .their sombre clothes, and slightly abstracted air. The best kind of Spanish painting is always marked by an intense realism. Geographically isolated from the rest of Europe, the meeting-place of Moor and Christian, of Fleming, Italian, and Frenchman, Spain has reflected the influence of most of the dominant political elements, but in every case has added something of its own particular quality.

Medieval Spanish painting – miniatures, frescoes, and panels – was a provincial version of the generally diffused Gothic styles; though it is slightly differentiated by a closer connexion with the Byzantine tradition – operating through Islam – and by a more emphatic use of gilding. The altar-pieces which spread from Catalonia throughout the peninsula pay more attention to the frame than the painting, and even the painting itself is usually encrusted with gilded ornaments and imitation jewellery – on the vestments, diadems, haloes, etc. The first creative influence was from Avignon, but by the fifteenth century Flemish influence was asserting itself, and in Bartolomeo Bermejo (c. 1450–95), who worked at Saragossa and Barcelona, Spain found her first important painter.

When Spain, under Charles V and Philip

II, became the centre of a world empire, however, she moved her artistic aspirations from Flanders to Italy, and until the end of the eighteenth century Rome and Venice dominated her artistic life. The first fruit of this new allegiance was the work of Alonso Sanchez Coello (1531–88), a court painter who was the pupil of Antonis Mor, a prolific and versatile Fleming whose influence was also felt in England. The first giant of Spanish painting, however, was a pupil of Titian – Domenikos Theotokopoulos, a Cretan settled in Toledo and more commonly known as El Greco (1541–1614). Reflecting the influence of his early Byzantine context, his art has only come to be widely appreciated in the course of this century, when his paintings have had a great influence. His curiously elongated figures, attributed by some critics to an ocular malformation, are immediately recognizable, and, in his later paintings, hover on the verge of the abstract. So personal an artist found no disciples nor imitators. His output was fairly limited; he is seldom to be found in old collections and his extant works are well documented.

Diego Velazquez (1599–1660) (Plate 304) was more of a realist. One of the most distinguished portraitists of all times, he often used a severely limited palette, creating harmonies of greys and blacks. His most famous portraits are those of the royal family, especially of Philip IV. They have found many copyists and imitators. But he was also a master of the still life, revelling in texture and in precise modelling, showing a passionate apprehension of visual reality. On close inspection his brushwork is revealed as remarkably free and vigorous, anticipating that of the Impressionists, and he was the ideal of many nineteenth-century painters. He usually painted directly on to light-brown priming, though there is occasionally greyish under-painting to be seen in parts of his works. He was always popular in England: Reynolds adored him, and some of his finest works are to be seen in London.

The works of Velazquez were never marked by that near fanaticism which is so characteristically Spanish. It is, however, a characteristic of two of his contemporaries whose work is now coming to be considered more seriously than ever before. Jiusepe Ribera (1589–1652) lived most of his life in Naples, which then belonged to Spain. His works are dramatic to the point of theatricality, the lighting strong and emphatic. They are concerned mostly with religious subjects. The colouring is simple and direct, the shadows and general tonality brown.

Francisco Zurbaran (1598–1664) was, again, a painter of religious subjects and of portraits, but he lacked Ribera's pomposity, and there is a certain freshness and innocence about his work which brings it close to that of such French contemporaries as the Le Nains.

The lowest common denominator of Spanish painting is Bartolomeo Esteban Murillo (1618–82), who dominated the eighteenth century in his country and also had a wide influence outside it. Occasionally a great painter, Murillo is often sentimental. His many religious paintings, sweet and appealing in their approach, and his many variations on the charms of childhood attracted scores of imitators and disciples who were rarely able to attain his great technical ability. He repeated several of his own subjects frequently. During the eighteenth and nineteenth centuries he was the most popular Spanish painter in the eyes of most English dealers and collectors. His markedly brown paintings, with their smoky atmosphere, are clearly distinguishable from the innumerable pastiches of them.

Goya (1746–1828) was the last of the great Spaniards, and once again an eccentric who, by his colourful personality and constant inventiveness, has come to grip the modern imagination. Commencing as an almost conventional eighteenth-century master, he soon developed a bold, vigorous style of his own, excelling in social reportage, political propaganda of a scarifying kind, and portraits of extraordinary penetration. Although his popularity has been bound up with the modern movement, his work became better known in England as a result of the Peninsular War, when he painted several portraits of Wellington. The best description of his technique is revealed by his own phrase: "There are no lines in Nature, only lighted forms and forms which are in the shadow, planes which project and planes which recede."

SPANISH STILL LIFE AND FLOWER PAINTINGS
seventeenth and eighteenth centuries

Towards the end of the sixteenth century still life, particularly the *bodegones* or kitchen pieces, flourished throughout Spain. Alonso Vazquez, an important exponent of it, was born at Ronda about 1600 and died in 1649. Pacheco, his rival, called him "the father of *bodegones*". But this may have been a diplomatic attempt to allot him a place in another field than that where they competed, for men of an earlier generation had already perfected the theme. Juan Sanchez Cotan (1561–1627) created strong images with a most convincing realism. The aspect of *trompe l'œil* is often not far behind still life, and there is a legend that this pious Spanish monk made a painting of the crucifixion so naturalistic that birds came to perch on the arms of the cross, while onlookers mistook it for sculpture. So when he painted a cabbage or an open melon they have this illusionist quality. He preferred to use only a few things in his compositions and set these against plain backgrounds. The thing in itself is all triumphant in this Spanish art at the turn of the century. So it is in the work of Juan Labrador. He was born at Badajoz as early as 1530 and died in Madrid in 1600, so that his painting belongs definitely to the sixteenth-century pioneers.

If the great Spaniards of the seventeenth century made their still life incidental to their splendid figure subjects, one has but to isolate details to see how important an influence this art of the *bodegone* was to them. Zurburan especially expends loving care to render plastically the bowls and fruit and baskets with which he embellishes his figure subjects, and sometimes he creates fine *bodegones* for their own sake. One has but to think, too, of Velazquez' *Christ in the House of Martha* in the National Gallery to remember that the sacred scenc is set back in another room reflected in a mirror behind a foreground of a kitchen table with wonderfully observed fish and eggs, dishes, jar and pestle obviously painted for their own sake and allotted one-fourth of the picture. They have no symbolic significance, and their prominence in this early work by Velazquez shows how influenced he was by the mode. All this is to some extent true of the Neapolitan School, where, of course, the tremendous influence of Caravaggio himself was creating a revolution as powerful as any in the whole history of European painting.

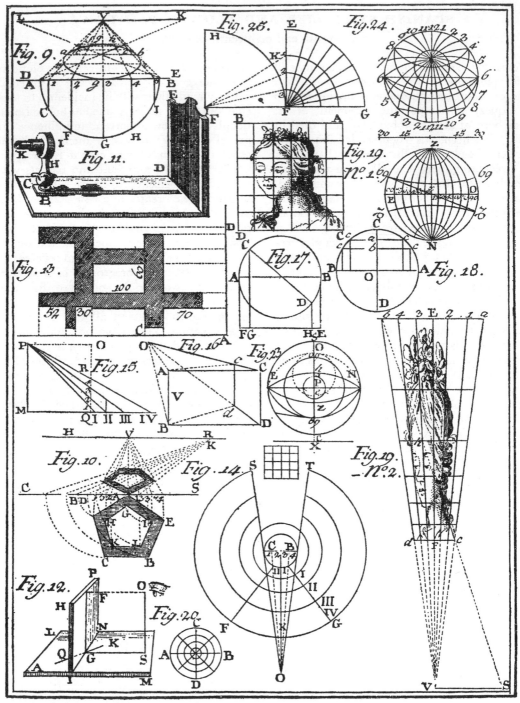

Perspective

POTTERY
AND PORCELAIN

As a craft, the making of earthenware vessels and effigies is as ancient as the recorded history of man. If, however, we exclude those examples which come chiefly within the province of the archaeologist, the general study and collecting of ceramics begins at a period not earlier than the T'ang dynasty (A.D. 618–906). This dynasty saw the full flowering of the art of the Chinese potter, and the invention of the beautiful translucent porcelain, that was to become at once a most prized and elusive material to its would-be imitators.

The following survey provides a concise and reliable guide for those who wish to trace the history and varied techniques employed in the making of pottery and porcelain throughout a period of more than a thousand years.

In the main text the dates, places of manufacture, materials, and characteristics of Chinese and European ceramics are set out in chronological order. There are also sections describing the productions of Russia and America. To this is added a glossary supplying copious additional information, together with the names of individual artists, technical terms, and methods of decoration. Line drawings illustrate examples of various types of ware and the principal marks of each factory.

American

POTTERY

"I Like fine things Even when They are not mine, And cannot become mine; I still enjoy them." This, translated from Pennsylvania dialect, appears on a *sgraffiato* plate signed by Johannes Leman, made before 1830 at the Friedrich Hildebrand pottery near Tyler's Port, Montgomery County, Pennsylvania.

Everything needed for the production of pottery was present in America – everything but the most important, enough encouragement. Potter's clays were abundant. The common red-burning clays (for bricks, roof-tiles, coarse redware) occurred in shales at or near the ground's surface, and their use since earliest days had called for only the simplest kilns and equipment. Buff-burning clays of finer texture were employed since the seventeenth century for experimental wares of every grade, and in the 1800s provided a range of factory-made wares from Bennington to Baltimore, and westward along the Ohio River.

White-burning pipe clay had been used by the aborigines. In a court trial of 1685, at Burlington, N.J., the potter, "Wm. Winn Attested sayth that hee can finde noe Clay in the Countrey that will make white wear", but white tobacco pipes were made as early as 1690 in Philadelphia, where in 1720 they were advertised by Richard Warder "Tobacco Pipe Maker living under the same Roof with Phillip Syng Gold Smith". And by 1738 "an earth" (the true kaolin, white chinaclay) was found by Andrew Duché "on the back of Virginia", a vein of unaker running through the Carolinas into Georgia, exposed on river-banks or along old stream beds.

Stoneware clays were absent in New England, but supplies were fetched by boat from northern New Jersey and Staten Island. At the Corselius (afterwards Crolius) pottery on Potbaker's Hill, "the first stoneware kiln or furnace was built in this year 1730" on lower Manhattan Island. In January of that year in Philadelphia, Anthony Duché and his sons had petitioned the Assembly for support in "the Art of making Stone-ware", to which they had been applying themselves "for severall Years past".

If the wanted clays were not near at hand, coastwise vessels and riverboats brought them. Materials for glaze or decoration were of simple and available sorts. Fuel for the potter's kiln was everywhere in this forested land.

Men with technical knowledge were here among the first. Brickmaking was reported by 1612 in Virginia, 1629 and 1635 in Salem and Boston. Rooftiles or "tile Earth for House covering" appeared in .Massachusetts court orders of 1646, and "tylemakers" prospered in Virginia by 1649. The potter Philip Drinker arrived in 1635 in Charlestown, and that same year at nearby Salem the "potbakers" William Vinson (Vincent) and John Pride were recorded. One "extraordinary potter"

came in 1653 to Rensselaerwyk (Albany) on the ship *Graef*, and a Dirck Claesen "Pottmaker" was established by 1657 at Potbaker's Corner, in New Amsterdam. The thumping of the potter's wheel was soon heard in every colonial town of consequence, and for New England alone (says Lura W. Watkins) two hundred and fifty potters were recorded by 1800, twice that number by 1850. How many more were never mentioned at all?

Place-names like Potter's Creek, Clay City, or Pottertown give a clue to the spread of activity – four states had a Jugtown, seven more a Kaolin.

All that was lacking was a proper market. In numbers the colonists were so few, a total of 200,000 by 1690 and the five leading towns accounting for only 18,600. The population nearly doubled every twenty years, so that by 1776 its total reached 2,500,000 (about equally divided between the five Southern and eight Northern provinces) and Philadelphia, with 40,000 souls, was the second city in the British dominions. Ninety per cent of the population was on the land, and for the most part comprised a sort of village society. The complaint was everywhere the same as in Virginia, that "for want of Towns, Markets, and Money, there is but little Encouragement for tradesmen and Artificers". It was all very well for a Boston official to say (1718) that "Every one Incourages the Growth and Manufactures of this Country and not one person but discourages the Trade from home, and says 'tis pitty any goods should be brought from England", but fashion preferred what was imported, and the colonial potter found little demand except for useful wares.

In the South (where tobacco was the cornerstone of the finances of Chesapeake society until 1750, followed by wheat and corn; where rice was the staple in Carolina from 1700, indigo from about 1745) the English character of plantation life was strongly marked. The local commodities were exchanged for English luxuries, and except for rude plantation crafts, nothing much was to be expected here. Andrew Duché and the mysterious Samuel Bowen, two early Savannah potters, were marvels who appeared far ahead of their time.

England's suppression of all colonial manu-factures was a sternly established policy. General Thomas Gage expressed the official attitude when writing to Lord Barrington in 1772 that it would be "for our interest to Keep the Settlers within reach of the Sea-Coast as long as we can; and to cramp their Trade as far as can be done prudentially". But he was unaware to what an extent people had al-ready moved inland, away from the agents who supplied English goods; nor had he per-ceived the rapid advance made in American manufactures since the French and Indian Wars of 1754–63.

Yet potmakers lagged in this general im-provement. Through the colonial years and far beyond, coarse red-clay pottery – jugs and jars, plates and bowls, mugs and milk-pans – formed the principal output of small potteries everywhere. New England's glacial clays made excellent redware, which was partly supplemented by grey stoneware from the time of the Revolution, or more extensively after 1800. Always popular, ordinary red-ware survived the competition offered by cheap and serviceable factory-made wares from the 1830s, and in country districts lasted through the nineteenth century, lingering within present memory.

REDWARE

In kitchen and dairy, or for table use along-side pewter and common woodenware or "treen", the simple forms of this sturdy folk pottery were washed or splashed with pleas-ant colour – glazed with browns and yellows, rich orange to salmon pink, copper-greens, a brownish black made from manganese. For this the least equipment was needed: a horse-powered mill for grinding and mixing clay, a home-made potter's wheel, a few wooden tools, with perhaps a few moulds as well. The maker might be no more than a seasonal or "blue-bird" potter who worked when his other affairs permitted, and carried his out-put by wagon through the near vicinity; or the larger and full-time potshops might em-ploy untrained lads (William Scofield of Honeybrook got "one skilled potter from every 16 apprentice boys") or migrant jour-neyman potters of uncertain grades.

There were no secrets in this simple manu-facture. Since 1625–50, at the Jamestown colony, potters everywhere had made useful everyday ware of much the same sorts, in its own time used up, smashed up, never re-garded as worth preserving.

Of this class, an early and curious milkpan pictured here for the first time (Plate 307A) is credited to Andrew Duché, who advertised (April 1735, the *South Carolina Gazette*) to sup-ply "Butter pots, milk-pans, and all other sorts of Earthenware of this country make". The story of its discovery over a decade ago was told by Ruth Monroe Gilmer in *Apollo* for May 1947.

Andrew Duché (1710–78), a Huguenot from Philadelphia, who worked in 1731–5 "on the Bay" at Charleston, South Carolina, and at New Windsor, South Carolina, from 1735 to 1737, finally enjoyed a short but important career 1738–43 at Savannah, Ga. (*see* Porce-lain, p. 871).

Found at Guyton (in the Salzburger area forty-five miles inland from Savannah) this heavy, thick and flat-footed pan was appar-ently made from riverbank clays, quoting its owner: "the body densely textured and mot-tled reddish brown, as if made from shale and ball clay . . . the glaze a clear straw-coloured lead used all over . . . the glazed bottom flat, without rim or ridge of any kind".

Not long after Duché's time, another Southern pottery was established by a colony of Moravians, who in 1753 moved from Beth-lehem, Pennsylvania, to the wilderness region of Wachovia, North Carolina. Here the United Brethren founded a communal society served by Brother Gottfried Aust as potter. He fired his first kiln at the village of Betha-bara in 1756, making redware, clay pipes, stove-tiles, and from 1761 conducted public sales which attracted buyers from a surprising distance (Rice, *Shenandoah Pottery*, pp. 271–7). The enterprise was transferred in 1768 to Sa-lem, N.C., where by 1774 far superior wares were achieved, and production lasted to around 1830.

Still another venture in this region was the so-called Jugtown Pottery, in a settlement peopled *c*. 1740–50 at Steeds, North Carolina, by a group of colonists from Staffordshire.

Apparently the plainest of "dirt dishes" were made here (1750?) by Peter Craven, first of his family, and latterly the place became known as Jugtown, for the common vessels it supplied to Southern distilleries. Languished and long forgotten, the pottery was revived in 1917 at a hamlet amusingly named Why Not?

Far north, New England must have been brimming with small but able potters. In 1775 (says John Ramsay in *American Potters and Pottery*) the two Essex County, Massachusetts, towns of Danvers and Peabody had seventy-five potters, and there were twenty-two Peabody potters at the Battle of Lexington.

Early New England potters and their wares were given ample and excellent record in Mrs Watkins's fairly recent book, in which the illustrations show what Puritan austerity characterized the general output. Simple and appropriate forms were enough, with richly coloured glazes to satisfy the eye and only with occasional attempts at further decoration. Pictured here (Plate 307c) is a basin with trailed lines of yellow slip; a cooky jar girdled with an incised rigaree; and herb-pot with *Edward Towle* (its owner?) scratched on the cover.

Pennsylvania-German. For the Pennsylvania-"Dutch" (that is, *deutsch* or German) Frances Lichten has provided a full report in her *Folk Art of Rural Pennsylvania*. In the "Dutch counties" settled in the eighteenth century by Swiss Mennonites, and by Germans from the Palatinate, pottery was made which was in wide contrast to New England work, marked by a love of colour, a play of ideas, an engaging humour.

The flat Pennsylvania fruit pie dish or *poischissel* was a distinctive article; or the pots for apple butter called *epfel buther haffa*; the saucered flower-pots or *bluma haffa*. Fluted turk's head cakemoulds were produced in all sorts and sizes, and there were standing pottery grease-lamps not seen in New England, quaint banks and bird-whistles, double-walled tobacco jars displaying skilful pierced work. (See *Pennsylvania-German Folk Art* by Frances Lichten, p. 401).

Shenandoah Valley. Just south of Pennsylvania, a numerous and flourishing group of potters worked throughout the nineteenth century in a hundred-mile stretch of the Shenandoah Valley. Foremost were the Bell family (Plate 306B), founded by Peter Bell, who from 1800 to 1845 produced "erthingwear" at Hagerstown, Maryland, and Winchester, Virginia. His oldest son, John Bell (1800–80), worked 1833–80 at Waynesboro, Pennsylvania, and was followed by five sons who continued the business until 1899. John's brothers, Samuel and Solomon, were in partnership from 1833 at Strasburg, Virginia, where the factory continued until 1908.

Mid-west. Fairly typical of what was made through Ohio and Indiana, where a variety of pottery and stoneware clays were abundant, a washbowl and jug, buff-glazed inside, is stamped on one handle *Zoar*, on the other 1840. The Society of Separatists (called Zoarites) were one of many religious sects gathered in communal settlements that flowered and died in the nineteenth century, themselves coming in 1817 from Württemberg and prospering in 1819–98 at Zoar, in Tuscarawas County, Ohio. In a long list of trades and crafts practised here, we find weavers and carpenters, a printshop and bindery, a fine black smith shop, and of course a pottery. Red roof-tiles (one is dated 1824) are still seen on a few houses, and in 1834 the Society was selling "porringers" to farm folk in the vicinity. The services of an outsider were engaged, Solomon Purdy, a potter recorded in 1820 at Putnam; in 1840 at Atwater. Until 1852–3 the Zoar associates still produced common brownware, and black- or buff-glazed redware.

Decoration: Last of the everyday wares, and different from the others, a buff pottery painted (sometimes stencilled) with manganese brown belonged to New Geneva, Pennsylvania. So wholly unlike the dutch-country pottery seen farther east, this sober stuff (Plate 306A) with hard, unglazed tan body was made in 1860–90 by James Hamilton of New Geneva, in the south-western corner of Pennsylvania, and very likely (see *Antiquarian* for September 1931) also across the river at the A. & W. Boughner pottery in Greensboro.

Long employed by redware potters everywhere, a simple and most effective method of

(A) The Madonna and Child by Dürer (or Dürer school). *National Gallery, London.*

(B) Christina of Denmark by Holbein. *National Gallery, London.*

(c) The Flight into Egypt by Elsheimer. *Munich, Pinakothek.*

PLATE 289

The Last Supper by Giotto. *Munich, Pinakothek.*

PLATE 290

(A) Madonna and Child by Filippo Lippi. *Munich, Pinakothek.*

(B) Ginevra dei Benci by Leonardo da Vinci. *National Gallery, Washington, D. C.*

(c) The Holy Family (Canigiani) by Raphael. *Munich, Pinakothek.*

(D) Mercury instructing Cupid before Venus by Correggio. *National Gallery, London.*

PLATE 291

St Jerome in the Wilderness by Mantegna. *São Paolo Museum. By courtesy of Frank T. Sabin.*

PLATE 292

(A) Danae by Titian. *Prado, Madrid.*

(B) Madonna with Canon van der Paele by Jan van Eyck. *Bruges Museum.*

PLATE 293

Vulcan surprises Mars and Venus by Tintoretto. *Munich, Pinakothek.*

PLATE 294

(B) Nativity by Botticelli. *National Gallery, London.*

(A) The Virgin appearing to St Bernard by Perugino. *Munich, Pinakothek.*

PLATE 295

(A) Majnūn entrusts a friend with a message for Laylā, from Amīr Khusraw's *Majnūn u Laylā, c* 1440. 4 × 3 ins. *Chester Beatty Library, Dublin.*

(B) The Fire Ordeal of Siyāwush, from the *Shāhnāma,* 1411. 6 × 4 ins. *British Museum, London.*

(C) The Birth of Rustam, from the *Shāhnāma, c.* 1450. 5½ × 5 ins. *Private Collection.*

(D) Kay Khusraw and his mother fording the Jihun, from the *Shāhnāma, c.* 1500. 6 × 6¼ ins. *Private Collection.*

PLATE 296

(A) Alexander and the Beggar, from the poems of Nawā'ī, 1485. 6¾ × 4½ ins. *Bodleian Library, Oxford.*

(B) An Angel descending upon Yūsuf, from Jāmī's *Yūsuf u Zulaykhā,* 1540. 6¼ × 4¼ ins. *Chester Beatty Library, London.*

(C) The Ascent of the Prophet to Heaven, from the poems of Hilālī, *c.* 1575. 7¼ × 4¾ ins. *Private Collection.*

(D) A young Dervish by Muhammadī, *c.* 1575. 8 × 4 ins. *India Office Library, Commonwealth Relations Office, London.*

PLATE 297

(A) A Youth Drinking, style of Riẓā-i 'Abbāsī, *c.* 1620. 7 × 3¾ ins. From the Clive Album. *Victoria and Albert Museum, London (loan).*

(B) Indians worshipping Fire by Muḥammad Qāsim, *c.* 1640–50. 7¾ × 5½ ins. *Chester Beatty Library, Dublin.*

(C) Khusraw spies Shīrīn bathing, from Nizāmī's *Khusraw u Shīrīn, c.* 1520. 10 × 7 ins. *Dr and Mrs Schott Collection, London.*

(D) Rustam and Kāmūs, from the *Shāhnāma, c.* 1590. 15 × 8½ ins. *Dr and Mrs Schott Collection, London.*

PLATE 298

Portrait of Fatḥ ʻAlī Shah by Mihr ʻAlī, 1805. 8 ft 9 ins × 4 ft 4½ ins.
Amery Collection, London.

PLATE 299

(A) *Left:* Icon of the Virgin of Vladimir. This Byzantine painting dates from *c.* 1130. It reached Kiev shortly after this date, but was moved to Vladimir within a few years. It remained there till early in the fifteenth century, when it was brought to Moscow by the Great Prince Dmitri to encourage his troops as they engaged in battle with Tamerlane. This rendering of the Virgin and Child is known iconographically as The Virgin of Tenderness. It was a favourite type in Russia, one of the finest versions being by the hand of Andrew Rublev. *Tretiakov Gallery, Moscow.*

(B) *Right:* Icon of Our Lady of Tolga. This panel formerly belonged to the Monastery of Tolga founded near Yaroslavl in 1314. The icon is probably to be assigned to much the same date and to the hand of a local artist. Professor Lazarev considers it one of the most moving of Russian icons. Its colours are particularly fine, for it is painted in shades of deep cherry red, pinks, dark blues, browny yellows, and emerald greens against a silver background. *Tretiakov Gallery, Moscow.*

(c) Icon of the Deesis: late twelfth century, school of Vladimir-Suzdal. This icon used to hang in the Cathedral of the Annunciation in Moscow. *Tretiakov Gallery, Moscow.*

PLATE 300

(A) *Left:* Icon of St Demetrius of Salonica. A late twelfth–early thirteenth-century painting of the Vladimir-Suzdal school. The saint was regarded in medieval Russia as the patron of soldiers. *Tretiakov Gallery, Moscow.*

(B) *Right:* Icon of an archangel from the Deesis row of an iconostasis: late fourteenth century, school of Pskov. *Russian Museum, Leningrad.*

(C) *Left:* Icon of St George. A magnificent example of twelfth-century Novgorodian work. *Palace of Arms Museum, Moscow.* (D) *Right:* Icon of St Nicholas. The panel belonged formerly to the Dukhov Monastery in Novgorod and dates from the mid-thirteenth century. *Russian Museum, Leningrad.*

PLATE 301

(A) Detail from Simon Ushakov's icon of the Virgin of Vladimir and the Tsar's family tree. The elder son shown in the group on the right was the future Tsar Alexis I. *Tretiakov Gallery, Moscow.*

(B) *Left:* Icon of the Birth of Christ. An excellent fifteenth-century painting from Novgorod. It reflects Muscovite taste, but is painted in a more robust manner than that which characterizes the work of the capital. *Tretiakov Gallery, Moscow.* (C) *Right:* A Stroganov school icon of the hermit Basil and Artemius of Vermolsk. *Tretiakov Gallery, Moscow.*

PLATE 302

(A) *Left:* An icon of the Novgorodian school showing the Raising of Lazurus. This lovely fifteenth-century panel displays the elongation of the figures and the love of linear rhythm which were characteristic of the period. *Museum, Novgorod.* (B) *Right:* The Saviour: an icon by Andrew Rublev. The panel has been adorned with a silver cover studded with jewels, which is of only slightly later date than the icon. *Tretiakov Gallery, Moscow.*

(C) *Left:* SS Boris and Gleb: a fourteenth-century icon of the Moscow school. The icon is painted in reds and browns against a white background. The saints wear national, secular dress which includes the red hose and long swords reserved for members of the ruling house. *Tretiakov Gallery, Moscow.* (D) *Right:* An icon by Simon Ushakov: Christ, not by the hand of man. *Tretiakov Gallery, Moscow.*

PLATE 303

Dona Isabel de Bourbon by Velazquez. *Frank T. Sabin.*

PLATE 304

(A) Blue-painted brown stoneware batter jug, "New York Feby 17th 1798 / Flowered by Clarkson Crolius / Blue". Height 11¾ ins. *The New York Historical Society.*

(B) Brown-stained stoneware 3-gallon jar stamped BOSTON. 1804. *Old Sturbridge Village, Sturbridge, Massachusetts.*

(C) Blue-painted grey stoneware crock and churn, Edmands & Co. (working 1850-68 at Charlestown, Massachusetts) and Madison Woodruff (working 1849–*c.* 1870 at Cortland, New York). Height 13 and 19¼ ins. *Henry Ford Museum, Dearborn.*

(D) Crock with blue-stencilled eagle, BROWN BROTHERS / HUNTINGTON, L.I. (working 1863–1904). Height 9 ins. *Samuel E. Kamens.*

PLATE 305

(A) *Left:* Pennsylvania Redware churn with brown and olive glaze, and wooden dasher; *Right:* brown-painted crock of unglazed tan pottery, made 1860–90 by James Hamilton at New Geneva, Pennsylvania. *Formerly Collection of Alfred B. Maclay, Parke-Bernet Galleries.*

(B) Bell Pottery, Shenandoah Valley: *Left:* Celadon-glazed jelly mould stamped JOHN BELL, made for his sister at Winchester, Virginia, *c.* 1825; *Left centre:* Frog glazed brown and green; *Centre:* Orange-glazed plate stamped JOHN BELL/WAYNESBORO; *Right:* Cup and saucer, *c.* 1860, and brightly splashed jug, both by Samuel and Solomon Bell of Strasburg, Virginia. Plate diameter 9 ins. *Private Collection.*

PLATE 306

(A) Detail.

(A) Brown pottery milk-pan; straw-coloured lead glaze. Detail of flat bottom. Credited to Andrew Duché, c. 1735–40. New Windsor, South Carolina, or Savannah, Georgia. Diameter 12½ ins. *Ruth Monroe Gilmer.*

(B) Pennsylvania Redware puzzle-jug; sgraffito decoration, inscribed SW 1775 and THIS AND THE / GEVER IS THINE / FOR EVER. Height about 8 ins. *Formerly Collection of Alfred B. Maclay, Parke-Bernet Galleries.*

(C) New England Redware: *Left:* Pan with brown-splashed light brown interior, lines of yellow slip; *Centre:* Black-glazed cup; *Centre:* Cooky jar with bright brown glaze, girdle of incised rigaree; *Right:* Herb pot splashed yellow, brown, and orange; and herb pot with salmon glaze, cover scratched EDWARD TOWLE. Cooky jar, Height 8 ins. *Private Collection.*

PLATE 307

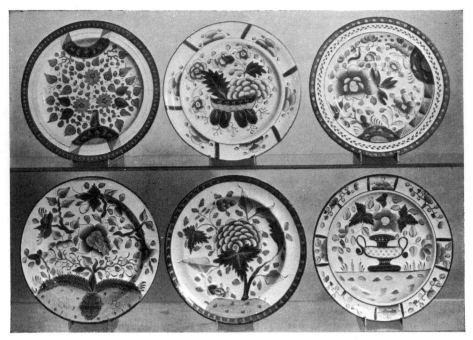

(A) Gaudy Dutch plates made *c.* 1820 for the Pennsylvania-German market, in order Strawflower, War Bonnet, Single Rose, Dove, Grape, Urn. Diameter 10 ins. *Formerly Yeager Collection, Parke-Bernet Galleries.*

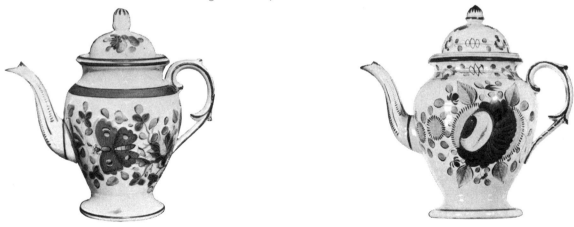

(B) Coffee-pot in Butterfly, most-sought-for of Gaudy Dutch patterns. Height 9½ ins. *Parke-Bernet Galleries.*

(C) Coffee-pot in King's Rose pattern. Height 10½ ins. *Parke-Bernet Galleries.*

(D) Gaudy Dutch plates in Oyster pattern, showing usual painted border and blue transfer-printed border. Diameters 7½ and 8¼ ins. *Formerly Yeager Collection, Parke-Bernet Galleries.*

PLATE 308

(A) and (B) Pair of bowls, mottled pink lustre with black-printed medallions of Franklin, Washington, Lafayette. U.S. Arms and REPUBLICANS [REPUBLICS] ARE NOT ALWAYS UNGRATEFUL. Diameter 8 ins. *Formerly Lorimer Collection, Parke-Bernet Galleries.*

(C) Liverpool jug, black-printed, *c.* 1790 SUCCESS TO THE CROOKED BUT INTERESTING TOWN OF BOSTON! Height 7¾ ins. *Formerly Lorimer Collection, Parke-Bernet Galleries.*

(D) Liverpool jug with U.S. Arms, reverse a frigate THE TRUEBLOODED YANKEE; rim and a large anchor below the spout in copper lustre. Height 8¼ ins. *Formerly Lorimer Collection, Parke-Bernet Galleries.*

PLATE 309

(A) Blue platter Harewood House, Yorkshire, with Erie Canal view at Albany, portrait medallions of Jefferson, Lafayette, Clinton, 1825; by Ralph Stevenson and (Aldborough Lloyd) Williams at Cobridge. Length 14¼ ins. *Formerly Hudnut and Hearst Collection, Parke-Bernet Galleries.*

(B) Blue plates Baltimore & Ohio Railroad (*c.* 1828 by Enoch Wood & Sons); Upper Ferry Bridge over the River Schuykill (before 1829 by Joseph Stubbs). Diameters 10 and 8¾ ins. *Parke-Bernet Galleries.* Blue plate Landing of the Fathers at Plymouth (2nd issue in 1821, Enoch Wood & Sons). Diameter 8¾ ins. *Los Angeles County Museum.*

PLATE 310

(A) The parent of Spatter wares, a painted Peafowl plate with blue frill edge, green sponged foliage. Impressed WEDGWOOD mark, *c.* 1800–20. Diameter 8 ins. *Formerly Lorimer Collection, Parke-Bernet Galleries.*

(B) Ironstone plate of the 1840s, blue spatter and colours, Bird on a Fence. Diameter 8½ ins. *Parke-Bernet Galleries.*

(c) Cup and saucer in Peafowl pattern, carmine spatter. *Parke-Bernet Galleries.*

(D) Spatter in typical patterns of 1820–40: The Star, Tulip, and Red Schoolhouse. Plates Diameter 8 ins. *Parke-Bernet Galleries.*

PLATE 311

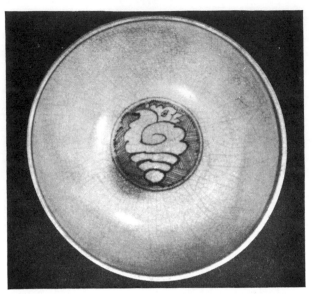

(A) Detail of the Duché bowl, interior with shell medallion perhaps from the Earl of Egmont's "sample" Chinese porcelains, sent in 1738.

(B) Blue-painted bowl of experimental porcelain, made 1738–43 by Andrew Duché at Savannah, Georgia. Diameter 5¾ ins. Height 3 ins. *Ruth Monroe Gilmer*.

PLATE 312

(A) Fine earthenware or "porcelain" teapot with blue painting, made 1771–2 in Philadelphia by Bonnin and Morris. Height 7 ins. Length 9 ins.

(B) Reverse with initials WP said to be for William Penn. *Mr and Mrs Arthur J. Sussel.*

(C) Blue-painted sweetmeat dish in style of Bow or Plymouth. Mark: P in blue. Bonnin and Morris of Philadelphia, 1771–2. Height 5¼ ins. Width 7¼ ins. *Brooklyn Museum.*

PLATE 313

(A) Parlour group The Elder's Daughter, issued October 1886 in New York by John Rogers; one of the popular Rogers Groups made 1859–93. Height 21 ins. *Los Angeles County Museum.*

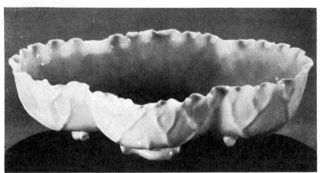

(B) American Belleek made 1891–8 at East Liverpool, Ohio, by Knowles, Taylor, and Knowles. Mark in green: K.T.K. CO. LOTUS WARE. Length 7½ ins. *Henry Ford Museum, Dearborn.*

(c) Belleek or "Lotus Ware" shell, same makers and mark as (B). Length 4¾ ins. *Clement Collection, Brooklyn Museum.*

(D) Cauliflower teapot, "Etruscan majolica", made 1879–90 at Phoenixville, Pennsylvania, by Griffen, Smith & Hill. Height 5¼ ins. *Clement Collection, Brooklyn Museum.*

PLATE 314

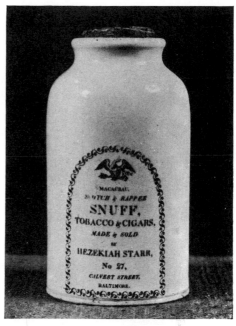

(A) Blue-printed creamware jar for snuff, and its mark: CLEWS'S MANUFACTURER'S. Made 1837–8 by the Indiana Pottery Co. (James Clews) at Troy, Indiana. *George William Bierce.*

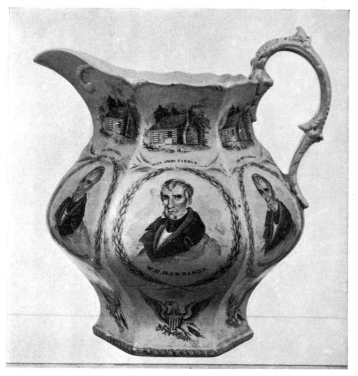

(B) Black-printed memorial jug, William Henry Harrison; made 1841 at Jersey City by the American Pottery Manufacturing Co. Height 10½ ins. *Formerly Collection of Alfred B. Maclay, Parke-Bernet Galleries.*

PLATE 315

(B) Toby jugs: the smaller one made 1852–8 at Bennington, Vermont, and the larger one 1838–45 at the Salamander Works at Woodbridge, New Jersey. Height 6½ and 12¾ ins. *Los Angeles County Museum.*

(A) Hot-water urn with pewter spigot, brown glaze flecked with green and blue, orange and yellow. Mark: FENTON'S ENAMEL / PATENTED 1849 / BENNINGTON v^t. Height 20¼ ins. *Bennington Museum.*

(C) The Bennington Lion, brilliant flint enamel and sanded or "Cole-slaw" mane, made 1851–2 and showing 1849 mark. Base 6 × 11 ins. Height 7¼ ins. *Bennington Museum.*

PLATE 316

(A) Bisque porcelain pitcher "The Poets", glazed interior with
leafage in gold and red; modelled in 1876 by Karl Müller,
marks of UNION PORCELAIN WORKS/GREENPOINT, N.Y. Height
7¾ ins. *Verna Ruth Quattlebaum.*

(B) Daisy and Tulip jug, raised mark FENTON'S
WORKS / BENNINGTON, VERMONT, made 1847–8.
Height 8 ins. *Formerly Collection of Alfred B. Maclay,
Parke-Bernet Galleries.*

(C) "Charter Oak" jug, white porcelain with
blue pitted ground, U.S.P. ribbon-mark, made
c. 1853 at Bennington by the United States
Pottery Co. *Formerly Collection of Alfred B. Maclay,
Parke-Bernet Galleries.*

PLATE 317

(A) Dam and Waterworks at Fairmount, and Old Schuylkill Bridge,
brown-painted *c.* 1827 by William Ellis Tucker, Philadelphia. Plate
Diameter 6¼ ins. *Mr and Mrs Arthur J. Sussel.*

(B and C) Tucker mug of the Hemphill period, about 1835, richly coloured view titled *Baltimore* and
gold scroll-work. Height 3⅝ ins. *Mr and Mrs Murray Braunfeld.*

PLATE 318

(A) "The Tucker Masterpiece", porcelain vase in salmon
and gold with colours, gilt-bronze handles. Made 1835
by Thomas Tucker. Height 21 ins. *Philadelphia Museum
of Art.*

Photo: Antiques.

(B) John Quincy Adams, Andrew Jackson, James Monroe, John Adams,
James Madison, portraits on violet-grey ground with wreath-moulded foot.
Tucker porcelain, 1835–8. *Formerly Collection of C. W. Lyon.*

PLATE 319

Painted earthenware. Han dynasty (206 B.C.–A.D. 220). *John Sparks Ltd.*

PLATE 320

decoration was by the use of diluted clay or "slip", which form a cup fitted with one or several quills was trailed on the surface of a piece in flourishes or perhaps words like *Lemon Pie*, names like *Louisa*. Made by George Wolfkiel at Hackensack, New Jersey, during the panic of 1837, were slipware platters woefully inscribed *Hard Times in Jersey*.

For such, a slab of clay was flattened with the wooden beater (one of them shows a beautifully worn and polished thumbprint) and smoothed like piecrust with a wooden rolling pin. When half-dried, the raised lines of slip would be pressed into the soft or "green" surface of the unfired dish, its edge would be trimmed and then notched with a wooden coggle-wheel.

Far more ambitious was *sgraffiato* (scratched) ornament, for which redware was thinly coated with cream-colour slip and this cut through to expose the darker body. Plates often showed a border inscription written with a sharp tool, and parts of the design might be enhanced with added colours (Plate 307B). Widely known in European peasant pottery, this technique was a favourite of the Pennsylvania-Germans from perhaps 1733 (a shaving basin, p. 197 in Barber's *Tulip Ware*) and furnishes surely the most decorative examples in American redware.

STONEWARE

The family of stonewares, a varied company, was made of finer and denser clays and fired in a kiln much hotter than for earthenware (above 2,000° F.), resulting in a hard body for which "no other glazing need be used than what is produced by a little common salt strewed over the ware" (1785). The salt vapour supplied a roughish, glassy coating that was colourless. According to the clays used and the temperature of the kiln, wares ranged from the familiar grey body to buff or cream, even a dark brown.

Fine grades of stoneware approached the quality of porcelain, such as the "white stone Tea-cups and sawcers" (thin-bodied white Staffordshire, later with scratch-blue decoration) sold 1724 in Boston, or the "Basketwork't plates" (of saltglaze with embossed and pierced lattice borders) which arrived from England in 1758 and 1764. Next century a middle grade of "figured stone pitchers" and Toby jugs of "superior stone" in buff and brown earned praise and awards in 1829–30 for David Henderson of Jersey City

The popular class of stonewares considered here were chiefly utility articles: common crocks, jugs, or churns, along with other things made for amusement, such as whistles and money-banks, bird or animal figures. Most of it was grey ware, and after about 1800 the vessels were usually coated inside with brown Albany slip.

The favourite decoration was freehand painting in cobalt blue, or rarely brown. Initials and dates, birds or flowers and scrolls, might be emphasized with scratched lines or die-stamped flowerets (Plate 305A), though after about 1850 stencilled designs were widely used (Plate 305D).

Many redware potters made stoneware also, and from *c.* 1800 often marked their work with a die-stamped name and perhaps the place. But later than 1850 and especially in the mid-west, crocks might show the name not of their maker but of some wholesaler to whom they were supplied.

Stoneware was developed because of fear of poison from lead-glazed wares. "Preceding the glorious Revolution", said a long notice in the *Pennsylvania Mercury* on February 4, 1785, "here and there, were a few scattered Potteries of Earthen-Ware, infamously bad and unwholesome, from their being partially glazed with a thin, cheap washing of Lead." This lead glaze, attacked by acid foods, "becomes a slow but sure poison, chiefly affecting the Nerves, that enfeebles the constitution, and produce paleness, tremors, gripes, palsies, &c." It was hinted that the Legislature should enact "discountenancing the use of Lead in glazing Earthen-ware", and further that "a small bounty, or exemption" might encourage stoneware potters.

Whatever justice there was in this alarm, it had long been discussed among potters. The apocryphal date 1722 appears on a large open-mouthed stoneware jar (Robert J. Sim, *Some Vanishing Phases of Rural Life in New Jersey*, p. 43). At least we have seen "the first stoneware kiln or furnace" erected 1730 near the Collect Pond in New York, by William Crolyas (Crolius). And we have heard Anthony Duché that same year claiming to have made stoneware "for severall Years past" in Philadelphia. Others soon sought to learn the mystery.

Isaac Parker of Charlestown (Boston) was one of these, a redware maker who eagerly sent for a man "trained in the stoneware potter's art". What arrived in Boston on July 14, 1742, aboard the brigantine *Mary* (Watkins, *Early New England Potters*, pp. 35–8) was James, son of Anthony Duché and brother of Andrew the porcelain maker. Two months later, Parker could report to the General Court that he had "now" learned the secret of stoneware making. Parker died forthwith; but by December 1742 his widow Grace with James Duché as co-partner was granted a fifteen-year monopoly, and in April 1745 their firm (called Thomas Symmes & Co.) advertised "blue and white stone ware of forty different kinds". Duché disappeared next year, probably returned to Philadelphia, and death in 1754 released Mrs Parker from a failing enterprise.

Nor was the failure surprising, since New England afforded no stoneware clay and was put to the expense of getting it from New York. Indeed, the major source of supply for all American stoneware was for many years the rich deposit of fine blue-clay centred at South Amboy, New Jersey, and extending to Staten Island and Long Island.

From this bed Adam Staats, a potter of Horse Neck (Greenwich), Connecticut, dug clay in 1751, on a five-year lease between "the Said adam States" and the town trustees of Huntingdon, Long Island. He knew its qualities, having worked at Cheesequake or "Chesquick" Creek (South Amboy) before appearing in 1743 in New York.

With seemingly one exception, other early stoneware makers, if not in the locality, were at least within easy range of the New Jersey blue-clay beds. This exception occurred far south, where the Moravians at Salem, North Carolina, burnt their first kiln of stoneware (according to Brother Aust's diary) in May 1774, instructed by an English journeyman

potter William Ellis, who came the year before from Pine Tree "where he had been working". At this inaccessibly inland town local clays must have answered.

Naturally, these opening years of the Revolution saw vigorous increase in stoneware potting. First by a boycott to express political discontent, and then by war itself, the domestic market was largely cut off from its accustomed foreign sources of supply, the Thames side potteries at Fulham and Lambeth, and the furnaces of the Rhine Valley.

Blue-painted grey stoneware shards carrying the dates 1775 and 1776 (*Antiques*, March 1944, pp. 122–5) have been found along Cheesequake Creek, presumably from a pottery operated by General James Morgan, who in 1779 filed a claim for "a kiln of Stoneware not burnt" that British soldiers had destroyed. Also dated 1775, *July* 18/*JC* is a stoneware jug (Metropolitan Museum) from the New York factory of William Crolius II. By 1778 a certain Bernard Hamlen advertised for return of a horse strayed from his "Stoneware Potting Manufactory at Trenton" (Clement, *Our Pioneer Potters*, p. 20).

By a potter who sometimes stamped his ware *C.Crolius Manhattan-Wells* and was working by 1794 (Plate 305A) is a brownish stoneware batter jug with die-stamped blue flowerets and leaves, scratched: *New York, Feby 17th 1798/Flowered by Clarkson Crolius/Blue*. The New York Historical Society, its owner, also possesses the maker's actual stamp and other tools. This was Clarkson, Sr (1773–1843), a grandson of William "Crolyas", the stoneware potter of 1730. Clement, *Our Pioneer Potters*, reviews (pp. 21–5) the complicated record of the Crolius dynasty (fifteen potters in all) who worked in New York until *c.* 1870 when Clarkson, Jr retired.

The first Corlius and one "Johannes Remmi" or de Remy (John Remmey I) married the Cornelius sisters, Veronica and Anna. But a supposed business partnership of Remmey & Crolius in 1742–4 finds no supporting records. The Remmeys followed their separate way from 1735 until today. When the New York factory failed in 1819–20 one great grandson continued at South Amboy until 1833; another had gone to Philadelphia about 1810, where (with a side venture at Baltimore from 1818 to *c.* 1835) the firm is still established.

A reason is easily seen for the flurry of new stoneware factories that appeared around 1805. From 1804 to 1812 the seizure and impressment of ten thousand American seamen into the British Navy led to a series of Congressional Acts (1806–9) that prohibited trade with England. With the Embargo Act of 1807 (one of the causes of the War of 1812) imports dropped to one-third, and American potters had to supply a domestic market cut off from foreign sources.

Xerxes Price, who stamped his jars *XP*, was working at Sayreville (South Amboy) as early as 1802 and until 1830. Peter Cross, whose mark was *P.Cross/Hartford*, appeared 1805 to *c.* 1818 in Connecticut. Samuel Wetmore in 1805 began the enterprise at Huntington, Long Island, that later would become Brown Brothers (Plate 305D). And from an unidentified maker (Watkins, *New England Potters*, p. 83) came sober brown-stained jars with "*BOSTON.1804.*" impressed (Plate 305B).

In Albany the able Paul Cushman from 1809 to 1832 made both redware and stoneware, on the hill "a half mile west of Albany Gaol". Not far east was Bennington, Vermont where Captain John Norton in 1793 had started a potworks continued by the family for a century, until 1894. By tradition, stoneware was made here in 1800; in 1810 wagons were fetching clay across the hills from Troy, and in January 1815 the diary of Hiram Harwood says the Nortons "were making ware of both kinds, stone and clay" (Spargo, *Potters of Bennington*, pp. 9, 11–13). But the flourishing period was from 1828 to 1832, when the proprietors had begun to use clays from South Amboy and Long Island.

In the Ohio country the earliest recorded stoneware potter was Joseph Rosier, working by 1814 near Zanesville; but by 1840 (says John Ramsay) there were more than fifty such potters through the area. Excellent clays were here in plenty, and potters of all sorts were attracted to the mid-west. East Liverpool with its fine Ohio River clays was to overtake northern New Jersey, which itself has been called "the Staffordshire of America".

By this time stonewares were a factory-made product that devoted less attention to form, more to decoration. Typical are a 4-gallon crock made in 1850–68 by Edmands & Co. (Plate 305C *left*) and the grey churn made in 1850–70 in the State of New York (Plate 305C *right*), a freely drawn, blue-painted deer on one, a whimsical bird on the other. Still later the decorations might be stencilled, to save labour, as in the case of the eagle of Plate 305D, in which is also seen the cylindrical shape much used for crocks after the mid-nineteenth century.

Government reports for 1900 showed an American output of stonewares valued at $1,800,000, but of redwares only $400,000 (Ramsay, p. 18), and the latter mostly from Ohio and Pennsylvania. The old order of work was indeed disappearing.

SOME BETTER WARES

In between the common grades of work, on one hand, and porcelains, on the other, American potters made constant boast of producing wares "allowed by the nicest judges to exceed any imported from England". These were always "on the very lowest Terms" – terms that were often based not on cash but barter, and perhaps "the potter will take in Pay, pork, tar, wheat, corn or tobacco" (Maryland, 1756). Though claiming so much, theirs were mostly small and experimental ventures, poorly financed and showing a high mortality rate. Edward Rumney in July 1746 bravely undertook "to sett up a Pottery" at Annapolis, having "furnished himself with Persons exceedingly well skilled (in the making of) all sorts of Potts, Pans, Juggs, muggs &c." Within four months his business was already offered at public vendue, even "two Potters and several Horses". A more ambitious project was that Factory in New Boston which advertised in October 1769 "for Apprentices to learn the Art of making Tortoiseshell, Cream and Green-coloured Plates" (or Queensware and so-called green-edge Leeds). After this solitary notice, only silence. From the dismal number of such failures, Lord Sheffield's *Observations on the Commerce of the United States* (1791) seems not too prejudiced in saying: "Manufactures of glass, of earthenware, and of stone mixed with clay, are all in an infant state." Yet across this fairly cheerless scene moved many potters of sound experience. Who were these lost men? Some are known only from one passing mention in early records, or for a solitary example of ware "said to be" by John Doe, a potter. Unlike the silversmiths, who were often men of public consequence, potters enjoyed relatively slight notice.

And where are their products, of which enormous amounts once existed? How to account for the total disappearance of examples from our first whiteware furnace (1688–92 at Burlington, New Jersey), where Dr Daniel Coxe said his agents made "a great quantity of White and Chiney ware"? What has become of all the "Pennsylvania *pencil'd* bowls and sugar dishes" praised for their "beauty of colours and elegance of figures", the work of Alexander Bartram who "has got a Pot-house" in Philadelphia and advertised 1767–73? Where is one specimen of "General Washington's bust, ditto in Medallions, several images part of them not finished", which in 1784 were offered at the sale of Jeremiah Warder's kilns in the North Liberties (Philadelphia)?

An answer might be that because American work of the better grades must compete with the imported, it attempted close imitation, and nowadays the American ware (so seldom marked, until after 1800) languishes unrecognized, mistaken for English. Thomas Baker who advertised 1756 in St Mary's County, Maryland, was only one who made "ware of the same kind as imported from Liverpool, or made in Philadelphia".

In their day the "compleat Setts of Bluechina, Enamuel'd ditto" shown in the Boston imports lists of 1737 probably had no equal here. But the "new fashion'd Turtle-shell Tereens" of Whieldon's ware (1754) were soon copied by colonial potters. The same were described as "Tortorise-ware" in Boston and New York lists of 1771, along with other Whieldon-Wedgwood types such as "Colly flower, Mellon, Pine-apple, Aggitt". Also in 1771 came "Queen's Ware" to Boston, the "Plain Cream-colour" to New York.

Creamware

Nothing approached the popularity of creamware, or lasted longer. Its inventor

Josiah Wedgwood called this (1767) "the Cream colour, alias Queensware, alias Ivory".

John Bartlem or Bartlam ("one of our insolvent master potters", complained Wedgwood in 1765, who was hiring hands to go to his "new Pottworks in South Carolina") was producing creamware by 1771 at Charleston. Messrs Bartlam & Co. in October 1770 had opened a manufactory on Meeting-street, "the proper Hands &c. for carrying it on having lately arrived here from England". Three months later it "already makes what is called Queen's Ware, equal to any imported". But a grant of £500 from the Assembly did not save it from disastrous labour troubles.

William Ellis, one of the Bartlam workmen, appeared in December 1773 at Salem, North Carolina, where Brother Aust's diary said "he understands how to glaze and burn Queens Ware". The Moravians built a suitable kiln, and the following May "Ellis made a burning of Queensware". He departed the same year and in 1783 Wedgwood referred to this Ellis as now "of Hanley" (Staffordshire), calling him the sole survivor of Bartlam's enterprise.

Philadelphia became the centre of creamware manufacture. Here in 1792 the Pennsylvania Society for Encouragement of Manufactures and the Useful Arts offered a $50 prize for specimens "approaching nearest to queen's-ware". John Curtis, having dissolved the partnership of Curtis & Roat in July 1790, continued with "the cream-color'd" from 1791 to 1811 at his Pottery-Ware Manufactory in Front Street, Southwark. Three others soon appeared: Alexander Trotter (who in 1809 had "lately established a Queens-ware pottery on an extensive scale"; the Columbian Pottery); Daniel Freytag (maker in 1810–11 of a "fine earthenware, the paste resembling queen's-ware"); and David G. Seixas (producing from 1816 a cream-colour "similar to the Liverpool").

In New York "a new Cream Ware Manufactory" was established in 1798 at Red Hook Landing, where J. Mouchet made Tivoli Ware "with colored edges". Nor had Alexander Trotter retired in 1812–13 (Spargo, p. 180), but reappeared 1815 in Pittsburgh, with Trotter & Co. advertising "Queensware similar to the Philadelphia".

The undiminishing popularity of this ware is reflected (*American Collector*, June 1940, p. 11) by one item in a ship's list of 1827: "532 doz. ordinary quality dinner plates, cream colored or blue and green edges", in a shipment of mixed pottery from Liverpool to Portsmouth, New Hampshire.

Another decade later, the Staffordshire potter James Clews arrived in 1836 at Louisville, Kentucky, where creamware had been made since 1830 by the Lewis Pottery Co. With the backing of Vodrey & Lewis, Clews built a large factory downriver at Troy, Indiana, and the first kiln of the new Indiana Pottery Co. was fired in June 1837. A blue-printed snuff jar seen here (Plate 315A) with the mark *Clews's Manufacturer's* is a good sample of the ware made here only in 1837–8, Clews then returning to England because the local clays proved disappointing.

After that time, fine creamware was scarcely heard of, though poor and coarser wares of cream or ivory colour were widely made, e.g. the "attempts at cream colored" reported 1850–1900 at the Shaker colony in Amana, Iowa. The Bennett Pottery might be listed in 1847 in the Pittsburgh directory as "makers of domestic Queensware", but through the Ohio country this name was understood to mean a cream-bodied earthenware with rich brown glaze.

Rockingham

This was the common utility ware made by everyone from the 1840s to 1900, a yellow-ware dappled or streaked with lustrous manganese brown glaze. Its quality ranged from coarse splattered yellow to a rich brown tortoise-shell, and this ware was used for every sort of article, doorknobs or pudding pans, hound-handled jugs or lamp bases, cuspidors or picture frames.

Little was marked, and "Bennington" as a generic name is wrongly applied to wares the bulk of which were made elsewhere, principally at East Liverpool and down the Ohio River, or by the Bennetts of Pittsburgh and Baltimore, by a hundred factories large and small. At Bennington Julius Norton first made Rockingham or "flint" glaze (as it was generally called) in 1841. Henderson had produced

it in 1829: "Flint Ware both embossed and plain", in what the New York *Commercial Advertiser* called "elegant pitchers . . . in a new style [which] if not too cheap will be accounted handsome".

As an improvement on quiet brown Rockingham, a brilliant glaze flecked and streaked with colours was patented by Lyman, Fenton & Co. in November 1849 and examples carried a special *Fenton's Enamel* mark (Spargo, *The A.B.C.*, p. 21, mark D). Oddly, this *1849* mark is found also on common Rockingham, or even on white Parian, and continued in use all through the U.S. Pottery Co. period (1853–8).

This colour-flecked glaze was not new; Fenton's patent referred only to a way of producing it with powdered colours. If an urn (Plate 316A) and the famous lion (Plate 316c) are examples of the best Bennington work, Fenton's enamel was widely pirated, being produced at East Liverpool as early as 1852 (Ramsay, p. 76). Pairs of Bennington lions in plain Rockingham or *1849* enamel, made with or without the platform and showing either a curly or the sanded "cole-slaw" mane, appeared 1851–2 and are attributed to Daniel Greatbach, though he did not arrive at Bennington until December 1851 or January 1852, remaining as chief modeller until the factory closed (Spargo, *Bennington Potters*, pp. 227–8).

PRINTED WARES

Doubtless because the Staffordshire and Liverpool makers supplied such a torrent of cheap and attractive printed pottery, in an endless range of patterns and colours, the development of printed wares made scarcely a beginning here. True, a "rolling press, for copper-plate printing; and other articles *made use of* in the China Factory" were advertised August 1774 when the Bonnin & Morris properties were offered. Apparently it was their intention to produce Worcester-type porcelains with printed blue decoration, but no examples are known today, if indeed they were made at all.

Not until 1839–43 are American-made subjects encountered (Clement, *Our Pioneer Potters*, Plates 10–13; the same as Nos. 128–32 in

Newark Museum catalogue *Pottery and Porcelain of New Jersey*), all four from the Henderson works, which since 1833 had been called the American Pottery Manufacturing Co.

In 1839 the pattern *Canova* was printed in light blue, cribbed from a design by John Ridgway of Hanley. The United States eagle and shield occurs on 6½-inch jugs also in light blue. In transfer print with added colours, the *Landing of Gen-Lafayette/at Castle Garden, New-York/16th August 1824* is seen on a larger jug and footed punchbowl at the New York Historical Society, the same jug with a 15½-inch oval cistern appearing No. 243 in the Van Sweringen sale of 1938 at Parke-Bernet Galleries. In *Antiques*, May 1931, p. 361, this view is assigned to 1843, when historic Castle Garden (formerly Fort Clinton) was leased to Christopher Heiser.

Pictured here (Plate 315B) is a black-printed W. H. Harrison memorial jug made in 1841, when the ninth president died after one month in the White House. Below the repeated portraits of Harrison (from the J. R. Lambdin portrait, engraved by R. W. Dodson and published 1836) is shown the American eagle; above is the "log cabin" symbol of the Harrison-Tyler presidential campaign, with *The Ohio Farmer*. When the same subject was issued a year before, during that campaign against the New York aristocrat Martin Van Brenu, the log cabin was lettered *To Let in 1841*.

The cabin so lettered, and the portrait entitled *Harrison & Reform*, occur on Staffordshire tea ware or copper-lustred mugs, the former marked *Manufactured/for Robt H. Miller/ALEXANDRIA. D.C.*, an importer who advertised October 30, 1840, that he was expecting "supplies of ware with Harrison and Log Cabin engravings, from designs sent out to the Potteries by himself" (*Antiques*, June 1944, p. 295, and February 1945, p. 120).

The Henderson jug carries a black-printed mark AM. POTTERY/MANUF^G C^O/JERSEY CITY, and for it (says Lura W. Watkins) "printing plates were executed by Thomas Pollock, an American engraver".

Slightly earlier (1837–8) is a blue-printed creamware jar for snuff (Plate 315A) made to order of Hezekiah Starr, a tobacconist at No.

27 Calvert Street, Baltimore. Its mark *Clews's Manufacturer's* is also pictured.

James Clews the English potter had a factory at Cobridge (Burslem) which "was noted for its cream-colored ware" in the 1820s, but to American collectors is chiefly known as a source of transfer-printed pottery showing American-historical views. When the J. & R. Clews factory closed in 1836, James (c. 1786–1856) came to America and at Louisville, Kentucky, found the firm Vodrey & Lewis, makers of creamware since 1829.

Clews, being "a man of fine presence and a fluent talker", persuaded Jacob Lewis and others to back him; the Louisville factory was closed, and a new Indiana Pottery Company established in January 1837 across the river at Troy, Indiana. Neither the workmen nor the Ohio River Valley clays suited him, and after disappointing efforts to make creamware in 1837–8 he returned to England. The factory under various proprietors made yellow and Rockingham wares until finally demolished in 1875.

Our pot for *Macabau, Scotch & Rappee SNUFF* (Plate 315A) is probably not unlike those creamware "pickle, pomatum & druggist pots" made in 1798 by J. Mouchet in New York. Another nearer its own time and area is the 10-inch brown-glazed jar, also found in Indiana, made for the tobacconist H. Thayer and carrying the mark of a Cincinnati maker *Franklin Factory/1834/S.Quigley/S.Quigley* (*Antiques*, August 1928, p. 162).

Only one more example of American printed ware deserves mention, a late blue platter, *Pickett's Charge, Gettysburg* (Ramsay, Fig. 86), with oak-leaf border picturing four generals who served that day in July 1863. Its blue eagle mark is for Edwin Bennett of Baltimore, who worked in 1841 at East Liverpool with his brother James (he was formerly with Clews at Troy) and from 1846 operated his own factory in Baltimore. His *Pickett's Charge* appeared in 1870 and was re-issued in 1901.

LATE WARES

It might be felt that Rogers Groups (Plate 314A) have no place here, being not of fired clay but plaster casts taken from clay models. But in their day these enormously popular figure groups were fondly accepted as ceramic sculpture, an "Art" expression that filled bare space in the Victorian parlour. And indeed they exerted a large influence upon potters who then produced Parian or other figure work.

John Rogers (1829–1904) created his patented story-telling groups in New York, from 1859 to 1893. Cast in reddish plaster and painted a sad putty colour, these low-priced groups were issued in vast editions, in 1886 *The Elder's Daughter* (Plate 314A) "weight 100 lbs packed, price $12". If sentimental, obvious, and sometimes silly, the subjects were well modelled; and their themes were from the Civil War, from domestic life of the time, or popular legends. Collections may now be studied at the New York Historical Society and at the Essex Institute, Salem.

Majolica

During this same period, a new pottery called majolica won wide favour; a coarse earthen body with coloured lead glazes, it appeared in useful wares, leaf-shaped dishes, and ornamental work of every description. In 1851 Minton had exhibited majolica at the Crystal Palace, and Wedgwood was producing it by 1860. Meanwhile, American potters adopted it; Edwin Bennett by 1853 at Baltimore, and Carr & Morrison of New York in 1853–5. In the 1880s it was a staple of potters everywhere, from the Hampshire Pottery (James Taft's) at Keene, New Hampshire, to the Bennett and Morley firms in East Liverpool. Best known is Etruscan majolica, made in 1879–90 by Griffen, Smith & Hill at Phoenixville, Chester County, Pennsylvania.

An excellent example of Etruscan majolica (Plate 314D) shows surprising likeness to the "Colly flower tea potts" imported a century earlier (Boston, 1771). Developed in 1754–9 by Wedgwood when a junior partner to Whieldon, cauliflower ware had a vogue in 1760–80. The match for our later teapot is seen in the Burnap Collection (No. 320, catalogue, 1953, the Nelson-Atkins Gallery of Art, Kansas City, Mo.). According to John Ramsay, "the first cauliflower teapot" was made by James Carr in New York, Dr Barber adding that Carr & Morrison (1853–88) only made majolica "for a period of about two years", 1853–5.

PORCELAIN

Allowance must always be made for the extravagant claims constantly offered by struggling potters who nervously looked for support. Small enterprises might make the loudest noise, asserting that they operated a China Manufactory and calling their ware porcelain, though they did not possess the requisite materials. Even if they did, it was one thing to know how, but another to produce a successful china.

The early "pottery att Burlington for white and chiney ware" (1688–92) surely achieved no more than white tin-glazed delftware. Indeed, England herself had done no better at that time. Half a century must pass before porcelains of even an experimental grade were actually made here.

The ideal, of course, was true hard-paste porcelain like the Chinese, with which all potters had long been well familiar. This was the ware always preferred by fashionable and wealthy persons, who bought so much of it that by 1754 the General Court of Massachusetts passed an Act placing special excise on "East-India Ware, called China-ware".

It should be noted that in August 1738 samples of this Chinese ware were sent by the Earl of Egmont (most active of the Trustees of the colony of Georgia) to a certain master potter in Savannah. These samples were to serve as models for one Andrew Duché, already mentioned, first of the three pre-Revolutionary porcelain makers.

Duché (sometimes Duchee, Deshee, Deusha) was third son of the stoneware potter Antoine (Anthony) Duché. Born in 1710 in Philadelphia, he married twice in 1731, worked first at Charleston (1731–5) and then at New Windsor (1735–7) across the river from Augusta, finally at Savannah (1738–43), where he had been assured that "all reasonable encouragement" would be given him by General James Oglethorpe, founder (1733) of the colony of Georgia. Indeed, he received a grant of £230 and built a pottery, where (say local records of 1743) he "found out the secret to make as good porcelain as is made in China".

Of his output, the "one or two specimens in the United States" mentioned by George Savage (*18th-Century English Porcelains*, p. 149) are pictured here (Plates 307A, 312). The late Mr Hommel and Mrs Gilmer have published extensive notes on Duché, the subject of happy excitement in research circles; and a further hoard of unpublished facts, graciously made available by Mrs Gilmer, might have assisted persons sceptical of Duché's true achievements.

As for his porcelains, Oglethorpe in 1738 already reported to the Trustees that Duché had found "an earth" (kaolin, china-clay) and baked it into china. By February in the next year he had discovered "a whole mountain of stone" (petuntze?) in the Salzburger area, near Ebenezer; and in 1740 Duché found "a quarry of Ironstone" on the five-acre lot of William Gough. For while conducting his experiments to perfect porcelain, Duché supplied the vicinity with useful articles of common earthenware or ironstone, and stove-tiles for the settlement forty miles inland.

On March 17, 1738, he had requested of the Trustees "two ingenious pot painters", and special supplies including "a Tun weight of Pig lead, 200 wt of blew smalt such as potters use, 300 wt of block Tin, and an Iron Mortar & pestle". The wanted materials (though skimped in their amounts) were sent him in August, and the "two servants" came in July 1739 on the ship *Two Brothers*. Duché here had all the requirements for blue-decorated porcelain, and skilled helpers to finish it.

Found in 1946 at Charleston, his unique bowl (Plate 312) is heavy for its size, slightly translucent but not resonant. Thanks to the Earl of Egmont's samples, its blue decoration resembles Chinese work but employs a local vernacular, with a band border of white oak leaves, a calyx of slim fern fronds below. If it bears no mark, Mrs Gilmer rightly asserts it is "marked" all over. This bowl of experimental grade is just such as Duché would produce

from the materials he had and working under the particular conditions.

The story of his after years belongs not here so much as in English accounts of porcelain making. Drawn into political squabbles, Duché came into disagreement with Colonel William Stephens, who was secretary to the Trustees; ostensibly to plead the cause of the dissatisfied settlers, he left Savannah in March 1743 and appeared in London by May the next year.

Our concern with him centres on his contact with the proprietors of the Bow factory, Edward Heylin and Thomas Frye, who obtained the following December a patent for "invention of manufacturing a certain material, whereby a Ware may be made of the same material as China". Their secret (apparently communicated by Duché) was "an earth, the produce of the Chirokee nation in America, called by the natives *unaker*".

This same year, Duché waited upon William Cookworthy, who in a letter of May 1745 discusses "the person who has discovered the china earth, calling it *kaulin* and saying that the finder is going for a Cargo of it". Cookworthy has seen "several samples of the chinaware of their making", and understands that the requisite earth is to be found "on the back of Virginia".

What profitable arrangements were made by Duché? We hear no more of him as a potter. From 1750 to 1769 he is a "merchant" and prosperous landowner in Norfolk, Virginia. In 1769 he returned to Philadelphia, and here (described as a "gentleman") he died in 1778.

Much briefer is the account of a second porcelain maker, the elusive Samuel Bowen. In 1745 one Henry Gossman, aged eighteen, and "son of a very poor helpless widow of Purisburg, South Carolina" (a Swiss Huguenot settlement on the river above Savannah), was apprenticed or "bound to a potter". This would appear to be Samuel Bowen, now occupying the potworks vacated by Duché two years before.

Not until November 1764 did an English newspaper (the *Bristol Journal*) report that "This week, some pieces of porcelain manufactured in Georgia was imported", but added that "the workmanship is far from being admired". Two years later (says Alice Morse Earle) Samuel Bowen was awarded a gold medal from the English Society for the Encouragement of Arts, Manufactures, and Commerce "for his useful observations in china and industrious *application of them* in Georgia" (italics ours). Two years later, in March 1768, he was thanking the Georgia Commons "for the Benefits he had received by their Recommendation of him". Nothing further is known of Bowen.

Bonnin & Morris

Recovering quickly from the French and Indian Wars (the American phase of the Seven Years War, 1756–63), the colonies had enjoyed since mid-century a rising prosperity, an established society, and a higher standard of living. Philadelphia in 1770 was a rich and fashionable centre, likely to support a porcelain factory. "The China-Works now erecting in Southwark" (January 1, 1770) was "compleated, and in motion" the following July, and for just short of two years gave continual report in newspaper advertisements (Prime, *Arts & Crafts*, pp. 114–24).

The China Proprietors were Gouse Bonnin (from Antigua) and a Philadelphia Quaker named George Anthony Morris. The latter retired in April/May 1771 and removed to North Carolina, where he died two years later while Bonnin in November 1772 was sulkily "embarking for England without the least prospect of ever returning to this continent".

They were financed by a £500 advance from the father of Dr James Mease (Barber, pp. 98–100), who got nothing in return but a blue-painted dinner service, from which one broken basket in the Worcester manner is all that survives (Philadelphia Museum). This piece and four others, all with a factory-mark *P* in blue, were the "known" output of Bonnin & Morris as fully reported in *Antiques* for January 1944, pp. 14–16, September 1946, p. 166, September 1950, p. 199 and February 1951, p. 139. The teapot here (Plate 313A, B) is a later discovery.

From the evidence, their ware seems to have been a fine grade of white earthenware, though their "first Emission of Porcelain" was

announced in January 1771, and that same month in an appeal to the Assembly they described the "Manufacture of Porcelain or China Earthen Ware . . . a sample of it we respectfully submit". Indeed, they achieved a translucent porcelain (the example in *Antiques*, February 1951).

Their clay came from White Clay Creek, near Wilmington (Barber, p. 99) and they advertised in July 1770 for "any quantity of horses or beeves shank bones", implying the attempt to make bone-china. But in August 1772 Bonnin had "lately made experiments with some clay presented by a Gentleman of Charles Town, South-Carolina". Could this have been John Bartlam? Although a few years earlier, Richard Champion of Bristol had received (1765) a "box of porcelain-earth" from his brother-in-law Caleb Lloyd of Charleston. The firm's first notice (January 1770) had referred to "the famous factory in Bow, near London", as if this were their ideal.

In October 1770 "nine master workmen" arrived in Captain Osborne's ship. Three months later "a quantity of Zaffer or zaffera" was wanted, and by July the factory could supply "any Quantity of Blue and White Ware". As their agent, Archibald M'Elroy in Second-Street was exposing a "General Assortment of AMERICAN CHINA" in January 1771 and next September "both useful and ornamental Enamelled China". The factory in January 1772 needed "Painters, either in blue or enamel".

Only their blue-printed wares are recognized today, such as a finely modelled sweetmeat dish (Plate 313C) found in New Jersey, or a teapot (Plate 313A, B) with charming *chinoiserie* and large initials *WP*. This latter came from a Philadelphia Quaker family in which it had always been known as "the William Penn teapot", unaccountably, since the Proprietor was in his grave by 1718.

To the next name in American porcelains it is a leap of forty years. Mentioned in 1810 as "of New Haven", a certain "Henry Mead, physician" appeared in the New York directory for 1816–17. This was the alleged maker of a solitary all-white vase (Plate 19, Clement's *Own Pioneer Potters*) on the evidence of a paper label: *Finished in New York* 1816. A little late then, "In 1819 the manufacture of Porcelain ... was commenced in New York by Dr H.Mead" (J.Leander Bishop, *History of American Manufactures*). No less confusing, the doctor's obituary notice (1843) said that "he commenced at Jersey City".

Records are far more satisfactory for the Jersey Porcelain & Earthenware Company, established in December 1825, in Jersey City and sold in September 1828 to David Henderson. In 1826 this firm won a silver medal at the Franklin Institute, for the "best china from American materials", though what competition might they have had? Fragments of hard-paste porcelain have been unearthed on the factory site, and praise of a visitor to the factory in 1826 (Clement, p. 68) was for articles "either of white biscuit, or of white and gold in the French style". Dr Barber in 1902 described one gold-banded white bowl "made in 1826", then in the Trumbull-Prime collection at Princeton but now lost.

Tucker porcelain

Coming now to the first really successful chinaworks, we need little more than to correct and abbreviate the oft-told accounts of that well-documented Philadelphia enterprise of 1826–38, Tucker porcelains. More than

FIG. 1. Tucker porcelain

half a century ago, Dr Barber devoted a chapter (pp. 126–53) to these well appreciated wares, *Antiques*, June 1828, pp. 480–4, adding further reports.

Born of a prosperous Quaker family, William Ellis Tucker (1800–32) began in 1826 his earnest experiments in porcelain making, at the Old Water-Works building in Philadelphia. That year he bought (in brief partnership with one John Bird) a property near Wilmington, Delaware, that yielded feldspar, and another at "Mutton Hollow in the state of New Jersey" that provided kaolin or blueclay. In 1827 his porcelains won a silver medal at the 4th Franklin Institute exhibition, and in 1828 another, for ware comparing with "the best specimens of French China".

Examples of his earlier work are three pieces *c.* 1827 (Plate 318A) with painted scenes not in the familiar sepia, but darker brown. A cup showing the *Dam and Waterworks at Fairmount* is apparently after the Thomas Birch drawing published 1824 (the same used on blue-printed Staffordshire pottery of 1825–30, Nos. 249–50 and 535–6 in Mrs Larsen's book). Seen here on a plate and cup, the *Old Schuylkill Bridge* occurs also on a cordate scent bottle owned by a Tucker descendant (*Antiques*, October 1936, p. 167). Again the subject (Plate 310B) is used on blue Staffordshire and in very rich taste was employed on a Hemphill jug of about 1835 (*Antiques*, June 1928, p. 481).

In 1828 a younger brother, Thomas Tucker (born 1812), became an apprentice, and William himself formed a partnership (1828–9) with John Hulme, as Tucker & Hulme. From this time came a large tea service factory-marked and dated 1828 (*Antiques*, October 1933, p. 134) with typical "spider" border in gold, wrongly said to enjoy "the distinction of being the first *complete sett* of china manufactured in this country".

In 1831 Tucker established still another partnership, Tucker & Hemphill (with Alexander Hemphill), and that year his porcelains won a silver medal at the American Institute, New York. William Tucker died in 1832, and from 1833 to 1836 the factory was continued by Alexander's father, Judge Joseph Hemphill, with Thomas Tucker as manager. The Hemphill period displayed rich taste, with enamel painting in Sèvres style and a lavish use of gold. Its masterpeice was a large vase (Plate 319A) made in 1835 by Thomas Tucker, the gilt-bronze handles designed by Friedrich Sachse and cast by C.Cornelius & Sons of Philadelphia.

The first quality of work about 1835 is seen (Plate 318B, C) in a mug with gold scrollwork and coloured scene entitled *Baltimore* in black script underfoot. Five cups from a set of *Presidents* (Plate 319B) must be dated towards the factory's close, since Jackson's portrait is from the *National Portrait Gallery of Distinguished Americans*, published in 1834–6. Judge Hemphill retired in 1837, and Thomas Tucker rented the factory a year, closing it in 1838.

After a curious lapse of a decade, when porcelains were wholly neglected, five factories deserve notice as producers of such ware on a commercial scale.

Bennington

In 1843 Julius Norton, a Vermont potter, brought from England one John Harrison, a modeller at the Copeland works, where the year before a waxy white porcelain called Parian or Statuary Ware had been perfected (*see* Glossary). Harrison's experiments from October 1843 to mid-1845 were interrupted by a disastrous fire, and he returned to Stoke. During 1845–7 the firm of Norton & Fenton set this work aside; but from 1847 to 1850 the reorganized Lyman & Fenton was producing successful white wares, including Parian. An example is the Daisy jug (Plate 317B) in white porcelain, showing the Fenton's Works mark of 1847–8, though variants of this design continued for some years.

With new financing and expansion in 1851–2, Christopher Webber Fenton developed blue-and-white porcelains (Plate 317C) or rarely tan, still rarer the green-and-white. Much work was unsigned, but the familiar *U.S.P.* ribbon-mark of the United States Pottery Co. (1853–8) is found "principally upon porcelain pitchers and vases, both the white and blue-and-white, and upon some Parian pieces" (Spargo, *The A.B.C.*, p. 19).

From the latter years of the factory, which closed in 1858, came whole dinner or tea services of heavy, gold-banded porcelain (Spargo, *Potters of Bennington*, Plate XXVII). Kaolin had been obtained from Monkton, Vermont. Pitchers displayed at the Crystal Palace exhibition in New York (1853–4) were "made of the flint from Vermont and Massachusetts, the feldspar from New Hampshire, and the china clays from Vermont and South Carolina".

Greenpoint

First of two factories at Greenpoint (now Brooklyn) was Charles Cartlidge & Co., operating 1848–56. The proprietor was a Staffordshire (Burslem) man, who at once brought over his brother-in-law Josiah Jones to model "biscuit busts of celebrated Americans". A 9-inch likeness of General Zachary Taylor in 1848 (Barber, pp. 446–7) was followed by Daniel Webster, John Marshall, and others, in what the firm always described as bisque porcelain. From buttons and cameos the firm's output ranged to inkstands and chessmen, cane heads and endless other novelties, which at the Crystal Palace in 1858 won a silver medal "for the excellence of the porcelain body and the gilding".

Second of the Greenpoint enterprises was that of William Boch & Brother, founded 1850, which exhibited at the Crystal Palace as makers of door hardware and bone-china table goods. Thomas Carl Smith, who became manager in 1857, acquired the shaky business in 1861, reopened it as the Union Porcelain Works in 1862, and by 1864–5 had changed over to hard-paste porcelain.

Karl Müller came to the factory in 1874, as chief designer and modeller, creating many once-famous subjects eyed nowadays with disfavour, and others of quality and virtue; among the latter was a bisque porcelain pitcher *The Poets* (Plate 317A), which in 1876 was a presentation piece to E. J. Brockett. Finely moulded heads of Milton, Ossian, Shakspeare (*sic*), Dante, Homer, and Virgil are seen with trophies and allegorical figures above and below. To the red-painted factory mark is added an impressed (later, printed) bird's head, the symbol adopted in 1876.

Other porcelain

Of minor importance is the Southern Porcelain Manufacturing Co., established in 1856 at Kaolin, South Carolina by William H. Farrar, who had been a Bennington stockholder. Numerous potters followed him here, the modeller Josiah Jones as manager in 1857, when the Cartlidge factory closed, and next year (when Bennington also failed), Fenton was there briefly on his way to Peoria, Illinois, where he built an unsuccessful works. Until fire destroyed the factory in 1863-4 only "a fair porcelain" was produced at Kaolin, such as the coarsely designed *Corn* pitchers of 1859-61 (Barber, pp. 188-9). But to this site six miles from Augusta, potters were still attracted as they had been in Duché's time more than a century before.

From an inconspicuous beginning in Trenton, New Jersey, in 1863 there grew two years later the firm of Ott & Brewer, whose workshop, called the "Etruria Pottery", proved the training ground for several potters of stature. For his own part, John Hart Brewer produced in 1875-6 a series of fine Parian portrait busts of Washington, Franklin, and U. S. Grant, modelled by Isaac Broome (Newark Museum, Clement's *Pottery and Porcelain of New Jersey*, Nos. 217-19 and Plate 44). The firm, dissolved in 1893, is especially remembered as a maker of American Belleek in the 1880s.

One of the Ott & Brewer apprentices was Walter Scott Lenox, later their decoration manager, who in 1889 formed the Ceramic Art Company, and in 1896 established the distinguished firm of Lenox, Inc. – since 1918 known as the makers of White House state services, and porcelains for the American embassies.

MOULDED WARES

The later porcelains (Plate 317) and the wares that follow (Plates 314, 315, 316) were of a new order. The factory period had arrived about 1830, product of an industrial revolution that showed a parallel in mechanization of the glass industry, as freeblown glass gave way to pressed. In the ceramics field new types of pottery were no longer thrown on the potter's wheel but shaped in moulds. Forms were now created by designers and mass-produced by professional workmen; the simple potshop was transformed into a factory, where output was large and the price small.

Parian

Being made from liquid clay, Parian ware had to be poured into moulds. Bennington had been first to introduce "this exquisite material, the happy substitute for marble in statuettes" – indeed, in 1852 had advertised it by the latter name, as "Figures in Parian Marble". The snowy ware was everywhere a favourite after the 1850s, made from Vermont to the Carolinas, or in Ohio by William Bloor of East Liverpool in 1860. And so much was its formula varied, one often doubts whether to call an example Parian or bisque porcelain.

But fear and outrage had swept the workers, at seeing "the old usages of the trade broken up" (Wedgwood and Ormsbee, p. 95). Labour strikes in 1834-43 were followed by a panic of Staffordshire workmen in 1845-6, when they thought their livelihood threatened by the invention of pot-making machines.

The nonpareil of all moulded work was a 10-foot monument made 1851-2 at Bennington and displayed 1853 at the Crystal Palace (Barber, Fig. 74). In three tiers of marbled or "scroddled" ware, of the colour-flecked Fenton's Enamel, and of brown-streaked Rockingham, it was topped with the Parian figure of a "woman in the act of presenting the Bible to an infant". Just below, a portrait bust also in Parian represented Mr Fenton himself, peeking through a classic colonnade.

In America David Henderson of Jersey City, who has been called "the Wedgwood of America", was pioneer in the manufacture of moulded wares. His fine buff stoneware jug marked *Uncle Toby/1829* was advertised as *Toby Philipot* (sic) in 1830. A very similar but larger one (Plate 316B) was made in 1838-45 at the Salamander Works (1825-96) in Woodbridge, New Jersey. This is a jug of rich chestnut-brown colour with yellow-glazed interior. Pictured alongside it is the Daniel Greatbach model with grapevine handle, made at Bennington, with normal Rockingham glaze but mis-marked *Fenton's Enamel/Patented* 1849.

American Belleek

Belonging with the porcelains, last of the late wares is American Belleek, a thin, highly translucent, feldspathic body which is cousin to Parian, finished with a pale pearly glaze. Irish Belleek (*see* Glossary) was seen at the Centennial Exhibition in 1876, and excited the admiration of American potters.

Some time between 1880 and 1882 the Trenton firm of Ott & Brewer brought over the potter William Bromley, who had developed Irish Belleek, and by 1882, produced "the first piece of belleek porcelain made in America" (a square tray, No. 223 in Newark Museum, *Pottery and Porcelain of New Jersey*). A fancy shell-shaped pitcher (*ibid.*, No. 233) marked *W.S.L./1887* was produced at their works by Walter Lenox, who later brought two Belleek workmen to his own Ceramic Art Co. (1889–96) and further developed the ware at Lenox, Inc., from 1896. Edwin Bennett had achieved the production of Belleek by 1886 at Baltimore, and the Columbian Art Pottery (established 1893) made it by 1895 at Trenton.

Perhaps best of the American Belleek was "Lotus Ware" (Plate 314B, C), a product of Knowles, Taylor & Knowles at East Liverpool, 1891–8. In 1887 Isaac W. Knowles had brought over Joshua Poole, manager of the Irish factory, and before 1889 made a finely moulded and fragile ware that in the 1890s earned much favour.

Belleek and Majolica, or the Art tiles and "studio wares" that flourished alongside Rookwood from the 1880s, cannot yet be classed as antiques. Yet with Tiffany glass and other late work of quality, they have gained wide acceptance among collectors. In 1879 the 3rd edition of W. C. Prime's *Pottery and Porcelain of All Times and Nations* (which devoted a total of six pages to "Pottery and Porcelain in the United States") began with these words: "Ten years ago there were probably not ten collectors of pottery and porcelain in the United States. Today there are perhaps ten thousand. . . ." What would he think of the range and vigour of collecting today?

Austrian

PORCELAIN

At Vienna Claudius Innocentius Du Paquier, assisted by Christoph Conrad Hunger from Meissen and Samuel Stoelzel, an arcanist Meissen, founded his own factory in 1717. He started by producing tableware derived from silver shapes, decorated with Chinese motifs and exotic flowers. About 1725 German flowers and European subjects were introduced in colours and in *schwarzlot*, a black monochrome heightened with gold. This technique, used earlier by Johann Schaper, of Nuremberg, for the decoration of glass and pottery, was first applied to porcelain by Daniel Preissler (1636–1733) in Silesia, whence it became a characteristic feature of Vienna ware. Du Paquier figures formed at first parts of vessels only, supports, handles, or finials, but gained independence about 1730 and came into their own. The mingling of rustic pottery tradition with the urbanity of Meissen models gives these wide-eyed figures an air of wondering surprise at their own appearance in crinolines rather than in peasant skirts.

Financial difficulties forced Du Paquier to sell his factory to the State in 1744, when a complete reorganization took place. At that time the Vienna mark, a shield incised or, more often, in underglaze blue, was first introduced (Fig. 2). New findings of kaolin in

 FIG. 2

Hungary (1749) and sound management finally brought prosperity to the enterprise. L. Dannhauser and J. J. Niedermeyer modelled figures of great charm, imparting the rhythmic grace of Austrian rococo to courtiers and market vendors alike. During the latter part of the century the transition to classicism took place under the direction of Konrad von Sorgenthal (1784–1805). Table wares in the manner of Sèvres have coloured grounds and gold decoration of restrained design, including medallions with portraits or landscapes. Figures of the period are often formed in biscuit to reproduce the effect of antique marbles. These figures are clad in stylized Greek gowns, and their timid character seems due to a certain slackening of creative power. However, the factory carried on until 1864.

Belgian

PORCELAIN

In Belgium, unaffected by the French Vincennes–Sèvres monopoly, the factory of Tournay was founded in 1751, under a monopoly granted by the Empress Maria Theresa. Robert Dubois, formerly at Chantilly and Vincennes, was appointed director in 1753, and the soft paste now produced, though not free from Meissen influences, is entirely French in spirit. The shapes of useful and decorative objects are simple and restrained, in spite of the flowering of the rococo style elsewhere. Much of the Tournay porcelain is left in white; and one wonders whether this is due to a genuine preference for the appealing pureness of the glaze, as it is in Nymphenburg, or whether coloured and gilt decoration was at times suppressed, out of reverence for the French crown. There is also a group of Tournay plates and dinner services with contemporary Dutch decoration, which the factory originally sold in white. They are easily recognized by the stork mark of The Hague, applied in overglaze blue (Fig. 3).

FIG. 3

FAÏENCE

Faïence has been made in Belgium from the sixteenth century onwards, at various places, including Antwerp, Liége, Tournay, and Brussels.

It is not widely known or collected, but the work of Corneille Mombaer's factory, founded in 1705, is of some interest and distinction.

No mark was used—but a rather streaky glaze, and the bold blue, green, and yellow colouring is distinctive. A few examples are signed and dated.

The most attractive pieces are tureens in the form of vegetables, fruits, birds, and fishes. Dishes with fruit modelled in the round and various figures were also made. Work continued here into the nineteenth century.

Chinese

POTTERY

Although Chinese pottery has only been effectively studied in quite recent times, our acquaintance with it is of far longer standing. Sung dynasty wares occasionally reached Europe from Near Eastern lands as early as the Middle Ages. By the late Renaissance the

Italians had already attempted to copy the blue-painted Ming porcelains, in their "Medici" ware; and from the seventeenth century onwards the East India companies brought shiploads of "china" for the mantelpiece or tea-table. But such imported wares were seldom comparable with the best productions; indeed, fine "antique" wares were scarcely known, and not readily available until the days of the great Victorian and Edwardian connoisseurs. Superb collections of Ch'ing dynasty porcelain were then formed, among them those of Salting and Grandidier, which are so well known to museum-goers in London and Paris. Since then, however, even earlier wares have been discovered. These have enabled us to complete our history, tracing the continuous development of the art from the earliest times. And it is among the earthenwares and stonewares of the T'ang and Sung dynasties, with their fine shapes and rich glazes, or among the brilliantly painted Ming porcelains, that the greatest masterpieces of Chinese ceramics are now sought.

The pleasure of exploring this new world fell to the last generation of collectors, among whom the names of George Eumorfopoulos and the scholar R. L. Hobson will be known to many. It is unlikely that comparable discoveries remain to be made today. The rarer wares, too, are now costly, and increasingly hard to find. Nevertheless, there are still many fine pieces on the market for a few pounds only, awaiting those who recognize their quality. In judging the merits of Chinese pottery, shape and finish, texture of materials, and aptness of decoration should all be considered, and for those who wish to learn there is no substitute for seeing the wares themselves, whether in museums (especially the Victoria & Albert and British Museums, the David Foundation in London, and Musée Guimet in Paris), or in the dealer's showroom, where they may be handled.

BRIEF HISTORY

Early Pottery

Some remarkable unglazed earthenware jars, painted in sombre colours with swirling abstract patterns (Fig. 4), are the earliest known Chinese pottery, made from about 2000 B.C. in the Neolithic period. The Shang and Chou dynasties (eighteenth to third century B.C.) laid the firm foundations of Chinese civilization, but we do not ascribe great importance to their pottery. Their superb ritual

FIG. 4

bronze vessels, however, exercised lasting influence on the sister art. By the time of the Han dynasty (206 B.C.–A.D. 220), roughly analogous to the Roman Empire, the skilful potter had mastered techniques with wider artistic possibilities, and notably that of glazing. A green or brown "lead" glaze (given a silvery patina by burial) was applied to a reddish earthenware. Vessels were still following metal forms, decorated with bands of animals and figures in moulded relief (Fig. 5). The Han tombs from which they come also contained model houses and farms, animals, and even human figures. Some grey earthenwares were left unglazed and adorned with unfired painting (Plate 320). Even more important from this time was the discovery of "felspathic"-glazed stoneware, which, with its hard, impervious body and strong, semi-transparent, olive-brown glaze containing felspar rock, foreshadows the invention of porcelain. The years of the Six Dynasties (220–589) saw the gradual refinement of the greyish, "porcellanous" Yüeh ware, with greyish-green glaze of this type. Although the lead glaze is not found during this period, painted grey earthenwares continue, notably in the tomb figures, which, like the contemporary Buddhist sculpture, steadily increase in human gracefulness.

The T'ang dynasty (618–906) is the golden age of China, great in literature and painting, and receptive and fertile in its contacts with the outside world. T'ang pottery conveys an unmistakable vitality and refinement, expressed in beautifully proportioned forms and a disciplined use of rich colour. The lead glaze was now revived, and applied over a fine white earthenware in green, golden-yellow, and blue colourings of great brilliance, which were often splashed on or mottled together (Plate 323A, B), or used to enliven designs incised into the surface. Designs were also impressed from moulds. Favoured subjects were stylized flowers and birds, and others – the palmette and vine – which, like some forms, were derived from Hellenistic sources. Among

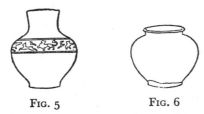

FIG. 5   FIG. 6

the tomb figures of the time are models of calm, smiling ladies, dancers (Plate 323A), ferocious warriors (guardians of tombs) and mythical monsters, and horses and camels with their riders and attendants, showing the most sensitive observation in their modelling. Some of unglazed earthenware were painted "cold", usually over a white "slip" of clay, which enhanced the colours. Apart from these, and the refined pale-green Yüeh ware already mentioned, the chief glory of T'ang potters is their invention of translucent white porcelain. This material, composed of the refined china-clay and china-stone fused at a high temperature, and covered with a glaze containing the latter, is found chiefly in small bowls. General indications of T'ang date are flat bases, and glazes which stop well short of the foot (Fig. 6).

FIG. 7

The Sung dynasty (960–1279) produced some of the most beautiful shapes and glazes of all pottery. It excelled particularly in felspathic stonewares of a more or less porcellanous nature, characteristic of which are the Lungchüan and "Northern" celadons, with their serene forms and soft jade-green depths of colour. Also of this kind are the rare Imperial Kuan, or Ko (Fig. 7), and Ju wares, and the opales-

cent blue and purple Chün. Very attractive, too, are the brown and black glazes of Honan and Tz'ŭ Chou in the north, and the Chien ware tea-bowls from southerly Fukien. All the above owe their colour principally to the presence of iron under varied kiln conditions. Among the vigorously shaped stonewares of Tz'ŭ Chou are those with skilful carved decoration relieving white, brown, or green glazes (Fig. 11); and on others bold floral painting in brown now makes its appearance (Plate 321A). Delightful incised designs of plants and animals are also a feature

SUNG DYNASTY

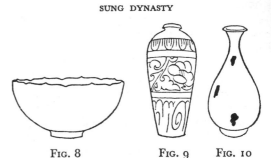

FIG. 8   FIG. 9   FIG. 10

of much Sung pottery (Plate 325A), and especially of the superb creamy-white Ting and bluish *ying ch'ing* porcelains (Plate 321B). Typical of Sung forms are the small-footed bowl, two-handled jar, *mei p'ing* vase, and graceful bottle shown in Figs. 8–10 and Plate 323C. Large dishes, jars, and bowls are found especially among the celadons exported in quantity throughout the Near and Far East.

The "Southern Sung" succeeded the "Northern" with the removal of the capital from K'aifeng (Honan) to Hangchow (Chekiang) in 1127 to avoid barbarian invaders. The irresistible onslaught of Genghis Khan was, none the less, to result in the establishment of the Mongol Yüan dynasty (1279–1368) by his famous descendant, Kublai. An important Yüan ware was the *shu fu* porcelain, decorated with designs in low relief. With the adoption of painting in underglaze blue, and the rise of the porcelain factories of Ching-tê-chên, a radical change in taste was now taking place.

The Ming dynasty (1368–1644), which began by overthrowing the Mongols, gave strong patronage to the porcelain industry, and in place of the variety of Sung wares and glazes developed a more or less standardized porcelain body as a vehicle for brilliantly coloured decoration. Its animated character, and the liveliness of the forms which it so admirably sets off, may be seen in the plates and Figs. 11–14. Ming glazes tend to be thick and "fat". Always popular, painting in underglaze blue was at its finest in the Hsüan Tê (Plate 323D) and Ch'êng Hua periods, since regarded as classic for perfection of material and harmonious proportion of forms and decoration. During the latter period painting in coloured enamels, requiring a second, low-temperature firing, is found in the delicate *tou ts'ai* class. In the sixteenth century the "red and green" family became conspicuous; but the Chia Ching and Wan Li periods are further noted for many rich combinations of enamels (Plate 324C), including with these colours yellow and turquoise. A rich violet-blue distinguishes the best blue-and-white of Chia Ching (Fig. 13). The Wan Li *wu ts'ai*, or five-colour decoration, employing overglaze enamels with underglaze blue, was to remain prominent until the reign of K'ang Hsi (Plate 321C). Coloured glazes, too, were used, either together or singly, and especially green with yellow. Of a somewhat different nature are the so-called *san ts'ai*, or "three-colour" wares; these are porcelain or stoneware, with designs incised or outlined in threads of clay and washed in with coloured glazes, among which a deep blue and turquoise are the most prominent (Plate 324A and Fig. 12). In the decoration of Ming porcelain much use was made of scrolling floral designs, flying dragons, and phoenixes taken from silk brocades, and of such pictorial subjects as landscapes with animals and garden terrace scenes with children. In later periods their execution becomes careless, and little of note emerges after Wan Li. Exports of blue-and-white were very considerable, however, and the crisp porcelains brought to Europe from 1600 and boldly painted "Transitional" wares may be very pleasing. These are not uncommon; but the finer Ming wares are almost as rare as the Sung. Apart from Ching-tê-chên wares, the Sung celadon and Tz'ŭ Chou types continued although declining in quality, and the Canton wares and Yi-hsing stoneware, as well as the *blanc-de-Chine* porcelain of Fukien, deserve mention.

Ch'ing dynasty (1644–1912). Under wise patronage the declining porcelain industry acquired new life during the long reign of K'ang Hsi (1662–1722), and its creations were realized with superb craftsmanship, which continued under his sons, Yung Chêng and Ch'ien Lung. The nobility and masculine elegance of the K'ang Hsi style is exemplified in Fig. 15 and in the forms of the "rouleau" vase and "trumpet" vase of Figs. 16 and 18; and the same strong-shouldered contours may be noted in Figs. 17 and 19. The ware now used was a most refined white porcelain, thinly and evenly glazed and with a meticulous finish, showing painted decoration to great advantage. For the best of the very numerous blue-and-white wares a brilliant sapphire blue was preferred, and designs, first drawn in outline and then washed in boldly in broad tones, are more precisely executed than hitherto. We find ambitious landscape or figure subjects. On some pieces there is also painting in copper-red, or a partial blue, celadon-green, or golden-brown glaze. For enamelled wares the brilliant *famille verte* palette, with its dominating greens and iron-red, soon replaced that of the Ming "five-colour" style (Plate 321C), and painting on this class was

MING DYNASTY

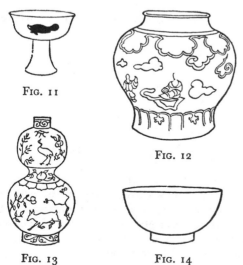

FIG. 11

FIG. 12

FIG. 13

FIG. 14

often of masterly quality, notably in plant or figure subjects (Plate 325B). The rare vases with black or yellow ground (*famille noire, famille jaune*) are generally enamelled "on the biscuit" – i.e. without intervening glaze; and this attractive technique distinguishes a whole *famille verte* group, which especially includes accessories for the tea-table, study, or studio. The third main group of K'ang Hsi wares are those with monochrome glazes, among them the *sang-de-bœuf* and peach-bloom red (Plate

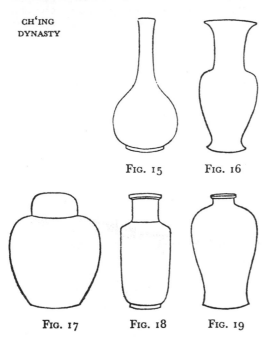

CH'ING
DYNASTY

FIG. 15   FIG. 16

FIG. 17   FIG. 18   FIG. 19

324B) and other high-temperature colours – blues, celadon-green, white, brown, and mirror-black – as well as many others. The beautiful *blanc-de-Chine* porcelain of Fukien (Plate 327B), and the unglazed red stoneware of Yihsing also flourished at this time.

The short reign of Yung Chêng (1723–35) brought a taste for softer colouring and some-

FIG. 20

what feminine refinement, the *famille verte* enamels giving way to those of the *famille rose*, with its prominent rose-pink (introduced from Europe) and other semi-opaque colours. Thin "egg-shell" plates and bowls (Fig. 20) were adorned with delicately drawn flowers or ladies (Plate 326A). Elegance of shape also distinguishes the monochromes (Figs. 21 and 22), again expanded in range of colours. The classic Sung and Ming styles, e.g. the Kuan and Ko, and the delicate *tou ts'ai* enamels were revived and imitated – and, indeed, most underglaze blue or red wares of the Yung Chêng and Ch'ien Lung periods reflect the fifteenth century (Hsüan Tê or Ch'êng Hua) style. From this time, too, wares with designs copied from European prints (Plate 326B) or with coats of arms supplied to order were much exported.

During the Ch'ien Lung period (1736–95) the antiquarian tastes of the Emperor were reflected in continued borrowings from the classical styles and from foreign techniques. The *famille rose* style went on, but often with crowded effects of design and less harmonious combinations of colour. Strong yellow or pink grounds (Plate 327C), or a celadon ground as in Plate 321D, may surround panels of delicate painting; and the rich effects of *cloisonné* enamel were sometimes sought. Some of the monochrome wares continue very fine in colour, notably the flambé copper-reds, and the soft, low-temperature enamels were much used as glazes. Shapes such as those in Figs. 21 and 22 are certainly not lacking in decided

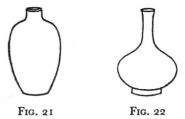

FIG. 21   FIG. 22

character. But the later wares of the reign undoubtedly show a marked decline in taste, inclining to fussiness and prettiness; and former standards were not to be recovered. Poorer-quality materials, slack shapes, uninspired drawing, and insipid colour are faults present to a greater or lesser degree in the wares of Ch'ien Lung's successors.

SUBJECTS OF DECORATION

Many of these are of a symbolic nature, associated with ancient myths and the principal religions – Buddhism, Taoism, and Confucianism. Certain symbols of supernatural forces have come down from very early times, e.g. the *yin yang*, a divided circle symbolizing the duality of things, as in male and female, and the Eight Trigrams (*pa kua*), representing the various elements.

Many groundwork and border designs on pottery, which were adapted from the traditional brocades of ceremonial robes, originally appeared on the ancient ritual bronze vessels: e.g. the swastika, the "key-fret" or "cloud-and thunder" pattern, petal-like motives, *ju-i* sceptre-head and *ling chih* sacred fungus, and the archaic characters *shou* (longevity) and *fu* (happiness).

The ever-popular dragon is of great antiquity; he signified the powers of the air and water, and is often depicted flying above the waves, or pursuing a flaming pearl, which may symbolize the sun. Other symbolic animals are the *kylin*, with dragon's head, deer's hooves, and bushy tail, signifying perfect Good; the tortoise of strength and longevity; and the phoenix, an emblem of the Empress. These, with the dragon, comprise the Four Supernatural Creatures (*ssŭ ling*). Animals associated with Buddhism are the familiar Lion, or Dog of Fo (Buddha), and the Hare, who offered himself as food to the Buddha; according to Taoist legend he now inhabits the moon and pounds the elixir of long life.

Taoism, founded on the precepts of Lao Tzŭ as a contemplative religion promising immortality, is in later times predominantly a cult of longevity; and the Taoist God of Longevity, Shou Lao – an old man with bulging forehead, holding a peach and riding on an ox – is often depicted. So are the Eight Immortals, with their various attributes (*see below*). Figures of the Buddhist Goddess of Mercy, Kuan-yin, are very popular, as are those of the Confucian God of War, Kuan-ti, and the corpulent apostle Pu-tai, with his bag.

Flowers, too, have their associations. The lotus-lily is a notable Buddhist emblem of purity, and the plum, peony, lotus, and chrysanthemum are the Flowers of the Four Seasons. Another groups are the twelve Flowers of the Months; and the Three Fruits (peach, pomegranate, and Buddha's Hand citron) symbolize the three Abundances of years, sons, and happiness. The prunus, pine, and bamboo trees often appear together as the Three Friends, symbolizing the three great religions. The following additional groups of emblems frequently appear singly:

The Four Accomplishments: Music (lyre-case), Games (checkers-board), Literature (pair of books), Painting (pair of scrolls).

The Eight Buddhist Emblems of Happy Augury (*pa-chi-hsaing*): Flaming wheel, Conch-shell, State umbrella, Canopy, Lotus flower, Vase, Pair of fishes, Endless knot.

The Eight Precious Objects (*pa-pao*): Jewel, Cash, Lozenge, Pair of books, Painting, Hanging jade musical stone, Pair of rhinoceros-horn cups, Artemisia leaf.

The Eight Immortals: Chung-li Ch'üan, corpulent, with fan and peach; Lü Tung-pin, with sword; Li T'ieh-kuai, a beggar with crutch and pilgrim's gourd; Ts'ao Kuo-ch'iu, with pair of castanets; Lan Ts'ai-ho, with basket of flowers and spade; Chang Kuo Lao, with two rods and a bamboo; Han Hsiang Tzŭ, playing a flute; Ho Hsien-ku, a lady with a lotus flower.

MARKS

Because of forgeries and repetitions, the evidence of marks on Chinese porcelain is very unreliable, and should always be confirmed by considerations of technique and quality. Calligraphy is highly regarded in China, and the finest pieces were carefully inscribed. But marks remained unusual until the Ming dynasty, when the six-character mark (*nien hao*) of the reigning Emperor, generally written on the base within a double ring, became fairly common. The most important of these marks are given below. They should be read from the right downwards, and the first example may be translated as follows: *Ta* (Great) *Ming* (Ming dynasty) *Hsüan Tě* (the reign-name of the Emperor) *nien* (period) *chih* (made). The four-character mark, omitting the first two characters, is shown for Ch'êng Hua. The final character is sometimes *tsao*.

Most Ming marks are written in underglaze blue. Those of Hsüan Tê and Ch'êng Hua often occur later, especially on K'ang Hsi wares. The genuine K'ang Hsi mark is comparatively rare; and that of Yung Chêng appears on wares of Tao Kuang date. From the time of Yung Chêng coloured enamel was often used, and "seal marks" in archaic characters were favoured. Those in red with turquoise ground are generally of Ch'ien Lung or later date.

The Chinese cyclical system of precise dating may occur in long inscriptions. For this, consult W. Burton and R. L. Hobson, *Marks on Pottery and Porcelain*, 1928. Here also are given many of the hall-marks, marks of good wishes and dedication, and symbols and emblems (such as those referred to above). Few of these, however, are of great assistance in identification.

FAKES

Modern imitations of eighteenth-century Chinese porcelain, painted with coats of arms, have been made in large quantities. Those made at Herend, in Hungary, are not so plentiful as those of Samson of Paris.

PRINCIPAL DYNASTIES AND REIGNS

SHANG-YIN	?1766–?1122 B.C.
CHOU	?1122–249 B.C.
HAN	206 B.C.–A.D. 220
SIX DYNASTIES	220–589
T'ANG	618–906
FIVE DYNASTIES	907–960
SUNG	960–1279
YÜAN	1279–1368
MING	1368–1644
Yung Lo	1403–24
Hsüan Tê	1426–35
Ch'êng Hua	1465–87
Hung Chih	1488–1505
Chêng Tê	1506–21
Chia Ching	1522–66
Lung Ch'ing	1567–72
Wan Li	1573–1619
T'ien Ch'i	1621–27
Ch'ung Chêng	1628–43
CH'ING	1644–1912
Shun Chih	1644–61
K'ang Hsi	1662–1722
Yung Chêng	1723–35
Ch'ien Lung	1736–95
Chia Ch'ing	1796–1820
Tao Kuang	1821–50
Hsien Fêng	1851–61
T'ung Chih	1862–74
Kuang Hsü	1875–1908
Hsüan T'ung	1909–12
CHINESE REPUBLIC	1912–
Hung Hsien (Yüan Shih-k'ai)	1916–

CHINESE LOWESTOFT AND EXPORT PORCELAIN

The first Chinese porcelain to leave the country where it had been made were pieces that had been manufactured for use in China itself. They had been brought home to the West by those few travellers who had penetrated the then unknown Orient. It was not until the seventeenth century that porcelain began to be made and decorated in China especially to the order of European buyers.

The Jesuit Fathers

The Europeans who were concerned in the first place with the production of porcelain in China were the French Jesuit Fathers. These

men, of whom the most famous in this connexion was Père D'Entrecolles, began to establish themselves in the country in about A.D. 1600. It was not until some fifty years after this date that a tangible result of their presence became apparent. This was the making of pieces of porcelain bearing representations of the crucifix accompanied, in many cases, by the letters *I.H.S.* It is uncertain whether they were made for export to Japan for the use of Christian converts in that country or for export to Europe. Whatever their intended destination, a few examples of these early wares, decorated in blue on a white ground, exist today, and their designs have an unquestionably European inspiration. However, in some instances, with a typically Chinese tolerance, Buddhist symbols have been incorporated in the patterns.

About half a century later there was a further output of religious designs. On this occasion there is no doubt that the products were made for export. Large quantities of porcelain were manufactured on which were painted copies of the Crucifixion and other Biblical scenes from both the Old and the New Testaments. Some were in full colours, but mostly they were in Schwarzlot. While the majority were in the form of plates and dishes, there are in existence also a number of secular articles, such as tea-sets, which were doubtless for display rather than for use, painted quite inappropriately with such designs.

Armorial decoration

Most popular form of decoration that was called for from China by patrons in England, Europe, and America generally, was heraldic. Just as it was then the fashion that silver plate should bear the arms or crest of the owner, so it was the same with porcelain. This may be accounted for by the fact that the shapes of the majority of the articles were copied from pieces of silver, which it was intended that the porcelain should replace, and it was not unnatural that such decoration as the originals bore should be copied in addition.

The making of porcelain in European forms commenced at the beginning of the eighteenth century. Such pieces can be dated by a combination of factors: the shape of the article; the style of decoration and the colours used in painting it; the type of porcelain used in the manufacture; and, in some cases, by the armorial bearings. With the aid of the latter it is possible sometimes to date a piece of china to within a few years. It may so happen that a marriage or a death caused a change to have taken place in the emblazoning of a coat of arms, and from this it can be found during which years the particular bearing was current.

In a few cases the original accounts have been preserved in a family, together with the china to which they relate. One such example is the bill, now preserved in the British Museum, referring to the service shipped from Canton in 1731 for a member of the Peers family. Two pieces of the actual china are in the same museum. Such careful and fortunate preservation of the original documents is, of course, very exceptional, and goes far to help in dating many other similar pieces.

Variety of articles

The output of porcelain for export was not confined by any means to articles solely for use at the table. Any attempt to provide a complete list of the many different things that were made would be doomed to failure. In this type of porcelain it is not untrue to suggest that there is nothing new under the sun, and frequently it is surprising to find what the Chinese potters and painters attempted to copy in a medium that was often completely unsuitable. However, although the result was usually a technical success, it must be agreed that it was far from being also an artistic one.

Next in popularity to table-services were punch-bowls. These were made in many sizes and decorated in an infinite variety of styles. Many bear the scene of an English fox-hunt round the outside, and some of these are completed by having the fox painted on the inside of the bowl. Others have accurate copies of European paintings and engravings, such as Hogarth's *Calais Gate*, of which a fine example in full colours is in the Victoria and Albert Museum, London. Others refer to political events, of which the bowl with caricature portraits of John Wilkes and the Lord Chief Justice Lord Mansfield (Plate 328B) is typical. Others bear externally, say, a group of flowers, but beneath the base is a well-painted amorous scene, best kept concealed from the general gaze.

A list of other utilitarian articles could be a lengthy one, and would include: candlesticks, cache-pots (in which a flower-pot stands), water-cisterns, shaving-bowls, chamber-pots, wall brackets, salt-cellars, pepper- and sugar-casters, knife-handles, snuff-boxes, tea-caddies, and beer tankards.

Figures

Apart from such articles intended for daily use in the home, pieces that could serve none other than a decorative purpose were also made. Figures with attempted European features and in Western clothing, such as the lady in Plate 329B, are typical. There are also figures of animals copied from Dutch Delft pottery, and from other originals. An interesting group is that of a man and woman dancing, illustrated in Plate 329D. This is known to have been first modelled at the Meissen (Dresden) factory about the year 1735 and, besides the Chinese copies, it was also imitated in England at both Chelsea and Bow. Few other groups can have been made at so many different factories in so many countries within the space of about twenty-five years. In the category of figures may be included jugs. Copies of jugs of the Toby type also exist in Chinese eighteenth-century porcelain.

The factories

The articles enumerated above were all made in one or other of the great factories grouped at Ching-Tê-Chên and decorated, with the exception of blue-and-white pieces, mostly at the port of Canton. Figures, groups, and other pieces were made also at the factories of Tê-Hua in the Province of Fukien. The porcelain made there was of a distinctive creamy-white colour, and was not usually decorated in the East. Much of it was imported into Holland and Germany and coloured in those countries. Small groups composed of figures wearing recognizably European costume are found in this ware, also tankards with rounded bodies and reeded necks taken from a model known in German stoneware. This type of porcelain, which dates from the mid-seventeenth century, is known as *blanc-de-Chine*.

One further group of eighteenth-century export porcelains was decorated in underglaze blue, together with touches of red and some slight gilding. It was based on that exported from Japan, and is known by the name of the port whence the original was sent to the West, Imari.

Late in the eighteenth century exportations from China included a large proportion of so-called Mandarin wares. These were painted with panels of figures within minutely patterned borders. In the next century came the Canton style, which features butterflies and flowers on a celadon-green ground.

Apart from a knowledge of the role played by the various East India Companies in trading with the Orient, little is known of the details of how this large trade was handled. The pattern plate illustrated in Plate 330D provides evidence that the business was not conducted in any haphazard fashion.

The Lowestoft myth

It must be admitted that the word *Lowestoft* applied to this section is something of a misnomer. In actual fact there is no real connexion whatsoever between Lowestoft, a fishing port in Suffolk on the east coast of England, and the porcelain produced in the factories of China. Certainly a type of porcelain was made for some years in a factory established at Lowestoft. The decoration applied to many of the productions of these minor works comprised bouquets of pink roses and groups of figures and was, by a coincidence, very similar to the decoration then current on porcelain from the Far East. This English porcelain itself does not compare at all with the hard Oriental product, and the two are not likely to be confused.

The widespread misapprehension over the origin of the Chinese pieces arose towards the end of the nineteenth century through a mistake in a book, and, in spite of repeated corrections over the past twenty-five years, collectors and dealers in both England and the United States continually refer to Chinese porcelain made to European order as *Lowestoft*. From being applied, in the first place, to pieces with a particular type of floral decoration, the term has been extended to cover the whole group of export porcelains, and today almost any piece of Chinese porcelain which displays in shape and decoration any obvious sign of European influence is designated by this inappropriate term.

The American China trade

Once the United States had won independence and was free to trade directly with other countries than England, Americans lost no time in entering the China Trade. They did not found an East India Company: individual merchants sent out their own ships and each was a separate venture. The first to sail to the East was the *Empress of China*, a former privateer, which left New York for Canton on February 22, 1784, and arrived during the summer. Major Samuel Shaw, former aide-de-camp to General Knox, was supercargo on this voyage – an extremely important post, for on the supercargo depended not only financial success of the venture but also diplomatic relations with the Chinese. Shaw acquitted himself well, laying the groundwork for future trade between his country and China, and bringing home a cargo that inspired many American merchants to join in the hazardous but lucrative China Trade.

Ships set sail to the Orient from New York, Philadelphia, Boston, Norfolk, Charleston, and other ports. By 1790 twenty-eight American ships had made the voyage. Before 1800 one merchant trader alone, Elias Hasket Derby of Salem, had sent out forty-five ventures. The China Trade became the most profitable branch of American shipping, and pre-sently threatened the monopoly of Britain's powerful East India Company. It reached its peak with the development of the clipper ship in the 1840s, and by the time steam replaced sail its great colourful days were over. But long before then literally tons of Chinese porcelain, along with tea and spices, silks and cottons, lacquer, and other exotic luxuries, had been brought into ports up and down the Eastern seaboard. Some survives still in the families for whom it was made.

Chinese porcelain for the American market

In general, American-market porcelain from China is less elaborate and less varied than what was made for Europe. This is partly because it covers a shorter period, partly because the taste of this period was for the neo-classic, more restrained than the rococo of the preceding era. Moreover, by the time Yankees were trading to the East, the production of export porcelain had become a highly developed commercial operation, and a large proportion of the ware was turned out in stock patterns of simple design instead of being specially made and decorated to individual order.

Danish

COPENHAGEN PORCELAIN

Attempts to make porcelain in Denmark did not meet with any real success until F. H. Müller, an extremely able chemist employed at the Danish Mint, began production in 1771.

The hard-paste porcelain made by Müller resulted from lengthy experiments with kaolin deposits discovered on the island of Bornholm in 1755 by Niels Birch.

An earlier undertaking by Louis Fournier, who had been at Sèvres in Chantilly, made only soft paste, and lasted no more than six or seven years (1759–66). Fournier's rare productions are usually marked with an "F" ac-companied by the number "5" (for Fredrick V of Denmark).

Various German workmen and arcanists, including the unreliable C. C. Hunger, had also offered their services, but these had been declined.

Müller was, however, assisted by J. G. von Langen, a mining engineer from Fürstenberg, who became advisor to the factory.

In 1774 a company was formed with Queen Juliane Marie as chief shareholder, and a year later it obtained a privilege.

On Langen's advice A. C. Laplau, a Fürstenberg modeller and arcanist, was employed in 1776, and with his help both the paste and techniques of production were much improved. In spite of this, financial difficulties caused the company to be taken over by the King in 1779. It then became the Royal Copenhagen Porcelain Manufactory (Den Kongelige Porcelainfabrik Copenhagen), a title retained until the present day; though Royal ownership ended in 1867.

The mark adopted from 1775 was three wavy lines, symbolizing Denmark's main waterways to the Baltic (the Sound, the Great and Little Belts). This, surmounted by a crown, and with varying inscriptions, has also been retained.

Twenty years of prosperity under the Crown was followed by a marked decline in the first half of the nineteenth century. Damage was caused to the factory during the bombardment by the British fleet under Admiral Gambier in 1807, and by 1822 the number of painters employed had dwindled to two. Modern revival dates from the appointment of Arnold Krog (1856–1931) an architect and designer of great ability, who became Art Director in 1885, following the removal of the factory from Købmagerade to Smallegrade, Frederiksberg.

Porcelain made during the first period (1772–9) was of a bluish-grey tone, but by 1780 it had become whiter and more translucent. The shapes and decoration in underglaze blue were at first much under the influence of Meissen and Fürstenberg. From the beginning of the Royal period a classical style prevailed and the palette was greatly increased. Rams' heads, architectural motifs, and pierced basket-work borders were favoured; also silhouettes in black or grey monochrome, historical portraits and landscapes with ruins. Some nineteenth-century biscuit figures and reliefs are after Bertel Thorvaldsen.

Copenhagen's greatest achievement was the famous "Flora Danica Service", probably intended for the Russian Empress Catherine II. It was started in 1789–90, but Catherine died in 1796, and the service, which was still incomplete in 1802, is now in the Rosenborg Castle, Copenhagen.

The decoration of the 1602 pieces was determined by the administrative director Theodor Holm, statesman and botanist, and the painting executed by J. C. Bayer, who had already illustrated Holm's book on Danish fungi. The shapes are neo-classical, painted with naturalistic botanical subjects taken from the earlier parts of a great work on Danish flora, started by Oeder and published between 1761 and 1883. Fruit and flower baskets are ornamented with flowers modelled in the round by Søren Preuss.

Dutch

POTTERY

When the name of a substance, such as nylon, or a product, such as Leica, is adopted immediately into the vocabulary of every civilized nation it is convincing proof of both its novelty and its world-wide appeal. The use of the name of a small Dutch town, Delft, spelt in a variety of ways, to describe more or less any blue-and-white earthenware in a score of different languages, leaves us in no doubt of the absolute pre-eminence enjoyed by the wares produced in that town over a period of some 150 years. It is the purpose of this chapter to give, briefly, the history of the evolution of those wares, to distinguish the various types, discuss their merits, and give some guidance to collectors.

Early Flemish and Dutch majolica

The technique of painting in high-temperature colours on a tin-enamel surface came north over the Alps from Italy early in the sixteenth century. We know that a potter from Castel Durante, Guido di Savino, who took the name of Guido Andriesz, settled in Antwerp in 1508, and we may take that date as the beginning of the school of South Netherlands majolica, which flourished for a hundred years and more. Other Italians, from Brescia and Venice, soon followed, and important commissions, especially for coloured tile pavements, have survived. Soon the drug pots and dishes began to acquire local characteristics which made them, in spite of their colouring, unmistakably non-Italian. The strong blue, green, deep orange, and yellow, with manganese outlines, were reminiscent of Urbino and Faenza, but were soon applied in characteristic groups of fruit, surrounded by circular bands of colouring. Two Italian motifs, which were to become Netherlandish specialities, were the strap-work, evolved from the cartouche, and the grotesques, derived via Urbino from Raphael's decorations in the Vatican – decorations themselves copied from ancient Rome. Unlike its Italian prototype, this Netherlands majolica seems to have been made only in "useful" wares.

By the third quarter of the century, Antwerp potters are known to have moved farther North, just as Jaspar Andries (believed to be a son or grandson of Guido di Savino) moved to England in 1567 and began the long history of "English Delft" some years before such wares were ever made at Delft itself. We have records of such Antwerp potters in Amsterdam (1584), Dordrecht, Middleburg, Rotterdam, Haarlem (1573), where they flourished, and eventually in Delft (1584).

It is extremely hard to classify these impressive early pieces, or to say with certainty that a particular piece was made in the North rather than in the South. The bold dishes, not unlike our "blue-dash chargers", were tin-enamelled on the front only, the back being covered with a transparent lead-glaze, showing the greyish yellow of the clay. There is no evidence, from excavation, that the wares decorated with "groteschi" of Urbino type were ever made in the North. Certain plain blue and white drug pots, with a gadroon border, are held to be Dutch (Plate 338B). A type of plate with birds and animals painted on a dark-blue ground seems, on the evidence of the large quantity of fragments excavated, to be exclusively North Netherlandish, and was probably made at Rotterdam, as were the majority of the plates with stylized rosettes or checkered patterns (Plate 338A and C). Pots and dishes in which the colours are exceptionally strong, and have been less well assimilated with the glaze, so that they seem almost to be in relief, are held, partly on the evidence of tiles, to be of North Netherlandish make, as are those which add dark-blue grapes to the conventional clusters of apples and pomegranates.

Northern also are the plates with raised knobs on the border and bearing pious inscriptions such as *Eert Godt altijt* (Honour God always) (Plate 339B), a type which, starting as early as 1580, even crops up in blue and white in the late eighteenth century. The palette used in these is unpleasing: a very strong blue, a pure bright ochreous orange, and a vivid opaque light green. It occurs in a number of plates with similar borders showing milkmaids (sometimes with a date) and coats-of-arms (generally imaginary), nearly all of which date from the first quarter of the seventeenth century. These, with the gadrooned albarelli and the blue-ground plates mentioned above, give us a fairly accurate picture of the North Netherlands majolica, which we can amplify by the study of the tiles. The few more elaborately decorated pieces which have survived seem to be almost certainly of South Netherlands and Antwerp origin, to which city may also be ascribed any pieces showing a pure, clear lemon yellow. It is worth commenting that an inscription in Dutch, or Flemish, cannot be considered as evidence one way or another.

Suffice it to say that by the close of the sixteenth century majolica was being made in a great number of Dutch towns, with Haarlem perhaps achieving the greatest technical perfection and Rotterdam producing the greatest quantity, especially of tiles. Dishes were still covered with lead glaze on the back: a practice which was not wholly abandoned until near the middle of the next century. Very little of it was marked, and none of the marks may be ascribed with any certainty to a particular maker, any more than pieces can be attributed, except by conjecture, to a particular place of origin.

All these early wares, the incunabula of Dutch pottery, are of Italian inspiration, however much design and colouring may have undergone a local modification. They are vigorous and confident, unsophisticated and unpretentious, attractive in their own artistic right as well as in the problem of origin which each separate piece poses to collector, dealer, and museum expert alike. Yet they remain essentially derivative, a late offshoot of a great tradition. Dutch majolica, in the making of which the Northern potters were building up an invaluable tradition of knowledge and skill, still awaited the external impulse which was to give it a new direction, a life of its own, and was to help it develop, with all the vigour of a young and prosperous nation, into something specifically and uniquely Dutch, one of the great monuments of ceramic art which, in its turn, fertilized and influenced the whole field of ceramic activity in Europe.

This external impulse came, in 1602, from the landing of the first large cargo of Chinese porcelain in Amsterdam. Chinese blue-and-white pieces had long been known and the material treated with awe as something well-nigh magical. This arrival in quantity, however, caused a revolution in taste. At first it was only the decoration which was imitated, and from about 1610 onwards we have a series of chargers with deep-blue borders on which appear, in reserves, the conventional Wan-Li designs of Buddhist emblems, etc. For a while these were combined with centre decorations done in the old Netherlands palette of blue, bright green, ochre, and reddish-brown, and the Chinese frame might surround a Dutch landscape, fruit bowls (Plate 339A), or a Madonna and Child. But soon the blue-and-white monochrome swept all before it, and a dish of that type appears in the arms of the Haarlem potters (1635). An important further consequence of greater familiarity with Chinese originals was that it became customary to apply tin-enamel to the back of the dish as well as the front, in order more closely to imitate porcelain. The earliest surviving fragment thus glazed back and front is dated 1622.

From now on, for over a hundred years, the decoration of by far the greater part of Dutch earthenware was to be Chinese in character. That it was not slavishly imitative but developed a character of its own is largely for technical reasons. The softness of the glaze, into which the decoration seemed to melt, was one such factor. More important, and more of an obstacle to any too minute copying, was the fact that the decorators were painting on to a highly absorbent ground, on which their colour dried instantly, allowing no retouching and demanding a swift and confident brush-stroke. Some pieces were indeed made which, at first glance or behind the glass of a museum cabinet, are impossible to distinguish from Kang Hsi originals. But soon the introduction of manganese outlines, the combination of Chinese with baroque motifs, the illustrating of scenes from Dutch life, all helped to create that intensely individual character which distinguishes Dutch Delft from the Chinese decoration which inspired it and from the innumerable imitations which were made, all over the rest of Europe, from the second half of the seventeenth century onwards (Plate 338D).

"Dutch Delft": it may seem doubly tautological to use the phrase, but one can avoid it no longer. The first of these Wan-Li dishes were probably made at Haarlem, whence the earliest recorded potters in Delft had come. Yet by 1650 Delft had established a predominance it was never to lose. Potteries continued to produce good work in Haarlem, Friesland, and elsewhere, while Rotterdam became the great manufacturer of tiles. Yet qualitatively and quantitatively, Delft stood alone in its high repute for the production of luxurious wares of every shape and every degree of elaboration. This was in part due to its convenient geographical position, between the estuaries of the Rhine and the Meuse and the rest of Holland, and near to the North Sea. But no town in Holland lacks access to the country's waterways. The rise of Delft must be ascribed to the chance of a combination of propitious circumstances. The geographical position, the arrival of large quantities of blue-and-white ware from China, the rapidly increasing prosperity of the country, seeking a new outlet for capital, and the sudden decline of the important Delft brewing industry, suffering from the competition with English beer (by 1667 only 15 of over 180 breweries were still working). This last was possibly decisive, as the buildings were thus made available for those who wished to set up a pottery. In fact, many potteries took over the names of the breweries they replaced: the Three Bells, the Rose, the Peacock, the Greek A, and many others which have become familiar to lovers of Delft. The new industry doubtless also profited by the rebuilding of much of the town after the explosion of the powder magazine in 1654. As the second half of the seventeenth century began, the industry at Delft was launched on the greatest period of its existence, in which it was to continue with unabated prosperity until well into the second quarter of the eighteenth century.

For convenience it will be best to discuss the wares produced at Delft according to types of colouring: blue and white, polychrome high temperature, and polychrome produced in the muffle kiln. This is, however, a division of convenience only. It should be remembered not only that blue and white remained the staple and most characteristic product right until the decline of the industry at the end of the eighteenth century but also that it was in blue and white, after the abandoning of the North Netherlandish majolica palette, that the first great triumphs of Delft earthenware were made.

Blue and white

In the second half of the seventeenth century the wares made fall into two main classes. Earliest perhaps were the large dishes known, from the Chinese porcelain brought round the Cape, as *Kaapsche Schotels*. These show the traditional late Ming border round a central octagon or hexagon in which are drawn water-fowl or deer of conventional Chinese pattern, or a bowl of peonies and other flowers standing on a low table on a terrace. One is immediately impressed by the great size of these dishes, most of which are at least 18 inches across, by the remarkable thinness of the potting, which is in fact as thin as the

porcelain it strives to imitate, and by the extreme delicacy with which the elaborate fretted backgrounds are drawn. It was on these dishes that the outlining in black or dark manganese was first applied, the *trek* which became so distinctive a feature of Delft. Here also we notice the introduction of the *kwaart*, the final coating of lead glaze, applied to the front only, giving a special brilliance to the finished article. Few of these pieces, which were mostly made between 1660 and 1700, are dated or marked, though the fine specimen here shown, unusual also in its brilliant white, as opposed to bluish, glaze, bears the exceptionally late date 1718 (Plate 339c).

Alongside these Oriental designs developed the wares whose decoration sought its inspiration nearer home, drawing especially on the vast wealth of engraving and etching produced as an offshoot of the great contemporary School of Dutch painting. Here we see the last vestiges, and the only undoubtedly Northern examples, of the Urbino grotesques so popular at Antwerp. In blue monochrome, they surround such pictures as the famous one of the young Prince of Orange (Plate 340A), and gradually fine down to a strip of decoration round some purely Dutch biblical scene (Plate 339D). Work of this quality was primarily meant for display, as is shown by the large number of plaques which have survived from the early period. The etchings of Berchem were specially popular sources, and a glance at the plaque illustrated in Plate 344A, which bears the early date 1658, as does a very similar plaque in Amsterdam, leaves one in no doubt as to the superlative quality of the workmanship.

In spite of all that enthusiastic perusers of marks have conjectured, it seems most likely that these finer works were executed as special commissions by special artists, working as *Hausmaler*. We know from inventories that there was a fashion for "porcelain landscapes" sometimes described as "in ebony frames". To these must be added the small, but often illustrated, group of portraits of protestant divines. These portraits are clearly the work of gifted artists, not of copyists, and the small hole at the top of each rectangular plaque makes it clear that it was meant to hang.

Supreme among these independents is Frederick Frijtom, whom we can trace as an immigrant to Delft in 1658, where he remained until his death in 1702. A number of highly elaborate landscape plaques have survived, such as we find mentioned as by him, in contemporary wills and inventories. They are of such quality as to expose the wishful thinking underlying the ascription to him of clumsier work. Even more remarkable are the plates, of which some two dozen have survived, showing simple landscape scenes of woodland and riverside within a broad border left severely unornamented (Plate 345B). Such unpretentious little views have a close affinity with the innumerable landscape etchings being produced at the time by Waterloo and others. Yet these are original works of art. On the exceptionally brilliant white ground the scenes are drawn in a series of lines and dots, distance being conveyed by a more delicate, finer touch and an ever paler blue. They are unlike anything else ever made and belong to the supreme ceramic masterpieces of all times and countries.

It was in the last twenty years of the century that the industry began to be organized into larger groups, and it is from then onwards that we find greater numbers of marked pieces. At one time it was believed that these marks were those of individual artists, but a closer examination has shown that the same mark occurs on pieces clearly by a number of different hands, or on pieces which, for stylistic reasons, must have been made long after a particular supposed author was dead. The marks are now taken to refer to the owners or lessees of the various potteries, the capitalists who were venturing into the rising industry. Some of these can be shown to have managed several different factories at different times.

In this first great period various marks are pre-eminent. Perhaps the earliest pieces are those marked *SVE*, in monogram. These date from the period 1675–86, when Samuel van Eenhoorn ran the "Greek A" factory – the only one with which his name is connected and one which had a long, distinguished history under a number of famous potters. The figures on *SVE* pieces are almost always outlined in black or purplish *trek*, and are mostly

decorated with Chinese scenes. The glaze is bluish, and the monochrome blue varied, in the same piece, from deep to pale, often with a strong mauve tinge (Plate 345A). Samuel van Eenhoorn was followed, in the same factory, by Adrianus Kocx, whose monogram *AK* is found on many of the most ambitious pieces made between 1690 and 1700, and who also produced, in a particularly brilliant blue, some of the closest replicas of K'ang Hsi blue and white. A closer study of *AK* pieces shows very clearly how these factories worked. Normally such pieces were made in standard baroque shapes and decorated with a mixture of baroque and Chinese designs. Special commissions were clearly farmed out to special decorators, men whose skill was something very different from that of the average workman (Plate 340B). Mr Arthur Lane has shown, in an article in *The Connoisseur* (March 1949) how special pieces commissioned by William and Mary for Hampton Court (for which the bills, dated 1695, have survived) were based on the designs of Daniel Marot, who also designed the parterres in the garden. The very delicate draughtsmanship on these famous vases, considered in conjunction with the finest landscape and portrait plaques and the work of Frijtom, suggests that quite apart from the standard pottery production, gifted artists, working rather in the manner of Hausmaler, frequently tried their hand in the new medium, just as, in 1711, Sir James Thornhill, Hogarth's father-in-law, decorated and inscribed a splendid series of plates with the signs and emblems of the Zodiac.

On Kocx's death in 1701, the factory was continued by his son Pieter Adriaensz Kocx, who died soon after. His widow continued the work, using his *PAK* monogram, far into the eighteenth century. We shall come across it again in discussing polychrome wares. It seems certain that the *AK* mark was widely copied by contemporaries (it is even found on Chinese porcelain) and probably that the factory continued to use it for some time after 1700.

The factory of Rochus Hoppesteyn, at the Moors' Head, produced some of the most distinctive, and most highly prized, work of the late seventeenth century. It is akin to that marked *SVE*, but the glaze is bluer and more brilliant, the *trek* darker, the drawing firmer, and many pieces are made notable by a skilful use of gold and an unusually clear and brilliant cornelian red. His mark was *RHS* in monogram, to which a Moors' Head is sometimes added. Closely associated with these pieces, and possibly produced in the same factory, is a series of large vases and fine dishes, ornamented in blue with scenes from Italian engravings, surrounded by arabesque borders in a paler version of the Hoppesteyn colours – including a foxy red and an olive green. The palette is distinctive, and once seen cannot be mistaken. Most of this group are marked with the monogram *IW*. For many years this was believed to refer to the father of Rochus Hoppesteyn, but that attribution is no longer considered tenable. It is more likely to be the mark of an independent decorator.

Perhaps most prolific of these early decorators and factories, was that which marked its productions with *LVE* in monogram. This mark, very often accompanied by numbers and by individual potters' monograms, occurs on innumerable pieces of blue and white made between 1700 and 1720. Most are of a bold and brilliant blue, with a highly shiny *kwaart*. The use of *trek* is rare, and the decoration tends to be crowded. It is also found on an important group of black-ground pieces. The mark is that of Lambertus van Eenhoorn. It has long been fashionable to divide this monogram between him and Louwijs Victoorsz. This theory, which still has its doughty champions, seems untenable. There is no clear stylistic break to suggest a dividing line; the monogram is clearly *LVE* or *LVF*, and Victoorsz never wrote, or could have written, his name with an F. The desperate suggestion that the F stands for *fecit* is irreconcilable either with what we know of factory practice or the non-existence of any other instance of the word being used by a Delft potter (Plates 340c and D, 341A).

Last, but among the very best of all, must be considered the wares made at the "Rose" factory, almost all of which are of quite exceptional quality. Most famous, perhaps, is a series of blue-and-white plates of New Testament scenes, within a border of cloud-borne putti. But there are also dazzling imitations of *famille verte*, a unique bottle with Near Eastern decoration, and a magnificent polychrome set of five massive vases of K'ang Hsi design, now in the Victoria and Albert Musem (Plate 341B). The factory mark was either the word "Roos" or a capital R, often surrounded by groups of dots, and sometimes, though more rarely, a stylized drawing of a rose.

Blue and white continued as the main product of the Delft factories throughout the eighteenth century. Designs became more stereotyped, Oriental being modified first with baroque motifs of lambrequins and the like, then with the more asymmetrical curls and graces of the Rococo. Artistically there was a decline in freshness and originality from about 1730, though much attractive earthenware continued to be made. In 1764, chiefly to protect themselves against "pirate" competition, the leading makers deposited their marks at the Town Hall. For that period, therefore, we have a reliable hand-list. The best makers in the second half of the century were:

The White Star	Mark:	a star
The Claw	„	a leg with claws
The Greek A	„	capital *A* with initials
The Porcelain axe	„	a hatchet
The Ewer	„	LPK
The Three Bells	„	three bells

Plates, jugs, and the like were produced decorated with scenes from various trades, or of the months, biblical scenes, shepherds and shepherdesses, coats-of-arms, beautiful interlaced ciphers, and loyal references to the House of Orange. In the sixties and seventies the repertoire became restricted and repetitive, and a few familiar designs, such as those of a large tree laden with fruit, of a "fan" of peacocks' feathers and of a goddess with a cornucopia were made indiscriminately by all the surviving factories. Special mention must be made of the large drug pots and tobacco jars, simple pieces with standardized decoration, but handsome and satisfying in both shape and design.

The Delft industry survived the twofold

competition of the enormously increased import from China and the rise of the German hard-paste porcelain. Yet by 1770 it was hard hit by a new rival: English cream wares, which captured the European market by their lightness, cheapness, and Louis Seize elegance. By 1790 only ten factories were still in production, and early in the nineteenth century only two were still making tin-enamelled wares, and the prosperity not only of the industry but also of the town whose name it had spread all over the civilized world had come to an end.

Polychrome wares

The coloured wares made in Delft fall into two main groups. Those fired in high-temperature colours and those fired in the muffle kiln.

(a) *High temperature*. From the late seventeenth century onwards the Delft potters added to their original blue and manganese a dull, coppery green, an iron red, and, rarely, a clear yellow. The red was a novelty in European ceramics, and was introduced at Rouen at about the same time. The whole Delft high-temperature colour scheme was, however, distinctive and unlike anything else. Many coloured replicas of Ming-Ching transitional pieces were made, the most popular being the sets of vases intended for the chimney-piece or the top of a Dutch cupboard. Of these the most famous were the reeded, octagonal vases, of great height, covered with a strewn decoration more reminiscent of Oriental embroidery than of any Chinese ceramic prototype. This design, in which the rusty iron-red predominates, was known as "cachemire", a name which suggests an Indian rather than a Chinese origin; a fine specimen is shown in Plate 343C. With the exception of *SVE*, the same factories produced these coloured pieces as made the blue and white, *LVE* being once again the most prolific. The peculiar palette of Hoppesteyn and the monogramist *IW* has already been discussed. The Rose factory, as ever, produced an exceptional variety, pieces having little in common except their high quality.

The high-temperature colours continued to be used far into the eighteenth century,

among other things on the rococo scroll work, in relief, surrounding plates, barber's bowls, plaques, etc., on which the main decoration was in blue or manganese.

(b) *Muffle kiln colours*. Quite apart from the wares more closely in line with the main trends of European faience, which attempted more and more to compete with the minutiae and brilliant colouring of hard-paste porcelain, Delft produced very early in the eighteenth century a special imitation of the Japanese porcelain made at Arita, and known throughout Europe as "Imari" ware. In these most distinctive Delft wares the iron red and blue predominate, supplemented by touches of pure lemon yellow, transparent manganese, and a translucent copper green. At first these were all fired in the high-temperature kiln, but as soon as gold was added to produce the "brocaded Imari", the muffle kiln was used increasingly, and the opaque colours of the *famille rose* were imitated more and more (Plate 342B). Plates, cruets, jugs, and the usual sets of five or seven vases were the main objects produced. Many bear in red the *PAK* mark of Pieter Adriaensz Kocx's widow. Others, including some of the most original and most brilliantly executed, the letters *AR* in monogram. Once again, a confident traditional attribution is found untenable, and the significance of the initials remains in doubt. In both these groups the paste is of a very brilliant and warm white, without a hint of blue in it, and the body itself is slightly pinkish.

It was after 1760 that attempts were made to rival the jewel-like brilliance of German porcelain. Small boxes, pipe stands formed as sleighs, pickle trays, butter dishes, and the like were made, decorated with "Watteau" scenes, or reminiscences of Herold or even – and it is almost the only time it is found on Delft – with a version of the "Kakiemon" designs so ubiquitous in European porcelain of every kind.

(c) *Coloured grounds*. In addition to the two main types of polychrome wares described above, must be described the important and highly prized group of coloured grounds.

The most famous, and most prized, of these are the black grounds. These are of two kinds.

The earlier type consists of a black enamel painted all over a dark-red clay body, and subsequently decorated in olive green and yellow, sometimes with touches of brilliant opaque light blue, red, and green. It seems that these were intended to imitate lacquer, a novel material enjoying an enormous vogue at the time, and that the olive green and yellow were meant to simulate gold. Such of these rarities as are marked mostly bear the *LVE* monogram.

The later type, closely associated with *Delft Doré* bearing the *PAK* and *AR* marks, has the black ground painted over the white body, leaving reserves to be painted in colours, the whole being fired in the muffle kiln. There are also pieces treated in this way but decorated in the usual high-temperature palette (Plate 342A and B).

Apart from the black grounds, there are pieces with deep olive, chocolate, emerald green (Plate 343D), yellow and turquoise grounds. Each colour seems to have been the speciality of one particular maker, though not all pieces are marked. Thus the turquoise and emerald green ground, with their ornamentation of brilliant opaque yellow, dark manganese lines, and occasional touches of underglaze blue, often bear the mark *IHL* in monogram. Chocolate grounds bear a CK in monogram, yellow grounds bear the *3 Astonne*, whereas the large and distinguished group of deep-olive-green pieces nearly all bear the mark *LVD*, the last two initials in monogram, as the evidence of the decoration. The olive and chocolate grounds would seem to date from the first quarter of the eighteenth century, the brighter grounds from the third quarter. Mention must also be made of the deep-blue ground pieces with white ornament, generally in conscious though heavy-handed imitation of a well-known Nevers type. Most of these were made early in the eighteenth century at the *Paeuw* pottery. The blue was painted over the white ground, the white decoration added next, no reserves being left uncovered by the deep cobalt blue.

Figures

Many figures were made at Delft, most of them in the middle fifty years of the eigh-teenth century. A distant echo of Meissen, these personages sit awkwardly round candle-sticks or small pots. They are much prized rarities, but to anyone not inflamed by a col-lector's cupidity they seem curiously bad for two reasons. The lesser plastic wares, such as lidded butter boxes, in the shape of boys on goats or eagles, or having the lid shaped as a plover, or grebe, or other marshland bird, are excellent in their simple way and far more pleasing than the analogous boxes made at Marieberg and elsewhere. A favourite type is where the box is in the shape of a curled pike (or even two) with a smaller fish in its mouth (Plate 344B). All these pieces are simply colour-ed with effective lines of colour over the main patches, to suggest feathers, features, and so on. Many bear the marks of the *Axe*, *LPK*, or the *3 Astonne*. The other reason for surprise at the feebleness of the more ambitious figures is that the Delft potteries showed no lack of plastic skill elsewhere. We do not refer to the very rare and rather absurd Delft violins. These were triumphs of misdirected cunning, only redeemed by the very high quality of the figure painting with which they are decorated or to the bird cages, which, again, are merely very rare. But plastic skill of a very high order is shown in the numerous types of complicated tulip vases, in which from pyramid and obe-lisk, or from less easily defined shapes, in-numerable orifices sprout upwards and side-ways. The masterpieces of the type may be seen in the Long Gallery at Hampton Court and are illustrated in the article by Mr Arthur Lane already referred to. But slightly less am-bitious pieces are by no means uncommon and may be seen in many museums and pri-vate houses (Plate 343A). It is perhaps signi-ficant that all these date from the earlier years, round 1700, whereas the pseudo-Meissen figures and the butter pots are later.

Dutch faïence made in other towns

Haarlem, as already stated, was early among the places where North Netherlands majolica was made, and a group of tiles with either simple patterns of small motifs ar-ranged in a diagonal cross or attractive ani-mal figures in blue surrounded by a wreath of blue and ochre "peacock's feathers", is, on slender evidence, associated with the town. There is no doubt that blue-and-white ware was made at Haarlem until late in the seventeenth century. A few signed pieces by M. van Eems have survived, and there is a record, dated 1642, of a dispute and an agreement between the Verstraetens, father and son, as to which should make majolica and which "Dutch porcelain" (i.e. blue-and-white faïence). The Haarlem plates tend to have Dutch scenes rather than Oriental designs, to be deep in the bowl, and to be painted in a very bright light blue, closely resembling that of Frankfurt. The town seems to have produced no wares in the eighteenth century, probably owing to the overwhelming competition of the Delft potteries.

Friesland, situated farther away from metropolitan Holland, and nearer the export market of Germany, produced a very great quantity of rather second-class goods throughout the eighteenth century.

The wares of Harlingen and Bolsward are difficult to identify. Harlingen is credited, among other things, with some very late teapot stands, in greyish-white faïence with simple Louis Seize and Empire decoration. Bolsward is even harder to identify, in spite of a magnificent document in the shape of a huge, widely reproduced, tile picture of the inside of a pottery on which one can study most of the processes involved. It is roughly painted in a pale and slaty blue. Much so-called "Peasant Delft" was undoubtedly made there, and production continued through the nineteenth century until the present day.

With Makkum it is possible to be more definite. Many plates are dated, and quite a few are inscribed. The painting is less fluent than that at Delft, but it is firm and convincing for all that. The blue is dark and slaty, and there is a preference for floral borders and firmly drawn biblical scenes. Marriage plates and alphabet plates were a popular line (Plate 343B).

Between 1755 and 1773 a faïence factory at Arnhem produced goods of the finest quality, in a fully understood rococo idiom, and entirely divorced from anything else made in Holland. The beautiful white enamel, decorated with flowers or scenes after French engravings, the amusing tureen shapes, and the firm, crisp lines of tripod coffee-pots, close to the admirable Dutch silver of the period, all combine to give Arnhem a high place among the faïence of rococo Europe. It can best be studied in the Musée du Cinquantenaire, Brussels, and the town museum at Arnhem (Plate 345C).

Tiles

Throughout the period under review an enormous number of tiles were produced in Holland and exported all over Europe in vast quantities. Indeed, for many people, these are the most characteristic examples of "Delft". Ironically, though produced to some extent in that town, by far the greater part were made in Rotterdam or in the various Friesland potteries.

The majolica tiles, dating from early in the seventeenth century (earlier types were almost certainly made at Antwerp), are of reddish clay and are well over half an inch thick. They show four-tile patterns of grapes, tulips, and pomegranates, in the usual Netherlands majolica palette, with blue and orange predominating. They were intended as wall tiles – a Spanish rather than an Italian use – and the designs may have been prompted by those used on Spanish leather. To these were soon added figures of animals in circles, with a simple dark-blue corner motif, the creatures rising on mounds of bright green and ochre, with occasional touches of manganese. The corner motifs soon became large fleurs-de-lis. By 1630 the Chinese fashion had radiated out from Delft, and blue-and-white tiles became universally popular, at first enclosed in a bold and effective late Ming fret. It is odd that actual Chinese scenes, so popular elsewhere, were always uncommon on tiles. At first large figures of animals, soldiers and officers, horsemen and ladies were the main subjects of decoration. As the seventeenth century moved on, these figures grew smaller and at the same time the corner motifs shrank and became insignificant. To the repertoire were added children, putti, marine monsters, innumerable and very attractive ships, from men-of-war to fishing smacks, and an immense variety of small landscapes. Round the turn of the century manganese replaced blue to some extent, especially in the Bible scenes, which from then on enjoyed enormous popularity. In the eighteenth century manganese, or more rarely blue, grounds were introduced, round a central scene painted in blue. All these types were imitated abroad, especially in England. A very few polychrome tiles in the colours of the muffle kiln have survived, but there is nothing to equal the extent or the quality of the polychrome tiles made in Liverpool in the second half of the eighteenth century, by which time the Dutch industry was declining both in quantity and in quality of output.

Tile pictures have always been popular. Apart from such masterpieces as the huge allegorical scene in the Victoria and Albert Museum – a special commission carried out, brilliantly, after a design by a stained-glass painter – there are innumerable harbour scenes and townscapes on quite a large scale. Most satisfactory are perhaps the huge flower pieces, in their baroque vases, which adorned the kitchens of several palaces in Germany and France. These are painted in the high-temperature colours and are akin in feeling to the "cachemire" vases.

Innumerable small scenes of six or eight tiles, showing cats, dogs, windmills, horses, bird-cages, in fact almost anything, were let into walls of plain tiles in kitchens and dairies, very much as pictures hanging on the wall.

In all their huge production it is difficult to be certain of date or provenance. Thin tiles are eighteenth century – the thinner, the later. Manganese is not much found before 1700. A slate blue and coarse white suggests Friesland. The subject is as inexhaustible as philately, with which it has points of affinity. Once one has felt the fascination of tiles one is an addict for ever, and one may promise oneself, with reasonable confidence, the discovery of an endless series of minor variants on the central themes. The collections at the Victoria and Albert Museum, at the Huis Lambert van Meerten, Delft, in the Boymans Museum, Rotterdam, and in the store rooms of the Rijksmuseum, Amsterdam, are the essential places of pilgrimage.

Forgeries

Few ceramic groups have been so extensively forged as Delft, and, for various reasons, faïence is easier to imitate convincingly than hard-paste porcelain. Hannover describes a visit to Samson's workshop in Paris, where he could compare original pieces side by side with the replicas, and all collectors would do well to heed his warning against buying important Delft pieces without a long pedigree.

The *AK* and *CK* monograms are the most frequently forged of the earlier marks, and the forgers show a strong preference for "important" reeded vases and for plates in sets, showing the months or some industry such as whale fishing or tobacco-curing (a famous faked set of this last, in the cellars of a great English national collection, is illustrated by Knowles). The *PAK* mark is also much forged, especially on *Delft Doré*. The standard of skill in the best forgeries is very high, but the following points may prove helpful.

Suspect any piece in which the blue has an ultramarine tinge, or in which the paste feels hard or faintly granular. In genuine pieces the exposed body of the clay feels soft to the fingernail. Suspect any *AK* mark followed by a group of numbers, and any *PAK* piece of "Imari" on which the painting is not convincingly neat and controlled.

There is the further problem of distinguishing Delft from German wares, such as those made at Frankfort and Hanau. It should be remembered that on the German wares the blue used is much starchier and brighter, the use of *trek* is rare, there is a preference for lobed dishes, which are uncommon in Holland, and that narrow-necked jugs are very common in Germany and very rare in Delft. It should also be remembered that Delft plates are remarkably thin and remarkably light.

Northern French wares, such as white-lobed plates with a central motif of a cherub, a fleur-de-lis or a portrait-head, and a frequently found series of puzzle jugs with blue and orange tulips, can soon be recognized by a family likeness and by the fact that the glaze is harder and more parchment-like to the touch.

Good-quality Delft is always very highly glazed yet soft to the touch, and it should be noted that crazing is very rarely found on any genuine piece.

PORCELAIN

In Holland Meissen workmen, unemployed during the Seven Years' War, helped to produce hard-paste porcelain at Weesp from 1759 on. The factory, with all moulds and plants, was transferred to Oude Loosdrecht in 1771, and thence to Amstel.

English

POTTERY

The making of pottery in England is continuous back to, and beyond, the Roman occupation. Before the later Middle Ages, however, the pots made were technically of the simplest. The dominant invention in the post-Roman period was the discovery of lead-glazing, by which clay, sprinkled with powdered galena of lead and fired at a reasonably low temperature, could be covered with a watertight glass-like coating. The decorative techniques used by the medieval potter were few and simple, and it is by their primary shapes that medieval pots make their greatest appeal. Since, however, they are seldom recovered intact, this quality can rarely make its due aesthetic impression, and medieval pottery is rather the preserve of the archaeologist than of the connoisseur and collector. Its technical character, however, is very important for the subsequent history of English pottery. By the sixteenth century a considerable degree of refinement had been achieved. Small, neat pots were now produced with a whitish buff body and a solid, satisfactory green lead-glaze; and a second class of pottery was made of a very hard red body with a dark brown, almost black, lead-glaze.

This century, however, also saw a notable innovation. Ever since the mid-fifteenth century Italian potters had been making an earthenware (*maiolica*) with a dense and smooth white glaze produced by the suspension in a lead-glaze of opaque white particles of oxide (ashes) of tin. This was not only more hygienic and cleaner-looking than ordinary lead-glaze, but served as an admirable base for painting in various metallic colours. The resultant popularity of *maiolica* induced Italian potters to follow their markets and settle in other European countries. One great centre of this transplanted industry was Antwerp, and from there in 1567 two potters came and settled in Norwich, moving to London in 1570.

Seventeenth-century delftware (Plate 347A)

The earliest dated piece of certainly English delftware (anachronistically so-called from the commanding position of Delft in the Netherlands tin-glazed pottery industry later in the century) is a dish of 1600 in the London Museum. Outside an Italianate arabesque border derived from *maiolica*, it has an edging of blue dashes, the earliest appearance of a motif which links together a large class of later polychrome dishes. These "blue-dash chargers" were used for decorative purposes, being placed on court-cupboards or hung on walls. The earliest are painted with fruit and floral designs based on foreign models, but figure designs appear at least as early as 1614. No specifically English type was evolved, however, until the 1630s, when, among other biblical subjects, the story of the Fall was represented, to be repeated in innumerable examples well into the eighteenth century. A characteristically English series of chargers bearing effigies of ruling monarchs or national heroes begins with a representation of Charles I dated 1653. Among the most striking "blue-dash chargers" are those decorated with boldly stylized tulips painted in green, blue, orange, yellow, and sometimes red. They are rarely dated, although there are examples of 1668 and 1676. The most characteristic specimens were made about 1650–80, but a piece dated 1628 is known. Equally effective are the rare specimens of similar date with abstract patterns, usually of spirals and feather-like groups of curves, painted in blue and purple.

The majority of the "blue-dash chargers" employed the polychrome palette taken over from Netherlands majolica. From the 1620s onwards, however, English delftware also began to imitate the blue-and-white colour-scheme, and the designs, of contemporary imported Chinese porcelain. This development appears to be connected with the opening of a pottery in Southwark, by one Christian Wilhelm about 1625. The earliest dated piece is a wine-bottle of 1628 painted with a design of birds, insects, and rocks in blue. Similar designs are found on spouted posset-pots (from 1631) and on mugs, whether barrel-shaped (from 1629) or tapering and straight-sided (from 1635). The blue of these Southwark wares was sometimes supplemented by purple. This and another Southwark pottery, together with the original Aldgate pottery founded in 1571, made all the English delftware of the second quarter of the seventeenth century, including many "Lambeth" types. The Lambeth potteries did not commence operations until about 1660.

One notable type of "Lambeth" delftware continued the blue colouring of the Chinese-imitated wares, but confined it to inscriptions or simple heraldic devices, leaving plain a large surface area of the incomparable dense smooth white glaze of the period. The forms most favoured were mugs (dated examples from 1650 onwards), stemmed goblets (from

1659), posset-pots (from 1650), and articles for the apothecary's shop – drug-jars for liquid and dry medicaments, and pill-slabs. The virtues of this type are best seen, however, in the wine-bottles, used for bringing the wine to table; numerous examples are known dating from the second and third quarters of the century. They normally bore no more decorations than the name of the wine, the date, and a simple calligraphic scroll.

Sometimes the beautiful glaze was left totally undecorated, as is sometimes the case with the horned biconical salt-cellars, the candlesticks, and other forms closely modelled on contemporary silverware or pewter.

It is difficult, and often impossible, to distinguish the London delftware of the later seventeenth century from that manufactured at the potteries founded at Brislington (near Bristol) about 1650 and in Bristol itself in 1683.

Seventeenth-century stoneware (Plate 348A)

Just as the importation of Netherlands majolica had brought the majolica-potters in its wake, so efforts were made in Queen Elizabeth's reign to start a manufacture of salt-glazed stoneware pots, to compete with those imported in great quantities from the Rhineland in the wine-trade. This is known from documentary sources only. It is only when we come to the patent taken out in 1671 by John Dwight, of Fulham, that actual pots can be associated with the documentary evidence.

A number of known types may be identified as Dwight's work. Two yellowish-brown mottled "bellarmines" were found on the site of his pottery and are preserved. Dwight must have made many more such under a contract to the Glass Sellers' Company in 1676. Akin to them, but more elaborate, are some brown and marbled pear-shaped bottles, with applied reliefs which roughly correspond with a set of brass stamps said to have come from the Fulham pottery-site. Of a similar material is a splendid series of figures of mythological personages, and portraits of royalty and of Dwight's own daughter, all now in public collections. Less rare are some small globular handled mugs with vertical reeded necks, made of mouse-coloured or marbled stone-ware. These are occasionally so thinly potted as to be translucent.

In 1693 Dwight brought a law-suit in defence of his patent rights against a number of defendants. It is clear from this that salt-glazed stoneware was being made in several parts of the country – Burslem in Staffordshire (by the brothers Thomas, Aaron, and Richard Wedgwood); Nottingham (by John Morley); Southampton and Southwark. The Staffordshire wares have been identified in a series of simple mugs with brown, grey, or speckled appearance. The Nottingham stonewares are marked by a peculiar lustrous brown surface, and were frequently decorated with incised or impressed designs. Small globular mugs, with decoration pierced through an outer wall, were characteristic of the seventeenth-century Nottingham products. The manufacture continued more or less unchanged throughout the eighteenth century (Plate 348B).

Dwight's most serious rivals, however, were the brothers John and David Elers, of Fulham, also cited in 1693. They appear to have had some connexion with Dwight, and their work at Fulham cannot be distinguished from his. Shortly after 1693, however, they migrated to Bradwell Wood, near Newcastle-under-Lyme in Staffordshire, and there started to manufacture unglazed tea-table ware from the local red clay. These imitated the red stonewares of Yi-hsing, imported in large quantities with the China tea itself during the seventeenth century. A number of globular mugs, cups, and teapots decorated with applied moulded relief have been identified as their work. Their clay had run out by 1699, but in that short time the clean quality of their workmanship seems to have made an impression in Staffordshire which contributed to the rise of the pottery industry there.

Seventeenth-century lead-glazed earthenware (Plate 347B)

Contemporaneously with the relatively refined wares described in the two foregoing sections, simple lead-glazed earthenware continued to be made in country districts in the sixteenth-century tradition. Thus at Wrotham

in Kent, there was a school of pottery which probably had its beginning in the sixteenth century, although the earliest dated piece is a tyg of 1612. The Wrotham wares were usually of red clay decorated with white pipe-clay, the former appearing red-brown and the latter straw-coloured under the lead glaze. The pipe-clay was either applied in pads and then stamped with small decorative motifs, or used as a "slip" for writing inscriptions, much as a cake is iced. The shapes of Wrotham pottery are primitive and without great distinction. Its greatest merits lie in the freedom and well-judged spacing of the trailed inscriptions, and in the warm colours of the clay. Similar virtues endow the pottery made in the London area about the middle of the seventeenth century ("Metropolitan" slipware).

The green-glaze tradition of medieval times was continued at York (Walmgate) throughout the seventeenth century, the forms made being large jars or milk-pots decorated with rosettes. A similar survival of green- and yellow-glazing is to be noted in the West Country, in Devonshire, Somerset, and Glamorgan, and continued into the eighteenth, and in some cases the nineteenth, century. Such pottery was often decorated with incised ("sgraffiato") designs.

In other parts of the country, however, the potters used no more than the natural colours of their clays. The Wrotham repertory of simple clay techniques was greatly extended, mainly in Staffordshire. The chief innovation was the use of a wash of white clay on which clays of various tones of red and brown (and, exceptionally, greenish-grey) could be trailed as desired. Areas of the darker colour could then be enlivened with dots of white. The resultant wares – notably the great dishes bearing the names of Thomas and Ralph Toft – have a freedom of design and a mellow vivacity of tone unsurpassed in peasant pottery. Their unsophisticated themes – mermaids, Adam and Eve, or King Charles in the oak tree – give them an added charm. Such dishes were also made by members of well-known potters' families in Burslem, such as Simpson, Glass, Meir, etc., and date from the 1670s until the first decades of the eighteenth century. Small cups, posset-pots, and various forms of jug were also made. These relatively elaborate wares were no doubt special commissions outside the potter's normal work on simple pots for kitchen and dairy (Plate 347B).

Yet more technical innovations followed, notably the use of various simple stamped devices, and (most effective of all) a technique of combing the trailed slip into feather- and arcade-patterns in dark and light tones.

Eighteenth-century earthenware and stoneware (Plates 346, 347D, 348, and 349A)

The refinements described in the preceding paragraph properly belong to the opening years of the eighteenth century, and the second and third decades of that century saw further innovations, which were clearly inspired by the whiteness and fineness of porcelain. The first step was the use of washes of imported white Devonshire clay laid over the local clay. The second was more fundamental, and consisted in adding calcined flint to a clay body, giving it lightness both of weight and colour, and a refractory character which enabled it to be fired at a high temperature, giving a stoneware which could be salt-glazed: at a lower temperature it became a cream-coloured earthenware, and from this point onwards (in the 1730s) there ceases to be a clear distinction between stoneware and earthenware potters.

The manufacturing methods of the period seem to derive from the tradition left behind by the Elers. Not only did the shapes employed stem from theirs (indeed, the whole idea of making tea-wares was an innovation in Staffordshire), but they were decorated by the applied relief technique. This was not only used on the red stoneware teapots but was applied to lead-glazed earthenware. In one class of wares, popularly attributed to John Astbury, but certainly also made by Thomas Whieldon, pads of pipe-clay stamped with a variety of simple designs were applied on a red ground. The same colour-contrasts were observed in tea-wares decorated with stamped flowers, vine-leaves, etc., in white placed on a darker ground, and joined together by freely-scrolled stems made of clay rolled between the palms. The spouts and handles, usually modelled to simulate a gnarled branch ("crabstock"), were also of white clay. The range of these colour-contrasts was extended by using glaze-colours applied in patches over the relief.

This art of colour-glazing was probably in some degree due to the generally improved control of glazes made possible by the substitution of a liquid glaze-mixture (in which the piece, lightly fired to an absorbent "biscuit" condition, could be dipped) for the powdered glaze which had previously been applied by sprinkling. The new colours included a mottled brown ("tortoiseshell") (Plate 346) and an all-over black, and added a range of soft tones of blue and grey, green and yellow. These colours were combined in delicate harmonies on the refined light-toned mid-eighteenth-century wares associated particularly with the name of Thomas Whieldon. Colours were also used to enliven the simple but animated figures made in this period – mainly clay-tones and occasional patches of green on the earlier pieces associated with Astbury, and the full range of glaze-colours in the figures of the "Whieldon" class (Plate 347D).

Colour-contrast was further exploited in a ware made by kneading together clays of contrasting colours, to produce marbled effects ("agate" ware). Since excessive manipulation spoiled the markings of these pieces, moulding was used, both for the lead-glazed tea-wares and the little figures (often cats) made in salt-glazed stoneware.

Moulding, indeed, was becoming increasingly important. The earliest form of this process was the pressing of clay into metal moulds but far more significant was the introduction, shortly before 1740, of the plaster-of-Paris mould. From a positive master-mould in alabaster or the like was taken an impression, from which in turn a number of mould-blocks were made in salt-glazed stoneware. From these were taken the final multiple plaster-of-Paris moulds, into which a liquid slip was poured. The water was absorbed by the plaster, leaving a fine film of clay adhering to the mould. This process enabled any number of pieces to be made from a single original, and was the crucial first step towards mass-production in the Potteries. It was particularly suited to the making of fine white stoneware for the tea-table, and it is mainly among the teapots of the period 1740–50 that the most original English moulded wares are to be found. These display a fantasy and humour which link them with the earlier slipwares, and which disappear in the more sophisticated second half of the century. These models are frequently attributed to the block-cutter Aaron Wood.

Thrown and turned stonewares, however, continued to be made and were decorated either with relief – in white on a drab body (often miscalled "Crouch" ware) or in white gilt on a white body – or by incised designs into which cobalt was rubbed to produce blue lines on the white ground ("scratch blue").

The appearance of this stoneware readily prompted comparison with porcelain, and it was natural that the decoration of porcelain should be copied. This enamelling technique (*see* Enamel) seems to have been introduced by immigrant artists from Holland, where English stoneware was much imported. In its developed form, however, it has an entirely English character, and employed a striking palette, which included blue, green, turquoise, and pink, often used in startling combinations (Plate 349A). Transfer-printing in a beautiful russet-red was also done on stoneware by John Sadler of Liverpool.

The whole of this phase is summed up in the career of Thomas Whieldon, of Fenton Low, near Burslem. On the site of his factory there have been found wasters of almost all the types described, and it is very likely that he was the great innovator of this intensely active period. It is perhaps significant that in 1754 he took as his partner the man who was to become England's most famous potter – Josiah Wedgwood (1735–95).

It is important to understand Wedgwood's contribution to English pottery. His greatest qualities were those of organizer, businessman, and technician. As an artistic influence he is less easy to assess. He was quick to associate himself with the incipient neo-classical movement in art of the 1760s, and he found a kindred spirit in Thomas Bentley, his partner from 1769 in the manufacture of ornamental wares. On these he now concentrated, in an effort to find ceramic bodies suitable for the incorporation of his classical ideals, and produced a whole series of fine-grained stonewares left unglazed. These included "black basaltes" (which when painted with matt red enamel could be used to imitate Greek red-figure vases), and *rosso antico*, resembling terra-cotta. In 1775 he finally perfected a body which would enable him to imitate the cameos of Antiquity – a fine-grained stoneware capable of being coloured by a number of different metallic stains ("jasper" ware – Plate 348c). Countless vases, cameos, medallions, mounts, etc., were made in it, and these are the productions most readily associated with his name. Although he employed the best artists he could find to model the reliefs with which these wares are decorated, and although he applied to them the most rigorous technical standards, they are to the modern taste rather cold in their devotion to classical purity, and sentimental in their rendering of more homely themes.

Alongside the decorative wares, however, Wedgwood continued the more practical wares of his partnership with Whieldon. One is of particular importance. This was cream-coloured lead-glazed earthenware, which he had perfected by 1760 and which was called "Queen's ware". This possessed the practical advantage of being tough but not excessively hard (salt-glazed stoneware tended to wear out silver spoons and forks), and added to this a slight fashionable ornamentation in the neo-classical style, painted in enamel. It was immensely popular, becoming the standard English body and being copied extensively on the Continent. Much was disposed of undecorated, to be transfer-printed by Sadler and Green, of Liverpool, or enamelled in independent workshops, where some of the most charming painting was carried out in red and black or polychrome.

Although Wedgwood was the outstanding figure in the history of English pottery, there were numerous other potters, in Staffordshire, Yorkshire, and elsewhere, who ran him close. The late eighteenth century was, in fact, characterized by mutual copying of materials and designs within the two main divisions of decorative stonewares and cream-coloured useful wares. There were some, however, who continued the older styles, notably the Ralph Woods, father and son. Their fame rests chiefly on the figures and groups, which, simply modelled with due regard to the limitations of lead-glazed earthenware in rendering sharp profiles or fine detail, are glazed in the harmonious quiet tones of the "Whieldon" palette. They are among the best things in English eighteenth-century pottery (Plate 347D).

Eighteenth-century delftware (Plate 349B)

The Chinese influence on English delftware becomes more pronounced in the late seventeenth and the eighteenth centuries. It shows itself not only in the blue-and-white palette but also in a polychrome scheme probably derived from the Chinese porcelain of the "famille verte". This colour-scheme, although used to render "Chinese" designs, was also employed for purely European themes (a windmill, a swan, etc.). The painting of this early eighteenth-century phase was broad and vigorous, the colours bold and strong. Towards the middle of the eighteenth century, however, when the baroque in art was giving way to the rococo, the painting becomes more delicate and the palette softer. The shapes often have the lobed and fretted outlines favoured in the mid-eighteenth century and were probably inspired by silverware. The subject matter of the painting is equally of the period, with fantastic Chinamen fishing or boating in imaginary landscapes, or tall elegant European ladies moving amidst slim trees in a landscape. The influence of Chinese procelain is everywhere noticeable, in the designs of peonies and bamboo, or the border-patterns of diaper or "cracked ice"; in ground colours of "powder-blue" (also much copied in manganese-purple) and *bianco-sopra-bianco* borders in imitation of the incised patterns on some Chinese porcelain. All these designs were executed in the "high-temperature" colours (those that are painted on the glaze-dipped "biscuit" and fired with it). Only in the second half of the eighteenth century were enamel-colours used and then only rarely, this development, like that of transfer-printing on delftware, being peculiar to Liverpool.

The rococo gave way to the neo-classical style in the course of the 1760s, but by 1770 the manufacture of delftware was on the wane and neo-classical decoration is therefore relatively rare, being restricted in the main to floral festoons.

Throughout the eighteenth century delftware was used for propaganda purposes, with inscriptions and themes reflecting the political passions of the moment ("God Save King George", "Calvert and Martin for Ever", etc.). It was also frequently topical, recording the taking of Chagre in 1740 or Lunardi's balloon ascent in 1783.

The repertory of forms of eighteenth-century delftware greatly extended that of the seventeenth century. Despite the unsuitability of the material, teapots, cups, etc., were made for the tea-table. Bowls, "bricks" (small perforated boxlike vases), wall pockets, and vases for flowers reflect the increased refinement of eighteenth-century living. "Puzzle-jugs" were made at all the main factories, and bottles and basins of exiguous dimensions answered the toilet needs of the period. The most numerous forms by far, however, were plates, dishes, and bowls. Tiles were made at all the factories.

By about 1790 the manufacture of delftware ceased. The Bristol potteries were all closed or turned over to other purposes before 1780, and those of Liverpool (begun about 1710) shortly afterwards. Only the Lambeth wares continued to be made into the 1790s, but they, too, were doomed by the competition of creamware.

The nineteenth century to 1830

By 1800 the pottery industry was well on the way to industrialization as we know it to-day. The different centres lost much of their individual character, and it is often impossible, in the absence of a mark, to say whether a piece was made in Staffordshire, Yorkshire, Liverpool, Scotland, or on Tyneside. Individual firms often copied shamelessly the materials and designs of their competitors.

The basic commodity on which this flourishing industry was built was cream-coloured earthenware in a wide range of varieties. Enamelling and printing were the chief methods of decoration, but in an atmosphere of breathless industrialization the quality of hand-painting was declining rapidly, being in some cases reduced to mere daubs of colour, as in the opaque dirty-coloured enamels which ousted the clear glaze-colours on figures of the type produced by the Woods (their final declension is seen in the wares of Walton, and others about the end of our period); or in the dabs of high-temperature colours (brown, green, and blue predominating) which emphasize the relief on wares of the "Pratt" type.

A method of decoration more in harmony with the spirit of the time was printing, and by the second quarter of the century underglaze-blue printing became the most widespread decorative technique in use, the wares so made having a world-wide market. Overglaze printing, mainly in brown and black, was also widely practised.

A fresh decorative resource of the nineteenth century was the use of "lustre" painting, the favourite colours being "silver" and pink. Lustre was frequently applied in solid areas, the pink sometimes in conjunction with black printing, but the most effective use of the medium was by painting designs in a "resist" which left them standing in reserve on the (usually silver) ground.

An innovation of this period was an earthenware body dubbed "stone china", more solid than cream-coloured earthenware and usually greyish in appearance. Similar in character, but patented at a later date, was the "ironstone china" of C. J. and G. Miles Mason (from 1813).

Stoneware went on being made up to the end of our period. The unglazed black basaltes and coloured jasper wares continued into the nineteenth century unaltered in technique but with decoration to suit the changing taste of the time. To Wedgwood's repertory of colours were added others, notably a green invented by Samuel Hollins of Shelton, a white associated with Castleford, and a drab much used at Herculaneum (Liverpool) and elsewhere. In the early nineteenth century it was a common practice to decorate these stonewares in opaque enamel colours.

The stoneware of the London area (Lambeth and Mortlake) continued in the crude style of the eighteenth century, with relief and incised decoration on unpretentious brown and grey wares, such as mugs for public-houses, spirit-flasks, and the like.

ENGLISH PORCELAIN

The eighteenth century (Plates 353-5, 356A and C)

The first porcelain known in this country was imported from China and, being rare, was very expensive. The high price was an inducement to imitate it. This was done in Italy in the sixteenth century, and again in France from 1673 onwards. The material made, however, was a "soft-paste" porcelain only in outward appearance like the Oriental. It was not until 1709 that true "hard-paste" porcelain was made in Europe, at Meissen (near Dresden). Meissen porcelain thenceforward became all the rage, and was imitated in its turn. The making of porcelain in England was part of this general imitative movement.

Although numerous experiments were made earlier, it was not until the 'forties of the eighteenth century that English porcelain is known to have been made. The earliest dated piece is a Chelsea jug of 1745, and although the Bow factory's patent dates from 1744, no specimen is known definitely dating from that year. Both these factories worked in the French soft-paste tradition, but at Bow was developed what proved to be England's greatest contribution to porcelain-chemistry – the use of bone-ash. This greatly reduced the risk of collapsing in the kiln, a fault to which soft-paste porcelain is particularly prone. A further novel ingredient was introduced at a factory founded at Bristol in 1749. This was soapstone (steatite), which made the porcelain body more resistant to sudden changes of temperature – a very desirable characteristic in tea-table wares.

Soft-paste porcelain alone was made in

England for the first twenty years. In 1768, however, William Cookworthy, of Plymouth, took out a patent for the making of true porcelain, and in 1770 transferred his factory to Bristol.

English porcelain was put to most of the uses for which china is employed today. In particular, it was devoted to the dinner-table and the tea-table

At first English porcelain tended to follow closely the forms of Meissen, and (often by way of Meissen) of Oriental china. Another potent influence on porcelain shapes, however, was that of silver. At Chelsea, perhaps because Nicholas Sprimont, the proprietor-manager, was a silversmith by training, this influence was particularly strong; and specific instances of exact copying can be cited. Tablewares (particularly tureens) made in the forms of animals, birds, and vegetables exemplify the contemporary rococo taste.

Although a fair proportion of the earlier porcelain was left undecorated (save, perhaps, for sprays of leaves and flowers applied in relief in imitation of those on the "blanc-de-chine" porcelain of Fukien), the greater part was "enamelled" (see Enamel) in various colours and styles. These, too, were imitated from Meissen, where, after a phase of close copying from the Oriental, a completely European manner of decoration was being evolved. As a complement to the "Indian" flowers of the Kakiemon porcelain was evolved a style of naturalistic European flower-painting ("Deutsche Blumen" – Plate 353A), at first stiff, formal, and large in scale, but later painted with greater fluency and less pretension. All these styles were taken up at Chelsea and Bow. From Meissen, too, was derived a manner of painting in which tiny figures were depicted against a background of landscape within panels. From the same source were derived the vignettes of gallants and ladies, or of grotesque Chinese, which were borrowed ultimately from Watteau.

Soon after the middle of the eighteenth century the role of Meissen as the fashion-leading European porcelain factory was assumed by the French royal factory at Sèvres, and the change is reflected in English porcelain. Notable among the styles borrowed were the rendering (both in painting and in gilding) of "exotic" birds in the manner of Hondecoeter, and the use of rich-coloured grounds, particularly a royal blue, a green, and a rich wine-red, the colours being further enriched by lavish gilding. These styles were particularly favoured at Worcester (Plate 353D) and at Chelsea in the "gold anchor" period. When French taste reacted from the lush exuberance of the rococo and entered upon the sober phase of the Louis XVI style, English porcelain followed suit. To the extravagances of the Chelsea "gold anchor" wares succeeded the restrained garlands, wreaths, and neo-classical urns of the combined Chelsea-Derby concern (Plate 356C), and this style was also followed at the recently founded Bristol factory.

One form of porcelain-decoration may confidently be claimed as an original English contribution. This was transfer-printing (Plate 353B), a process first introduced in the enamel factory at Battersea before 1756, but was then used at Bow in that year. By 1757 its chief exponent, Robert Hancock, had moved to Worcester, where it was to be most extensively used. A similar process was used at Liverpool to decorate tiles at about the same time, but its application to porcelain there probably dates somewhat later. Transfer-printing is also occasionally to be seen on Chelsea, Derby, Longton Hall, and even Bristol porcelain. The prints were sometimes washed over with colours to give the effect of polychrome painting. The overglaze method of transfer-printing was before long adapted for printing in underglaze cobalt blue.

Most characteristic of all in an art which catered for the extravagant and carefree taste of the rich in the eighteenth century were the figures in porcelain (Plates 354 and 355). These, too, were the invention of Meissen. In Germany porcelain figures and groups were used to replace the sugar and wax figures which were combined into scenes and panoramas on the tables at great banquets. This idea, as well as the actual Meissen models, was transplanted to England, and porcelain figures were used for table-decoration until almost the end of the century. Such figures had to be modelled so that they could be viewed from any point, but from about 1760 figures and groups became popular also as ornaments for chimney-pieces and cabinets, and these, being intended for a front-view only, were modelled accordingly, and were often provided with a leafy bower or background ("*bocage*").

Figures were (and are) made by cutting the original model into parts suitable for making moulds. The corresponding clay parts taken from the moulds were reassembled by the "repairer", who, although not necessarily a modeller of any originality, needed special aptitude for the work. The "repairers'" marks sometimes found on figures do not, therefore, indicate the identity of the original modeller. When not derived directly from Continental originals, English porcelain figures were frequently inspired by engravings, and sometimes by sculpture in other materials. They were seldom entirely original work.

Figures were usually decorated in enamels, and, in the appropriate period, gilt. Sometimes, however, they left the factory in the white, in which state they are usually found today (Plate 355B). The original intention was almost certainly to paint them in unfired ("cold") colours, traces of which may sometimes be noted on otherwise plain pieces. Such work was probably done outside the factories by independent decorators.

The neo-classical movement of the later eighteenth century inspired the use of an unglazed "biscuit" porcelain to resemble marble. Figures and groups in this material were the speciality of the Derby factory (Plate 354C), but were also made elsewhere.

The nineteenth century to 1830 (Plate 356B and D)

Of the great eighteenth-century factories, only Worcester and Derby survived into the nineteenth century. The neo-classicism of the previous century lingered on and developed into the heavier Regency style. In this field there seems to have been some borrowing from the greater Continental factories. There was a general tendency to use heavy all-over decoration, and this is seen most clearly in the gaudy "Japan" patterns common to Derby and the Staffordshire factories, of which many began to manufacture porcelain about or soon after 1810. In Staffordshire much of the decoration common on pottery was extended to porcelain – lustre-painting, overglaze printing, etc. Nearly everywhere the English bone-china body as finally evolved by Josiah Spode II was becoming standard, and this fact and the general mutual copying of designs make for a certain monotony in the porcelain of this period.

A notable exception was provided by the beautiful glassy soft-paste porcelain made at Nantgarw and Swansea (Plate 356D) by William Billingsley, and later at Coalport. These porcelains were much sought after by the independent London dealers and decorators. To Billingsley was also due a naturalistic manner of flower-painting in which the highlights were wiped out with the brush (Plate 356D). This style, although evolved at Derby before 1800, only became general after that date. In the hands of subsequent painters it hardened into a somewhat arid formalism, and the flowers were often rendered against a heavy-coloured ground.

Towards the end of our period the rococo style was revived, and porcelain was decorated with asymmetrical scrollwork, often emphasized by brassy gilding. Beige, grey, maroon, and other coloured grounds, were favoured and are commonly associated with the Rockingham factory, although used elsewhere (Plate 356A). Much use was also made of elaborate incrustations of flowers, particularly at the Coalport factory.

French

FAÏENCE

The art of tin-enamelling earthenware was probably introduced into France during the sixteenth century by migrant potters from Spain and Italy. Early French wares, such as those made at Lyons, show the dominating influence of Italian majolica techniques, and both Florentine and Genoese artists are recorded as having worked there in the first half of the sixteenth century. The term faïence, derived from the Italian town of Faenza, was, however, not in general use until about 1610.

The development of an independent style began at Nevers, which was the last city to receive the wandering Italians. From 1632 onwards new establishments sprang up there, and from then until the end of the eighteenth century the industry continued to thrive, notably at Rouen, Moustiers, Marseilles, and Strasbourg.

Nevers had carried forward the finest Italian traditions, as a result of privileges granted to three brothers of the Conrade family, who came from Albrissola near Genoa. A departure is first seen in a well-defined type decorated in imitation of Chinese blue-and-white porcelain, imported into Europe in the seventeenth century. Another innovation for which the potters of Nevers became famous was a deep-blue glaze, on to which was painted in opaque white, yellow, and orange, the so-called "Persian" motifs of flowers and birds. Their pseudo-Oriental character led Brongniart (Director of the Sèvres Museum) to classify them as Persian, and the ground colour is generally known as *bleu persan*. The shapes were either Oriental or baroque, and coinciding with the Chinese imitations, were beautiful pictorial subjects, painted from engravings after Raphael, Frans Floris, and the baroque masters Poussin, Van Dyck, and Simon Vouet.

In 1847 the factory at Rouen, owned by Edme Poterat, obtained a fifty-year monopoly for the whole of Normandy. A very distinctive kind of ornament originating there was the somewhat monotonous repetition of symmetrical patterns painted in blue on a white ground. Known as *style rayonnant*, it consists of elaborately scrolled and foliate decoration converging inwards in pendants (*lambrequins*) towards the centre of a dish or plate: alternatively, the pattern was "reserved" in white on a blue ground. Variations, introducing *ferronnerie*, figures, and slight architectual motives, were taken from engravings by Jean Bérain (*style Bérain*).

Faïence was at first regarded as only suitable for use by the bourgeoisie, and below-stairs in the houses of noblemen. At the beginning of the eighteenth century, however, a national emergency caused Louis XIV and his courtiers to send their silver plate to be melted down at the Mint, and this provided the faïenciers with an unexpected opportunity to sell their wares in a very different market. Those nearest Paris naturally benefited most, and numerous Rouen services painted with the arms of famous families testify to the patronage of the nobility.

In the south, Moustiers and Marseilles at first adopted the prevailing styles. Pierre Clerissy, assisted by a painter François Viry and his sons Gaspard and Jean Baptiste, founded the industry at Moustiers in 1679. Through successive generations the business was handed down to his grandson Pierre II, who, until 1757, continued it with such success that he became a landed nobleman. His enterprise also attracted others to the district.

The fashionable blue-and-white palette used on early Moustiers shows great distinction. Some fine dishes painted by Viry depict hunting scenes taken from engravings by

Antonio Tempesta, also biblical subjects after Leclerc's engraved illustrations in the Bible de Sacy, published in Paris, 1670. The early eighteenth century saw the adoption of the *style Bérain*.

Foremost among the other factories was that of Jean Baptiste Laugier and his brother-in-law Joseph Ollerys. It lasted from 1738 to 1790. The use of polychrome was introduced to Moustiers by Olerys, who had already worked at the Alcora factory in Spain (1727–37). From the *style Bérain* it passed to a phase characterized by elaborately framed pictures and festooned borders *décor à guirlandes*. Biblical and allegorical scenes with figures painted in small detail are believed to have been executed by Olerys. Emerging from this came a period of grotesque figures, dwarfs, clowns, birds, etc., scattered irregularly among fantastic vegetation. The painting is sometimes in orange, purple, or yellow monochrome.

From the latter part of the seventeenth century until the time of the French Revolution, faïenciers were thriving in or near Marseilles, its maritime trade providing great opportunities for expansion. An establishment in the suburb of Saint-Jean-du-Desert was directed by Joseph Clerissy, brother of Pierre, who came from Moustiers to take over in 1679 a factory started by potters from Nevers. Joseph died in 1685, but the family retained control of the business until it closed in 1748. Its connexions with Nevers and Moustiers are obvious, and were reflected in its productions. In the town of Marseilles an important factory was run by Joseph Fauchier, whose management dates from 1710. Here too the influence of the earlier factories was evident, though the interpretation was more robust. In addition to other wares Fauchier made some excellent large figures, wall-fountains, and crucifixes. He died in 1751, and his nephew Joseph II, who carried on the business, was elected an Associate of the Academy of Painting and Sculpture at Marseilles. He is also credited with the invention of a very fine yellow ground colour, though this feature is common to all the Southern factories.

Other important establishments were those of Leroy, Bonnefoy, Savy, and Perrin (the last-named was known as Veuve Perrin, be-cause it was carried on by the widow of the founder). Savy, who was in partnership with her from about 1761 to 1764, invented a green enamel, used as a wash over drawings in black outline. Chinoiseries after Pillement were particularly well done at Veuve Perrin.

Somewhat straggling flowers in green monochrome are common on Marseilles wares. Excellent marine subjects arranged as still-life typify its marine environment.

Eighteenth-century faïence colours were of two kinds. Those known as *grand feu* were painted on to the glaze and fired with it. Blue, copper-green, manganese-purple, orange, and antimony-yellow withstood this high-temperature firing. Others proved intractable, and in order to include them, pieces were first glazed and fired. Enamel colours fluxed with glass and lead could then be applied and fixed at a low-temperature *petit feu*. These provided varying shades of red, crimson, pink, etc. The most famous, "purple of Cassius", was obtained from gold.

Perhaps the best known of all French faïence was that made at Strasbourg, where, in 1732, C. F. Hannong conveyed to his sons Paul and Balthasar the factories at Strasbourg and Haguenau, which he himself had founded. Paul at first managed the main branch, but in 1738 both establishments passed into his hands.

The interchange of French and Germanic rococo styles was particularly noticeable at Strasbourg, owing to its close proximity to the German border. This influence was further heightened by the arrival of A. F. von Lowenfinck and his wife Seraphia from Hochst in 1749, followed by that of J. J. Ringler in 1753. Another German, W. Lanz, was chief modeller between 1745 and 1754.

Hannong showed great capabilities. Besides increasing the *grand feu* palette, he was the first French faïencier to adopt the full range of *petit feu* colours; among which the "purple of Cassius" has already been mentioned. Gilding was first used in 1744 on pieces presented to Louis XV. Modes of decoration between 1749 and 1760, the year of Hannong's death, begin with borrowed Chinese and Japanese motives. Stylized *fleurs des Indes*, introduced by Lowenfinck, were followed by naturalistic *fleurs fine*, the *deutsche Blumen* of Meissen.

The forms are mostly rococo, employing elaborate scrolls, shells, etc. A great variety of articles was made, including clock-cases, vases, figures, wall-fountains, and tureens modelled in the form of vegetables.

Offshoots of Strasbourg were at Niderviller, Les Islettes, Luneville, and Saint Clement.

Of the others, Sceaux, near Paris, was by far the most important. Its first owner, De Bey, an architect, made nothing significant, but in 1749 he enlisted the services of an itinerant craftsman Jacques Chapelle, who became sole proprietor ten years later. An application to make porcelain had been suppressed owing to Vincennes' monopoly, but Chapelle succeeded in making a quantity of admirable faïence, which was, by intention, closely akin to Sèvres porcelain. The shapes were at first mostly rococo. Tureens of animal and vegetable forms were also made. Later the neoclassical style of Louis Seize prevailed. Sceaux colours were strong and of excellent quality.

At the close of the eighteenth century the coming of the French Revolution, combined with competition from Wedgwood's cream ware, spelt ruin for the faïence industry.

For lead-glazed wares see glossary under *Palissy*.

PORCELAIN

In France soft-paste porcelain, decorated with underglaze blue arabesques in the style of Bérain, had been made at Rouen since 1673. During the early eighteenth century new factories were established at St Cloud, Chantilly, and Mennecy, which all centred in and around Paris. St Cloud porcelain, rarely pure white but of soft ivory tonality, continues at first with traditional underglaze blue lacework borders. Thereafter a distinctive raised and tooled gold decoration, heightened with coloured enamel, was introduced, which the young Hunger copied at Meissen, Vienna, and Venice, as mentioned earlier. Contemporary silver determines the shape of useful articles, bowls, covered jars, and cache-pots with reeded or gadrooned borders and mask handles. Applied plumblossom relief in white after the Chinese, and painted Kakiemon motives after the Japanese, are additional features. At Chantilly, which the Prince de Condé chose as a place for a factory in 1725, white tin glaze on softpaste porcelain forms the background for simplified Japanese decorations in asymmetrical order, expressive of the playful mood of French rococo (Plate 360E). Snuff-boxes and fashionable pieces for the tea-table are covered with these slight but clearly defined and self-confident designs in bright colours, which establish perfect balance of form and decoration. Mennecy, the last of these earlier factories, was founded in 1734, at the rue de Charonne in Paris, whence it moved to Mennecy in 1748, and later to Bourg-La-Reine. Imitating St Cloud and Chantilly at first, they soon attained great technical skill, but the primeval freshness of earlier patterns was not always maintained (Plate 360A). The mature style of Mennecy was chiefly inspired by that of Vincennes. Few figures were produced in these three factories up to the middle of the century, since soft paste did not lend itself easily to moulding in the round, and there was danger of collapse in the kiln during the firing.

The factory of Vincennes, installed in 1738 in an abandoned royal palace, was transferred to Sèvres in 1756, where it flourishes to this day. A monopoly protecting the factory from competition, allowed Vincennes exclusive rights in the making of porcelain and in decorating it with figure subjects and gilding. This monopoly forbade the engagement of

FIGS. 23 and 24

Vincennes workmen elsewhere and provided for the punishment of deserters. As further protection, a factory mark, consisting of the royal cypher, two crossed *L*s, was introduced in 1753, and a date letter added at the same time (Fig. 23). Thereafter the name *Manufacture royale de porcelaine* was assumed well before the time (1759) when the King finally bought the concern. In spite of the original intention to rival Meissen, a desire intensified after the exchange of presents between Augustus III and Louis XV on the occasion of the marriage of the former's daughter, Maria Josepha, to the Dauphin in 1748, Vincennes did not produce hard paste for years. But in 1753, when P. A. Hannong's factory at Strasbourg was affected by the monopoly granted to Vincennes, the opportunity of learning the secret presented itself. However, only some of it seems to have been extracted from Hannong, and no French sources supplying kaolin and petunse had as yet been discovered. These difficulties prevailed until 1769, when the right clay was found near Limoges. Meanwhile Hannong had to destroy his porcelain kilns at Strasbourg and founded the factory at Frankenthal. The new hard-paste porcelain, made concurrently with soft paste, was marked with a crowned version of the crossed *Ls* and named *Porcelaine Royale* to distinguish it from the *Porcelaine de France* (Fig. 24).

The earliest Vincennes, which is unmarked, includes *jardinières*, jugs, ice-pails, and trays of simple shape. Among the factory's first achievements are decorations in blue monochrome with flesh tones added, and the earliest of the many famous ground colours, a dark and sometimes mottled *gros bleu*. Occasionally gold decoration is used alone, but more frequently in combination with *gros bleu* grounds and reserved panels, which are painted with figures and birds in landscapes, or with silhouetted birds among blossoms (Plate 363B). And while, as yet, there are but few figures, the modelling of naturalistic flowers in imitation of "Saxe" proved to be the factory's greatest success, forming five-sixths of the total sales value. Such flowers were used for *bocages*, they formed parts of candelabra, clocks, and other decorative objects, which often included porcelain figures. Occasionally we hear also of a whole bouquet of these flowers; there is one at Dresden which the Dauphiness Maria Josepha sent to her royal father in 1748–9, to show that Vincennes could equal Meissen.

Biscuit porcelain, as a medium for figure modelling, was first mentioned in 1753, and soon began to displace glazed and coloured kinds. The influence of Boucher upon early biscuit groups of children and pastorals is felt strongly until such time as the sculptor E. M. Falconet entered the factory. During his nine years at Sèvres Falconet created models which were entirely original and belong to the best in the factory's history (Plate 365B). After his departure for Russia in 1766 it became an established practice to employ sculptors as modellers, who made reduced versions of well-known monuments, and adapted classical models for reliefs. By 1780 pastorals had completely gone out of fashion, superseded by mythological and contemporary literary subjects, presented in a somewhat lifeless manner, following neo-classical taste.

The most characteristic of all Sèvres decorations are paintings enclosed in panels, reserved upon various coloured grounds, each shade in succession a triumph: turquoise (*bleu celeste*) in 1752; yellow (*jaune jonquille*) the following year; pea-green in 1756; and the pink known as "*rose Pompadour*" again a year later. Finally, the strong, even *bleu du roi*, of such unequalled brilliance that an all-over pattern called "*œil-de-perdrix*", consisting of tiny gilt dots within rings and white circlets, was often applied to soften the effect. Festoons of flowers were also popular (Plate 364B). Landscape and figure decorations, which are frequently signed at Sèvres, tend to become more sumptuous than they had been on early Vincennes porcelain. They adopted the manner and style of oil painting, surrounded by a framework of richly chased and burnished gold. A rare form of decoration, from about 1781–4 onwards, is the so-called jewelled Sèvres, with drops of translucent coloured enamel fused over gold or foil, simulating precious stones.

The breakdown of the Sèvres monopoly about 1770 gave other French factories their long-expected chance. Henceforth hard-paste porcelain was made in various small centres at Paris, some under the protection of the Royal family. In the east Strasbourg and Niderviller opened factories, and at Luneville soft paste was made of the famous *terre de Lorraine*, concurrently with hard paste called *pâte de marble*. The discovery of kaolin in the vicinity of Limoges prompted the brothers Grellet to establish a hard-paste porcelain manufacture in 1771, and with it a flourishing industry in the Haute-Vienne district of France.

German

FAÏENCE IN THE SEVENTEENTH AND EIGHTEENTH CENTURIES

The extraordinary variety and complexity of German faïence derives from the central position of the country, open to influences from Western, Eastern, and Southern Europe, and from the fact that, until well into the nineteenth century, it was divided into innumerable independent states, free cities, and principalities, many of them no bigger than an English parish, few larger than an English county.

It will simplify matters if the productions of North and South Germany are considered separately. This is, however, a division of convenience. All over Germany potteries were exposed, in different degrees of intensity, to the same influences and caprices of fashion, and especially in the eighteenth century, influenced and imitated each other. There is no region of European ceramic study where questions of provenance and attribution can prove more difficult. It is this quality of uncertainty, this wide scope for further research, that makes German faïence such a peculiarly attractive field for the collector.

NORTH GERMANY

Hamburg

No documentary evidence survives to give details of the seventeenth-century Hamburg potteries, which were among the very earliest faïence factories in all Germany. Yet we know from dated specimens, which are numerous (the earliest known being dated 1624), that there was a flourishing production in the middle fifty years of the seventeenth century. The wares are very characteristic, strongly painted in a good, sometimes rather blackish, deep blue. Many pieces bear coats-of-arms, with bold mantling, sometimes the arms of the city itself, more often the pseudo-heraldic achievement of some non-armigerous merchant. Dates and initials are very common, as are merchants' marks. Plates and chargers are sometimes scalloped and almost always decorated with the typical Wan-Li export ware border of alternate segments of flowers and scrolls, precious objects and the like (Fig. 25).

FIG. 25. Hamburg, dated 1643

These contemporary Oriental porcelains enjoyed an immense vogue and were copied in many places, most notably, besides Hamburg, in Holland and Portugal. The Dutch versions, known as Kaapsche Schotels, are larger and more finely drawn. The Portuguese are more difficult to distinguish from the Hamburg dishes, except by the mercantile decoration mentioned above, which strongly suggests Hamburg. An unusually wide foot-rim and a hint of blackish purple in the blue generally denotes a Portuguese origin, as does a more granular glaze. There is no doubt that there was a close trading and artistic connexion between these two maritime states.

Most characteristic of all are the Hamburg jugs. These stand a foot high and are shaped like a pear with the point downwards, leading into a broadly splayed circular foot. The neck of the jug is high, narrow, and slightly tapering. The front, where not decorated with the arms and merchants' marks referred to as occurring on the plates, bears vaguely allegorical figures. The painting is predominantly blue, enlivened occasionally with touches of a very pure, strong yellow, and more rarely with green and red. These jugs, clumsy yet vigorous, are much sought after.

No factory mark, as opposed to potter's mark, is recorded, and the Hamburg factory seems, for some reason unknown, to have ceased production about the year 1670.

In the eighteenth century a Hamburg faïence factory specialized in the production of blue-and-white tiled stoves. Very few "useful wares" can be ascribed to it with certainty, but the tiles made were of the highest quality – perhaps the most successful rococo tiles made anywhere – and one would expect an equally high standard of decoration of any other productions of the factory.

Berlin and Potsdam

There were four factories in Berlin and its immediate neighbourhood during the period under review. The wares are difficult to differentiate, since the craftsmen copied one another. There are no definitive factory marks and, in all cases, the body is reddish in tone. The two earliest factories were founded by Dutchmen: one, by Pieter van der Lee, in Potsdam (1678), which soon moved into the town and continued well into the eighteenth century; the other, founded in 1699 by Cornelius Funcke, came to an end by 1760. A third factory was started in the middle of the eighteenth century by Lüdicke, who later moved to Rheinsberg and in the end specialized in cream wares to rival English products. In Potsdam itself Rewend's factory prospered for some thirty years from 1739.

The products of these factories form a curious group. There is a distinct preference for bold baroque shapes and reeded bodies, for double gourds with unusually narrow necks, and for combinations of cylinder and octagon not seen elsewhere (Fig. 26). Yet throughout this ambitious variety runs a marked vein of provincialism. The shapes themselves are seldom convincing, the waisted foot misses the elegance to which it aspires: lids, especially, often look absurdly small for the vase they crown.

Most of the decoration is in a strong rather matt blue, with ever-recurring motifs of swans and pea-

FIG. 26. Berlin

cocks, sometimes in a reserve of scroll cloud which must derive from Isnik ("Rhodian") wares of the previous century. A similar Near Eastern source must account for a remarkable group of vases, in a variety of typical Berlin shapes. Here, on a turquoise ground, are portrayed Levantine ships with their lateen sails left white, or, more rarely, reserves with chinoiseries in manganese. These are attributed to Funcke's factory and are quite unlike anything else in European faïence.

Hannoverisch-Münden

The most notable wares from this Northern pottery, with its easily recognized mark of three crescent moons (drawn from the arms of its founder, von Hanstein), are vases and, more rarely, tureens, with double walls and panels of open basket work (Fig. 27). These are painted in rather pallid high-temperature colours, as are the vaguely pastoral scenes, a very long way removed from the "Watteau" originals which inspired them. There was also much blue-and-white, only distinguishable from the main bulk of North German eighteenth-century faïence when it bears the factory mark.

FIG. 27. Hannoverisch-Münden

Brunswick

The elder of the two Brunswick factories – the Herzogliche Fabrik, whose wares are generally marked V H in monogram – began by producing pottery which was clearly Dutch-inspired. Some immensely tall tulip vases exist, remarkably well potted and painted with schematized trees with sponged foliage. The factory produced a number of figures, no coarser than those made at Delft, most occurring in blue monochrome as well as in simple high-temperature colours. This same predilection for plastic effects is shown in various baskets and plates with open basket-work edges and, more notably, in the relief ornament

FIG. 28. Brunswick, marked B. C.

on various covered vases of heavy rococo shape, generally painted in blue and manganese (Fig. 28). The Brunswick factory, with its

early date and attractive, simple colouring, in which a curiously flat cobalt blue is characteristic, exerted a wide influence, and mention must also be made of jugs and mugs on which the crowned monogram AR, sometimes in cobalt blue, is shown on a powdered manganese ground. These are often, wrongly, associated with Queen Anne: the cypher is that of Augustus Rex.

A rival to the Ducal factory was Chely's pottery, which after a short career (1745-57) amalgamated with it. Here again the local enthusiasm for plastic shapes was in evidence, and work of a high standard was produced, including figures of blackamoors and street-vendors, rather thickly coloured, and some excellent butter-dishes in the form of a duck brooding a clutch of fruits and nuts (Fig. 29).

FIG. 29. Brunswick, marked Ŏ.

Chely's mark was a monogram of crossed cs, like that later used at Ludwigsburg and Niderviller. In vases and useful wares ornamented in cobalt blue a similarly high standard of painting was maintained, distinguishing the work from the superficially similar productions of other factories.

Schleswig-Holstein

Until 1848 Schleswig-Holstein belonged to Denmark, and the important group of factories in this area is sharply differentiated from the main stream of German eighteenth-century faïence. As ever, once the borders of Scandinavia are approached, a lively and sophisticated understanding of and feeling for rococo is immediately noticeable. The faïence produced in this Northern outpost is among the most charming ever produced anywhere. The shapes are original without being provincial, the painting is fully worthy of the Strasbourg and Marseilles work which inspired it, yet distinctive and excellent in its own right.

A Scandinavian characteristic of these factories is that their marks tend to consist of groups of two or, more often, three or four letters, placed underneath one another and separated by horizontal lines.

Thus: Schleswig

$$\frac{S}{R} \qquad \frac{S}{L}$$

Criseby and Eckernförde

$$\frac{S}{\frac{L}{\frac{O}{\frac{E}{\frac{B}{Z}}}}}$$

Kiel

$$\frac{K}{\frac{B}{L}}$$

It will be seen that the factory initial comes first – below are mainly potters' marks.

Schleswig, perhaps the least impressive of the major factories in the group, produced mainly useful wares, including the "Bishop" bowls, painted in manganese and colours, as blue-and-white was a jealously guarded monopoly at Copenhagen.

Johann Nikolai Otte, who had been involved in the founding of the Schleswig factory, was also responsible for the founding of a factory on his own estate at Criseby, near Eckernförde. His initial is the o above the E in the mark given. Otte's masterstroke was the engagement of two important artists: Johann Buchwald and his son-in-law, Abraham Leihamer. Buchwald had had experience at Höchst and Fulda, at Hölitsch in Hungary, and Rörstrand in Sweden. He was later to leave Eckernförde for Kiel and Stockelsdorff, and in all three places was responsible for the peculiar distinction of the work produced. At Eckernförde were made admirable tureens and plates of French silver shape, *surtouts de table* and tureens with heavy relief ornament. All were of excellent quality. The white glaze has a mauve tinge: the decoration is mostly of "natural" flowers, freely and brilliantly painted in muffle colours in the Meissen manner.

Buchwald moved on to Kiel in 1769, remaining there, with his son-in-law, until 1772, and this brief reign marks the golden age of the factory founded by Tännich in 1763. Yet the whole ten years of the Tännich–Buchwald dynasties rank very high in the history of European faïence.

The tin-enamel at Kiel was of exceptional whiteness, and the colours, applied in the muffle kiln, were of astonishing brilliance. A bold crimson, close to that of Strasbourg, was used for flowers and for picking out detail left in relief. A violet, a clear yellow, and a very pure copper green, shaded with black, added further to the palette.

In addition to useful wares, all sorts of elaborate shapes were made: watch-holders, inkstands, barber's bowls, baskets, and tureens. Among the most characteristic were the punch bowls in the form of a mitre (for the popular drink "Bishop", a sweet punch made with spice and oranges): these are plump and roundly confident in shape, with true ceramic feeling (Fig 30.). The Kiel pot-pourri jars, or "Lavendelkrüge", are of a shape which does not occur elsewhere: a pear-shaped, flat-shouldered body rises above a spreading foot, with a high-

FIG. 30. Kiel, signed *Leihamer fecit*

domed, fluted, and pierced lid covered with applied twigs and flowers. Finally, one must mention the wall-cisterns and bowls, in wavy variations of a basic shell-pattern. A famous polychrome set, in the Copenhagen Museum, illustrated in colour by Hannover, must rank as one of the supreme masterpieces of European faïence – or indeed of all ceramic art.

The factory at Stockelsdorff produced many wares akin to those of Kiel, coming under the same management and similar influences. Special lines were plates with basket-work edges, helmet-shaped jugs, and a form of pear-shaped covered vase (Plate 367B) more controlled and more deeply satisfying than that of the Kiel pot-pourriers. These are often decorated with religious and other scenes after engravings by Nilson, and the knob on the lid is frequently in the form of a figure. This was sometimes humorous, sometimes a cloaked madonna or a nun. But the great glory of Stockelsdorff both was and is in its faïence stoves, of which there are a number at Hamburg and in other North German museums. The factory was founded in 1771, when already the springs of rococo inspiration were running dry, and many of the Stockelsdorff stoves were of an opulent neo-classicism. Yet the finest were the late rococo ones, either decorated in the delicate chinoiseries by Leihamer or left plain, rising tall and elegant above their cast-iron foundation in an exquisite balance of contrasting curves.

In all these factories a main source of design lay in the work of the Augsburg engraver, J. E. Nilson, and it was in part through him that they reached, in their Northern fastness, so high a pitch of sophistication. One more Holstein factory must be mentioned, Kellinghusen. Here the pottery is far from sophisticated; it is in fact peasant ware, but so individual and decorated with so sure a sense of ceramic values, that it merits a place in any collection. The best-known type consists of useful wares – most frequently plates, decorated in high-temperature colours with stylized flowers and leaves, within a densely designed border of foliage. The dominant colours are an ochreous yellow and a yellowish green, with blues and brownish reds to add the stronger touches. Both design and colour scheme are unlike anything else, and once seen can never be mistaken. These delightful things continued to be made until half-way through the nineteenth century.

With the remaining Northern factories it is only possible to deal selectively. On the Eastern frontier, projecting right into Poland, the Upper Silesian factory at Proskau enjoyed a brief heyday in the third quarter of the eighteenth century, as did the closely associated Glienitz. Both produced wares in a derivative Strasbourg style, Glienitz boasting a particularly fine crimson and a deep copper green, shown to best effect by the black outlining and shading. Proskau colours were

more delicate. Here, as at Glienitz, a speciality was vases with highly modelled naturalistic flowers and in a number of figures, including one of a monk in a white habit. During the earlier years the factory mark was a rather florid P: from 1770 to 1783 a D:P:.

A forest region with unlimited fuel and plentiful clay, it was inevitable that Thuringia should have as many faïence as it had porcelain factories. Apart from some fine baroque tureens, most of the work is undistinguished and, unless clearly marked, indistinguishable. The Erfurt factory may be taken as typical. In addition to much robust blue-and-white of manifestly Dutch inspiration, some of it is decorated with amusingly naïve chinoiserie, the main productions were the familiar *Kruge*, or beer mugs. No problem in German faïence is more difficult than that of assigning these to their various factories, for they were made everywhere, and are seldom marked otherwise than with a potter's initial. Yet certain characteristics suggest Erfurt, or more certainly Thuringia: bold drawing, thick manganese outlines, trees of olive green with highly stylized leaves outlined in dark manganese, and a general *art paysan* character. The typical Thuringian high-temperature palette, in which cobalt and manganese predominate over a muddy yellow, a green made from mixing blue and yellow rather than from copper, and a dry "sealing-wax" red which lies on top of the glaze. A word of caution must be given against dating such pieces by the pewter lids with which they are nearly always fitted. Old lids were often used again for new pots,

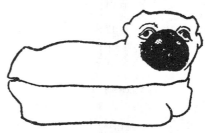

Fig. 31. Erfurt pug-dog.

and new inscriptions as often added to mark the presentation of a piece already ten or fifteen years old. Erfurt also produced the oblong boxes in the shape of pug-dogs, coloured olive green and black, ugly but entertaining and endearing, which were also made at Bayreuth (Fig. 31).

Near the Southern limits of Northern Germany, in Hesse, the short-lived factory of Fulda (1741–58) produced wares of the most consummate brilliance, worthy of the exquisite porcelain to be made later. The famous Meissen painter Löwenfinck came to Fulda from Bayreuth and must be held responsible for much of the sophisticated accomplishment of the work produced.

Over a rather dark-red material Fulda spread a very pure white enamel. Much of the decoration was in muffle colours, heightened with gold, and both the painting and the firing were of superlative quality. Vases were decorated in a transposed *famille verte* style of great individuality, notable for a brilliant emerald green, while in reserves are harbour scenes, based on and in no way inferior to those made popular by Herold at Meissen. Blue-and-white wares were produced in a vivid violet-blue, often described as "copying ink-coloured", outlined with manganese. Two splendid altar candle-sticks, over 2 ft 6 ins high, in the Cassel Museum are masterpieces of baroque in shape and ornamentation. Simpler objects, such as plates, showed a sensitive appreciation of K'ang Hsi blue-and-white, far closer to the original in spirit than most of its innumerable imitators could achieve. Some of the finest pieces were signed by Löwenfinck or his wife. But the usual factory mark consists of the letters F. D. over some other initials. The F. D. mark is also found on a few of the famous *famille verte* plates of a Chinese fairy riding on a roebuck, traditionally ascribed to Bayreuth.

SOUTH GERMANY

The great seventeenth-century factories founded at Frankfort-am-Main and the nearby Hanau were for long considered to have been the earliest in Germany. Though they have now yielded pride of place to Hamburg, their importance, both in output and influence, remains unchallenged. Yet before we consider them we should glance briefly at two other factories which produced, as it were, the incunabula of German faïence. Nuremberg,

with its strong trading link with Venice, is considered as the source of a group of mid-sixteenth-century South German majolica, painted mainly in blue and characterized by carefully drawn arabesque foliage borders. Most of the known pieces are dated from the middle years of the century and are safely tucked away in German museums, though a famous small plate in the Victoria and Albert Museum shows their quality and the strongly German character of the drawing, clearly derived from Northern woodcut or engraving. Nuremberg majolica seems to have been made well into the first twenty years of the seventeenth century, but to have left no direct progeny, though much interesting and attractive South German peasant ware, including the splendid Habaner dishes from Moravia, shows a kindred Italianate inspiration.

The other group of German faïence "primitives" is that frequently signed L. S. and ascribed to Lorenz Speckner. Most unmistakable of this group are the flat-sided square bottles, the earliest of which is dated 1618. Such pieces are often inscribed with bold square lettering and coats-of-arms and decorated with strongly stylized flowers of possibly Near Eastern origin, drawn as if with a pen and heavily cross-hatched. It is, among other things, this highly characteristic drawing which links the bottles to a group of *albarelli* and spouted drug-jars, on which it is combined with the spiral whorls which have given the type its name. They appear to have been made until after 1668, though in the later wares the glaze is coarser and the drawing, created for penmanship, has lost its tense vigour when applied with a brush. It seems certain that this group was a faïence side-line of the Kreussen stone-ware factory, possibly made to meet specific orders for the furnishing of apothecaries' shops.

Hanau

The factory was founded in 1661 by two Dutchmen, Behagel and van der Walle, who had first tried to obtain permission to set up shop in Frankfort. With Frankfort, it was perhaps the most productive of all the German factories. Its rather coarse blue-and-white wares were made in most of the usual shapes, specializing in the various ribbed and pleated dishes, in the narrow-necked jugs known as *Enghalskrüge* and rather squat pear-shaped pitchers and tankards. The standard cylindrical beer-mugs do not seem to have been made there.

The Hanau wares, naturally enough, showed strong traces of their Dutch foundation and have indeed often been mistaken for Delft. Yet the pottery produced is thicker, less deftly painted, and lacks the lead over-glaze, or *Kwaart*, which gave the finest Delft such brilliant finish. The subjects, too, are easily distinguishable. The direct imitation of Chinese designs was soon abandoned and never wholly assimilated. Vaguely turbaned figures with their hands in their sleeves and a generally low standard of painting are indices of Hanau origin. Chinoiserie was soon discarded for isolated flowers and birds interspersed with groups of four or five dots to suggest smaller flowers. Some of the flower-painting, in cobalt blue and outlined with manganese, has the pedantic charm of early illustrations to herbals and must have been inspired by engravings.

The factory soon evolved its own special bunch of flowers, arranged symmetrically round a central large-petalled flower left white, above which rises a second flower, while others radiate to left and right. The whole is highly stylized, and a characteristic feature is the drawing of the leaves, carefully hatched with the final third, towards the point, filled in in monochrome. The total effect is of a robust peasant art, instinctively skilful but in no way sophisticated. To the mid-twentieth-century eye by far the most satisfying Hanau wares are the armorial jugs and pitchers. The heraldic decoration, with rich mantling or supporters, is neat and small, showing a firm sense of spacing and allowing the blue painting to be set off to best advantage by the excellent white of the tin enamel. The charm of these pieces is much akin to that of the similarly decorated Lambeth Sack bottles, but the drawing is firmer and the result more confident and thus more convincing.

Hanau continued right through the eighteenth century, attempting a variety of baroque shapes with some agreeable but unsensational decoration in muffle-kiln colours. There was at first no factory mark, though a roughly shaped incised crescent occurs so frequently that it may be accepted as a sure sign of Hanau origin. Later a monogram of A and V, for van Alphen, and the word Hanau itself, are often found.

It has been claimed that the spiral fluting of the *Enghalskrüge*, their rope-twist handles and the manner in which the handle is impressed into the main body are signs of Hanau origin, but Riesebieter and others have shown that identical evidence might be brought forward in support of a number of other South German factories.

In distinguishing the wares of Hanau from those of Frankfort it is safer to judge by the less brilliant glaze, by the preference for certain designs outlined above, by the fact that Frankfort hardly ever used the four-and-five-dot flowerets, by a strong suspicion that dark manganese outlining indicates Hanau, and finally by assuming that coarser quality and inferior painting are a pointer to Hanau rather than Frankfort, to which splendid factory we can now turn.

Frankfort-am-Main

In 1666, five years after Behagel and van der Walle, the founders of the Hanau factory, had been refused leave to found a pottery in Frankfort, a French workman from Hanau succeeded in obtaining permission. He was financed by Johann Christoph Fehr, who by the next year was the sole proprietor of the factory. It was during the ownership of Fehr and his sons, between 1666 and 1723, that the finest wares were made, though production continued until about 1770.

The faïence of Frankfort is, at its best, characterized by great brilliance of colouring and materials, combined with superb drawing. A final lead glaze, or *Kwaart*, was sometimes added to the enamel, as was done at Delft. This gave an almost glassy finish and imparted a rich depth to the colour. The blue most often used was an exceptionally bright cobalt, so striking that once seen it is always recognizable, and this blue is set off by the pure milky whiteness of the tin enamel. The drawing is hardly ever outlined by the black or deep manganese *trek* so often used in Delft.

Most of the shapes favoured resemble those of Hanau. The decoration of the *Enghalskrüge* tends to be spread over the whole jug, whereas at Hanau it is usually divided into three zones: neck, body, and foot. Moreover, the body of the Frankfort jugs is pear-shaped, narrowing down bit by bit towards the foot, while the Hanau body is more often spherical, separated from the splayed foot by a narrow waist. Double and treble gourd vases were popular at both factories, but the Frankfort type has a straight cylindrical neck, the Hanau showing a preference for a spreading trumpet. Beer mugs were made with necks only just narrower than the swelling bodies, and these were not often made elsewhere. Frankfort showed two other marked preferences: many very large vases were made, some standing a full 3 feet high and more, impressive objects, though the swelling shape is often inflated and clumsy, lacking the controlled baroque excellence of the larger, architectural pieces made in Holland. There was also a fondness for eight- or nine-lobed dishes, the lobes being decorated with alternating motifs, which never quite worked out when nine lobes were involved. One final shape must be described as being very much a Frankfort speciality and one which one often sees attributed to Lambeth, Bristol, or Delft. We refer to the circular, lidded, two-handled posset bowls, some 3 inches deep. The majority are decorated with pseudo-Chinese scenes, and most are in blue-and-white. Yet there is a large class where the painting is in very pale manganese with either an equally pale sage green or lemon yellow, or a combination of both. The motif is generally that of the "philosopher squatting in a rocky landscape", always a great favourite at Frankfort, and the glaze is more often a greenish blue, common to many potteries in the last decade of the seventeenth century, rather than the dazzling white for which the factory is famous.

Like innumerable seventeenth-century factories, Frankfort began by more or less faithful copies of Wan-Li export wares. These Chinese motifs were agreeably rendered and show us either the familiar solitary sage or parties of vaguely dallying Orientals, grouped among boldly painted trees and plants. Among these the most typical are well-drawn and well-understood clumps of giant plantain, very close to their late Ming originals, and fir trees whose foliage, shown by curious six-fold palmettes of radiating strokes, repeated over and over again, is almost a guarantee of Frankfort draughtsmanship. Yet the great splendours of the factory arose only when it broke away from direct copying and evolved a style of its own. This had as its central theme the widespread lotus leaf on its tall stem, like an elegant parasol being blown inside out.

A series of great dishes, intended for display rather than use and measuring 18–20 inches across, bears witness to the standard reached. At first glance they are difficult to distinguish from the equally imposing *Kaapsche Schotels* being produced in Delft at much the same time. Yet the thicker body, the colouring and, it must be admitted, a certain controlled elegance in the drawing, betray the Frankfort dishes, as does the broad flat brim round the strongly recessed centre. The masterpieces of the series, still very close to their Chinese originals, are two splendid specimens in the Hamburg Museum. Of these one can only say that the drawing reaches a pitch of combined strength and delicacy which was never equalled in any other blue-and-white earthenware.

For many years the lotus leaf remained, on dishes, gourd vases, and jugs, the dominant Frankfort motif. Gradually the designs of which it was a component became simpler, the drawing less refined, and the lotus leaf itself more highly stylized, until in the end it resembled two symmetrical bunches of holly leaves round a central flower, boldly drawn by artists who no longer had any clear idea of what it was they were drawing. Other effective borders of flowers and leaves, painted freely and without hard outlines, were evolved from Dutch and Italian sources, and a notable series of plates with biblical subjects was based on baroque engravings. The factory closed in the 1770s, having never produced inferior work and, in its prime, earned its place among the greatest of European potteries.

Höchst

In 1746 two Frankfort businessmen, Göltz and Clarus, founded a faïence factory at Höchst, near the electoral city of Mainz. As their chief associate they had the Meissen porcelain painter Adam von Löwenfinck, of whom we have already heard at Fulda. Löwenfinck's peregrinations through the faïence and porcelain factories of the eighteenth century make a fascinating chapter in the art history of the period. He was a highly skilled painter and produced admirable work wherever he went. Short though his stay was, for he deserted to Strasbourg in 1749, he may be considered as largely responsible for the exceptional quality of the faïence made at Höchst. He brought with him from Fulda Georg Friedrich Hess, and soon summoned further painters, including his younger brother, from Meissen.

From the first, very little blue-and-white was made at Höchst, the painting being chiefly in enamel colours and with a conscious imitation of porcelain. Many decorative shapes were made, besides plates and dishes. Specially common were rococo tureens and sauce-boats of a shape familiar in Strasbourg and North-Eastern France, and wide-mouthed, pear-shaped vases of a shape not found elsewhere. In all these the glaze is of a brilliant, milky white. The rocaille work on the tureens is picked out in crimson and blue, the vases are often decorated with delicate landscapes, either in polychrome or in black, the whole surrounded with an elaborately asymmetrical rococo frame, later to become familiar on the useful wares made in Höchst porcelain.

The factory was also renowned for those essentially rococo *trompe-l'œil* pieces, dishes formed as turkeys, capercailzies, pheasants, jays, pug-dogs, boar's heads, or cabbages, artichokes, and bundles of asparagus. The drawing is delicate and refined, the stylization controlled: nowhere else, except in Strasbourg, were these amusing objects so beautifully made.

Many Höchst pieces are marked with the wheel, generally six-spoked and rather roughly drawn. To this are often added the initials of the painter, Friedrich Hess and his son Ignaz, Johannes Zeschinger, and others who have not been identified. Production seems to have ended early in the 1760s, but in its short life the factory produced wares of exquisite quality, very close to porcelain in inspiration and effect, which deservedly hold a proud place in any private or public collection and are fully worthy of the famous Höchst porcelain to which they formed in some sort the prelude.

As was stated in the introduction, the traditional ceramic division into North and South Germany is a division of convenience only. Fulda in the North, Hanau and Frankfort in the South, all belong to Hessen-Nassau and to Prussia, and Höchst lies but some 20 miles from Frankfort. But with Ansbach, 100 miles to the South-East, we are well into Bavaria. Here the Southern-ness is no longer a convenience of cataloguing, but a solid geographical and ethnological fact, and we can state without fear of contradiction that, of all the South German faïence factories, four reign supreme: Ansbach, Nuremberg, Bayreuth, and, farthest South of all, Künersberg.

Ansbach

The factory was founded early in the eighteenth century, shortly after 1708, under the special protection of the Margrave of Brandenburg, who soon forbade the sale of Frankfort and Hanau wares within his territories. The dominating figures in its history were the various members of the Popp family, associated with it from about 1727 and in sole charge from 1747 until the turn of the century. In the earlier period no factory mark was used, but from the sixties the signature A.P. (=Ansbach. Popp) was adopted.

The factory began by making blue-and-white wares of Dutch type, often on a bluish ground similar to that favoured at Bayreuth. In the 1720s a restrained variant of the Rouen *lambrequins* was invented, and subsequently introduced, by an Ansbach potter, Wackenfeld, to Strasbourg, where it enjoyed great popularity. During this early period were made the *Enghalskrüge*, decorated with the small birds and groups of dots typical of the Hanau prototype, and only distinguishable by the hue of the bluish glaze, and a less spherical body.

The two chief glories of the Ansbach factory date from the second third of the century. The first of these was a version of "brocaded Imari", not unlike the famous *Delft Doré*, though less successful. Ornamental pieces, including some vases 2 ft 9 ins high, were painted in strong underglaze blue and then lacquered with red and gold. These colours were insecure, indeed the muffle kiln seems never to have been used at Ansbach, and the gold is often badly worn. The second, and more famous, speciality was the so-called Ansbach *famille verte*. This seems to have been a closely guarded secret and to have been made during a short number of years only, possibly only during the thirties, though a reference in a contemporary book of travel suggests that the secret had been known at least ten years before. The characteristic colours of this type are a transparent viridian green and a strong violetish blue, both lying thick upon the paste and translucent as enamel. To these are added a yellowish green, red-brown, sulphur-yellow, and a liberal use of manganese, successfully re-creating the aubergine of the Chinese originals. The designs are mostly Oriental, but the colouring is also applied with baroque formal strap-work. The effect is extremely rich and much admired, though often the decoration is overcrowded and provincial in character. The shapes were mainly Oriental, lidded or beaker-shaped vases, often with part of the design in relief.

In later years the factory continued to make wares painted in underglaze blue, notably some very tall twelve-side vases (just under 3 feet high) painted in a local and strongly characteristic version of Delft–Oriental.

One cannot leave Ansbach without mentioning the polychrome tiles, painted in the green, yellow, blue, and manganese of the high-temperature palette. Though ultimately derived from the Dutch, these tiles show an extreme originality with their gay portrayal of local characters, huntsmen, landed gentry, chinoiseries based on the engravings of J. Chr. Weigel, stags, peasants, parrots, and, in one case, a pottery vendor in his booth, inscribed "A.P. 1763". They are 7½ inches wide, half as wide again as the standard Dutch tiles, and are indeed unique in every way. An entire room in the Residenz at Ansbach is lined with them, a bewildering and enchanting spectacle for anyone who has once succumbed to the lure and fascination of the study of tiles.

Nuremberg

With its strong trading connexion with Italy it had already produced, in the middle of the sixteenth century, the earliest truly German majolica. Yet production had died away by the middle of the next century and when in 1712 two merchants decided to follow the fashion of the day and embark upon a faïence venture, they had no thread of tradition to guide them. Their first technical expert was J. C. Ripp, who had been apprenticed in Delft, and came to Nuremberg via Frankfort, Hanau, and Ansbach. We trace him later at many factories, but he seems to have been a quarrelsome man and he only stayed at Nuremberg for a year. This was enough to launch the pottery on safe Delft–Frankfort lines. Yet it soon deserted these and developed a baroque style of decoration more peculiarly its own than any other factory. One characteristic was a tendency to cover as much of the surface as possible with painting. It is not indeed until the full tide of rococo that European ceramic art rediscovers the knack of leaving areas unadorned. At Nuremberg, as at Bayreuth, every available square inch was covered with the so-called *Fiederblätter* or feathery leaves of fern or hemlock, curling this way and that in balanced symmetry. The best years of the factory were still dominated by the *"Laub und Bandelwerkstil"*, the formal foliage and strapwork of the baroque age. Much of the work was still in underglaze blue, most often on a bluish ground, and a favourite motif is that of a basket of fruits and flowers, crowned with birds. When high-temperature colours were attempted they were confined to a bold blue, a dull green, brilliant lemon yellow, and a manganese varying from pale lilac to near-black. Red was seldom used. The glaze is often so brilliant as to suggest the use of *Kwaart*, though that technique is not known to have been employed.

The usual wine-jugs of Hanau–Ansbach type were made either with the birds and dots decoration and thus almost indistinguishable or with a bold and lavish all-over design of flowers. The painting on the cylindrical mugs is superior to that done in most places. Well-drawn scenes from the Bible or classical mythology, splendid coats-of-arms, or landscapes set in a formal frame-work of debased *lambrequins* are the best-known types. In addition to large reeded dishes, Nuremberg created two highly original shapes. The first was that known as the *Sternschüssel*, or Star dish (Fig. 32). In these a central depression in

FIG. 32. Nuremberg *Stern-schüssel*

the shape of a large or small six-pointed star is surrounded by heart-shaped hollows, in between the points of the star, the whole being covered with lavish decoration of curling foliage. Nothing quite the same seems to have been made elsewhere, though Bayreuth, too, made imitative star dishes of its own. Although they resemble sweetmeat or pickle dishes, they were probably meant for show only. Remembering the brass dishes for which Nuremberg was long famous all over Europe, we may conjecture a metal origin for this curious design. The other peculiar pattern was that of small, squat teapots, shaped as eight-sided pyramids on ball feet, and equipped with a fanciful spout and even more flamboyant handle. The shape does not occur elsewhere except in Böttger's red stoneware, and must originally have been designed by some Dresden court silversmith, such as Irminger.

No factory mark was used at first, but from about 1750 a monogram of NB is often found, as are the signs for the planets Jupiter, Venus, and Mars. On the other hand, painters' signatures or initials are extremely common, the most familiar being that of Kordenbusch, who was also the factory's most important artist. The mark, a capital K, is nearly always accompanied by three dots, arranged as a tri-

angle standing on its apex, and these are also found unaccompanied. So many pieces, of such different degrees of accomplishment, are found with these marks that they most probably indicate Kordenbusch's workshop rather than that the pieces came from his hand. The earlier years of the factory were the best and, though it continued production until as late as the middle of the nineteenth century, the quality of the wares declined steadily from about 1770.

It was in Nuremberg that the majority of the *Hausmaler* worked, independent painters and enamellers who decorated jugs, tankards, and dishes bought undecorated from the potteries. They showed a preference for the wares of Hanau, with their very white glaze, and of Frankfort and Ansbach. The whole subject of *Hausmalerei* is extremely complex, and we cannot here do more than refer the inquirer to the standard work on the subject, by Pazaurek, published in Leipzig in 1925. These outside decorators were in the main recruited from those who had enamelled glass or silver, and they do not all show an equal appreciation of ceramic values. Yet at their best, in black or purple monochrome at the end of the seventeenth century, in the rich autumn-tinted fruits and flowers which followed, or the delicate muffle-kiln colours of the mid-eighteenth century, their works count as among the most desirable of all ceramic objects, and are as highly valued as they are rare. The collector should bear in mind, when confronted with a German faïence object of unusually rich decoration, the names of such *Hausmaler* as Schaper, Heel, and Helmack, and the Augsburg engraver Bartholomäus Seuter. He should also bear in mind the possibility of forgery.

Bayreuth

The factory was founded in 1713 and for some sixty years was one of the best known and most productive of all German potteries. The brown-glazed and rarer yellow-glazed wares, delicately decorated with silver or gold arabesques and chinoiseries, were made in the earliest years of the factory and are justly famous. The type is often confused with Böttger's stoneware, but a brief examination will show that it is not a stoneware at all, but a porous, reddish earthenware, covered with a coloured lead glaze. The manufacture of faïence began slightly later. Throughout, the major part of the production was in blue-and-white, the blue being distinguishable for the minute bubbles within the pigment, which give a milky brilliance to the whole.

All the usual South German shapes were made, and some which are not so usual, such as candle-sticks, butter-dishes disguised as fruit, birds, logs and the like, and hideous jugs in the form of top boots. The standard of painting was very high. On more ordinary wares, sometimes in high-temperature colours, often in a combination of blue and manganese, the favourite decorations were groups of tall, vaguely italianate castles and a boldly effective design of flowers, highly stylized and almost chintzy in appearance. In such wares broad bands of blue gave strength to the ensemble. The "birds on basket" motif was also very popular at Bayreuth. The more ambitious wares included tall, covered cups and dishes with strap-work borders surrounding monograms, notably that of Georg Friedrich Carl, Margrave of Brandenburg–Bayreuth, and coats-of-arms brilliantly executed and showing the innumerable quarterings of which the German nobility was so notoriously enamoured.

Two groups of Bayreuth wares must count as its masterpieces, each produced by a peripatetic painter whom we have met elsewhere. Adam von Löwenfinck was at Bayreuth from 1736 to 1741 and must be held responsible for a group of *famille verte* dishes, trays, and tankards, dispersed among various German museums. These pieces are unsigned, but in their drawing and colouring, in the spacing of that drawing upon the object decorated, they show a sophisticated control and elegance that makes the *famille verte* of Ansbach, for instance, seem clumsy and countrified and has won for these rarities a place among the masterpieces of all European chinoiserie. During the same period, but more briefly, the Vienna painter Dannhöfer worked at Bayreuth. He too created an intensely personal group of objects, decorated with the black-and-red baroque arabesques familiar on Vienna porcelain of the Du

Paquier period. More recently, some German experts attribute Löwenfinck's *famille verte* to Dannhöfer, working at Fulda, but the attribution is not yet definitely established. Of pieces manifestly by the same hand (and not, as it seems to us, Dannhöfer's) some bear the Fulda mark, F D, and at least one that of Bayreuth, BK.

Towards the end of its time the Bayreuth factory broke with its past and produced some charming wares with moulded decoration, notably dinner plates and tureens with a border pattern in pinks and greens, of sprays of wild flowers springing from a rococo shell, centred round a charmingly drawn moss-rose, and even more notably a looking-glass frame in the Neues Schloss at Bayreuth.

The factory's period of greatest prosperity was during the direction of Knöller (1728–44). Its wares are recognizable by the quality of the blue, by the type of design, and by the odd fact that the spur marks on the underside of plates and dishes have been filed flat, the resulting scratches still showing on either side, though sometimes covered with a final coat of glaze. At Bayreuth, however, the marks are uniquely helpful and for once give a sure aid in dating pieces. For the earliest period no marks are known, but from Knöller onwards all is simple. The marks, often over a line below which are painters' initials, are as follows:

Knöller period.	1728–44.	B. K.
Fränkel and Schreck.	1745–47.	B. F. S.
Pfeiffer and Fränkel.	1747–60.	B. P. F.
Pfeiffer.	1760 onwards.	B. P.

Künersberg

This factory is the southernmost and also the latest founded of the factories we describe in detail. Küner, a successful financier of the small town of Memmingen, had founded a new town outside its gates and named it Künersberg and here, in about 1745, he set up a faïence factory. Not much is known of its short history, but it had almost certainly closed down by 1770. The earlier pieces are often, but not always, marked either KB or Künersberg, in full. The first dated piece (1745) is a tankard in the Hamburg Museum. Against a rambling landscape and a white-clouded sky of almost urbinesque brilliance, a sheep, a goat, and a kid are shown cropping the grass or munching the shoots of a vine. The combination of delicate drawing and broad brushstrokes, of warm colours with colder greys and blues give this famous specimen an altogether exceptional quality and lead one to think that it was probably a trial piece, a demonstration of what the new factory and its first manager, Conradi, could do. Though seldom resembling it, the subsequent wares were of great excellence. The *Enghalskrüge* are elongated, slender variants on a familiar theme. Two-handled vases and wall sconces, both decorated in relief, formed part of the wares painted in underglaze blue, as did plates and dishes decorated in dark blue with a very clearly drawn version of the Rouen *lambrequins*, transmuted by Ansbach and Strasbourg. Yet with its brilliant white enamel Künersberg was bound to yield to the mid-eighteenth century feeling for the elegant colours of the muffle kiln, and it is here that its most charming productions were made. Vases and plates were painted with porcelain-style landscapes, in vignettes surrounded by delicate gilding. Plates of French or North Italian "silver" shape were decorated with flowers or coats-of-arms similar to those made later at Lenzburg in Switzerland, as were

FIG. 33. Künersberg

dishes with still-life scenes of fruit, tumbling out of upset hampers (Fig. 33). Most delightful of all, and peculiar to Künersberg, are the

coffee jugs and teapots decorated with sporting scenes in two shades of green, black, or characteristic nut-brown, and pale blues and yellows. Nor must one forget the small patch-boxes, their lids decorated on each side, sometimes with "souvenir" views of Memmingen, sometimes with little "Watteau" figures which recapture, in their discreet colours, not only the gaiety of the rococo but also something of its tenderness.

In this first survey of German faïence in the seventeenth and eighteenth centuries we have had to omit much. Strasbourg, intensely Germanic both in its antecedents and its personnel, is universally accepted, outside Germany, as one of the glories of French ceramic culture. We have considered the principal productions of some twenty-five leading factories out of a total of something like eighty. Of those omitted Abstbessingen, Crailsheim, Jever, and Durlach appeal strongly to the writer's affection, but the majority are minor factories, some of them excessively short-lived and most of them producing derivative work under the shadow of the greater centres. Those discussed will suffice to show how wide is the variety, and how great the riches, of the German faïence achievement. Less confident, but also less standardized and less mass-produced than Delft, less urbane than French faïence, less intimate than English Delft, it must be considered in its own right, standing in the centre of European culture, sincerely individual, as a major branch of European ceramic art. When we consider how few of the pieces in this enormous production are marked, how much uncertainty still exists and to what extent experts still disagree, we may realize that here is a vast field calling for exploration, for all those delights of recognizing similarity in difference, of attribution and counter-attribution, of hope deferred and unexpected good fortune, which are the lifeblood of collecting and compared with which progress through some more accurately charted ceramic region is as a stroll, pleasurable but unexacting, through the known niceties of a municipal garden.

GERMAN PORCELAIN

The foundation of the Saxon factory at Meissen in 1710 marks the actual beginning of porcelain-making in Europe, where its commercial value to a court in need of money was at once recognized. Johann Friedrich Boettger, an alchemist in the service of Augustus the Strong, Elector of Saxony and King of Poland, discovered in 1710 a red stoneware "which surpasses the hardness of porphyry", as he reports to the King in March 1709 (Plate 359). During the following year this red stoneware was offered for sale at the Leipzig Easter Fair. Almost immediately rival factories appeared, one at Plaue on the Havel, where a Prussian minister found red clay on his estate, another at Potsdam, encouraged by the King of Prussia himself. But neither of these factories was progressive, whereas Boettger succeeded in replacing the red clay with white kaolin. Thus he produced the first real porcelain in Europe, called Boettger ware, after the inventor, and sold at the Leipzig Fair from 1713 on. Above the entrance of Boettger's laboratory, where the King had virtually kept him a prisoner, there is a significant inscription: "God, our creator, has made of a goldmaker a potter" (*Gott unser Schoepfer hat gemacht aus einem Goldmacher einen Toepfer*).

The earliest porcelain tableware followed the shape of contemporary silver, and the first modeller, Johann Jacob Irminger, was a Saxon court silversmith. Some of this porcelain is decorated with applied floral motifs, some with enamel, gilding, or lustre colour, which is a pale mother-of-pearl coating obtained from gold, the outcome of another of Boettger's experiments. The earliest figures show dependence upon ivory statuettes, and ivory carvers are known to have found employment at the Meissen factory. A figure of the King himself, in heroic attitude, made first in red Boettger ware and later in white with enamel colouring, belongs to this period, and is attributed to the Saxon ivory carver Johann Christoph von Luecke.

With the rediscovery of underglaze blue at Meissen, the first factory marks were introduced. A pseudo-Chinese sign of square shape is the earliest mark recorded, followed by the so-called Caduceus, in turn replaced by the letters K P M (*Koenigliche Porzellan Manufaktur*) (Fig. 34), until, in 1724, the Crossed Swords,

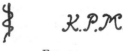

FIG. 34

taken from the King's arms, were permanently adopted (Fig. 35). Special commissions

FIG. 35

executed for the King himself bear his initials AR (*Augustus Rex*) in underglaze blue (Plate 360D). Incised signs are usually factory assembly marks, for the convenience of workmen or "repairers" rather than for individual distinction.

Meanwhile Johann Gregor Herold experimented with colours and, among others, produced a clear yellow ground which found the King's special favour, since it recalled the Imperial colour of China (Plate 358B). Herold's chinoiserie subjects, based upon engravings, became an established fashion (Plate 360B), followed in the later thirties by harbour views with figures which reveal the influence from Delft (Plate 365C). In spite of the complete anonymity which Herold enforced upon his workers, it is sometimes possible to trace the style of individual artists, such as Hunger and Löewenfinck (Plate 358A), since they were able to sign work done elsewhere, when visiting other factories. Such moving about by porcelain workers was often caused by financial gains resulting from the disclosure of the technical secrets of one factory to another.

Painted porcelain was more costly than white ware, and outside painters, called *Hausmaler*, often executed private orders upon request. The Meissen factory suffered from such competition, and introduced measures to prevent the further sale of undecorated porcelain, unless imperfect or of a discontinued pattern. But we may be glad that the competition existed, for some of the *Hausmaler*, mainly those centred at Augsburg and Dresden, display an originality of design which would have been difficult to attain under the levelling influence of Herold's strong personality.

With the employment at Meissen of Johann Gottlob Kirchner in 1727 the great period of porcelain sculpture begins. Misled at first by his ambitious royal patron, who commissioned large-scale statues for the Japanese Palace, Kirchner modelled figures which did not obey the innate laws of the new material. His powerful, fantastic animals, in white, are again more distinctive as remarkable *tours de force* rather than as cabinet pieces for the porcelain collector.

J. J. Kaendler, who became chief modeller at Meissen in 1733, was the first to recognize the possibilities of the new material, and to exploit its inherent qualities. His Italian Comedy figures seem to dance on the shelves of china cabinets, and his fashionable ladies to swing their crinolines in rhythmic movements, anticipating Mozart's minuets (Plate 363A). Even conventional tableware takes a share in plastic decoration, and the "Swan Service", which Kaendler modelled for Count Bruehl (1737–41), reveals his creative genius in the many variations on the theme of swans. Kaendler's birds were all studied from nature, since Augustus the Strong kept a large collection of domestic and rare specimens at the Moritzburg.

Meissen figures and groups served often as table decorations, replacing earlier ones of wax or sugar. The themes are suggested by court amusements, from theatrical characters performing with baroque exuberance to disguised princesses and shepherds of sophisticated elegance. Mythological and allegorical subjects are never absent: river-gods, seasons, continents, or the arts, all richly endowed with the graces of eighteenth-century society. Watteau scenes begin to appear on Meissen porcelain about 1738–40. At that time the

King's daughter, Maria Amalia Christina, married Charles IV, King of Naples, and the famous service with green monochrome Watteau decoration, made as a wedding gift, established the new fashion. The increased demand for French engravings as sources of designs was satisfied by J. C. Huet, brother of the painter, who became the factory agent in Paris. Kaendler himself did not undertake the journey to Paris until 1749, when Maria Josepha, another of the King's daughters, married the Dauphin. After Kaendler's return, French influence gained in intensity at Meissen. Elongated figures, painted in soft colours, turn into pleasing conversation pieces and an air of sentimentality pervades, replacing the whimsical mood and vigour of earlier days.

Kaendler was assisted by a few gifted modellers, and Peter Reinicke, as well as Johann Friedrich Eberlein, deserve special credit. Friedrich Elias Meyer, appointed after Eberlein's serious illness in 1748, belonged to a younger generation, and the ageing Kaendler had some difficulty in ruling this self-willed pupil. Meyer's figures are easily recognized by their small heads and slender proportions, to which richly moulded and gilt scroll bases lend additional height. The young artist did not stay at Meissen for long, but in 1761 followed a call to the newly established Prussian factory at Berlin.

With the outbreak of the Seven Years' War in 1756, the Meissen factory suffered a heavy blow. The Prussians occupied the town, and the King and his ministers fled to Warsaw. Frederick the Great had thirty boxes of porcelain dispatched to Potsdam, and placed further orders for table services and snuff-boxes at the factory, some of which were copied later on at the Berlin factory. After the war Meissen never regained its former unchallenged lead. A number of other factories, patronized by German rulers and princes, had meanwhile been established, producing porcelain of local character and refreshing charm. They add much variety and colour to the gay company of German eighteenth-century porcelain figures, and enhanced the attractions of the tea-trays and dinner-tables of contemporary society. At Meissen an academic (neo-classical) period followed under the French modeller Acier and the director, Count Camillo Marcolini, with an ever-increasing production of dinnerware. The disaster of the Napoleonic Wars brought these activities to an end.

In spite of all efforts to keep the secret of porcelain-making as a source of wealth for Saxony alone, itinerant technicians (arcanists) would offer information for sale. Thus the Saxon enameller and goldworker Christoph Conrad Hunger, having been at St Cloud first, made his way from Meissen to Vienna and Venice, each time taking an active part in the establishment of a new factory.

The factory at Hoechst started in 1750, at the place where Fr A. von Löewenfinck, the migrant Meissen painter, had founded a faïence factory four years earlier, but he had left for Strasbourg shortly before. The factory was granted a monopoly by the Elector of Mainz, who later on subsidized it. Meissen influence is obvious in pieces produced in the initial years, and some early figures are copies. But the modellers J. Chr. L. Luecke and Simon Feylner show independence. The set of Italian Comedy figures, attributed to Feylner, is remarkable for freedom of movement: each actor is placed upon a high pedestal, in the manner of contemporary garden sculpture, taking a bow in the limelight. As the rococo period advanced J. Fr Lueck created idyllic groups on richly scrolled openwork bases, similar to those he designed at Frankenthal a few years later (Plate 361). L. Russinger (1758–65), afterwards at Fulda, modelled the famous table decoration known as "The Chinese Emperor", while J. P. Melchior, a friend of the young Goethe, finished some of the figures which formed part of the group after 1765. Melchior's own works include portrait medallions, busts, and reliefs, some produced in biscuit. After Melchior's departure for Frankenthal and Nymphenburg, the factory closed down. The mark applied to Höchst porcelain and faïence is the wheel of Mainz, either incised or in colour, above or below the glaze (Fig. 36).

In 1751 the Berlin merchant W. K. Wegely, helped by workers from Meissen and Höchst,

started a factory which produced tableware, often in white, as well as figures after Meissen and Höchst models (Plate 365A). Frederick the Great encouraged Wegely at first, but later on showed dissatisfaction with his results, whereupon the factory closed down in 1757. One of the modellers, E. H. Reinhard, sold the secret of porcelain to Gotzkowsky, who started production in 1761, assisted by artists who had fled from Meissen during the Seven Years War. In 1763 the Berlin factory was sold to Frederick the Great, and it became State property, which it has remained ever since. F. E. Meyer, from Meissen, and his brother, W. Chr. Meyer, modelled at Berlin some of the best figures made during the third quarter of the eighteenth century; otherwise the factory is better known for tableware. Wegely's mark is a W and numerals in underglaze blue (Fig. 37), Gotzkowsky's a G. Subsequent marks include a sceptre and the letters K P M (*Koenigliche Porzellan Manufaktur*), again in underglaze blue.

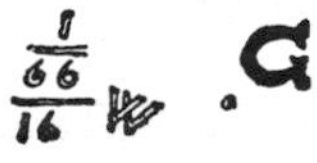

FIG. 37

At Neudeck, near Munich, porcelain was made from 1753 on, due to the initiative of Count Sigmund von Haimhausen and the arcanist Ringler. In 1761 the factory moved to a building in the palace grounds at Nymphenburg, where it continues to this day. The first two modellers, Ponhauser and Haertl, were succeeded in 1754 by Anton Bustelli of Locarno (1723–63), the greatest creative genius in porcelain. He recaptured the playful mood of the rococo period and gave it permanence in figures, often rendered in pure white, or in restrained colours, so that light and shade bring out the innate charms of the new material (Plate 362D). Bustelli's figures show great affinity of style with those of Ignaz Guenther and other contemporary Bavarian sculptors; whereas C. Lindeman and C. Purtscher painted on tableware figure subjects which were inspired by J. E. Nilson and Augsburg engravers of the period. Bustelli's successor, D. Auliczek, continued along established lines, but showed his originality by modelling animal groups of a type not hitherto attempted. In 1797 J. P. Melchior, formerly at Höchst and Frankenthal, came to Nymphenburg, where, following the taste of the time, he modelled his sensitive portrait busts and medallions in biscuit. The Nymphenburg mark, the "Rautenschild" from the arms of Bavaria, is usually shown upon the base, impressed as part of the decoration (Fig. 38).

The factory at Frankenthal, founded in 1755 by P.A.Hannong from Strassburg, owes its existence partly to the French monopoly protecting Vincennes, which prevented the foundation of similar privately owned ventures. Hannong crossed the Rhine and was granted a monopoly by the Elector Palatin. He started his factory near Mannheim; it was sold to the Elector Carl Theodor in 1755, and was closed in 1799, in consequence of the war with France. Among the gifted modellers attracted to Frankenthal, I. W. Lanz (1755–61) and Konrad Link (1762–6) are noted for large allegorical groups and hunting scenes of great originality. Link was succeeded by K. G. Lueck in 1766 (Plate 364A). With Melchior as modeller (1779–93) the influence of Höchst is felt, and the fashion for biscuit portrait medallions was introduced. The tableware of Frankenthal owes much to France, repeating popular bird patterns of Vincennes and Sèvres. The marks on Frankenthal porcelain vary, showing Hannong's initials until 1756, and thereafter a quartering from the arms of the Palatinate, occasionally also the lion from the same arms (Figs. 39 and 40). The

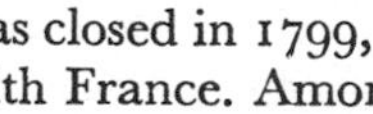

FIG. 39 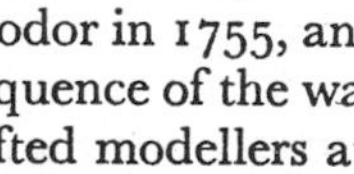   FIG. 40

initials of the Elector Carl Theodor, with or without crown, appear after 1762, all in underglaze blue.

The factory at Ludwigsburg near Stuttgart was founded in 1758, with the help of the arcanist Ringler, who had previously made porcelain at Höchst, Strasbourg, and Mu-

nich. The best work belongs to the period of 1760–7, while the change from rococo to classicism took place under G. F. Riedel and the court sculptor W. Beyer (Plate 362c), who left in 1767 for Vienna. Of real originality are miniature groups by J. Jean Louis, ranging from allegorical and satirical subjects to representations of the "Venetian Fair", depicting tradesmen in their booths. The latter became popular after the return of the Duke from Venice, and were modelled on actual fairs held at Stuttgart from 1767 on. Ludwigsburg tableware, made under G. F. Riedel, is often decorated with birds and flowers: the jugs and teapots are usually supported upon three legs. The manufacture came to an end in 1824. The early mark of Ludwigsburg porcelain consists of interlaced Cs with or without crown, substituted by the stag's horns, from the arms of Wuerthemberg (Fig. 41).

Other factories under princely patronage founded in Germany during the third quarter of the eighteenth century include Ansbach (1758–1860), Kelsterbach (1761–8), (1789–1802),Ottweiler (1763–c. 1770), Fulda (1765–90), Cassel (1766–88), Kloster Veilsdorf (1760), Limbach (1762), and Wallendorf (1763). The misfortunes of Meissen during the Seven Years' War made their sudden growth possible, but few outlasted the founder's personal interest. The demand for porcelain decreased with the change from an extravagantly decorative style, for which porcelain was eminently suited, towards the pale tranquillity of neo-classical marble and biscuit sculpture. During the last quarter of the century, and after the conclusion of the Prussian war, Meissen, rivalled by Vienna only, continued under Count Camillo Marcolini to supply the German market with tableware and decorative porcelain. But change of taste and lack of inspiration forced the factory to follow other styles created at the royal manufactory at Sèvres and elsewhere.

Italian

MAJOLICA

The name *maiolica*, first applied to the lustred Spanish pottery of Valencia, imported into Italy via the Balearic Island of Majorca, later became a generic term, embracing not only the whole range of tin-glazed Italian earthenwares but also those of other countries working in the same tradition.

The growth of the industry in Italy dates from about the second half of the fifteenth century, when there were already establishments at Orvieto (Umbria), Florence and Siena (Tuscany); Pisa was the port to which the Spanish wares were shipped, and Faenza (Emilia). The great influence of the latter place has caused the term faïence to be adopted for another large class of tin-enamelled pottery, particularly on the Continent. Rome, Padua, Cortono, and Todi have also been identified as places of manufacture.

Very early Italian majolica shows a marked Spanish influence, employing the same palette of green and purple applied to a white ground. Some "Florentine green" dishes, and the famous "impasto-blue-painted" Tuscan "oak-leaf-jars" are notable but very rare examples. There are, however, numerous blue-and-white and blue-and-lustred pieces, together with exceptionally fine tile-pavements, in the Spanish manner. This influence is seen principally in the painting, as the shapes adhered more or less to native traditions.

Towards the end of the fifteenth century Italian majolica developed a new and indigenous style, and for the next fifty years or so there was produced some of the most beautiful examples of European painted pottery.

Faenza has already been mentioned as one of the most important centres. From the last quarter of the fifteenth century to the end of the sixteenth, its output was copious and of an extremely high quality. Moreover, emigrant workmen, establishing themselves elsewhere,

helped to spread its influence. A documentary piece, now in the Musée de Cluny, is a magnificent plaque inscribed with the name "Nicolaus de Ragnolis" and dated 1475. There are also many tiles bearing similar inscriptions. Some pieces are decorated with gothic scrolls and foliage, others have peacock-feather motifs and varied diapering. Inverted-pear-shaped vases with flat handles; tiles and drug-jars (*albarelli*) painted with grotesques, busts, or coats-of-arms in rich polychrome, are typical. A method known as "contour-framing" outlined a design by surrounding it with a white halo. In some instances the whole ground was stained with a single colour. The palette is manganese-purple, dark blue, orange, yellow, and copper-green. Seven or eight highly accomplished artists, identified on stylistic grounds and by monograms, painted many wonderful panels and dishes with mythological and Biblical subjects; some of the latter are after Raphael. A quantity of commoner wares was also made.

At Deruta (Umbria), where potteries exist to the present day, fine polychrome and lustred pottery is known to have been made between about 1490 and 1545, though the earliest is hard to distinguish from that of Faenza. The style was much under the influence of the Umbrian school of painters. Characteristic colouring, besides a warm yellow and manganese-purple, was a strong blue in combination with lustre. The colours were inclined to run, and, as has been pointed out by Bernard Rackham, the tin-glaze is sometimes cut through to the clay body (*sgraffiato*) to obviate this difficulty. Many dishes and plates have profile busts painted in circular reserves surrounded by intricate designs, and in a class known as "petal-back" the lead-glazed reverses are decorated with imbricated floral patterns. Deep shading in blue to accentuate

(A) Painted Tz'ŭ Chou stoneware. Sung dynasty (960-1279). *Victoria and Albert Museum, London.*

(B) Ying ch'ing porcelain. Sung dynasty (960-1279). *Mrs Alfred Clark Collection.*

(c) Porcelain painted in underglaze blue and enamels. K'ang Hsi period (1662-1722). *Sydney Moss.*

(D) Porcelain with celadon ground and enamels. Ch'ien Lung period (1736-95). *Victoria and Albert Museum, London.*

PLATE 321

Famille verte porcelain. K'ang Hsi period (1662–1722). *Bluett & Sons.*

PLATE 322

C

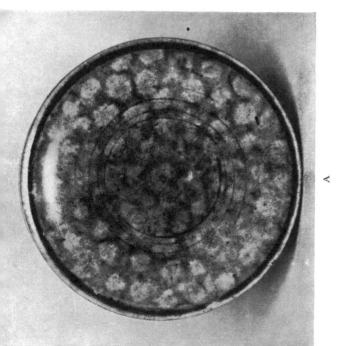

A

B

D

(A–B) Covered box. Earthenware with coloured glazes. T'ang dynasty (618–906). *Mrs Alfred Clark Collection.* (C) Chün ware. Sung dynasty (960–1279). *Mrs Alfred Clark Collection.* (D) Porcelain painted in underglaze blue. Mark and period of Hsüan Tê (1426–35). *H. R. Norton.*

PLATE 323

(A) "Three-colour" stoneware. Fifteenth century. *Musée Guimet, Paris.*

(B) Porcelain with "peachbloom" red glaze. K'an Hsi period (1662–1722). *Chinese Government.*

(C) Enamelled porcelain. Chia Ching period (1522–66). *Hamburg Museum.*

(D) Porcelain painted in underglaze blue. About 160 *H. R. Norton.*

PLATE 324

(A) Northern Celadon bowl with incised decoration. Sung dynasty (960–1279). *Bluett & Sons.*

(B) *Famille verte* porcelain. K'ang Hsi period (1662–1722). *John Sparks Ltd.*

PLATE 325

PLATE 326

(A) Painted earthenware, T'ang dynasty (618–906). *Mrs Alfred Clark Collection.*   (B) Bodhidarma. White porcelain (*blanc-de-Chine*) of Fukien. Seventeenth century. *Chinese Government.*

(C) "Dogs of Fo." *Famille rose* porcelain, Ch'ien Lung period (1736–95). *Sydney Moss.*

PLATE 327

(A) Bowl decorated in blue with a scene of the Crucifixion. Early eighteenth century. Diameter $5\frac{7}{8}$ ins. *Victoria and Albert Museum, London.*

(B) Punch-bowl painted with caricature coats-of-arms of John Wilkes and Lord Mansfield. The former with Lord Camden and Lord Temple as supporters, and the latter with King George III and the Devil. About 1770. Diameter $10\frac{1}{2}$ ins. *Private Collection.*

PLATE 328

(A) Fukien group of Europeans with a dog. Height
6½ ins. *Victoria and Albert Museum, London.*

(B) Candlestick in the form of a European lady.
First half of eighteenth century. Height 7¾ ins.
Victoria and Albert Museum, London.

(c) Candlestick, about 1770. Height 6⅝ ins. *Private
Collection.*

(D) Man and woman dancing, after a Meissen
model of about 1735. This was made also at Chelsea
and Bow. Mid-eighteenth century. Height 5½ ins.
Victoria and Albert Museum, London.

PLATE 329

(A) Dish with the Royal arms of England and inscription in Dutch. Early eighteenth century. Diameter 15⅛ ins. *Victoria and Albert Museum, London.*

(B) Dish decorated in blue with figures of European musicians; the border with Chinese landscapes. Early eighteenth century. Diameter 13¾ ins. *Victoria and Albert Museum, London.*

(C) Plate painted with two figures of Scotsmen; the border with vignettes of birds and landscapes. Mid-eighteenth century. Diameter 9 ins. *Victoria and Albert Museum, London.*

(D) Pattern plate. The back inscribed with the name of a dealer in Canton: SYNGCHONG. About 1790. Diameter 9¾ ins. *Victoria and Albert Museum, London.*

PLATE 330

(A) Part of a tea set painted with a scene of the Crucifixion in schwarzlot. First half of eighteenth century. *Boston Museum of Fine Arts.*

(B) Covered vase of European form. About 1800. Height about 13 ins. *Boston Museum of Fine Arts.*

(C) Part of a dinner service painted with the coat-of-arms of Newman. About 1790. *Boston Museum of Fine Arts.*

PLATE 331

(A and B) Ship decoration: the Grand Turk punch bowl, with view of interior inscribed SHIP GRAND TURK AT CANTON 1786. *Peabody Museum, Salem, Massachusetts.*

(C) Emblematic: insignia of the Society of the Cincinnati, with monogram of original owner, Dr David Townsend of Boston, and floral motifs; 1790. *Henry N. Flynt.*

PLATE 332

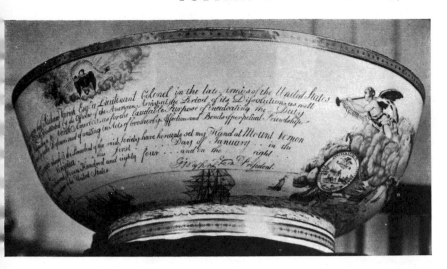

(A) Richard Varick punch bowl; motifs and inscription from Varick's certificate of membership in the Society of the Cincinnati. *Washington Association of New Jersey, Morristown.*

(B and C) Punch bowl presented to the Corporation of the City of New York by General Jacob Morton, 1812. Interior shows view of city after engraving by Samuel Seymour. *Metropolitan Museum of Art, New York.*

PLATE 333

(A) Underglaze decoration: Fitzhugh pattern in green with enamelled American eagle. *Metropolitan Museum of Art, New York.*

(B) Underglaze decoration: Canton type with scene in blue. *New York Historical Society.*

PLATE 334

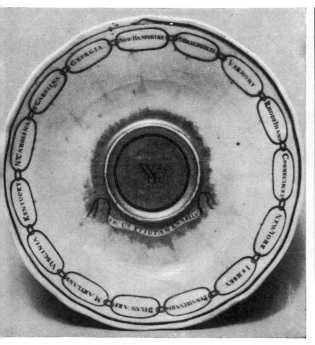

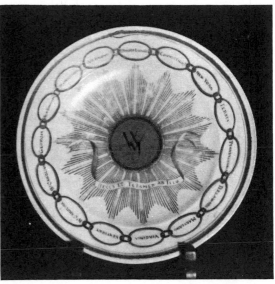

(B) French reproduction of "States", probably 1876.
Antiques, xxi, 172.

(A) "States" pattern, presented to Martha Washington, 1786.
Metropolitan Museum of Art, New York.

(C) Tureen; orange-peel texture. This, with *famille rose* decoration, is one of the
European market types sought by American collectors today. *McCann Collection,
Metropolitan Museum of Art, New York.*

PLATE 335

Flagon with ship decoration; reverse shows the ship in fair weather, flying American flag. *New York Historical Society.*

PLATE 336

(A) Monogram and mythological; brought on the "Grand Turk", 1786, for Deborah Fairfax Anderson. *Essex Institute.*

(B) Floral: wide dark blue border with floral reserves and gilt stars; early 1800s. *Mottahedeh; Antiques,* xxviii, 121.

(C) Pseudo-armorial; monogram in mantled shield; ship with American flag. Privately owned; *Antiques,* xix, 442.

(D) Armorial: arms of Pennsylvania. *New York Historical Society.*

PLATE 337

(A) Polychrome on blue ground, North Netherlands, probably Rotterdam, *c.* 1620. *Victoria and Albert Museum, London.*

(B) Blue monochrome, North Netherlands, *c.* 1620. Height 7½ ins. *Rijksmuseum, Amsterdam.*

(C) Polychrome, North Netherlands, probably Rotterdam, *c.* 1600. *Victoria and Albert Museum, London.*

Photo: Thomas Fall.

(D) Blue monochrome, Delft, late seventeenth century. Mark: LV monogram. *Glaisher Collection, Fitzwilliam Museum, Cambridge.*

PLATE 338

(A) Dutch, probably Haarlem, first half of seventeenth century. *Glaisher Collection, Fitzwilliam Museum, Cambridge.*

Photo: Thomas Fall.

(B) Polychrome and dark blue, Dutch, early seventeenth century. *Victoria and Albert Museum, London.*

(C) Blue monochrome, Delft, dated 1718. *Rijksmuseum, Amsterdam.*

Photo: Thomas Fall.

(D) Blue monochrome, Delft, mid-seventeenth century. *British Museum, London.*

PLATE 339

(A) Blue monochrome, Delft, dated 1661. *British Museum, London.*

(B) Blue monochrome, Delft, late seventeenth century. Mark: AK. *Glaisher Collection, Fitzwilliam Museum, Cambridge.*

Photo: Thomas Fall.

(C) Blue monochrome, Delft, c. 1700. Mark: LVE. *Glaisher Collection, Fitzwilliam Museum, Cambridge.*

(D) Blue monochrome, Delft, c. 1710. Mark: LVE. *Private Collection.*

PLATE 340

(A) Blue monochrome, Delft, *c.* 1710. Mark: LVE WK. *Private Collection.*

(B) Polychrome, Delft, *c.* 1710. Mark: ROOS. *Victoria and Albert Museum, London.*

PLATE 341

Photo: Thomas Fall.

(A) Teapot, yellow on black, LVE factory, Delft, *c.* 1720. Unmarked. *Glaisher Collection, Fitzwilliam Museum, Cambridge.*

(B) Delft caddies, *c.* 1720. Mark: LVE. "Delft Doré" plate, *c.* 1720. Unmarked. *Victoria and Albert Museum, London.*

PLATE 342

A   B

(A) Blue monochrome tulip vase, Delft, *c.* 1715. *Victoria and Albert Museum, London.*
(B) Blue monochrome, Makkum, dated 1787. *Private Collection.*

C   D

(C) Polychrome, Delft, *c.* 1710. Mark: LVE. *Victoria and Albert Museum, London.*
(D) Plate, yellow and manganese on turquoise ground, Delft, *c.* 1765. *Private Collection.*

PLATE 343

Photo: Thomas Fall.

(A) Blue monochrome, Delft, dated 1658. *Glaisher Collection, Fitzwilliam Museum, Cambridge.*

Photo: Thomas Fall.

(B) Polychrome butter pot, Delft, *c.* 1770. Mark: HVH. *Fitzwilliam Museum, Cambridge.*

PLATE 344

(B) Blue monochrome, Delft, Frijtom. *Victoria and Albert Museum, London.*

(c) Arnhem, *c.* 1770. *Museum Boymans, Rotterdam.*

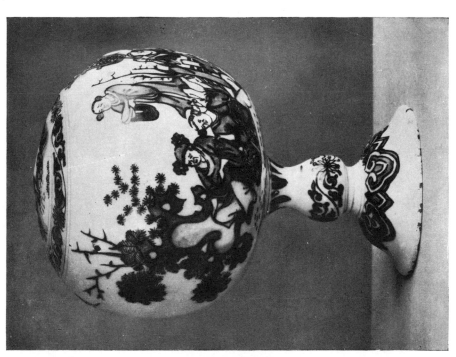

(A) Blue and purple, Delft, late seventeenth century. Mark: SVE. *Victoria and Albert Museum, London.*

PLATE 345

Coffee-pot, earthenware with mottled glaze ("tortoiseshell" ware). Staffordshire, about 1760. Height 8½ ins.
Schreiber Collection, Victoria and Albert Museum, London.

PLATE 346

Photo: Fine Art Engravers Ltd.

(A) Covered posset-pot, delftware painted in blue with darker outlines. Lambeth, 1691. Height 7¾ in. *L. Lipski.*

(B) Honey-pot, lead-glazed earthenware with slip decoration. Staffordshire, late seventeenth or early eighteenth century. Height 5⅝ ins. *A. J. B. Kiddell.*

(C) Figure of a shepherd, earthenware with lead-glaze variously coloured. Ralph Wood, Burslem, *c.* 1770–80. Height 9⅛ ins. *Glaisher Collection, Fitzwilliam Museum, Cambridge.*

(D) Group, earthenware with mottled lead-glaze. Staffordshire ("Astbury-Whieldon" type), *c.* 1740. Height 8¼ ins. *Willett Collection, Art Gallery and Museum, Brighton.*

PLATE 347

(A) Mug, of unglazed red stoneware. Perhaps made by John Dwight of Fulham, c. 1690. Height 4 ins. *Victoria and Albert Museum, London.*

(B) Loving-cup, brown salt-glazed stoneware with incised decoration. Nottingham, 1719. Height 9 ins. *Museum and Art Gallery, Nottingham.*

(C) Vase, black stoneware with white reliefs ("jasper" ware) Wedgwood, late eighteenth century. *Museum and Art Gallery, Nottingham.*

(D) Coffee-pot, cream-coloured earthenware. Leeds, about 1770. Height 9¾ ins. *D. Towner.*

PLATE 348

(A) Tea- or punch-pot, white salt-glazed stoneware painted in enamel-colours. Staffordshire, about 1765. Height 8 ins. *Victoria and Albert Museum, London.*

(B) Punch-bowl, delftware painted in blue, yellow, and manganese. Lambeth, about 1760. Diameter 12 ins. *Private Collection.*

PLATE 349

(A) Jar and cover on tripod support, lustre glaze. Marked JOSIAH WEDGWOOD FEB 2ND. 1805. Height 5¾ ins. *Victoria and Albert Museum, London.*

(B) Figure of a triton, forming a candlestick. Designed by John Flaxman. Height 11⅛ ins. *The Castle Museum, Nottingham.*

(c) Meat dish with printed decoration in blue. Marked WEDGWOOD. Width 20⅝ ins. *Victoria and Albert Museum, London.*

PLATE 350

(A) Plaque in blue jasper ware with relief in white of The Sacrifice of Iphigenia, modelled by Pacetti from a Roman original. This plaque also exists with the figures undraped. *The Castle Museum, Nottingham.*

(B) Teapot of jasper ware; the body white, the festoons green, and the medallions lilac. Marked WEDGWOOD. Height 3½ ins. *D. M. & P. Manheim.*

(C) One of a pair of vases and covers of blue jasper ware with reliefs in white. Marked WEDGWOOD. Height 13 ins. *D. M. & P. Manheim.*

(D) One of a pair of vases and covers of blue jasper ware with reliefs in white. The gilt bronze mounts made by Matthew Boulton at Soho, Birmingham. Marked WEDGWOOD. Height 11¾ ins. *D. M. & P. Manheim.*

PLATE 351

(A) Doulton stoneware modelled by George Tinworth. The boy musicians are part of a charming set. *Private Collection.*

(B) Large terra-cotta panel by George Tinworth: The Sons of Cydippe (from a poem by Edmond Gosse), c. 1880

Courtesy of the Royal Doulton Potteries.

PLATE 352

an outline was another device. Subjects were also rendered in relief. After the middle of the sixteenth century the quality declined and was never revived.

By the beginning of the sixteenth century the industry had become well established. Pharmacies were adorned with beautiful sets of drug-vases and jars, and the great dishes, *piatti da pompa*, were displayed on sideboards and tables.

Castel Durante (near Urbino), renamed Urbania in 1635, was probably under the patronage of the Dukes of Urbino. The earliest dated specimen, 1508, bears the arms of Pope Julius II. It is also signed by Giovanni Maria, recognized as one of the great painters of majolica. Perhaps the most notable contribution of Castel Durante was the *istoriato* painting of Nicola Pellipario, working there between about 1515 and 1527. This kind of narrative painting is usually spread across the whole surface of a dish or plate. It was brought to its highest state of perfection by this master, and extensively copied elsewhere.

Gubbio, also in the Duchy of Urbino, was famed for its magnificent gold and ruby lustres. The best period comes within the first thirty years of the sixteenth century. Some of the finest pieces were gadrooned or embossed to give full play to the refulgent brilliance of the lustre colours. The master of this art was Giorgio Andreoli, "Maestro Giorgio", a native of Intra in Lombardy, who became a citizen of Gubbio in 1498. Much already decorated majolica was sent to Gubbio to be enriched with lustre.

Caffaggiolo (near Florence), a renowned centre of Tuscan potting, was, for a time, under the patronage of the Medici family, whose arms and mottoes appear on some of its wares. The earlier work shows the influence of the Florentine masters, particularly Botticelli; Donatello's work was also copied. A family named Fattorini made pottery in the neighbourhood in 1469, and were at Caffaggiolo from about 1506 onwards. The subjects are boldly painted in strong colours. They reflect Florences's individual status and depict, besides religious and classical subjects, scenes of pageantry, triumphs, shields of arms, and trophies. "Peacock-feather" ornament was also used here. Typical themes are: a rich blue, used as a background; lemon-yellow, orange, and green; also lustre, and a dark cherry-red peculiar to the factory. The best work was done between 1506 and 1526.

The painter Titian is recorded as having supervised the making of majolica at Venice in 1520. Much that was made there from about 1530 is characterized by the admixture of cobalt blue with the white enamel glaze. This produced a greyish-blue surface called *smaltino*, on to which were painted designs in dark blue and opaque white. Their Chinese origin shows the influence of Oriental importations. *Istoriato* painting in the manner of Urbino was developed later.

ITALIAN PORCELAIN

The first successful attempt to produce porcelain in Europe was made at Florence about 1575 under the patronage of Francesco de' Medici. Inspired by contemporary blue-and-white Ming ware, an artificial porcelain was produced for a short time only, which contained some kaolin, the pure infusable clay used in China, mixed with powdered glass and frit. Medici porcelain, proudly marked with the cupola of the cathedral and the "F" of Florence, is decorated in underglaze blue of varying intensity, which gently melts into the glaze. The flowering of the faïence industry during the seventeenth century is due in no small measure to the untiring quest for the secret of porcelain manufacture. This faïence, or earthenware, which fuses at a low temperature in the kiln, is usually dipped into opaque tin glaze, which, while hiding impurities of texture, is admirably suited to be the recipient of coloured decoration.

Venice, with its great glass industry, is also an early centre for true porcelain. Chr. C. Hunger, the Meissen goldworker and arcanist, reached Venice from Vienna in 1720, bringing with him the secret of porcelain-making. This he disclosed to the brothers Francesco and Giuseppe Vezzi, former goldsmiths, who launched an enterprise which flourished until 1727. Cups without handles and saucers with coloured decoration, and teapots with acanthus-leaf reliefs are characteristic of this factory, which took as models not only Meissen and Vienna porcelain but also Italian silver. Monochrome or coloured decoration reveals that lightness of touch which one has come to associate with Venetian art in general. Vezzi porcelain is marked va, VENA, or VENEZIA, in underglaze blue or overglaze red (Fig. 42).

FIG. 42   V.ᵈ VEN: Venezia

N. F. Hewelcke and his wife, Dresden dealers who had left Saxony during the Seven Years' War, secured rights to manufacture porcelain "in the style of Meissen" at Venice in 1758. Thus the market continued until 1764, when Geminiano Cozzi started to manufacture aided by the Venetian senate. From then on, figures, snuff-boxes, cane-handles, and table-wares were made; the latter all marked with an anchor in red. This enterprise lasted until 1812. Porcelain was also made at Lenove (1762–1825) and Este, from 1781.

The most beautiful and important Italian porcelain was made at the Royal Palace of Capodimonte, where Charles, King of Naples, established a factory in 1743.

His interest in the project was aroused through his marriage to Maria Amalia of Saxony, daughter of Augustus III of Poland, who brought him as part of her wedding dowry a great quantity of Meissen porcelain.

Attempts to rival the German production were at first frustrated by an inability to discover the secret of making a suitable paste. Following unsuccessful attempts to lure arcanists from the Doccia and Vienna factories, a chemist of Belgian extraction, Livio Ottavio Schepers, was employed. He too proved unsatisfactory and was dismissed in 1744, when his place was taken by his son, Gaetano, who supplied a successful recipe for the making of soft paste.

Giuseppe Gricci was the chief modeller and Giovanni Caselli remained in charge of the painting until his death in 1754. Both Gricci and Schepers continued at Buen Retiro when the manufactory was removed there in 1759.

In addition to the table-wares, snuff-boxes, cane-handles, and vases were made from an early period, when the influence of Meissen was still a factor. Tea-services are recorded as having been painted with figure subjects, seascapes, landscapes, battle scenes, etc., by Guiseppe della Torre. Oriental designs included the raised prunus motif of *blanc-de-Chine*, common to most early European factories.

The porcelain is frequently unmarked, but the Bourbon fleur-de-lis in blue or gold was used both here and at Buen Retiro. It is generally impressed on figures.

Capodimonti's greatest achievement was the decoration of a porcelain room at the Palace of Portici (1757–59). Removed to the Capodimonte Palace in 1805, it has remained there to the present day.

Many beautiful figures were modelled by Gricci; they include subjects from the Italian Comedy and peasant types. A very noticeable characteristic is the extreme smallness of the heads. The colouring and soft creamy quality of these pieces is something which has never been surpassed.

Contrary to popular belief, the white or coloured figure subjects in relief on vases and other wares have nothing to do with Capodimonte. They originated at Doccia, and have since been widely reproduced in debased forms. Nineteenth-century Doccia examples are marked with the crown N of Naples, but crude copies are still made elsewhere.

The Doccia factory was founded by the Marchese Carlo Ginori in 1735, and carried on by his son Lorenzo from 1757 to 1791.

Karl Anreiter, an independent decorator from Vienna, was engaged in 1737. His son, Anton, later became a painter at the factory. Both left in 1746. The chief modeller was Gaspare Bruschi.

By 1740 good progress earned Ginori a privilege for making porcelain in Tuscany. The best period was 1757–91.

Small figures of the Italian Comedy among

other subjects are particularly attractive, though on the whole Doccia colouring is inclined to be hard and the glaze rather dry in appearance. A hybrid hard-paste body was very liable to fire-cracks.

About 1770 white tin-glaze was used. Large white groups of biblical and mythological subjects, mounted on rococo bases, were well modelled in the Italian baroque manner. In these pieces the fire-cracking is usually extensive.

The factory mark of a star, taken from the Ginori arms, was introduced towards the end of the eighteenth century.

The concern remained in the hands of the Ginori family until 1896, and still bears their name.

Porcelain marked with an N surmounted by a crown, together with the monogram F.R.F., was made at the Royal Naples factory, started in 1771 by Ferdinand IV, as an attempted revival of his father's enterprise at Capodimonte.

The porcelain is of a soft, glassy paste and highly translucent. Early products recall those of Capodimonte, where some of the painters had worked. An Academy of the Nude was started in 1781, when a classical style was adopted. Many of the later figures are in biscuit. Large services were decorated with scenes and neo-classical subjects.

The original factory lasted until 1807, when it was sold to the French firm, Jean Poularde Prad & Company.

Russian

PORCELAIN

Russian porcelain, being little known or collected in the West, has often been mistakenly judged as an inferior imitation of the more famous German, French, and Austrian factories which preceded it, and therefore hardly worthy of being studied as a ceramic art with a character, artistic quality, and history of its own. Closer acquaintance, however, reveals many distinct and individual qualities, which at their best can rival the standard set by the finest West European products, although the first Russian factory started later, and only began to flourish after a series of calamities.

Peter the Great had sent scientific experts on Russian trade caravans to Peking, with strict instructions to find out from the secretive Chinese the exact manner in which they made their porcelain. But his emissaries returned home none the wiser. It was not until 1744 that his exuberant daughter, the Empress Elizabeth, entrusted a vagrant German, C. K. Hunger, then employed in Stockholm, with a written contract to "found in St Petersburg a factory for making Dutch plates and pure porcelain, as it is made in Saxony". Hunger had started life as a goldsmith's apprentice, later sought out Böttger, the famous director of the first hard-paste Meissen factory, and was employed as a gilder there in 1727. He wrote to the Empress Elizabeth that he had been responsible for organizing the Rörstrand ceramic factory in Sweden (whence he had in fact been summarily dismissed).

He belonged to that familiar class of restless international adventurers, in which even the eighteenth century abounded. Lavish in promises, he knew how to advertise his very scanty talents, and thereby win the confidence of highly placed people. From the start, his behaviour in Russia aroused suspicion. His first firing in the kiln was a total failure, but he always found plausible excuses. Eventually he exhausted the patience of the director, Baron Cherkasov, who complained that during three years Hunger had turned out barely a dozen cups, and even they were crooked and discoloured.

A Russian priest's son, Dmitri Vinogradov,

who had studied chemistry in Marburg, was then ordered to extract from Hunger all the secrets of porcelain manufacture, to supervise him, and never to leave him alone for a single moment. In 1747 he replaced Hunger, who was dismissed. Undoubtedly Vinogradov gave himself heart and soul to experimental work, especially with the ingredients of the paste and glaze, and scientific methods of firing in the kiln. He produced some good though limited results, but he suffered from bouts of drunkenness, which made him violent and unreliable. In 1752 Baron Cherkasov, who took porcelain seriously, had Vinogradov fastened to an iron chain, perpetually watched and in his turn forced to write down every technical recipe that he knew. He died in 1758 at the early age of thirty-nine.

After this painful initiation the Imperial Factory came into its own during the reign of Catherine II (1762–96). She made a thorough personal inspection of the factory in 1763, and at once ordered highly skilled painters, modellers, and craftsmen to be engaged, regardless of expense, from Germany, Austria, and France. Catherine had a passion for building, and for filling whatever she built with beautiful and magnificent objects, without any prejudice about their national origin. For her new Imperial Hermitage and Tsarskoe Selo she collected pictures, sculpture, and porcelain from all over Europe.

Reacting against the lush and gaudy baroque encouraged by her predecessor, she promoted a sterner classical temper in architecture, and admired an architectural dignity in decorative art. Her best and favourite architects were Italians. "I want Italians," she told her agent, Grimm, "because we already have enough Frenchmen who know too much and design ugly buildings." She bought up all the portfolios of Clérisseau's drawings and aquatints, made during a tour of Italy, minutely depicting Italian ornamental plaster work, arabesques, vase construction, and Pompeian detail. This decorative Italian strain, often nostalgically reflected by northern temperaments, also found expression in Russian porcelain, where it recurred throughout the following century. At the same time Catherine herself, being a pure German and a usur-

per, tried hard to personify some more ideal aspects of her adopted country, and was keen on giving scope for native Russian themes in art.

Many West European porcelain factories had begun by working in the manner initiated either by the Chinese or by their immediate predecessors. The first Russian factory was no exception, for it frankly emulated Meissen, as the best and leading European exponent of ceramic art. Catherine ordered a well-known dinner-service from Meissen ("The Hunter's Service", because it was decorated with diverse hunting scenes). But characteristically, as soon as some plates and dishes became broken, she insisted that the Imperial Factory should make all replacements. And these turned out hardly inferior to the originals, although the paste was less uniformly white, showed the bluish tint of Russian kaolin, and the painting was recognizably freer and more naïve.

The Chinese Empire, being uncomfortably close, appeared less romantic to Russia than it did to Western Europe at that time. And the Western fashion for fantastic whimsical *Chinoiseries* found less favour there. Moreover, in Russia, any craving for the exotic could be fully gratified at home. A book by the German traveller, J. Georgi (translated into Russian in 1776), called *Description of the Races inhabiting the Russian Empire*, attracted attention chiefly by its lively coloured illustrations. These formed the starting-point for a whole new series of porcelain figures, showing many characteristic types, wearing picturesque national or regional costumes.

Perhaps they were partly inspired by earlier racial figures from the Meissen modeller, Kaendler, but they drew upon original and local raw material. Their striking success led to the creation of a further series, illustrating Russian peasants, tradesmen, craftsmen, etc., wearing their professional clothes and carrying the emblems of their work. These provide delightfully idealized *genre* studies of Russian life in the late eighteenth and early nineteenth centuries.

Jean Rachette, son of a French sculptor but born in Copenhagen, came to the Imperial Factory as a modeller in 1779. He took responsibility for launching both these series of porcelain figures, which were often as remarkable for their balanced rhythmical composition as for their pure and sensitive modelling and colourful brilliance. This foreigner's talented interpretation of native Russian themes launched a new tradition, which was drawn and enlarged upon by later Russian porcelain factories throughout the nineteenth century. Rachette remained active until 1804, when he was granted the rank of State Counsellor in recognition of his great services to art. Paradoxical though it sounds, foreign artists who came to work in Russia were often more inspired by original Russian subjects and environment than native artists, who went out of their way to imitate the latest Western fashions, whether they were bad or good.

Another line, developed in the Imperial Factory at this time, glorified Catherine and the achievements of her reign. On many vases her head appears in medallion form with the helmet of Minerva. On another a Cupid crowns with a laurel wreath her interlaced initials, while a double-headed eagle holds out an olive-branch of peace. A vase at Gatchina depicts her greeted by a whole group of allegorical female figures, *Abundance, Humanity, Science, Justice,* and *Industry,* while *Chastity,* with modest downcast eyes, holds up a mirror to the Empress. The so-called "Arabesque Service", though decoratively inspired by frescoes excavated at Herculaneum, also served to illustrate Russian naval victories.

But the majestic dinner-services and vases, ordered by Catherine, already differed both in colouring and form from the Meissen porcelain of the period. They were severer, more compact in line, less elaborate and mannered in execution. In the "Cabinet Service" (first ordered as a present for her favourite, Count Bezborodko) the artistic splendour of luxuriant Italian ornament prevailed over national self-glorification. Together with exquisite detail, similar to that in the Arabesque service, it is distinguished by a broad gold band, encircled by garlands of delicate flowers, with oval medallions in the centre, depicting Italian architectural scenes, sometimes with human figures.

Having mastered ceramic technique and

form in the eighteenth century, the art of modelling, painting, and gilding porcelain reached its high point and boldest native originality in the first half of the next century under Alexander I and Nicolas I. At the same time preoccupation with new experiments in colour contrast was accompanied by a diminishing concern with purity of form. This led to a looser relationship between sculptural design and painted decoration. The latter tended to predominate. Intense malachite and emerald greens, rich lapis-lazuli blue, delicate mauves and buffs and deep maroon, more and more took the place of pure and dazzling white as favourite colours for the background. But exquisite miniature painting, often framed in white panels, was made to blend effectively with these coloured grounds (Plate 376A *right*).

Catherine's son, the Emperor Paul (1796–1801), although he was a certifiable megalomaniac and hated his domineering mother, inherited her passion for good porcelain. He particularly liked medallions with paintings of landscapes and fine buildings, and he started a branch of the Imperial Factory near his own palace at Gatchina. It is recorded that, the day before he was murdered, he received a new dinner-service he had ordered, painted with Russian architectural scenes, and, admiring it together with members of his family, pronounced that day to be the happiest in his whole life.

Alexander I (1801–25), despite the Napoleonic Wars which dislocated his reign, did not neglect the factory, which continued to recruit first-class artist craftsmen, regardless of nationality. As a rule each new foreign craftsman was (very sensibly) put under contract to teach two Russian apprentices. The most important foreign painter, Schwebach, who had worked for twelve years at Sèvres, was prominent in launching a new *genre* of decoration, depicting soldiers in battle scenes, and Asiatic figures seen against Russian landscapes.

In 1806 Alexander was persuaded to issue a decree imposing a prohibitive tariff on the import of foreign porcelain into Russia. By stimulating internal competition, this measure made private porcelain factories start to multiply. Some were straightforward business ventures, run by enterprising merchants. Others, like that run by Prince Yusupov at his palace of Arkhangelskoe, were designed to gratify the taste of wealthy connoisseurs, and to provide unique presents for their personal friends. The Miklashevsky factory, started by a landowner who had found china-clay on his estate, and employing his own serfs, won a gold medal at an exhibition in Petersburg in 1849. Its most striking work was a huge porcelain iconostasis with blue and gold columns, made for the owner's village church at Volokhitin. One generous landowner, who detected a natural talent for modelling and carving in a young serf called Kudinov, arranged for him all facilities to start his own porcelain factory in 1818, and later gave him his freedom. This factory was managed by the Kudinov family, whose name it bore, until 1881, lasting longer than many others founded in the same period, which did not survive the Emancipation of 1861.

The main difference between Russian and European porcelain at this time depended less on style (which was everywhere neo-classical) than on choice of themes and mode of artistic interpretation. While the Sèvres factory concentrated on glorifying Napoleon and his deeds, the Imperial factory started to specialize in majestic and graceful vases, with an astonishing variety of shapes and decoration. Events of the patriotic war in 1812 also provoked a vogue for battle scenes with soldiers and officers wearing splendidly gay uniforms.

In 1814 the Russians learned from a French prisoner of war the process of making transfer prints of colour blocks on porcelain. This practice was later adopted by private commercial concerns; but the directors of the Imperial factory rejected it as a semi-mechanical device, good enough for the quick salesmanship required by Western bourgeois mass production, but unworthy of the Russian court and aristocracy, which demanded and appreciated first-class hand-painting.

Nicolas I (1825–55) was more exacting than his predecessor. He required splendid and dignified porcelain to decorate the royal palace, examined every piece personally, and gave little encouragement to his director's scheme to make the Imperial factory pay its way by selling surplus products to the public. During his reign the vases were superbly painted, although they began to show too many scenes directly copied from Old Master paintings in the Hermitage. But some of the most lively and exquisite original paintings depicted flowers, fruit, or exotic birds, and were made on the flat centres or borders of plates and dishes (Plate 375B right). One of the Russian painters, Paul Ivanov, excelled in modelling porcelain flowers and foliage in high relief. At the 1851 Crystal Palace exhibition in London the Imperial Factory was awarded a medal for its exhibit.

During the reign of Alexander II (1855–81) orders for the palaces and members of the Imperial family rapidly declined. Emancipation of the serfs in 1861 also led to the closing down of numerous private factories, which had depended on serf craftsmen, formerly trained by their masters and foreign artists. Taste grew more stereotyped and stale, and art began to be overshadowed in importance for its patrons by the fashionable concentration on social reforms.

In 1871 the Empress told the director of the factory that he must fight against academic stagnation, and aim at more vitality, diversity of shapes, painting, and style. She suggested he might start to take some helpful examples from English porcelain. The chief sculptor, Spiess, was thereupon dispatched to England, whence he brought back many specimens from English factories. Despite the decline of interest among its patrons, the Imperial Factory still had superb artists, and the flower painting on some of its vases remained as perfect as in the earlier period, reminiscent of the most luxuriant Dutch seventeenth-century "still life" style (Plate 374A).

Alexander III (1881–94), on his accession gave orders for the Imperial Factory to be given the best possible technical and artistic opportunities. A survey taken at this time admitted that a quite disproportionate number of administrative officials demoralized the best craftsmen, and that many incompetent workmen were engaged or retained, merely because they happened to be children or relatives of members of the staff. Regularly once a year Alexander gave instructions about projects submitted to him. Far from being a stuffy philistine, his own taste was definite. He encouraged a dignified and massive simplicity (Plate 376B *right*). Towards the end of his reign, however, he showed a preference for the pale, cold blues and greys of the late Copenhagen style. He ordered one important and elaborate painted dinner-service for the court. This was described as the "Raphael Service" because the motifs in it were taken from Raphael's Vatican decorations, which had been copied in the eighteenth century for the Hermitage in Petersburg.

Under Nicolas II (1894–1917), who had inferior personal taste and no love for art, the standard rapidly declined. During his reign little original work was done, except perhaps in Easter eggs, and the best porcelain consisted of replacements or additions to services previously commissioned by his more cultured predecessors.

The first mark of the Imperial Factory in the reigns of Elizabeth and Peter III consisted of a black or impressed double-headed eagle, and, more rarely, an impressed anchor. From the time of Catherine II, and under all subsequent emperors, the mark consisted of the reigning sovereign's initials painted under the glaze, usually in blue, but sometimes in black or green. Except in the reign of Catherine, these initials are surmounted by the Imperial crown. Some pieces, made in the reign of Alexander II, have the Emperor's initial surrounded by a circular wreath. Many pieces are unmarked, since marking was first made compulsory by Nicolas I (Fig. 43).

Though the Imperial factory usually launched the style and themes for other Russian porcelain manufacture, it was followed and frequently surpassed in quality by several private factories. The most notable of these was started about 1756 by an Englishman, Francis Gardner, who appears to have first settled in Russia in 1746. It was successfully carried on by his descendants until 1891, when it was sold to the giant Kuznetsov porcelain and faïence combine. The factory was situated in the Gjelsk region, near Moscow, where local clay, which proved suitable for

FIG. 43. Imperial Porcelain Factory marks, 1744–1917

porcelain, could be used. Gardner started with a German manager called Gattenberg, who later joined the Imperial Factory, and he employed a well-known German painter, Kestner. But these and other foreigners taught many Russian craftsmen, principally serfs, who gradually replaced them, as soon as they had mastered the various techniques; so that the number of foreigners employed in key positions steadily diminished in course of time.

Eighteenth-century Gardner groups and figures of a sentimental pastoral character are still close to Meissen prototypes, and so are its rare figures representing characters from the Italian *Commedia dell' arte*. The academician, G. Miller, who visited the Gardner factory in 1779, noted that "its quality is equal to that of any foreign factory". He found only one defect: "that its glaze is less white than the Saxon. But they are trying to remedy this, and have gone quite far towards success". (A. Selivanov: *Farfor i Fayans Rossiyskoy Imperii* (Vladimir, 1903, p. 22). Not only did Gardner already compete with the Imperial Factory, but he even obtained orders from the court of Catherine II for specially designed services.

Miller remarked with admiration on the beauty of one of these, decorated with architectural scenes and classical ornament. Gardner also produced for the Court four separate dinner-services decorated with emblems of the Russian orders of knighthood.

By the beginning of the nineteenth century the work of the Gardner factory had grown emancipated from imitation of foreign models. In particular, its figures of Russian peasant types and craftsmen reveal a dignified simplicity, remote from the increasing sophistication of Sèvres and Meissen figures that were being made at that time. The best of these also show a mastery of sensitive modelling and sculptural poise, accompanied by a bold and brilliant range of colour combinations, and frequently by skilful contrasts between matt and glazed painting used on the same figure. All these innovations and refinements illustrated how Russian modellers and painters were freshly and independently inspired by this new art, and were reaching beyond what they had learned from foreign masters, while introducing native themes and decorative colouring drawn from their traditional Russian background.

The Gardner factory could not escape the general decline in visual art which oppressed the second half of the nineteenth century throughout Europe. But in a number of its individual products it still maintained the exacting standards of an earlier age. Some of its figures of national types, especially Asiatic ones, are modelled with extraordinary finesse,

even in the 1880s, though the colouring tended to be cruder than it was in the previous decades. But many of the peasant figures of this late period are mannered and "literary". Some are painfully coarse and clumsy, and seem like drunken caricatures of their serene and charming predecessors. In this period Gardner also embarked on mass-produced tea-services, gaily painted with roses in white medallions against deep blue, red, or green grounds. Many of them were for export to the Turkish Empire or Central Asia, and carry Arabic lettering under the Gardner factory mark. They are widespread enough to be familiar to many people who have never seen the rarer and finer kinds of Russian porcelain.

Gardner porcelain had a wide variety of marks in the hundred and forty years of its existence. Different shapes of the Latin letter G, painted underglaze in blue or black, were most frequent in the late eighteenth and early nineteenth centuries. Occasionally the mark is similar to the Meissen crossed swords with a star. In the first quarter of the nineteenth century the full name of the factory, impressed either in Cyrillic or Latin characters, becomes more frequent. In the second half of the nineteenth century the mark is usually the Moscow St George and Dragon crest, surrounded by a circle, bearing the full name of the factory, at first impressed, and later painted in green or red. In the last decades of the factory's existence the double-headed eagle was added to the design, and this elaborate mark continued after the Gardner firm had been absorbed by Kuznetsov (Fig. 44).

One of the most important factories, stimulated by the protective tariff of 1806 was started in that year in the village of Gorbunov near Moscow, by a certain Karl Milli. It was taken over in 1811 by a Moscow merchant, A. Popov, who gave his name to the factory, which, together with his son, Dmitry, he personally built up and directed until he died in the 1850s. A decade later it was sold by the Popov family, and passed rapidly from one new owner to another. In the 1870s it belonged to an Armenian, and finally to a Russian merchant who liquidated the whole enterprise.

FIG. 44. Gardner Factory marks, *c.* 1765–1870

Large-scale ceremonial bread and salt dishes with brilliant floral borders, were another speciality of Popov. The mark of this factory during the whole period of its existence consisted of an impressed or underglaze blue monogram, showing the initials of the founder (Fig. 45).

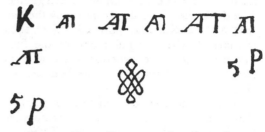

FIG. 45. Popov Factory marks, 1811–1872

The Kornilov factory, started in 1835 by two brothers of a merchant family in Petersburg, engaged skilled artists and craftsmen from the Imperial, Gardner, and Popov factories. It quickly acquired a reputation for artistic excellence, and as early as 1839 won a gold medal at the Moscow ceramic exhibition. The owners spared no expense and trouble to bring their products to perfection, and for this

FIG. 46. Kornilov Factory marks, *c.* 1830

This factory made most money out of porcelain services designed for country inns. But it also specialized in a small output of extremely fine artistic pieces (Plate 374B). The Popov porcelain highly valued by collectors consists of figures of Russian types, dancing peasants, and elaborate dishes featuring flowers or fruit in high relief, which in the quality of their modelling and painted designs are equal to the best of the Gardner and Imperial factories. There is a remarkable figure of a negro in the Sèvres museum, illustrating Bernardin de St Pierre's novel, *Paul et Virginie.*

purpose commissioned original drawings from leading artists of the day. The gorgeous colouring, rich gilding, and decorative finesse of

Kornilov products soon became well known, and they were sought after by collectors. But they remained much more expensive than the corresponding Gardner porcelain.

In the last decades of the nineteenth century this factory started mass production of cheap porcelain wares for export. Connoisseurs can detect the difference at a glance. The distinction is made still easier by the fact that all the Kornilov porcelain after 1861 is marked with the full name of the firm in underglaze blue, whereas prior to that date similar marks had always been in red (Fig. 46).

In 1817 there were about forty-five porcelain factories in Russia, many of them very small. In the 1870s the number had risen to seventy, and it fell to fifty towards the end of the century. As time went on the larger factories swallowed up the small ones, or forced them out of business. By the beginning of the twentieth century, the giant M. Kuznetsov combine had eliminated so many competitors that it was responsible for about two-thirds of the total quantity of pottery and porcelain produced throughout the Russian Empire.

Only the Imperial Factory, which remained outside commercial competition, escaped from the degeneration of a period in which cheapness and transient popular novelty were rapidly conquering pure artistic quality. Working solely for the court, it maintained a surprisingly high level of craftsmanship and decorative brilliance up to the very end of the nineteenth century, and even during the uninspiring reign of Nicolas II.

Spanish

BUEN RETIRO PORCELAIN

There is so little Buen Retiro porcelain outside Spain that the proper place to study it is in that country. This fact is remarked by Arthur Lane in his fine monograph on Italian Porcelain, which includes a section on Buen Retiro, as an extension of the Capodimonte factory.

When Charles III, Bourbon King of Naples, inherited the crown of Spain in 1759 he transported to Madrid artists, workmen, and materials from Capodimonte, where he had started a factory in 1743.

The new establishment was erected in the grounds of the royal palace of Buen Retiro, and by May 1760 work began there under the administrative direction of Giovanni Bonicelli who in 1781, was succeeded by his son Domingo.

The actual making of porcelain was at first in the hands of the chief arcanist Gaetano Schepers and the artistic director Giuseppe Gricci. Schepers died some time after 1764 and Gricci in 1770, after which the manage-ment passed successively into the hands of their sons.

Production was much hampered by difficulties arising from the composition of the paste, a situation further complicated by a feud between the Gricci and Schepers families. These factors, together with enormous costs, brought about a steady decline. Disastrous experiments between 1798 and 1802 caused the abandonment of soft-paste manufacture, and after 1805 the wares were hard paste and of utilitarian character. Occupation by French troops in 1808 finally brought about the closing of the factory, and an attempted revival at La Moncloa between 1817 and 1849 was of no artistic importance.

The finest period was during the lifetime of the founder, who died in 1788. Rococo and chinoiserie styles were quickly superseded by the early neo-classical (Louis Seize) influence of Sèvres, though the interpretation is unmistakably Spanish.

The earlier paste, which has a beautifully

soft brilliance, is often slightly yellow in tone; latterly it became of a hybrid variety owing to difficulties experienced with the composition and materials.

Gricci's first great undertaking was the Porcelain Room in the Palace of Aranjuez (1763–65). Here, the magnificent mirror-frames, brackets, vases, groups of putti, and Chinese figures among elaborate scroll work, remain to the present day. A great chandelier in the form of a Chinaman and a monkey holding a palm tree is now in the Royal Palace on the outskirts of Madrid.

Many of the figures, which formed a great part of the factory's output, were modelled by Gricci himself. Naked infants, often representing the continents and seasons, were grouped on scrolled rococo bases; others are of rustic subjects. Table-ware, snuff-boxes, holy water stoups, and a variety of trinkets were also made.

The colouring is soft and the painting particularly characterized by stippling. Where gilding is used it has a warm and distinctly mellow tone. The eighteenth-century mark was the Bourbon fleur-de-lis, either painted or incised, as at Capodimonte. From 1804 to 1808, it was an MD surmounted by a crown.

SPANISH POTTERY

The history of Spanish pottery goes back to medieval times, when it was dominated by Islamic traditions, imposed by Arab and Moorish invaders, who brought with them the art of making tin-glazed and lustred earthenware. The best known and most important type dates, however, from the period of re-conquest, when a synthesis of Near Eastern and European styles is seen in the so-called Hispano-Morsque wares.

From the beginning of the fifteenth century onwards Valencia, and particularly the suburbs of Paterna and Manisses, were the chief centres of the industry. Here, under Christian rule, Moorish potters produced wares decorated in a hybrid style, in blue and white, and blue enriched with gold-lustre.

Arabesques and inscriptions in Arabic gradually merged with Christian emblems and epigraphs in gothic lettering; together with bold heraldic devices and foliate patterns of great power and distinction. Human figures were more rarely depicted.

Albarelli and great dishes, superbly painted with the armorial bearings of famous French and Italian families, such as those of René of Anjou and Lorenzo de' Medici, indicate the high esteem in which these wares were held; indeed, it was asserted in a contemporary writing that "Manisses work was gilded and painted in masterly fashion, with which the whole world is in love—pope, cardinals and princes ordering it by special favour, and marvelling that things of such excellence and nobility could be made from clay". Gadrooned and relief-decorated pieces appeared towards the end of the fifteenth century, while arabesques and diapered patterns of Persian origin were still in use.

The diminishing number of coats-of-arms appearing in the sixteenth century prove the decline in aristocratic patronage, and, though the manufacture has continued, there has been no revival of its previous excellence.

ALCORA

An important factory making faïence at Alcora (Valencia) was founded in 1726–7 by the Count of Aranda, who secured the services of Edouard Roux and Joseph Olerys, formerly of Moustiers.

On the death of the founder the factory was carried on by his son, and continued to make fine-quality faïence, together with some porcelain, until the latter half of the eighteenth century; after which, nothing of any merit was produced.

During the period of Olerys' employment (1727–37), the style was very similar to that of Moustiers (*see under* French Faïence).

Some fine pictorial painting on large panels and oval plaques with moulded frames was done by Miguel Soliva. After Olerys' departure, elaborate rococo forms were adopted, and a recipe for lustre was obtained from nearby Manisses in 1749.

A number of excellent busts was made at Alcora, and a magnificent portrait of the Count of Aranda is in the collection of the Hispanic Society of America, New York.

Swiss Porcelain

Switzerland has not produced much porcelain, and since it is bordered by Germany and France it is not surprising that Zürich porcelain is of the German type and Nyon porcelain of the French type.

ZÜRICH

At Schooren near Zürich, a company, including the poet Salomon Gessner, started to produce soft paste in 1763, and two years later hard paste, with kaolin brought from Lorraine. Gessner occasionally supplied his own designs for the decoration of plates, which bring to mind the vignettes in his *Idyllen*, published in Switzerland about this time. Whether he actually painted some himself is uncertain. The factory's best period lasted up to 1790; its output included original figures of great charm, some influenced by artists from Lorraine, others closer to Ludwigsburg, from whence the modeller J. V. Sonnenschein had come (Plate 362B).

From 1766 to 1790 the factory was under the technical direction of Adam Spengler, whose son John was a modeller at the Derby factory (1790–95).

NYON

Hard-paste porcelain was also made at Nyon, near Geneva, from about 1780, by Ferdinand Müller of Frankenthal and Jaques Dortu, who had been at Berlin and Marieberg. Dortu, whose technical knowledge provided a good-quality white paste, eventually became sole director, 1809–13. In the latter period English-style earthenware was made.

A variety of pieces were competently painted in the current Paris mode, with scattered sprigs of flowers, butterflies, beribboned trophies, garlands, and diapers. The coloured grounds of Sèvres and commoner Meissen patterns were also imitated. Figures are very rare.

The mark of a fish in underglaze blue has been used by Hamann of Dresden (1866), also as a rebus in the perch (fish) of the Paris decorator Perche (about 1825).

Glossary

Absolon. *See* Independent decorators.

Adam and Eve. A favoured subject on delftware "chargers" (first dated example 1635, but continued well into the eighteenth century) and slipware, also for stoneware "Pew" groups.

Adam. A number of potters of this name worked in Staffordshire in the late eighteenth and early nineteenth centuries.

"AF" mark. *See* Bow.

Agate. Wares made in imitation of this stone. They were made either of differently coloured clays, mixed, and with the colours going right through the body of the piece, or the effect was achieved by means of coloured clays on the surface of plain pottery.

Albany slip. The diluted, creamy state of a fine clay found on the Hudson river-bank near Albany, New York. Of rich dark-brown colour, sometimes used as a glaze, or after *c.* 1800 for coating the interior of salt-glazed stoneware vessels. In 1843, the New York Geological Survey said it was "known and shipped all over the country".

Albarello. A cylindrical jar made to contain ointments or dry medicaments. The neck is grooved for tying on a parchment cover. Those with a spout were for liquids.

Allen, Robert (1744–1835). An artist at the Lowestoft, Suffolk, porcelain factory from 1757, and manager there from about 1780. On the closing of the works in 1802 Allen set up as an enameller of white porcelain on his own account. A Chinese teapot and cover in the Schreiber Collection at the Victoria and Albert Museum, London, has the body painted with a Crucifixion scene, the cover bears some flowers, and the base is signed: *Allen, Lowestoft.* The religious scene was painted in China, and the flowers probably in Lowestoft by Allen, who added his name to the whole.

"A" mark. *See* Bow.

Anchor mark. *See* Chelsea, Bow, Derby, Davenport.

An hua ("secret") decoration. Faint engraving or painting in white slip, visible only against the light; found especially on early Ming and eighteenth-century white porcelain.

Arcanist. Workman knowing the secret of pottery-making in general, and of porcelain-making in particular.

Arcanum. Chemical composition and technique of porcelain-making.

Arrow mark. *See* Worcester and Pinxton.

Art pottery. Also called Studio Ware. Much ornamental work in what Dr Barber (writing in 1893) considered "elegant decorative forms" appeared after the Centennial, 1876. Rookwood faïence (*q.v.*) was especially admired, also the wares of Chelsea Keramic Art Works (1872–89 at Chelsea, Massachusetts, U.S.A.) developed by Hugh C. Robertson from 1891 as the Chelsea Pottery, from 1895 as Dedham Pottery. Art Tiles (*see* Barber, pp. 343–84) flourished in the 1880s, notably John G. Low's from 1789 at Chelsea, Massachusetts.

Astbury. A family of Staffordshire potters. To John A. (1686–1743) were attributed (questionably) the first use of white clay washes and of calcined flint in earthenware manufacture. The name "A." is applied to red earthenware with applied white reliefs, and to small figures in white clay enlivened with touches of red clay and dabs of colour in the glaze. Both were probably also made by other potters.

Wares marked "Astbury" impressed were made by a later A. (after *c.* 1760).

"Astbury" type. Classification of Staffordshire pottery in which red and white clays are combined under a transparent lead glaze. Similar wares covered by a glaze splashed with metallic oxides are generally styled "Astbury-Whieldon".

"B" mark. *See* Bow, Bristol (hard-paste porcelain), Worcester (Dr Wall and Flight & Barr) and Pinxton.

Ballot box. A common name for a salt kit.

Bamboo-ware. A variety of stoneware, of a darker tint of brown than the cane-ware, introduced by Josiah Wedgwood in 1770.

Barm pot. Pot for storing barm or yeast (*see also* salt kit).

Basaltes. The name given by Josiah Wedgwood to his fine-quality black stoneware introduced in 1766.

Batavia. A trading station of the Dutch East India Company in Java (*see* Batavian ware).

Batavian ware. Porcelains with lustrous brown-glazed ground and panels of *famille rose* decoration; named after the Dutch trading station in Java through which they reached Europe in the first half of the eighteenth century.

"Battle for the Breeches." Theme of popular imagery concerning marriage occurring on seventeenth-century slipware and as a subject for nineteenth-century spill vases. Possibly made by Obadiah Sherratt.

Baxter, Thomas (1782–1821). Painter, worked independently (*see* Independent decorators), and at Worcester (1814–16 and 1819–21) and Swansea (1816–19): painted figure-subjects, landscapes, shells, flowers, etc.

Bear jug. Model in the form of a bear hugging a dog, illustrating the sport of bear-baiting. The detachable head serves as a cup. Made in Staffordshire and Nottingham, eighteenth century.

Bellarmine. Big-bellied stoneware bottle with a bearded mask in relief, named after Cardinal Bellarmine (1542–1621). Frequently cited in contemporary literature and used in magic and witchcraft. Also called "Greybeards".

Belleek. A light, fragile feldspathic porcelain cast in moulds, with lustrous pearly glaze. Invented c. 1860 by William Goss of Stoke, improved by William Bromley at the Irish factory of David McBirney & Co. (founded 1857 at Belleek, Co. Fermanagh), which by 1865 won a medal at the Dublin Exhibition. Produced at many American factories 1882–1900 and called *Lotus Ware* by Knowles of East Liverpool (Plates 314B, C).

Bellringers' jugs. Jugs for serving ale to bellringers, kept in the church tower, as at Macclesfield, or in the home of a ringer.

Belper (Derbyshire). *See* Bourne.

Bennington. A name widely, and wrongly, applied to brown Rockingham wares in general. The Vermont town had two establishments, a lesser stoneware works of the Norton family (1793–1894) and the enterprising factor of Christopher W. Fenton, 1845–58 (called the U.S. Pottery Co., from 1853). Fenton produced a diversity of wares, from common yellow and Flint Enamel

FIG. 47

(q.v.) to porcelains and Parian (Plates 317B, C and 316A, B, C).

Bérain, Jean (1637–1711). French engraver and draughtsman. Dessinateur to Louis XIV. Creator of a style of ornament used on French faïence and porcelain. Also his son, Jean II (1674–1728).

"BFB" mark, impressed. *See* Worcester.

"Bianco-sopra-bianco." An opaque-white pigment used for decorating a tin-glaze of slightly contrasted colour.

Billingsley, William (1758–1828). Porcelain-painter and maker. B. originated a style of flower-painting with the high-lights wiped out with the brush. Painted at Derby 1775–96, leaving to join Pinxton (q.v.) as technician; independent decorator at Mansfield c. 1800, painting landscapes; at Worcester 1808–13. In 1813 he started the Nantgarw factory, and in 1819 went to Coalport.

Bird call. Pottery whistle in the form of a bird. Sometimes built into old chimneys as a charm against evil spirits.

Bird fountain. Wall bracket with a projecting socket for water, made in blue-printed, lustred, or enamelled earthenware, eighteenth and nineteenth centuries.

Biscuit. Unglazed porcelain or, more rarely, pottery, as a medium for statuettes and reliefs, used since the middle of the eighteenth century under the influence of the classical revival. The material more nearly resembles marble than porcelain. Falconet created some of the earliest Sèvres models, Melchior some of the later portraits, at Höchst, Frankenthal, and Nymphenburg. (*See* Derby, Bristol.)

Bisque. Unglazed or "biscuit" porcelain (Plate 317A).

Black. *See* Brown and Black glazes.

"Black basaltes"
"Black Egyptian". An unglazed line-grained black stoneware perfected by Wedgwood c. 1769 and much imitated elsewhere. Decorated with relief, gilding, or enamelling.

Black-printing. "A term for applying impressions to glazed vessels, whether the colour be black, red, or gold" (William Evans, 1846).

Blake, William. The artist, poet, and visionary, was employed to draw and engrave a catalogue of Wedgwood cream-coloured wares in the year, 1815 and 1816. The engravings run to eighteen in number and illustrate 185 pieces of domestic china. Eight of the actual copper-plates are still in existence, but have been altered since they left Blake's hand. Some correspondence between the artist and Josiah Wedgwood is printed by Geoffrey Keynes in *Blake Studies* (1949). Sixteen of the engravings are reproduced in W. Mankowitz's *Wedgwood*, Keynes gives two, one of which is not in the latter volume.

Blanc-de-Chine. The porcelain known as

blanc-de-Chine was made at Tê-Hua in the Province of Fukien. This china, in which the white varies in colour from a deep ivory to the starkest bluish white, was first manufactured some time during the Ming dynasty (1368–1644). The factory specialized in figures of the numerous deities and sages of the Buddhist faith, and there must be few persons interested in Oriental china who have not seen one of the typical graceful statuettes of Kuan-yin (Goddess of Mercy) that were made in great quantities.

From about 1650 this factory began to make pieces that show European influence. A soldier, perhaps Dutch, dates from this time; another well-known figure of a man wearing a tricorn hat is probably rather later. It has been pointed out that the inhabitants of Fukien Province are extremely superstitious, and it has been suggested that this may explain why there exist *blanc-de-Chine* groups and figures of Europeans placed in typically Chinese settings and attitudes. For example, there is a group in which a European is seen standing on the head of a dragon, which symbolizes the attainment of the highest literary honours. The small mugs of stoneware form are thought generally to be of Western origin, and to have been copied from a German specimen.

Tê-Hua porcelain was occasionally painted in China, but when coloured is found to have been decorated more often in Holland or Germany during the eighteenth century than in its country of origin. The ware was exported principally from the port of Amoy.

"Blue-and-white" porcelain. Decoration with painting in cobalt blue under the glaze has continued ever since its introduction. It is both attractive and economical, requiring one firing only. Some fourteenth-century wares depict plants and animals within floral scroll borders. The classic fifteenth-century Ming reigns of Hsüan Tê and Ch'êng Hua produced perhaps the finest of all "blue-and-white", with perfect forms, superb glaze, rich colour, and lively yet restrained painting of dragons and floral scrolls. A deep violet-blue was used in the Chia Ching period, and sixteenth-century painting is freely executed in "outline and wash" technique. As well as the traditional subjects, ladies on garden terraces,

playing boys, and animals in landscapes are now depicted. Much Ming porcelain now in European collections comes from the Near East or South-East Asia, whither it was exported in many styles and qualities. From about 1600 the East India Companies imported into Europe thin porcelain plates and bowls with indented edges, painted with emblems and figures in wide panelled borders. The "Transitional" period wares of the mid-seventeenth century, e.g. cylindrical vases and bottles with tulip designs, bold landscapes and figure subjects, are often finely painted. The paste of K'ang Hsi period wares is fine and white, and for the best pieces a brilliant sapphire blue was used, applied in overlapping flat strokes, as on the famous "prunus jars", with sprays of plum-blossom reserved in white. Decorative vases and "useful" wares are extremely various in shape and decoration. Landscapes and scenes from literature, with elegant ladies or huntsmen, are common, and a great variety of panelled, brocaded, and bordered designs with flowers (aster and tiger-lily patterns, lotus, chrysanthemum, etc.), as well as the traditional animals and emblems. Ming reign-marks were often used; that of K'ang Hsi rarely. The Yung Chêng and Ch'ien Lung periods produced little besides revivals of early Ming styles, and export wares of declining quality. Later eighteenth-century services made to European order ("Nankin china") are rather coarse, with thick glazes, and crowded designs of the "willow-pattern" type.

"Blue-dash chargers." *See* p. 898, English pottery.

Blue or lavender glazes. Especially fine porcelains with the high-temperature cobalt-blue glaze were made during the Ming reigns of Hsüan Tê and Chia Ching; it was also used in coarser wares decorated with raised white slip designs, and in the "three-colour" class. During the Ch'ing dynasty the colour was varied by dilution or addition of manganese purple to produce a variety of tones. K'ang Hsi deep-blue glazes are generally overpainted with gilt designs, or appear beside underglaze blue or red painting; they include the "powdered" blue (*q.v.*). Several shades of lavender and pale blue, such as the *clair-de-*

lune, were at their best under Yung Chêng and Ch'ien Lung; when fine imitations of the crackled Sung Kuan and Ko wares were also made.

"Bocage." A background of flowers and leaves, usually on figures and groups intended for a frontal view only.

"Boccaro" ware. A misnomer for Yi-hsing stoneware.

Body. The composite materials of which potter's clay is made – the ware itself, usually pottery or stoneware; for porcelains the word *paste* is preferred (as hard-paste, soft-paste).

Bone-ash
Bone china. The white ashes of bones were used in Bow porcelain from 1748, and subsequently in the modified hard-paste porcelain which from *c.* 1800 became the standard English body.

Boulton, Matthew (1728–1809). In partnership with John Fothergill (to 1781), and with John Watt, was a manufacturer of metalwork at Soho, Birmingham. He mounted Wedgwood cameos, etc., in cut-steel and in gilt-bronze. Writing to Bentley in 1768 Wedgwood said: "We have an order from Mr Boulton for some bodys of vases for mounting, which I must either comply with or affront him, and set him a-trying to get them elsewhere . . ." One of a pair of jasper-ware vases, with gilt metal mounting, is shown in Plate 351C.

Bourne & Co. Stoneware-potters at Belper (from *c.* 1800), Codnor Park (from 1833), and Denby (from 1812) in Derbyshire. Mark: "Bourne".

Bow (soft-paste porcelain). The B. factory, possibly active in 1744 (when E. Heylyn and Thomas Frye took out a patent), was certainly working before 1750. In 1748 Frye took out a second patent, the ingredients including bone-ash; the resultant phosphoric acid in the paste is diagnostic. Frye remained manager until 1759. After 1763 the history of the factory is uncertain, but it is stated to have closed in 1775 or 1776, the moulds being removed to Derby.

B. specialized in useful wares, but many figures were also made. The porcelain is characterized by a creamy colour, a tendency to stain brown, and an occasional black speck-

ing. The early (*c.* 1750) white wares were often decorated by applied moulded sprigs.

The colours on the earlier B. porcelain (to *c.* 1765) include a characteristic rose-purple and opaque light-blue. Imitation *Kakiemon* and *famille rose* painting was much practised; since much B. porcelain, however, was outside-decorated (*see* Independent decorators), the painting is a fallible guide. Much porcelain painted in underglaze blue of a vivid, intense tone was made. Transfer-printing, mainly in russet and purplish-black, was employed *c.* 1756 (*see* Hancock).

B. figures may often be distinguished by the modelling of the head, rather small and doll-like, with only slightly modelled chin and cheeks, and a *retroussé* nose. They are rather heavy, and often have a square hole cut behind for an ormolu embellishment. The characteristic rococo vase, from *c.* 1755, has four feet and in front a pendant scroll, all picked out in rose-purple (Plate 353B).

Towards the end a palette including a pink and a watery green was adopted; the opaque blue enamel was replaced by a darker translucent colour.

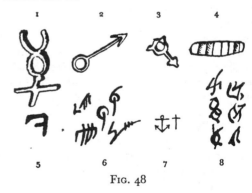

FIG. 48

MARKS: 1–3 above *c.* 1750; CT, R, W, AF & D (incised), B, T°, T, and 4 above (impressed) are probably repairers' marks of *c.* 1750–60; B, G, "13", various simulated Chinese characters (e.g. 6 above), and 5 above, in blue, occur on blue-and-white porcelain *c.* 1755–65; various numerals and initials in enamel were used on useful wares; I, A, a crescent, two dots, and 7 above, in blue, and various forms of 8 above in brownish-red occur on late figures, etc., *c.* 1760–75.

Brampton (Derbyshire). Brown stoneware

pottery, second half of eighteenth and nineteenth century.

MARKS: "Oldfield & Co.", "S. & H. Briddon".

"Brinjal bowls." K'ang Hsi porcelain bowls with incised flower-sprays coloured yellow and green on an aubergine (Anglo-Indian: *brinjal*) purple ground, in glazes applied "on the biscuit".

Brislington. Delftware pottery from *c.* 1650 to 1750 (*see* Bristol, delftware).

Bristol (delftware). A pottery at Brislington, near B., was founded by Southwark potters *c.* 1650; it in turn colonized a factory in B. (Temple Pottery, 1683–1770, when delftware was abandoned). Others were St Mary Redcliffe's (*c.* 1700–77) and Limekiln Lane (*c.* 1700–54).

Early B. delftware is difficult to distinguish from Lambeth, and the later from that of Liverpool. The B. glaze, however, often had a distinctive lavender-blue tone, and the early red (*c.* 1700) stands out in appreciable relief. The B. *bianco-sopra-bianco* borders usually include a cone motif and curved sprays of leaves. Characteristic B. shapes include a plate with straight sides forming an obtuse angle with the bottom; puzzle-jugs with openwork necks formed by intersecting circles; flower-"bricks" pierced with a square hole at the top and mounted on small bracket feet, and (seventeenth-century) porringers having a circular handle with corrugations radiating from a central hole.

Bristol (hard-paste porcelain). About 1770 the Plymouth factory moved to B. In 1773 the factory and rights were bought by Richard Champion, and in 1781 sold to a combine of Staffordshire potters (*see* New Hall). The Plymouth models were continued, and it is sometimes impossible to distinguish the work of the two factories. Both suffered from technical defects (*see* Plymouth), and B. thrown wares show in addition spiral marks known as "wreathing". Useful wares were, exceptionally, painted or printed in underglaze blue, or printed in overglaze enamel. The more normal enamelling was in perceptible relief; the colours included a characteristic "juicy" red, clear yellow, and bright translucent green. The decoration reflected Sèvres styles. Figures

were much made (Plate 355B) often with a rockwork base. "Biscuit" presentation plaques, with applied flowers framing portraits, coats-of-arms, etc., were a speciality.

MARKS: a cross or B (sometimes both), in greyish-blue enamel; crossed swords imitating Meissen, in underglaze blue or greyish-blue enamel, T° impressed.

Bristol (soft-paste porcelain). In 1749 a factory using soapstone as an ingredient was founded in B. Until recently called "Lowdin's", it is now known to have been started by William Miller and Benjamin Lund. In 1752 it was advertised as transferred to Worcester, and it is usually impossible to distinguish B. from the earliest Worcester porcelain. Certain sauce-boats, however, and figures of a Chinaman, bear the mark BRISTOL(L) in relief, impressed. Underglaze-blue (and occasionally manganese-brown) and enamel painting were practised, usually in styles copying Chinese export porcelain. (*See also* "Scratch cross".)

MARKS: *see* Worcester.

Brown and black glazes. These colours derived from iron are among the high-temperature glazes of Sung stonewares (e.g. Chien ware); and coffee-brown glazes occur on Ming porcelain. The lustrous glazes of the Ch'ing dynasty – the Chinese *tz'ǔ chin* ("brown gold") – range from pale *café-au-lait* to deep golden brown. "Nankin yellow" is the pale golden-brown added to some blue-and-white; the darker "dead leaf brown" framing *famille rose* painted panels is Batavian ware; and *café-au-lait* was sometimes overpainted in *famille verte* enamels. All appear also as monochromes. The superb glossy K'ang Hsi "mirror black" was generally enamelled with gilt designs. Produced by an admixture of manganese with iron, it should not be confused with the *famille noire* black (*q.v.*). During the Yung Chêng and Ch'ien Lung periods mottled or speckled brown glazes such as the "iron rust" and "tea dust" were favoured, and another class faithfully imitate the character and patina of archaic bronze and silver vessels. Crackled wares with transparent brownish glaze, often with stamped designs in unglazed relief, are principally nineteenth century.

Bull-baiting. Pottery groups showing a bull goring or tossing a dog, often upon table bases supported by six legs, popular *c.* 1830–

FIG. 49

35. Said to have been made by Obadiah Sherratt (Fig. 49).

Bussa. Large earthenware pot commonly kept in old Cornish cottages for salting down pilchards.

Butter-pot. Cylindrical earthenware vessel made to hold fourteen pounds of butter, made at Burslem in the seventeenth century for use at Uttoxeter market. An Act of 1661 regulated abuses in the manner of making and packing the pots.

"Cadogan" tea or hot-water pot. A copy of the Chinese peach-shaped wine-jug, filled through an orifice in the base and constructed on the principle of a non-spillable inkwell. (*See* Rockingham.)

Café-au-lait. *See* Brown glazes.

Calligraphy. Chinese copying of European handwriting was purely mechanical and, as may be expected, many mistakes occurred in the transcription of verses, mottoes, and inscriptions sent from the West. Letters were omitted, or formed into unpronounceable diagraphs, and the letter *N* was rendered frequently as ᴙ. A typical mistake of another type was the careful copying of a coat-of-arms on each piece of a service, with the addition of the words *These are the Arms of myself and my wife*, which had been written on the pattern sent from England.

Cane-coloured ware. Unglazed fine-grained buff stoneware, sometimes decorated with blue, etc., enamels, made by Wedgwood, Turner, Elijah Mayer, etc., late eighteenth century.

Canton potteries. Chün-type wares reputedly made here from Sung times remain unidentified, but may include the soft-glazed, sandy-bodied Ma Chün. Certain wares with opaque, crackled grey, purple, and blue glazes are possibly as old as Ming. Stonewares with grey or brown bodies and various glazes, ranging from opaque grey or blue to the streaked flambés of purple, red, and green, continue till the present day. Very large jars, vases, etc., were made for outdoor use, sometimes with elaborate applied work, and numerous small animal figures serve as incense burners, water-pots, etc. Enamelling workshops at Canton decorated porcelain in the *famille rose* style for export, as well as the "Canton enamels" painted on copper.

Canton. The principal port on the coast of China for trade with Europe in the eighteenth and nineteenth centuries (*see* East India Company). Porcelain was brought to Canton by river from Ching-Tê-Chên. From the middle years of the eighteenth century increasing quantities of the porcelain were sent unpainted, and decoration was applied to order by artists in enamelling shops at the port. *Canton* is the familiar name for a nineteenth-century Chinese porcelain exported to Europe. It bears a decoration of butterflies, flowers, etc., on a celadon-green ground.

Capacity mug. Cylindrical measure made in stoneware, earthenware, mocha ware, etc., from the seventeenth century. The presence of a Royal Cypher or an Excise Stamp provides a clue as to date.

Carpet balls. Used in the Victorian game of carpet bowls, made in brown stoneware or white earthenware coloured with starry, ringed, or flowery patterns. A set comprised six patterned and one white or self-coloured balls. Made in Scotland and Staffordshire. The Parr family of Burslem specialized in them.

Castleford (Yorkshire). Pottery founded by David Dunderdale *c.* 1790, making creamware, black basaltes, and other characteristic Leeds and Staffordshire wares. Best known for unglazed relief-decorated white stoneware, usually called "Castleford" but certainly also made elsewhere. Wares marked "D.D. & Co., Castleford" are authentic productions: these do not include pieces with enamelled landscapes within blue-outlined panels.

Castle Hedingham. Pseudo-medieval and Tudor pottery was made here by Edward Bingham (b. 1829). Sometimes mistaken for authentic, fifteenth-, sixteenth-, and seventeenth-century wares.

Cats. Figures made in striped salt-glazed stoneware ("agate" ware) and earthenware in the mid-eighteenth century (Staffordshire); also in delftware.

Caughley (soft-paste porcelain). This Shropshire factory did not make porcelain until acquired by Thomas Turner (previously at Worcester) in 1772. In 1799 it was amalgamated with Coalport. The wares were mainly blue-and-white, often printed in the Worcester manner (towards the end of the century often combined with gilding), but elaborate enamel-painting, mostly of tightly packed flowers, was also done. C. porcelain resembles Worcester, but is brownish by transmitted light. Characteristic are two shades of blue, one markedly mauvish, the other greyish; a foot-rim of approximately rectangular section; an incised circle beneath the foot. C. porcelain was frequently outside-decorated.

MARKS: s, c, a crescent, or 1–4 below, in blue; SALOPIAN, impressed.

FIG. 50

"Cauliflower ware." Green- and yellow-glazed earthenware, often in the form of cauliflowers, pineapples, etc., made by the Whieldon–Wedgwood partnership about 1750–70.

"CD" mark. *See* Coalport.

Celadon wares. Wares with felspathic glaze of characteristic pale-greyish or bluish green tone derived from iron; the name was apparently taken from the character Céladon in Honore D'Urfé's early seventeenth-century

pastoral romance *L'Astrée*, and not from *Saladin*, as sometimes supposed. Typical are the early Yüeh ware, and the much-exported Lung-chüan celadons of the Sung and Ming dynasties. Ch'ing dynasty celadons generally differ from these in their white porcelain body, even glaze, and careful finish. But some Sung wares were skilfully copied, and the bluish and lavender-toned Kuan and Ko glazes, their crackle, and even their dark body, were reproduced. In eighteenth-century France the later celadons were sometimes mounted in ormolu.

Chaffers, William. Editor of the famous works *Marks and Monograms on Pottery and Porcelain*, first published in 1863. He was responsible for the error by which a great quantity of Chinese porcelain was ascribed to the English Lowestoft factory. At this distance of time it seems strange that such a mistake ever should have occurred, and even stranger that some of the greatest ceramic experts of the period should have joined the argument, and produced complicated theories that were no less remote from the truth.

Champion, Richard. *See* Bristol.

Chelsea (soft-paste porcelain), 1745–84. The finest and most significant English eighteenth-century porcelain. The earliest wares ("triangle" period: *see* Marks) were of a milk-white glassy porcelain showing "moons". They were often left white, and decorated only with moulding, frequently closely imitating silverware. Small flower-sprays to conceal blemishes in the paste, and occasionally rather stiff "botanical" flowers drawn in Meissen style were sometimes added in enamel.

In the succeeding "raised anchor" phase (*see* Marks) the use of painted decoration was greatly extended, the Japanese *Kakiemon* manner being much copied. Meissen porcelain inspired other decorative styles; these include a more developed flower-painting and harbour scenes (to which are related Æsop's Fables subjects). A warm brown is characteristic. The extremely rare transfer-prints were perhaps done at the Battersea enamel factory. Figures are rare – mainly dwarf-like ("Callot") or Italian Comedy types, characterized by bright-red cheeks. Bird-figures were suggested by Meissen. From 1749 at latest C.

was managed by Nicholas Sprimont (1716–71), a silversmith from Liége, and the continuity of the Chelsea style is unbroken in the succeeding "red anchor" period.

In this period the repertory and skill of the C. painters were increased to include figures and landscapes in purple monochrome; "botanical" flowers (Plate 353A) copied from illustrated herbals or even from nature; polychrome figural compositions derived through Meissen from the French Masters. Underglaze blue was used, but rarely. Characteristic of the useful wares were three small projecting "spur-marks" within a ground-down foot-rim. Tureens and dishes simulating birds, animals, vegetables, etc., were much favoured. Most notable, however, were the very numerous figures. Their subjects may be roughly divided into mythological and "abstract" (e.g. Sciences, Seasons); trades (Plate 354A), hunting and pastoral life; Italian Comedy characters and "exotics" (e.g. Turks, Chinese). They are superbly modelled and sparingly coloured, so as to reveal the beautiful porcelain material. A plain mound-base is normal. Mainly of this period also were the "Chelsea toys" – tiny étuis, scent-bottles, patch-boxes, etc., exquisitely modelled and painted, and showing a rich fancy in the invention of (mostly amorous) conceits.

In 1758 bone-ash was introduced in the C. body. The frequently "crazed" glaze tends to run into greenish glassy pools; the grinding of foot-rims persisted. This "gold anchor" period is marked by ever-increasing sumptuousness. Coloured grounds (royal or "Mazarin" blue, pea-green, turquoise, and claret) were copied from Sèvres, and gilding was lavishly used. Elaborate rococo scrollwork was used on figures and vases, etc. (Plate 356A). The painters' repertory was enlarged to include elaborate mythological scenes after Boucher or Rubens, or Pillement chinoiseries; "exotic" birds in polychrome enamels on white or in gilding on a ground were inspired by Sèvres; groups of fruit became favourite subjects. The Kakiemon subjects were discarded, but Japanese patterns resembling elaborate textile-designs ("brocaded Imari") continued in favour. In figure-modelling a broader style and a larger scale were introduced. Elaborate "bocages"

were made and the figures were richly and elaborately painted and gilt.

In 1769 the factory and its contents were sold, in 1770 passing into the possession of Wm. Duesbury and John Heath, of Derby.

MARKS: 1 below, incised (c. 1745–50); 2, in relief (c. 1749–53); 3, in red (c. 1753–60), in gold (c. 1758–69); "R", impressed, a repairer's mark (c. 1760–5).

FIG. 51

1 2 3

Ch'êng Hua period (1465–87). The rarest porcelains of this classic reign employ coloured enamels over sparing underglaze blue outlines ("tou ts'ai" enamels); and this style was much imitated from the seventeenth century. The blue-and-white "palace bowls" were more slightly potted and decorated than previously. The reign-mark is much used on later wares.

Chesterfield (Derbyshire). Brown stoneware pottery, second half of eighteenth and nineteenth centuries.

Chia Ch'ing period (1522–66). Ming reign noted for painted blue-and-white of rich violet tone, and the development of brilliantly coloured enamel painting, chiefly in red, green, yellow, and turquoise. Coloured glazes, too, were used, sometimes in combination (e.g. yellow and green), covering incised designs "on the biscuit". Heavily potted blue-and-white jars and dishes were much exported to the Near East. The reign-mark was used in K'ang Hsi times.

Chia Ch'ing period (1796–1820). In this period the later Ch'ien Lung styles continued, but with poorer glaze and less lively drawing in enamelled wares. Iron-red enamelling was popular, and heavily-potted wares with thick blue or celadon-green glazes may be mentioned.

Ch'ien Lung. During the reign of this emperor, who was on the throne from 1736 to 1795 and who abdicated at the advanced age of eighty-six, was produced much of the porcelain decorated to the order of Europeans. The Emperor Ch'ien Lung was a noted patron of the arts, and encouraged the making of porcelain in his country. He was interested in Western culture, and there is no doubt that he encouraged the making of many pieces of china based on the design of French articles sent as presents to Peking from the King of France, or ordered from Paris by the Jesuits at the command of the Emperor.

Chien ware. This production of Fukien Province during the Sung dynasty consisted principally of small conical tea-bowls. A very granular grey-black stoneware, with thick treacly brown or black glaze, often streaked with fine golden lines ("hare's fur"), or spotted and dappled, and arrested above the foot. These effects result from the varied response of iron to kiln conditions. Known to the Japanese as "*temmoku*" ware. Other brown and black wares from Kiangsi, Honan, or Tz'ŭ Chou, have a lighter body.

Chill. Earthenware oil lamp shaped like a large candlestick with a lipped cup large enough to hold two cups of "train" (pilchard oil), used in Cornwall before candles. Sometimes rendered STONEN CHILL.

China-clay. A white-burning natural clay (kaolin) used with china-stone (petuntze, *q.v.*) to produce true porcelain. It was the *unaker* of the Cherokees, found "on the back of Virginia" and through the Carolinas, into Georgia. Wedgwood imported "the Cherokee earth", and in 1777 wrote to his partner saying that "it is really used in all the Jaspers".

"China" dogs. Mantelpiece ornaments in the form of spaniels, Welsh sheep dogs, French poodles, greyhounds, etc., made in earthenware, and sold extensively in Wales and the West Country. Made by Sampson Smith, James Dudson, William Kent, and many others in Staffordshire and Scotland; rarely marked.

China-stone. Feldspar, decomposed granite (petuntze). Fuses at great heat, combining with china-clay to produce porcelain.

Chinese export porcelain.
Decoration.
1650 The earliest designs on Chinese export porcelain were of a religious character. The blue-and-white pieces, dating from this time, painted with religious scenes

and emblems, are the subject of some argument as to whether they were made for use by Christian converts in China and Japan rather than for export to the West (*see* Plate 328A).

1700 Still with decoration in blue are cups, saucers, etc., painted with European figures, and inscriptions in French. Coloured figures were made (Plate 329B).

1725 At about this time the first pieces painted with English and other coats-of-arms in colours began to be made in quantities. In these early importations the coat-of-arms is usually of a large size with elaborate mantling. (Mantling: the scrollwork, etc., surrounding the actual coat-of-arms.)

Schwarzlot decoration, especially of religious subjects, was also exported.

1750 The coat-of-arms grew smaller and the mantling was simplified.

1770 The coat-of-arms was usually in a simple shield.

1790 The coat-of-arms was in a spade-shaped shield, and the rest of the piece is plainly decorated with the Gold Star, or some similar bordering. The surface of the china is often of the texture of an orange skin. The pattern-plate (Plate 330D) is of this date. In contrast, the complicated Mandarin patterns were also being made.

1825 Butterflies and flowers painted on a celadon-green ground were becoming popular, the so-called Canton style (*see* Blanc-de-Chine).

Marks. Marks are not generally to be found on Chinese porcelain made for export. Two pieces of blue-and-white in the Victoria and Albert Museum are marked; a bottle bears a capital G and beneath a plate is the word "BEVERE". The plate illustrated in Plate 330D bears the name *Syngchong* on the back. There is a plate, also in the same museum, inscribed *Canton in China 24th Jany. 1791* (*see* Syngchong).

China "Imari". Imitations of the Japanese export porcelain, with strong decoration in greyish underglaze blue and enamel colours, especially iron-red, and prominent gilding; made in the first half of the eighteenth century.

"Chinese Lowestoft." A misnomer for Chinese export porcelain.

Ch'ing Dynasty 1644–1912, reign marks.

Shun Chih (1644–61)

K'ang Hsi (1662–1722)

Yung Chêng (1723–35)

Ch'ien Lung (1736–95)

Chia Ch'ing (1796–1820)

Tao Kuang (1821–50)

Hsien Fêng (1851–61)

T'ung Chih (1862–74)

Kuang Hsü (1875–1908)

Ching-tê-chên. The town situated on the south bank of the River Ch'ang, where pottery and porcelain has been made, almost without cessation, for many centuries. In the early years of the eighteenth century the population ran to a million persons, all of whom were employed, it was stated, in the production of porcelain that was fired in some three thousand kilns. Rare Ching-tê-chên porcelain figures are those with *famille verte* or early *famille rose* enamelling. Fine models of birds and animals with coloured glazes were made during the eighteenth century, and especially those in turquoise have been imitated.

Chinoiserie. Fantastic decoration in gold, silver, or colours, depicting an exotic world with Chinese figures, surrounded by flowers, birds, and animals, attending court ceremonies or pursuing such diversions as are centred around the tea-table. These decorations were in no way indebted to Oriental sources, but to European engravings and travelogues published in Holland and Germany in the second half of the seventeenth century and later. The Augsburg *Hausmaler* of the early eighteenth century developed a distinct style of "Goldchinesen", occasionally in silver, whereas Johann Gregor Herold, at Meissen, preferred to work in bright colours from his own etched designs. A later type of *chinoiserie* adopted in the thirties shows larger figures of Europeans in Chinese guise, taken from French sources, including Pillement, Watteau, and Boucher.

Christening goblets. Footed four-handled loving cups with whistles attached for calling for replenishment, specially associated with Wiltshire, and used for christenings, harvest homes, etc. A favourite inscription is HERE IS THE GEST OF THE BARLY KORNE GLAD HAM I THE CILD IS BORN. Dates from 1603 until 1799 recorded (Fig. 52).

FIG. 52

Chün ware. Sung stoneware, more or less porcellanous, usually burnt buff at the foot, with thick, opalescent glaze ranging from pale lavender to deep blue, sometimes with crimson splashes; from Chün Chou (Honan Province). Frequent shapes are spreading bowls, two-handled jars, and flat dishes. There is also a green variety. Large flower-pots and bulb-bowls often have streaked flambé glazes. "Soft Chün" wares (Ma Chün) have a sandy buff body and soft crackled glaze. The similar stonewares of Canton and Yi-hsing are seldom earlier than the seventeenth century.

"Church Gresley." A factory was apparently working at C.G. (Leics.) 1794–1808, but its porcelain remains virtually unidentified.

Clair-de-lune. *See* Blue glazes.

"Claret" ground. *See* Chelsea, Worcester.

Clay. Special plastic earths of varying grades and colours, from coarse red-burning clay fit for bricks or tile-making to the blue-clays required for stoneware, the fine white kaolin used for porcelains.

Cloisonné ware. Enamelled metal on which the colours of the design are separated by thin metal "*cloisons*". A similar technique employing clay "*cloisons*" was used in the Ming "three-colour" pottery.

"C" mark. *See* Caughley.

Coalport (soft-paste porcelain). John Rose started a pottery at Jackfield about 1780, and shortly afterwards moved it to C. (Shropshire) almost opposite the Caughley factory, acquired in 1799. The Swansea and Nantgarw moulds and stocks were bought up (1819–24), and W. Billingsley's services obtained (1819). The C. porcelain, previously indistinguishable from that of Caughley, became white and translucent like the Welsh porcelain. Billingsley's style of flower-painting was introduced, but much C. porcelain was painted by independent decorators. The "revived rococo" style (Plate 356B) at C. (*c.* 1830) was characterized by lavishly applied flowers, bright green enamel, light-coloured gilding, and flower-decoration with pink-printed outlines washed over in colours. C. copied Chelsea porcelain.

MARKS: the name, or script "CD", in blue.

Cockpit Hill, Derby. Probably made slip-wares, early eighteenth century; from *c.* 1751 to 1779 Staffordshire-type pottery, latterly printed creamware.

Codnor Park. *See* Bourne.

Combed slip. A technique in which a marbled or feathered effect is achieved by brushing together, while wet, two or more different-coloured slips.

Compagnie Dessin (French: Company pattern). The French name for porcelain made to European order in the Far East, and imported by the *Compagnie des Indes*, the French East India Company.

Contour-framing. A method of emphasizing a design by means of a line following the edge, but leaving a white margin.

Cookworthy, William. *See* Plymouth.

Copeland. *See* Spode.

Copper-red glazes and painting. When successful, the fugitive high-temperature copper-red is one of the most splendid glazes in Chinese porcelain. Fourteenth-century painted wares were often imperfect in colour, but both painted and colour-glazed wares succeeded brilliantly in the fifteenth century. In later Ming times the iron-red enamel is more common. A triumphant revival was, however, achieved by the K'ang Hsi potters. Justly famous are the brilliant *sang-de-bœuf*, or "ox-blood", monochromes (Chinese: *lang yao*); other shades are the ruby-red and cherry red, and those of a paler or browner colour, e.g. the "liver-red" and pale "ashes of roses". The apple-red and rare brownish pink "peachbloom" often show brown or green mottlings. Yung Chêng and Ch'ien Lung pieces in general show more regular, even glazing and a neatly finished foot. Flambé effects of red streaked with purple or blue become more common; and are imitated in the flambé Canton stonewares. Nineteenth-century pieces are distinguishable by poorer shape and finish, especially of the foot.

Painting in underglaze red, again popular from the K'ang Hsi period, includes more or less exact copies of the early Ming, especially in combination with underglaze blue.

Costrel. Flat, circular bottle with loop handles for suspension from the shoulder, used by field workers.

Cottages. Used as night-light shields, pastille burners, and mantelpiece ornaments. The latter frequently represent the scenes of sensational crimes, such as the Red Barn at Polstead (Maria Marten) or Stanfield Hall (the Rush murders). Porcelain models were made at Rockingham, but probably far more frequently in Staffordshire, mainly second quarter of the nineteenth century.

Cow milk-jug. Model of cow with mouth and tail forming spout and handle. Filled from an aperture in the back. Based upon a Dutch model introduced into England about 1755. Made in Staffordshire, South Wales, Yorkshire, and Scotland.

Crackled glazes. Crackle was intentionally produced – e.g. in the Sung Kuan wares – by causing body and glaze to contract unevenly after firing. The unintentional "crazing" which particularly affects low-temperature glazes may occur naturally with age.

Cradle. Presentation piece for a newly married couple, having the same significance as the "La Fécondité" dish. Slipware specimens recorded from 1673 until 1839. Used as a hold-all or pipe-tray.

Crazing. Fine network of cracks in the glaze caused by unequal shrinkage of body and glaze.

Cream-coloured earthenware
Creamware. A lead-glazed earthenware with light body made of pale clay and usually containing calcined flint, perfected in Staffordshire about 1740–50. It began to oust other tablewares about 1760. It was made extensively in Staffordshire, Yorkshire, and elsewhere, and enjoyed a world market in the late eighteenth and early nineteenth centuries. It could be decorated with pierced, moulded, enamelled, or printed designs. It was the most mentioned of American imports, their potters constantly claiming to equal the English (Plate 315A).

Crescent mark. *See* Bow, Caughley, Worcester.

Crich (Derbyshire). Brown stoneware portery, second half of eighteenth century and perhaps earlier.

Cross mark. *See* Bristol (hard-paste porcelain), Plymouth, Worcester.

"Crouch" ware. Staffordshire ware said to have been made before the mid-eighteenth century, sometimes wrongly identified with stoneware having white reliefs on a drab ground. Perhaps a variegated stoneware or an earthenware imitating it. "C." is sometimes identified with "Crich".

"CT" mark. *See* Bow.

Cuckoo. Bird call in the form of a large spotted bird perched upon a fence, with four smaller birds. Commonly made in slipware, nineteenth century (Fig. 53).

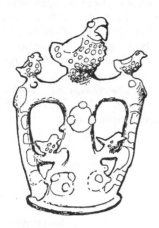

FIG. 53

Dagger mark. *See* Bow.

Daniel, Ralph. A Staffordshire potter credited with the introduction, before 1750, of plaster-of-Paris moulds, and with being the first English enameller of salt-glazed stoneware.

Davenport. Family of potters at Longport (Staffordshire). From 1793 made cream-coloured and other earthenware, and, from the early nineteenth century, porcelain.

MARKS: an anchor or "Davenport", sometimes both.

Delftware. Earthenware coated with a glaze made opaque by the addition of tin ashes, named after Delft in Holland, which became an important centre of manufacture in the seventeenth century.

Denby (Derbyshire). Brown stoneware pottery, late eighteenth and nineteenth centuries (*see* Bourne).

Dendritic. Having tree-like markings.

D'Entrecolles, Père François Xavier. A Jesuit missionary who went out to China in the year 1698. At a time when all the nations of Europe were trying actively to discover the secrets of porcelain manufacture he informed his compatriots of the methods of the Chinese potters. Two long letters, detailing with accuracy all that he had seen and heard, were written by him in 1712 and 1722, and published later in Paris. These documents are still the basis of much of our knowledge of porcelain-making in China. Père D'Entrecolles died in Peking in 1741.

The letters have been translated into English, and are most accessible in *Porcelain: its Nature, Art and Manufacture* by William Burton, London, 1906.

Derby (soft-paste porcelain). Porcelain was made in D. by 1750, and by 1756 there was a prolific factory, established by W. Duesbury and John Heath. Many figures were produced, often avowedly copying Meissen. The early figures are characterized by bases having a "dry edge" (bare of glaze) and a hole underneath formed as if countersunk for a wood-screw; light weight, pale colours, and often a blue-toned glaze. About 1760–70 a richer palette (including a characteristic dirty brownish turquoise) was used, with gilding; the figures almost always have three or four dark patches below the base. The early tablewares were characterized by painting of flowers with stems rendered as trembling hair-lines, and of birds and moths by a distinctive hand (the "Moth-painter").

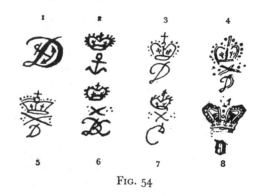

FIG. 54

In the early period blue-and-white and printed decoration are rare. There was no regular factory mark.

In 1770 the Chelsea factory was acquired. Although some work continued there, the Chelsea style was largely abandoned. The figures of this "Chelsea–Derby" period are characterized by rather weak modelling, and a lighter palette of pink, pale green, and a *clear* turquoise. Many were made in "biscuit" (Plate 354c). The tablewares were finely potted and fastidiously painted, mainly with neo-classical designs (Plate 356c), but fine flower-painting was also done. On more elaborate pieces coloured (opaque bright blue and brownish claret are characteristic) and striped grounds were combined with miniature-like painting of landscapes and classical subjects. The porcelain of this period is commonly marked (*see* below).

Duesbury died in 1786 and was succeeded in turn by his son (d. 1796 or 1797) and Michael Kean (until 1811). This (1786–1811) is the "Crown Derby" period proper. The figures continued the old models, and "biscuit" was extensively used. The useful wares are characterized by the use of figure- and landscape-subjects on diapered or pale-coloured grounds. Naturalistic flower-painting was introduced (*see* Billingsley).

In 1811 the factory was bought by Robert Bloor (went insane, 1826), and the period 1811–48 is known by his name. The figures (mainly old models) have opaque paint-like enamels and profuse brassy gilding. On useful wares the elaborate "revived rococo" and Japanese "brocaded Imari" styles largely supersede the neo-classical.

MARKS: script "Derby", incised (*c.* 1750); (at left) 1, in gold or red ("Chelsea–Derby" period); 2, in gold (*c.* 1770–80); 3, in enamel or gold (*c.* 1784); 4, incised on figures, and 5, in enamel or gold (*c.* 1784–1810); 6, in purple (1795–6); 7, usually in red, and 8, printed in red (Bloor period).

Derbyshire. Slipware was made at Bolsover until about 1750; brown stoneware at Brampton and Chesterfield from the second half of the eighteenth century; at Crich somewhat earlier, and by Bourne & Co. at Belper (from *c.* 1800), Denby (from 1812), and Codnor Park (from 1833). (*See* Tickenhall, Cockpit Hill.)

Devonshire. Rustic lead-glazed earthenware was made (mainly at Barnstaple, Bideford and Fremington) from the seventeenth century onwards. The characteristic ware was of red clay with designs incised through a white slip, under a yellow green glaze.

"D" mark. *See* Bow, Derby.

DK mark. *See* Derby.

"Doctor Syntax." Fine underglaze blue transfer-prints representing the adventures of Doctor Syntax, used as tableware decorations by James and Ralph Clews, Cobridge, *c.* 1821. Pottery figures were also popular. *The Tours of Dr Syntax in Search of the Picturesque* by Dr Clombe, with illustrations by Thomas Rowlandson, published 1815–21, were a satire upon the writings of the Rev. William Gilpin.

Don Pottery (Swinton, Yorks.). Made creamware and other Leeds-type pottery, early nineteenth century.

Dots mark. *See* Bow.

Doulton (Lambeth). Stoneware pottery, founded 1818, making mainly industrial brown ware.

Duesbury, William (1725–86). Independent decorator in London 1751–3; controlled porcelain factories at, successively, Derby (1756–86), Chelsea (1770–84), and perhaps Longton Hall (1760) and Bow (1763 onward). His son, Wm. D. (1763–96 or 97) owned the Derby factory 1786 until his death.

Dwight, John (*c.* 1637–1703). Potter, of Fulham, from about 1671.

Easter eggs. "Nest" eggs decorated, inscribed with the name of the recipient, and given as Easter and birthday gifts.

East India Company. The Honourable East India Company was incorporated in 1600, and had a monopoly of trade between England and the East. Factories (warehouses) were established for trading with China during the second half of the seventeenth century at Tongking, Amoy, Tainan (on Formosa), and at Gombron in the Persian Gulf. None lasted for more than a few years. In 1715 Canton became the principal port, and the Chinese side of all business came under the regulation of the *Co-hong*, a closed corporation of the local merchants. The Company formed a Council of Supercargoes to deal with them.

In addition to the ships belonging to the East India Company, licences were granted to the vessels of other traders, and there were in addition numerous unlicensed and unprincipled interlopers. Before long the vessels of the licensees and the unlicensed outnumbered those of the Company and, in turn, the total number of British vessels outnumbered those of all the other trading companies of the European nations. The factories of the various trading nations fronted the Pearl river, and contemporary views of them are found on porcelain and in paintings on canvas and glass. The East India Company was dissolved in 1858.

East India Company china and "Compagnie des Indes" china. The wares imported by these trading companies. The former continued till 1854.

"Egg-shell" porcelain. *See* Famille rose. Thin-bodied white bowls of Yung Lo (1403–24), with faint incised or slip-painted designs, were copied in the K'ang Hsi period. Some modern Japanese porcelains are egg-shell thin.

Egyptian black. Hard stoneware body heavily stained with manganese.

Ehret, G. D. Born at Heidelberg in 1708, became one of the most celebrated botanical artists of the eighteenth century. His work inspired some of the botanical designs on Chelsea porcelain. He died in 1770.

Elers, John Philip and **David.** Stoneware potters, originally silversmiths, of German extraction, settled in England before 1686. Worked in Fulham about 1690–3, at Bradwell Wood about 1693–8.

Enamel. Enamel-painting on porcelain, a decoration in vitreous colours which fuse upon the glazed surface in the muffle kiln at a low temperature. On soft-paste porcelain the enamel sinks deeply into the fusible lead glaze. On hard-paste porcelain it is not absorbed.

Encaustic painting. Josiah Wedgwood was granted a patent in 1769 for: "The purpose of ornamenting earthen and porcelaine ware with an encaustic gold bronze, together with a peculiar species of encaustic painting in various colours in imitation of the antient Etruscan and Roman earthenware." He prepared a number of substances by which were produced the following colours: red, orange, white, green, blue, yellow, and both a matt and a "shineing" black. The principal use for these colours was in the decoration of the basaltes body, which was modelled and painted in imitation of ancient Greek ware.

Engine-turning. Process of turning a dried but unfired pot on a lathe to produce a relief pattern, often of an irregular basket-work design ("rose-engine-turning"); probably introduced by Wedgwood about 1760.

Etruria
"Etruscan" vases. *See* Wedgwood.

"F" (and F reversed) **mark.** *See* Bow, Worcester.

Faïence also **fayence.** The term, derived from the Italian town of Faenza, was adopted in France at the beginning of the seventeenth century to describe tin-glazed earthenware. It has since been loosely applied to all kinds of white pottery.

Famille noire. K'ang Hsi wares enamelled in *famille verte* style, generally "on the biscuit", with dry black ground colour, made lustrous by a covering of green glaze. The large vases with superb floral designs have fetched great sums, encouraging forgeries and skilful redecoration of old pieces. Cups and bowls are less rare. A few marked examples are of the Yung Chêng period.

Famille rose. A class of enamelled wares characteristic of the reigns of Yung Chêng and Ch'ien Lung, named after the prominent rose-pink introduced from Europe. The rose, blue, and yellow were often thickened with opaque white. A new delicate painting style began to oust that of the *famille verte* about 1720, and was applied especially to plates, bowls, and cups and saucers of "egg-shell" thin porcelain. The "ruby-back" variety is coloured deep rose-pink on the reverse. Frequently painted subjects are scenes with ladies and children, birds or flowers, often framed in elaborate diapered borders. Pieces with European figure subjects, often imitated from engravings, were made to order for export. Many Ch'ien Lung and later wares employ the *famille rose* enamels, but with diminishing delicacy and taste.

Famille verte. A large family of wares of the K'ang Hsi period painted in a harmonious palette of brilliant green and red, yellow, aubergine-purple, and violet-blue enamels, the strong iron-red being almost as characteristic as the green. The blue enamel replaces the underglaze blue of the late Ming and seventeenth-century "five-colour" palette. The full range of colours were not always used. To heighten the effect, gilding was sometimes added. The paste of these wares is fine, white, and excellently potted, and a great variety of plant, landscape, animal, and romantic or historical figure subjects, as well as emblematic designs and elaborate borders and panel-work, were employed in their decoration. The best examples exhibit superb painting on the finest materials, but others were only sketchily executed. A more delicate style appears towards the end of the reign, e.g. on the Imperial "birthday" plates, foreshadowing the *famille rose* wares. The rarer examples with yellow or black grounds are known as *famille jaune* and *famille noire*, and there are wares with celadon or coffee-brown grounds, or with "powdered blue" surround. Imitations of Japanese "Imari" porcelains should also be mentioned.

Painting "on the biscuit", i.e. without intervening glaze, principally in yellow, green, and aubergine, provides a distinct group developed rather from the Ming "three colour" type. Besides large, finely painted vases there are delightful small objects for the scholar's table: brush-rests, water-pots, small figures, tea- and wine-pots, and stands, etc.

"Fazackerley" colours and patterns. *See* Liverpool (delftware).

FBB mark. *See* Worcester.

Feeding-bottle. Flattish oviform article with a small circular aperture at the top and a small nozzle.

"Felspathic glazes." Those containing felspar rock, an essential ingredient of porcelain glazes; but used also on stonewares (*see* main article).

"Female archer." Subject of "Pratt" type jugs and earthenware figures intended as satire upon the smart archery parties popular in "high" society, 1800–50. Sometimes known as the "fair toscopholite" or "toxophilite".

Ferronnerie. A style of ornament resembling wrought-iron work.

Ferruginous. Containing iron rust and, therefore, reddish brown in appearance.

Ferrybridge (near Pontefract, Yorks). Pottery making Wedgwood-style stoneware and creamware, late eighteenth and early nineteenth centuries. From 1796 to 1806 the firm had Ralph Wedgwood as partner, and used the mark "Wedgwood & Co", impressed.

Fitzhugh. A Chinese pattern very popular in America was the profuse floral arrangement known as Fitzhugh (said to be a Yankee version of Foochow) (Plate 334A). The wide, distinctive border is composed of pomegranates, butterflies, and latticework, and the centre is filled with four large medallions of flowers and emblems. The border alone sometimes frames enamelled motifs, as on George Washington's Cincinnati service. Enamelled decoration is also combined with the complete design, usually in the form of a monogram, occasionally of an eagle, placed in the centre. Though most often in underglaze blue, Fitzhugh occurs also with overglaze colour – green, brown, or orange.

Flambé glazes. Glazes in which kiln conditions produce variegated colour effects, e.g. on some Chün wares of the Sund dynasty, the eighteenth-century copper-red wares, and Canton stonewares.

Flasks. In form of fish, mermaid, constable's baton, horse-pistol, boot, potato, cucumber, barrel, or a figure of some royal or political celebrity, commonly made in brown stoneware or "Rockingham"-glazed earthenware, early nineteenth century. Chief centres: Denby, Chesterfield, Brampton, Lambeth. (*See* Reform Flasks.)

Flaxman, John, R.A. A well-known sculptor who was employed by Josiah Wedgwood from 1775 to 1787. Much of his work has been identified; it includes a number of plaques in relief, some portraits, and a set of chessmen. His father, also named John, supplied plaster casts of antique busts to Wedgwood, and some confusion has resulted in the classification of the work of father and son.

Flint enamel. *Fenton's Enamel*, an improvement on the brown Rockingham glaze, patented 1849 by Lyman, Fenton & Co. of Bennington, Vermont, U.S.A., but soon copied by East Liverpool and other factories. Metallic powders dusted on the glaze produced streaks and flecks of colour (Plate 316A, C). *See* Rockingham.

Flight & Barr; Flight, Barr & Barr. *See* Worcester.

"Florentine green" dishes. Mid-fifteenth-century majolica dishes painted in green, orange, and purple, at Florence.

Flowers. Porcelain, usually mounted on ormolu branches, were made at Chelsea and Derby as embellishments for porcelain figures, etc.

"Fretted square" mark. *See* Worcester.

Fuddling-cups. Cups of three, five, or more conjoined compartments communicating internally, made at Donyatt and Crock Street, Somerset, seventeenth and eighteenth centuries (Fig. 55).

FIG. 55

Fukien. *See* Blanc-de-Chine.

Fulham. *See* Dwight, Elers. In the eighteenth century massive mugs of brown-and-grey salt-glazed stoneware were made, with applied reliefs of hunting-scenes, topers, etc.

Garniture de Cheminé. Set of five vases, two trumpet-shaped beakers, and three covered vases, usually of baluster shape, a combination originating in China, whence adopted by most European faïence and porcelain factories.

Gaudy Dutch. The popular name for a gaily decorated Staffordshire pottery produced *c.* 1810–30 for the American trade.

Gaudy Welsh. Also gaudy ironstone. Later wares (*c.* 1830–45 and 1850–65) made in England for the American trade.

"German flowers" (deutsche blumen). Contemporary name for naturalistically painted flowers, introduced as porcelain decoration at Meissen about 1740. "Ombrierte Teutsche Blumen", flowers with shadows, are a variation. Later the treatment became freer, and smaller flowers, arranged in sprays or bouquets, were scattered over the whole surface until, under classical influence, they were confined between conventional rims and borders.

Giles, James. Owned a decorating establishment in London about 1760–80, where

much Bow and Worcester porcelain was painted.

"Girl in a swing" family of early porcelain figures (mostly white) having Chelsea affinities; by some conjecturally ascribed to dissident workmen from Chelsea, *c.* 1750.

Glaze. A shiny coating, rendering porcelain impervious to liquids while lending brilliance to its surface. In China body and glaze were fired together. At Meissen the body was fired first at a low temperature (Vergluehbrand), then dipped in a liquid glaze mixture and subjected to firing at a higher temperature. Glazes can be translucent, opaque, or coloured. The chemical composition is dependent upon that of the body beneath, lead and salt glazes being applied to pottery and soft-paste, feldspathic glazes to hard-paste porcelain.

"G" mark. *See* Bow.

Gold star. A pattern commonly used as a border for tea and dinner services, etc., towards the end of the eighteenth century, and in the early years of the century following. It is in the form of a band of dark-blue overglaze enamel, with small gold stars set on it at intervals. It was, and is, very popular in America.

Gombron. In the early part of the seventeenth century the English East India Company established a factory at the port of Gombron, in the Persian Gulf. As a result of this, native Persian ware and Chinese porcelain imported into England from this source were referred to indiscriminately as *Gombron ware*. As late as the 1770s Horace Walpole wrote of *two basins of most ancient Gombron china*, which may have been either Persian or Chinese. The modern name of the port is Bandar Abbas.

Gotch. East Anglian word for a large stoneware jug.

"Granite" ware. A creamware with minutely speckled glaze resembling granite, late eighteenth and nineteenth centuries.

Greatbach, William. Potter, of Lane Delph, Staffordshire. Some creamwares with black transfer-prints washed over in colours bear his name, probably as maker (some dated 1778).

Green glazes. Apart from the celadon wares, *see* Medium- and Low-temperature glazes.

Gretna Green. Popular black-print showing a runaway couple being married by the Gretna blacksmith, accompanied by the verse, "Oh! Mr Blacksmith, ease our pains:/ and tie us fast in Wedlock's Chains". Known alternatively as "The Red Hot Marriage".

"Greybeards." *See* Bellarmines.

Grey hen. Stoneware liquor bottle.

"Greyhound" jugs. Jugs with greyhound handles and relief decorations of sporting subjects.

Griffin mark. *See* Rockingham.

Ground-colours. Areas of coloured glaze as a background to painted or gilt decoration, often in reserved panels; chiefly yellow, deep blue, claret, green, and turquoise.

Hackwood, William (*d.* 1839). Wedgwood's principal modeller from 1769 to 1832. Hackwood spent much of his time in adapting the antique, but is known also to have done some original work. Occasionally he signed his work with his name in full, or with initials.

Hancock, Robert (1730–1817). Engraver. H. probably learned transfer-printing at the Battersea enamel factory (1753–6), subsequently practising it at Bow (1756), Worcester (1757 at latest, until 1774), and Caughley (1775).

Han dynasty (206 B.C.–A.D. 200). *See* p. 879.

Hard-paste (or "true"). Porcelain is compounded of "china-clay" (kaolin) and "chinastone" (petuntse), and glazed with petuntse made fusible with a "flux". Being wholly vitrified, it shows a shining fracture and resists a steel file (*see* Bristol, Plymouth, New Hall).

Hausmaler. Independent faïence and porcelain painter of Germany, working on white porcelain from Meissen, Vienna or on Chinese export ware, in competition with legitimate factory decorators. Hence the reluctance of the Meissen factory to sell white porcelain, and the introduction of the K P M mark as protection against outside painters. At Augsburg Johann Aufenwerth, his daughter Sabina, members of the Seuter family and others painted chinoiseries in gold and silver, framed by conventional lacework borders, which occasionally include contemporary scenes. In Silesia and Bohemia *schwarzlot* and coloured monochrome decoration are more

characteristic, originally derived from Dutch glass workers. Jacobus Helchis and Ignaz Bottengruber excelled in these techniques on Vienna porcelain. At Dresden Christoph Conrad Hunger combined the gold relief technique of St Cloud with that of Saxon glass decorators. There also seems to be proof that Meissen factory workers occasionally undertook outside work. During the second quarter of the century Johann Friedrich Metzsch and R. Chr. von Drechsel, of Bayreuth, painted figures in landscapes with palace architecture or harbour views, enclosed in ornamental borders with shell motives, sometimes painted in purple monochrome.

Hearty good fellow. Toby jug in form of a swaggering standing figure clasping a jug.

Hen and chickens. Emblems of Providence, hence frequent use as adornments of money-boxes (Fig. 56).

FIG. 56

Hen dish. Oval, basket-shaped egg-dish with cover in the form of a sitting hen (Fig. 57).

FIG. 57

Herculaneum. *See* Liverpool (cream-ware).

Historical blue. Also "Old blue". Staffordshire pottery transfer-printed with scenes of actual places, notable persons, historic events. These deep-blue prints of the 1820s were followed by light colours about 1830 and into the 1840s (Plate 310).

Ho-ho bird, or *fêng-huang.* The phoenix.

Hollins, Samuel. Potter of Shelton, Staffordshire, late eighteenth century. Made chiefly Wedgwood-type stonewares.

MARK: S. HOLLINS (impressed).

He was succeeded by his sons.

MARK: T. & J. HOLLINS (impressed).

Honan wares. Black- and brown-glazed wares of the Sung dynasty, probably made in Honan Province.

Horn mark. Imitated from Chantilly, at Worcester and Caughley.

Hsüan Tê period (1426–35). Classic reign for "blue-and-white" porcelains of very fine, richly glazed material. A certain rhythmic vitality is found alike in the contours of vessels and in their painted lotus scrolls, flying dragons, etc. Blackish spots sometimes mottle the cobalt pigment. Underglaze copper-red painting, white wares with faint incised or slip designs (*an hua*), blue or red monochromes, and the use of yellow enamel grounds, are found. Later times (especially the eighteenth century) "borrowed" the reign-mark, and also made admirable copies of the wares.

Hull (Yorks). Pottery founded 1802, making Staffordshire-type earthenware.

MARK (from 1825): "Bellevue Pottery Hull" and bells.

"Image toys." Contemporary designation of mid-eighteenth century Staffordshire figures.

Imari. A port in Japan which gave its name to a porcelain made in that country and decorated in a distinctive style in underglaze blue, iron red, and gold. Similar patterns in these colours on Chinese porcelain are known also as *Imari,* or *Chinese Imari.*

"I" mark. *See* Bow. Wrongly attributed to Isleworth.

Impasto. A method by which the colour is applied thickly so that it stands out in relief.

Imperial Russian service. Known also as the "Frog" service. Josiah Wedgwood received the order to make this enormous service of cream-coloured earthenware in March 1773. It was for the Empress Catherine of Russia, and was to be placed in her palace near St Petersburg (Leningrad), known as "La Grenouillière". The device of a green frog was painted in a shield in the border of each piece. The service numbered more than nine hundred pieces, each of which bore at least one painting of an English view, the obtaining of which caused a great deal of difficulty. The cost of the actual ware came to £51 8s 4d, but the decoration and other charges raised the final total to nearly £2,500. The Empress is believed to have paid £3,000 for it, and Wedgwood wrote: ". . . there will not be near the proffit upon this service that we have upon our commonest painted goods".

The painting of the service was done at Chelsea, where Wedgwood had an enamelling establishment under the supervision of Thomas Bentley. It was commenced in April 1773, and when the newly acquired show-rooms at Portland House, Greek Street, were ready for opening in June of the year following it was found that a sufficient number of pieces of the service had been completed for an exhibition to be made of it. The service was shown there with success, and was seen by many famous people, including Queen Charlotte. It is at present in the Winter Palace at Leningrad.

Independent decorators. Porcelain in the eighteenth and early nineteenth centuries was often obtained in the white and decorated by enamellers working outside the factory. Notable were W. Duesbury; J. Giles; Baxter (father of Thomas Baxter), who decorated Caughley and Coalport porcelain in a workshop near Fleet Street (early nineteenth century); T. M. Randall and R. Robins, of Spa Fields, decorated Coalport, Swansea, and Nantgarw for the London dealers (*c.* 1815–25).

Salt-glazed stoneware was also enamelled outside the factory (e.g. by Wm. Duesbury), as was creamware (e.g. by Robinson and Rhodes at Leeds about 1760–70 and by Absolon at Yarmouth). (*See also* Pardoe.)

India ware. The term in general use in England during the eighteenth century for imported Chinese porcelain. It gained currency owing to the fact that the East India Company held a monopoly of trade with the East. It sold the goods it imported by auction at India House, London. This building in the City was demolished in 1861.

Inlaid decoration. Process used by medieval potters for decorating paving tiles (Cleeve Abbey, Westminster Abbey) and by Sussex potters, *c.* 1790–1850, for useful and ornamental wares. The decoration was formed by impressing the body with punches or with printers' types, and filling in with clay of a contrasting colour, usually white on red.

Iron red. A red pigment made from an oxide of iron; used to decorate ceramics.

"Ironstone china." Variety of "stone china" (*q.v.*) (*see* Mason). Produced experimentally 1740–3 by Andrew Duché at Savannah. Wares of heavy grade similar to the Mason ironstone were a staple of American makers from 1860 to 1900 under such names as white granite, opaque porcelain, flint china, with so-called hotel china and semiporcelain appearing about 1885.

Isleworth (Middlesex). Pottery run by Joseph Shore and R. and W. Goulding, making Staffordshire-type pottery, late eighteenth century. Relief-decorated teapots, etc., marked "S. & G." and some Worcester blue-and-white porcelain have been wrongly attributed to I.

"Istoriato" painting (Lit. storied). It is especially associated with Urbino, though not invented there. Essentially pictorial, it frequently covers a whole plate or dish, leaving no border.

Italian Comedy figures. Characters from the I.C. were popular as porcelain models, mid-eighteenth century, chiefly Pantaloon, Isabella, Cynthio, Pierrot, Harlequin, Columbine, Captain, Doctor, Advocate.

Jackfield (Shropshire). Old-established pottery, making (*c.* 1750–75) black-glazed earthenware, usually decorated with unfired painting and gilding.

"Japan" patterns. Term indiscriminately used of both Chinese and Japanese designs in the eighteenth century. Chinese *famille verte* and *famille rose* patterns were copied, as well as the Arita wares known as *Imari* (often with sumptuous floral and "brocaded" designs in underglaze blue, enamels, and gilding) and *Kakiemon* (enamelled in red, green, blue, turquoise, and yellow).

Jasper-dip
Jasperware. A fine-grained unglazed stoneware perfected by Wedgwood in 1775. Normally white, it could be stained with different metallic colours (chiefly blue, lilac, sage-green, and black). From about 1780 this colouring could be superficial only ("jasper-dip"). Wedgwood's jasperware was much copied elsewhere.

"Jesuit" china. Porcelains of the first half of the eighteenth century painted with Christian subjects supplied by Jesuit missionaries, principally in black monochrome or *famille rose* enamels. The Jesuits brought to bear the first Western influence on the Chinese potters and painters. They first came to reside in the country towards the end of the sixteenth century.

Johanneum. The Dresden building containing the porcelain collection started by Augustus the Strong. Inventory marks, begun 1721, engraved on the wheel and coloured black, show numbers and letters to classify the type of porcelain, including Chinese and Japanese export ware.

Joney or joney grig. A dialect term for a chimney ornament in the form of a dog. A well-known Burslem pottery in the nineteenth century was known as a "doll and jona" (figure and dog) works.

Ju-i. A sceptre with cloud-scroll head, emblem of fulfilled wishes.

Ju ware. Rare Imperial ware of the early twelfth century, with buff body and crackled lavender-blue glaze.

Kakiemon. Japanese potter of Arita, credited with the first application of enamelling to Japanese porcelain (*c.* 1600). A class of Japanese ware with subtle asymmetrical decoration, named after him, and much copied in Europe during the eighteenth century, particularly at Meissen, Chantilly, and Chelsea.

Kaolin. *See* China-clay.

Photo: Fine Art Engravers Ltd.

(A) Finger-bowl, cup and saucer, porcelain painted in enamel-colours. Red anchor mark on saucer. Chelsea, about 1755. Height of finger-bowl 2⅝ ins. *Schreiber Collection, Victoria and Albert Museum, London.*

(B) Jug, transfer-printed in black, with a man kissing a woman's hand ("L'Amour"). Worcester, *c.* 1765. Height 7 ins. *H. R. Marshall.*

Photo: Fine Art Engravers Ltd.

(C) Cup and saucer, hard-paste porcelain with polychrome painting. New Hall, *c.* 1790. Diameter of saucer approximately 5⅛ ins. *G. E. Stringer.*

(D) Vase with polychrome painting reserved in panels on a dark blue ground reticulated in gilt. Mark: a "fretted square", in blue. Worcester, *c.* 1770. Height 10⅝ ins. *H. R. Marshall.*

PLATE 353

(A) Fiddler, Map-Seller, and Rat-Catcher. Red anchor marks. Chelsea, *c.* 1755. Height of central figure 7 ins.
Cecil Higgins Museum, Bedford.

(B) Figure of a Turkish Dancer. Mark: two dots in blue. Bow, *c.* 1765. Height 7¾ ins. *Victoria and Albert Museum, London.*

(C) Biscuit porcelain group, "Graces distressing Cupid" (after Angelica Kauffmann). Derby, late eighteenth century. Height 14¾ ins. *Victoria and Albert Museum, London.*

PLATE 354

(A) The Continents. Derby, about 1800. Height 9 ins. *Museum and Art Gallery, Derby.*

(B) Figures of Spring and Summer, and a frill vase, of hard-paste porcelain. Bristol, *c.* 1770–5. Height of vase 11¼ ins., *Glaisher Collection, Fitzwilliam Museum, Cambridge.*

PLATE 355

(A) Covered vase, with polychrome painting reserved on a crimson ground, and gilding. Gold anchor mark. Chelsea, *c.* 1765. *His Grace the Duke of Northumberland.*

(B) Vase, porcelain painted in colours, with a green ground, and gilt. Coalport, 1830–40. Height 8½ ins. *Museum and Art Gallery, Nottingham.*

(C) Sugar basin and cover. Mark: D intersected by an anchor, in gold. "Chelsea–Derby", *c.* 1770–80. Height 4⅞ ins. *Victoria and Albert Museum, London.*

(D) Sugar-bowl, cover, and stand, porcelain painted in colours and gilt. Mark: NANT-GARW C.W., impressed. Swansea, *c.* 1815. Height of bowl 5¼ ins. *Victoria and Albert Museum, London.*

PLATE 356

(A) Abrotanum humile, Plate II, Vol. I, of Philip Miller's *Figures of Plants*, by G. D. Ehret.

(B) A Chelsea plate painted with Abrotanum humile, formerly in the Bellamy Gardner Collection.

(c) A Chelsea plate painted with Antholyza, formerly in the Bellamy Gardner Collection.

(D) Antholyza, Plate XL, Vol. I, of Philip Miller's *Figures of Plants*.

PLATE 357

(B) Meissen cup and saucer, c. 1740, decorated with landscapes on a yellow ground. *H. E. Backer, London.*

(D) Meissen cup and saucer of Boetger porcelain, c. 1715–20, with

(A) Meissen bowl, c. 1735, painted by A. F. von Löewenfinck. *H. E. Backer, London.*

(C) Meissen teapot, 1739, painted by G. B. Haeuer. *H. E. Backer, London.*

PLATE 358

Early Meissen coffee-pot, *c.* 1715. Black glaze with gold decoration on Boettger stoneware. *Collection of Dr Syz, Westport, Connecticut.*

PLATE 359

(A) Mennecy covered jar, *c.* 1760. *Collection of Dr Syz, Westport, Connecticut.*

(B) Meissen tankard, *c.* 1725, painted by Johann Gregor Herold. *H. E. Backer.*

C

D

E

(C) Meissen tea-caddy, *c.* 1750. *H. E. Backer.* (D) Meissen vase, *c.* 1730, bearing the AR (Augustus Rex) mark. Decorated with chinoiseries by A. F. von Loewenfinck. *H. E. Backer.* (E) Chantilly vase with cover, *c.* 1740. *Antique Porcelain Co., London.*

PLATE 360

Hoechst, *c.* 1755. Freemasons group. *Collection of Dr Syz, Westport, Connecticut.*

PLATE 361

(A) Capo di Monte, c. 1755. *H. E. Backer.*

(B) Zürich, c. 1765. *Antique Porcelain Co., London.*

(C) Ludwigsburg. Model by Wilhelm Beyer, c. 1766.
H. E. Backer.

(D) Nymphenburg, Italian Comedy figure. Model by
F. A. Bustelli. *Rosenberg and Stiebel, Inc., New York.*

PLATE 362

(A) Meissen. Lady with a Blackamoor. Model by J. J. Kaendler. 1737. *Rosenberg and Steibel, Inc. New York.*

(B) Vincennes jardinière, 1755. *Antique Porcelain Co., London.*

PLATE 363

(A) Frankenthal. La Bonne Mère. Model by K. G. Lueck, *c.* 1765. *H. E. Backer.*

(B) Sèvres ewer and basin, marked 1759 and 1775. *Antique Porcelain Co., London.*

PLATE 364

(A) Berlin, Wegely factory. 1752–7. *Collection of Dr Syz, Westport, Connecticut.*

(B) Sèvres biscuit figure, Le Baiser Donné. Model by Falconet, 1765. *H. E. Backer.*

(C) Meissen tureen and cover, *c.* 1730, decorated with chinoiseries and port scenes by Christian Friedrich Herold.

(D) Vienna, Du Paquier period, *c.* 1730–40. *H. E. Backer.*

PLATE 365

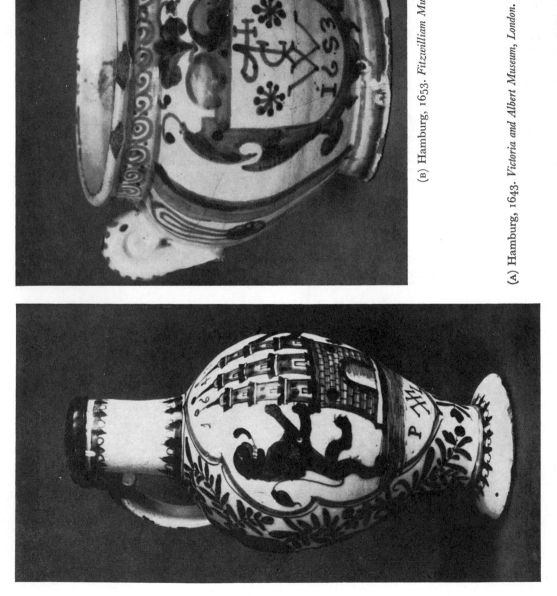

(B) Hamburg, 1653. *Fitzwilliam Museum, Cambridge.*

(A) Hamburg, 1643. *Victoria and Albert Museum, London.*

PLATE 366

(A) Kiel, *c.* 1770. *Victoria and Albert Museum, London.*

(B) Stockelsdorff, *c.* 1775. *Victoria and Albert Museum, London.*

(C) Hoechst, *c.* 1750. *Victoria and Albert Museum, London.*

(D) Stockelsdorff, *c.* 1780. *Private Collection.*

PLATE 367

(A) Kellinghusen, *c.* 1800. *Fitzwilliam Museum, Cambridge.*

(B) Proskau, *c.* 1775. *Private Collection.*

(C) Glienitz, *c.* 1775. *Private Collection.*

(D) Fulda, *c.* 1750. *Victoria and Albert Museum, London.*

PLATE 368

(A) Hanau, c. 1700. *Fitzwilliam Museum, Cambridge.*

(B) Hanau, mid-eighteenth century. *Private Collection.*

(C) Hanau, 1765. *Fitzwilliam Museum, Cambridge.*

(D) Hanau, c. 1750. *Fitzwilliam Museum, Cambridge.*

PLATE 369

(A) Frankfort, *c.* 1680. *Private Collection.*

(B) Frankfort, *c.* 1680. *Private Collection.*

(C) Frankfort, *c.* 1680. *Private Collection.*

(D) Frankfort, *c.* 1700. *Private Collection.*

PLATE 370

(B) Ansbach, *c.* 1733. *British Museum, London.*

(A) Nuremberg, *c.* 1720. *Frank Tilley Collection.*

(C) Nuremberg, *c.* 1730. *British Museum, London.*

(D) Erfurt, mid-eighteenth century. *Private Collection.*

PLATE 371

(A) Bayreuth, *c.* 1735. *Fitzwilliam Museum, Cambridge.*

(B) Bayreuth, *c.* 1755. *Fitzwilliam Museum, Cambridge.*

(C) Bayreuth, *c.* 1740. *Private Collection.*

(D) Bayreuth, 1745–7. *Private Collection.*

PLATE 372

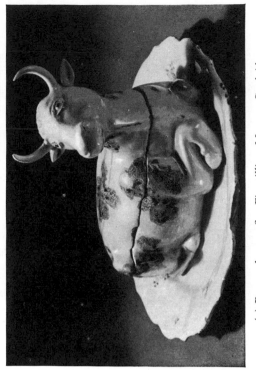

(B) Bayreuth, c. 1765. *Fitzwilliam Museum, Cambridge.*

(D) Künersberg, c. 1765. *Private Collection.*

(A) Bayreuth, c. 1765. *Fitzwilliam Museum, Cambridge.*

(C) Frankfort, c. 1700. *Fitzwilliam Museum, Cambridge.*

PLATE 373

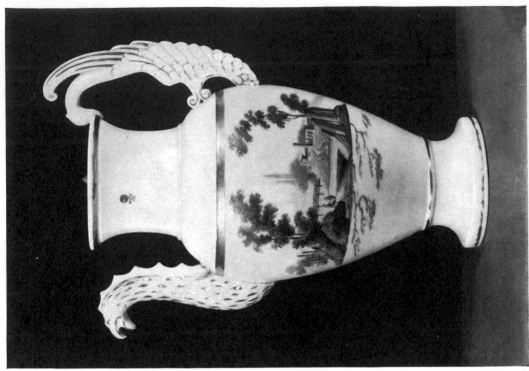

(B) Coffee-pot, painted with delicate landscape scene, contrasting with vigorous spout and handle, modelled in the shape of stylized birds, Popov Factory, early nineteenth century. *Private Collection.*

(A) Monumental vase, painted with flowers and foliage on a maroon ground, Imperial Factory, mid-nineteenth century.

PLATE 374

(A) *Left:* Plate depicting a woman carrying laundry shown against an Italianate background, Gardner Factory, . 1800. *Right:* Plate with coloured rim painted with a picture of a Yakut woman in national costume, Imperial Factory, *c.* 1820. *Private Collection, London.*

(B) *Left:* Plate painted with iron-red monochrome portrait of Anna Petrovna, Imperial Factory, late eighteenth century. *Right:* Plate painted with multi-coloured flowers, butterflies, and exotic bird, Imperial factory, *c.* 1840.

PLATE 375

(A) *Left:* Hot-water jug showing Eastern influence on design, painted with airily floating flowers and gilded arabesques, Kornilov Factory, mid-nineteenth century. *Right:* Coffee-pot painted with scenes on white medallions against an emerald green ground, Imperial Factory, *c.* 1830.

(B) *Left:* Teapot painted in purple and gold with bouquets of flowers in oval medallions, Imperial Factory, mid-nineteenth century. *Right:* Coffee-pot bearing monogram of Alexander III in purple and gold against pure white ground, Imperial Factory, late nineteenth century.

PLATE 376

(A) Portrait of Rev. Jonathan Mayhew by Paul Revere. Line engraving. *Prints Division, New York Public Library.*

(B) Portrait of John Jay by Cornelius Tiebout. Stipple engraving. *Prints Division, New York Public Library.*

(C) The Country Store by Alexander Anderson. Wood-engraving. *Prints Division, New York Public Library.*

PLATE 377

(A) View of the Battle at Concord, Massachusetts, 1775, by Amos Doolittle. Coloured line engraving after Ralph Earl. *Prints Division, New York Public Library.*

(B) Newburgh. Coloured aquatint from the *Hudson River Portfolio*, after W. G. Wall, by John Hill. *The Old Print Shop, Harry Shaw Newman.*

PLATE 378

(A) Buffalo from Lake Erie, 1836, by William J. Bennett. Coloured aquatint after a sketch by J. W. Hill. One of the series, *Views of American Cities. The Old Print Shop, Harry Shaw Newman.*

(B) City Hall (New York) by John Hill. Coloured aquatint after W. G. Wall. Published 1826. *The Old Print Shop, Harry Shaw Newman.*

PLATE 379

Photo: Culver Service.

(A) Washington by Rembrandt Peale. Pendleton Lithograph. *Library of Congress.*

(B) Passed midshipman, U.S. Navy. *U.S. Military Magazine. P. S. Duval lith. Phila. The Old Print
Shop, Harry Shaw Newman.*

(C) Osceola. Drawn and on stone by George
Catlin, 1838. The greatest life portrait of an
Indian. *The Old Print Shop, Harry Shaw Newman.*

PLATE 380

(A) Wall Street from Trinity Church, New York, 1834. Lithograph by Peter Maverick after Hugh Reinagle. *New York Historical Society.*

Photo: Antiques.

(B) Great Fire, New York, 1835. One of the first "disaster" prints. Published by H. R. Robinson, New York.

PLATE 381

(A) Castle Garden, *c.* 1825. Early lithograph of Imbert & Co., New York. Drawn by A. J. Davis. *New York Historical Society.*

(B) Preparing for Market. After L. Maurer. Lithograph N. Currier, 1856. *The Old Print Shop, Harry Shaw Newman.*

PLATE 382

(A) East View of Faneuil Hall Market. Boston 1827. Early Pendleton lithograph; drawn by J. Andrews. *New England Historical Art Society.*

(B) National Lancers with the Reviewing Officers on Boston Common, 1837. Moore's Lithography, Boston. On stone by F. H. Lane after C. Hubbard. *Library of Congress.*

PLATE 383

(A) De Witt Clinton (Mohawk & Hudson). Lithograph by Leggo & Co., Montreal, Canada, 1869, from Brown's silhouette of 1832 in the Connecticut Historical Society. *The Old Print Shop, Harry Shaw Newman*.

(B) Ellicott's Mills; end of first section of Baltimore & Ohio Railroad. Drawn and lithographed by Ed. Weber, Baltimore, *c.* 1837. *The Old Print Shop, Harry Shaw Newman*.

PLATE 384

"Keep within compass." A popular "morality" used as decoration for earthenware by John Aynsley (1752–1829), showing the rewards of virtue and the punishments of sin.

Kiln. Used to fire body and glaze of hardpaste porcelain at about 1,200–1,400° C. (*grand feu*).

"Kinuta" celadon. *See* Lung-chüan celadon.

Ko ware. Crackled Sung celadon ware of Kuan type.

Kuan ware. Rare Sung celadon patronized by the Emperor, with dark-grey porcellanous body and thick, often crackled glaze of pale greyish-blue or greyish-green colour, suggesting marble or jade; made at Hangchow (Chekiang Province) from the twelfth century. Creditable imitations were made during the eighteenth century.

Kü Yüeh Hsüan ware. A group of eighteenth-century porcelains of Imperial quality, carefully painted with flower and landscape subjects in coloured enamels, principally of the *famille rose*, sometimes with coloured grounds. They are often inscribed with a poem. The title more properly belongs to some later painted glass vessels.

Lambeth (delftware). "Lambeth" is often used to denote the London delftware potteries generally, namely: Aldgate (1571–*c.* 1780), Southwark (Pickleherring Quay, *c.* 1620–1770, and St Saviour's, *c.* 1630–*c.* 1760), Vauxhall (perhaps late seventeenth century–*c.* 1800), and Lambeth (Howard House, Church Street, *c.* 1665–1770, and Fore Street, first half of eighteenth century–late eighteenth century).

Characteristic of L. are (seventeenth-century) porringers with oval handles having a central oval hole or heart-shaped perforations; posset-pots with curved profile (Plate 347A); plates (*c.* 1690 onwards) having a sloping rim, and almost vertical sides curving into a flat base; (eighteenth-century) flat-based flower "bricks" perforated with round holes; puzzle-jugs with narrow in-curved necks, often with V-shaped perforations; wall-pockets somewhat resembling a rain-water drainhead; trinket-trays of one central star-shaped and five outer lobed compartments.

The L. *bianco-sopra-bianco* design usually includes flattened spirals.

Lambrequins. Originally applied to drapery, but later extended to all forms of pendant, lace-like (vandyked) decoration.

Lang yao. *See* Copper-red glazes.

Lead. Was employed for lead-glazing either as a dry powder (galena, native lead sulphide) or a liquid (litharge, lead oxide). "Baron" Stiegel the glassmaker was buying "Litterage" for lead-glass in 1772. In scarce times one Ohio potter obtained lead by collecting and burning the lead-foil with which Chinese tea was packaged.

Le Compte, Père Louis. A Jesuit missionary who published in Amsterdam in 1697 *Memoirs and Observations made in a late Journey through China*. The book was issued in translation in London in the same year. Le Compte devotes several pages to porcelain and mentions that blue-and-white was the principal product. He adds that the European merchants foolishly bought anything that the Chinese were willing to sell.

Leeds (Yorks). A pottery was founded about 1760 by two brothers Green. Fine creamware, frequently enamelled outside the factory, was a speciality (Plate 348D). Pierced decoration was common. Most of the late eighteenth-century Staffordshire-type wares, including a few simple figures, were made.

MARKS: HARTLEY GREENS & CO. and LEEDS POTTERY, either alone or repeated in a cross. The old moulds were reused at Slee's pottery (Leeds) from 1888, and were marked like the original wares.

Leeds horse. Large model of horse on a rectangular plinth made specially at Leeds, and probably used as the sign of a horse leech.

Limehouse. A short-lived porcelain factory before 1750. Its productions are unidentified.

Ling lung. Pierced openwork, as found on some seventeenth- to eighteenth-century blue-and-white porcelain bowls, and on elaborate vases of Ch'ien Lung and later date.

Littler, W. See Longton Hall.

Liverpool (creamware). A pottery, founded 1793–4, and in 1796 renamed "Herculaneum", made creamware, often transfer-printed in blue or black, and other Staffordshire-type wares. MARK: HERCULANEUM (impressed). In U.S.A. Liverpool was a generic name given to creamware made 1780–1825 by Liverpool but also certain Staffordshire potters, especially in jugs black transfer-printed with American-historical subjects (Plate 309).

Liverpool (delftware). Delftware began in L. in 1710 and was thereafter manufactured at numerous potteries (eight in 1750 and twelve by 1760), including some making porcelain. After about 1770 the industry declined, until by 1780 there were only three potteries. L. delftware is often indistinguishable from Lambeth and Bristol. Typical of L. is a foxy red, often used, together with blue, yellow, and green, in designs of flowers and Chinese lattice fences ("Fazackerléy" colours). Red was also frequently used to edge rims. The L. blue sometimes tends to cause a depression in the glaze. L. *bianco-sopra-bianco* borders consist of rosettes separated by curved sprays of leaves. Characteristic L. shapes are: plates with sides forming an obtuse angle with the bottom; mugs, both bell-shaped and cylindrical, with a spreading foot; bottles with a distinct foot-rim; large vases painted in blue; puzzle-jugs with neck-perforations of rosettes with heart-shaped petals; cornucopia wall-pockets for flowers; trinket-trays, some with dishes fitting into an outer lobed tray; flower-bricks with large, round (sometimes square) holes on top and a waved edge below or four solid ball feet; round dishes with low vertical rims painted with fishes ("charpots"); bowls decorated with ships. L. delftware was occasionally decorated in overglaze enamels and gilt. Transfer-printing was also employed, particularly on tiles.

Liverpool (soft-paste porcelain). (1) Richard Chaffers (1731–65) from at latest 1756 made porcelain of Worcester type, a common form being a bulbous mug with an incised cordon above the foot, enamelled with a Chinese scene in polychrome. C. was succeeded by Philip Christian. (2) Seth, James, and John Pennington made porcelain, especially bowls, painted in a bright "sticky" blue. (3) To Zachariah Barnes are traditionally ascribed pieces roughly printed in a smudgy dark blue. (4) Samuel Gilbody was making porcelain by 1761 at latest, and (5) W. Reid, by 1756. In general, L. porcelain is characterized by foot-rims vertical or undercut on the inner surface; flat bases to mugs; areas of blue ground marbled in gold; a blued glaze giving a "thundercloud" effect where thick under the base.

"L" mark. *See* Worcester, Longton Hall.

"Long elizas." A corruption of the Dutch "*lange lijzen*", the gawky ladies often depicted on K'ang Hsi blue-and-white.

Longton Hall (soft-paste porcelain). Excavations on the site of this factory, together with documents traced by Dr Bernard Watney, prove that it was founded 1749–50 by William Jenkinson, who, in 1751, took into partnership William Nicklin and William Littler. Nicklin took no part in the work of the factory, which was managed throughout by Littler. In 1755 Jenkinson sold the majority of his shares to Nathaniel Fermin, who died soon afterwards. Robert Charlesworth also became a partner in this year, obtaining a major financial interest in the establishment. He dissolved the partnership in 1760, causing the factory to close down. Dr Watney's discoveries show that the wares thought typical of L.H., including the "snowman" family, were in fact made there, while many of its useful wares have been wrongly attributed to other factories. Characteristic of L.H. porcelain are a rich blue used as a coloured ground, sometimes over-painted in opaque-white enamel; vessels simulating melons or formed of overlapping leaves; a distinctive yellowish green; painting with roses delineated by a trembling outline; and a relief border-design of strawberries and leaves. The porcelain is commonly heavy and glassy, with a palish-green translucency betraying large bright flecks and frequent imperfections. The L.H. figures have been identified in a class characterized by poses half-turned to right or left; scrolled bases, often picked out in red; costume diapered with stars and small formal motifs, rather than flowers; and outlining of eye-lashes, often in red. The rare gilding is usually poor.

Mark: As diagram in blue.
(*See also* "Snowman" family.)

Lotus ware (Plates 314B, C). *See* Belleek.

"Lowdin's" factory. *See* Bristol.

Lowestoft (soft-paste porcelain). This factory (1757–*c*. 1802) specialized in table- and tea-wares, usually decorated with Chinese-derived patterns in underglaze blue or enamels. There is a strong affinity with Bow, their blue-and-white porcelain being sometimes almost indistinguishable. Both used bone-ash. The Chinese and rococo styles persisted longer at L. than normally elsewhere, but towards 1800 slight "sprig" patterns became popular. Primitive underglaze-blue printing was done. L. characteristics are wedge-shaped foot-rims, and workmen's marks in blue inside them. There was no recognized factory mark, but (e.g.) Meissen and Worcester marks were copied. The very rare L. figures include swans, sheep, cats, and putti. Paris fakes of L. and genuine L. pieces redecorated are occasionally found.

"Lowestoft" china. Chinese porcelain of the eighteenth century with European-style decoration, once mistakenly attributed to this English factory.

"Lund's" factory. *See* Bristol.

Lung-chüan celadon. This great centre for celadon wares in Chekiang Province flourished during the Sung dynasty. The greyish-white porcellanous body often appears brown where exposed raw to the fire. The characteristic glaze is thick, smooth, and translucent, varying principally between a cool greyish and deep grassy green, the colour being derived from iron. Best known are the stoutly potted, large, heavy dishes, jars, and vases exported in quantity throughout the Near and Far East. Finer wares are various in shape, often with freely carved or incised designs, or decoration impressed from moulds of fishes, dragons, or plants, sometimes left unglazed and burnt an attractive red. The *kinuta* celadon, a subdued bluish green in colour, is of outstanding quality. Another type with brown spots is the Japanese *tobi seiji*. Early Ming celadons are similar, but often more elaborately decorated. Quality then declined rapidly.

Lustre. A sheeny surface-film deposited on pottery or porcelain by firing metallic pigments in a "reducing" (smoky) atmosphere (early nineteenth century). "Silver" l. was made with platinum and pink and mauve l. with gold, which on a red body also produced copper. L. could be either applied in "solid" areas or used for painting, often combined with printing. Alternatively, designs were painted in a glycerine or shellac medium and the piece dipped in lustre mixture. On removal of the medium, the pattern remained in negative on a l. ground ("resist" process).

Lustre colour. A pale mother-of-pearl shade containing some red, found on early Meissen porcelain, used either as background colour, for painted designs, or for overglaze marks. Probably the outcome of one of Boettger's experiments in search of the Chinese underglaze red.

Majolica (from *maiolica*), the name first used in Italy to describe the lustred wares of Valencia. It was later extended to all varieties of Italian tin-glazed earthenware. By a further extension, it was applied to the pottery of other countries, painted in the traditional colours. Majolica is a nineteenth-century English name for lead-glazed pottery of sixteenth-century French style. Enormous quantities were distributed as premiums in the 1880s in America.

Manchu dynasty. The Ch'ing dynasty (1644–1912).

Mandarin. Late eighteenth-century decoration of groups of figures wearing official dress, painted in panels within borders of elaborate diaper and other patterns.

"Mandarin" china. Porcelains imported during the second half of the eighteenth century and later, with predominantly pink, red, and gold enamelling of floral or figure subjects, often framed in underglaze blue scrollwork; frequently with undulating glaze.

"Marbled ware." *See* "Agate ware".

Marks. Signs of origin on porcelain, applied either in underglaze blue, impressed, incised, or painted above the glaze. Marks are usually applied beneath the base, though occasionally, as for instance on Nymphenburg figures, they may form part of the decoration. Generally they indicate the factory, but marks can also refer to a painter or "repairer", some are factory *assemblée* or warehouse signs for the convenience of workers, as are the early Herold period lustre marks; or else they may help to control gold supplies handed to individual decorators, as do gold numerals on tea services with *chinoiserie* decoration.

Martha Gunn. Female Toby jug modelled in the likeness of Martha Gunn (1727–1815), the Brighton bathing-woman.

Mason. Potters of Lane Delph (Staffordshire and Liverpool). Miles M. (d. 1822) made porcelain. His son, C. J. M., patented "Ironstone China" in 1813, commonly blue-printed or painted with "Japan" patterns.

MARKS: usually the name in full.

"Mazarin" blue. *See* Chelsea.

Medium- and low-temperature glazes. Certain coloured glazes are applied to the already baked biscuit porcelain, which is then refired at "medium" temperature. Such were the glazes of the Ming "three-colour" class; monochromes, among which the yellow and turquoise-blue were especially popular; and bowls and dishes with coloured glazes covering incised designs of dragons, flower sprays, etc., which were still made throughout the following dynasty. The K'ang Hsi, Yung Chêng, and Ch'ien Lung monochromes are remarkable for their wide range of rich, luminous colours and fine shapes. Turquoises are particularly distinguished from the Ming and more modern pieces by their clear brilliance. Greens include a leaf colour, dark green, olive-green, and speckled cucumber-green, as well as the much-prized apple-green, which is applied over a crackled white glaze. Various light yellows are distinguishable, and one with a deeper, brownish tint. A deep purple and paler, brownish aubergine were produced with the aid of manganese. Occasionally glazes are splashed with two colours – e.g. turquoise with purple, and green with yellow (tiger-skin or "egg-and-spinach").

Low-temperature glazes are the familiar enamels of overglaze painting, and were fired in the "muffle-kiln". Very various in shade, they include most of the colours of the *famille verte* and *famille rose*, and are often opaque. A mustard yellow and opaque light green, for example, resemble colours found on Ch'ien Lung painted wares. The opaque, mottled

"robin's-egg" blue, spotted with lavender and crimson, is one much revived during the nineteenth century.

In dating these wares shape and finish, especially of the foot, should be carefully considered: for the same quality is not achieved in nineteenth-century and later pieces.

Mei p'ing. "Prunus" vase, with small mouth to hold one spray of plum-blossom.

"Merry man" plates. Delftware plates, usually simply decorated, forming a series of six, normally inscribed: (1) "What is a merry man"; (2) "Let him do what he can"; (3) "To entertain his guests"; (4) "With wine and merry jests"; (5) "But if his wife do frown"; (6) "All merriment goes down". Late seventeenth and first half of eighteenth century.

"Metropolitan" slipware. Lead-glaze red-bodied earthenware with white slip-decoration (inscriptions, simple rosettes, stars, coils, etc.), made in the London area about 1630–70.

Mille fleurs. Decoration with panels of growing plants reserved on a flower-covered ground: employed from the Ch'ien Lung period.

Ming dynasty (1368–1644). *See* Chinese Pottery.

Ming dynasty 1368–1644, reign marks.

Hsüan Te
(1426–35)

Ch'êng Hua
(1465–87)

Hung Chih
(1485–1505)

Chêng Tê
(1506–21)

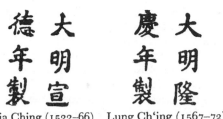

Chia Ching (1522–66)   Lung Ch'ing (1567–72)

Wan Li (1573–1619)   T'ien Ch'i (1621–7)

Minton, Thomas (1765–1836). After apprenticeship at Caughley,. M. worked for Josiah Spode. In 1796 he set up for himself at Stoke, first making pottery only (much blue-printed), but from 1798 to 1811, and again 1821–5, porcelain too. Excellent transfer-printing in black and brown was done.

MARKS: "M" or as diagram, in blue.

"M" mark. *See* Minton, Pinxton.

Mocha. Ware decorated with coloured bands into which tree, moss, or fern-like effects have been introduced by means of a diffusing medium, described by William Evans (1846) as "a saturated infusion of tobacco in stale urine and turpentine", made from about 1780 until 1914. Named from mocha quartz.

Moco, moko. Buff or redware mottled by spattering various coloured slips over the surface before glazing. A cheap nineteenth-century substitute for mocha.

Money-boxes. Made at most country pot-

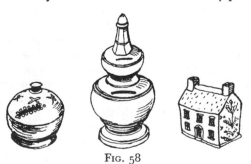

FIG. 58

works from medieval times. Usual forms comprise houses, chests of drawers, globes, fir-cones, pigs, and hens and chickens. Associated with the custom of the "Christmas box" (Fig. 58).

Monochrome-glazed porcelain. These are divisible into two classes: (i) with high-temperature glazes, fired in one process at the full heat of the kiln – namely, white, blue, copper-red, celadon-green, and brown or black; (ii) the remainder, with medium- or low-temperature colours (*q.v.*).

"Moons." Specks of higher translucency observable in some porcelains.

"Mr and Mrs Caudle." Relief decoration on brown stoneware spirit flasks, made about 1846 by Doulton of Lambeth, and based upon Douglas Jerrold's *Punch* papers ("Mrs Caudle's Curtain Lectures"). One side shows "Mr and Mrs Caudle in Bed", the other "Miss Prettyman".

Muffle. Kiln used for low-temperature firing (*petit feu*) of about 700–900° C. The porcelain piece is enclosed in an inner chamber "muffle", out of contact with flames or smoke, hence the name. It is used to fuse enamel painting into the glaze of faïence and porcelain, and for the firing of soft paste in general.

"Nankin" china. Blue-and-white porcelain of the late eighteenth and nineteenth centuries which was shipped from Nanking.

"Nankin yellow." Lustrous pale golden brown glaze used in association with K'ang Hsi underglaze blue painting, especially in export wares for the Near East.

Nantgarw (Glamorgan, soft-paste porcelain). A porcelain factory at N. was started in 1813 by W. Billingsley and, after transfer to Swansea (1814–16/17), continued until Billingsley left for Coalport (1819), and afterwards (probably for decoration only) until 1822 under W. W. Young.

At Swansea (*q.v.*) the beautiful but uneconomic N. material (white, glassy, and translucent) was adapted to produce: (1) a body with a greenish translucency ("duck's egg"), and then (2) one with a minutely pitted surface and yellow translucency (*c.* 1817).

The porcelain of both factories, although often simply decorated on the spot with

"Billingsley-style" flowers, birds, etc. (*see* Pardoe, Baxter), was keenly sought after by London dealers and decorators, who were responsible for much elaborate decoration (Plate 356D). A raised border-pattern of floral panels was favoured at both factories.

MARKS: NANT-GARW C-W impressed, used at both N. and Swansea; "Swansea" impressed or written in red or gold, on (1) above; SWANSEA with a trident, impressed, on (2) above.

Neale, J. *See* Palmer.

Newcastle-on-Tyne. Potteries here (St Anthony's 1780 onwards, and St Peter's about 1817 onwards) made inferior creamware.

New Hall (Shelton, Staffordshire). In 1781 the Bristol patent for hard-paste porcelain was bought by a Staffordshire combine, which in 1782 established a factory at N. H. Hard-paste porcelain decorated with simple, mainly floral, patterns was produced until about 1810, when a glassy bone china was adopted.

MARKS: pattern-numbers prefaced by "N" or "N°"; on bone china, "New Hall" within a double circle, printed.

Nien hao. *See* section on Marks.

"N°" mark. *See* New Hall.

"N" mark. *See* New Hall.

Northern celadon. Sung wares probably from Honan Province, with grey porcellanous body burnt brown where exposed, and usually glazed base. The glaze is often glassy and olive-green to brown in tone. They include beautifully shaped bowls, pear-shaped vases, and small shallow dishes superbly carved with plant forms or free designs incised with a comb.

Nottingham. Stoneware pottery from late seventeenth century to about 1800, making wares thinly potted and overlaid with a lustrous ferruginous wash. Pierced, impressed, or incised decoration was common. Latterly almost indistinguishable from Derbyshire stoneware (Plate 348B).

"Oak-leaf-jars." Mid-fifteenth-century Tuscan drug-jars decorated with foliage in impasto-blue.

"Oilspot" glaze. Some of the so-called Honan brown and black glazes of the Sung dynasty bear attractive silvery spots, caused by precipitated iron crystals.

On-glaze. Decoration applied after the ware has been glazed and fired.

"Opaque china." *See* Swansea.

"Orange-jumper." Local subject on Yorkshire cream-coloured earthenware made at the Don pottery, *c.* 1808, depicting a coarse-featured local horse-breaker who acted as messenger for Lord Milton in the 1807 election. He is clothed in orange, the "colour" of Lord Milton. Orange-tawny was considered the colour appropriate to the lower classes.

Owl jug. Jug with a separate head forming a cup, made in slipware, *c.* 1700, and white salt-glazed stoneware, *c.* 1720–75. The proverb "Like an owl in an ivy bush", used of a vague person with a sapient look, may explain its convivial associations (Fig. 59).

FIG. 59

Palissy, Bernard. A celebrated French potter (b. *c.* 1510, d. *c.* 1590). Palissy's great reputation rests on the fine coloured glazes used on his wares. He was originally a painter of glass, and after a period of travel in France, settled at Saintes. His ambition to become a potter was aroused, according to his own account, by the sight of a beautifully decorated cup. After many costly experiments he succeeded in making pottery and decorating it with mingled colour glazes. His *figulines rustiques* (pottery with rural subjects modelled in relief) brought him the patronage of the Constable de Montmorency, who, on one occasion, had him released from prison by declaring him *inventeur des rustiques figulines du roi*. The subjects of these "figulines" include snakes, lizards, shells, fishes, etc., modelled on a ground of rock-work and moss. The glazes provide a harmonious blending of blue, purple, brown, yellow, and green. He decorated a grotto at the Tuileries in this manner to the order of Catherine d' Medici; but, as a Huguenot, was obliged to flee from Paris in order to escape the massacre of St Bartholomew's day. Eventually imprisoned in the Bastille de Bucy, he died there about 1590. Genuine specimens of his work are extremely rare, but it has been extensively copied.

Palmer, Humphrey. Potter of Hanley (Staffordshire), 1760–78, rivalled Wedgwood in making black basaltes (1769) and jasperware. Bankrupt in 1778, he was helped by J. Neale ("Neale & Co.", subsequently (1784) "Neale & Wilson"). Their lead-glazed earthenware figures are notable for neat modelling and clear, bright enamel-colours.

Pancheon. Large shallow earthenware bowl with sloping sides used for settling milk.

Pap-dish. A shallow boat with a tubular spout for feeding infants.

Pardoe, Thomas (1770–1823). Painted porcelain at Derby and Worcester, pottery at Swansea (1797–1809); became independent enameller in Bristol (1809–21); decorated Nantgarw porcelain (1821–?1823). Painted mainly "botanical" flowers.

Parian or statuary ware. Fine-grained, waxy feldspathic porcelain resembling white Parian marble, developed in the 1840s by Copeland and Minton; much admired at the Crystal Palace exhibitions in London and New York (1851 and 1853). Soon a favourite of American makers, chiefly for portrait busts and parlour ornaments.

"Parson and clerk." Figure group showing a drunken parson being led home by the faithful Moses, first made by Enoch Wood (1759–1840) as a sequel to the "Vicar and Moses". A satire on the drinking, hunting squarson type of incumbent (Fig. 61).

FIG. 61

Pastille burners. Box-like containers, often in the form of cottages, churches, or summer-houses, with detachable perforated lids for burning cassolette perfumes. These consisted of finely powdered willow-wood charcoal, benzoin, fragrant oils, and gum arabic. Extremely popular, 1820–50 (Fig. 62).

FIG. 60

"Patch family." *See* Derby.

"Paul Pry." Model for pottery figures and

FIG. 62

Toby jugs based upon the meddlesome hero of John Poole's comedy of that name, 1825.

"Peachbloom" glazes. *See* Copper-red glazes.

Pearl-ware. A white variety of the cream-coloured pottery ("Queen's Ware") introduced by Josiah Wedgwood about 1779. It had a nacreous glaze, hence the name given to it.

Peasant style. Ornament derived from peasant art: specifically earthenware painted in the "resist" lustre style with a restricted palette of colours.

"Pebbled" vases. Vases with marbled surface (*see* "Agate-ware", Wedgwood).

Peever. A piece of slate or stone used in the game of hopscotch, also a disc of pottery, so used, coloured and lettered with the name of the owner. Made at Alloa and elsewhere in Scotland, nineteenth century.

"Peggy Plumper." Crude decoration showing Peggy Plumper sparring with Sammy Spar for mastership of bed and board, accompanied by a long rhyme "about wearing the breeches".

Peking bowls. Bowls of Ch'ien Lung or later date, with painted *famille rose* medallions reserved on a single-coloured ground covered with engraved scrollwork; said to have been sent as yearly tribute to the Emperor at Peking.

"Pelican in her piety." A Christian emblem representing the old popular fallacy that the pelican feeds her young with her own blood. Used on Staffordshire slipware.

Penny bank. Earthenware money-box in the form of a house or chest of drawers.

Petuntze. *See* China-stone.

"Pew groups." In salt-glazed stoneware depicted seated figures, sometimes playing instruments (*see also* Adam and Eve). Conjecturally attributed to Aaron Wood.

"Piatto da pompa." An elaborately decorated dish made entirely for ornamental display.

Piggin. A small milk pail. A pig-wife is a woman who sells crockery.

Pilchard pots. Made in North Devon, South Wales, and Cornwall for the West Country fishermen, and known by size as "gallons", "bussas", and "great crocks", etc.

Pilgrim-bottle. *See* Costrel.

"Pine-apple" ware. *See* "Cauliflower" ware.

Pinxton (soft-paste porcelain). The P. (Derbyshire) factory (1793–1813) was started with the technical assistance of W. Billingsley, a fine translucent white porcelain being made. In 1799 Billingsley left, and a coarser Staffordshire-type porcelain was made. The decoration followed Derby styles. A yellow ground is notable.

MARKS: "T" and "M", impressed; "P", in various enamels; 1 below in blue, 2 in purple, 3 and 4 in red enamels.

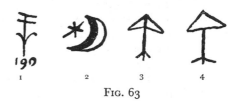

FIG. 63

Pipkin. Earthenware cooking vessel.

Pirlie-pig. Earthenware money-box. "Pig" is a North Country word for an earthen jar: "pirlie" is a diminutive indicating something of slight value.

Pitcher mould. Mould made of clay and fired.

Plymouth (hard-paste porcelain). In 1768 William Cookworthy, a Plymouth apothecary, took out a patent for hard-paste porcelain. The factory was moved to Bristol about 1770. P. porcelain suffers from technical defects – smoky glaze-discoloration, fire-cracks, warping, etc. The enamels (often of a dirty tone) frequently stand out in relief. A characteristic brownish-red was much used on the rococo bases of figures. These formed an important part of the factory's production. Painting in blackish-toned underglaze-blue was practised.

MARKS: (1) as diagram, in underglaze blue, blue or red enamel, or gold; (2) occasionally a cross, alone or with (1), either incised through the glaze or in enamel or gilt; (3) "T" and "T°" impressed.

"P" mark. *See* Worcester, Pinxton.

Porcelain. Translucent, vitrified ware made of china-clay and china-stone fused at great heat – the "true" or hard-paste porcelain. Soft-paste and "artificial" porcelains are of white clay with glassy frit, sometimes soaprock (steatite, soapstone) or later bone-ash. From continual experiments, the formulas varied endlessly, and many marginal "porcelains" are accepted if they show translucence.

Pope and Devil. Reversible bell-shaped cup showing the Pope in his triple tiara when held one way up, and the Devil when reversed. Sometimes inscribed "When Pope absolves, the Devil smiles". Late eighteenth century.

Porringer. Child's basin for broth or porridge.

Portland Vase. This vase, which is in the British Museum, London, is in the form of an *amphora* about 10 inches in height. It is made of glass of a deep blue colour, over which is a layer of white glass. The body of the vase is cut in relief with scenes from the story of Peleus and Thetis. It dates from the first century A.D. The base, which does not belong to the vase, is of the same materials, and is carved with the bust of a youth wearing a Phrygian cap. When in the possession of the Duke of Portland it was loaned to Wedgwood, who made many successful copies.

"Portobello" ware. Made at Tunstall, Staffordshire, *c.* 1830, in imitation of banded and "Pratt" type wares made at Portobello in Scotland.

Posset. Beverage comprising hot ale, milk, sugar, spices, and small pieces of bread, toast, or oatcake, said to have been a common supper beverage in Staffordshire and Derbyshire on Christmas Eve. Enjoyed widespread popularity.

Posset-pot. Straight- or curve-sided vessel

FIG. 64

with loop handles and spouts, generally covered with a slanting or dome-shaped lid, and occasionally crowned with an elaborate knob, used for posset, and made in delftware and slipware, seventeenth and eighteenth centuries (Fig. 64).

Potiche. Large, broad-mouthed jar of "baluster" shape, with cover; favoured from Ming times.

Pottery. In the broadest sense is "any receptacle or vessel made of clay" by the potter. But the name is saved for earthenwares fired at low temperature (600° C. or more) as distinguished from stoneware or porcelain, fired at much greater heat.

Pottle-pot. Quart pot.

Powder-blue. Blue ground, produced by spraying colour through a tube closed with gauze. This process allowed the reserving of panels, to be painted in colours. A Chinese invention, copied at Meissen under Herold. Occasionally green is used instead of blue.

"Powdered" (**soufflé**) **blue.** Mottled blue glaze of K'ang Hsi period produced by blowing on dry pigment through a tube. It was adorned with gilded designs (often since restored) or used as a surround for underglaze blue or *famille verte* enamel painting.

"Pratt" type. Wares made at the end of the eighteenth and the beginning of the nineteenth centuries, decorated in a distinctive palette of colours, consisting of drab blue, dirty brown, ochre, orange, yellow, and dull green. Made in Staffordshire by Pratt and others; also in South Wales, Liverpool, Sunderland, and Prestonpans.

Printing. The process of printing, or transfer-printing, on pottery and porcelain is carried out by means of "inking" an engraved metal plate. An impression is then taken on thin paper and applied to the article to be decorated. The engraving, being printed with a special ink and used while it is still wet, is thus transferred. This is done on a piece that has been glazed already, and when it is fired the printing sinks into the glaze and a smooth surface results.

The invention is an English one, and its use was practised in the first place at the Battersea enamel works, near London, in 1753. Shortly afterwards it was in use at Worcester and at Liverpool. John Sadler and Guy Green, of the latter town, claimed credit for the original invention, stating that they had made it in 1749. No evidence in favour of this claim has come to light.

The invention proved a workable and economical one, Sadler and Green stating that they had within the space of six hours "printed upwards of twelve hundred tiles of different colours and patterns, which, upon a moderate computation, was more than one hundred good workmen could have done of the same patterns in the same space of time by the usual way of painting with the pencil".

By the year 1764 Wedgwood is known to have been sending plain cream-coloured pottery to Liverpool to be decorated by Sadler and Green by the transfer process. A typical example, a tankard dating from about 1775, is in the Victoria and Albert Museum.

Printing in blue, which was done by a similar process but prior to the application of glaze to the article, was developed at Worcester soon after the invention of the first process, and outstripped the latter in popularity. It was employed extensively at Caughley and by Spode, but an example bearing the Wedgwood mark, dating from about 1840, is shown in Plate 350c.

Punch. Beverage consisting of spirits blended with hot milk or water, sugar, and flavoured with lemon and spice.

Punch-bowl. Large basin for serving hot punch, sometimes called a "jorum".

Purple of Cassius. Discovered by Andreas Cassius of Leyden, in the middle of the seventeenth century. It involved dissolving gold in nitric acid and sal ammoniac.

Puzzle jug. Vessel made in earthenware, delftware, or stoneware with a hollow tube round the lip opening into three or more spouts, and connected with the inside by the hollow handle. Sometimes there is a hole under the top of the handle. The neck is pierced with ornamental motifs, and usually inscribed with a challenge to the drinker. To empty the vessel without spilling the contents it is neces-

FIG. 65

sary to stop all the apertures except one, and to drain it by suction.

Queen's wares. Cream-coloured earthenware improved and marketed by Josiah Wedgwood. He named it "Queen's ware" in honour of Queen Charlotte, the wife of George III.

Red glazes and enamels. The copper-red glazes (q.v.) and underglaze pigment should be distinguished from the vermilion-toned iron-red enamel colour. This was much used in Ming times, is prominent in the K'ang Hsi *famille verte*, and appears also on some *famille rose* wares, and as a monochrome glaze from Yung Chêng.

Redware. Or red-clay pottery. Simple lead-glazed wares of soft, porous body ranging in colour from pinkish buff to reds and brown. (*See also* Slipware, Sgraffiato.)

FIG. 66

Reform flasks. Brown salt-glazed stoneware spirit flasks made by Doulton (Lambeth), Stephen Green (Lambeth), Oldfield (Chesterfield), and Joseph Thompson (Wooden Box Pottery, Hartshorne), in the form of prominent politicians and royalty, at the time of the Reform Bill, 1832. Personalities portrayed included William IV, Queen Adelaide, Lord Grey, O'Connell, Brougham, Richard Cobden, and Lord John Russell (Fig. 67).

FIG. 67

Registry mark. Appearing on English wares in two cycles, 1842–67 and 1868–83. A lozenge with code-letters and numerals assigned by the "Registration of Designs" Office (*see Antiques*, March 1931, pp. 204–6).

Relief decoration. There are various ways of producing relief decoration: by free-hand modelling, free-incising or piercing, or, more frequently, by pressing soft clay in plaster moulds; also by impressing the surface of soft clay objects with cut metal stamps. Occasionally separately moulded low reliefs are applied to the surface.

Repairer. Repairer, or *bossierer*, workman responsible for assembling the porcelain clay impressions from moulds, attaching heads, limbs, etc., and finishing the figure, which was usually modelled by another artist. Incised and impressed marks on figures and groups often refer to these repairers.

Reserved. A surface left plain to receive decoration.

"Resist" lustre. On-glaze decorative process used generally with silver lustre, giving an effect of a light or coloured decoration against a metallic background. The ornament is painted on the ware with a "resist", covered with the metallic solution, and fired; the infusible "resist" being removed by polishing with whiting afterwards.

"Rice-grain" decoration. Small perforations filled with transparent glaze; a technique adopted from Persian pottery, popular during the eighteenth century.

Ridgway. Staffordshire potters at Hanley (1794 onwards) and Cauldon Place, Shelton (from 1812), making mainly stone-china, but also porcelain.

"R" mark. *See* Chelsea, Bow.

Rockingham (England). Little is known about "The R. Works" (near Swinton, Yorks) founded about 1750, but from 1787 to 1806 it was allied to the Leeds Pottery, after which it passed to the Brameld family. The wares are almost indistinguishable from those

FIG. 68

of Staffordshire or Leeds. Distinctive, however, were a streaky dark-brown glaze, and a special ("Cadogan") type of teapot. Porcelain (soft paste) was made from 1820 in the contemporary florid taste (*see* Introduction, English porcelain). Some figures were made, including dogs, models of cottages, etc.

MARKS: BRAMELD and ROCKINGHAM, impressed, and as diagram overleaf.

Rockingham (U.S.). A common yellow ware with lustrous brown manganese glaze, mottled or streaked. The popular misnomer is "Bennington ware", but it was made at

FIG. 69

countless American factories from the 1840s onward. East Liverpool produced "probably fifty per cent of the total" (*see Antiques*, Jan. 1946, pp. 42–4) (Plate 316B).

Rookwood faïence. *See* Art Pottery. The Rookwood Pottery at Cincinnati, Ohio, was founded in 1880 by Mrs Maria L. Nichols (later Mrs Bellamy Storer), first making table-wares, but by 1889 receiving a gold medal at the Paris Exposition for its now widely recognized Art wares.

"Rose-engine-turning." *See* Engine-turning.

Rosso antico. The name given by Wedgwood to his red stoneware, which was a successor to imitations of the "Boccaro" ware imported from China in the seventeenth century. It was decorated by being polished on a grindstone and by means of "engine-turning" applied on a lathe.

"Ruby-back" plates. *See* Famille rose.

Sadler, John (1720–89), of Liverpool. Decorated with transfer-prints pottery, porcelain, and enamels obtained from various sources – notably delftware tiles (from 1756) and Wedgwood's cream-coloured earthenware (from 1761).

Salt-glazed stoneware. Stoneware in which the glaze is formed by throwing common salt into the kiln when it reaches the maximum temperature. The salt decomposes, forming sodium oxide and hydrochloric acid, the former combining with the alumina and silica of the surface of the wares to form a thin coating of glass.

Salt kit. Dome-topped ovoid jar surmounted by a knob and loop-handle with a wide circular aperture at one side; used for storing salt, etc.

Samson. This Paris porcelain factory is well known for clever copies of old armorial Chinese porcelain, which have been made there for more than half a century. The coats-of-arms are often those of Great Britain or of France, or of some famous person, such as Lord Nelson. Examined closely, these copies should not deceive the collector, but in an ill-lighted room a costly mistake might easily be made. Samson's productions sometimes bear a simulated Chinese "seal" mark or a disguised "S" beneath the base in red.

"S. & G." mark. *See* Isleworth.

Sang-de-bœuf. *See* Copper-red glazes.

San ts'ai (three-colour) ware. Generally implies the Ming three-colour ware, but also describes porcelains enamelled "on the biscuit" in *famille verte* yellow, green, and purple during the K'ang Hsi period, and hence also Ming porcelains with this technique.

"Scratch blue." Decoration characteristic of white salt-glazed stoneware comprising incised floral arabesques and inscriptions into which clay stained with cobalt was rubbed. Examples dated from 1724 to 1776 recorded.

"Scratch cross" porcelain. Mainly mugs and jugs, marked underneath with an incised cross and/or strokes inside the foot-rim. Analogies with Worcester and Bristol (soft-paste) porcelain suggest that they were made at one or both of these factories, probably about 1751–5.

Schwarzlot. Black monochrome decoration, sometimes heightened with iron-red or gold. This technique, originating with Dutch glassworkers and Nuremberg faïence painters, was probably first applied to porcelain by Daniel Preissler (1636–1733), of Bohemia, whence it became characteristic for the decoration of Du Paquier porcelain, executed by Jacobus Helchis and others.

Sgraffiato. Cutting away, incising, or scratching through a coating of slip to expose the colour of the underlying body. Popular technique in South Wales, Devonshire, Somerset, and Staffordshire. In the U.S.A. used on redware, especially the Pennsylvania–German show plates (Plate 307B).

An important class of lead-glazed earthen-

FIG. 70

ware of this type was made in Italy from the fifteenth century onwards. The great centre was at Bologna. Incised patterns were sometimes reinforced by adding touches of coloured pigment, and by staining the glaze with metallic oxides.

Shrinkage. The contracting of porcelain after firing by about one-seventh of the size of the mould. Hence the supports, in the shape of tree-trunks or rockery, to prevent contortion after the cooling process.

Shu fu ("Privy Council") ware. Yüan dynasty porcelain of Ching-tê-chên with slightly opaque, bluish-tinged glaze covering moulded relief designs of flying cranes, lotus sprays, and the characters "*shu fu*".

Siamese twins. The "monstrous" birth in Somerset, May 19, 1680, recorded on a *sgraffiato* dish and Bristol Delft platter. The Kentish Siamese twins, Eliza and Mary Chulkhurst (d. 1734, aged 34), occur on red-ware copies of the "Biddenden" cake.

Skillet. Earthen saucepan with three legs.

Slip. A clay watered down to a creamy consistency and normally used either to coat a pot of another colour or to decorate it with lines or dots produced by means of a spouted can.

Slipware. Earthenware decorated with white or coloured slip. (*See also* Combed slip, Sgraffiato, Trailed slip, and Inlaid decoration.) (Plate 307c.)

FIG. 71

"S" mark. *See* Caughley.

"Smaltino." The contemporary Italian name for a pale blue tin-glaze on sixteenth-century Italian *maiolica*; especially at Venice.

"Snowman." Family of porcelain figures, with glaze partially obscuring the modelling.

Mainly of animals, often with a clumsy rosette on the base, made at Longton Hall about 1750.

Snufftaker. Standing Toby jug in the form of an ugly man taking a pinch of snuff, usually with a deep purple-brown lustrous "Rockingham" glaze.

Soapstone. An ingredient in Bristol (soft-paste), Worcester, Caughley, and Liverpool porcelain. (*See* English porcelain, p. 904.)

Soft-paste ("frit" or "artificial") porcelain. Is compounded essentially of white clay mixed with a glassy substance. In England soapstone and bone-ash were also used.

Somerset. Lead-glazed pottery, with incised designs and glaze stained green in patches, was made at Donyatt from mid-seventeenth century onwards, and at Crock Street in the eighteenth and nineteenth centuries.

Southwark. *See* Lambeth.

Spatter. A cheerful range of wares with sponged colour and painted designs, made *c.* 1820–50 in Staffordshire for the American market (Plate 311).

Spinario. Figure of boy extracting a thorn from his foot, copied from statue in the Capitoline Museum, Rome.

Spode. Josiah S. I (1733–96), once a work-man of Whieldon, started a pottery at Stoke-on-Trent about 1770. His son, Josiah S. II (1754–1827) added porcelain (*c.* 1810) to the productions, and is considered the inventor of "bone china"; in 1805 "stone-china" was manufactured. W. J. Copeland became a partner in 1813 and manager in 1829.

MARKS: "Spode", impressed, in blue and red, blue-printed, etc., and as diagram, blue-printed.

"Sponged" ware. A crude, easily recognized peasant style originally made by Adams of Tunstall, and, because of its "bright fancy character" (Jewitt), extensively exported.

Sprigging. The term used to describe the method of ornamenting wares by means of applied reliefs. The "sprigs" are moulded separately and attached to the plaque, vase, or other object by means of water or thinned clay. Wedgwood used sprigging for the decoration of his jasper-ware.

Steen. Originally an earthen vessel with two ears to hold liquids, later used for bread, meat, or fish.

"Stone China." A hard white earthenware containing china-stone, made as a cheap substitute for porcelain in Staffordshire from 1805.

Stoneware. A variable family of hard, high-fired wares mostly salt-glazed, from the

FIG. 72

thin white Staffordshire stonewares of 1720–50 to heavy crocks and jugs of blue-painted grey stoneware so common in the nineteenth century (Plate 305).

Stubbs, George, R.A. The painter who excelled in the delineation of the horse was an acquaintance of Josiah Wedgwood. In 1777–8 the latter was attempting to assist the painter, who wished to attempt enamel-painting by using large plaques of china for the purpose. Three of these made of creamware, one of which is a panel 36 inches in height, painted with a portrait of the potter by Stubbs, are in the Lady Lever Art Gallery, Port Sunlight. Stubbs also designed some cameos with equestrian subjects, and painted on canvas a characteristic "conversation" portrait of Mr and Mrs Josiah Wedgwood and their family. This was exhibited at the Royal Academy in 1780.

Sunderland (Co. Durham). Several potteries here made creamware, often decorated with transfers and/or pink lustre (late eighteenth and early nineteenth centuries).

Sung dynasty (960–1279). *See* Chinese pottery.

Supper-set. For this style of article there is a contemporary notice from which its introduction can be dated with reasonable accuracy. Mrs Philip Lybbe Powys, who carefully recorded the events in her daily life in a series of Diaries covering the years from 1755 to 1809, entered under the year 1797:

> "August 31st. – In the morning we went to London a-shopping, and at Wedgwood's, as usual, were highly entertain'd, as I think no shop affords so great a variety. I there, among other things, purchas'd one of the newly-invented *petit soupee* trays, which I think equally clever, elegant, and convenient when alone or a small party, as so much less trouble to ourselves and servants."

Sussex. Rustic lead-glazed earthenware was made in S. (at Cadborough, Chailey, Brede, Rye, Wiston, Dicker, Burgess Hill, etc.) from the second half of the eighteenth century onwards. The characteristic ware was a red pottery decorated by incisions or stamped depressions (often printer's type) filled with white clay.

Sussex pig. Pottery jug with a loose head used as a cup, enabling the user to drink a hogshead of liquor without disquieting aftereffects. Peculiar to the Sussex factory of Cadborough, Rye, nineteenth century (Fig. 73).

FIG. 73

Swansea (Glamorgan). (1) "The Cambrian Pottery" (1765 onwards), mainly run by L. W. Dillwyn from 1812 until 1831, made most of the typical contemporary Staffordshire wares, including a white earthenware ("opaque china") and a creamware with a rippling surface, blue-printed or painted in lustre or colours (botanical painting done by Thos. Pardo; birds, butterflies, and flowers by

W. W. Young). At this factory was made the Swansea porcelain (*see* Nantgarw). (2) "The Glamorgan Pottery" (*c.* 1813 onwards) made earthenwares of the same types as (1) above.

"Swatow" ware. Porcelains with thick, "fat" glaze and roughly finished, glazed, gritty base, made in S. China and probably exported from Swatow, especially to Japan. Dishes, with wild, powerful painting in red, green, and turquoise enamels and similar underglaze blue wares date from the late sixteenth to seventeenth centuries; also celadon, light-brown and pale-blue monochromes with white slip flowers.

Syngchong. A dealer in Canton *c.* 1800. A large bowl belonging to the Corporation of the City of New York, bearing a view of the city and the arms of the corporation, and dated 1802, is inscribed on the outside of the rim of the base: *This bowl was made by Syngchong in Canton, Fungmanhe Pinxt.*

"T" and "T°" marks. Probably for the modeller Thibaud (Bow, Bristol, Plymouth).

T'ang dynasty (A.D. 618–906). *See* Introduction.

Tao Kuang period (1821–50). Characteristic wares are those minutely painted in *famille rose* style, employing low-toned enamels, and *graviata*, coloured grounds. *Tou ts'ai* decoration was also popular. The body is coarser than in eighteenth-century wares, and the glaze has an oily sheen.

Taws. Marbles or small balls made in earthenware.

Teapoy. An incorrect name for a tea caddy.

Temmoku. Japanese name for wares with lustrous brown glazes, especially Sung Chien wares.

Texts. Wall plaques with lustre "frames" and cottage mantelpiece ornaments in the shape of pedimented façades enclosing a clock, sun, and moon, and boldly lettered scripture verses ("PREPARE TO MEET THY GOD"), nineteenth century.

"TF" mark. *See* Bow, Worcester.

Tickenhall (Derbyshire). Pottery has been made at T. since the Middle Ages, but "T" ware usually connotes a hard, dark-brown lead-glazed earthenware decorated with shaped applied pads of white clay (seven-teenth century), although the name is some-times loosely applied to other slip-wares.

Tiles. All the main English delftware factories made tt. (Lambeth and Bristol, late seventeenth and eighteenth centuries, Liverpool and Wincanton, eighteenth century). Some very rare relief-moulded salt-glazed stoneware tt. are known. Creamware tt. were made at Liverpool and in Staffordshire (late eighteenth century).

Ting. The small three-footed cauldron used as an incense-burner.

Tin glaze. Lead glaze made opaque by the addition of tin ashes.

Ting ware. Light, fine-grained, creamy-white porcelain of the Sung dynasty, with ivory-toned glaze often running into gummy drops; from Ting Chou (Chihli Province). Common forms are shallow-lobed bowls and rimless dishes. The finest examples have decoration of plants or flowers, fish, swimming ducks, etc., freely incised under the glaze. Designs were also impressed from moulds. Ting type wares were also made elsewhere, and at later dates – for example, the "Kiangnan Ting" of S. China, with softer, sandy body and crackled glaze, probably of the Ming dynasty and later. Eighteenth-century imitations of Ting at Ching-tê-Chên do not resemble it in quality.

"Tithe pig." Figure subject in porcelain and earthenware, also used as decoration of mugs and jugs accompanied by such rhymes as "In Country Village lives a Vicar/Fond as all are of Tithes and Liquor". A well-known Toby jug is inscribed "I will have no child tho the X pig". The collection of tithe in kind was abolished by the Tithe Commutation Act, 1836.

"T°" mark. *See* "T".

Toad mug. Surprise mug with a large toad inside, seen only as the vessel is emptied, and causing consternation because of popular superstitions connected with toad poison. Often inscribed "Tho' malt and venom seem united, etc." Made at Sunderland, late eighteenth to the end of nineteenth centuries.

Tobi seiji ("**buckwheat celadon**"). Japanese name for brown-spotted Sung celadon wares of Lung-chüan.

Toby Fillpot. Nickname of a noted toper, Harry Elwes, who, through contemporary engravings, served as model for the original Toby jug.

Toby-jugs. Are shaped like a man seated holding a mug of beer and a pipe, his tricorn hat often forming a detachable lid. Made by Ralph Wood and numerous Staffordshire and Yorkshire imitators, late eighteenth and nineteenth centuries. Many variants are recorded. Also produced at various U.S. factories.

Toft. An often-recurring Staffordshire name on slipware (late seventeenth and early eighteenth centuries), probably that of the potters (*see* Introduction, English pottery).

Torksey (Lincs). W. Billingsley is supposed to have made porcelain here (1802–3). Some rare pieces of coarse material and primitive decoration (cup and saucer in the Victoria and Albert Museum) have been identified.

Tortoiseshell glaze. Mottled glaze stained with manganese and cobalt used by Thomas Whieldon, of Fenton.

"Tortoiseshell ware." A Staffordshire earthenware with mottled, usually brown, lead-glaze (mid-eighteenth century).

Tou ts'ai ("contrasting colour") enamels. Delicate, sparing designs in underglaze blue set off by transparent enamel colours, chiefly red, yellow, and green; their jewel-like quality was perfected under Ch'êng Hua (1465–87). Deceptive imitations and new-style wares were made under Yung Chêng and Ch'ien Lung; and again revived under Tao Kuang (1821–50).

Trailed slip. Slip applied by trailing it from a spouted or tubular vessel.

"Transitional" period. The years of the seventeenth century between the Ming period of Wan Li and the K'ang Hsi revival, when blue-and-white and Ming "five-colour" style wares of some quality were made.

Turner, John (d. 1786). Potter of Stoke and Lane End (Staffordshire), made fine creamware and Wedgwood-type stonewares. His sons continued until 1803.

MARKS: TURNER and TURNER & CO., impressed.

Turquoise blue glazes. *See* Medium-temperature glazes.

Tyg. Beaker-shaped drinking vessel with from two to twelve handles.

Tz'ŭ Chou ware. The Tz'ŭ Chou neighbourhood (Chihli Province) has made stonewares from the Sung dynasty until the present day. The characteristic body is hard and greyish white, covered with slips and glazes of creamy-white, brown, or black, and occasionally green colour, often ingeniously combined. The Sung wares are remarkable for bold, sensitive shapes – especially tall, swelling vases and jars with loop-handles at the shoulder. Plates and dishes are rare. One type of decoration has leafy floral designs strongly incised or carved through the glaze to reveal another colour beneath. Another is bold painting in brown or black. Black painting under a turquoise glaze was popular about the fourteenth century. Red, green, and yellow enamel painting is sometimes of Sung date. Ming wares employed similar techniques, and elaborate landscape and figure subjects became more common; but there is a marked decline in their vitality.

Unaker. See China-clay.

Underglaze blue. Well known from Chinese porcelain, particularly of the Ming period. David Koehler, assisted by Johann Georg Mehlhorn, both working under Boettger at Meissen, rediscovered the secret of applying blue colour beneath the glaze. Apart from its decorative qualities, their discovery made it possible at Meissen to introduce the well-known factory mark of two crossed swords in underglaze blue in 1724.

Underglaze colours. Only a few metallic oxides, notably cobalt, stand the high temperature of the glaze-firing. Manganese-purple was occasionally used. (*See* Underglaze blue.)

Underglaze decoration. Decoration applied to biscuit pottery before the addition of glaze.

Venisons. Bowls "made to fit into one another . . . in capacity ranging from a pint to a peck" (George Bourne), made at Frimley, Cove, and Farnborough, *c.* 1800–50.

"Vicar and Moses." Popular satire on the drinking parson, showing a clergyman asleep in the pulpit with the parish clerk conducting the service. First made by Ralph Wood of Burslem, *c.* 1775.

Wall, Dr. *See* Worcester.

Wall pocket. Flower or spill vase shaped as a mask, fish, or cornucopia, made in Staffordshire salt-glaze, and in Liverpool and Lambeth Delft, eighteenth century.

Walton, John, Burslem. Made small earthenware figures, often with *bocages* and painted in opaque enamels (*c.* 1820–30).

MARK: WALTON, impressed.

Wan Li period (1573–1619). Most of the Chia Ching styles were continued. Porcelain with enamels and underglaze blue painting (the *wu ts'ai*) are especially characteristic. The numerous blue-and-white export wares are very variable in quality, often with poor blue and careless drawing. Pieces expressly intended for Europe become common.

Warburton. Family of potters of Hot Lane, Cobridge (Staffordshire), late eighteenth century. Made creamware.

MARK: WARBURTON, impressed (rare).

Wassail bowl. Two-handled loving cup passed clockwise around the company on convivial occasions.

"Wassailing." Originally a rite to ensure fertility in cereals, fruit crops, and cattle, but later a term of abuse to describe Christmas revels.

Webber, Henry. A modeller employed by Josiah Wedgwood between the years 1782 and 1794, both at Etruria and at Rome with John Flaxman. He was engaged in the copying of the Portland Vase.

Webber received a gold medal from the Royal Academy in 1779. On that occasion he gave his address as "Etruria", and his association with Wedgwood may be ante-dated perhaps from the accepted period given above.

"Wedgewood" mark. Used by W. Smith, Stockton-on-Tees, mid-nineteenth century.

"Wedgwood & Co" mark. *See* Ferrybridge.

Wedgwood, Josiah W. (1730–95), after apprenticeship with his brother and participation in a works at Stoke, entered into partnership with Thomas Whieldon in 1754. These associations made him master of the contemporary Staffordshire pottery techniques in most branches, and in 1759 he set up for himself, first at the Ivy House, Burslem, subsequently at the Brick House Works (1764). In 1768, in partnership with Thomas Bentley (1730–80), he built a new factory, called "Etruria", for making ornamental wares. At these two works he produced: (1) green and yellow-glazed "cauliflower", etc., wares; (2) creamware from about 1765, called "Queen's Ware", enamelled either in the factory or at an establishment in Chelsea, or sent in the white to various outside enamellers or to Liverpool for transfer-printing (*see* Sadler); (3) "marbled" wares; (4) "pearlware", from about 1779; (5) unglazed stonewares: (*a*) black basaltes from about 1767, (*b*) red (*rosso antico*) often rose-engineturned, from about 1763, (*c*) cane-coloured, (*d*) "jasper" in various colours, from about 1774 and "jasper-dip" from about 1780.

Additions to the repertory after W.'s death were "silver"-lustred pottery (up to about 1810), pink lustreware, and bone-porcelain (1812–16).

W. wares after *c.* 1770 were nearly always marked "WEDGWOOD" impressed; "WEDGWOOD & BENTLEY" or "W. & B" occur on decorative pieces 1768–80.

(*See also* English porcelain.)

"Welsh" ware. Shallow meat dishes with feathered slip decoration, in form like a gardener's trug, commonly made in Staffordshire, Sunderland (Scott's "Superior Fireproof") and Isleworth, under this name.

Whieldon, Thomas (1719–95): potter of Fenton Low, Staffordshire, from 1740–80, one of the foremost makers of his day, manufacturing all the known contemporary types of ware – "agate" and "marbled", "tortoiseshell", "Astbury", and "Jackfield" wares; earthenware with dappled coloured glazes, unglazed red stoneware and salt-glazed stoneware, sometimes with "scratch-blue" patterns.

(*See also* English pottery: eighteenth-century earthenware and stoneware; Wedgwood.)

"Whieldon" ware. Ware made in creamcoloured earthenware under a glaze splashed with metallic oxides to give tortoiseshell or mottled effects, made by Thomas Whieldon (1719–95) at Fenton, and others.

White porcelains. White porcelain was

first made during the T'ang dynasty. To the Sung period belong the creamy-white Ting and bluish-tinged *ying ch'ing* wares, with their lively incised or impressed decoration. The Yüan "*shu fu*" ware marks the growing importance of the porcelain manufacture at Ching-tê-chên.

Despite the Ming predilection for colour, excellent white wares were still made, notably during the fifteenth century, with "*an hua*" (secret) decoration. During the Ch'ing dynasty white was the colour of court mourning and not greatly employed. Decorated with incised designs and carved or applied relief work, wares are often reminiscent of the Sung and Ming.

Much use was made of "soft paste" opaque glazes and painting in opaque white slip (*pâte-sur-pâte*), and small pieces were made with "soft-paste" body.

The technique of pierced openwork (*ling lung*), as in the "rice-grain" decoration, was employed with considerable ingenuity. Unglazed (biscuit) porcelain vases with landscapes or figures carved in relief are of Ch'ien Lung or later date. Wares with intentionally crackled glazes and the numerous "*blanc-de-Chine*" wares are discussed elsewhere.

"Willow-pattern." A blue-printed pseudo-Chinese design, traditionally ascribed to T. Minton at Caughley, *c.* 1775–80. Many variants were made elsewhere.

Wincanton (delftware). A pottery was run by the Ireson family between at least 1737 and 1748. Blue and manganese painting only are known. A powdered manganese ground is characteristic.

Wirksworth. W. porcelain, probably made about 1800, remains unidentified. New Hall wares are often mistakenly attributed to W.

"W" mark. *See* Worcester.

"W(***)" mark. *See* Wood, Enoch.

Wood, Aaron (1717–85). The most renowned mould-cutter for Staffordshire salt-glazed stoneware. (*See* Pew-groups.)

Wood, Enoch (1759–1840). Son of Aaron W. Modeller and potter of Burslem, in partnership with Ralph W., 1783–90, and with J. Caldwell, 1790–1818 ("Wood & Caldwell"); thereafter the firm was "Enoch

Wood & Sons". Most of the current types of stoneware, earthenware, and probably also porcelain, were made; notably earthenware figures with enamelled decoration.

MARKS: the various styles of the firm, and probably W(***) on porcelain, all impressed.

Wood, Ralph (1715–72) and his son, R.W. (1748–95). Potters of Burslem. The elder R.W. made salt-glazed stoneware from at least 1749 until 1770. Later productions were figures, reliefs, and Toby-jugs in lead-glazed earthenware (Plate 347c) with soft colours.

MARKS: R. Wood, RA. WOOD, BURSLEM, impressed.

Worcester (soft-paste porcelain).

"Dr Wall" period (1751–1783)

A factory was founded in 1751, and in 1752 incorporated the Bristol factory. The period 1751–83 is called after Dr John Wall (d. 1776), a leading partner, although, in fact, William Davis (d. 1783) managed the factory.

Soapstone was used in the porcelain, and is revealed on analysis by a high percentage of magnesia. The porcelain is greyish (greenish by transmitted light) with a thin, hard-looking, and "close-fitting" glaze, which often shrinks away from the foot-rim underneath. The potting is fine and "crisp". In the early period moulding, after silver models, was much used. The earliest painting, indistinguishable from the Bristol, is characterized by "chinoiseries" in polychrome enamels or underglaze blue. By about 1760 a distinctive W. style evolved, including European figure- and landscape-subjects, often in a soft purple monochrome; polychrome flower-sprays and birds; fantastic Chinese landscapes in panels on a yellow ground; and pseudo-Chinese subjects painted in a thin linear style in black ("pencilled"). Transfer-printing in overglaze black, lilac, and brownish red was much used from 1756/7 (*see* Hancock); underglaze-blue printing was occasionally practised from 1759.

The period about 1765–75 is characterized by the adaptation of *Kakiemon* and "brocaded Imari" designs.

In 1769 Chelsea painters migrated to W. and elaborate decoration in Sèvres style dates from this time, with figure-subjects and particularly exotic birds, in panels on coloured (blue, claret, "apple green", turquoise, and lavender) grounds, which were frequently diapered, the commonest pattern being an imbricated dark-blue ground ("scale blue"). Fine, slightly dull gilding is characteristic, painted in lacy scrollwork designs. Much porcelain was decorated in the workshop of J. Giles.

Towards 1780 neo-classical designs (urns, festoons, etc.) and modified Sèvres *Louis Seize* styles were introduced. Landscapes and classical figure-subjects within medallions were favoured. A bright-blue enamel like that of Chelsea–Derby was used, and gilding was frequently employed alone in floral, etc., designs.

Blue-and-white porcelain characterized by a deep indigo tone formed a large part of the output, whether painted or (from 1759) printed.

Figures are exceptionally rare (a Turk, a Gardener, and a Sportsman, with their companions, and a Nurse and Child).

Imitations are known both in soft- and hard-paste, and in Staffordshire earthenware.

MARKS: 1 and 10 below (in red), 2–12 (in blue), probably workmen's marks, on Bristol

FIG. 74

or early W. (*c.* 1750–2); 13, in red, 14–16 and 18, in blue, painters' marks, *c.* 1752–70; 17, in blue, 19 in various colours (chiefly blue), much used to about 1795; 20, in blue, much used (1755–83).

(*See also* Scratch-cross *and* W.)

"*Fight*", "*Flight & Barr*", *etc.* (1783–)

In 1783 the W. factory was bought by Thomas Flight. In 1792 Martin Barr was taken into partnership, and with the admission of other members of the family the firm became successively "Barr, Flight & Barr" (1807) and "Flight, Barr and Barr" (1813–40).

The style of this period reflected the prevailing neo-classical taste, with areas of marbling and figures in panels, the best by James Pennington and Thomas Baxter. The gilding became brassy and unsympathetic.

MARKS (apart from names written in full): "B" or "DB", incised (to 1809); the initials of the partners, "BFB" and "FBB" under a crown, impressed.

Chamberlain's

In 1783 Robert Chamberlain left the W. factory and set up as a decorator. From about 1800, however, a greyish porcelain resembling Flight and Barr's was manufactured.

C.'s work reflects the contemporary styles, but is notable for profuse gilding, and the production of vases, etc., in the most florid "Japanese" taste.

MARKS: the name.

Grainger's

Thomas Grainger at first (1801) decorated porcelain obtained elsewhere, but latterly manufactured a fine white and translucent porcelain.

MARKS: the name.

"Wreathing." See Bristol.

Wrotham (Kent). Slipware pottery (seventeenth and early eighteenth centuries). (*See* Introduction, English pottery.)

Wu ts'ai (five-colour) wares. This generally implies the characteristic Wan Li period wares, painted in underglaze blue and enamel colours (red, green, yellow, and purple). Some, however, date from Chia Ching; and they continue into K'ang Hsi's reign, when the *famille verte* was introduced.

Yellow. *See* Medium- and low-temperature glazes.

Yellow ware. Utility ware moulds, baking dishes, etc.) of cream or buff clays with transparent glaze ranging from pale straw colour to deep yellow; it became Rockingham (*q.v.*) when given a mottled brown manganese colouring. Widely made *c.* 1830–1900.

Yi-hsing stoneware. Here in Kiangsu were made the unglazed red and brown stoneware teapots which accompanied the new drink to late seventeenth-century Europe. They are often beautifully shaped, rounded, or faceted, with incised or moulded relief decoration. Less pleasing are over-naturalistic forms of tree-trunks or fruit. Signatures of Ming potters are too common for credence; dating is difficult, but later pieces are generally of poorer quality. Crudely enamelled pieces are probably nineteenth century. Glazed imitations of Sung Chün ware are spoken of.

Ying ch'ing ("shadowy blue") ware. Porcelain with brilliant transparent glaze of a pale bluish or greenish tinge, made in Kiangsi and other provinces chiefly during the Sung dynasty. The best examples are of a sugary fracture, thinly and delicately potted: lobed bowls, cups, or vases. Freely incised or moulded designs often resemble those of Ting ware.

Yorkshire. Trailed and marbled slipwares were made at Howcans, Swill Hill, Burton-in-Lonsdale, Midhope (eighteenth century onwards). (*See also* Leeds, Don Pottery, Castleford, Ferrybridge.)

Yüeh ware. Celadon ware with grey porcellanous body and thin, pale, greyish-green, or buff glaze, made in Chekiang Province from about the third to eleventh centuries. Early examples often borrowed forms and moulded decoration from bronze work. Later pieces may be delicately potted, with lobed sides and delicately incised designs.

Zaffer. Cobalt oxide in powder form, from which was made *smalt* (a powdered blue glass) the blue colouring used by potters. Bonnin & Morris in January 1771 wanted "a quantity of Zaffre" for their blue-painted porcelains. The potter John Bell wrote to his brother Samuel in 1848 that "graffree is calcined cobalt or fly stone which is the same thing", warning him that this "coulering matter is rank poison".

PRINTS AND DRAWINGS

The collecting of prints and drawings is one of the oldest pastimes of amateur and connoisseur alike. The reasons are not far to seek. It is one of the most rewarding: there can be few fields of collecting where an ever-widening knowledge can yield treasures acquired for an ever-diminishing outlay; prints and drawings can be easily stored, and the choicest can adorn the walls. And then there is the variety, both in media and kind; lovers of prints can never tire of the incisiveness of a fine proof etching or engraving, where the ink has a deeply satisfying richness and clarity. A collector of prints usually knows exactly what he is looking for; and when he has acquired an impression of a long-sought print the pride of possession gives way to a desire to obtain a yet finer and rarer impression. It must never be forgotten that many of the greatest masters of European painting regarded the print as a worthy medium for their genius.

To a collector of drawings the keenest pleasure lies in the revelation of the unexpected: the vigorously or sensitively drawn figure subject, when subjected to the scrutiny of a scholar, may become indisputably a rare little gem by an Old Master, perhaps only sparsely represented in museums.

There is yet another variety, ranging from Japanese colour prints to American silhouettes, the etchings of Rembrandt, the drawings of Tiepolo to English mezzotints. The field is so inexhaustible that the collector of prints and drawings can decide for himself whether to specialize or to sample all the delights in every sphere.

American

ENGRAVINGS AND WOODCUTS

For the collector, American prints in the wider sense of the word begin with the views of the second half of the sixteenth century, engraved and published in Europe from 1590 onwards; while in the narrower sense they are restricted to prints produced in America, beginning in the middle of the seventeenth century. John Foster of Boston illustrated the books he printed with woodcuts which are the first American prints to which a maker's name can be attached; they hardly merit the word artistic. However, his name stands out in the anonymity of seventeenth-century American engravings, surrounded, as it were, by a number of crude productions by unknown craftsmen who were most likely printers or silversmiths working with simple tools and having little or no training.

Theodore de Bry, a Flemish engraver and copperplate publisher who resided in Frankfurt, Germany, from 1588 until his death in 1598, engraved for his collection of *Great Voyages* the first views and pictorial accounts of the North American mainland with its native inhabitants, their tribal customs, their villages and the flora and fauna of the newly discovered country. Some of the engravings were made after the paintings by Jacques Le Moyne de Morgue, the French explorer who had journeyed to Florida with the Huguenots under René de Laudonnière in 1564. Twenty years later Le Moyne wrote a narrative of his explorations and illustrated his account, entitled *Brevis Narratio*, with forty-three sketches which de Bry engraved and published in 1591. A year earlier de Bry had engraved the drawings by John White, the artist who had accompanied Sir Walter Raleigh on his unsuccessful expedition to Virginia in 1585, and a second time as "Governor of the Colonie" in 1587. Of the seventy-five water-colours by John White – the "first" English water-colours – de Bry engraved twenty-three to illustrate Thomas Hariot's account, *A Briefe and True Report of the New Found Land of Virginia*, for his Virginia volume of the *Great Voyages*, and later two others for the work on Florida. The twenty-three water-colours by John White are now preserved in the British Museum, while of Jacques Le Moyne's small paintings only one is known to exist, in the possession of an American collector; the others are presumed lost. De Bry's collection of *Great Voyages* was issued in a number of editions and translations. Some of the later publications based their illustrations on those which appeared in de Bry's work, but, in addition to these, other travel books written by European explorers and travellers were illustrated with new pictorial material. In Sir Francis Drake's *Expeditio* of 1588 appears the first view of a town within today's limits of the United States, the town of St Augustine in Florida; while the earliest known engraved view of New York, the so-called Hartger's view, was issued with the small book entitled *Beschrijvinghe van Virginia, Nieuw Nederlandt, Nieuw Engelandt ...* published in Amsterdam in 1651. John Ogilby's *America* (London, 1671) contains views of a number of ports in this hemisphere, and in Father Louis Hennepin's *New Discovery of a Vast Country* (London, 1698) there is possibly the earliest view of Niagara Falls. Not only do the early views appear in books, but also as insets on handsome maps like the important maps of the Visscher series published in the middle of the seventeenth century.

Parallel, although on a very different level artistically, was the production of illustrated books in colonial America. The crudity of the early cuts, either wood or type-metal, is more than made up for by their historical importance in the development of the American graphic arts. Their naïve charm somewhat compensates for their lack of artistic quality. It is to John Foster of Boston, who established his printing shop in 1675, that the credit goes for being the first American-born "artist" to have made engravings in this country. His woodcut portrait of Richard Mather, the Massachusetts clergyman (1670), is known in only five impressions. Almost as rare are his other woodcuts, a seal for the Massachusetts Bay Colony in 1675 and a map of New England which appeared in William Hubbard's *Narrative of the Troubles with the Indians* (1677).

It was not until the beginning of the eighteenth century that single prints were published, apart from book illustration. Again the earliest were published in Europe, although drawn in America and advertised for sale in the colonial newspapers. William Burgis was the first to supply large single views of American cities. Very few copies of these views, however, are known to exist, either in first states or in later, second, states, but they can be studied in public collections which are fortunate enough to own them. William Burgis' panoramic views of New York (1719) and Boston (1722) were engraved by John Harris of London and published there, copied and plagiarized by later engravers, no doubt to satisfy the great demand of a curious public eager to know what the new country looked like. In studying these early views we find that some are fairly accurate renderings, others slightly fictitious, while still others, like the colourful *vues d'optique*, show a remarkable fantasy and lack of knowledge of conditions in a pioneering country. These hand-coloured – amusing rather than puzzling – peepshow prints, with reversed lettering in the top margin, and the text often in both German and French, were published in the second half of the eighteenth century in Augsburg and Paris to be used in mirrored boxes and carried around by itinerant showmen.

Not more than about a dozen engravers were working in colonial America in the eighteenth century, and these were primarily engaged in illustrating books, including several Bibles and periodicals. It was from Europe that the colonists received their large prints to be hung on the walls of their homes or, in some few cases, kept in portfolios.

The post-Revolutionary period brought a radical change in the conditions in the field of print-making in this country. Professionally trained painters and engravers arrived in increasing numbers from England and Scotland and settled in Boston, New York, or Philadelphia, where publishers were ready to employ them. Among these was John Hill (Plate 378B). The English artists brought with them the knowledge and techniques of the highly developed art of water-colouring, which had such a vogue in eighteenth-century England, while the engravers were equipped to handle the aquatint process, so well suited to reproduce the water-colours. The beginning of the nineteenth century saw an increased production in the numbers of town and local views and, because of their artistic and picturesque quality, these views are among the most attractive to today's collector. The aquatints were coloured, either by hand or printed from several plates, limiting the use of the process usually to topographical work – to the picturesque rather than mere landscape. Very few attempts were made to use this technique for portraits, which are more suitably engraved in either stipple or mezzotint.

The growing periodical literature gave increasing opportunity for employment to engravers. This had already been done by American editions of British encyclopaedias published in Philadelphia, although there was little chance given for artistic development and imagination. Bank-note engraving was another field for many excellent engravers, who had to meet the high standards of workmanship required for such meticulous work. The first half of the nineteenth century has been called the "Golden Age of Engraving", brought to a close by the activities of a number of art societies which sponsored annual distribution of large engravings to their membership, the most prominent being the Apollo Association, later called the American Art Union, 1839–51. Unfortunately the invention of a number of mechanical ruling devices for use in engraving began to spoil the artistic quality of many of the prints produced towards the middle of the century, which deteriorated to mere hack work. Finally, the photomechanical processes liberated the engravers from mere reproductive work and gave the field of print-making a new lease of life.

Views

The earliest views of American towns appeared in books published in Europe, but they can often be found as separates, either with or without the accompanying text. Single prints of American scenery were not published till the early eighteenth century, and among the earliest are the very rare Burgis views of New York (1719) and Boston (1722), the Boston Lighthouse and the view of the New Dutch Church in New York, dedicated to Governor Rip van Dam. Of equal importance are the panoramic views of Charleston, South Carolina, by B. Roberts (1739) and the Scull-Heap view of Philadelphia (1754). The Carwitham views of Boston, New York, and Philadelphia, published for Carington Bowles of London some time after 1764, are based chiefly on earlier views, although with a character of their own.

These coloured line engravings, signed by John Carwitham, are among the most attractive, although very scarce; later states with alterations exist: however, they are not as valuable.

In 1734 the earliest view of Savannah was engraved by Pierre Fourdrinier after a drawing by Peter Gordon, a bird's-eye view, showing the newly settled town with its straight streets and large squares for markets amidst a wilderness. The view of Philadelphia depicting the House of Employment, Alms House, and Pennsylvania Hospital, about 1767, was engraved by John Hulett after a drawing by Nicholas Garrison, and is another of the important early views of an American city.

One of the handsomest of large collections of topographical prints of North America and the West Indies in the middle of the eighteenth century is the *Scenographia Americana*. This collection, which was published in London in 1768, contains twenty-eight engraved plates. In some cases it has been augmented to include as many as seventy-four, reproducing the drawings made by British army and navy officers. Matching in importance the *Scenographia Americana* is another set of views, the *Atlantic Neptune*, a collection of as many as 275 maps, charts, and views brought together for the British Admiralty by J. F. W. Des Barres during the years 1763–84. This publication includes aquatinted views of American ports.

Following the Revolution a number of very beautiful views were executed by newcomers to America, some using the relatively new aquatint process for reproducing water-colours. Saint-Mémin, in addition to his prolific output of profile portraits, made two charming etchings of New York in 1796. The well-known London aquatinter Francis Jukes reproduced four water-colours by Alexander Robertson, the Scottish artist who had come to New York around 1794 and opened the Columbian Drawing Academy together with his brother Archibald. Included in this set of four views are *New York from Hobuck Ferry* and *Mount Vernon* in 1799.

At the turn of the century William and Thomas Birch, father and son, drew, engraved, and published a set of twenty-eight line engravings entitled: *The City of Phila-*

delphia as it appeared in 1800. The dates on individual plates range from 1798 to 1800. A later edition was published by Birch in 1806 and re-issued by Desilver in 1841. The aquatints by J. Cartwright in the Atkins and Nightingale series of American views are all very rare. They were made after the paintings by George Beck of Philadelphia and published in London between 1800 and 1810. A decade later W. G. Wall executed his water-colours for the justly famous *Hudson River Portfolio* (Plate 378B), a series of twenty aquatinted views engraved by John Hill and published by Henry J. Megarey in New York about 1825. Together with William J. Bennett's nineteen views of American cities (Plate 379A) published in the 1830s, they make up the finest and most desirable group of coloured aquatints in America. In a different style altogether are two other publications containing views of the city of New York. These are the small, well-executed engravings of the Bourne *Views of New York City* (1831) and the Peabody *Views of New York and Environs* (1831–4). Both series contain double plates with accompanying text and were issued in parts.

Among the last aquatinters in this country who engraved views of American scenery were Robert Havell, Jr, who had come to New York after completing the engravings of Audubon's *Birds of America* in London. Havell made two panoramic views of New York, one from the North River (1840), the other from the East River (1844); a view of Hartford, Connecticut, and a view of Niagara Falls. Another was Henry Papprill, who engraved the Catherwood view of *New York from Governor's Island* in 1846, and in 1849 his bird's-eye view of New York from the steeple of St Paul's Church, after a drawing by John W. Hill, published by Henry J. Megarey. Modern impressions, or re-strikes, exist of many of the listed views, and in some cases the original copperplates have been preserved and are owned by public institutions. It is, therefore, advisable for collectors to study the literature on these prints before buying any of them. Sidney L. Smith re-engraved a number of rare American views, but these are all clearly signed and identified; in themselves they are very attractive and in some instances also rare.

Woodcuts and wood-engravings

Mention may be made of the extremely rare, crude, anonymous German woodcut of about 1505 which depicts the Indians of the northern shores of South America and is "the first pictorial representation of any part of the mainland of the western hemisphere". This cut is known in two states and shows the Indians with fearful evidence of cannibalistic habits.

It was not until the middle of the seventeenth century that woodcuts were first printed in colonial America by John Foster of Boston. Not till the eighteenth century, and well into the middle of it, did the artistic quality of the woodcuts improve, decorating pages of farmers' almanacs and broadsides describing cruel deeds and crimes or advertising travelling entertainers. Crude as they are, these cuts have a quaint charm and may attract the collectors of folk art as well as the social historian. James Franklin of Boston and his younger brother Benjamin in Philadelphia are both credited with having made some woodcuts and metalcuts in their printing shops. The Revolution inspired broadsides in the nature of political caricatures, while the post-Revolutionary period created pictorial evidence of the growing national strength and geographical expansion. At the turn of the century Alexander Anderson, a New Yorker, introduced to this country Thomas Bewick's white-line technique of cutting the design on the end-grain of the woodblock instead of on the plank. In this manner Anderson executed nearly ten thousand cuts during his lifetime, for books, periodicals, and commercial ephemera; even if not of great artistic quality, they reflect a certain high standard of craftsmanship (Plate 377C). Among the few other known wood engravers of the first half of the nineteenth century is Abel Bowen, who is known for his large historical woodcut in three sections, *View of Colonel Johnson's Engagement near the Moravian Town*, October 5, 1812, as well as for some cuts for book illustration. Other wood engravers active in the second quarter of the century, supplying illustrations for books and magazines, were Alfred A. Lansing, John H. Hall, Abraham J. Mason, Joseph Alexander Adams, and Benson J. Lossing.

Historical subjects

The first historical print produced in America was Samuel Blodget's *Battle of Lake George*, September 8, 1755, which was published in Boston, December 22 of that year. An English copy was published a year later in London, and like the American edition was accompanied by a pamphlet describing this battle of the French and Indian war. Henry Dawkins' *Paxton Expedition* in Philadelphia in 1764 records an historical event in which Benjamin Franklin played an important part. It is also the earliest known street view of this city. Paul Revere's engravings of the British ships landing their troops in Boston Harbour, 1768, and his print of the "Bloody Massacre" in Boston on March 5, 1770, are foundation stones of American historical engraving. The original copperplate of Revere's *Boston Massacre* is still preserved in the office of the State Treasurer of Massachusetts.

During the Revolution a set of four crude, but highly important historical prints were engraved by Amos Doolittle, showing the *Battles of Lexington and Concord* in 1775 (Plate 378A) after paintings by Ralph Earl. Doolittle also engraved a view of the façade of Federal Hall in New York City after a drawing by Peter Lacour, depicting George Washington's first inauguration in 1789 on its balcony. Another print of the Revolutionary period was made by Bernard Romans, whose *Exact View of the Late Battle of Charlestown* (Bunker Hill), 1775, was re-engraved by Robert Aitkin on a reduced scale and published in the latter's *Pennsylvania Magazine* for September 1775 (issued probably in October of that year) and called a *Correct View* ... Robert Edge Pine's painting of *Congress Voting Independence* exists in an unfinished line and stipple engraving by Edward Savage, *c.* 1794.

The war of 1812 produced the following prints: *The Capture of the City of Washington by the British Forces*, August 24, 1814, a line engraving by an unknown engraver published by John Ryland; John Bower's rather crude prints of the *Battle of Patapsco Neck*, September 12, 1814 and the *Bombardment of Fort McHenry near Baltimore*, on September 13, 1814; a pair of aquatints by Robert Havell, Sr, of the *Attack on Fort Oswego, Lake Ontario*, May 6, 1814 and *Storming of Fort Oswego*, published in 1815; *The Battle of New Orleans*, 1815, *and Death of Major General Packenham*, a line engraving by Joseph Yeager of Philadelphia. Historical prints of the Mexican War were executed almost entirely in lithography.

College views

Among the earliest college views is the Burgis view of Harvard, *Prospect of the Colledges in Cambridge in New England*, in 1726; another early Harvard view was engraved by Paul Revere in 1768. *William and Mary, c.* 1740, the second oldest college view in America, was engraved after a drawing possibly made by the colonial botanist John Bartram. The earliest view of Princeton appears in the New American Magazine for 1760 entitled *Auld Nassovica*, while the second oldest view of this college was engraved by Henry Dawkins (*North-West Prospect of Nassau-Hall*), and was published as a frontispiece to *An Account of the College of New Jersey* (Woodbridge, N.J., 1764). Yale College is first shown in an engraving by Thomas Johnston from a drawing by John Greenwood and published by James Buck, *c.* 1749. King's College (Columbia) is shown prominently in a view of New York from the collection of the *Scenographia Americana* (1768). One of the last college views in the eighteenth century appeared in the *Massachusetts Magazine* for February 1793; this is a view of Dartmouth College in New Hampshire. Beginning with the nineteenth century, the number of college views increases rapidly. Alvan Fisher drew a "North East View" of Harvard as well as a "South View", which were engraved and published in 1823. The University of Virginia appears as an inset on a map of the state published in 1825 and engraved by B. Tanner. J. H. Hinton, in his *History and Topography of the United States* (1830–1), included views of Amherst College, Massachusetts, and Kenyon College, Ohio. William Henry Bartlett drew a view of Yale College in 1839 which was engraved

and issued in N. P. Willis' *American Scenery* (1840). J. W. Barber's view of *New Haven Green with Buildings of Yale College* is much sought after by collectors, as is the view of Dartmouth College by Christian Meadows, 1851.

Portraits

From among the great number of portraits executed in America in the period under discussion a few may be mentioned here either for their historical importance or for their artistic merit. The first woodcut portrait produced in America was made by John Foster, the Boston printer, in 1670. This is the portrait of Richard Mather, the New England clergyman and grandfather of Cotton Mather, whose portrait was engraved in mezzotint by Peter Pelham, a London-trained engraver who had come to America and executed a series of mezzotint portraits of clergymen about 1727. Paul Revere engraved the portraits of Samuel Adams, Benjamin Church, John Hancock, Jonathan Mayhew (Plate 377A), and others. Amos Doolittle, the engraver of four important battle scenes of the Revolution, also engraved a number of small portraits. Late in the eighteenth century Charles Willson Peale made a few and very rare mezzotint portraits of Benjamin Franklin, Lafayette, William Pitt, and George and Martha Washington. John Norman is credited with having made the first engraved portrait of George Washington in 1779 as well as a series of other historical portraits. H. Houston of Philadelphia did some meritorious portrait engravings in stipple, as did Edward Savage, a native American engraver who had studied in London. His important portraits are those of John Adams, Benjamin Franklin, and George Washington. Cornelius Tiebout is called the first American-born engraver of any artistic talent. He engraved portraits of George Washington, John Jay (Plate 377B) after Gilbert Stuart, and the generals of the American Revolution. Charles B. J. Févret de Saint-Mémin, a French nobleman who, while earning his living in New York and Philadelphia by making profile crayon drawings with the aid of the *physionotrace* and reducing them with a pantograph on to the copperplate which he then etched and aquatinted, executed about eight hundred portraits of distinguished American ladies and gentlemen. Another engraver who used the aquatint process for portrait work was William Strickland. David Edwin was an excellent and prolific engraver of stipple portraits and has been called "the American Bartolozzi" by Stauffer. James Barton Longacre executed some very fine stipple portraits, among them one of Andrew Jackson after a painting by Thomas Sully (1820). Longacre is also responsible for many of the plates in the *National Portrait Gallery* (1834–9), in four volumes, which he published together with the painter James Herring. Asher Brown Durand, before becoming known as the father of American landscape painting, was a very fine engraver of portraits in line. J. F. E. Prud'homme did fine portrait work in stipple, while John Rubens used both stipple and mezzotint for his many portrait engravings.

No other person in America has been so much portrayed as George Washington. Hart, in his catalogue of the engraved portraits of George Washington, lists eight hundred and eighty entries with several states adding up to a number close to fifteen hundred. The largest number of these are engravings after the paintings by Gilbert Stuart.

AMERICAN LITHOGRAPHS

Lithography began to be used in the United States soon after the painter Bass Otis did two drawings on stone in 1819–20. Otis apparently had no idea of the possibilities of lithography, but they were soon realized and utilized. Only about seven years later Rembrandt Peale, in his copy of his own painted portrait of Washington, showed real understanding of what could be done by this new process (Plate 380A).

That the new process had importance through possible service to business appeared from the start. What concerns us here is that this exploitation for profit has provided a very large storehouse of documentary material. And historical documentation is an important function of antiques.

It is an impressive, many-sided picture of American life and its rural and urban setting that is presented in this mass of publications serving popular interest and demand.

Portraits there are in large number, including many good ones. Among those who signed them were Henry Inman, Albert Newsam, Charles Fenderich, F. D'Avignon (who did a series of drawings in delicate, silvery grey, after daguerreotypes by Brady), L. Grozelier, C. G. Crehen (portrait of the painter W. S. Mount) and Fabronius. There are also the numerous portraits of North American Indians by J. O. Lewis, King, and Catlin (Plate 380C).

Views of natural scenery were done by Charles Gildemeister, E. Whitefield, Mrs Frances F. Palmer (who drew a number of country scenes for Currier & Ives), Charles Parsons, and others. Pictures of rural life were offered by various artists, among them Louis Maurer (his *Preparing for Market*, 1856 (Plate 382B), is full of detail in picturing farmyard appearance, wagon construction, harness). In these the life of the gentleman farmer is often accentuated, and they present also an interesting record of suburban architecture.

City views were numerous, naturally, giving expression to local pride in urban development. Avoiding a catalogue, here are a few names: Maverick (Plate 381A, view of Wall St, New York), A. J. Davis the architect (Plate 382A), C. W. Burton (panoramic view of New York), Max Rosenthal (Independence Hall, Philadelphia, 1846, printed in colours by L. N. Rosenthal). Interest in the city and its life brought also pictures of city types, including such valuable items as the series on New York's volunteer firemen, by Louis Maurer. Other human figures thus preserved are the "Bowery B'hoy", and people skating on ponds in parks and elsewhere, with a show of changing fashions in dress. Dress brings to mind the uniforms of military companies, of which there is a notable array in drawings such as those by A. Hoffy and F. J. Fritsch.

(The latter's large prints of the 38th Regiment, Jefferson Guards, 1843, and the First Division, 1844, have been collected as highly interesting New York views.) To this record of military dress are to be added the many illustrated sheet-music covers of marches dedicated to various military companies, many of them grenadier guards wearing the French high bearskin shako. These covers usually show uniformed members of the company in question, and they give a valuable record of militia uniforms that is scattered and apparently cannot be found in any collected form.

Transportation is another speciality dealt with in lithographs. Railway prints are numerous; Gen. Wm. Barclay Parsons brought together a considerable number of them. Sailing vessels were portrayed by Charles Parsons and others in good number.

Sports were also much pictured. Hunting and fishing scenes, ably done by A. F. Tait and Louis Maurer, bear the stamp of actual experience and interest and add their part to the colourful panorama of our social life. Horse-races were naturally a popular subject. Pictures of trotting races and trotters show changes in the form of vehicle used. The numerous portraits of individual horses, running and trotting, included one of Hambletonian, the famous sire of trotting horses, shown with his owner at Chester, New York.

There was also the separately published political caricatures of obvious importance to the historian. Large collections of these may be seen in the New York Historical Society, the American Antiquarian Society, Worcester, the New York Public Library, the Library of Congress, and other institutions.

Theatre posters illustrate still another phase of American social life. Designed by Matt Morgan, H. A. Ogden and H. F. Farny, among others, and printed by various firms such as the Strobridge Lithographic Co., many of these productions are so large as to make preservation a problem. However, they have been collected, and towards the end of the nineteenth century there came a vogue, almost a craze, which resulted in numerous articles and books, exhibitions, and much collecting activity. Advertising art also made use of lithography, and examples of this are finding their way into collections of industrial subjects. Still other specialities come to mind, for instance Christmas cards, for the designing of which Louis Prang enlisted the services of well-known artists.

All this pictorial material evidently had its appeal, to which the public made a response that is reflected in the productiveness of the many lithographic printing firms. The name of Currier & Ives is apt to come first and most easily to mind, but there were plenty of others competing with them.

In the enormous mass of material here hinted at there is very much of great interest and value to collectors and historians, and in fact to anyone interested in the development of American social and political life. It is to be noted also that from the 'forties and 'fifties drawings of similar subjects and interest, engraved on wood, were appearing in illustrated weeklies and comic papers.

Quite naturally he who collects as well as he who writes history should carefully examine this output of the nineteenth century before choosing. For instance, the sentimental bits relating to domestic life have no great interest save in showing what the public bought. The Civil War battle scenes put out by Currier & Ives are quite negligible. But when the same firm issued pictures based on actual contact of the artist with the scene depicted, as in the pictures of New York City's volunteer firemen, or hunting subjects, or country life, we were given valuable pictorial illustration of social history.

Here, then, is a rich field to delve into. Critical discrimination in choice will still leave a full storehouse, a crowded one, of pleasure and profit.

AMERICAN MARINE PRINTS

Naval pictorial art emerged in America as soon as national pride demanded it. It was not until the country became a nation on its own, with a navy of its own, that pictures of naval and maritime accomplishments were created. American primitive art had started in colonial days, but its subjects were those close to the hearts of the people and their everyday life.

The task of recording pictorially the history of the country from its colonial days until after its independence from England fell upon artists and engravers of foreign lands. There was a dearth of material produced even in the mother country.

The Revolutionary War

It was not until the outbreak of the Revolutionary War that an American warship sailed the seas, and it was later before there appeared an American picture of an American ship. The people were too busy fighting the war to have time to paint or engrave its events. It fell upon well-established British and French artists and engravers to be the "combat artists" of the American Revolution.

Joseph F. W. Des Barres of London published *The Atlantic Neptune* in 1777, a book of charts "for the use of the Royal Navy of Great Britain". Among the charts appeared sketches of landfalls and port views. One of the most handsome of these aquatints shows *The "Phoenix" and the "Rose" Engaged by the Enemy's Fire Ships and Galleys on the 16 August, 1776*. This naval action was the first important one of the American Revolution, and the print the first view of the war to be published.

Naval historians consider the Battle of Lake Champlain in October 1776, early in the war, to rank in importance with Admiral De Grasse's fleet action off Chesapeake Bay at the war's end. Although lost by the Americans, the Lake Champlain action was important because it delayed the advance of British troops until winter set in. Contemporary engravings published in London by Robert Sayre and John Bennett record this battle.

Naturally enough these prints published in England generally record British victories. Other examples are two prints which appeared in *The Naval Chronicle* in 1814 showing the disembarkation of British troops on Long Island on August 22, 1776, and Sir George Collier's victory over a small Continental fleet in Penobscot Bay, August 13, 1779. A map,

engraved by William Faden, London, 1778, is illuminated with drawings of warships which took part in the action off Mud Fort in the Delaware River on October 22, 1777. Lieutenant W. Elliott, Royal Navy, also produced an aquatint of this attack, an action not entirely favourable to the British.

Pictures of naval engagements of the Revolutionary War were few, indicative perhaps of the lack of importance which the British placed upon the war. There was one engagement, however, which is generously depicted, the battle between the *Bon Homme Richard* and the *Serapis*, off the coast of England on September 23, 1779. Although it was a victory for Captain John Paul Jones, it is also remembered with pride in England because the *Serapis*, although sunk, achieved its purpose of protecting a convoy of merchant ships, and because of the gallantry of the British commander, Captain Richard Pearson. British artists produced pictures of the battle, the most notable of which is the line engraving published by John Boydell after a painting by Richard Paton.

The quasi-war with France

It was not until the quasi-war with France, 1799–1801, that the first completely American prints appeared. Edward Savage, an American-born engraver of Philadelphia, brought out a pair of aquatints in 1799 depicting the action between the *Constellation* and the *Insurgent*, the principal engagement in this naval war.

The war with Tripoli

Several naval subjects appeared at the time of the romantic war with Tripoli (1801–5). This war was the result of attacks by the Barbary pirates on American shipping in the Mediterranean, and in it the United States managed to convince the Barbary States that she was an established nation. There were incidents in the Tripolitan War which captured the imaginations of Americans interested in the fortunes of their young navy. Print-makers were ready with depictions of Stephen Decatur's bold destruction of the captured frigate *Philadelphia*, and of the unfortunate explosion of the fireship *Intrepid* before she was able to destroy enemy ships in the harbour of Tripoli. The former is recorded in an aquatint by Francis Kearny, published in New York in 1808. An illustration of the *Intrepid* incident appears in *The Port Folio* in 1810. Charles Denoon drew interesting views of the loss to the Tripolitans of the *Philadelphia*, and Preble's bombardment of Tripoli.

The War of 1812

The war of 1812 was principally a naval war, and from the pages of its history emerge names of naval engagements which have been pointed to with pride by Americans ever since. Artists and print-makers have not been the least among the naval historians to make these battles famous.

The city of Philadelphia was the centre of artists and engravers of naval pictures at the time of the war of 1812. Thomas Birch (1779–1851), who had taken up marine painting in 1807, was the artist of many well-known engagements of the war: the *Constitution* and the *Guerrière*, August 1812; the *Wasp* and the *Frolic*, October 1812; the *United States* and the *Macedonian*, October 1812; the Battle of Lake Erie, September 1813; the *Peacock* and the *Epervier*, April 1814; and the *Constitution* versus the *Cyane* and the *Levant*, February 1815; all American victories.

Engravers of these Birch views were Cornelius Tiebout, Francis Kearny, Denison Kimberly, Samuel Seymour, Benjamin Tanner, Alexander Lawson, William Strickland, P. S. Duval, and Abel Bowen, most of them of Philadelphia, and all of them well known in the world of print-makers.

The battles named above were also painted by J. J. Barralet, Michèle Corné, Thomas Sully, Thomas Chambers, W. A. K. Martin, and George Thresher. Prints were published by Freeman and Pierce, William Kneass, J. R. Smith, Samuel Walker, William Smith, Joseph Delaplaine, H. Quig, J. Baillie, D. W. Kellogg and Cammeyer & Acock.

Other well-remembered American victories have been recorded in prints and paintings, such as the engagement between the *Constitution* and the *Java*, December 1812; the *Hornet* and the *Peacock*, February 1813; the *General*

Pike and the *Wolf*, September 1813; the *Enterprise* and the *Boxer*, September 1813; Macdonough's victory on Lake Champlain, September 1813; the bombardment of Fort McHenry, September 1814; and the battle of Lake Borgne, Louisiana, December 1814. Outstanding among the pictures of these battles is an engraving by Benjamin Tanner after a painting by Hugh Reinagle of Macdonough's victory; a lithograph by H. R. Robinson of the victory of the *Enterprise*, and an aquatint of the bombardment of Fort McHenry by J. Bower showing "the bombs bursting in air", as seen on that occasion by the writer of the *Star Spangled Banner*, Francis Scott Key.

A number of naval prints originated in periodicals contemporary with the war of 1812. *The Naval Monument* was one of these. Most of the engravings are by Abel Bowen, W. Hoogland, W. B. Annin, and Wightman after originals by Michèle Corné. Works of Corné are also reproduced in *The Naval Temple*. Thomas Birch drew for another periodical, *The Port Folio*, and Samuel Seymour did the engraving. Printed later (1840) was the *United States Military Magazine*, which carried lithographs by J. Queen after J. Evans and Thomas Birch. This magazine specialized in pictures of uniforms. Portraits of naval officers are reproduced in the *Analectic Magazine* appearing in 1813.

The war with Algiers

The fifth war fought by the U.S. Navy was brief and almost bloodless. Algiers attempted extraction of tribute money from American ships, as had her neighbour, Tripoli. She had a free hand in such practice until the war with England ended. In June 1815, however, squadrons under Decatur and Bainbridge appeared off Algiers, as the result of which threat the Dey released American prisoners and signed a treaty. This short chapter in our naval history is illustrated with several small prints, principally appearing in magazines of the day. One of the best shows *The U.S. Squadron, under the Command of Com. Decatur at anchor off the City of Algiers, June 30th, 1815*, published in New Haven by N. Jocelin and G. Munger.

Portraits of naval ships

A classification of naval picture, different from the "naval action picture", is the ship "portrait" which shows the likeness of a ship when not engaged in battle.

The best known and most frequently painted ship of the U.S. Navy is the *Constitution*. She was one of a group of frigates to be built by the Congress when the infant republic first realized the need for a regular navy, and she remains afloat today, 160 years after her launching.

One of the earliest portraits of the *Constitution* is an engraving by Abel Bowen (1790–1850) of Boston, the publisher of *The Naval Monument*. The artist was William Lynn. The Senefelder Lithographic Company produced another portrait of "Old Ironsides" about 1830 after a drawing by William Marsh, Jr, copied on stone by James Kidder. The same print appeared later under the name of William S. Pendleton, who took over the Senefelder presses after 1831. Other portraits of this famous ship are: lithographs by J. Baillie, three by P. S. Duval after J. Evans, 1840; engravings by J. Thackara; a drawing by O. E. Linton.

Just as there was a surge of shipbuilding activity a few years after the Revolutionary War which added famous frigates to the American Navy, so was the War of 1812 followed by the creation of great ships-of-the-line. Four of these, the *Washington*, *Independence*, *Franklin*, and *Columbus*, were built in the last years of the war. The names of later ones indicate the start of the practice of naming battleships after states. They were the *North Carolina*, launched in 1820; *Delaware*, 1820; *Ohio*, 1821; *Pennsylvania*, laid down in 1822 but not launched until 1837, and *Vermont*, launched in 1845 after twenty-seven years' building.

These impressive ships were popular subjects with artists, engravers, and lithographers. The *Delaware* seems to have been the most popular of all. J. Hill shows her on the stocks at Gosport (now Norfolk), Virginia. A pair of lithographs published by Childs & Inman after J. G. Bruff show her entering America's first dry dock (still in use) at Gosport Navy Yard in 1836. There are three oil paintings by James C. Evans and an Endicott lithograph after an Evans painting. A tempera in the Roosevelt Collection shows the *Delaware* off Naples. N. Currier produced a small folio print. A lithograph by F. W. Moore seems to be after an Antoine Roux painting.

The *Ohio* was lithographed by J. C. Sharp, Endicott & Co., and N. Currier. A view of the launching of the *Pennsylvania* appears as a lithograph published by Lehman & Duval, and there are portraits by Gibbs & Co. and N. Currier. Currier, in fact, published prints of all these ships-of-the-line. A spirited view of the *Pennsylvania* in a storm is in an aquatint by W. J. Bennet after J. Pringle. The *North Carolina* was painted by Henry Walke and Cammillieri. She was lithographed by Ensign & Thayer and appears on a sheet-music cover.

The peacetime Navy

During some eleven years scattered throughout the country's first forty years, the American people had been at war. The period of quiet which followed gave the nation three decades in which to build up its economy. The navy was active during these years, playing its part in the protection of merchant marine and the expansion of American trade.

One phase of this period had to do with the opening of the Far East to American trade. In 1842 Commodore Lawrence Kearny sailed to China to protect interests of the United States in incidents connected with the British–Chinese Opium War. Kearny's work extended further and before he was through he had done much to increase China's trade with America. A formal trade treaty was made the following year by Caleb Cushing, who sailed for China in the steam frigate *Missouri*. A pair of lithographs published by Day & Haghe, London, and one by N. Currier, show the untimely end of the *Missouri* by fire at Gibraltar while on the way to China. Cushing continued his voyage in the frigate *Brandywine*.

The treaty which Cushing brought back was ratified by Congress and was returned to the Chinese Government by Commodore Biddle in the ship-of-the-line *Columbus* in company with the sloop-of-war *Vincennes*. Before returning to the United States, Biddle made the first attempt to open the fast-closed trade door to Japan. A lithograph by Wagner & McGuigan after drawings by John Eastley shows the *Columbus* and *Vincennes* in the Bay of Jeddo (Tokyo), surrounded by hundreds of Japanese craft. These boats finally helped to tow the American ships out of the Bay, "rejoicing", as the title puts it, "that they had rid themselves so easily of such a number of Barbarians".

Although Biddle's visit to Japan failed, he learned customs and protocol which were valuable to Commodore Matthew C. Perry in his successful venture on the same mission in 1853. Lithographs by Sarony & Company and others by Hatch and Severin show Perry's imposing squadron at Jeddo and details of the theatrical pomp which the astute Perry knew would appeal to the Japanese. Perry's official report, a two-volume publication, is generously illustrated with lithographs by Sarony & Company.

Two prints, one by J. L. Keffer and one by J. H. Bufford, Boston, bring to mind one other incident which occurred in this period when the door to the Orient was being opened. Commander A. H. Foote with the sloops-of-war *Portsmouth* and *Levant* was attempting to withdraw American neutrals from Whampoa lest they become involved in British–Chinese hostilities in 1856. Despite an understanding with Chinese authorities, the American ships were fired upon and denied passage beyond the "barrier forts". The prints show the exchange of fire and the landing of a force of Americans to attack the forts from land.

Captain Ingraham Vindicating American Honor is the title of a lithograph by Endicott & Company recalling an incident which took place in the harbour of Smyrna in July 1853. Martin Koszta, a naturalized American citizen, was arrested by Austrian officials and held aboard a warship in the harbour. Commander Ingraham, of the sloop-of-war *St Louis*, took the initiative in the situation, anchored abreast of the Austrian warship and, with loaded guns, demanded Koszta's release. As a result, the man was placed in neutral hands ashore.

The Boston lithographers, Lane & Scott,

brought out a print of the departure from Boston of the sloop-of-war *Jamestown* for Ireland, laden with food for the relief of victims of the Irish famine. The Irish people replied with a lithograph (published by W. Scraggs) of the *Jamestown* entering the Cove of Cork, April 13, 1847. The caption states the print to be "commemorative of the splendid generosity of the American government in dismantling a ship of war for a Mission of Peace and Charity".

A handsome lithograph was published in England at the time of the joint British–United States venture of laying the Atlantic telegraph cable in 1856. This print, published by W. Foster, London, shows the U.S. Steam Frigate *Niagara* together with H.M.S. *Agamemnon* laying the cable.

The Mexican War

In 1846 the controversial Mexican War broke out over the disputed Texan frontier and ended in the annexation of the territories of Texas, New Mexico, and California, and the establishment of the Rio Grande River as the United States–Mexican border. The U.S. Navy's principal part in this war was to transport General Wingfield Scott's army to Vera Cruz, whence it could move on Mexico City, carrying the war to the heart of Mexico.

Lieutenant H. Walke, U.S.N., served aboard the bomb-brig *Vesuvius* in the naval operations against Mexico. Possessed of artistic talents, he made paintings of the movements of the ships in this expedition. Eight of his views were produced as lithographs by Sarony & Major under the title *Naval Scenes of the Mexican War*.

Another U.S. Navy lieutenant, Charles C. Barton, drew Mexican War scenes of the landing of General Scott's army which P. S. Duval, Philadelphia lithographer, reproduced on stone. In Frost's *Pictorial History of the the Mexican War* appeared a spirited picture of the Vera Cruz landing, lithographed by Wagner & McGuigan. Nathaniel Currier, alert as ever for news pictures, secured from a midshipman a sketch for his lithograph, *Attack of the Gun Boats upon the City and Castle of San Juan de Ulloa* (Vera Cruz).

(A) Twenty five ton Passenger Engine. Made by Lawrence Machine Shop, Lawrence, Massachusetts. Drawn by A. Lederle; lithograph, S. W. Chandler, Boston, 1853. *Collection of C. L. Winey.*

(B) The Arkansas: built by McKay Iron & Locomotive Works, Jersey City, Lithograph, Charles H. Crosby & Co., Boston. No date. *Collection of C. L. Winey.*

PLATE 385

(A) Carrolton Viaduct. Drawn on stone by Moses Swett. Lithograph, Endicott & Swett, *c.* 1831. *Kennedy Galleries.*

(B) Portage Bridge. Lithograph, Compton & Co., Buffalo, New York, from drawing by J. Stilson, *c.* 1865. *Kennedy Galleries.*

PLATE 386

(A) American Autumn. Starucca Valley viaduct, Erie Railroad. Painted by Jasper Cropsey; chromolithograph, T. Sinclair, Philadelphia, 1865. *Kennedy Galleries.*

(B) Across The Continent, Westward The Course of Empire Takes Its Way. Drawn by F. Palmer after J. M. Ives; large folio; Currier & Ives, 1868. *Collection of C. L. Winey.*

PLATE 387

Original silhouette of an unknown man, by William H. Brown, 1808–82. The subject is shown against a background drawn in crayon. *Collection of C. F. O'Connor, New York.*

PLATE 388

(A) The Town Crier and John Bowen of Barnstable by William James Hubard. *Valentine Museum, Richmond, Virginia.*

(B) Dr E. A. Holyoke of Salem, 1728–1829, by Master Hankes. *Essex Institute, Salem, Massachusetts.*

(C) Equestrian subject by William James Hubard. *Valentine Museum. Richmond, Virginia.*

PLATE 389

(A) Painted silhouette of Robert Bolling, Peters-berg, Virginia, 1781, signed Chapman. *Collection of Mrs Francis Hartman Markoe, née Rebecca Bolling.*

(B) Silhouette of Titian R. Peale, Philadelphia, against a lithographic background, by Édouart, 1842. *The Old Print Shop, Harry Shaw Newman.*

PLATE 390

(A) David Wadsworth by William Bache. *Wadsworth Atheneum, Hartford.*

(B) Painted and shaded profile signed by Bache. *Essex Institute, Salem, Massachusetts.*

(C) Hollow-cut Peale silhouette with the rare PEALE stamp. *Library of Congress.*

(D) A Peale head, the curls delicately executed; hollow-cut. *Library of Congress.*

PLATE 391

(A) Landscape Composition (pencil and wash) by Alexander Cozens. *Victoria and Albert Museum, London.*

(B) Holt Bridge on the River Dee (black chalk heightened with white) by Richard Wilson. *Birmingham Museum and Art Gallery.*

PLATE 392

(A) Landscape (black chalk) by Thomas Gainsborough. *Victoria and Albert Museum, London.*

(B) Cart and Team (pencil) by John Constable. *Victoria and Albert Museum, London.*

PLATE 393

Summer Morning (mezzotint) by David Lucas, after John Constable. *P. & D. Colnaghi & Co. Ltd.*

PLATE 394

(B) Lt-Col. Banastre Tarleton (mezzotint) by John Raphael Smith, after Reynolds. *P. & D. Colnaghi & Co. Ltd.*

(A) Margaret Smith (line engraving) by William Faithorne, after Van Dyck. *P. & D. Colnaghi & Co. Ltd.*

PLATE 395

(A) Three Heads (pencil) by Sir David Wilkie. *Victoria and Albert Museum, London.*

(B) Alinda (mezzotint-stipple and crayon) by William Ward.
P. & D. Colnaghi & Co., Ltd.

PLATE 396

(A) The Interior of the Fives Court with Randall and Turner sparring (aquatint) by **Charles** Turner, after T. Blake. *Vicars.*

(B) Epsom, Settling Day at Tattersall's (aquatint) by Charles Hunt, after **James Pollard.** *Fores & Co.*

PLATE 397

(A) First Introduction to Hounds (aquatint) by J. Harris, after H. Alken. *Parker Gallery*.

(B) A Sudden Squall in Hyde Park drawn and etched by Thomas Rowlandson, aquatinted by
T. Malton. *Frank T. Sabin*.

PLATE 398

(A) Battle of Trafalgar (aquatint) by J. Jeakes, after T. Whitcombe. *Parker Gallery*.

(B) Entrance to the Strand from Charing Cross (lithograph) by T. S. Boys.

PLATE 399

(A) Charles XII of Sweden, engraved by John
Smith after David Von Krafft, 1701. *Private
Collection.*

(B) John Philpot Curran, Esq., engraved by
John Raphael Smith after Sir Thomas Lawrence, 1801. *Frederick B. Daniell & Son, London.*

(c) The Gower Family, engraved by John Raphael Smith after George
Romney, 1781. *Frederick B. Daniell & Son, London.*

PLATE 400

Mary, Duchess of Ancaster, engraved by James McArdell after Thomas Hudson, 1757. *Private Collection*.

PLATE 401

(B) Diana, Viscountess Crosbie, engraved by William Dickinson after Sir Joshua Reynolds, 1779. *Private Collection.*

(A) Lady Elizabeth Keppel, engraved by Edward Fisher after Sir Joshua Reynolds, 1761. *Private Collection.*

PLATE 402

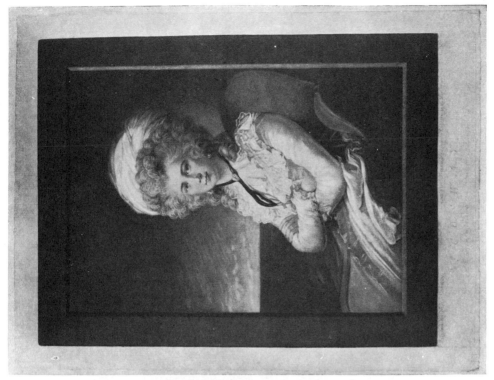

(A) Miss Cumberland, engraved by John Raphael Smith after George Romney, 1779. *Frederick B. Daniell & Son, London.*

(B) Mrs Cosway, engraved by Valentine Green after Maria Cosway, 1787. *Frederick B. Daniell & Son, London.*

PLATE 403

Wild Turkey. Hand-coloured aquatint. Drawn by Titan Peale, *c.* 1825. Engraved by Alexander Lawson.

PLATE 404

Cockerel. Hand-coloured engraving. Drawn by F. H. Frisch, *c.* 1740.

PLATE 405

Wood Duck. Hand-coloured engraving. Drawn by X. Manetti, *c.* 1770.

PLATE 406

(B) Parakeet. Hand-coloured engraving. Drawn by P. Brown, 1776.

(A) The Dodo. Hand-coloured engraving. Drawn by G. Edwards, 1757.

PLATE 407

(B) Oiseau de Paradis Rouge. Engraving printed in colour and finished by hand. Drawn by J. Barraband, *c.* 1810.

(A) Colombe Muscadivore. Engraving printed in colour and finished by hand. Drawn by P. de C. Knip, *c.* 1810. Engraved by C. Macret.

PLATE 408

(B) Der Pirol – Oriolus Galbula. Hand-coloured engraving. Drawn by J. C. Susemihl, c. 1800.

(A) Finches. Hand-coloured engraving. Drawn by P. Paillou, c. 1765.

PLATE 409

(B) The Golden Winged Woodpecker. Hand-coloured engraving by M. Catesby, c. 1735.

(A) Geay Bleu du Canada. Hand-coloured engraving. Drawn by F. Martinet, c. 1770.

PLATE 410

Avocet. Hand-coloured lithograph. Drawn and lithographed by J. Gould and H. C. Richter, c. 1870.

PLATE 411

(A) St Christopher: woodcut, dated 1423. The earliest dated European print. *John Rylands Library, Manchester.*

(B) Death, Famine, War and Plague: from the Apocalypse, woodcut by Albrecht Dürer, *c.* 1495–1500. *British Museum, London.*

(C) The Battle of Ten Nudes: line engraving by Antonio Pollaiuolo, late fifteenth century, *Metropolitan Museum.*

PLATE 412

(A) The Flagellation: line engraving by Andrea Mantegna, late fifteenth century. *Boymans Museum, Rotterdam.*

(B) Diogenes: chiaroscuro woodcut after Parmigianino by Ugo da Carpi, early sixteenth century. *British Museum.*

(C) The Death of Lucretia: line engraving by Marcantonio Raimondi, probably after a drawing by Raphael, early sixteenth century. *British Museum, London.*

(D) Line engraving from the Apocalypse series by Jean Duvet, mid-sixteenth century. *British Museum, London.*

PLATE 413

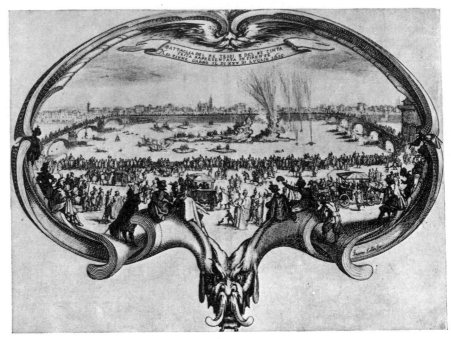

(A) L'Eventail: etching of a fête given on the River Arno in 1617, by Jacques Callot.
British Museum, London.

(B) Landscape with a Sportsman and Dogs: etching by Rembrandt van Rijn, *c.* 1652.
City Art Gallery, Leeds.

PLATE 414

(A) The Port of Dolo on the Brenta: etching by Antonio Canale, called Canaletto, 1741. *Craddock and Barnard, London.*

(B) Satyrs and a Nymph: etching by Jean Honoré Fragonard, 1763. *Fitzwilliam Museum, Cambridge.*

PLATE 415

(A) *Top:* View of Paestum: etching by Giovanni Battista Piranesi, 1778–9. *Boymans Museum, Rotterdam.*

(B) *Left:* The Boxers: lithograph by Théodore Géricault, 1817–21. *British Museum, London.*

PLATE 416

Civil War

The story of the navies of the Civil War is one of blockade and blockade running, a few engagements between individual ships, river warfare, some "amphibious" operations, and attacks from the sea on near-impregnable forts.

When President Lincoln ordered the blockade of Southern ports the Union Navy consisted of scarcely twenty-five vessels.

The New York lithographers Endicott & Company have left a telling record of the Union Navy's answer to Lincoln's order for the blockade. With what soon amounted to monotony, the Endicott lithographic stones rolled out print after print of newly constructed gunboats. The portraits themselves vary little, and the names even were similar, being of Indian origin: *Winooski, Ascutney, Lenape, Mackinaw*, to mention but a few, with *Grand Gulf and Fulton* added for variety.

The answer of the Confederates to the blockade was the "blockade runner", which dashed through the blockade with greater speed than the Federal guard ships could muster, to bring the South imports necessary to carry on the war. Unfortunately there were few artists to record these craft and their existing exploits.

Some Confederate vessels acted as privateers. The U.S. Revenue Cutter *Aiken*, seized in Charleston at the outbreak of the war, was converted to the privateer schooner *Petrel*. On her first cruise she was chased by the U.S. Frigate *St Lawrence*. After a brief action the schooner sank. The Philadelphia lithographer, L. Haugg, published a handsome print to commemorate this incident.

One of the most notable exploits of the war was the cruise of the Confederate Raider *Alabama* under Raphael Semmes. During this eleven-month cruise the *Alabama* captured sixty-nine prizes. The successful voyage was brought to an abrupt end in June 1864, when the raider was cornered in Cherbourg harbour by the U.S. Sloop-of-War *Kearsarge*. The Confederate ship unhesitatingly went forth to meet her opponent, but after a battle of less than two hours, she struck her colours and sank. This, one of the few duels of the war,

was popular in story, song, and picture. An artist named Xanthus Smith, an enlisted man in the U.S. Navy, has left several paintings of the engagement, and W. F. Mitchell and C. Oliver did water-colour drawings of it. Prints include French lithographs, a pair of small folios by Currier & Ives, a chromolithograph by L. Prang & Co., and a sheet-music cover by L. R. Rosenthal.

The renowned battle between the first ironclads, the *Virginia* (ex-*Merrimac*) and the *Monitor*, was a popular subject for prints and paintings. The *Merrimac*, as a steam frigate before conversion by the Confederates, appears in a portrait lithographed by L. H. Bradford & Company. Currier & Ives have pictured her on her first appearance as the ironclad ram *Virginia*, sinking the frigate *Cumberland*.

The fight of the *Virginia* and *Monitor*, which revolutionized naval history, took place on March 9, 1862. Among the many contemporary pictures it inspired are lithographs by Casimir Bohn, Henry Bill, Endicott, Hatch, and Currier & Ives. The battle though not in itself a decisive one, was ostensibly a victory for the *Monitor*. A lurid print published by Currier & Ives shows *The Destruction of the Rebel Monster MERRIMAC off Craney Island, May 11, 1862*.

There followed the construction or conversion of ships of the types of both of these vessels. The rams, similar in appearance to the *Virginia*, were later seen particularly on the Mississippi River and are recorded especially in lithographs by Currier & Ives. Vessels of the design of the *Monitor* were built in numbers by the Federal Navy. Endicott published a series of lithographs, over a dozen, of monitors also having Indian names, as *Manhattan, Weehawken, Monadnock*, and *Wassuc*.

The firm of Currier & Ives, lithographers, was in its prime at the time of the Civil War. The six thousand-odd titles published by these prolific print-makers cover a wide range of subjects. Many had to do with current events and were, in effect, forerunners of the present-day newspaper pictures. In consequence we find the firm furnishing its "readers" with views of the latest developments at the "front", including the naval "front". Thus a list of Currier & Ives naval prints, in order of publication, becomes a chronology of the naval war.

The Mississippi River was the Confederate front in the west. Important naval operations took place on the river and its tributaries. One of the key points first to be won with the aid of Commodore Foote's fleet of Union gunboats was Fort Henry, Tennessee, on February 6, 1862. This action is recalled in a Currier & Ives print, as is the Battle of Shiloh, April 6, 1862. Middleton, Strobridge & Company, lithographers of Cincinnati, who produced a series of Civil War battle scenes, also depicted this battle. Proceeding southward, the fleet engaged in *The Bombardment and Capture of Island Number Ten, April 7, 1862, by the Gunboat and Mortar Fleet*, another Currier & Ives title.

Meanwhile a fleet under Admiral Farragut entered the mouth of the Mississippi. A woodcut published by Howard Brown after a drawing by William Waud records the *Bombardment of Forts Jackson and St Philip*. A drawing by William McMurtrie shows the fleet lying before New Orleans, before proceeding northwards to "engage the Rebel Batteries at Port Hudson (Louisiana) March 14th, 1863", as the Currier & Ives title reads. A dramatic chromolithograph by L. Prang shows the Union fleet as from a Confederate battery near Port Hudson. The last major engagement on the Mississippi was the Battle of Vicksburg, in which the Naval forces took part, as is evidenced by the title, *Admiral Porter's Fleet Running the Rebel Blockade of the Mississippi at Vicksburg, April 15th, 1863*. Other naval operations followed but with the river opened and the Confederacy divided, the navy had done most of its work in the west.

A "combat artist" of the Civil War, worthy of special mention, was Alfred Waud. He was employed by *Harper's Weekly* as a "war correspondent". Most of Waud's pencil sketches had to do with the operations of the army, but there were many drawings of naval activity done in his admirable style. The Library of Congress owns most of his work.

It was difficult to blockade the coast off Hatteras, North Carolina, owing to generally

unfavourable weather, so the Federals decided early in the war to get a foothold on shore in order to prevent blockade runners from bringing supplies in at this point. Currier & Ives recorded this operation in a print entitled *The Bombardment and Capture of the Forts Hatteras and Clark at Hatteras Inlet, N.C., by the U.S. Fleet under Commodore Stringham and the Forces under Genl. Butler, August 27th, 1861*.

The Victorious Bombardment of Port Royal, S.C., November 7, 1861, by the United States Fleet under the Command of Commodore Dupont, a Currier & Ives print, depicts the action which gave the South Atlantic Blockading Squadron a much-needed base of operations at a point between Charleston and Savannah.

The Savannah River was closed to Confederate use after *The Bombardment of Fort Pulaski, Cockspur Island, Georgia, 10th and 11th of April 1862*, as the title of the Currier & Ives lithograph puts it.

We turn to prints by Endicott and W. H. Rease to give a prelude to the siege of Charleston. These lithographs show the monitor *Weehawken* fighting rough weather on the way south to attack, with other monitors, the invulnerable Fort Sumter. The action was disastrous to the Union naval forces and proved an unfounded reliance on this new type of vessel.

Fort Sumter proved a stronghold hard to silence. Other Currier & Ives prints show that it was "bombarded" frequently. The print, *The Siege of Charleston, Bombardment of Fort Sumter and Batteries Wagner and Trigg ... August 1863* depicts the climax of the naval war at Charleston and the silencing of Sumter, though the town was not abandoned until General Sherman's arrival by land.

Wilmington, North Carolina, was one of the last important strongholds on the coast to be captured. A fleet, comprising over 150 warships and transports, was assembled for the amphibious assault which the Currier & Ives print, *The Bombardment and Capture of Fort Fisher, N.C., January 15, 1865*, depicts. Endicott & Company also produced a print of this battle, which took place three months before the Confederate surrender at Appomattox.

AMERICAN RAILROAD PRINTS

The beginnings

The first incorporated railroad to perform transportation service in the United States was the Granite Railway, organized in Quincy, Massachusetts, in 1826: it was horse-drawn. The first full-sized steam locomotive to operate on rails here was the *Stourbridge Lion*, brought from England in 1829. As early as 1825 Colonel John Stevens demonstrated a steam railway in Hoboken, New Jersey. The *American Railway Journal*, which began publication in 1832, carried a wood engraving of the *Stourbridge Lion* on its mast for several years. Otherwise there are no contemporary prints of these interesting "firsts".

The *De Witt Clinton* was the first practical American steam locomotive to operate. It ran from Albany to Schenectady, beginning July 31, 1832. On that day a dextrous observer, William H. Brown, cut a silhouette of the train. In 1869, Leggo & Company of Montreal made a lithograph (Plate 384A) from the silhouette. Although not contemporary, the lithograph gives a clear picture of the first locomotive of the New York Central.

Equally important is the lithograph by Ed. Weber of a view of Ellicott's Mills (Plate 384B), the first stopping place of the Baltimore & Ohio Railroad. Begun in 1828, the road was used as horse-drawn means for carting granite blocks from which, incidentally, the Carrollton Viaduct was built. A print of this viaduct shows one of Ross Winans' locomotives with steam up and two cars attached, ready to leave for Baltimore. The print dates from about 1837.

With the full development of lithography in the United States, railway prints came into their own. It is interesting that this process, easier and cheaper than the etching and engraving processes favoured in Europe, formed the bulk of American railroad prints. A list of known early American railway prints was published by the Railway and Locomotive Historical Society in 1934. 326 items are listed. By far the greater number are litho-graphs, only fifteen having been executed in other techniques.

Locomotive prints

Among the most prized items on the lists of collectors of railroad subjects are prints of early locomotives. They are actual portraits of the engines themselves. They were engineer scale-drawings transferred to the lithographic stone and include a mass of detail often showing even the decorative panels which had been painted on the engine and tender. The prints were large and bright and bold in colouring, but the engine is not shown in motion. They were used as advertisements by the builders and were circulated among their agents and railroad companies (Plate 385A, B).

One hundred and fifty of these locomotive prints are included in the Railway and Locomotive Historical Society list. Forty-four builders are listed. Often the same lithographer was employed over a period of years by a firm, and we find the same print-maker's name appearing again and again. J. H. Bufford is one of these. He lithographed the *Auburn, Amoskeag, Ontario, Gazelle, Jervis* and *Saturn* for the Amoskeag Manufacturing Company. For the Boston Locomotive Works he did the *Buffalo, Norwalk, Lisle, Rapid, Sacramento, Boston, Fashion, Ysabel,* and *Marquette*. For other manufacturers he did the *Express, Janus, State of Maine, Forest State, Shelburne, Minnehaha, Rough and Ready, Calumet and Tender, President and Tender, New Englander and Tender,* and *Northerner* (*sic*).

Julius Bien did the following lithographs for M. W. Baldwin: *Locomotives* 4-4-0, 4-6-0, and 0-8-0, *Baldwin & Co. Locomotives, Baldwin's Coal Burning Boiler, Baldwin Engines Types C, D,* and *E, Thomas Rogers*. Bien's partner, Sterner, did *Baltic, Young America,* and *Superior* for Breese & Knowland. Richard Norris & Son, locomotive builders in Philadelphia, hired L. N. Rosenthal and A. Brett to portray the *Auburn, Meredith, Sagua la Grande, Wyoming, Union,* and at least four others.

Thomas S. Sinclair lithographed the

Massachusetts for Hinkley & Drury of Boston; the *John C. Breckenridge and Tender*, for the Lancaster Locomotive Works; the *Assanpink* for the Trenton Locomotive Works; and a miscellaneous lithograph called *Track Across the Susquehannah River*. The lithography firm of Tappan & Bradford published some of the finest examples of the locomotive print: *General Stark* for the Amoskeag Manufacturing Company; *Columbia*, *Mercury*, and *Ariel* for other manufacturers. Charles H. Crosby and also Tappan & Bradford worked on the stone for William Mason, the builder in Taunton, Massachusetts, and brought out the *Armstrong*, *Phantom*, *Highland Light*, and *Janus*. John Sartain, probably the leading mezzotint engraver in the United States in his time, scraped *Three Locomotives with Baldwin Plant in Background*; *The Baldwin Works*; and *Certificate of the Franklin Institute*, which is, technically, a railroad print.

Donald McKay built the *Arkansas*, and C. H. Crosby's lithograph of this engine is a gem (Plate 385B). The *Arkansas* is shown in the Far West. Two U.S. troopers appear lower right. Indians, of which there are seven, are in a state of agitation occasioned by this, their first view of a locomotive. The most remarkable figure in the piece is the fireman, who is wearing a pigtail and Chinese dress. He is one of the thousands of Chinese who were encouraged to emigrate to the United States, where they played an important part in the construction of the railroads in the West.

No doubt the very popularity of these gay and decorative prints accounts for their scarcity today. Cheaply framed, if at all, they were hung in railroad stations, offices, barns, bedrooms, and bagnios, where they were thrown away when damaged. Those kept in the files of the manufacturing firms were discarded as their prototypes were replaced by newer and better models.

Viaducts and bridges

When the roadbeds were laid out bridges and viaducts were required. They were viewed as wonders at the time of their building, and shared some of the enthusiasm accorded the locomotives. The type of construction varied according to the materials available locally. There is a peculiar satisfaction in contemplating the old prints and reflecting that our ancestors' ingenuity served them well in overcoming obstacles to their progress.

In the vignette of *The Carrolton Viaduct* (Plate 386A) published by Endicott & Swett in 1831, we see the solidly constructed viaduct straddling the glen, its beautiful arch and well-built buttressed walls made of granite from the quarry at nearby Ellicott's Mills. The horse-drawn railway coach is practically bursting with passengers as it proceeds majestically.

Thirty years later we find a larger print lithographed by Compton & Company after a drawing by J. Stilson. It is called *Portage Bridge* (Plate 386B) and represents a bridge of the Erie Railroad in Western New York. Of timber construction, it had a cross walk from which pedestrians could contemplate the waterfalls below. The legend on the print states that 1,602,000 feet of timber and 108,862 pounds of iron were used in its construction. In the picture a steam locomotive chugs across this wonder of engineering, pulling two freight and five passenger cars.

Currier & Ives' *Railroad Suspension Bridge near Niagara Falls* appeared at the same time as the *Portage Bridge*. Lithographed from a painting by Charles Parsons, it designates as engineer John A. Roebling, whose name was to become a household word in America after the building of Brooklyn Bridge. Across the Niagara Bridge, suspended by cables from huge stone towers, goes the train, while below, on the underpath, horse-drawn carriages proceed.

A beautiful chromolithograph done in 1865 by Thomas Sinclair is entitled *American Autumn* (Plate 387A). It shows the Starucca Valley Viaduct on the Erie Railroad, which was said to be the longest viaduct in the country at that time.

Railroad accident prints

Lithography lent itself well to tabloid reporting, and John Collins published *Accident on the Camden and Amboy Railroad near Burlington, New Jersey*, August 29, 1855, shortly after the disaster. *The Abolition Castastrophe*, a political cartoon published by Bromley & Company is another story. Hullmandel & Walton published *Accident on the Baltimore and Ohio Railroad* in 1853. John L. Magee published *The Dreadful Accident of the North Pennsylvania Railroad, 14 Minutes from Philadelphia*, July 17, 1856.

Prints with historical significance

Charles Parsons' *Panama Railroad – View of the Culebra or the Summit* shows the first railroad which operated between the Atlantic and Pacific Oceans. It is dated 1854. Currier & Ives' *Across the Continent* (Plate 387B) commemorates the completion of the railway across the North American Continent. Schile & Company also issued no less than three coloured lithographs under this title. These prints are more noted for dash than accuracy.

Railroad scenes of the Civil War include: *The Invasion of Pennsylvania*, a coloured woodcut by Berghaus; *Volunteer Refreshment Saloon, Supported Gratuitously by the Citizens of Philadelphia, Pa.*, published by B. S. Brown and printed in colour by W. Boell; *Lookout Mountain near Chattanooga, Tennessee*, by Donaldson & Elmes; *Military Post, Cowan, Tennessee*, by Henry Eno; *Tracy City, Tennessee*, also by Eno; *Away to the Front*, by MacClure, MacDonald & MacGregor; and *Camp at Melville, Md.*, by Sachse & Company.

Western print-makers of railroad items

Information concerning Western print-makers is small, and examples of their work are much appreciated by collectors. A few titles are: *The Way Not to Build the S.P. Railroad* – anonymous and with no date; *What we want in California. From New York Direct, Family and Fireside*, by Britton & Rey; *San Diego, Cal.*, by George H. Baker. This is an interesting field for collectors with pioneer instincts.

Strangely enough, early railroad prints before 1860 were comparatively few among the Currier & Ives' productions. The first railroad print issued by Nathaniel Currier is a small folio entitled *The Express Train*, and was taken from a bank-note of the Fort Jervis Institution. Undated, it shows the engine before the addition of a headlight. *The American Express Train*, after Charles Parsons, published

in 1855, is a large folio. It was re-issued with an overprint in the sky, *Adams Express Co.*, with that company's advertising legend in the margin. The large *Express Train*, published in 1859 after a painting by Parsons, is almost a duplicate of the former, but in reverse. All of these prints show entire trains in motion with smoke issuing from the stack and with landscape backgrounds.

The most important railroad prints done by Currier & Ives, however, were those issued towards the end of or shortly after the Civil War. These are imaginative to the point of being theatrical, are not accurate as to detail, are well drawn and highly coloured, and seek to dramatize some important railroad incident. We find such titles as *The Lightning Express Trains Leaving the Junction*; *Night Scene at an American Railway Junction*; *The Great West*; *American Railroad Scene, Snow Bound*; *Through to the Pacific*; *Prairie Fires of the Great West*; and *Across the Continent, Westward the Course of Empire Takes its Way* (Plate 387B). The Currier & Ives' productions are among the most charming of the railroad prints.

Mention should be made of the long series of "comics" issued by Currier & Ives, those caricaturing new railroad conveniences such as the "accommodation train", stops for refreshments at the station, entanglements with cattle, and so on, plus the amusing group of *Darktown* prints.

Music sheets, bank-notes, and stock certificates

Any event which kindles public interest and enthusiasm is usually a theme of popular poetry and song. Railroading was no exception. One finds numerous titles referring to this industry, and most have lithographed representations of railroads on their covers. Perhaps the earliest in this field are the marches dedicated, at the time of the inception of the Baltimore and Ohio Railroad, to Charles Carroll of Carrollton, the last surviving Signer of the Declaration of Independence. The marches were dedicated to him and the other directors of the company. The event took place on the Fourth of July 1828 and *The Carrollton March* and *The Baltimore and Ohio March* were sold on the streets on that

momentous day. *The Lion Quickstep* was played for the first time at the opening of the railroad to Westborough (Boston), November
15, 1834. *The New Orleans and Great Northern
Railroad Polka* was published in 1854. The
galops, polkas, quicksteps and even "steam
galops" generally bore names at least as
exuberant as the pictures on their covers.
Amusing collectors' items, they yet offer important sources for certain elusive railroad
data.

Bank-notes and stock certificates of the
early period utilized railroad material for decoration. On its notes of 1833 the Bank of Te-
cumseh, Michigan, used a picture of a railroad
train with a sharp-pronged cowcatcher on
little wheels. This device was actually used by
Isaac Dripps of the Camden and Amboy Railroad in 1832. The engraving also shows the

iron bonnet on the smokestack devised to ar-
rest the burning embers belched forth from
the engine. The first trip of the *De Witt Clinton* and the near incineration of the passengers
had made the necessity for such an invention
obvious. There is no doubt that the engravers
of the notes, Rawdon, Wright & Hatch of
New York, had actually seen this train in
operation and have left us an accurate picture of it.

Catalogues of railroad subjects offered for
sale often list old stock certificates which have
a current value only because of the railroad
items engraved on them. These vignettes have
a charm of their own, which comes from the
fact that the spectator generally holds them
and looks at them close up. The New York
Public Library has a fine collection of vignettes, many of which portray railroads.

AMERICAN SILHOUETTES

In 1767 Benjamin Franklin wrote home from
London: "I send you the little shade that
was copied from the great one." This "great"
shade – presumably life-size – was a silhouette of Franklin, now lost, made by Patience
Wright, the New Jersey Quakeress then established in England. However, the earliest
mention of silhouette work done in America
is found in a letter written in 1799 by Harriet
Pinckney, a South Carolina belle, in which
she mentions her "shade" by Thomas Wollaston. The whereabouts of the profile are unknown; it is probable that the artist was an
amateur.

Foremost among the notables of the period,
George and Martha Washington were in-
numerably portrayed by amateur silhouettists, among whom were their granddaughter
Nelly Custis, Samuel Powell, Mayor of Philadelphia, and Miss Sarah de Hart, of Eliza-
bethtown, New Jersey. The work of Major
André – his own self-portrait, his studies of
General Burgoyne, Major Stanley, "Becky"
Stedman – is naturally of high historical
interest. Such "shades" when encountered
speak for themselves eloquently enough. An
eighteenth-century silhouette signed Chapman, 1781, showing a Virginia subject,

Robert Bolling of Petersburg, Virginia, still
in the possession of the family, is illustrated
(Plate 390A).

However, with the advent of the nineteenth
century, the growing popularity of silhouette
soon created a real demand, and the sporadic
manifestations of amateurs were supplemented by the steady production of a group of professionals. One of the earliest among these was
Moses Chapman of Salem, Massachusetts (*c.*
1780–1821), no relation to Chapman of Virginia so far as is known. The Salem silhouettist was not a particularly gifted artist; his
work is correct but undistinguished. But he
was an innovator in the sense that he made
use not of the silhouette proper but the outer
contour usually discarded by the cutter. This,
placed on a black ground, paper, silk, or any
other material, furnished a striking effect.
Chapman employed the tracing and cutting
machine invented by Chrétien in France, the
physionotrace, but occasionally still cut free-
hand.

The possibilities of silhouette work by this
"hollow-cut" process were to be fully realized
by Charles Willson Peale (Plate 391C and
D) (1741–1827), the extreme example of
Yankee ingenuity and business sense, who

resolved to bring about the mass production of silhouettes. He actually achieved this by means of the *physionotrace*, complemented by an ingenious stencil machine (invented by his assistant Isaac Hawkins) which is described as enabling "any steady hand in a few moments" to "produce a correct indented outline". Peale was eminently successful financially, but it is obvious that the works executed entirely by this means are almost devoid of artistic value. The work of Peale himself must, at least in some cases, be excepted. He was a serious, really excellent artist and craftsman, having been in succession, though more often simultaneously, a saddler, clockmaker, silversmith, taxidermist, soldier, legislator, educator, and scientist (naturalist and archaeologist). He established his own museum in Philadelphia, largely devoted to natural history. Of the three stamps he used on silhouettes, *Museum* is the most usual; *Peale's Museum* comes next, and rarest is the plain mark, *Peale*; all three are embossed in roman capitals.

Peale's nephew, Charles Peale Polk (1767–1822), made profiles on gold background, the rarest type of American silhouettes.

Not on a level with Peale the elder, but something more than an amateur was Samuel Folwell (1765–1813), whose first avocation had been the engraving of bookplates in New Hampshire. Having moved to Philadelphia, then the metropolis of the arts in America, Folwell, in order to meet active competition, turned to various occupations, among them miniaturist, profilist, worker in hair (as were most profilists), and in his spare time, school teacher. His most famous work, the profile of George Washington, is firm and delicately chiselled. A Folwell silhouette is *rarissima avis*.

William Doyle was born in Boston in 1769, the son of a British soldier. He divided his admiration equally between Peale and Miers. To Miers he paid artistic homage, and he strove to emulate him, but never attained to the subtle effects of the English artist. He did rival Peale, if not as an artist, at least as a museum founder. His business enterprises, in co-operation with another silhouettist, David Bowen (whose only date, 1791, is found on a portrait, *George Washington and his lady*), were quite successful, in spite of disaster by fire. Doyle generally copied the Miers bust curve, but interrupted it half-way with an odd little nick that is extremely characteristic. He was known to have done some works on plaster, but none was thought to exist until a unique discovery of such a profile on "composition". He signed in careful script, but never stamped.

Henry Williams (Boston, 1787–1830) was fully as versatile as any of his colleagues, and in addition was a professor of electricity and a modeller in wax. His method was the usual hollow-cut technique, and his advertisements offered "16 different sizes down to a quarter of an inch", this last no doubt intended for setting in jewellery. His work is very rare.

"Todd" must remain just that; his first name is not known. He was approximately a contemporary of Doyle and Williams, and an album with about two thousand examples of his work is in the collection of the Boston Athenaeum. It provides a delightful and lively record of costumes and types, in an unpretentious and effective clean-cut style without any pen flourishes. The stamp *Todd's Patent* is the only signature. Most valuable perhaps, Todd kept a meticulous record of his sitters' names, with dates of posing.

William King (active 1785–1805) wielded his magic "Patent Delineating Pencil" in Salem and vicinity. Possibly it may have been his own invention; he is spoken of as "an ingenious mechanic but full of projects & what he gains in one he loses in the other". In an advertisement published in 1806 King claimed to have executed upwards of twenty thousand silhouettes. Yet today it is rare to find even one.

In perfect contrast to King was the serious and honest William Bache, who was to raise hollow-cutting (Plate 391A and B) to the level of art. Born on December 22, 1771 (at Bromsgrove in Worcestershire, England), Bache emigrated to Philadelphia when he was twenty-two years old. His career as a profilist took him far and wide through the south, particularly Louisiana, where he did some excellent work, and later to the West Indies. In his short career as a profilist he produced much and created a new style, being the first hollow-cutter to paint on his paper backings details of dress such as the transparent collar ruffle worn by the lady in Plate 391B. At his hands, hollow-cutting lost rigidity and coldness. A true artist, he was equally skilful in cut-and-pastel work and in painted silhouettes.

The last days of silhouette, before the advent of daguerreotype sounded its doom, saw its richest flowering. Among a host of lesser lights, which limitations of space preclude mentioning, there emerges William Henry Brown, who was born in Charleston, South Carolina, in 1808, died there in 1883. Brown was something of a prodigy; his first silhouette, of Lafayette, was executed at the age of sixteen. In contrast to the usual American practice, Brown was a free-hand cutter. His style is pure and severe, without extraneous embellishments of gold or colour. This is silhouette in the finest sense of the word, which implies denudation to the point of artistic asceticism. The characterization of subjects is superb, but is always rightly held subservient to the artistic conception. Brown was an artist and social observer, and, as a result of this, has given us a more enduring record of his age than the most slavish hollow-cutter.

Brown's greatest accomplishment was the compilation of the *Portrait Gallery of Distinguished American Citizens*, published at Hartford, Connecticut, in 1846. To this album of lithographs he furnished both text (biographical notes) and illustrations, the subjects being shown against backgrounds which he did not execute himself, but must have supervised and in many cases suggested. These are of great historical interest. Almost the entire edition of the *Portrait Gallery* was destroyed by fire shortly after publication, so that copies are of the utmost rarity (Plate 388).

The prestige of free-hand cutting quite did away with the hollow-cutting by machine that had satisfied earlier: silhouettists now were "scissorgraphists". William James Hubard ("Master Hubard", born in England in 1807, died 1862) was advertised as a child prodigy, starting on his career at the age of twelve. There is scepticism on this point now, and it is thought, on good grounds, that he

may actually have been fifteen at his debut. He later became a pupil of Sully and a competent portrait painter in his own right. His highest success was won in Charleston, and he finally settled in the south. The Valentine Museum in Richmond, Virginia, has a collection of his work (Plate 389A and c).

A successor, Master Hankes, was also born in England. Hankes' career started in Salem, Massachusetts, in 1828. He may have been an early anonymous associate of Master Hubard, helping to satisfy the press of business. When he appeared under his own name he was only moderately successful, doing best of all in Baltimore. Returning to New England after this tour, Master Hankes disappears from view. His talent, however, was not mean, as seen in the portrait of Dr Holyoke (Plate 389B).

Phenomenal also, but far inferior artistically, were Miss Honeywell and Master Nellis. The first, born without arms, contrived to cut with scissors held in her mouth. Her work may have fully satisfied many, but it is probable that most of her patronage was due mainly to compassionate interest. Little of it has survived.

Of Sanders K. G. Nellis we know nothing but his name from an advertisement. Also armless, he made use of his toes in place of fingers. Mention is made merely on the chance that some vestige of his pathetic industry might turn up at some future date.

A history of silhouette in America must necessarily include mention of the work of visiting artists from abroad, whose works represent a documentary study of national interest.

Charles Balthazar Julien Févret de Saint-Mémin (born in Dijon in 1770, died 1852) was a French *émigré* originally destined to a military career. A gifted amateur artist in happier days, he developed under pressure of financial necessity into a masterly professional. Although he undertook to furnish the American market with silhouettes, his most important work was in the related form of coloured profiles in life size, and engravings, of which he executed a large number during his stay. In style, he combines eighteenth-century grace and the cold intensity of

Davidesque neo-classicism. Much of this is reflected in his silhouettes, which have purity of line and a very special flavour of French elegance.

Augustin Amant Constant Fidèle Édouart (1789–1861) was the universal silhouettist – his subjects ranging all the way from dignified historical portraits to humorous genre scenes. In addition to his huge European output (see the article on British and Continental silhouettes), his ten years' stay in America resulted in a unique and priceless record totalling upwards of ten thousand silhouettes. Much of this was lost in a shipwreck, that is, the careful record of duplicates kept by the artist; many of the originals have survived. But Mrs Nevill Jackson was still able to refer to her photographic files of the remaining thirty-eight hundred American Édouart silhouettes as "in such number as no other nation possesses". His portrait of Titian Peale, son of Charles Willson Peale, is illustrated (Plate 390B).

Édouart's style was that of a purist of genius: no adornments, no shading of any sort, gold or otherwise. He allowed himself at most a slit of white for the gentlemen's neckcloths, but within the bounds of this self-imposed economy achieved extraordinary linear expressiveness.

British

PRINTS

Reduced to its simplest analysis, a print is merely a drawing or a painting transferred to a plate of copper or zinc, a block of wood, or a stone. The word "print" is a generic term applying to several methods – line-engraving on wood and copper, etching, soft-ground etching, drypoint, aquatint, mezzotint, and lithography, and some knowledge of each technique is an aid to appreciation.

Engraving had reached a state of perfection on the continent of Europe at least a hundred years before its advent in England; but it was not long before an indigenous school was established.

During the last years of the sixteenth century William Rogers the first important native-born engraver, was busy with plates expressive of a glorious reign and event. Appropriately, one of his most famous works was in honour of Queen Elizabeth I. It commemorated the victory over the Spanish Armada, and was called *Eliza Triumphans*. It is a full-length effigy of the Queen, elaborating details of her fantastic costume, and is dated 1589. More historic than aesthetic, it is none the less a landmark in English engraving.

Working contemporaneously with Rogers was Thomas Cockson, who illustrated Sir John Harrington's metrical translation of Ariosto's *Orlando Furioso*. His best plates, however, are the equestrian portraits of the Earls of Devonshire, Essex, Cumberland, and Nottingham. Carefully cut after good drawings, these engravings, if somewhat formalized, have considerable distinction.

Rogers and Cockson set a course for portrait engraving in England. Unlike portrait painting, it was an art that could be shared by many, and print-sellers and publishers were not slow to take advantage of a profitable accessory to their trade. William Hole, another engraver of that time, is also remembered for his portraits, including that of George Chapman used in the 1616 edition of his translation of Homer.

With William Faithorne (1616–91) the engraved portrait reached a splendour that loses nothing by comparison with the work of any other master of the burin or graver. He cut many plates after Van Dyck, Dobson, and Walker. Faithorne understood the painter's mood and interpreted it as one might translate a poem from one language into another, without losing its original inspiration. Faithorne's print represented a warm and intimate personality. His line is bold and vital, and his feeling for character, colour, and texture is absolutely convincing. The artist's life was not without adventure, for he took up arms in defence of the Royalist cause, was captured at Basing House garrison and confined in Aldersgate. On being released, Faithorne went to France, where he was fortunate in making friends with the Abbé de Marolles, who allowed him to study his enormous collection of about 120,000 prints by all the great masters of engraving and etching. While in France Faithorne also worked with the famous engraver Robert Nanteuil, thus consummating his own style. He returned to England with the Protector's permission, and enjoyed many years of success in his profession. Notable plates by him are portraits of Prince Rupert, Oliver Cromwell, William Sanderson, Charles II, Barbara Villiers, William Prince of Orange, and Margaret Smith (Plate 395A).

The artists so far mentioned cut direct on the copper, a method known as line-engraving, which, after being inked, was put under the press.

A line-engraver and etcher of much originality in animal, bird, and fish subjects was Francis Barlow (1626–1702). His 110 etchings for Æsop's Fables are of exceptional interest to students and collectors.

It was Wenceslaus Hollar (1706–77) who introduced the art of etching into England. He came here with the Earl of Arundel, whom he met at Cologne. A Czech from Prague, Hollar adapted himself to English ways, married an English woman, attached himself to the Royalist cause, and was taken prisoner, strangely enough, at the same time as Faithorne at Basing House. Retiring to Antwerp, whither his patron, the Earl of Arundel, had withdrawn, Hollar lived there from 1644 to 1652, after which year he returned to England, where he spent the rest of his life. A versatile and spirited artist, Hollar etched over 2,500 plates – interpretations of religious and classical paintings, portraits, and townscapes. His great panorama of London, views of other cities, and studies of feminine costume form a microcosm of England and Europe as they were during the seventeenth century. Essentially a realist, Hollar's accurate yet vibrant line is instinct with acute, if unimaginative, observation.

An amateur of some importance who was a friend of Hollar's, and influenced by him, was Francis Place (1647–1728). Among the first of the English topographical artists, Place toured the country recording views in monochrome, which he afterwards etched in a style akin to Hollar's. He also engraved mezzotint portraits.

Etching differs from line-engraving in that the drawing is not incised in the copperplate but produced by the biting effect of hydrochloric or nitric acid. The plate is first covered with a thin ground of wax. The drawing is done on the wax, the etching needle sufficing only to open lines or channels into which the acid will bite when the plate is immersed therein. The strength of the bitten line depends upon the length of time the plate is left in the mordant. Lines that have been bitten deeply enough are "stopped out", i.e. protected by a special varnish while other lines, in their relative degrees of strength or delicacy, are brought to completion.

A variant of the etching method is known as soft-ground etching, which, in printing, suggests the grain and texture of the paper on which the drawing is made. In this method the drawing is transferred to the etching ground by a tracing.

The evolution of the English print in the seventeenth century, whether line-engraved or etched, is concentrated in the work of Faithorne, Hollar, Barlow, and Place, all of whom were associated with one another.

Though George Vertue (1684–1756), himself a competent artist and esteemed historian of art, deplored the decline of engraving in the first half of the eighteenth century, the century as a whole produced a veritable flood of prints of every conceivable subject in every kind of technique. For separate prints, and as illustrations for books, the copperplate had become indispensable. It was William Hogarth (1697–1764), however, who proved that the engraving which reproduced the subject-picture could be of immense monetary gain to artist and print-seller alike. Twelve hundred persons are said to have subscribed a guinea each for a set of *The Harlot's Progress*. Thus the commercial value of the print became paramount and resulted in an ever-increasing number of clever craftsmen. Hogarth's own line-engravings had no other purpose than to translate the painting as obviously as possible in all its details. His prints were designed to gratify popular taste in its widest sense. As an engraver, therefore, he is not in the first class.

If Hogarth was a rapid worker with the burin, William Woollett (1735–85) was slow and deliberate, and would take many months on a plate, which no doubt accounted for his feeling such intense relief when the work was finished that he signalized it by firing a cannon from the roof of his house. His engraving after Richard Wilson's picture *The Destruction of the Children of Niobe* set the seal on the fame of one of the most prominent reproductive landscape engravers. Woollett's chiaroscuro effect, wrought with an infinity of intricate lines, especially in his plates from Wilson's pictures, catches some of the poetic solemnity of Wilson's mood. Woollett was also a portrait and animal engraver. A well-known print by him is *The Spanish Pointer*, and he did many others after George Stubbs. Woollett, like other eighteenth-century line-engravers, started his plates with a preliminary etching as a guide to the general design.

Equally celebrated in his time, but principally for historical and religious subjects, was Sir Robert Strange (1721–92), who gained an international reputation as well as a knighthood for his plates after Van Dyck and other Dutch and Italian masters.

Of the same period were William Sharp, who began as a craftsman engraving guns and pewter, and later achieved a position in the art comparable with Woollett's; Richard Earlom, celebrated for his plates after Claude; and William Pether, interpreter of Rembrandt. These three used the mezzo-tint method.

While so many eighteenth-century engravers were engaged in reproducing paintings, either by old or contemporary masters, William Blake (1757–1827) relied on his own

mystical mind for invention and ideal imagery. At his best an inspired poet, Blake was eminently gifted for the task of illuminating Holy Writ and the poetry of his time. For original composition, devout feeling, and refinement of line his designs for *The Book of Job* are outstanding in the history of the art. They should be studied in conjunction with the earlier plates for Young's *Night Thoughts* and the seven for Dante's *Divine Comedy*, on which Blake was working during the last year of his life. An unusual and little-known line-engraving is that entitled *Christ with a Bow Trampling on Satan*, believed to be one of the poet-painter's last works.

Another supreme artist in the creative style was Thomas Bewick (1753–1828). Regarded as the restorer of the art of engraving on wood, he designed a vast number of prints of birds and animals.

Prints from copperplates reached a crescendo in the late eighteenth and early nineteenth centuries. Portrait, classical, historical, topographical, genre, architectural, marine, sporting, and satirical subjects found a ready market. Novel variants known as the crayon or chalk and pastel manners further stimulated public interest. A charming example of the crayon or pastel style is the print entitled *Alinda* (Plate 396B) by William Ward (1762–1826). The object was to suggest the graceful texture of the chalk drawing, and the etching ground was perforated with various needles and other tools. Ward was a pupil and assistant of John Raphael Smith, and he engraved works after Sir Joshua Reynolds, and George Morland, who was Ward's brother-in-law. He was equally skilled in what is known as the stipple engraving, the main technique of which is the use of innumerable dots and flicks to suggest modelling and gradation.

The stipple method was also practised by L. Shiavonetti and A. Cardon, who collaborated in one of the most successful series of prints ever created, *The Cries of London*, after Francis Wheatley, R.A. Schiavonetti was greatly influenced by, and worked for some time with, Francesco Bartolozzi, who enjoyed phenomenal success with his stipple engravings, notably a set of portraits of the time of Henry VIII, after drawings by Holbein, published by John Chamberlaine in 1792–1800.

Yet another novelty was the aquatint, introduced into England by the Hon. Charles Greville, who communicated the principle to Paul Sandby, R.A. Greville is said to have bought the secret from Jean Baptist Le Prince, a French engraver. As soon as Sandby had shown the way by publishing *Twelve Views in Aquatinta from Drawings taken on the Spot in South Wales* (1775), he had many followers. The name of James Malton is familiar to collectors, for his aquatinted Dublin views, published 1792–9, while his brother, Thomas Malton, is known for his London and Westminster views, dated 1792–1801, and Oxford views dated 1802. Other accomplished aquatinters were William Daniell and his uncle, Thomas Daniell, for Oriental scenes and views of Great Britain. D. and R. Havell and J. C. Stadler were also masters of this method of engraving.

Boxing, racing, hunting, and other sports attracted scores of aquatinters. *The Interior of the Fives Court with Randall and Turner Sparring* (Plate 397A) is crowded with interest. Many of the foreground figures are portraits of personalities connected with the "fancy". We learn from a key that Jem Belcher is among them, but the famous pugilist died long before the print was made. Lifeguardsman Shaw, also a champion boxer, and one of the soldiers in uniform, was killed at Waterloo; but it was not infrequently the convention to commemorate in prints the figures of celebrities who had been popularly connected with sport. The painting of the Fives Court is by T. Blake, the print by Charles Turner, who among other important works, engraved twenty-four plates after J. M. W. Turner's *Liber Studiorum*.

What better impression could be gained of Tattersall's as it was in the last years of William IV than from the print entitled *Epsom* by Charles Hunt, after J. Pollard? It is an aquatint full of figure, sartorial, and architectural ingenuities (Plate 397B). Charles Hunt (*fl.* 1820–50) has about 120 plates to his credit, including many of racehorses.

Sporting art and the Alken family are synonymous, and they exhausted every aspect of the subject. Henry T. Alken (1785–1851) was the best artist in several generations, and certainly no other sporting painter expressed with keener fun and more accurate knowledge the "ritual" and predicaments of hunting, racing, fishing, and shooting. To detail all the prints, either by Alken himself or other engravers after his pictures and drawings, would necessitate volumes. Dates appear on prints from 1813 to 1859 inclusive. Some interesting examples are *Shooting Discoveries* (1816); *How to Qualify for a Meltonian*, aquatinted by "Ben Tally Ho", Alken's pseudonym; *On the Road to the Derby* (1819); *The High Mettled Racer*, in which set he collaborated with T. Sutherland (1821); *First Steeplechase on Record, or the Night Riders of Nacton*, engraved by J. Harris (1839).

First Introduction to Hounds (Plate 398A) is also by J. Harris, dated 1850, and is probably from a picture by Samuel Henry Alken, Henry T. Alken's son, who signed himself H. Alken, thereby causing no little confusion to students of this family of sporting artists.

James Pollard was another versatile painter who provided engravers with plenty of sporting "copy". F. Rosenberg's plate of *The Yard of the Swan with Two Necks*, showing the Royal Mails preparing to start for the West of England, is a very rare print.

Coaching, which reached its zenith during the time of George IV, provided many lively subjects for the engraver, and a splendid coaching print is T. Sutherland's *The Peacock, Islington*, after Pollard (1823). Sutherland is a very subtle master of aquatint. Another coaching subject of exquisite quality is T. H. A. Fielding's *Elephant and Castle* (1836), also after Pollard.

The heroic and hazardous years from 1793 to the eclipse of Napoleon at Waterloo brought a patriotic sentiment into the print world, and many plates were made with a naval interest, such as *Representation of the Battle of Trafalgar* by J. Yeakes, after T. Whitcombe (Plate 399A). The antics of Napoleon repeatedly touched off "salvoes" of satirical squibs, and two contemporary geniuses who delighted the public by "despoiling" the Corsican ogre, when they were not ridiculing home affairs, political and social, were Joseph

Gillray (1757–1815), and Thomas Rowlandson (1750–1827), some of whose plates can be very coarse and violent. An amusing Rowlandson drawing, etched also by him for the purpose of the aquatint by Thomas Malton, is *A Sudden Squall in Hyde Park* (Plate 398B). It shows the panic among "fashionables" caught in a shower. Joseph Grego, in his book on Rowlandson, identifies the figure on horseback as the Prince of Wales, and that standing in the lofty phaeton is Lord Barrymore. Prints after Rowlandson should be studied in *The Microcosm of London* series (1808–10), *Dance of Death* (1815–16), and other publications by the enterprising Rudolph Ackermann.

Aquatinting is a method of etching in tone. In pure aquatint no lines are necessary, but most of the specimens mentioned above and those generally in vogue during its hey-day included the use of line. The copperplate must first be prepared with a ground either of powdered asphaltum or resin dust or a spirit solution, which produces a tiny porous, reticulated surface into which the acid bites, leaving a tone so minutely even all over as to print like a wash drawing. Variety of tone in aquatint, like degrees of strength in line-etching, is obtained by "stopping out". The Malton print after Rowlandson is a typical example of the method. The general effect is as of a water-colour. Pure aquatint tones make up the sky. Figures and buildings are delineated.

By the turn of the nineteenth century the craft had become crystallized in the works of many gifted performers who supplied the print-sellers and public. They served a utilitarian purpose. Here and there a few great original artists – John Crome, Thomas Girtin, and J. M. W. Turner – made use of the copperplate with individual distinction. Crome's *Mousehold Heath*, Girtin's softground *Views of Paris and Its Environs*, aquatinted by F. C. Lewis and other engravers (1802–3), Turner's pregnant outlines as the basis for full-tone plates, may be cited as masterpieces of creative engraving.

The medium of the copperplate, however, was temporarily superseded by lithography, the new invention for multiplying prints. Lithography, as its name implies, means writing, or drawing, on stone. Brought to England in the first decade of the nineteenth century, it particularly attracted the water-colour painters, notably Richard Parkes Bonington. His best lithographs are to be found in that sumptuous publication *Voyages pittoresque et romantiques dans l'ancienne France*, sponsored by the French Government, the first volume of which was published in 1822. Among other English artists who contributed to this work were Samuel Prout, J. D. Harding and Thomas Shotter Boys. No lithographer excelled Boys in his handling of this method of art expression. Two classics on the subject are his *Picturesque Architecture in Paris, Ghent, Antwerp, Rouen, etc.* (1839) and *London as it is* (1842). *Entrance to the Strand from Charing Cross* (Plate 399B) is one of many superb architectural lithographs by Boys.

The virtue of lithography is that the print from the stone has the appearance of an original drawing, and many lithographers drew direct on the stone. The line is neither incised nor raised. The chalk or crayon used must contain a certain amount of grease. The drawing completed, the stone is sponged with acid, which fixes the drawing, but the acid is removed before it has time to bite into the stone. The stone is then moistened with water, and as grease and water will not mix, the greasy drawing rejects the water, while those parts of the stone untouched by the chalk absorb it. Greasy ink on a roller is then passed over the stone and adheres to the drawing only for the purpose of the print.

An important figure in lithography was Charles Joseph Hullmandel (1789–1850), who is credited with having invented the method whereby lithographs could be printed with oil colours direct from the stone instead of being tinted afterwards by hand. He thus developed a method that made the chromolithographic print the most popular style of reproduction during, at least, the second quarter of the nineteenth century.

BRITISH DRAWINGS

"Drawing" and "water-colour" are sometimes interchangeable terms, but for the purpose of this encyclopaedia drawings are taken to be those works that are created mainly in monochrome. Media used are pencil, pen-and-ink, charcoal, and chalk, either black or red. Sometimes they are washed over with indian ink, sepia, grey, or blue.

The cult of collecting drawings in England began in the seventeenth century, when one of the first connoisseurs, the Earl of Arundel, acquired works by famous Continental masters. Whereas it has always been the pride of the collector to possess drawings by great foreign masters, it is mostly during the present century that specimens by English artists have found a wider appreciation worthy of their merits.

For example, Alexander Cozens (?1717–86) has emerged from comparative obscurity into a position that makes a knowledge of his work indispensable to students and collectors. He was the son of Richard Cozens, a shipbuilder, who worked for the Tsar of Russia in St Petersburg. He studied in Italy, came to London, and was a fashionable teacher. His book, the *New Method for Assisting the Invention in the Composition of Landscape*, shows that Cozens' method was to develop any landscape suggestion inherent in haphazard washes put on the paper. Only a great draughtsman could avail himself of such fortuitous means, and that Cozens was a master is clear from his magnificent drawing *Landscape Composition* (Plate 392A). On a darkly tinted paper this landscape, which loses nothing by comparison with the best drawings by Claude, is a poetic dream rather than a literal transcript of Nature. Any known Alexander Cozens is rare and very costly. To discover one would be a triumph of discernment and good fortune.

Contemporary with Cozens was Richard Wilson, R.A. (1713–82), famous landscape painter. His drawings are sensitive impressions of Italian and other scenes, such as *The Temple of Venus, Bay of Baie* (Victoria and Albert Museum), and *Holt Bridge on the River Dee* (Plate 392B), and essentially memoranda to help the artist in the construction of paintings. Pictures in black and white, yet with all the tonal values, atmospheric unity, and harmony of design truthfully suggested.

Thomas Gainsborough, R.A. (1727–88), eminent both as portrait and landscape painter, was a prolific artist with pencil and chalk, sometimes heightened with white, on grey paper. He made use of some of these drawings to help him in his pictures, but his landscapes in this medium, generally speaking, were executed mostly for the sheer enjoyment of the rustic scene and as a relief from the ardours of professional portrait work. Gainsborough achieved hundreds of them as a lyrical poet throws off verses. A Gainsborough drawing, apparently so effortless, broad in touch, and distinguished in feeling, ennobles any wall space. The *Landscape* (Plate 393A) is typical of his way of massing trees in black chalk on grey paper. Gainsborough also drew with lead pencil on white paper.

Lead-pencil drawing has no subtler master than John Constable, R.A. (1776–1837). His skill in this difficult medium resulted in that perfect technique which, allied with intense curiosity for everything that interested him, made the merest note memorably beautiful. Careful as he was in his finished drawings, conscientious to the last line and most delicate tone, Constable used the pencil with a kind of reverence for its potentiality as an instrument of expression. His drawings aided him in his paintings, but they are none the less complete works of art in themselves. The *Cart and Team* (Plate 393B) is an example of Constable's power to suggest light, shade, and colour in monotone. The meridian sun illuminates the vehicle and backs of the horses. The deep shadow in the foreground contrasts with the gentler note of the bank and trees in the background.

An artist dominant in the English school is William Hogarth (1697–1764), and it is owing to the popularity of his engravings, and the paintings from which many derived, that his drawings were more or less forgotten until recently. A sketch by Hogarth is worth having, even if it does not offer the unique pleasure of a Constable or Gainsborough; and the reason is that Hogarth's sketches in pen, ink, and wash are merely utilitarian working material for paintings and engravings. It is instructive to observe how closely he followed the preliminary sketch in carrying his ideas to completion. As can be seen from the series entitled *Industry and Idleness* (British Museum), Hogarth was in the habit of making a rough sketch and a finished drawing as a guide for the engraving. Such quick notes as *The Fellow 'Prentices at Their Looms* and *The Idle 'Prentice at Play in the Churchyard* survive almost intact, as to composition, in the finished versions. The known drawings by Hogarth are few in relation to the enormous amount of work that the artist did, but that a Hogarth sketch is still lurking in some "junk" shop, neglected attic, or even between the covers of an eighteenth-century folio, is the not impossible dream of the ardent collector.

In the eighteenth century the public interest in topography gave new opportunities to English artists. A large number of drawings made in this period were townscapes, views of country houses and architectural antiquities. They were intended to represent the scene before the eyes in simple elementary lines and washes, and if some of them are negligible as works of art, the topographs drawn by such accomplished performers as Thomas Hearne (1744–1817) and Michael "Angelo" Rooker (1743–1801) are artistically charming as well as informative. Hearne's and Rooker's drawings are often on the market, and may be recognized by their neat pen-lines conveying the architectural facts, trees, and figures, reinforced with clear blue-grey or sepia washes. Another topographical draughtsman of conspicuous ability was Joseph Farington (1747–1821), who relied on an accurate and fluent pen-line, and a chiaroscuro effect with washes in dark grey, sepia, or blue. A painstaking limner, as may be seen from such drawings as *Lancaster, North-east View* and *The Old Water-tower, York Buildings, Whitehall* (Victoria and Albert Museum), Farington extracted the essentials of architecture and landscape with lineal precision.

His work was thus suited as a basis for coloured illustrations. Farington's *Views of Cities and Towns in England and Wales* (1790), *History of the River Thames* (1794), *Views of the Lakes, etc., Cumberland and Westmorland* (1789, new edition 1816), should be studied to gain an idea of his topographical style. Many of his drawings were engraved in aquatint. Other artists whose monochrome drawings are worth collecting are William Gilpin, Anthony Devis, H. S. Grimm, P. S. Munn, J. B. Malchair; F. L. T. Francia, and J. C. Ibbetson.

The collector will want to vary his landscapes and building subjects with figure-drawings; and an artist with an original style is Henry Fuseli, R.A. (1741–1825). His works in pen-and-ink and pencil-and-wash are singularly imaginative. Inspired by Michelangelo and Shakespeare, he is a weird reflection of Michelangelo's overwhelming technical power and the Bard's dramatic genius. Fuseli's best-known drawings are his illustrations to Shakespeare.

As to book illustrations generally, the collector has a vast choice of drawings by many eighteenth- and early nineteenth-century artists. Examples by Richard Westall, R.A. (1765–1836), who illustrated classic and contemporary literature, T. Stothard, R.A. (1755–1834), and John Masey Wright (1773–1866), similarly engaged over a long period of time, help to make a collection fully representative. By reason of their abundance, the drawings of the last three artists have been purchased in the salerooms for a few shillings, but they are none the less charming examples of graphic art.

Finally, there are miscellaneous odd sketches by celebrated painters, done either for practice or as notes for possible pictures, and these too are procurable at modest prices. The pencil drawing of three heads by Sir David Wilkie (Plate 396A) is a case in point. The aesthetic value of a drawing is not any the less because it is picked up among twenty others of no interest whatever in a portfolio for a pound or so. It will remain a drawing of superlative skill, and the amateur soon learns that an apparently derelict and worthless bundle can contain a treasure worthy of his attention,

BRITISH MEZZOTINTS

The mezzotint was brought to its highest point of perfection in England during the second half of the eighteenth century, and although its depth and subtlety of tone, delicacy and velvet-like texture had always been admired, it was only during the last three decades or so of the nineteenth century that the first large collections began to be formed – notably those of Lord Cheylesmore (the whole of which was left to the British Museum), H. S. Theobald, Fritz Reiss, and Martin Erdmann, not to mention countless smaller collections. During the first thirty years of this century mezzotints enjoyed a reputation in the art auction rooms of London bordering on absurdity: in 1923 £3,045 was paid for Valentine Green's *The Ladies Waldegrave*.

The best mezzotinters have highly individual styles; yet it must be emphasized that the mezzotint is essentially an interpretive print: the original is generally an oil-painting, usually a portrait. There is little doubt that many mezzotints, in so far as two media are comparable, are superior to their originals: compare, for example, John Raphael Smith's *Mrs Carnac* with Reynolds' original in the Wallace Collection. Although many mezzotints have been printed in colours, the effect being often very impressive, the mezzotint depends on its rich tonal qualities for its effect of colour, thus rendering real colours superfluous, even distracting: so one must expect a mezzotint to be printed in black or deep shades of brown. Anyone who has seen a row of well-framed mezzotints ranged along a wall cannot fail to have been impressed by their decorative effect; their purely tonal colouring seems to enhance nearly all normal colour patterns of the average interior.

A mezzotint is produced by roughening, or grounding, a highly polished sheet of copper all over with a rocker, an instrument resembling a chisel but having a curved serrated edge with cutting teeth. The blade of the rocker is rocked to and fro in hundreds of criss-cross lines until the plate is so roughened that there is no discernible pattern. The grooves caused by laying the ground hold the ink. If the plate were inked over at this stage and an impression taken on a sheet of paper a uniformly deep black image would result. In order to produce a mezzotint the ground has to be scraped. With a scraper, a tool with a flat, curved blade finely sharpened, the engraver scrapes away at the ground on to which the design has been sketched, smoothing down those portions which are to be lighter than the rest, and continuing until the right contrast of light and dark tones has been produced to complete the design. If the engraver wants a highlight he polishes that particular part of the surface with a burnisher. It will have become apparent from the process described that the mezzotint is ideally suited to effects of moonlight, the representation of dress and velvet hangings, and softness of facial expression: in fact, all the trappings of a portrait.

The mezzotint was invented by Ludwig von Siegen (1609–76), a soldier in the service of William VI, Landgrave of Hesse-Cassel. Von Siegen was a lover of the arts and particularly of engraving. The first finished mezzotint was a portrait of the Landegrave's mother, *The Landegravine Amelia Elizabeth* done in the year 1642. Von Siegen kept the process secret until twelve years later when he met a fellow soldier artist and engraver, none other than Prince Rupert. The Prince at once saw the possibilities. Before long he produced a mezzotint, *The Executioner of John The Baptist* after Ribera, the intensity and power of which has seldom been equalled in this medium. The quality of this print may in part be due to the strange appearance of early mezzotints, which have all the primitive force of an entirely new medium, but more particularly because of obvious indications that the process was different from that commonly used during the next two hundred years. Thus it was that Prince Rupert introduced the art to England, where it rapidly took roots. Abroad, where the line-engraving held first place, the mezzotint flourished little and indeed became known as "the English Manner".

One of the first to work in "The English Manner" was a Dutchman named Abraham Blooteling (1634–98), already distinguished abroad for his line-engravings. During his four years in England from 1672 he engraved a number of mezzotint portraits after Lely with considerable success; perhaps the finest was his *James, Duke of Monmouth*. The honour of producing the first dated mezzotint by an Englishman falls to William Sherwin (*fl.* 1669–1711). This was a portrait of Charles II dated 1669. The weakness of this print is its coarse texture, a fault with most early mezzotints. Sherwin was a talented amateur. Another was Francis Place (1647–1728), who was quickly drawn to the new medium, producing a few smooth-toned mezzotints. With Isaac Beckett (1653–1719) we come to the first English mezzotint engraver who practised extensively and may be said to have founded a school. As with most mezzotinters of this period, a large proportion of his prints are after the fashionable portraitists of the day, first Lely, then Kneller. He engraved about a hundred known plates in which he shows a skilful use of the scraper, although tending at times to a deadly monotony. Occasionally he achieved sufficient grace to rival John Smith. A typical example of Beckett at his best may be seen in his *Lady Williams* after Wissing. One of the most interesting of this early group was George White (1684–1732). He tended to use the etched line in combination with the scraper, a practice common to both the earliest and the latest mezzotint engravers. He was, perhaps, the first to show the affinity between artist and engraver which characterizes the best mezzotints, in his broad, fluent strokes, which catch the spirit of brush work in oil-painting. This is particularly evident in his *William Dobson* after Dobson.

John Smith (*c.* 1652–1742), the first of the great masters of the mezzotint, produced nearly three hundred portraits, ranging in quality from dull to excellent. Unfortunately a great number of Smith's plates were extensively printed from after his death. Thus impressions from these plates, faded and ghostly, are commonly met with, and others, when he destroyed the plates, are extremely rare. An early impression of one of his prints, such as *Mrs Arabella Hunt* after Kneller or *Charles XII of Sweden* after Von Krafft (Plate 400A), shows Smith to have been master of his medium. In the latter print the sensitive face of the great soldier set in the flowing curls of his periwig and the steely glint of the armour are engraved with refinement and vigour, characteristic of the subject of the portrait. Indeed, the qualities of John Smith's style at its best are sensitivity, strength, and a kind of watery lucidity, which can be most readily admired in some of the very small subject plates after Titian, Coreggio, and other Italians. These tiny crystallizations from great originals are among the most lovely of all mezzotints.

If Smith dissipated his energy in over-production, John Faber the younger (1684–1756) spread his rather meagre talent over more than four hundred plates. Occasionally, in prints like his *Lady Christiana Moray Abercairny* after Davison and his very rare *Lute-player* after Franz Hals, he was equal to the best of John Smith. He is chiefly remembered for his forty-eight portraits of the Kit-Kat Club after Kneller and the twelve *Beauties of Hampton Court*. He lived to engrave portraits after Sir Joshua Reynolds.

During the first forty years of the eighteenth century the mezzotint went into a decline; for the stiff and awkward style of the fashionable portraitists of that period gave little encouragement, and it was due to the work of two engravers in Dublin, Andrew Miller and John Brooks, that the art was kept alive. The rise of Reynolds, Romney, and Gainsborough gave the mezzotint exactly the kind of stimulus it needed, and one by one the Dublin engravers came to London, so that in a short time the mezzotint flourished again until it quickly attained a glory never surpassed.

Of the Irish group, James McArdell (1729–65) was the greatest. In his short life of thirty-six years he engraved over two hundred plates, and he is the first to have engraved to any great extent after Reynolds. Scarcely any of his plates are without distinction, and the finest have few equals. He was matchless in his ability to stimulate the actual texture of costumes. His best plates glow with the most radiant kind of virtuosity, so that one is compelled to turn to them again and again. His *Duchess of Ancaster* (Plate 401) after Thomas Hudson is one of the most beautiful female portraits and one of the greatest mezzotints ever engraved. This must always be one of the first to be sought by the collector. The sweetness of expression, elegance of pose, and the luxuriant dexterity with which the dress is engraved combine to produce a print of consummate brilliance. The same power may be seen in his *Lady Mary Coke* after Ramsay, and again in his *Lords John and Bernard Stuart* after Van Dyck. Others of special quality are *Lady Charlotte Fitzwilliam* after Reynolds and *Mrs Middleton* after Lely. McArdell's contemporary and fellow Irishman Richard Houston (1721–75) is chiefly remembered for his powerful interpretations of Rembrandt. Of his prints after Reynolds, *Harriet Powell* has always been popular.

With Edward Fisher (1722–85), another of the Irish school, we come to a powerful engraver who earned Reynolds' unfair rebuke that he paid too much attention to unnecessary details. On the contrary, Fisher showed great skill in his handling of tone-surfaces. Of his sixty-odd plates one must single out *Lady Elizabeth Keppel* (Plate 400A) after Reynolds. This plate went through five states. In the third state the inscription was carefully erased so as to stimulate a first state. An early state will reveal the true richness and variety of this dignified print, in which Fisher makes skilful use of the etching needle. His *Hope Nursing Love* after Reynolds combined strength with sweetness, and has a sumptuous tonal quality. Yet another Irishman, John Dixon (1730–1800), had great merit. His *Duchess of Ancaster* after Reynolds is a powerful print. The same must be said of his *Rembrandt's Frame-maker* after Rembrandt. The last of the Irish group, James Watson (1739–90), was an engraver of considerable delicacy and technical skill, though sometimes lacking in strength. His many plates have a consistently high quality, and he is said to have always destroyed an unsatisfactory plate rather than re-engrave on it. Of his male portraits *Dr Johnson* and *Thomas Burke* after Reynolds and *Augustus Hervey* after Gainsborough are noteworthy. Among the women, prints like his *Countess of Suffolk* after Read and *Mrs Hale* after Reynolds are typical.

William Pether (1731–1821) is placed slightly apart from the main stream. He engraved some very powerful mezzotints, few of them portraits. His best are after Rembrandt and Joseph Wright of Derby. *A Philosopher giving a Lecture on the Orrery* shows him to be a master of brilliant artificial light effects. Richard Earlom (1743–1822), an engraver justly famous for his versatility and skill, produced some fine mezzotints after Van Huysum, Snyders, and Mario di' Fiori. These flower-pieces, market scenes, and *The Concert of Birds*, in particular, after the last of these make a welcome break from the tradition of portraiture.

The great period of the mezzotint may be said to fall between approximately 1770 and 1810, and we come now to the school of mezzotinters who brought the medium nearest to perfection during the time of Reynold's mature period.

Few names shine as brightly in the history of the mezzotint as that of Valentine Green (1739–1813). A native of Worcestershire, he learnt to engrave in mezzotint after a short spell of line-engraving, and during his life produced some hundreds of plates. His style, at its best, is distinguished by the utmost delicacy and smoothness, and by the most meticulous handling of tone-surfaces: at its worst his prints are flat to the point of monotony. The brilliance of his best plates and the skill with which Reynolds' portraits are translated to the engraver's medium have placed his plates among the most highly prized of all, a fact once reflected in the auction rooms, where hundreds of pounds were paid for single impressions. Out of a score of outstanding plates may be mentioned his *Maria Cosway* after herself (Plate 403B) a portrait of haunting beauty, *Valentine Green* after Abbott, a fine male portrait, and of the many portraits after Reynolds: *The Duchess of Rutland* (for which £1,555 has been paid in the auction room), *The Duchess of Devonshire* (£1,333 was paid in 1924), *The Ladies Waldegrave*, a lovely but rare print, *Lady Elizabeth Compton*, and the sensitive and sophisticated print of *Louise, Countess of Aylesford*. From a host of prints after other artists one might add the suavely executed *General Washington* after Peale.

The name of Thomas Watson (1748(43?)–81) also stands high among mezzotinters. His powerful style is characterized by great depth and warmth of tone. His famous *Lady Bampfylde* after Reynolds for long held the record auction price of 1,200 guineas in the Huth sale of 1905. The large triple portrait known as *The Three Graces* after Reynolds is a print of most impressive richness and dignity. *Warren Hastings* after Reynolds is a notable mezzotint. In a set of six prints entitled *The Windsor Beauties* after Lely, Watson engraved with the assurance of a master. In 1778 Watson took William Dickinson (1746–1823) into partnership. Dickinson was a fine engraver with a stylistic affinity to Watson. The treatment of backgrounds, in the suggestion of thundery skies, rich foliage, and streaks of light became a convention with later engravers. Dickinson had the lighter touch, and in two full-length portraits after Reynolds, *Diana Viscountess Crosbie* (Plate 401B) and *Mrs Mathew*, he placed himself in the first rank. Characteristic of his grace and vigour are *Miss Benedetta Ramus* and *Mrs Pelham feeding Chickens*.

With one or two notable exceptions, John Jones (1745–97) is chiefly remembered as an engraver of male portraits. He had a bold painterly style which may be seen in his many portraits after Romney, of which his *Edmund Burke* is a fine example. The fascination of *Madame Giovanni Baccelli* is vividly conveyed in his full-length portrait after Gainsborough.

By far the most generally talented of them all is John Raphael Smith (1752–1812). An artist in his own right, J. R. Smith handled the mezzotint with the freedom and assurance of an original artist. His powerful style, changing with ease from boldness to restraint according to the nature of the subject, leaves mere interpretation far behind. Of the many superb prints after Reynolds, Romney, and Gainsborough, one can only list a few. The serenely beautiful print of *Mrs Carnac* (with an erstwhile sale record of £1,218) deserves pride of place; not far behind is his *Mrs Musters*; *Lady Catherine Pelham Clinton* and *The Children of Walter Synnot* are very appealing

child subjects; and *Colonel Tarleton* is a vigorous portrait. Romney is no less well served in his large *The Gower Family* (Plate 400C); the stylish costume in *Miss Cumberland* (Plate 403A) is accomplished with wonderful *panache*. Out of dozens of equally desirable prints may be mentioned *Lady Elizabeth Compton* after Peters, *The Fruit Barrow* after Walton, typical of his many genre pieces, and lastly his immensely powerful *John Philpot Curran* (Plate 400B) after Lawrence. George Morland's bucolic scenes were ably translated by J. R. Smith.

John Dean (1750–1805) was a mezzotinter of unusual refinement, whose few plates have more charm than vigour. James Walker (1748–1808) engraved one or two fine plates, notably *Mrs Musters* and the rare *Admiral Sir Hyde Parker*. John Young (1755–1825) is chiefly remembered for his attractive plates after Hoppner, including the famous *The Godsall Children*. Gainsborough Dupont (1767–97) engraved twelve of his uncle Thomas Gainsborough's works, of which *Colonel St Leger*, pendant to J. R. Smith's *George, Prince of Wales*, is a fine example. Charles Phillips (1737–73) is remembered solely for his rare and lovely print *Nelly O'Brien* after Reynolds.

Even during J. R. Smith's lifetime, the mezzotint was on the decline. This was partly due to a similar decline in portraiture: the latent harshness and facility of Lawrence's portraits were less suited than the softer and richer tones of Reynolds' canvases to translation into the medium of mezzotint. William Ward (1766 and 1826) was scarcely less good than his master J. R. Smith. While he excelled at portraiture he is chiefly remembered for his fine prints of farmyard and ale-house scenes after his brother-in-law George Morland. His many portraits include the rare circular print, *Elizabeth, Countess of Mexborough*, the very popular *Daughters of Sir Thomas Frankland*, and *The Salad Girl* (*Mrs Phoebe Hoppner*), all after Hoppner. The full-length portrait of *Henry Beaufoy* is an attractive print after Gainsborough. James Ward (1769–1859), in his life of ninety years, engraved only in his early period. He at least equalled his brother in quality, if not in output, producing mezzotints in a vigorous and powerful style. The affectations first noticeable in Thomas

Watson's prints are more pronounced in James Ward's. His extremely rare and beautiful print *Mrs Michael Angelo Taylor as "Miranda"* after Hoppner is one of the most desirable of all mezzotints. A fine portrait of *Joseph Wright of Derby* after himself is also worthy of note.

S. W. Reynolds (1773–1835) produced a great number of plates, the best of which are his earliest. His *Duchess of Bedford* (1803) is perhaps the last of the great full-length portraits of women in mezzotint. Charles Turner (1774–1857) engraved a variety of subjects on a very large number of plates. Only his earliest work is of real interest, and shows him to be a good interpreter of Raeburn. His *Lord Newton* after this artist reveals Turner at his best. Samuel Cousins (1801–87) engraved a great quantity of plates after Lawrence, many

of them on steel, the pernicious invention of a certain William Say (1768–1834) dating from 1820. This invention may be said to have dealt the death blow to the mezzotint as a medium. A print engraved on steel, a harder-wearing metal than copper, will produce well over a thousand good impressions, but the result lacks the marvellous quality of a mezzotint engraved on copper, which can produce only about two dozen perfect impressions before the plate begins to wear. A brief and final mention must be made of David Lucas (1802–81), whose talented plates after Constable's landscapes, seem to underline the suitability of the medium to portraiture.

Mezzotints are fragile and should be well cared for, and protected against dirt, exposure, or too much handling. It is then that they will give most pleasure.

European

PRINTS

"Almost every man of taste is in some degree a collector of prints," wrote Joseph Strutt in 1785, when the vogue for print collecting was at its height and no gentleman's library was considered complete without a bulging portfolio of etchings and engravings. The same could hardly be said today, but there are signs that the tide of taste is changing once again. Now that paintings and drawings of high quality are becoming annually scarcer and more expensive, an increasing number of collectors are turning their attention to works by the outstanding etchers and engravers of the past, and discovering that these prints are no mere "second best" alternatives, but individual works of art of considerable interest and great beauty.

Prints may be divided into two main categories, the original and the reproductive, the former being those etched, engraved, or lithographed by the artists who provided the designs, and the latter those executed by one

artist after the paintings or drawings of another. The appeal of original prints need hardly be laboured, for they often form as important a part of an artist's output and give as clear an impression of his personality as his work in other mediums. Indeed, many great artists found in print-making, usually in etching, an alternative means of self-expression. Reproductive prints should not, however, be slighted. Dürer usually and Holbein invariably employed skilled craftsmen to transfer their designs to the printer's block, and throughout the subsequent centuries artists who were uncertain of their abilities as cutters and engravers called on specialists to perform these technical parts of their work. The process of reproductive engraving is a difficult one, requiring not only a virtuoso's command of the burin but also an intuitive understanding of the master's painting or drawing. Great reproductive engravers (like Marcantonio Raimondi) have possessed both technical ability and also a high degree of interpretative artistry. Both reproductive and original prints were widely collected in the past, and both types were extensively faked. The collector must therefore be on his guard against forgeries, especially of the most valuable prints.

Fakes

"Woe to you! you thieves and imitators of other people's labour and talents. Beware of laying your audacious hands on our works," wrote Dürer at the end of a series of woodcuts, but his words were little heeded, and few artists have suffered more than he from the wiles of thieves and imitators. Even in his own time his woodcuts were plagiarized with varying degrees of fidelity and his monogram was freely applied to indifferent works by other artists. The simple lines of the woodcut provided fakers with some of their easiest work, and early prints have been imitated in freehand by the use of new blocks which reproduce the old designs, by lithograph, and by zincograph. Most of these fraudulent prints were copies of well-known works, but one nineteenth-century forger was sufficiently enterprising and, we may now say, sufficiently rash, as to fabricate a whole series of cunning pastisches called the *Saints of Basle*, which he dated 1414 and which enjoyed such a success among unsuspecting collectors of incunabula that it went into three editions, marked by minuscule differences of state. Rembrandt's etchings were copied free-hand and in the mid-eighteenth century Benjamin Wilson etched an "original" Rembrandt landscape which hoaxed Thomas Hudson. But his reputation has suffered more harm from his own plates, some fifty of which survived him and were unscrupulously used to multiply impressions long after his death. To repair the damage of frequent use these plates had to be heavily re-worked, and the prints made from them have none of the sparkling freshness of those Rembrandt pulled himself. In the detection of forged prints the study of watermarks is, alas, of little avail, since most competent fakers took the precaution of printing or drawing their impostures on paper of the correct period. The only sure method of showing up a dubious print is to compare it with a similar work of undoubted authenticity in one of the great collections of Europe or America.

The prints mentioned in this section are those valued primarily for their aesthetic or technical merits, but there are, of course, many others, the main interest of which lies in their subject matter. These include portraits, topographical views, caricatures, and representations of historical events, many of which have great charm. Their importance to the historian is obvious, but the collector of fine prints concerns himself with them only if they have independent artistic qualities.

Incunabula

The earliest surviving European prints date from the first half of the fifteenth century. They represent religious scenes and were mostly printed in monasteries, usually from wooden blocks (Plate 412A) but sometimes from metal plates. Designed principally for an unlettered public, they have none of the sophistication of contemporary manuscript illuminations, but are characterized by an engaging peasant *naïveté* of conception and rustic virility of line. By 1457, however, the art of the wood-block carver had developed to such a degree that he was able to produce the superb two-colour initials to Fust and Schoeffer's Latin Psalter. In the 1450s and 1460s fine line-engravings were being printed in Germany not only of religious themes such as *The Death of Mary* but also of such decidedly secular subjects as *The Gardens of Love*.

Martin Schongauer (*c.* 1430–91), the first great German line-engraver, emerged at Colmar in about 1453. A master of his medium, able to give his prints a greater subtlety of tone than any of his predecessors, he was also a religious artist of great power, as is shown by his brilliant engraving of *Christ Falling Beneath the Cross*. His near contemporary, Israhel van Meckenem (d. 1503) executed a number of religious engravings as well as a series of a dozen very attractive genre scenes. Meanwhile, the art of line-engraving had been introduced into Italy by Maso Finiguerra (1426–64), a Florentine niellist whose work shows the strong influence of Antonio

Pollaiuolo (1432–98). Unfortunately Pollaiuolo's own graphic work is known by only one plate, the superb and mysterious *Battle of Ten Nudes* (Plate 412C), which shows his complete mastery of the medium and is drawn with the same sinewy strength as his paintings. In northern Italy, Andrea Mantegna (1431–1506) (Plate 413A) was producing engravings in a similarly fine but somewhat harder style. Before the century had ended the *Hypnerotomachia Poliphili* illustrated with numerous highly sophisticated and elegantly simple woodcuts was published in Venice. Within a hundred years the art of the woodcutter and engraver had developed from infancy to maturity.

Sixteenth-century prints

First among early sixteenth-century print makers was Albrecht Dürer (1471–1528), who executed etchings, line-engravings, and drypoint engravings as well as designing the woodcuts for which he is principally remembered. His prints are technically flawless, having an elegant sensitivity of line and subtlety of tone which demonstrate his perfect understanding of the potentialities of each medium he employed. Moreover, the extraordinarily wide range of their subject matter – religious, mythological, and allegorical – reveals him as one of the great personalities of the age of Humanism and the Reformation. As to the aesthetic value of his prints, suffice it to say that he is the only major European artist whose stature would be undiminished if he were known only by his graphic work (Plate 412B). Hans Holbein (1497–1543) showed a similarly nice regard for the wood-block medium in his *Dance of Death* series, and in the Netherlands Lucas van Leyden (1494–1533) adapted his style to the needs of the copper plate. Among Italian line-engravers of this period Marcantonio Raimondi (1480–*c.* 1530) (Plate 413C) is probably the greatest, though his work was largely reproductive. Notable French engravers do not appear until later in the century, the earliest of interest being Jean Duvet (1485–*c.* 1561), whose works, especially the *Apocalypse* series (Plate 413D), seem to recreate the fervid mysticism of the Middle Ages.

The art of etching, which was developed in Germany at the beginning of the century and practised by Dürer, was introduced into Italy in about 1520. Here it was taken up by Parmigianino (1504–40) and later by Federigo Barocci (1528–1612), who executed a few exquisite plates in this medium. The most notable etchers of the later sixteenth century were, however, the group of Netherlandish landscape painters which included Pieter Breughel (1525–69), Jan Breughel (1568–1625), and Paul Bril (1554–1626). The chiaroscuro process also originated in Germany and was introduced by Ugo da Carpi (*fl. c.* 1455–1527) (Plate 413B) into Italy, where it was found a perfect means for the reproduction of mannerist designs. Towards the end of the century it was much used in the Netherlands by Hendrik Goltzius (1558–1616) and Abraham Bloemaert (1564–1661).

Seventeenth-century prints

The seventeenth century may well be regarded as the golden age of etching which was practised by a considerable number, one might almost say the majority, of leading painters. Moreover, the period is marked by the emergence of a number of highly interesting artists who are known principally, if not solely, for their works in this medium. At the beginning of the century in France, Jacques Bellange (*fl.* 1600–16) evolved a highly sophisticated and fantastic personal style, based on a strange medley of mannerist influences, which he expressed in a few etchings of scenes (mostly religious) populated with small-headed, long-necked women in sweeping robes. Another latter-day mannerist etcher was Jacques Callot (1592–1635) (Plate 414A), who worked from 1611 to 1621 at the Medici court, where he executed vast plates of Florentine festivities and tiny grotesques of prancing, gesticulating, and grimacing pantaloons, hunchbacks, and dwarfs. A note of seriousness crept into his work after his return to France and in 1633 he etched the terrifying yet very beautiful *Grandes Misères de la Guerre*, which eloquently expressed his horror at the atrocities of the Thirty Years' War. Callot's Florentine pupil, Stefano della Bella (1610–64), brilliantly developed the fantastic strain in his master's work and also executed some delicate topographical plates. Abraham Bosse (1602–76), who collaborated with Callot in Paris, applied himself to the semi-satirical rendering of genre scenes. A French artist of a very different stamp, Claude Lorrain (1600–82), etched some of his idyllic visions of the Roman Campagna and that more volatile landscape painter, the Neapolitan Salvator Rosa (1615–73), etched a few plates of bloodthirsty *banditti* and *Landsknechte*.

In the Netherlands Sir Anthony van Dyck (1599–1641) showed himself a masterly etcher in twenty-two prints (mostly portraits) which he produced in the late 1620s. Another notable Flemish etcher of this period was Hercules Seghers (c. 1590–c. 1635), who executed prints of landscapes and other subjects in a wholly individual manner and experimented by printing them on tinted paper or linen. But the outstanding figure of the century is, of course, Rembrandt (1606–69) (Plate 414B), who began his work as an etcher in about 1628.

More than any other great artist, Rembrandt found an ideal means of self-expression in the art of etching, and for a full understanding of his personality his works in this medium must be given as much prominence as his paintings and drawings. Tireless in his search for expression, he experimented not only with problems of composition and form but also with technical matters, combining the dry point with the etching needle to obtain some of his finest effects. His three hundred-odd prints, varying in size from the tiny *Beggars* to such grandiose plates as *The Death of the Virgin*, testify to his remarkable virtuosity as a craftsman no less than to his fecundity as an imaginative artist. With equal success he was able to represent the icy calm of a Dutch winter landscape and the stormy drama of *The Descent from the Cross*, the beautiful and resigned face of his mother and the angry countenance of a starving beggar. Furthermore, his etchings supplement the incomparable autobiography presented by his self-portraits in oil, showing him truculent in youth, pompously prosperous in maturity and utterly disillusioned in his last years. Few

artists have rivalled the technical perfection of Rembrandt's etchings, and none has approached his ability to express the profoundest thoughts and emotions in this medium.

Eighteenth-century prints

At the beginning of the century, in France, Antoine Watteau (1684–1721) made a few etchings of gossamer delicacy; many of his drawings were etched by his pupil François Boucher (1703–70), who also did original work in this medium. Later, Jean Honoré Fragonard (1732–1806) etched a few plates of nymphs and satyrs which have the same gay lightness of touch as his drawings (Plate 415B). But the greatest French contribution during this period was in book illustrations printed from line-engravings designed by such master hands as H. F. Gravelot (1699–1773), Charles Eisen (1720–78), Charles N. Cochin (1715–90), and a host of others, some of whom engraved the architectural fantasies of Lajoue, the rococo furniture designs of Meissonnier, and the gay chinoiseries of Pillement. To obtain their effects of cobweb brittleness most of these artists employed a mixture of etching and engraving.

In Italy the most productive centre of print-making was Venice, where Giovanni Battista Tiepolo (1696–1770) and his son Giovanni Domenico Tiepolo (1727–1804) produced many lovely etchings of *capricci* and religious scenes. Canaletto (1697–1768) (Plate 415A) also etched *capricci* and some shimmering views of the lagoon. Moreover, a group of line-engravers, of whom Marco Pitteri (1707–86) was probably the ablest, produced admirable prints after the drawings of G. B. Piazzetta and other contemporary masters. The most remarkable of Venetian graphic artists was, however, Giovanni Battista Piranesi (1720–78) (Plate 416A), who spent most of his working life in Rome, where he etched phantasmagoric scenes of imaginary prisons and scarcely less imaginative and dramatic views of classical ruins.

Nineteenth-century prints

The cult of the picturesque greatly increased the demand for topographical prints in the early nineteenth century. Perhaps the most notable artist to produce such works was Bartolomeo Pinelli (1781–1835), whose etchings, engravings, and aquatints of Rome and the Campagna populated with picturesque bandits fighting, peasants gaming, and spruce young couples dancing the *saltarello* have greatly contributed to the northerner's romantic vision of Italy.

Soon after the beginning of the nineteenth century, lithography ousted nearly all other means of colour reproduction and provided artists with an alternative to etching. Many great artists, including Géricault (Plate 416B), Delacroix, and Blake, essayed the new medium, but none as successfully as Francisco Goya (1746–1828) (Plate 417A). Goya found both lithography and aquatint excellent mediums in which to express his devastatingly satirical message, and his prints are among the finest ever made. Later in the century, lithography was employed by the two great French masters of caricature, Gavarni (1804–66) and Honoré Daumier (1808–79).

The mid-nineteenth-century interest in the past brought about the revival of nearly all the old methods of reproduction for "artistic" purposes. After about 1850 the lithographic and line-engraving processes were principally used for commercial purposes, while the crafts of wood-block cutting, etching, and dry-point engraving were reserved for artists; though relatively few of them attained an understanding of the mediums in which they worked. However, some revivalist engravers like William Hooper (1834–1912), who cut the Renaissance style wood-blocks for books printed at the Kelmscott Press, achieved very fine effects. Several Impressionist painters, including Edgar Degas and Édouard Manet, created prints of exquisite quality.

EUROPEAN SILHOUETTES

Although its origins go back to classical antiquity, the silhouette as we recognize it today most likely originated at the end of the seventeenth century. Doubtless various influences contributed to its subsequent popularity, but probably the greatest stimulus it received came from the publication of Johann Kaspar Lavater's *Essays on Physiognomy* in the 1770s, in which, as well as claiming the silhouette to be the most faithful of all types of portrait, the author used many such portraits for illustrating his work.

At about this time silhouettes became fashionable and their popularity spread everywhere, finding admirers so diverse in character as Johann von Goethe, King George III of England, and the Empress Catherine the Great of Russia.

The earliest silhouettes were probably scissor-cuts. One was that of William and Mary, said to have been cut by Elizabeth Pyburg (*fl.* 1699). Indeed, these early cut silhouettes have great charm, and are much sought after by collectors. Some of them – especially those of Francis Torond (1743–1812) – are of great rarity.

But charming though these old cut silhouettes are, the art's highest peaks have undoubtedly been reached by artists producing painted work. It is generally agreed that one of the greatest silhouettists of all was John Miers (1758–1821), whose work is painted as finely as the most delicate miniature. Although not so prolific a worker as Miers, Isabella Beetham (*fl.* 1750), whose work was painted mostly on the reverse side of convex glass, is, so far as quality is concerned, at least his equal.

At the end of the eighteenth century the silhouette went into a period of decline, from which it was rescued mostly through the efforts of Augustin Amant Constant Fidèle Edouart and the French refugee who came to England in 1814. Edouart, a free-hand cutter, initiated the second and last great period of English silhouettes. His output was enormous (he cut something approaching a quarter of a million likenesses), and this fact, coupled with the publication of his (now excessively rare) *Treatise* on the subject, published in 1835, gave a great impetus to the numerous and often very able school of amateur silhouettists that arose at the time.

The Continent, too, produced a large number of good silhouettists during the eighteenth and nineteenth centuries. The art particularly flourished in Germany. Goethe himself was a cutter, and mention must also be made of the delicate and lacy cut-work of Christina Luise Duttenhofer (1776–1829) and that of Philipp Otto Runge (1776/7–1810). France produced A. Forberger (1762–1865) and E. P. Sideau (*fl.* 1782); and Austria H. Loeschenkohl (*fl.* 1780) and Leopold Gross (*fl.* 1790). In fact, most European countries can boast at least one or two silhouettists of some standing.

Although silhouette work continues to be used even today, its heyday as a form of portraiture ended with the invention of photography. It is one of the few fields still open in which the collector can obtain genuine rarities at reasonable prices.

Italian

EIGHTEENTH CENTURY

There can be no doubt that the greatest *settecento* draughtsmen were the Venetians: G. B. Piazzetta, G. B. Tiepolo, Canaletto, G. B. Piranesi, and Francesco Guardi. It is naturally the aim of every collector of Italian eighteenth-century drawings to obtain specimens of their work. The steadily rising prices of the art market have, however, placed the best drawings of these masters beyond the pockets of all but the most affluent or the most fortunate. Collectors of moderate means will therefore be well advised to turn their attention to the work of less well-known artists. Many of the minor painters of the Venetian school were exquisite draughtsmen: indeed, their works often pass under the names of their greater contemporaries. Painters working in other cities, especially Bologna, Turin, Florence, Rome, Naples, and, towards the end of the century, Milan, also deserve more attention than they have hitherto received. But collectors need not confine their attention to the drawings of painters. Architectural drawings of this period depicting the vast façades of palaces or churches richly embellished with statuary – many of which appear to have been day-dreams of over-ambitious architects – are often of fine quality. So, too, are the many designs for stage sets drawn by the members of the Bibiena family and their imitators. Caricatures present a fascinating glimpse of Italian life as its most exuberant. And the gouache views of Venice, Rome, and the Bay of Naples, with their cloudless skies and gaily dressed figures, originally painted for northern grand tourists, still serve as delightful souvenirs of an Italian visit.

Old master drawings of all periods may roughly be divided into two categories: those executed as studies for works in other mediums, and those which were created as an end in themselves. The former group includes studies for parts of paintings and ideas (or *pensieri*) for compositions, the architect's first rough designs for his buildings and the details of their ornament, and the sketches of sculptors. In the latter class there are portraits, caricatures, fancy pieces, and topographical views. But the dividing line between these groups is often difficult to draw, and it is a matter of opinion whether certain of Tiepolo's drawings of *putti* and mythological scenes, though they do not differ in style or handling from his sketches for identifiable paintings, were not executed for the portfolios of the *cognoscenti*. Nor is it easy to determine whether many drawings of single figures were done simply as academic exercises or to provide the artist with a guide for his work in fresco or oils. The following account of the principal types of drawings which the collector is likely to encounter is therefore arranged according to their subject matter rather than their intention.

Sketches for religious and mythological paintings have probably won the attention of collectors more than any other type of drawing, for they give a glimpse of the artist's creative imagination at work. If, as is rarely possible, a group of drawings for a single picture can be assembled, they reveal the artist struggling with both the problem of his general composition and the details of its various parts. Very seldom do these preliminary sketches tally precisely with the painting itself. An inventive artist would naturally make alterations, however slight, as he transferred his design on to canvas. Highly finished drawings which exactly correspond with painted compositions or parts of them are therefore more likely to have been executed (sometimes by the artist himself) as a record rather than a design. In style these sketches reflect the artistic currents of eighteenth-century Italy. Most of those produced in the first quarter of the century continue the baroque tradition of the previous period. Though even the earliest eighteenth-century Venetian drawings have a hint of that rococo elegance which was to mark the work of this school until the very end of the century, long after the rest of Italy had succumbed to neo-classicism. In Rome the first breath of neo-classicism was felt before the middle of the century, and its influence grew steadily stronger in the succeeding fifty years, during which it spread to other parts of the peninsula. Under the influence of this new movement drawings lost much of their exuberance, the figures in them became increasingly statuesque and solid, details of classical costume and architectural backgrounds were drawn with greater regard for archaeological accuracy. Drawings of this later period are often of fine quality, and as they have been very little studied up to now, they provide a very rich field for the collector.

The gradual transition from baroque to rococo and the more sudden break between the latter style and neo-classicism may similarly be seen in the drawings of sculptors, of which all too few survive (save those of Canova). Drawings for sculpture raise a difficult problem, however, for many of those recorded were executed by painters or architects who in this period often designed the sepul-chral monuments which were then carved in marble by the sculptor. Architectural drawings are far more numerous, including rough sketches for whole buildings and their decorations, and highly finished projects. The most notable are, perhaps, those of Filippo Juvarra, which have a brilliant bravura and reveal as complete a command of pen and ink as any contemporary painter. The more meticulous designs of later architects, especially those of the Lombard school – Quarenghi, Piermarini, and Cagnola – though less spirited, have great charm and elegance. Some of the architects, including Juvarra, provided designs for furniture, but this seems to have been an unusual practice. A few craftsmen's drawings have, however, survived, notably a series by the silversmith Giuseppe Valadier in the Cooper Union Museum, New York.

Closely connected with the more grandiose mid-eighteenth-century architectural drawings are the theatrical designs: prospects for vast and impractical palaces, all colonnades and *cortili* and flights of steps. The most famous Italian stage designers of the eighteenth century were the various members of the Galli di Bibiena family, whose name has been indiscriminately applied to the majority of drawings of this type. Somewhat similar architectural fantasies, or *capricci*, were executed for their own sake by a number of artists including Juvarra and Piranesi.

Capricci of a somewhat different type were drawn (and painted) by the Venetian *vedutisti* (view painters), who occasionally represented imaginary groups of buildings gathered together from various islands in the lagoon and even from the mainland. Some of these (Plate 427) are so deceptively realistic that students have sought in vain for actual views in Venice which correspond with them. In style they are indistinguishable from the same artists' topographical views, for which there was a steady demand, especially among visiting grand tourists, throughout the eighteenth century. Venetian artists were the most accomplished at this type of work, but very attractive views were produced in nearly all Italian towns. In the mid-century, topographical artists began to produce gouache views which seem particularly to have appealed to those who were unable to afford large paintings but wanted more colourful records of their Italian tour than could be provided by pen-and-ink drawings. The production of such gouaches was developed as a minor industry in Venice and Naples towards the end of the eighteenth century.

Among the finished drawings perhaps the most interesting are those which, for want of a better name, may be called Fancy Pieces. They include heads of Orientals, children, and peasants, either single or in groups of two or three. Sometimes these drawings appear to have been executed for engravers to copy (a series by G. B. Piazzetta at Windsor, for example), but others were probably made and sold simply as drawings. G. B. Tiepolo's heads and G. B. Piazzetta's heads of children are the most notable examples of this type of work. Many of G. B. Tiepolo's little mythological scenes and drawings of hunchbacks seem also to have been executed for a market in drawings – it is perhaps significant that they are nearly always signed in full.

Portrait drawings, as distinct from ideal heads, are rare in eighteenth-century Italy, unless we include under this heading the numerous pastels of Rosalba Carriera and her followers. Caricatures are much commoner and provide the collector with a singularly rich and as yet uninvestigated field. The art of caricature seems to have been developed in the studio of the Carracci at Bologna early in the seventeenth century, and during the next hundred and fifty years several artists applied themselves to it – though never, it seems, as a principal occupation. Most famous among them is P. L. Ghezzi, who drew caricatures of nearly all the leading personalities – artistic, social, ecclesiastical – in early eighteenth-century Rome. He was followed by Giuseppe Marchionni, who, however, lacked his wit and ability. G. B. Tiepolo drew caricatures with his accustomed brilliance. Marco Ricci and A. M. Zanetti also drew amusing caricatures, principally of opera singers. The larger caricatures, representing groups of men and women, present engaging pictures of *settecento* life, which were also provided, more seriously, by the drawings of such genre painters as Pietro Longhi.

The training of a painter in eighteenth-century Italy placed great stress on the art of drawing. Early in his career the young artist would begin drawing both nude and draped figures in the life class at his local academy. Many drawings executed at the life class, called Academy Drawings, have survived, some of high quality which are well worth the collector's attention, though it is seldom possible to attribute them to individual artists. They are usually executed in charcoal or red chalk, then on tinted paper, and show models placed in the attitudes of celebrated classical statues or the figures in High Renaissance paintings. Closely allied with them are the drawings after antique statues (though some of these were executed as archaeological records), paintings, and prints. Although they lack the interest of wholly original works, these drawings are not to be despised if they are of good quality.

To distinguish good eighteenth-century copies of earlier drawings from originals is not always easy. And it is also difficult to recognize these drawings which pupils executed after their masters' work; though they are usually given away by an initial hesitancy of line harshly redrawn. Such works were not originally intended to deceive, and cannot therefore be regarded as fakes. So far the fakers seem to have confined their attention to a small circle of artists whose drawings command sufficiently attractive prices: G. B. Piazzetta, G. B. Tiepolo, Francesco Guardi, and the Bibiena family. Copies and fakes can usually be unmasked by comparing them with drawings of undoubted authenticity in the great public and private collections.

In order to attribute a drawing to a particular master it should be compared with undoubted specimens of his work, and not with the large number of drawings which, in ever-widening circles, have accumulated around a few autograph sheets. Unfortunately it is rarely possible to document the history of drawings from the day they left the artist's studio, as may often be done with paintings. Occasionally sketch books of known provenance have come on to the market and their leaves have been dispersed. G. B. Tiepolo made a selection of his own drawings which were bound into nine volumes and, after passing through the hands of several collectors, dismembered. But attributions of drawings must usually be made on stylistic grounds. Inscriptions and signatures which appear to be in the artist's hand may be of help, though they must always be treated with suspicion if they are applied to drawings which differ widely in style or handling from undoubted autograph works. A further aid is provided by collectors' marks. These are little stamped marks, usually to be found in inconspicuous corners, applied by collectors to drawings in their possession. The identification of a mark may not only give the modern collector some indication of the date of a drawing (providing at any rate a *terminus ante quem*) and, occasionally, help in tracing its earlier provenance, but may also remind him that he, too, is a member of the great tradition of amateurs of draughtsmanship to whom the modern world owes the preservation of old master drawings.

Materials: most of the drawings of this period were executed either in pen and ink, charcoal or chalk. The ink normally used was iron gall black, which has faded to a brown colour. Brown ink (either sepia or bistre) was, however, used in the eighteenth century, and Canaletto, for example, occasionally drew his outlines in it and then applied shading with grey Indian ink washes. Charcoal and red and black chalk was much used, especially for academy drawings and rough sketches. Sometimes the charcoal was steeped in oil to make it indelible, though unfortunately this process leaves a slight yellow streak on either side of the line. Black and red chalks were used in conjunction by some artists, and G. A. Pellegrini sometimes combined them with pen and ink and washes. Water-colour was very rarely used in Italy except for architectural drawings. But body colour, usually known as gouache (water-colours mixed with Chinese white to provide opaque pigments), was much used for small landscapes, especially those of famous monuments and views produced for the foreign tourists.

Japanese Prints

SEVENTEENTH AND EIGHTEENTH CENTURIES

The Japanese print was "discovered" soon after the opening up of the country to foreign visitors in 1854, and considerable impetus was given to the formation of collections later in the century by the enthusiasm of the French Impressionists and their protagonists, who found much that appealed to their aesthetic senses, ever tuned to receive the new, the adventurous, the unacademic, in the calculated design and arbitrary use of form and colour, of the Japanese print designers. The most immediately attractive of these exotic engravings were the colour-prints of the late eighteenth century, but in the methodical way of the European art-historian it was not long before the origin of these gay pictures was traced back to black outline prints of the seventeenth century.

Indeed, the earliest wood-engravings made in Japan belong to a very remote period. Some can reliably be given to the eighth century and, as wood-engravings are still being published in Japan, the term "Japanese print" might conceivably embrace everything from the crude Buddhistic cuts of an almost legendary antiquity to the pseudo-Picasso abstractions of post-war Tokyo artists. Specifically, however, the term is usually held to apply to the productions of a certain school of mainly Yedo artists, the Ukiyo-ye, which arose in the mid-seventeenth century, and whose work was virtually ended by the time of the Restoration in 1868.

The collector may not wish to limit himself strictly to this school: book illustrations of great beauty and originality were designed during the Tokugawa or Yedo period (1615–1868) by painters of various other schools whose styles differ vastly from the Ukiyo-ye. Nor need strict regard be given to the limits of the period: one needs to study the illustrated books of the early seventeenth century for the light they throw on the development of the designer's art; and though it is convenient to consider 1868 as a date closing a particular chapter of Japanese art, specimens of the work of artists who flourished thereafter may well be included in a collection, if for no other purpose than to exhibit the changes the "Western invasion" brought about.

At the outset it should be remarked that Japanese prints are all wood-block prints and were issued as much in bound or book form as in the form of separate broadsheets. Folding albums (gwajo) and picture books (yehon) must come within a collector's purview, for no study of the art of the Japanese print as a whole can be complete unless the prints in books are considered side by side with those published as separate sheets. Moreover, whereas practically all the broadsheets were produced by the Ukiyo-ye school, artists of the classical, naturalistic, and impressionistic schools were responsible for some of the loveliest and most remarkable picture books ever printed, East or West.

Technique

Wood-engraving is the traditional, and almost exclusive, means of reproduction in Japan, as in the East generally. By the inheritance of the centuries-old lore of the craft, and by a rigorous apprenticeship, engravers were capable of almost incredible feats in making a facsimile of an artist's brush-drawing. The painter-engraver was unknown: the engraver was a skilled craftsman whose sole task was to make a faithful reproduction of the artists' designs, just as the German engravers made facsimiles of Dürer's designs.

The wood used was normally cherry-wood "on the plank", in contrast to "on the end grain" as in Europe since Bewick's day. The drawing, made on thin paper, was usually pasted face down on to the block, and the paper then scraped to render the drawing

perfectly visible. The engraver or, more properly, cutter, for he used a cutting knife not an engraving tool, made incisions along both sides of the lines, afterwards removing the wood between, leaving the lines in relief.

The printer was, in his way, as much artist-craftsman as the engraver. The ink was brushed on to the block pigments being mixed with a little rice paste to give them consistency, and the impression taken by placing paper over the face of the block and burnishing the back with a rubbing implement called a *baren*. When colour-printing from blocks was introduced a great deal devolved upon the printer. Black ink proofs were taken from the "key-blocks" prepared from the artist's drawing, and the proofs then pasted down on to additional blocks, a separate one for each colour to be printed, the artist indicating on each proof, for the engraver's guidance, the area to be printed in the chosen colour.

In making a colour-print, the same sheet of proofing paper had to pass first over the "key-block" and then over each colour-block in turn. Accurate "register" was achieved by a simple arrangement of a right-angle cut in the blocks at one side with a corresponding guide-line cut at the opposite side.

In addition to the increase in the number of colour-blocks used, various refinements were introduced to embellish the prints, mentioned in the account that follows:

The "Ukiyo-ye" or "Passing world" school

The greatest single impetus to the development of Japanese print came from Hishikawa Moronobu (1626–94). Though not the titular founder of the Ukiyo-ye school (which came to be the Popular school identified with the common people, notwithstanding the fact that its founder was an aristocrat named Matabei), Moronobu came at a time when there was a rapidly expanding demand for illustrated literature of every kind – classical poetry, legend, novel, everyday happenings, descriptions of the well-known landmarks of the country, and especially of the capital, Yedo. Owing to his tutelage in several different schools of Japanese painting, he was capable of drawing in a number of styles, but his most justifiably admired prints and book illustrations show the early Ukiyo-ye style at its best. The bold line and undulating swing in the drawing, coupled with a compact and rhythmic pattern in the design, are characteristics that mark the work of all succeeding Ukiyo-ye artists, and in his treatment of his subject matter we discern already the sophistication, the raciness, and the vulgarity that, in greater or lesser degree, are in the make-up of all subsequent prints of the school. Apart from his development of book illustration as an art, Moronobu is also credited with the production of the first separately printed sheets, called *ichimai-ye.*

Contemporaries of Moronobu, responsible for much fine work in book illustration, were Hinaya Ryūho, Yoshida Hanbei, Ishi-Kawa Ryusen, and Sugimura Jihei, all more or less independent of Moronobu. A little later there were Moronobu's direct pupils, Moroshige and Morofusa.

Towards the end of the seventeenth century prints began to be issued to record the *Kabuki* drama, the popular plays that were filling the Yedo theatres with devotees whose fanaticism was not only equal to the strain of day-long performances but also gave rise to a demand for pictures of favourite actors in their roles in the latest "thriller". Women were debarred from the stage, and female parts were played by men, some actor families specializing in women's roles. It was natural that the People's Theatre should have been recorded by the Ukiyo-ye artists, and actor-prints are as numerous in their output as portraits of the reigning courtesans, the other principal subject.

Among the earliest to make these prints was Torii Kiyonobu (1664–1729), a great artist who had much influence on the development of the actor-print, and whose own gift of expressive draughtsmanship and swirling design was never equalled. His pupils and followers include many of the best designers of the early eighteenth century – Kiyomasu I (1696?–1716?); Kiyomasu II (1706–65); Kiyonobu II (1702–52?), Kiyoshige, Kiyotada, Kiyotomo, and Terushige.

Most of these early prints were hand-coloured, at first with *tan*, a strong red-lead pigment, later with more elaboration. Printing of colours by wood blocks did not occur until many years later.

Other powerful "Primitives", as artists up to the introduction of colour-printing in 1764 are called, are a group of four or five artists bearing the name Kwaigetsudō, whose superb *kakemono-ye* are among the rarest and the most coveted of all Japanese prints; and Nishikawa Sukenobu (1674–1754), whose work is almost confined to book illustrations, in which the rough boldness of his contemporaries is tempered with a grace and gentleness that was to have an immense effect upon aftercomers. Another great artist, a publisher, too, with a flair for technical devices, was Okumura Masanobu (1686–1764). Owing something to Moronobu, Kwaigetsudō, and Sukenobu, and passing through phases when the influence of each of these masters predominated in turn, Masanobu's fusion of strength and grace produced some of the loveliest prints of the first half of the seventeenth century. To him is probably attributable the introduction of *urushi-ye*, the "lacquer-prints" with applied metal dusts, whose glint still catches the eye, as it was meant to catch the eye of the Yedo purchaser over two hundred years ago. His pupil Toshinobu (active 1725–50) also made some very attractive prints of this type.

About 1740, or soon after, occurred the momentous substitution of block-printing of the colours for the hand application that had prevailed hitherto.

Okumura Masanobu has been credited with the introduction of the two-colour process, but by 1740 a number of gifted artists were working in the medium, any one of whom was capable of making the innovation. The most prominent were the Torii masters, Kiyonobu II, Kiyohiro (active 1737–68), and Kiyomitsu (1735–85), all carrying on in the family tradition of actor-print designing, and Nishimura Shigenaga (1697–1756), whose later work shows the trend towards a new ideal of womanhood that was to lead to the exquisite fragility of Harunobu's child-woman. The prints of the Ukiyo-ye school were not only a mirror of the life of the time, the daily events, the customs and festivals but also the glass of fashion. In them one follows the changing predilection of the Yedo male for women of Junoesque amplitude of form in the early years of the eighteenth century, garbed in clothes decorated with patterns that have large pictorial motifs, to the diminutive *musume* of the 'sixties, disporting herself in silks that have the most intricate of pretty designs worked upon them. With this change, quite a gradual one, but speeded up after the introduction of the *beni-ye* prints, came another, no less significant, in the subjects portrayed, an introduction of a more domestic setting, of scenes from play or legend or even daily life, that are in some way made to seem idyllic, to belong to a never-never land of the Japanese artists' imagination.

This magical world is perhaps most the creation of Shigenaga's pupils – Ishikawa Toyonobu (1711–85), Suzuki Harunobu (1739?–70), Isoda Koryūsai (active 1764–80), and Kitao Shigemasa (1739–1819). Toyonobu was the earliest, and, under the name of Shigenobu, designed hand-coloured prints before 1737. His later work, contemporary with that of Kiyomitsu and Kiyohiro, has an individual charm that has caused one Japanese enthusiast to call him the "lyric poet of Ukiyo-ye". Harunobu has been accredited – rightly or wrongly, it hardly matters – with the introduction of the full colour-print which made its appearance about 1764. The innovation coincided with the issue of a flood of calendar prints for the year 1765, a number of which are known to have been designed by Harunobu. Between 1765 and his premature death in 1770 Harunobu designed hundreds of prints that design, colouring, and an exquisite fancy combine to render among the most charming of all the prints of this school.

The introduction of polychrome printing was more the culmination of a gradual development than a sudden innovation, for three and four blocks had been used with entrancing effect by Toyonobu, Kiyomitsu, and Kiyotsune between 1760 and 1765, but the year 1765 is used as an arbitrary line between the "Primitives" and their successors. Thereafter, while there is little new technically in the production of the print once Harunobu

and others had introduced a whole range of lovely colours hitherto untried, and the printers had perfected relief-printing, blind-printing or *gauffrage* and the use of gold and silver dusts and mica backgrounds, many great artists arose to make the fullest use of the perfected medium.

Koryūsai was not only a master of that most typically Japanese, and most exacting, format the *hashirakake*, the long panel print designed to hang on pillars, but he also popularized the large *ōban* sheet with pictures that are really "fashion-plates" showing the reigning beauties in the latest creations of the *haut-couturiers*. Katsukawa Shunshō (1726–92) brought to the narrow *hoso-ye* actor-print wonderful powers of dramatic design, and tutored a whole school of artists, most of whom, like Shunkō, Shunjō, Shundō, Shunyen, and Shunsen, repeated almost exactly the style of their master, while Shunyei, though associated with the theatre, developed on more individual lines. Ippit-Susai Bunchō (active 1760–79) is sharply distinguishable from all his contemporaries, however similar his subject matter, for qualities that spring more, we feel, from an unusual personality than from any especial adroitness of hand. He was equally at home in the theatrical print as in the idyllic composition in Harunobu's vein.

After Harunobu's death in 1770 and Koryūsai's retirement about 1780, Torii Kiyonaga (1752–1815), came to the fore, and in the 'eighties was responsible for a vogue for tall women of regal mien, who now ousted the diminutive *musume* from favour. The diptych and triptych forms, in which the design is carried over two or three sheets, had an especial appeal to Kiyonaga, and through his magnificent example became popular formats with all succeeding Ukiyo-ye artists. As the creator of the currently fashionable feminine "type", Kiyonaga influenced practically all his contemporary print designers, except perhaps the conservative, Shunshō, Shunchō, and Shunzan, originally pupils of Shunchō, and Shunman, who had studied under Shigemasa, were perhaps the most successful followers of the Kiyonaga model, the work of each having certain distinguishing traits, the recognition and identification of which is one of the subtler pleasures of connoisseurship. Kitao Masanobu (1761–1816), another pupil of Shigemasa's, designed some splendid prints in the early 'eighties and seemed to vie for a time with Kiyonaga as the arbiter of fashion in Ukiyo-ye, but deserted painting for literature when quite a young man.

Throughout its history, the Ukiyo-ye school received the stimulus from a new genius in its midst just when the influence of the last was beginning to wane. So now, as Kiyonaga went into retirement about 1790, Kitagawa Utamaro (1753–1806) became this new and revitalizing force. Beginning as a devotee to the Kiyonaga manner, and producing many lovely prints before 1790 rather in his style, Utamaro was afterwards responsible for a number of innovations – three-quarter-length "portraits" with mica backgrounds; large portrait heads in which the design relies on the outlined features of the face and the decoratively coiffured hair; and, for a time, affectedly elongated girls whose extravagant height he used both to show to best advantage the glorious clothes they wear and to create sweeping and decorative compositions.

Chōbunsai Yeishi (active 1780–1800) was another artist who came to his maturity under the benign influence of Kiyonaga. He brought to his designs a refinement that makes his courtesan of the hour and his princess of olden times indistinguishable. His pupils, Yeishō, Yeiri, and Yeisui, were also responsible for prints of unusual refinement.

Two artists stand somewhat apart from their fellow print-designers of the last decade of the eighteenth century: Toshūsai Sharaku (active 1794–5) and Yeishōsai Chōki (active 1782–95). The actor prints of Sharaku are phenomenal, even in company with the most powerful productions of such gifted contemporaries as Shunshō, outstanding in this field, or Shunyei, whose large "portrait heads" preceded those of Sharaku by several years. His sudden emergence as a print-designer, his short career, and his *faire brutale*, constitute the great mystery of the Ukiyo-ye. Chōki, much influenced by Kiyonaga, Utamaro, and Sharaku, designed a small number of prints

of beauties, mostly printed on mica backgrounds, that are as distinctive among the *bijin-ye*, from subtleties of design and vague distortion of forms, as Sharaku's are among the theatrical prints.

The last years of the eighteenth century saw the beginning of a deterioration in the standard of print- and picture-book production, which seems to have been a reflection of changing social conditions in Yedo, the growth of the demand for prints, a consequent increase in the output of the artists, and a coarsening of the fibre both of those that purchased and those that made the prints. Certain it is that stronger causes than a simple failure of powers in the artists have to be found for the degeneration which set in at the end of the century. It infected the later work of Utamaro and of his pupils Hidemaro, Tsukimaro, and Kikumaro, and of his followers like Yeizan, Bunrō, and Ryōkoku, but it is most glaring in the prints of Utagawa Toyokuni (1769–1825) and his pupils.

Toyokuni (a pupil of Toyoharu (1733–1814)), founder of the Utagawa sub-school and himself principally remembered for *Uki-ye* (or "perspective pictures"), was an accomplished artist who, in the 'nineties, designed many fine prints, though one thinks of him more as a plagiarist of Utamaro, Sharaku, and Shunshō than as an artist of originality. Some of his early actor-prints, however, are superb, and it is in comparison with these that his later work, almost entirely theatrical, seems so slipshod and vulgar.

Of the vast number of pupils of Toyokuni, it is possible to mention only a few. Apart from Kunimasa, whose "large heads" are as rare and as much sought after as Sharaku's, most of the pupils were prolific and their prints are common. Kunisada (1786–1864), who later took over the name of Toyokuni (being the third of the name, since Toyoshige, another pupil, had already used it from the death of Toyokuni I in 1825 until his own death in 1835), produced enough fine prints to prove he was capable of great things, but his enormous output of actor-prints succeeds only in overpowering us with a welter of riotous pattern and colour.

Kuniyoshi (1797–1861) is more interesting,

and is justifiably renowned for his great battle-pieces founded on the events of the clash between warring clans in medieval Japan. His landscapes are also noteworthy.

But the first half of the nineteenth century produced its own great master – Katsushika Hokusai (1760–1849) and Andō Hiroshige (1797–1858). Hokusai's life spans a vast number of changes in the art of the Ukiyo-ye school, and his own early work, contemporary with that of Kiyonaga and Shunshō, has something of the style and much of the charm that was in the air they breathed in that halcyon period. But his finest work was in landscape, a new development in Ukiyo-ye art, and in prints of birds and flowers that take something from the *kwachō* of the aristocratic masters of China and Japan. These prints are probably the best known of all Japanese prints and maintain their hold upon us whatever fashions in collecting may decree: "others abide our question . . ."

Hiroshige is another artist whose work of most account is in landscape and whose lovely renderings of the Japanese scenery, his capture of transient atmospheric effects by the skilful use of the utmost art at the colour-printer's command, has endeared him to most Western collectors. Keisai Yeisen (1790–1848) was also capable of fine things in landscape, but his *bijin-ye* suffer from the faults of vulgarization that vitiate so many of these late artists' gifts.

Most of Hokusai's pupils developed a talent, which Hokusai had had in large measure for designing *surimono*, and collections can be formed of these enchantingly conceived and exquisitely printed little sheets of greeting, invitation, or commemoration. Shinsai, Taitō, Hokkei, Gakutei, and Shigenobu excelled in this miniature art.

Disparagement of the prints of the "decadence" has become what has been called the "correct" view of Japanese prints. On the other hand, the wholesale condemnation of everything produced after 1800 is manifestly wrong, and many things of real merit can be collected from the vast mass of prints surviving from the period. Picture-books, for reasons hard to find, were often much better printed during this period than the prints,

and offer a rich mine of material to the collector.

Collecting

"Orthodox lines" would probably be a matter for dispute, for collecting today is conditioned largely by what remains to collect. Even a great fortune, and a long period of patient collecting, would not be able to bring together collections on the scale and of the scope of those of, say, Hayashi or Happer. One tendency nowadays is for small but select collections to be formed of a hundred or two outstandingly lovely prints, with no particular deference to chronology or completeness, or even to artists' traditional reputations – the supreme example of this type is the famous Ledoux Collection. Another method is for specialization, with a focus either on one period or one artist, or even on a particular type of print, for instance, *surimono*, or illustrated novels, or landscape prints.

Condition and "state" are naturally of the utmost importance. Much reprinting from the original blocks was done contemporaneously, and many of the best prints have been copied, with intent to deceive or otherwise. Expertise in distinguishing the genuine first impression from reprints and facsimiles comes only through seeing and handling multitudes of specimens of all kinds, so that one learns the tell-tale variations in colour and in the texture of the paper, the surest guides where it is not possible to compare the actual woodcut lines with those of a known authentic impression.

The collector's ideal should, of course, always be a first impression in immaculate, unfaded condition, but very few prints, and even fewer *yehon*, have survived in that state. Originally they were sold to the commoners of Yedo, the prints to be exposed to the light and to the discolouring fumes of charcoal fires, the picture-books to be thumbed through, often without the care we pay to them as "works of art".

Value of prints and books, therefore, turns on three things: the stature of the artist; the comparative rarity of his work; and condition. A few artists' prints could only be secured – if ever the chance occurred – at something over

£500; any print by Kwaigetsudō and certain rare masterpieces of Toyonobu, Kiyonaga, and Utamaro are of this order. Fine prints by most important artists of early period vary from, say, £25 up to several hundreds of pounds, but hosts of good prints can be obtained for far less than £25. The finest *yehon* may well fetch £25 to £150, but those who

collect with an eye to acquiring representative examples of an artist's work (and are not too concerned about the charge of "heresy" that some will make against them) can pick up odd volumes and detached sheets for a modest outlay. Every collector will find his own level of outlay and his own particular sphere for specialization.

Glossary

TERMS

Aquatint. A colour print which emulates the pale washes of water-colour and was sometimes finished by hand in water-colour. Jean Baptiste le Prince (1734–1784) is usually credited with having invented the process in about 1768, but an aquatint background appears to have been used in a portrait of Oliver Cromwell, signed *Velde sculp.* in the seventeenth century. Ploos van Amstel (1726–98), who imitated old-master drawings, L. M. Bonnet (1735–93), and P. G. Floding (1731–91) were producing prints which closely resemble aquatints in the 1760s. Le Prince contented himself with monochrome, usually sepia, washes, but his follower, François Janinet (1752–1813), initiated the practice of printing in several colours which was successfully developed by P. L. Debucourt (1755–1832) for his scenes of high life. The one great artist to make use of aquatint was Goya, who employed it for his *Caprichios* and *Proverbios*. The process won great popularity in England.

Black line. In the black-line process of engraving, used mainly for woodcuts, the white or negative parts of the design are cut away from the block.

Block book. A type of book produced before the invention of movable type in which each page was printed from a single block on which both text and illustration had been cut. The recto and verso of each page were printed on separate sheets, which were stuck together. Among the earliest of such volumes

are the *Exercitium super Pater Noster* and an *Apocalypse* printed between 1430 and 1450. The *Ars Moriendi* appeared a little later. A few block books, including the *Biblia Pauperum*, the *Canticum Canticorum*, and *Speculum Humanæ Salvationis*, were produced after movable type had come into use.

Broad manner. The name given to a style of line-engraving practised by certain Florentine craftsmen in the later fifteenth century. Broad-manner engravings imitated the style of open-pen drawings with lines drawn in parallel strokes having light return strokes between them.

Burin or **graver.** A sharp metal instrument used to incise lines on metal; made in many sizes and forms.

Chiaroscuro. Chiaroscuro prints are made from a number of wood-blocks to show several tones of a single colour. Black outlines are provided by the first or key block and degrees of colour by two or three successive blocks. The process demands care to ensure that the blocks are correctly superimposed. In Germany this method of making prints was practised after 1508 by Lucas Cranach (1472–1553), Hans Baldung Grün (*c.* 1476–1545), Johann Wechtlin (*fl.* 1506–26), and others. It was introduced into Italy by Ugo da Carpi (*fl.* 1455–1527) and extensively practised throughout the sixteenth century by such artists as Antonio da Trento (*fl.* 1510–50) and Andrea Andreani (1584–1610). Netherlandish artists who produced chiaroscuro prints included Hendrik Goltzius (1558–1616), Abraham Bloemaert (1564–1651), and Frederick Bloemaert (1610–69). The process was revived in the eighteenth century in England, notably by J. B. Jackson (*fl.* 1701–54) and John Skippe (1742–96). Chiaroscuro blocks were sometimes used in combination with etched or engraved plates in both England and France at this period. In Venice the process was used by Antonio Maria Zanetti (1680–1757) to execute a series of reproductions of drawings by Parmigianino. Towards the end of the nineteenth century chiaroscuro was again revived by Charles Shannon (1863–1937) and others.

Bronzing. The name of the metallic shading on some silhouettes. In some cases this was used with beautiful effect, particularly by John Miers, who used real gold. It was usually, though not exclusively, used on painted work.

Colour print. The earliest colour prints were made from a series of wood-blocks like those used for chiaroscuro prints but each impregnated with ink of a different colour. This process was first used for the bichromatic initials in Fust and Schoeffer's Latin Psalter (1457), and later for illustrations to books published by Ratdolt at Venice (*c.* 1482–6) and for liturgical books published at Augsburg (1487–1516). During the eighteenth century various attempts were made to print in the full range of colours from metal plates, and J. C. Le Blon developed an unsatisfactory process depending on Newton's theory of the three cardinal colours. At the end of the century more successful colour-prints were produced by aquatint and later by lithography. The art of colour-printing from wooden blocks was revived at the end of the nineteenth century, notably by Camille Pissarro (1831–1903). Colour-prints made from a single plate repainted after every printing were produced by a few seventeenth-century line-engravers (notably Johannes Teyler) and later by stipple engravers and mezzotint scrapers.

Conversation. A silhouette representation of a group of people – usually a family – engaged together in some domestic pursuit.

Some of its finest exponents were Francis Torond, a French refugee who worked in Bath and London, Johann Friedrich Anthing (1753–1823), a native of Gotha, who produced some outstanding conversations of the Russian Imperial Court, which he cut or painted at St Petersburg, August Edouart, William Wellings (late eighteenth century), Charles Rosenberg (1745–1844), and J. Dempsey (early nineteenth century).

Counter-proof. A print made from a damp impression and not a plate. It is much weaker than an ordinary impression and presents the subject in reverse. Artists usually made counter-proofs in order to have a print in the same direction as the plate to assist them in making alterations to the plate.

Crayon engraving. A process in which etching and engraving were combined to render the lines of a chalk drawing. Roulettes with heads designed to reproduce the grain of a chalk line were used to prepare the plate for biting with acid. After the plate had been etched, burin, dry-point, and roulette were used direct on its surface. This process was much employed for the reproduction of Old Master drawings, mainly by artists who otherwise worked in stipple or mezzotint.

Decorative border. These were sometimes used as settings for silhouettes. They were of two kinds: (*a*) *Printed*. These were used in much the same way as the nineteenth-century photographers' cards, as cheap settings for the cut portraits which were pasted on them. They were particularly favoured by Continental silhouettists. (*b*) *Painted*. These were usually painted as an intrinsic part of the silhouette portrait, but sometimes were painted under frame-glass in *verre églomisé*.

Del. Short for *delineavit* or *delineaverunt* – Latin for he or she or they drew. To be seen after the artist's name, usually on the left-hand side of the print.

Dry-point. A process of engraving on a metal plate with a solid rod of steel shaped like a pencil which is drawn (not pushed like the burin) across the plate and throws up a rich burr. This burr is allowed to remain on the plate, holds the ink, and imparts a velvety tone to the print, but is soon worn down. Only the first fifty impressions, or even fewer, show the full effect. The first prints scratched in a manner similar to that of dry-point were made by the anonymous German *Master of the Amsterdam Cabinet* in about 1480. Dürer engraved three outstanding dry-point plates, and in Italy Andrea Meldolla (Schiavone) (d. 1582) used dry-point in conjunction with etching. The process was brought to a high pitch of perfection by Rembrandt, who occasionally produced pure dry-points but more often used the dry-point pencil to finish his etchings. In the late eighteenth century dry-point was revived in England by Thomas Worlidge (1700–66) and Benjamin Wilson (1721–88): and in the early nineteenth century by David Wilkie (1785–1841), Edward Thomas Daniell (1804–42), and many others. It has been much used by modern etchers.

Engraved background. These were used by some cutters as settings on which to mount their portraits. A. Edouart used them widely and even used printed accessories such as newspapers, scrolls, etc., to place in the hands of his subjects.

Engraved silhouette. Books of printed silhouettes were popular in the eighteenth and nineteenth centuries, and the collector should be cautious of any such portraits framed up to look like genuine cut or painted examples. The books themselves are well worth collecting. On the other hand, it must be remembered that some silhouettes of celebrities were printed especially for framing.

Etching. A process of print-making in which the plate is not engraved or cut with a tool but bitten (etched) with acid. The artist draws with an etching needle on a copper plate which has been covered with a ground composed of various waxes, gums, and resins. The needle cuts through the ground to expose, without incising, the plate, which is then immersed in acid (usually nitric) until the lightest lines have been sufficiently deeply etched. These lines are then covered with protecting varnish and the plate is replaced in the acid bath until the darker lines have been etched. This process is repeated as often as the artist desires. Sometimes the plate is finished in dry-point. The process of etching allows the artist a greater freedom of hand than that of engraving, but also demands a high degree of proficiency. Etchings by the greatest masters have a lightness of touch and depth of tone which can otherwise be obtained only in a drawing.

As a method of decorating iron, etching was extensively used by armourers, especially in Germany, in the second half of the fifteenth century, and the first etched prints were probably made by Daniel Hopfer (*fl.* 1493–1536), an armourer of Augsburg, in about 1500. The earliest dated etching was made in 1513 by Urs Graf (*c.* 1485–1529). Dürer etched a few plates between 1515 and 1518, and many minor German engravers occasionally worked in this medium during the first half of the sixteenth century. Etchings were first produced in Italy in about 1520 by Parmigianino and Schiavone, but the most notable sixteenth-century Italian etcher was Federigo Barocci (1528–1612). In the Netherlands etchings were executed in the first half of the sixteenth century by Lucas van Leyden (1494–1533) and Dirick Vellert (*fl.* 1511–44) who were followed by an important group of painters, including Pieter Breughel (1525–69), Jan Breughel (1568–1625), Hans Bol (1534–93), and Paul Bril (1554–1626), all of whom etched landscapes. From the beginning of the seventeenth century until our own times many of the greatest European painters have occasionally practised etching, while many artists of noteworthy ability have confined themselves almost exclusively to this medium.

Fine manner. The name given to a style of engraving practised at Florence in the later fifteenth century, notably in the workshop of Maso Finiguerra (1426–64). Fine-manner prints have something of the appearance of washed drawings with close lines of shading and cross-hatching. The style is distinct from broad manner practised at the same time.

Glass-coloured print. Painted copies of prints which enjoyed much popularity in England in the eighteenth century. A glass-coloured print was made by pasting a print – usually a mezzotint – on to a sheet of glass, and then rubbing the paper away. The sheet of glass was then painted on the inner side.

Glass-print. Certain nineteenth-century artists, including Corot, Daubigny, Théodore

Rousseau, and J. F. Millet, produced "glass-prints" by exposing sensitized photographic paper beneath sheets of glass covered with an opaque ground from which the required design had been removed with an instrument like an etching needle. Such prints closely resemble etchings in effect.

Glass silhouette. Silhouettes painted on to glass by one of the following methods: (*a*) *Verre églomisé* and *gold-glass engraving.* Silhouettes of this kind were produced by the Parisian artist A. Forberger (1762–1865), who backed his portraits with gold leaf or blue wax and often gave them floral borders, and W. A. Spornberg, a Swede, who worked at the end of the eighteenth century in Bath, and whose profiles are backed with red pigment and usually surrounded by a geometrical border. (*b*) *Painting on to the reverse side of flat or convex glass.* This was a common form of silhouette painting, and one capable of giving very effective results, particularly on those painted on convex glass, mounted over white backgrounds on to which their shadows could be thrown. Work of this kind was painted by Walter Jorden (late eighteenth century), Isabella Beetham, Charles Rosenberg (1745–1844), W. Rought (early nineteenth century), and many others.

Several silhouettists, among them John Miers, mounted their ordinary painted work beneath convex glass with *églomisé* borders, and Mrs Beetham often combined *églomisé* mounts with portraits in plain black painted on the underside of the same glass. At least one silhouette in a glass millefleurs paper-weight is on record.

Impression. Any print made from a block, plate, or stone is termed an impression. The number of impressions that can be pulled depends upon the fineness of the artist's technique and the softness of the medium he employs. Whereas one of Rembrandt's more delicately etched plates or a dry-point plate yielded barely fifty impressions, a steel engraving might produce several thousands. Some recent artists have destroyed their plates or stones after taking a limited number of impressions.

Incunabula. Prints or printed books produced before 1500; also called incunables.

Ivory was sometimes used as a ground for silhouettes. It was particularly favoured for silhouettes intended for insertion in jewellery.

Jewellery and trinkets. Some of the art's most pleasing examples are set in jewellery and trinkets. Rings, brooches, and snuff-boxes were particularly favourite repositories for shades. Some of John Miers' tiny shades, some less than half an inch high, are in such settings under coverings of rock crystal. Silhouette jewellery is of the greatest rarity.

Line-engraving. Line-engravings are printed from finely polished metal plates, usually of copper but sometimes of iron, pewter, silver, or steel, on which the engraver has incised the design with a burin. At the side of the line the burin leaves a burr of displaced metal which would hold ink and is therefore cut away with a scraper. In dry-point engravings the burr is left on the plate.

Decorations were incised on gold, silver, and base-metal surfaces from the earliest times and throughout the Middle Ages, but not until the first half of the fifteenth century were plates engraved for the purpose of printing on paper. The earliest dated line-engraving is one of a series of prints of the *Passion* executed by an anonymous craftsman in 1446. Many similar prints dating from the same period or a little later have also been preserved, but the names of their engravers and the exact dates of their production are unknown. The first major artist in this medium was Martin Schongauer (*c.* 1430–91), whose works stand between the somewhat primitive engravings of such anonyms as the *Master of the Banderoles* or the *Master E.S.* and the highly polished works of Albrecht Dürer and Lucas Van Leyden. The earliest known Italian line-engraver was Maso Finiguerra of Florence, who began his career as a goldsmith working in *niello*. Two notable *quattrocento* artists, Antonio Pollaiuolo and Andrea Mantegna, executed works of superb quality in this medium, and Leonardo da Vinci has occasionally been credited with line-engravings, though only one has even a slight claim to be by him. The art of line-engraving was practised by several north Italian artists in the early sixteenth century, notably Jacopo de' Barbari (1450–c. 1516), Benedetto Montagna (1480–1540), Giulio (*fl.* 1482–1514), and Domenico Campagnola (*fl.* 1511–63).

Whereas etchings were frequently executed by painters, line-engravings made after the early years of the sixteenth century were usually the work of specialists who copied the designs of greater artists. Some, like Marcantonio Raimondi (1480–c. 1530), were interpretive artists of genius, but the majority were humble craftsmen able to achieve little more than the rough outlines of the works they copied. Perhaps the most notable and original were those who engraved perspective views of architecture. Fine original engravings were produced in France in the 1550s by Jean Duvet (1485–1561) and Étienne Delaune (1518–95), while certain artists, such as Domenico del Barbieri (1506–70) and Jean Viset (*fl.* 1536), executed fine prints after Fontainebleau school paintings. In the early seventeenth century Abraham Bosse (1602–76), who wrote an important treatise on the art of etching and engraving, showed himself a master of the burin, as well as the etching needle, especially in his original genre scenes. Most other seventeenth-century engravers confined themselves to reproductive work, and Rubens employed several in his studio to make plates after his paintings. In England line-engravings were produced in ever-increasing quantities after 1540. Most are, however, book illustrations, and very few are of conspicuously high quality.

The widespread vogue for the collection of prints, especially those after the most famous paintings by Old Masters and portraits of contemporary celebrities, gave a great impetus to the production of line-engravings in the eighteenth century. Several artists, as for example, Sir Robert Strange (1721–92), subsisted solely by making engravings after portraits and Old Masters, while some advanced neo-classical painters, such as Gavin Hamilton, found that they could make more money and secure a far wider reputation from the sale of engravings than from the pictures that provided the designs. Most of these painters, however, employed engravers rather than applying themselves to the burin, and some suffered from the diffusion of piratical prints after their works. Among the most notable eighteenth-century engravings were those produced as illustrations to books by such artists as H. F. Gravelot (1699–1773), Charles Eisen (1720–78), and Jean Michel Moreau (1741–1814). The art of the line-engraver deteriorated sharply after the beginning of the nineteenth century with the increased use of steel plates.

Lithograph. Lithographs are printed from absorbent stone blocks impregnated with chalk and have the effect of chalk drawings. The artist may either draw his design in specially prepared greasy lithographic chalk directly on to the stone or on paper with a gummed surface from which it can be transferred to the stone. In the latter instance the impressions are usually pulled by a craftsman.

The lithographic process was at first used only for making black-and-white prints, but its possibilities for colour-printing were developed early in the nineteenth century. In Germany lithography was much used for reproducing the more famous pictures in the Munich and Dresden galleries between 1820 and 1850. Perhaps the greatest artist to employ lithography was Francisco Goya, but Théodore Géricault (1791–1824) and Eugène Delacroix (1798–1863) were among many others who designed for the medium. Later in the century Édouard Manet (1832–83) and Fantin-Latour (1835–1904) both produced notable lithographs. The greatest modern master of the medium was probably Pierre Bonnard (1867–1947).

Lithotint. When the design was washed on with a brush and greasy ink the effect of a water-colour was produced, and this was by some firms named a "lithotint".

Machine-cutting. Silhouettes produced by a mechanical profile machine, of which there were many forms. Such work may usually be distinguished by a certain hardness and lack of freedom in its outlines. There were, however, a few machine-cutters who produced commendable work. One such was Mrs Sarah Harrington (*fl.* 1775), whose shades are full of vivacity. On the whole, however, machine-cutting is the art's most debased form.

Maculature. A weak impression. The

copper plate or block from which prints are taken must be inked after each impression has been pulled; a maculature is a second impression taken without re-inking, usually to extract the rest of the ink from the lines.

Manière criblée. Prints in the *manière criblée*, sometimes called "dotted prints", are taken from a metal plate engraved in the same manner as a white-line wood-block. The name is derived from the groups of dots made on the plate with a punch to break up otherwise black areas of background. Prints of this type were made in the late fifteenth and early sixteenth centuries, especially in Florence, and there are isolated examples of *manière criblée* prints by Giuseppe Scolari of Vicenza and Urs Graf. The method was revived in England towards the end of the eighteenth century.

Mezzotint. Literally "half tint"; a method of engraving which renders tone rather than line. The process is as follows: a copper plate is roughened with a mezzotint rocker which makes a series of uniform indentations, each with a burr to hold ink, and provides the black background; the artist then removes the burr with a scraper where he wishes to obtain the lighter portions of the print, and polishes portions of the plate with a burnisher to obtain highlights. As the quality of the print depends on the delicacy of the burr, few impressions can be taken before the plate is flattened in the press. Finished prints are somewhat delicate and liable to deteriorate.

The mezzotint process was extensively practised in the Netherlands, but became so popular in England before the end of the seventeenth century that it acquired the name, *la manière anglaise*. In the late seventeenth century and throughout the eighteenth century mezzotints after paintings (usually portraits and later of genre scenes often executed primarily for reproduction by this means) were produced in considerable quantities by English artists, including Isaac Beckett (1653–1719), John Smith (1652–1742), John Faber the elder (*c.* 1660–1721), John Faber the younger (1684–1756), James McArdell (*c.* 1729–65), John Dixon (*c.* 1730–1800), Richard Earlom (1743–1822), Valentine Green (1739–1813), and John Raphael Smith (1752–1812). In the nineteenth century Turner's *Liber Studiorum* was executed by a combination of mezzotint and etching, and David Lucas (1802–81) scraped a series of landscapes after Constable.

Monotype. Plates painted with oil colour instead of ink yield a single impression which is called a monotype. This process was occasionally used by G. B. Castiglione (1616–70), William Blake (1757–1827), and Edgar Degas (1834–1917).

Niello. A method of ornamenting metal work used by goldsmiths in the second half of the fifteenth century. A small metal plate, usually of silver or gold, was engraved and the lines filled in with a black substance composed of lead, silver, copper, and sulphur. The plates were an end in themselves, but occasionally their makers seem to have taken prints from them, or from sulphur casts of them, probably as records of their work. The art of *niello* was closely bound up with the development of line-engraving in Florence, and its most notable exponent was the engraver Maso Finiguerra.

Paste print. Paste prints were made in the fifteenth century from metal plates, similar to those used in the *manière criblée* process, on which a glutinous ink or paste was used, so that gold leaf or tints of colour could be added.

Painted silhouette. These were produced in a number of techniques on various materials, ranging from paper to glass.

Plaster shade. Shades painted on slabs of plaster, often with beer as the medium. This was at one time a common background, and it undoubtedly was effective, its snowy depth giving the greatest possible contrast and sharpness to the black of the shade. Probably the greatest master of this type of silhouette was John Miers. Another was W. Phelps (*fl.* 1788), although shades by the latter are excessively rare. Great care should be exercised in handling shades painted on plaster, as they are exceedingly fragile and will often crack at the smallest impact. Neither should any attempt be made to brush off dust that may have accumulated on them through the years, as they scratch very easily. If a plaster shade requires attention, it should be given to a specialist to do what is necessary.

Plate mark. The name given to the indentation made by the edges of the plate on the print. This mark forms the frame of an etching or line-engraving, but is rarely visible on woodcuts or lithographs. Impressions of etchings or engravings cut within the plate mark are said to be clipped and are of considerably less value than those on which the mark is to be seen.

Porcelain. Porcelain was sometimes, particularly at the end of the eighteenth century, decorated with silhouette portraits, usually of royalty, though sometimes of other celebrities. The factories of Royal Worcester, Royal Copenhagen, Dresden, Meissen, Berlin, and Sèvres all produced porcelain of this type. And objects so decorated include mugs, chocolate pots, jardinières, cups, saucers, plates, vases, and simple plaques. No silhouette porcelain is common, and most of it is rare.

Profile. A silhouette portrait in which features other than the outline are drawn, sometimes in great detail. Silhouettes in which features and hair are drawn in gold paint on a black ground come into this category. Some profiles are merely miniatures painted in sharp outline. Edward Foster of Derby (1761–1865) painted many portraits of this type.

Remarque proof. A print on which the engraver or etcher has added a little sketch or token in the margin as a sign of state. This practice of marking prints was fashionable in the late nineteenth century.

Samt-teigdrucke. Known in French as *empreintes veloutées* and occasionally referred to in English as "flock prints". They were printed from ordinary black-line wood-blocks on which a glutinous ink or paste had been used. Before the ink dried the impression was sprinkled with powdered colour, which gave it a velvety surface. Such prints were executed only in the fifteenth century and are very rare.

Sand-grain. A sand-grain aquatint is obtained from a plate which has been pulled through the press with a piece of sandpaper to roughen its surface.

Scissor-work. Silhouettes cut freehand from paper. Although this technique is not capable of giving such great refinements of finish as any of the painting methods employed, it is nevertheless capable of giving very striking effects of a different kind. Its most notable quality is the uncompromising sharpness it gives to the outlines of its subjects. It is possible for a cutter, by holding several thicknesses of paper together, to cut as many duplicates at the same time, thus giving several "originals". The most prolific cutter of all was A. Edouart. Other noteworthy cutters were Francis Torond, "Master" William James Hubard (1807–62), who achieved notoriety as a protégé, and the ill-fated Major John André (1751–80), who was hanged by the Americans as a spy in the Civil War. One method of cutting was to cut out the portrait as a hollow from a piece of white paper and then mount it over a piece of black paper or material.

Scraped lithograph. A lithograph executed by a reverse process which gives the impression the appearance of a mezzotint. The whole surface of the stone is covered with lithographic chalk, which the artist scrapes away to bring out highlights and on which he draws with a point to obtain white lines.

Shade. A silhouette portrait in which the face is painted in black. Ideally, the whole portrait should be in black, but sometimes clothes, nosegays, or other details are inserted in colour, but the face itself must have no detail at all apart from that of its outline. J. Buncombe, who practised from *c.* 1745 to *c.* 1825 at Newport, Isle of Wight, painted fine shades of soldiers in which the uniforms are shown in colour and in great detail. Edward Foster of Derby often painted faces in brown, blue, or some other colour, and unless details are shown in the faces, such may also be termed shades. But this treatment is really a departure from the best practice. The most effective shades are those with faces painted in pure black on an unadulterated white ground.

Silhouette. The name usually given collectively to shades and profiles. It is derived from that of Étienne de Silhouette (1709–67), the parsimonious finance minister of Louis XV. He was an amateur cutter of shades. As such portraits were cheap, they were dubbed à la Silhouette, as indeed at the time were all cheap objects. He was not the originator of the art.

Soft-ground etching. A soft-ground etching imitates the effect of a pencil or chalk drawing. The soft ground, a mixture of ordinary etching ground with tallow, is laid on the plate and a sheet of paper stretched over it. The design is then drawn on the paper in pencil in such a way that the ground adheres to the paper beneath each stroke. The plate is then immersed in acid. Soft-ground etchings are often difficult to distinguish from crayon engravings, which obtain a similar effect by different means.

State. At various stages in the making of a print a single impression or group of impressions may be pulled. Each such group of impressions is termed a state. Rembrandt, for instance, made numerous alterations to his etchings, some of which exist in as many as five states. The term state 1 is given to the earliest group of impressions pulled from the plate; state 2 to those pulled after the first alterations have been made; and so on. It is often difficult to ascertain which state was considered final by the artist, as some later alterations were made to repair damage to a worn plate. State 1 usually provides the rarest but not necessarily the most satisfactory group of impressions; the later states were often pulled after the plate had been heavily worn and had been reworked, sometimes by another hand. Connoisseurs of states should, however, be warned that, even in the eighteenth century, unscrupulous dealers were not above creating unique first-state impressions of Rembrandt etchings by deleting details from an ordinary first-state print.

Steel engraving. Steel plates which suffer less wear in the press and thus yield a greater number of impressions than copper plates were first used by line and mezzotint engravers in the early nineteenth century. Such plates are, however, difficult to work, and the resulting impressions – known as steel engravings – are somewhat harsh. Later in the century it was discovered that a steel facing applied by electrolysis to a copper plate added equal durability without cramping the engraver's style.

Stipple engraving. On stipple engravings depths of tone are shown by conglomerations of dots and flicks of varying density. The plates from which these prints are obtained are covered with an ordinary etching ground through which the darkest portions of the design are picked out with an etching needle or roulette. The plate is then steeped in acid until the dots are sufficiently deeply bitten, and is finished with a stipple graver used directly on the metal.

Stippled shading (applied without the aid of acid) was occasionally used by sixteenth-century Italian engravers, including Giulio Campagnola, Marcello Fogolino, and Ottavio Leoni, but the stipple process was not fully developed until the mid-eighteenth century. It was then taken up by Francesco Bartolozzi (1728–1813), a Florentine who executed most of his work in this medium in England, where it enjoyed great popularity. Indeed, most late eighteenth-century stipple engravings were executed by English artists or foreign artists working in England, and the process remained popular throughout the nineteenth century.

Sulphur-tint. Sulphur-tint aquatints are produced by dusting powdered sulphur above a layer of oil on the surface of the aquatint plate. Particles of the sulphur corrode the plate in a delicate grain, which gives the appearance of a colour wash to the prints.

Trade label. Silhouettists, particularly in the eighteenth and early nineteenth centuries, often used trade labels which they fixed on the back of the frames containing their works. These labels in themselves form a fascinating subject for study. If still in place, covering the aperture at the back of a frame, a label can often be taken as at least a partial guarantee that the original contents of the frame have not been tampered with.

White-line engraving. The reverse process to black-line engraving. The block provides a black background on which the white lines of the design are incised.

Woodcut. Woodcuts or xylographic prints are obtained from blocks of wood, usually a soft wood like beech, apple, pear, or sycamore, sawn with the grain and about seven-eighths of an inch thick (thicker blocks were used for the earliest prints). The woodblock process developed out of the medieval practice of printing patterns on textiles from wooden forms, but it does not seem to have been used for printing on paper or parchment until the late fourteenth century. As early as 1377 playing cards were in use in Germany, but none has been preserved, and it is not certain whether they were printed from woodblocks or painted individually. The earliest surviving woodcuts, dating from the first half of the fifteenth century, are of scenes from the Passion of Christ and the lives of the Saints which were distributed to pilgrims at various shrines and seem to have been printed in monasteries. Early in the fifteenth century volumes of woodcuts, known as block books, were produced in Germany. After the invention of movable type (at a date which has never been ascertained, but probably in the 1450s) woodcuts were extensively used for book illustrations; the earliest-known date from between 1460 and 1464. Among the first major artists whose works were reproduced in woodcuts were Albrecht Dürer (1471–1528), Hans Burgkmair (1473–1531), Albrecht Altdorfer (c. 1480–1538), Lucas Cranach (1472–1553), Lucas van Leyden (1494–1533), and Hans Holbein (1497–1543). These artists seldom cut their own blocks, however, and names of the most of the carvers are lost. One of the most notable was Hans Lutzelburger (d. 1526), who made some of the blocks for Holbein's *Dance of Death* and illustrations to the Old Testament. Mid-sixteenth-century woodblock cutters included Giuseppe Scolari (*fl. c.* 1580), Jost Amman (1539–91), Virgil Solis (1514–62), Tobias Stimmer (1539–84), and Bernard von Salomon (c. 1508–61). The popularity of woodcuts waned towards the end of the sixteenth century, and the medium was little employed until the late eighteenth century, when it was taken up by William Blake and others. In the late nineteenth century black-line woodcuts based on fifteenth-century prototypes were extensively used to illustrate finely printed books; some of the most notable were cut for the Kelmscott Press by William Hooper (1834–1912) after designs by William Morris and Edward Burne-Jones.

Wood-engraving. The wood-engraving differs from the woodcut in being taken from a block of hard box wood cut across the grain. This process permits finer effects than those obtainable from woodcut blocks. Thomas Bewick (1753–1828) developed the art of wood-engraving (by the white-line process) towards the end of the eighteenth century. He was followed by three pupils: Charlton Nesbit (1775–1838), Luke Clennell (1781–1840), and William Harvey (1796–1866).

AMERICAN ENGRAVERS

Aitken, Robert (1734–1802). Printer and publisher, originally from Scotland, who issued the *Pennsylvania Magazine* 1775–6. He supposedly re-engraved on a reduced scale the view by Bernard Romans of the Battle of Bunker Hill: *A Correct View of the Late Battle at Charlestown*, June 17, 1775, which appeared in the *Pennsylvania Magazine* for September 1775.

Allen, Luther (1780–1821). Engraved *A South West View of Newport, R.I.*, after a drawing by S. King, 1795.

Anderson, Alexander (1775–1870). Wood-engraver, born in New York of Scottish parents, studied medicine, but turned to wood-engraving, introducing to America the "white-line" technique of Thomas Bewick. He made about 10,000 cuts for books, periodicals, bill-heads, advertisements, etc. (Plate 377c).

Atlantic Neptune. A large collection of about 275 views, maps, charts, etc., of ports in North America, published for the British Admiralty under the direction of Joseph F. W. Des Barres during the period 1763–84.

Bakewell, Thomas. London publisher of the 2nd state of the famous Burgis view of New York, called the Bakewell re-issue of 1746.

Barber, John Warner (1798–1885). Engraver and publisher of New Haven, Conn., whose interest in history led him to illustrate and publish the following books: *History and*

Antiquities of New Haven (1831); *Connecticut Historical Collections* (1836); *Views in New Haven and Vicinity* (1825). Very much sought after by collectors is his view of New Haven Green with the buildings of Yale College.

Barralet, John James (1747?–1815). Philadelphia painter and engraver; chiefly a designer of views engraved by others. Came to America in 1795 from Ireland.

Bartlett, William Henry (1809–54). Artist, whose numerous sepia drawings were engraved by others for books such as N. R. Willis' *American Scenery* (1840), which was issued in parts.

Beck, George. Landscape painter, located in Philadelphia from 1798 to 1807, drew the views of American scenes published by Atkins & Nightingale in London, *c.* 1801–9.

Bennett, William James (1787–1844). Painter and engraver of aquatints, born in England. A pupil of the Royal Academy and of Westall, he came to America in 1816. Known for his series of *Views of American Cities* (Plate 379A), the finest colour aquatints in this field; also for the three *Street Views in the City of New York* published by H. J. Megarey in New York in 1834; two views of the Great Fire of New York in December, 1835 (after N. V. Calyo), and *The Seasons* after George Harvey (1841).

Bingham, George Caleb (1811–79). Portrait and genre painter whose paintings were engraved by John Sartain, Gautier, and Thomas Doney, and widely distributed, especially to the members of the American Art Union.

Birch, Thomas (1779–1851). Landscape and marine painter, son of William, with whom he worked. Later became known for naval subjects of the war of 1812, which were engraved by Tiebout, Tanner, and Lawson.

Birch, William (1755–1834). Born in England, active as an enamel painter, engraver, and print publisher. He came to Philadelphia in 1794. His earlier engraved work was done in stipple. Drew and engraved, together with his son, a series of twenty-eight views of the City of Philadelphia issued in 1800, either plain or coloured; also a series of small views of the *Country Seats of the United States* (1808).

Blodget, Samuel. First American-born artist to draw an eye-witness account of an historic event, the view of the *Battle of Lake George*, engraved by Thomas Johnston, Boston, 1755, also published by Thomas Jefferys in London, 1756. This is the first historical print engraved in America. Both the English and American issues were accompanied by a pamphlet describing the battle.

Bourne, George M. Publisher of the so-called Bourne *Views of New York City*, 1831. There are nineteen double plates, all but the first six copyrighted in 1831. Charles Burton drew most of these views, while James Smillie engraved the greater number of the plates. The New York Historical Society owns original drawings of eighteen of the views, while fifteen of the remaining twenty are in the Smillie Collection of the New York Public Library. The New York Historical Society owns all but three of the copperplates.

Bowen, Abel (1790–1850). Copper- and wood-engraver, known for his line and stipple engravings of public buildings in Boston for Snow's *History of Boston* (1825) and for a woodcut in three sections of the *View of Colonel Johnson's Engagement with the Savages near the Moravian Town*, October 5, 1812. Publisher of the *Naval Monument*, partly illustrated by him.

Bower, John (*fl.* 1809–19). Philadelphia engraver who executed two important battle scenes of the war of 1812: *The Battle of Patapsco Neck*, September 12, 1814, and *The Bombardment of Fort McHenry near Baltimore*, September 13, 1814.

Bry, Theodore de (1528–98). Flemish engraver and publisher of the earliest prints depicting North American Indians, their villages and customs, appearing as part of his collection of *Great Voyages* published in 1590 and 1591.

Buck, James. Boston publisher of the first view of Yale College in 1749, engraved by Thomas Johnston after a drawing by John Greenwood.

Burgis, William. Early eighteenth-century publisher of maps; an artist whose panoramic views of New York and Boston were engraved by John Harris of London and published in 1719 and 1722 respectively. He also drew a view of Harvard College, issued in 1726, a view of the Boston Lighthouse and the New Dutch Church in New York. These views are among the most sought after by collectors; only a few recorded impressions are known.

Burt, Charles (1823–92). Engraver, born in Edinburgh, came to New York in 1836. Engraved portraits and illustrations for books, some large "framing" prints for the American Art Union; after 1850 worked almost exclusively on banknote engraving.

Calyo, Nicolino V. (1790–1884). Painter who came to New York from Italy and is known for two aquatint views of the Great Fire in New York in 1835 engraved by William J. Bennett; also for a series of Street Cries of New York (now at the Museum of the City of New York).

Cartwright, John. English engraver of the aquatint series of American scenes by George Beck of Philadelphia, published by Atkins & Nightingale of London from 1801 to 1809. (Not to be confused with T. Cartwright.)

Carwitham, John. Active 1723–64. London engraver for Carington Bowles: his name appears on three important and attractive views of New York, Boston, and Philadelphia. His name appears on the second states only of these prints, which were issued after 1764, although the three cities are depicted between 1731 and 1755. The Boston view is probably based on the Burgis view of 1722, while the Philadelphia view seems to copy the Scull-Heap view of c. 1754.

Casilear, John W. (1811–83). A good line-engraver who turned to painting of landscapes.

Catherwood, Frederick (1799–1854). English artist, architect, and engineer, known for his views of Central America and his view of *New York from Governor's Island*, 1846, which was engraved in aquatint by H. Papprill.

Charles, William. Engraver and etcher who came to America from Scotland in 1801 and died in Philadelphia about 1820. Known for his caricatures of the war of 1812.

Clover, Lewis P. New York publisher of William J. Bennett's aquatints, 1834–8.

Cooke, George (1793–1849). Maryland

artist, known for the four views in the Bennett series of American Cities: Charleston, S.C., Richmond, Washington, and West Point.

Copley, John Singleton (1737–1815). Painter (stepson of Peter Pelham), who is known to have made only one mezzotint, the portrait of the Rev. William Welsteed of Boston, 1753.

Davis, Alexander Jackson (1803–92). New York architect whose drawings of private homes, towns, and colleges from 1820 to 1850 were engraved by a number of different engravers.

Dawkins, Henry. Active in New York by 1754, also in Philadelphia, as an engraver of bill-heads, maps, caricatures, but known chiefly for his *View of Nassau-Hall* (Princeton College) which appeared as a frontispiece in Blair's *An Account of the College in New Jersey* (Woodbridge, N.J., 1764). Dawkins died probably in 1786.

Des Barres, J. F. W. English cartographer and artist who prepared the *Atlantic Neptune* for the British Admiralty, 1763–84.

Dewing, Francis. English engraver and printer in Boston who engraved and printed the earliest and most important plan of Boston, the *Bonner Map* of 1722, known in five states and republished three times: in 1733, 1743, 1769.

Doney, Thomas. New York mezzotint engraver whose print after Bingham's *Jolly Flatboatmen* was distributed by the American Art Union to its members in 1845. Contributed mezzotints to periodicals.

Doolittle, Amos (1754–1832). Engraver of New Haven, Connecticut, known for his crude but important set of four views of the Battles of Lexington and Concord (Plate 378A) in 1775 after Ralph Earl, as well as a view of Federal Hall in New York, after a drawing by Peter Lacour, showing George Washington's first inaugural ceremony on its balcony, April 1789.

Durand, Asher Brown (1796–1886). Engraver of portraits, subjects (John Trumbull's *Declaration of Independence*, 1820), and banknotes. In 1836 he turned to painting and came to be known as the "Father of American Landscape Painting".

Earl, Ralph (1751–1801). American portrait painter whose original drawings of the Battles of Lexington and Concord, 1775, were engraved by Amos Doolittle.

Edwin, David (1776–1841). Engraver, born in England, came to Philadelphia in 1797. Excellent engraver of portraits in stipple, including portraits of generals.

Fay, Theodore Sedgwick (1807–98). Editor of *Views in New York and its Environs* published by Peabody & Co., New York, 1831–4, a collection of thirty-eight engraved views on sixteen plates, including a map and descriptive text, issued in parts (only eight of the proposed ten were published) after drawings by J. H. Dakin, A. J. Davis, and others, and engraved by A. Dick, among others.

Foster, John (1648–81). Boston printer and engraver, credited with the first signed portrait in colonial America, the portrait of Rev. Richard Mather; also a seal of the Massachusetts Bay Colony and a map of New England which served as a frontispiece for William Hubbard's *A Narrative of the Troubles with the Indians in New England* ... Boston, printed by John Foster, 1677. These are woodcuts.

Greenwood, John (1727–92). American-born artist who did etchings and mezzotints in eighteenth-century Europe. There is no record of his having made prints in America. Born in Boston, he worked in Holland and England.

Harris, John. London engraver of the William Burgis views of New York and Boston.

Harvey, George (c. 1800–c. 1877). English painter who resided in America between 1820 and c. 1842. Known for his *Atmospheric Views of North America* in water-colours, of which only four were engraved in aquatint by William J. Bennett and published under the title: *Primitive Forest in America, at the four seasons of the year*, London, 1841.

Havell, Robert, Jr (1793–1878). English engraver who came to America after completing Audubon's *Birds of America* published in London. He engraved in aquatint a number of views of American cities, among them two panoramic views of New York, one of Hartford, Conn., Boston, and Niagara Falls in 1845.

Heap, George. Map-maker, map-seller, and surveyor who drew one of the most important early views of Philadelphia, the so-called Scull-Heap view of 1754.

Hill, John (1770–1850). London-born artist who came to New York in 1816. Known for the aquatint plates in the *Hudson River Portfolio* (Plate 378B) after the paintings by W. G. Wall, published by Megarey, New York, c. 1825; also engraved Joshua Shaw's *Picturesque Views of American Scenery* (Philadelphia, 1819) and seventeen aquatints for *Lucas' Progressive Drawing Book* (Baltimore, c. 1827).

Hill, John William (1812–79). Son of John Hill; made some aquatints, but known chiefly for the views which were engraved by others.

Hill, Samuel. Boston engraver of portraits and views for the *Massachusetts Magazine* between 1789 and 1796.

Hornor, Thomas. English water-colour artist and engraver who came to New York in 1828. *Broadway, New York* (c. 1834) was drawn and etched by this artist, but aquatinted by John Hill. An unfinished etching of a panoramic view of New York from Brooklyn, c. 1837, and an unfinished wash drawing of a bird's-eye view of City Hall Park, are in the collection of the New York Public Library.

Hudson River portfolio. A series of twenty views drawn by W. G. Wall and engraved by John Hill (Plate 378B). Four of the first issued views were engraved by J. R. Smith. Published by Henry J. Megarey, New York, c. 1825. "The finest collection of New York State views"; originally planned to include twenty-four plates, issued in six numbers of four views each. Only five numbers with a total of twenty views were actually published.

Johnston, Thomas (1708–67). Boston engraver of the *Prospect of Yale College*, 1749, after a drawing by John Greenwood, published by J. Buck; also of *The Battle Fought near Lake George*, 1755; *Plan of Boston* after Wm Burgis, and a *View of Quebec*, 1759.

Jones, Alfred (1819–1900). English-born engraver who worked in New York, known for some large engravings distributed by the Apollo Association, among them Mount's

Farmers Nooning, engraved in 1836, distributed in 1843.

Jukes, Francis (1747–1812). London aquatint engraver, specializing in views and marine scenes. Engraved Henry Pelham's *Plan of Boston*, 1777; four aquatints after water-colours by Alexander Robertson, including the views of *New York from Hobuck Ferry* and *Mount Vernon*, 1799.

Krimmel, John Lewis (1787–1821). Philadelphia artist, whose *Election Day at the State House, Philadelphia*, 1815, was engraved, but left unfinished, by A. Lawson. Joseph Yeager made an aquatint after his *Procession of Victuallers of Philadelphia*, 1821.

Lawson, Alexander (1773–1846). Born in Scotland, came to Philadelphia in 1793. Engraved plates for A. Wilson's *Ornithology* and a number of periodicals; *Perry's Victory on Lake Erie*, 1813, after a painting by T. Birch; *Election Scene at the State House, Philadelphia*, 1815, after J. L. Krimmel (unfinished plate).

Longacre, James Barton (1794–1869). Engraver specializing in stipple portraits. Noteworthy among these is the portrait of Andrew Jackson after the painting by T. Sully, 1820. Together with James Herring, a portrait painter, published the *National Portrait Gallery of Distinguished Americans*, 4 vols, 1834–9.

Maverick, Peter (1780–1831). Son and pupil of Peter Rushton Maverick, 1755–1811. Conducted a large engraving and publishing business in New York, turning to lithography about 1824. Best known for his view of Wall Street (lithograph) after Hugh Reinagle.

Meadows, Christian. New England engraver and apparently a counterfeiter, active about 1840–59; known for one of the most desirable college views, the Meadows' View of Dartmouth College, Hanover, N.H., 1851.

Megarey, Henry J. New York publisher of *The Hudson River Portfolio* (Plate 378B), a set of twenty aquatint views engraved by J. R. Smith and John Hill after the water-colours by W. G. Wall, 1821–5; Street Views in the City of New York (Fulton Street and Market, South Street from Maiden Lane, Broadway from Bowling Green), a series of three views engraved by W. J. Bennett, *c.* 1834.

Mount, William Sidney (1807–68).

America's first genre painter, whose paintings were reproduced by a number of engravers as well as lithographers and widely distributed in America and in Europe.

Norman, John (1748–1817). Architect and landscape engraver from London who worked in Philadelphia and Boston. Engraved portraits of heroes of the Revolution and a portrait of George Washington in 1779. Worked also for New York publishers.

Okey, Samuel. Mezzotint engraver from London who worked in Newport, R.I., 1773–5; is known for having been America's first engraver to reproduce old master paintings.

Papprill, Henry. Aquatint engraver who worked in New York in the 1840s. He engraved two large views of New York, one after F. Catherwood called *New York from Governor's Island*, 1846 (the Papprill–Catherwood view) and *New York from the Steeple of St Paul's Church*, after a drawing by J. W. Hill, 1849, re-issued in 1855.

Parkyns, George Isham (*c.* 1749/50–after 1820). English artist and aquatint engraver who came to Philadelphia in 1795, planning a series of twenty aquatint views, of which, however, only four were executed. These are: *View of Mount Vernon, Annapolis, Md*, and two views of *Washington*. Parkyns is also the author of *Monastic and Baronial Remains*, 1816.

Peale, Charles Willson (1741–1827). Painter and founder of a museum in Philadelphia; he engraved a few, rare, mezzotint portraits.

Pelham, Peter (*c.* 1684–1751). Earliest engraver in America; came from England to Boston in 1726 as an experienced mezzotint engraver; did a series of portraits of American clergymen, among them the portrait of Cotton Mather, 1727. Stepfather of John Singleton Copley.

Prud'homme, John Francis Eugène (1800–92). Engraver of stipple portraits, and plates for periodicals and banknotes for the U.S. Treasury Dept. in Washington.

Revere, Paul (1735–1818). Boston's most famous silversmith and a patriot who was also an engraver of three important historical prints. These are: *The Landing of the British Troops in Boston* (1768) issued in 1770; the so-called *Boston Massacre* in 1770; a *View of Harvard College* in 1768. He also engraved a number of plates for the *Royal American Magazine*, 1774–5; the Massachusetts paper currency, 1775–6, and some portraits (Plate 377A) and political caricatures.

Roberts, Bishop. English artist who drew the most important early view of Charleston, South Carolina, in 1739, which was engraved by Wm H. Toms and published in London. Roberts died in October 1739.

Robertson, Alexander (1772–1841). Scottish artist who established, together with his brother Archibald, the Columbian Drawing Academy in New York, c. 1795. Four of his water-colour views were engraved in aquatint by Francis Jukes of London.

Robertson, Archibald (1765–1835). Painter and etcher, born near Aberdeen, Scotland. Studied in Edinburgh and London from 1782 to 1791, when he came to New York. Painted a portrait of George Washington at the request of the Earl of Buchan. From 1792 to 1821 he worked in New York as a painter, chiefly in water-colour, and as a teacher of drawing. Established the Columbian Drawing Academy in New York, c. 1795.

Robertson, Archibald (c. 1745–1813). British naval officer during the Revolutionary period, who, like several fellow officers, made sketches of American ports and naval engagements. The Spencer Collection of the New York Public Library owns a large part of these original drawings. He is not to be confused with the aforementioned artist.

Rollinson, William (1762–1842). English-born engraver of stipple portraits for magazines, who became interested in bank-note engraving, inventing a mechanical ruling device. Best known for his portrait of Alexander Hamilton, published in 1804, after a painting by Archibald Robertson; and for his aquatint view of New York, 1801, which was printed in colours.

Romans, Bernard (1720–84). Engraver, engineer, and cartographer from Holland whose eye-witness view of the Battle of Bunker Hill, Boston (*Exact View of the Late Battle at Charleston, June 17th, 1775*) was published in America in 1775; an almost identical engraved plate was published in London in 1776; a reduced re-engraving was made by Robert Aitkin for the *Pennsylvania Magazine* for September 1775.

Saint-Mémin, Charles Balthazar Julien Févret de (1770–1852). French émigré who came to the United States in 1793, staying in New York and Philadelphia, earning a living by making crayon profile drawings with the aid of the *physionotrace* and reducing them with the pantograph to fit a circle of about 2 inches in diameter on to a copper plate which he then etched and finished in aquatint and some roulette work. In this manner he made about 800 portraits of distinguished Americans; he is also known for two views of New York. Returned to France, where he became the director of the Museum of Dijon in 1817.

Sartain, John (1808–97). Prolific engraver in mezzotint who came to America from England in 1830 and settled in Philadelphia where he died in 1897. He was also a publisher of several illustrated magazines. His larger plates are in line, among them the engraving after Bingham's *County Election* and *Martial Law* (Order No. 11).

Savage, Edward (1761–1817). Painter and engraver, generally credited with the first aquatint made in America: *Action between the Constellation and L'Insurgent*, 1798, published 1799. Originally a goldsmith, he learned to engrave portraits in stipple and in mezzotint in London. Known for his portraits of George Washington and an unfinished engraving of the *Congress Voting Independence* after a painting begun by Robert E. Pine.

Scenographia Americana. A collection of views in North America and the West Indies, engraved by Sandby, Grignion, Rooker, Canot, Elliot, and others from drawings taken on the spot by several officers of the British navy and army. Printed in London for John Bowles, Robert Sayer, Carington Bowles, Henry Parker, 1768. This collection contained originally twenty-eight plates, but was in some cases augmented to as many as seventy-four plates.

Scull, Nicholas (d. 1762). A native of Pennsylvania who became a cartographer and Survey-General of the Province of Pennsylvania in 1748, under whose direction the so-called Scull-Heap *East Prospect of the City of Philadelphia*, 1754, was made.

Seymour, Samuel. Philadelphia engraver, active 1797–1820, who engraved portraits and views after the paintings by Thomas and William Birch, among them views of Philadelphia, New York, and Mount Vernon.

Shaw, Joshua (1776–1860). Landscape painter who came to America in 1817 and drew the originals for *Picturesque Views of America* which were engraved in aquatint by John Hill (Philadelphia, 1819–20) and published by Moses Thomas and M. Carey & Son.

Smillie, James (1807–85). Born in Scotland, came to New York in 1828. Engraved a great number of fine landscapes, largely after his own drawings; a series of four allegorical prints of the *Voyage of Life* after Thomas Cole. From 1861 he worked almost exclusively on banknote engraving. Some of his large plates were issued as membership prints by the American Art Union.

Smith, John Rubens (1775–1849). Born in England, son of the engraver John Raphael Smith, 1752–1812. Worked first in Boston and then in New York where he painted, engraved, and directed a drawing school. For a while he worked also in Philadelphia. He engraved portraits in stipple and mezzotint and did some views in aquatint for the Hudson River Portfolio, as well as naval subjects.

Strickland, William (1788–1854). Philadelphia engraver and architect who was one of the first to engrave in aquatint in America; executed some small views and a few portraits. Although unsigned, except for the vignette on the title page, Strickland did the ten plates for *The Art of Colouring and Painting Landscapes in Water Colours*, published by F. Lucas, in Baltimore, 1815.

Tanner, Benjamin (1775–1848). Engraver in both line and stipple; publisher in Baltimore. He engraved some large plates of portraits and naval subjects relating to the Revolution and the war of 1812. Among these are *Macdonough's Victory on Lake Champlain*, *Perry's Victory on Lake Erie*, published January 1, 1815.

Tennant, William. Princeton graduate, class of 1758, who drew the view of *Nassau Hall* (Princeton), 1764, which was engraved by Henry Dawkins.

Tiebout, Cornelius (c. 1773–1832). The first American-born engraver who produced good stipple portraits; also some small landscape prints for the *New York Magazine* (Plate 377B).

Toms, William Henry (c. 1700–c. 1750). London engraver of the important Roberts' view of Charleston, S.C., published in 1739.

Trenchard, James. Engraver, active in Philadelphia in the 1770s, who did some portraits and views, among them a view of the State House in Philadelphia after a drawing by Charles Willson Peale, 1778, as well as illustrations for the *Columbian Magazine*.

Trumbull, John (1756–1843). Painter of historical subjects, among them the *Declaration of Independence*, which he commissioned A. B. Durand to engrave in 1820. Trumbull is credited with engraving a caricature depicting the Loyalists, published in New York in 1795. Elkanah Tisdale engraved nine satirical copperplates for Trumbull's *M'Fingal, a modern epic poem in four cantos* (New York, printed by John Buel, 1795).

Turner, James. Engraver who moved from Boston to Philadelphia, where he died in 1759. Engraved portraits and views for books and magazines and is known for his maps of Boston, the Middle Colonies (1755), and Philadelphia.

Wall, William Guy (1792–after 1862). Dublin-born landscape artist who resided in New York from 1818 till 1836, returning once more in 1856. In the 1820s he painted the water-colours which were engraved for Megarey's *Hudson River Portfolio*; also known for views of New York: *New York from Weehawk*, and *New York from Brooklyn Heights*, 1823, *City Hall*, 1826 (Plate 379B).

Yeager, Joseph (c. 1792–1859). Engraver in Philadelphia from 1816 to 1845, who worked for Philadelphia publishers. Known for his aquatint of the *Procession of Victuallers of Philadelphia*, 1821, and his line-engraving of the *Battle of New Orleans and Death of Major General Packenham*, 1815. Together with William H. Morgan published many children's books.

AMERICAN LITHOGRAPHERS

Autenrieth, C. Name appears on a set of lithographs of New York views in decorative borders published by Henry Hoff, New York, 1850.

Barnet & Doolittle, New York. First American lithographic firm, 1821-2.

Beyer, Edward (1820-65). Drew originals for Beyer's *Album of Virginia*, a desirable set of views containing representations of the fashionable spas of the ante-bellum South, drawn in America but lithographed Berlin, Dresden, 1858.

Bien, J. New York lithographer, active 1850-68. In 1860 issued Audubon's *Birds of America*, elephant folio, in chromolithography.

Bowen, J. T. Lithographer, New York, 1835-8. Moved to Philadelphia, 1838-44; issued a good series of twenty views of Philadelphia after J. C. Wild.

Britten & Rey. San Francisco lithographic firm, c. 1849-c. 1880; of great importance for scenes of the Gold Rush.

Brown's Portrait Gallery of Distinguished American Citizens. Lithographs from twenty-six silhouettes cut by W. H. Brown, published with decorative backgrounds by Kellogg, Hartford, 1845. Most of original edition destroyed by fire; has been published in facsimile about 1930.

Burton, C. Artist, active 1830-50, New York. Did work for Sarony & Major, Pendleton, Michelin.

Buttersworth, James. Marine painter whose subjects were lithographed by Currier & Ives.

Cameron, John. Lithographer and artist, active 1852-62, New York; best known for horse subjects done for Currier & Ives, but did work independently, or with other lithographers.

Castelnau, Francis. French traveller in · America, 1838-40; published *Vues de l'Amérique du Nord*, Paris, 1842; illustrated in lithography.

Catlin, George (1796-1872). Artist and lithographer, traveller in Far West in the 1830s. Best known for *North American Indian Portfolio*, folio, with lithographs (London,

England, published by the author, 1844); later published in America.

Childs, Cephas G. Philadelphia lithographer, active 1823-58; associated at various times with Pendleton, Kearny, Inman, and Lehman.

Currier & Ives. The leading American lithographic firm, founded by Nathaniel Currier in New York in 1833. James M. Ives became a partner in 1857. The firm was in existence until 1906. Publishers of popular subjects, including sporting subjects, genre, comics, etc., and employing such artists as Louis Maurer, A. F. Tait, Fanny Palmer, Charles Parsons, Thomas Worth, and James Buttersworth.

Durrie, George H. (1820-63). Painter, born and worked in Connecticut. Did the originals of the best-known farm and winter scenes published by Currier & Ives.

Duval, Peter S. Philadelphia lithographer, active 1831-79; associated at times with Lehman, Huddy, Prang and others.

Endicott. An important name in American lithography. Firm began as Endicott & Swett in Baltimore, 1828, and moved to New York 1830; active under various names until 1896.

Hoff, Henry. New York lithographer, active 1850.

Hoffy, Alfred. Philadelphia artist and lithographer, active 1840-60; best known for his drawings of military costume in Huddy & Duval's *U.S. Military Magazine*.

Huddy & Duval. Philadelphia lithographers, 1839-41; published *U.S. Military Magazine*, 3 vols, prized for costume plates.

Imbert, Anthony. Active 1825-35 as pioneer lithographer, New York. His work for Colden's *Erie Canal Memoir*, 1826, the first outstanding American work.

Inman, Henry (1801-46). Painter; member of Philadelphia lithographic firm, Childs & Inman, 1831-33.

Jevne & Almini. Leading Chicago lithographic firm, established about 1866. Publishers of *Chicago Illustrated* 1830.

Kearny, Francis. Philadelphia engraver

and lithographer; member of the firm of Pendleton, Kearny & Childs, c. 1829–30.

Kellogg, D. W., later **E. B. & E. C. Kellogg.** Lithographic firm of Hartford, also in New York and Buffalo; the most prolific firm after Currier & Ives; established 1833; subjects included sentimentals, portraits, book illustrations.

Klauprech & Menzel. One of the best Cincinnati lithographic firms; active 1840–59; views of Ohio a speciality.

Koellner, August (1813–c. 1878). Artist and lithographer, best known for fifty-four well-drawn views of American cities lithographed by Deroy, Paris, published by Goupil, Vibert, 1848–51.

Lane, Fitz Hugh (1804–65). Marine artist, born in Gloucester, Massachusetts. Did originals of town views; having worked at the lithographic firm of Pendleton in Boston, he put some of his own work on stone (Plate 383B).

Lehman, George (c. 1800–70). Painter, engraver in aquatint, lithographer; worked in Philadelphia with Duval and also with Childs.

Leighton, Scott. Painter of horses for Currier & Ives.

Mathews, A. E. Artist, known for *Pencil Sketches of Colorado*, 1865, lithographs by J. Bien, New York, and *Pencil Sketches of Montana*.

Maurer, Louis. One of the Currier & Ives artists, whose speciality was sporting subjects, including field sports, represented by *Deer Shooting, On the Shattagee*, and horse subjects, such as *Trotting Cracks on the Snow*.

Michelin, Francis. Lithographer, Boston 1840; moved to New York 1844; worked to 1859.

Milbert, J. French artist, in America 1815–23. Author of the *Itinéraire Pittoresque du Fleuve Hudson* . . . issued in Paris in thirteen parts beginning 1826 and containing fifty-three numbered views in lithograph.

Nagel, Louis. Lithographer, in New York 1844; Nagel & Weingaertner, 1849–57. Went to San Francisco in 1862, where he was associated with Fishbourne & Kuchel.

North American Indian Portfolio, 1844. Lithographed in England by Daye & Haghe, after George Catlin.

Otis, Bass. Made the first American lithograph, Philadelphia, 1818–19.

Pendleton. Important lithographic firm, Boston, New York, Philadelphia, 1825–c. 1866.

Robinson, H. R. New York lithographer, active 1832–51. Showed the news value of the lithograph with his view of the New York Fire, 1835 (Plate 381B), issued a few weeks later; also the arrival of the steamship *Great Western* in New York harbour, 1838; his *Peytona and Fashion* was the first print of an American horse-race, 1842 (also issued by N. Currier).

Sarony, Napoleon (1821–96). Expert lithographer and artist working in New York alone and with others, as Sarony & Major, also Sarony, Major & Knapp; withdrew from lithography about 1867.

Tait, A. F. (1819–1905). Leading sporting painter of the nineteenth century; not a staff artist of Currier & Ives, but many of his scenes of field sports were issued in lithograph by them.

Walton, Henry. English artist known for attractive town views in New York State, such as Ithaca, Elmira, Binghampton, and Watkins Glen; was in Ithaca 1836–46. Work issued in lithograph by Bufford and others.

Whitefield, Edwin. Active 1854–5, artist and publisher of largest series of American city views in lithograph, printed by F. Michelin, Endicott & Co., Lewis & Brown.

Wild, J. C. Artist, came to Philadelphia in 1838. The firm of Wild & Chevalier issued lithographs of Philadelphia. Later Wild went to Ohio, St Louis, and Davenport, Iowa, where he died in 1845. Wild drew originals for *The Valley of the Mississippi*, published 1840 by Chambers & Knapp, St Louis.

Worth, Thomas. Artist, worked for Currier & Ives; best known for horse subjects, such as *Trotting Cracks at the Forge*; also comics.

AMERICAN RAILROAD-PRINT MAKERS

Bien, Julius. Active New York 1850–68.

Brett, Alphonse. Active Philadelphia and New York 1852–64.

Bufford, John H. Active Boston and New York 1835–1870s.

Crosby, Charles H. Active Boston 1852–72.

Currier & Ives. Active New York 1834–1907.

Duval, Peter S. Active Philadelphia 1831–93.

The Endicotts. Active New York 1830–96.

Rosenthal, Louis N., and family. Active Philadelphia 1852–70.

Sartain, J. Born 1808 and died 1897.

Sinclair, Thomas. Active Philadelphia 1839–89.

Swett, Moses. Active New York, Boston, and Washington 1830–7.

Tappan & Bradford. Active Boston 1848–53.

AMERICAN SILHOUETTISTS

Andrews, Mrs M. (Died 1831). Illustrated reminiscences of Washington, D.C.

Banton, T. S. Early nineteenth century, New England.

Bascom, Ruth (1772–1848). Gill, Massachusetts. Her silhouettes are frequently adorned with details of metal foil.

Brooks, Samuel. Boston, 1790.

Brown, J. (*c.* 1812–20). Salem, Massachusetts.

Chamberlain, William (*c.* 1824). New England.

Colles, J. (*c.* 1778). New York.

Cottu, M. (*c.* 1811). A French *émigré*.

Cummings, Rufus (*c.* 1840s). Boston.

Doolittle, A. B. (*c.* 1807). Son of Amos Doolittle, the engraver.

Doolittle, S. C. (*c.* 1810–20). Worked in South Carolina.

Edwards, Thomas (1822–56). Boston.

Ellsworth, James (*c.* 1833). Worked in Connecticut.

Griffing, Martin (1784–1859). Cripple, itinerant. New England.

Harrison, A. H. (1916). St Louis, Missouri.

Howard, Everet (*c.* 1820).

Jones, F. P. (early nineteenth century). New England.

Joye, John? (born Salem, March 14, 1790). Active, Salem 1812.

Letton, R. (*c.* 1808). Showman and silhouettist.

Lord, Philip (1814–40). Born in Newburyport, Massachusetts. Active 1830–40. Made use of silver and gold in shading.

Metcalf, Elias (1785–1834). New York. Travelled in Guadeloupe, Canada, New Orleans, and West Indies.

Mitchell, Judith (born 1793, married 1837). Quakeress, Nantucket, Massachusetts. .

Perkins, George (*c.* 1850–55). Salem. Did some original work and numerous replicas of the silhouettes of William Henry Brown. Often confused with the originals.

Rogers, Sally. Armless cutter. Active New York, 1807.

Rossiter (active 1810–11). Hanover, N.H.

Seager (*c.* 1834). Cutter, New Bedford, Massachusetts. Halifax, Nova Scotia, 1840, Boston, 1845–50.

Stewart, Rev. Joseph (active 1806). Hartford, Connecticut.

Valdenuit, M. de. Assistant to Saint-Mémin. Silhouette work is often signed *Vnt & S. M.* or *Drawn by Valdenuit and Engraved by St. Mémin.*

Vallée, Jean-François de la (1785–1815). Portrayed Washington. Active Virginia, Philadelphia, New Orleans.

Waugh (active 1835). North Carolina.

Way, Mary (active 1811). New London, Connecticut.

Williams, Henry (1787–1830). Boston.

BIRD PRINTS

History. All, or almost all, bird prints were to start with part of a book. Whether it is ethically agreeable to pull books to pieces and to sell their engravings separately need not affect the collector so much as the print dealer. Some books such as Dr Thornton's *Temple of Flora* or Audubon's *Birds of America*, were in effect collections of prints which have finally found their way into book form.

Bird books with coloured plates make an interesting subject for collectors, but they demand a very considerable capital outlay and a library of some size. The individual coloured prints take up little space and can be collected reasonably cheaply. Furthermore, it is possible to specialize and to collect, for example, prints of, say, a robin or a bird of paradise, or to limit oneself to English, French, or German prints.

Coloured bird prints started to appear in books around 1730, with hand-coloured copper engravings which continued until about 1830, though at the beginning of the nineteenth century the French produced wonderful stipple engravings of birds and flowers, partially printed in colours by a method unequalled before or since and touched up by hand. Hand-coloured lithographs began to appear around 1830, and chromolithographs, printed in colour, after 1850. All these types have their own special interest, while Audubon's *Birds of America*, giant aquatint engravings which appeared between 1827 and 1838, are unique.

Almost all bird prints come from Germany, France, or Great Britain; a few from Italy and Holland, some of very good quality. And a very few, not very interesting, from Scandinavia. The Germans excelled in copperplate engravings, the French in stipple engravings partly printed in colour, and the British in lithographs. Audubon's aquatints stand above all competition, but as loose plates are on sale almost exclusively in the United States, they are not easy to collect, as well as being very expensive.

Prices of individual prints naturally vary from a few shillings for the smaller and more common prints up to fifty pounds and more for Audubons; but most other large prints can be bought for well under ten, often for under five pounds.

Most, but not all, prints have the name of the artist on them, usually but not always in the bottom left-hand corner; and again most, though slightly less often, have the name of the engraver, this usually in the bottom right-hand corner. In addition, the name of the printer sometimes appears, under the title or elsewhere. A list of the abbreviations used to indicate artist, engraver, or printer will be found below. Meanwhile it must be pointed out that some confusion can be caused to the collector by the naming of complete sets of prints after the author of the book rather than the artist. Thus bird prints painted by Barraband are usually referred to as Levaillant's birds, since Levaillant's name is on the title-page of the books in which these prints appeared. Quite often, however, the author was the artist.

Albin, Eleazar. Author and artist. His *Natural History of Birds*, 3 volumes, quarto, 1731–8, is the earliest of all collections of coloured bird prints, with 306 in hand-coloured engravings. Also produced in 1737, twenty-three engravings, very small, of British songbirds.

Audebert, Jean Baptiste. Author and artist. Produced *Les Oiseaux Dorés ou à Reflets Metalliques*, 1802; 190 very fine engravings printed in colours by a method invented by Audebert himself. There were two sets of these plates, the ordinary one with lettering in black, the superior in gold. Printing in colours had been performed in various ways since 1730. It consists basically only of putting the colours on to the engraved plates and pressing them on to the paper, rather than printing the paper in monochrome and colouring it later. The French, however, performed feats of colour printing which gave us these prints, almost all Redouté's flower books and the illustrations to Levaillant's bird books, which have never been surpassed.

Most of these engravings, however, were printed in colours and finished by hand.

Audubon, John James Laforest. The author and artist of the most famous of all collections of bird prints, *The Birds of America from Original Drawings made during a Residence of Twenty-five years in the United States*, published between 1827 and 1838 in four volumes, size double elephant folio, easily the largest bird prints ever done. There were 435 hand-coloured aquatints, of which Lucy Audubon drew Plate 404, but Audubon himself the rest. The first ten were engraved by W. H. Lizars, and the remainder by Robert Havell and Robert Havell Junior, who also revised later editions of the first ten plates, adding their name. It is likely that not more than 300 copies of each print were produced. This is by far the most valuable of any collection of bird prints, and a complete set fetches around £10,000 to £12,000. This means that individual copies of the most sought-after prints sell for over £100, while the general level is around £50. For a collection of this size the capital value is therefore staggering, and no other bird prints are in the same class. The most expensive flower prints, the engravings from Dr Thornton's *Temple of Flora*, number only thirty-five, of which the first and only good printing comprised not more than 400 copies of each, but the prints sell for – on average – £30 apiece. Audubon prints are very rarely on sale individually in Britain, and are, moreover, outside the scope of the ordinary collector.

Barraband, Jacques. Artist. Drew most of the pictures reproduced by François Levaillant in his very important series of exotic birds published between 1796 and 1816.

Bessa. Artist, mainly famous for his drawings of flowers, which were almost comparable to Redouté, but drew some of the pictures for R. P. Lesson's *Histoire des Oizeaux Mouches*, 1828–33, and *Illustrations de Zoologie*, 1832–35.

Bock, Johann Carl. Artist. Helped to illustrate Bernhard Meyer's *Naturgeschichte der Vögel Deutschlands*.

Bolton, James. Author and artist for *Harmonia Ruralis*, 2 volumes, quarto, 1794–6, with 80 hand-coloured engravings. Other editions

of this well-known collection appeared until 1845.

Bonaparte, Prince Lucien Charles Laurent. Author of *American Ornithology or the Natural History of Birds inhabiting the United States not given by Wilson*, 4 vols., folio, 1825–33, with twenty-seven hand-coloured engravings by T. R. Peale, A. Rider, and J. J. L. Audubon; and of *Iconographie des Pigeons*, large folio, 1857–9, with fifty-five hand-coloured lithographs by P. L. Oudart, F. Willy, and E. Blanchard.

Borkhausen, Moritz Balthasar. Author of *Deutsche Ornithologie*, 2 vols., folio, 1800–17. Illustrated by H. Curtmann and the Susemihl family. A very rare collection, reprinted 1837–41.

Boucquet, Louis. Artist. Illustrated L. J. P. Vieillot's *Histoire Naturelle des Plus Beaux Oiseaux Chanteurs de la Zone Torride*, 1805–9.

Brookshaw, George. Author and artist of *Six Birds accurately Drawn and Coloured after Nature*, folio, 1817; six hand-coloured lithographs. Brookshaw also drew the famous "Pomona Britannica" series of fruits.

Brown, Peter. Part author with Thomas Pennant and artist of *New Illustrations of Zoology*, quarto, 1776; fifty hand-coloured engravings.

Buffon, Comte Georges-Louis Leclerc de. Author of the famous *Histoire Naturelle Générale*, 1749–1804. Many editions of this book, a number with coloured plates, were published, but the important illustrations to it are those drawn by François Nicholas Martinet, which numbered 1,008 in all, appearing between 1770 and 1786. Size: small folio, and de luxe edition, larger folio. Attractive plates with a gold-panel line drawn round each, they represent one of the largest of all single collections.

Catesby, Mark. Author and artist of *The Natural History of Carolina, Baltimore and the Bahama Islands*, large folio, 1731–43; 220 hand-coloured engravings (109 of which are of birds). These are the earliest of all American bird prints. Reprinted in 1748–56 and in 1771; and in Germany in 1750 and 1757.

Chromolithograph. The lithograph only requires one stone for printing, but the chromolithograph needs as many stones as colours are to be used on the finished print. A different colour is applied to each stone, and the various stones are applied in succession to the same paper until the complete picture is achieved. It is obvious therefore that to produce a really fine chromolithograph was both a cumbersome and an expensive process, so that while some magnificent examples appeared, there were far more prints which tended to be cheap and nasty. The very important series of illustrations by Keulemans and others for the works of Richard Bowdler Sharpe were all reproduced in chromolithography, but in most cases the printing and colouring leave much to be desired. A comparison of one of these prints with one of the hand-coloured lithographs from Gould's *Birds* will make this inferiority immediately plain.

Copper engravings. Until the arrival of the lithograph all bird prints, save the few reproduced by aquatint, were taken from copper plates on which the necessary lines had been scratched with an engraving tool. The results naturally varied according to the skill of the artist or the engraver; in many cases the artist was his own engraver. Almost all bird prints, then, from 1730 to 1830 are copper engravings, and some later still, though the hand-coloured lithograph was responsible for the important work in the later period.

Descourtilz, Jean Theodore. Author and artist of two works on Brazilian birds. The earlier published in Paris in 1834 with sixty-six hand-coloured lithographs: the later published both in Rio de Janeiro and London in 1856 with forty-eight hand-coloured lithographs. Both large folio. These prints are much sought after, as they stand almost alone in portraying only South American birds.

Donovan, Edward. Author and artist of several collections between 1794 and 1826; all octavo size and depicting both British and exotic birds.

Edwards, George. Author and artist of *A Natural History of Uncommon Birds and Gleanings from Natural History*, in all seven volumes, quarto. With 362 very fine hand-coloured engravings, mostly of birds. Edwards' bird prints are some of the most important, and were reprinted in London, Amsterdam, and Nurem-

berg, the last edition being in 1805. The colouring of these printings varies, but even the later ones are still good, while the printing of 1802–5, which produced only twenty-five of each print, is perhaps the best coloured of all.

Elliot, Daniel Giraud. Author and part artist of a number of important collections of bird plates published in New York and London. All hand-coloured lithographs, large folio size, and showing grouse, pheasants, birds of paradise, hornbills, and other birds. The other artists were P. L. Oudart, J. Wolf, J. Smit, E. Shephard, W. S. Morgan, and J. G. Keulemans.

Frisch, Johann Leonard. Author of one of the most enjoyable of all bird books, *Vorstellung der Vögel in Deutschland*, containing 255 hand-coloured engravings, folio size, drawn by F. H. Frisch, P. J. Frisch, and J. C. Frisch. Published Berlin 1733–63, and re-issued 1764 and 1817. These lovely prints are unfortunately very rare.

Gabler, Ambrosius. Part artist of Bernhard Meyer's *Naturgeschichte der Vögel Deutschlands*, 1799–1807.

Gould, John. Author and also largely artist of the most complete and most famous collection of bird books, depicting over 3,000 different birds. All Gould's plates are folio and all are hand-coloured lithographs: the principal subjects are British Birds, European Birds, Humming-birds, Birds of New Guinea, Birds of Australia, Birds of Asia, Toucans, Trogons, Partridges of America, and Himalayan Birds. His fellow artists were: his wife, E. Gould; Edward Lear, H. C. Richter, William Hart, and Joseph Wolf. The artists did their own lithography, and the printing was done by C. Hullmandel and, to a lesser extent, by Walter and Coln. The dates of the prints, which are all of very fine quality, range from 1831 to 1888. Gould himself died in 1881.

Graves, George. Author and artist of *British Ornithology*; 144 octavo hand-coloured engravings, 1811–21.

Gray, John Edward. Author of *Gleanings from the Menagerie and Aviary at Knowsley Hall*, containing seventy-nine hand-coloured lithographs. Nine of these are of birds and are drawn by Edward Lear, who was at that time

(1846–50) curator to Lord Derby at Knowsley.

Hart, William. Artist of a number of the plates in Gould's *Birds*.

Hayes, William. Author and, with the other members of his family, artist of *A Natural History of British Birds*; forty hand-coloured folio-size engravings, 1771–5; and of *The Birds of Osterley Park*; 101 hand-coloured engravings, quarto size, 1794–9. Both very attractive series. Many of the plates are signed in ink by the artists.

Hergenroder, J. M. Part artist of Bernhard Meyer's *Naturgeschichte der Vögel Deutschlands*.

Huet, Nicholas. Part artist of Temminck's *Nouveau Recueil de Plantes Coloriées d'Oiseaux*.

Hullmandel, C. Printer of almost all the lithographs for Gould's *Birds*.

Jardine, Sir William. Author of Jardine's *Naturalist's Library*, published in forty volumes between 1833 and 1843. Size small octavo. The first fourteen volumes were devoted to various sorts of birds, and the plates were drawn by Edward Lear, William Swainson, James Stuart, and others; each volume contained about thirty plates. Not very exciting to look at, they have been used a great deal in recent years to cover tablemats.

Keulemans, John Gerard. Artist and lithographer. Produced about 800 plates of birds altogether during the latter part of the nineteenth century, notably for D. G. Elliot and R. Bowdler Sharp.

Knip, Antoinette Pauline Jacqueline Rifer. Artist. Illustrated *Histoire Naturelle des Tongoras, des Manakins et des Todiers*, by Desmarest with seventy-two plates, 1805, printed in colour and produced herself *Les Pigeons*, large folio, 1809–11, with 147 coloured plates. Madame Knip, who was the accredited Natural History Painter to Queen Marie-Louise, produced in *Les Pigeons* one of the finest of all sets of bird prints. The first eighty-seven are printed in colours and finished by hand, engraved by J. C. Macret. The remainder are lithographs, hand coloured except for a few engravings by Dequevaubiller or Guyard.

Langlois. French printer, who printed partly or wholly in colours, very finely, many books, notably among bird books those by Levaillant and Vieillot.

Latham, John. Author and artist of *A General Synopsis of Birds*, quarto, 1781–5, with many supplements and reprints. The final total of hand-coloured engravings was 193.

Lear, Edward. Lear wrote and illustrated the famous *Nonsense Rhymes*, limericks, etc., and produced many books with topographical plates. He was also famous as a painter of birds. His own illustrations of the family of Psittacidae, or Parrots, folio, 1830–2, with forty-two hand-coloured lithographs, are very fine plates. He also did many of the drawings for Gould's *Birds*, for Jardine's *Naturalist's Library*, and J. E. Gray's *Knowsley Menagerie*.

Lesson, Rene Primevere. Author of many bird books published between 1828 and 1839. All fairly small octavo or royal octavo, illustrated with plates printed in colour and and finished by hand, drawn by J. G. Prêtre, P. L. Oudart, A. G. Bevalet, Bessa, and others. In all responsible for more than 700 bird plates, of which the best known are of birds of paradise, fly-catchers, and colibris.

Levaillant, François. Producer until surpassed by Gould of the largest series of works on exotic birds, including the parrots, birds of Africa, birds of paradise, birds of America, etc. In all nearly 700 engravings, printed in colour and finished by hand. Most of his collections were published in two editions, a folio and a larger folio, the latter "grand papier" edition being the better coloured. The artists were J. F. L. Reinold and J. Barraband, with various engravers, but almost all were printed magnificently by Langlois.

Lewin, William. Producer and artist of several bird books. His *Birds of Britain*, 1795–1801, quarto, with 336 hand-coloured engravings, is of moderate interest, but the first edition of this work, 1789–94, limited to sixty sets, is unique, in that all the illustrations are water-colours drawn and painted by Lewin himself.

Lizars, W. H. Engraver of the first ten aquatints in Audubon's *Birds of America*.

Lord Thomas. Artist and author of Lord's *Entire New System of Ornithology*, folio, 1791; 111 hand-coloured engravings.

Lorenzi, Lorenzo. One of the artists for Manetti's *Storia Naturale Degli Uccelli*.

Manetti, Xaviero. Author and part artist of *Storia Naturale Degli Uccelli*. Large folio, Florence, 1767–76; 600 magnificent hand-coloured engravings. A superb collection of bird prints: the other artists were L. Lorenzi and V. Vanni.

Martinet, François Nicholas. Artist. Drew the 1,008 pictures for the great edition of Buffon's *Histoire Naturelle*. Martinet also drew and engraved thirty-one plates for François Salerne's *Histoire Naturelle*, a French edition of John Ray's *Synopsis Methodica Avium*.

Meyer, Bernhard. Author of *Naturgeschichte der Vogel Deutschlands*, folio, Nuremberg, 1799–1807. A very fine collection of engravings drawn by A. Gabler, J. M. Hergenroder, and J. C. Bock.

Meyer, Henry Leonard. Author and artist of *Illustrations of British Birds*, folio, 1835–41; 313 hand-coloured lithographs; and *Coloured Illustrations of British Birds and Their Eggs*, octavo, 1841–50; 432 hand-coloured lithographs.

Miller, John Frederick. Author and artist of the *Cimelia Physica*, large folio, 1796, with sixty hand-coloured engravings (forty-one of birds).

Morris, Francis Orpen. Author of *A History of British Birds*. Originally published 1851–7, 6 vols., royal octavo, with 358 hand-coloured lithographs, and reprinted often. The illustrations are disagreeable in all editions.

Murray, G. Engraved some of the pictures for Wilson's *American Ornithology*.

Nozeman, Cornelis. Author of *Nederlandsche Vogelen*, 5 vols., large folio, Amsterdam, 1770–1829; with five hand-coloured title-pages and 250 hand-coloured engravings by J. C. Sepp. A splendid collection of prints.

Oudart, Paul Louis. Artist. He did illustrations for Prince Bonaparte, D. G. Elliot, and R. P. Lesson.

Pennant, Thomas. Author of the *British Zoology*, folio, 1761–6; with 132 hand-coloured engravings, 121 of birds, all engraved by P. Mazell; drawn by various artists, including P. Paillon and George Edwards.

Reinold, Johann Friedrich Leberecht. Artist. Drew the pictures for Levaillant's *Birds of Africa*.

Richter, H. C. Artist. Drew some of the pictures for Gould's *Birds*.

Rider, A. Artist. Helped to illustrate Bonaparte's *American Ornithology*.

Selby, Prideaux John. Drew illustrations of *British Ornithology* – 222 huge double-elephant folio hand-coloured engravings (nearly as large as Audubon's *Birds of America*). Issued between 1821 and 1834.

Sepp, Jan Christian. Illustrated Nozeman's *Nederlandsche Vogelen*.

Sharpe, Richard Bowdler. Author of a number of works issued between 1868 and 1898 and illustrated in chromolithography by J. G. Keulemans, William Hart, J. & P. Smit, and others. Quarto or folio, they show birds of paradise, kingfishers, swallows, etc. The plates are interesting ornithologically but not aesthetically.

Smit, Josef. Artist. Drew some of the illustrations for Elliot's *Pheasants and Birds of Paradise*, for Gould's *Birds*, and for R. Bowdler Sharpe.

Susemihl, Johann Conrad, Johann Theodor and Erwin Eduard. Drew between them most of the illustrations to Borkhausen's *Deutsche Ornithologie*.

Swainson, William. Drew many of the illustrations for Jardine's *Naturalist's Library*; also produced *Zoological Illustrations* with 334 hand-coloured lithographs, 1820–33, and *A Selection of the Birds of Brazil and Mexico*, seventy-eight hand-coloured lithographs all drawn by himself.

Temminck, Coenrad Jacob. Author of *Nouveau Recueil de Planches Coloriées des Oiseaux*, a tremendous, but not so attractive sequel to the edition of Buffon's *Natural History*, with plates by Martinet. The plates, 600 hand-coloured engravings by N. Huet and J. G. Prêtre, were issued in both quarto and folio size between 1820 and 1839.

Vanni, Violante. Artist. Drew many of the plates for Manetti's *Storia Naturale Degli Uccelli*.

Vieillot, Louis Jean Pierre. Author of several works published in Paris between 1805 and 1830, with folio coloured plates by P. L.

Oudart and J. G. Prêtre. The most important are *Les Oiseaux Chanteurs de la Zone Torride* (seventy-two engravings printed by Langlois), *Les Oiseaux d'Amérique* (131 plates printed by Langlois) and *La Galerie des Oiseaux* (324 hand-coloured lithographs). All very fine plates.

Walter. Printed a number of the plates for Gould's *Birds*.

Warnicke, J. G. Engraved some of the illustrations to Wilson's *American Ornithology*.

Watermarks. It is sometimes possible to date a print which is not otherwise dated by inspecting the watermark. Most hand-made paper had a watermark in it, and this watermark often included the date. It is a fair inference, though not quite always true, that the date of the watermark will be little if any before the time of the making of the print. To inspect the watermark hold the print up to a strong light, when it will at once stand out.

Wilson, Alexander. Author and artist of the fine folio work in nine volumes, published in Philadelphia 1808–14, called *American Ornithology*, with seventy-six hand-coloured plates engraved by A. Lawson, J. G. Warnicke, G. Murray, and B. Tanner. Though not comparable artistically to Audubon's *Birds of America*, these plates were considerably earlier and were the first done of American birds in America. Bonaparte's book was a supplement to this.

Wolf, Joseph. Artist. Drew many of the illustrations for Gould's *Birds*.

ITALIAN DRAUGHTSMEN OF THE EIGHTEENTH CENTURY

Appiani, Andrea (1754–1817). Born at Milan and first achieved prominence in 1778 with a series of paintings of the *Rape of Europa* which reveal a debt to the Bolognese school of the early seventeenth century. He later developed a strongly neo-classical style which was destined to dominate Lombard painting for several decades. His large religious, mythological, and allegorical paintings have a certain mannered charm, but he is principally remembered today for his portraits. His sketches for history pieces are very vigorous (much more so than the finished paintings), and his portrait heads have a rare and subtle delicacy. A large number of his drawings are to be found in the Brera at Milan and the Pinacoteca Tosio Martinengo at Brescia.

Bartolozzi, Francesco (1727–1815). A Florentine whose fame derives mainly from his engravings. He was trained in Venice, and in 1764 went to England, where he became engraver to the King and was among the foundation members of the Royal Academy. In 1802 he was appointed Director of the Academy of Arts at Lisbon, where he spent the rest of his life. The majority of his drawings are associated with his engravings and include some clever copies and imitations of Guercino.

Batoni, Pompeo (1708–87). Born at Lucca and studied painting at Rome under Sebastian Conca and Agostino Masucci. He acquired a European reputation as a portrait painter, specializing in depicting the rich young grand tourists who flocked to Rome each year. But he was also a history painter of outstanding ability and one of the originators of the neo-classical style. Numerous drawings of nude figures (academy studies) have been attributed to him on very slender evidence, and only a few sketches for his altar pieces (in private collections) can with certainty be ascribed to him.

Beaumont, Francesco Claudio (1694–1766). Most notable Piedmontese painter of the first half of the eighteenth century. He was born at Turin and trained in Rome under Francesco Trevisani. From 1731 he was employed principally in working for the Royal House of Savoy. His paintings and drawings reveal an almost French *rocaille* elegance and delicacy (Plate 425c). His drawings are well represented in the Biblioteca Reale and the Museo Civico, Turin.

Bellotto, Bernardo (1720–80). A Venetian, was the nephew and pupil of Canaletto, and like him became a view painter. Most of his career was passed outside Italy, working for the courts of Dresden, Vienna, Warsaw, and St Petersburg. His drawings – of which the best collections are those in the National Museum, Warsaw, and the Landesmuseum at Darmstadt – include sketches for views and *capricci* and also some rather hard studies of figures.

Bibiena. The name, from their place of origin, given to members of the Galli family, who were the greatest stage designers, theatre architects, and *quadraturisti* (painters of *trompe l'œil* architecture) of eighteenth-century Italy. The most notable members of the family were the brothers Ferdinando (1657–1743) and Francesco (1659–1739) and Ferdinando's two sons Giuseppe (1696–1757) and Antonio (1700–74). All the Bibiena seem to have produced drawings of fantastic architecture either as theatrical designs or simply as *capricci*. Most of the larger public collections of drawings include specimens of their work.

Bison, Giuseppe Bernardino (1762–1844). The last of the Venetian rococo painters. He was born at Palmanova and trained at Venice, where he spent the first stage of his career, working mainly as a painter of views (somewhat in the style of F. Guardi) and fresco decorations. In 1807 he settled at Trieste, but in 1831 moved to Lombardy, where he passed the rest of his life, dying in Milan. His drawings contain echoes of his greater predecessors, G. B. Tiepolo and F. Guardi. He is represented in the Ashmolean Museum, Oxford, and the Albertina at Vienna.

Bonomino, Paolo Vincenzo (1756–1839). Born at Bergamo, where most of his work was executed. He is best known for his Dance of Death paintings (Church of S. Grata, Borgo Canale, Bergamo), which reveal a macabre wit, but he also executed neo-classical history and decorative paintings. A large collection of his drawings is in the Castello Sforzesco at Milan.

Bortoloni, Mattia (1696–1750). A somewhat obscure but highly interesting Venetian painter whose principal works are a ceiling in the church of the Tolentini at Venice and a large cycle of frescoes in the Villa Cornaro at Piombino Dese. His figures have an almost mannerist attenuation and elegance. Drawings by him are in the Albertina and the Ashmolean Museum.

Bossi, Giuseppe (1777–1815). A Milanese who went to Rome in 1795 and became a member of the circle of leading neo-classical artists and amateurs. After returning to Milan in 1801 he executed numerous allegorical and mythological paintings in a strongly neo-classical style and also some portraits similar to those of Appiani. His figure drawings, of which numerous examples are in the Brera and Castello Sforzesco at Milan, have a serene statuesque quality.

Busiri, Giovanni Battista (c. 1698–c. 1757), nicknamed **Titarella.** A view painter who worked in Rome and Naples. He executed numerous oil and gouache views of classical ruins, for which he based his style on the great seventeenth-century landscape painters, and was patronized especially by grand tourists. One of his sketch books is in the Fitzwilliam Museum.

Cades, Giuseppe (1750–99). A painter of French extraction, was born at Rome, where he passed most of his life. He never wholly succumbed to the "Grecian" style of neo-classical painting, and his costume pieces of sixteenth-century subjects have a rococo sense of movement. Two of his drawings are in the Ashmolean Museum.

Cagnola, Conte Luigi (1762–1833). One of the most notable Milanese architects of the Empire period, was born into a noble family and did not take to the practice of architecture till 1801. A large number of his drawings, which include highly finished designs as well as lightly touched rough sketches, is in the Brera.

Canal, Antonio, known as **Canaletto** (1697–1767). The outstanding Venetian view painter of the first half of the eighteenth century. He also worked in England (where much of his loveliest work was done) between 1746 and 1755. His drawings, which are represented in nearly all the larger public collections, may roughly be divided into two types: very faint and exquisite sketches which appear to have been executed in connexion with his paintings, and some rather bold *capricci* and views which seem to have been done as an end in themselves (Plate 427).

Canova, Antonio (1757–1822). Greatest of Italian eighteenth-century sculptors, was born near Venice and moved in 1780 to Rome, where most of his career was spent. A vast collection of his drawings, including academy studies, drawings after the antique, and sketches for his own work, is in the Museo Civico at Bassano. They reflect his style as a sculptor, though they reveal little of his superb technical accomplishment in the handling of terracotta and marble. See E. Bassi, *Il Museo Civico di Bassano, I Disegni di Antonio Canova* (1959).

Carlevaris, Luca (1663–1729). First of the eighteenth-century painters to specialize in Venetian views, was born at Udine and went to Venice in 1679. His views are principally distinguished for their lively figures, which present an enthralling picture of *settecento* life. His figure drawings are similarly vivacious. One of his sketch books is in the British Museum.

Cignaroli, Giambettino (1706–70). Born at Verona and worked in many north Italian cities, including Venice and Florence. His drawings and paintings owe much to his master Antonio Balestra, though they reveal a wholly eighteenth-century sweetness and elegance.

Crespi, Giuseppe Maria (1665–1747). The last of the great Bolognese painters. He produced both religious paintings and genre scenes distinguished for their rich, almost Rembrandtesque, use of paint. His work exerted a profound influence on two Venetian painters, G. B. Piazzetta and Pietro Longhi. There are two figure drawings attributed to him at Windsor Castle, but disappointingly few others have been identified.

Creti, Donato (1671–1749). A Bolognese painter who continued the seventeenth-century traditions of his school into the eighteenth century. He is represented at Windsor by some attractive feathery landscape drawings and sketches for some of his many history paintings.

Crosato, Giovanni Battista (1685–1758). A minor but very attractive painter of the Venetian school, who worked much for the court at Turin. His paintings and drawings have an elegance and grace characteristic of the Venetian *settecento*, though they lack the brilliance of his greater contemporaries.

Diziani, Gaspare (1689–1767). Born at Belluno and went to Venice, where he studied under Sebastiano Ricci. He worked mainly in Venice, but also for several north European courts, including that of Dresden. His paintings, mainly religious subjects, are reminiscent of Ricci, though less accomplished. In his drawings the influence of Pellegrini is strong. He is represented in the print room at Warsaw and the Correr Museum, Venice.

Fontebasso, Francesco (1709–68/9). A Venetian artist, was strongly influenced by G. B. Tiepolo, as is revealed by both his paintings and drawings. He worked at Venice, Petersburg, and Milan. Drawings by him are in the Ashmolean Museum and several other collections.

Francheschini, Marco Antonio (1648–1729). A very prolific Bolognese painter who was trained under Carlo Cignani and worked in Rome, Genoa, Piedmont, Germany, and Spain, as well as his native city. His most notable work is in the church of Corpus Domini, Bologna. Many of his sketches for paintings are at Windsor.

Fuga, Ferdinando (1699–1782). One of the leading architects in Rome and Naples, was born at Florence. He was much employed at Rome during the 1730s and early 1740s, when he executed most of his outstanding works. A good collection of his drawings, most of which are highly finished, is in the Gabinetto Nazionale delle Stampe at Rome.

Gabbiani, Domenico (1652–1726). Leading Florentine decorative painter of the late seventeenth and early eighteenth centuries. Working in a somewhat restrained late baroque style he enriched the ceilings of many a Florentine palace. Some of his sketches for these works (Plate 425A), and also a volume of caricatures, are in the Uffizi print room.

Gandolfi, Gaetano (1734–1802) and his brother **Ubaldo** (1728–81). Bolognese painters who worked principally in their native city. Most of their drawings reveal the same slightly sentimental and affected grace as their paintings, though they derive from the great tradition of Bolognese draughtsmanship. Gaetano also, on at least two occasions, executed sets of drawings of *seicento* pictures in

Bolognese churches. Similar copies of paintings were drawn by J. A. Calvi (1740–1815) and, probably, other draughtsmen of this school.

Ghezzi, Pier Leone (1674–1755). A Roman painter of large altarpieces and decorations for villas. His present fame rests mainly on his many vivacious caricatures, which are among the best produced in eighteenth-century Italy (Plate 429B). They are usually drawn in pen and brown ink and sometimes inscribed by the author with lengthy descriptions of the people represented. The best collection of them is in the Vatican library, others are in the British Museum.

Giaquinto, Corrado (1603–1765). A Neapolitan painter, was a pupil of Solimena. He worked also in Rome, Turin, and Madrid. His large paintings of religious and mythological scenes have a characteristically Neapolitan baroque vigour, which is also evident in his drawings.

Guardi. An outstanding family of Venetian painters consisting of the brothers Giovanni Antonio (1699–1760) and Francesco (1712–1793) and the son of the latter, Giacomo (1764–1835). The drawings of these three artists, who worked in similar styles, are often difficult to distinguish. Giovanni Antonio worked solely as a history (mainly religious) painter, and the drawings that can securely be attributed to him show little of the brilliance of his younger brother. Francesco was also a history painter, but achieved fame on account of his views, which perfectly capture the sparkling light effects of Venetian sunshine playing on marble and water. His rapidly executed drawings, whether of figures (Plate 428A) or buildings, have a vitality which is hard to parallel even in eighteenth-century Italy. Giacomo was an able imitator of his father's style, though later in his life he took to producing large quantities of views, either in pen and ink or gouache (Plate 428B), which were sold to visitors. Such views were, almost invariably, signed with the painter's name and address on the back.

Juvarra, Filippo (1676–1736). Was undoubtedly the greatest early eighteenth-century Italian architect. Born at Messina, he worked in Rome, Lucca, Turin, and in Spain.

His drawings, which are very well represented at Turin, are mostly rapid sketches of whole buildings or decorative details, but he also executed some architectural fantasies which seem to foreshadow the *Carceri* of Piranesi.

Longhi, Pietro (1702–85). Venetian genre and portrait painter, was trained under G. M. Crespi at Bologna. Most of his drawings – which are well represented in the Museo Correr at Venice and the print room at Berlin – are careful studies of figures similar to those in his paintings of Venetian life.

Magnasco, Alessandro (1677–1749). A Genoese painter who specialized in grotesque subjects. He worked in Milan and Florence as well as his native city. Most of his drawings are connected with his paintings and reflect their bizarre charm.

Mengs, Anton Raphael (1728–79). A German painter trained in Rome, where most of his work was executed. He also worked in Madrid. One of the founders of the Roman neo-classical style, his most famous work is the *Parnassus* ceiling in the Villa Albani. His figure drawings reflect the statuesque Graeco-Roman style of this painting. Numerous academy studies have also been attributed to him.

Nogari, Giuseppe (*c.* 1700–63). A Venetian who studied under Antonio Balestra. He worked in Venice and for the Court at Turin. His paintings reveal the influence of Piazzetta, which is also notable in the few drawings which have been attributed to him.

Pannini, Giovanni Paolo (1691/2–1765). Born at Piacenza, but spent most of his career in Rome, where he became the most celebrated painter of the ancient and modern monuments. He also painted *capricci*, in which ruins from various parts of the city were grouped together. His surviving drawings, of which good examples are in the Ashmolean Museum, appear to be sketches for paintings.

Pellegrini, Giovanni Antonio (1675–1741). Born in Venice, but worked principally in northern countries: France, Germany, Holland, and England. His importance as one of the originators of the Venetian rococo style has only recently been recognized. Most of his drawings are *pensieri*, sudden thoughts for compositions great and small worked out with lightning rapidity. Very few of them can be connected with finished paintings (Plate 426c).

Piazzetta, Giovanni Battista (1683–1754). One of the greatest Venetian painters of his time. His work provides a striking contrast with that of G. B. Tiepolo, for in his paintings he used a richly coloured palette with thick impast, while Tiepolo strove after an increasingly light effect. Tiepolo's drawings have a lightning rapidity and economy of line; Piazzetta's a carefully worked richness of tone. Piazzetta characteristically used black and white chalks as his favourite medium, and few have equalled him in his command of it. The gentle strokes seem to caress the snub-nosed and remarkably solid faces of the boys and girls he usually depicted (Plate 426A). Many of his drawings were executed for engravers, but there can be little doubt that others were sold as finished works. He is represented in all the main public collections of drawings.

Piermarini, Giuseppe (1734–1808). Born at Foligno, was the first and one of the best architects of the neo-classical buildings in Milan (including the Teatro della Scala). His drawings, most of which are highly finished designs for his many buildings, garden layouts, and projects, are well represented in the Biblioteca Civica at Foligno.

Piranesi, Giovanni Battista (1720–78). Born near Venice and trained as an architect. In 1740 he went to Rome, where he spent most of his life. Unsuccessful as an architect (he obtained only one commission), he turned his attention to producing prints of Roman ruins which stressed their dramatic grandeur. He etched a series of plates of imaginary dungeons – the famous *Carceri* – and also produced a volume of designs for interior decoration almost as fantastic. His drawings were prized by his contemporaries, and many of them survive: views of Roman ruins, fantastic architectural *capricci* (Plate 431B), and some figure studies which remind one that he was a Venetian.

Pittoni, Giovanni Battista (1687–1767). A history painter, born in Venice. He first fell under the influence of Balestra, then of G. B.

Tiepolo. Much of his work was executed for foreign Courts. He specialized in grandiose, mythological, and religious scenes, which he painted with great charm and refinement though they are usually touched with a slight air of sentimentality. Many drawings by Pittoni and members of his studio – mostly sheets of studies – have survived.

Quarenghi, Giacomo (1744–1817). Born near Bergamo and went to Rome in 1763, where he studied under Mengs. He abandoned painting for architecture before 1770, and six years later obtained employment as architect to the Russian court at Petersburg, where he spent most of the rest of his life. Many of his drawings have been preserved, both rough sketches of buildings seen or projected and highly finished coloured designs for architecture and schemes of decoration. The largest collections of his work are in the Hermitage, Leningrad, and the Biblioteca Civica, Bergamo.

Ricci, Marco (1676–1730). Born at Belluno and worked mainly in Venice and England. Primarily a landscape painter, he was influenced by Salvator Rosa and Magnasco. He also worked for the theatre and drew caricatures (Plate 429c). His landscape drawings reveal the influence of Dutch etchings as well as seventeenth-century Italian works. His work of all types is well represented at Windsor.

Ricci, Sebastiano (1639–1734). Uncle of Marco Ricci; was born at Belluno. He worked in many Italian towns, also Vienna, Paris, and London. A painter of grandiose history scenes, he was an accomplished eclectic, deriving most of his ideas from High Renaissance and *seicento* masters. Towards the end of his career he seems to have fallen under the spell of Pellegrini and the young Tiepolo. His drawings, which are well represented in the Accademia at Venice, and at Windsor, reveal the many changes of his style.

Solimena, Francesco (1657–1747). Outstanding Neapolitan painter of the early eighteenth century. He broke away from the somewhat heavy baroque tradition of this school and infused his works – mostly large religious paintings – with an eighteenth-century elegance. Most of his drawings are sketches for his paintings. A characteristic example is in the Ashmolean Museum.

Tesi, Mauro Antonio (1730–66). Stage designer, engraver, and decorative painter, who worked mainly in Bologna and Florence. He came under the influence of Count Algarotti, the theorist who inspired him to work in a classicizing style. Many of his drawings of architectural fantasies have survived and have sometimes been confused with those of the Bibiena family.

Tiepolo, Giovanni Battista (1696–1770). Undoubtedly the greatest Italian painter of the century. He was born in Venice, where a large proportion of his paintings were executed. He also worked in Germany and Spain. His drawings of mythological subjects have the same elegance, gaiety, and brilliance as his paintings (Plate 430A), while those of religious themes have an intensity of feeling hard to parallel in the eighteenth century (Plate 426B). A large number of his preparatory sketches has survived, and also some drawings of ideal heads and *capricci* executed either for prints or for their own sake. He was, in addition, a master of caricature, able to give more expression to a man's back than most artists can give to a face. He is well represented in most public collections.

Tiepolo, Giovanni Domenico (1727–1804). Was both the pupil and assistant of his father, Giovanni Battista, with whom he travelled to Germany and Spain. After 1784 he worked mainly in Venice. His paintings and drawings may be divided into two distinct categories: those which show him as an able imitator of his father, and wholly independent works. The independent drawings are marked by a genius for fantasy and include numerous representations of *pulcinelli* and mythological beings. Many, drawn with a somewhat hard line, are very highly finished and may have been intended for sale simply as drawings

(they are usually fully signed). Most public collections include examples of his work.

Trevisani, Francesco (1656–1746). Born in Capodistria and received his artistic training at Venice, but went at an early age to Rome, where he passed most of his life. He painted in a classicizing baroque style, and on the death of Carlo Maratti became the unquestioned leader of the Roman school. All his surviving drawings are connected with his paintings (Plate 425B). Examples of his draughtsmanship are to be found in the Louvre, British Museum, and other public collections.

Visentini, Antonio (1688–1782). Architect, draughtsman, decorative painter, and engraver, was born in Venice, where he worked for most of his life. As a painter he specialized in prospects of imaginary architecture, the most notable being those which adorn the Villa Giustiniani at Noventa Padovana. He provided delicate rococo illustrations, title-pages, and devices for numerous books published in Venice by Pasquali. A protégé of Consul Smith, he is very well represented at Windsor Castle.

Zanetti, Antonio Maria (1679/80–1767). Venetian engraver, connoisseur, and art dealer. He produced some beautiful chiaroscuro woodcuts after Parmigianino. As a draughtsman he is known only for his caricatures, in the manner of Marco Ricci, which are well represented at Windsor Castle.

Zuccarelli, Francesco (1702–88). Born near Siena and worked as a landscape painter in north Italy and England, where he attracted the patronage of George III. His drawings are mostly ideal landscapes (Plate 430B), with picturesque peasants tending their herds, and have the same quiet charm as his numerous paintings. Good examples of his work are in the Ashmolean Museum and at Windsor Castle.

JAPANESE PRINTS

Ban. Size (*see* Chūban, Kōban and Ōban).
Baren. The burnisher used in hand-printing from blocks.

Beni. A pink or red pigment obtained from saffron flowers.
Beni-ye. Pink picture: generally applied to

two-colour prints, in which the *beni* was used with one other colour, usually green.

Beni-zuri-ye. Pink-printed pictures, a more correct term for the two-colour prints.

Bijin-ye. Pictures of beautiful girls.

Chūban. A vertical print about 11 × 8 inches; medium-sized.

Fude (or **Hitsu**). A brush; also painted with a brush.

Gauffrage. Blind-printing, producing an embossed effect without colour.

Gwa. Picture or drawing; drew (at the end of an artist's signature).

Gwafu. Book of sketches.

Gwajō. Album of folding pictures.

Harimaze. Sheets printed with two or more irregularly shaped subjects, to be divided up by the purchaser.

Hon. A book.

Hoso-ye. Small, vertical, narrow picture, about 12 × 6 inches.

Ichimai-ye. Single-sheet pictures.

Ishi-zuri. Stone-print.

Kabuki. Dramatic performances.

Kakemono. Hanging picture, rolled up when stored.

Kakemono-ye. Prints in the form of hanging pictures, usually about 26–28 × 10–12 inches.

Key-block. The engraved block from which the outline of the picture was printed.

Koban. A size smaller than the chūban, about 8 × 7 inches.

Kwachō. Bird and flower pictures.

Meisho-ki. Guide-books to famous places.

Mon. Badge or device serving as a sort of heraldic emblem for actors, courtesans, and others.

Naga-ye. Kakemono-ye.

Nishiki-ye. Brocade pictures, colour-prints.

Ōban. Full-size, 15 × 10 inches.

Sumi-ye. Ink-pictures, i.e. printed in black only.

Surimono. Literally "printed things", especially prints used for greetings or to mark special occasions.

Tan-ye. Pictures coloured by hand with *tan*, a red-lead pigment.

Tanzaku. Narrow, vertical prints, inscribed with verses, about 14 × 6 inches.

Tate-ye. Upright pictures.

Uchiwa-ye. Fan-shaped pictures.

Uki-ye. "Perspective" prints.

Urushi-ye. Lacquer prints.

Ye-goyomi. Pictorial calendars.

Yehon. Picture book.

Yoko-ye. Horizontal pictures.

(B) Rotherhithe: etching by James McNeill Whistler, 1871. *Craddock and Barnard, London.*

(A) Pobrecitas: aquatint from Los Caprichios by Francisco Goya y Lucientes, *c.* 1797. *Victoria and Albert Museum, London.*

PLATE 417

(A) Portrait of a gentleman by A. Forberger. *Verre églomisé.* 2⅛ × 2¾ ins. *Private Collection.*

(B) Silhouette portrait painted on a plaster slab by John Miers. *Verre églomisé.* 4 × 5 ins. *C. H. Stockbridge, Cambridge.*

(C) Conversation by Francis Torond. Cut work. 12¾ × 10¼ ins. *Private Collection.*

PLATE 418

(B) The actor Bandō Mitsugorō as a Daimyō. Polychrome by Katsukawa Shunshö, c. 1775–80. *British Museum, London.*

) Pillar print by Koru-
. *Honolulu Academy of
Arts.*

(C) Girl closing her umbrella by Ishikawa Toyonobu. Three-colour print. *Hashirakake, c.* 1760. *British Museum, London.*

PLATE 419

(A) A page from the picture-book of woman's occupations, *Yehon Tokiwa Gusa*, by Nishikawa Sukenobu. Published 1731. *British Museum, London.*

(B) Evening under the murmuring pines by Chōbunsai Yeishi. Triptych, part of a series called a "Popular Version of the Romance of Genji". Polychrome, *c.* 1793–4. *British Museum, London.*

PLATE 420

(A) Travellers crossing the sand at low tide to the island of Enoshima by Katsushika Hokusai. One of the "Thirty-six Views of Fuji". Polychrome, 1823–8. *British Museum, London.*

(B) The Soga Brothers' Revenge by Utagawa Kuniyoshi. The fight of the two brothers against the retainers of Suketsune during a rainstorm. Triptych, *c.* 1845. *British Museum, London.*

(C) Beggars importuning travellers at Takasaki by Ando Hiroshige. One of the Sixty-nine Stations on the Kisakaido. Polychrome, *c.* 1840. *British Museum, London.*

PLATE 421

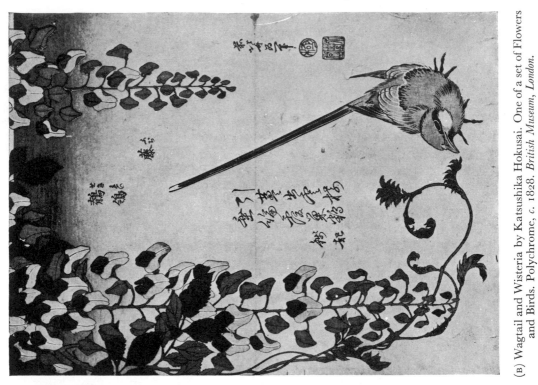

(B) Wagtail and Wisteria by Katsushika Hokusai. One of a set of Flowers and Birds. Polychrome, c. 1828. *British Museum, London.*

(A) Pheasants and Peach Blossom attributed to Isoda Koryūsai. Polychrome, c. 1775. *British Museum, London.*

PLATE 422

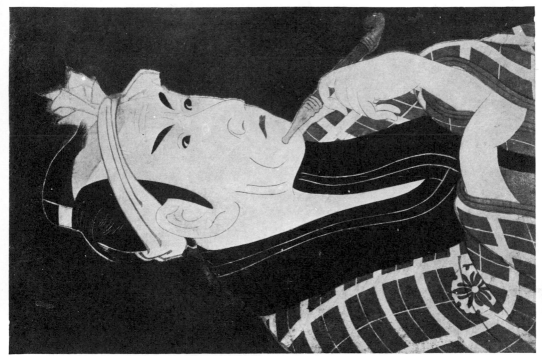

(B) The actor Matsumoto Kōshirō IV in rôle by Tōshūsai Sharaku. Polychrome, with mica background, 1794. *British Museum, London.*

(A) Two geisha girls and a maidservant by Kitao Shigemasa. Unsigned. *c.* 1778. *British Museum, London.*

PLATE 423

(B) Two actors as a man and a woman in a scene from a play by Utagawa Toyokuni. Polychrome, *c.* 1795–6. *British Museum, London.*

(A) Mother and Daughter by Kitagawa Utamaro. Polychrome, *c.* 1795. *Honolulu Academy of Fine Arts.*

PLATE 424

(A) The Apotheosis of Hercules by Anton Domenico Gabbiani, pen and brown ink sketch for a ceiling in the Palazzo Corsini at Florence. *Uffizi, Florence.*

Photo: Fondazione Giorgio Cini.

(B) A sheet of studies by Francesco Trevisani for The Massacre of the Innocents in the Gallery at Dresden, black chalk. *Janos Scholz Collection, New York.*

(C) Study of girl's head by Claudio Francesco Beaumont, red chalk sketch for an overdoor in the Palazzo Reale, Turin. *Museo Civico, Turin.*

PLATE 425

(A) The Procuress by Giovanni Battista Piazzetta, drawing in black and white chalk on brownish paper for an engraving. *Reproduced by gracious permission of Her Majesty The Queen.*

Photo: Fondazione Giorgio Cini.

(B) Abraham and the Angels by Giovanni Battista Tiepolo, sketch in pen and ink heightened with white-lead connected with a large painting in the Scuola di San Rocco, Venice. *Museo Civico, Bassano.*

(C) Study for a composition by Giovanni Antonio Pellegrini, pen and ink with brown wash, squared for enlargement in red chalk. *Kunstmuseum, Dusseldorf.*

PLATE 426

Photo: *Fondazione Giorgio Cini*.
An imaginary Venetian view by Canaletto, pen and brown ink with grey wash. *Janos Scholz Collection, New York*.

PLATE 427

(A) The Polignac Wedding by Francesco Guardi, pen and brown ink with wash. *Biblioteca Correr, Venice.*

(B) View of Venice by Giacomo Guardi, gouache. *Marlborough Fine Art Ltd, London.*

PLATE 428

(A) Seven men standing on a quay by Antonio Maria Zanetti, pen and brown ink. *Reproduced by gracious permission of Her Majesty The Queen.*

(B) Caricature of C. L. Clérisseau by Pier Leone Ghezzi, pen and brown ink. *British Museum, London.*

(C) Caricature of an opera singer, possibly the *castrato* Senesino, by Marco Ricci, pen and brown ink. *Reproduced by gracious permission of Her Majesty The Queen.*

PLATE 429

(A) The Rape of Deianira by Giovanni Domenico Tiepolo, pen and brown ink with brown wash. *National Museum, Warsaw.*

(B) Landscape by Francesco Zuccarelli, pen and brown ink and grey wash. *Janos Scholz Collection, New York.*

PLATE 430

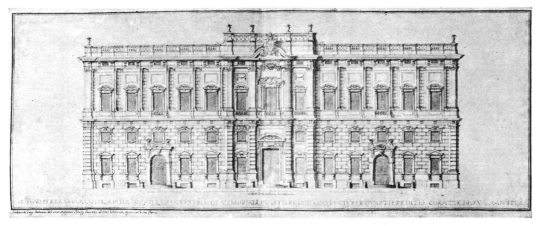

(A) Project for the façade of the Palazzo della Consulta, Rome by Ferdinando Fuga, pen and brown ink with grey wash. *Gabinetto Nazionale delle Stampe, Rome.*

Photo: Fondazione Giorgio Cini.

(B) Architectural fantasy by Giovanni Battista Piranesi, pen and brown ink. *Janos Scholz Collection, New York.*

PLATE 431

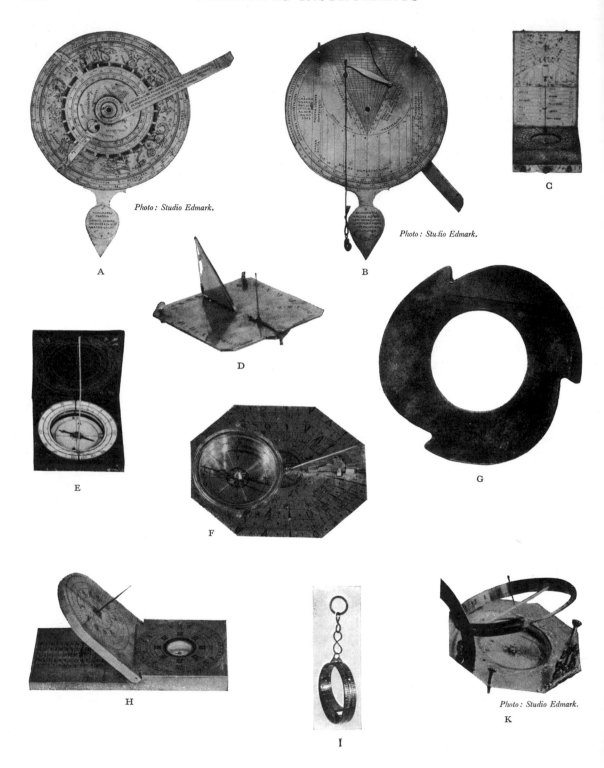

Photo: Studio Edmark.

A

Photo: Studio Edmark.

B

C

D

E

F

G

H

I

Photo: Studio Edmark.

K

PLATE 432

Description of Plates

PLATE 432

(A) German Nocturnal and Regiomontanus Dial made by Caspar Vopel in Cologne, brass, 1552 – front, showing nocturnal, which includes a lunar volvelle and *aspectarium*. *Museum of the History of Science, Oxford.*

(B) Back of (A), showing Regiomontanus dial. *Museum of the History of Science, Oxford.*

(C) German Diptych Dial, signed with the punch-mark, a crowned serpent, of Hans and Thomas Tucker of Nuremberg, ivory, c. 1600. The following can be seen in the photograph: (i) a vertical pin-gnomon dial for Italian and Babylonian hours and showing solar declination; (ii) a table of latitudes; (iii) a horizontal string-gnomon, dial, and compass; (iv) two *scaphe* for Italian hours. Not visible are: (i) a wind-rose and (ii) a lunar volvelle and table of Julian and Georgian epacts. *National Maritime Museum, Greenwich.*

(D) French Analemmatic Dial, made by E. Baradelle (Baradelle the younger) in Paris, brass, late eighteenth century. *National Maritime Museum, Greenwich.*

(E) French Horizontal String-Gnomon Dial, unsigned, ebony and ivory, c. 1620. *National Maritime Museum, Greenwich.*

(F) French Butterfield-type Dial made by Nicolas Bion in Paris for the Eastern (probably Turkish) market, silver, c. 1700. The maker signed in Arabic script within the hour scales. Note the adjustable "bird"-gnomon. *National Maritime Museum, Greenwich.*

(G) Chinese Circumpolar Constellation Template or Hsüan-Chi, jade, date unknown. This instrument was probably used in conjunction with a sighting tube for finding the position of the pole (at a time when the present pole star was not close to the pole) and the direction of the solstitial colure (indicated in this instrument by the line of grain in the jade); the instrument was held up like a nocturnal and the outer edge aligned on certain circumpolar stars, the position of the pole being determined by successive observations of a bright star (β *Ursae minoris*) viewed in the centre hole. *Museum of the History of Science, Oxford.*

(H) Chinese Universal Equinoctial Dial made by Fung Shu Sui in Tsinan, lacquered wood, nineteenth century. Needham's type B (4,310 ff.), possibly indigenous to China and dating back to the Sung period. *National Maritime Museum, Greenwich.*

(J) Ring (Poke) Dial, origin unknown, unsigned, ? c. 1700. Not to be confused with the universal equinoctial ring dial (Plate 435C). *National Maritime Museum, Greenwich.*

(K) German Universal Equinoctial Dial (Augsburg-type) made by Georg Friedrich Brander in Augsburg, gilt and silvered brass and silver, c. 1750. *Museum of the History of Science, Oxford.*

PLATE 434

(A) (a) German Globe Dial, unsigned, gilt-brass, sixteenth century. (b) German Cruciform Dial by Marcus Purman, gilt-brass, 1596. (c) German Vertical Disc Dial, unsigned, gilt-brass, eighteenth century. (d) Russian Inclining Dial, signed by Morgan, St Petersburg, brass and silvered brass, eighteenth century. (e) Italian *Scaphe* by Hieronymus Vulpariae (compare Plate 435A), brass in turned wood box, 1588. (f) French Cylinder Dial, unsigned, ivory with silver gnomon, seventeenth century. (g) English Polyhedral Dial made for Cardinal Wolsey, perhaps by Nicolaus Kratzer, or to his design, between 1518 and 1530. *Museum of the History of Science, Oxford.*

(B) Persian Celestial Globe made by Ja'far b. 'Umar b. Dawlatshâh al Kirmânî in 764 A.H. (i.e. A.D. 1362/3), brass. The constellations with their names are engraved on the globe and the stars are marked by inlaid silver points. *Museum of the History of Science, Oxford.*

(C) Surveyor's and Gunner's Triangulation Instrument made by Erasmus Habermel of Prague (compare Plate 437F), late sixteenth century. *Museum of the History of Science, Oxford.*

(D) French Graphometer made by Canivet, "à la Sphere", in Paris, brass and silver brass, with verniers on the alidade, c. 1760. *M. D. C. Forrer Collection.*

(E) (a) Italian Refracting Telescope made by Leonardo Semitecolo, vellum and paper covered pasteboard tubes, horn mounts, brass stand, c. 1760. The telescope is held by a brass sleeve on a ball and socket mounting. (b) English Gregorian Reflecting Telescope made by James Mann and James Ayscough of London, brass, red shagreen-covered tube, c. 1740–50. The telescope is focused by turning the knob at the end of the threaded rod at the side of the tube. Compare the mounting with that of (a). *Museum of the History of Science, Oxford.*

(F) (a) German Astronomical Compendium made by Christoph Schissler in Augsburg, gilt-brass, 1557, including (from left to right) (i) a universal astrolabe using the projection associated with Juan de Rojas, (ii) universal horizontal string-gnomon dial, (iii) geographical astrolabe, (iv) wind-vane. *Museum of the History of Science, Oxford.* (b) German Mechanical Equinoctial Dial made by Godfried Weiss, early eighteenth century, gilt-brass in leather-covered wood box. *Museum of the History of Science, Oxford.*

Photo: Studio Edmark.

A

Photo: Studio Ed

B

Photo: Studio Edmark.

C

Photo: Studio Ea

D

Photo: Studio Edmark.

E

Photo: Studio E

F

For captions see page 1169.

PLATE 434

B

Photo: Studio Edmark.

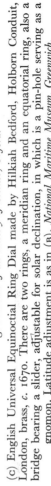

C

(A) Italian Ptolemaic (geocentric) Armillary Sphere made by Hieronymus Volpariae Girolamo della Volpaia in Florence, brass and gilt-brass on marble base, 1571. The small globe in the centre of the sphere represents the earth and the small crescent the moon; the symbol of the sun is not visible in the photograph. The broad band, engraved with the names of the signs of the zodiac, represents the ecliptic. The horizon, the meridian, the equator, the tropics, and other great circles are also shown. *C. H. Josten Collection.*

(B) Flemish Astronomical Ring, unsigned but perhaps by Johann Motter, brass, dated 1602. There are three rings, a meridian ring, an equatorial ring, and a movable ring with sights. The instrument is adjusted for latitude by moving the position of the suspension ring in relation to the latitude scale below. The relative positions of several fixed stars are engraved on the movable ring. *Museum of the History of Science, Oxford.*

(c) English Universal Equinoctial Ring Dial made by Hilkiah Bedford, Holborn Conduit, London, brass, c. 1670. There are two rings, a meridian ring and an equatorial ring, also a bridge bearing a slider, adjustable for solar declination, in which is a pin-hole serving as a gnomon. Latitude adjustment is as in (B). *National Maritime Museum, Greenwich.*

A

Photo: Studio Edmark.

PLATE 435

Photo : Studio Edmark.

Photo : Studio Edmark.

A

B

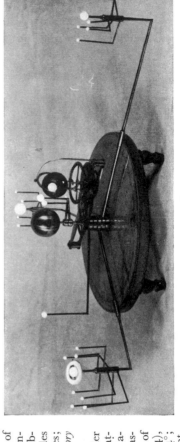

C

(A) English quadrant made by John Prujean of New College Lane, Oxford, printed from an engraved plate and pasted on wood, brass plumb-bob and sights, *c*. 1690. The side shown includes quadrants of both Gunter and Allen types; made for latitude 51° 45'. *Museum of the History of Science, Oxford.*

(B) *Maghribī* Astrolabe-quadrant made, under the guidance of the *mu'addil* al-Mu'tī b. aṭ-Ṭayyib, by 'Abdallah Aḥmad b. 'Ali an-Anda-lusī, for the *faqīh* Muhammad b. Hajj 'Abd as-Salām as-Salāwī, in Rabat, on the last day of Jumādā I, 1219 A.H. (i.e. 6 September, 1804); brass. Made for use at Meknès, latitude 34°; the side not shown is a sinecal quadrant. *Museum of the History of Science, Oxford.*

(c) English Orrery, published for and sold by J. Addison, Regent Street, London, Globe-maker to George IV, brass, ivory, printed and coloured paper scale and star-map mounted on wood base, *c*. 1800. The planets and their satellites up to and including Uranus are shown, the earth and moon are modelled in greater detail than the other heavenly bodies and are linked to each other and the sun by gear work. *National Maritime Museum, Greenwich.*

PLATE 436

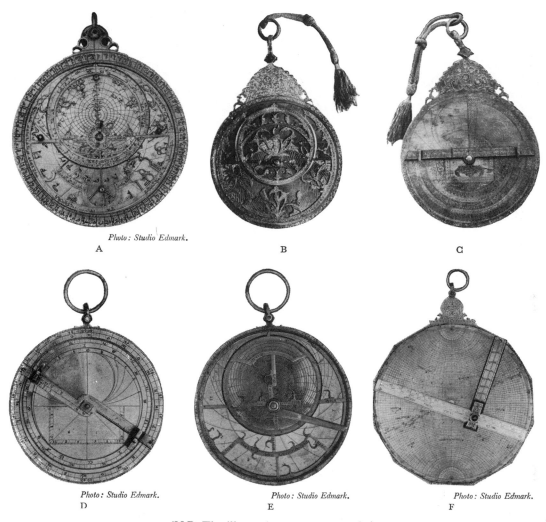

Photo: Studio Edmark.

A

B

C

Photo: Studio Edmark.
D

Photo: Studio Edmark.
E

Photo: Studio Edmark.
F

(N.B. The illustrations are not to scale.)

(A) *Maghribî* (Hispano-Moorish) Astrolabe, signed by Muḥammad b. Saʿîd aṣ-Ṣabbân in Madînat al-Faraj (i.e. Guadalajara, Spain) in 474 A.H. (i.e. A.D. 1081/2), brass, showing the characteristic *maghribî* type *ʿankabût* (cut-away "star-map") over one of the six plates. *Museum of the History of Science, Oxford.*

(B) Persian Astrolabe made by Khalîl Muḥammad b. Ḥasan ʿAlî and decorated by Muḥammad Bâqir Iṣfahânî, probably in Isfahan, 1119 A.H. (i.e. A.D. 1707/8), brass – front, showing the typical Persian foliate pattern *ʿankabût* and decorated *kursî* (throne) and the suspension cord or *ʿilâqa* (the plate is inverted in this photograph). *National Maritime Museum, Greenwich.*

(C) Back of (B), showing the diagram of sines, the graphs of arcs of the signs of the zodiac and azimuths of the *Qibla*, shadow-square, astrological tables, and the signatures (in the two cartouches below the alidade, pivot). *National Maritime Museum, Greenwich.*

(D) Medieval European ("Late Gothic") Astrolabe, perhaps French, unsigned, brass, c. 1430 – front, showing characteristic "wavy flame" star-pointers. *Museum of the History of Science, Oxford.*

(E) Back of (D), showing scale of degrees, Zodiac/calendar scale, unequal honour diagram and shadow-square. *Museum of the History of Science, Oxford.*

(F) European Astrolabe made by Erasmus Habermel of Prague for Franciscus Paduanus of Forlì, physician to the Emperor Rudolf II, whose arms appear on the front of the throne, gilt brass, late sixteenth century – back, which is engraved with a universal astrolabe projection, the *astrolabum catholicum* of Gemma Frisius, and the rule and cursor for use with this projection (a hinged arm on the cursor – *brachiolus* – is missing). *Museum of the History of Science, Oxford.*

PLATE 437

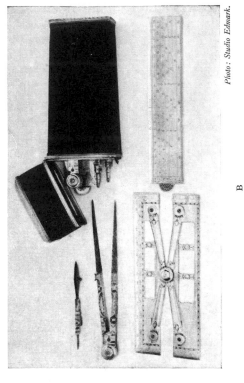

A

B

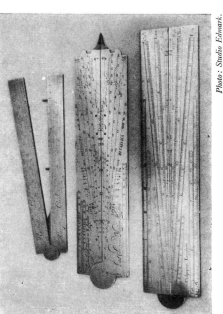

C

D

(A) Sectors: (a) French type made by Rochette in Paris, brass, c. 1750. *M. D. C. Forrer Collection.* (b) Dutch type, unsigned, brass with steel points, c. 1750. *Museum of the History of Science, Oxford.* (c) English type made by Edmund Culpeper in London, brass, c. 1700. *Museum of the History of Science, Oxford.*

(B) English set of Drawing Instruments by Richard Glynne of London, silver and gold with steel points in silver-mounted fish-skin case, early eighteenth century. Among the instruments is a combined protractor and parallel ruler. *Museum of the History of Science, Oxford.*

(C) Napier's bones: (a) "rotating" type, unsigned, in boxwood box, c. 1700; (b) "loose" type, unsigned, ivory in wood slip-in case, c. 1700. *Museum of the History of Science, Oxford.*

(D) German Miner's Compass and accessories, signed HW, ivory and wood in wooden case, dated 1689 on the compass and 1690 on the

PLATE 438

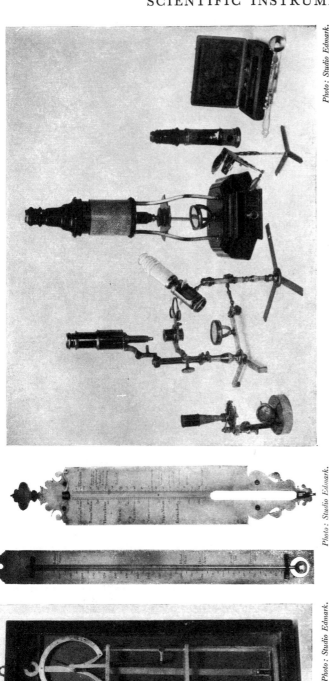

C

B

A

(A) English Hygrometer made by Dollond, London, brass and silvered brass in glazed mahogany case, *c.* 1800. *Museum of the History of Science, Oxford.*

(B) (*a*) English Thermometer made by John Bird of London, brass register plate, Fahrenheit scale, *c.* 1750. (*b*) Register plate from a Dutch Thermometer, the tube is missing, made by P. Wast in Amsterdam. Réaumur and Fahrenheit scales, 1758. Certain extreme temperatures, with the dates when and the places where they were recorded, are noted on the right-hand side of the scale. *Museum of the History of Science, Oxford.*

(C) Microscopes: (*a*) Gould-type by William Cary of London, brass, stage-focusing and mechanical stage, *c.* 1790; (*b*) Universal, invented and made by Benjamin Martin of London, brass, stage has coarse (rack) and fine (screw) focusing, *c.* 1760–70; (*c*) Screw-barrel by Edmund Culpeper of London, brass and ivory, attached to the stand by a ball and socket joint, *c.* 1700; (*d*) Culpeper-type by Matthew Loft of London, red shagreen body, green vellum draw-tube marked for five *foci, lignum vitae* mounts, brass and wood stand, *c.* 1745; (*e*) Lindsay's Patent, invented and made by George Lindsay of London, coarse adjustment by a slide and clamp, fine by a lever, three powers in a brass slide, *c.* 1750; (*f*) Drum made by Benjamin Martin of London, shagreen outer body on brass foot, green vellum inner body, *lignum vitae* mount, *c.* 1750; (*g*) Compass, unsigned, ivory and brass with silver *lieberkühn,* fish-skin case with accessories, screw fine-adjustment, four objectives, each with *lieberkühn,* early eighteenth century. *Museum of the History of Science, Oxford.*

PLATE 439

A

B

C

E

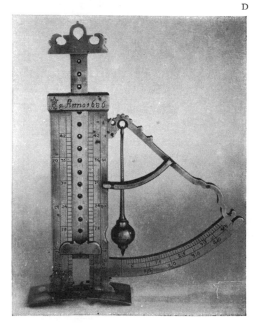

D

(A) Loadstone, origin unknown, mounted with steel pole pieces in gold, eighteenth century. *Museum of the History of Science, Oxford.*

(B) ? German Pedometer, unsigned, brass, dated 1667. The two dials on the other side of the instrument record units and tens; in use a thread is attached to the lever on the left-hand side and to the wearer's knee. *Museum of the History of Science, Oxford.*

(C) English Frictional Electrical Machine made by Edward Nairne of London, brass, c. 1780. *Museum of the History of Science, Oxford.*

(D) German Gunner's Level, inscribed HR and ME surmounted by a crown, with the date 1686, brass. *Museum of the History of Science, Oxford.*

(E) Scandinavian Clog Almanac inscribed "IC 1660", wood, presented to the Ashmolean Museum, Oxford, by John Heysig in 1683. *Museum of the History of Science, Oxford.*

All photos: Studio Edmark.

PLATE 440

(A) Cycladic marble idol, third millennium B.C.; height 12 ins.

(C) The "Auxerre statuette" of limestone in Paris. Probably Cretan, seventh century B.C.; height 25½ ins.

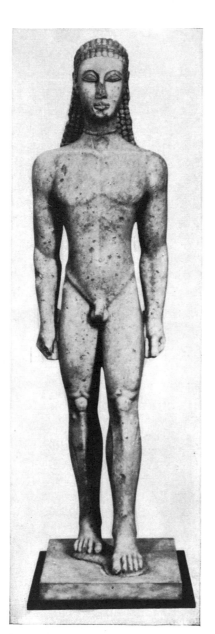

(B) Marble kouros from Attica; in New York, about 600 B.C.

PLATE 441

(A) Head of a girl, from Miletus (E. Greece), in
Berlin, late sixth century B.C.

(B) Metope relief, from near Paestum (Italy), late sixth
century B.C.

(C) Head of the Peplos Kore, from Athens, about
530 B.C.

(D) Head of the Rampin horseman from Athens, in Paris,
mid-sixth century B.C.

PLATE 442

(A) Head of Athena, from the Temple of Zeus at Olympia, mid-fifth century B.C.

(B) Head of the Hermes of Praxiteles, in Olympia, mid-fourth century B.C.

(c) Head of Demosthenes, in Oxford; copy of a work of the early third century B.C.

(D) Bust of the Emperor Lucius Verus (A.D. 161–9), in Oxford.

PLATE 443

(A) Statuette of a horse from a cauldron handle, from Olympia, eighth century B.C.

(C) Late Etruscan statuette of Hercules, in Oxford; height 6 ins.

(D) Graeco-Roman statuette of Mercury, in Oxford; height 6 ins.

(B) Etruscan statuette of a warrior, in Oxford, fifth century B.C.; height 11 ins.

(E) Graeco-Roman statuette of Minerva, in Oxford; height 4 ins.

(F) Graeco-Roman statuette of Venus, in Oxford; height 4 ins.

PLATE 444

(B) Boy jockey from the *Artemision* wreck, in Athens, third century B.C.

(A) God from the *Artemision* wreck, in Athens, mid-fifth century B.C.

PLATE 445

(B) Bronze of Apollo, North Italian, proba
by Girolamo Campagna, last quarter of
sixteenth century. *Collection of John Gere*

(A) Bronze of Seated Female Satyr, school of Riccio, late fifteenth
century. *Alfred Spero*.

PLATE 446

(A) Bronze of Rape of the Sabine Women, school of Giovanni Bologna, late sixteenth century. *Wallace Collection, London.*

(B) One of a Pair of Fire-dogs, showing Jupiter Victorious over the Titans, by M. Anguier after A. Algardi. French, mid-seventeenth century. *Wallace Collection, London.*

PLATE 447

(A) William Pitt, 1807, by Joseph Nollekens.
Private Collection.

(B) Sir Isaac Newton, *c.* 1739, plaster copy
after Michael Rysbrack. *Private Collection.*

(C) Louis F. Roubiliac. Self-portrait. *National
Portrait Gallery, London.*

(D) The First Duke of Wellington by J. Francis.
National Portrait Gallery, London.

PLATE 448

SCIENTIFIC
INSTRUMENTS

The scope of this chapter

Contemporary interest in the history of science has led to a wider appreciation of early scientific instruments. These, until fairly recently, were collected and studied by only a few pioneers. This field, almost as extensive as science itself, includes medical and dental instruments, pharmaceutical equipment, chemical and physical apparatus, all of which, however, must be excluded, because of their rarity or specialized appeal, from a brief article addressed primarily to collectors. Large astronomical instruments from observatories, whose size alone would deter most collectors, are also omitted. This chapter is confined to those instruments comprised in the old phrase, "mathematical instruments" – the smaller astronomical and surveying instruments, drawing and calculating instruments, microscopes, and some of the apparatus used by the natural philosophers of the eighteenth century. Most of these instruments were made by professional instrument-makers to accepted designs for use by the practitioners of some profession (such as surveying) or for the interested layman.

History

(*i*) *The Islamic East*. Very few scientific instruments have survived from Babylonian, Egyptian, Greek, or Roman antiquity. The Muslim conquest of Syria in the seventh century A.D. brought the Islamic peoples into contact with Hellenistic scientific knowledge, which was soon made available in translation and supplemented by further mathematical knowledge from India. The flowering of Islamic scientific activity in the succeeding centuries involved a development of the craft of instrument-making and resulted in improvements of the classical instruments.

The earliest surviving Islamic instruments are astrolabes. The astrolabe (Plate 437),[1] a complicated observational and computing instrument, was for many centuries the most important precision instrument available to astronomers. Until about the sixteenth century in Europe, centres of instrument-making are associated with schools of astronomers: for example, the Toledo astronomers in Muslim Spain in the eleventh century. The history of the astrolabe will serve here as an illustration of the spread of astronomical and mathematical knowledge and of the making of associated instruments, such as celestial globes, sundials, and quadrants.

The earliest extant astrolabes[2] were made in Syria in the late ninth century. Based on

[1] For notes on the various instruments mentioned in this introduction, see *Glossary*.
[2] There are examples in the Museum of the History of Science, Oxford, the Bibliothèque Nationale, Paris, the Museo Nazionale, Palermo, and the Museum of Islamic Art, Cairo.

Hellenistic models, the early astrolabes were soon improved by the addition of scales using trigonometrical knowledge derived from India. At the beginning of the tenth century the manufacture of astrolabes had already begun in Persia, at Isfahan, and certain stylistic features of the earliest Persian astrolabe remained typical of eastern Islamic astrolabes throughout their history. During the succeeding nine centuries, Persia remained an important centre of instrument-making. Scientifically the astrolabe remained unchanged. Such improvements as there were were mainly in the decoration of the instruments, which, by the seventeenth and eighteenth centuries, were lavishly ornamented with engraving. In the middle of the sixteenth century there appears to be a break in the tradition of astrolabe-making in Persia. A revival in the latter part of the century may have derived its inspiration from Mogul India, where astrolabes were first made about 1570. Certain European influences are to be seen on Persian astrolabes about this time.[1] This is a complex and unstudied aspect of the instrument's history.

In Muslim India the history of the manufacture of astrolabes and other scientific instruments runs parallel to its history in Persia from the late sixteenth century until the early nineteenth century, by which time in both regions the craft had degenerated. In non-Muslim India there was what was probably an independent tradition of instrument-making. The astrolabes are engraved in Sanskrit and appear to derive from an early Islamic source, perhaps from the instruction which the eleventh-century Islamic scientist, al-Bîrûnî, gave to the Brahmins, and of which he speaks in his history of India.[2] However, the surviving Sanskrit instruments are all later than Jai Singh's revival of Hindu astronomy in the late seventeenth and early eighteenth centuries.

(*ii*) *The Islamic West* (*the maghrib*). Islamic science spread westwards to Spain about two centuries after the Muslim conquest. The ninth Umayyad Caliph at Córdova, akl-Haam II, (961–76), imported books from Syria and Egypt and encouraged the public teaching of science. Maslama b. Ahmad al-Majritî, (d. *c.* 1007), the first great Spanish scientist, wrote a treatise on the astrolabe, from which the whole tradition of western Islamic (and therefore European) astrolabe-making probably stems. The earliest known western Islamic astrolabes date from the eleventh century.[3] After the Christian reconquest of Toledo in 1085 the way was open for an unchecked transmission of Islamic knowledge to medieval Christian Europe.

(*iii*) *Europe.* The work of the early translators from Arabic, who had begun to acquaint Europe with the achievements of Islam (if only in order to be able to combat the heresy more effectively), was reinforced by the translations sponsored by Alfonso el Sabio of Castile (1221–84) in the *Libros del Saber*, and the scientific activity in Catalonia and southern France. The Sicilian court of Frederic II may also have played an important part.

Some of the earliest instruments engraved in Latin script may indeed have been made in Spain by Muslim, or recently Christianized, craftsmen. Soon, however, France, Germany, Italy, and England had their own centres of instrument-making. The work of the Judaco-Provençal mathematician, astronomer, and zoologist, Prophatius (*c.* 1236–*c.* 1304), Johannes Regiomontanus (1436–76), Georg Hartmann of Nuremberg (1489–1564), Gemma Frisius (1508–55) of the University of Louvain, and others led to the introduction of new instruments and the improvement of older instruments. The Arsenius family at Louvain, relations of Gemma Frisius, made instruments to his design which were sold throughout Europe, partly through the agency of the Plantin printing-house. The exquisite craftsmanship of the Arsenius workshop perhaps reached its peak in the work of Erasmus Habermel, at the Court of Rudolph II in Prague, and was reflected in the work of

---

[1] See below, p. 1185 and footnote, *ibid.*

[2] Edward C. Sachau (trans. and ed.), *Alberuni's India. An Account of the Religion, Philosophy, Literature, Geography, Chronology, Astronomy, Customs, Laws, and Astrology of India about* A.D. *1030*, 2 vols., London, 1910, vol. I, p. 137.

[3] There are examples in the West-Deutsche Bibliothek, Marburg, the Museum of the History of Science, Oxford, the British Museum, London, and in the Royal Scottish Museum, Edinburgh (dated A.D. 1026–27 and therefore the earliest dated maghribî astrolabe; see *Illustrated London News*, October 19, 1957).

the Fleming, Thomas Gemini, and of Humfrey Cole, the two greatest instrument-makers in England in the sixteenth century. Already, at the beginning of the sixteenth century, workshops of craftsmen who specialized in the manufacture of the popular types of instrument, such as the ivory diptych dials, had been established at Nuremberg and Augsburg. The latter town, to which the beautiful work of the two Schisslers had brought fame in the sixteenth century, is especially associated with the manufacture, during the seventeenth and eighteenth centuries, of the small octagonal universal equinoctial sundials which bear its name. The manufacture at Dieppe, c. 1660, of a particular type of magnetic azimuth sundial by Charles Bloud and others, and the small universal horizontal sundials of the type associated with the name of Michael Butterfield of Paris about the same time, are further examples of the production in quantity of small popular instruments by the craftsmen instrument-makers, who had replaced the scholar or astronomer who either made his own instruments or closely supervised their construction by an artisan who might specialize in some other field. The finest instrument-makers of the seventeenth and early eighteenth centuries – such as Elias Allen (*fl.* 1606–54), Henry Sutton (d. 1665), and John Rowley (d. 1728), of London, and Pierre Sevin (*c.* 1665–83) of Paris – not only produced excellent examples of the popular instruments but also collaborated with scholars (e.g. Allen's association with the mathematician William Oughtred, 1575–1660) to produce new types of instrument.

By the end of the seventeenth century a number of factors had produced a fundamental change in the work demanded of the professional instrument-makers. The development of the telescope, the enhanced accuracy of clocks and watches, the influence of the work of Tycho Brahe, who had realized the need for more accurate astronomical observations, and above all the increasing momentum of scientific discovery, made many of the traditional instruments outmoded and required an increasing specialization if the desired precision of ever more complex new instruments was to be achieved. The fate of

the astrolabe in Europe is illustrative of the change. As a time-telling instrument it was no longer required. Telescopes had replaced it for astronomical observations, and, for surveying, specialized instruments, such as the circumferentor and theodolite, were favoured. The dawning "Age of Reason" had no use for an instrument conceived by astrologers.

After the work of Isaac Newton and the publication of several popular works explaining his scientific ideas, the eighteenth century finally accepted the Copernican (heliocentric) system. The simple armillary sphere, designed to illustrate the Ptolemaic (geocentric) system, for centuries had been the universal instrument for the demonstration of cosmological theory. It was superseded by the complicated orrery with its trains of gears for showing the movements of the planets around the sun. The orrery, together with the airpump, the loadstone, and the frictional electrical machine, served to demonstrate the "New Philosophy" and to satisfy the popular interest in the natural sciences. The development of the dividing engine and other aids to precision helped to produce a class of professional instrument-makers who were technologists and scientists rather than merely embellishers of traditional designs, applying themselves, like Tycho, to the solution of problems in the very design of the instruments. Such were men like John Bird (1709–1776) and Jesse Ramsden (1730–1800); others like Benjamin Martin (1704–82) and George Adams (*c.* 1704–73) made a wide range of instruments and wrote on associated scientific subjects.

(*iv*) *Islamic countries in the eighteenth and nineteenth centuries.* In Islamic countries, where the impetus had gone out of scientific discovery since medieval times, the traditions lingered on, encouraged by occasional influences from Europe.[1] Many of the latter Islamic instru-

[1] European influences on later Islamic instrument-making have been unjustly neglected. Two examples may be mentioned. A Persian astrolabe, in the National Maritime Museum, Greenwich (No. A. 35–36.678), has obviously been influenced by the work of the Arsenius family at Louvain in the sixteenth century (see above). The *rete* has the characteristic Arsenius pattern, and a small compass has been inserted in the bracket; the latter feature is also found on a few other late Islamic astrolabes. Another Persian astrolabe, in the Hermitage

ments are of considerable interest. An early nineteenth-century quadrant from the *maghrib* should be despised by no collector. It may well prove as good an example of a Prophatius astrolabe-quadrant as he is likely to find.

(*v*) *The Far East*. Few important Chinese or Japanese instruments are found in the European market. Chinese geomancers' compasses of lacquered wood are not rare, and other types of compass are found. Chinese and Japanese sundials of lacquered wood, ivory, or metal are somewhat rarer. They are mostly based on European models, though one particular type seems to be of Chinese origin. A hitherto unrecognized scientific instrument is the *hsüan-chi*, a circum-polar constellation template (*cf.* the European nocturnal), formerly sought only by the jade collector (Plate 432G).

Materials

The interdependence of the concentration of instrument-making at certain places and the convenient supply of materials is an interesting line of inquiry which has been suggested by Monsieur Henri Michel of Brussels. For instance, he has pointed out that southern Germany and the Netherlands developed as such centres in the late sixteenth century in connexion with the trade in rolled (as opposed to beaten) brass plates, a monopoly of the Fugger family; similarly, the availability of a very large quantity of ivory at Dieppe, brought there by ship in the fourteenth century, led to the development of an ivory-carving industry, and later, in the latter half of the seventeenth century, to the manufacture of ivory sundials.

Most instruments are of brass or bronze, which in the late eighteenth and the nineteenth centuries was usually lacquered. In view of the great variety of alloys used for the older instruments, it is sometimes difficult to distinguish between brass and bronze. Copper has occasionally been used. It is also notably the material of which a number of faked instruments were made. All three metals were often silvered or gilded.

The scales, especially of many European instruments of the seventeenth, eighteenth, and nineteenth centuries, are silvered in the same way as the chapter-rings of old clocks. Fire-gilding is not infrequently found on instruments of the sixteenth and seventeenth centuries, and was used with beautiful effect by Erasmus Habermel.

Iron and steel were rarely used except for small parts. Silver was popular in the seventeenth centuries for finely made small sundials. It was the most commonly used material for Butterfield-type sundials and for the hour-scales and calendar scales of the ivory magnetic azimuth dials of Bloud type. Other small instruments frequently made of silver were universal equinoctial sundials and equinoctial ring-dials. From Islam, only one instrument, an astrolabe, is known which is made entirely of silver,[1] but silver and gold were some used for damascening.[2]

Stone has mostly been used for large outdoor sundials, but several small seventeenth- and eighteenth-century German horizontal table sundials were made of Solenhofen stone, the inscriptions and decoration being very finely carved.

Wood, after brass and silver, is probably the most common material and has been used in many ways. Many instruments exist of plain incised wood. Pear-wood and box-wood, for instance, are characteristic materials of one type of English nocturnal of the seventeenth and eighteenth centuries. Sets of Napier's bones and mathematical rules and scales are also commonly of wood, covered with a thin layer of plaster. Wood was an obvious choice for the cores of globes. The gores, printed from engraved plates, were posted on the plaster, coloured with water-colour and finally varnished. A similar technique was

Museum, Leningrad (No. VC512), is engraved with the projection associated with Juan de Rojas, a pupil of Gemma Frisius. At a later date further European influences penetrated to Islamic science through the attempt in Turkey, in the early eighteenth century, to study European science aided by the work of a renegade Hungarian printer and publisher, Ibrahim Mütaferrika.

Of similar interest is the revival of Hindu science by Jai Singh (1686–1743), who used European as well as Islamic and Hindu works, and sent a mission to Europe in quest of astronomical knowledge. This resulted in a curious blend of old and new learning.

[1] Museum of the History of Science, Oxford, No. 55–6, dated A.D. 1350–51 or 1311–12.

[2] E.g. on the astrolabe of 1227/28 by 'Abd al-Karîm al-Misrî, in the Museum of the History of Science, Oxford, No. G(1C), 103.

used to produce instruments which could be sold more cheaply than those made of brass, or which could be made by a layman. Astrolabes and quadrants, for instance, were made by engraving the instrument (or its component parts) on copper-plates from which many copies could be printed. The printed sheets were pasted on to wooden boards or paste-boards which were cut to the desired shape. Georg Hartmann of Nuremberg, (c. 1530), Johann Krabbe of Münden (c. 1580), Phillipe Danfrie of Paris (c. 1590), Henry Sutton of London (c. 1650), and the unfortunate John Prujean of Oxford (c. 1690) were makers who occasionally used this technique. It was also used in Italy in the eighteenth century for small quadrants and vertical sundials. Some of the early books on scientific instruments, such as those of Peter Apian (1495–1552) of the University of Ingolstadt, and Johann Krabbe, include full-size plates which may be cut out by the reader in order to make instruments in this way. Certain woods were especially suitable for particular uses. Boxwood was ideal when scales had to be engraved on the wood itself, as in the manufacture of mathematical rules. *Lignum vitae* was found to be excellent for the lens mounts of microscopes and telescopes and was commonly used for this purpose in the seventeenth century. In the following century mahogany was favoured for the tubes of telescopes.

In Persia and Turkey, during the eighteenth century and the early part of the nineteenth, quadrants, *Qibla*-indicators, sundials, and dialling instruments were made of wood and lacquered in yellow, red, black, and gold. (Dealers and collectors have unjustly neglected the attractive and interesting instruments made in this way.) Chinese geomancer's compasses were similarly made.

Paste-board (which has been mentioned as a support for printed scales), together with papier mâché, covered with tooled leather or vellum, was used in the seventeenth century for the tubes of microscopes and telescopes.[1] These materials, with coverings of fish-skin and shagreen, served also in the eighteenth

century for the small cases containing drawing instruments or pocket sundials.

Ivory and bone have been used for instruments since medieval times, and are the usual materials for the diptych, or book, dials of the sixteenth century. In combination with wood, they were used with most satisfying effect for the inlay of German miners' compasses of the late sixteenth and seventeenth centuries.

The instrument-makers

Numerous techniques and disciplines are involved in the design and construction of scientific instruments. Much work still remains to be done on the more detailed aspects of their history, especially on the instrument-makers themselves. A large proportion of instruments were not signed or dated by their makers. In particular, the earliest non-Islamic instruments of Europe are anonymous; the first of such instruments to bear their maker's name are those by Hans Dorn (c. 1480), Georg Hartmann, Pier Vincenzo Danti (c. 1490), and Euphrosynus Vulpariae (c. 1520). The late Professor L. A. Mayer showed that most Islamic instruments were made by men who were, in a sense, professional astronomers. In Europe, in recent periods, instruments were mostly the work of professional instrument-makers who often specialized in narrow fields. In other periods the situation is more complex. In medieval times, in the sixteenth and seventeenth centuries, and even later, the craftsmen were often masters of several disciplines, enabling them not only to produce works that combined scientific precision with ornamental beauty but also sometimes to improve the design unaided by professional mathematicians. Yet most early instruments of the western world were made by metal-workers carefully instructed by an astronomer or a mathematician. Such were the Arsenius, who followed the designs of their uncle, Gemma Frisius. Perhaps it was the lack of such supervision that caused Erasmus Habermel, a maker of the greatest ability and aesthetic sense, to perpetrate the same gross error on every one of his astrolabes. The link between those craftsmen who engraved copper-plates for printing and those who engraved brass plates as instruments has already

[1] E.g. the fine instruments by John Marshall of London (1663–1725).

been mentioned. Thomas Gemini, for instance, is remembered not only as the maker of two fine astrolabes for Queen Elizabeth I and of other fine instruments but also as the engraver of the plates for the first English edition of Vesalius. A seventeenth-century Spanish engraver, Juan Batista Morales, made in his later years one of the finest known universal equinoctial dials. Conversely, in the eighteenth century, Edmund Culpeper (1660–1738), famed for his microscopes and sundials, appears also as the engraver of an ecclesiastical monumental brass. Another versatile maker of this type was Philippe Danfrie, who wrote and printed, in Robert Granjon's *caractères de civilité*, a book on a surveying instrument (*graphomètre*) he had designed. Collaboration between different trades is also suggested by the use of bookbinders' tools on the leather and vellum coverings of microscope and telescope tubes.

Restoration and cleaning

Any historical object should be restored as little as possible. Under-restoration is decidedly the lesser one of two evils.

There is no point in leaving instruments in a dirty condition, though most collectors will prefer a little dullness on an instrument to the glare of shiny brass. A rub with a clean soft cloth, perhaps after careful application of some soap and water, is often sufficient and is the only appropriate treatment for gilt or silvered brass and copper. A form of liquid cleaner made for use with fine silverware can, however, be safely used on silvered brass and copper to remove the tarnish. Seriously tarnished brass or silver work should be cleaned with a non-abrasive cleaner, e.g. of the impregnated wadding type. Decayed lacquer on nineteenth-century brass work may be removed with a suitable organic solvent, followed by further cleaning as described above.

For the leather tube coverings of microscopes and telescopes, and for leather instrument-cases, the use of the British Museum leather dressing[1] is recommended, preceded, if the leather has suffered from acid decay, by a previous application of a $7\frac{1}{2}$ per cent aqueous solution of potassium lactate.

[1] Available from Messrs Baird & Tatlock, London.

Fakes

Faked scientific instruments, made with sufficient skill to deceive the specialist, are uncommon. The majority of fakes are crude. A large group of reasonably skilful fakes including many instruments attributed to Habermel) have been described by Price, and examples of this group of fakes still occasionally appear on the market. In recent years several faked Persian astrolabes have been sold and are of sufficient quality to pass unnoticed, except by those familiar with details of the mathematical designs and the traditional Arabic epigraphy.

Collections and sources of information

Nothing can replace a detailed study of the important collections of instruments. In the British Isles there are comprehensive or otherwise notable collections in the Museum of the History of Science, Oxford;*[2] the National Maritime Museum, Greenwich;* the British Museum and the Science Museum, London;* the Whipple Museum of the History of Science, Cambridge; and the Royal Scottish Museum, Edinburgh. Abroad, the Conservatoire des Arts et Métiers, Paris,* the Museo di Storia della Scienza, Florence,* the Deutsches Museum, Munich, the Mathematisch-Physikalischer Salon, Dresden, the Rijksmuseum voor de Geschiedenis der Natuurwetenschappen, Leiden,* the Musée de la Vie Wallone, Liége,* the Adler Planetarium, Chicago,* the New York Historical Society,* the Museum of Islamic Art, Cairo, the Przypkowski Collection, Jedrzjow, and the firm of Nachet, Paris,* have valuable collections. Important instruments, however, are found in many other museums, such as the Benaki Museum, Athens; the Arab Museum, Baghdad;* Harvard University, Cambridge (Mass.);* the Museum of the Jagiellonian University, Cracow; the Musées Royales d'Art et d'Histoire, Brussels; the Landesmuseum, Innsbruck; the Hessisches Landesmuseum, Kassel; the Hermitage Museum, Leningrad; the Wellcome Historical Medical Museum,

[2] Asterisks by the names of museums indicate that partial catalogues or useful descriptive guides are available of the collections in these museums. The instruments at the British Museum have been catalogued, but the catalogue has not yet been published.

London (whose collection includes a few astronomical instruments); the Lüneburg Museum; the Victoria and Albert Museum; the Museo Naval, and the Museo Arqueológico Nacional, Madrid; the Germanisches Museum, Nuremberg; the Bibliothèque Nationale, Paris; the Národní Techniké Museum, and the Umělecko-průmyslové Museum, Prague; the Kunsthistorisches Museum, Vienna; and many others.

There are a few good books of a general nature on various classes of instrument, and these are listed in the bibliography at the end of this book. These are often the main source of information for the serious student. Many of the old books on instruments are of much more than historical interest and remain of great practical use to the collector. An extensive bibliography of the ancient and modern literature of the subject may be compiled by consulting the bibliographies in the works of R. T. Gunther, L. A. Mayer, D. W. Waters, E. Zinner, the Supplement to the Catalogue of the Billmeir Collection,[1] also the catalogues of such booksellers as Messrs William Dawson & Sons, Malcolm Gardner, Maggs Bros., Henry Sotheran, and E. Weil (all of London), and Herbert Reichner (Stockbridge, Mass.), F. & G. Staack (Camden, N.J.), and Zeitlin & Ver Brugge (Los Angeles). The Science Museum, London, and the Museum of the History of Science, Oxford, both have excellent libraries, which include most of the important books. The latter also possesses the Lewis Evans Library, probably the finest collection of the older literature on astrolabes, dialling, and mathematical instruments generally.

The available lists of instrument-makers do not entirely cover the field, and there are some serious gaps. Islamic makers have been exhaustively treated by L. A. Mayer. German and Dutch makers of the eleventh to the eighteenth centuries and their instruments have been listed by E. Zinner. There is also a useful list of makers from the northern Netherlands in M. Rooseboom. English mathematical practitioners of the sixteenth and seventeenth centuries are well covered by

E. G. R. Taylor. French instrument-makers may be found in M. Daumas. Many European astrolabe-makers are listed in H. Michel.

English makers of the eighteenth and early nineteenth centuries, French makers of the sixteenth century, and American, Italian, and Spanish makers have not been adequately studied. Some information on English makers of the eighteenth and nineteenth centuries, Italian makers in general, and American makers in Philadelphia may be found in Clay & Court, M. L. Bonelli, and H. E. Gillingham respectively. There is a useful general list of makers in the Nachet catalogue. Otherwise recourse must be had to the instruments themselves, to the indexes of makers at the Museum of the History of Science, Oxford, and the Science Museum, London,[2] and to such original sources as trade-cards.[3]

As might be expected, the dating of unsigned instruments involves a combination of the comparative study of instruments, an assessment of their place in the history of artistic design, and, occasionally, scientific aids.[4]

Collecting today

Scientific instruments are much more sought after than even a few years ago. Consequently their rarity and prices have increased. Most of the finest instruments pass through the hands of a few specialist dealers or are sold by auction, mainly in London and Paris. It is, however, still possible to find at modest prices many of the more common instruments. The low price of sectors and Islamic quadrants, for example, is not in proportion to their historical interest.

N.B. No attempt is made in the following Glossary to list all early scientific instruments or the many technical terms associated with them. The glossary is merely a selection of some of the most interesting and least familiar instruments and of some of the terms likely to be encountered in descriptions of them.

[1] Now in the Museum of the History of Science, Oxford.

[2] The Science Museum has in preparation a comprehensive list of English instrument-makers.
[3] The Gabb Collection included many trade-cards of instrument-makers (now in the Science Museum).
[4] E.g. the use of the precession (52) protractor for astrolabes, and the magnetic variation marked on the compasses of sundials.

Glossary

Alidade. A rule with sights for use with a plane-table; on astrolabes, etc., a rotatable diametrical or radial arm, sometimes equipped with sights, for measuring altitudes, etc. (Plates 437C, D, F, 434C, D).

Armillary sphere. An instrument for demonstrating cosmological theory, consisting of a skeleton celestial sphere composed of rings representing the meridian, the equator, the tropics, the ecliptic, etc., on which various fixed stars are usually marked by pointers. Within the sphere are representations of the planets. Most armillary spheres are constructed according to the Ptolemaic (geocentric) system and have a small terrestrial globe in the centre. Examples survive from medieval times to *c.* 1700, when a few Copernican (heliocentric) armillary spheres were made (Plate 435A).

Astrolabe. The most important astronomical and astrological computing and observational instrument from Hellenistic times to *c.* 1700; also used for surveying. It consists essentially of (i) a thick plate with a cavity (Latin: *mater*; Arabic: *umm*) on one side, into which fit (ii) one or more plates (Latin: *tympanum*; Arabic: *safiha*); the latter are engraved with stereographic projections of the celestial sphere for various latitudes. Over the uppermost plate is (iii) a rotatable star-map (Latin: *rets*; Arabic: *'ankabût*). (i), (ii), and (iii) are assembled by a pin and wedge ("horse") which also hold the alidade on to the back of (i), where are engraved scales of degrees and other scales and tables of use to the astronomer or astrologer. A bracket or "throne" (Arabic: *kurst*) and ring attached to (i) enable the whole instrument to be suspended vertically when in use.

Stylistically and historically, astrolabes fall into several distinct groups. It is usual to distinguish among Islamic astrolabes, the Syro-Egyptian, the Persian, the Indo-Persian, and the Hispano-Moorish (*maghribî*) instruments, all of which have their own characteristics. Medieval European instruments are classified as Hispano-Moorish, "semi-quatrefoil" or "trefoil", Y-type, and late Gothic.

Some astrolabes (known as "universal astrolabes") use a projection which may be used in any latitude. Such are the projections associated with az-Zarquellu (the *sapha arzachelis*), Gemma Frisius, and Juan de Rojas (Plate 437).

The mariner's astrolabe was a deliberate simplification of the astrolabe made for nautical use in Portugal towards the end of the fifteenth century. The *rete* and plates of the usual astrolabe are omitted; the instrument consists essentially of a heavy pierced disc with a suspension ring. Around the edge of the disc are engraved scales of degrees, and the instrument is equipped with an alidade. It was used solely for measuring altitudes.

Astrolabe-quadrant. *See* Quadrant.

Astronomical compendium. A small rectangular, circular, hexagonal, or octagonal box, usually of gilt-brass, sometimes in the shape of a book with clasps, containing several astronomical devices, such as sundials, a nocturnal, a lunar volvelle, a wind-rose, a compass, and tables of latitudes. In addition, it may include an astrolabe, a quadrant, tide-tables, a map, or a set of drawing instruments. Mostly of the sixteenth and seventeenth centuries (Plate 434F).

Astronomical ring. A rare observational instrument, derived from the armillary sphere, which may be used to perform some of the functions of an astrolabe for time-telling and surveying. Revived by Gemma Frisius (Plate 435B).

Circumferentor. A surveying instrument consisting of a graduated circle of degrees over which moves an alidade. The Holland circle type has four sights (separated by 90°) on the main circular plate. A semicircular version of a circumferentor is known as a graphometer. Both usually have a ball-and-socket joint for tripod mounting: sixteenth to eighteenth century (Plate 434D).

Compass, magnetic. Among special

types of compass are the meridian (or trough) compass, which is in a narrow rectangular box and the needle of which can move only a few degrees on either side of the meridian, the surveyor's compass, which is made for use with or attachment to a plane-table and has often a reversed compass-card, and the miner's compass used in the surveying of mines and the charting of mineral rights, which has a characteristic numeration of the points of the compass (Plate 438D).

A particular type of Islamic compass, often combined with a sundial, is the *Qibla*-indicator (*Qibla-numa*) giving the azimuth of the Qibla (i.e. the direction of Mecca) when the instrument is aligned on the meridian at various places inscribed on the instrument.

The Chinese geomancer's compass consists of a small magnetic compass set in the centre of a round lacquered wooden board. Surrounding the compass are circular scales of cyclical characters and *kua* symbols used in the art of geomancy (*feng shui*).

Cross, surveyor's. A simple sighting instrument, often combined with a compass, consisting of a cylinder or box with slit sights at 90°, sometimes 45°, intervals.

Dial or **sundial.** The terms used in classifying the numerous types of sundial often overlap, as some of the terms refer to the scientific principle of the dial's design, others to the form of the instrument. Universal dials are those which may be adjusted for use in more than one latitude. Altitude dials and directional dials constitute the two main classes of dial. The former depend for their operation on the variation of the sun's altitude during the day; the latter on the variation of its azimuth or its hour-angle measured along the equinoctial circle. Dials which are not self-orientating include compasses and must be aligned on the meridian; dials which are neither fixed nor suspended when in use must also be levelled, and sometimes include plummets or spirit levels for this purpose. A few of the terms used in describing the dials in each class are listed in alphabetical order below (those marked * are altitude dials; those marked †, directional dials).

Analemmatic.† A self-orientating dial (therefore requiring no compass) which includes an hour-arc and an azimuth dial on the same hour-plate.

Azimuth.† A pin-gnomon dial with concentric hour-scales graduated in the solar azimuth angles for each month of the year; *see* Magnetic azimuth.

Augsburg.† Pocket octagonal universal equinoctial dials, particularly associated with the town of Augsburg in the seventeenth and early eighteenth centuries. Also popular in France in a slightly different form.

Bloud.† A form of diptych dial, usually of ivory, associated with Charles Bloud and other Dieppe makers, *c.* 1660; the main feature is a magnetic azimuth dial, but usually polar, equinoctial, and string-gnomon dials are also included.

Butterfield.† A small octagonal, oval, or rectangular universal horizontal dial, often of silver, associated with Michael Butterfield and other Paris makers of the seventeenth and early eighteenth centuries. Similar horizontal dials, but without the adjustable gnomon with the latitude index in the form of a bird's head and beak, are also found.

Compass.† A compass, usually in a round box with a screw-on lid, with a horizontal dial fitted over the compass; the hour-plate is cut away to reveal the compass below. *See also* Magnetic dial.

Crescent.† A self-orientating small pocket dial of silver and gilt-brass associated with Johann Martin and Johann Willebrand of Augsburg (early eighteenth century); it derives from the universal equinoctial ring-dial. The hour-ring is cut into two semi-circles set back to back. There is a crescent-shaped gnomon which slides on a declination scale.

Cruciform (or *crucifix*).† A multiple universal dial of cruciform shape in which the arms of the cross form the gnomons.

*Cylinder.** Also known as shepherd's dial, particularly the unsophisticated wooden versions which were made until recently in the Pyrenees. The hour-scale is marked on the outer surface of a vertical cylinder. The gnomon projects horizontally from the top of the cylinder.

Diptych.† A dial made of two hinged leaves, usually of ivory, sometimes with coloured engraving, sometimes in the form of a book with clasps. Contains usually universal equinoctial, vertical, and horizontal string-gnomon and pin-gnomon dials. Mostly made at Nuremberg in the late sixteenth and early seventeenth centuries.

Equatorial. *See* Equinoctial.

Equinoctial.† A dial the hour-scale of which is set parallel to the plane of the equator. As the hour-scale is circular, it may be simply and accurately divided; one of the most common forms of dial, usually made universal.

Geminus. *See* Rojas.

Globe (or *spherical*).† An equinoctial dial consisting of a sphere on which the hour circles are engraved: often made of stone.

Horizontal.† A dial in which the hour-scale is horizontal, and which has a gnomon of which the shadow-casting edge is parallel to the Earth's axis – the usual garden sundial is of this type.

Inclining.† A horizontal dial made universal by including a means of tilting the hour-plate from the horizontal for adjustment to different latitudes. Most inclining dials of the eighteenth century resemble large compass dials, but small versions for use in a few latitudes are often included in the small gilt brass *victoria* (small pocket dials usually of gilt-brass) and astronomical compendia of the sixteenth and seventeenth centuries.

Magnetic (compass).† A small dial, mostly of the eighteenth and nineteenth centuries, wherein a magnetic compass-card is marked with hour-lines (as for an ordinary horizontal dial) and also carries the gnomon. As the compass-card aligns itself on the meridian, so the dial is orientated.

Magnetic-azimuth.† A dial in which a magnetic compass needle indicates the time, when the dial is directed towards the sun; instead of having separate hour-scales for the varying azimuth of the sun throughout the year, some dials of this type have an elliptical hour-scale, or the pivot of the compass needle is adjustable by means of an index moving over a calendar scale. Bloud dials have an adjustable hour scale.

Mechanical. Used of an equinoctial dial, having a radial index which is turned towards the sun; the tip of the index then shows the hour, and a small hand, geared to the equinoctial hour-plate (which is toothed), shows the minutes on a smaller dial-face.

Navicula. *See* Regiomontanus.

Pin-gnomon. Any dial whose gnomon consists of a short vertical or horizontal pin; the shadow of its tip indicates the time.

Poke. *See* Ring.

Polar.† A dial of which the plane of the hour-scale is parallel to the Earth's axis; rare, usually found only on polyhedral and Bloud dials.

Polyhedral.† A multiple dial, usually cube-shaped, but other polyhedra and the surfaces of caskets were used; a dial was drawn on each face. In eighteenth-century Germany D. Beringer and others made cube dials of wood on which were pasted coloured printed scales: large polyhedral dials of stone were used as garden dials.

Rectilinear. *See* Regiomontanus.

Ring. The simplest form of ring dial (also called poke dial)* consists of a single ring with a sliding collar in which is a small hole; the collar was adjusted to the solar declination and the ring suspended and turned towards the sun so that sunlight passing through the hole indicated the time on an hour-scale engraved within the ring. An equinoctial ring† dial is a self-orientating universal dial, consisting of a meridian circle and an equinoctial hour-ring within which is a gnomon consisting of a pierced slider on a declination scale ("bridge"); after adjustment for latitude and solar declination, the dial is suspended and turned until sunlight passing through the hole in the slider falls on the equinoctial ring where it indicates the time.

*Regiomontanus.** Also known as universal rectilinear dial; a complex vertical dial sometimes found on the back of a nocturnal in the sixteenth and seventeenth centuries; also separately, especially in Italy in the seventeenth and eighteenth centuries with a particular (i.e. for one latitude only) rectilinear dial on the reverse. A very rare form of Regiomontanus dial in the shape of a ship is known as navicula.

*Rojas.** Also called Geminus; a vertical universal dial based on a simplification of the universal astrolabe projection associated with

Juan de Rojas, a pupil of Gemma Frisius; often found on the back of nocturnals.

*Scaphe (cup-dial).** A dial with the hour-lines engraved on the inner surface of a hemisphere, shallow bowl, or a goblet.

Shepherd's. See Cylinder.

String-gnomon (string-style). Any dial in which the gnomon is a taut thread.

Universal ring. See Ring.

Vertical. Any dial in which the hour scale is vertical (e.g. vertical disc* dial, vertical plate* dial, and the vertical form of an ordinary horizontal dial†).

Window. A vertical dial painted on a pane of glass for insertion in a window (Plates 434, 435c).

Gunnery instruments. Many instruments were made for the use of gunners, e.g. levels, combined with sights, for use with cannon; sectors and rules with scales correlating the weight and sizes of shot of different materials and showing the necessary charges; and calipers for measuring bore and shot (Plate 441D).

Hours. Not all horary systems divide day and night into twenty-four equal hours, numbered in two series of twelve. Among other systems used on Islamic and European astrolabes, quadrants, and sundials, the following may be mentioned: planetary (unequal or Jewish) hours resulting from a division of the periods from sunrise to sunset and from sunset to sunrise each into twelve equal hours (noon and midnight are therefore the sixth hours), the hours vary in length from day to day, and except at the equinoxes, day hours differ in length from the night hours; Babylonian hours (*horae ab ortu solis*), which are equal hours counted up to twenty-four from the first hour after sunrise; and Italian hours (*horae ab occasu solis*), which are similarly counted from the first hour after sunset. In the pre-1873 Japanese system of time-keeping the periods from sunrise to sunset and from sunset to sunrise were each divided into six equal *toki*. The *toki* were numbered, starting at midnight and again at midday, 9, 8, 7, 6, 5, and 4. The "hour"-lines on Japanese sundials are, therefore, marked with numerals indicating the 5th, 4th, 9th (midday), 8th, and 7th *toki* of the day.

Loadstone. A piece of magnetic iron ore, magnetite, usually ground symmetrically, equipped with steel or iron pole-pieces and a keeper, and mounted in a metal frame with a suspension ring. Popular in the seventeenth and eighteenth centuries for "philosophical" experiments and for magnetizing the compass-needles of pocket compasses and sundials (Plate 440A). A spherical loadstone reproduces in miniature the magnetic system of the Earth and is known as terella.

Microscopes are either simple (with one lens) or compound (with several lenses). The earliest simple microscopes, such as those of Leeuwenhoek or Musschenbroek type, and the earliest compound microscopes, such as those made by John Marshall, *c.* 1700, are very rare. In the eighteenth and nineteenth centuries there were many types of compound microscope, known by names derived from their function (e.g. botanic, universal), their form (e.g. drum, chest-type, screw-barrel), their place of origin or a maker associated with them (Cuff, Culpeper, Gould, Joblot, Lyonnet, Nuremberg), or some variation of the normal form (aquatic, lucernal, reflecting, solar) (Plate 439c).

Napier's bones. A pocket calculator, for multiplication and division, invented by John Napier of Merchiston. The commonest type consists of loose square-sectioned "bones" or rods, with a series of numbers divided by diagonal lines on each of the four sides of each "bone"; the "bones" lie on a small tray which slides into a case. Another type has rotatable cylindrical "bones" fixed in a box (Plate 438c).

Nocturnal. An instrument used to find the time by night. It consists usually of a disc with a handle, with a smaller disc and an index arm attached to the centre of the main disc by a pierced rivet. The small disc is set to the date; the pole star is sighted through the hole and the index arm moved until it cuts a particular star of the Great or Little Bear, when it will indicate the time (Plate 434A, B). Regiomontanus or Rojas dials are often found on the backs of nocturnals.

Orrery. The eighteenth-century successor to the armillary sphere; a hand- or clockwork-driven machine for demonstrating the motion of the planets about the sun, and in the larger and more elaborate types showing also the movements of the satellites of the planets. Usually the earth and moon are made to a larger scale than the other planets so as to show their motions relative to each other and to the sun in greater detail. Orreries were especially popular in England. The first true orrery appears to have been made by George Graham and Thomas Tompion, *c.* 1709. Inspired by this machine, John Rowley made, *c.* 1712, a similar instrument for Lord Orrery, which, according to Richard Steel, the essayist, was named "orrery" by Rowley in honour of his patron (Plate 436c).

Quadrant. Consists essentially of a flat plate (of wood or metal) in the shape of a quarter of a circular disc; the simplest form has a scale of 90° along the curved edge and a plumb-line and bob suspended from the apex of the right-angle. Equipped with a pair of sights on one radial edge, it could be used for finding angular elevations of heavenly bodies or in surveying. Islamic quadrants usually have on one side a nomograph of the sines and cosines of the angles marked on the arc. This is known as a sinecal quadrant (*quadrans canonis* or *vetustissimus* in medieval Europe). Another type of quadrant had a diagram of planetary hours above the scale of degrees. This required a sliding bead on the plumb-line and was improved by the addition of a zodiacal scale for ascertaining solar declination. An adjustable zodiacal scale rendered the quadrant universal (*see above s.v.* Dial). This was the medieval *quadrans vetus*. European quadrants of the sixteenth, seventeenth, and eighteenth centuries were made with hour-lines for ordinary Italian and Babylonian hours, and include many ingenious new designs. Seventeenth-century English quadrant designs include those associated with Allen, Collins, and Gunter (Plate 436A).

An astrolabe-quadrant is a reduction to a quarter of a circle of the essential lines of the stereographic projection on the rete and plates of an astrolabe. The commonest type is that described by Prophatius in the thirteenth century (the medieval *quadrans novus*). The typical Islamic quadrant is engraved on one side as a Prophatius astrolabe-quadrant, and on the other as a sinecal quadrant (Plate 436B).

Qibla-indicator. *See s.v.* Compass.

Sector. A mathematical instrument consisting of two flat equal arms hinged together as in a joint rule. The arms bear various scales which were used for the solution of numerous problems in practical geometry, surveying, dialling, and gunnery. For instance, to divide a given line into the same proportions as a scale on the sector, it is only necessary to open the sector until the ends of the two arms are as far apart as the length of the line and to drop verticals from the scale to the line: hence the French name, *compas de proportion* (which must not be confused with the English proportional compass). Three main types of sector are distinguishable by the types and lay-out of the scales engraved on them, viz. the English, French, and Dutch types. Surveyor's sectors are equipped with sights and sometimes a ball-and-socket mounting. Some of the fine sixteenth- and seventeenth-century triangulation instruments are also based on the principle of similar triangles (Plate 438A).

Sundial. *See* Dial.

Telescopes are either refracting or reflecting. In the latter type the light is focused by means of a speculum mirror. In the Newtonian reflecting telescope the mirror reflects the light through a prism to an eye-piece mounted at the side of the upper end of the telescope tube. In the Gregorian reflecting telescope the light is reflected on to a second smaller mirror at the upper (open) end of the tube and thence back to an eye-piece mounted behind a hole in the centre of the mirror. Unlike terrestrial telescopes, astronomical telescopes give an inverted image (Plate 434E).

SCULPTURE AND CARVING

Sculpture

ANCIENT GREEK AND ROMAN SCULPTURE

It is unlikely today that major works of ancient Greek or Roman statuary will come the way of the ordinary collector, and in the rare instances in which they are found the advice of an expert must be sought to distinguish originals from ancient, or modern, copies. Minor works are, however, not uncommon, especially in bronze and, to a lesser extent, in marble. These, in detail and style, closely reflect the major sculpture of their day, and can only be appreciated and understood in the light of the development of major sculpture in the ancient world.

STONE SCULPTURE

The ready accessibility of fine white marble which could easily be quarried from the ground surface was a prime factor in the development of stone sculpture in Greece. As early as the third millennium B.C. marble from the islands of the Cyclades was being used for female statuettes, either of the type illustrated in Plate 441 A or of a simple "fiddle" outline. These had, however, no immediate successors in the Aegean world.

By the eighth century B.C. renewed contact with the Eastern countries, Assyria, Phoenicia, and other states, led to a revival of interest in carved work as opposed to the simple clay figurines of animals and human beings which had been made to serve as votive offerings. In the seventh century the island quarries were also rediscovered and schools of marble sculpture arose, first perhaps on the Cyclades, then on the East Greek islands and in mainland Greece. The island marble was exported to other parts of Greece, but local resources of limestone were often used as well. Simple canons of proportion for the human figure were observed, and the triangular faces with large eyes and the layer "barrister-type" wigs are distinctive of the style called Daedalic. Male figures (*kouroi*) are generally nude, occasionally wear a belt, and stand with their hands to their sides and one foot slightly advanced in a pose which has for a long time been familiar in Egyptian statuary. Women are clothed in simple pleatless dresses (*peploi*). Details of the body are rendered, if at all, in a simple formal manner, and it is clear that the figures were first sketched on the surface of the unworked block, which was then cut back to the outline, for there is no concession to any view other than the strictly frontal, or side – certainly none to three-quarter views (Plate 441c).

By about 600 B.C. a little more realism appears in the carving of head and body, well shown in a fine series of statues from Athens and Attica (Plate 441B). The triangular outline of the face softens into more of an oval, and the corners of the lips are raised in an "archaic smile". Body markings are still rudimentary and shown by a formal pattern of grooves or sharply intersecting planes. Through the sixth century the strict frontality of the figures is gradually abandoned and more ambitious poses attempted, particularly in relief sculpture. This was generally reserved for architectural decoration – for the metope panels in Doric buildings or the friezes of Ionic buildings. The use of overlapping figures in such reliefs, together with more skilful carving, lends an impression of depth. Frontal figures are attempted, but not three-quarter views, and even in profile views of the human head the eyes are shown as if seen from the front (Plate 442B). In the sixth century the East Greek (Ionic) styles of sculpture also become more differentiated from the mainland schools, and generally favour more rounded and fleshy profiles, as on Plate 442A. From the island of Samos comes an important series of marble statues distinguished by their columnar bodies and rounded heads. Around the middle of the century a greater naturalism in the representation of drapery appears, with formal patterns of pleats and hem-line folds. This accompanies the adoption of the more sophisticated Ionic costume, the short-sleeved *chiton*, which replaced the severe Doric *peplos* as the usual dress for women, at least in sculpture. A superb series of maidens (*korai*) from the Acropolis at Athens illustrates the fussy decorativeness of the new fashion. They are the work of both Attic and Ionian artists, and form the most important group of archaic statuary preserved. Beside them were statues of horsemen and animals. Plate 442D shows the head of one of these horsemen, and Plate 442C the head of a *kore*, who was dressed in the earlier Doric manner with a foldless *peplos*. Their hair is represented in tight formal curls and crimped waves; the eyes are wide and staring, the lips set in an archaic smile.

With the fifth century, the classical period, almost full naturalism is achieved, at least in the representation of the human body. This generally means the male body, which, through the characteristic Greek interest in athletics, presented a more ready model for the artist, and which, in the gymnasium or stadium, offered difficult poses and torsions to tax his skill. The nude female body was hardly ever represented in art before the fourth century. Fuller naturalism in the carving of heads is also apparent, but the features are usually composed and idealized, with no hint of portraiture and little attempt to represent emotion. The hair is carved in a more naturalistic manner in individual locks with a combed crown, and in reliefs the eyes appear now in a properly foreshortened side view.

The decoration of buildings was still a major concern of the sculptor, but occasionally his figures also fulfilled a structural function. Thus the Caryatids of sixth-century treasuries at Delphi and in the Erechtheum porch of fifth-century Athens serve as columns. In the same spirit are the great Atlas-pilasters on the Temple of Zeus at Acragas (Agrigento), and, much later, the crouching satyrs which support the stage of the Theatre of Dionysos at Athens. It is a motif which has long been popular. Of the middle of the fifth century is the sculpture from the Temple of Zeus in Olympia, in which violent action and composed "classical" features sometimes contrast strangely. Plate 433A, the head of a young Athena on a metope, typifies the new spirit. Now, too, the names of artists can be associated with preserved works or (more often) copies of their originals. Myron's Diskobolos is a good example of a difficult athletic pose successfully rendered. Polyclitus' Diadoumenos and other figures show how well understood now is the anatomy of a relaxed figure standing with his weight on one leg, far removed from the archaic *kouros* pose with straight back and one leg slightly advanced.

It is perhaps in the reliefs which decorate the gravestones (*stelai*) of the fifth century that this classical calm is at its most expressive; the dead woman looks for the last time at the jewels her maid has brought her, parents take leave of their son, a girl bids farewell to her pet doves. In the middle and second half of the century falls the work of the school of Phidias, designer of the marble sculptures on the Parthenon at Athens, now largely in the British Museum, and of colossal gold and ivory cult statues, now known only in much reduced and adapted copies. Drapery in particular is more realistically rendered, and the relief figures from the balustrade around the Nike Temple at Athens show how well it could be carved to reveal the contours of the limbs and body beneath.

In the fourth century there was added to the sculptor's established command in representing the human body an interest in expressing emotion and individuality. Portraits appear, both of dead poets and politicians and of contemporary notables. Portraits of philosophers and orators, for instance the Demosthenes of Plate 443C, are familiar from several ancient copies. Local schools and the work of individual sculptors can again be recognized. To Scopas is attributed the type of head with intense deep-sunk eyes; to Lysippus new canons of proportion, and the expression of incipient movement and contrasting lines of composition in single figures which led to the more complicated and restless groups and figures of the succeeding "Hellenistic" age. Now, too, the statuary is successfully designed to be viewed satisfactorily from any angle. The nude female body becomes a popular motif for the first time in Greek art, and in the fourth century are evolved many of the Aphrodite types which were so often copied and adapted in the following centuries. The name of Praxiteles is particularly associated with these, and his lithe figures created a profound effect on contemporaries and later critics. An original from his hand may be preserved in the Hermes from Olympia (Plate 443B).

The Hellenistic period, of the third and second centuries B.C., sees the logical fulfilment of the novelties and experiments of the preceding two centuries. Portraiture, expression of emotion and violent exertion, compositions of several figures, are developed to a point beyond which there was little more to be attempted in the way of representational plastic art.

The individual styles of local schools can, to some extent, be distinguished. The Pergamene school is thus best represented in the reliefs from the Great Altar of Zeus at Pergamum, where the contorted bodies of fighting gods and giants are closely knit in the composition of a frieze. Rhodes and some of the cities of the Asia Minor coast favour a baroque style of changing rhythms and restless drapery. Two-figure compositions are successfully attempted, of wrestlers, warriors, or the like. The bronze boxer and jockey (Plate 445B) exemplify the new command of movement and expression. No subject is shirked, from old age or deformed grotesques to the mannered prettiness of muses and nymphs, which was more popularly reflected in the "Tanagra" figurines of clay.

The conquest of Greece by the Romans and the emergence of the Romans as art patrons whose tastes created a constant demand for statuary forms a significant stage in the history of ancient sculpture. Very much of the work of this "Graeco-Roman" period, both in Italy and in the Empire, can be classed as copy or adaptation of classical or Hellenistic Greek original. It is clear, too, that Greeks were still for the most part the artists; the Roman genius lay elsewhere.

Italy had already some local traditions in statuary which may have conditioned Roman taste. The Etruscans evolved an archaic "graecising" style, but lacking good marble, their statuary was virtually confined to small bronzes and impressive but graceless terracotta figures, often over life-size. The traditional practice of making portraits of the dead also bred a taste for what often seem cruelly accurate likenesses with none of the idealizing spirit which imbues most Greek work. The most important innovation in the Roman period is the historical, narrative relief, as those of Trajan's column in Rome. Portraiture of both imperial (Plate 443D) and private persons reached its peak in the first and second centuries A.D., although the combination of a matron's head with the copied torso of a buxom Hellenistic Aphrodite sometimes produces a mixture of frankness and flattery which we find unhappily incongruous. Relief sculpture of the Roman period is probably best known from the marble *sarcophagi*, or coffins, which are carved on one or all sides with mythological scenes, cupids, and the like, often including a medallion with the bust or head of the dead person.

Of the sculpture in this country, and, indeed, in most European collections outside Greece and Italy, most Greek originals have arrived untouched from excavations or enterprising purchase. The Graeco-Roman statues have, however, had a more chequered career. Many were recovered from the soil of Italy in the sixteenth to eighteenth centuries and sold to foreign noblemen, but before they left Italy they were "treated" in Roman workshops and studios, where missing limbs and heads were supplied, pastiches of different originals composed, and original parts often worked over to suit current tastes in "antique marbles". Even afterwards they were commonly subjected to repairs, overworking, and drastic cleaning, or sometimes, what is worse, neglect. Thus, the Aphrodite of Arles in the Louvre had her bust remodelled by Louis XIV's sculptor Girardon to suit the more elegant contemporary fashion.

MATERIAL AND TECHNIQUE

The white marble of the Greek islands (Naxos, Paros) used for the earliest statuary, but still popular and much exported later, is distinguished by its relatively large crystals, which lend considerable translucency. Pentelic marble, from Attica, has a finer grained, "hard" appearance, while other white marbles from the Asia Minor coast and islands are intermediate. Limestone or other local stones were sometimes employed, especially in the archaic period, but never in later centuries for major works. Carrara marble has very small crystals and a dull white colour which blackens with age; it cannot compare with the Greek marbles for translucency. Only in the Roman period are coloured marbles widely used for statuary. Occasionally in late works the hair is modelled separately in plaster and then painted. It was a common practice, too, in all periods of antiquity to make statues in separate pieces – head, limbs, etc. – which would then be dowelled together.

Traces of working are still apparent on many pieces. The prehistoric statuettes were painstakingly worked with emery. Archaic statuary often shows the marks of claw chisel and rasp, particularly on the backs of figures and in less conspicuous parts of the body. In later times different chiselling was deliberately employed to give different surface qualities to flesh and drapery. Later classical, Hellenistic, and Roman work often carries a highly polished surface which had been waxed to lend added translucency and an almost sensual quality to parts representing bare flesh. In the Roman period the drill and deep undercutting which produce heavy shadows were often employed to excess. The metallic glaze which appears on pieces in many collections is the result of drastic cleaning.

Colour was regularly used on Greek statues for the drapery, eyes, lips, and hair. Most of this has usually disappeared with time or cleaning, but traces can still be observed on excavated statues which had not been too long exposed before they were buried. The practice continued in Roman Imperial times, and from the second century A.D. the pupil of the eye is regularly also represented by an incised circle. Gilding is often apparent on the hair. We owe most of our misconceptions about the appearance of classical statuary to the disappearance of the colour from the originals. Metal diadems, jewellery, weapons, etc., were also regularly attached, but of these their holes for fastening are usually all that is preserved.

Accurate copies of earlier statues were made in the Roman period by means of the "pointing" process, which is still practised today. Occasionally the traces of the basic "points" remain on the surface of the copy in the shape of small pierced mounds. The extraordinary accuracy of this process is attested by the uniform size of many different copies, and by the rare instances in which the original itself is also preserved.

BRONZE SCULPTURE

Because of the value of the material very little bronze statuary has survived from antiquity except for minor objects and some fortunate major discoveries in excavations or wrecks (as Plate 445); the rest went to the melting-pot in the intervening centuries, even more readily than the marble statuary did to the limekiln. This easily leads to an under-estimate of the importance of bronzes. The original of a bronze statue, being plastically built up by hand in clay, gave more scope to the sculptor's inventiveness than did the carving techniques required by ivory, wood, or stone. It is the plastic quality of the small solid-cast statuettes which is most apparent. In the Late Bronze Age (about 1600–1200 B.C.) minor bronzes representing animals, men, and women were being made, notably in Minoan Crete, where the distinctive dress is a loincloth for the men and flounced skirt for the women. In Geometric Greece of the eighth century B.C. similar subjects are treated in no very different style, the most popular figures being lanky warriors, naked but for their helmets and spears, and bulls, which serve as humble substitutes for richer animal offerings. Particularly distinctive horses are made from hammered bronze strips which are welded together; these either decorated cauldron handles (as Plate 444A) or, on flat openwork stands, served as independent votive offerings. Some complicated small groups were attempted, such as a lion hunt or ring dance. With the seventh century the Daedalic style, which we have already met in stone sculpture, is equally well represented in bronze statuettes that observe the same canons of proportion and detail, but their plastic quality makes them often more satisfying, as they are less rigidly frontal. A small group of bronzes from Crete is executed in the *sphyrelaton* technique of hammered bronze plates fastened on to a wooden core.

The development of major bronze sculpture from this time on runs parallel to that of stone sculpture; in fact, in many ways it precedes it, and in marble statuary many details reveal in their treatment and execution the decisive influence of bronze work. This is particularly true of hair represented in irregular tufts and curls which can be easily modelled in clay but which could hardly recommend themselves to the stone carver otherwise (Plates 443B and 445B). Bronze also enabled the sculptor to attempt bold compositions of flying figures with outstretched limbs which could not safely be executed in stone. This explains many of the gratuitous tree-trunks and similar supports which appear on Graeco-Roman marble copies of Greek bronze originals whose slender ankles need no reinforcement to carry the weight of the body above.

It is the smaller bronzes which are most likely to come into the purview of the collector today. Through the archaic period, the seventh and sixth centuries B.C., bronze statuettes were made in styles closely resembling the larger marble statuary. As well as independent figures, usually votive offerings, of youths, women, or animals, human figures and animals are found serving as the supports for bronze mirrors or the handles of bronze vases. In miniature they reproduce the details of the life-size stone *korai* and athletes of their day. Some local schools and classes can be distinguished among these statuettes, such as the Arcadian shepherds with their pointed caps, and the stocky Spartan warriors. The most important sources of bronzes in this period are the sanctuaries of Zeus at Dodona and Olympia.

From the classical and Hellenistic period there is preserved an occasional statuette which reflects vividly the excellence of the lost major sculpture in bronze of the day. There are some fine animal bronzes in this period. The famous bathing-girl statue in Munich is an unusually good example of a type which, in variants, became popular in the fourth century. It is hollow-cast (by the "cire perdue" method), though most statuettes of all periods are cast solid.

In Italy local traditions die hard in many classes of bronze statuettes, and the Greek motifs are sometimes drastically refashioned. Campania and south Italy have produced important groups of bronzes, but it is in Etruria that most have been found. As well as close imitations and derivations from Greek types, there are individual groups of small "match-stick" figures, or slim warriors like Plate 444B, which are characteristic of this part of Italy. Later come the common statuettes of votaries wearing radiate crowns and holding bowls (*paterae*) in their hands, of divinities and of heroes. Hercules is particularly popular with his raised club, and lionskin draped over his left arm (Plate 444C). These are types which seem to have been made outside Etruria also, and they long remained popular; their execution is sometimes extremely crude.

The bronze statuettes of the Roman period are often technically superior. The same types are current, especially Hercules, Mercury with purse and caduceus, helmeted Minerva (Athena), and Venus (Plate 444D–F) – all in poses which reflect major Greek originals. These have been found in all parts of the Roman Empire, from England to Egypt.

Just as the marble statues were usually painted, the bronzes, too, were embellished. Eyes, lips, nipples, finger- and toe-nails could be inlaid with paste, stone, or with strips of a contrasting metal like silver. Detailed patterns on drapery and the like might be treated in a similar way, but it is rarely that such details are preserved. When they are, as on the Delphi charioteer, they are startlingly effective.

Most ancient bronzes have been excavated from the soil, and are consequently coated with a patina and incrustation. In some cases the patina is so light and of so attractive a colour that it enhances rather than detracts from the appearance of the piece. This is, however, rarely true, and much delicate chasing and modelling, to say nothing of incised inscriptions, may be hidden by it. It is clear that in antiquity pains were taken to see that the bronze statues were kept bright and free from rust.

ANTIQUE EUROPEAN BRONZES

Bronze, an alloy of copper and tin, was the earliest metal to be used by man, and the ease with which it can be cast, chiselled, chased, and engraved, and the fine patina it acquires with age, have assured its popularity ever since, both for utilitarian and artistic work. There are many aspects of this vast field open to collectors – from prehistoric axes to the great portrait busts of eighteenth-century France or from Greek lamps to fine decorative plaques made to decorate eighteenth-century furniture; though much of this material is no longer within the reach of collectors today – the collecting of Greek and Roman or Medieval bronzes can only be attempted by the really wealthy connoisseur. In spite of his, much still remains to interest the collector of modest means: the small statuettes and figure groups of Italian and French, as well of rarer Flemish and German origin from the late fifteenth to the eighteenth centuries; the fine household articles of the same period, such as ink-stands, fire-dogs, and door-knock-

ers; the delicate bronze-gilt mounts made in the seventeenth and eighteenth centuries to decorate furniture or clock-cases; the fine mortars of the late medieval period and later centuries from Italy or Flanders and even England and France; the plaquettes made for the decoration of furniture or household articles, such as ink-stands, as well as for acquisition by connoisseurs and collectors since the late fifteenth century.

A difficulty which confronts the collector of bronzes is to discriminate between the work of, say, the sixteenth century, and later casts after the same model, varying from work of the master's followers or his workshop to copies made as late as the nineteenth century. Only the handling of many bronzes and the careful study of the best work in public collections, will enable the aspiring collector to recognize quality of casting, the type of finish achieved by individual chiselling and chasing or polishing of the figure, and the correct patina appertaining to individual periods.

Small bronzes are rarely signed and are usually attributed to individual artists on style or, when possible, by the direct relation the small work may bear to documented major sculpture by known masters.

Sculpture in bronze, of such importance to Antiquity, saw its great revival in Italy during the Renaissance of the fifteenth century. At first the medium was used solely for major works under the patronage of the Church, like the two pairs of bronze doors for the Baptistry of Florence. The open competition for the first pair of these doors, held in 1401 and won by Lorenzo Ghiberti, heralded the beginning of the Renaissance.

Donatello, the giant of Italian sculpture of the next generation, was responsible for the revival of the conception of a free-standing figure, released from the subservience to any architectural setting, not practised since antiquity. He was probably also responsible for the revival of the small statuettes so beloved in the guise of little gods or ornamental detail in the Greek and Roman period, which were henceforth to decorate the rooms of Italian humanists and wealthy patrons. While in Florence in the studios of Verrochio, A. Pollaiuolo, and especially Bertoldo, this new cult of an aspect of the antique was further developed, it was in the university city and centre of learning, Padua, under the influence of Donatello's stay from 1443 to 1453, that a school of bronze casters developed which first fully exploited the possibilities of small bronzes for decorative and utilitarian purposes. The production of statuettes, often directly inspired by the antique, of ink-stands, handbells, salts, small caskets, fanciful and grotesque oil-lamps, candlesticks, mortars, and animals of powerful and, at times, almost hideous realism, began in the last decades of the fifteenth century, and the prolific production was carried on well into the sixteenth century. Outstanding among the many artists who must have been employed in their manufacture was Andrea Briosco, called Riccio. Works attributed to him, especially examples of a great variety of male and female satyrs made by him and his school, may be seen in some private and most public collections. In the snakes, toads, and crabs, one of the popular products of the Paduan school which were probably cast from Nature herself, one can see the emphasis on naturalism in this school and their desire to re-create, rather than slavishly follow, the work of Antiquity. At the smaller courts of northern Italy, however, the fashion for the Antique was stronger. At Mantua, for example, under the patronage of Isabella d'Este, Pietro Ilario Bonacolsi, who went to the extreme of using the pseudonym "l'Antico", produced finely chiselled copies of the Antique almost exclusively for the Mantuan Court. A number of artists from the late fifteenth century onwards were engaged in producing small-scale, straightforward copies of the Antique for collectors. Among the most popular models were the *Youth removing a Thorn from his Foot*, after the original in the Capitoline Museum in Rome, and *Hercules resting on his Club*, after the colossal statue in the Naples Museum. After other sculptors produced fragmentary casts – for example, the Venus by the Venetian Tullio Lombardi – the imitation of the Antique could go no further.

The creation of the High Renaissance in the early sixteenth century by Leonardo da Vinci, Michelangelo, and Raphael had both a direct and an indirect influence on the production of small bronzes. The indirect influence was a negative one. The new search for the revival of the grandeur as well as the forms of Antiquity forced the intimate art of the statuette temporarily into the background. The direct influence was, of course, the tremendous impact of Michelangelo's sculptural genius on Italian art.

In Florence his influence was almost disastrous and resulted in merely superficial imitation. Less overpowering, though strong, was Michelangelo's influence on Jacopo Tatti, called Sansovino, after his master, Andrea Sansovino. When after the sack of Rome in 1527 he settled in Venice, he formed a school which dominated the second half of the sixteenth century as Riccio's had dominated the first half. On his arrival in northern Italy, Sansovino found that the naturalism and rather laboured appreciation of the Antique as exemplified in Riccio's school and the naïve and somewhat dry antique-inspired art of the

Lombardi had already been redirected in the work of the Paduan Francesco da Sant' Agata and the Brescian Maffeo Olivieri, who worked in Venice. Both had sought to infuse a new dramatic sense of movement into the dry bones of Antiquity, an intention parallel to the new mannerist tendency in Michelangelo. Francesco achieved this by an elongated and elegant figure style, resulting in highly polished statuettes; Olivieri by a more thick-set and dramatic style, in which the original wax modelling is left more apparent, the unevenness of the surface being retained in the finished work and not chiselled and polished down as in most of the work of his contemporaries. With Sansovino a new phase begins in north Italian sculpture. The unmistakable influence of Michelangelo, which he was the first to translate into the medium of the statuette, can be seen in his work. The powerful modelling of the anatomy of his figures, now more directly inspired by Nature than by the Antique, and the strong *contra-posto* movement point to it. His own contribution may be seen in the more delicate rendering of surface, the thinner, richer treatment of drapery and the full acceptance of the elegance and elongated proportions characteristic of sixteenth-century Mannerism. These latter tendencies were developed to full Mannerism in his pupils, Danese Cattaneo and, especially, Alessandro Vittoria. Characteristic of the transition in Venice from Mannerism to Baroque is the work of Nicolo Roccatagliata, who was active from the late sixteenth into the seventeenth century. His many variations on the theme of small child-statuettes has given him the title "Master of the Putto".

In Florence the best exponent of the Mannerist style was Benvenuto Cellini. His famous golden salt-cellar, a work of great elegance made for Francis I and now in Vienna, shows the abilities of this sculptor in work on a small scale. Unfortunately, it has not been possible to attribute any small bronzes to him. The most important sculptor of the later sixteenth century in Florence, however, was to be the Flemish-born Giovanni Bologna. Under him, aided by the lavish patronage of the ruling Medici princes, Florence again became the most important centre for bronze sculpture in

Europe, and developed from the Mannerist to the Baroque style. His work was continued by his school, if anything even more prolific than Riccio's had been, well into the seventeenth century. The mannered elegance of his famous Neptune, designed in 1563 to crown the fountain for the Piazza Maggiore in Bologna (now in the Museo Civico), gives way in his later work to the intricate, spiral-like composition of Baroque vigour, like the group of the *Rape of the Sabines*, the original marble of which was set up in the Loggia dei Lanzi at Florence in 1583. Many small bronzes, often with slight variations in composition, of these as well as most of Bologna's major works are known: the most famous among them, no doubt, is the *Flying Mercury* first cast in 1564. His most important pupil and follower was Antonio Susini, whose workshop was continued by his nephew, Francesco Susini. With the end of the sixteenth century the importance of the small, free-standing bronze statuette diminishes. In the baroque conception of decoration everything is subordinated to an all-enveloping theme of grand dimensions, and the intimacy and individuality of the Renaissance figurine is no longer at home.

German Renaissance bronzes are rarer than Italian, and therefore a more difficult subject for systematic collection. The popularity of bronzes, never as great as it had been in Italy, began in the early sixteenth century under Italian influence, and their production was mainly undertaken in southern Germany, with Nuremberg as its centre. The first half of the century was dominated by the Vischer family workshop, under the direction of Peter Vischer the Elder. Their major work, the Sebaldus Tomb in Nuremberg, shows the new interest in small figures and groups in its details, but the making of free-standing figures was attempted only by his sons, Peter and Hans. Their small statuettes of antique subjects, often adapted as ink-stands, clearly betray Italian, especially Paduan, inspiration. But they never descend to mere imitation. The naturalism they employ is of a northern and a Germanic kind, often still reminiscent of Late Gothic rhythms, and it is always further removed from antique formulas than their

Italian counterparts. After the Vischer workshop was dissolved in 1549, Pankratz Labenwolf's workshop takes over the leading position until his death in 1563. His most famous production is the *Man with the Geese* fountain in Nuremberg. It is also typical of the period, with attention given to the naturalistic rendering of genre figures, especially peasants, and not even an echo of the interest in Antiquity portrayed by the Vischer school. Small bronzes identical with and closely related to the "Gooseman" have survived in numbers. At much the same time as Labenwolf's naturalism we also find Wenzel Jamnitzer, active mainly as a goldsmith, working wholeheartedly in the elegant style of the Italian mannerists for aristocratic and wealthy families.

During the seventeenth century, while Italy, in the field of small bronzes, does little more than continue to exploit her late sixteenth-century traditions, France takes over the leadership. Since the direct influence of Italian art at the time of Francis I and the school of Fontainebleau, French art had been closely connected with the royal Court and the servant of the lavish tastes of succeeding monarchs, culminating in the "Grand Siècle" of Louis XIV (1638–1715). The small, intimate bronze had no place in their tremendous decorative schemes. Only one or two functions remained for original work on a comparatively small scale, such as the magnificent fire-dogs needed for the decoration of fireplaces. A pair crowned by the figures of Jupiter and Juno, cast by M. Anguier, after his master A. Algardi, are in the Wallace Collection. The style of such work did not accept the full religious fervour of the Baroque, but retained a more disciplined and colder classicism favoured at the Court of Louis XIV. There also survive a large number of bronzes representing small workshop copies of major works by leading sculptors of the period: for

example, the equestrian statue of Louis XIV by F. Girardon or the *Chevaux de Marly* by G. Couston.

In the eighteenth century the light-hearted quality and feminine elegance that is characteristic of Rococo art under Louis XV and Louis XVI resulted in a new fashion for the small intimate decorations which were to be found in every well-to-do home. The small porcelain figurines of the eighteenth century are another aspect of this revival of intimate decoration, and small bronzes are often closely related to the productions of the Sèvres factory. In some cases we can see in these bronzes the models made for the porcelain factory. One such piece is L. S. Boizot's group of Pluto carrying off Proserpine, in the Wallace Collection. In the utilitarian field fine bronze candelabra, usually with elegant figures supporting bronze-gilt candle-holders of foliate form, and the fine bronze-gilt decorative mounts applied to furniture, are typical of the period. One sculptor, J. J. Caffieri, a member of the family famed for the production of the latter, has left us a signed and dated group of *Cupid Vanquishing Pan* (Wallace Collection), showing the playful and delicate style of the Rococo.

First signs of the renewed classicism characteristic of the period during and after the French Revolution appear shortly before that event, but the new style was consciously developed first by the bourgeois republicanism of the revolutionary period and later under the new Empire. Characteristic bronzes were produced by A. Canova, the first sculptor to aim at the revival of the purer Greek values rather than those of Rome, and by Claude Michel, called Clodion, who designed decorative accessories as well as producing major sculpture, both before the Revolution, in a vivid and sensuous style, and after the Revolution, adapting himself to the new taste, in the severe style of the Greek revival.

ANTIQUE STATUARY AND WAX-MODELLING

ANTIQUE STATUARY

Sculpture, in some form or other, goes back to the very beginnings of history: and there is

practically no civilization which has not attempted to carve, model, or cast in some material or other – whether it be marble, stone, clay, ivory, wax, wood, or bronze – the representation of the human form. Such attempts range from the crude clay figures of the early Cypriote Bronze Age to the superb art of Praxitiles, and from the wooden carvings of the untrained Bantu to the works of Henry Moore.

Sculpture in all its forms, save for modern works, is neither difficult nor expensive to collect, and a bust by Nollekens which, a hundred and fifty years ago, cost the sitter one hundred guineas can today, with luck, be purchased for as many shillings, while wax portraits and bronze busts are equally reasonable. The collector of sculpture will find he has advantages over his friends who search for the more popular forms of art, since he is far more likely to discover a bargain.

Fortunately, the majority of British sculptors signed their names on the back or side of a bust, and it is therefore easy to discover the name of the artist. Bronze and wax busts in the round (the best of which date from 1790 to 1840) are frequently signed on the back, and the majority have the words "Published by", showing that a number of copies of this work were made.

Foreign portrait busts of any merit, especially eighteenth-century French ones, are not often to be discovered in England. On the other hand, busts by nineteenth-century Italian artists are only too frequent. Most of them are either copies of classical works or imaginary portraits mass produced by firms in Pisa, Florence, or Rome.

In England during the last half of the eighteenth century a number of firms produced plaster copies, usually coloured black, of busts of famous writers, statesmen, soldiers, etc., or copies of Greek and Roman poets, emperors, etc. They were intended to stand on top of bookcases in country-house libraries, and were usually sold in sets, the "moderns" consisting of Pope, Locke, Inigo Jones, Newton, etc., while the "antique" set contained busts of Homer, Virgil, Horace, Socrates, etc. When these busts went out of fashion at the beginning of the Victorian age, a number of sculptors modelled for various firms, such as Copeland and Minton, busts and figures made in white china or "Parian", which is the finest type of biscuit china made. It differs only from porcelain in the use of a more fusible felspar instead of Cornish stone, and Parian figures of Wellington, Nelson, Queen Victoria, Wilberforce, and others are not infrequent.

It is not perhaps generally realized that all eighteenth-century sculptors, and most early nineteenth-century ones, produced, in addition to likenesses of their living clients, an even larger number of posthumous portraits. Indeed, the largest part of their business was carving commemorative busts or monuments to be placed in churches, the former being either based on portraits or death-masks. Nollekens' best-known bust, that of the younger Pitt, of which he carved nearly a hundred replicas, was made from a death-mask, which the sculptor waited outside the dying statesman's house to take. The student of English sculpture will be well advised not only to study the collections in public galleries and museums but also to visit Westminster Abbey (and provincial cathedrals and parish churches), if he wishes to understand and learn about this art. Nor should it be forgotten that no church is too obscure to visit in the hope of discovering an unrecorded bust. It is only by studying the signed and documented works of the great sculptors that the collector will be able to recognize the unsigned ones by the same artists. At the same time it must be remembered that some of the most popular busts were frequently reproduced by minor sculptors and copyists. Sir Francis Chantrey produced only three versions of his famous bust of Sir Walter Scott, yet there are a large number of copies of this work in both private and public collections, nearly all of them, however ill carved, masquerading as Chantrey's work.

WAX-MODELLING

Beeswax is possessed of properties which make it the most convenient medium for making portraits either by modelling or by casting in moulds, for it melts easily, mixes with any colouring matter, and can be tinted. Figures of wax were used by the Ancient Egyptians at their funerals, while wax dolls were known to the Hellenistic world, and waxen masks in Ancient Rome.

Wax-modelling can be traced from the Middle Ages, when it was chiefly in use for votive offerings to churches, though it first became of artistic importance in the Italy of the Renaissance. Owing to the fragility and rarity, few wax portraits earlier than the eighteenth century have survived. Indeed, it was well after 1700 that the art reached its greatest popularity, both in England and on the Continent.

Wax portraits are not infrequently signed, often on the truncation, and it is sometimes possible also to find the artist's trade card in the back of the frame.

Like almost everything else one can collect, wax portraits have been copied, while those which represent famous persons, such as Nelson, Washington, Wellington, and others, have been at one time or another mass-produced in large numbers. But most of these works are so coarse and clumsy that the beginner-collector will soon learn to recognize and spurn them. If he is starting to acquire wax portraits he would be well advised to study the large series of documented portraits in the Victoria and Albert Museum. Luckily for such a collector, wax portraits and busts are not in very great demand. This is curious, for they are small and decorative and grace almost any room.

ENGLISH GARDEN STATUARY

Chaste sphinxes, monitory gods and goddesses, over-indulged putti, coy country maidens, and leering satyrs, all delicately mossed and lichened, people our more formal parks and gardens, where, like foreign trees, they have been naturalized to the English soil and climate. Pedestalled beneath dripping beeches or niched in obscure yew hedges, the "Apollo Belvedere" and the "Venus de Medici" guard the northern arcadia of which they form so important and so delightful a part. Never so numerous as in Italy, they look perhaps a little lonely, for, as Hugh May told Pepys, "a little mixture of statues and pots which may be handsome" is sufficient to ornament a garden. Too dense a population can only give an impression of vulgarity.

The phrase "garden statuary" is inclined to give an impression of a minor art, practised by masons rather than sculptors. It should, however, be remembered that much sculpture of the highest order was intended to grace the garden. In England, as well as in France, Italy, and Germany, the best sculptors of the day were commissioned for such works. Bernini's *Neptune*, in the Victoria and Albert Museum, and Giovanni Bologna's *Samson and the Philistine*, in the same collection, were both designed as the centre-pieces of fountains for private gardens. It was for Fontainebleau that Benvenuto Cellini designed his *Colossus*, and Giovanni Bologna erected his giant *Appenino* in the garden of the Villa Pratolino. Versailles is peopled with figures by Pierre Le Gros, Girardon, G. B. Foggini, and Bernini; the walks of Vietshöchheim are lined by the grotesques of Ferdinand Dietz. Here we are concerned mainly with Britain, where garden sculpture was never as important and rarely as fantastic as it was abroad. "A little mixture of statues and pots" has generally been preferred.

ENGLISH GARDEN SCULPTURE

Garden statuary first became popular in England in the sixteenth century. When Henry VIII took over Hampton Court in 1526 he set about the transformation of the royal privy garden, for which he ordered thirty-eight stone statues of kings and queens, a quantity of dragons, lions, greyhounds, harts, and unicorns, sixteen of the "King's Beasts" and sixteen sundials – all to be crowded into an area of a few acres. The fashion for this form of statuary in wood and stone appears to have been current throughout the century and to have diminished only with the introduction of a more classical taste in the Stuart period. Nicholas Stone the elder supplied statues of Cupid, Venus, Ceres, Hercules, and Mercury for the Paston family in 1632. But it was not until after the Restoration that the great age of the formal garden, and consequently of garden sculpture, dawned. A neat geometrical lay-out intersected with balustrades provided excellent opportunities for the placing of statues, sun-dials, urns, and fountains. As the century drew to its close, these enclosures were superseded by the landscaped parks modelled on Le Nôtre's Versailles, and great urns were often used to terminate the vistas hacked through the woods. Figures were placed on the parterre, and sometimes introduced to give interest to a general scheme. Elaborate fountains, like that at Blenheim (a small copy of Bernini's *Fontana Navona*), were erected by those rich enough to afford them. As at Versailles, figures and urns were occasionally gilded, but this distasteful ballroom fashion seems to have declined in the late 1720s, for William Kent, and others, had "leaped over the fence and saw that all nature was a garden". Kent did not eschew the use of statues, terms, and pots, which he used sparsely but effectively, circling the neat exedrae and standing in the glades. But their popularity diminished as "Capability" Brown transformed the parkland of England, and sculptors who had specialized in supplying lead figures for gardens fell upon hard times in the 1760s. There was, indeed, little room for statuary on Brown's shaven lawns, though figures were still needed to stand in the niches of temples and to flank the doorway to the house. Heraldic beasts, carved in stone or cast in lead, held their appropriate place on the park gates, where they were often joined by the more fashionable sphinxes. When the parterre was politely grassed over lead Fames and deities seem to have been banished to the "wilderness". The invention of Coade stone in 1769 brought statues within the reach of modest purses, and they must frequently have found a place in smaller gardens, even if they were little used in the grander lay-outs (Plate 450D). Humphrey Repton seems to have had still less room for them than Brown, but they returned to popularity with the revival of the formal garden in the nineteenth century.

MATERIALS

Various materials have been used for garden sculpture, stone being most popular as the cheapest of the more durable substances. Wood was used in the sixteenth century and probably in succeeding ages, but naturally no complete statues have survived. Figures in marble appear to have been imported more frequently than carved in England. Marble was, of course, an expensive substance and weathers badly in the British climate. The most durable of metals, bronze, was also costly. Richard Osborne (*fl.* 1691–1715) made bronze statues, and so did Grinling Gibbons; others, such as the figures Massimiliano Soldani supplied for Blenheim, were imported.

Lead is one of the most satisfactory substances for garden statuary, although it limits the sculptor by its weight and is not capable of fine effects. It was greatly favoured, especially in the early eighteenth century, on account of its comparative cheapness and immunity to weather – it is actually improved by patination. Most of the best English garden statues and urns have been made of it. In the 1760s, however, it was falling into disrepute, and William Shenstone pleaded for its use in his *Unconnected Thoughts on Gardening*. It was revived in the last century when copies of many late seventeenth- and early eighteenth-century statues and pots were put on the market – some carefully patinated. The invention of Coade stone, a moulded artificial stone impervious to frost but capable of delicate effects, caused a minor revolution in garden sculpture. The Coade factory at Lambeth could supply anything from an Ionic capital (ten shillings) or a frieze of griffins (fifteen shillings a foot) to "A River God 9 feet high, with an urn through which a stream of water may be carried" (one hundred guineas). Many prominent sculptors were commissioned to design objects in Coade stone, which were produced both individually and in stock patterns. Its fashion lasted until the 1840s, when its place was taken by cheaper and generally less attractive substances.

STATUES
Copies after the antique

Of all the types of figure used for the decoration of British gardens, copies of the well-known Roman and, as was believed, Greek statues in Italy were most favoured, especially in the eighteenth century.

The Venus de Medici, the clapping Faun, the fighting Gladiator, and the dying Gaul were frequently cast in lead or carved in stone for English parks. Such figures were probably copied from plaster casts made in Italy, and some were faithful, if somewhat heavy-handed, versions of the originals. Modifications were occasionally made for convenience or, towards the end of the century, for the sake of modesty; and some figures are derivations from rather than copies after the antique. The category of figures derived from the antique also includes terms – armless busts on pedestals tapering towards the base – which enjoyed a great vogue in the first half of the eighteenth century.

Copies after modern statues

The sculptor whose works were most frequently copied for eighteenth-century gardens was Giovanni Bologna, the Fleming who worked in Italy from about 1545 until his death in 1608. It may seem strange that a mannerist artist should enjoy so much favour at this time; but he stood supreme among modern sculptors, and the patron who lived in a house based on a design of Palladio and whose gallery was filled with copies of pictures by the Italian painters of the sixteenth and seventeenth centuries would naturally wish to have copies of figures by Giovanni Bologna in his garden. His most popular figure was the Mercury at Florence, which, despite the unsuitability of so heavy a metal for the graceful tip-toe poise, was often cast in lead, subsequently acquiring a drunken stagger. His famous groups of the *Rape of the Sabines* (at Florence) and *Samson and the Philistine* (formerly at Hovingham and now in the Victoria and Albert Museum) were also popular; there is a copy of the former at Painshill and of the latter at Harrowden. Another Flemish sculptor who worked in Italy and was copied in England was François Duquesnoy, called Il Fiammingo. John van Nost adapted his works on occasion, and was paid ten guineas in 1706 for "two boys after Flamingo modelled apurpose and cast in a hard metall". The only other foreign sculptor who appears to have been fashionable in eighteenth-century England was François

Girardon (1628–1715), who was responsible for much of the statuary in the gardens of Versailles; copies of his figures of *Winter* and *The Rape of Proserpine* by John Cheere are now at Southill. In the early nineteenth century the vogue for Antonio Canova produced a number of his coy Graces, in marble and Coade stone.

Original works

Statues of notable people were occasionally set up in gardens, either designed expressly for that purpose or copied from public monuments. There are lead figures of Prince Eugene and the Duke of Marlborough at Glenham Hall, and at Wrest Park there is a fine statue of William III which bears a suspicious likeness to Grinling Gibbons' bronze of James II. At Hartwell, in Buckinghamshire, there is an equestrian statue of Frederick Prince of Wales also in lead. Lord Burlington commissioned a small population of statues for the gardens of his elegant villa at Chiswick in Middlesex, where a semicircle of sombre Romans stands in the exedra, and Rysbrack's Palladio and Inigo Jones appropriately guard the portal. Busts of Roman and British worthies mounted on pillars also decorated the classical landscaped garden.

Gods, goddesses, and personifications in the classical taste were made for gardens throughout the eighteenth century. Peter Scheemakers (1691–1781) executed groups of Cain and Abel, Apollo with a Muse, and a Satyr for the grounds of Chiswick House. A lead group of Perseus and Andromeda by John van Nost is at Melbourne, Derbyshire; a live lead Pan is at Glemham; and there are personifications of the arts at Hardwick Hall, Derbyshire. In the grotto at Stourhill, Dorset, there is a large River God by Scheemakers. *Amorini* or winged putti were also much in demand, the finest being those made for Melbourne, Derbyshire, by John van Nost, some cavorting in pairs and others single – the most endearing shows an inquisitive child who has disturbed a hornets' nest and is suffering the consequences. Other amorini made by Nost or his successor, John Cheere, are at Wilton, Wiltshire, and a good set from Stowe,

Buckinghamshire, was, until recently, in the possession of Messrs Crowther (Plate 450A).

Blackamoors appear to have been popular throughout the first half of the century, not only as sundials but also as independent ornaments. At Melbourne, Derbyshire, that *locus classicus* for the study of garden sculpture, there is a fine early-eighteenth-century pair of kneeling figures, one a blackamoor, the other an Indian, each supporting rather perilously upon his head a tray that carries a small urn. Shepherds and shepherdesses, which were popular after the turn of the eighteenth century, were a speciality of John Cheere, who had taken over Van Nost's yard and effects in about 1739. Normally of lead, they were occasionally painted and are not lacking in rustic elegance (Plate 450B, C).

Animals

Animals and birds in lead and stone were not infrequently made for the garden in the eighteenth century. Naturally enough, the Roman boar in the Uffizi was popular, and its progeny are occasionally to be seen in English glades. Dogs and lions were often made, but a lead cow, reproduced by Weaver, must be numbered among the rarities. Throughout the century heraldic beasts held

lions, and lionesses for Castle Hill in Devonshire, and he was also responsible for the sphinxes placed on the bridge at Blenheim in 1773. There are many statues of dogs – some derived from the famous dog of Alcibiades at Duncombe Park, Yorkshire – but none is more charming than the Coade-stone memorial to Jock, a favourite spaniel, made for Southill in 1806 to the design of George Garrard (1760–1826).

Sundials

Sundials have held their popularity as garden ornaments from the sixteenth century to the present day. Most are of a fairly simple baluster shape, but more elaborate patterns have occasionally been used. Heraldic beasts were sometimes made to support the dial – a very fine seventeenth-century example at Glamis Castle, Angus, has four rampant lions each holding a dial in its paws. A sundial in the form of a lead *amorino* who holds the dial above his head was made in the eighteenth century and extensively copied in recent times.

Urns and vases

According to William Shenstone, the owner of Leasowes, poet, theorist, and practitioner

FIG. 1. Mid-eighteenth-century lead Sphinx

their popularity for the decoration of gates – two of the best being the large wyverns made for the entrance to Glynde Place, Sussex, by John Cheere in 1759, for £48 5*s*. The sphinx appears to have been brought to wide popularity by the neo-classical revival, and it held its place at the gate, the entrance to the house, and on the balustrade of the bridge until the Victorian era. Cheere supplied sphinxes,

FIG. 2. Early eighteenth-century lead urn

FIG. 3. Late eighteenth-century urn

of the eighteenth-century picturesque garden, "urns are more solemn if large and plain; more beautiful if less and ornamented. Solemnity is perhaps their point, and the situation of them should still co-operate with it". They have, indeed, been the most popular of all items of garden statuary, and some are among the very finest. In the formal garden they stood at the focal-points of the lay-out; in the early landscaped gardens they were placed at the heads of vistas to act as eye-catchers; in the picturesque garden they found a place beneath the trees, and were often engraved with lines calculated to summon up the sweet tear of Sensibility. Among the best are the magnificent specimens carved in marble by Caius Gabriel Cibber (1630–1700) and Edward Pearce (*fl.* 1658–95) between 1690 and 1700 for the gardens of Hampton Court.

FIG. 4. Early eighteenth-century lead vase

These vast works, seemingly based on French designs, were enriched with carvings of classical subjects around their bodies, and cost more than £400 apiece; they are now at Windsor Castle. Scarcely less fine is John van Nost's richly ornamented lead urn supported on four monkeys and crowned with a fantastic bouquet of flowers at Melbourne; a similar one with a fox sitting on the top was until recently in the possession of Messrs Crowther. Less grandiose urns made in the early eighteenth century often have a fluted base and cover, a plain body, and are topped with a flame-like motif. Globe-shaped urns enriched with swags of heavy fruits and flowers were also popular at this time. With the change in taste in the middle of the century, simpler patterns became the rule, and in the last

three decades the Adamesque type predominated (Fig. 3). In the later part of the century urns were used for the decoration of the balustrades by the house or raised on columns in the park, to commemorate a person or a pet.

Seventeenth-century vases or pots were often in the shape of baroque urns without covers, and were generally provided with two handles of human or animal shape. Lead was much used for making these vessels, which vary in height from 1 to 3 feet. In the eighteenth century their decoration varied with the taste of the time, and after the 1760s they were frequently modelled on Greek and Roman vases. Some are, indeed, copies of classical vessels; the famous Vasa Medicea in the Uffizi and the great Warwick Vase were particularly popular as models, and are to be found in lead and stone as well as marble. Vases and urns were also made in Coade stone and, in the nineteenth century, in various types of hard earthenware.

Cisterns

Rain-water cisterns made of lead and decorated in low relief survive in not inconsiderable numbers from the seventeenth and eighteenth centuries. Generally the work of provincial craftsmen, their decoration is often

FIG. 5. Mid-eighteenth-century lead vase

a little behind the times. The surface was usually divided into sections, each of which contained an heraldic device, initial, or monogram; many are dated. Occasionally they were decorated with bunches of fruit and flowers or personifications of the seasons. A particularly fine example of 1750 is in the courtyard of Sackville College, East Grinstead; its relief panels are identical with those on one of 1725 in the possession of Bert Crowther Ltd.

TERRACOTTA

Terracotta statuettes are to be numbered among the most beautiful and fascinating works of sculpture on a small scale. The medium itself is of peculiar delicacy, and when handled by an artist sensitive to the charms of *matière* can provide an astonishing variety of both colour and texture. Colour ranges from a soft powdery grey, slightly flushed with pink, to a raw and earthy red; while the texture may be as smooth and brittle as Sèvres biscuit or as soft and malleable as the wet clay itself, so the imprint of the artist's hand remains as fresh as in a Tiepolo sketch. Most of the great European sculptors used terracotta for the *maquettes* or *bozzetti*, and these possess the same appeal as the drawings of great painters. As manifestations of an artistic personality at work the terracotta *bozzetti* of Bernini or Canova are as revealing as the rapid pen drawings of Rembrandt or Guardi. There is, however, another class of terracotta sculpture – the small groups and figures produced mainly during the eighteenth century by such artists as Clodion. These were intended as independent works of art, and the finest of them attain an elegance and refinement which is naturally lacking in the *bozzetti* even of the greatest sculptors. Like old master drawings, therefore, terracottas may be divided into two distinct categories: those modelled by the sculptor as sketches for works to be executed in other less malleable mediums – usually marble or bronze – and those intended as fully realized works of art.

Terracotta figures are modelled from wet clay which may be found in most parts of Europe but which differs in colour and fineness of texture from region to region. Before it is moulded the clay is prepared and freed from impurities. The figures are usually modelled by hand and retouched with a variety of blunt, rounded, or sharp-pointed instruments. Once the sculptor has finished the work of modelling, the figures are allowed to dry and are then baked in a kiln. Afterwards they may be left in their natural state or painted and gilded or covered with enamel. The enamelling process was much practised by the Della Robbia family of sculptors at Florence in the fifteenth and sixteenth centuries, but works treated in this way are more properly to be considered under the heading of ceramics.

Renaissance terracottas

In classical Greece terracotta seems to have been used mainly for the fabrication of small cult images, toys, and ornaments. The Etruscans used it for the same purposes and also for the construction of cinerary urns. In ancient Rome terracotta was used for ornamental figures, some of which were of considerable size, like those found at Pompeii. Classical sculptors may, perhaps, have used terracotta models to assist them in their works in marble and bronze, but none is known to have survived.

After the fall of the Roman Empire the artistic use of terracotta seems to have been abandoned until the later Middle Ages, when it was employed primarily for architectural decorations rather than for independent sculptures. Only with the advent of the Renaissance was this medium at all widely used by sculptors, and thereafter it has been constantly employed. The finest and most interesting of fifteenth-century terracottas are, without doubt, those produced at Florence, where nearly every prominent sculptor worked on occasion in this medium, while many anonymous modellers appear to have been engaged in reproducing the marble reliefs of such artists as Rosselino and Donatello in this cheaper substance (a workshop which seems to have turned out a large number of devotional reliefs was that now associated with the name of the shadowy Michele da Firenze).

The reliefs, usually of a Madonna and Child, enjoyed a particularly wide popularity and were used for the decoration of churches, private chapels, and, sometimes, the exteriors of houses. They seem usually to have been painted, though few now retain more than fragmentary traces of their original pigmentation. Good examples of such works may be found in the Museo Nazionale at Florence, the Victoria and Albert Museum, and the Kaiser Friedrich Museum, Berlin. Similar reliefs were made of painted stucco, which has so nearly the appearance of painted terracotta that it may well be treated under the same heading.

In the later fifteenth century terracotta was also used for portrait busts, some of which are among the finest ever modelled. Two in the Museo Nazionale at Florence – a young man in armour usually ascribed to Verrochio and a widow variously attributed to Donatello, Vecchietta, and Antonio Pollaiuolo – indicate the liveliness, realism, and subtlety which a master can obtain in this medium. Indeed, they demonstrate the full potentialities of terracotta as a medium for sculpture on the scale of life. Outside Florence, at Siena, Jacopo della Quercia made occasional use of terracotta for statues of saints. At Naples Guido Mazzoni also made use of clay for figures on a large scale, the most notable being the magnificent and disturbingly life-like *Deposition* group in the church of Monte Oliveto. Slightly later Antonio Begarelli (1479–1565) modelled the powerful dramatic groups in terracotta which are among the principal treasures of the churches of Modena and Bologna.

High-Renaissance sculptors seem to have regarded terracotta as a means to an end rather than as a suitable medium in which to create the works which they hoped would rival the statues of antiquity. Michelangelo, to quote the most celebrated instance, made use of terracotta, as well as terrasecca and other mediums, such as wax, to sketch out his first thoughts for his grandiose marbles. He also made, or had made in his studio, large-scale models in terracotta. Examples of his sketches are in the Casa Buonarotti, Florence, and the Victoria and Albert Museum, but the only large-scale *modello* known to have survived is the reclining male figure in the Accademia at Florence. At an intermediary stage in the creation of his monumental marbles Michelangelo also produced highly finished terracotta models on a small scale, and these seem to have been in demand among collectors during the artist's lifetime. It is significant that when his pupil Antonio Mini went to France in 1531 he took with him a case of such works to sell to the *virtuosi*, thus defraying the cost of his journey. These models were widely copied in various mediums, and many found their way into artists' studios, where they supplemented the usual range of casts after the antique. Moreover, although Michelangelo ordered the destruction of all the sketches for sculpture and paintings in his house, shortly before his death, a number survived the holocaust and found their way into the collections of those who treasured the least performances of so great a master. There is no evidence that Michelangelo considered any of his works in terracotta as finished works of art. His example was followed by nearly all the major sculptors of Europe (e.g. Giovanni Bologna).

In the sixteenth century the self-conscious distinction between the major and the minor artists becomes clear for the first time in the history of European art. The major sculptors felt that bronze or marble were the only fitting substances for their grand conceptions and looked down on terracotta as a medium suitable only for *bozzetti*. Humbler artists devoted themselves wholly to this medium, however, especially in the production of devotional figures for the less wealthy churches. These inspired artisans had no apparent desire to rival the marbles of their greater contemporaries, but aimed at producing a life-like effect in their finished works, which were coloured and sometimes adorned with real hair and beards. The best examples of this type of terracotta are to be found in the *Sacri Monti* of northern Italy, where between the mid-sixteenth and the late eighteenth centuries, chapels were filled with large groups of realistically modelled and painted terracotta figures enacting scenes from the Bible and the lives of the Saints.

Baroque terracottas

In the seventeenth century sculptors seem to have made a greater use of terracotta *bozzetti* than ever before, and a large number dating from this period has survived. To enumerate the names of the sculptors whose terracotta sketches are known would, however, serve little purpose. It is hardly surprising that the most notable was also the greatest sculptor of the period – Gian Lorenzo Bernini. He appears to have found in the wet clay an ideal medium for the first realization of his incomparable marbles. Several of them have indeed a greater interest than the finished works, for while the terracottas were the production of the master's own hand and brain working in rapid harmony, the finished marbles were frequently executed in great part by studio assistants working under his direction. This same quality distinguishes the terracottas of many later sculptors, some of whom are said never to have set hand to chisel once their reputations were secure, but to have relied entirely on their studios to carve and finish the marble.

Baroque *bozzetti* naturally vary in style according to the countries in which they were created, and express the individual mannerisms of their modellers. Generally speaking, Italian examples have a lightly touched and hastily worked character, typical of the national genius for improvisation. South German sculptors were strongly influenced by the Italians, but contrived to give to their terracottas a sense of greater solidity. French terracotta *maquettes*, on the other hand, often show the classicizing influence of Poussin's paintings and generally appear to have been more carefully and thoughtfully finished. In the Netherlands Rubens exerted as strong an influence on the modellers of terracottas as on artists in other mediums. And here, moreover, *bozzetti* seem to have been collected for their own sakes – and not merely as mementoes of great sculptors – from the seventeenth century onwards. Many a Dutch studio interior of this period includes a number of terracotta or plaster figures. It is interesting to note that before the end of the seventeenth century Walter Pompe was doing a brisk trade in terracottas which have the sketchy quality of the *bozzetto* but which were in fact made expressly for sale as independent works of art.

Eighteenth-century terracottas

In the eighteenth century the new fashion for living in smaller rooms and reserving the grandiose apartments solely for special occasions created a demand for smaller and more exquisite works of art. The *sculpture d'appartement* created for these rooms included small works in marble, bronze, and especially terracotta. Clodion was perhaps the sculptor who most notably produced terracottas of this type, but he had a number of imitators. Other, anonymous, artists produced small terracotta replicas of antique and modern statues. Occasionally these copies of seventeenth-century statues have been mistaken for *bozzetti*, though they possess little of the distinction of the original works. In England little modern sculpture apart from portrait busts and statues was appreciated during the eighteenth century. There was, however, a vogue for terracotta replicas of Rysbrack's and Roubiliac's portraits of notabilities, and these were among the furnishings of many a gentleman's library. Some were, probably, executed by the artists themselves (not necessarily as preliminary sketches), but the majority were the work of assistants or imitators.

The terracottas of the eighteenth century are among the finest and most fascinating of all, for during this period the full beauty of the substance itself came to be appreciated for the first time. The French works of this period are perhaps the most exquisite, as they are certainly the most eagerly sought by collectors. Yet the reader's attention is also directed to the Italian sculptors, many of whom executed admirable work in this medium and are still too little known.

Fakes

A word of warning should, perhaps, be added on the subject of fakes and imitations. Terracottas have been the object of many collectors' ambitions for several centuries and consequently have often been faked, especially in the nineteenth and present centuries. Hellenistic figures of the type usually known as Tanagra have suffered most, but Renaissance and baroque *bozzetti* have also been fabricated in considerable quantities. Clodion, who is probably the greatest of French eighteenth-century terracotta modellers, has been most skilfully imitated. Close comparison of suspect statuettes with known originals will, however, reveal the inadequacy of the bogus article. A different problem is posed by the eighteenth-century reproductions of seventeenth-century and earlier statues to which reference has been made above, but the dead hand of the copyist is generally apparent and easily recognized.

Carving

ALABASTER CARVING IN BRITAIN

Speaking chemically, alabaster, commonly called gypsum, is only sulphate of lime which, crushed and calcined, makes admirable plaster.

In England alabaster was first used decoratively[1] round about A.D. 1160 on the west door of Tutbury's Norman parish church in Staffordshire. The parish church of Hanbury in the same county provides the earliest datable example of alabaster figure[2] carving: namely, the tomb-figure of a knight of c. 1280–1300. The alabaster used was quarried at Chellaston, Derbyshire, and at Tutbury, Staffordshire.

From the former site alabaster, both worked and unworked, was sent abroad[3] and to other parts of England – London,[4] for example. The affinity between tomb-carvers and these medieval workers of alabaster images, altar-pieces, and residual plaques is very marked.

It is quite possible the altar-piece and plaque carvers sprang from the carvers of "tomb-weepers", clearly inferior craftsmen to the effigy-carvers, whose apprentices they could have been.

In any event, the carvers of plaques and altar-pieces were originally attracted by the semi-translucent, creamy whiteness of this English alabaster, and the aesthetic appeal of the vellum page bedight with gold, red, blue, and green accented by the packed "black letter", quill-pen, Gothic writing of the period under review – c. 1340 to the Reformation.

During this fourteenth century, even when the influence of French ivories (Plate 453c) seems to be felt, the sculptor is always aware that his medium is stone and respects it. Nevertheless, by the mid-fifteenth century this approach is being rapidly superseded by much blunter carving (Plate 453B) and, as far as "the images" are concerned, all-over colouring, thus producing an effect very similar to that of the great Flemish and German polychromed and gilded altar-pieces of carved wood, their contemporaries.

Alabaster – Clientele and Transport

(a) **The Home Market.** The material sold was composed of "images" (Plate 453A, B, C), individual plaques in painted wooden shrines, and, by the late fourteenth century, altar-pieces, at which point in time the foreign trade rapidly increased. Nevertheless, the only properly documented home commission is Edward III's[5] to Peter the Mason of Nottingham for an altar-piece of the life of St George for St George's Chapel, Windsor. This no longer exists.

Records of two important commissions from Durham and Ripon[6] and the Suppression Inventory of the London Charterhouse (1538–9) show that, at one time or another, these monasteries had acquired both alabaster "images" and altar-pieces. Wills, bequests, and individual church inventories also show the consumption level of these objects, and considerably justify calling this craft a

Nottingham one, despite production at York, Burton-on-Trent, and Leicester. On this last point the existing vagueness is considerably the outcome of referring in legal[7] documents to any and everybody involved in this craft, from the actual alabaster carver to the mere travelling salesman, as an "alablasterer".

Today there are only five altar-pieces in England – three in the Victoria and Albert Museum and two[8] in private collections.

(b) **The Foreign Market.** Foreign trade is better documented. First there is Richard II's permit of 1382 to Cosmato Gentilis – Pope Urban II's agent for collecting Peter's pence – to take out of England an "image of the Virgin, St Peter,[10] St Paul and a small Trinity". This was via Southampton.

Then there is the famous altar-piece of 1456 which was given to the Cathedral of St James at Compostella[11] by a priest named John Goodyear, Rector of Chale, Isle of Wight. There are also references to alabaster "images" in the medieval import tax returns of Iceland. There is also one mid-fifteenth-century five-plaque altar-piece in that country.

The further extent of this foreign trade may be measured by there being at least fourteen complete altar-pieces in France, three in Italy, two in Denmark, and one in Holland and Germany, not to mention many detached and widely dispersed plaques contributing to the approximately estimated total of 4,000.

Since single-figure carvings have not as yet been definitively collated, it will here suffice to refer the reader, by way of a reminder of their existence, to the Boston *Trinity* (Plate 453A) found in Spain and *St Anne instructing the Virgin* (Plate 453B) found in Portugal in 1934, and the Flawford *Madonna and Child* (Plate 453C).

In short, it was no mean trade which extended from Iceland to Italy and from Portugal to, perhaps, as far to the east as Russia.

In France the distribution centre seems to have been Bordeaux and the main transport route the River Garonne. Germany and the Netherlands were doubtless contacted through the Kentish ports and over the trade routes of the Hanseatic League. Trade with Scandi-navia, many of whose medieval bishops were English, was apparently conducted through Yorkshire ports.[12]

Dating of images, plaques and altar-pieces

Unless these are documented the dating is perforce deductive, partly stylistic, and in any event tentative. It is rarely that an accurate rendering of costume – as in the *St Anne instructing the Virgin*[13] (Plate 453B) – solves one's dating problems.

The First period, c. 1340–80. To it belongs such superb carvings as the Boston *Trinity*[14] (Plate 453A) and *The Madonna and Child* (Plate 453C), found in 1779 at Flawford, near Nottingham.

Both give the impression of serene happiness, smiling through that complete sculptural integrity destined to disintegrate during the fifteenth century. In this period individual plaques of various shapes were also made – apparently horizontals more often than uprights. Their carving is in low relief with an "edging" having the appearance of a frame. Such plaques have also been found pierced and with latten[15] attachments for hanging. It is therefore reasonable to assume that such work was inspired by private devotion.

Aesthetically, the fourteenth century is the best period, the easiest to identify, the most rare and, consequently, the most costly to acquire.

Second Period, c. 1380–1420. In it plaques become permanently upright, with average size $17\frac{1}{2}$ inches high by $10\frac{1}{2}$ inches wide, and, when not the central plaque from an altar-piece, often much larger. Further, the "picture-frame" edging is replaced by a thin edge, which is sometimes bevelled. This facilitated the placing of these plaques side by side in a painted and gilded wooden framework. Add a saint at each end, and phase one of the altar-piece has been evolved, probably around 1400. This was also stage two in building up a foreign market, the "images" being most probably the first objects to be sold abroad in any quantity.

Low relief is now replaced by shallow carving rather than deep, and the plaques or "tables" now have gilded backgrounds diapered with studs and "embattled" tops. Finally, towards 1420 five of these plaques are now assembled with an extra large one in the middle: stage two in the evolution of the altarpiece.

Third Period, c. 1420–60. In this period the altar-pieces are more and more characterized by uprights dividing the panels, the former rapidly becoming ornately decorated with small saints standing under canopied niches.

Hitherto the subject-matter has been mainly "Scenes from the Passion" and from "The Life of Our Lady". Now lives of the saints are added, those of St Thomas à Becket and the very apocryphal St George being the most popular. Finally, shallow carving is replaced by very deep cutting; large "floppy-hat" haloes become fashionable, together with much painting of flowers, sprigs and general decoration on dresses and furniture.

Last Period, c. 1460–80. This period could just as well be called "from 1460 to the Reformation". It is a period of rapidly degenerating craftsmanship, over-crowded compositions, general bad taste and, even, total iconographical confusion. The only triumph is the "two-row" altar-piece, such as the superb example now in the Musée Vivinelle at Compiègne and, until the French Revolution, in the Church of St Germain l'Auxerrois, Paris.

Iconography

It should be remembered that during the Middle Ages some 90 per cent of mankind was totally illiterate, theocentric and acquiring its information from word of mouth when not from works of art. In addition, some of their religious beliefs were acquired both from, and expressed through, a dramatically presented liturgy.

It was, therefore, virtually inevitable that Mystery[16] and Morality plays, at the height of their influence in England by about 1450, should have contributed so much, though not everything, to the iconography of these particular medieval craftsmen. For example, the Crucified Christ on the stem of a lily is purely English symbolism. But its source – some hymn now lost? On the other hand, the three-flowered lily consistently rendered in "Annunciations", is a clear allusion to Christ as a Person of the Trinity. Such an adequate symbol as this must surely have grown from direct clerical inspiration.

Two alabaster carvings of the *Coronation of the Virgin* show two other methods of symbolizing the Blessed Trinity. The Nyköping Museum "Coronation" has a dove above the Madonna's head, and to the left Christ, nimbed, wearing only the crown of thorns, whereas God the Father to the right has a golden crown. In the very lyrical "Coronation" (Plate 454), owned by Mrs Anthony Norman, all three persons are identically crowned, though God the Father is the least in size.

Since size and lack of it were both symbols, the diminutive God the Father was clearly embarrassing, and this Trinity problem was never really satisfactorily solved despite the frequent presentation of all three persons on the same scale.

Another subject popularized through stained glass and painting, especially that of the fourteenth century, is *The Judgement of Souls by St Michael*.[17] But at that date and in those media the Madonna does not cast her rosary over the beam of the Archangel's scales. This is undoubtedly a dramatic contribution from the mystery players. St Michael's scaly legs should be understood as feathered tights recording a theatrical convention so ubiquitous as to figure in the presentation of him on those coins of Henry VI called angels. This subject in alabaster is comparatively rare. However, the two subjects with the best documented evidence of mystery play influences are *The Adoration of the Magi* and *The Resurrection*. All "Adorations of the Magi" are from "Life of the Virgin" altar-pieces, and the one from the Sir Alfred Bossom Collection, because of the surviving colour and good condition, is a particularly fine example of its kind.

The iconography of the Resurrection, very frequently a plaque from a "Passion" altar-piece, is provided by the Chester[18] mystery plays in the following instruction (in Latin) to the "Christus" player: "Jesus rising crushes the soldier with his foot." The complaining words from the soldier which follow make this gesture quite clear and that the emphasis is on a corporeal resurrection. This particular convention, of a foot placed directly on a sleeping soldier, is extremely rare in Continental art.

One also wonders whether or not the royal regalia in any way contributed to the current iconography. The crowns worn by the Trinity (Plate 453A and c) and the Madonna in *St Anne instructing the Virgin* (Plate 453B) are, for example, very close to those on some of the contemporary coins; and when crosses on orbs have survived they are usually very long stemmed, as in the portrait of Richard II in Westminster Abbey.

The invariable "daisy-dotted" green foregrounds began as decoration derived from manuscripts such as the fourteenth-century "Queen Mary Tudor psalter" in the British Museum. When, however, this decoration occurs on the Cross[19] itself it may well be an allusion to the medieval[20] legend that the wood of the Cross was of the dead wood from the forbidden tree in Eden and that it flowered anew at the Redemption.

The present state of our alabaster knowledge suggests that further documentary information is now much more likely to be found abroad than at home, and that a thorough and systematic stylistic analysis of the known material of all types would very probably lift much of the mist of uncertainty still overhanging this aesthetically erratic, though historically important, medieval English craft.

NOTES

[1] (a) The whole door in *Staffordshire*, by Arthur Mee (Hodder & Stoughton, 1937), p. 209. (b) The alabaster detail in *English Mediaeval Sculpture*, by Gardner (Cambridge University Press, 1951), p. 315, Fig. 619.

[2] *English Mediaeval Sculpture*, by Gardner (Cambridge University Press, 1951), p. 324, Fig. 641.

[3] For export to Nantes *vide* T. Rymer, *Foedera*, O. VIII, 540; for export to Fécamp *vide* Bilson, *Archaeological Journal*, Vol. LXIV, pp. 32-7 (1907), and the same in *Transactions of the Thoroton Soc.* (Nottingham), Vol. XIV, 1910.

[4] For examples of worked alabaster sent from Derbyshire to Newcastle via London *vide Historiae Dunelmensis Scriptores, tres* (Surtees Soc. 9), 135, 136.

[5] Issue Rolls of 42 Edward III (1367/68-6869) and 45 Edward III (1370/71-71/72).

[6] For Durham, see *Historiae Dunelmensis Scriptores,*

tres (Surtees Soc. 9), 131, 135, 136. For Ripon, see *Memorials of Ripon* (Surtees Soc. 8), III, 18, 38, 39.

[7] *Vide* the references to these craftsmen in *Nottingham Borough Records*, II & III.

[8] (a) *The Last Supper*, Victoria and Albert Museum (48-1946). (b) *The Five Joys of Mary* (also called "The Swansea" altar-piece) – from Singleton Abbey, though bought in Munich – Victoria and Albert Museum (89-1919). (c) *The Twelve Apostles* (an altar-piece that has lost its "howsing"). Victoria and Albert Museum (148/59-1922).

[9] One of these, the mid-fifteenth-century altar-piece in the chapel of Haddon Hall, Derbyshire. *Vide Antiquaries' Journal*, XVII, Plates 49-51.

[10] T. Rymer, *Foedera*, O. VII, 357.

In *Antiquaries' Journal*, Vol. XXV (1955), p. 185 (with reproductions) Hildburgh argues convincingly that this St Peter and St Paul are now in the Church of Santa Croce in Gerusalemme, Rome. His arguments would have been conclusive had he contrasted this St Peter in Rome with the Flawford *Madonna and Child* (Plate 2). The cutting of the heads of both is identical and therefore the work of the same hand. Further, this St Peter holds a small symbolic church identical with that held by the (Nottingham) Flawford *St Peter as Pope*, reproduced in *The Connoisseur*, May 1954, Fig. 4. It can also be remarked here that the seated *Madonna and Child* in the Burrell (Glasgow Gallery) Collection (reproduced in *Scottish Art Review*, Vol. V, No. 4, p. 4) is also, on technical grounds, quite clearly from the same hand.

[11] *Vide Antiquaries' Journal*, Vol. VI (1926).

[12] The whole transport question is variously discussed in (St John Hope) *Archaeological Journal*, Vol. LX (1904); (Destrée) *Annales de la Société d'archéologie de Bruxelles*, Vol. 23 (1909); (Nelson) *Archaeological Journal*, Vol. XXV (1918); and (Rostand) *Bulletin Monumental*, Vol. 87 (1928).

[13] This attire, the adapted habit of a religious, was worn by "vowesses", i.e. women vowed to maintain their widowhood. See, for example, the brass of Matilda Burghurst (1436) in Ewelme Church, Oxfordshire, reproduced on p. 252 *English Church Monuments*, by F. H. Crossley, F.S.A.

[14] Boston Trinity: whether, or not, such figures *without* a dove and *with* souls in a napkin can rightly be called "Trinities" is discussed (Hildburgh) in *Folklore*, Vol. XI.IV, March 1933, pp. 50 et seq.

[15] See authority referred to under note 15, and a fifteenth-century "Trinity" in a shrine with such attachments in the Burrell (Glasgow Gallery) Collection.

[16] *Re* mystery plays – in France: Emile Mâle in *Gazette de Beaux Arts* (1904); in England: (Hildburgh) *Archaeologia*, Vol. XCIII (1949), pp. 51-101.

[17] See (Hildburgh) *Folklore* (March, 1933), p. 48; (June 1949), p. 260.

[18] *Chester Plays* (Shakespeare Society) (London, 1843-7), Vol. II, p. 89.

[19] Such a "daisy pattern" cross occurs on *Christ Carrying his Cross* in York Museum, for example (reproduced in *Preview*, No. 54, July 1954), and on central "Trinity" on *The Swansea Altar-piece* (Victoria and Albert Museum, 89-1919). The practice is not extremely rare and leaves the impression that originally it was the norm.

[20] The legend referred to discussed in (Miss M. R. Bennett) *Archaeological Journal*, Vol. LXXXIII. *The Kettlesbaston Trinity* (fragment) in the British Museum has only a green cross.

ESKIMO SOAPSTONE CARVING

For many hundreds of years the Eskimo has produced, out of the unlikely background of the arctic night and the frozen wilderness, an art form of extraordinary strength and compulsion. Yet its best products have only lately begun to be sought after in the United States, in Canada, and in western Europe.

The origin of Eskimo art is obscure, although it has been established with reasonable certainty that soapstone has been carved in the Arctic for many centuries. The pieces illustrated in the accompanying plates are enough to establish the sympathy in both spirit and manner between traditional Eskimo work and some of the best of contemporary European sculpture. Yet the similarity in feeling and execution remains a mystery. The Eskimo carver is totally apart from European influences. His work is based on the traditional carving of his ancestors, on his inherited skill, on his own observation, and on the limitations of the tools and material available to him.

Study of the origin of the Eskimo himself provides a few clues to the source of his highly developed art. It is generally agreed that Eskimos are Asiatic in origin, but there is no certainty at all as to whether, in the remote past, he arrived in the Arctic with his civilization and his art-forms already established, or in a more primitive state and then developed his civilization to meet the climatic challenge. Significantly, many collectors on seeing the polished Eskimo carving for the first time remark on its resemblance to some types of Chinese work in jade. The Eskimo sculptor, in his attitude to his art, shows one other notably Chinese characteristic. Etiquette demands that on producing a piece of carving for examination by a visitor, the Eskimo must decry his own work, saying what a poor thing it is and how unwise he has been to try his hand at something so plainly beyond him.

Because white men have been in contact with the Eskimos since the days of the Vikings they no doubt have, over many centuries, as traders, seen and handled examples of Eskimo art. Only within recent decades, however, is any reference to be found in the records of Arctic voyagers.

From the turn of the century a few traders, government officials, and Christian missionaries began to collect and treasure the soapstone carvings, but outside this small circle the excellence of Eskimo art remained unknown. It was not until the summer of 1948 that the Canadian artist James Houston went on an expedition to Port Harrison and Povungnetuk on the north-eastern coast of Hudson Bay. There he was shown a few of the stone carvings. He immediately recognized their exceptional quality and – equally significant – their potential value to the Eskimo economy if they could be taken south for sale. Houston arranged with the Canadian Handicrafts Guild that next summer he would return north and make a test purchase, exchanging cartridges, tea, and other commodities for soapstone figures.

In the autumn an exhibition was held in the Guild's gallery in Montreal, and within three days every piece had been sold. Since that first sale the demand has increased rapidly, as the work has become more widely known, and today the buying, bringing south, and marketing are handled by the Department of Northern Affairs, still under the guidance of James Houston and with the co-operation of the Guild.

Among Eskimos there are no professional artists. All carving is done by men and all Eskimo sculptors are hunters first and artists second.

Soapstone, or steatite, is the material used in the carvings here illustrated (Plates 455 and 456), though ivory from walrus tusks is used to supplement the stone from time to time. Carvings in ivory alone are by no means uncommon, and carvings are also made of driftwood and antler, but it is only in soapstone that the characteristic quality is attained.

It has been used by the carvers for many centuries. No precise date can be put to the earliest-known work; but there is at Churchill, on Hudson Bay, a collection of ancient carvings, excavated in the Igloolik area on the extreme northern horn of Hudson Bay, which are similar in many ways to contemporary work.

The choice of steatite for carving must originally have been made because it is a stone soft enough to be carved by tools made of other, harder stone. The mallet and chisel of the European sculptor are unknown to the Eskimo. His traditional tools for all purposes are the adze (originally with a stone blade and bone handle), a short knife, a hand drill or bow drill, and a saw originally made by notching a flat stone such as slate. Today many of the stone tools have been replaced by tools made of scraps of iron or steel, fitted to handles of ivory or antler. White men's tools are used when they can be obtained.

Because the Eskimo is a nomad, his carvings are small and easily portable. Eight or ten inches is an average height for a standing figure, and all Eskimo work is intended to be enjoyed by passing it from hand to hand, rather than by standing it on a shelf. Therefore the quality of the stone to the touch is as important as its appeal to the eye. The pieces are intended to be seen from every angle, including being held upside down. In the igloo, or in the summer tent, carvings are not kept on display. They are put away wrapped in fur or skin and only brought out, after a proper show of modesty, for the benefit of a visitor.

As will be seen from the plates (455, 456), the Eskimo carver chooses for his subjects the familiar things of everyday life. The mother and child, the hunter, the seal, and other animals of the chase, these are the subjects that occur again and again. It is probable that soapstone carving originally began with the forming of purely utilitarian objects, such as the familiar half-moon-shaped blubber lamp, used for both cooking and lighting, which is still made of soapstone in the regions where the stone is to be found. A next step may have been the carving of small models of such valuables as sleds or kayaks for putting on the graves of the dead, the original objects being too precious to abandon at the death of the owner if a model would serve the needs of his spirit equally well. Even today the carving of seals, bears, and other animals of the chase has a ritual significance, the belief being held that a well-carved model of a bear will in some way please the bear and persuade it to allow itself to be killed, but there is no doubt that Eskimo carvings are now made primarily as works of art, to give aesthetic pleasure to the sculptor and his friends. Nevertheless, some very poor work has already found its way on to the market, turned out presumably by men with little natural talent but a keen eye for an easy dollar. It remains to be seen whether the standard shown here will be maintained by the next generation.

IVORY CARVING IN EUROPE

Ivory has been used as a medium for carving since the palaeolithic age. The primitive arts of the earliest dynasties of Egypt and Assyria are known through ivories. The Greeks made use of carved ivory for some of their greatest works of sculpture, including the vast Olympian Zeus and the vast Athena of the Parthenon, which both had ivory faces and hands. Ever since Roman times the same substance has been used for small statues, ornaments, boxes, and articles of personal adornment. It would, indeed, be possible to trace the history of European taste from Imperial Rome to the late nineteenth century solely in carved ivories. Hence their great importance to the

historian of art and their enduring fascination to the collector; for these miniature works show every vagary of style which has been expressed by European sculptors in the past two thousand years. Moreover, this precious substance has in itself a charm, and when carved by a master hand permits a delicate precision of detail which can hardly be obtained in any other medium.

Strictly speaking, ivory is derived solely from the tusk of the elephant, though several similar substances, which are often difficult to distinguish, have been used in the same way, including rhinoceros horn, the tusks of fossil mammoths, hippopotami, walruses (morse ivory), and narwhals. Ivory is a substance hard to work and takes a highly polished finish. With time it discolours and acquires a pleasantly golden tone, occasionally marred by dark streaks. It is translucent, and very finely carved sheets are almost transparent. Many attempts to imitate ivory by chemical processes have been made, but none has been successful.

Fakes

As ivories have been among the most jealously collected works of sculpture, so they have been the most extensively faked. The nineteenth-century interest in medieval sculpture which was combined with a passion for exquisite miniature *objets d'art*, created a demand for ivories far greater than the supply. Obliging craftsmen therefore filled the breach by the production of numerous carvings skilfully patinated by artificial means. Most forgers confined themselves to fabricating copies – with minor variations – of impeccable but not too widely known originals; one is known as the Trivulzio forger from the number of imitations he made of ivories in the Trivulzio Collection. But although they followed their originals as faithfully as they could, these forgers were unable to avoid endowing their impostures with certain features – too coy a smirk on the face of a Virgin or too mechanical a treatment of foliated ornament – which we may now recognize as characteristically nineteenth century. In the works of more enterprising fakers, who either invented Gothic compositions or derived their designs from paintings or large sculptures of the correct period, nineteenth-century mannerisms are of course, more glaringly obvious. It should, however, be pointed out that many genuine early ivories have been "restored" in such a heavy-handed manner that they have taken on the appearance of fakes. But as they have lost all, or nearly all, their beauty, they will be of little interest to collectors. Fakers seem to have applied themselves less extensively to the fabrication of seventeenth-century ivories, save for richly carved tankards which enjoyed some vogue in the nineteenth century, and miniature reproductions of the more notable baroque statues.

Early Christian, Byzantine, and Romanesque ivories

A comparatively large number of ivories have survived from the period between the end of the fourth and the middle of the seventh century, and these carvings are among the most important documents for the study of late antique and early Christian art. Unfortunately it is seldom possible to date them with great precision, and eminent authorities have differed over the dating of individual examples by as much as three hundred years. Nor has there been any unanimity among scholars about the places where various groups of ivories were carved. Constantinople, Rome, Antioch, Alexandria, lower Egypt, and Milan were probably the most important centres, but ivories have also been assigned to Ravenna and Jerusalem, and there is reason to believe that some were carved in Provence. The high standard of work produced at Rome in the fifth century is demonstrated by the lovely diptych of the Symmachi and Nicomachi families, of which one leaf is in the Musée de Cluny, Paris, and the other in the Victoria and Albert Museum. This work is entirely pagan in feeling and is executed in the idealistic and decadent style of late antique sculpture. The more realistic style of carving practised at Antioch may be illustrated by the magnificent fourth-century casket in the Museo Civico, Brescia. Egyptian work, as Professor Talbot Rice has pointed out, "was characterized by a rather florid naturalism and by very full designs; by the sixth century its products had become easily distinguishable, being rather coarse and essentially provincial". Carvings executed at Constantinople reveal an eclectic blending of numerous styles, both classical and Oriental.

Three main types of ivory carvings survive from this period: diptych, caskets, and pyxes. Among the most interesting are the Consular diptychs, of which some fifty are known, dating from 406 to 541, when the anachronistic office of Consul was merged in that of the Emperor. As these diptychs were issued by the newly elected consuls at the beginning of their year of office and are usually inscribed with their names, they may be dated with greater precision than most other ivories of the period. Diptychs carved to commemorate personal events had first become popular in the fourth century. They were usually of wood or ivory decorated with appropriate subjects on the outer sides of the panels and inscribed on the inner sides (the inner sides were hollowed out to receive a thin layer of wax on which the message could be written with a stylus). A law of 384 confined the use of ivory diptychs to the two consuls, who were alone granted the privilege of sending "their names and portraits, engraved on gilt tablets of ivory, as presents to the provinces, the cities, the magistrates, the senate and the people". The most interesting diptychs are carved on each panel with a full-length portrait of the consul seated on the curule chair and holding in his right hand the *mappa circensis*, the handkerchief thrown down as a signal for the games in the arena to begin. Beneath his feet there is sometimes a carving of an incident in the arena or a symbolical arrangement of money bags to proclaim the consul's intended generosity. Simpler diptychs were carved with medallion portraits or inscriptions and floriated motifs. The earliest surviving consular diptych is that of Probus (406) at Aosta, which is wholly Roman in feeling; that of Boethius (487) at Brescia gives some indication of the style of carving that was practised in Italy (probably at Rome) in the late fifth century. All the surviving sixth-century diptychs derive from the Eastern Empire and were issued at Constantinople, though some may well have been carved at Antioch. Among the most notable are those of Areobindus (506) in the Landesmuseum, Zürich, and Magnus (518) in the Castello Sforzesco, Milan. Numerous copies of each diptych were issued by the consuls, varying in size and richness according to the rank of the recipient. Some have been preserved in several versions. Other secular panel carvings of the same period include a remarkable wing of a diptych carved with a stag hunt in the museum at Liverpool; a similar panel representing a chariot race at Brescia; and a complete diptych carved with a spirited lion fight in the Hermitage, Leningrad.

Closely associated with the consular diptychs are the religious diptychs which were carved on the outer sides of the two panels with religious scenes while the inner sides were inscribed with the names of the living and dead for whom prayers were asked during the Eucharist. There is an exceptionally fine religious diptych in the Museo Nazionale, Florence, carved with Adam in the Garden of Eden on one panel and with scenes from the life of St Paul on the other. It is probably of Italian workmanship and dates from the late fourth or early fifth century. A single leaf dating from about the same period, in the Castello Sforzesco, Milan, represents the two Maries at the Sepulchre and is generally regarded as Roman work, though a Palestinian origin has sometimes been suggested. Another single leaf of outstanding importance is that carved with a figure of St Michael in the British Museum, which was almost certainly executed at Constantinople in the early sixth century. Large diptychs, each wing of which consists of five panels of ivory, were made for both secular and ecclesiastical purposes. Among the most notable are those in Milan Cathedral (late fifth-century Italian work); the Museum at Ravenna (early sixth-century Egyptian or Palestinian work); and the Bibliothèque Nationale at Paris (late sixth-century Egyptian or Gaulish work). All are decorated with scenes from the life of Christ.

A few early caskets have also survived, of which the finest is that dating from about 370 in the museum at Brescia. This exquisite little work, decorated with scenes from the Old and New Testaments, is of the highest quality and has the sophisticated refinement of a late Roman sarcophagus. Pyxes, small round boxes originally made for domestic use but also extensively used in the Church as receptacles for the Eucharist, were carved in quantity in Egypt, and a comparatively large number has survived. They were decorated with somewhat roughly carved religious or mythological scenes. Notable examples are in the Musée de Cluny, the Museo Nazionale, Florence, the Landesmuseum, Zürich, and the British Museum. Other objects made in ivory include combs and tiny medicine boxes. But the most remarkable sixth-century ivory, or group of ivories, is the throne made up of numerous richly carved panels for Maximilian, Archbishop of Ravenna, between 545 and 556 and still at Ravenna. This extraordinary work has been ascribed to the artists of practically every school where ivory was carved in the sixth century, but there is good reason to suppose that it is of Constantinopolitan origin.

In the seventh century the centre of ivory carving passed to Constantinople. The most notable works produced here were caskets, which were decorated with secular or religious themes depending on whether they were intended for domestic or ecclesiastical use. In the Musée de Cluny there is a fine tenth-century casket decorated with a relief of soldiers fighting. An eleventh- or twelfth-century example carved with scenes from the life of David, for which an Armenian origin has been suggested, is in the Palazzo Venezia, Rome. Horns decorated with animals and used for hunting were produced in great quantities; other horns, intended for liturgical use, were ornamented with carvings of religious subjects. But the largest group of ivories surviving from this period are the religious diptychs and triptychs, from which standing figures of saints stare out at one with the same impassive countenance as their brethren on contemporary mosaics. Traces of paint reveal that these panels were usually coloured. A very notable tenth-century triptych is in the Palazzo Venezia at Rome.

The Carolingian renaissance of the late eighth and early ninth centuries brought about a revival of ivory carving in western Europe. The principal centres of activity seem to have been near the Rhenish monasteries of Trèves, Lorsch, Cologne, and Aix-la-Chapelle, but ivories were also carved at Rheims and Metz. Carolingian carvers took their inspiration from early Christian ivories and manuscripts, and certain of their works have in the past been confused with fifth-century carvings. Notable examples include a book cover in the Bodleian Library, the cover of the Psalter of Charles the Bold in the Bibliothèque Nationale, Paris, several panels and a remarkable cylindrical reliquary in the British Museum.

English ivories carved in the tenth and eleventh centuries stand apart from those of Continental Europe, for they show the blending of the Byzantine style with the native Anglo-Saxon tradition. This is particularly marked in a *Crucifixion* relief in the Victoria and Albert Museum. A more pronouncedly English style is evident in such works as the whale-bone *Adoration of the Magi* panel in the Victoria and Albert Museum, the Alcester Tau in the British Museum, and the famous crozier head in the Victoria and Albert Museum, which, as Professor Talbot Rice has pointed out, suggests a relationship with paintings of the Winchester school.

Gothic ivories

The artistic force of Byzantium was spent before the late twelfth century, when the Gothic style began to emerge in northern Europe. This new style brought with it a great revival in the art of ivory carving, which was practised in every European country, though most notably in France. During the thirteenth and fourteenth centuries, indeed, ivories helped to diffuse the French Gothic style throughout Europe, in the same way that Constantinopolitan ivories had spread Byzantine influence in earlier periods. Remarkably few ivories carved in a transitional Romanesque-Gothic style have, however, survived. Perhaps some of the ivories usually attributed to late twelfth-century artists should be assigned to the early thirteenth century, although they show no traces of Gothic influence. One of the earliest known carvings to show Gothic characteristics is the magnificent large morse Crucifix at Herlufsholm Church in Denmark, which significantly, is French work and may be dated between 1220 and 1240. Very few other ivory carvings which can be securely dated in the first half of the thirteenth century are recorded.

The great period of Gothic ivory carving, which may well be considered the golden age of the ivory, began shortly after 1250 and lasted until the end of the fourteenth century. Paris has generally been regarded as the principal centre for works carved in ivory during this period. But although archives record the names of numerous ivory carvers resident in and around Paris, none of these artists can be credited with surviving works, and it seems highly probable that many of the ivories attributed to the "School of Paris" were in fact carved elsewhere. Groups of ivories may, however, be attributed to distinct studios or even hands who are known by the names of their most prominent works, like the Master of the *Death of Mary* or the Master of the Kremsmünster diptych.

Book-covers and reliquaries of carved ivory, or of metal embellished with carved ivory, which were popular in previous periods, do not seem to have been made after the beginning of the thirteenth century. Gothic ecclesiastical ivories are confined almost exclusively to diptychs and triptychs, little statues which usually appear to have formed part of triptych shrines, and the heads of croziers. Secular Gothic ivories include caskets, combs, mirror cases, and writing tablets, of which numerous examples have survived. The iconographic patterns on which the carvings were based were established in the late thirteenth century and persisted unaltered until the fifteenth century. Religious ivories were nearly always decorated with the same series of New Testament subjects, while secular ivories illustrated a limited number of scenes of chivalry and courtly love. Neither group of carvings shows even the changes of costume which took place in the fourteenth century, for drapery was treated in a wholly conventional fashion. These ivories have an ethereal quality and reflect a predilection for the charming and romantic. Brutality and grotesqueness are conspicuously lacking from them. Individual figures seem occasionally to have been inspired by statues in the great Gothic cathedrals, but ivories, which were invariably coloured and gilded, show closer affinities with contemporary paintings and manuscript illuminations. The triptychs and diptychs formed part of the furnishing of houses rather than of churches, and it is significant that they went out of fashion at the moment when small religious paintings intended for the house came into vogue.

Among free-standing Gothic ivories perhaps the most notable is the famous *Deposition* group in the Louvre (Plate 457B), which may be dated between 1260 and 1270. At once supremely graceful and deeply moving, this little work is carved with a perfect understanding of the potentialities and limitations of the medium. Dating from about the same time is the very simple and lovely *Coronation of the Virgin* group, also in the Louvre (Plate 457A). This preserves much of its original painting and gilding. Numerous ivory figures of the Madonna and Child have survived from this period; gracious, sweetly smiling figures of which the best examples are probably the *Vierge de la Sainte-Chapelle* (Plate 457C) in the Louvre and the slightly later *Madonna and Child* in the collegiate church of Villeneuve-les-Avignon.

The largest group of Gothic ivories is composed of low relief panels, usually arranged as diptychs, triptychs, or tabernacles, in which a niche holding a statue of the Virgin is flanked by two or four hinged panels. As these diptychs and triptychs were valued for their decoration, they were arranged to fold – unlike the early Christian diptychs – with the plain surface on the outside and the carved surface inside. The smaller diptychs usually have on each panel a single figure or scene framed in a Gothic arch which is sometimes surmounted by turrets and towers. Larger panels, which became increasingly popular in the fourteenth century, are decorated with a number of New Testament scenes, usually the Passion, arranged one above another in tiers, separated by lines of arches, and crowned by a row of richly crocketed gabled arches. In the later thirteenth century the figures in each scene were shown standing against a blank background, almost as if they were taking part in a miracle play performed, most improbably, in a cloister. Notable examples of this type of carving are the "Salting leaf" in the Victoria and Albert Museum; the complete diptych by the same master in the Wallace Collection, both carved between 1270 and 1290; the Soissons diptych of about 1300 in the Victoria and Albert Museum; and the triptych with scenes from the life of the Virgin and Christ of the same date in the Instituto de Valencia de Don Juan, Madrid. The early fourteenth-century style of relief carving is best exemplified by the works of the anonymous Master of *The Death of Mary*, who flourished from about 1300 to 1330, and whose finest achievement is probably the triptych from St Sulpice de Tarn in the Musée de Cluny. He is also represented in the Louvre – by a lovely triptych of scenes from the life of the Virgin – the Victoria and Albert Museum, the Martin Le Roy Collection in Paris, and the Wernher Collection at Luton Hoo. His work is characterized by the light dancing movement of his figures, which was exaggerated to the point of grotesqueness by his many followers and imitators.

In the course of the fourteenth century the style of relief carving underwent a change. Architectural motifs began to assume a far less important role and the elaborate Gothic arcades were replaced by a simple series of arches, often in no more substantial form than a wavy line separating the scenes, or straight borders decorated with bands of roses. At the same time details of architecture and landscape connected with the scenes themselves – a bastioned gateway in the *Entry into Jerusalem* and a row of trees in the Garden of Gethsemane – began to appear among the figures. This development was, no doubt, occasioned by a greater demand for realism, which was satisfied in other arts, and to some extent in ivories, by the treatment of religious subjects as if they were genre scenes. The later fourteenth-century style may be seen in the diptych with scenes of the Passion in the Kaiser Friedrich Museum, Berlin. Each wing has three tiers of carving separated by rows of shallow arches. The scenes themselves are somewhat overcrowded with gesticulating figures in crumpled drapery, and the narrative is confused, though the carving is both fine and vigorous. The Master of the Kremsmünster diptych, who is often regarded as the last important Gothic ivory carver, worked with a greater fluency of line and simplicity of composition, almost in opposition to the spirit of the time. The work from which his anonym is derived is still in the Abbey at Kremsmünster, and he is also represented in the Kaiser Friedrich Museum and the Wernher Collection, Luton Hoo. During the fifteenth century ivory relief carvings of religious subjects became increasingly elaborate and detailed.

Other ecclesiastical objects made of ivory in this period included paxes and pastoral staves. The pax, a tablet usually made of silver, wood, or ivory, was used in the Mass, when it was kissed by the celebrant, the other priests, and, occasionally, the communicants. Ivory paxes were decorated with low relief carvings in the same style as contemporary diptychs and triptychs. Pastoral staves were often very elaborate and sheltered in the curve of their volutes single figures of saints of New Testament scenes – usually the Madonna and Child or the Crucifixion.

Of secular Gothic ivories, the mirror backs or cases are among the most attractive. They are usually circular plates of ivory given a square outline by four beasts or stylized vine leaves on the rim, to the back of which a disc of polished metal, the mirror itself, was attached. Sometimes the mirror may have been held between two carved panels of ivory, but no complete example of this type is known to have survived. As befitted their purpose, mirror cases were usually decorated with low relief carvings of scenes of courtly love – knights and ladies riding out together or playing at chess, or simply flirting; knights jousting or storming the Castle of Love (Plate 458B). Good examples are in the Victoria and Albert Museum, the British Museum, the Louvre, and the Museo Nazionale, Florence. Similar scenes were carved on combs made at the same period (Plate 458A). Caskets were also decorated with representations of knights enjoying the pleasures of the tilt-yard or the arbour. A very fine example carved with the pathetic tale of the Châtelaine of Vergy is in the Metropolitan Museum (other caskets illustrating the same story are in the British Museum and the Kunsthistorisches Museum, Vienna). Incidents of this type and also religious subjects were used to decorate the covers of writing tablets which were formed out of several sheets of ivory bound together.

Certain ivory carvings produced in England in the fourteenth century are of conspicuously high quality. Indeed, some are well worthy of comparison with French productions of the same period. Generally speaking, they are distinguished by a greater severity of style and solidity of composition. Perhaps the most notable is the early fourteenth-century "Salting leaf" diptych in the Victoria and Albert Museum, which shows the Madonna and Child on one wing and Christ blessing on the other. English ivory carving of a slightly later date may be exemplified by the two triptychs in the British Museum and the diptych divided between the British Museum and the Louvre which were executed for John Grandisson, who was Bishop of Exeter from 1327 to 1369. These works are, however, of a more pronouncedly provincial character than the "Salting" diptych.

Italian ivory carvings of the later thirteenth century show dependence on French models, which are, however, treated with a greater monumentality. The most important is the somewhat heavily restored Madonna and Child by Giovanni Pisano in the Cathedral at Pisa, which was probably carved in 1299. In the late fourteenth century Baldassare degli Embriachi founded a large school of carvers in bone, and more rarely ivory, which flourished in Venetia and Lombardy in the first half of the fifteenth century. Their works are usually composed of numerous long, narrow, carved bones and are often of considerable size. A large altar-piece carved by Baldassare himself between 1402 and 1409 is in the sacristy of the Certosa at Pavia. Other works attributed to him, or to his followers, are in the Museo Nazionale, Florence, the Musée de Cluny, the Louvre, the Metropolitan Museum, New York, and the Victoria and Albert Museum. The Embriachi School were also responsible for numerous bone and ivory caskets decorated with religious or mythological subjects. German ivory carvers who had closely imitated French models in the thirteenth and fourteenth centuries developed an independent style in the middle of the fifteenth century. They seem to have specialized in the production of small figures and groups which were carved in the minutest detail, like the *St George* in the Wallace Collection, London.

Renaissance ivories

The art of ivory carving had declined before the middle of the fifteenth century and received little stimulus from the Renaissance. In fact, Renaissance sculptors seem to have despised a substance which could only be worked on so small a scale. Many ivory statuettes have, from time to time, been attributed without a shred of evidence to the greatest sixteenth-century sculptors, Benvenuto Cellini, Giovanni Bologna, and even Michelangelo. Such little figures were often copied from the greater Renaissance statues but were invariably the work of minor craftsmen.

In Germany and the Low Countries carvings of religious subjects were executed in a *retardataire* Gothic style until well into the sixteenth century. Similarly in France late Gothic style ivories seem to have been carved in the first half of the sixteenth century. The most notable French ivories of the period are, however, two Renaissance style statuettes of the Virgin and Child by the same anonymous artist. One is in the Victoria and Albert Museum, the other in the Metropolitan Museum. Italian ivories in the Renaissance style are less rare. Low reliefs of religious subjects carved in ivory and mounted on horn backgrounds enjoyed some popularity in northern Italy at the end of the fifteenth century. Two examples of this type of work, an Annunciation diptych and a St Sebastian, are in the Victoria and Albert Museum. Ivory statuettes of saints and of naked putti were also carved in Italy in the late fifteenth and early sixteenth centuries. The finest Italian renaissance ivory carvings are probably those which decorate the two coffers made on the occasion of the marriage of Paola Gonzaga to Leonhard Duke of Goerz in 1477 and now in the Cathedral of Graz in Styria. These *cassoni* are decorated with low relief carvings of the *Triumph of Petrarch*, which may, perhaps, have been designed by Andrea Mantegna. Several contemporary copies of individual panels are known, notably the fine *Triumph of Love* in the Museo Nazionale, Florence (Plate 458D), the *Triumph of Fame* in the Louvre, and the somewhat weaker and badly damaged *Triumph of Divinity* in the Victoria and Albert Museum.

In the sixteenth century ivory seems to have been regarded less as a suitable medium for small-scale sculpture than as a valuable substance which could give an air of opulence to an article of everyday use. Rosaries of minutely carved ivory beads and chaplets made of somewhat larger beads terminated by a Crucifix or a *memento mori* death's head enjoyed a wide popularity, especially in France. Mirror cases, memorandum tablets, hunting horns, powder flasks, seals, the handles of daggers and table knives, the pommels of swords, and the decorative parts of saddles were also made of ivory and decorated with characteristically Renaissance motifs. An early-sixteenth-century comb in the Museo Nazionale, Florence (Plate 458c), is decorated with Venus and two *amorini* on the central band and grotesques at the ends. It may be compared with a comb made some fifty years before (Plate 458A) and decorated with Gothic scenes of courtly love. Some of the memorandum tablets worked in low relief with allegorical figures have great charm. A good German example of the later sixteenth century is in the Wallace Collection. As in the Gothic period, chess-men and chess-boards were often made of carved ivory.

Baroque ivories

The birth and diffusion of the baroque style in the early seventeenth century brought about a great revival in the art of the ivory carver. We may indeed consider the seventeenth century as the third important period in the history of European ivories, for the best works reveal impeccable standards of craftsmanship even if they do not rival the masterpieces of early Christian or Gothic carvers. Ivory was more widely used than ever before to embellish everyday objects. Decorative reliefs and statuettes of ivory also returned to favour in all parts of Europe. The great innovation of this period was the ivory crucifix, which had hitherto been rare but now acquired a widespread popularity (Plate 459A). Some crucifixes, especially the smaller ones, were wholly carved in ivory, but it became a more usual practice to carve the Body of Christ alone in ivory and mount it on a wooden cross. Iconographically the crucifixes adhere to the patterns set by baroque painters, the Van Dyck type with upstretched arms being one of the most usual. Among the finest is that carved by Jean Guillermin of Lyon (1622–99) for the Confrérie de la Miséricorde of Avignon and now in the Musée Calvet, Avignon. Another notable example is that carved by Balthazar Stockamer in the Palazzo Pitti, Florence.

After the beginning of the seventeenth century the art of ivory carving ceases to be anonymous, and the student must therefore turn his attention to the styles of individual masters, only a few of whom can be mentioned here. Most of these masters are known by a few signed or documented works which provide a basis for a study of their styles, but many indifferent ivories have been, and still are, attributed to a few great names, notably François Duquesnoy, Gerard van Opstal, and Lucas Faid'herbe. The most celebrated was François Duquesnoy (1594–1643), known as *Il Fiammingo*, a Flemish-born sculptor of the first importance who spent most of his working life in Rome. His large-scale statues in marble are among the masterpieces of restrained baroque sculpture, but unfortunately no documented ivory carving by him is known. Six bacchanalian scenes, often known as "Fiammingo's boys", in the Victoria and Albert Museum, were for long ascribed to him, but are now generally regarded as copies after lost originals (Bellori describes a series of such ivories in his life of Duquesnoy).

Gerard van Opstal (*c.* 1597–1668) was also of Flemish origin and, like Duquesnoy, a sculptor in marble as well as ivory. He went to Paris in about 1643, became an academician in 1648, and was appointed sculptor to the King. His work in ivory is known by five bacchanalian scenes, two of which are signed, in the Louvre (Plate 458E). On the basis of these works a number of similar reliefs have been attributed to him, notably those in the Musée de Cluny, the Kunsthistorisches Museum, the Rijksmuseum, the Institut Staedel, Frankfurt, the Museum at Brussels, and the Wallace Collection. Lucas Faid'herbe (1617–97) worked under Rubens, who wrote a certificate of his ability in 1640, declaring that he had executed several fine works in ivory for him. His only signed work is a low relief of children dancing (in the Prado), but numerous ivories have been attributed to him. Another important Flemish ivory carver of this period was François van Bossuit (1635–92), who spent much of his life in Italy and is known by several signed works, among which the most notable are the *Death of Adonis* and *Music* in the Rijksmuseum and the *Toilet of Bathsheba* in the Wallace Collection.

Numerous fine ivory carvers flourished in Germany in the seventeenth century. One of the most interesting was Georg Petel (*c.* 1590–*c.* 1634), who also worked in other mediums. He is represented in the Bayerisches Nationalmuseum, Munich, by a fine statuette of St Sebastian carved in about 1627 and in the National Museum, Stockholm, by a *Triumph of Venus*. Christof Harrich (d. 1630), a virtuoso craftsman, applied his skill to the repellently realistic treatment of decomposing flesh on *memento mori* figures, for which there was a great demand in Germany. His contemporary, Christof Angermair (d. 1632–3), employed a scarcely less remarkable talent for the carving of minute details in obtaining more attractive decorative effects. His best-known signed work is an elaborate coin cabinet in the Bayerisches Nationalmuseum. A fine little relief of the *Judgement of Paris* in the Victoria and Albert Museum has also been attributed to him (Plate 459C). Adam Lenckhart (*fl.* 1632) is known by signed reliefs carved in a strongly Italianate style in the Victoria and Albert Museum and the Metropolitan Museum. The late seventeenth-century sculptor Balthazar Permoser (1651–1732) occasionally worked in ivory, and is represented by two exquisite little figures of *Spring* and *Winter* in the Germanisches Museum, Nuremberg. Of the many carvers who produced ivory tankards heavily decorated with figures on the drum, one of the most notable was the Augsburg craftsman Bernard Strauss (*fl.* 1651), who is represented by signed examples in the Victoria and Albert Museum, the Rijksmuseum, and in the Kunsthistorisches Museum. J. M. Maucher (b. 1645) specialized in the production of elabor-

ately carved cups, of which there are signed examples at Berlin and in the Hohenlohe Collection at Neuenstein. A fine cup in the Victoria and Albert Museum (Plate 459D) has also been attributed to him. Two other distinguished German ivory carvers, F. Senger (*fl.* 1681) and Balthazar Stockamer (*fl.* 1666–1700), worked principally for the Medici Court at Florence. The former, who styled himself Ivory Turner to Cosimo III, Grand Duke of Tuscany, is represented by a turned cup supported by a naked youth in the Victoria and Albert Museum. The latter carved the exceptionally fine crucifix (Plate 459B) and a *Hercules Killing the Hydra* in the Palazzo Pitti. German influence was strongly felt in Scandinavia and is evident in the work of the Norwegian Magnus Berg (1666–1739), who is represented by a figure of *Venus* and group of *Venus and Adonis* at Cassel.

French ivory carvers of this period are most notable for their crucifixes and for their portrait busts and reliefs. Jean Cavalier (*fl.* 1686–1707), who was of French origin but passed a roaming life working in England, Sweden, Denmark, Bavaria, Austria, and Russia, seems to have confined his attention to small portrait medallions, which he carved in low relief with exquisitely fine precision. He is represented in the museums of Stockholm, Copenhagen, Cassel (some thirty medallions), Berlin, Munich, Dresden, Brunswick, and the Victoria and Albert Museum. The Dieppois David le Marchand (1674–1726), who worked principally in England, executed a number of medallions in the style of Cavalier (now in the Museum at Brunswick, The Royal Observatory, the British Museum, and the Victoria and Albert Museum). He also worked in the round and occasionally carved subject groups, two of which are in the Victoria and Albert Museum – a charming *Time and Opportunity* and a somewhat weak *Venus and Cupid*.

Among the numerous small articles carved out of ivory by anonymous craftsmen in the seventeenth century the snuff rasps are probably the most interesting. These were bars of ivory about 2 inches wide and 6 or 7 inches long carved in relief on one side and fitted with perforated iron graters on the other.

They were used for grating tobacco to make snuff. Great ingenuity was shown in the treatment of the carved surface, which was either decorated with a group of figures or formed in the shape of a single figure. Dieppe was the most notable centre for the production of these rasps, or rapps as they were usually called. They were also made in England, Germany, and the Low Countries.

Rococo ivories

Ivory presents an ideal medium for the sculptor of exquisitely elegant statuettes, and it is therefore surprising that more rococo artists did not apply themselves to it. The most distinguished ivory carvers of the eighteenth century were the Germans. Carl August Lücke (1668–1730) and the younger members of his family produced many fine portraits and statuettes. In the Victoria and Albert Museum there is an arresting low relief bust of George II, carved by L. von Lücke. The outstanding ivory carver of the eighteenth century was, without doubt, Simon Troger (1693 or 4–1769), who executed a number of large groups in ivory and hard wood. By using ivory only to represent flesh he was able to work on a much larger scale than the size of tusks will normally permit. He was, moreover, a minor rococo sculptor of genius, and his works have a graceful vitality hardly paralleled in any other ivory carvings of the period. Good examples of Troger's work are to be seen in the Victoria and Albert Museum, the Residenz at Wurzburg, the Bayerisches Nationalmuseum, and in the Palazzo Madama, Turin. Another master of rococo ivory carving was Joseph Teutschmann (1717–87), who was responsible for such charming little objects as the heads of pastoral staves in the Victoria and Albert Museum and the Bayerisches Nationalmuseum. The brothers Sebastian Hess (b. 1733) and Paul Johann Hess, who were born in Bamberg but worked principally in Brussels and Vienna, carved little landscapes and other scenes on a microscopic scale.

The most distinguished French ivory carver of the eighteenth century was Joseph Rosset (1706–86), who executed a number of fine religious statuettes – as, for example, that of St Teresa in the Louvre – but is more notable for his portraits of Voltaire, Montesquieu, Jean-Jacques Rousseau, and d'Alembert, of which numerous versions are known. He also carved snuff rasps and snuff-boxes decorated with medallion portraits of contemporary celebrities. In his work he was assisted by his sons Jacques Rosset (1741–1826) and Antoine Rosset (1759–1818). In England Rysbrack's pupil Van der Hagen (*fl.* 1766–79) occasionally worked in ivory and is represented by a few portraits in the Victoria and Albert Museum.

Many of the most attractive eighteenth-century ivories are the work of anonymous craftsmen. They include a wide variety of small objects, snuff-boxes, snuff rasps, fans, fan cases, bodkin cases, and the handles of canes, all embellished with elegantly fantastic decorations.

Nineteenth-century ivories

The art of ivory carving declined sharply after the end of the eighteenth century. The most interesting nineteenth-century ivories are undoubtedly the portrait busts and medallions. In England Benjamin Cheverton (1794–1876) executed a few good original busts, including one of William Huntington in the Victoria and Albert Museum, and miniature copies after antique sculptures and the works of such masters as Roubiliac and Chantrey. In 1828, together with a Mr Hawkins, he invented a machine which enabled him to produce miniature facsimiles in ivory of large-scale busts and reliefs in marble or other materials. Another notable English ivory carver was Richard Cockle Lucas (1800–83), who sprang to posthumous notoriety on account of his terracotta bust which was acquired by Dr Bode for the Kaiser Friedrich Museum as an original work by Leonardo da Vinci. He produced numerous small ivory carvings, mainly copies after the antique and portraits.

Ivory carvings were produced in great quantities on the Continent, especially in Germany, during the nineteenth century. The vast majority of them were, however, derivative in design and mechanical in execution. Towards the end of the century certain French carvers were producing works of a mildly erotic nature in which all the least-attractive qualities of ivory were emphasized.

Such works have, however, a certain interest as period pieces.

JADE CARVING IN CHINA

No stone other than jade has had so continuous a relationship with man in his social and religious development. Centuries before the Christian era we find it emerging as the visible and tangible – if somewhat arbitrary – symbols of his Heaven and Earth, and in one instance, at least, of a famous constellation. These arbitrary forms have been handed down through the ages to modern times, even when their original significance has become no more than a tradition: and this applies not only to objects of a strictly ritual character but also to those more intimately connected with everyday life.

As early as the seventh century B.C. jade was looked upon as containing in *itself* – that is, in its actual mineral structure – parallels to certain virtues. They were enumerated in a contemporary ritual as follows: "If jade is highly valued, it is because, since very olden times, the wise have likened it to virtue. For them, the polish and the brilliancy of jade represent the whole of purity; its perfect compactness, and its extreme hardness represent the sureness of the intelligence; its angles – they do not cut although they seem sharp – represent justice; the pure and prolonged sound which it gives forth when one strikes it represents music. Its colour represents loyalty; its interior flaws, always showing themselves through the transparency, call to mind sincerity; its iridescent brightness represents Heaven; its admirable substance, born of mountain and of water, represents the Earth. The price which all the world attaches to it represents the truth."

The interest in jade is, in the great majority of cases, kept within the boundary of personal taste and inclination, and he to whom the early – often called "tomb jades" – appeal, rarely seems to have an equal appreciation of the masterpieces of later centuries. The reason for this is undoubtedly the allure of age felt by some minds, and the quite sincere conviction that the earliest Chinese jades have the most

personality. The inexperienced collector should train himself to refrain from thinking that great age is *in itself* to be blindly accepted as a proof of artistic or aesthetic superiority.

"The preponderance," says Professor Hansford, "among jades attributable to pre-Han periods of plaques designed for attachment to other materials, bears witness to their widespread use as jewels or embellishments." These thin, flat plaques, whose outlines include formalized birds, animal masks, dragon motifs, etc., are of necessity of quite small size.

From time to time, however, there appeared carvings which were strikingly different, such as the standing courtier (11 inches high) and the fine green head and shoulders of a horse (7 inches high), both dating from the Han Dynasty (206 B.C.–A.D. 220). But the most impressive example in Great Britain of simplicity of treatment is unquestionably the magnificent reclining buffalo (Fitzwilliam Museum, Cambridge), which at one time was said to be "possibly Han" but is now considered to be some centuries later. It has an unchallengeable pedigree in Chinese history since 1422, when it was then taken to Pekin by the Emperor, Yung-lo.

This bold simplicity of treatment seems to have continued down through the T'ang Dynasty (A.D. 618–906), and appeared intermittently through succeeding centuries, particularly those which covered the Sung, Yuan, and perhaps the beginning of the Ming.

The evolution of a style – more naturalistic and more detailed – must have been a very gradual process: and the beginnings can only be suggested from the study of some well-known sculpture, such as, for example, the unique black horse of the ninth century, whose mane and tail, and indeed the whole modelling, seem to suggest a breaking away from formal conventions (Fitzwilliam Museum, Cambridge).

Through the three centuries of the Ming Dynasty, stretching from 1368 till 1644, the process went on, and a magnificent illustration are the dragons on the huge jade basin in Pekin, which was carved not later than the middle of the fourteenth century and is one of the largest specimens in the world. It measures 26 inches high by 70 inches long.

There are unlikely to have been any fixed rules of treatment, and the carver would study the colour and shape of the jade in order to give full value to its individual quality. The Ch'ing Dynasty, which assumed imperial power at the fall of the Mings, had as its second ruler the great Emperor K'ang-hsi, whose reign, which began in 1666 and continued until 1722, was a period of great prosperity. Oddly enough, very little definite data seems available as to what jade carvings were produced during these sixty years. The one example about which there can be no doubt is the white jade dragon-headed horse (lung-ma) carrying the Books of Knowledge across the waves of the Yellow River. This was executed at the express command of the Emperor K'ang-hsi (*c.* A.D. 1670), to complete the animal trilogy of the large jade buffalo and black jade horse previously mentioned. With them this is also now at Cambridge.

The general opinion seems to be that some of the numerous jades now classified as Ch'ien-lung (1736–95) may belong to the two previous reigns: and against this view there is at present no way of definitely deciding. It seems justifiable to think that any carvings done during the short but artistically brilliant reign of Yung Ching (1722–35) (the son of K'ang-hsi) would not have been at variance with the aesthetic quality of the delicate egg-shell porcelains, probably the most sophisticated of Chinese ceramics.

It was, however, on the accession of his son, the Emperor Ch'ien-lung, that the golden age of decorative jade dawned, and during his long reign, which lasted from 1736 until 1795, many examples of outstanding quality and beauty issued from the jade-carvers *ateliers*. The choice of subject was now free from the fetters of ritual compulsion. Apart from those done to imperial command, they would obviously illustrate the line of preference of wealthy and cultured patrons, who would be wise enough to commission artists according

to the bent of their individual genius, and would not expect an incense-burner or a bowl from one whose skill was as a carver of animals or birds, or vice versa.

Among figures the favourite was *Kuan-Yin*, Goddess of Mercy, who is often shown with a vase in her hand from which she was supposed to pour the elixir of peace on the troubled waves of the world. Others represented are *Shou-lao*, God of longevity, with a stag and often holding a peach, sundry of the Taoist immortals, seated and holding their appropriate emblem, and *Pu-Tai* (the Japanese Hotei), with his well-known corpulency, his happy smile, his bag, and often one or two children, and fully justifying his title of "god of contentment". Occasionally one meets with a figure of the Buddha, although he is generally sculptured in the Indian tradition with broad shoulders and constricted waist and closely fitting garments. Domestic scenes are comparatively rare, and when found are almost invariably of a mother and children or children alone – two or three of them – climbing in or out of a large shallow bath. Occasionally a child is used as the body of a snuff-bottle.

As symbolism has been an integral part of Chinese mentality since its earliest days, it seems appropriate to indicate briefly such symbolism as is associated with some of the objects favoured by the jade-carver. Foremost among these are four mythical creatures, representations of which far exceed those which have the advantage of an actual existence.

Firstly, the dragon, which needs no introduction, as it has at all periods lent itself uniquely to representation in jade, since dragons among swirling waves and clouds recall their heavenly power as the bringers of beneficent rain as well as forming an artistic motif capable of a varied presentation. It was also the personal attribute of the Emperor in the same way that the Phoenix was of his consort. The kylin, that attractive and elegant product of imagination, with its slender, stag-like legs and bushy tail, was a creature of good omen, appearing only during the reign of a virtuous ruler, while the Buddhist lion, a fearsome beast but gentle, was the guardian of

Buddhist temples and the prototype of the Pekinese dog.

And now to the natural creation. Longevity was characterized by the stag, the peach, the fir tree, the lotus, and the tortoise. Conjugal felicity by the mandarin duck and also by two fish – usually carved with extreme formality at the bottom of a bowl – while the bat stood for happiness. The horse has often been carved, usually reclining, and sometimes is shown resting on waves and with the books of Buddhism on its back. The elephant is another animal fairly frequently carved in jade, sometimes richly caparisoned and bearing on his back a vase of auspicious emblems, or alternatively free from all trappings, when it has a more sculptural effect.

Among other subjects with a less-emphasized symbolism were the so-called "longevity" mountains, with their rugged pine-clad sides and often inscribed with an Imperial poem and a somewhat similar type of decoration, e.g. views in the fabled Western Paradise, with sages seated by pavilions amid trees and waterfalls, which could be used to

advantage for the cylindrical spill-vase and for table-screens. Bowls, of course, allowed a wide range of decoration, such as the Eight Emblems of Happy Augury, among scroll foliage on the exterior and a fine floral design in relief on the interior. The long, slender sceptre, or *ju-i*, which was supposed to grant every wish, although they had a general similarity of outline, allowed for many variants of enrichment, from dragons and fruiting branches of peach or pomegranate to simple linear designs.

The one series which allowed of little or no latitude were the replicas of early bronze vases, incense-burners, and other ritual objects which were reproduced with great fidelity and at times of imposing size.

The question "How was jade carved?" is one that cannot be answered simply and satisfactorily. No reference is to be found in the classical writings, nor in those of the Han and T'ang dynasties as to the way jade was ground and cut. Even in later days and right down to modern times, allusions are extremely scarce, and those that exist are often misleading.

WOOD-CARVING

AMERICAN

The term "folk art" as used in Europe is often synonymous with peasant art. In the United States the term is apt to be less specific; it often refers to primitive or untutored art. When the early settlers came to America they brought with them their own folk heritage, which was at times modified by the changing conditions of the new country. This was true of wood-carving, perhaps the most widely distributed American folk art. The ready supply of wood and the ease with which it was possible to acquire some elementary skill must have contributed historically to the continuity and geographically to the wide distribution of wood-carving.

American wood-carvings are of the eighteenth century and, to a larger extent, of the nineteenth. As carvers did not sign their works, they are mostly anonymous. But the discerning student of wood-carving can dif-

ferentiate between the professional and the amateur carver. Since folk art may include both the amateur and the professional, well-known carvers are here represented only by those works which are closer to folk than to academic art. Early American wood sculpture was usually painted or gilded. White was used in imitation of stone, or various colours to represent costume and flesh tints.

Early figures and busts

Other examples of carving of this period survive; sometimes the original location and carver are known. A small figure of *Justice* by John Fisher, privately owned, was in a courtroom in Pennsylvania at the time of the Revolution. The head of a statue of *Minerva* (Historical and Philosophical Society of Ohio, University of Cincinnati), carved in 1822 by one Schafer (anglicized to Shepherd) of Cincinnati, is in the traditional eighteenth-century classical manner. Joseph Wilson, a carver of Newburyport, Massachusetts, around 1810 may have carved two near-life-size reclining female figures, *Peace* and *Plenty* (for "Lord" Timothy Dexter). They appear to have been used one on either side of some central feature. In these figures, privately owned, a traditional style has received a vigorous expression.

A trend towards carved life-size wooden statues continued into the second half of the nineteenth century. David G. Blythe (1815–65) of East Liverpool, Ohio, is known to have carved the figure of General Lafayette in walnut, 8 feet high; Herman D. A. Henning of Baltimore (*c.* 1875) carved the 4-foot figure of the Civil War General of the Union forces, John A. Dix. A bust of Franklin in the post office of Newport, Rhode Island, was carved by Alexander Swasey (1784–1864) in the manner of marble sculpture. Carved portrait busts parallel portrait busts in painting. More like a realistic portrait painting is the painted head of a boy by Alexander Ames (d. 1847) in the New York State Historical Association (Plate 462B). The carver probably had little if any academic training, as is indicated by the lack of correct anatomy, even though he achieved a general semblance of the structure of the head. Definitely in the folk-art manner is a 12½-inch figure of a seated woman (Colonial Williamsburg, Virginia). The motif of the raised arms is a device to suggest animation; the skirt, left in the cubical shape of the block, suggests the folk carver; the dress with its rickrack braid suggests the nineteenth century. It was found near Ephrata, Pennsylvania, and is Pennsylvania-German.

Figureheads and ship carvings

The figurehead was a carved and painted decoration placed under the bowsprit of the old sailing vessels. It was the most important part of ship carving. During the early period of the newly formed republic figurehead carving took on a native expression. The typical American full-length, life-size figurehead is slightly detached from the hull and stands with head erect, as if peering into the distance. Another American characteristic is the variety of subjects chosen. American carvers selected motifs from contemporary

life, and used as models the ship owner, his wife and daughter, figures from history and literature, and American generals and admirals, as well as figures of *Liberty*. In addition to the full-length figure, busts, heads, and half and three-quarter-length figures were used, as well as eagles and occasionally animals, such as serpents' heads. Where individuals were represented the intent was to achieve a portrait-like character in the head, as in those of George Washington, Benjamin Franklin, and Andrew Jackson. The classic influence produced *Hercules, Julius Caesar,* and *Galatea*; an American Indian contribution is noted in *Tamanend, Minnehaha,* and Indian chiefs and princesses. Of celebrated contemporaries we have portraits of Jenny Lind, the singer, and shipbuilders like Donald McKay.

A unique ship carving in a vigorously naturalistic style is a figure from the American Civil War, a Negro mascot of the Union Army (City Art Museum, St Louis, Mo). It was dredged from the Missouri River in the early 1870s. A figurehead about contemporary with the Negro mascot, carved in Boston for *The Highlander* (built in 1868), shows a Scot in native dress (Peabody Museum, Salem, Massachusetts). The timidity of the carving, lacking the skill of the earlier work, suggests that in this late period some work was also entrusted to less-competent carvers. Even so, excellent work was still being done, as shown by the *Cassandra Adams* figurehead carved about 1876.

The smaller vessels used busts as figureheads, growing out of scroll and leaf carving, or resting on scrolled shelf-like supports. Billetheads consisted of voluted scrolls gilded and painted. This particular type is close to the architectural carving of the classic and baroque periods.

Eagles used on whalers show variety in the carved details. They were gilt or painted to set off eye and beak against the colour of the feathers. Eagles on pilot houses of tugboats, river craft, or other steamers have been preserved. They were carved in the round, at times with a wingspread of several feet. Examples are preserved in the Museum of the City of New York (tugboat eagle) and the Public Museum of Davenport, Iowa. Such eagles are usually poised on a globe-and-rope base. Small eagles cut board-like from the same pattern and used originally on ships were carved by John Bellamy of Maine, the well-known ship carver, to be given away to his friends. They were painted red, white, and blue, and have been imitated. The template he used has been preserved by Joseph W. P. Frost, a descendant.

Carved eagles, gilt and painted, and combined with flags, shields, and scrolls in the manner of ship carving, were also used architecturally in pediments over doorways (Library, Goshen, Connecticut) or as finials on flagpoles and fence posts. The boom, used on sailing vessels as a derrick for the raising of the anchor, at times terminated in a carved cat's head.

Shop figures and tavern signs

An earlier type of shop figure and tavern sign existed during the eighteenth century, and the tradition was continued into the nineteenth. Such shop signs as wood-carved boots and gloves, mortars and pestles, spectacles, razors, clocks, and other forms continued almost to our own day; the striped barber pole is a remnant of this tradition. The eighteenth-century shop sign is represented by a man dressed in uniform in a style which for ease and competence is above the usual level of the later cigar-store Indians. The date 1720 on his belt probably refers to the year in which the business, tailor shop or tavern, was established. A well-known figure (Old State House, Boston), the so-called *Little Admiral* with *1770* on the base, served as a sign for William Williams, a mathematical instrument maker in Boston. The same date appears on an early tobacconist's figure in an eighteenth-century costume for Demuth's Tobacco Shop in Lancaster, Pennsylvania.

Several tavern figures carved in a bold manner with dramatic expression suggest a European tradition. Well known is the *Bacchus* of the Windham, Connecticut, Library, the work of John Russell, an English ship carver, who, with his assistants, was held prisoner during the Revolutionary War. The same lusty naturalism pointing to the experienced carver who worked in the English tradi-

tion is shown in two tavern busts of a man (Plate 462C) and woman, in the Waters Collection (1936) in Grand Rapids, Michigan. Derived from the Hogarthian tradition, both could have been imported, or carved in America. Such bold characterization, showing massive features with broad grins bordering on the grotesque, represents a mature art.

A ship-chandler's figure in the New York State Historical Association belongs to a tradition that existed before the appearance of the cigar-store Indian. Other ship figures of the same tradition had their individual motifs. An interesting shop sign is one carved in 1835 for a Fairhaven, Massachusetts, slaughterhouse. It represents a man driving a pig, both placed on top of a huge butcher's knife (New Bedford Whaling Museum). A drug store in Salem, Massachusetts, had a bust of *Paracelsus*, the sixteenth-century Swiss physician, in which a classicizing style shows the influence of sculpture. A coachman over 2 feet high (privately owned, 1938) with extended arms to hold the reins, and dressed in a blue coat, yellow trousers, high boots, and a three-cornered hat, may have been an early shop sign. Horses' heads carved in the round were placed over entrances to livery stables, and large wooden horses stood in show windows of saddlers. A figure of a Negro porter carved about 1850 (arm restored) stood for years in the Old Trenton, New Jersey, Hotel. The ingratiating porter about to welcome his guests is vividly expressed in pose and facial expression.

An early nineteenth-century sign was made for a Boston hardware dealer by the figurehead carver Isaac Fowle. Out of a single semicircular panel to fit in an arched opening, Fowle carved a collection of carpenter's tools. Saws and planes are skilfully arranged within the available space.

Cigar-store Indians

As sailing-ships were replaced by steamships and iron supplanted wood, figureheads disappeared. Some of the figurehead carvers turned to the growing craft of tobacconists' figures. Thomas W. Brooks of New York was a ship carver who carved and sold cigar-store

Indians for at least thirty-five years. A relation to ship carving is occasionally suggested in a tobacconist figure in its posture with raised head and chunky modelling. As a group, the tobacconist figures appear to be independent of an earlier traditional ship-figure type carried over from the eighteenth century. Though an English custom of using small counter figures preceded the use of the American life-size tobacconist figures, the latter bear no stylistic relation to the English counter figures.

The man credited with having introduced tobacconist figures into New York after 1850 was named Chichester. Of the carvers, few names are known; but occasionally a figure is known to have been carved by a professional sculptor, like Herman Matzen of Cleveland or Julius Theodore Melchers of Detroit, who carved the figure of a Scot (about 1868) for Tom Dick's saloon in Detroit.

With exceptions, cigar-store figure carving was a business geared to mass production. In place of a master craftsman taking commissions for individual figureheads, the owner of the business hired carvers to produce figures for sale. The cigar-store Indian carving was divided among half a dozen firms, which are said to have produced from two hundred to three hundred wooden Indians a year. When eventually an old figure was replaced by a new one the old figure might be repaired, repainted, and sold.

The life-size cigar-store Indian suggests the handiwork of the less skilled artisan; repetitions of a few typical poses are characteristic, but occasionally we see academic influences, particularly from well-known classic sculpture. This influence resulted in freer movement and a more individual style in the exceptional figure. In the usual cigar-store Indians there are perhaps half a dozen standard postures; the simplest of these consists of a flat profile sawed out of a thick board. In the fully developed figure the right arm may be raised to the forehead in Indian salute. Extended arms were carved separately and dowelled in. There was no intention to imitate the Indian of the plains in realistic fashion, either in dress or physiognomy. Cigar-store Indians were white man's creations, excepting

those instances where a specific Indian chief was carved in a portrait-like manner.

Butter moulds

The greatest variety of wood-carvings is to be found in household articles and small carvings related to the home. Carvings in intaglio include butter moulds and moulds for marzipan boards, moulds used by tailors for the steaming of cloth, and occasionally stamps used for burlap bags for grain, as well as relief-carved maple sugar moulds.

Butter moulds, known in England and on the continent of Europe, were turned out on a lathe, knob and carved disc in one piece. Circular bell-shaped covers (plunger type) used to cut and shape the butter have occasionally been preserved. The design which printed the butter was also carved on a separate disc or stamp, to which a handle was attached which worked plunger-like within the "skirt". The flat or slightly concave disc was chip-carved with a symmetrical and compact design of tulips, hearts, cows, and other motifs (Pennsylvania-German type), or with floral and animal motifs in a more open style (New England type). The former point to a German Swiss, the latter to an English, origin. Some of these butter stamps may have been originally combined with a skirt, and were a part of the plunger type.

In a box-mould type the mould consists of a box with hinged sides so that it could be opened. The design was carved on a removable bottom. There are even hollow cylinder moulds made from six strips of wood fastened together so that they could be opened and cleaned. The inside was hexagonal, and removable stamps were fitted into each end. This mould produced a six-sided column 6 inches high with designs impressed on the ends.

Marzipan boards

Marzipan moulds are rectangular intaglio-carved mahogany boards, from 14 to 30 inches long. They were used for large cakes baked for special celebrations or in memory of historical events. Cake and cookie moulds are known in European countries, and no doubt these American moulds are a continuation of the

European practice. For excellence in design and craftsmanship the marzipan moulds are of the best.

Toys

Home-made hobby-horses were carved out of solid wood with legs made separately and attached. Small toy horses on platforms with wheels were made commercially, but others of a Pennsylvania-German type have a less professional, folk-art look, and were probably made by wood-carvers as a hobby.

Dolls of various types have found favour with collectors and some dolls were carved of wood. An early example, about 13 inches high, in the Philadelphia Museum of Art, shows a little girl in hoop skirt and tight bodice. She was carved in 1776 in Philadelphia.

Wooden dolls were carved regionally, as in New England and the Southern Highlands; others achieved a general vogue and were carved in many places. A primitive type of doll with a wooden head and kid hands may go back to colonial days, and is believed to be from the mountains of western Virginia. The round head shows a minimum of detail, a peg nose in a head that otherwise depends on painting and a cloth dress.

A group of Swiss settlers in New Hampshire carved dolls about 6–12 inches high in solid pine. They were not painted, but were left in the natural wood. These New Hampshire dolls are entirely carved, from head to foot. Dress, shoes, and costumes are carved in the wood, and hands and features are individually expressed; no special emphasis is given the head. The carving is a little wooden figure, fully rounded, as only a trained wood-carver would attempt. The forms are simplified; realism is modified by an insistence on near-cylindrical and spherical volumes.

There are other more individually conceived dolls like two named *Emma* and *Jim* which James Rich of Bedford, Ohio, carved for his daughter in 1859. They conform to the type that emphasizes the head and allows the dress to conceal the body. In contrast to this type carved by a father for his children is the so-called "Dutch" doll or "penny wooden". It came originally from Germany and Switzerland, but was imitated in the United States and exists in many examples. "Penny woodens" are jointed dolls, arms and legs are pegs. They are made movable by having wood joints which connect arms and legs to a torso and head carved in one piece. The egg-shaped head has a peg nose and painted hair and features. "Penny woodens" are still being made today.

Decoys and weathervanes

The history of carving decoys and wild fowl, ducks, geese, and other water-birds out of solid blocks of wood goes back to the colonial period and reached its maturity at the time of the Civil War. Decoys were painted and set with glass eyes; at times the heads were carved separately. They are still available for collectors. A flat stick-up type shows the profile only. The bird is attached to a stick which is stuck in the grassy marsh to attract the wild fowl.

Roosters, horses, and cows were also favoured by weathervane carvers, but they also carved more unusual subjects, such as serpents, dragons, grasshoppers, and fish. This variety appears to have been an indigenous American development which was continued in metal weathervanes. The usual type of wooden weathervane sawed out of a board is to be differentiated from the more elegantly carved weathervane that served as a pattern for a metal vane. Examples of this type, a cow and a figure of *Columbia* holding a flag, are in the New York State Historical Association.

Whirligigs from 2 to over 4 feet high come from Pennsylvania. They are figures with paddle-like arms that rotate with the wind, a revolving rod being set through arms and shoulders. The cylindrical figure is slightly shaped to differentiate the coat-tailed upper part from the legs fitted with knee-high boots. A uniform is indicated largely by painting. Whirligigs as toys have an old European ancestry, to which these Pennsylvania-made examples may also be linked.

Religious carvings

The regions important for religious wood-carving, particularly in the south-western states, are those once held by Catholic France and Spain. The south-west may be divided into two parts: New Mexico (including Arizona) with a background of two and a half centuries of Spanish–Mexican rule; and California, where white settlement did not begin until 1769. In California wood-carving is largely confined to church furnishings.

New Mexico has produced the largest number of wood-carved saints or *bultos*, dating back as early as 1750. The early religious carvings, *santos*, were made by priests; they show lively gestures and expressive features. As the native craftsman became independent during the early decades of the nineteenth century he developed a folk art or *santero* style of his own which, however, perpetuated a Mediterranean tradition. These statuettes of patron saints, usually under 2 feet high, are serious and dignified, with an emphasis on simplicity. The *bultos* are carved of cotton-wood and painted in tempera over a gesso ground. The upper part of a *bulto* may be solid and the lower part made up of a hollow framework of an armature of sticks covered with cloth dipped in gesso and painted.

A different type of wood-carving of nearly life-size figures shows the influence of French Canada. Examples (mostly privately owned) have been found in Illinois and Wisconsin. A *Virgin and Child* from Sullivan, Wisconsin, shows a Gothic element in the posture and the backward tilt of the figure. A figure of *St Joseph*, about 4 feet high and 7 inches thick, shows a slight backward tilt due to the contour of the board.

EUROPEAN

Carved wooden figures exhibit all the styles employed by sculptors from the twelfth century to the present day. Ranging from the hieratic Madonnas and Christs of the romanesque era to the abstract fancies of Miss Barbara Hepworth, they vary in size from great religious images larger than life to little cabinet ornaments 3 or 4 inches high, and include the masterpieces of Donatello and Ignaz Günther and the spare-time achievements of provincial carpenters.

Although it must have been the earliest of media employed by sculptors (an ancient Egyptian figure in wood is in the Gizeh Museum at Cairo), we cannot speak with any authority of wood-carving before the twelfth century.

Naturally enough, the art of wood-carving has flourished where timber is most easily available and, more notably, where other materials are scarce, as in Bavaria. But the availability and tractability of wood have not been its sole advantages; its lightness has recommended it for figures that must be moved about and permitted effects that may hardly be achieved in stone.

Materials

Nearly every type of wood has been employed by carvers. Oak, because of its hardness and durability, has been much used for large figures in northern Europe, but in the south, where it is scarce, carvers have worked in walnut, cedar, cypress, and pine. In Germany lime, which permits an exquisite finish and presents a good surface for paint, has been extensively used. For small figures hard, close-grained box-wood and pear-wood, unobtainable in large pieces, have usually been preferred. Generally speaking, these little statuettes were polished to resemble bronze and occasionally gilt, while large figures were nearly always painted.

Although the collector of wooden figures is unlikely to find outstanding examples of the work of the greatest artists mentioned below, he may frequently be able to acquire beautiful statues by minor artists, most of whom are likely to remain anonymous. Fine Flemish and German carvings of the sixteenth century are occasionally available; baroque angels and putti are often to be met with, but fakes abound. Many a genuine but uninteresting early carving has been ruined by the faker's desire to make it conform with some trend of modern taste in art. Giovanni Bastianini (1830–68) and Alceo Dossena (1878–1937) were among the more gifted forgers of wooden sculpture, and their works were until recently (to be studied as originals) in several notable public collections.

The Romanesque period

The earliest considerable groups of wood-carvings date from the twelfth century, and were executed in Spain, France, southern Germany, and Italy. As far as may be judged, they were limited almost exclusively to figures of the Virgin and Christ, many of which have been treasured as images and copied throughout subsequent ages. Some were as large as, or larger than, life, but the clean, unbroken lines give the smallest figures of the Virgin a grand statuesque appearance. The Virgin is normally enthroned holding the Child on her knee, the figures being painted and, occasionally, enriched with precious stones. A rare dated example of 1199, formerly at Borgo San Sepolcro and now in the Kaiser Friedrich Museum, Berlin, shows a strong Byzantine influence. Another Italian example of about twenty years later is in the Museo di Palazzo Venezia, Rome. Both are the work of a school of wood-carvers who flourished in Tuscany, Umbria, and Lazio from the middle of the twelfth to the end of the thirteenth century. The late twelfth-century Deposition group at Tivoli, one of the masterpieces of Italian sculpture, shows the great ability of these anonymous artists, who interpreted the revolutionary style of the Emilian Benedetto Antelami in wood. Stiff and unbending, the tall, slender figures assist at the removal of Christ from the Cross, showing in their sombre ineloquent faces a depth of compassion rarely met with in the art of any other period. A similar but later group is in the cathedral at Volterra. The type was apparently popular in Spain at the same period; one formerly at Tahull is now in the Plandiura Collection at Barcelona, and another, dated 1251, is at San Juan de las Abadesas (Gerona).

Several large, carved-wood crucifixes of the twelfth century have survived, invariably showing the living Christ with open eyes. German examples dating from about 1180 are in the Bayerisches Nationalmuseum at Munich. In Spain and in Italy the *Volto Santo* type, supposedly derived from the crucifix carved by Nicodemus and probably originating in the eastern Mediterranean, showing Christ in majesty dressed in the long *colobium* or seamless garment, enjoyed great popularity in the late twelfth century. The most famous of these is the *Volto Santo* at Lucca, which is, however, of a slightly later date, and was probably made to replace one of great antiquity. This most beautiful of all carved crucifixes is imbued with a new sense of naturalism, which endows the figure of Christ with a suggestion of His earthly nature, as well as giving the hieratic impression which was one of the great achievements of romanesque sculpture.

The Gothic period

From the greater quantity that survives, it is possible to obtain a wider impression of Gothic than of romanesque wood-carvings. Large figures naturally follow the general current of sculptural taste from the early thirteenth to the late fifteenth centuries, but small groups, like those made in the Low Countries and Germany, demonstrate the medieval love of realistic incident applied to religious scenes which reflect the common life of the period. French figures of the Virgin show the same smiling face and meticulously creased drapery as the stone carvings, and also the small ivories from which the Gothic bend, or backward stoop, is said to have been derived. The beautifully coiffed head, delicately fragile wings, and slightly affected gesture of an angel in the Victoria and Albert Museum exemplify the style of the French school towards the end of the fifteenth century. It should be compared with the etiolated and supremely elegant figure of an angel (in the same collection) by a Pisan artist of the mid-fourteenth century – one of many figures which express the high achievement reached by Italian Gothic sculpture. Such figures, deriving from the school of Nino Pisano, are well represented in the Museo Civico at Pisa. An interesting school of wood sculptors flourished at Siena in the late fourteenth and early fifteenth centuries, its most notable member being Domenico di Niccolo (c. 1362–c. 1450), whose expressive figure of St John in S. Pietro Ovile, Siena, hesitates upon the brink of the Renaissance. Other prominent Sienese sculptors who occasionally worked in wood included Jacopa Della Quercia (1374–1438) and Francesco di Valdambrino (fl. 1401–35).

The richly ornate Gothic of Spain and Portugal was fully exploited by the wood-carver in agonized Christs, dripping with blood, in prettified long-faced Virgins and angels and in massive, intricate altar-pieces. Here again wood-carving follows sculpture in stone, except where a greater delicacy might be achieved in the lighter medium. The most notable sculptor of retables and single figures was Damian Forment (*c.* 1480–1541), who had absorbed a certain amount of Italian influence, but worked in a predominantly Gothic style. In the museum at Coimbra, Portugal, an early fourteenth-century crucifix expresses the sharp, tormented line of Iberian Gothic. The style remained popular up to the first decade of the sixteenth century.

In the Low Countries an important school of wood-carvers rose to prominence in the middle of the fifteenth century, and was particularly notable for little altar-pieces of oak which were disseminated throughout Europe. Full of life and charm, they have an appealing naïveté which has long endeared them to collectors. Most of the artists were anonymous, and many did little but copy the familiar patterns, though some, like the author of the lovely *Meeting of Joachim and Anne*, in the Rijksmuseum, Amsterdam (Plate 463B), were artists of fine sensitivity. In the same collection there is a lovely *Death of the Virgin* and a group of blithe musician angels by Adriaen van Wesel, of Utrecht, who carved them between 1475 and 1477. Similar carvings of peasants enacting religious scenes – the Nativity, the Flight into Egypt – were executed in the Rhineland.

Towards the end of the fifteenth century tiny tabernacles and altar-pieces a few inches high, carved in exquisite detail with numerous minute figures, became popular for devotional use in the home; though one may suspect that their principal charm lay then, as it does now, in the technical virtuosity of their workmanship. A Flemish tabernacle of 1511, in the British Museum, has a triptych crowded with scenes from the life of Christ and a Last Supper, in the round, all fitted into the compass of 9.9 inches. In the Wallace Collection there is a German box-wood group of St George Killing the Dragon, with the princess standing on a rock and a castle in the background, only 3¾ inches high.

Our knowledge of English wood-carving in the Middle Ages relies principally on the choir-stalls of cathedrals and great churches, for comparatively few independent figures whose origin is certain have survived. At Wells there is an Annunciation group of the fourteenth century, displaying a somewhat alien French elegance. In the next century the dominant influence seems to have been Flemish.

There can be no doubt that the most important school of Gothic wood-carving was that established in southern Germany and flourishing from the early fourteenth to the end of the fifteenth century. In the fifteenth century two cults were productive of particularly fine wooden figures. That of the Schöne Madonna demanded the image of a pretty if somewhat mincing Virgin, holding a lively, kicking child; she was frequently shown standing on a crescent moon supported by cherubim. Early examples are delightfully fresh, but towards the end of the period the Gothic bend and the elaborately creased draperies became exaggerated (Plate 463D). In direct and pathetic contrast, the very popular Pietà figures, which seem to have been particularly numerous in Germany, showed a grief-stricken Virgin seated with the emaciated dead body of Christ stretched across her knees. One of the best examples of this powerful but not very attractive group is that of about 1400, carved in lime-wood, in the museum at Frankfurt-am-Main. A small Pietà of this kind, for which an English origin has been suggested, is in the Victoria and Albert Museum.

The glory of German Gothic wood-carving is, however, in the large altar-pieces like those executed by Michael Pacher at St Wolfgang, by Veit Stoss at Crakow (Plate 463A), and by Tilman Riemenschneider at Creglingen and Rottenburg. Michael Pacher (*c.* 1435–98) worked in a somewhat prickly Gothic fashion, crowding his figures beneath heavily interlaced tracery and surrounding them with little angels who hold up their garments, sing, and trumpet. In the carvings of Veit Stoss (1447–1533) there is a greater simplicity and a closer attention to the naturalism of the heads. His early work was purely Gothic, but his masterpiece, the Annunciation group which is suspended above the choir in the Church of St Lorenz at Nuremberg, has been affected by a strong breath of the Renaissance from Italy. Stoss also worked on a small scale, and is represented in the Victoria and Albert Museum by a little box-wood statuette of the Virgin and Child, who are both as lively as they are plain. The greatest of the three artists, Tilman Riemenschneider (c. 1460–1531), demonstrates a combination of Gothic and Renaissance elements which make it difficult to fit him into either movement (Plate 463C). His beautiful clear-cut faces, beneath their masses of minutely carved locks, are on bodies clothed with rippling Gothic robes; his altar-pieces are crowned by intricate patterns of flamboyant tracery. Among other prominent late-Gothic carvers mention must be made of Erasmus Grasser (1450–1526), who made the two lively, smirking dancers at Munich; Simon Lainberger (*fl.* 1475–1503), who is responsible for a lovely walnut Madonna and Child of about 1485, in the Kaiser Friedrich Museum, Berlin; Hans Lainberger, the author of the comely peasant-faced Madonnas at Munich, and H. Yselin (*fl.* 1478–1513), the carver of the arresting bust of a carpenter, also at Munich. The best of these figures eschew the idealized and somewhat vapid beauty of the late-Gothic Virgin while retaining the traditional poses and crinkly garments. At the same time, and until well into the sixteenth century, an empty and exaggerated Gothic style, devitalized by constant repetition, persisted in conservative studios.

The Renaissance

The emergence of the Renaissance style in Italy in the fifteenth century did little to stop the production of predominantly Gothic figures for churches. Indeed, the majority of Renaissance sculptors, fired with a zeal for the antique, appear to have spurned so humble a material as wood, though it was used by some of the greatest. Donatello (c. 1383–1466) carved his Magdalen in the Baptistry at Florence and the St John in the Frari at Venice in wood, which was also used for the St Jerome at Faenza which has been attri-

buted to him. His follower, Desiderio da Settignano (1428–64), also used wood for the Magdalen in Sta Trinità at Florence. Furthermore, Brunelleschi (1377–1446) carved his great crucifix, in Sta Maria Novella at Florence, in wood, making a figure which, in its accurate anatomy and calm beauty, contrasts with the tortured Christs of the Gothic period. In north Italy wood-carvers of the early sixteenth century were influenced by their German contemporaries, as is evident in the fine altar-piece of the Crucifixion in pear-wood, in the Victoria and Albert Museum.

Purely ornamental, secular wood-carvings, principally of classical subjects, first became popular in the Renaissance period. It has been suggested that many of these were made as models by goldsmiths and sculptors in bronze. One of the finest, the box-wood *Hercules* in the Wallace Collection, was certainly the work of a goldsmith, Francesco da Sant' Agata of Padua (*fl.* 1520), to whom bronzes have also been attributed on stylistic grounds. Many figures of this type appear to have been carved in Germany, where one of the most notable sculptors was Konrad Meit (c. 1470–c. 1550), who is principally famous for his work in marble at the church of Brou. That he was strongly influenced by Dürer is demonstrated by his box-wood statuettes of Adam and Eve at Vienna, which also show his strict adherence to the practice of modelling from the life. Flemish and German artists who had specialized in religious *genre* scenes also turned their attention to the carving of individual figures, such as that of an old man in the Wallace Collection.

It was not until the end of the fifteenth century that the Renaissance spirit began to reach Germany, and only in about 1510 did it achieve any prominence. Two of its earliest exponents, Sebastian Loscher (1482/3–1551) and Adolf Daucher (op. 1491–1524), who worked on the famous Fugger Chapel at Augsburg, both carved in wood, tending to use the late-Gothic style for traditional religious subjects, but following the new manner where the occasion allowed, in figures of putti, for instance. In Spain the Renaissance style in sculpture seems to have been introduced by Felipe de Vigarni (d. 1543) and, more notably, Alonso Berruguete (1480–1561), who was strongly influenced by Michelangelo. With the growth of Mannerism in the sixteenth century, the style of wood-carvers naturally changed, and from this period we may date the widespread copying in box-wood of Italian bronzes.

The Baroque period

After something of an eclipse in the later Renaissance, the wood-carver returned to prominence in Italy with the birth of the baroque style. Vast altars crowded with figures of saints and cherubim demanded a material cheaper and more easily worked than marble. Stucco was used extensively, but in those districts where wood was readily available – Piedmont, for example – figures and sometimes whole altar-pieces were carved in it. A yet uninvestigated school of wood-carvers, the most notable of whom were Carlo Plura (1655–1737), Stefano Maria Clemente (1719–1794), and Antonio Maria Maragliano (1719–1739), flourished in Piedmont and Liguria throughout the later seventeenth and eighteenth centuries. They executed decorative carvings of angels and putti, life-sized crucifixes and images which could be carried in processions. The processional figures were usually made in groups for such lay orders as the *Confraternità della Misericordia*, and represent saints or scenes from the Passion; their brightly coloured drapery is arranged in baroque flounces, but the figures themselves seem to derive from the realistic terracottas in the Sacro Monte chapels.

In the Iberian peninsula somewhat heavy-handed baroque sculpture was very popular throughout the seventeenth century, and many a great altar was enriched with wooden angels attired in billowing drapery. Small box-wood figures were also popular; a fine statuette of Christ at the Column, typically Spanish in the nervous tautness of its line, is in the Victoria and Albert Museum. It also owns a bust of the Virgin of Sorrows in painted wood, attributed to Pedro de Mena (1628–88). The most notable Spanish sculptors in wood of this period include Gregorio Fernandez (1566–1636) and J. Martinez Montanez (1564–1649).

The baroque marks a period of transition between two greater epochs in the history of German sculpture. There is a lingering flavour of Mannerism in the work of Martin and Michael Zurn (op. 1624–65), who carved a number of altar-pieces in Bavaria. On the other hand, a box-wood group of Salome and St John, in the Victoria and Albert Museum has a touch of fantasy which seems to anticipate the rococo. Most female statuettes have a greater solidity, like those by Leonard Kern (1588–1663). Georg Petel (1590–1633) worked in an uncompromising baroque style which he had acquired in Italy.

Rococo

In the eighteenth century the history of wood-carving is dominated by Germany, where a school of unparalleled excellence flourished. The rococo pilgrimage churches of Bavaria, which are among the greatest masterpieces of the period, demanded the most delicate and the most sophisticated ornaments and statues in both stucco and wood. Johann Baptist Straub (1704–84) worked much for the Bavarian Court, and employed so large a staff of assistants that his personal style is hard to distinguish. His celebrated putti in the church at Berg-am-Lain perfectly express the wit of the rococo in their playful allusions to the statues by which they stand – one child, accompanying the Archangel Raphael, wears a vast hat and sports upon the back of a dolphin, while Gabriel's companion, bubbling with laughter, supports an open book. Straub's pupil, Ignaz Günther (1725–75), is probably the greatest of these sculptors, for he alone realized all the potentialities of wood as a medium. Without straining his material he drew from it all that it was capable of yielding. In the large figures he carved for the church of Rott-am-Inn in 1762 one sees the crystallization of the rococo in all its eloquence, grace, wit, and supreme elegance. Although his statues are painted, no effort has been made to disguise their medium, which gives the lie to the usual implication in the adjective "wooden" (Plate 464).

Of the many sculptors who worked on a small scale in box-wood and pear-wood, the most important is Ferdinand Dietz (or Tietz) (1708–77), who also executed larger figures in stone, including those for the gardens of Vietshöchheim; indeed, many little figures he carved in lime-wood are models for garden sculpture. In his work the gay spirit of comedy frequently borders on the grotesque but never approaches the ugly. His lime-wood models have a somewhat sketchy, impressionistic finish, but his figures in box-wood are carved with a nice precision.

Among the other wood-carvers who worked in Germany in the eighteenth century, the following should be mentioned. Aegid Verhelst (1696–1747), a native of Antwerp, worked principally in Bavaria in a late-baroque style, specializing in large figures, the most notable being those of Peace and Love in the throne-room of the Old Residenz,

Kempten, and the fine Pietà group at Friedberg. Paul Egell (1691–1752) also worked on a large scale, but is represented in the Wurzburg Museum by a charming little group, possibly a sketch, of St Francis Xavier baptizing a blackamoor. Daniel Köhler (*fl.* 1751–78) is represented in the same collection by a statuette of St Sebastian. Towards the end of his career, Köhler forsook the rococo for a neo-classical style, which found fuller expression in the work of Christian Jorhan (1727–1804).

A flourishing school of wood-carving at the end of the eighteenth century existed at Turin, where it centred around Giuseppe Maria Bonzanigo (1744–1820), who was also a cabinet-maker and worked on a very small scale, with the greatest delicacy, treating his medium as though it was ivory.

Glossary

Abbott, George (1803–83). In 1850 he executed bronze cabinet busts of Peel and Wellington. A large number of replicas of both these works were made, those of Peel being manufactured by Messrs Hetley of Soho Square.

Adams, George Gamon (1821–98). Made a number of busts of the first Duke of Wellington, both in bronze and marble, some executed from life and others based on the death-mask. Copies of both these are not rare, and the one from the death-mask was considered by the Iron Duke's family to be the best likeness of the numberless busts made of him.

Angermair, Christof (d. 1632–3). Wood-carver, employed his remarkable talent for the carving of minute details in obtaining more attractive decorative effects. His best-known signed work is an elaborate coin cabinet in the Bayerisches Nationalmuseum. A fine little relief of the *Judgement of Paris* is in the Victoria and Albert Museum (Plate 459c).

Artists in bronze

Italian School

Ghiberti, Lorenzo, 1378–1455
Donatello, ?1386–1466
Bertoldo di Giovanni, ?1425–91
Pollaiuolo, Antonio, 1429–98
Verrochio, Andrea, 1436–88
Vinci, Leonardo da, 1452–1519
Lombardi, Tullio, c. 1455–1532
Bonacolsi, Pietro Ilario, called l'Antico, c. 1460–1528
Belli, Valerio, 1468–1546
Briosco, Andrea, called Riccio, 1470–1532
Michelangelo Buonarotti, 1475–1564
Raphael Santi, 1483–1520
Olivieri, Maffeo, 1484–after 1534
Tatti, Jacopo, called Sansovino, 1486–1570
Francesco da Sant'Agata, active c. 1520
Bernardi da Castelbolognese, Giovanni, 1496–1553
Cellini, Benvenuto, 1500–71

Cattaneo, Danese, 1509–73
Leoni, Leone, 1509–90
Bologna, Giovanni, 1524–1608 (*see* Plate 447A)
Vittoria, Alessandro, 1525–1608
Campagna, Girolamo, 1549–after 1626 (*see* Plate 446B)
Roccatagliata, Nicolo, active *c.* 1600
Duquesnoy, François, called Fiammingo, 1594–1643
Susini, Antonio, d. 1624
Susini, Francesco, d. 1646
Algardi, Alessandro, 1602–54
Canova, Antonio, 1757–1822.

German School

Vischer, Peter the Elder, *c.* 1460–1529
Vischer, Peter, 1487–1528
Vischer, Hans, *c.* 1489–1550
Flötner, Peter, *c.* 1493–1546
Labenwolf, Pankratz, d. 1563
Jamnitzer, Wenzel, 1508–85.

French School

Goujon, Jean, 1510–68
Pilon, Germain, 1537–90
Anguier, Michel, 1612–86 (*see* Plate 447B)
Lebrun, Charles, 1619–90
Girardon, François, 1628–1715
Coustou, Guillaume, 1677–1746
Falconet, Etienne Maurice, 1716–91
Caffieri, Jean-Jacques, 1725–92
Michel, Claude, called Clodion, 1738–1814
Boizot, Louis Simon, 1743–1809.

Baily, Edward Hodges (1788–1867). Best known for his statue of Nelson in Trafalgar Square. He produced a large number of busts, many of which had great charm. He was for many years chief modeller to the famous silversmiths Rundell & Bridge, designing racing trophies, presentation plate, candelabra, etc.

Behnes, William (1795–1864). Probably the greatest of the early Victorian portrait sculptors, and at his best a very fine artist. Unfortunately his extravagance forced him into the hands of money-lenders, and some of his later works were not worthy of him, though even towards the end, when penniless, harried by bailiffs, and seeking refuge in drink he could still turn out work of great beauty and charm.

Berg, Magnus (1666–1739). A Norwegian ivory-carver, strongly influenced by German masters. He is represented by a figure of *Venus* and group of *Venus and Adonis* at Cassel.

Berge (**Berger** or **Verger**), **Jacques.** Born at Brussels in 1693 and died there in 1756. Studied at Paris under N. Coustou and later in Italy. He returned to Brussels in 1722. His style is remarkably classical for its date. His best known work is the monumental fountain in the Place du Grand Sablon, Brussels, commissioned by the British Ambassador Sir Thomas Bruce in 1751. Several of his terracottas are in the Brussels Museum.

Berruer, Pierre-François. Born and died in Paris 1733–97. Studied under Michel-Ange Slodtz and then at Rome, where he was a *pensionnaire* at the French Academy from 1759 until 1763. He exhibited regularly at the Salons between 1765 and 1793 and was admitted an Academician in 1770. He worked mainly as a decorative sculptor on public buildings in Paris and in the provinces, but he also made terracotta groups and statuettes, good examples of which may be seen in the Musée de Bescançon.

Boizot, Simon-Louis. Son of the painter Antoine Boizot. Born and died at Paris, 1743–1809. Studied first under Michel-Ange Slodtz, then at the École Royale, and finally at the French Academy in Rome, having won the Prix de Rome in 1765. He remained in Italy until 1770. In 1778 he was admitted an Academician, his *morceau de réception* being the statue of Meleager now in the Louvre. He exhibited regularly at the Salons from 1773 until 1806, often showing terracotta statuettes and small groups and occasionally busts in the same medium. He also executed much decorative sculpture, for example at the Château de Fontainebleau and the Palais Bourbon in Paris. From 1774 to 1785 he was in charge of the sculpture section of the Manufacture Royale de Sèvres, for which he executed many models, usually in terracotta. During the Revolution he escaped the eclipse that befell so many of the royal sculptors and was made a member of the commission appointed to take over the protection of works of art. He also contributed to the decoration of the column of the Grande Armée in the Place Vendôme.

Bossuit, François van (1635–92). Flemish ivory-carver. Spent much of his life in Italy and is known by several signed works, among which the most notable are the *Death of Adonis* and *Music* in the Rijksmuseum and the *Toilet of Bathsheba* in the Wallace Collection.

Bouchardon, Edmé. Born at Chaumont en Bassigny (Hte Marne) in 1698 and died at Paris in 1762. Studied first under G. Coustou the younger, then at the École Royale and later in Rome, where he was a *pensionnaire* at the French Academy from 1723 until 1732. After his return to Paris he was extensively employed by the King. His early works (e.g. the Neptune Fountain at Versailles, 1736–9) are strongly influenced by Roman baroque sculpture, but he later developed strong classical tendencies, as is shown in his fountain in the Rue de Grenelle, Paris, and the equestrian statue of Louis XV in the Place de la Concorde. He was also an accomplished draughtsman and issued several series of prints, e.g. the *Cris de Paris*, which came out between 1737 and 1746. His terracottas are generally sketches for marble figures or groups, but he occasionally used this medium for independent works of art, and these were avidly collected by French connoisseurs during the eighteenth century.

Bouchardon, Jacques-Philippe. Born at Chaumont en Bassigny (Hte Marne) in 1711 and died in Stockholm in 1753. Studied under his brother Edmé's guidance at Rome. Returned to Paris about 1730. In 1741 he was called to Stockholm and remained there for the rest of his life, working mainly for the Swedish Court and nobility. Good examples of his terracottas are in the Nationalmuseum, Stockholm.

Breton, Luc-François. Born at Besançon in 1731 and died there in 1800. Studied under C. Attiret at Dôle and then at Rome, where he won the first prize for sculpture at the Accademia di San Luca in 1758. He re-

mained in Rome until 1771. A large collection of his terracottas is preserved in the museum at Besançon.

Bronze disease. Natural patina formed in the soil, often of a soft and porous nature, tends to retain some of saline constituents of the soil. These salts, together with the moisture in the atmosphere, may form bright-green spots, which are sometimes dry or moist, a condition called bronze disease. The disease, if not attended to, spreads quickly and has a destructive corrosive action. Its cure by chemical processes is perhaps too complicated to be attempted by collectors, but is easily accomplished by an expert restorer.

Caffieri, Jean-Jacques. Son of the famous *ciseleur* and bronze worker Jacques Caffieri. Born in Paris in 1725 and died there in 1792. Studied under his father and Jean-Baptiste Lemoyne II. Later he entered the Academy, and between 1749 and 1753 studied at Rome. Admitted an Academician in 1757 and appointed *Sculpteur du Roi* to Louis XV. He exhibited regularly at the Salons from 1757 until 1789. Caffieri is now best known for his portrait busts in marble and terracotta, such as those of the French dramatic poets which he made for the foyer of the Comédie Française. Those in terracotta, which he handled with great sensitivity, are outstanding even in an age of portrait busts. During the revolution he was put in charge of the paintings and works of art preserved in the old Académie Royale, but he died almost immediately. Good examples of his terracotta busts may be seen in the museum at Dijon and in the Louvre.

Campbell, Thomas (1790–1858). Spent most of his life in Rome and was much influenced by the classical school. Though now a forgotten and neglected artist, he deserves a better fate. He was a careful worker and took an infinity of trouble to give a characteristic likeness to each of his sitters. (Plate 449B.)

Cavalier, Jean (*fl.* 1686–1707). Was of French origin, but passed a roaming life working in England, Sweden, Denmark, Bavaria, Austria, and Russia. He seems to have confined his attention to small portrait medallions, which he carved in low relief with exquisitely fine precision. He is represented in the museums of Stockholm, Copenhagen,

Cassel (some thirty medallions), Berlin, Munich, Dresden, Brunswick, and the Victoria and Albert Museum.

Chantrey, Sir Francis, R.A. (1781–1841). The most popular sculptor of the Late Georgian era and his energy must have been heroic. From his studio flowed an almost ceaseless flood of busts and monuments, the former, considering the rapidity with which they must have been modelled, extremely good, some almost inspired. His busts of men are better than those of women. In his lifetime nearly everybody of importance sat to him.

Chasing or **chiselling.** The *cire-perdue* process of casting leaves roughness and poor finish, as well as often resulting in the loss of detail. It is therefore necessary to work over the rough-cast with steel chisels and gravers. The absence of such evidence of individual treatment of bronzes may be taken at best as a sign of a poor workshop production, at worst as a sign of modern after-casting.

Chaudet, Denis-Antoine. Born in Paris in 1763 and died there in 1810 Studied first under J. B. Stouf and E. Gois, then at the École Royale and later at the French Academy in Rome, where he was a *pensionnaire* from 1784 until 1788. In 1791 he was made a member of the Gobelins and exhibited at most of the Salons between 1789 and 1810. He worked at the Panthéon under Quatremère de Quincy and received several important commissions from the Imperial Government: e.g. the statue of Napoleon on the summit of the column of the Grande Armée in the Place Vendôme. He was also a painter. He executed many small groups and statuettes in terracotta, and these were highly valued by the leading collectors of his day.

Cheverton, Benjamin (1794–1876). English sculptor. He executed a few good original busts, including one of William Huntington in the Victoria and Albert Museum, and miniature copies after antique sculptures and the works of such masters as Roubiliac and Chantrey. In 1828, together with a Mr Hawkins, he invented a machine which enabled him to produce miniature facsimiles in ivory of large-scale busts and reliefs in marble or other materials.

Chinard, Joseph. Born at Lyons in 1756 and died there in 1813. Studied first at Lyons under B. Blasie and then at Rome, where he won a prize for sculpture at the Accademia di San Luca in 1784. Returned to Lyons in 1787, but was back in Rome by 1791. In the following year he was arrested and imprisoned in Rome as a revolutionary. On his return to Lyons in 1793 he was again imprisoned, this time as a counter-revolutionary. After his release in 1794 he rapidly achieved fame for his busts and medallion portrait heads of patriots and *Conventionnels*, ultimately becoming a protégé of Napoleon and almost the "official" portraitist of the Bonaparte family. In 1800 he made a third visit to Italy. He is best known for his portraits, such as that of Madame Récamier, which he executed in both marble and terracotta. Excellent examples of his terracottas may be seen in the museum at Lyons, in the Musée Carnavalet at Paris, and in the Louvre.

Cire-perdue. The "lost-wax" method of casting, used for all casting of work of any complication from ancient to modern times. Its processes are, briefly, this: the work is modelled on a clay core in wax of a thickness intended in the final bronze product. The finished wax model, to which vents and pouring channels are added, is then surrounded by an envelope of finely ground clay mixed with sawdust, chopped straw, or some such inflammable material, which will burn out when the mould is fired, giving the envelope the necessary porosity. In the firing process the wax melts and leaves the mould through the vents and pouring channels – and the metal may be poured in to take the place of the wax. The mould is then broken off the bronze and the core removed by breaking it up. It is, of course, obvious that only one bronze can be cast from each wax model by this method. For each of the workshop productions of the Renaissance there must therefore have been a wax model first, and this explains the infinite slight variations in each example made after the master model produced by the head of the workshop. Moulds which may be taken apart in small sections are called piece-moulds, and have perhaps been known since the sixteenth century. They were probably never used for bronze sculpture until the nineteenth century, and the presence of small ridges, that are the result of the tiny gaps between each section of the mould, may be taken as the surest evidence of modern manufacture.

Collino, Ignazio. Born at Turin in 1724 and died there in 1793. Studied under F. Beaumont and F. Ladatte. In 1749 he was sent to Rome by the King of Sardinia and studied under Maini. He also worked at Rome as a copyist after the antique. In 1760 he was elected to the Accademia di San Luca. His younger brother Filippo, with whom he later worked in partnership, joined him at Rome in 1754. In 1763 Ignazio was appointed *Scultore del Re* at Turin, and thereafter he and his brother worked extensively for the King of Sardinia's villas and palaces in Piedmont. Excellent examples of their terracotta statuettes are preserved in the Accademia Albertina at Turin.

Cyfflé, Paul-Louis. Born at Bruges in 1724 and died at Ixelles in 1806. Studied under B. Guibal at Lunéville and later succeeded his master as *sculpteur ordinaire* to the King of Poland, for whom he executed the remarkable fountain in the Place d'Alliance at Nancy. In 1768 he obtained permission to set up a factory for making faïence in *terre de Lorraine*, and it was during the next few years that he made the small groups and figurines in terracotta which are now so highly valued by collectors of eighteenth-century French art. In 1777 Cyfflé abandoned his factory at Nancy and returned to Bruges. In 1785 he set up a new factory at Namur, but this did not survive the Revolution. Good examples of his terracottas may be seen in the museum at Nancy, in the Musée de Cluny, Paris, and in the museum at Sèvres.

Dardel, Robert-Guillaume. Born at Paris in 1749 and died there in 1821. Studied under Pajou, and from 1780 until 1788 worked for the Prince de Condé. He later became an active supporter of the Republic and, unlike so many of his contemporaries, escaped any suspicion of royalism, partly through the patronage of David. In 1793 he was appointed member of the Commission des Arts, and in 1796 became Director of the Musée de

Versailles. He specialized in retrospective studies of historical personages. He exhibited regularly at the Salons, often showing terracotta statuettes. Good examples of these may now be seen in the Musée Condé, Chantilly, and in the Wallace Collection.

Delvaux, Laurent. Born at Ghent in 1696 and died at Nivelles in 1778. Studied at Ghent, Brussels, and London, and later in Italy, where he lived from 1718 until 1732. In 1733 he was appointed court sculptor to the Regent Marie Élizabeth in Brussels. He settled at Nivelles in 1734 and became court sculptor to the Duke of Lorraine. Delvaux worked in the late Italian baroque style, which he infused with certain characteristics of his native Flemish idiom. Good examples of his terracottas may be seen at the Musées Royaux des Beaux Arts, Brussels, and in the Victoria and Albert Museum.

Dumont, Jacques-Edmé. Son of the sculptor Edmé Dumont. Born in Paris in 1761 and died there in 1844. Studied under Pajou and later at Rome, where he was a *pensionnaire* at the French Academy from 1788 until 1792. Returning to Paris during the revolution he won immediate success with such works as *Le Peuple français vainqueur du despotisme* and *La Liberté*. Examples of his terracotta groups and statuettes are in the Musée Carnavalet, Paris, and in the museums at Semur and Sèvres.

Duquesnoy, François (1594–1643). Known as *Il Fiammingo*, a Flemish-born sculptor of the first importance who spent most of his working life in Rome. His large-scale statues in marble are among the masterpieces of restrained baroque sculpture, but unfortunately no documented ivory carving by him is known. Six bacchanalian scenes, often known as "Fiammingo's boys", in the Victoria and Albert Museum, were for long ascribed to him but are now generally regarded as copies after lost originals.

Faid'herbe, Lucas (1617–97). Worked under Rubens, who wrote a certificate of his ability in 1640, declaring that he had executed several fine works in ivory for him. His only signed work is a low relief of children dancing (in the Prado), but numerous ivories have been attributed to him.

Figurehead Carvers (American). Over seven hundred names of ship carvers are known, and in some instances carvings have been related to particular artists. Among those whose work is known are Charles A. L. Sampson of Bath, Maine (d. 1881), who carved the figurehead for the *Belle of Oregon*; and John Haley Bellamy (1836–1914) of Kittery Point, Maine, Portsmouth, New Hampshire, and Boston, especially known for his great eagle with a wing-spread of 18 feet, carved as a figurehead for the U.S.S. *Lancaster* (Mariners' Museum, Newport News, Virginia). Other carvers were William S. Gleason & Sons of Boston (clipper *Minnehaha*); William Luke of Portsmouth, Virginia (*Tamanend* bust, U.S. Naval Academy); Laban S. Beecher of Boston (*Jackson* figurehead of the frigate *Constitution*); Dodge & Son of New York, carvers of a later *Jackson* figurehead; Woodbury Gerrish of Portsmouth, New Hampshire (*Franklin*); Jacob S. Anderson of New York City (*David Crockett*); Hastings & Gleason of Boston (*Indian Chief*); Emery Jones of Freeport, Maine (*Samuel Skolfield*); William Southworth of Portland, Maine; J. E. Verrill of Rockland, Maine; and John W. Mason of Damariscotta, Maine. Ship carvings today are in historical and marine museums, in private collections, and in gardens of private estates. Although figureheads belong to sculpture, few are in art museums.

Edbury Hatch (1849–1935), one of the later ship carvers of Newcastle, Maine, continued to carve after ship carving as a craft had come to an end. From his later years are a number of his carvings of fine quality now privately owned around Wiscasset, Damariscotta, and Newcastle, Maine. He embellished his house with wood-carvings and carved a fine coat-of-arms of the state of Maine, privately owned since 1949. His style is characterized by boldness and simplicity, as yet without the self-conscious stylization of our own day.

Foucou, Jean-Joseph. Born in 1739 and died in Paris in 1815. He studied first at Marseilles, then in Paris under Caffieri, and finally in Rome between 1771 and 1775. Admitted an Academician in 1785. Exhibited regularly at the Salons from 1771 until 1814. He worked extensively as a decorative sculptor in Paris and also executed several fine portrait busts. His terracottas may be seen in the museum at Aix.

Francis, John (1780–1861). His small cabinet busts are admirable. Many were of politicians; for Francis was a keen Whig and was called the "official sculptor" of that party. His sitters used to order a number of replicas of their busts to present to their friends. Francis' work is therefore not rare, but that does not make it any the less attractive. (Plate 448D.)

Garden furniture. The earliest garden seat seems to have been made of turf.

This type has been revived in recent years in the thyme seat. Benches were also found in the arbour, and in the early seventeenth century Bacon recommended "seats set in some decent order". It seems probable that wood was generally used for garden furniture, which has subsequently perished. Stone benches were, however, in use by the end of the seventeenth century, and have held their popularity ever since, more for their looks than comfort. Usually simple, they were occasionally supported on figures of lions or other conveniently shaped animals. Lead might also be used for a small bench – there is a ponderous classical example at Castle Hill in Devonshire. In the eighteenth century the design of garden seats naturally followed that of interior furnishings. Marble thrones in the Grecian taste were also popular at the end of the century.

It is difficult to determine when the rustic garden seat first appeared; it was probably made of wood. In the late 1740s Gainsborough painted Mrs Andrews sitting upon what appears to be a rococo iron seat designed for the garden, but in Zoffany's picture of the Garrick family taking tea at the river-side, some thirty years later, the chairs look as if they have been brought out from the dining-room. Rustic conversation pieces suggest that boulders and fallen trees were sometimes used by the hardy aristocrat.

As far as may be judged, the great age of garden furniture came only with the increased use of cast-iron in the nineteenth century. In 1818 John Papworth set about the design of charmingly elegant garden seats, "claiming a share of novelty" in the Regency taste; one was beneath an umbrella of iron and thin copper plates, the other, "of the marquee character", was covered with cloth upon an iron frame (Fig. 6). Simpler seats of the period were made out of twisted and twirled iron wire. With the ripening of the nineteenth century, garden furniture naturally became heavier and more elaborate. A good Gothic settee in cast-iron illustrates the change in taste.

FIG. 6. Regency garden seat designed by J. B. Papworth

Rustic seats, made to look as if they had been assembled out of odd fragments of wood, probably originated in the hermitages of the eighteenth-century park, but were never so popular as in the Victorian era. The catalogue of the Great Exhibition lists a number of more grandiose items of garden furniture, such as vast fountains, coy figures, huge forbidding park gates, and an "ornamental rustic dome, in cast-iron bronzed", an erection of great complexity which sheltered John Bell's heroic statue of the Eagle Slayer. Towards the end of the Victorian period the interest in formal gardening brought about a revival of seventeenth-century ornaments and discreet stone furniture.

Garrard, George, A.R.A. (1760–1826). Though he produced a number of skilfully carved busts, Garrard will be best remembered for his accurate small-scale models of animals, particularly of dogs and cattle, which he executed both in bronze and plaster.

Gois, Étienne-Pierre-Adrien. Born in Paris in 1731 and died there in 1823. Studied under Michel-Ange Slodtz and later in Rome, between 1761 and 1764. He exhibited regularly at the Salons between 1767 and 1804.

Worked mainly as a decorative sculptor in Paris. He was also a skilled engraver. During the Revolution Gois became Professeur des Écoles Nationales. He frequently worked in terracotta, using the medium for life-size busts and decorative low-reliefs, as well as for statuettes and small groups.

Gosset, Isaac (1713–99). Wax-modeller. His portraits are nearly always in a yellowish wax (invented by himself) and modelled in a low relief, which thins at the extremities of the profile, so that the nose, hair, and other features appear almost to be painted on the background.

Hardy, B. C. (1726–1819). German wax-modeller working in Britain whose superb portraits are modelled in so deep a relief as to be almost in the round.

Harrich, Christof (d. 1630). Wax-modeller, a virtuoso craftsman, applied his skill to the repellently realistic treatment of decomposing flesh on *memento mori* figures for which there was a great demand in Germany.

Hess, Sebastian, and **Paul Johann.** Brothers, both ivory carvers, were born in Bamberg, but worked principally in Brussels and Vienna, carved little landscapes and other scenes on a microscopic scale.

Houdon, Jean-Antoine. Born in Versailles in 1741 and died in Paris in 1828. Studied first at Versailles and then in Paris under Slodtz, Lemoyne, and Pigalle. He later attended the École Royale and won the Prix de Rome in 1764. The next four years were spent at the French Academy in Rome, where he executed several remarkable works, including the famous marble statue of St Bruno in Sta Maria degli Angeli. On his return to France he rapidly achieved renown, especially for his portrait busts, and during the next few years he travelled widely in Europe to execute commissions. He became the leading portraitist in the round, and nearly all the celebrities of the day sat to him. In Houdon the great tradition of French eighteenth-century portrait sculpture may be said to have culminated. In 1785 he was invited by Franklin to visit America to execute the now famous whole-length portrait of Washington in the Capitol at Richmond, Virginia. He also went to Germany and executed several commis-

(B) Sarah Siddons (marble) by T. Campbell. *National Portrait Gallery, London.*

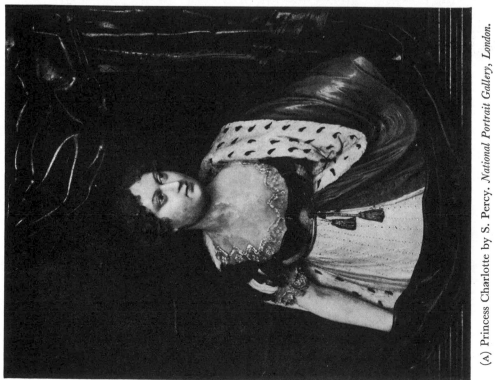

(A) Princess Charlotte by S. Percy. *National Portrait Gallery, London.*

PLATE 449

(A) Group of lead *amorini* in the style of John van Nost. Formerly at Stowe.

(B) Lead shepherd in the style of John Cheere.

(C) Shepherdess in the style of John Cheere.

(D) Classical figure in Coade stone, dated 1803.

PLATE 450

(B) Bacchante by Joseph-Charles Marin. *Victoria and Albert Museum, London.*

(A) St Joseph and Child by Giuseppe Mazza. *Pinacoteca, Bologna.*

PLATE 451

(A) Philosopher (or River God?) by Augustin Pajou. Height 7½ ins. *Cailleux Collection, Paris.*

(B) Mythological scene by Claude Michel, called Clodion, signed. Length 32¼ ins. *Cailleux Collection, Paris.*

PLATE 452

Holy Trinity (alabaster), *c.* 1380–1410.
Museum of Fine Arts, Boston.

(c) "Flawford" Madonna and Child (alabaster), *c.* 1380. *Nottingham Castle Museum and Art Gallery.*

(B) St Anne instructing the Virgin (alabaster), *c.* 1436. *National Museum, Lisbon, Portugal.*

PLATE 453

Coronation of the Virgin (alabaster). Between 1420 and 1440. *Mrs Anthony Norman Collection.*

PLATE 454

(A) Sling shot thrower by Isacee of Povungnituk. *Canadian National Film Board.*

(B) Polar bear having caught a seal, from Cape Dorset, Baffin Island. *Private Collection.*

PLATE 455

Eskimo carving given to the Queen (as Princess Elizabeth) during her visit to Canada in 1951. It is the work of Munamee, an eskimo from Nuvojjak, a camp in the Cape Dorset region of Southwest Baffin Island. *Reproduced by gracious permission of Her Majesty the Queen.*

PLATE 456

(A) The Coronation of the Virgin, French, mid-thirteenth century. *Louvre, Paris.*

(B) The Deposition, French, *c.* 1265. *Louvre, Paris.*

(C) La Vierge de la Sainte-Chapelle, French, early fourteenth century. *Louvre, Paris.*

PLATE 457

(A) Comb, decorated with scenes of courtly love; French, fourteenth century. *National Museum, Florence.*

(B) Mirror case decorated with the Assault on the Castle of Love; French, fourteenth century. *National Museum, Florence.*

(D) The Triumph of Love, North Italian, probably Mantuan, second half of the fifteenth century. *National Museum, Florence.*

(C) Comb, decorated with Venus and amorini; Italian, sixteenth century. *National Museum, Florence.*

(E) Silenus by Gerard van Opstal, mid-seventeenth century. *Louvre, Paris.*

PLATE 458

(A) Crucifix, French or Flemish, 1670. *S. W. Wolsey, London.*

(B) The Crucifixion by Balthazar Stockamer, late seventeenth century. *Palazzo Pitti, Florence.*

(C) The Judgement of Paris, attributed to Christof Angermair, early seventeenth century. *Victoria and Albert Museum, London.*

(D) Carved cup, attributed to J. M. Maucher, late seventeenth century. *Victoria and Albert Museum, London.*

PLATE 459

(A) Chinese horse's head and neck about 12 ins in height. Han dynasty. 206 B.C.–A.D. 220. *Victoria and Albert Museum, London.*

(B) Celadon jade mountain with two poems by the Emperor Ch'ien Lung, 1736–95. Length 12½ ins. *Spink & Son Ltd.*

(C) Jade Tsung. Early C dynasty, *c.* 1122–249 *Eumopolos Collection, B Museum, London.*

(D) Pale grey jade incense burner and cover, copied from an early ritual bronze. Ch'ien Lung, 1736–95. Height 4¼ ins. *Spink & Son Ltd.*

(E) An old Chinese plainly carved spina h jade bowl. Ch'ien Lung period, 1736–9 meter 8½ ins, height 3½ ins. *John Spark Lt*

PLATE 460

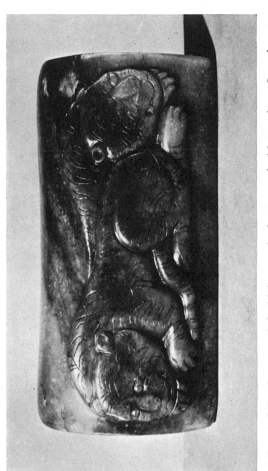

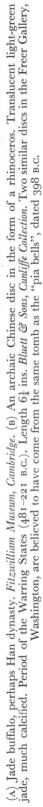

(A) Jade buffalo, perhaps Han dynasty. *Fitzwilliam Museum, Cambridge.* (B) An archaic Chinese disc in the form of a rhinoceros. Translucent light-green jade, much calcified. Period of the Warring States (481–221 B.C.). Length 6¼ ins. *Bluett & Sons, Cunliffe Collection.* Two similar discs in the Freer Gallery, Washington, are believed to have come from the same tomb as the "pia bells", dated 398 B.C.

(D) Grey jade head-rest mottled with brown, the front carved with two tigers. Sung dynasty, A.D. 960–1279. Length 10½ ins. *Spink & Son Ltd.*

(C) Jade dragon-headed horse. K'ang-hsi A.D. 1662–1722. *Fitzwilliam Museum, Cambridge.*

PLATE 461

(A) Ceres by Simeon Skillin, 1756–1806. Height 24 ins. *New York State Historical Association, Cooperstown, New York.*

(B) Head of a Boy, dated 1845, by Alexander Ames. *New York State Historical Association, Cooperstown, New York.*

(C) Tavern Bust. Height 19 ins. *Collection of Mrs Dudley E. Waters, 1936 (Index).*

(D) Ship Figurehead, about 1825. Height 27½ ins. *Abby Aldrich Rockefeller Folk Art Collection, Williamsburg, Virginia.*

PLATE 462

(A) St James supporting the Virgin by Veit Stoss.
From the Crakow altar.

(B) Joachim and Anne. North Netherlandish
carving in oak, 1470–80. *Rijksmuseum, Amsterdam.*

(C) Tilman Riemenschnieder. Angel in lime-wood,
early sixteenth century. *Victoria and Albert Museum,
London.*

(D) Late fifteenth-century
Virgin. *Gerald Kerin.*

PLATE 463

St Kunigunde, carved in lime-wood by Ignaz Günther, 1762. *Church of Rott-am-Inn.*

PLATE 464

(A) and (B) Octagonal waste bowl and sugar bowl by Joseph Richardson (1711–84), Philadelphia. Cypher of Margaret Wistar. Width (waste bowl) 5¾ ins. Height (sugar bowl) 4¾ ins. *Collection of Mrs Charles H. Taylor.*

(C) Coffee-pot and sugar bowl by Simeon Soumain (*c.* 1685–*c.* 1750), New York. Straight sides indicate first half of the century; rare to have accompanying sugar bowl. Height (pot) 10⅜ ins. *Museum of Fine Arts, Boston.*

PLATE 465

(A) Coffee-pot by Daniel Henchman (1730–75), Boston. Height 10⅞ ins. *Collection of Philip H. Hammerslough.*

(B) Coffee-pot by Joseph Anthony, Jr. (1762–1814), Philadelphia. Coffee-pots "single and double belly'd" advertised 1760s. Height 13 ins. *Henry Ford Museum, Dearborn, Michigan.*

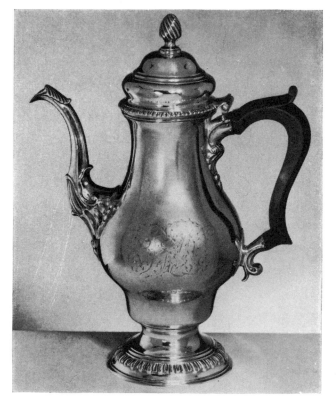

PLATE 466

(A) Sugar caster with the Schuyler arms, by Pieter Van Dyck, 1684–1750. Height 7¾ ins. *Garvan Collection.*

(B) Early eighteenth-century spout-cup with cover, by Jacob Boelen, New York, 1654–1729. *Metropolitan Museum of Art, New York.*

(C) The William III tankard persisted in New York well into the eighteenth century. Adrian Bancker made this in 1735 for the marriage of John and Anne (Jacobs) Gillingham of Philadelphia. It shows a typical New York decoration, a cipher of imposing proportions. Height 6½ ins. *Ginsburg & Levy, New York.*

Loving cup, by Jacob Hurd, Boston, 1744. Presented to Edward Tyng for a naval victory in King George's War. Height 15½ ins. *Garvan Collection.*

PLATE 467

(A) Tea-set by Paul Revere, Boston, presented 1799 to Edmund Hartt, builder of the frigate *Constitution*.
Museum of Fine Arts, Boston.

(B) Tea-set by Abraham du Bois, Philadelphia, *c.* 1790, showing the ovoid forms and pierced gallery favoured
in Philadelphia in the classic period. *Garvan Collection.*

PLATE 468

(B) John Coney's monteith was made for John Colman, a Boston merchant, in the early eighteenth century. The rim is not detachable as on English monteiths. Diameter 11 ins. *Garvan Collection.*

(D) New York cup and footed cover showing English and Dutch influence. Made by Gerrit Onckelbag for the christening of Judith Bayard, December 13, 1696. Height 5¾ ins. *Garvan Collection.*

(A) Boston salver with chinoiserie decoration in late Stuart style; made by Timothy Dwight who died 1691–2. Diameter 11 5/16 ins. *Museum of Fine Arts, Boston.*

(C) New York punch-bowl of pumpkin shape and panelled sides with *repoussé* and chased floral ornament. By Cornelius Kierstede, *c.* 1698. Diameter 9¾ ins. *Metropolitan Museum of Art, New York.*

PLATE 469

(A) Transition, rococo to classic; sugar bowl, by William Gilbert, New York, c. 1785. *Museum of the City of New York*.

(B) Fluted oval teapot with accompanying stand; ornament in bright cut engraving. By Ebenezer Moulton of Boston and Newburyport, Massachusetts, 1768–1824. *Minneapolis Institute of Arts*.

(c) One of a pair of salvers, by Myer Myers of New York, showing the Phillipse arms, c. 1770. Diameter 8 ins. Spoons from set of six, made for same family by Simeon Soumain, New York. *Ginsburg & Levy, New York*.

PLATE 470

A

B

C

D

(A) Exceptional example of the globular teapot in the work of John Potwine, Boston, *c.* 1730; shows arms of Samuel Welles, 1660–1731; cover has a rare bayonet fastening. *Robert Ensko, Inc.*

(B) Two-handled cup by John Dixwell, Boston, 1722. Height 5¼ ins. *Spalding Collection, Museum of Fine Arts, Boston.*

(C) Typical New York teapot, by Adrian Bancker, *c.* 1740. Height 8 ins. *Tiffany & Co.*

(D) A masterpiece of the rococo is this Philadelphia tea-kettle on stand with spirit lamp, by Joseph Richardson, Sr, before 1760. Height 14½ ins. *Garvan Collection.*

PLATE 471

Tigerware jug with silver mounts, 1560. *E. T. Biggs & Sons.*

PLATE 472

(A) Wine-cup, 1641. Maker's mark I over w between two pellets. *Crichton Bros.* (B) Silver-mounted coconut cup, *c.* 1650. Maker's mark WR, possibly for William Rainbow. *H. R. Jessop.*

(C) Covered tankard, 6¼ ins high, 1672. Maker's mark IN, a mullet below. *E. T. Biggs & Sons.* (D) Covered tankard by Philip Easton, Exeter 1726. *Brufords of Exeter.*

PLATE 473

(A) Pair of sauceboats by John Gilpin, 1746. *Crichton Bros.*

(B) Chased rococo coffee-pot by William Cripps. 1753; plain coffee-pot by John Payne, 1774.
Thomas Lumley.

PLATE 474

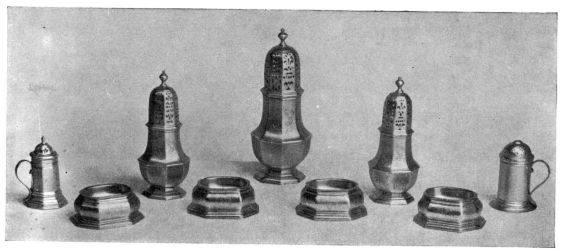

(A) Three casters $5\frac{3}{4}$ ins and $7\frac{1}{4}$ ins high by Charles Adam, 1716; four octagonal trencher salts by Glover Johnson, 1724; octagonal dredger $3\frac{1}{4}$ ins high by Glover Johnson, 1724; cylindrical dredger $3\frac{1}{4}$ ins high by John Gibbons, 1728. *Crichton Bros.*

(B) Four mugs. *Left to right:* 1704, 1725, 1744, 1739. *Crichton Bros.*

(C) Four cream-jugs: *Left to right:* James Manners, 1739; George Jones, 1742; Thomas Williamson (Dublin), 1735, and John Munns, 1764. *Spink.*

PLATE 475

(A) Old English pattern table silver and pistol-handled knives from 1730 to 1757.
W. H. Willson.

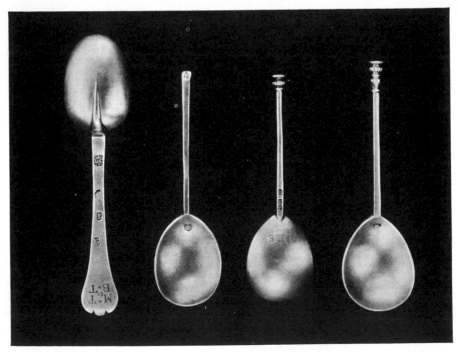

(B) Four early spoons: *Left to right:* (i) Trifid top, Lawrence Coles, 1694; (ii) Slip
top 1669, maker's mark I.K., rose and two pellets below; (iii) Seal top 1600, maker's
mark a crescent enclosing a w; (iv) Seal top, Benjamin Yate, 1627. *W. H. Willson.*

PLATE 476

(A) Pair of candlesticks by Francis Page, 1749; inkstand by William Robertson, 1755. *H. R. Jessop.*

(B) Set of three silver-gilt sugar vases by Pierre Gillois, 1777; pair of Corinthian column candlesticks by John Carter, 1773. *H. R. Jessop.*

PLATE 477

(A) Shaped square salver, 1729. *S. J. Phillips.*

(B) Pair of covered sauce tureens by Thomas Heming, 1775. *Thomas Lumley.*

PLATE 478

(A) Oblong entrée dish and cover by Thomas Robins, 1810. *Brufords of Exeter.*

(B) Oval soup tureen and cover, Dublin 1820. *Thomas Lumley.*

PLATE 479

(A) Quaich, Edinburgh, 1736, maker Charles Blair. *Royal Scottish Museum.*

(B) Two-handled cup, Edinburgh, 1709, maker James Symp-sone. *Earl of Haddington.*

(C) A Scottish silver tankard, Edinburgh, 1728, maker James Mitchellsone. Weight 32 ozs. *Thomas Lumley.*

PLATE 480

sions for the Empress Catherine of Russia. In 1777 he became a member of the Académie. The fall of the *ancien régime* was a turning-point in Houdon's career, and though he escaped imprisonment through the influence of friends, his position was never the same again. He continued working in obscurity, however, and executed a few commissions for Napoleon. During his last years he taught at the École des Beaux Arts, only retiring in 1823. Houdon's most celebrated work is the *Frileuse* in the Montpellier Museum, but it is as a portraitist that he is now chiefly valued, especially for his terracotta busts. Unlike his predecessors, he was more successful with his male than with his female sitters, though he made some charming heads of young girls, especially those of his own family. Examples of Houdon's terracotta busts may be seen in most public collections in France – in the Louvre and in the museums of Toulouse, Grenoble, Dijon, as well as in Berlin and Neufchâtel in Switzerland.

Julien, Pierre. Born at S. Paulien (Hte Loire) in 1731 and died in Paris in 1804. Studied in Lyons under Perrache and then in Paris under G. Coustou II. He was a *pensionnaire* at the French Academy at Rome between 1768 and 1773. On his return to Paris he worked for a time as Coustou's assistant but soon established his own reputation, being elected an Academician in 1779. He received many Royal commissions and worked extensively for the Pavillon de Flore in the Tuileries and for the Dairy at the Château de Rambouillet. He used terracotta for both *sculpture d'appartement* and for portrait busts. Good examples of his terracottas may be seen at the museums of Angers and Le Puy, Paris.

Kerriex, Guillaume. Born in 1654 and died at Antwerp in 1719. One of the leading Flemish sculptors of the late seventeenth century, his work is somewhat Frenchified and rococo in style. Good examples of his terracottas may be seen in the museum at Brussels and at the Victoria and Albert Museum.

Ladatte, Francesco. Born at Turin in 1706 and died there in 1787. Studied first in Turin and then in Paris, where he attended the École Royale. He exhibited at the Salons between 1737 and 1743. In 1741 he was admitted an Academician. He returned to Turin in 1744, having been appointed *Scultore del Re* by the King of Sardinia. His best-known work in France is the bronze relief representing the Martyrdom of St Philip in the chapel of Versailles. In Turin he carried out many decorative works in bronze, both as garden sculpture and for interior decoration. He also worked as a *ciseleur*. He exhibited many terracotta groups and statuettes in the Paris Salons, and good examples of his work in this medium may be seen in the Musée des Arts Décoratifs in Paris and in the Museo Civico at Turin.

Larmier, Pierre-Philibert. Born in Dijon in 1752 and died there in 1807. Studied first in Dijon and later in Paris under G. Coustou. He exhibited at the Salons from 1791 to 1793, and in 1804 was appointed keeper of the museum at Dijon, where he remained for the rest of his life. He worked almost exclusively in terracotta or plaster, in which mediums he attained the utmost dexterity and lightness of touch. The best examples of his work in terracotta may be seen at the Musée de Dijon.

Lecompte, Félix. Born in Paris in 1737 and died there in 1817. Studied under Falconet and Louis-Claude Vassée. He won the Prix de Rome and was a *pensionnaire* at the French Academy at Rome from 1761 to 1768. Elected an Academician in 1771. Lecompte exhibited regularly at the Salons from 1769 to 1793. The King gave him several commissions for portraits in marble, both busts and full-lengths, and he also worked extensively as a decorative sculptor for various prominent architects, including the ultra neo-classic Ledoux. His terracottas were collected by many of the leading connoisseurs in Paris during the late eighteenth century. Good examples may now be seen in the Louvre and in the chapel of the École des Beaux Arts, Paris, and in the museum at Le Mans.

Lemoyne, Jean-Baptiste. Born in Paris in 1704 and died there in 1778. He was the son of Jean-Louis Lemoyne and a member of a distinguished family of French sculptors. Studied under his father and Robert le Lorrain. He won the Prix de Rome, but did not go to Italy on account of his father's failing eyesight. Elected Academician in 1738 and exhibited regularly at the Salons between 1737 and 1771. His larger works were nearly all destroyed during the Revolution, and he is now remembered mainly for his busts, both in marble and terracotta, which form a remarkable gallery of portraits of all the leading figures in the world of fashion. He was especially successful with his female sitters. Several good examples of his terracotta busts may be seen in the Musée des Arts Décoratifs, Paris, and in the Museums at Tours and Toulouse.

Lochee, John Charles. Born in 1751, studied at the Royal Academy, and was, like a number of other wax-modellers, employed by Wedgwood. His portraits are usually in pink wax painted with colours, and the details, hair, uniform, etc., in considerably higher relief than the face of the sitter. Unfortunately, he does not seem to have been a good man of business. He was declared a bankrupt in 1791, and after that trace of him is lost.

Lucas, Richard Cockle (1800–83). Sculptor. His portraits (generally ivory-coloured) are mounted on chocolate-coloured wax, while the frames, which he designed himself, have an inside edging of a very unattractive brown plush. A large collection of his works can be seen at the Bethnal Green Museum, London. He sprang to posthumous notoriety on account of his terracotta bust which was acquired by Dr Bode for the Kaiser Friedrich Museum as an original work by Leonardo da Vinci. He produced numerous small ivory carvings, mainly copies after the antique and portraits.

Lücke, Carl August (1668–1730). With the younger members of his family produced many fine portraits and statuettes. In the Victoria and Albert Museum there is an arresting low relief bust of George II by L. von Lücke, carved in 1760.

Macdonald, Laurence (1799–1878). A prolific artist who spent much of his life in Rome, where his work was sought by the fashionable English visitors, his studio being described as containing "the peerage done into marble". Macdonald flattered his sitters,

making all the men appear noble and all the women beautiful, with the result that his busts are inclined to be tame and insipid.

McIntire, Samuel (1757–1811). Of Salem, Massachusetts, was an architectural carver who occasionally carved figures. He began in the eighteenth-century tradition and developed a style of his own. Though he was a master craftsman of interior woodwork of houses, McIntire is close to folk art in his busts, such as *Voltaire* and *Governor John Winthrop*, painted to suggest stone. His emphasis on meticulous detail may be as much due to his decorative bent as to his lack of experience with the living figure.

Marchand, David le (1674–1726). Of Dieppe, who worked principally in England, executed a number of medallions in the style of Cavalier (in the museum at Brunswick, The Royal Observatory, the British Museum, and the Victoria and Albert Museum). He also worked in the round and occasionally carved subject groups, two of which are in the Victoria and Albert Museum – a charming *Time and Opportunity* and a somewhat weak *Venus and Cupid*.

Marin, Joseph-Charles. Born in Paris in 1759 and died there in 1834. Studied under Clodion, whose style he imitated with great virtuosity. He first exhibited at the Salon in 1791. In 1797 he travelled in Italy and returned there in 1801. In 1813 he was appointed Professor of Sculpture at the École des Beaux Arts, Lyons, but later returned to Paris, where he died in penury. Marin was a prolific artist in all manner of decorative accessories, but is best known for his terracotta groups and statuettes representing satyrs, fauns, and nymphs in the style of his master Clodion. He also executed portrait busts and occasionally monumental figures in marble, such as that of the Admiral de Tourville in the Cour d'honneur, Versailles. Good examples of his terracottas may be seen in the Louvre and Musée des Arts Décoratifs, in the museums at Besançon and Bordeaux, in the Victoria and Albert Museum (Plate 451B), and in the Metropolitan Museum.

Masson, François. Born in Vieille-Lyre and died in Paris in 1807. Studied under Charles-Guillaume Coussin and Guillaume

Coustou. In 1765 he designed and executed the fountain at Noyon. From 1771 until 1775 he studied in Rome. On his return to France he worked mainly as a decorative sculptor on such neo-classical buildings as the Palais du Gouvernement at Metz and the Panthéon at Paris. He was awarded several honours under the Empire. He used terracotta both for sketches and for independent works of art, many of which he exhibited at the Salons.

Maucher, J. M. (b. 1645). Specialized in the production of elaborately carved cups, of which there are signed examples at Berlin and in the Hohenlohe Collection at Neuenstein. A fine cup in the Victoria and Albert Museum (Plate 459D) has also been attributed to him.

Mazza, Giuseppe. Born in Bologna in 1653 and died there in 1741. He first studied painting, under Canuti and Cignani, but later turned to sculpture and quickly achieved prominence in his native city. Apart from a brief period in Rome in about 1722, he is not known to have worked outside Bologna. Mazza specialized in terracotta low-reliefs, though he also produced figures in the round and worked in marble and bronze. As a technician he was the equal of all but the best French artists in terracotta of his period. Most of his work is still *in situ* in the Bolognese churches and palaces for which it was designed. Good examples of his terracottas may also be seen in the museums of Berlin and Frankfurt (Plate 451A).

Melchior, Johann Peter. Born at Lintorf in 1742 and died at Nymphenburg in 1825. Studied under Boos and later in France, where he was living c. 1762. In 1765 he was working at Mainz, and from 1770 to 1797 was Modellmeister at the Nymphenburg factory. In 1802 he was appointed Porzellanfabrikinspektor. He produced a considerable quantity of *sculpture d'appartement* in terracotta, good examples of which may be seen in the museum at Mainz.

Michel, Claude (called **Clodion**). Born at Nancy in 1738 and died in Paris in 1814. Studied first in the studio of his uncle Lambert-Sigismond Adam and then for a short time under Pigalle. Later he entered the École Royale, won the Grand Prix de Sculpture, and from 1762 until 1767 was a *pension-naire* at the French Academy at Rome. His talent for witty invention and his extraordinary technical virtuosity in the handling of terracotta were already apparent by this date, and he began to receive commissions from various prominent collectors, such as the Empress Catherine of Russia, which enabled him to remain in Italy for several years after leaving the Academy. On his return to Paris in 1771 his genius was immediately recognized, and he soon became one of the most eagerly sought-after sculptors of his time. He was never admitted to the Academy, however, perhaps because his constant preoccupation with private commissions prevented his ever finishing a diploma work or perhaps because of matrimonial difficulties which had antagonized his father-in-law, Pajou, who was an influential member of the Academy. In any event, his fashionable success was in no way affected by this professional set-back. Specializing in *sculpture d'appartement*, Clodion worked in various mediums and was a prolific designer of all kinds of decorative accessories. But his fame has always rested mainly on his terracotta statuettes and low reliefs representing dancing fauns and nymphs and the pagan deities. In this type of sophisticated and supremely elegant *objets d'art* Clodion still remains supreme, both as artist and as craftsman. In addition to his consummate dexterity in the handling of terracotta, he managed to infuse into his works a light-hearted and apparently spontaneous spirit of pagan sensuousness which raises them above the general level of work of this nature turned out during the last years of the *ancien régime*. His career suffered a great blow at the Revolution, and he never succeeded in adapting his style to the new climate of taste, with its passion for the severe forms affected by the Republican era. Clodion died in penury, and the contents of his studio were sold for prices which would have been thought derisory a few years previously. Fifty years later, when French eighteenth-century art returned to fashion, Clodion's work was widely and sometimes very skilfully copied and faked. Examples of Clodion's work in terracotta may be seen – in the Louvre, the Musée des Arts Dècoratifs, Musée de Cluny, Paris, in the Victoria and Albert

Museum, and in the Metropolitan Museum, New York.

Moitte, Jean-Guillaume. Born in Paris in 1746 and died there in 1810. Studied first under Pigalle and Jean-Baptiste Lemoyne, then at the École Royale, and finally in Rome, where he was a *pensionnaire* at the French Academy from 1771 until 1773. On his return to Paris he worked for a time with Auguste the *orfèvre du roi*, and thereby exerted some influence on *orfèvrerie*. He later developed a considerable practice as a decorative and monumental sculptor, and his surviving terracottas are generally sketches for such large-scale works. He occasionally used terracotta for small, independent works of art. Good examples may be seen in the Louvre and in the museum at Besançon.

Morlaiter, Giovanni Maria. Born at Villabassa in 1699 and died at Venice in 1781. Perhaps the best-known eighteenth-century Venetian sculptor, Morlaiter executed numerous statues and altar-pieces in marble for churches in Venice (notably for Sta Maria del Rosario), and he also worked for the Elector of Saxony and for the Empress Catherine of Russia. A large number of terracottas originally in the Donà dalle Rose Collection and now in the Correr Museum, Venice, have been attributed to him. Morlaiter was the leading exponent in sculpture of the Venetian rococo style.

Mortars. In Antiquity mortars were usually made of stone or heavy pottery, but during the Middle Ages they were normally cast in bronze. Their use was widespread, both in the apothecaries' laboratories for the grinding and pounding of chemicals and in the home for the pounding of condiments and spices. In the painter's studio it might also have found its use in the pulverization of pigments. From the fourteenth century onwards mortars survive in considerable numbers, especially from Flanders and England, and later from Germany and Italy. With the exception of Italy, where they were produced by such schools as Riccio's, they seem to be mainly the work of the bell foundries, and, because the alloy used is so often close to that employed by these foundries, they are normally said to be made of "bell metal". An inducement to the collecting of this class of objects, rarely of any great artistic merit, is the fact that they more often than not bear inscriptions in raised lettering, usually pious in intention or giving the owner's or maker's name as well as the date of its production. Among the earliest of such mortars is the fine Gothic example in the York Museum, dated 1308 and signed "Frater William de Towthorpe". Flemish signed and dated mortars are more common, especially from the sixteenth century. But collectors should beware of the many nineteenth-century after-casts of these, usually of very crude quality and slurred definition. Mortars of the fourteenth and fifteenth centuries are rare, the bulk being of the sixteenth and seventeenth centuries. During the eighteenth century their manufacture ceased.

Mountsteven, Eley George. Wax-modeller. Was born in Ireland and worked in England between 1781 and 1791. He used a white wax, and his portraits are very fine – indeed, it was said of him that he brought wax-modelling to "a higher degree of perfection than ever it had obtained before". He left England in 1791 and died abroad.

Nollekens, Joseph (1737–1823). The greatest portrait sculptor of his time. Doctor Johnson said, on hearing a rival sculptor praised, "I think my friend Joe Nollekens can chop out a head with any of them." Even Nollekens' acid biographer, J. T. Smith, wrote: "His fame for bust-making will never be diminished." His most popular busts were those of the younger Pitt and Fox, the former based on the death-mask, while of the latter there are two completely different versions. Of the bust of Pitt over ninety replicas were made by the sculptor, and practically as many of each of the busts of C. J. Fox. (Plate 448A.)

Opstal, Gerard van (*c.* 1597–1668). Of Flemish origin, was a sculptor in marble as well as ivory. He went to Paris in about 1643, became an academician in 1648, and was appointed sculptor to the King. His work in ivory is known by five bacchanalian scenes, two of which are signed, in the Louvre (Plate 458E). On the basis of these works a number of similar reliefs have been attributed to him, notably those in the Musée de Cluny, the Kunsthistorisches Museum, the Rijksmuseum, the Institut Staedel, Frankfurt, the museum at Brussels, and the Wallace Collection.

Ormolu. Ormolu is the French name, first used in the seventeenth century, for the applied decoration, always of bronze-gilt, found on clock cases and furniture from the seventeenth to the eighteenth centuries.

Pajou, Augustin. Born in Paris in 1730 and died there in 1809. Studied first under Jean-Baptiste Lemoyne, then at the École Royale, and finally in Rome, where, from 1752 until 1756, he was a *pensionnaire* at the French Academy. He quickly achieved prominence after his return to Paris and was elected to the Academy in 1760. From 1768 to 1770 he was in charge of the decoration of the Opera House at Versailles. He also executed several busts of Louis XVI. His daughter married Clodion. During the revolution Pajou was appointed a member of the commission for the preservation of monuments. His works in terracotta date from throughout his career, and he produced both *sculpture d'appartement* and portrait busts in this medium. His terracotta busts are outstanding, notably those of Madame Dubarry, the Dauphin, and the Comte d'Artois. His work in terracotta may be seen in the Louvre and Musée Carnavalet, Paris, in the Musée Bonnat, Bayonne, and in the museum at Nantes.

Percy, Samuel (1750–1820). Wax-modeller, an extremely versatile artist. He could produce either a simple portrait or an animated group, consisting of a number of miniature figures. His portraits are frequently in white wax, though most of his groups are brightly coloured.

Pigalle, Jean-Baptiste. Born in Paris in 1714 and died there in 1785. Studied under Robert le Lorrain and Jean-Baptiste Lemoyne and later at the French Academy at Rome between 1736 and 1739. He returned to Paris in 1741 and was admitted an Academician in 1744. He was a protégé of Comte d'Argenson, and from 1750 to 1758 worked for Madame de Pompadour. His best-known work is the large monument in marble to the Maréchal de Saxe in St Thomas at Strasbourg (1776). He frequently used terra-

cotta, especially for busts, and his work in this medium may be seen in the Musée des Arts Décoratifs and the Musée de Cluny, Paris, the Musée d'Orleans, and the Musée Saint-Jean at Angers.

Pinelli, Bartolommeo. Born in Rome in 1781 and died there in 1835. Studied at the Accademia di San Luca at Rome and then at Bologna. He is best known for his drawings and prints of Roman scenes and of Roman types, but he also executed many charming terracotta groups and statuettes of the same subjects – peasants playing *morra*, picturesque *banditti*, and, of course, the *pifferari*. His terracottas have the same "Trastevere" charm and brio as the Roman dialect poems of his contemporary Belli. An excellent collection in the museum of the Palazzo Venezia, Rome.

Pio, Angelo. Born at Bologna in 1690 and died there in 1770. Studied first under Andrea Ferrari and then under Mazza. In about 1718 he went to Rome and studied under Camillo Rusconi. After his return to Bologna he executed many statuettes and small groups, especially *presepio* groups and figures, in terracotta. Examples may be seen in the Museo Davia-Bargellini, Bologna.

Plaquettes. Plaquettes are found cast in lead and silver as well as in bronze, and were used to decorate household utensils and furniture from the fifteenth century onwards. They have also been collected for their own sakes by connoisseurs since the sixteenth century, and formed part of collector's cabinets, together with medals, intaglios, and cameos. It is not always easy to distinguish between medals and plaquettes, but basically the medal has an obverse and a reverse and is circular, whereas the plaquette is one-sided and square, oblong, or oval. More precisely, the medal is commemorative or historical in character, bearing on its obverse the portrait of a notable personage, usually surrounded by an inscription, while plaquettes are purely decorative in intention, with mythological, historical, or religious subjects depicted. Plaquettes belong to the category of reproducible objects, and one may almost speak of different "states", as in the case of prints. In each reproduction it tends to lose some of its definition, and poorer, often modern, copies show little of the sharpness and individual chasing hat characterize the first few to leave the ar- ist's workshop. Plaquettes are more closely connected with painting than with sculpture, and their compositions can be related to the various Renaissance schools of painting – and especially to the engravings which gained in popularity during the sixteenth century. They were mostly issued from the schools of bronze casters beginning with Donatello's in the fif- teenth century. In the first half of the six- teenth century the work of Valerio Belli of Vincenza and Giovanni Bernardi is worthy of note. They, like a number of the sculptors who issued plaquettes, also produced some fine engraved gems. In the second half of the sixteenth century Leone Leoni worked in this field among the Mannerist followers of Michelangelo, although he is more famous for his medals. Plaquettes of religious subjects were made north of the Alps from the fifteenth century onwards, and in the early sixteenth century, under Italian influence, secular sub- jects began to be produced in southern Ger- many, especially Nuremberg, in the Vischer school and by Peter Flötner, who is not known to have worked in the round at all. Plaquettes never attained the popularity in the Netherlands and in France which they enjoyed in Italy and Germany.

Ramey, Claude. Born in Dijon in 1754 and died in Paris in 1838. Studied first at Dijon, then in Paris under Gois, and finally in Rome, where he was a *pensionnaire* at the French Academy from 1782 until 1786. After his return to Paris he worked extensively as a decorative sculptor on public buildings. He obtained several important official commis- sions under the Empire. He exhibited many terracotta statuettes and low reliefs at the Salons between 1793 and 1827. Examples of his work in terracotta may be seen in the Musées de Beaune and Coutances.

Rosset, Joseph (1706–86). The most dis- tinguished French ivory carver of the eigh- teenth century, who executed a number of fine religious statuettes – as, for example, that of St Teresa in the Louvre – but is more not- able for his portraits of Voltaire, Montes- quieu, Jean-Jacques Rousseau, and d'Alem- bert, of which numerous versions are known.

He also carved snuff rasps and snuff-boxes decorated with medallion portraits of con- temporary celebrities. In his work he was assisted by his sons **Jacques Rosset** (1741– 1826) and **Antoine Rosset** (1759–1818).

Roubiliac, Louis François (1705?–1762). Probably the grandest sculptor to work in England during the eighteenth century. His busts are superb, since he had both the seeing eye as well as the skilled hand. Vertue said of him that "his inventions were copious and free, picturesque – so light and easy – as painting", and those who have seen his terra- cotta busts in public or private collections cannot fail to agree with this criticism. (Plate 448c). Good examples may be seen in the Victoria and Albert Museum and in the National Portrait Gallery, London.

Rouw, Peter (1770–1852). A wax-model- ler, a versatile artist, for he was also a sculptor and a gem modeller, produced a large num- ber of admirable portraits, mostly modelled in pink wax. He is also known on occasions to have used colour or painted wax.

Rue, Louis-Félix, De la. Born in Paris in 1731 and died there in 1765. Studied under Lambert-Sigismund Adam and also at the École Royale. He won the Prix de Rome, but stayed only one year (1754–5) at the French Academy at Rome. Before leaving for Italy he had already executed several groups of putti, after drawings by Boucher, for the Manufac- ture Royale de Sèvres, and on his return to France he continued to produce similar groups and other *sculptures d'appartement*, generally *à la* Clodion, whose manner he anticipated, especially in low-relief. His terra- cottas were collected during his lifetime by such French connoisseurs as Julienne and Livre de Jully.

Rush, William (1756–1833). Of Philadel- phia, who is rightly claimed as the first Ameri- can sculptor, was trained in the European tradition. Though much of his work has not been identified or has disappeared, his known works indicate that he transcends the limits of folk art. His signed bust of Samuel Morris (1812) conveys a definite personality in a style which shows that Rush had an easy com- mand of the tradition of sculpture. An eagle in the Philadelphia Museum of Art, carved for a volunteer fire company and attributed to him, could perhaps be classified as folk art. Even here the composition and vigour of carving suggest the academic background fused with a personal style.

Rysbrack, John Michael. Born at Antwerp in 1694 and died in London in 1770. Studied under Van der Voort and then came to England in about 1720, where he was employed by the architect James Gibbs on funeral monuments. Thereafter he worked on his own account and was eventually acknowledged the head of his profession in England. Rysbrack specialized in portrait busts and monumental sculpture in marble, but he used terracotta both for sketches and for independent works of art, such as the five charming low reliefs at Stourhead. Some of his terracottas may be seen at the Victoria and Albert Museum and in the National Portrait Gallery, London.

Sculpture d'appartement. A term often applied to the pairs, or groups, of figures, usually rather larger than the small bronzes we have discussed and made for the decoration of the great *salons* and galleries of the time of Louis XIV. They were normally enriched by much gilding and the use of coloured marbles.

Sonnenschein, Valentin. Born at Stuttgart in 1749 and died at Berne in 1828. Studied under Luigi Bossi in the 1760s and subsequently under Wilhelm Beyer. Worked extensively as a stuccoer, and in 1773 was appointed professor at the Stuttgart Academy. In 1775 he went to Zürich, where he was patronized by Lavater. Good examples may be seen in the museums of Berlin, Berne, and Zürich.

Stockamer, Balthazar (*fl.* 1666–1700). Worked principally for the Medici Court at Florence. He carved the exceptionally fine crucifix (Plate 459B) and a *Hercules Killing the Hydra* in the Palazzo Pitti.

Strauss, Bernard (*fl.* 1651). Ivory carver of Augsburg, produced ivory tankards heavily decorated with figures. He is represented by signed examples in the Victoria and Albert Museum, the Rijksmuseum, and in the Kunsthistorisches Museum.

Tassie, James (1725–1799). Wax-modeller, born in Scotland. As a young man he moved to Dublin and worked with the physician Henry Quin. Together they invented an enamel or vitreous paste, in which Tassie cast his wax medallion portraits. In 1766 Tassie came to London, where he was employed by Wedgwood and later by Catherine, Empress of Russia. Tassie modelled portrait medallions in wax from life and then cast them in his hard, white-enamel paste. A large collection of these can be seen in the Scottish National Portrait Gallery. They are admirable works, since Tassie took infinite pains to get accurate likenesses.

Teutschmann, Joseph (1717–87). A master of rococo ivory carving who was responsible for such charming little objects as the heads of pastoral staves in the Victoria and Albert Museum and the Bayerisches Nationalmuseum.

Troger, Simon (1693 (or 94)–1769). The outstanding ivory carver of the eighteenth century who executed a number of large groups in ivory and hard wood. By using ivory only to represent flesh he was able to work on a much larger scale than the size of tusks will normally permit. He was, moreover, a minor rococo sculptor of genius, and his works have a graceful vitality hardly paralleled in any other ivory carvings of the period. Good examples of Troger's work are to be seen in the Victoria and Albert Museum, the Residenz at Wurzburg, the Bayerisches Nationalmuseum, and in the Palazzo Madama, Turin.

Turnerelli, Peter (1774–1839). He was son of an Italian sculptor, but was born in Dublin. His busts are careful likenesses and have considerable merit. He was the first British sculptor completely to break away from the convention of portraying his sitters in classical costume, and to show them instead in everyday dress. His best-known work is the bust of Daniel O'Connel (1828), of which it was said ten thousand plaster copies were sold.

Van Der Voort, Michel. Born at Antwerp in 1667 and died there in 1737. Worked in Italy, France, and England, as well as the Low Countries. Good examples to be seen in the Brussels Museum.

Wagner, Johann Peter. Born at Ober-theres in 1730 and died at Würzburg in 1809. Trained under his father and subsequently at Vienna, Salzburg, and at Munich. Worked mainly as a decorative sculptor and frequent-ly collaborated with the architect Balthasar Neumann. His terracottas are outstanding for their dramatic power and exuberant hand-ling. A large collection of his terracottas is preserved at the Mainfränkisches Museum, Würzburg.

Wax modellers (British)

Andras, Catherine (*fl.* 1795–1824)
Bally, William (*fl.* 1832–46)
Bouquet, W. V. (*fl.* 1782–98)
Burch, E., R.A. (b. 1730, d. 1814)
Cave, J. (*fl.* 1820–30)
Coffin, Edmund (*fl.* 1783–1803)
Cornman, H. (*fl.* 1799–1821)
Cramphorn, William (*fl.* 1807–19)
Cunningham, Patrick (d. 1774)
Dell, J. (*fl.* 1793–97)
De Vaere, John (b. 1755, d. 1830)
De Veaux, John (*fl.* 1821–36)
Engleheart, Thomas (b. 1745, d. 86)

Flaxman, John, R.A. (b. 1755, d. 1826)
Giannelli, J. G. (*fl.* 1808–29)
Hackwood, James (*fl.* 1770–90)
Hagbolt, T. (b. 1773, d. 1849)
Henderson, J. (*fl.* 1782–97)
Hepstinstall, J. (*fl.* 1818–22)
Lyon, Edwin (d. 1837)
Morison, David (*fl.* 1821–50)
Peart, Charles (b. 1759, d. 98)
Pingo, Lewis (b. 1743, d. 1830)
Pistrucci, Benedetto (b. 1784, d. 1855)
Plura, Giuseppe (b. 1753)
Poole, T. R. (*fl.* 1791–1809)
Smith, Joachim (*fl.* 1758–1803)
Smith, Thomas (*fl.* 1830–50).
Stothard, Alfred Joseph (b. 1793, d. 1864)
Webber, Henry (b. 1754, d. 1826)

Woolner, Thomas (1825–1892). One of the best of Victorian artists, he was the sculp-tor member of the pre-Raphaelite brother-hood, and his busts are carefully, even pain-stakingly, modelled. Though without doubt admirable likenesses, they seem to lack the spark of true genius.

SILVER

Egyptians, Assyrians, Phoenicians, Greeks, Romans, all the ancient civilizations delighted in the splendour of wrought silver. The Old Testament abounds in references; Homer wrote of silver wine-bowls; Horace of the silver brilliance in the Roman home. Long before the Romans came to Britain the Celts were embossing, chasing, punching, and engraving their magnificent silver ornaments and drawing wire for exquisite silver filigree. Gold may suggest greater magnificence, but silver has always offered peculiar opportunities to the creative artist-craftsman, and specimens remain representing every period and style from the Gothic to the present day.

Entirely pure silver is too soft to work and other white metals render it brittle, but copper proved a satisfactory alloy, in the proportion of 11 oz. 2 dwts silver to 18 dwts copper – the quality recognized in Britain and known and revered throughout the world as sterling. Unfortunately, however, it is difficult to detect far larger proportions of alloy in the silver, and in London, Paris, and other Continental centres the master silversmiths early formed themselves into guilds for protection from such unfair competition. The London Goldsmiths' Company, especially, has proved remarkably successful in upholding the sterling quality ever since its establishment in the thirteenth century. In the early sixteenth century a Continental visitor exclaimed that all the shops of Rome, Milan, Venice, and Florence together could not rival the gold and silver work on sale in London, and English hall-marked silver retains a unique position to this day.

American

The art of the silversmith (or goldsmith, as the craftsmen called themselves) flourished early in colonial America, with a skill and sophistication not found in the other crafts. The styles were basically English, as the earliest goldsmith whose work has come down to us was, like many subsequent ones, trained in London. Robert Sanderson emigrated after a nine years' apprenticeship to arrive in Massachusetts in 1638. Richard Storer had served only five years in a London goldsmith's shop before he came to Boston in 1635, yet he was able to instruct his young half-brother, John Hull, in "the trade of a goldsmith", until he "through God's help obtained that ability in it, as I was able to get my living by it". Storer's work, and that of John Mansfield, the first trained goldsmith in New England, are unknown today. Hull was one of the most active early Boston citizens, and upon being appointed mintmaster recorded again in his diary that the Court permitted him to take his friend, Robert Sanderson, to be his partner. Most of the silver fashioned by these men bears the mark of each partner, and most of it survives from having been given to churches. Marks were not a requisite on plate fashioned in the colonies, and wrought plate was a commodity as valuable as its weight in coin, and more useful. Hence, a good proportion of the silver owned by the first churches had served a period of domestic use; and the tankard, caudle cup, beaker, and standing cup are ecclesiastic as well as secular forms. Porringers are unknown today in church services; it is probable that this shallow bowl with a flat, pierced, horizontal handle was always a domestic piece. Inventories disclose that it was always a popular one, whereas the seemingly equally domestic dram cup lost favour in the early eighteenth century.

Spoons, too, a household's first possession in the precious metal, followed English styles; although those with slipped in the stalk or puritan handles are rare today, suggesting re-fashioning into the ensuing forms. Another seventeenth-century Boston worker in precious metal, William Rouse, has left a few pieces in distinctly English style; yet the journal of Jasper Danckaerts, visiting in Boston, reveals that he was "Willem Ros, from Wesel. He had married an English-woman and carried on his business here. ... We were better off at his house, for although his wife was an Englishwoman, she was quite a good housekeeper."

The first native craftsman was Jeremiah Dummer, born of English parents in 1645 and recorded as his apprentice in Hull's diary of 1659. Indentures for apprentices followed

those of England, and in Boston the legally required term was seven years. Dummer's contract called for eight years. His work, too, was largely in English styles; exceptions are his seventeenth-century columnar candle-sticks like earlier French ones copied in England, and his punch bowl of 1692, which is Portuguese in derivation. He is credited with having introduced cut-card work and gad-rooning into colonial silver-smithing. Some of his contemporaries, documented apprentices of Hull as were the Samuels, Paddy, and Clark, have left no known work; Timothy Dwight, similarly trained, is known by only two pieces, yet each of a skill to make the scarcity of his work the more surprising. John Coney, whose work survives in greater quantity and variety than any of the others, reasonably seems to have learned his craft from the same source. His earliest sugar boxes are in rich Charles II style, as are his cherub-laden caudle cups or punch bowls, yet the majority of his pieces are simple.

Sanderson had three sons whom he trained, yet only one is known by his work today. Hull's sons all died in infancy; his daughter Hannah, however, married Samuel Sewall, who has been called the colonial Samuel Pepys; his diary records activities of "Cousin Dummer", "Mr Coney", "Tim", and their successors. Thomas Savage, whose small porringer's handle is very much like the simple early ones by Dummer, was by witness of Sewall's diary the master of Samuel Haugh.

Dummer's generation saw the beginning of the craft in New York, which, although then under English rule, still held to Dutch traditions. The very names of the earliest crafts-men, Van der Burgh, Onckelbag, Kip, and Kierstede, proclaim their origin. Cornelis van der Burgh was the first native New York goldsmith, and one who worked entirely in the seventeenth century, for he died in 1699. His best-known beaker – the basically Dutch form which had, however, been incorporated into English plate in Jacobean days – was engraved with illustrations by Adriaen van der Venne from a Dutch book of poems; his broad two-handled panelled bowl shows the form most characteristic of New York plate. A simpler one, yet characteristically New

York by its six embossed panels and similar caryatid handles, was made by Jesse Kip, who is thought to have taught the craft to Cornelius Kierstede.

The Huguenot, Bartholomew LeRoux, who is known to have been working in New York in 1689, wrought similar handles for his generous "brandy bowl" now owned by Yale University, but left the sides similarly unadorned save for the grooves to indicate panels. LeRoux trained his own sons, John and Charles, and the Dutch-named Peter Van Dyck, who, in the manner of apprentices, married his master's daughter. Onckelbag and Kierstede in New York's first generation vie for the richest productions, although Jacobus van der Spiegel's tankard at Yale University has no rival in its intricacy of engraving. Tankards were fashioned with great skill by all the Dutch New Yorkers, although the form was not one found in their homeland. To the English vessel, elaboration of handle and base moulding, and frequently of the cover too, gave a distinctly local style well exemplified in the one by Peter Van Dyck.

When, in the last years of the seventeenth century, the craft developed in Pennsylvania, the first tankards had simplified New York base mouldings, although porringer handles were derived from New England styles. New York porringers almost always show a regional character; the first handles had intricate cuttings that left no room for the owners' initials proudly proclaimed on others, and in the eighteenth century cuttings were starkly simple in a handle of distinct solidity. New York spoons, too, had been different in their first styles of case shaped handled with hoof or caryatid terminal, whereas Philadelphia's earliest are the trifid-ends, of which the greatest surviving number in the colonies are from New England.

Rhode Island, at the turn of the eighteenth century, was training goldsmiths, probably in Boston. Samuel Vernon, the first from that colony whose work has survived, occasionally employed the meander wire and stamped base moulding of New York derivation. Connecticut became the home of Boston-trained John Potwine and the New Yorker, Cornelius

Kierstede, who was without doubt that colony's unsurpassed craftsman. In the south, although English goldsmiths, apparently seeking metal, had arrived in Virginia earlier even than in New England, no goldsmiths are known to have plied their craft until the eighteenth century. In Virginia, which still preferred to order its fine plate in London, small wares and repairs continued to be the goldsmith's chief role until Revolutionary days. Cesar Ghiselin, who was Philadelphia's first goldsmith, moved to Annapolis to become Maryland's first – as Johannis Nys, in Philadelphia in the late 1690s, went on to start the craft in Delaware. In South Carolina the Legares from New England and Stoutenburghs from New York started a craft of which little now remains.

Meantime, in the city of Boston, John Coney had taken a Huguenot lad to be his apprentice. Apollos Rivoire anglicized his name and as Paul Revere became famous through his son and namesake. Coney had had no sons to carry on; but John Burt, believed to have been his apprentice, had three sons to continue the proud craft, one of whom worked throughout the second half of the century. Although there were numerous goldsmiths in Boston at that period, the patriot Revere and Benjamin Burt seem to have shared the earlier importance of John Coney and Jacob Hurd. Edward Winslow had been an apprentice of Jeremiah Dummer, as had, undoubtedly, John Noyes and, probably, John Edwards. No parallel is found for Winslow's four sugar boxes, all dated in the early 1700s. Dummer, Winslow, and Edwards, in partnership with Allen, fashioned the three surviving standing salts of colonial make. A third maker of sugar boxes in the early 1700s is thought to have been Daniel Greenough of New Hampshire where, for the most part, less ambitious pieces were fashioned. Early in the eighteenth century, Salem, Newburyport and other towns supported goldsmiths, but important works seem to have been largely restricted to the main centres of the craft.

John Edwards was the scion of a three-generation craft tradition; his sons, Thomas and Samuel, were almost exact contemporaries of Jacob Hurd. The last, by the

quality and variety of his work and importance of his clients, seems to have taken
Coney's place in Boston for approximately a
quarter of a century. His sons, Nathaniel and
Benjamin Hurd, and his apprentice, Daniel
Henchman (Plate 466A), all worked in the
third quarter of the century and left an occasional rococo piece, though New England
obviously still preferred simple lines and fine
proportions. Jacob Hurd was commissioned
by the maritime court to make its admiralty
oar; the Court of Vice-Admiralty in New
York ordered one from Charles LeRoux. The
latter fashioned a gold box for Andrew
Hamilton, an official presentation piece now
owned by the Historical Society of Pennsylvania. An earlier gold gift had been made
in 1693 by Cornelis van der Burgh for
Governor Fletcher, but it is known only by
documentation.

In Albany the Ten Eyck family of goldsmiths was flourishing; the early Koenraet
had sent his son Jacob to be an apprentice of
Charles LeRoux. A generation earlier Kiliaen
Van Rensselaer, apprenticed to Jeremiah
Dummer in Boston, had found living in that
staid town to be rather simple. Kiliaen's
work in unknown, but Koenraet and his sons,
Jacob and Barent Ten Eyck, have left examples of their fine workmanship. Barent
fashioned for Daniel Cruyn in 1755 a gorget
engraved with the British Royal arms, also
engraven on the Admiralty Oars. Throughout the eighteenth century, and in all colonial
centres, British designs set the styles for
colonial craftsmen. Samuel Sympson's *Book
of Cyphers*, published in London in 1736, is
known to have been used in New York and
Rhode Island. John Singleton Copley painted
Nathaniel Hurd with the 1724 edition of
Guillim's *Display of Heraldry* at his elbow, and
many craftsmen followed the heraldic designs
in this oft-published work.

There are more portraits of silversmiths
than of other craftsmen. Copley painted
Revere in his shirt-sleeves, though at a highly
polished work-bench, with a pear-form teapot in his capable hand; and depicted Rufus
Greene, an apprentice of William Cowell,
who, in turn, had learned his craft with Dummer. Nathaniel Hurd sat for his miniature

portrait on copper to Copley, and to an unidentified limner in water-colour on ivory.
William Gilbert of New York sat to James
Sharples, as did Joseph Anthony of Philadelphia to Gilbert Stuart; but none of these
portraits proclaim the sitter's profession as
Copley twice had done.

The shift to English styles in New York was
undoubtedly broader in scope than the influence of such London-trained craftsmen in
that town as Simeon Soumain (Plate 465C)
and Daniel Christian Fueter, two well-known
names in its goldsmithing annals. The latter
advertised employing a chaser from Geneva,
yet the average goldsmith was still carrying
on his trade in all its branches. Many were
also spreading into other fields which were
then, but not now, allied to it. Dentistry was
an achievement of several goldsmiths, best
known among them, no doubt, the patriot
Revere. Nathaniel Hurd had turned to engraving so that, at his early demise in 1777, it
was as an "ingenious engraver" that he was
extolled. Revere's engravings were sometimes executed carefully, but the best known
of his were political cartoons, carelessly and
hastily executed. He gave up his craft entirely
for the five years of the Revolution, but resumed to work in the newest English fashion
practised also by Benjamin Burt, both of
whom continued into the early years of the
1800s. Revere printed continental currency;
Ephraim Brasher of New York minted the
famous and now very rare Brasher doubloon.
Like the earliest mint in Massachusetts, it was
not entirely legal, but extremely convenient.
Myer Myers of New York, whose work also
spanned the rococo through classic styles,
showed usually a preference for simplicity.
His dish ring is unique in known American
silver, and his cake basket made for the same
patrons, Samuel and Susanna Cornell, has
come to public attention since the publication
of Mrs Rosenbaum's recent book on Myers.

Philadelphia had three families of three-
generation craftsmen who almost spanned the
eighteenth century. Philip Syng, Jr, fashioned
the standish used at the signing of the Declaration of Independence; his father and
son, both of the same name, owe their present-
day reputation to him. Francis Richardson

had a namesake and a Joseph (Plate 465A, B) among his sons. The latter – who imported much English plate and worked in richest styles – had sons Joseph and Nathaniel as successors. Peter, David, and his son and grandson John were capable craftsmen, but probably owe their reputation today to their family adherence to the craft rather than to their individual practice of it. Richard Humphreys was selected by the Continental Congress to fashion its rich presentation urn to Charles Thomson, Secretary of the Congress, and by George Washington to make camp cups.

The silversmithing family of Faris in Annapolis was founded by William, who has been characterized as "the most picturesque figure among eighteenth-century Maryland silversmiths". His accomplishments included clock and watch making, portrait painting, and work as a cabinet-maker, dentist, innkeeper, and tulip grower. He has left the only known manuscript book of silver designs in the colonies, and had three sons whom he trained in silversmithing.

Unique in America was Baltimore's endeavour in the early 1800s to establish a guild-system similar to that so long in existence in England and on the Continent. For a brief time, starting in 1814, silver made in Baltimore was marked at a hall and identified by a date letter; this compulsory marking was abolished in 1830. By coincidence, perhaps, this is the period when American silver was becoming, through the taste of the time and introduction of machinery, a commodity of far less appeal than that of the previous two centuries

British

The collector who turns his activities to the silver wrought in the British Isles in past centuries enters a field of exploration in the antique which yields to no other sphere of collecting in extent and interest, and is indeed of greater range and possessed of more possible varieties of specialization than many other forms of applied art. This breadth of subject may well be a discouragement to the beginner as he comes to realize that English plate survives from the sixteenth century downwards in great quantity on account of its intrinsic value, which has encouraged its safe keeping, and of its comparative indestructibility. But this same high rate of survival affords a reasonable prospect, whatever particular form a collection may take, that sufficient examples will appear in the market to make pursuit and selection of desirable pieces a practical and enjoyable pastime.

Many ardent collectors must have had their first interest in the subject aroused by stumbling attempts to decipher the hallmarks on some inherited piece of plate, and by the subsequent realization that every normal piece of English silver bears its own documented evidence of age and origin. To this, no doubt, may have succeeded a rush of marks to the head and an attempt to acquire every piece that falls in one's path for the pleasure of identifying and labelling it. Slowly a deeper appreciation of the subject grows as more pieces are handled, standard works consulted, and museums and exhibitions visited. The pieces of the puzzle fall into shape and the collector sees his subject as a whole and realizes the often quite small part of it he can expect to make his own particular sphere. There are, of course, lovers of old silver who never become real collectors on a set plan. They merely acquire pieces which please the eye and for which they have some specific domestic need. They are not greatly exercised over questions of period, style, or craftsmen, so long as the piece "goes" with their general taste and decor; though it is true that appreciation of the quality of workmanship, line, and proportion will be sharpened with practice, despite any indifference to the historical relationship of the piece. From this general interest, however, a more particular study may easily spring, once the first general "furnishing" phase is over.

What lines is specialization likely to take in silver? There is first the national division of England, Scotland, and Ireland. The silver of each country shows distinct characteristics and certain specific forms which do not occur, unless as exceptions, in either of the other types, and many collectors like to concentrate on the native work of their own country. The study of Scottish silver is perhaps the most rewarding, since there was a smaller output of silver in Scotland at all periods. Up to the mid-eighteenth century at least any piece, however simple, possessed a sharp individuality which often seems to vanish into the smoothness of repetition in its English counterpart produced in far greater numbers.

Inside national divisions it will always be possible to focus attention on the other methods of specialization to be considered. The most obvious is undoubtedly that of period: and so inherently of style. A study of the trend of prices in relation to the comparative number of pieces of any particular period available will show that it is not necessarily scarcity alone that determines a price or the demand for the period which the price reflects. There are distinct fashions in collecting as there are in every other form of activity. These trends in popularity move slowly, and there are crosscurrents which at times may confuse the direction of the main stream. But if we stand far enough off we can see the movement. The serious collector of a chosen period will rise above popular fancies of the moment and find his own reward.

The next form of specialization is that of a particular type of piece as it was made at different periods, allowing a study of its development, decoration, and social use. The enormous varieties of form which wrought plate has taken makes this a very worthwhile pursuit. Here, again, one may detect fashion. At present tankards are out of, and teapots in, favour. This form of collecting is undertaken perhaps less seriously than others, but it has its devotees. I have seen a collection of taper-sticks of all dates and styles; a whole herd of cow cream-jugs; a large array of casters, and so on. The assembly of a particular class of object in sufficient numbers to form comparisons contributes a great deal to knowledge of the subject and reveals aspects of workmanship and design not immediately recognized from isolated examples seen at intermittent intervals.

The most highly specialized form of collecting is that of early spoons. These, from their personal associations and their usefulness, have survived in greater numbers than any other single form of wrought plate, and provide a very wide field for collectors. Since the spoon is naturally the first piece of plate required, it early became the established christening gift and was made in many small provincial centres where little other silver was ever made. It thus provides by far the greatest number of examples of rare provincial silversmiths' marks. Much work has been done and much remains to establish the definite ascription of many of these marks. Spoon-collecting therefore brings an extra reward to its devotees in the study the subject entails. The main types of spoons are indicated in the glossary to follow, but the present scope cannot permit of any detailed account of rare provincial types or the larger subject of the marks on such pieces. The established collector will know where to turn for his information. The beginner is advised to take the advice of an established collector or specialist dealer.

Perhaps the most rewarding form of specialized collecting, and one practically ignored, is that of studying the work of one maker. This has been done as regards the whole Huguenot school of the early eighteenth century, in the incomparable Farrer Collection now in the Ashmolean Museum, Oxford. Few attempts have been made to assemble the work of one craftsman, other than that of Paul Lamerie or Paul Storr. There is now an enthusiasm in America for Hester Bateman's work. But there seems a certain frenzy in the scramble for pieces by her which suggests that keenness has swamped discrimination. One other individual family of silversmiths, that of Augustine Courtauld, his son Samuel, and the latter's wife Louisa, has received worthy attention promoted by the interest of his present-day descendants. But there are very many other excellent craftsmen of whose work never more than a few pieces have been seen together at a time, and who would be worthy of greater attention. This interest can scarcely be extended to pieces made before 1697, from which date the surviving records at Goldsmiths' Hall provide the identification of makers' marks. The maker's name provides the personal touch which seems necessary to an appreciation of his work; though there are outstanding silversmiths, particularly of the seventeenth century, known only by their marks, such as the maker who used a hound sejant and whose work possesses great individuality and outstanding merit worthy of special attention.

Those who prefer to collect silver, not as specialists but simply to enjoy the use of beautiful plate, will find their opportunities widened by the exercise of ingenuity in transforming the original purpose of a piece to a modern use. The late eighteenth-century Argyle or gravy-warmer serves excellently for a small coffee-pot; the sharp-pointed skewer opens letters as if made for the purpose; the pierced mazarine or dish strainer, mounted on a dark wood tray can be enjoyed afresh for the intricacy of its arabesque piercing; large oval tea-caddies or early tankards make excellent biscuit-boxes, wine-coolers can be used as flower vases, and so on. Few pieces, except the rarities of the sixteenth century, need be considered purely as cabinet or decorative items.

The would-be collector may well be attracted by the study of hall-marks, and it is often apparent how a facility for interpreting these indications of age and provenance excites the envy of the beginner. The scope of this guide to silver precludes any serious attempt to explain the system or to show examples to illustrate its working. But there is room for brief advice. Most important factor is that no one mark, whether it is date-letter, town, or maker's mark, should ever be relied upon alone for evidence of date or provenance, or forced to support some point of view which has no other evidence of style, workmanship, or period to back it. Even when a complete set of marks is present it is easy to misread them by overlooking relative evidence. For example, although the cycles of London date letters are varied in succession, certain superficial resemblances occur at various periods. The capital Roman O, for instance, for 1809, is not very dissimilar from the small o for 1829. Whereas with the former letter the leopard's head used is crowned, that of the latter cycle is uncrowned. Once this is appreciated, confusion becomes impossible. Again, two Court letter cycles were used, commencing respectively in 1638 and 1697. In the former the Sterling Standard marks of leopard's head and lion passant were in force, whereas the latter cycle began with the introduction of the Britannia Standard with the figure mark, from which it takes its popular name, accompanied by the lion's head erased. The only time the second Court cycle of letters can occur with leopard's head and lion passant is on gold plate of the time. Other examples of this nature could be adduced, but enough has been said to point to the need for a careful weighing of all the evidence provided by the marks. In this respect collectors would be well advised to avoid the use of pocket lists of marks which provide the cycles of date-letters alone without the accompanying standard marks. A counter check should always be made with the maker's mark, which can be identified in the standard works of Sir Charles Jackson, Chaffers, or Cripps. The date at which the mark was entered at Goldsmiths' Hall or of incorporation in a provincial guild provides a *terminus a quo* for the piece. Latest possible date for a maker is less easily determined. But without definite evidence to the contrary, a working life of thirty years should be considered long enough, and many makers seem to have a shorter working time than this. A further check is provided by re-entry of a mark in a new form at a known date.

Even such a brief discussion as this cannot overlook the matter of false and transposed marks. These two categories must be distinguished. By the former is meant reasonably close imitations of old marks made by fakers in the late nineteenth century for the express purpose of deceiving. It is almost impossible to recommend any firm method of detecting such imitations. Their recognition must spring from the experience of much handling of plate. This promotes an "eye" for a genuine mark, either in its fresh, clearly struck state in some position not subject to wear or in an exposed position which has suffered the wear and polish of centuries. On the other hand, we may note certain points which may lead to the detection of a false mark. Many deliberate forgeries appear to have been perpetrated by fakers whose lack of knowledge led them to use marks of some date at variance with the style of the piece they were attempting to reproduce, or even to invent some new form of vessel which has no authentic prototype of the date to which the marks would assign it. Here a knowledge of the characteristics of the particular period suggested by the marks is essential. Again, a certain type of false mark, struck with soft metal punches, gives the appearance of wear, often in positions normally protected from rubbing, such as the bases of jugs or tankards. Common sense will raise immediate doubts of such pieces. Marks obtained from castings of genuine examples are harder to recognize at first sight. Comparison of presumed date and style may still provide the first clue. Sets of table silver, spoons, and forks sometimes bear cast marks. A close examination of a number of the suspects side by side will often reveal that the marks are spaced and related to each other in exactly the same degree in each piece, revealing a master die for all, in place of the infinite variations obtained in genuine individually struck marks.

Transposed marks fall into two categories. There are, first, the genuine old pieces of plate, known colloquially as "duty dodgers", made by a silversmith working in the contemporary style of his day, who, to avoid the expense of submitting his work to the Assay, inserted into the new piece a set of marks taken from some old and possibly worn-out piece on his hands. Often he completed the deception by adding his own mark, striking it over the earlier maker's mark, if this was visible. Such pieces were felonious evasions of the hall-marking laws at the time, and, although clearly genuine examples of antique plate of their period, remain illegal in the eyes of the unaltered law of today.

The other form of transposed mark is the nineteenth-century faker's device, usually handled with more cunning than the imitative forging of marks, and needs constant watchfulness to detect. It is possible, particularly when the piece is oxidized by lack of cleaning, to detect the solder line surrounding marks let into a plain surface. But when the joint of the applied plate of marks is masked, for instance, by a separate cast base applied to a coffee-pot or sauceboat, detection may be harder. There may possibly be a small pinhead blowhole to allow the imprisoned air expanded by the heat of the solder to escape. This is an invaluable clue. This may, however, be dispensed with by a clever craftsman and detection will be increasingly harder. Mistakes of style, form, and decoration will probably also occur in such pieces.

A further type of illegal plate must also be mentioned. This is represented by pieces which have either been altered in form, though retaining their original metal and marks, or have had additional sections added to change their decoration or purpose. They are also illegal, since additions made to hall-marked plate should also be marked at the time they are added. Often such alterations were carried out to private order so as to provide a new purpose for an outmoded or disused piece. The commonest example is that of a seventeenth- or eighteenth-century covered tankard with a spout added at the front to convert it to a jug. If the spout, in the hands of an honest silversmith who knew the law, was made of standard silver and the piece sent to the Assay office for the additions mark to be impressed, this would be in order. But the great majority of such pieces, having been privately ordered, possibly from the local country silversmith, were not so marked, and remain illegal. The discerning collector will not be interested in such pieces, but the beginner should be warned.

Another form of alteration which is not illegal is that of the addition of later decoration. Plain pieces of the seventeenth and eighteenth centuries in every form were the prey of the prevailing Victorian taste for lavish embossing of fruit, flowers, animals, and other motifs with which the craftsmen of the time fondly hoped to enrich their predecessors' handiwork. The recognition of such later work can be achieved only by the experience of handling; by seeing as much genuine period decoration as possible; by a study of the essential forms of plain pieces which the student must learn to perceive below the overgrowth of later years. This is sometimes complicated by pieces with some original decoration to which later work has been added. Again, there exists the necessity for continual handling of every type of piece and the slow cultivation of an eye for what is and what is not original.

Much has been heard in recent years of the value of antiques as an investment. In precious metals there is an underlying feeling of security in the intrinsic value of the pieces apart from any rarity value in the collector's market. On the other hand, it is apparent from a study of prices over a wide range of years that changes in fashion can affect values very considerably. The genuine enthusiast will scarcely consider the question of a potential return or profit on his outlay. No monetary value can be put to the intangible assets his collecting activities will produce for him in the thrill of the chase and in pride of possession. Even allowing for the decline in the purchasing power of money, it is growing more and more apparent that there is an ever-widening circle of appreciation for the beautiful products of past centuries. So long as a civilized existence continues, such appreciation must promote the desire to share in inherited treasures. The collector links the past with the future and is happy in the part he plays.

Scottish

For the purposes of the collector, Scottish silver spans a period from the late seventeenth to the early nineteenth centuries. Pieces dating from the sixteenth century or before are rare indeed; although the craftsmanship reflected by some of them is of a standard that suggests long experience and a considerable output, while the appearance of anything hitherto unknown from the first half of the seventeenth is an event. Most of the choicer things which now come on the market belong to the eighteenth century.

The general characteristics of Scottish silver are not obvious ones. If anyone new to the subject thinks he will be able to recognize what is Scottish by its manifestly Celtic shape or by the crop of thistles engraved on it, he is mistaken. There are only two or three types of vessel which are exclusively national. On the other hand, the Scottish goldsmith had an outlook and an approach quite different from those of his colleagues south of the Border. In the first place there lay behind him no sumptuous tradition such as produced the extravaganzas of Cellini or the Nuremberg craftsmen. He had not even the elegant patrons to foster in him any of the assured, sophisticated design-sense of a Lamerie. The virtues which his circumstances developed in him were directness, a canny respect for the metal, and a real love for its beauty unadorned. Simplicity and functionalism are therefore the marks of Scottish silver at least until a taste for the rococo spread northwards in the mid-eighteenth century, and they laid a restraining hand on ornament for another generation or two after that. The ornament, when it is present, is often heavy-handed by English or foreign standards. Yet if it has not the crispness or the precision, at least there is nothing stereotyped about it, and this often lends a life and sparkle which make the piece good to live with.

Foreign influences were numerous. Silver mirrors the country's social history. French imports probably dominated the late medieval scene, if the Gothic tabernacle heads of the St Andrews' University maces or verges are significant. Low Countries influence is marked among the Communion plate of the east coast in the seventeenth century, and the Scandinavian link in some of the tankards of the Restoration period. In 1707 the Union opened the door wide to an English impact which inevitably, although only after a century, imposed itself completely on the Scottish goldsmiths.

Scottish silver was perhaps at its most distinctive in the second half of the seventeenth century. This is the period when the quaich was being translated from wood into silver, when the so-called "thistle" cups were being made, when sugar-casters and tankards and, above all, spoons still had an unmistakably Scots accent. For the collector, however, it is a period which demands a fairly long purse, as well as a good deal of patience. Quaichs of various sizes do turn up at intervals. It is rather less difficult to find a silver-mounted wooden quaich, transitionary pieces which have a peculiar charm, especially those in which the staves are of alternating woods. Unfortunately shrinkage has often rendered the staves loose, and even the silver mounts, and to tighten them permanently and satisfactorily is very difficult indeed. Nothing in all the range of treen is more graceful, however: and this grace is inherited by the earliest of the all-silver quaichs, becoming lost as the more sophisticated goldsmiths of the eighteenth century turned the quaich into a mere twin-handled bowl. The thistle cup is perhaps even more rare and expensive. What it was used for has never been clear. It was certainly not made in sets like tea-cups, though pairs are found occasionally. It seems to have come into fashion about the end of Charles II's reign. The exuberant ornament which was such a feature of this reign in England is not nearly so marked in Scotland, incidentally. The Scots possessed less high hopes of the restored monarchy than did their neighbours.

The massive simplicity so characteristic of the best Scottish silver achieved its peak in the early years of the eighteenth century. Men like Colin McKenzie and James Sympsone in Edinburgh were making sober pieces of considerable importance, such as tankards, two-handled cups, fruit-dishes, and coffee-pots (Plate 480B). As a rule they are devoid of any ornament except for such details as thumb-pieces and finials and the coats-of-arms which are not excelled by Scots engravers of any other period. The coffee-pots, whether octagonal or round in section, are among the loveliest things of their kind. They are, however, excessively rare. Spoons, commonly of the rat-tail form, offer more hope for the collector, but even these are not numerous of such early date. It should be remembered that a fair proportion of the energies of the goldsmiths was being diverted to the manufacture of Communion plate, since many churches were still not properly equipped in the reign of Queen Anne.

The 1730s and '40s are in many ways the Golden Age of Scottish silverware. At the same time modest, domestic pieces were being produced in large numbers in Edinburgh, Glasgow, Aberdeen, and to some extent in smaller places. Collectors can still secure prizes belonging to this period. Teapots are eagerly sought after, notably those by such makers as James Ker and William Aytoun. They are variations of the "bullet" type, sometimes flattened a little, sometimes nearly spherical, and in earlier examples the spouts are usually quite straight. A few still have their stands, which greatly enhance their appearance – and their value. The corresponding cream-jugs and sugar-basins are as difficult to find as the teapots. Local lairds and ministers often had their domestic silver made in the nearest city, even in burghs of the size of Banff or Elgin, and a small amount of this probably remains in the districts where it has always been. The best hunting-ground used to be, and possibly still is, the north-eastern counties, which were fairly prosperous towards the close of the eighteenth century and yet isolated enough from Edinburgh to make it possible for the burgh craftsmen to develop their trade. The simple pieces which resulted have great charm, and are well suited to the collector who wants good old craftsmanship with which he can live.

In Edinburgh and Glasgow the second half of the eighteenth century brought closer imitation of southern styles, and elaborate ornament makes it much less easy to distinguish what is Scottish. The swing of fashion can be traced even in the output of a single maker, such as Patrick Robertson (Plate 483B). His rococo of the 'sixties becomes classicism in the 'seventies, when Craig's New Town was beginning to take shape and Robert Adam was building his Register House. The more recognizably Scottish work from now right on into the nineteenth century came from centres such as Aberdeen, Perth, and Inverness, where styles were conservative and treatment more individualistic than in the sophisticated south. Much table silver was made in small places as far north as Tain. These attractive provincial pieces ceased to be made after 1836, when a Statute required all Scottish silverware to be assayed in Edinburgh or in Glasgow.

With Scottish as with English silver, almost the first thing the collector looks for is the hall-mark. The standard reference work is still the Scottish section of Sir Charles Jackson's *English Goldsmiths and Their Marks*; although a great deal has been learned since it was written, especially about the provincial goldsmiths. Briefly, the Edinburgh hall-marking system has been in operation since the middle of the sixteenth century. When the date-letter was added in 1681 this brought the normal complement of marks on Edinburgh silver to four, at which it remained until the sovereign's head was added in 1784. Glasgow instituted the date-letter in the same year as Edinburgh, so far as we know, but its appearance was most irregular until as late as 1819. Aberdeen and the other burghs do not seem to have had a regular date-stamp. Indeed, the hall-marking of all places other than Edinburgh is full of pitfalls for the collector. The form of the town-mark is only of very general help in dating a piece, a matter which really has to be decided by the maker's punch. Sometimes the town-mark has such a range of variations that it opens wide the door of speculation, as when the dromedary mark of Inverness beguiled Jackson into including the Calcutta elephant among the symbols of the Highland capital. Many small provincial pieces, however, have no "hall-mark" other than the maker's punch carrying his initials. This is true of a high proportion of the table silver, and then only familiarity with the actual punch, considered in relation to the style of the piece, enables one to hazard an identification at all. This is perhaps not quite such wild guess-work as it may seem at first sight, since the makers in towns such as Banff or Elgin were few, and it is possible to acquire a "feel" for their products. A few of those in the north and east of the country were itinerant, and stamped pieces now in one town, now in another, which adds to the problems of the collector.

Dutch

If all the Dutch silver of the sixteenth and seventeenth centuries had been melted into bullion, as indeed the greater part of it was, hardly a single fashionable style would have been lost. The Dutch masters of painting so faithfully recorded the tradition of contemporaneous silverware in such minutely detailed domestic scenes that reproductions of old silver have been made directly from pictures in museums. This was a great creative era during which Dutch silversmiths wrought their fashionable plate into designs of almost riotous magnificence.

Some of this silver is still in existence. The Earl of Yarborough, for instance, possesses a celebrated historic tazza-shaped cup and cover of the sixteenth century. This cup, commemorating the naval victory of the Dutch over the Spanish in the Zuyder Zee on October 11, 1573, was made in 1574, probably as a thanks-offering from the citizens of Enkhuisen to William the Silent for their deliverance from Spanish domination. It is elaborately embossed and chased with marine scenes, including a view of the Zuyder Zee with ships and towns. The ornament includes sea monsters and tritons and the arms of William the Silent.

Dutch silver of the early seventeenth century was richly chased with scenes of farm life, domestic themes, rural landscapes, and other homely subjects. Then, from the 1640s until the end of the century, fashion demanded symbolical, allegorical, legendary, mythological, and classical subjects. Ornamental motifs were acquired from every possible source, resulting in a motley assemblage of escutcheons in Renaissance styles, such as winged heads, cherubs, satyrs, acanthus leaves, heraldic shields, all surprisingly well harmonized.

Distinguished among the many Dutch silversmiths of the late sixteenth and early seventeenth centuries were Adam van Vianen, the elder, and Johannes Lutma. The former sponsored grotesque designs, and his fantastic enrichments influenced silversmiths in London of Charles II's reign working from his book of designs engraved by Th. van Kessel and published in 1641: a ewer in the collection of the Marquess of Sligo is illustrated in this work.

Although van Vianen was born in about 1555, none of his work made before 1610 is known to have survived. His masterpiece is the noble rose-water ewer and basin belonging to the City of Amsterdam. The basin is exquisitely chased with scenes from the Dutch and Spanish War, enclosed in panels on the wide rim; in the depression is a representation of the battle of Nieuwpoort, 1600, and the raised centre displays the arms of Amsterdam and the date 1614. The ewer is enriched with three panels depicting similar scenes. A second member of this celebrated family, Christian van Vianen, entered the service of Charles I, for whom he made, in 1637, vessels for St George's Chapel, Windsor. These, unfortunately, were melted for bullion during the civil war. A large dish, decorated with dolphins and dated 1635, is in the Victoria and Albert Museum.

Dutch connoisseurs consider Johannes Lutma to have been a greater silversmith than Adam van Vianen, but surviving works are too few for accurate judgement. Lutma delighted in depicting marine life, adapting it most gracefully to his patterns. Remaining pieces include two funeral shields dated 1633, intended to be deposited on the coffins of Guild Masters in accordance with Dutch custom; a famous ewer and basin commemorating the opening of Amsterdam Town Hall in 1655; and a dish signed by him in 1641 similar to one shown in his etched portrait of his close friend Rembrandt.

Handsome drinking-horns have been recorded in paintings by Dutch artists. Horns were costly gifts presented to Guilds by prominent members and used at Guild banquets. The most celebrated drinking-horn belonged to the Guild of St Sebastian in 1565. This horn, richly mounted with figures in the round representing the saint's martyrdom, is seen in Bartolomew van der Helst's portrait group of the Guild officers painted in 1653. Three years later the artist included it again on a canvas portraying four high officers of the Archers' Guild. The magnificent horn presented to the Guild of St George in 1566 also takes its theme from the story of its saint. This was recorded by van der Helst in his painting of the banquet held in the hall of St George's Guild to celebrate the Peace of Munster in 1648.

Silver beakers were important articles of plate. First they were used as drinking-vessels commemorating peaceful achievements or events. After the Reformation they were used also as sacramental cups engraved with conventional arabesques and flower sprays, sacred subjects, Biblical scenes, symbolical personifications, and views of churches. Sacramental beakers, usually gilded, are recorded in the still-life paintings by Pieter Claesz and Willem Heda.

In the seventeenth century the beaker, with a moulded circular foot and slightly spreading sides, was usually decorated with all-over engraving. Typical is a beaker struck with the Delft hall-mark for 1633: it is divided horizontally by a central corded rib, the upper part engraved during the second half of the century. By 1700 and during the eighteenth century decoration was commonly chased.

Silver galleons or nefs on wheels were made by Dutch silversmiths in enormous numbers from the 1660s for use in the service of wine.

Such a vessel was fully rigged: and the wine was contained in the hull and was poured into glasses through the wide-open mouth of the figurehead. Richly ornate examples were made throughout the eighteenth century.

Dutch silver tankards are now comparatively rare, yet they are conspicuous in still-life paintings, notably those by Willem Heda. It was fashionable for them to be engraved with historic scenes, many taken from prints by the engraver Bastiaen Stoopendaal. The engravings depict Queen Mary, consort of James II of England, with her infant son, later known as the Old Pretender; the escape of James II, represented by three figures in a barge; the departure of the Prince of Orange for England in 1688; and William III opening the English parliament in 1689.

Characteristic of Holland and not made by silversmiths elsewhere were the tall, elegant holders for single glasses of wine. These were made in sets of a dozen. They are seen in many paintings, notably those by Jan Steen and Willem van Aelst. The City of Amsterdam possessed a set of five stamped with the Amsterdam date letter for 1609 and the maker's monogram L.C. Others have been noted made two centuries later.

The three cups most representative of Dutch conviviality are the windmill cup, the bridal cup, and "Hans in the cellar", made from the sixteenth to the nineteenth century and exported profitably to other European countries. The windmill cup was filled with wine and handed to the guests of the party who, by blowing through a slender tube, set in motion the sails of a tiny windmill which operated a pointer around a numbered dial. The wine had then to be consumed in a single draught before the windmill sails ceased revolving. Failure to accomplish this feat involved drinking as many cupfuls as were indicated on the dial. A variant contained a globular openwork cage containing a silver die placed between the windmill and the bell-shaped cup. One of Johanne van Haensbergen's paintings illustrates a wager cup in use. Windmill cups might be engraved with the figures of Faith, Hope, and Charity.

The bridal cup, more often used as a wager cup, was in the shape of a young woman with both arms raised, holding aloft a swinging bowl. Her wide skirts formed a drinking-cup which the bridegroom was expected to empty without spilling any wine from the smaller vessel now swinging perilously below. He would then hand his bride her share of the wine.

Hansje in den kelder or "Hans in the cellar" was brought out when a birth was expected in the family, so that host and friends could drink the health of the mother and her baby. As the wine was poured into the cup, its increasing weight lifted a domed lid in the centre, and to the delight of all a tiny silver model of a child would automatically emerge.

The brandy bowl is another characteristic piece of seventeenth- and eighteenth-century plate expressive of the Dutchman's native sociability. This vessel was reserved for intimate family gatherings and was filled brimful with brandy and raisins, eaten direct from the bowl with silver spoons. Its early shape was octagonal or heptagonal, and it was engraved with symbolical figures, sometimes associated with the family, and often fitted with mask handles. An oval form evolved in the 1670s and continued throughout the following century, the handles flat and chased, as seen in Metsu's *The Collection*.

Few early Dutch salts and casters remain, and reliance regarding their shapes must be placed on paintings by Heda, Pieter Claesz, Jan Steen, de Heem, and Dou. Silver candlesticks are rare, too, but they can be seen, for example, in Jan Steen's *Physician's Visit* and Terborch's *Guitar Lesson*. Those with clustered columns appear over and over again on Gerard Terborch's pictures. Boxes, often gilt, were made specially for costly peppers and spices.

Ordinary domestic silver made in large quantities during the eighteenth century was influenced by French design, and much gilded. There was a great demand for table bells, tobacco boxes, charcoal braziers, tea canisters, teapots, kettles, tea urns (from 1760), trays and waiters, cake baskets, and candlesticks. When it is realized that fine silver was made in at least thirty-four different towns in Holland before 1800, it became obvious that many silversmiths concentrated on plain domestic ware for everyday use by the gentry.

Dutch silver was of sterling quality for finely wrought ware: ordinary domestic plate contained 9 per cent more copper alloy.

French

French silver plate until the mid-sixteenth century was dominated by the formal restraint of Gothic design, decoration being chiefly confined to wide bands of lettering. The centre of the silversmiths' craft was in Paris, where workshops were originally established near the Pont-au-Change, a covered bridge which ended at the steps of Notre-Dame Cathedral. Early in the fifteenth century silversmiths gradually moved to the section of the River Seine bank now known as the Quai des Orfevres. Little French silver of the Gothic period now remains. The British Museum houses a gold and enamelled cup attributed to about 1380, decorated with scenes from the life of St Agnes. Although altered from time to time, enough of the original remains to show that these French silversmiths were superb craftsmen.

The Italian Renaissance influence was introduced by Benvenuto Cellini late in the reign of Francis I (1515–47). He visited Paris in 1540 and was persuaded to establish a school for silversmiths, where for five years under his vigorous guidance pupils wrought magnificent ecclesiastical and domestic plate so that the Gothic formality was soon superseded by silver embossed with intricate and fanciful designs often containing human figures. The demand by the French nobles for silver plate enriched in the Italian manner became so immense that Paris attracted many master silversmiths from Italy.

Little now exists, however, of the gorgeous silver designed and made during this period: to gain an idea of its exact appearance students refer to the many contemporaneous prints of domestic scenes. The engravings by J. A. Ducercean (1510–84) and René Boyvin (1530–98) illustrate an extensive array of

fashionable silver, its surfaces virtually covered with strapwork and elaborate repoussé figures.

When Henri III founded the Order of the Saint Esprit in 1578 he presented a silver-gilt bottle in the Italian style, believed to have been made by the master silversmith Noel Delacroix and now in the Musée du Louvre. In the same year Henri levied a high tax on silver plate, his purpose being to discourage the manufacture of luxurious services, and so direct more silver to the Royal Mint to remedy the drastic shortage of bullion.

Elegance of form characterized French plate of the seventeenth century, plain surfaces contrasting with lavishly florid covers and handles. Immense numbers of *écuelles* were made, tableware peculiar to France but closely resembling contemporaneous English porringers and used for serving spoon meat. The *écuelle* was a two-handled shallow bowl raised from thick-gauge plate, with cover and standing plate. The majority were enriched with engraved cut-card work and ornamental finials. Handles usually projected horizontally, either decoratively pierced or engraved on the upper surface: others were wrought in the shape of leaves or other motifs, such as the coiled snakes associated with wine tasters.

Most of France's finest domestic silver was sacrificed in 1681, when Louis XVI commanded a nation-wide melting at the behest of the powerful group of bullionists. Few outstanding pieces of plate escaped the general confiscation, apart from those that had been sent abroad. These included the magnificent silver-gilt toilet set, covered almost entirely in repoussé work, made by Pierre Prevost in 1670 and now in the possession of the Duke of Devonshire. This set once belonged to William of Orange and Princess Mary, who were married in 1677: their arms are engraved on each of the twenty-two pieces. Louis XIV's melting did not prevent silversmiths from producing plate as handsomely wrought as formerly. A pair of octagonal stands, pierced and chased with foliage, strapwork, and medallion heads, formerly in the collection of Lord Brownlow, were made at Bayonne in 1690.

At the opening of the eighteenth century French silversmiths were continuing fashions in plate evolved over a long period, but when Louis XIV moved his Court to the splendour of Versailles, French taste under the influence of Daniel Marot, developed for massive, heavily decorated plate, including toilet tables with matching stools and mirror frames, as well as extensive toilet services. Applied ornament included arabesques, lambreauquins, and masks. Superb craftsmanship was carried out under the masters Sebastien Leblond and Jean Baptiste. The death of Louis XIV in 1715 began a short era of simplicity, with piercing a fashionable style of ornament.

This trend was succeeded by forty years of showy rococo design. This greatly appealed to hostesses eager to load their tables with glittering arrays of plate. The outstanding master in this work was Justin Aurèle Meissonier, who interpreted the rococo at its most florid. Under his influence the decoration of French domestic plate reached a high standard of radiance. Louis XV appointed him royal silversmith. Other celebrated silversmiths of this period were Claud Ballin, the younger; Paul Charvel; Robert Joseph Auguste, a prolific worker; Antoine Boullier; Edmé Balzac; and Claud Augustus Aubry. Thomas Germain and his son François were accounted high among the silversmiths of Paris. The elder possessed a flair for bold design and skilful handling of the sumptuous and ornate. An immense tureen made for Louis Duc d'Orleans, son of the Regent, is a notable feat of craftsmanship. The cover is piled high with all kinds of game, meat, fish, and vegetables, with boars' heads for handles, and the stand supported by boars' feet. François rivalled him in creative skill and in the quantity of his

productions, which were in continual demand at the Continental Courts. Little remains of the plate produced by Thomas, but several sumptuous pieces by his son have survived, notably at Lisbon and Leningrad. Louis Lenhendrick, a contemporary, supplied fantastic plate in the rococo style to the Russian Court.

Rococo was succeeded by neo-classicism, a style thoroughly suited to the French temperament. These new patterns acquired fashion appeal when the celebrated Delafosse published designs which overcame early prejudice and influenced silversmiths throughout France. The neo-classic continued until the Revolution, when once again fashionable domestic plate was confiscated by the Government for conversion into bullion. The result is that French silver wrought earlier than 1790 is extremely scarce, much scarcer than that of other Continental countries. Many people, however, possessed no more than a single lightweight article of undecorated silver such as a spoon, beaker, wine taster, or écuelle. Little of this fell into the hands of the bullionists, and examples are plentiful.

Prior to the Revolution enormous quantities of silver plate had been made, much of it with consummate skill. Paris alone supported more than five hundred master silversmiths, and in every town throughout the country at least one member of the craft was fully occupied. A law was enacted in 1784 requiring each of the 176 silver communities or guilds in France to register in Paris an invariable mark by which their work could be identified, with the date indicated by the last two cyphers of the year. Such a community mark was usually identified with the region in which the silversmith operated: such as a rose for Provence, a grape cluster for Theims, an artichoke for Laon, a cannon for Mezieres, scissors for Thouars, lace bobbins for Valenciennes, a lion's head for Lyons, a rock for Rochfort, a bear for Vesoul, a squirrel for St Germain-en-Laye, a ship for Brest, a fish for Dieppe, and a cat for Meaux.

The provincial silversmiths were not slavish imitators of the Parisian designers and craftsmen; many of them established less lavish localized styles. These were too widespread to be much affected by competing models, and each jealously guarded autonomy discouraged any tendency towards uniformity. Each community restricted membership, and no trained craftsman was permitted more than one assistant.

The period of Napoleon's Empire emphasized the elegance of classicism in silver plate by such masters as Marc Jacquart, Martin Biennais, Henri Auguste, and J. B. Odiot. The Château de Malmaison houses four pieces from a silver-gilt dinner service made by Auguste to the command of Napoleon I, who presented it to the City of Paris. The soup tureen and stand are typical of Empire classicism: the bowl is encircled with a border of classical figures in relief, repeated on the stand, which is supported by four figures of winged lions. The cover finial consists of a seated classical figure. The Emperor's favourite was Biennais: many historic services by this master have survived.

During the next thirty years or so there was a close resemblance between French and English silver plate. An English silversmith's catalogue published in about 1850 illustrates numerous designs found also struck with French hall-marks. For instance, a silver-gilt vase-shaped coffee-pot made in 1825 by Marc Augustin Lebrun, Paris, was constructed of units of plate – none of it hand-raised – to which cast and chased ornament was soldered, such as palm leaves and bulrushes, swans, fountains, and dolphins.

The *Jury's Report of the Great Exhibition*, 1851, records in connexion with French silver plate: "The beauty of elegance of the individual forms and ornamental details is a thorough study of ornamentation; figures are perfect parts of many compositions and might be oxidized to emphasise their beautiful workmanship. Ornament is in low relief over the surface generally and parcel gilding gives expression when design is confused by excess. The plateaus on which tea cups, cream and sugar vessels are arranged are ornamented in niello." The electrotype process of reproducing elaborately worked silver was now in use: the copies were, of course, in unalloyed silver. A pioneer of this branch of silver-working was F. A. Thouret, Paris, who produced replicas of many cups, including one representing the "Rape of the Sabines" and the "Cup of Fulda".

One of the most prolific of Parisian silversmiths during this period was J. F. Rudolphi. One fashionable piece, of which he made many, was a round tripod work-table constructed entirely from units of cast silver. The top consisted of a hollowed flat plate with a mask of a Naiad in the centre surrounded by Titans and Naiads, the rim ornamented with applied masks, birds, and foliage. The pillar resembled a stem of reed foliage, ornamented with kingfishers: upon the three claws were a bird's nest being attacked by a rat, and an intoxicated infant Bacchus.

In France it is compulsory for a standard mark, either 950 or 800, to be struck by the State Assay Office, and it is illegal to sell below these standards in France, although silver of lower quality may be exported. The maker is also required to strike his mark.

German

Vienna, home of the German emperors from the time of Rudolf IV in the fourteenth century, was the centre of early silversmithing. Here assembled the craftsmen whose brilliant wares eventually brought fame to the German states. It was the custom in Vienna to provide Court appointments to master goldsmiths resident within the city. These men were exempt from guild regulations, and none was compelled to strike his plate with any mark.

The German Gothic period in silver, about 1150–1550, was one of exceptional magnificence. Crocketed and pinnacled, enriched with exquisite figurines of saints, gilded and enamelled, set with precious stones and gems, much of this silver was designed for ecclesiastical purposes, such as monstrances and reliquaries, huge candlesticks and chalices. A favourite cup form late in the period was the small castle on slender stem and lobed foot.

Mazers and drinking-horns were mounted in silver and usually engraved with Gothic lettering or leaf ornament. Mazers were often elaborate, the wooden bowl being fitted with a silver foot bearing the arms of its owner in enamel and the cover being surmounted by a silver figure, such as a falcon holding an heraldic shield upon which the arms were repeated.

By 1500 the free city of Nuremberg and the German town of Augsburg were supporting many prosperous master silversmiths with an enormous output of Gothic plate, much of it exported. Wenzel Jamnitzer, who went from Vienna to Nuremberg as late as 1534, became one of the most celebrated silversmiths in the Gothic style. Many German silversmiths had been apprenticed in or near Vienna, and consequently produced plate now counted as German, although very few pieces exist. These prove beyond doubt that no other European country made silver plate of comparable workmanship.

The Italian renaissance affected the design of domestic plate during the sixteenth century, making it renowned for its gorgeous ornamental detail, including new motifs, such as putti, urns, satyrs, nymphs, and acanthus leaves: the Church authorities preferred the formality of Gothic design until about 1600. Pineapple cups and columbine cups of superb craftsmanship were made by every aspirant to mastership. These were constructed according to guild rules and were masterpieces to prove dexterity of hammerwork and a sensitive touch in the chasing.

Germany's well-organized guild life favoured the production of plate such as wine-cups, tankards, beakers, wager cups, and the like. There was little ecclesiastical patronage after the Reformation, and silversmiths found their profits among the solidly prosperous burghers. Every collection of German plate inevitably contains a preponderance of drinking-vessels.

Doctors from the fifteenth century advised every man who could afford it to drink from vessels of precious metals as a protection against infection.

Certain drinking-vessels were used exclusively by Germans, mostly at their guild meetings. These include the giant *Riesenpokal* and the *Jungfrauenbecher*, a double cup – that is, one-stemmed cup supporting a precisely similar cup brim to brim. Some fantastic cups were fashionable in the shape of figures, birds, and animals, such as the parcel gilt lion *passant*, its tongue formed as a spout and the tail reflexed over the back; and the lion *sejant* with a detachable head and a finely chased mane.

Specialist designers working on a free-lance basis became established in the sixteenth century and included Albrecht Altdorfer (1480–1538); Peter Flütner, whose Kunstbuch was published in 1549; Virgil Solis (1514–62); Hans Rosamer (*fl.* 1520–34); Bernard Zan (*fl.* 1580s); Hans Sibmacher (*fl.* 1555–95); Georg Wechter; Paul Flindt. Ornament on English Elizabethan and Jacobean silver was influenced by these German artists.

Cups were often masterpieces of lavish design, but their stems might be wrought of copper and heavily gilded. In others the cover, stem, and foot were in gilded copper, only the bowl being in silver, and that of quality lower than sterling.

Cups in which the liquor was held in nautilus shells were in great demand. The shell was cleaned by grinding until its mother of pearl surface showed unflawed and iridescent: it might then be all-over engraved. The upper curve was decorated with silver such as with the reptiles associated with Jacob Frick of Constanz. The shell bowl was held firmly by four hinged straps of silver rising from an expansive oval base of embossed silver. Many handsomely engraved examples were made at Augsburg for a century from the 1550s.

Silver-mounted coconut cups were largely exported during the same period. In these the bowl was meticulously carved with religious or personal subjects and held by three silver straps. Daniel Michael, Augsburg, from 1580 made silver-gilt mounted figures of cocks, the body consisting of a coconut, the head detachable to form a drinking-vessel, and the hinged wings and tail in openwork silver.

Globe cups, German productions of the seventeenth century, were never very fashionable. They resembled terrestrial and celestial globes and were sold in pairs. The globes were supported by carefully modelled figures of Atlas kneeling on plinths of baroque design, often chased with dolphins and shells. These cups appear to have been used mainly for ornament.

Wager cups of the type associated with Dutch silversmiths were produced prolifically in Germany, particularly in Augsburg. Both those in the form of a windmill and those shaped as a woman holding aloft a swinging cup were made from the late fifteenth century until the 1850s.

Nefs of richly wrought silver were produced in hundreds of patterns from the fourteenth century, and one maker exhibited at the Great Exhibition, 1851. They were originally in almost universal use among the nobility and higher clergy. Until the mid-eighteenth century these sometimes massive pieces of plate, resembling perfectly rigged galleons, were often the work of specialist nef workers in Nuremberg and Augsburg. In the British Museum is an example made in 1581 by Hans Schlott, Augsburg, with a clock incorporated in its design.

Tankards were fashionable from the sixteenth to the eighteenth centuries, many of them parcel-gilt. The beaker-shaped body was decorated with masses of chased embossments and engraving, virtually no plain space being left on body or lid; the handle was an elaborate casting such as caryatic or claw. A 7-inch tankard made by Kaspar Bauch, Nuremberg, 1580, is covered with strapwork, masks, birds, and bunches of fruit, with a female bust handle and with a thumbpiece in the shape of an infant bacchanal. There was also a vogue in Danzig for setting the body with numerous coins, all from a single state such as Brandenberg, or Prussia, and chasing the intervening spaces with foliage and scrollwork on a matted ground. Several struck with the mark of P. Overdieck, Hamburg, late in the seventeenth century, are encircled with frieze designs of bacchanalian figures and have grotesque scroll handles. Others by Cornelius Poppe, of the same period, are encircled with Roman emperors' heads.

Beakers were made throughout the collector's period of German silver plate, invariably in thick-gauge metal, Hamburg, Breslau, and Strasbourg being the specialist centres. Many are fitted with finialled lift-off covers, and their capacities are usually pint or half-pint, although other sizes are found. Early beakers might have ball feet, but a moulded or gadrooned foot rim was more usual. A typical beaker by Matthias Gelb, Augsberg, 1670, is worked in *repoussé* and chased with amorini astride dolphins in a seascape. Many in the eighteenth century were engraved with inscriptions in praise of wine.

The baroque and rococo styles extending from 1600 to 1760 were recognized by the Church, and their architects realized the decorative value of silver and designed handsome altar frontals, delicate monstrances, and enormous candlesticks. Silversmiths during this period made full use of the baroque flame-like curve on which they based many of their designs and ornaments.

German silversmiths excelled the Dutch until early in the seventeenth century, when the latter began embossing plate in a style acknowledged to be the finest in European silver of the period. This fashion was superseded by the Louis XIV style during the third quarter of the century. The Germans then turned their attention to much plainer domestic plate, producing small wares in enormous quantities in a metal less than sterling, but also making huge wine fountains and cisterns, magnificent centrepieces, and entire dinner services and tea equipages.

There was a late seventeenth-century and early eighteenth-century vogue for associating agate with silver mounts, such as candlesticks and drinking-cups, later copied by Wedgwood in agate ware with silver rims. Silver gilt and agate tea services made from agate ware consisted of a teapot with hexagonal sides, each set with a pink and brown agate medallion, two oval boxes for tea and sugar, and four brown agate tea-cups and saucers, the cups with moulded silver feet and the saucers in fluted silver.

Ordinary domestic ware continued as the

mainstay of the German silversmiths during the eighteenth and nineteenth centuries and included teapots, jugs, tea canisters, coffee-pots, tazzas, ewers, and basins in styles little different from the English rococo, neo-classic, and regency, but always in metal of a quality lower than sterling.

The cathedral city of Osnabruck in Hanover, of which George IV was created archbishop a few days after his birth, wrought much domestic silver for the English royal family. Examples have been noted engraved with the crest of George II as Prince of Wales, and with the arms of George III; but none of this is of sterling quality.

The German standard for silver is 800 parts per thousand, compared with 925 parts per thousand for sterling, the alloy being copper.

The German silversmith may strike his personal mark and the standard mark, but neither of these is compulsory. It is not illegal in Germany to sell silver plate below recognized standards. German silver plate could be imported freely into Britain, but was difficult to sell owing to the absence of the sterling hallmark. The Foreign Plate Act of 1842 required German plate, if it were to be sold, to be assayed and struck with a mark if it is of sterling quality: any found to be below sterling was to be rejected and battered. By rigid adherence to their demand for sterling quality the Goldsmiths' Company successfully prevented the entry of German silver for sale. This Act, and the low standard of German silver, accounts for its absence from the Great Exhibition, 1851.

Italian

Italian silver and gold of the Renaissance and earlier periods has for long been admired by all connoisseurs. Such works as the Pistoia altar, numerous reliquaries, processional crosses and croziers, the exquisite gold roses given by the popes to various sovereigns (Plate 493c), and Benvenuto Cellini's magnificent gold salt-cellar at Vienna, are among the outstanding examples of the European goldsmiths' and silversmiths' craft. But only in recent years has the silver of late periods won the attention of collectors. One of the chief reasons for this neglect was probably the difficulty which collectors experienced in their attempts to identify the marks on Italian silver. Two books published in 1959 – Signor C. G. Bulgari's dictionary of Roman silversmiths and the catalogue of an exhibition held at the Poldi Pezzoli Museum, Milan – have, however, made it possible to identify most of the town marks and the Roman makers' marks. It may safely be predicted that the new interest in Italian silver of the seventeenth, eighteenth, and early nineteenth centuries will soon spread from col-lectors in Italy to the rest of Europe and America.

To eyes trained on the relative severity and solidity of the best English plate, much Italian baroque and rococo silver may, at first, seem a little too showy, not to say meretricious. Although Italian silversmiths produced numerous vessels marked by a restrained elegance of design, they excelled in the production of richly ornamented and often fantastic works. It must also be admitted that very few pieces of Italian silver reveal that exquisitely controlled sense of form and decoration which marks the finest works of French silversmiths. However, the same might be said in a comparison of any of the arts of eighteenth-century Italy and France. Exuberance is the outstanding quality of the best seventeenth- and early eighteenth-century Italian silver. And even in their later, severer, neo-classical works, the *argentieri* seem to have had difficulty in restraining their sense of fantasy, making coffee-pots in the form of urns with leaping greyhounds or goats as handles, crowning tureens with statuettes of river gods, fashioning lamps as Egyptian slaves.

There is a bold virility in the curves which decorate many large and small examples of Italian plate of the late seventeenth and eighteenth centuries. These pieces are also marked by a sculpturesque quality which is the other distinguishing feature of the best Italian silver. Such a relief as that by Luigi Valadier (Plate 496c) and many crucifixes and giant candlesticks like those at Lisbon, may indeed be regarded as minor masterpieces of Italian sculpture. But this sculpturesque quality is also evident in much domestic plate: the magnificent tureens made at Turin and Genoa (Plates 499b and 500a), for instance, or such a boldly modelled object as the oil lamp in a private collection at Milan (Plate 495c).

Marks and regional characteristics. Silver objects produced in different parts of Italy naturally show variations of style similar to those which mark the regional schools of sculptors and painters. The five most important centres for the production of silver were Rome, Turin, Venice, Genoa, and Naples, where the practice of hall-marking silver of approved quality seems to have been almost invariable in the eighteenth century. The study of marks has, however, revealed that fine work was produced in many other places. The silver coffeepot seen in Plate 496b, for example, was regarded as an outstanding specimen of Genoese silver until the hall-mark was shown to be Maltese: though its maker may, of course, have come from Genoa. The list of notable Italian silversmiths printed below reveals how many, born and trained in various parts of Italy, worked principally in Rome. It is therefore rash to attribute silver to different regions purely on stylistic grounds. Silversmiths of the five main centres of production did, however, have their specialities.

Roman silversmiths naturally specialized in ecclesiastical plate, for which there was a particularly brisk market not only among the prelates resident there but also the numerous visitors. The Roman hall-mark – the crossed keys of St Peter with either the Papal tiara or the ceremonial umbrella – may thus be found on much ecclesiastical silver in all parts of Europe. Silver reliefs and statuettes, of mythological as well as religious subjects, seem to have been made in Rome more frequently than elsewhere. It is interesting to note that Roman silversmiths adopted the neo-classical style in the early 1770s, a decade or more before their colleagues in other towns.

At Genoa the art of making silver filigree flourished as nowhere else in Italy, though unfortunately few pieces bear the city's mark (a tower). Another speciality of Genoese silversmiths were *trembleuses* (Plate 499a), which appear to have been made nowhere else. Much mid-eighteenth century Genoese plate reveals the influence of France. The French influence on the silversmiths of Turin was stronger and eighteenth-century Turinese *écuelles* might easily be mistaken for French work (Plate 497b). The Turin hall-mark – the arms of the House of Savoy – may also be found on many tureens, coffee-pots, and sugar bowls which have a French elegance of design. Venetian silversmiths seem to have specialized in rather highly embossed decorations, and they produced some of the finest book bindings and *cartagloria* frames made in Italy. The Venetian hall-mark – the winged lion of St Mark – also appears on many simple domestic objects, some of which seem to show the influence of English plate. Many objects bearing the Naples hall-mark – the first three letters or the full name of Napoli, with a crown above – are also very simple. But Neapolitan silversmiths are more famous for such exuberant and sometimes rather gimcrack productions as vases of silver flowers. Other towns where fine silver was produced included Bologna, Florence, Mantua, Messina, and Palermo.

SOME NOTABLE ITALIAN SILVERSMITHS

Agricola, Giuseppe (1717–1804). A German originally named Bauer who began to work in Rome in 1739 and obtained his patent in 1745. His mark (initials) is to be found on several pieces of domestic plate dating from the second half of the century. Two of his sons Luigi (1759–1821) and Vincenzo (b. 1769) became gem engravers.

Arrighi, Giovanni Francesco (1646–1730). Roman, obtained his patent in 1683. He worked much for Cardinal Cybo and provided plate for several Roman churches. His mark (a lion's paw) appears on a pair of candelabra in the church of S. Maria Assunta at Capranica (Viterbo). His sons Agostino (1682–1762) and Antonio (1687–1776) were also silversmiths, employing marks similar to his. Antonio obtained his patent in 1733. His most notable work is the magnificent silver and lapis lazuli altar frontal, made to the design of Agostino Corsini and Bernardo Ludovisi for the royal chapel in Lisbon, between 1747 and 1749. He also produced grandiose works for Roman churches.

Bartalesi, Urbano (1641–1726). Sienese, was in Rome by 1660. His mark (a wolf, the Sienese arms) is found on domestic and ecclesiastical plate. His son, Stefano (1692–1737), took over his workshop in 1726 and employed the same mark.

Bartolotti, Giuseppe (1709–75). Roman, obtained his patent in 1731. His mark (a fish) is found on several pieces of mid-eighteenth-century domestic plate. The same mark (changed in 1790 to an upright fish between the initials C B) was used by his son, Carlo (1749–1834), who obtained a patent in 1777. A very handsome tureen with ram's head handles and a river god seated on the cover, made c. 1785–95, is in the collection of Dr Massimo Spada.

Belli, Vincenzo (1710–87). Founder of a very important family of silversmiths working in Rome, was born in Turin. He is first recorded at Rome in 1740 and obtained his patent next year. His mark (initials) is to be found on much ecclesiastical and domestic plate, a fine example being the ewer and basin (1772–83) in the Palazzo Venezia in Rome. His son Giovacchino (1756–1822) followed his calling, obtaining his patent in 1788, and produced some very fine silver in a strongly neo-classical style. Giovacchino's son, Pietro (1780–1828), also became a silversmith, obtaining his patent in 1825. Many of his designs for silver are in the Cooper Union Museum, New York. In the fourth generation Vincenzo II (*fl.* 1828–59), Pietro's son, took over the workshop, obtaining the patent in 1828. Among his numerous works (marked either with his initials or full name) one of the most outstanding is a coffee-pot,

based on one of his father's designs, with a handle in the form of a greyhound and a triton as spout (collection of G. Colonelli, Rome). He also produced a silver statuette of Menelaus with the body of Patroclus (modelled on the antique group at Florence) which was bought by the Earl of Jersey in Rome between 1828 and 1848, and is now in the collection of Dr Massimo Spada.

Benzi, Tommaso (1644–1723). Born in Genoa but went to work in Rome, where he obtained his patent in 1697. His mark (the head of a bearded man) appears on a monstrance in the church of S. Giovanni dei Genovesi, Rome.

Birelli, Bernardino (1707–67). A Roman, he obtained his patent in 1733. His mark (a lion with a book) has been found on several pieces of plate, including a pair of candlesticks in the collection of Professor Carlo Pietrangeli.

Boroni, Bartolomeo (1703–87). Born in Vicenza but was working in Rome by 1725. He obtained his patent in 1730. Among other works he provided the gilt-copper crown and sceptre for the coffin of the Young Pretender, made two reliquaries of solid gold to the design of Piranesi, and in 1774 produced several "decorazione" for the Vatican after designs by Mengs. Three of his sons became silversmiths: Giuseppe, who used his father's mark (a monogram of Maria), was responsible for much work that has survived, including a Crucifix and six candlesticks of silver and lapis lazuli in the church of S. Biagio at Fabriano.

Carlier, Michele (1665–1741). Born in Ath in France, but had settled in Rome by 1688. Two years later he received his patent. He was much employed by Cardinal Camillo Cybo, for whom he made, among other objects, a gold reliquary adorned with diamonds and amethysts which was given to the Duke of Gordon in 1726. His mark (a cross on a pedestal) appears on three *cartagloria* frames in the cathedral at Poggio Mirteto.

Cellini, Benvenuto (1500–69). Born in Florence, was probably the greatest of all Italian goldsmiths and one of the most notable sixteenth-century sculptors. His famous autobiography presents a fascinating account of an artist's life in the late Renaissance. His literary fame has naturally attracted numerous attributions to his name, but the magnificent salt in the Kunsthistoriches Museum, Vienna, is the only surviving work in precious metals that can with certainty be ascribed to him.

Cervosi, Angelo (1661–1720). A Roman who obtained his patent in 1690. A fine engraved salver in the collection of Mr Edward Burnett Lawson bears his maker's mark (a stag).

Chiocca, Matteo (1702–58). A Roman who obtained his patent in 1737. In 1739 he became silversmith to the city of Rome and the producer of chalices for the Camera Capitolina. In this capacity he made the chalices (varying from thirty-four to forty-three per year) which were given by the Magistrato to the various churches of Rome on their patronal festivals. His mark is therefore found on much ecclesiastical plate in the city (a sun with initials). He was succeeded by his son Giuseppe (1743–1812), who obtained his patent in 1739 and also produced numerous chalices for the Magistrato.

Colleoni, Corinzio (1579–1656). Born in Gallese, working in Rome by 1596, obtained his patent in 1612. Between 1616 and 1654 he made numerous chalices given by the Magistrato to the churches of Rome. In this work he was followed by his nephew Bartolommeo (1633–1708), who provided chalices between 1658 and 1701. The third Colleoni to hold this post of silversmith to the Magistrato was Bartolomeo's nephew, Agostino (1663–1746), who made many chalices between 1714 and 1738. The three Colleoni used as a mark a leopard's head rendered in different ways.

De Alessandris, Flavio (1668–1744). Born at Narni and obtained his patent at Rome in 1692. He worked also in Naples. His mark (a spread-eagle) appears on six large candlesticks in the church at Polaggia. His son, Paolo (1696–1773), obtained his patent in 1739 and made for the church of São Roque, Lisbon, six large candelabra between 1748 and 1750. A *cartagloria* frame in the convent of S. Caterina at Fabriano also bears his mark (the diadem of the Holy Trinity).

De Caporali, Lorenzo (*c.* 1712–77). Born

at Civitavecchia and worked in Rome, where he obtained his patent in 1745. His son, Antonio (1755–1832), obtained his patent in 1783. Several pieces of neo-classical silver bear his mark (a halberdier which was used by his father, the initials R. L. C., another which reads D. N. D./Vedov L. C., and finally, A 42 C.).

De Castro, Antonio (*fl.* 1565). A Portuguese silversmith who made for Franco Lercaro in 1565 the magnificent ewer and basin now in a private collection in Venice, and another in the Wallace Collection.

Fedeli, Stefano (1794–1870). A Roman who obtained his patent in 1815. Among his works the most notable is a statuette representing *The Return of Ulysses*, formerly in the collection of the Earls of Jersey, now in that of Dr Massimo Spada, Rome.

Fornari, Antonio (1734–1810). A Roman who obtained his patent in 1760. His mark (initials with a star beneath or full name) has been found on ecclesiastical and domestic plate (Plate 495c).

Gagliardi, Giuseppe (1687–1749). A Roman who obtained his patent in 1742. For the King of Portugal in 1745 he made a magnificent pair of silver gilt *tochères* more than 9 feet high, now in the Museum of Religious Art, Lisbon. He also made for this patron a silver-gilt statue of the Madonna, some 6 feet high, on a model provided by G. B. Maini. His son, Leandro (1729–1804), also worked for the King of Portugal, making four reliquaries, holy water bucket, censer, and incense boat which were sent to Lisbon. The reliquaries have vanished, but the other objects survive.

Gentili, Antonio (1519–1609). Born in Faenza and went to Rome in about 1550. In 1582 he made for Cardinal Alessandro Farnese a silver-gilt crucifix and pair of candlesticks now in the Treasury of St Peter's, Rome.

Ghini, Simone (1410–*c.* 1475). Born in Florence, in about 1435 he went to Rome, where he was employed in making ceremonial swords and also papal roses, one of which survives in the Palazzo Communale, Siena.

Giardini, Giovanni (1646–1721). Born at Forlì, he was in Rome by 1665, and ten years later obtained permission to open a workshop.

Together with his younger brother Alessandro (1655–1718), he made the bronze relief for the monument of Queen Christina of Sweden in 1700. His mark (a basket of flowers) is to be found on a reliquary at Gubbio and several vessels in the treasury of St Peter's. In 1714 he published a book of somewhat fantastic designs for silver.

Giardoni, Francesco (1692–1757). A Roman who obtained his patent in 1729. His mark (a bee) appears on a statue of San Felice in the cathedral at Foligno. He also made two statuettes of silver on models by Bernardino Ludovisi. His brother Carlo (1693–1764) appears to have specialized in making silver statues, but none is known to have survived.

Grazioli, Giuseppe (1717–92). Born at Fermo, obtained his patent at Rome in 1749. His mark (initials) has been found on a reliquary in the cathedral at Piperno and on domestic plate.

Guizzardi, Martino (1561–c. 1652). A Roman, who obtained his patent in 1583. In 1614 he made the silver case for the body of St Agnes in the church of S. Agnese, Rome.

Jacomini, Samuele (1625–1707). Born at Manzan in Lorraine, he was working in Rome in 1653 and obtained his patent there in 1661. A jeweller rather than a silversmith, he specialized in the production of rings, jewelled crosses, and reliquaries. A richly worked baroque chalice by him, dated 1690, is in the Cathedral at Gnesen.

Ladatte, Francesco (1706–87). Born in Turin and trained in Paris and Rome. Most of his life was passed in his native city, where he worked much for the House of Savoy as sculptor and *ciseleur*. He is also known to have produced works in silver, notably a monstrance for the basilica at Superga, but none of these survives.

Landi, Marc' Antonio (1688–1732). A Roman who obtained his patent in 1716. His marks (a heart and later a bunch of grapes) have been recognized on several pieces of ecclesiastical plate.

Lorenzini, Nicola (1710–67). A Roman who obtained his patent in 1756. In 1759 he made a magnificent silver lamp for the church of the Consolazione at Todi, now in the Museo Civico, Todi.

Lotti, Santi (1599–1659). Born at Viterbo, he was in Rome by 1621 and obtained his patent in 1629. He made chalices for the Magistrato of Rome to give to churches in the city. In the cathedral of S. Severino (Macerata) there is a large silver statue of St Severino made by Lotti in 1659.

Mariani, Domenico Gabriele (1697–1756). Born at Ronciglione and worked in the shop of Giuseppe Nipote at Rome from 1725 until 1753 when he obtained his own patent. His mark (three stars) has been found on some fine domestic plate (Plate 496A).

Mascelli, Luigi (c. 1770–1825). A Roman who obtained his patent in 1804. He seems to have specialized in the production of small gold boxes which are marked with his initials.

Menniti, Giacomo (1643–1714). A Roman who obtained his patent in 1668. His mark (the shield of the city of Rome) is found on ecclesiastical and domestic plate, notably a fine simple ewer in the collection of S. E. Silvio Innocenti.

Merlini, Lorenzo (1666–c. 1745). Born in Florence, he went to Rome in 1694, returned to his native city in 1702, and went back to Rome in 1715. A sculptor and architect, he occasionally worked in silver and obtained his patent as a silversmith in Rome in 1719.

Miglié, Natale (1649–1720). Born at Dôle in Burgundy, he was in Rome by 1665 and obtained his patent in 1673. A holy water bucket dated 1710 in the church of S. Maria Assunta, Rome, bears his mark (an anchor). His son, Simon (1679–1752), who used the same mark, made three lamps for the church of São Roque, Lisbon, between 1745 and 1749.

Mola, Gaspare (1567–1640). Born at Coldrè (Como), he went to Rome and was working for the mint there by 1625. His masterpiece is a large, elaborately worked plate of silver, partly gilt, made for the Boncompagni family to record the reform of the calendar and now in a private collection in Venice (Plate 494B).

Monti, Francesco (1662–1708). A Roman who obtained his patent in 1696. His mark (a rampant unicorn) has been found on six reliquaries in the church of S. Giovanni dei

Portoghesi, Rome, and several other pieces of ecclesiastical silver.

Moretti de Amicis, Antonio (1611–87). A Venetian, was in Rome by 1640 and obtained his patent in 1652. He worked much for the Chigi family, and many pieces of the silver for their chapel in the cathedral at Siena bear his mark (the heads of two Moors facing each other).

Ossani, Francesco (*fl.* 1800–29). Obtained his patent in Rome in 1801. His mark (initials) appears on several pieces of domestic plate of great elegance and simplicity.

Petroncelli, Lorenzo (1724–1801). A Roman who obtained his patent in 1758. His mark (a bee) has been found on several very fine pieces of domestic plate.

Pieri, Pietro Paolo (1658–1718). Born in Villach, Germany, and went to Rome before 1671, obtaining his patent there in 1685. His mark (a dove) is found on silver in the cathedrals of Sutri and Pergola.

Reali, Raimondo (*c.* 1714–78). A Roman who obtained his patent in 1742. His mark (initials) is found on a reliquary in the cathedral at Pisoniano and the bust of a Saint at Capranica Prenestina.

Sangeni, Carlo (*c.* 1770–1836). A Roman who obtained his patent in 1815. He worked much for the Vatican and made an elaborately engraved walking stick for Pius VI. This is now in the Vatican Museum.

Sanini, Giovanni Felice (1727–87). Born at Lucca and went to work in Rome in 1741, obtaining his patent in 1747. He provided silver for the King of Portugal, and several of his works are now in the Museum of Religious Art, Lisbon, notably a crucifix on which the figure of Christ was made by G. B. Maini.

Scarabello, Angelo (1711–95). Born at Este. His most famous work is the gilt-bronze doorway to the chapel of the relics in the Santo at Padua. He also made the *cartagloria* frame illustrated here (Plate 494C).

Spagna, Paolo (1736–88). A Roman who obtained his patent in 1772. His mark (a pair of dividers with an S between them) appears on much domestic and ecclesiastical plate, including the silver bust of St Rufino in the cathedral at Assisi.

Spezzani, Giuseppe (1627–1710). A Flo-rentine who went to Rome in 1640 and obtained his patent there in 1654. Two of his sons, Cosimo (1663–1717) and Giovanni Girolamo (1665–1748), became goldsmiths using similar marks (a centaur). Cosimo made four reliquaries now in the Cathedral at Sezze.

Spinazzi, Angelo (*fl.* 1720–85). Born at Piacenza, obtained his patent at Rome in 1721. He made two large candelabra for the King of Portugal (Museum of Religious Art, Lisbon), worked much for the Vatican and made the large silver altar frontal now in the Cathedral at Siracusa.

Taglietti, Fantino (1574–*c.* 1650). A Roman. Between 1627 and 1647 he was employed in making chalices to be given by the Magistrato to the churches of Rome. His masterpiece is the silver statue of St Ambrose on horseback, of 1641, in the Cathedral at Ferentino, which bears his mark (a rose).

Valadier, Andrea (1695–1759). Founder of a very important family of Roman silversmiths, was born at Aramont in the south of France and began to work in Rome in 1720, obtaining his patent in 1725. Two sons, Giovanni (1732–1805) and Luigi (1726–85), both became silversmiths. Giovanni's mark (initials beneath a fleur-de-lis) is found on much fine silver of the Pius VI period. Luigi (his mark was either initials between three fleurs-de-lis, or his full name) made numerous domestic and ecclesiastical vessels, also the model of Trajan's Column (together with B. Hecher) now in the Residenz at Munich. Both his marks were used after his death by his son, Giuseppe (1762–1839), who was also an architect. Both father and son produced silver in the neo-classical style (Plates 496c and 497A). Many of Giuseppe Valadier's designs are in the Cooper Union Museum at New York.

Vendetti, Antonio (1699–1796). Born at Cotanello in Sabina and obtained his patent in Rome in 1737. He is represented in the Museum of Religious Art, Lisbon, by three *cartagloria* frames made for the church of São Roque between 1744 and 1749. They bear his mark (a spread-eagle).

Venturesi, Mattia (*c.* 1719–76). Born at Forlì, was in Rome by 1738 and obtained his patent there in 1762. His mark (a lion's paw

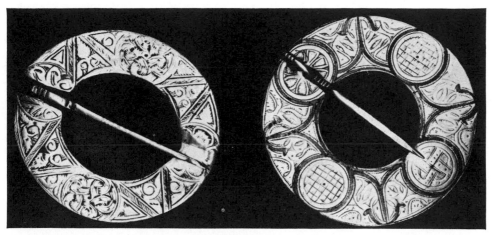

(A) Silver brooches, with *niello* inlay: eighteenth century. *National Museum of Antiquities, Scotland.*

(B) Earliest silver club of the Royal and Ancient Golf Club of St Andrews, *c.* 1754. *Royal and Ancient Golf Club.*

(C) Trifid spoons from set of four earliest known: Edinburgh, 1665–80, maker Alex Reid. *Lt-Col. J. N. Price Wood.*

PLATE 481

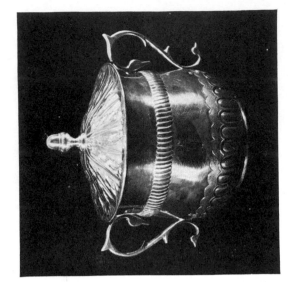

(A) Communion cup of Ellon: seventeenth century, maker Walter Melvil.

(B) A Charles II Scottish silver tumbler cup: Glasgow, c. 1680, maker Thomas Moncrur. Maker's mark only. The arms are those of the Scottish family of Crockett. Weight 5 ozs, 12 dwts. *Thomas Lumley.*

(c) Covered cup (one of pair): Perth, c. 1790, maker Robert Keay. *Royal Scottish Museum.*

PLATE 482

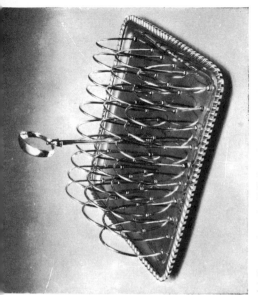

(B) Bannock-rack, Edinburgh, 1773, maker Patrick Robertson. *Royal Scottish Museum.*

(C) Salver, one of two; Aberdeen, *c.* 1730, maker George Robertson. *Royal Scottish Museum.*

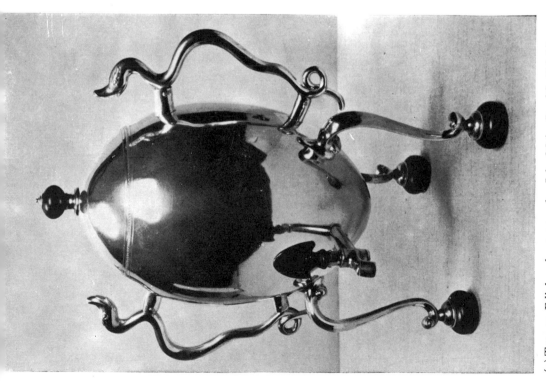

(A) Tea urn, Edinburgh, 1732, maker John Main. *Royal Scottish Museum.*

PLATE 483

(A) Sugar casters: Edinburgh, 1728, maker B. and W. Penman. *Private Collection.*

(B) A set of three Queen Anne silver casters: Edinburgh, 1706, maker Patrick Murray. Weight 25¼ ozs. *Thomas Lumley.*

(C) George II Scottish silver teapot: Edinburgh, 1746, maker William Gilchrist; Assay Master, Hugh Gordon. *Harvey and Gore.*

PLATE 484

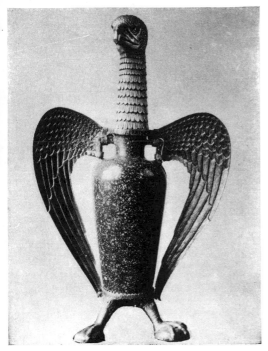

(A) Ewer made in about 1140. Silver-gilt and por-phyry. *Louvre, Paris.*

(B) The Reliquary of the Holy Thorn. Gold, enamelled, and set with jewels. French work of the late fourteenth century. *British Museum, London.*

(C) *Left:* The Belem Mon-strance. Gold and enamel. Por-tuguese work of the early six-teenth century. *Museu de Arte Antigua, Lisbon.*

(D) *Right:* Monstrance in the gothic style, late sixteenth cen-tury, Dutch. *St Amelberga's Church, Zandhoven.*

PLATE 485

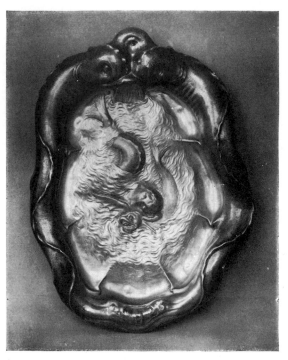

(A) Large dish. Made by Van Vianen in 1635. *Victoria and Albert Museum, London.*

(B) Tankard. Partly gilt. Made by Albrecht Biller at Augsburg, *c.* 1690. *S. J. Phillips.*

(C) One of a pair of salts in the Van Vianen style. Made at Utrecht, *c.* 1620. *S. J. Phillips.*

(D) One of a pair of candlesticks made by Jacques Nicolas Roettiers at Paris in 1771 and hall-marked at Leningrad in 1784. *S. J. Phillips.*

PLATE 486

(A) Centre-piece by Thomas Germain of Paris, 1730–1. *Museu de Arte Antigua, Lisbon.*

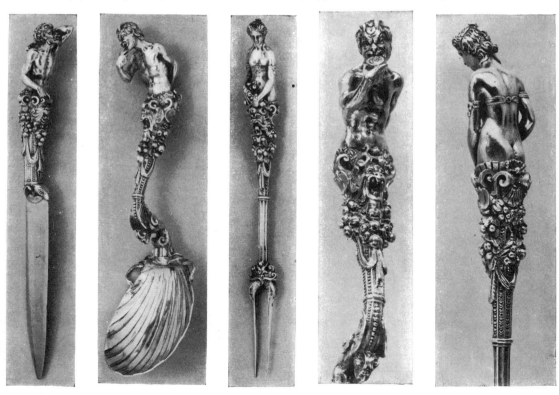

(B) Knife, fork, and spoon (and two details of handles). Italian, sixteenth century, attributed to **Antonio Gentili.** *Metropolitan Museum of Art, New York.*

PLATE 487

(A) Salt. Silver-gilt, decorated with Limoges-enamel plaques. French, late sixteenth century. *Wallace Collection, London.*

(B) Columbine cup made at Nuremberg in about 1572. *Victoria and Albert Museum, London.*

(C) Bason and ewer. Silver-gilt. Made by the Genoese Franco Lercaro and the Portuguese Antonio de Castro in 1565. *Wallace Collection, London.*

PLATE 488

(A) Stag cup. Silver-gilt. Made at Augsburg in the late sixteenth century. *British Museum, London.*

(B) Nef. Silver partly gilt. Made by Esias Zur Linden at Nuremberg, *c.* 1620. *S. J. Phillips.*

(C) Windmill-cup. Made at Enkhuizen in 1621. *S. J. Phillips.*

(D) Nautilus-shell cup. Mounted in silver-gilt. Made by Hans Anthony Lind, Nuremberg, *c.* 1590. *S. J. Phillips.*

PLATE 489

(B) Covered beaker. Silver parcel-gilt. German, late fifteenth century. *Victoria and Albert Museum, London.*

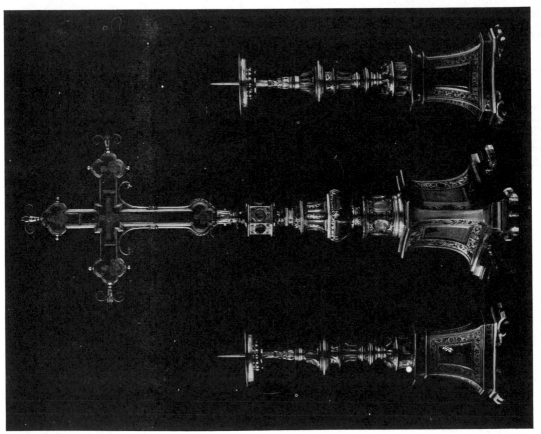

(A) Crucifix and candlesticks. Crystal and silver, gilt and enamelled. North Italian, c. 1520. *Victoria and Albert Museum, London.*

PLATE 490

(B) Monstrance. Silver-gilt, set with precious stones. Made at Munich in about 1740 by J. C. Steinbacher to the design of Aegid Asam. *Johannes Nepomuk-Kirche, Munich.*

(A) Chalice. Silver-gilt, enamelled and set with precious stones. Made by F. A. Gutwein at Augsburg, 1765–8. *Benediktiner-Abtei, Ottobeuren.*

PLATE 491

(B) Part of a tea-set. Made by Augsburg, 1771-3. *S. J. Phillips.*

(D) Folding spoon and fork. Silver parcel-gilt. Flemish, sixteenth century. *British Museum, London.*

(A) Travelling table service made for Cardinal York by L. Valadini at Rome, *c.* 1790. *By gracious permission of Her Majesty the Queen.*

(C) Drinking horn. Mounted in copper-gilt. Danish, fifteenth century. *British Museum, London.*

PLATE 492

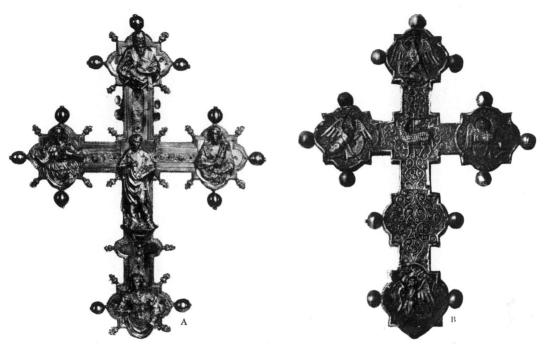

(A) Silver party gilt processional cross attributed to Francesco Marti of Lucca, 1489. Height 18¼ ins.
SS Lorenzo e Barbara, Seravezza.
(B) Processional cross, North Italian, probably fourteenth century. Height 19⅝ ins. *SS Giusto e Clemente,*
Partigliano.

(C) Papal rose, gold and sapphires, presented in 1562 by Pius VI to Duchess Anna, wife of Albrecht V
of Bavaria. Height 32¼ ins. *Residenzmuseum, Munich.*
(D) Silver-gilt chalice, Lombard, late fifteenth century. Height 13 ins. *Museo d'Arte del Castello, Milan.*

PLATE 493

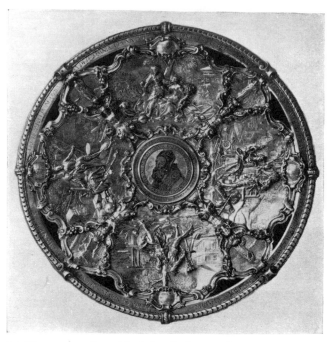

(A) Silver-gilt chalice made at Palermo, sixteenth century. Height $11\frac{3}{8}$ ins. *C. G. Bulgari Collection, Rome.*

(B) Silver party gilt and lapis lazuli plate made to commemorate the reform of the calendar by Gaspare Mola, early seventeenth century. Diameter $21\frac{1}{4}$ ins. *Private Collection, Venice.*

(C) *Cartagloria* frame by Angelo Scarabello, mid-eighteenth century. Height 31 ins. *Private Collection, Genoa.*

(D) Vase made at Venice, early seventeenth century. Height $14\frac{5}{8}$ ins. *Dr Aldo Crespi Collection, Milan.*

PLATE 494

A   B

(A) Oil lamp made at Naples, mid-eighteenth century. Height 20¼ ins. *Bacchi Collection, Milan.*
(B) Oil and vinegar bottle stand made at Genoa, 1768. Height 5¾ ins. *Basevi-Gambarana Collection, Genoa.*

C   D

(C) Oil lamp made by Antonio Fornari at Rome, mid-eighteenth century. Height 12¼ ins. *Private Collection, Milan.*
(D) Candelabrum made at Genoa, 1743. Height 12⅜ ins. *Secondo Galtrucco Collection, Milan.*

PLATE 495

A   B

(A) Coffee-pot made by D. G. Mariani at Rome, 1753–6. Height 10¾ ins. *Private Collection, Milan.*
(B) Coffee-pot made at Malta, early eighteenth century. Height 10⅝ ins. *Dr Aldo Crespi Collection, Milan.*

C   D

(C) The Crucifixion of St Peter, high relief by Luigi Valadier, Rome, c. 1780. Width 20⅞ ins. *Private Collection, Rome.*
(D) Coffee-pot made at Turin, mid-eighteenth century. Height 10¾ ins. *F. Fossati Bellani Collection, Milan.*

PLATE 496

(A) Tureen made at Rome by Luigi or Giuseppe Valadier, 1784–90. Height 19¼ ins.
Fassio Martelli Collection, Genoa.

(B) *Ecuelle* made at Turin, *c.* 1760. *Private Collection, Turin.*

PLATE 497

A   B

(A) Holy-water bucket made at Venice, *c.* 1700. Height 5¼ ins. *Gatti Casazza Collection, Venice.*
(B) Sugar bowl made at Genoa, probably in 1768. Height 5½ ins. *A. Robiati Collection, Milan.*

(C) *Garniture de cheminée* of filigree vases made at Genoa, 1771. Heights 12¼ and 10¼ ins. *Basevi Gambarana Collection, Genoa.*

PLATE 498

(A) Pair of *trembleuses* made at Genoa; 1765, with cups of Savona porcelain. Height 3½ ins. *G. M. Gardella Collection, Milan.*

(B) Tureen made at Turin, mid-eighteenth century. Height 11 ins. *Private Collection, Turin.*

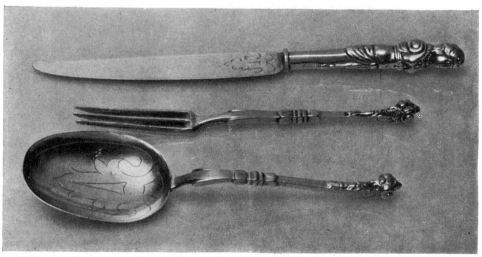

(C) Knife, fork, and spoon (a *posata*), made at Venice, sixteenth century. Length of knife 7⅞ ins. *Gatti Casazza Collection, Venice.*

PLATE 499

(A) Tureen made at Genoa, 1776. Height 19¼ ins. *Marchesi Antonia Serra and Mina Serra Balduino Collection, Genoa.*

(B) Standish made at Naples, 1740. Length 11¾ ins. *Private Collection, Biella.*

PLATE 500

(A) Tureen by Jacob Steen, Christiania, 1787. *Private Collection.*

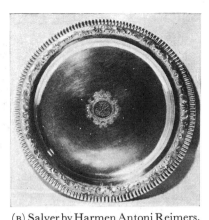

(B) Salver by Harmen Antoni Reimers, Bergen, *c.* 1715. *Kunstindustrimuseum, Oslo.*

(C) Bowl by Oluf Jörgensen, Bergen, 1669. *Kunstindustrimuseum, Bergen.*

(D) Dish by Jens Christensen Seested, Trondhjem, *c.* 1690. *Kunstindustrimuseum, Trondhjem.*

(E) Beaker, *c.* 1740. *Private Collection, Östfold.*

(F) Welcome cup, Bergen, *c.* 1740. *Victoria and Albert Museum, London.*

(G) Mirror-frame by Jens Kahrs, Bergen, *c.* 1745.

PLATE 501

(A) Beaker, Hanseatic type, Bergen, sixteenth century. *Victoria and Albert Museum, London.*

(B) Gold smelling-bottle by Jens Kahrs, Bergen, *c.* 1750. *Kunstindustrimuseum, Bergen.*

(C) Flagon by Jan Reimers, Bergen, 1661. *St Mary's Church, Bergen.*

(G) Brooch with heraldic animals, seventeenth to eighteenth century. *Victoria and Albert Museum, London.*

(D) Spoon by Lucas Steen, Bergen, after 1620. *Private Collection, Bergen.*

(E) Spoon by Michel Plumeion, Bergen, 1618. *Univeristy Collection, Bergen.*

(F) Spoon by Jacob M. Steen, Bergen, *c.* 1730. *Kunstindustrimuseum, Bergen.*

(H) Pyx box of Andreas Kierumgaard Seebye, Bergen, 1778. *Naustdal Church.*

PLATE 502

(A) Jewel-box by Jens Kahrs, Bergen, 1753. *Kunstindustrimuseum, Oslo.*

(B) Coffee-pot by Andreas Blytt, Bergen, 1801. *Kunstindustrimuseum, Bergen.*

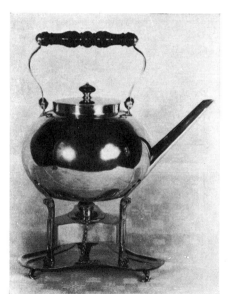

(c) Kettle by Baard Gandolphi Bonsach, Christiania, *c.* 1700. *Private Collection, Östfold.*

(D) Coffee-pot by Daniel Schebs, Brevik, *c.* 1760. *Kunstindustrimuseum, Oslo.*

PLATE 503

(A) Engraved lid of tankard by John J. Reimers Jr, Bergen, *c.* 1730. *University Collection, Bergen.*

(B) Tankard by Jan Reimers, Bergen, *c.* 1660. *Private Collection.*

(C) Spoon by Jonas Andersen, Bergen, 1625. *Kunstindustrimuseum, Bergen.*

(D) Beaker with lid by Albert Groth, Christiania, *c.* 1710. *Kunstindustrimuseum, Oslo.*

(E) Engraved lid of tankard by Oluf Jörgensen, Bergen, 1652. *Victoria and Albert Museum, London.*

(F) Tankard by Hinrich Meyer, Bergen, 1632. *National Museum of Wales, Cardiff; Sir J. J. Jackson Loan Collection.*

PLATE 504

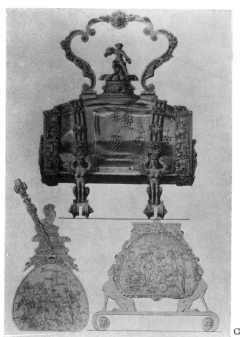

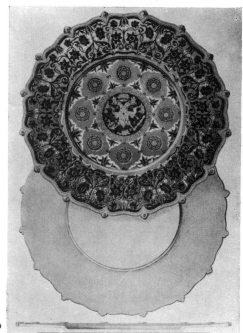

(A) Silver gospel cover chased with sacred figures in bas-relief against smooth backgrounds, surrounded by filigree scrolls, from the Kyrillo-Byeloserski Convent, c. 1534. Illustrated in *Art Treasures of Russia*, Volume I, St Petersburg, 1901.

(B) Silver-gilt *Zion* (casket for holy relics) made for the St Sofia Cathedral, Novgorod; fourteenth century. The inscriptions show a blend of Greek and Church Slavonic lettering, but the style of the fine embossed figures of evangelists is strictly Byzantine.

(C) Crystal barrel in unique silver-gilt setting, presented by the Metropolitan of Novgorod to Tsar Ivan III, when he annexed that city. Probably made by North German silversmiths in Novgorod; fifteenth century. Bacchanalian scenes reveal the penetration of pagan Renaissance motifs to the Hanseatic towns.

(D) Majestic gold plate of Tsar Alexei Mikhailovich decorated with flowers and interlacing foliage in coloured enamel. The curly border is set with sixteen rubies; mid-seventeenth century. *Kremlin, Moscow.*

PLATE 505

(A) Plate made for the Empress Maria Temrukovna in 1561. This bold but austere design, with flat *nielloed* border, became a classic example, copied frequently. *Orujeinaya Palata, Kremlin, Moscow.*

(B) Silver dish painted with tulips etc. in enamel colours, seventeenth century. Formerly in the collection of Prince M. Kurakin at Kosatskoe.

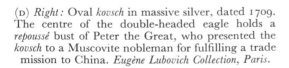

(C) *Above:* Silver *bratina* of Emperor Ivan IV (the Terrible); second half of sixteenth century. *Kremlin, Moscow.*

(D) *Right:* Oval *kovsch* in massive silver, dated 1709. The centre of the double-headed eagle holds a *repoussé* bust of Peter the Great, who presented the *kovsch* to a Muscovite nobleman for fulfilling a trade mission to China. *Eugène Lubovich Collection, Paris.*

PLATE 506

(A) Lid of silver sarcophagus of Prince Dmitri, made by the court silversmiths, 1630. *Kremlin, Moscow.*

(B) Ikon of the Virgin of Vladimir. The elaborate setting, with jewelled medallions and embossed figures, was made in the early seventeenth century. Illustrated in *Antiquities of the Russian Empire*, St Petersburg, 1852.

(C) Ikons of Madonna and Child, demonstrating unique use of silver to adorn paintings and add sculptured detail, crowns, drapery, etc.: *Left:* characteristic mid-seventeenth-century design of finely chased foliage. *Centre:* early-eighteenth century silver surround, combining floral pattern with precious stones, river pearls, and beads. *Right:* mid-nineteenth century, with whole drapery modelled in silver. *Private Collection, London.*

PLATE 507

(A) *Centre:* cup and cover, richly engraved, with *repoussé* busts of Peter the Great and his daughter, the Empress Elizabeth, dated 175 (last figure erased). *Private Collection, London. Left:* silver beaker, with embossed heads, Moscow, dated 1745. *Right:* silver beaker *nielloed* with human figures and cupids, Moscow, dated 1802.

(B) Three pieces illustrating mid-nineteenth century revival of Eastern styles: *Left:* silver-gilt coffee-pot with Turkish motifs, made by Sazykov, Moscow, 1864. *Centre:* pot engraved with figures and wild animals in Sassanian style, mid-nineteenth century. *Right:* covered jug with massive bosses and coiled dragon handle, made by Sazykov, Moscow, 1856. *Private Collection, Paris.*

PLATE 508

(A) *Left:* massive engraved coffee-pot with inscription, made by Sazykov, Moscow. *Right:* covered wine jug with embossed scene of peasant driving a horse and harrow. Base engraved with heads of Alexander II and his consort, probably made to celebrate their coronation: Sazykov, Moscow, 1856. *Private Collection, London.*

(B) Silver-gilt teapot, chased with floral pattern in coloured *cloisonné* enamel, Moscow; mid-nineteenth century. *Left and right:* two chalice-shaped enamelled wine cups, 1870. *Beneath:* silver cigarette-case with miniature peasant dance-scene painted in enamel colours on red lacquer, Moscow, *c.* 1880. *Private Collection, Paris.*

PLATE 509

(A) Mid-nineteenth-century teapots, showing a blend of Russian and West European styles: *Left:* traditional Russian scene and decorative engraving. *Right:* more Western shape, except for spout and handle. *Centre:* massive hexagonal tray with finely chased foliage border, made by Gubkin, Moscow, 1844.

(B) Silver box *nielloed* with Russian architectural scene, St Petersburg, *c.* 1820. Snuff-box to commemorate the wedding of Grand Duke Paul and his second wife, Maria Fyodorovna, St Petersburg; eighteenth century. Box with *nielloed* sporting scene, St Petersburg, *c.* 1800. *Bottom row, left to right: nielloed* box showing Russian country house, mid-nineteenth century. Box with mythological scene, box with a view of Rumyantsev Museum (now part of the Lenin Library), St Petersburg, mid-nineteenth century. *Private Collection, London.*

PLATE 510

(A) Examples of *kovsh* made by Fabergé in the late nineteenth century, but inspired by ancient Russian styles: *Above:* contrast between austere body and elaborate handle. Heraldic birds embossed on latter resemble seventeenth-century Moscow designs. *Below:* modern adaptation of massive traditional forms, discreetly set with jewels. *Private Collection, Paris.*

(B) Silver-gilt tea-caddy decorated with coloured enamel and filigree spirals. Square bosses and winged mythological figures show free adaptation of old Russian motifs, Fabergé; late nineteenth century. *Left and right: nielloed* wine cups of customary bulbous shape, *c.* 1870.

PLATE 511

(A) *Centre*: cup and cover with high-relief *troika* applied in centre and gilded prancing horse on top, late nineteenth century. *Left*: *bratina* with peasant scene and arabesques in *nielloed* medallions, *c.* 1840. *Right*: beer tankard with view of Moscow Kremlin, *c.* 1850.

(B) Five glass-holders for drinking tea, showing rich variety of silver designs made for this purpose throughout the nineteenth century. The gilded glass and spoon in centre were made for their holder.
Private Collection, London.

PLATE 512

with a star below) has been found on a great many pieces of domestic and ecclesiastical plate.

Vincenti, Giovanni Antonio (1636–95). Born at Perugia, was in Rome from 1655 to 1659 and returned in 1672, when he obtained his patent. His mark (a unicorn) has been noticed on several pieces of ecclesiastical plate, including the reliquary of the Holy Shroud in the Cathedral at Amelia.

Norwegian

A limited amount of Norwegian silver from the Middle Ages – spoons, jewellery, church plate, and drinking-vessels – still exists. But as most of it is now kept in churches and museums in Norway, it is of little interest to the collector. Post-Reformation silver made in Norway is, on the other hand, eminently collectable. There is a lot of it about, and important pieces frequently come on the market in Norway and Denmark and in Britain.

The fact that so much old Norwegian silver can be found in Britain can to some extent be explained from the very close contacts which have always existed between the two countries, especially in the fields of commerce and shipping. Most pieces of Norwegian silver in Britain seem, however, to have found their way there during the nineteenth century as tourist souvenirs for British visitors to Norway. Especially important are the activities of English-born Thomas Bennett (b. 1814), who settled in Oslo in 1848 and founded Norway's first travel agency. Bennett transformed travelling in Norway from being a dangerous job for intrepid and hardy explorers to a comfortable pastime for people of leisure. Early in his career the sale of Norwegian antiques (some genuine, others copies) to his customers, the vast majority of whom were British, had become an important part of his business. A description of Bennett's premises in Store Strandgade 17, in Oslo, in 1873 tells of an extensive stock of Norwegian silver tankards, jugs, belts, woodcarvings, paintings and etchings, maps, books: anything, in fact, that demonstrated Norwegian life in ancient and modern times to the foreign visitor.

The more quaint and picturesquely "Norwegian" the souvenirs were, the more they were sought after by the Victorian travellers, and it is easily noticeable that most Norwegian antiques found in Britain today are of types with no close English parallels. During the 1920s Norwegian silver began to trickle back to its country of origin, and when finally the Norwegian museums began an organized campaign to bring back the more important pieces from Britain, no less than three of the tall Welcome cups (*q.v.*), which are the most picturesque of all silver types made in Norway, were brought to light, apart from any number of peg tankards and spoons of medieval type (though mostly of later make: *see* Spoons). In spite of the many antique-dealers and private collectors from Norway who have been looking for Norwegian silver in Britain since, pieces still continue to appear, both in the art auction rooms and in private collections.

Guilds

The earliest silver made in Post-Reformation Norway was produced during the early and middle part of the sixteenth century by German goldsmiths, working for the Hanseatic merchants in Bergen. Their products were naturally very closely related in style to contemporary north German silver. Not until the late sixteenth century did an indigenous goldsmith's art develop. The goldsmiths in Bergen organized themselves into a guild as early as 1568, and at the beginning of the seventeenth century the activities of goldsmiths working everywhere in the Danish–Norwegian kingdom were regulated through a series of royal decrees. The craft was to be carried on in the towns only, and the goldsmiths in all the major cities were organized in guilds. The system of masters, journeymen, and apprentices was properly regulated and the standard of the metal fixed. Hall-marking was made compulsory (*see* Marks). Powerful guilds now developed both in Christiania (as Oslo was then called) and Trondhjem. By far the strongest guild, with the greatest number of members, was that in Bergen. Until about 1840 Bergen was the biggest city in the country, and old Bergen silver is preserved in greater quantities and in more varied styles than that from any other town. During the eighteenth century loosely organized guilds appeared in some of the medium-sized towns like Stavanger and Bragernes (Drammen today), and even in some of the smaller townships on both sides of the Oslo fjord. These smaller guilds seem to have worked under the supervision of the guild in the nearest big city.

The guilds in Bergen, Trondhjem, and Christiania seem to have worked in comparative isolation from each other, and the silver from each of the three towns has its own stylistic peculiarities and its own chronological development. During the Renaissance, and for a time between 1740 and 1790, Bergen silver was of quite exceptional quality (Plate 501C), while the guild in Trondhjem seems to have had a particularly fine period during the latter part of the seventeenth century. The finest Christiania silver was made during the early part of the eighteenth century (Plate 504D) and during the decades preceding 1800 (Plate 501A).

All the goldsmiths' guilds in Norway worked in close connexion with the large and powerful organizations on the Continent. The guilds in Norway, Denmark, and Germany worked according to similar rules and had the same ceremonial at their meetings. German was the common language spoken by all members, and journeymen from all three countries travelled over the whole area. That there should be important stylistic similarities in the products of German, Danish, and Norwegian goldsmiths is only natural. The guild system was abolished in Norway in 1839.

Social backgrounds

Norwegian silver from the sixteenth to the nineteenth centuries has essentially a bourgeois character. During the four hundred years of political union with Denmark (1397–1814) the monarch of the "Twin Kingdoms" resided in Copenhagen, and the spectacular orders for silver from the King and his Court were given to the goldsmiths of the capital. The most important patrons of the Norwegian goldsmiths were officers, clergy, civil servants, and the merchants in the coastal towns. Some of the latter had great wealth. They lived elegantly in their spacious town houses and comfortable country homes, and their collaboration with the goldsmiths was sometimes unusually inspiring (Plate 501G). Some encouraging orders were also occasionally given for church plate (Plates 501D, 502C and H).

Marks

The earliest marked silver made in Norway is that produced by the German goldsmiths

FIG. 1. From the beginning of the nineteenth century: the seven balls only

for the Hanseatic merchants in Bergen during the early and middle part of the sixteenth century. The chief trading commodity of the

FIG. 2. *Christiania.* From *c.* 1630 to *c.* 1820; a crowned C, sometimes with the last two figures of the year fitted into the bend of the letter

Hansa merchants was dried cod from Arctic Norway. Their coat-of-arms was a crowned fish with an eagle, their goldsmiths' mark a

FIG. 3. From *c.* 1820; the city arms, i.e. a sitting St Halvard contained in a shield

crowned fish. Sometimes their works also carried a maker's mark, but none of these can now be identified.

The rules about marking laid down during the seventeenth century do not seem to have been very strictly enforced, but quite a lot of silver from the period is marked with town and maker's mark. During the early and middle part of the eighteenth century wardens were appointed in the various guilds to ensure that the marking was properly carried out.

From then on we find occasionally, though not always, complete sets of marks with town mark, maker's mark, warden's mark, and the mark for the year and the month of production. Gold products of the proper metal standard are marked with an impressed *c.*

The chief town marks are: *Bergen.* From *c.* 1580 until the middle of the eighteenth century: a crowned B. Occasionally the figures of the year are applied to the top or sides of the letter.

From the middle of the eighteenth century

FIG. 4. *Trondhjem.* From *c.* 1700: a rose or six-pointed star

to the beginning of the nineteenth: the city gate with seven balls in two rows underneath, four in the top row and three in the bottom. On late eighteenth-century pieces are sometimes found the figures of the year applied to the sides of the gate.

Russian

The knowledge and aesthetic reputation of Russian metalwork have suffered, like those of other Russian arts, from the scanty interest shown by many *Westernized* Russians, overcorrected later by an unnecessary attempt to demonstrate unique gifts and dazzling national originality, peculiar to Russian craftsmen. In fact, the best Russian plate assimilated a bewildering variety of influences, both from East and West, and foreign artists of diverse nationalities appear to have played a prominent part in its creation from earliest times.

That artificial controversy, involving national vanity, as to whether foreign or native craftsmen, imported fashions or tradition,

predominated, is less important than clear visual evidence that many talented foreigners worked in a different manner when they were employed in Russia, that they taught Russian apprentices (who might surpass their masters), and did more to stimulate than impede the growth of some characteristic styles and techniques while on Russian soil. The French architectural historian, Viollet le Duc, likened Russia to a vast laboratory, in which the art of contrasting races mingled in the creation of something intermediate between Asia and the West. Exuberant bejewelled magnificence from India and Sassanian Persia, curly calligraphic motifs from Islam, the naïve wooden crafts of a changeless Slav peasantry, combined with a sternly ascetic Byzantine strain and with many refined secular fashions from Italy, Germany, and France.

Three of the most typical and striking genres brought to perfection by silversmiths in Russia were of course practised previously in the Byzantine Empire, namely niello, filigree work, and patterns in coloured enamel, especially *cloisonné*. Niello, in the characteristic manner used in Russia, demanded an expert draughtsman as well as a master engraver; for the design was first drawn upon the silver, then chased, so as to lower the pattern, after which the hollowed sections were filled with a black enamel alloy. The article was then heated in a kiln until the enamel fused with the silver. Finally, it was polished, until the black design or lettering became flush with the surface of the silver.

Filigree, the art of making intricate patterns out of malleable gold or silver wire, was known from ancient times in Russia as *skan*. It was favoured for decorating the covers of sacred books and the surrounds of ikons, and the silver wire was usually soldered against a solid silver background. Nineteenth- and twentieth-century excavations from burial mounds and the sites of ruined towns have also revealed many early filigree ornaments dating from the ninth to the thirteenth centuries. The Russian style of filigree developed a strikingly compact geometrical composition of spiral scrolls merging in a rhythmic flow against smooth or embossed surfaces (Plate 505A).

Many Greek enamellers worked in Kiev prior to the Mongol invasion, but the Russian iconographic expert, P. Kondakov, maintained that in the eleventh and twelfth centuries Russian enamellers on precious metals under the Kiev Grand Princes did work as fine as that of the best Byzantine Greeks. He proved that a princely diadem, excavated in 1889, had *not* been made by Greeks, because of obvious mistakes in rendering classical draperies on the enamelled figures, and because it introduced a turquoise blue unknown in Byzantium.

The destructive lust of Mongol hordes, who overran and occupied the greater part of Rus-

sia in the mid-thirteenth century, obliterated much of early Russian art, and most of all gold and silver vessels, which were easily looted, broken, or melted down. In Kiev alone six hundred churches were left as smoking ruins by the Mongols. But after the sack of Kiev, the chief centre of fine silver craftsmanship shifted to Novgorod, which escaped the Mongols, and where many specialized artists continued to work for the monasteries and churches until the end of the fifteenth century, when it was annexed by resurgent Moscow. The silver work of Novgorod, and that of Kostroma, another local centre, is generally regarded as cruder and more provincial than that of earlier Kiev or later Moscow, but first-class specimens, both of sacred and lay silver, have survived (Plate 505B).

Novgorod's close trade relations with the Hanseatic towns attracted North German artists to work in Russia, where scope seems to have been given to their talents. This may be the origin of a crystal barrel in an elaborate silver-gilt setting, presented by the Metropolitan of Novgorod to the Tsar Ivan III when he annexed that city in 1478. This exuberantly pagan work illustrates the extent and power of Renaissance influence in northern Europe during the fifteenth century. The sides of the mount are chased with bacchanalian scenes, and a nude young Bacchus sits on the lid, pouring wine into a beaker (Plate 505C).

Moral servitude to copying Byzantine models and paralysing fear of cunning Tartar conquerors were overcome in integrated Moscow, though it had taken two centuries to shake off the Tartar yoke. The healthier, more self-confident Russian state of mind was reflected in a vigorous upsurge of decorative art in the sixteenth century. Foreign envoys who visited Russia at this time bore witness to the dazzling splendour and abundance of gold and silver vessels, encrusted with precious stones as large as nuts, used at royal receptions and feasts in the Moscow palaces. The Church was equally lavish in using the precious metals to make its ceremonies more majestic and impressive. Unfortunately much of this gorgeous work was in its turn destroyed during the anarchic *Time of Troubles* in the early seventeenth century.

After the Poles had been driven out, the more stable Moscow period of the early Romanov Tsars enabled Russian work in precious metals to reach a high peak of artistic style and a distinct kind of international originality. Within the recently consolidated Empire, artists of all races and skilled in all techniques, flocked to the new capital. But the Moscow Tsars (long before Peter the Great) also invited silversmiths from Holland, Germany, and England, and even from India and Persia.

One striking feature of early seventeenth-century Russian silver is the chasing of finely stylized foliage and flowers in all-over patterns, which became thicker and more complicated as the century proceeded (Plate 505D). Filigree was now rarely plainly soldered on sheets of metal, but was filled with polychrome enamels, in which white, blue, and yellow tones predominated. Towards the end of the century geometrical *cloisonné* began to give place to miniature portrait painting in enamel colours, a *genre* which became widespread in the eighteenth century.

Some provincial towns also began to flourish artistically at this time. Solvychegodsk, largely belonging to the great merchant family, the Stroganovs, who opened up trade in Siberia, produced superb examples of free painting with enamel colours direct on silver surfaces (Plate 506B). The Stroganovs educated their town by bringing to it exemplary specimens of silver from abroad, and they appear to have encouraged Ukrainian artists, who painted silver bowls and boxes with the most luscious foliage, huge tulips, garlands of daisies and sunflowers, and also with designs of swans, turkeys, lions, and stags.

Ceremonial dishes played an important part in the marriage ceremonies of old Russia. A grandiose specimen (Plate 506A), dating from 1561, has survived in the Orujeinaya Palata of the Moscow Kremlin. Its interior is chased with a simple but dynamic design of curved concave spirals, radiating from a central double-headed eagle, engraved in niello. The flat rim is adorned with a fine network of stylized foliage, varied by an old Slavonic inscription. Just as in ancient China certain forms in jade or porcelain became revered as

classical standards of perfection, repeated with slight variations from one century to another, so did silversmiths in Russia repeat the refined simplicity of this circular dish, its interior curves and flat nielloed rim, right up to the early eighteenth century, when more sophisticated Western fashions prevailed.

Such unique gold and silver vessels were highly cherished by their owners, and hardly ever sold. They changed ownership chiefly by inheritance, or by passing as gifts from Tsar to Patriarch, or to deserving Boyars and other citizens. Sometimes from a disgraced Boyar they would find their way back into the Imperial Treasury. Or, after the death of a conscience-stricken owner, they would be bequeathed to some monastery to promote the repose of his soul.

Two traditional vessels, the *kovsch* and the *bratina*, derived from earlier models made in wood by Slav peasants, had characteristic shapes. These were different to any metalwork made outside Russia. The *kovsch* was a low almost boat-shaped drinking-vessel, with a raised handle, like a ladle, principally used at feasts for drinking mead, *kvass*, or beer. Gradually it lost its practical importance, and became a decorative symbol of honour awarded for some outstanding service to the State. It could also be a reward for some military feat, or for a successful diplomatic or commercial mission (Plate 506D). For a long time its shape maintained the same severe simplicity, but during the eighteenth century Western fashions made it more ornate and complicated. Later, in the nineteenth century, came another reaction in taste, which led Fabergé and other eminent silversmiths to produce numerous ceremonial *kovschy*, evidently inspired by older seventeenth-century styles.

The *bratina*, a loving-cup without handles, was always globular in shape, with a flat band-like lip, usually inscribed with stylized old Slavonic lettering (Plate 506C). On the death of a royal prince, a favourite *bratina* of his was often placed on his tomb in a church, and could afterwards be consecrated for use there as an incense-burner. A *bratina* which originally belonged to Tsar Michael, the first Romanov, bears an inscription that it was placed on the coffin of the Tsarevich Ivan

Ivanovich to commemorate the murder of that prince by his father (Ivan the Terrible). Though the inscription round the rim sometimes records the name of the owner, or the purpose for which it is dedicated, more often it is a simple toast, or poetic axiom, such as: "True love is a golden cup, which can never be broken; the soul alone can change it."

Many persons of high rank had their own *bratina* made for them, and a few notable early specimens have survived. An exceptionally elaborate one, made for Peter Tretyakov, a state official in the first quarter of the seventeenth century, is illustrated in *Antiquities of the Russian Empire* (1852). Its foot is supported by miniature human caryatids, who appear to uphold the bowl on their heads and outstretched hands. The surface of the bowl is richly embossed with an arabesque of flowers and foliage and four heraldic plaques. It is also remarkable in having a coved cover finishing in a long-stemmed silver flower, identical to the one used on Persian and Chinese perfume-sprinklers of the same period. The edifying inscription round the rim reads: "As arms are needed by the warrior in battle, as rain in time of drought, as drink to the thirsty, and as a sincere friend to console in time of misfortune and sorrow, so concord and friendship are demanded from all those who would drink from this cup." It should be remembered that old Russian drinking customs were embellished by a lot of ritual. The man who proposed a toast had to stand with his head uncovered, empty the cup to the dregs, then turn it upside down over his head, so that all could see that he had emptied it and thereby sincerely wished the health of the person he had toasted.

Though the Orthodox Church resembled Islam in frowning on sculpture of the human figure in the round, as an instrument of idol worship, it permitted carving and chasing in high relief. In this way silver ornament of many kinds, especially the surrounds of ikons, allowed remarkable sculptural gifts to be expressed, so long as they were consecrated by a genuine religious purpose. One of the finest surviving early specimens of this kind is the lid from the silver sarcophagus of the Tsarevich Dmitri, made in 1630 by the chief Kremlin silversmith to be placed in the Archangel Cathedral in Moscow (Plate 507A). In 1812, when Napoleon occupied Moscow, the body of the sarcophagus disappeared, but the superb gilded lid with its life-size figure of the young prince, embossed in high relief, is now in the Orujeinaya Palata. The head is worked out with a severe but sensitive fullness, and the whole silver background, partly granulated and partly smooth, is filled in with rich patterns of interlacing foliage.

Until the middle of the seventeenth century the masters of the Kremlin Gold and Silver Chambers served not only the Imperial Court but also the wealthy Patriarchate, which kept a huge staff of artists, craftsmen, and jewellers employed in making church adornments, mitres, crucifixes, censers, and covers for church books. But in the 1650s the Patriarch Nikon organized his own workshop for this purpose near the Patriarchal palace. About the same time, an exceptionally able and cultured nobleman, the Boyar Khitrovo, was appointed by the Tsar Alexei Mikhailovich to take charge of the Kremlin gold and silver work, a post which he retained for over twenty years. Talent and creative enterprise meant far more to him than national origin. Records show that he employed Poles, Germans, Tartars, Greeks, and Swedes. This happy combination of factors helps to account for the high quality of Russian silver work during that period. Much of its ornament was derived from Italian Renaissance motifs, especially in its treatment of foliage, figuring graceful main stems, from which sprang numerous symmetrical side-shoots. But the increasing representation of animals and birds more probably derived from Persia, and the love of niello from Greek artists on Mount Athos.

At the turn of the seventeenth century drinking-cups of Western European design, and huge covered tankards, like those from Augsburg, appeared more frequently in Russia. The early eighteenth century saw the start of St Petersburg silver, which flourished in the hands of many foreign craftsmen brought by Peter the Great to work in his new capital. But one must remember, as had happened often before, that artists from abroad worked differently in their new environment. The Russian Government was strict about maintaining the purity of precious metals, as they were about measures to safeguard against debasement of the currency. Though marking of silver vessels started in the seventeenth century, Peter first made it systematic and universal by a decree in 1700. In 1714 he also allowed foreign craftsmen in precious metals to form their own separate guild. The majority were then from Germany, and their records were kept in German. Swedes took second place, and a number came from Finland.

Catherine II gave the same guilds more definite rules in a decree issued in 1785. The guild consisted of masters, journeymen, and apprentices, as in the West; a "master" had to have a "masterpiece" of his work approved, after serving not less than three years as a journeyman. In 1793 the guild of Russian craftsmen in St Petersburg had forty-four masters, and that of foreign craftsmen fifty-nine. The number of masters rose to about one hundred and fifty at the beginning of the nineteenth century. They often had foreign pupils, but also many Russian ones. The native Russian craftsmen had for long tended to specialize in work for churches, crosses, lamps, and surrounds for ikons (Plate 507A). A few outstanding artists, like the Frenchman, Ador, who made exquisite jewelled boxes for Catherine II, did not belong to any guild. The Swiss, J. Pauzié, who worked for Peter's daughter, the Empress Elizabeth, completely remodelled the Imperial crown, to "modernize" it for Catherine's coronation. But, tired of being exploited, as he said, by many of his Russian patrons, he left in 1764, and spent the remainder of his life in his calmer native land. A number of beautifully embossed tall cups and covers in silver-gilt were made for the Court during this period (Plate 508c).

Towards the end of the eighteenth century, and more markedly in the early nineteenth century, there started a reaction against conventionally classical and stereotyped Western styles, and a reversion of taste to earlier models, to the use of filigree, niello, and coloured enamel, sometimes combined with traditional shapes, and painted directly on medallions. It was by order of the Emperor Nicolas I that the Imperial Academy of Sciences undertook the first large-scale attempt to catalogue and illustrate widely scattered and hitherto little known masterpieces of ancient decorative art and ikons preserved in the Russian Empire. The result emerged in the massive illustrated volumes *Antiquities of the Russian Empire* already referred to. These are still the best records available. It is also to the credit of Nicolas I that he had the building of the Orujeinaya Palata in the Kremlin completely renovated and enlarged so that the whole Imperial collection of Moscow gold and silver vessels should be transferred and properly displayed there.

While the range of articles which they made was widening, the best Russian silversmiths in the second half of the nineteenth century returned increasingly for inspiration to Byzantine Muscovite motifs, in particular to more grandiose and massive shapes and to a revival of the old techniques of filigree, niello, and coloured enamel. The latter became a speciality of the Moscow jewellers and silversmiths, Ovchinikov, Klebhikov, and Sazykov, but it was also pursued by Morozov and Fabergé in St Petersburg. Three pieces by Sazykov made between 1856 and 1864 (Plate 508B) illustrate the revival of the older Oriental strain in decorative silver. The massive coffee-pot and wine jug made in the same period (Plate 509A) show how the old Slavonic type of ornament could be skilfully adapted to contemporary civilized objects of utility. The brilliantly enamelled but dignified teapot and wine goblets seen in Plate 509B are a fine example of slightly later work from Moscow silversmiths, and the box shown below on the same plate reveals the exquisite painting of miniature peasant scenes on silver. This work reached a high level during this period.

Delicately incised or *nielloed* architectural scenes, landscapes with figures, on cigarette-cases and snuff-boxes, were also produced by many good silversmiths at this time (Plate 510B). With individual variations, they continued a tradition established in the late eighteenth and early nineteenth centuries. Certain domestic utensils, like teapots and trays, achieved a harmonious fusion of contemporary European and Russian styles (Plate 510A), whereas objects like silver or silver-enamelled glass-holders for tea, primarily used in Russia, retained a distinctive Russian character right up to the early twentieth century (Plate 511B). The old *bratina* shape was still produced, with certain changes, as can be seen from a *nielloed* specimen decorated with peasant scenes. The same plate shows a typically European tall cup and cover decorated with a characteristic Russian prancing *troika*.

There is no space to do justice in this context to the master silversmith and jeweller, Carl Fabergé, whose superb work, while justly famous, has rather overshadowed that of other fine Russian silversmiths. His fantastic Imperial Easter eggs, his elaboration in *bijouterie* of classical French styles, have already been well described and documented. But it is sometimes forgotten that he also instilled into old Muscovite Byzantine traditions that fresh touch of Russian idiom, that stimulating *genius loci*, which exercised such a powerful spell over the best foreign artists who worked in Russia. And the "neo-Russian" products of Fabergé show a classical restraint which is absent from the flamboyant extravagances of some Russian seventeenth-century silver. Both the large and small *kovsch*, seen in Plate 511A, are good examples of this skilful Fabergé adaptation. So, too, is the elegant tea-caddy, shown in Plate 511B, which uses old Slav folk-lore motifs, filigree spirals, and massive bosses.

This internal renaissance of decorative art in nineteenth-century Russia becomes more understandable when one bears in mind that West European taste, from which Russia had drawn so much, was at the same time going through a series of eclectic revivals. By contrast the best nineteenth-century Russian silver work preserved an integrity of style, grandeur of design, and finesse of craftsmanship which approximated to eighteenth-century European standards, more rapidly disappearing in the fluid industrial society of the modern West. Of course there is a striking unevenness about the quality of "neo-Russian" work produced at this time, whether by Moscow or Petersburg silversmiths. While at its best, it is bold, brilliant, and refined, at its worst it can be coarse, gaudy, heavy, and monotonous. But its best is far better than has yet been widely recognized.

Systematic marking and control of objects made in precious metals came into force in 1700 under Peter the Great. The silver standard is represented by the numerals 84, 88, or 91, which mean the number of *zolotniks* of pure silver in ninety-six parts (equivalent in weight one continental pound). The standards for gold are represented by the numerals 56, 72, and 92, indicating the proportion of pure gold in ninety-six *zolotniks*. The four regulation marks were: the maker's initials (sometimes his full name), second, the crest of the city where the silver was tested, third the initials of the assayer (the latter was often followed by the date), fourth, the figures showing the proportion of pure silver. The St Petersburg town mark shows two crossed anchors with a sceptre in the centre, and the Moscow mark a St George and Dragon. After 1896 the town marks were dropped, and a woman's head with a headdress was adopted as a general hall-mark both for gold and silver objects.

MINIATURE SILVER

Miniature silver toys, replicas of furniture, table accessories, and other household equipment, have delighted the children of noble families for at least 500 years. The daughter of Henry II in 1576 commissioned a set of silver toys including "buffet pots, bowls, plates and other articles such as they make in Paris", to be sent to the children of the Duchess of Bavaria. In the wealthy homes of Holland and Germany miniature silver toys were already commonplace. The plate inventory of the mother of Henry IV of France (1553–1610) records "a doll's set of silver plenishments set with diamonds".

In England miniature toys of gold and silver delighted rich Stuart and early Georgian sophisticates, but such trinkets were for adult enjoyment, with an adult subtlety about their very childishness. Today they are particularly fascinating as meticulous records of passing vogues in innumerable household details from rocking horse to foot warmer. Few early Stuart examples remain, but Christie's on May 7, 1952, sold a miniature goblet, its bowl formed from a nut held in scalloped straps engraved with foliage, supported on a wire scroll tripod stem and a circular pierced foot. This was attributed to about 1630.

Miniature silver in the late seventeenth century closely followed the Court fashions for silver furniture and magnificent toilet sets. Many of these were imported from Holland, but hall-marks prove their manufacture in London for at least a century from 1665, and again in the nineteenth century. Few examples have been noted struck with provincial hall-marks.

Towards the end of the seventeenth century there began a half-century vogue for superb dolls' houses, then known as "baby houses". These were individually designed for the rich by architects who might also supervise their construction by cabinet-makers. But in those days, when a homely occupation was essential to fill the long hours of the evening, it was not uncommon for them to be made at home. In 1750 the Prince of Wales was "building baby houses at Kew".

Miniature furniture and all the accessories found in contemporaneous homes of the rich were bought from specialists in this work, in wood, silver, and other metals. An extensive range might be accumulated over the years, and those in precious metal were treasured and handed down from one generation to another. Modern children would find little to admire in a pair of snuffers and a tray, just large enough to snuff the tiny candles in their miniature candlesticks; but in those days such toys were highly appreciated.

An essential part of the charm of silver toys is their close adherence to the fashions and customs of the time when they were made. The range of objects includes furniture, everything for the tea equipage, tankards and mugs, monteiths and punch bowls, cruet stands, table baskets, salvers, candlesticks, warming pans, and a numerous array of other perfectly constructed miniatures reflecting the tastes of wealthy silver-flaunting families. Toilet sets are superb treasures complete with

silver-framed mirror and receptacles for trinkets, soap, unguents, and the rest. Even the men and women, their horses and carriages, soldiers, beggars, parrots, and dogs were fashioned as silver toys. But scarcely less beguiling is, say, a frying pan complete with fish.

George Middleton, a descendant of Sir Hugh Middleton, the celebrated goldsmith and jeweller to James I and Charles I, appears to have been the first London silversmith to become a specialist in the manufacture of miniature silver. He was followed by innumerable other specialists, but few achieved comparable quality.

Miniature silver was sold at the spas, but this was probably the work of London silversmiths. Lady Mary Wortley Montagu wrote in her *Farewell to Bath*, 1736:

> "Farewell to Deards' and
> all her toys which
> glitter in her shop.
> Deluding traps to girls and boys. . . ."

The Deards' trade card published by their shop in St James's, London, during the mid-1760s, refers to a "Variety of Fine Toys", showing that fashionable demand continued.

Much of the existing early miniature silver was made as carefully as jewellery, every piece worked by hand. These silversmiths were notably accurate in copying detail and proportions, and the consistent careful construction and meticulous finish, including engraved ornament and dainty *repoussé* work, suggests the nimble fingers of women assistants. The majority was shaped and wrought from flat plate with the addition of small castings. Wall sconces, for instance, were perfect replicas, the smooth reflecting surface being surrounded by intricate embossed work: a tankard would be rolled from flat plate, seamed vertically and a base inserted. Some of the most attractive hollow-ware was hand-raised from the plate: later in the eighteenth century hollow-ware was shaped by spinning in a lathe in the style current with factory-made silver. Candlestick stems might be turned from slender cast rods, and applied details, such as handles, feet, and so on, might be midget castings.

Early in the nineteenth century miniature silver consisted of castings, and gilding was frequent. The early Victorians reverted to fine toys, however, entirely hand-made. So far as tableware was concerned, these copied the so-called Queen Anne styles.

Some important makers of miniature silver were John Clifton, Augustine Courtauld, Edward Dobson, Anthony Ellines, Joseph Lowe, Isaac Malyn, George Middleton, John Sotro, Viet and Mitchell, and Wetherell and Janaway.

FILIGREE

In the ancient world it must be supposed that the art of working in filigree was mastered at an early stage, at least where the technique of working in silver and gold had attained a reasonably high level. We know that excellent filigree jewellery was produced by the Egyptians, and even in the Far East a very early mastery of the craft must be taken for granted. To Mexico and South America, however, a knowledge of it was first implanted by Spanish and Portuguese craftsmen. There have, moreover, been times when filigree was highly prized. Today, little is seen of it other than as souvenir pieces or products of peasant art.

Filigree is a Latin word, a combination of *filum* (wire) and *granum* (grain). It seems difficult, however, to arrive at a general agreement to the exact etymological implications of the term. In the modern usage followed in this chapter it should be understood to comprise all works in silver or gold (or, rarely, even other metals), in which either the form or merely the ornamentation has been effected by means of thin wire, frequently with the addition of minute grains or balls. Granulation or granulated work remain the correct terms where these grains or balls are used alone, either placed in rows or grouped together, on a solid surface, for decorative purposes.

TECHNIQUE[1]

It is known with certainty that at any rate for the last thousand years filigree wire has been produced by means of the draw-plate, a method which was described for the first time by the versatile monk and craftsman Theophilus Presbyter in his *Schedula diversarum Artium*, written probably about 1100.[2] According to him, a thin bar of silver or gold would be drawn by hand with a pair of strong pliers through successively smaller holes in a solid piece of flat iron, the draw-plate. This resulted in a thin wire several yards long. During the fifteenth century the process was made less complicated by the introduction of the draw-bench, where a small pulley was used.[3] In both cases the process calls for repeated annealing of the wire.

It is calculated that the process of drawing wire was known much earlier than the ninth or tenth centuries, when, according to my knowledge, the earliest existing draw-plate was made.[4] It was found in a Norwegian grave, and indicates an earlier mastery of draw-plate technique in the more advanced countries of classical antiquity either round the Mediterranean or in the Near East. Here the earliest draw-plates may even have been made of hard stone.[5]

However this may be, it is also certain that wire was not produced by means of the draw-plate alone. On jewellery found in Norwegian graves dating from the late Roman Empire, wire of extreme fineness is found to have been produced from thin, narrow sheets or strips of silver or gold. These strips have been coiled spiral-wise into long tubes, similar to the insulating sheath coiled round an electric cable, to form thin pieces of wire on which very fine spiral lines may be observed even without a magnifying glass.[6] A similar kind of wire is found in Etruscan jewellery,[7] and the French *savant* Édouard Salin has observed the same on Merovingian pieces.[8] A close examination of antique jewellery would probably show this to be a method generally adopted, at least for very thin wire, by the earliest filigree-workers.[9]

Yet a third form of wire was employed by filigree workers of the Migration period, and of the Carolingian and Romanesque centuries. This is the so-called pearl-string wire. During the long span of time already referred to filigree ornamentation was among the forms of embellishment most commonly used: not only in jewellery, bookbindings, crucifixes, and reliquaries, but, for example, in the making of Emperor Otto's crown in A.D. 962. The above-mentioned Theophilus Presbyter also taught how this pearl-string wire was made:[10] with the aid of small, grooved irons the drawn wire was transversely impressed with grooves, one beside the other, to form a series of balls or pearls. The efficiency of the method has been proved through recent experiments carried out by Mr Oscar Sørensen, head of the goldsmiths' class at the Governmental School of Arts and Crafts in Oslo. His experiments have also shown the frequently discussed equatorial grooves (which may be observed encircling the broadest part of each "pearl", or thickened ball, on a piece of pearl-string wire) to be a natural outcome of the process itself – not, as has been repeatedly argued, a result of aesthetic consideration, a means to "catch the light" or in any other way enhance the effect. Numerous pieces of Migration and Viking Age jewellery examined by myself prove this beyond doubt.[11]

The use of pearl-string wire was universal until the end of the Romanesque era, but during the eleventh century we meet the first pieces of jewellery in which a twisted, two-cord round wire takes its place. Interesting examples are illustrated by Dr Joan Evans.[12] Now linear surface ornamentation may also be built up by means of single, smooth wires of a rectangular section, placed on end and soldered to the underlying metal – in the manner of metal ribs of *émail cloissonné* left without their enamel fillings. The last and so far final step in this technical development was taken some time before the sixteenth century. After this date, wire of two different kinds are generally seen combined in the same work: for the main lines of the design, a fairly heavy drawn wire of a square or rectangular section was used. For the more detailed parts, or fillings, two thin, round wires were twisted together, then rolled or possibly hammered flat, thus producing a flat wire with a diagonally serrated edge. A similar effect may be obtained by passing a round wire through a screw-die, afterwards rolling it flat. The last method produced a slightly mechanical, dry effect. It has been used sporadically in eighteenth-century pieces. But its employment became general, at least in Scandinavia, only after 1800. Several other forms of twisted or plaited wire are also used, mostly for decorative rims and borders.

The *grani* or grains used in filigree work, or in granulated work, are best produced as described by Benvenuto Cellini.[13] He mixed tiny pieces of silver or gold with charcoal in a crucible, and heated it until the metal melted. At that point each little particle contracted into a ball, the balls being sorted according to size by means of a series of riddles.

The complicated and numerous parts which made up a piece of filigree-work were kept together by means of solder. It also seems evident that at least the Etruscans employed a simple technique of welding for the granulated work. As these details are not of great importance for the present understanding of the subject, it is sufficient to refer to more detailed treatises.[14] A further study of the technical niceties of filigree may reap rich rewards. It has been suggested that the various forms of wire are typical each of its separate period. Yet an examination of further material over a wider field may well reveal unknown lines of influence and new important centres of technical as well as aesthetic innovation.

HISTORY

Filigree jewellery of the Ancient World may be studied in several large collections on both sides of the Atlantic. Already in Egyptian pieces the intricacies of granulated work and wire ornamentation have been mastered. Greek, and still more Etruscan work must be placed in a class by itself, because of its singular forms and the unparalleled perfection of its granulation. In this last respect, the quality of pieces like the lion-clasp in the Pigorini Museum, Rome, has never been equalled.

During the early centuries of the Middle Ages new forms were fostered by the Germanic tribes of the north and west, and important finds from Gotland indicate that during the Viking age this island may have been an important centre of production.[15] A solid gold tenth-century spur and harness trappings covered with granulated work (from Rød,

Østfold, Norway) are exceptional pieces.[16] In the Celtic areas of Britain filigree was known, but apparently more sparingly used. In the Byzantine Empire, on the other hand, classical traditions must have been kept alive for a considerable time.

However, precise knowledge of the development is incomplete, mainly because proper attention has never been given to the subject. It must suffice to demonstrate the preference shown in Migration jewellery for pearl-string wire ornamentation, and to suggest a direct link between this and the best period of pearl-string filigree during the subsequent Carolingian and Romanesque eras. From the ninth century on, filigree achieved a place of eminence even in monumental pieces of goldsmithing. Reliquaries, bookbindings, and regalia have been handed down to us, in which jewel-studded wirework enriched with granulation is the chief feature of ornamental design. Outstanding and unique pieces are the gold Imperial Crown and the Imperial Cross and Orb of the Holy Roman Empire, in the Schatzkammer, Vienna. In construction they span from the middle of the tenth until the twelfth centuries.[17]

It seems that in the northern and western countries of Europe this great period of filigree ended as the Gothic style advanced. Now, finely cast architectural detail and twisted and bent scrollwork in stylized imitation of foliage satisfied the demand for intricate and profuse ornamentation. It would seem a reasonable assumption that the strong position of filigree in popular jewellery all over Europe marks a continuation, on a lower social level, of the great age which had lasted from the early Middle Ages until the advent of the Gothic style.

Only in a few centres did the production of high-class filigree continue to prosper. One of the most prominent among them was Venice. While superb pieces remain to us from the Romanesque period in Italy, and sporadically even from the subsequent centuries of the Middle Ages, the Venetian art of filigree held a prominent position even as late as the sixteenth century, when the goblet with silver wirework on a ground of silver gilt now in the Museo di Palazzo Venezia, Rome, was made. The reliquary of St Louis of Toulouse in the Museo degli Argenti, Florence, also gives a fine example of the combination, according to Filippo Rossi so typical of Venice, of filigree and crystal.[18] Signor Rossi dates this piece to the sixteenth century. It seems as likely that the gold filigree, at least, might be placed around 1600 or a little into the seventeenth century. Possibly, also, the "chrystalline glasse and cover garnished with wyer work of gold, appraised at £30" in the treasury of Charles I, was closely related.[19] It should now be realized that, in Venetian pieces like the ones just mentioned, a new and important stage of technical development had been reached. Between smooth, rectangular-sectioned wire that marks the main lines of the composition, the intricate lines of the fillings are made up of a doubly twisted wire rolled flat. This development marks a crucial change, and much would be gained if we knew how, when, and where it first took place.

Siebenbürgen was another important centre for the production of filigree throughout the late Middle Ages. Here filigree was still popular among the farming population and the nobility of the surrounding principalities, and granulated wire ornamentation was employed on a distinguished series of altar-cups. Their bases, stems, and the lower part of the cup were covered with an ornamental display of filigree. This style continued into the sixteenth century.[20]

Besides filigree from Siebenbürgen and Venice, a group of German tankards should be mentioned among the comparatively rare sixteenth-century examples of the craft. Many of them are of the "poison tankard" type. That is, they have crystal drums set in silver, covered with a mesh of granulated wirework. If the drink were poisoned, the crystal was supposed to burst. Some of the tankards date from the seventeenth century. The earlier ones, however, prove that the art of working in filigree was far from unknown during the Renaissance, even if, possibly, it was less universally practised. The famous poison tankard owned by Clare College, Cambridge, belongs to this group.[21]

With few, if any, exceptions it seems that before the seventeenth century filigree was conceived as a decorative adjunct, as something added or applied to objects of art. The poison tankards are excellent examples of this. However, this conception was soon to be changed. When, during the seventeenth century, a positive vogue for filigree became manifest in all European countries this not only marked the revival of a technique which apparently, in most places, had been out of fashion for several hundred years, but it was clear that with the old craft everywhere returning to favour, a completely new and intriguing style was also rapidly taking shape.

It is now that we meet, for the first time in Europe, the delicate open lacework which most of us associate with the word filigree. It is no longer used merely as a means to decorate something else, but assumes the character of a constructive material in its own right. Furthermore, it expresses in a rare manner the stylistic ideals of its time. Few branches of the decorative arts are more baroque in their wealth and complexity than filigree, when its web-like flowers and leaves are moulded into plastic shape, enamelled, and then set with coloured stones.

The new way of exploiting an old craft achieved immediate success. It created a demand, as far as can be judged, in all countries of Europe. So popular did the new fashion become that in some countries a new class of worker in filigree was admitted to the trade guilds. In her book *Hispanic Silverwork*, Ada Marshall Johnson has given some details about the production of filigree in Spain. She explains how, in the archives of Sevilla and Toledo, several goldsmith's names occur followed by the word *Filigranero*. At the same period the guilds instituted special test pieces in the form of ear-rings and rosaries.[22] Statutes of a similar kind were known in Sweden[23] and Norway,[24] and it will probably in due course be found that similar arrangements existed in other countries on the Continent at about the same period.

Equally significant is the fact that the very word filigree was only at that time introduced into the Spanish, French, and English languages. In the two latter the word is first encountered in the 1660s, in Spanish it is known somewhat earlier. Introduced from Italy, it was at first given a varied spelling, as in *filagramme* and *philigrin*. Throughout the latter half of the seventeenth century we meet it in contexts which indicate its growing familiarity. This also proves that objects of filigree were of quite common usage.[25]

A new fashion, a new style, a new name to describe it, special craftsmen to cater for the new whim of a sophisticated public. Why and how did it all arise?

It must necessarily be stressed that existing knowledge on this point is very incomplete. It may seem far from unlikely that seventeenth-century filigree was born in Italy. The importance of Venice has already been referred to, and it is well known that, at least during the eighteenth century, Genoa was famous for its products.[26] There is another possible solution, however, which may not even exclude the first. What if the original impulse for the new fashion in filigree came from the Far East?

Very little is so far known about the early filigree of the Orient. The Chinese Emperor Wan-Li (1573–1619) was buried with his two wives, each skull carrying "a high curved crown, black with gold filigree set with jewels".[27] These were not European, and it seems unlikely that they represent an influence from one of the few centres where the art may have been practised at that early date. During the latter half of the seventeenth century the Siamese Ambassador to Louis XIV brought splendid pieces of filigree among his gifts.[28] Also, among seventeenth-century references to filigree is one where Lady Ann, wife of Charles II's Ambassador to Spain, Sir Richard Fanshawe, records that among several gifts of filigree which she and her daughters received from Spanish dignitaries or from English countrymen settled in Spain, was a silver box and a small trunk of *filigrana*, made "in the Indies". This was in 1665, when she accompanied her husband to his embassy at the Spanish Court. Objects in silver and gold made "in the Indies" are mentioned by her on several occasions, along with pieces of furniture, such as "three pair of Indian cabinets of Japan".[29]

It has to be admitted that no investigation

has as yet been undertaken to confirm the validity of what might be called the Oriental theory. Indeed, since filigree has never been seriously studied, such an investigation would have to start with the most elementary examination of museum pieces, few of which are known to exist except by museum curators. They are very rarely published, probably because marked pieces are scarce, and also because somehow the general lack of knowledge about them seems to prevent their inclusion in books on gold and silverwork.

It will therefore be understood that further research is needed before the main events in the history of filigree can be established with certainty. Until then, the theory of a strong Oriental impulse at the base of its surprising development in the seventeenth century must stand as a fascinating possibility.

Whatever the original impulse for its expanding popularity, the art of filigree *did* flourish: first and foremost, it seems, in Spain. According to Ada Marshall Johnson, Spanish filigree, especially of the north-west, is well known and is of a very fine quality. Fine pieces are found in several churches, the cathedral treasure of Santiago da Compostela in particular being well supplied. There are caskets, reliquaries, chrismatories, and Saints' crowns.

Swedish filigree has lately been treated by Dr Carl Hernmarck,[30] who points to its formal reliance on German prototypes. Many leading masters were, in fact, German immigrants. Swedish filigree is conservative and continues the older tradition of wirework used as a decorative foil on a solid base. Famous masters worked in Stockholm and Gotenburg, and filigree cups and mirrors were presented as royal gifts to Tsar Peter of Russia.[31] The craft lasted until the early part of the eighteenth century.

Filigree has been popular in Germany, where Augsburg seems to have specialized in sets of knives, spoons, and forks with filigree handles. As far as is known, however, no special literature exists on the subject, which doubtless deserves wider treatment. The same is true of other European countries, with the exception of Sweden and Norway.

In Norway, research undertaken in connexion with a recent exhibition of filigree sponsored by the Museums of Applied Art in Bergen and Oslo, has brought to light a school of masters who produced excellent pieces, starting during the latter half of the seventeenth century, and carrying on through the next.[32] The most prominent among them worked in Bergen, and their production was quite varied: bookcovers, caskets, or miniature chests for keepsakes or jewellery, and many small boxes, oval, round, rectangular or square. A number of curiosities were also made. These included such things as miniature chests of drawers, small filigree ships, a complete, miniature set of furniture – chairs, stools, gueridons, table, all fully equipped with tea-cups, tea-pots, sugar-basins, trays, and candle-sticks. These are stamped pieces, made by Johannes Johannessen Müller of Bergen, working from 1723 to 1739. The *pièce de résistance* of this school, however, is a truly monumental piece of work. It is the great filigree casket, formerly owned by the aristocratic Knagenhielm family, now in the Historic Museum, Bergen University measuring 43 by 29.5 cm. and 20 cm. high it is, as far as is known, unequalled for size, while the workmanship displayed is of a very high order. It is unmarked, but its Bergen origin can now be considered certain. A similar, if smaller, piece in the David Collection, Copenhagen, confirms the impression that the type was by no means confined to Norway. In short, as more and more objects come to light, many of them sumptuously decorated with floral ornamentation rendered in the subtlest of silver filigree, our conception of silversmithing, especially from the seventeenth and eighteenth centuries, is that much advanced. A factor of equal importance is that what has already come to light suggests that a similar and probably even richer variety may be found to have existed in other countries from which Norwegian craftsmen drew their inspiration.

Although in leading countries like Spain the *grand époque* of filigree ended as the eighteenth century progressed, its popularity continued. In 1718 Mme de Montespan was amusing herself by harnessing six white mice to a carosse of *filagramme*,[33] and throughout the century the material continued to be put to a great variety of uses. From the neo-classic period until the end of the Empire, a more particular style *à l'antique* became universally favoured for gold jewellery. Light ear-rings were common, crescent-shaped or constructed like flower-baskets or cornucopia, or with side-split filigree drops. Delicate gold wire frames were designed for the miniature medallions then universally in use, whereas boxes, caskets, and so forth no longer seem to have been equally in favour.

Like the products of other crafts, much nineteenth-century filigree made after 1830 was of a revivalistic kind. In Italy, Castellani recovered the Etruscan method of granulation, and delicate gold bracelets and brooches with filigree ornamentation soldered on in the shape of fine wire or grains became fashionable all over Europe. With an increasing interest in folk-lore and prehistoric styles, various other branches were studied and refined, prominent among them the ancient Celtic and Scandinavian styles. Various forms of peasant filigree jewellery were re-introduced, and exploited commercially by various firms. Jacob Citroen of Amsterdam carried on a large production, and from the 1850s Jacob Tostrup of Christiania (now Oslo) produced large quantities of provincially inspired filigree jewellery. He was soon followed by others, whose products soon became well known abroad. At the same time, however, a naturalistic style imitating flowers and vegetable forms was also highly popular. The experiments which from the 1880s were carried out to master the technique of *émail au jour* were based on a thorough mastery of filigree.

Filigree is being produced in many parts of the world today, but mostly, it seems, along less ambitious lines. Souvenirs from the Far East or from the Mediterranean countries may be of very fine workmanship, but apart from this there is little to qualify them as works of art. Even from a technical point of view, modern pieces rarely equal the delicacy of fine antique work. With the advance of mechanization, it is probable that filigree will never again resume its old position among the crafts.

NOTES

1. For a detailed, illustrated treatise see Riisøen and Böe, *Om Filigran. Teknikk, historikk, filigran i norsk eie* (Filigree, its Technique and History. Filigree in Norwegian Ownership), Oslo, 1959.
2. Vol. I. *Revidirter Text, Übersetzung und Appendix* von Albert Ilg, Vienna, 1874. See pp. 160, 162, 260.
3. Numerous illustrations from Delaunay and others reproduced by Marc Rosenberg, *Geschichte der Goldschmiedekunst auf technischer Grundlage*, Frankfurt a.M. 1907–22, "Einführung". The earliest-known reference to a draw-bench is stated by him to date from 1498 (pp. 94–6).
4. Found in a Viking Age burial mound at Bö, Löten, Hedmark, in the south-eastern part of Norway. Exhibited at the Oslo University Collection of Antiquities, No. U.O. – C.9553.
5. As suggested by H. Wilson, *Silverwork and Jewellery*, 2nd ed. in collaboration with Professor Unno Bisei, London, 1951, p. 390.
6. Oscar Sørensen, "Gullsmedteknisk vurdering av enkelte funn", *Viking*, XV, Oslo, 1951, pp. 204–9.
7. Øyvind Modahl, "Hvorledes fikk de det til?", *Gullsmedkunst*, No. 6, Oslo, June, 1956, pp. 73–6.
8. Edouard Salin, *La Civilisation Mérovingienne*, Paris, 1957, IIIe Partie, Les Techniques, pp. 44 ff.
9. A possible connexion between this process and the methods used by medieval makers of gold or silver thread for the textile industry might well be sought. See Sofus Larsen, "Kvindeligt Haandarbejde i Middelalderen med særligt Hensyn til Folkeviserne", *Aarbøger for nordisk Oldkyndighed og Historie*, III Række, 5. Bind, Copenhagen, 1915, pp. 56 f. My attention was directed to this reference by Dr Odd Nordland.
10. *Op. cit.*, p. 164.
11. See Thale Riisöen and Alf Böe, *op. cit.*, footnote 23. Oscar Sørensen, *op. cit.*
12. Joan Evans, *A History of Jewellery 1100–1870*, London, 1953, pls. 1–3.
13. *Opere di Benvenuto Cellini*, Milano, Dalla Società Tipografica de' Classici Italiani, 1806–11, Vol. III, capitolo iii: "Dell' arte del lavorare di filo, del modo di fare la granaglia, e del saldare", p. 38. Interesting supplementary explanation of Cellini's text is offered by Marc Rosenberg, *op. cit.*, Abteilung: Granulation, p. 10.
14. The problem has been thoroughly discussed by Marc Rosenberg, *loc. cit.* A modern English patent No. 415181, March 1933, may have a bearing on the problem. Our attention was drawn to this reference by the goldsmith Øyvind Modahl, Oslo.
15. M. Stenberger, *Die Schatzfunde Gotlands der Wikingerzeit*, Lund 1947.
16. Illustrated in *The Connoisseur*, October 1958,

Vol. CXLII, No. 572, p. 104. On Scandinavian filigree from Carolingian times until the end of the Middle Ages, see Aron Anderson and Alf Böe's articles under Filigran, in *Nordisk Kulturleksikon*.

17. See Hermann Fillitz, *Die Insignien und Kleinodien des Heiligen Römischen Reiches*, Vienna and Munich, 1954.

18. On the position of Venice, see Filippo Rossi, *Capolavori di Oreficeria Italiana* (Swedish edition, Malmö, 1958).

19. J. Starkie Gardner, *Old Silver-Work chiefly English from the XVth to the XVIIIth Centuries*, London, 1903, p. 18.

20. See Charles Pulsky, Eugène Radisics and Émile Molinier, *Chefs-d'œuvre d'orfèvrerie ayant figuré à l'exposition de Budapest*, Paris, Budapest, London, New York, no date; Julius Bielz, *Die sächsische Goldschmiedekunst Siebenbürgens*, Bukarest, 1957.

21. Marc Rosenberg, "Studien über Goldschmiedekunst in der Sammlung Figdor, Wien", *Kunst und Kunsthandwerk*, Wien, 1911, pp. 354 ff. The Clare College tankard has been studied and described by J. E. Foster and T. D. Atkinson in *An illustrated Catalogue of the Loan Collection of Plate exhibited in the Fitzwilliam Museum, May* 1895, Cambridge, 1896, Cat. No. 28.

22. Ada Marshall Johnson, *Hispanic Silverwork*, New York, 1944, pp. 110 ff.

23. Carl Hernmarck, "Trådarbeten", *Svenskt Silversmide*, Vol. I, pp. 232–4, Stockholm, no date. Ed by Olle Källström and Carl Hernmarck.

24. Riisöen and Böe, *op. cit.*, p. 56.

25. *Ibid.*, p. 26 f.

26. Examples illustrated in *The Connoisseur*, November 1959, Vol. CXLIV, No. 581, p. 156.

27. Miss Ella Winter in *Illustrated London News*, April 11, 1959, p. 617.

28. We are grateful to Dr Carl Hernmarck for this information. Dr Hernmarck refers to Guiffrey, *Inventaire Général du Mobilier de la Couronne sous Louis XIV*, which it has not been possible to consult.

29. *The Memoirs of Ann Lady Fanshawe*, London and New York, 1907, pp. 139 f., 147, 189.

30. *Op. cit.*

31. E. Alfred Jones, *Old Silver of Europe and America*, London, 1928, pp. 325 f. Jones refers to Filimonows catalogue of the Kreml Collections, and to F. R. Martin, *Schwedische königliche Geschenke an Russische Zaren, 1647–1699*, pl. 50 and p. 21. We have not found occasion to consult these works.

32. Riisöen and Böe, *op. cit.*

33. Letter from Mme de Maintenon to Mme de Caylus, January 24, 1718, referred to in E. Littre, *Dictionnaire de la langue française*, 1863, Filigrane.

SHEFFIELD PLATE

Georgian Sheffield plate is beautiful and distinguished, its range of design rivalling that of eighteenth-century hand-wrought silver. Shortcomings in the processes involved, however, made it difficult to follow the florid cast silver patterns introduced by the silversmiths from 1797 after the Goldsmiths' Company had complained to Parliament that "plated manufacturers have produced articles of the highest elegance and fashion, many of which are now made with solid silver – borders, shields, ornaments, finished in exact resemblance of real plate – and which do material injury to the sale of wrought plate".

Beautiful table accessories were no longer the prerogative of the rich. Families of moderate means were now dining from Wedgwood's creamware or Spode's bone china, graced with elegant accessories in radiant Sheffield plate. The effect of this was so devastating upon the silversmith's craft that for the next half-century little wrought plate was made in England.

The fact that Sheffield plate reacted like a single piece of metal when shaped by silversmiths' tools, raised it to an important position during the reign of George III (1760–1820). Skill and time expended upon it by the craftsmen were no less than for solid silver, however. The tax of sixpence an ounce levied upon manufactured silver plate from 1782 had the effect of enabling Sheffield plate to be sold at one-third the price of silver: in 1815 the silver tax was increased to eighteen pence an ounce.

Many enthusiastic collectors prefer the peculiar lustre radiating from plate made by fusing silver over copper to the brilliance of silver plate. Similar patterns were made over such long periods that only a detailed knowledge of the processes involved in Sheffield plating will enable a collector to place examples within closely defined periods.

Sheffield plating is one of the many industries entirely English in origin. The discovery that silver and copper could be united by fusion was made in 1743 by Thomas Bolsover (1704–88), a Sheffield cutler. It is uncertain how Bolsover's achievement came about: the story of the broken silver knife handle and the copper penny bears no investigation, for such a coin was not included in the English coinage until 1797.

Aware that silver and copper would fuse together, he experimented with rolled copper plates and sheets of silver foil. These he fused together as a single entity. With borrowed capital of £170 and Joseph Wilson as partner, Bolsover began to manufacture silver-plated buttons. The venture prospered, and within a year the loan had been repaid with interest. During the following twelve months he experimented further, fusing a plate of silver to an ingot of copper and reducing them to plate thickness by passing between heavy spring rollers. The relative proportions of silver and copper remained unaltered and the copper was silvered on one side only. Bolsover named his production Copper Rolled Plate, and although he did not patent the process, it appears to have remained under his sole control until 1758. During this period he manufactured small circular and oval boxes with pull-off lids hand-embossed in low relief.

Joseph Hancock, a former apprentice of Bolsover's, discovered the single-lapped edge and, aware of its potential value, had established himself as a competitor by 1758. His vision carried him further, and by installing horse- and water-power he rolled heavier ingots into plates large enough for him to enter the field formerly the prerogative of silversmiths. He issued a wide range of domestic ware, including tea- and coffee-pots, hot-water jugs, saucepans, all tin-lined, as well as candlesticks. Bolsover, already a rich man, made an unsuccessful effort to follow suit, and eventually sold his business to Hancock.

It was probably to Hancock's workshops that Matthew Boulton (1728–1809) was sent in 1760 by his father, a Birmingham toy-maker, who appreciated the potentialities of the silver-plated ware. After mastering the technique, Matthew Boulton returned to Birmingham, and by 1762 was producing plated ware at Soho, two miles to the north. Three years later he founded the Matthew Boulton

& Plate Company in Birmingham to organize the sale of silver and plated ware, issuing an ever-increasing stream from his factory.

The wide variety of ware issued by the Sheffield platers is shown by illustrated pattern books dating from about 1790. In the Victoria and Albert Museum are several such books, the earliest a folio of eighty-four plates issued by John Green, Sheffield. On the first page is written his name and the year 1792, with a note to the effect that a discount of 30 per cent was allowed. Unfortunately, however, the articles are not priced. The objects illustrated are tea- and coffee-sets, cake-baskets, hot-water jugs, tea-caddies, tankards and beakers, teapots, wine-bottle corks, bottle labels, waiters and trays, cruet frames with glass accessories, toasters, breakfast dishes and covers, soup tureens, chamber candlesticks, wax-taper holders, snuffers and snuffer trays, toast-racks, standishes, wine funnels, sand boxes, salt-cellars, candelabra, spoons and forks, fish servers, sauce-boats and sauce tureens, tumbler stands, egg-cups, mustards, sugar-basins, table-heaters and stands, ladles, oil-bottle stands.

Another catalogue, issued in 1797 by John Cadman, Sheffield, is a folio of seventy plates illustrating similar objects in different patterns, but showing, in addition, tea-urns, candlesticks in perspective and half section, and this firm's well-known telescopic candlestick marked "patent". Prices have been written in with pen and ink.

A further catalogue, undated but with pages watermarked 1811, illustrates a widening range of ware with the addition of cigar-cases, oil lamps to fit candle-sockets, combined egg-cup holders and muffineers, tea-bells, spirit-frames and bottles, knife-rests, wine-coolers, beefsteak dishes, saucepans, cream-buckets, cream-ewers, argyles, strainers, and plate-covers.

These pieces continued in production throughout the traditional period to the establishment of Elkington's electroplate, during which German silver gradually superseded copper as the foundation for Sheffield plate. The decline was slow, for in 1865 there were nine platers operating in Birmingham, using between them about ten tons of plate annually.

Glossary

Acanthus. Conventional foliage adapted from the capitals of Corinthian columns, used extensively throughout the Renaissance period, sixteenth to seventeenth centuries, chiefly in embossed technique.

Almsdish. Circular dish with broad, flat rim, plain or decorated in prevailing style of period. Single examples of seventeenth-century domestic plates sometimes mistaken for almsdishes.

Altars. Since the early Middle Ages, altar frontals, and sometimes whole altars, have occasionally been made in silver. At Città di Castello, in Umbria, there is a fine twelfth-century frontal which is an important specimen of late romanesque sculpture. One of the best examples of a complete silver altar is that of St James made, between the thirteenth and the fifteenth centuries, for Pistoia Cathedral (cf. *The Connoisseur*, November 1956). Among numerous seventeenth- and eighteenth-century altars that by G. B. Foggini for the Corsini Chapel in the Carmine at Florence, and that of 1730 at Frieburg (near Augsburg), should be mentioned.

Andirons. On the Continent were frequently made in silver for palaces, but few of these heavy pieces of furniture have survived. In the Victoria and Albert Museum there is a very fine rococo one made by Philip Jacob Drentwitt of Augsburg (1747–79). In England rare in silver, but examples occur from Restoration period. Usually of richly chased baluster or vase form and occasionally as caryatid figures. Either cast from solid metal or built up in sections on iron cores.

Annealing. Process of softening the silver by heating over red-hot charcoals, as it became brittle under hammering during the process of raising from a flat sheet.

Anthemion. Conventional foliage resembling honeysuckle blossom found as ornament on pieces in the classical idiom (Greek).

Applied. A term used in connexion with ornament; certain parts, such as spouts, handles, covers, were made separately and applied with solder.

Arabesque. Interlaced patterns of flowers and foliage often combined with Strapwork (*q.v.*) in sixteenth century and in pierced work of eighteenth century.

Argyle. Gravy container, cylindrical or vase-shaped, resembling small coffee-pots with either outer lining or central container (sometimes detachable) for hot water. Introduced about 1770; in favour until the 1820s. Not made in Sheffield plate until the late 1780s.

Armour. In the sixteenth century it was not uncommon for the pageant armour of great princes to be made either wholly or partly of silver. The Louvre has a magnificent enamelled gold shield and morion made for Charles IX between 1560 and 1574. A great shield of iron, in the British Museum, damascened with gold and plated with silver, was made by Giorgio Ghisi of Mantua in 1554, and is a notable example of Mannerist art.

Asparagus tongs. Introduced in late eighteenth century. Derived from fish-slice with spring-hinged upper jaw. Later form of spring-bow form with pierced flat grips. Handle patterns conform to table services. Rare in U.S. silver.

Aspergill. The orb-ended rod or brush used for sprinkling holy water; the handle is often of silver and made to match a holy-water bucket (*q.v.*).

Assay. In silver, the test made to prove that the metal was of required quality.

Assay-groove. The wriggled groove by which metal was taken for purposes of assay. Occurs usually in proximity to hall-marks up to the late seventeenth century. This method was practised on the Continent, and is an interesting minor reflection of close historical link between Scotland, where it was also used, and certain European countries.

Bannock-rack. Resembles an outsize in toast-racks, the silver tray secured to a wooden base. Few examples known date from the second half of the eighteenth century (Plate 483B). Bannock is a flat home-baked Scottish cake made from oatmeal, barley, or peasemeal, generally the first, broken into pieces when removed from the girdle and served hot.

Baptismal basin. While many baptismal basins were made specifically for the purpose, there are instances of the bequest of rose-water basins to churches to serve in this capacity, such as the one now belonging to the First Parish Church, Cambridge, U.S.A., which was made by Jeremiah Dummer of Boston. Earliest baptismal basins are of the seventeenth century.

FIG. 5. Baptismal Basin, 1716

Baroque. The generic title for the late Renaissance flamboyant style of scrollwork and naturalistic ornament.

Basket. Variously used for bread, cake, or fruit. Early examples rare and usually circular. Oval form introduced about 1730 with pierced bodies and swing handles. Wirework bodies with applied foliage, wheat, and flowers popular about 1770. Later examples have solid bodies, engraved decoration, and gadrooned or reeded rims. Circular gilt baskets return after 1800 for dessert use (*see* Cream, Dessert, and Sugar baskets).

Basins. Were frequently made in gold, silver, or mounted crystal, and the decoration of some is so elaborate that one suspects that they were intended primarily for display on the sideboard. A fairly simple Flemish example, of about 1560, with a raised centre, belongs to the Corporation of Guildford. In the Louvre there is a magnificent basin (with its ewer), made at Antwerp 1558–9, chased with scenes of Charles V's expedition to Tunis in 1535. A large Portuguese basin in the Wallace Collection (*c.* 1565) is richly embossed with symbols of the seasons, the ele-

ments, and the planets. Basins were used for the essential hand-washing before and during meals, but their popularity as decorative pieces lasted until after the introduction of forks and declined in the early eighteenth century (Plate 492C).

Bat's-wing fluting. Graduated gadroon-

FIG. 6

ing curved to resemble the outline of a bat's wing and encircling hollow-ware.

Beading. A border ornament composed of small contiguous half-spheres resembling pearls or beads. Commonest in late eighteenth century.

Beakers. Stemless drinking-cups were popular in various parts of Europe from the fifteenth until the eighteenth century. In the fifteenth century they were especially popular in Germany, where they usually had covers

FIG. 7

decorated with over-hanging Gothic leaf decoration around the rim. A superb nielloed example of about 1480 is in the British Museum. Some were made in fantastic shapes, like the copper-gilt one in the Victoria and Albert Museum, which is very intricately fashioned to resemble a castle. Norwegian beakers of the sixteenth century usually rest on feet in the form of lions or female busts. Simple, uncovered beakers, much like those made in England at the same time, reached the height of their popularity in the sixteenth and seventeenth centuries in Holland (Fig. 7), where they also served as communion cups in Protestant churches. In Hungary very tall beakers, decorated in national fashion, were favoured, and in Italy they were occasionally covered with filigree work (Plate 490B). In the United States the early ones were straight-sided with flaring rim, followed by a Queen Anne bell-shape on low moulded foot; the body became ovoid in Federal period, *c.* 1800.

Bedwarmers. Were made in silver, but few have survived. One by the French craftsman Charles Petit in 1661 was in the Puiforcat Collection.

Beefsteak-dish. Similar to an entrée dish, and described in the 1797 catalogue as fitted with "the handle to screw off to make a pair of dishes occasionally".

Beer bowles and **beer cupps.** Encountered in inventories but not distinctly recognizable today.

Beer jugs. *See* Jugs.

Bekerschroef. A stand for a wine-glass, shaped like the stem of a large cup. These objects are peculiar to Holland, where they were made in the early seventeenth century.

Bells. Table bells of silver have been made since the sixteenth century, varying in style with the taste of the times. A famous bell, decorated with snakes, lizards, and insects, made by Hans Jamnitzer at Nuremberg in about 1558, is in the British Museum, and a similar one attributed to the same craftsman, is in the Schatzkammer der Reichen Kapelle at Munich. In England they were rare before the eighteenth century. Usually found with baluster handles, frequently as centrepiece of inkstands until mid-eighteenth century. Later

examples have wood or ivory handles. In Scotland it is doubtful if any handbells survive earlier than 1800, with the notable exception

FIG. 8. Ivory-handled bell, 1806

of the Holyrood Mass Bell. Two examples of racing bells are preserved from seventeenth century.

Bezel. The added inside rim to make a cover fit more firmly.

Biggin. A form of cylindrical coffee-pot with short spout, often with stand and spirit-lamp.

Blackjack. Leather tankard occasionally mounted with silver rim, of seventeenth- and eighteenth-century date. Certain examples bearing pretentious historical inscriptions should be viewed with scepticism.

Bleeding-bowl. *See* Cupping-bowl.

Blowhole. A small hole pierced in hollow castings or seamed hollow members as handles, finials, etc., to allow escape of the air expanded by heat when soldered to the main body. Tankards with this feature have long been mistakenly known as "whistle" tankards, to be used for calling for another drink. This fantasy dies hard.

Bookbindings (*rilegature*). In Italy, from a very early period, books, especially liturgical books, have occasionally been bound in precious materials. In the seventeenth and eighteenth centuries the entire bindings were sometimes made of embossed silver plates. A more usual practice was to decorate the leather- or velvet-covered boards with silver edges and a pattern of scrollwork with central medallion of a religious subject or the arms of the owner. Bindings of this type rarely bear hall-marks.

Bottle tickets. Small plaques, plain or ornamented, engraved or cut with the name of a beverage, with a chain to be hung on the neck of a decanter. Date from the 1730s.

Bowl. An unknown item is the "silver Bowl with two wooden handles" in a U.S. inventory of 1728; "a wrought bowl which will hold five pints, with handles" is mentioned in 1758. Slop bowls and slop basins appear in inventories early in the eighteenth century, but are identifiable chiefly in the second half.

Box. Small circular and oval boxes occur from seventeenth century onward, made for patches, comfits, pomades, and other feminine needs (*see also* Snuff and Tobacco Boxes, Pomanders, Vinaigrettes, and Étui).

Brandewijkom. An oval, two-handled bowl peculiar to Holland, where it was made in the seventeenth and eighteenth centuries. It was used on festive occasions to hold raisins steeped in brandy.

Brandy-bowls. Flat, two-handled bowls called *orekovsken* in Denmark, *oreskaal* in Norway, and *dopskal* in Sweden, used for serving hot brandy, were popular throughout the Scandinavian countries in the seventeenth century.

Bratina. A globular, covered cup with a contracted lip (usually decorated with a sententious inscription), peculiar to Russia. It was a form of loving-cup, intimately associated with its owner and used at his funeral feast. Sometimes they were richly enamelled and begemmed; a rare example in gold is in the museum at Vienna.

Brazier. Circular bowl with pierced plate in base for burning charcoal as heaters for kettles or dishes. Found late seventeenth century and occasionally in eighteenth, but supplanted by spirit-lamp stands (*see also* Chafing stand).

Bread baskets. The opulent form, usually of pierced work and on feet, although a U.S. example by Myer Myers is on a baseband, with bail handle; today called a cake basket, as in the will of Dorothy Quincy Hancock Scott (1830): "My large silver cake basket

requesting her to have it used at the weddings .... as it has been heretofore."

FIG. 9. Bread basket; D. C. Fueter

Bridal crowns. The custom for Norwegian brides to wear a crown at their wedding probably goes back to the Middle Ages, but all the examples which now exist in Norway must have been made in post-Reformation times. One particular example, which has names of saints engraved on it, may date from *c.* 1550. Some specimens go back to the seventeenth century, while the majority of existing crowns must have been made in the eighteenth and nineteenth centuries. The crown is made of a ring, from which rise the ornamental parts. From them again ornaments are suspended, which glitter and tinkle when the wearer moves about. On some of the best examples the ring (which rested on a padded cushion) is divided into sections, and the ornaments above are cut out into heraldic figures of decorative patterns. These are repeated in identical form with each section. Another type consists of a plain cylinder, the top of which has been cut out into the patterns desired, and to them the hanging ornaments are attached. The cheaper specimens are made of silver-gilt copper. Crowns seem to have been most widely used in western Norway. In fact, the bridal crown is still in use in that part of the country, but, like the national costume with which it is usually worn, its traditionalism seems a little self-conscious.

Bright-cut engraving. A particular form of engraving popular about 1790 in which the metal is removed by bevelled cutting, giving a jewel-like, faceted sparkle to the surface.

Britannia metal, plating on. Introduced in the early 1820s by Kirkby, Smith & Company, Sheffield. A sheet of pure silver was laid on a flat surface and well heated. Molten Britannia metal was poured over this. When cold it was found to have picked up the silver. The two were then rolled into sheets as for plated copper. Owing to difficulties in assembling, the method was soon abandoned, but examples are to be found from time to time.

Britannia Standard. The Higher Standard for wrought plate introduced in 1697 to prevent the melting down of coinage by silversmiths. It consists of 11 oz 10 dwts fine silver in the Pound Troy (12 oz). Named from the mark of Britannia replacing Sterling mark of lion passant. In force till 1720, when Sterling or Old Standard was restored, the Higher being left as optional, which it still is.

Brooches. The heavy silver Norwegian specimens, made by country goldsmiths or by guild masters for provincial customers, are of special interest. They were used either to hold together the standing collar on the blouse of the national costume (and some of these were worn by both men and women) or rested on the bosom of the wearer as a magnificent ornament. It is among the latter group that the most interesting types are found. Some of these "sölje" brooches are made to patterns that go back to medieval times, like the very fine example with heraldic animals in a circle which is in the Victoria and Albert Museum (Plate 502G). Others rely for their effect on hanging ringlets, which are suspended from the edges of the brooch and give a glittering, shimmering effect of a certain primitive beauty. Other examples are made in a mould. Finally there are the filigree specimens, which are lighter and more elegant than any of the other types. Some of the latter are made of very white metal.

Peasant brooches were particularly sought after by English tourists in quest of souvenirs from Norway, and quite a number of them have been found in Britain. It should always be remembered that they have been much copied for tourists during the last eighty to a hundred years. Some of them have very close parallels in Scotland, like the little heart-shaped "Luckenbooth" brooch or the circular moulded type with the pin to catch (not to stick) into the material of the blouse.

Buckles. For knees, shoes, girdles, and stocks were recorded in great quantity in the United States in gold, silver, paste, etc., but comparatively few have survived, and even fewer with maker's marks.

Burnishing. Polishing with a hand tool containing a hard, smooth stone or, in modern times, steel; used to remove planishing marks from the "planishing teast" or hammer.

Butter tester. A device found in silver from the mid-eighteenth century akin in shape to a modern apple corer, and sometimes thus called erroneously.

Butter-dish. Oval pierced bowl and cover with glass liner, usually Irish, dating from the second half of eighteenth century. English examples rare till nineteenth century, when circular tub-shaped examples occur.

Butt joint. A joint made by soldering two ends of silver on the flat without fold or overlap.

Cake basket. *See* Basket.

Candelabrum. A branched candlestick. In England virtually no survivals before eighteenth century. Stems and base conform to candlestick design. Detachable or fixed scroll branches for two or more lights with finials of various forms. Late examples highly elaborate and many-branched, sometimes with interchangeable *épergne* dishes. In the Portuguese royal collection there is a magnificent rococo one by the French craftsman François Thomas Germain whose pupil, Robert Joseph Auguste, made three great candelabra for the Winter Palace at Petrograd. Silver wall-sconces of the seventeenth and eighteenth centuries are commoner, especially in Holland and Germany. A pair of fine candle-brackets with tulip-shaped holders, made by Nicholas Verhaar at Utrecht, is in the Brum Collection in that city.

Candlestick, altar. Either larger version of domestic examples of the period or of Italian Renaissance design with tripod bases. Prickets (spikes) occur in place of sockets.

Candlestick, chamber. Also known as flat candlestick. Usually circular, flat base. Early examples have cast pear-shaped handles, later of scroll or ring form. Extinguishers fit in slots on sockets or handle. Late examples often with snuffers carried in opening in stem. Found from late seventeenth century onwards.

Candlestick, table. In England found in pairs and sets of four or more from Charles II onwards. Stems either of cast baluster form or classical columns in sheet metal, the latter in Adam period die-struck at Sheffield and loaded with resin or lead. Telescopic stems rare in silver but frequent in Sheffield plate. Single candlesticks of silver have been made on the Continent since the sixteenth century in all sizes, for use in churches and houses, varying with the stylistic trends of the times. In the seventeenth century domestic candlesticks were normally square and solid, like the Dutch examples in the Victoria and Albert Museum (Fig. 10). They provided great scope for the rococo silversmiths and designers like Meisonnier, who made roses sprout and blossom from the hollows of the contorted pillars. In the United States the earliest, 1686, by Jeremiah Dummer, Boston, shows architectural influence, continued in a different form in baluster stems of the early eighteenth century, used by Coney in Boston and

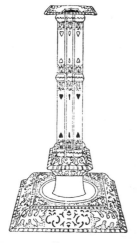

FIG. 10

George Rideout in New York; fluted columns on square or octagonal bases are seen in work of Boelen and Kierstede. After about 1715 candlesticks were cast in moulds, being raised from a flat piece of silver in the earlier period. Baluster forms continued to be most popular throughout the eighteenth century.

Canes. Inventories from 1697 refer to "silver-headed canes"; in 1719 the Boston gold-

smith, Samuel Haugh, had "a silver ferril upon an Agget Canes head", and Revere's day-book in 1786 mentions a gold cane head. Many English examples exist.

Canister. A receptacle for tea; Edward Franklin's inventory of 1725 listed "a Canister Boat for spoons". This was a wicker basket.

Cann. Drinking-vessel, usually of one-pint capacity, like a mug, but always having rounded sides, and standing on a moulded base. The term "cann" appears in old inventories of the late eighteenth century.

Canoe shape. A piece oval on plan with the two ends, seen in elevation, higher than

FIG. 11. Canoe-shaped cruet-stand

the centre, such as in some standishes and cruet frames.

Canongate silver. Calls for separate mention, since Canongate is now merged in Edinburgh, but until the nineteenth century formed independent burgh with its own trade guilds. Finest period sixteenth century, when some elaborate mazers crowned its output, but good work still done in seventeenth. By end of eighteenth century main output was table silver. Feature of list of Canongate goldsmiths is number of apparent foreigners. Close proximity to gates of Holyrood Palace may account for place's prosperity. Canongate silver (mark: stag's head lodged) is comparatively rare and much sought after.

Canteen. Small individual set of knife, fork, and spoon with beaker and condiment box, contained in shagreen case, used for travelling, dating from late seventeenth to late eighteenth centuries.

Caryatid. The cast thumb-grips on the handles of caudle-cups generally take this form, derived from the classic draped female figure used as a support for an entablature.

Caskets. Large caskets of silver were made in Germany in the sixteenth century, but elsewhere they were usually of other materials, mounted in silver, like the famous Renaissance *Cassetta Farnese* in the Naples Museum. Small wedding-caskets for jewellery, no more than 3 inches high and fashioned like miniature chests, were made in Holland in the seventeenth century.

Cast. To shape in a mould, which was generally of brass. Certain small parts, thumb-pieces, finials for covers, hinge-plates, handles for cups, etc., were given their form in the molten state. These were finished by filing and chasing after removal from the mould.

Caster. Found singly or in set of three for sugar, pepper, and with unpierced cover for mustard. Seventeenth-century form cylindrical. In eighteenth century pear-shaped and later of vase form, polygonal or circular in outline. Largely replaced in late eighteenth century by cut-glass examples with silver covers (*see also* Cruet frame, Dredger, Muffineer).

FIG. 12. Pierced Caster Cover, 1716   FIG. 13. Caster, 1715

Castwork. Decoration or parts of a vessel cast in a mould and soldered to the main body. Principally used for handles, feet, spouts, and finials. Complete castings occur in candlesticks built up in various sections and in some other pieces.

Celtic decoration. After, perhaps, ninth century anything which can really be called Celtic decoration is most rare on silver, except for some jewellery (*q.v.*). Touches of Celtic feeling occur on croziers and on Dunvegan Cup (fourteenth century), but latter is Irish. Also on Macleod Cup, of late sixteenth century, but this fundamentally Renaissance.

Censer. Occasionally called a thurible. The vessel in which incense is burnt; it is more frequently of base metal than silver. Gothic examples are usually architectural in form,

FIG. 14

and resemble fantastic spires or octagonal chapter-houses. In Renaissance times a simpler, vase-shaped type came into use, and in subsequent periods its decoration varied with current trends in architectural taste. A very fine silver censer of 1767–79 in the Bayerisches Nationalmuseum echoes in its broken curves the decoration of the rococo pilgrimage churches of Bavaria (Fig. 14). A few English examples late seventeenth to eighteenth centuries have survived, and the Ramsey Abbey example (fourteenth century).

Centre-piece. A large and often fantastic object, sometimes called a *surtout de table*, used to decorate the centre of a table; in some ways it took the place of the ceremonial salt. One of the most famous is that made by Wenzel Jamnitzer (1546) in the form of a woman, standing on a mound covered with leafy plants, holding on her head a covered dish crowned by a vase of flowers (Rijksmuseum, Amsterdam). A Swedish example of the late seventeenth century has four candle branches, a dish supported by a five-headed dragon, casters for sugar, and shell-shaped dishes for sweetmeats. Rococo silversmiths allowed their ingenuity to run riot when designing such objects, and one of the finest of all was that made in 1730 by Thomas Germain, now in the Museum de Arte Antigua, Lisbon, which stands some 3 feet in height, bears two three-branch candleholders, and is enriched with putti, dogs, tortoises, and hunting-horns (Plate 487A; *see also The Connoisseur*, December 1954, p. 259). *See* Épcrgne.

Chafing-dish. A general term, covering various forms of dishes for hot foods. A familiar form in Boston work, at least two dozen

FIG. 15

being known, also made in simpler form in New York; possibly their popularity was result of Huguenot and Dutch influence. Chafing-dishes are made for the use of charcoals, and the dish supports are continued downward to form the foot.

Chafing-stand. A similar word for brazier or spirit-lamp stand for the above.

Chalice. The cup in which wine is consecrated at the Eucharist. When intended for the use of the Roman Catholic Church it was invariably made of gold, silver, or silver-gilt, frequently enriched with enamel and relief decoration and occasionally encrusted with precious stones. The earliest chalices have a hemispherical bowl on a spreading, knopped stem, and some romanesque examples, like that at Kremsmünster, are decorated with Christian symbols amid interlaced decoration (Fig. 16). In the Gothic period the stems were occasionally enriched with buttresses and pinnacles, like the fifteenth-century Venetian one in the Victoria and Albert Museum, but such becrocketed vessels must have been diffi-

cult to handle, and a simpler, more practical type, in which the decoration was limited to engraving on the bowl with enamelling on the knop and foot, was generally preferred (Fig.

FIG. 16

17). In the fourteenth century a deeper form of bowl came into use, and a pattern was established that did not alter radically until the nineteenth century, when the hemispherical bowl was revived; but the decoration of both bowl and stem varied considerably with the times. In the seventeenth and eighteenth centuries the lip of the bowl was normally left

FIG. 17

free from the baroque or rococo decoration, which swirled round the lower part to riot on the stem and foot (Plate 491A). Many chalices of these periods were enamelled and some decorated with stones; one in the Vatican, made in Rome for the Cardinal of York, being studded with diamonds. Rococo craftsmen occasionally made the stem in the form of a standing figure, as in the example of 1707 in the Church of St Paul, Antwerp. Large numbers of chalices were made by English silversmiths in the mid-nineteenth century.

Chandelier. Hanging candle branches to be distinguished from the standing candelabrum. The two words are the French and Latin forms of the same word. The above distinction is usually observed in English for clarity.

Charger. *See* Sideboard dish.

Charka. A small cup with a single handle, peculiar to Russia; it was used for drinking strong liquors. A characteristic, richly enamelled example is in the British Museum.

Chasing. Relief decoration raised by surface hammering of the metal. Also applied to the finishing given to cast or *repoussé* work, in which former case roughnesses or projections may also be filed or cut away (*see also* Flat chasing).

Cheese-scoop. Introduced in late eighteenth century for serving cheese. Consists of a short, curved blade with silver shaft and ivory or wood handle. Later examples have silver handles conforming to table service patterns.

Cheese warmers. Shallow, rectangular trays with rounded corners and projecting handles of turned wood. From second quarter of eighteenth century. Attractively simple, but rare.

Cherub's head. A cast cherub mask appears on the curve and at the tip of the handle of New York tankards, at tip in Boston work. The European source of design was identified by Marshall Davidson (*Antiques*, April 1940) in cast ornament of spandrels of Dutch and English clocks of the late seventeenth century. The cherub mask with pendant leafage on handles duplicates a French seventeenth-century *applique de cabinet* (*see* "Le Bronze", second part of a catalogue of metalwork, Musée des Arts Décoratifs, Plate 26, Fig. 256). Masks and pendants as used by different silversmiths are so similar as to suggest the moulds were imported.

Chinoiserie. Decoration of pseudo-Chinese inspiration. Occurs at three periods: (i) from about 1680 to 1685 in engraved form; (ii) about 1750 chiefly in *repoussé* and chased form; (iii) about 1820 in the same technique with cast details.

Chocolate-pot. Of the same basic form as the coffee-pot, from which it can be distinguished by the detachable or sliding cover finial concealing the hole for insertion of the swizzle-stick for stirring the chocolate. Many pieces must have been used indiscriminately for both liquids.

Chop dish. Small, flat, two-handled, oblong dish occurring from about 1750 to the 1850s.

Ciborium. The receptacle used for the reservation of the Eucharist. It is normally provided with a hinged cover and a lock. Gothic examples usually have a spire-shaped cover above a cylindrical (occasionally polygonal), font-shaped bowl (Fig. 18). Flatter covers, usually crowned by a cross, were introduced at the Renaissance.

FIG. 18

Clasps. For books, pocketbooks, and cloaks were shaped plaques on which, to judge by the few remaining ones, a goldsmith could show his imagination and skill in engraving. Clasps for necklaces and bracelets were usually oblong or elliptical and engraved. These are sometimes called lockets.

Coaster. *See* Wine coaster.

Coat-of-arms. Arms on earliest pieces were engraved in a flat-topped shield (on a lozenge for widows or spinsters), surrounded with a plumed mantling. A baroque form with broad, curling acanthus leaves was favoured in New York in early eighteenth century. About 1740 a new style was adopted with imbrication in the framework surrounding the arms; then followed the Chippendale rococo, well exemplified by Revere and Nathaniel Hurd; Guillim's *Display of Heraldry* was largely used by American silversmiths. In the classic period, 1785–1810, the shield showing the arms has floral garlands suspended on either side.

Cobbet pot. In Boston in 1667 John Wilson left "one chased cobbet pott & Cover" of silver. The *Oxford Dictionary on Historic Principles* lists *Cobbit* as an obsolete form of *Cobbard*, or fire dog.

Coffee-pot. Introduced about 1680. In England early examples basically of straight tapering form, later polygonal. Pear-shaped bodies appear about 1730 and classical vase forms in the Adam period. Later cylindrical forms often provided with spirit-lamp stands (*see also* Biggin). On the Continent they vary but slightly from one region and date to another. They were normally vase-shaped with a spout, but exotic patterns also occur, like that entwined with snakes and crowned with a toad, which was made at Dresden in about

FIG. 19. Coffee pots, 1720 and 1770

1700 by J. M. Dinglinger. In the United States the earliest coffee-pots, *c.* 1700, were of severe tapering form like the earliest English type, followed about twenty years later by a modification of the tapering form, being rounded at the base, and standing on a narrow moulded foot. The rococo coffee-pot was, like the English, pear-shaped and tall, stood on a spreading foot, and had a domed cover. In the Federal period (late eighteenth and early nineteenth centuries) the coffee-pot was an inverted pear with a simple scroll handle of wood; some were made in classical urn shape.

Coin. Inlaid in lid of tankards; German and Scandinavian practice, followed in New York and England.

Coin silver. In the United States the stamp, coin, after 1850, signified pieces made from silver coin, 900 parts pure silver, 100 alloy, or less than sterling.

Communion silver. A very important branch of Scottish silverware, although unlikely to have much immediate concern for collectors, as most pieces are still in the hands of the kirks for which they were made. Reformed church demanded entirely new types of vessels, owing nothing to traditional forms, and earliest cups – late sixteenth and early seventeenth centuries – seem to have been modelled either on standing mazers or on secular wine cups. Presbyterianism required participation of all communicants in Sacrament, and cups in populous parishes are frequently large-bowled, and occur in pairs or even fours. Graceful shapes, but little or no ornament. Cups become more stereotyped with advance of eighteenth century. Names or initials and coats-of-arms of donors commonly engraved on bowls, with date of gift. On north-east coast and inland typical cup is of beaker type, modelled on Dutch and German secular beakers, which themselves are sometimes adapted for sacred use and then copied by local goldsmith (Plate 482A). A number of handsome basins and lavers from the seventeenth century are still in use in the churches. Earliest is baptismal basin of St John's Kirk, Perth (1591).

Compostiera. A container for stewed fruit, usually in the form of a salver carrying a pair of silver jars normally having glass linings. The containers are often richly worked and have elaborate knobs on their covers. An example made at Turin (now in a private collection at Milan) has a barking dog to serve as the knob of one lid and a cat arching her back on the other.

Corkscrew. A thumb-piece of twisted shape derived from the Dutch form, used especially on New York and English tankards.

Cow cream-jug. Small model of cow with open mouth and lid in back. Introduced from Holland about 1755 by John Schuppe, probably a Dutchman. Later examples occur by other makers.

Cream basket. Small vase or boat-shaped basket, pierced or plain, introduced about 1760, often matching larger examples for sugar.

Creamer. In the United States earliest cream-pitchers are of second quarter of the eighteenth century and are pear-shaped with collared foot and domed cover. Next came a higher form with larger lip, three cabriole legs, double-scroll handle. This was followed by the inverted pear-shape; then the classic helmet.

Cream-jug. Early examples of plain pitcher form from Queen Anne to George II. Mid-eighteenth century, pear-shaped bodies on three feet, plain or chased. Classical vase or helmet shape introduced about 1780. Flat-bottomed examples about 1800. After this

FIG. 20. Cream-jug, 1753

usually part of tea service *en suite* with teapot and sugar-basin.

In Scotland a most unusual type is the very rare, spherical covered jug of about 1730–40, matching bullet teapots (Fig. 21). Helmet-

FIG. 21. Cream-jug, Edinburgh, 1730.
Maker, William Aytoun

shaped jug with upstanding handle, of same period, is equally attractive, but almost as rare. Otherwise development of styles follows southern fashions.

Crozier. The head of the crozier, or bishop's pastoral staff, has often been made of silver. Gothic examples usually have a circle of crocketed niches beneath the volute which contains the figure of a saint. The sinuous

curve of the crook naturally appealed to eighteenth-century silversmiths; there is a fine rococo example at Eichstätt.

Crucifixes. Altar crucifixes and processional crosses (which are decorated on both sides) generally follow, somewhat tardily, the stylistic development of sculpture. The Gothic type of cross, which had arms terminating in trefoils or quatrefoils enclosing symbols of the evangelists or half-figures of saints, persisted into the sixteenth century. Italy is particularly rich in silver crosses, some of which were designed by great artists like Antonio Pollaiuolo, who was responsible for the magnificent altar cross in the Museo dell' Opera del Duomo at Florence. A simpler type, introduced at the Renaissance, has generally persisted ever since.

Cruet frame. First examples date from Queen Anne. Made with open rings and central or side handle to hold sets of casters with or without glass oil and vinegar bottles. Later form oblong or boat-shaped, containing silver-mounted glass bottles, casters, and mustard-pot (*see also* Oil and Vinegar frame, and Soy frame).

Cruets. The vessels containing the wine and water for use at the Eucharist. Sometimes wholly silver, they are frequently of glass with silver mounts, and follow the patterns prevalent in domestic plate. A fourteenth-century Burgundian cruet in the British Museum is quite plain except for the animal head at its spout. There is a curious pair of fifteenth-century workmanship in the Victoria and Albert Museum – one labelled A for *acqua*, the other V for *vinum*.

C-scroll. A term applied usually to the

FIG. 22. Two-handled cups, 1701 and 1720

shape of a handle in form like the letter C; also called "single scroll".

Cupping-bowl. Flat, shallow, circular

bowl with one flat, pierced, and shaped handle. Believed to have been used for cupping or bleeding, but more probably a form of individual porringer, by which name they are always called in America and in England. The covers of early skillets or saucepans are of the same basic form.

FIG. 23. Pierced cupping bowl handle, 1698

Cups. Silver and gold cups have been made from very early times until the present day, but after the mid-eighteenth century their popularity as drinking-vessels declined, and they have since been used mainly for presentation. So great was the diversity of cups in the sixteenth and seventeenth centuries, that no account of all the patterns made can be attempted here, but a list of the principal types would include the following.

ANIMAL CUPS. Covered cups fashioned like animals – foxes, hounds, deer, unicorns, dragons, elephants, etc. – were made in Germany between the sixteenth and eighteenth centuries, being at the zenith of their popularity from about 1575 to about 1650. Some, made principally at Augsburg, were in the form of groups, St George and the Dragon or Diana riding a Centaur, and a few were fitted with clockwork mechanism so that they could be made to run across a table (Plate 489A).

BIRD CUPS. In the form of owls, larks, griffins, pelicans, etc., enjoyed the same popularity as animal cups, but seem to have been more widely made. A Portuguese owl-cup of the seventeenth century is in the collection of Comandante Ernesto de Vilhena, and at Clare College, Cambridge, there is a falcon cup made at Antwerp in about 1555.

CAUDLE-CUPS. Two-handled cups with or without cover, generally of gourd-shape; used for caudle, a thin gruel mixed with spiced

wine or ale; also used for other drinks; frequently left to churches, they became communion cups. An alternative name for porringer.

CHOCOLATE CUPS. Boston's famed Peter Faneuil left "6 Lignum Vitae chocolate cups lin'd with Silver" in 1743, but they are unknown today.

CHURCH CUPS. A designation in bequests for standing cups and beakers diverted from domestic to ecclesiastical use.

COCONUT CUPS appear to have been made as early as the thirteenth century, but the oldest survivors are those made in Germany in the sixteenth century. Coconuts, polished and occasionally carved, were enclosed in delicate silver mounts and set upon stems (Fig. 24). They appear to have been popular in Holland in the sixteenth century, and to have been introduced into Russia in the seventeenth, shortly before they went out of fashion in western Europe. In Scotland they occur from sixteenth to eighteenth centuries. Nuts never carved as on Continent, and mounts of simplest, with vandyked edges and usually only small amount of engraved pattern, if any. Seem to have attracted provincial makers especially; some of the finest are Dundee

FIG. 24

products (Bute Collection) of early seventeenth century. Mounts are in most cases crude.

COLUMBINE CUPS were often, but not invariably, trial pieces made by candidates for admission to the goldsmiths' guilds of Germany. Their complicated form (Plate 488B) tested the skill of the young craftsman without trying his ingenuity. Nuremberg was probably the first town to define the form in the sixteenth century.

COMMUNION CUPS. The Protestant equivalent of the chalice (q.v.). Introduced under Edward VI and continued as basic form till the end of the eighteenth century. Deep, beaker-shaped bowl, spool-shaped stem, with compressed central knop and circular foot. The accompanying paten usually fits the lip to form a cover (*see also* Paten).

CRYSTAL AND HARD-STONE CUPS were mounted in silver and gold from the end of the fifteenth century. In the sixteenth century Prague and Vienna were notable centres for this work, which was also practised in Germany and Italy. Rock-crystal was much favoured as it was believed to act as a poison detector, but all manner of precious and semi-precious stones – emerald, agate, onyx, chalcedony, jasper, etc. – were also used. The precious nature of the material which could not be wasted in making regularly shaped vessels determined some of the most bizarre patterns and tested the invention of the craftsmen.

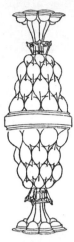

FIG. 25

DOUBLE CUPS are intimately identified with Germany, and became increasingly popular there from the end of the fifteenth century. Formed out of a cup of normal pattern with a cover that could be used as a second one, usually a smaller cup intended for the mistress of the house (Fig. 22), they were occasionally shaped like double mazers. Hans Petzolt, a conspicuous Nuremberg silversmith of the sixteenth century, made several double cups. Such vessels are rarely found to date from after the middle of the seventeenth century.

FEEDING-CUP. Small, plain, saucepanlike cup with one or two handles and curved or straight spout designed for child or invalid feeding. Found from mid-seventeenth century onwards.

FONT-SHAPED CUPS. A form of low, circular wine-cup on spreading foot, with or without cover, occurring in the first half of the sixteenth century. Extremely rare.

GLOBE CUPS, in the form of terrestrial globes, usually supported by a human figure, were made in France, Germany, and Switzerland in the sixteenth and seventeenth centuries. Abraham Gessner of Zurich appears

to have specialized in making these vessels, some of which were as much as 20 inches high (Fig. 26).

FIG. 26

GOURD-SHAPED CUPS were made in Germany in the late sixteenth century, inspired by the design of Brossamer and Solis. They frequently stand on twisted tree stems.

GRACE CUP. *See* Wine-cup.

NAUTILUS SHELLS, elaborately mounted as cups in gold or silver, were very popular in Germany some hundred years after 1550. An unusual example of 1580, in the British Museum, is mounted on a foot fashioned like the claw of a bird, and has a shell which was engraved in China. They were introduced into Holland in the sixteenth century. The greatest ingenuity was used in mounting the shells, which were sometimes made to resemble birds and beasts. It must be assumed that these vessels were intended for display rather than use. On occasions, nautilus shells were also made into flasks or cups (Plate 489D).

OSTRICH EGGS, sometimes supposed to be

the eggs of griffins or phoenixes, were often mounted as cups (and occasionally made into flasks) in the later Middle Ages. Most surviving specimens are German and date from the sixteenth or early seventeenth centuries. A notable example is mounted as an ostrich, the egg serving as the body.

PINEAPPLE CUPS, with covered bowls, in the shape of stylized pineapples, were distinctive products of Germany (called *ananaspokal*), where they were made in the seventeenth century. Some stand as much as 30 inches in height (Fig. 27).

SPOUT-CUP. *See* Feeding-cup.

STANDING CUPS. Large ceremonial or decorative cups on high stems and feet found in every variety of style and decoration down to the end of the seventeenth century, after which they were replaced by the two-handled cup on low foot without stem. Examples without covers have probably lost them in the past.

FIG. 27

FIG. 28. Cup and cover, 1590

STEEPLE CUPS. The popular term for a particular form of standing cup surmounted by an obelisk or pyramid finial found in the reign of James I and early years of Charles I.

STIRRUP-CUP. Handleless and footless drinking-cup in the form of a fox's or greyhound's

mask, based on the classical rhyton and introduced about 1770 for sporting prizes and commemorative trophies.

THISTLE CUPS. An exclusively Scottish type, rather like tea-cup, with single S-shaped handle and everted lip. Principal decoration is calyx-like arrangement of *appliqué* lobes rising from foot towards waist, and waist is also encircled by fillet. Handle sometimes enhanced with beaded ornament. Precise use obscure, but cups seem to have been made

FIG. 29. "Thistle" type cup, Edinburgh, 1696. Maker, Alexander Forbes

in some numbers in Edinburgh (also Canongate), Glasgow, Aberdeen, and Inverness. A miniature version also occurs. Range in time short: from about 1690 to beginning of eighteenth century (Fig. 29).

TWO-HANDLED CUPS. Introduced in the late seventeenth century, developing from porringer form and gradually replacing the earlier standing cup on high stem (*q.v.*). Normally found with cover. Of great variety of size and decoration. Used for "loving cup" ceremonies in corporate bodies, race prizes, and display generally.

TUMBLER CUP. Small, plain drinking-bowl with rounded base and straight sides. Extant from mid-seventeenth century onwards.

WAGER CUP. *See* Jungfrauenbecher.

WINDMILL WAGER CUPS were shaped like model windmills so that when they were inverted the body of the mill acted as the bowl. They were used for wagers on festive occasions, the drinker having to consume the contents before the sails had stopped revolving (Plate 489c). (*See also* Jungfrauenbecher.)

WINE-CUP. Small, individual goblet on high stem, surviving from the late sixteenth to seventeenth centuries. Also known as Grace Cup. Very small examples of mid-seventeenth century have no stem but a small, trumpet-shaped foot (*see also* Goblet). A wine-cup of tumbler form was popular in New York.

MISCELLANEOUS. Among many other types of cup the following may be mentioned. They were occasionally made in the form of human heads, one, made by Albrecht Biller of Augs-burg between 1696 and 1700, being that of a hideous witch. Cups fashioned like peasants carrying barrels, which act as the bowls, are not uncommon. Presentation cups given to distinguished Dutch sailors in the seventeenth century were often enamelled with sea-fights. (For other drinking-vessels see: Beakers, Brandy-bowls, Bratina, Chalices, Charka, Goblets, *Haufenbecher*, Horns, *Jungfrauen-becher*, Mazer, *Prunkgefass*, *Riesenpokal*, Tan-kards, Tazza, and Wine-tasters.)

Cut-cardwork. Flat sheet metal cut into foliage and strap outline and soldered to the main surface to produce relief decoration. Of French origin, introduced in late seventeenth century and later built up in various planes to greater relief.

Cypher. Double monogram, especially popular on New York tankards. Sympson's *Book of Cyphers*, published in London about 1726, was widely used in America.

Date letter. The specific mark of a letter of the alphabet used at the various Assay Offices to distinguish the year of hall-marking. There are no date letters on American silver.

Deacon. In Scotland the chief office-bearer of the craft or guild. In Edinburgh the dea-con's mark appeared as proof of test among the hall-marks, normally in third place, from the sixteenth century down to the institution of the date-stamp in 1681–2, when the assay-master's punch replaced the deacon's.

Decanter stand. *See* Wine-coaster.

Dessert basket. Oval or circular in form, usually pierced. Met with in sets of various sizes and numbers, the larger often with separate plinth. Introduced in the late eight-eenth century. Usually gilt.

Dessert service. Gilt set of plates, dishes, and baskets, following the pattern of the con-temporary white dinner service. Not common before the late eighteenth century.

Dessert table service. Set of gilt dessert spoons, knives, and forks, either of similar styles to the white table services (*q.v.*), or also found in a number of ornamental vine, foliage, and bacchanalian patterns.

Dinner service. The total assemblage of everything required for the banquet table. Plates, dishes (oval and circular), soup and sauce tureens, entrée dishes, vegetable dishes, and many other items are all found made *en suite* and of the same date.

Dish. Vast dishes, intended for display rather than use, were a speciality of Augsburg in the seventeenth century (of the nineteen gigantic dishes in the Kremlin, fourteen are of Augsburg manufacture). A fine early seven-teenth-century Italian example, embossed with the departure of Christopher Columbus, is in the collection of the Marchese Spinola at Genoa. Circular dishes embossed in the centre with flowers or birds, frequently peacocks, were popular in Portugal in the second half of the seventeenth century. A large dish de-corated with dolphins by Christopher van Vianen, a member of the famous family of Dutch seventeenth-century silversmiths, is in the Victoria and Albert Museum (Plate 486A). In the United States Revere made "4 silver dishes" in 1796 for presentation to the First Church in Boston in the form of the six given in 1764 by Thomas Hancock to the Brattle Street Church. These in turn are similar to the wholly domestic ones of Winslow's and Coney's make, which have been erroneously called "alms dishes". The royal gifts to estab-lished churches included a "receiver" in plate form. "Issue plates" and "trencher plates" of silver were recorded in private possession in the 1690s. *See* Entrée, Meat, Second-course, Soufflé, Toasted cheese, Vegetable, and Venison Dish.

Dish cross. Spirit-lamp stand with two adjustable arms revolving around the lamp with sliding feet. The lamp sometimes omitted and replaced by a pierced plate for use with separate lamp below. Found from about 1750 to 1850s.

Dish ring. Also called "Potato ring". Of Irish origin. Circular dish or bowl stand with straight or incurved sides usually pierced and chased with pastoral or classical motifs. Found from about 1740 onwards, many dating from about 1770. Modern copies should be carefully distinguished.

Dish stand. Importation of "ex-s with slides and lamps for dish stands" and "table crosses" with and without lamps were advertised in the second half of the eighteenth century, and a few, also known as dish crosses, with local maker's marks are known.

Dish-strainer. *See* Mazarine.

Dolphin. A thumb-piece design, generally on Boston tankards, showing addorsed dolphins with a mask.

Domed. Spheroid form of cover, used on tankards, teapots, coffee-pots beginning in the 1690s.

Double-scroll. A sinuous line of S-shape, or composed of reverse curves, employed especially in design of handles.

Doune. Small town on Highland border where making of steel flourished in seventeenth and eighteenth centuries. Pistols were skilfully inlaid with silver, occasionally with gold.

Douters. Scissor-like implements with flat, elliptical "blades" for extinguishing candles. Not to be confused with snuffers, which have a cutting edge. Douters are comparatively rare and not always recognized as such (*see* Snuffers).

Dram cup. A small, two-handled, shallow bowl, similar to a wine taster, seldom made after the second decade of the eighteenth century.

Drawing benches. Used in forming applied mouldings and strap handles.

Dredger. Small, cylindrical pepper-pot with side scroll handle of early eighteenth century date. Also called "Kitchen pepper".

Dutch silver marks. Dutch miniature silver was struck with the town mark, maker's mark, date and a letter, such as on the three following beakers: Amsterdam, ewer in a shaped shield, 1622; The Hague, wing, 1666; Dordrecht, bunch of grapes, 1653. Of more than two hundred eighteenth-century specimens examined more than 90 per cent bore the town mark of Amsterdam, the Hague, or Leeuwarden: others displayed marks of Utrecht, Haarlem, and Rotterdam.

Silversmiths whose miniature ware has been noted included: *Amsterdam:* sugar bowl by Samuel Strik, 1793; bowls, Lucas Claterbos, 1756 and 1758; set of four table candlesticks, Jan Pondt, 1733; table bell, Hendrik Swiering, 1738; candlestick, Jan Buysen, 1804; teapot of inverted pear shape, Hendrik Griste, 1776; brazier on three feet, J. P. Dell, 1792; two-handled tray, Roelof Helwig, 1780; pear-shaped coffee-pot, H. Nieuwenhuyse, 1762; cruet frame with casters, Reynier Brandt, 1753; oval tray with handles, D. W. Rethmeijer, 1806; caster and mustard pot, W. Warneke, 1771. *The Hague:* cruet frame and casters, Nicholas Radijas, 1764; pear-shaped caster, Cornelis de Haan, 1766; bowl, Reynier de Haan, 1738; vase-shaped casters, C. van der Toorn, 1750; oval tea-caddy, J. van de Toorn, 1803; salver, Godert van Ysseldijk, 1753; kettle and stand, F. M. Simons, 1791; pair candlesticks, Jacques Tuiller, 1710. *Leeuwarden:* pair of sauce boats, W. Dominicus, 1767.

Dutch miniature silver imported during the eighteenth century bore the marks of origin, but was also on occasion struck with an English silversmith's mark, showing that Dutch silver was retailed by English makers. Since 1867 all imported plate of sterling or Britannia standard has been struck with a capital F, and from 1904 with an assay office mark, fineness mark and date letter. The plate laws are strictly enforced in Holland, where there is no legal obligation for the maker's mark to be present.

Dutch toys. These were sold side by side with English productions and for comparable work were slightly less expensive. A collection of Dutch miniature silver might include plain, engraved, or embossed work: pear-shaped coffee-pots, money boxes, cups and saucers, sweetmeat baskets, milk cans, braziers, flatirons, frying pans, mortars, mustard pots, chairs, settees, bookcases, toilet mirrors, vases and covers, and many other pieces.

Écuelle. A shallow, two-handled, covered dish peculiar to France, where it was a favourite piece of plate in the Régence and rococo periods. Late seventeenth-century écuelles usually had flat covers with a handle on top, but in the eighteenth century the covers were usually domed and surmounted by finials (Fig. 30). A fine silver-gilt example of 1672 is in the Victoria and Albert Museum. Some were provided with a dish, knife, spoon, and fork enclosed in a leather case for travelling.

FIG. 30

In spite of the strong influence exerted by French silversmiths, écuelles were rarely made in other countries, though a few German and Italian (Piedmont) examples are known.

Edgings. *See* Mounts.

Egg and dart. A sixteenth-century border ornament composed of alternating ovolos (*q.v.*) and arrowheads.

Egg and tongue. A similar border ornament of alternating ovolos and pointed mouldings. Usually stamped from a die, but in important pieces may be chased by hand.

Egg-frame. Open-work frame holding two and more eggcups with spoons and, occasionally, a salt-cellar above. Introduced *c.* 1785.

Embossing. A general term to describe reliefwork on metal. Strictly applicable only to hammered work (*repoussé*), but extended to cover any technical method resulting in relief.

English plate. A term used by Sheffield platers to distinguish ware in which the silver was plated on copper from that plated on white alloy such as German silver.

Engraving. Flat line decoration incised on the surface with a cutting tool. The normal method of rendering inscriptions and armorials. Also used at all periods for every variety of ornament. Sometimes combined with "Flat chasing" (*q.v.*) (*see* Bright-cut engraving).

It was customary for Sheffield plate to be engraved with the coat-of-arms or crest of its owner the more nearly to complete its semblance to silver plate. From about 1815 tea and coffee services, kettles, trays and waiters,

and other articles of the tea equipage might be engraved all over with complicated patterns surrounding the heraldic device. To prevent the copper from showing when the silver was cut with a graving tool the whole surface was coated more thickly than usual.

Where only coats-of-arms and the like were to be engraved it was at first customary to cut a suitable area of metal clean out of the article and insert a thickly silvered section of metal. The scarcely perceptible join was masked by wavy borders, but examination of the reverse of a coat-of-arms will show if insertion has been effected.

This method was discarded between 1810 and 1815 in favour of "sweating-on" or "rubbing-in" a circle or shield of four-gauge pure silver of suitable size. The plate to receive the extra silver was heated over a clear charcoal fire, then placed in position and rubbed vigorously with a steel tool until it adhered to the plated copper. After burnishing it was impossible to detect the join except by warming the piece, when a difference in the colour of the silver is noted, the sweated-on piece then showing lighter in hue than the surrounding metal. A small dot was always made in the centre of such shields so that the engraver was sure of his mark.

Entrée dish. A covered dish, early examples usually circular or polygonal. Later chiefly of oblong form or occasionally oval. The covers may have detachable handles, enabling their use as separate dishes. Later examples have silver or, more commonly, plated heater stands *en suite*.

Épergne. Table centrepiece of elaborate design incorporating numerous dishes for fruit, pickles, or sweetmeats. Early examples also fitted with candle-branches, casters, and other accessories. Rococo models festooned with flowers, swags, pierced and boat-shaped forms, Chinese pagodas, and Classical temples are all recognized examples (*see also* Centrepiece and Dessert basket).

Etching. Surface decoration bitten-in with acid as in the print process of the same name. Rare in English silver, but occasionally found in the sixteenth century.

Étui. Small case usually of tapering oval form fitted with scissors, bodkin, snuff-spoon, etc., for ladies' use. Silver examples chiefly found first half of eighteenth century and in the mid-nineteenth century.

Ewers. Large jugs to carry water for the ablutions at meal-times were essential items of plate in the later Middle Ages and the sixteenth century; they were often made of silver and intricately wrought. The most popular type was vase shaped with a grotesque handle, and German examples frequently had disproportionately narrow necks (Fig. 31). A fine German ewer of 1559 in the British Museum has a low relief of the Rape of Helen on its body and a handle fashioned like a satyr leaning backwards. They were usually matched with basins, many of which have since disappeared. Spanish ewers of the late sixteenth and early seventeenth centuries tended to be rather small and to stand on short feet. Like cups and basins, they were frequently made in rock crystal or hard stone. Later French and Spanish examples were helmet shaped, but their popularity declined as a result of the change in eating habits occasioned by the introduction of the fork.

FIG. 31

Feather edge. Decoration of edge of spoon-handle with chased, slanting lines.

Filigree work (*filigrana*). Genoa was the most renowned centre for the production of filigree work in eighteenth-century Italy. A large variety of such objects were produced here, from tall Chinese-shaped vases (Plate 498c) to tiny toys and ornaments.

Finial. The small cast ornament at the top of a cover; sometimes acorn-shaped in early eighteenth century; flame-shape in rococo period, urn-shape in classic period. Pineapple used also in rococo period, and pine-cone, beginning *c.* 1782.

Firedog. *See* Andiron.

Fireplace furniture. In English minia-

ture silver dates from the late seventeenth century, when fireplace sets composed of fire-basket and fireback, firedogs, fender, tongs, shovel, and poker were made. A number of these by Middleton still remain, in the Westbrooke Baby House and various museums. A collection of eighteenth-century specimens displays chronologically their changes of form and dimensions.

Fish-slice. Introduced in mid-eighteenth century. Early examples finely pierced and engraved in fish and floral patterns. Later

FIG. 32

and soberer models conform to standard table service patterns and have little decoration. Also found with ivory or wood handles. Accompanying fish-fork made from *c.* 1800.

Flagon. Large vessel for serving wine or other liquors. Pear-shaped and cylindrical bodies occur contemporaneously at most periods and are always closely related in form

FIG. 33. Flagon, 1710

and decoration to tankards. Except for ecclesiastical use, the flagon is rare after the mid-eighteenth century.

Flagons. Were usually much like those made in England, but fantastic shapes were also used; in about 1610 Melchior Gelb of Augsburg made one in the form of a vine-covered head of Silenus.

Flat chasing. Surface decoration in low

relief produced by hammering with small blunt tools. Popular in the early eighteenth century combined with engraving for borders to salvers and other pieces. Widely used in the United States, 1750–85.

Flute. A concave channel originating in classical columns, used either as detached decorative element or in close repeated formation as a border or body ornament. Found extensively on bodies of cups, tankards, and other vessels in late seventeenth century alternating with gadroons (q.v.) to form corrugated surface.

Forks. In the later Middle Ages small forks were made in most countries, but they do not appear to have been used for eating meat; it is significant that they were frequently made to match spoons, never knives. Some late fifteenth-century examples are of great delicacy, like that of Flemish workmanship with a rock-crystal handle in the Victoria and Albert Museum. Folding forks were frequently made in conjunction with spoons (q.v.). The use of forks for eating meat seems to have originated in Italy in the sixteenth century, and to have spread through the rest of Europe in the course of the next hundred years. A fine sixteenth-century set, consisting of a fork, knife, and spoon, each with a handle in the form of a human figure, attributed to Antonio Gentili, is in the Metropolitan Museum, New York (Plate 487B). The earliest forks were two-pronged, the three-pronged type being introduced in the early eighteenth century. In the eighteenth century the handles of forks, as of spoons and knives, varied slightly with the changes in taste. No English silver forks have survived before the early seventeenth century. Early examples two-pronged, followed by three-pronged form till about 1750 and, occasionally, later. After this four prongs are standard. Stems follow spoon models throughout. Sets of twelve or more survive from Charles II onwards, but are very rare before the eighteenth century.

Forks are extremely rare in American silver, but mentioned in old inventories.

Fountains. Made to stand in the centre of a table and dispense scented water or wine in the course of a meal, enjoyed some popularity in the richest households of the sixteenth century; but few have survived. In the British Museum there is a German example, dating from about 1580, which is formed out of a Seychelle nut with silver-gilt mounts.

Frames (*cornici*). The frames of small pictures were occasionally made wholly or partly of silver in the seventeenth and eighteenth centuries. More familiar are the large *cartagloria* frames designed to stand on altars and hold cards inscribed with prayers. They are often richly embossed with rococo scroll work (Plate 494C). Many examples in private collections have been transformed into looking glasses.

Freedom box. Small circular or oblong box, usually gilt, when not gold, presented with script conferring the freedom of a town. Particularly popular in Ireland late eighteenth to early nineteenth centuries. In Scotland, on rare occasions at least, a much larger, silver box seems to have been made to contain the parchment.

Frosting. A rough or mat white surface produced by acid fuming or scratch brushing. Not found before the early nineteenth century, principally used on ornamental and figure work on centre-pieces.

Furniture. Silver furniture in the form of sheet metal overlaid on wood survives from the Restoration period, and may have been made earlier. Examples are rare and confined to the Royal Collection and one or two famous houses: Ham, Knole, Boughton. George Middleton made miniature chairs and daybeds of the Charles II type during the 1680s, the "woodwork" in flat plate silhouettes and chased to resemble turned uprights and stretchers, the seat and back panel pierced to look like woven cane. Gate-leg tables were made by Isaac Malyn and other early eighteenth-century toy makers. Tripod tables by Augustine Courtauld are known with stem and feet cast, the rim of the round top chased to resemble a pie-crust edge. Later chairs in the style of Hepplewhite have cast legs and backs.

Gadroon (French: *Godron*). A border ornament either hammered or cast composed of radiating lobes of curved or straight form. Principally used on rims and feet of cups and other vessels or to borders of plates and dishes from late seventeenth century onwards.

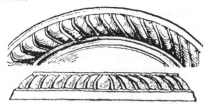

FIG. 34. Gadrooning: (*a*) Salver border, 1694; (*b*) candlestick base, 1762

Geometric. Pierced handle of early eighteenth-century porringer; in Boston and Philadelphia, crescent, heart, and tulip; in New York, cross, heart, and diamond.

German silver. Introduced to the plating trade by Samuel Roberts, who was granted a patent in 1830 by which "a layer of German silver or other white or light-coloured metal was introduced between the silver and copper". A coating of silver could thus be applied with the knowledge that if it were thin the defect would be far less perceptible than if applied direct to the copper. This method was superseded in 1836 by Anthony Merry's patent by which the copper was omitted, plating the silver direct to a foundation metal of German silver. Stronger and more durable than copper, German silver consisted of nickel, copper, and zinc in varying proportions. Workers in this medium described themselves as "platers on white metal".

Gilding. *See* Silver-gilt.

Goblets. Silver goblets, closely imitating

FIG. 35

German glasses with heavy bases and bulbous tops, were popular in Scandinavia in the late sixteenth and early seventeenth centuries. Two Swedish examples in the British Museum have bosses typical of glass decoration (Fig. 35). Imitations of glass in silver do not appear to have been usual after the middle of the seventeenth century.

Goldwork. Rare, but appears in New York. Garvan Collection at Yale has eight gold teaspoons and strainer by Soumain, child's spoon with bells by Vanderspiegel, rattle by Fueter, necklace by Van Dyck, freedom box by Samuel Johnson; all of New York.

Golf-clubs. Practice of reproducing full-sized golf-clubs in silver, as trophies, appears to date from about the middle of the eighteenth century. Several of such clubs are still preserved, notably those of the Edinburgh Burgess Golfing Society and of the Royal and Ancient Club at St Andrews (Plate 481B). Captains or tournament-winners attached silver balls to the shafts, engraved with name. Clubs and balls were quite well modelled, even to reproduction of spiral grip; but unfortunately hall-marks and makers' punches have not been added, so that nothing is known of where they were made.

Granulated band. A form of decoration, generally on beakers, derived from Scandinavian and German work.

Graver. Tool used to engrave silver with initials, coats-of-arms, etc., or to sharpen the chased ornament.

Guilloche. A border moulding composed of interlaced ribbon enclosing foliage rosettes, chiefly used early eighteenth century. Simpler forms occur in sixteenth century.

Hall-mark. Strictly speaking, the distinguishing mark of the Hall or Assay Office at which the piece so marked is assayed, e.g. Leopard's head for London, Crown for Sheffield, etc. Used generally in the plural to denote the whole group of marks employed, viz. Hall, maker's, standard, date-letter, and, between 1784 and 1890, the monarch's head duty mark.

There are no hall-marks on American silver. In 1918 Maryland established an Assay Office at Baltimore, but other Assay Offices were non-existent, although in Pennsylvania, beginning in 1753, many attempts were made to have the Assembly enact legislation (*see* Pseudo hall-marks).

Hammermen, Incorporations of. These were the craft-guilds to which the goldsmiths in Scotland belonged. They were influential bodies which looked after the interests of all metal-workers, among them blacksmiths, cutlers, pewterers, and armourers. Like the great guilds elsewhere, they were highly organized, with strict control over the conduct of their members and apprentices. Religion played an important part in their activities, and they had their own altars or chapels in the Middle Ages, under the patronage of St Eloi. Strict religious control continued after the Reformation.

Hammers. Coney's inventory in 1722 contained "112 Hammers 'for Raising, Pibling, Swolling, Hollowing, Creasing, Planishing &c." as well as several "Two-hand hammers" to give an idea of the painstaking care in hand-wrought silver.

Hanap. The medieval name for "standing-cup" (*q.v.*).

Handles, Bail. A half-hoop or semicircle hinged on a pair of pivots or looped ears on hollow-ware, such as a basket or cream-pail.

Fig. 36. Bail-handle

Hash-dish. Circular dish with straight sides, close-fitting cover, and loop or dropring handles. Similar to and probably used also as vegetable dish. Often found with open-frame stand and spirit-lamp.

Haufenbecher. Alternatively called a *Setzbecher*: literally a piling cup. Beakers that could be fitted into one another, in pairs and in sets of six or twelve, popularized by the designs of Virgil Solis, were made in Germany in the late sixteenth century, but appear to have gone out of fashion before 1650. Each beaker has a band of moulded decoration around its rim, like a modern picnic cup. They were much used for hunting parties.

Hinges, Book. Found on lids of coffee-pots, jugs, and so on. They have a round back resembling a book spine, and the pin-joints, where the base metal is left bare, are con-

cealed beneath slightly ornamental silver caps.

Holy-water bucket. The receptacle for the holy water sprinkled in the *asperges* at the beginning of the Mass. Early examples are normally straight sided, polygonal or cylindrical, and occasionally waisted; the bombé-vase shape came into fashion in the seventeenth century. Handles were occasionally terminated with dragon heads. A good Spanish example of about 1500 is in the Victoria and Albert Museum.

Holy-water stoups (*acquasantiere*). These were made for the house as well as the church. Some are in the form of a large framed relief of the Madonna and Child or other sacred subject, with a small shell-shaped container.

Honey-pot. Jar formed as skep beehive with detachable cover and circular dish-stand. Made by Paul Storr and others from about 1795 into the nineteenth century.

Hooped cans. The shape is copied from a wooden type, made on the principle of a barrel and with a broad, bulbous body, a narrow cylindrical neck, a thin, straight spout, and a lid. The wooden can was probably in its turn

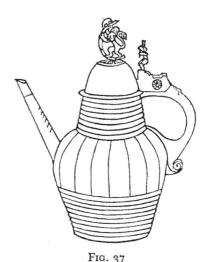

FIG. 37

a copy of a metal form. In wood it can be traced back to the seventeenth century. An early eighteenth-century example, with silver mounts, is in the Kunstindustrimuseum in Oslo, but the plain wooden types must at that time have been used mainly in the country.

Silver copies are known from Copenhagen as well as from Norway. Both the Danish and the Norwegian examples have a moulded lion on a hallberd as handle to the lid. The presence of this symbol from the Norwegian coat-of-arms seems to indicate that the type was meant to be romantically "Norwegian". The shape was also copied in Danish pewter and faïence and in Norwegian pewter, faïence, and glass. The silver examples are gilt or partly gilt, and sometimes they were made in pairs and accompanied by beakers, shaped like small barrels. They are comparatively rare (Fig. 37).

Horns. In the *De Bello Gallico*, Caesar observed that the Germans drank from horns tipped with silver, and this practice persisted in Scandinavia, and less extensively in Germany, until the close of the Middle Ages. Originally the normal drinking-vessels, they acquired in time an almost ritualistic significance, were carried into the hall for the assembled guests by girls, and used for mead and wine rather than ale. The majority do not seem to have been mounted in silver – eighteen out of the twenty-four horns in the Copenhagen Museum have mounts in copper-gilt. Normally the mounts are simple, but a Norwegian example of 1300 (in the Copenhagen Museum) is decorated with Gothic architectural features, and a Danish one in the British Museum has been made to resemble a bird, mounted on claw feet, the point of the horn fashioned into a tail (Plate 492C).

Hot-milk jug. Small pear-shaped or polygonal jug and cover similar in form and decoration to the larger contemporary coffee- or chocolate-pot but with beak spout. Also found with egg-shaped body on three feet.

Ice-pail. *See* Wine-cooler.

Incense boat. The vessel in which the incense is carried before it is placed in the censer to burn. Normally it is a fairly simple boat-shaped vessel, and it was occasionally made to match a censer. Many were of base metals or of other materials mounted in silver; a crystal incense boat mounted in silver-gilt is in the Victoria and Albert Museum.

In Italy the Gothic tradition of making these vessels in the form of model ships standing on baluster stems survived until the late seventeenth century. The form of the boat was then swallowed up in baroque scroll-work. In the late eighteenth century a simpler outline became popular.

Inkstand. Early name Standish. A few examples have survived from pre-1650, but not many recorded before 1680. "Treasury" type an oblong casket with two centrally hinged lids. Tray form in prevailing style of period persists throughout eighteenth century. Fittings include inkpot, sand and/or pouncebox, bell, and taperstick in varying combinations. Glass bottles appear about 1765, together with pierced gallery sides. About 1790 small globe-shaped form introduced. Mahogany desk models with silver tops appear from 1800 onwards.

Instruments for surgery. Made by silversmiths for the wealthy practitioners who could afford this most hygienic material. "Rasors and Scissors tipt with silver" in the seventeenth century; spatulas and probes, the former perhaps another name for tongue depressors, were common in the eighteenth century, towards the end of which speaking trumpets were made which survive. Spectacle frames were made in gold and silver.

Jewel-boxes. Rectangular, low boxes with hinged lids, usually rather ornate, with chased or moulded decorations, more rarely engraved work. Because of their luxury purpose, the jewel-boxes are always important pieces, richly ornamented and prettily finished. They came into use in Norway during the early eighteenth century, and the majority of the existing examples are in an elegant rococo style (Plate 503A). It has been suggested that the moulded parts may have been imported.

Jewellery. Beads, bracelets, buttons for shirts and cuffs, necklaces, and rings are the most frequently found. In Scotland simple and somewhat crude silver brooches were made in large quantities in the Middle Ages. Usually round or octagonal, with swinging pin. Commonly they have talismanic inscriptions, hailing Christ or the Virgin Mary. Niello decoration sometimes introduced. There is a small group of elaborate brooches mounted with charm-stones, which belongs to the sixteenth century: family heirlooms, and it is unlikely any more will turn up to tempt collectors. Field in which collectors may still hope to find a few good things is that of seventeenth- and eighteenth-century Highland brooches. Larger, usually of brass. Smaller silver brooches, which may have been worn by women, are much more rare. Decoration rather crude, chevrons or zig-zags, occasionally plant or zoomorphic forms, deteriorating in interest with advance of eighteenth century. The silver brooches all seem to be betrothal tokens, as they carry two sets of initials scratched on. Fairly valuable. Type of brooch most easily acquired is Luckenbooth, heart or double-heart shaped little ornament, sometimes set with garnets, related to Scandinavian type. These are also betrothal pieces. Made down to nineteenth century as far north as Inverness. (*See also* "Mary" brooches.)

Jug. Large jugs, probably used for numerous purposes and variously called beer, wine, claret jugs, or ewers, occur from the early eighteenth century onwards. Usually with pear-shaped bodies plain or chased, circular feet, and finely moulded scroll handles (*see also* Cream, Hot-milk and Water, and Tigerware).

Jungfrauenbecher. A wager-cup in the form of a girl with a wide-spreading skirt

holding a bowl above her head (Fig. 38). The bowl is pivoted so that when the figure is inverted the skirt forms an upper cup and the bowl a lower one. Such vessels were used specially at wedding feasts, when the groom was expected to drink the contents of the larger cup without spilling any of the contents of the smaller, which he passed to his bride. They first appeared in Germany in about 1575,

FIG. 38

and their fashion continued throughout the seventeenth century, when many were made at Nuremberg. A simpler form, apparently popular in Holland, replaced the head and

shoulders of the girl with a mesh ball, which occasionally contained a die.

Kettles and urns. The earliest vessels made for heating water at the tea-table are the kettles with a handle and a spout, fitted over a small spirit lamp. A remarkably early example dates from *c.* 1700 and appears strongly influenced by the English Queen Anne style (Plate 482c). Some very fine kettles of the same basic shape have twisted ribs in mature rococo. Another type from the same period (about the middle of the eighteenth century) stands on three tall feet and has a pear-shaped body with twisted ribs and a tap. With neo-classicism real urns are introduced. They stand firmly on a base and have internal heating and a tap. Some examples are in the rich and exuberant Louis XVI style.

Keyhole. The name given to the pierced handle of a porringer which has a central pierced design similar to a keyhole, surrounded by interlacing scrolls; introduced first half of eighteenth century and continued in more delicate form to about 1810.

Knife. Silver-handled knives occur at all periods from late seventeenth century onwards, and single rare specimens from earlier dates. Earliest form found in sets has tapering round or polygonal handle about 1690, followed by the pistol handle, its form becoming more decorated in mid-eighteenth century. Later handles of thin stamped sheet metal filled with resin, in many designs, finally about 1800, being made *en suite* with main table service. In Italy knives of the Renaissance period often had silver handles cast in the shape of human figures.

Knife-rests. Were of two types and sold by the dozen: (*a*) cross-ends joined from their centres by a short rod: in 1797, of Sheffield plate, priced 20s a dozen and with ball centres 24s a dozen; (*b*) solid or pierced triangular ends joined from each angle by short rods.

Knope. Word used in medieval period to denote finials to cups or spoons. Modern use refers to flattened spherical or polygonal bulbs at centres of stems in Communion cups and candlesticks.

Knurling. Show ridges or bead tooled on borders and handles from early in the eighteenth century.

Kovsh. A boat-shaped vessel with a single handle used for ladling out drinks, such as *kvass* and beer. It is peculiar to Russia, where its popularity lasted until the middle of the eighteenth century. There is a silver example in the Victoria and Albert Museum, and a rare gold one was in the Green Vaults at Dresden.

Ladle, cream. Small ladle with circular bowl and curved handle, similar to sugar-sifter and found associated with the latter in sets of sugar and cream vases and baskets.

Ladle, punch. Long-handled ladle for serving punch into glasses. Early examples have oval bowls and tapering silver handles. Eighteenth-century handles usually of horn or whalebone, the bowls sometimes inset with or beaten out of a silver coin. Also known as "Toddy ladle". The first had hollow handles of silver, followed by horn handle. Bowls might be double-lipped from 1725.

Ladle, sauce. Basic form has deep, circular bowl and curved stem. In mid-eighteenth century decorative forms with shell bowls and foliage or bird's-head handles occur. Later examples match table service patterns.

Ladle, soup. Similar in form to sauce-ladles, but with long stem. Early examples have hooked ends, sometimes formed as eagle's head, etc.; later models match table services.

Lamps. Were occasionally made in silver, conforming in design with those made in glass or other materials. A fantastic Genoese example of the eighteenth century, shaped like a pagoda, is in the collection of Dott. F. Fassio at Genoa.

Lanterns (*lanterne*). Large lanterns, for use on ceremonial occasions, were sometimes made partly or (very rarely) wholly of silver. An outstandingly fine example, apparently made for use at the celebration of the Farnese–Spanish marriage of 1714, is in the Costantino Nigro Collection, Genoa.

Larding pine. A pointed instrument, angular in section, seemingly dating from the late eighteenth century.

Lemon-squeezer. A hinged instrument with cuplike depressions to contain the fruit, leverage being supplied by wood handles. Early nineteenth century.

Limmel. The early form of *lemail*, or scrapings or filings of metal.

Lion passant. The lion walking with dexter paw raised appears in relief on seventeenth-century tankard handles by New York makers. This is not an English style and it is likely that it comes from a Continental source.

Luckenbooths. Wooden booths once situated in the High Street of Edinburgh, near St Giles' Church. Many of city's goldsmiths had shops here, though booths were of small size. Heart brooches associated with name, since no doubt sold here.

Mace. Civic, university, or State emblem of authority derived from medieval war weapon. Usually surmounted by royal arms and crown. Examples date from fifteenth century onwards.

Maker's mark. The distinguishing mark of the individual goldsmith, device or initials struck on every piece of plate from his workshop. First enforced in London in 1363. In the United States marks were not required, but they were usually used. The early marks are composed of the first letters of the maker's given name and surname, generally in a shaped shield, and frequently with some device, such as a fleur-de-lys. In the eighteenth century the full name or the surname and initial were used.

At least fifty London silversmiths' marks have been noted on miniature silver made between 1665 and 1739. These include: *RD* crowned, 1665; *FC* 1669; *G* crowned, 1670; *EM* in monogram, 1677; *CK* under a mitre, 1686; *WP* with a mullet below, 1689; and *IC* over a star, 1691. Later were Edward Jones, 1696; Jonathan Bradley, 1696; Matthew Marden, 1697; John Cole, 1697; William Matthew, 1698; Nathaniel Green, 1698; Matthew Pickering, 1703; Joseph Smith, 1707; Jacob Margas, 1708; James Godwin, 1710; George Smart, 1715; James Morson, 1720; Edward Coven, 1724; John le Sage, 1725.

"Mary" brooches. A double-M brooch usually surmounted by a crown. Scottish betrothal type, early nineteenth century, or later. Thought vainly by many possessors to have been gifts from Mary Queen of Scots to her Four Maries.

Masking spoon. A slender Scottish spoon intended for stirring the tea when "masking" (Scots for infuse).

Matting. A dull, roughened surface produced by repeated punching with a burred tool. Much used in mid-seventeenth century on tankard and cup bodies.

Mazarine. Pierced, flat straining plate for use with fish dishes, supposedly named after Cardinal Mazarin.

Mazer-bowls. Made of spotted maple wood and mounted in silver, silver-gilt, or base metals, appear to have originated in Germany, and were popular throughout northern Europe in the later Middle Ages. Double mazers (Fig. 39) in the form of a large

FIG. 39

one with a single handle surmounted by a smaller were occasionally made, and this pattern was sometimes copied for double cups. Handles were often richly fashioned; a double mazer in the Wallace Collection has a handle shaped like a Gothic chapel. Large standing examples on high feet found in Scotland and a few in England. Rare after the sixteenth century.

Meat-dish. Oval in form. Survivals rare before eighteenth century. Early examples have moulded rims. After 1730 the rims are shaped and gadrooned. From about 1775 beaded rims occur and later shaped mouldings or reed-and-tie patterns. Found in all sizes from about 10 to 30 inches long.

Meat-plate. Also called Dinner-plate.

Made in large sets throughout the eighteenth and early nineteenth centuries. Examples of the seventeenth century occur, but practically only as single specimens. Borders conform to those of meat-dishes.

Midband. A moulded band slightly below centre of a tankard to strengthen as well as ornament; introduced in late sixteenth century. Also used on large two-handled covered cups.

Milk potts of silver seem to have been the same as cream-jugs.

Mirror. *See* Toilet service.

Monstrance (occasionally called an **Ostensory**). The vessel in which the Host is displayed or, less frequently, in which a relic is shown. They vary in size according to whether they were intended primarily to be placed on an altar or carried in procession. Frequently enriched with enamelling and precious stones, they are among the most magnificent pieces of church plate. Gothic monstrances tended to be of architectural design with a cylindrical container for the Host in the centre. The famous Portuguese Belem monstrance (Plate 485c), of the early sixteenth century, shows little figures of the Apostles kneeling in adoration of the Sacrament. In many countries the Gothic pattern persisted until the end of the sixteenth century, when it was superseded by a baroque pattern in which the Host is placed in a cylinder flanked by angels or framed by a flaming sun, the rays of which were often decorated with jewels. A Spanish chalice of about 1600 (in the Victoria and Albert Museum) has a detachable monstrance as a cover; both parts being lavishly decorated with Renaissance motifs. A fine Flemish example of 1670, by Joannes Moermans, is in the Church of Notre Dame at Rupelmonde. One of the most beautiful (Plate 491b) was designed in about 1740 by the great Bavarian architect, Aegid Asam, for the little Church of St Johannes Nepomuk, which he and his brother built in Munich. A diamond-set monstrance made by Johann Baptist Känischbauer von Hohenreid and Mathias Stegner, in 1699, is (or was) in the Church of St Loretto at Prague.

Monteith. Wine-glass cooler with indented rim. Introduced in early 1680s. The rim at first part of the body, made detachable about 1690. The name said to be derived from that of a Scottish adventurer with notched cloak, although it is very rare indeed in Scotland. Edinburgh example of 1719 belongs to Royal Company of Archers, and is hung with gold archery medals.

Morse. A clasp for fastening a cope, occasionally made of gold or silver and decorated with jewels. The most famous was that made by Benvenuto Cellini for Pope Clement VII.

Moulding. Cast or hammered border or body girdle composed of various arrangements of convex and concave members based on architectural models. Also applied to castings from the mould.

Mounts and edging. A basic problem facing the early Sheffield platers was that of concealing the dark reddish streak of copper visible when the silvered plate was sheared. This problem was never satisfactorily solved by Bolsover, and his ranges of productions were drastically limited.

(a) *Single-lapped edge* (1758–1780s). Joseph Hancock introduced the single-lapped edge in 1758. This required a thicker coating of silver to be applied to the copper than had been customary. The edges of the plated copper were cut with a blunt tool so manipulated that the layer of silver was extended sufficiently beyond the edge of the silvered copper to lap over and effectively conceal the raw edge.

(b) *Double-lapped copper mount* (1768–early nineteenth century). This followed as a direct result of George Whateley's patent of 1678, by which he "plated silver upon mettal wire and drew the same into small gauge wires". A thick cylindrical ingot of copper-brass alloy was plated with rolled silver and passed through a series of holes in a draw-plate until reduced to the required gauge: the thicknesses of the copper and silver remained in their original proportions. This wire was then passed between polished steel pressure rollers, thus forming a thin, flat ribbon of plated metal silvered on both surfaces and the edges. This was the immediate forerunner of plating on both sides of the sheet.

This paper-thin ribbon was soldered to the silvered edge of the plate, so that it protruded sufficiently over the edge to permit it to lap over the raw edge and be flat against the underside. So skilfully was lapping carried out that upon the plated surface it was difficult to detect the joins.

(c) *Silver-lapped mount* (1775–1815). This followed the introduction of double-plated copper in the early 1770s. A narrow ribbon of paper-thin silver, which might measure as little as one-sixteenth of an inch wide, was passed through a small round hole in a draw-plate, thus making a fine-bore tube. The seam was then opened throughout its length to the same width as the gauge of the plate upon which it was to be mounted. This was accomplished by fixing into a vice a steel plate of the same gauge as the plated copper. The seam of the tube was inserted into this and opened by drawing the silver along. The resulting U-shaped silver wire was then fitted to the plated edge and soldered into position on both surfaces. These were vigorously burnished until the joins were invisible.

(d) *Solid silver mounts* (c. 1780–c. 1830). These ornaments for fine Sheffield plate were cast and hand-chased by silversmiths. They were hard-soldered into position. These hand-chased mounts are sometimes difficult to distinguish from blurred stamped work finished by chasing.

(e) *Drawn silver wire mounts* (1785–c. 1820). Valentine Rawle in 1785 patented a method by which the joints of articles made from Sheffield plate could be strengthened "by covering the mitres, angles and joints with drawn silver wire, the invention being likewise applicable to wares made round and oval". Silver wires were drawn in a range of decorative cross-sections – flat, half-round hollow U, sharp L, angles, and curves. These were filled with a mixture of lead and tin, and could be easily shaped by the hand to fit the piece they decorated. Before such mounts were applied to edges, silver wire measuring one thirty-second of an inch in thickness was soldered beneath the rim. Rawle licensed his patent to other platers.

(f) *Silver stamped mounts* (from early 1790s). These first appeared on Sheffield plate during the early 1790s, following the introduction of a hard steel capable of making profitable runs on the press when cut in deep, sharp relief. As in drawn silver-wire mounts, the silver was either pure metal or alloyed with brass, but better than sterling. Sterling silver produced finer work both as to colour and durability, but unfortunately wear on the tools was much harder, considerably reducing their useful life. Pure silver mounts were used on common ware as it could be rolled much thinner for stamping without danger of splitting in the tools.

The first mounts to be stamped in silver included bead, thread, and a variety of gadroon patterns. Early in the nineteenth century technical improvements permitted the stamping of mounts composed of festoon and bead, leaf and scroll, laurel leaf, egg and dart, scallop shell and scroll, and others. The under seam was made invisible by vigorous burnishing.

Wide, deeply struck mounts in elaborate rococo designs seldom date earlier than about 1815. Earlier mounts had been struck from silver so thick that the sections could be hard- or silver-soldered into position after filling back hollows with soft solder. From about 1815 thinner silver and soft solder were used.

These mounts were applied to edges in which the copper was already concealed by a silver-lapped mount. The division between the two mounts is unmistakable.

(g) *Improved silver stamped mounts* (from 1824). This method of applying elaborate rococo mounts to Sheffield plate in such a way that the junction between body and mount was rendered invisible, was patented in 1824 by Samuel Roberts of Sheffield, who licensed the process to other platers of repute. After shaping the edge of the ware to be ornamented to follow the indentations of the mounting, drawn silver wire was hard-soldered over the bare copper edge. This was flattened with a hammer until it extended a little beyond the ornamental silver edge. The projecting part of the soldered silver edge was then filed off. Burnishing made the join invisible, even to the inquiring fingernail.

Muffineer. Name for caster (*q.v.*) with low, slightly domed cover. The derivation indicates their use for sprinkling cinnamon on muffins. In the United States a tall caster

with high pierced dome, for sugar and cinnamon, a quite different use of the term from the English. Caster is the more common term for all types and sizes in American silver.

Mug. Small-handled drinking-vessel conforming mainly to tankard shape. A late seventeenth-century form has bellied body and cylindrical neck similar to pottery of the period. Cylindrical forms follow, to be superseded in mid-eighteenth century by bellied bodies and later by hooped barrel forms. Shaped forms return in nineteenth century.

Mustard-pot. Mustard taken dry and mixed on the plate was contained in casters with unpierced covers until well into the eighteenth century. A few vase-shaped pots have survived from time of Queen Anne. After about 1760 pierced or plain cylindrical forms appear, to be followed by oval and later spherical bodies. Glass liners, usually blue, are commonly used.

FIG. 40. Mustard-pot, 1796

Nef. A vessel shaped like a ship and used in the later Middle Ages for the lord's napkin, knife, and spoon. In 1392 a nef on wheels was recorded in the papal collection. In the sixteenth century ornaments, jugs, and cups were made in the same form, notably in Germany and Switzerland. Many were very elaborate and accurate models, richly enamelled and peopled with little figures of sailors. A Swiss example is in the British Museum, and a wheeled nef, made at Nuremberg in about 1620 and probably intended as a jug, is in the Rothschild Collection on show at the Victoria and Albert Museum (Plate 489B). In the eighteenth and nineteenth centuries they were adapted for use in England as wine servers and bottle coasters.

Niello. A black composition composed of silver, copper, lead, and sulphur frequently employed to fill in engraved lines on surface of silver brooches from the Middle Ages to the nineteenth century (Plate 481A).

Night light. A square, oval, or circular tray having a central cylindrical candle-socket enclosed within-in a gallery pierced with a double circuit of crosses towards the lower edge. This was fitted with a glass chimney. By burning a fine wax night light, no snuffing was required. An extinguisher was hooked to the handle, a rod extending from its apex enabled it to be inserted down the chimney without lifting it off.

FIG. 41

Nutmeg grater. Found from the late seventeenth century onwards. Formed as circular, oval, spherical, or cylindrical boxes fitted with a steel grater under the cover or down the side, or in hanging form with curved grater at front.

Oar. Civic emblem of authority in ports over local waters. Admiralty examples also survive.

Oil and vinegar bottle stands. These are usually in the form of small salvers with containers for the bottles and a tall handle to which the stoppers are attached by chains. In Italy mid-eighteenth century examples are often a riot of rococo curves (Plate 495B), but in the neo-classical period a severer type with a central column crowned by an urn came into favour.

Onslow pattern. Design for flatware copied from English design in which the handle is shaped as an Ionic volute.

Ostensory. *See* Monstrance.

Ovolo. A small oval convex moulding chiefly used in repetition as sixteenth-century border ornament. Some use also made of the device in late eighteenth to early nineteenth centuries.

Pannikin. A small silver drinking-vessel.

Pap-boat. Small, shallow, oval bowl with tapering lip at one end for feeding infants.

Surviving examples date from early eighteenth century onwards.

Parcel-gilt. Descriptive of plate decorated by the partial application of gilding (*see also* Silver-gilt).

Paten. Small circular plate for Communion bread. Medieval examples have shaped central depression and flat rim. Elizabethan paten-covers fit the cup and have flat seal foot. Later examples follow this pattern until the entry of the Gothic revival. Small circular footed waiters of *Tazze* should not be confused with ecclesiastical pieces.

Pax. A tablet with a projecting handle behind, used in the Eucharist, when it is kissed by the celebrant, the other priests, and, very occasionally, the communicants. It is usually decorated on the front with a sacred symbol, a scene from the Gospel (usually the Crucifixion), or the lives of the saints, engraved, nielloed, or enamelled. A large silver-gilt Spanish pax of about 1530 in the Victoria and Albert Museum has a low relief of St Idelfonso receiving the chasuble from the Virgin.

Peace medal. Late eighteenth-century medals were engraved for presentation to Indian chiefs on occasion of ceremonial visits to the national capital, then in Philadelphia. They are dated between 1792 and 1795, and were the work of Joseph Richardson, Junior, of Philadelphia, who was assayer of the United States Mint.

Peg tankards. The tankard was a communal drinking-vessel, and most of them have a row of pegs set in a vertical row inside the drum on the side where the handle is fixed. This was supposed to mark exactly how much each drinker was supposed to consume of the contents. Collectors therefore call them peg tankards.

Although rare in the rest of Europe and the United States, during the greater part of the period under discussion the tankard was the most usual silver vessel of importance to be made and used in Norway. A tankard was a favourite present at weddings, and engraved with the names or initials of the married couple it remained a family memory and a treasured possession for generations.

The Norwegian Renaissance tankard (Plate

504F, Fig. 42) is tall and thin and rests on a base of concave form, which on the more elaborate examples is decorated with chased ornaments. Round the lower part of the drum

FIG. 42

is a decorative belt, usually moulded into the shape of a rope, while the smooth part of the drum above might be decorated with engraved ornaments. The lid rises in steps to the centre, where a coin is sometimes inserted. Some of the steps may have chased decoration that harmonizes with that on the base. The thumb-piece is moulded into a flat ornamental shape or has the form of a plain turned knob. The late sixteenth-century examples have an almost Gothic slimness, but during the early seventeenth century the shape becomes slightly broader and more sturdy.

A completely new type of tankard was introduced during the latter part of the seventeenth century. The baroque tankard (Plate 504B) is broad and squat, has a rounded bottom and rests on three feet, moulded into the shape of a lion, a pomegranate, or a ball and claw. The thumb-piece is of a similar shape (Fig. 43). The earliest specimens date from the 1650s and 1660s and are quite plain, except for an engraved border round the centre of the lid, which is decorated with an engraved inscription or an inserted coin (Plate 504E). Some tankards have a small leaf ornament

soldered on to the drum where the feet join it, or the same area may be engraved. During the last quarter of the seventeenth century chased ornamentation was increasingly used. This gave a richer and more truly baroque general effect. Chased decoration first be-

FIG. 43

came obligatory for the drum round the three points where the feet join it, and soon the border round the central part of the lid became decorated with wreaths of flowers or leaves, chased out into high relief. A number of tankards from Christiania and a few from Bergen have the whole of the drum covered in chased decoration (Fig. 44). A few examples

FIG. 44

have human figures introduced into the composition.

The basic form of the baroque tankard remained popular until the middle of the eighteenth century, with some modifications in the ornamentation according to the change of taste, from baroque to *Régence* (Plate 504A). For provincial customers tankards of the basic baroque shape were made well into the latter part of the eighteenth century with rococo or neo-classical decorations.

Apart from the standard Renaissance and baroque types described, Norwegian tankards can be seen in more unorthodox shapes, with a polygonal body, set with coins or decorated with engravings with a topical significance. A few examples from the middle of the seventeenth century have a plain drum, slightly tapering, which rests on a broad plinth. The type is closely related to the contemporary counterpart in England.

Spice Dredger. A small cylindrical or octagonal piece with a pierced cover and single handle. More survive from the early than the late eighteenth century.

Perfume-burner. Pierced baluster form vase on scroll feet of late seventeenth-century date. Rare. Less lavish examples made in England until mid-nineteenth century.

Pibling. An obsolete form of pebbling. Coney's inventory included hammers for pibling, undoubtedly to produce the matted surface found on some of his early work.

Pierced work. Fretwork decoration cut with saws, used alone or combined with embossed work. Found at most periods in naturalistic or formal lattice and diaper designs. The application of ornamental piercing to Sheffield plate was governed by the development of hard-steel tools. The fret-saw was useless, because such cutting exposed the cen-

Fig. 45. Pierced salt

tral core of copper in such a way that it could not be concealed. Shortly after the introduction of double plating in the early 1770s, fly presses were used with hardened punches so designed that a layer of silver protruded very slightly beyond the copper, enabling it to be lapped over and thus conceal the tell-tale line.

With adequate burnishing the laps were virtually invisible. At first each pierced motif was pressed singly: by the mid-1790s they were produced in small groups, and the collector will easily detect this work. After about 1820 piercing machines with hard-steel tools did this work much more quickly.

Pin-cushion. Silver-framed examples survive from late seventeenth century in toilet services or separately and continued to be made by England until 1850s.

Pine-tree shillings. Made by John Hull and Robert Sanderson of Boston, 1652; first silver currency in Massachusetts. Hull was appointed mint-master of Colony in that year.

Pipkin. Small vessel, like saucepan with spout and turned wooden handle, for warming brandy.

Pitchers. Early in the nineteenth century Paul Revere adapted in silver the Liverpool pottery pitchers favoured by sea-captains;

Fig. 46. Pitcher; Paul Revere, c. 1800

copied copiously today for water pitchers, and in small sizes for cream, one can only speculate on their original use. Revere left three sizes of them in his own inventory, to judge by the listing; and large ones survive from his household.

Planishing. Making flat by hammering with an oval-faced punch, called in the old days a planishing teast.

Plate. The generic term for wrought silver or gold. Later applied by transference to the imitative wares of Sheffield and electroplate (*see also* Meat- and Soup-plate).

Plateau. A shallow dish on a short stem. A type characteristic of Spain and Portugal in the sixteenth century is derived from Valencia pottery.

Plating. Until the 1790s copper was silver-plated in the actual factories in which the ware was fabricated. Afterwards plating became a specialist trade, being made and stocked in three standard qualities, according to the thickness of the silver. This was sold to the plate workers.

An eight-pound copper ingot alloyed with about one-fifth its weight in brass, and measuring 8–10 inches long by about 3 inches wide and 2 inches thick, was smoothed and cleaned on the upper and lower surfaces. At first this was done by hand-filing; from about 1820 by steam-driven planing machines.

An ingot of silver was rolled to the required thickness, as needed for varying qualities of metal, the lowest weighing 16 dwt, to cover one face of the copper. This was increased to as much as 8 oz for the very rich plating used before the introduction of silver mountings and for the lavishly engraved work from 1820. The coating of silver required to be more than a mere film, otherwise it discoloured when heated by the soldering iron. A rectangle of silver plate, flawless in texture and unpitted, measuring about one-eighth of an inch less each way than the surface of the copper ingot, was cleaned on one side. The two bright surfaces were then placed together and bedded by placing a heavy iron upon the silver and striking it with a sledge-hammer until every part of the two surfaces was in close contact.

A heavily whitewashed piece of thick sheet copper was placed over the silver and firmly bound to the ingot with iron wires, burnt borax and water being applied to the edges of the silver to act as a flux. The ingot was now placed in an oven containing a charcoal fire and its door pierced with a small hole through which the plater could observe its progress. A bright line encircling the edges of the silver told him when fusion had taken place. He immediately removed the ingot and plunged it into diluted spirits of salt. After cutting the wires the ingot was compressed in a rolling machine, repeated annealing being required as it was gradually converted into sheets of specified width and gauge. These sheets, in which silver and copper were perfectly united, were not silvered on both sides until the early 1770s.

Pomander. From the French "Pomme d'ambre". Small box for sweet-smelling spices carried to ward off infections. Formed as segmented spheres, skulls, fruits, or other fancies. Used up till the seventeenth century. Partially superseded by vinaigrettes (q.v.).

Porringer. Two-handled bowl with or without cover for porridge and spoon meat. Survivals date from the first half of seventeenth century and last into the nineteenth. Shallow bowls with flat handles commonly called cupping- or bleeding-bowls (q.v.), probably also used as small porringers. The

FIG. 47. Porringer, 1699

two-handled seventeenth-century form in its largest size is the most important form of decorative vessel of its day. In the United States the term applies only to cupping- or bleeding-bowls. Porringers were popular in miniature during the period of Britannia standard silver.

Potato ring. *See* Dish ring.

Pouncebox or **Pot.** Baluster or vase-shaped bottle for sprinkling powdered gum-sandarac (pounce) on writing-paper. Indistinguishable from Sandbox (q.v.).

Pricking. Delicate needle-point engraving used principally for armorials and inscriptions in sixteenth to seventeenth centuries and also to a limited extent for naturalistic decoration on small scale.

Prunkgefass. A cup intended for display rather than use. A typical example is the gold cup supported somewhat insecurely on a coral figure, made by Peter Boy in about 1700, in the Schönborn Collection at Pommersfelden.

Przeworsk. A Polish method of decorating belts with chased silver plaques sewn on to the leather.

Pseudo hall-marks. Devices were occasionally adopted by individual makers of

British plate (not silver) from 1835, to suggest English hall-marks.

Punch-bowl. Large circular bowl with or without drop-ring handles for preparing punch. Used contemporaneously with Monteiths (*q.v.*) from the seventeenth century onwards.

Punched work. Elementary form of embossing struck with blunt punches grouped in primitive floral designs, principally used in mid-seventeenth century.

Punch-ladle. *See* Ladle, punch.

Purchase. *See* Thumbpiece.

Pyx. A small vessel, usually a round silver box, in which the sacrament is carried to the sick. They were frequently richly decorated, like the French one of 1562 in the Victoria and Albert Museum, embossed with the Last Supper and other Biblical scenes, and crowned by a standing figure of Christ at the column. Only one authenticated English medieval example has survived; now in Victoria and Albert Museum.

Quaich. A Scottish drinking-cup with two or more handles (der. Gaelic *cuach*). Originally probably hollowed from solid, by the seventeenth century quaichs were built up from neatly carved staves, beautifully feathered together, the vessels being bound around with withies. Woods often of different kinds, alternating. Handles in this phase formed part of staves and had characteristic "dip", which should be studied by those wishing to be judges of a good quaich of any period. By latter part of century wood quaichs were being mounted in silver (handle, foot, rim, sometimes plate inside). By third quarter of century quaichs were being made in silver. Stave construction nearly always recalled by incised lines on body, commonly with floral engraving in alternate panels (Tudor rose and tulip; thistles exceptional). Initials of original owners usually appear on handles. In late eighteenth and nineteenth centuries quaich degenerated into mere bowl with handles, often fancifully decorated, sometimes with Gaelic motto. Though sold as quaichs, they should be avoided by connoisseurs. Delightful miniature quaichs were made in the earlier part of the eighteenth century, some in Aberdeen and Inverness.

Prices more moderate than those of full-sized examples, which run well into three figures. Quaich had a very special place in Highland social ritual. Primary use for drinking rather than for food, but some adopted by churches for Communion, and even for offertory purposes (Plate 480A).

Raising. The normal technique of forming a hollow vessel from sheet metal by successive rows of hammering on a wood block, stretching and curving the metal. The silver, hardening by the hammering, is annealed or softened by repeatedly being raised to red-hot heat as required.

Ram's-horn. Thumb-piece of twisted form seen on early Boston tankards. It differs from the New York corkscrew.

Rapiers. With silver hilts were fashionable for dress occasions in England, America, France, Russia, and elsewhere in the eighteenth and nineteenth centuries. American examples show little variety whether made by early or late men of New England or New York.

Reedings. A border moulding composed of contiguous parallel convex members. Derived from the convex filling to the lower part of fluting in classical columns.

Reed-and-tie. A similar moulding to the above with the addition of crossed straps simulating ribbons binding the reeding together.

Regency. Miniature silver made in the early nineteenth century was of smaller dimensions than formerly and confined largely to tea-table ware. Whereas seventeenth- and eighteenth-century productions averaged between $1\frac{3}{4}$ inches and $2\frac{1}{2}$ inches in height, the Regency series was normally no more than a third of these measurements. For the most part they were cast with turned interiors and conformed with fashionable plate of the period with all-over decoration in relief. They were never heavy enough to demand hallmarking, and because of the chasing might lack even the maker's mark. They are found fully gilded: gilded within and in white silver.

Reliefs (*rilievi*). Silver reliefs, usually of religious subjects, enjoyed great popularity in Italy from the Renaissance to the late eighteenth century. Many are of such high quality that they may be regarded as minor works of sculpture (Plate 496c). Small reliefs were made to decorate paxes in the Renaissance period.

Reliquary. The vessel in which a relic or relics of the saints are kept. Reliquaries have been made in a great variety of patterns, offering the maximum scope for the invention of the goldsmith. Early examples were generally of architectural design, like the reliquary of Pepin d'Acquitain in the treasury of Ste Foy at Conques, which dates from the ninth century and, with its high roof and round-headed niches, resembles a shrine. Some made in the Rhineland in the twelfth century (one is in the Victoria and Albert Museum and another at the Schlossmuseum, Berlin) were made as model romanesque churches. Church-shaped reliquaries followed, a little tardily, the changes in architectural taste, and the shrine of St Elizabeth at Marburg (1236–9) is decorated with a mixture of romanesque and early Gothic ornaments. Reliquaries in the form of limbs and busts were also made as early as the eleventh century, and held their popularity for some five hundred years. They were frequently enriched with precious stones, which have in some instances (the bust of St Agatha at Catania) been so richly augmented by the offerings of the pious that the original work is now practically obscured. The early busts were normally stylized and expressionless, but during the Renaissance period they were treated with greater naturalism. One of the most famous medieval reliquaries is that of the Holy Thorn in the British Museum, which was made of gold richly decorated with enamel and precious stones by a Burgundian craftsman of the fourteenth century (Plate 485B). (This object may also be called an Ostensory, as it is intended for the display of the relic.)

During the Renaissance the architectural type of reliquary developed into the coffer-shaped, of which the best example is that of St John the Baptist in the Cathedral at Siena. This type, richly ornamented with reliefs and statuettes, was normal throughout the baroque period. Among the curiosities is the early eighteenth-century reliquary of St Anthony in the Victoria and Albert Museum, which is shaped like a spire.

Replating. The problem of detecting Sheffield plate replated during mid-Victorian days is difficult to solve. Advertisements were consistently inserted in newspapers and elsewhere from 1849 offering to replate at one-third of the original cost. Such pieces have toned down with a century of cleaning and now closely resemble genuine plating. Fused plate is much harder than electroplate, the effect of introducing alloy into the silver, this being plus rolling and hammering. Electroplating tends to soften the foundation metal. Electroplated silver is always white; Sheffield plate has a faintly bluish hue owing to the presence of alloy.

Repoussé work. Relief ornament hammered from the under or inner side of the metal. Usually given added sharpness of form by surface chasing of detail and outline. Common at all periods.

Reproductions. Precautions need to be taken when acquiring miniature toys lacking a full series of marks. Modern copies struck with a bogus date letter or lion passant gardant are far more numerous than originals. Shapes are important: it is, for instance, inconsistent to find a ball-shaped tea-urn with a pre-1739 hall-mark, as they were not designed for a full quarter century later.

Riesenpokal. Literally a travelling cup. The name is usually given to the vast cups, standing up to 40 inches in height and usually gilt, intended for ostentation rather than use, and made in Germany in the sixteenth century.

Rings. To commemorate special occasions, and particularly as funeral mementoes, were a common task of the goldsmith.

Rococo. The generic title for the eighteenth-century style of ornament based on shellwork and scrolls (French "rocaille").

Roses. Golden roses were sent by the popes to princes who had rendered signal service to the Roman Church and, later, to important ecclesiastical bodies. Of the many made in the fourteenth and fifteenth centuries few survive; one of the most notable, the gift of Pius II, is at Siena. All were made by goldsmiths working in Rome.

Rosewater ewer and dish (or **Basin**). Used for finger-washing at table. Extant examples from early sixteenth century onwards. Dishes usually circular or occasionally oval. Ewers of various form, chiefly vase- or helmet-shape. Important pieces of decorative plate displaying the highest standards of ornament and design of their periods.

Salad-servers. Introduced about 1800 to conform with main table services. Spoons with flattened bowl ends, forks with deep prongs cut into bowl of spoon form.

Salt-cellar. Early form known as Trencher Salt (*q.v.*). Basic form in eighteenth century a shallow circular bowl, first on moulded base, later on three or four feet. Oval pierced examples with glass liners introduced from about 1765. Plain boat-shaped model about 1780. Early nineteenth-century examples revert to earlier models, and sometimes match tureens of dinner services.

FIG. 48. Salt-cellar, 1735

Salts. The ceremonial salt occupied a prominent position on the medieval dining-table, and its importance did not decline until the seventeenth century; but the surviving French and German salts of the sixteenth century look plain and insignificant beside English examples of the same date. Some French salts were of great delicacy enriched with Limoges-enamel plaques, like the one in the Wallace Collection (Plate 488A); and German salts were occasionally fantastic, as may be seen from one in the British Museum, which is in the form of a whale supporting a shell on its tail. An exotic pair made at Breslau in about 1600 are fashioned like turkeys with spotted shells for their bodies. The most famous of all salts is, of course, that made in gold by Benvenuto Cellini for Francis I. Dutch silversmiths of the seventeenth century occasionally used human figures or fish for

decoration (Plate 486c); a beautiful example of about 1625 by Thomas Bogaert of Utrecht, supported by a kneeling girl, is in the collection of the Duke of Buccleuch. In spite of their diminished importance, French rococo craftsmen saw the decorative value of salts as table ornaments, and one of the finest sets ever made, consisting of four double and three single cellars supported by putti with feathered Red Indian head-dresses, by François Thomas Germain, was in the Portuguese Royal Collection. (*See The Connoisseur*, December 1954, p. 264.) Salts of Sheffield plate were sold in pairs and catalogued in three qualities, the first two fitted with blue-glass liners: (*a*) tinned inside; (*b*) plated inside with silver edges; (*c*) gilt inside with silver edges. Until 1820 they were made with three or four feet.

FIG. 49

Salver. Flat circular plates for presenting other vessels. Early examples have central spreading foot and are often erroneously called *tazze* (*q.v.*). From about 1725 small feet applied at circumference. Circular, oval, and polygonal forms all found, with chased or plain centres. Early borders plain mouldings, followed by shell and scroll, pierced, beaded, or gadrooned patterns (*see also* Waiter).

Samovars or **tea-urns.** Though principally connected with Russia, were also made in other countries. A fine rococo specimen by François Thomas Germain was in the Portuguese Royal Collection.

Sandbox. Baluster or vase-shaped pot used for sprinkling sandarac on wet ink. Found as part of inkstands or separately (*see also* Pounce-box).

Sauceboat. Introduced in early eighteenth century. First examples have oval-moulded bases, later replaced by individual scroll or

FIG. 50. Double-lipped sauceboat, 1722

hoof feet. Handles formed as scrolls, dolphins, eagles' heads, etc. Largely supplanted by tureens in late eighteenth century, with some revival of the boat form in the early nineteenth.

Saucepan. Found throughout eighteenth and early nineteenth centuries. Cylindrical or bellied bodies with projecting wood handles, with or without cover (*see also* Skillet).

FIG. 51. Saucepan, 1730

Save-alls. Are recorded with snuffers and extinguishers suggesting use with lighting equipment; Revere recorded in 1797 two with a total weight of 1 oz 16 dwt, so it is not surprising that none are known to have survived.

Scaldini (portable braziers). These were often made of silver and enjoyed more popularity in Italy than elsewhere in Europe. In shape they generally resemble tureens with flat perforated tops. They have hinged handles with wooden centrepieces.

Scent-bottle. Of small size for personal use, usually of pear-shaped form with chased or engraved decoration of the period. Very common in mid-nineteenth century. Larger examples in seventeenth-century toilet services.

Sconce. Wall-light for candles extant from the Restoration into the eighteenth century. The wall-plate usually of cartouche form with embossed decoration and branches for one or more candles. A plain form with rounded top to wall-plate and flat pan with single low socket also occurs. The name also used in the past for the normal candlestick.

Seal-box. A flat circular or oval box for containing the seal attached to important documents as royal warrants, university degrees, etc. The covers embossed or engraved with appropriate armorials.

Sechielli. Vessels shaped like holy water buckets (Plate 498A), but not necessarily in-

tended for ecclesiastical use. The body of the vessels was usually embossed or engraved. They were used for carrying liquids or ice, and the same Italian word is used for wine-coolers.

Second-course dish. Circular dish for serving entremets and puddings. Conforms in style and pattern to meat-dishes and plates of the period, throughout eighteenth and early nineteenth centuries. Sizes range from 10 to about 16 inches.

Serrated. Knotched, used especially of the shaped edge of the rim of tankard lid.

Sewing equipment. Thimbles, scissors, bands on pin balls, hooks, needle cases, bodkins, in gold and silver are known by record more than by surviving specimens.

Shaving-dishes. Kidney-shaped bowls, usually accompanied by helmet-shaped ew-

FIG. 52A

ers, enjoyed great popularity in Spain and Portugal in the eighteenth century (Figs. 52A and 52B).

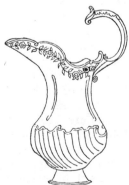

FIG. 52B

Shaving-pot. Small cylindrical or tapering vessel, usually with detachable ivory or wood handle, stand, and spirit-lamp. Introduced in late eighteenth century. Found in fittings of men's dressing sets.

Sheffield plate. The earliest and most effective substitute for wrought silver. Invented by Thomas Bolsover about 1743. Composed of copper ingot fused to a thinner one of silver and rolled to requisite thickness, the metals remaining in the same relative proportions when rolled. First used for buttons and other small articles, but from about 1765 onwards a serious rival to silver in every type of vessel.

The silvered copper could be shaped by any of the hand-raising processes customary in silversmithing, by stamping, or by spinning.

The exterior of Sheffield plate was rarely, if ever, gilded. Sugar-basins, cream-jugs, mustard-pots, and salt-cellars were gilded inside as protection against the foods concerned, which tended to corrode silver and produce black spots difficult to remove. In tea services the teapots were also gilded to match.

It was illegal until 1784 to strike a name or mark upon Sheffield plate. In that year the law was amended so that reputable platers "working within one hundred miles of the town of Sheffield" might be enabled to distinguish their work by name and emblem.

In England it is an offence to describe as Sheffield plate any ware which has not been manufactured by actually laying silver upon copper. Among the subterfuges adapted to keep within the law is to add the letter "d" and thus label pieces electrically plated in Sheffield as "Sheffield Plated". Some of the original tools are still in use for making Sheffield plate by the original methods.

Collectors of Sheffield plate should be aware that during the 1820s and 1830s large quantities of cheap, thin-gauge, poorly plated ware was imported from France. The copper, which was quick to spin and required no annealing, contained less alloy than its English counterpart, and consequently was of a redder tinge, which imparted a faintly pinkish hue to the thin film of silver.

Shell. Small dish of life-size scallop shell form introduced about 1700 for butter and other uses. Usually raised, but fine examples occasionally cast from nature.

Shield. The handle frequently terminated in a shield on tankards.

Sideboard dish. A large circular dish primarily designed for display, usually enriched by finely engraved or embossed armorials. Probably derived from the rose-water dish (*q.v.*). Later versions take the form of convex shields richly ornamented for special presentation, e.g. the Waterloo Shield of the Duke of Wellington. Also known as Chargers.

Silver-gilt. Silver with an applied surface of gold. Traditional technique known as fire, water, mercury, or wash gilding consists of painting on an amalgam of mercury and gold. The former is driven off with heat and the gold combines with the silver. Modern method of electro-gilding employs the use of electric current in a bath of gold solution, producing a deposition of the latter as in electro-silver-plating.

Silver guns. Only two of these silver guns are known, at Dumfries and Kirkcudbright. James VI and I presented them to the incorporated trades of the two burghs for annual shooting competitions. Dumfries gun still being shot for in 1813. No hall-marks on either.

Skewer. Extant meat-skewers date from the early eighteenth century. Normally provided with ring or shell top to afford a grip. Later examples conform to table service patterns.

Skillet. Seventeenth-century form of saucepan on three feet for heating gruel or other liquids. Covers of flat cap form with flat pierced handle resembling cupping-bowls.

Snuff-box. Found in great variety of forms from late seventeenth century onwards, both in solid silver and wood, tortoiseshell, and other materials mounted with silver.

Snuffers. Scissor-like implement for trimming candlewicks. The cutting blade fits into shallow box when closed for holding the snuffed wick, the box having a pricket end for lifting bent-over wire. Survivals common from late seventeenth century.

Snuffer-stand. Upright container on stem and moulded base into which snuffers fit.

Introduced in late seventeenth century, but superseded by trays in the early eighteenth.

Snuffer-tray. Oblong or oval tray with or without small feet and scroll or ring handle at side for holding snuffers. Not to be confused with spoon trays (*q.v.*).

Soap-box. Spherical box for soap-ball, standing on moulded base with screw-on or hinged pierced or plain cover. Can be mistaken for pounce- or sand-box (*q.v.*), but the spherical form appears to have been peculiar to soap-box.

Soufflé dish. Cylindrical bowl with liner, usually two-handled, to hold soufflés, introduced in early nineteenth century.

Soup-plate. Similar to Meat-plate (*q.v.*) but with deeper centre.

Soup tureen. *See* Tureen.

Soy frame. Oblong or oval stand with ring frame for holding soy or sauce bottles. Introduced in late eighteenth century. Found *en suite* with larger cruet frames (*q.v.*).

Spectacle frames and cases. Appear in inventories in the seventeenth and throughout the eighteenth centuries, and in nineteenth-century silversmiths' catalogues.

Spice-box. A general name for caskets of indeterminate purpose of the early seventeenth century, usually of shell outline with scallop lid and shell or snail feet. Later applied to oval caskets of the Charles II period which may also have served as tobacco boxes. An eighteenth-century version has centrally hinged twin lids with or without a detachable nutmeg-grater in the centre.

Spinning. Much miniature hollow-ware dating from the 1750s onwards was shaped by spinning in the lathe. This was much less expensive than hand-raising with the hammer. It is particularly noticeable among Dutch miniature silver. From the 1770s light domestic hollow-ware might be spun by factory methods. Almost invisible circular marks were made on the interior by the tools.

Splayed. A candlestick or other foot is termed splayed when the top and bottom diameters are different.

Spoons. In medieval times spoons, used for consuming thick, sweet liquids, were usually carried as personal possessions and not provided on the table. Some very elaborate early examples have survived, with bowls of shell, agate, or other hard stones, exquisitely mounted in gold or silver. Occasionally they were combined with forks; in the British Museum there is a folding spoon and fork in a Gothic handle which also contains two dice and a pen (Plate 492D). With the general introduction of forks, the variations in pattern became fewer. Generally speaking, the fig-shaped bowl remained normal until the middle of the seventeenth century, when it was superseded by the egg-shaped. Incense spoons, used for placing incense in the censer, usually had spade-shaped bowls.

APOSTLE SPOON. Early type of spoon with full-length figure of an apostle or Christ (The Master) as finial. Extant examples date from late fifteenth century till Charles II period. Complete sets of thirteen of very rare occurrence.

BASTING SPOON. Long-handled, with nearly oval bowl, early examples rat-tailed, presumed to have been used for basting. Similar in form to early punch-ladles and probably of general domestic use.

CADDY SPOON. Small spoon with short handle for measuring tea from the caddy. Made in numerous fancy forms, leaf, jockey cap, hand, etc., from about 1780 onwards.

CHERUB SPOON. A genuine creation of the Renaissance in Norway is the cherub spoon with a drop-shaped bowl and a thin stem which tapers towards the cherub's mask which forms the knob.

DESSERT SPOON. Introduced in early eighteenth century. Has a parallel development to the tablespoon.

DISC-END SPOON. In fashion in Scotland 1575–1650, or thereabouts. The main feature varies considerably, but there is always a disc, cushioned from the stem by anything from a short bar to an elliptical member, all cut with the stem in one piece. A set of six of these, inscribed 1575, is in the Bute Collection. The disc-end grows into a Puritan type of spoon in the second half of the seventeenth century by merging its members into a simple broadening of the stem, ornament being confined at most to some shallow notches in the top of the stem and some simple line engraving on the face of it. Stem joins bowl without rat-tail or other type of reinforcement.

EGG SPOON. Not recognized before late eighteenth century. At first found in egg-frames and later as part of complete table services.

GRAPE SPOON. Norwegian type, simple and elegant with a drop-shaped bowl and a long thin stem terminating in a bunch of grapes. A similar type is sometimes found, with the knob of the stem shaped like a shell instead of a bunch of grapes.

GRAVY SPOON. Long-handled spoon similar to basting spoon and indistinguishable in early eighteenth century. Later forms follow main table service patterns.

LION SEJANT SPOON. Early form surmounted by a small figure of a seated lion, sometimes supporting a shield at the front. Extant examples date from fifteenth to early seventeenth century.

MAIDENHEAD SPOON. Early form with finial formed as a female head with long hair rising from Gothic foliage. Extant from fifteenth to seventeenth centuries.

MARROW SPOON. Long, narrow-bowled spoon, usually double-ended with two widths of bowl for eating bone-marrow. Alternative version has normal tablespoon bowl and marrow-bowl in place of handle. Found from early eighteenth century onwards.

MULBERRY SPOON. *See* Straining Spoon.

MUSTARD SPOON. Not recognized before mid-eighteenth century. Early examples have long curved stems and deep circular bowls. Later versions conform to main table service patterns with egg-shaped bowl.

OLIVE SPOON. *See* Straining Spoon.

PURITAN SPOON. Mid-seventeenth-century form with flat stem with straight top edge, and nearly oval bowl. The earliest form of English flat-stemmed spoon.

RAT-TAIL SPOON. The principal form of the late seventeenth to early eighteenth centuries, distinguished by tapering rib running down back of bowl. Found with trifid (*q.v.*), dog-nose, and rounded top stems.

SALT SPOON. Early examples either small versions of contemporary rat-tailed type or formed as shovels. Many fancy varieties occur in mid-eighteenth century. Later examples conform to main table service patterns.

SEAL-TOP SPOON. The commonest surviving form of early spoon with flat, seal-like finial placed on short turned baluster of oval, circular, or polygonal section, and with hexagonal stem. Examples range from fifteenth century till Charles II period. In Scotland the rarest type, of sixteenth and early seventeenth centuries, has been called the seal-top, but has little or no resemblance to English spoon of this name. "Seal" is little wedge-shaped member with projecting collar where it joins the stem, which is flat instead of hexagonal in section. Bowls also distinctive, and have undeveloped rat-tail. Only four examples known at present.

SLIP-TOP SPOON. Early form with hexagonal stem with sloping or bevelled end. Examples occur from medieval period until mid-seventeenth century.

SNUFF SPOON. Miniature version of larger contemporary spoons found in snuff-boxes and *étuis* for taking snuff.

STRAINING SPOON. Spoon with pierced bowl, found either in large sizes for gravy or similar use or in teaspoon size with thin, tapering stem with pricket top, used for skimming motes from tea-cups. These latter have been called Mulberry or Olive spoons, but have no possibly explicable function for such fruits. Their purpose as tea-strainers is exemplified by their conjunction with teaspoons in fitted tea-caddy caskets.

STUMP-TOP SPOON. Seventeenth-century form with octagonal stem swelling at the end and diminishing to a flattened point. Rare.

TABLE SPOON. Developed as a specific size contrasting with dessert spoon in early eighteenth century. The main constituent of table services and the prototype for the various patterns evolved (*see* Table service).

TEA SPOON. Rarely found in sets before 1700. Conform in general to prevailing styles of larger spoons, but individual patterns in mid-eighteenth century occur, e.g. foliage stems and bowls, shell bowls, and many small devices stamped on bowl backs.

TREFID or TRIFID SPOON. Also known by the French term, "Pied de biche". Late seventeenth-century form with flat stem widening to a lobed outline at the top, split by two cuts forming three sections suggestive of a cleft hoof. The ends sometimes curve upwards. Normally found with rat-tailed bowls.

VOLUTE SPOON. The stem ends in a palmette with a protuberance below, shaped like a volute.

WRITHEN-TOP SPOON. Rare medieval form surmounted by spirally fluted ovoid finial.

Spoon-tray. Small oval or oblong dish of early eighteenth-century date used for holding teaspoons in the absence of tea-cup saucers. Usually with scalloped and fluted or moulded rims.

Stake. An iron tongue or anvil, on which the silver object is formed. Many kinds of stakes are used, shaped for certain purposes, such as to give an inward curve, a flat surface, etc.

Stamped work. Relief ornament produced by hammering from reverse of the metal into an intaglio-cut die. Commonly used in sixteenth century for strapwork and ovolo borders, and occasionally for larger surface patterns. In late eighteenth century developed on a commercial scale with large dies at Sheffield and Birmingham for candlesticks, dish-borders, et.

Standing Dishes. Occasionally, and incorrectly, called *tazze*, have shallow bowls on baluster stems, and were used for sweetmeats

FIG. 53

or fruit. The interior of the bowl is often richly adorned with relief decoration, and some have standing figures in the centre (notably those made by Paul Hubner of Augsburg between 1583 and 1614) (Fig. 53). They were popular, especially in Germany and Holland, from the late sixteenth to the early eighteenth centuries. The British Museum possesses an exceptionally fine set of a dozen made at Augsburg, and there is a notable example, made by Adam van Vianen at Utrecht in 1612, in the Victoria and Albert Museum.

Standish. Early name for ink-stand (*q.v.*).

Statuettes (*figurine*). Italian silver statuettes of saints and mythological beings correspond closely with contemporary bronzes on which some appear to have been modelled. Early in the nineteenth century statuettes were occasionally based on Graeco-Roman figures or the works of such neo-classical sculptors as Canova and Thorvaldsen.

Stepped. A term indicating the elevations on a lid, as "single-stepped" or "double-stepped".

Sterling Standard. The normal standard for wrought plate in the British Isles. Established in London in 1300 and in force till 1696. Then replaced by Britannia Standard (*q.v.*) till 1720, when Sterling was restored as legal. Consists of 11 oz 2 dwt of fine silver in every pound Troy (12 oz) of wrought metal, or 925 parts in 1,000. In the United States the word Sterling appears on Baltimore silver, 1800–14, and, after 1860, elsewhere. However, eighteenth-century silversmiths used the same standard as English Sterling, and so advertised their wares.

Stoning. Polishing with an emery-stone.

Strainer. Rare survivals of the seventeenth century have circular bowls and tapering hollow handle. Of common occurrence in eighteenth century with two open scroll handles for use as lemon-strainers in punch-making and for other purposes.

Strapwork. Arrangements of interlaced ribbon and scrollwork mixed with naturalistic foliage and floral patterns, either engraved or *repoussé*, common in sixteenth century. The name is also used for the cast and applied vertical ribs and scrollwork derived from the earlier cut-cardwork (*q.v.*) much used by the Huguenot school in England in the eighteenth century.

Strawberry-dish. A name given to small saucer-like dishes of seventeenth- and early eighteenth-century date, the early examples with punched decoration, the latter with fluted scalloped borders. Probably used for a variety of purposes.

Sucket-fork. Two-pronged fork with flat stem, a spoon at other end, used for eating sweetmeat. A rare example by William Rouse, Boston, was made before 1689.

Sugar-basin. The later form of sugar-bowl or basket, with two handles and of oblong, circular, or oval form, usually part of a matching tea service from about 1790 onwards.

Sugar-basket. Pierced or plain vase or boat-shaped basket dating from about 1760 onwards with swing handle and glass liner in the pierced examples. Often made with matching cream basket.

Sugar-bowl. Found as separate piece in the early eighteenth century of plain circular or polygonal form, usually with low cover. Later combined with two tea-caddies matching to form set contained in casket. Small covered bowls for sugar, usually in the form of miniature tureens, were as popular in eighteenth-century Italy as tea-caddies were in England. The knobs are fashioned in the form of animals, squatting Chinamen, flowers, nuts, and pineapples, while their bodies are enriched with every type of embossed or engraved, floral, foliated, and abstract rococo ornament (Plate 498B).

Sugar-box. Like British Charles II sweetmeat-box; term adopted in America because of its use in old inventories, with "sugar chest" or "sugar trunke". Seven Boston examples known.

Sugar-nippers. An early form of scissor-like sugar-tongs with scrolling stems and shell grips of George I and II date.

Sugar-shifter. Small ladle with pierced bowl for sprinkling sugar over fruit, etc. Introduced about 1750.

Sugar-tongs. Early eighteenth-century examples modelled as minature fire-tongs. Later examples of spring bow form with pierced or solid stems, subsequently conforming to table service patterns. In the United States tongs appear about mid-eighteenth century in a scissor-form ending in cast shell grips; after 1760, bow-shaped "spring tongs", in which a spring joins the arms.

Swage. A form into which silver might be stamped as the "2 Tests with plaine and flower'd Spoon Swages" of Edward Webb's inventory in 1718 (U.S.).

Sweetmeat basket. Small oval or circular basket introduced about 1740, found separately or on *épergne* branches. Early examples mostly pierced with cast floral borders. Later ones solid and decorated with engraving.

Sword-hilts. In Scotland a small number of solid silver basket-hilts has survived from the eighteenth century. One by Robert Cruickshank of Aberdeen is in the collection of Her Majesty the Queen. The account-book of John Rollo lists sword-hilts, including one of basket type for the Duke of Perth.

Table decorations. Small silver objects, figures, animals, miniature coaches, etc., were occasionally made as table decorations in the eighteenth century; in style they are similar to contemporary porcelain figures. Genoese craftsmen appear to have specialized in these objects, which they decorated with filigree work.

Table services. Complete table services in silver did not come into any general use until the eighteenth century, when those made for princely houses were often of the greatest magnificence. Small travelling table services were occasionally made, the most notable being the Italian one which belonged to Cardinal York and is now at Windsor (Plate 492A). For main patterns see below.

FEATHER-EDGED. Found in the second half of eighteenth century. Stems filled with a narrow border fluting resembling the edge of a feather.

FIDDLE PATTERN. Stems shaped with broad upper section and notched shoulders at bowl end, resembling slightly the basic form of violin body. Introduced early nineteenth century. Found plain, with threaded edges or with stamped shells at top.

HANOVERIAN. Stems with central longitudinal ridge on the front and upcurved ends. The common form from about 1720 to 1740.

KING'S PATTERN. Early nineteenth-century form with shaped stems with waisted hourglass tops decorated with scrolls, shells, and anthemion-like foliage.

OLD ENGLISH PATTERN. Perfectly plain form

with flat stems spreading slightly to the rounded ends. Common form from mid-eighteenth century onwards. Scottish and Irish varieties show a tendency to more pointed ends to stems.

ONSLOW PATTERN. Rare mid-eighteenth century form of stem with upper third decorated with radiating fluting and cast and applied corkscrew-like scroll tops.

QUEEN'S PATTERN. A less elaborate form of King's pattern, the decoration struck only on the upper surface of the stem and without a shell on the bowl.

Tankard. Drinking-vessel for beer with single handle, with or without hinged or, rarely, detachable lid. Appear to have been among the most popular silver vessels made in northern Europe, especially Scandinavia, in the seventeenth and eighteenth centuries. The type that first appeared in Germany in the sixteenth century had a small tapering body, but in the next hundred years patterns became larger and more ornate (Plate 486B). In the late seventeenth and early eighteenth centuries tankards set with coins were in demand. In Scandinavia and the Baltic states tankards with tall cylindrical bodies were favoured in the late sixteenth and early seventeenth centuries. Later Swedish examples tended to have shorter bodies which tapered downwards, lower and broader covers projecting over the lip and larger thumb-pieces. Heavy, squat ones standing on ball feet were usual in the Baltic states in the later seventeenth century; five massive examples of this type being in the collection of the Kompagnie der Schwarsen Haupter at Riga. In Hungary, tall, hexagonal, octagonal, or cylindrical tankards narrowed in the middle of the body and sometimes decorated with medalions of Roman heads were popular during the seventeenth century.

In England embossed examples occur in sixteenth century. From seventeenth century of strictly plain functional form with cylindrical tapering barrel. Mid-eighteenth century form with bellied barrel and domed lid.

In the United States, in Nonconformist New England, tankards were used rather than flagons in communion service. In New York the tankard was larger and heavier than in New England. Early forms were tapering and cylindrical; the flat-top cover (like English Stuart form) persisted in New York, but Boston adopted a domed cover about 1715 and used a midband on the body. The New York tankard is distinguished by an applied foliated band at the bottom. New York silversmiths frequently used a corkscrew thumb-piece, Boston a dolphin, and many American makers used for ornament on handle a cast cherub's head (*q.v.*). Tankards of pear-shape body and domed cover were made in the rococo period, 1750–85, but the flat-top, Stuart tankard was continued in New York past mid-eighteenth century. The tankard went out of fashion in late eighteenth century.

Taper-box. Small cylindrical box with handle and hole in lid to contain coiled sealing-wax taper. Found from about 1700 onwards (*see also* Waxjack).

Taperstick. Small version of contemporary candlestick to hold sealing taper. Found both in vertical form and with flat

FIG. 54. Taperstick, 1734

base similar to chamber candlestick. Extant from late seventeenth century onwards. In eighteenth century found as central fitting to inkstands.

Tassie. Scots for a drinking cup (French *tasse*).

Tazza (Italian; cf. French *tasse*; Scottish *tassie*). Wine-cup with shallow circular bowl. The name, correctly applied to such pieces of sixteenth to seventeenth century, has become erroneously extended to cover flat dishes and salvers on central foot. Its derivation is clear, however, and can have no connotation with the latter pieces.

Tea-canister. A small oblong or octagonal

canister with cap-cover, with or without sliding base, and kept in a tea-chest. Vase forms introduced in mid-eighteenth century and accompanied by similar sugar-bowls in sets in fitted wood, ivory, or shagreen caskets, to which the name was transferred. Later examples of oval, circular, or oblong form with lock, and interior division to hold two qualities of tea. Were known as caddies.

FIG. 55. Tea-canister, 1739

Teacup. Rare examples of silver handleless teacups and saucers survive from *c.* 1700.

Teacup-stand. Circular saucer dish with detachable open frame for holding porcelain cup, found in first two decades of eighteenth century. Very rare.

Tea-kettle. Introduced about 1690, the bodies conforming nearly to teapot form. The early examples have brazier-like stands for charcoal or spirit-lamp, later replaced by open frame stand. A very rare feature is the accompanying silver tripod table to hold kettle and stand. Late eighteenth-century examples occasionally have tap in lieu of spout. Tea-urns (*q.v.*) largely replaced kettles from about 1765.

Teapots. Modelled on those made in ceramics and imported from China, appear to have been made in all countries in the eighteenth century. A very early tea-set of Augsburg craftsmanship (Plate 492B) shows the application of rococo motifs to a pot and jugs. Towards the end of the century, English patterns were occasionally used on the Continent. In England bodies were of pear shape under Queen Anne, spherical from George I to II, followed by inverted pear form early George III and oval flat-bottomed model with stand about 1780. Squat circular forms were introduced in early nineteenth

century, with matching sugar-basin and cream-jug. Teapots of Sheffield plate were made in shapes following those of the silversmiths, with handles of ivory, ebony, horn, or hardwood.

Tea service. Few examples of matching tea-sets before 1785 in England. Some evidence of earlier fashion in Scotland. Services of teapot, sugar-basin, and cream-jug common from 1790 onwards with or without coffee-pot or hot-water jug with stand and lamp. Kettles very rarely form matching part of service until nineteenth century.

Tea-tray. Large, two-handled oval or oblong trays introduced *c.* 1780. Earlier the purpose was served by handleless salvers used in conjunction with tripod mahogany tables. Trays are among the rarities in American silver, but nine were made by Jacob Hurd, Boston, while Paul Revere's large oval tray made for Elias Hasket Derby in the Garvan Collection is one of the masterpieces of American silver.

Tea-urn. Large vase-shaped hot-water urn introduced about 1760 in lieu of tea-kettle (*q.v.*). A few earlier examples found in Scottish silver. Body fitted with a compartment at base or suspended in mouth for red-hot heating iron.

Teasts. Coney's inventory (U.S.) in 1722 had "spoon teasts"; *see also* Swage.

Threading. One or two narrow lines engraved as a border to spoon and fork stems and other small pieces.

Thumbpiece. The projecting part above the hinge of a covered vessel whereby the cover might easily be opened with the thumb. On tankards these showed greater variety than on flagons; on a few early chocolate pots a thumbpiece is found. Corkscrew, cusped, dolphin and mask, scrolled, and open thumbpieces denote periods and places.

Tigerware jug. German stoneware bellied jug of the sixteenth century mounted with Elizabethan silver or gilt embossed and engraved neckband, cover, foot, and handle mounts. Rarer examples of this technique are the coloured Turkish faïence jugs and a few English pottery jugs similarly mounted.

Tinkers. Known in Gaelic as *ceardan*, these had a long tradition of metal-working in the

Highlands, and some were considerable craftsmen. Responsible for many of the early brooches, and probably for most of the brass and silver brooches of the seventeenth and eighteenth centuries. Sometimes made domestic articles of silver, but in nineteenth century degenerated into menders of pots and pans.

Tinned. Sheffield plate coated with pure tin, deposited on the copper surface by first sprinkling it with sal ammoniac, and then washing with molten tin. Early hollow-ware was tinned inside: after the introduction of double-faced plate the backs of large trays and waiters were usually tinned, and the interiors of tea-urns, dish-covers, coffee-pots, and hot-water jugs. Even in the 1820s catalogues describe trays, snuffer-dishes, and so on as having either "tinned" or "plated" backs.

Toasted-cheese dish. Oval or oblong dish with hinged cover and hot-water compartment below. Sometimes fitted with separate pans to hold the cheese. Introduced in late eighteenth century.

Toast-rack. Introduced about 1770. Early examples have detachable wires on oval base. Boat-shaped form *c.* 1790 followed by oblong examples, usually on four feet with ring handle above.

Tobacco-box. Flat oval or circular box with hinged or detachable lid, dating from late seventeenth century onwards. Often finely engraved with armorials or ciphers.

Toddy-ladle. *See* Ladle, Punch.

Toilet-sets. Of gold or silver were made for the *grandes dames* of the seventeenth and eighteenth centuries. They might contain as many as fifty-three pieces, as did the gold one made for the Empress Maria Theresa by Anton Mathias Domanek in about 1750, and sometimes included, besides pots, brushes, and combs, such objects as bodkins, tongue scrapers, and combined tooth- and earpicks.

Toothpicks and **toothpick cases.** Of silver and gold are not known to have survived in the United States, although mentioned in the seventeenth and eighteenth centuries.

Touch. Maker's mark, impressed with a punch.

Touchstone. A piece of polished "stone" on which a piece of silver of known quality could be rubbed to compare its mark with that of a piece being assayed.

Toy silver. Miniature models of every form of wrought plate made for children and doll's-house use. Sometimes considered to be travellers' sample pieces, but the evidence of maker's marks indicating specialists in this genre makes this unlikely. Rare in America, but a set made for Bethea Shrimpton by an unidentified silversmith is in the Garvan Collection at Yale.

Trembleuses. Little silver trays with stands, usually in the form of leaves, to hold porcelain cups. These objects, which were probably derived from a French pattern, appear to have been a speciality of Genoese silversmiths and to have been made only in the 1750s and 1760s (Plate 499A) and in mid-nineteenth century.

Trencher salt. Small individual salt-cellar with solid sides lying flat on the table. Earliest examples date from about 1630. The standard form of table salt till about 1725. Of circular, oval, square, or polygonal form with oval or circular well.

Tulip design. Floral decoration in form of a tulip is found in Boston and New York silver, known through both Dutch and English precedent.

Tumblers. Are the rounded based cups familiar in various sizes.

Tureen. Circular or oval bowl and cover for soup introduced in early eighteenth century. Richly decorated in rococo period. Later of plain classical vase form, becoming elaborate again in the nineteenth century. Small versions of matching design to the soup tureen introduced about 1760 in sets of two or four as alternative to sauce-boat.

Eighteenth-century tureens are among the most magnificent examples of Italian plate. Some of them are as much as 18 inches high. The knobs on their covers were often modelled in the form of human figures or delicately wrought still-life groups of dead game or vegetables. Usually they were provided with large shallow dishes in which to stand (Plates 497A, 499B, and 500A).

Tureen ladles. Appear in Revere's ledgers, but silver tureens of colonial make are rare if existent. A few from the Federal period follow classic forms. John Singleton Copley wrote from Paris of "Soupp . . . in Silver Turenes" in 1774, which probably would not have been noteworthy had he known them at home.

Urn. *See* Tea-urn.

Vase. Sets of large, richly decorated vases and bottles for chimney display date from the Restoration. In the late eighteenth century large models of classical form appear for presentation purposes. In the early nineteenth century the Warwick Vase was reproduced in this way.

In the south of Italy altar vases were often provided with bouquets of paper-thin silver or, more usually, silver-gilt, flowers and foliage (Plates 494D and 498C).

Vegetable-dish. Of circular or oval form with straight, deep sides and cover, introduced late eighteenth century (*see also* Hash-dish).

Venison dish. Similar to meat-dish with channels and well for collecting gravy.

Vinaigrette. Small box with hinged lid and inner pierced grille holding sponge for aromatic vinegar. For ladies' use against faintness and megrims. Introduced late seventeenth century in many varieties of forms, e.g. books, purses, eggs, etc.

Voyding dish or **voyder.** Large dish for collecting broken meats and table remnants. A medieval term. The only known surviving example, a seventeenth-century replacement of an earlier dish, belongs to the Drapers' Company.

Waiter. Small tray for handing wine-glass, letter, etc. Conforms generally to salver form (*q.v.*). In eighteenth century often found in pairs *en suite* with the larger salver. The small, early, footed form often misnamed *tazza* (*q.v.*).

FIG. 56. Footed waiter, 1724

Warming-pan. Rarely found in silver, but several late seventeenth and early eighteenth century English examples have survived with pierced, engraved covers.

Water pots. Seemingly appear first in an advertisement in Philadelphia in 1782 as "milk pots, water ditto . . ." but the beverage was not catered for by colonial goldsmiths.

Waxjack. Open-frame stand for coil of sealing taper threaded on central pin and led through nozzle above. Found late seventeenth century onwards. Several enclosed types made after *c.* 1750.

FIG. 57. Waxjack, 1795

Welcome cups. The welcome cup was a communal drinking-vessel used at the guild ceremonies to celebrate the acceptance of a new member, the reception of a visitor, or some other solemn occasion. It was used in guilds of all kinds, by bakers and tailors, coopers and shoemakers as well as by the goldsmiths themselves, in the organizations for both masters and journeymen. The welcome cups were used all over Scandinavia and in many parts of the Continent, and were among the most prized treasures of the guilds. To the members it symbolized the unity of their organization. At the guild meetings it stood in a prominent place, and when the guild changed its premises the cup was proudly carried at the head of the procession.

Occasionally ordinary beakers or tankards did service as welcome cups, but mostly they were tall goblets with ornate stems and lids with elaborate handles in pewter, copper, or, usually, silver. The details of the shape changed with the varying fashions, but generally speaking they were conservative in style. An early eighteenth-century type, with a marked horizontal division of the bowl, rich chased decoration, and a gay figure in mould-ed work as handle to the lid, was made over a period of forty years in Bergen. Apart from being the traditional welcome cup of the period, it seems to have been the set master-piece for Bergen goldsmiths. A fine example of this type, unfortunately unmarked, is in the Victoria and Albert Museum (Plate 501F).

Sometimes, but not always, the welcome cup carries inscriptions that describe its purpose. Members and friends of the guild had badges made with their names and appropriate inscriptions to be hung on the cup on special occasions. When all the badges were in place the cup was more or less covered. Welcome cups were made in Norway well into the nineteenth century.

Westbrooke baby house. A superlative collection near Baldock, Hertfordshire, of more than fifty miniature silver toys has accompanied this doll's house, which, for nearly 250 years, has been handed down from mother to daughter as an heirloom. The majority of these are struck with London hall-marks of the Britannia standard. A grate with a fire-back in *repoussé* work included in this collection is struck with the maker's mark *ID.*, also found on a mug, six plates, and four chargers. This is the mark of John Deard, toyman and goldsmith of Fleet Street, who died in 1731. A wall-down hearth with fire-dogs, tongs, shovel, and poker bear the London hall-mark for 1718 and the maker's mark *CL*, showing them to have been made by John Clifton, Foster Lane, a well-known silver toy-maker. There are two chairs in the late seventeenth-century style bearing the mark of Matthew Madden of Lombard Street, registered in 1696, and a three-legged pot made by Thomas Evesdon in 1713. A rare detail is a foot stove, such as were used in wealthy homes, in plate silver decorated with orna-mental piercing, "to laye under their feete when they write, or studie, in cold weather, or in their coaches to keep their feet warm".

"Whistles." The hole at end of a tank-ard handle, mistakenly called a whistle, was actually a vent for hot air to be expelled during soldering.

Whistles. With corals and bells for chil-dren are depicted in gold and silver in por-traits and survive of eighteenth-century crafts-manship from the three centres: Boston, New York, and Philadelphia.

Whistle tankard or **cup.** *See* Blow-hole.

Wine-bottle stand. Oval bowl on mould-ed base for holding the early form of glass wine-bottle with rounded base of early eigh-teenth century. The very rare examples that survive are sometimes mistaken for sugar-bowls.

Wine bowls, wine-cups, and **wine tumblers.** Are recorded in American silver annals of colonial time, but not identified in form.

Wine-cistern. Large oval vessel on base or separate feet for keeping bottles in cold water or ice. Survivals date from Charles II to the mid-eighteenth century. Important decorative pieces of a high standard of design and ornament.

Wine-coaster. Circular decanter or bottle stand for table use. Pierced or solid silver sides, usually with turned wood base. Intro-duced about mid-eighteenth century. Occur in pairs, set of four, or greater numbers.

Wine-cooler. Also known as ice-pail. Vessel for holding single bottle. A few sur-vivals from early eighteenth century, but not common till about 1780. Vase or tub shape, and occasionally of double oval form. Occur in pairs or sets of four or more. Usually fitted with liner and flat rim.

Wine-fountain. Large vessel-shaped urn with tap in body.

Wine-funnel. Tapering funnel with de-tachable strainer for decanting. Circular stands of saucer form with domed centres were used with the funnels.

Wine-label. Pierced or chased label with the name of the wine hung by chain round decanter neck. A rarer form have neck ring in place of chain. Many varieties of form and name, including plain initials, occur from mid-eighteenth century onwards.

Wine-tasters. Small vessels, usually two-handled, found in all wine-growing coun-tries, though the Portuguese type with a domed centre, to reflect the colour of the wine, is said to be of English origin.

Wire work. Among the rarest pieces of Sheffield plate are those constructed from plated wires, dating chiefly between 1785 and 1815. They were a direct result of George Whateley's patented invention of 1768, by which copper rods, round, flat, square, and triangular, could be silver-plated. Not until after the expiry of the patent in 1782 was this work carried out on a considerable scale, the demand being chiefly for a wide range of inexpensive table baskets, toast-racks, and *épergnes*. The wires at first were cut into short lengths, fitted into holes drilled into rim and base, and soldered into position. Early in the nineteenth century less-expensive wire ware was made by bending lengths of wire into continuous curves forming patterns. These were soldered to rim and base, thus saving the cost of drilling. Ball handles might consist of flat wire curved and spaced with balls or other ornament, or of twisted wire of various sections.

Collectors should realize that dessert, cake, and sweetmeat baskets in many period styles have been made by the twentieth-century copyists. Wires in sections other than round are not found in this series, in which the soldering lacks the experience of the old workers.

Wrigglework. A form of engraving employing a zig-zag line cut by a rocking motion. Used in conjunction with line engraving at certain periods, principally late seventeenth century, for filling in spaces between engraved lines. Its use may have been copied from the more extensive practice in pewter.

Der Rotschmidt.

FOR FURTHER READING

LIST OF MUSEUMS AND GALLERIES

INDEX

For Further Reading

Arms and Armour
European Armour by Claude Blair, Batsford, London, 1958.
Armour by J. F. Hayward, Victoria and Albert Museum, London, 1951.
Swords and Daggers by J. F. Hayward, Victoria and Albert Museum, London, 1955.
European Firearms by J. F. Hayward, Victoria and Albert Museum, London, 1955.
A Record of European Armour and Arms through Seven Centuries (5 vols) by Sir Guy Laking, G. Bell & Sons, London, 1920–2.
The Age of Firearms by Robert Held, Harper Bros, New York, 1957.
Arms and Armor in Colonial America 1526–1783 by Harold L. Peterson, Harrisburg, Pennsylvania, 1956.

Barometers, Clocks, and Watches
Old English Barometers by G. H. and E. F. Bell, The Wykenham Press, Winchester, 1952.
The Story of Watches by T. P. Camerer Cuss, MacGibbon and Kee, London, 1952.
English Domestic Clocks by Cescinsky and Webster, Routledge, London, 1913.
The Evolution of Clockwork by J. Drummond Robertson, Cassell, London, 1931.
A Book of English Clocks by R. W. Symonds, Penguin, London, 1947.
Thomas Tompion, His Life and Work by R. W. Symonds, Batsford, London, 1951.
Old Clocks for Modern Use by Edward Wenham, Bell, London, 1951.
Watchmakers and Clockmakers of the World by G. H. Baillie, 2nd ed. N.A.G. Press, London, 1947.
The English Domestic Clock by Alan Lloyd, privately printed, 1938.
The Book of American Clocks by Brooks Palmer, Macmillan, New York, 1950.
American Clocks and Clockmakers by Carl Drepperd, Branford, New York, 1955.
Time and Timekeepers by Willis I. Milham, Macmillan, New York, 1941.
Connecticut Clockmakers of the Eighteenth Century by Penrose R. Hoopes, Dodd, Mead & Co., New York, 1930.
The Clock Book by Wallace Nutting, Doubleday, New York, 1935.

Books and Bookbindings
ABC for Book-Collectors by John Carter, Hart-Davis, London, 1952.
Books and Book-Collectors by John Carter, Hart-Davis, London, 1956.
New Paths in Book Collecting by John Carter, John T. Winterich, and P. H. Muir, Constable, London, 1934.
Talks on Book-Collecting by Percy H. Muir, Cassell, London, 1952.
Taste and Technique in Book-Collecting by John Carter, C.U.P., Cambridge, and Bowker, New York, 1948.
The Book-Collecting Game by A. Edward Newton, Little, Brown, New York, 1928.
End Papers by A. Edward Newton, Little, Brown, New York, 1933.
London Bookbinders by Charles Ramsden, Batsford, London, 1956.
English Bookbindings in the British Museum, 1893.

Carpets and Rugs

Rare Hook Rugs by William Winthrop, Tudor, Springfield, Mass., 1941.

American Rugs by Estelle H. Ries, Cleveland, Ohio, 1950.

Collecting Hooked Rugs by Elizabeth Waugh and Edith Foley, New York, 1927.

Homecraft Rugs by Lydia LeBaron Walker, New York, 1929.

Handwoven Carpets, Oriental and European (2 vols) by A. F. Kendrick and C. E. C. Tattersall, Benn, London, 1922.

A History of British Carpets by C. E. C. Tattersall, F. Lewis, Leigh-on-Sea, 1934.

Le Manufacture de le Savonnerie by L. Bracquentié and J. Magnac, 1924.

Les Tapis Roumains by Henri Ernst (edition), Paris, 1928.

Cairene Rugs and Others Technically Related by Ernst Kühnel and Louise Bellinger, Textile Museum, Washington, D.C.

How to Identify Persian and other Oriental Rugs by C. J. Delabere, Crowell, New York, 1953.

Oriental Rugs by Hermann Haack, translated by George and Cornelia Wingfield Digby, London, 1960.

The Carpets of Persia by C. E. C. Tattersall, London, 1931.

Antique Rugs from the Near East by Wilhelm von Bode and Ernst Kühnel, revised ed. translated by C. G. Ellis, 1958.

Notes on Carpet Knotting and Weaving by C. E. C. Tattersall, Victoria and Albert Museum, 4th ed., 1949.

Oriental Rugs and Carpets by Arthur Urbane Dilley, New York, 2nd ed., 1959.

Coins and Medals

Historia Numorum: A Handbook of Greek Numismatics by Barclay V. Head, O.U.P., Oxford, 1911.

Greek Coins by Charles Seltman, Methuen, London, 2nd ed., 1955.

Some New Studies of Roman Republican Coinage by H. Mattingly, O.U.P., Oxford.

Coins of Roman Empire by H. Mattingly, British Museum, London.

English Coins by G. C. Brooke, Methuen, London, 1950.

The Scottish Coinage by I. H. Stewart, Spink, London, 1955.

Traité de numismatique du moyen âge by A. Engel and R. Serrure, Paris, 1891–1905.

Traité de numismatique moderne et contemporaine by A. Engel and R. Serrure, Paris, 1897–9.

The Coinage of the European Continent by W. C. Hazlitt, London, 1893.

Indian Peace Medals Issued in the United States by B. L. Belden, American Numismatic Society, New York, 1927.

Fractional Currency by Neil Corothers, New York, 1930.

Early Coins of America by S. S. Crosby (reprinted 1946).

State Coinages of New England by H. C. Miller *et al.*, American Numismatic Society, New York, 1920.

Biographical Dictionary of Medallists by L. S. Forrer, London, 1902–30.

Furniture

American Furniture, Queen Anne and Chippendale by Joseph Downs, Macmillan, New York, 1952.

Cabinetmakers of America by Ethel Hall Bjerkoe, Doubleday, New York, 1957.

Colonial Furniture in America (2 vols) by L. V. Lockwood, New York.

Standard Book of American Antique Furniture by Edgar G. Miller Jr, 1950.

American Furniture 1650–1850 by Charles Nagel, 1949.

Fine Points of Early American Furniture by Albert Sack, 1950.

Eighteenth-Century American Arts, a catalogue of the M. & M. Karolik Collection, E. J. Hipkiss, 1941.

Handbook of the American Wing, Metropolitan Museum by R. T. H. Halsey, C. O. Cornelius, and J. Downs, 7th ed., 1942.

John and Thomas Seymour: Cabinetmakers in Boston by Vernon C. Stoneman, 1959.

The Arts and Crafts of Newport by Ralph E. Carpenter Jr, 1954.

Blue Book of Philadelphia Furniture by William M. Hornor, 1931.

Duncan Phyfe and the English Regency by Nancy McClellan, 1939.

Charleston Furniture 1700–1825 by E. Milby Burton, Livington, Narberth, Pa., 1955.

Pine Furniture of Early New England by Russell H. Kettell, Dover, New York, 1949.

Field Guide to American Victorian Furniture by Thomas H. Ormsbee, Little, Brown, Boston, Mass., 1951.

Handbook of Antique Chairs by Carl Drepperd, Doubleday, New York, 1948.

Furniture Treasury (3 vols) by Wallace Nutting, Macmillan, New York, 1948–9.

Second Treasury of Early American Homes by Richard Pratt, Hawthorn Books, New York, 1954.

The People Called Shakers: A Search for the Perfect Society by Edward Deming Andrews, O.U.P., New York, 1953.

Early American Furniture by Charles O. Cornelius, New York, 1926.

English Chairs by Ralph Edwards, 2nd ed., Victoria and Albert Museum, London, 1957.

Georgian Furniture by Ralph Edwards, 2nd ed., Victoria and Albert Museum, London, 1957.

Georgian Cabinet-Makers by Ralph Edwards and Margaret Jourdain, Country Life, London, 1946.

English Furniture Styles from 1500 to 1830 by Ralph Fastnedge, Penguin, London, 1954.

A Short Dictionary of Furniture by John Gloag, Allen and Unwin, London, 1954.

English Furniture with some furniture from other countries in the Irwin Untermyer Collection by John Gloag and Yvonne Hackenbroch, Thames and Hudson, London, 1958.

The London Furniture Makers (1660–1840) by Sir Ambrose Heal, Batsford, London, 1953.

Treen by Edward H. Pinto, Batsford, London, 1949.

Furniture Making in the Seventeenth and Eighteenth Century in England by R. W. Symonds, Connoisseur, London, 1955.

A History of English Furniture, Victoria and Albert Museum, London, 1955.

English Furniture Designs of the Eighteenth Century by Peter Ward-Jackson, Victoria and Albert Museum, London, 1959.

Dictionary of English Furniture (3 vols) by P. McQuoid and R. Edwards, Country Life, 1954.

French Furniture and Decoration in the Eighteenth Century by Lady Dilke, Bell, London, 1901.

Le Style Louis XVI, "Arts, Style, and Techniques" by Emile Dacier (Collection publiée sous la direction de Norbert Duforq), Larousse, Paris, 1939.

Sheraton Furniture Designs with a Preface by Ralph Edwards, Tiranti, London, 1948.

Le Style Louis XV. Origine et évolution de Rococo by Fiske Kimball, A. et J. Picard, Paris, 1949.

Le meuble léger en France by Guillaume Janneau and Pierre Devinoy, P. Hartmann, Paris, 1948.

Il Mobile Veneziane, Milan, 1958, *Il Mobile Italiano*, Florence, 1940, *Il Mobile Genovese*, Milan, 1949, by Guiseppe Morazzoni.

Lo Stile dei Mobile by Terisio Pignatti, Verona, 1951.

Europäische Lackarbeiten by Hans Huth, Darmstadt.

Lacche Veneziane del Settecento by G. Lorenzetti, Venice, 1938.

Glass

Two Hundred Years of American Blown Glass by G. S. and H. McKearin, Crown, New York, 1950.

American Glass by G. S. and H. McKearin, Crown, New York, 1948.

Milk Glass by E. M. Belknap, Crown, New York.

Cut and Engraved Glass 1771–1905 by Dorothy Daniel, Barrows, New York, 1950.

Sandwich Glass by Ruth Webb Lee, Pittsburgh, Penn., 1931.

Early American Pressed Glass by Ruth Webb Lee, Northboro, Mass., revised ed., 1946.

Stiegel Glass by Frederick W. Hunter, Dover, New York, 1950.

Old Glass Paperweights by Evangeline G. Bergstrom, New York, 1948.

The Story of American Pressed Glass of the Lacy Period by James H. Rose, Corning, New York, 1954.

Rare English Glasses of the Seventeenth and Eighteenth Centuries by Joseph Bles, Bles, London, 1926.

History of Old English Glass by Francis Buckley, Benn, London, 1925.

The Art of Glass by Wilfred Buckley, 1939.

Handmaid to the Arts (2 vols) by Robert Dossie, 1758 and 1764.

English and Irish Cut Glass 1750–1950 by E. M. Elville, Country Life, 1953.

English Tableglass by E. M. Elville, Country Life, 1951.

Scottish and Jacobite Glass by A. Fleming, 1938.

Old English Drinking Glasses by Grant R. Francis, 1926.

Old English Glasses by Albert Hartshorne, 1897.

Glass Through the Ages by E. B. Haynes, 1948.

Old English, Irish, and Scottish Table Glass by G. Bernard Hughes, Batsford, London, 1956.

The Glass Collector by Percival MacIver, 1918.

English Glass by W. B. Honey, Collins, London, 1946.

English Glass by W. A. Thorpe, Black, London, 1949; Macmillan, New York, 1961.

A History of English and Irish Glass (2 vols) by W. A. Thorpe, Medici Society, London, 1929.

L'opaline française au 19ième siècle by Yolande Amic, Paris, 1952.

La verrerie en France de l'époque Gallo-Romaine à nos jours by James Barrelet, Paris, 1953.

L'art française depuis vingt ans. La céramique et la verrerie by René Chavance, Paris, 1928.

Ecrits pour l'art by Emile Galle, Paris, 1908.

La verrerie française depuis cinquante ans by L. Rosenthal, Paris and Brussels, 1927.

Paperweights and other Glass Curiosities by E. M. Elville, Country Life, 1954.

Irish Glass by M. S. Dudley Westropp, Herbert Jenkins, London, 1920.

Äldre svenska glas med graverad dekor by H. Seitz, Stockholm, 1936.

Gammelt norsk glass by A. B. Polak, Oslo, 1953.

Il Vetro di Murano by A. Gasparetto, Venice, 1959.

L'Arte del Vetro by G. Mariacher, Verona, 1954.

Jewellery

English Jewellery 1100–1870 by J. Evans, Faber, London, 1953.

English Jewellery from the Fifth Century A.D. to 1800 by J. Evans, London, 1921.

Magical Jewels of the Middle Ages and the Renaissance, particularly in England by J. Evans, Oxford, 1922.

Jewellery by J. Clifford Smith, London, 1908.

Victorian Jewellery by Margaret Flower, Cassell, London, 1951.

English Painted Enamels by Therle and Bernard Hughes, Country Life, London, 1951.

Der Schmuck by E. Bassermann-Jordan, Leipzig, 1909.

Geschichte des Kunstgewerbes aller Zeiten und Völker (vol. 5) by H. Th. Bossert, Berlin, 1928–35.

Grünes Gewëlbe Dresden by W. Holzhausen, Führer, Dresden, 1937.

Der Schmuck der Sammlung W. Clemen by E. Moses, Cologne.

Vienna, Kunsthistorisches Museum by A. Weizgärtner, Weltliche Schatzkammer, Führer, Vienna, 1929.

Oeuvres de bijouterie et joaillerie des XVIIe et XVIIIe siècles by A. Guérinet, Paris.

Argentiere Gemmari e Orafi D'Italia: Parte Prima-Roma by C. G. Bulgari, Rome, 1959.

Notizie Storiche sull'origine e progressi dei Lavori di commesso in Pietre Dure by A. Zobi, Florence, 1853.

Il Museo dell'Opificio delle Pietre Dure di Firenze by Bartole and Maser, Florence.

Metalwork

Early American Decoration by Esther Brazier, Pond-Ekburg Co., 1947.

The Art of Coppersmithing by John Fuller, David Williams Co., New York, 1911.

Early American Copper, Tin and Brass by Henry J. Kaufmann, Medill McBridge, New York, 1950.

English Domestic Metalwork by R. Goodwin Smith, F. Lewis, Leigh-on-Sea, 1937.

The English Brass and Copper Industries to 1800 by Henry Hamilton, Longmans, London, 1926.

Knives and Forks by C. T. Bailey, Medici Society, London, 1927.

Tutenag and Paktong by A. Bonnin, Oxford, 1924.

Guide to the Medieval Room, British Museum, 1st ed., 1907.

Spanish Ironwork by A. Byrne and M. Stapley, The Hispanic Society of America, 1915.

Histoire de luminaire by H. R. de l'Allemagne, Paris, 1891.

Les accessoires du costume et du mobilier (3 vols) by H. R. l'Allemagne, Paris, 1928.

Old French Ironwork by E. B. Frank, Harvard U.P., Cambridge, 1950.

Handbook on Ironwork (3 vols) by J. Starkie Gardner, Victoria and Albert Museum, London, various editions.

Colonial Lighting by A. H. Hayward, Boston, 1923.

Serrurerie du moyen âge et de la Renaissance by I. H. Hefner-Alteneck, Paris, 1870.

The Story of Cutlery by J. B. Himsworth, Benn, London, 1953.

Die deutschen Meister des Eisengusses im 16 Jahrhundert by A. Kippengerger, Marburg, 1931.

Iron and Brass Implements of the English House by Seymour Lindsay, Medici Society, London, 1927.

Dinanderie by J. Tavenor-Perry, London, 1910.

English Metalwork by W. Twopeny, Constable, London, 1904.

English Church Fittings, Furniture & Accessories by J. Charles Cox, 1933.

"English Brass Chandeliers" by C. C. Oman, in *Archaeological Journal*, vol xciii, 1936.

"A Pair of Chandeliers" in *The Connoisseur*, December 1956, "Churches and Candlelight" in *The Connoisseur Year Book*, 1958.

"Chandeliers and the Scrap-Yard" in *The Connoisseur Year Book*, 1959, "Chandeliers and Posterity", *The Connoisseur Year Book*, 1960, "Chandeliers, Fine and Handsome", *The Connoisseur Year Book*, 1961, "In Search of Chandeliers", *The Connoisseur Year Book*, 1962, all by Robert Sherlock.

The English Fireplace by L. A. Shuffrey, 1912.

The History and Origin of Horse Brasses by R. A. Brown, 1952.

Horse Brasses and Other Small Items for the Collector by G. Bernard Hughes, Country Life, 1956.

Antique Locks from the Collection of Josiah Parks & Sons Ltd, Willenhall, Staffs, 1955.

Pontypool and Usk Japanned Wares by W. D. John, Ceramic, Newport, Mon., 1953.

Story of Japan and Tin-plating by W. H. John, London, 1900.

History of Bilston by G. T. Lawley, 1893.

Japanned Work in Wolverhampton by Gerald Mander, 1925.

English Papier-Mâché, London, 1925.

Scottish Pewterware and Pewterers, by L. Ingleby Wood.

National Types of Old Pewter by H. H. Cotterell, 1925.

Pewter Down the Ages by H. H. Cotterell, 1932.

Old Pewter, Its Makers and Marks by H. H. Cotterell, 1929.

American Pewter by J. B. Kerfoot, 1924.

Guide to American Pewter by Carl Jacobs, 1957.

Pewter in America by Leslie I. Laughlin, 1940.

Bulletins of the Pewter Collectors' Club of America, 1934 to date.

Pewter Plate by H. J. L. J. Massé, 1910.

The Pewter Collector by H. J. L. J. Massé, 1921.

Causeries on English Pewter by A. F. de Navarro, 1911.
Old Base-metal Spoons by F. G. Hilton-Price, 1908.
History of the Worshipful Company of Pewterers (2 vols) by C. Welch, 1902.
Old British Pewter, 1500–1800 by A. V. Sunderland-Graeme, Connoisseur, London, 1951.
The Colonial Craftsman by Carl Bridenbaugh, New York U.P., New York, 1950.
Pioneer America – Its First Three Centuries by Carl W. Drepperd, Doubleday, New York, 1949.
Wrought Iron in Architecture by Gerald K. Geerlings, Scribners, New York, 1929.
Iron and Brass Implements of the English and American Home by J. Seymour Lindsay, The Medici Society, Boston.
Early American Wrought Iron by Albert H. Sonn, Scribners, New York, 1928.

Needlework and Embroidery

Early American Textiles by Frances Little, New York, 1931.
American Samplers by Ethel Standwood Bolton and Eva Johnston Coe, Massachusetts Society of the Colonial Dames of America, 1921.
American Needlework by Georgiana Brown Harbeson, Coward-McCann, New York, 1938.
Needlework as Art by Lady Marian Alford, 1886.
Mediterranean and Near Eastern Embroideries (2 vols) by A. J. B. Wale Haltan, 1935.
The Shuttle-craft Book of American Hand-weaving by Mary Meigs Atwater, New York, 1928, 1946.
Old Quilts by M. D. Junton, Jr and William Rush, Contonville, Maryland, 1946.
Old Patchwork Quilts and the Women who Made Them by Ruth E. Finley, Philadelphia, 1929.
The Romance of the Patchwork Quilt in America by Carrie Hall and Rose G. Kretsinger, Idaho, 1935.
A Book of Handwoven Coverlets by Eliza Calvert Hall, Boston, 1912.
The Standard Book of Quilt Making and Collecting by Margeurite Ickis, New York, 1949.
Historic Quilts by Florence Peto, New York, 1939.
American Quilts and Coverlets by Florence Peto, New York, 1949.
Yearbook of the Pennsylvania-German Folklore Society by Guy F. Reinert, 1948.
American Quilts by Elizabeth Wells Robertson, New York, 1948.
Quilts – Their Story and How to Make Them by Marie D. Webster, Doubleday, New York, 1915.
The Lace Book by N. H. Moore, 1937.
The History of Lace by F. B. Palliser, 1869.

Painting

Counterfeit by Sonia Cole, London, 1955.
Genuine and False by Hans Tietze, London, 1948.
Van Meegeren's Faked Vermeers and De Hooghs by P. Coremans, London, 1949.
Die Wandmalerien der Marienkirche zu Lübeck by H. A. Gräbke, Hamburg, 1951.
Vincent? A new method of identifying the artist and his work and of unmasking the forger and his products by H. M. van Dantzig, Amsterdam, 1953.
Publications in the Fogg Art Museum (U.S.A.).
The Story of the Old English Glass Pictures, 1690–1810 by H. G. Clarke, Courier Press, 1928.
Pictures on Glass by L. Loewenthal, privately printed, 1928.
Seventeenth-century Painting in New England by Louisa Dresser, Worcester Art Museum, 1935.
America's Old Masters by J. T. Flexner, New York, 1939.
The New York Historical Society's Dictionary of Artists in America, 1564–1860 by G. C. Groce and D. H. Wallace, New Haven and London, 1957.
First Flowers of our Wilderness by J. T. Flexner, Boston, 1947.
The Light of Distant Skies, 1760–1835 by J. T. Flexner, New York, 1935.
John Singleton Copley by B. N. Parker and A. B. Wheeler, Boston, 1938.
Charles Willson Peale (2 vols) by C. C. Sellers, Philadelphia, 1947.

Portraits and Miniatures by Charles Willson Peale by C. C. Sellers, Philadelphia, 1952.
Frederic Remington by Harold McCracken, Philadelphia, 1947.
The Charles M. Russell Book by Harold McCracken, New York.
The West of Alfred Jacob Miller by Marvin C. Rose, University of Oklahoma Press, 1951.
Artists and Illustrators of the Old West 1850–1900 by Robert Taft, New York, 1953.
Westward the Way, Catalogue of an exhibition at the City Museum, St Louis, 1954.
Early American Portrait Painters in Miniature by Theodore Bolton, New York, 1921.
John Singleton Copley: American Portraits in Oil, Pastel and Miniature by B. N. Parker and A. B.
    Wheeler, Boston, 1938.
The Life and Work of Edward Green Malbone, 1777–1807 by R. P. Tolman, New York, 1957.
American Miniatures, 1730–1850 by H. B. Wehle, New York, 1927.
American Sports, 1785–1835 by Jennie Holliman, Seeman, Durham, North Carolina, 1931.
"American Prize-fight Prints" by Paul Magriel in *Antiques*, November 1959.
Sport in Art, Catalogue of an exhibition, Albright Art Gallery, Buffalo, February 1948.
American Painting by Virgil Barker, New York, 1950.
A History of American Landscape Painting by Alan Burroughs, New York, 1942.
After the Hunt: William Harnett and Other American Still Life Painters by Alfred Frankenstein,
    University of California Press, 1953.
Winslow Homer by Lloyd Goodrich, New York, 1944.
The History of American Painting by Samuel Isham, New York, revised ed., 1927.
Art and Life in America by Oliver W. Larkin, New York, 1949.
Painting in America by E. P. Richardson, New York, 1956.
Book of the Artist: American Artist Life by Henry T. Tuckerman, New York, 1867.
American Pioneer Art and Artists by Carl Drepperd, Springfield, Mass., 1942.
American Primitive Painting by Jean Lipman, New York, 1942.
American Decorative Wall Painting by Nina Fletcher Little, Old Sturbridge Village, Mass.,
    1952.
History of the "Old Water-Colour" Society by J. L. Roget, 1891.
The English Water-Colour Painters by C. E. Hughes, Benn, London, 1950.
Water Colour Painting by A. W. Cundall, Seeley, London, 1951.
British Miniaturists by B. S. Long, London, 1930.
*Sea Painters of Britain. From Van de Velde to Turner, Part I; Sea Painters of Britain. From Constable to
    Brangwyn, Part II* by F. G. Roe, Leigh-on-Sea, 1947.
An Introduction to British Marine Painting by Oliver Warner, London, 1948.
British Sporting Artists from Barlow to Herring by W. S. Sparrow, London, 1922.
Joseph Crawhall by Adrian Bury, London, 1958.
Animal Painters by W. Gilbey, London, 1900.
Sport in Art by W. B. Groham, London, 1919.
The Horse in Art by D. L. Learmouth, London, 1959.
The Melton Mowbray of John Ferneley by Guy Paget, Leicester, 1931.
Sporting Prints of the 18th and early 19th centuries by R. G. Roe, London, 1927.
The Story of British Sporting Prints by F. Siltzer, Hulton, London, 1925, 1929.
The Autobiography of Sir Alfred Munnings, London, 1950, 1951, 1952.
English Art 1800–1870 by T. S. R. Boase, Oxford, 1959.
A Century of British Painters by R. and S. Redgrave, London, 1947.
Painters of the Victorian Scene by G. Reynolds, London, 1953.
French, Flemish and British Art by Roger Fry, London, 1951.
Holbein by Paul Ganz, Phaidon, London.
Van Eyck by Ludwig Baldass, Phaidon, London.
Die Altniederländische Malerie (14 vols) by Max J. Friedländer, Berlin, 1924, to Leiden, 1934.
Geschichte der Deutschen Kunst by Georg Dehio, Leipzig, 1930.

Dürer by Wilhelm Wätzold, Phaidon, London.

A New History of Painting in Italy (3 vols) by Crowe and Cavalcaselle, London, 1909.

The Italian Painters of the Renaissance by Bernard Berenson, London, 1952.

Caravaggio by Bernard Berenson, London, 1953.

An Introduction to Italian Painting by Charles Holmes, London, 1929.

The Mind of Leonardo da Vinci by Edward MacCurdy, London, 1952.

Pierro della Francesca by Kenneth Clark, Phaidon, London.

Tinteretto by Eric Newton, London, 1952.

Fra Angelico by John Pope Hennessy, Phaidon, London.

Titian by Hans Tietze, Phaidon, London.

Bellini by Philip Hendy, Phaidon, London.

Raphael by W. E. Suida, Phaidon, London.

Descriptive Catalogue of the Persian Painting in the Bodleian Library, Oxford, 1958.

Art Treasures of Soviet Russia by M. I. Conway, London, 1925.

Masterpieces of Russian Painting edited by M. Farbman, London, 1925.

The Art and Architecture of Russia by G. H. Hamilton, Pelican History of Art, London, 1954.

The Russian Icon by Minns-Kondakov, O.U.P., Oxford, 1927.

Russian Icons by D. Talbot Rice, Penguin, London.

Russian Art by T. Talbot Rice, Penguin, London, 1949.

Russian Icons by P. Schweinfurth, Batsford, London, 1953.

Pottery and Porcelain

The Pottery and Porcelain of the United States by E. A. Barber, Putnam, New York, 1893, 1902, 1909.

Tulip Ware of the Pennsylvania-German Potters by E. A. Barber, Pennsylvania Museum, 1903, 1926.

The Colonial Craftsman by Carl Bridenbaugh, New York U.P., New York, 1950.

Our Pioneer Potters by A. W. Clement, The Author, New York, 1947.

The Potters and Potteries of Chester County, Pennsylvania, Chester County Historical Society, West Chester, Pa., 1945.

Folk Art of Rural Pennsylvania by Frances Lichten, Scribner, New York, 1946.

American Potters and Pottery by John Ramsay, Hale, Cushman and Flint, Boston, 1939.

The Shenandoah Pottery by A. H. Rice and J. B. Stoudt, Shenandoah, Strasburg, Pa., 1929.

The A.B.C. of Bennington Pottery Wares by John Spargo, Bennington Historical Museum, Bennington, Vt, 1948.

Early American Pottery and China by John Spargo, Century, New York, 1926.

The Potters and Potteries of Bennington by John Spargo, Houghton Mifflin, and Antiques Inc., Boston, 1926.

Early New England Potters and Their Wares by Lura Woodside Watkins, Harvard U.P., Cambridge, U.S.A., 1950.

Notes on American Ceramics 1607–1943 by Arthur W. Clement, Handbook to the Museum Collections, Brooklyn Museum, Brooklyn, 1944.

The Pottery and Porcelain of New Jersey, 1688–1900 by Arthur W. Clement and Edith Bishop, Exhibition Catalogue, Newark Museum, Newark, N.J., 1947.

Loan Exhibition of Early American Pottery and Early American Glass by G. S. McKearin, from the Collection of George S. McKearin, held 1931 at the Grand Central Palace, New York, The Author, Hoosic Falls, 1931.

Early American Pottery and Porcelain by Helen McKearin, Foreword to sales-catalogue of the Alfred B. Maclay Collection, Parke-Bernet Galleries, New York, 1939.

Antiques, Boston, 1922–9, and New York, 1929 to date.

The Blue-China Book by A. W. Camehl, Dutton, New York, 1916; Tudor, New York, 1946.

China Collecting in America by E. M. Earle, Scribner, New York, 1892, Empire State Book Co., New York, 1924.

Pictures of Early New York on Dark Blue Staffordshire Pottery by R. T. Haines Halsey, Dodd, Mead, New York, 1924.

Anglo-American China, Parts I and II, Sam Laidacker, The Author, Bristol, Pa., 1951.

American Historical Views on Staffordshire China by E. B. Larsen, Doubleday, New York, 1939, revised ed., 1950.

Les porcelaines de Tournay by E. J. Soil de Moriamé, Tournay, 1910, 2nd ed. by L. Desplace de Formanoir, 1937.

La céramique bruxelloise du bon vieux temps by J. Helbig, Brussels, 1946.

Early Chinese Pottery and Porcelain by Basil Gray, Faber & Faber, London, 1953.

Concise Encyclopedia of English Pottery and Porcelain by Wolf Mankowitz and Reginald Haggar, Deutsch, London, and Hawthorn, New York, 1957.

Handbook of the Pottery and Porcelain of the Far East by R. L. Hobson, 3rd ed., British Museum, London, 1948.

Chinese Pottery and Porcelain (2 vols) by R. L. Hobson, Cassells, 1950.

Later Chinese Porcelain by W. B. Honey, Victoria and Albert Museum, London, 1927.

Ceramic Art of China by W. B. Honey, Faber, London, 1945.

Later Chinese Porcelain by Soame Jenyns, Faber, London, 1951.

Oriental Lowestoft by J. A. Lloyd Hyde, 2nd ed., Newport, Mon., 1954.

Chinese Export Art in the Eighteenth Century by Margaret Jourdain and Jenyns Soame, London, 1950.

China-Trade Porcelain by J. G. Phillips.

Pottery and Porcelain by E. Hanover, translated from the Danish by B. Rackham, London, 1925.

Dansk Porcelainsfabrik by Den Kyl Christensen, Copenhagen, 1938.

Royal Copenhagen Porcelain by A. Hayden, London, 1911.

La céramique hollandaise by H. Harvard, Amsterdam, 1909.

Het Oud-Hollandsch Porselein by C. H. C. A. van Sypesteyn, Hilversum, 1933.

The Ceramic Art of Great Britain (2 vols) by Llewellyn Jewitt, London, 1878.

British Pottery Marks by G. W. Rhead, London, 1910.

Catalogue of the Glaisher Collection (2 vols) by B. Rackham, Cambridge, 1934.

The Pottery and Porcelain of Swansea and Nantgarw by E. Morton Nance, London, 1942.

English Pottery and Porcelain by W. B. Honey, 3rd ed., London, 1947.

English Ceramic Circle, English Pottery and Porcelain Exhibition Catalogue, London, 1948.

Nineteenth Century English Pottery and Porcelain by G. Bembrose, London, 1952.

Catalogue of the Collection of English Pottery in the British Museum by R. L. Hobson, London, 1903.

Catalogue of an Exhibition of Early English Earthenware, Burlington Fine Arts Club, London, 1914.

English Pottery by B. Rackham and H. Read, London, 1924.

Catalogue of the Schreiber Collection, Vol. II by B. Rackham, London, 1929.

Staffordshire Pottery Figures by H. Read, London, 1929.

Wedgwood Ware by W. B. Honey, London, 1948.

English Delftware by F. H. Garner, London, 1948.

Early Staffordshire Pottery by B. Rackham, London, 1951.

Handbook of Leeds Pottery and Catalogue of the Exhibition Material at the Leeds City Art Gallery by D. Towner, Leeds, 1951.

Catalogue of the Collection of English Porcelain in the British Museum by R. L. Hobson, London, 1905.

Catalogue of the Herbert Allen Collection of English Porcelain by B. Rackham, London, 2nd ed., 1923

English Porcelain Figures of the Eighteenth Century by W. King, London, 1925.

English Blue and White Porcelain of the Eighteenth Century by J. L. Dixon, London, 1952.

Old English Porcelain by G. Savage, London, 1952.

English Porcelain of the Eighteenth Century by J. L. Dixon, London, 1952.

Eighteenth Century English Porcelain by G. Savage, London, 1952.

Champion's Bristol Porcelain by F. S. Mackenna, Leigh-on-Sea, 1947.

Caughley and Coalport Porcelain by F. A. Barrett, Leigh-on-Sea, 1951.

French Faïence by Arthur Lane, London, 1948.

Les faïences primitives, d'après apothicaireries hospitaliers by J. Chompret, Paris.

La faïence antique de Moustiers by C. Damiron, Lyons, 1919.

Nevers Faïence: the High Renaissance and Baroque Styles by A. Lane, Faenza, 1946.

Festive Publication to commemorate the 200th Jubilee of the oldest European China Factory by K. Berling, Dresden, 1911.

Dresden China by W. B. Honey, London, 1934 and 1946.

Meissner Porzellanmalerei des XVIII Jahrhunderts by G. E. Pazaureck, Stuttgart, 1929.

Meissner Porzellan by E. Zimmermann, Leipzig, 1926.

Deutsche Fayence und Porzellan-Hausmaler by G. E. Röder, Mainz, 1930.

Berliner Porzellan: Die Manufaktur Friedrich des Grossen (3 vols) by G. Lenz, Berlin, 1913.

Frankenthaler Porzellan by F. H. Hofmann, Munich, 1911.

Ansbacher Porzellan by A. Bayer, Ansbach, 1933.

A descriptive Catalogue of the Maiolica in the South Kensington Museum by C. D. E. Fortnum, Oxford, 1873.

Maiolica by C. D. E. Fortnum, 1896.

Catalogue of Maiolica in the Ashmolean Museum by C. D. E. Fortnum, Oxford, 1897.

Guide to Italian Maiolica by B. Rackham, Victoria and Albert Museum, London, 1933.

Catalogue of Italian Maiolica in the Victoria & Albert Museum by B. Rackham, London, 1940.

Corpus della maiolica Italiana: (I) Le maioliche datate fino al 1530; (II) Le maioliche datate al 1531–1535, Rome, 1933, 1938.

La maiolica italiana dello origini alla fino del cinquecento by G. Ballardini, Florence, 1938.

Catalogue of the Italian Maiolica in the Walters Art Gallery by Joan Prentice von Erdberg and Ross Marvinc, Baltimore, 1952.

European Ceramic Art by W. B. Honey, London.

Le Porcellane di Capodimonte by Barone Angelo de Eisner Eisenhof, Milan, 1925.

Russian Art Porcelain by B. Emme, in Russian, Moscow–Leningrad, 1950.

Russisches Porzellan by G. Lukomsky, Berlin, 1924.

Les marques sur la porcelaine russe by A. Rozembergh, Paris, 1926.

The State Porcelain Factory edited by I. Rodin, in Russian, Leningrad, 1938.

Spanish Arts by J. F. Riaño, South Kensington Museum Handbook, London, 1879.

Hispano-Moresque Ware: Supplementary Studies by A. Van de Put, London, 1911.

The Valencia Styles of Hispano-Moresque Pottery 1404–1454 by A. Van de Put, New York, 1938.

Lustre Ware of Spain by Alice Wilson Frothingham, New York, 1951.

Artes e Industrias del Buen Retiro by M. Perez, Madrid, 1904.

Capodimonte and Buen Retiro Porcelain: Period of Charles III by Alice Wilson Frothingham, New York, 1955.

Zürchner Porzellan des XVIII Jahrhunderts by S. Ducret, Zürich, 1944.

Die Zürchner Porzellanmanufaktur und ihre Erzugnisse, im 18 und 19 Jahrhundert by S. Ducret, Zürich, 1958–9.

Histoire documentaire de la manufactaire de la porcelaine de Nyon, 1781–1813 by A. De Molin, Lausanne, 1904.

Prints and Drawings

Paul Revere's Engravings by C. S. Brigham, American Antiquarian Society, Worcester, Mass., 1954.

Early American Prints by C. Dreppard, New York Public Library, New York, 1950.

American Woodcuts 1670–1950 : A Survey of Woodcuts and Wood-engravings in the United States by U. S. Johnson, Brooklyn Museum, New York, 1950.

American Graphic Art by Frank Weitenkampf, Macmillan, New York, 1924.

American Engravers upon Copper and Steel (2 vols) by D. M. Stauffer, The Grolier Club of the City of New York, 1907.

American Lithographs by Helen Comstock, New York, 1950.

America on Stone by H. T. Peters, New York, 1931.

California on Stone by H. T. Peters, New York, 1935.

Currier and Ives : Printmakers to the American People (2 vols) by H. T. Peters, New York, 1929 and 1931.

American Historical Prints, Stokes and Haskell, New York, 1933.

History of the First Locomotives in America by W. H. Brown, Appleton, New York, 1871.

American Lithographs of the 19th Century by Helen Comstock, Barrows, New York, 1950.

The William Barclay Parsons Railroad Prints, Columbia University Library, 1935.

Wax Portraits and Silhouettes by E. S. Bolton, Boston, 1914.

Shades of our Ancestors by Alice van Leer Carrick, Little, Brown, Boston, 1928.

A History of Silhouette by E. N. Jackson, Connoisseur, London, 1911.

Ancestors in Silhouette by E. N. Jackson, New York, 1921.

Silhouette Notes and Dictionary by E. N. Jackson, London and New York, 1938.

Engraving in England in the 16th and 17th Centuries (2 vols) by A. M. Hind, Dent, London, 1926–31.

Aquatint Engraving by S. T. Prideaux.

The Print Collectors' Quarterly by Campbell Dodgson.

English Coloured Books by Martin Hardie.

The Art of Etching by E. S. Lumsden.

Mezzotints by Cyril Davenport, London, 1904.

John Raphael Smith by Julia Frankau, London, 1902.

James McArdell by Gordon Goodwin, London, 1903.

A Short History of Engraving and Etching by A. M. Hind, London, 1921.

English Mezzotint Portraits (2 vols) by C. E. Russell, London, 1926.

Old English Mezzotints by M. C. Salaman, London, 1910.

British Mezzotinto Portraits (4 vols) by J. C. Smith, London, 1884.

The Masters of Mezzotint by Alfred Whitman, London, 1898.

Bird Books and Bird Art by Jean Anker, Copenhagen, 1938.

Fine Bird Books by S. Sitwell, H. Buchanan, and J. Fisher, London and New York, 1953.

Le peintre graveur by A. Bartsch, Vienna, 1803–21.

Le peintre graveur italien by Baudi de Vesme, Milan, 1906.

Early Italian Engraving by A. M. Hind, London, 1938–48.

The Processes and Schools of Engraving by A. M. Hind, London, 4th ed., 1952.

The Art of Silhouette by Desmond Coke, Secker, London, 1913.

Silhouettes by Raymond Lister, Pitman, London, 1953.

A Catalogue of Japanese and Chinese Woodcuts in the British Museum by L. Binyon, London, 1916.

Japanese Colour Prints by L. Binyon and J. J. O'Brien Sexton, London, 1923.

Block Printing and Book Illustration in Japan by L. N. Brown, London, 1924.

Japanese Masters of the Colour Print by J. Hillier, London, 1954.

Japanese Colour Prints by A. W. Ruffy, Victoria and Albert Museum Picture Book, London, 1952.

Japanese Colour Prints by E. F. Strange, Victoria and Albert Museum Handbook, London, 1910.

Scientific Instruments

Surveying Instruments. Their History and Classroom Use by E. R. Kiely, New York, 1947.

Cristoph Schissler der Ältere und der Jüngere by Maxmilian Bobinger, Augsburg and Basle, 1954.

The History of the Microscope by R. S. Clay and T. H. Court, London, 1932.

Les instruments scientifiques aux XVIIe et XVIIIe siècles by Maurice Daumas, Paris, 1953.

Catálogo crítico de astrolabios existentes en España by Salvador García Franco, Madrid, 1945.

"Some Early Philadelphia Instrument Makers" by H. E. Gillingham in *The Pennsylvania Magazine of History and Biography*, October 1927.

"The Classification of Sundials" by Kathleen Higgins in *Annals of Science*, Vol. IX, no. 4.

The History of the Telescope by H. C. King, London, 1956.

Islamic Astrolabists and their Works by L. A. Mayer, Geneva, 1956.

Practical Astronomy by W. Schroeder, London, 1956.

The Mathematical Practitioners of Tudor & Stuart England by E. G. R. Taylor, Cambridge, 1954.

The Art of Navigation in England in Elizabethan and Early Stuart Times by D. W. Waters, London, 1958.

A History of Science, Technology and Philosophy in the 16th & 17th Centuries by A. Wolf, 2nd ed. revised by Douglas McKie, London, 1950.

Sculpture and Carving

The Sculpture and Sculptors of the Greeks by G. M. A. Richter, New Haven, 1950.

Kouroi by G. M. A. Richter, New York, 1942.

Archaic Greek Art by G. M. A. Richter, New York, 1949.

Ancient Italy by G. M. A. Richter, Michigan, 1955.

Greek and Roman Bronzes by W. Lamb, Methuen, London, 1929.

Classical Sculpture by A. W. Lawrence, London, 1929.

Archaic Marble Sculpture from the Acropolis by H. Payne and G. M. Young, London, 1936, 1952.

La sculpture antique by C. Picard, Paris, 1935.

Ancient Marbles in Great Britain by A. Michaelis, Cambridge, 1882.

Die Italienischen Bronzen der Renaissance und des Barock. Zweiter Teil: Reliefs und Plaketten by E. F. Bange, 1922.

Die Deutsche Bronzestatuetten des 16 Jahrhunderts by E. F. Bange, 1949.

Italian Bronze Statuettes (3 vols) by W. Bode, 1907–8.

J. Pierpont Morgan Collection of Bronzes (2 vols) by W. Bode, 1910.

Sculpture by J. G. Mann, Wallace Collection Catalogue, 1931.

Die Bronzeplastiken by L. Planiscig, 1924.

Andrea Riccio by L. Planiscig, 1926.

Piccoli Bronzi Italiana by L. Planiscig, 1930.

The Gustave Dreyfus Collection: Reliefs and Plaquettes by S. de Ricci, 1931.

Life and Works of Louis François Roubiliac by K. Esdaile, O.U.P., Oxford, 1928.

Dictionary of British Sculptors, 1660–1815 by Rupert Gunnis, Odhams, London, 1953.

Michael Rysbrack, Sculptor by M. I. Webb, Country Life, London.

Portrait Waxes by D. R. Reilly, Batsford, London, 1953.

The English Garden by Ralph Dutton, 1945.

English Leadwork by L. Weaver, 1909.

English Art 1307–1451 by Joan Evans, Batsford, London, 1921.

Alabaster Tombs by A. Gardener, C.U.P., Cambridge, 1940.

Mediaeval Figure Sculpture in England by E. S. Prior and A. Gardener, C.U.P., Cambridge, 1912.

Introduction to "English Medieval Alabaster Carvings", York Festival Exhibition, 1954.

Die Consulardiptychen by R. Delbrück, 1929.

Elfenbeinarbeiten der Spätantike und des frühen Mittelalters by W. F. Volbach, 1952.

The Andrews Diptych by J. Beckwith, 1958.

Les ivoires gothiques français (3 vols) by R. Koechlin, 1924.
Elfenbein by O. Pelka, 1923.
English Ivories by M. H. Longhurst, 1926.
Ivoires français by L. Grodecki, 1947.
Popular Art in the United States by E. O. Christensen, Penguin, London, 1948.
Wild Fowl Decoys by J. D. Barber, Windward House, 1934.
Saints and Saint Makers by E. Boyd, Sante Fe, 1946.
"Schimmel the Woodcarver" by M. E. Flower in *Antiques*, February 1942.
Hunting Indians in a Taxicab by Kate Sanborn, Gorham, Boston, 1911.
La Scultura Lignea Senese by Enzo Carli, 1951.
Scultura Medioevale in Legno by Geza de Francovich, 1943.
Wood Sculpture by Alfred Maskell, 1911.
Ignaz Günther by A. Schönberger, 1954.

Silver
Early American Silver by C. L. Avery, Metropolitan Museum of Art, New York, 1920.
Historic Silver of the Colonies by F. L. Bigelow, Macmillan, London, 1914.
American Silver by K. H. Buhler, Cleveland, Ohio, 1950.
John Coney, Silversmith by H. F. Clarke, Boston, 1932.
Marks of Early American Silversmiths by Ernst M. Currier, 1938.
American Silversmiths and their Marks, privately printed, 1948.
Jacob Hurd and his Sons, Hollis French, 1939.
The Old Silver of American Churches by E. Alfred Jones, privately printed.
Maryland Silversmiths 1715–1830 by J. Hall Pleasants and Howard Sill, 1930.
Old Silver of Europe and America by E. A. Jones, London, 1922.
American Silver by J. M. Phillips, London and New York, 1949.
Guide to Marks of Origin on British and Irish Silver Plate, 1544–1946, 7th ed., 1947.
Gilda Aurifabrorum by W. Chaffers, 1899.
Old English Plate by W. J. Cripps, 11th ed., 1926.
English Goldsmiths and their Marks by C. J. Jackson, 1949.
An Illustrated History of English Plate (2 vols) by C. J. Jackson, 1911.
English Domestic Silver by C. C. Oman, 2nd ed., 1947.
Paul de Lamerie, His Life and Work by P. A. S. Phillips, 1935.
Old English Silver by W. W. Watts, 1924.
Argentiere Gemmarie Orafi D'Italia: Parte Prima – Roma by G. C. Bulgari, Rome, 1959.
Argenti Italiani by G. Gregorietti, Milan, 1959.
Gammel bergensk gullsmedkunst, Catalogue, Vestlandske Kunstindustrimuseum, Bergen, 1937.
Kristiania-sölv 1604–1854, Catalogue, Oslo Kunstindustrimuseum, 1954.
Gammel guldsmedkunst, Catalogue, Oslo Kunstindustrimuseum, 1909.
Bergen Silver from the Guild Period (2 vols) by R. Kloster and Thv. Krohn-Hansen, Bergen, 1957.
"Bergen Silver of the Guild Period" by N. M. Penzer in *The Connoisseur*, April 1958.
Peter Carl Fabergé, His Life and Work by H. C. Bainbridge, London, 1949.
Art Treasures of Russia edited by A. Benois, in Russian and French, St Petersburg, 1901.
Russian Art by C. Bunt, London, 1949.
Inventaire des palais impériaux by A. Foelkersam, St Petersburg, 1907.
Argenterie russe ancienne de la collection Eugène Lubovich, privately printed, Paris, 1932.
Guide to Artistic Silver in the Hermitage, in Russian, Moscow, 1956.
Russian Art by A. Maskell, London, 1886.
Russian Silver and Enamel, Russian Museum, Leningrad by N. Porfiridov, Leningrad, 1956.

List of Museums and Galleries

The following list is arranged under the main subject headings in the book – Furniture, Glass, etc. It does not seek to be exhaustive and covers only major museums and galleries and a few provincial ones which contain a certain number of good examples of the objects indicated; however, many provincial galleries can show one or two good specimens and are usually worth a visit.

ARMS AND ARMOUR
GREAT BRITAIN
City Museum and Art Gallery, Birmingham
Blair Castle and Atholl Museum, Perth
Admiral Blake Museum, Bridgwater
City Museum, Bristol
The West Gate, Canterbury
Chiddingstone Castle, Edenbridge
Royal Scottish Museum, Edinburgh
Farleigh Castle Museum, Hungerford
The Scott Collection, Glasgow Art Gallery and Museum, Glasgow
The Whitelaw Collection of Scottish Arms, Glasgow Art Gallery and Museum, Glasgow
Ilfracombe Museum, Ilfracombe
Inverness Museum, Inverness
Dick Institute Museum, Kilmarnock
Abbey House Museum, Leeds
Lichfield Museum, Lichfield
Lincoln Municipal Museum, Lincoln
Rapallo House Museum and Art Gallery, Llandudno
The Royal Artillery Museum, Woolwich
Imperial War Museum, London
Tower of London
Victoria and Albert Museum, London
British Museum, London

Wallace Collection, London
Ludlow Museum, Ludlow
Laing Museum, Newcastle-upon-Tyne
Padiham Memorial Park Museum, Padiham
Thrope Prebend House and Museum, Ripon
Preston Hall Museum and Art Gallery, Stockton-on-Tees
St Edward's Hall Museum, Stow-on-the-Wold
Henry Stilby Fire-arm Collection, Wyndham Museum, Yeovil

EUROPE
Musée des Arts Décoratifs, Paris
Louvre, Paris
Musée de l'Armée, Paris
Museum für Deutsche Geschichte, Berlin
Deutsches Klingenmuseum, Solingen
Bayerisches Nationalmuseum, Munich
Deutsches Museum, Nuremberg
Veste Coburg, Coburg
Schweizerisches Landesmuseum, Zurich
Historisches Museum, Basle
Landeshaus, Graz
Kunsthistorischesmuseum, Vienna
Tajhusmuseum, Copenhagen

Kunzl Livinstkammarenm, Stockholm
Musée de la Porte de Hal, Brussels
Het Legersche museum, Leiden
Real Armeria, Madrid
Museo Stibbert, Florence
Bargello, Florence
Castello Sant Angelo, Rome
Palazzo Venezia, Rome
Armeria Reale, Turin
Palazzo di Capodimonte, Naples
Museo Poldi Pezzoli, Milan
Palazzo Ducale, Venice

U.S.A.
United States National Museum,
  Washington
Metropolitan Museum of Art, New York
Cincinnati Art Museum, Ohio
Cleveland Museum of Art, Ohio
West Point Museum, N.Y.

BAROMETERS, CLOCKS AND WATCHES
Clocks and Watches
GREAT BRITAIN
British Museum, London
Science Museum, London
Victoria and Albert Museum, London
Clockmakers Company, Guildhall, London
Wallace Collection, London

EUROPE
Bayerisches Nationalmuseum, Munich
Germanischesmuseum, Munich
Germanischesmuseum, Nuremberg
Hessisches Landesmuseum, Cassel
Herzog Anton-Ulrich Museum, Brunswick
Kunsthistorischesmuseum, Vienna
Conservatoire des Arts et Métiers, Paris
Louvre, Paris

U.S.A.
Old Sturbridge Village, Sturbridge,
  Massachusetts
Boston Museum of Fine Arts, Boston,
  Massachusetts
Bristol Clock Museum, Bristol, Connecticut
California Academy of Sciences,
  San Francisco
Essex Institute, Salem, Massachusetts
Metropolitan Museum of Art, New York

Newark Public Library, Newark, New York
New York University (the James Arthur
  Collection)
Pennsylvania Historical Society,
  Philadelphia
Smithsonian Institute, U.S. National
  Museum, Washington D.C.

Barometers
GREAT BRITAIN
Science Museum, London
Wallace Collection, London
Victoria and Albert Museum, London
Royal Scottish Museum, Edinburgh
Museum for the History of Science, Oxford

EUROPE
Conservatoire des Arts et Métiers, Paris
Deutschesmuseum, Munich
Zeylers Museum, Haarlem
Rijksmuseum for the History of Science,
  Leiden

BOOKS AND BOOKBINDINGS
GREAT BRITAIN
British Museum, London
Bodleian Library, Oxford
University Library, Cambridge
National Library of Scotland, Edinburgh
National Library of Wales, Aberystwyth
John Rylands Library, Manchester
The College Libraries of Oxford and Cam-
  bridge and collections at the other uni-
  versities, such as the Brotherton Library,
  Leeds
The Libraries of Eton College and
  Winchester College
The Cathedral Libraries throughout the
  country

EUROPE
Deutsche Staatsbibliothek, Berlin
Landes- und Stadt-Bibliothek, Düsseldorf
Westdeutsche Bibliothek, Marburg
Württembergische Landesbibliothek,
  Stuttgart
Stadbibliothek Trier, Trier
Kestner-Museum Hanover
Bibliothèque Calvet, Avignon
Musée et Château de Chantilly, Paris

Biblioteca Ambrosiana, Milan
Biblioteca Nazionale Centrale, Florence
Biblioteca Nazionale Braidense, Milan
Biblioteca Nazionale, Naples
Athenaeum-Bibliotheek, Deventer
Koninklijke Bibliotheek, The Hague
University Libraries of Padua, Bologna,
    Leiden, Utrecht, Barcelona, Uppsala, and
    many other towns

U.S.A.

Folger Shakespeare Library, Washington
Newberry Library, Chicago
Pierpoint Morgan Library, New York
New York Public Library
Free Library of Philadelphia
Harvard University Library, Cambridge
University of Virginia Library
Nelson-Atkins Gallery of Art, Kansas City
Walters Art Gallery, Baltimore

CARPETS AND RUGS
GREAT BRITAIN

Victoria and Albert Museum, London
    (general)
Ham House, nr Richmond, Surrey (English)
Osterley Park, Osterley (Gobelins and
    Beauvais)
Hampton Court Palace, London (late
    medieval)
City Museum and Art Gallery, Birmingham
Burrell Collection, Glasgow
Bowes Museum, Barnard Castle
Wernher Collection, Luton Hoo
Knole, near Sevenoaks, Kent
Hatfield House, Hatfield

EUROPE

Louvre, Paris (general)
Musée de Cluny, Paris (medieval)
Musée des Arts Décoratifs, Paris (medieval
    and later)
The Castle, Angers (15th–16th centuries)
The Cathedral and Museum, Rheims (late
    medieval)
Rijksmuseum, Amsterdam
Musée du Cinquantenaire, Brussels (general)
Historischesmuseum, Basle (15th century)
Historischesmuseum, Berne (15th century,
    Tournai)

Landesmuseum, Zurich (15th–16th century)
Palaces and Galleries, Florence (especially
    16th century)
Museo Vaticano, Rome (Sistine Chapel)
Palaces and Galleries, Rome (16th–18th
    centuries)
Palazzo Real, Madrid (Flemish 16th century
    and Spanish 18th century)
La Seo Catedral Museo, Saragoza (medieval)
La Catedral Museo, Zamora (medieval)
Kunsthistorischesmuseum, Vienna (general)
Hofburg, Vienna (general)
Österreichischesmuseum für
    Angewandtekunst, Vienna
Germanischesmuseum, Nuremberg
    (15th–16th centuries)
Bayerisches Nationalmuseum, Munich
    (general)
Schloss Nymphenburg, Munich (18th
    century)

U.S.A.

New York State Historical Association,
    Cooperstown, New York
Winterthur Museum, Delaware
Shelburne Museum, Shelburne, Vermont
Metropolitan Museum, New York

COINS AND MEDALS
GREAT BRITAIN

Ashwell Village Museum, Ashwell, Herts
The Holburne of Menstrie Museum of Art,
    Bath
Victoria Art Gallery, Bath
Modern School Museum, Bedford
Public Library, Museum and Art Gallery,
    Blackburn
Fitzwilliam Museum, Cambridge
National Museum of Wales, Cardiff
Victoria Jubilee Museum, Cawthorne
Gorey Castle Museum, Jersey
Chelmsford and Essex Museum, Chelmsford
Colchester and Essex Museum, Colchester
National Museum of Antiquities, Edinburgh
The Hunterian Museum, Glasgow
Gloucester City Museum, Gloucester
Charterhouse School Museum, Godalming
King's Lynn Museum and Art Gallery,
    King's Lynn
Library of the Thoresby Society, Leeds

Lichfield Museum, Lichfield
Lincoln Municipal Museum, Lincoln
British Museum, London
Lord Wandsworth College Museum, Long
    Sutton, Hants
Philpot Museum, Lyme Regis
Athelstan Museum, Malmesbury
Manchester Museum, Manchester
Art Gallery and Museum, Merthyr Tydfil
Castle Museum, Norwich
Library and Museum, Oswestry
Ashmolean Museum, Oxford
Arbuthnot Museum, Peterhead
Poole Museum, Poole
Public Museum, Rochester
City Museum, Sheffield
Marlipins Museum, Shoreham, Sussex
Spalding Museum, Spalding
Swindon Museum, Swindon
Somerset County Museum, Taunton
Ancient House Museum, Thetford, Norfolk
Museum and Art Gallery, Tunbridge Wells
Wells Museum, Wells
Public Library and Museum, Whitehaven
Church Porch Folk Museum, Winchcombe
Yorkshire Museum, York

EUROPE
Cabinet des Médailles, Bibliothèque
    Nationale, Paris
Cabinet des Médailles, Bibliothèque Royale,
    Brussels
Koningklijk Kabinet van Munten, The
    Hague
Koorgelige Montsamling, Copenhagen
Statens Historiska Museum, Stockholm
Universitets Museum, Oslo
Museum für Hamburgische Geschichte,
    Hamburg
Staatliche Münzsammlung, Munich
Musée d'Archéologie, Geneva
Historischesmuseum, Basle
Castello Sforzesco, Milan
Museo Nazionale, Rome
Museo Nazionale, Naples
National Museum, Athens
National Museum, Zagreb
National Museum, Budapest
National Museum, Prague
Bundessammlung von Münzen, Vienna
Hermitage Museum, Leningrad

U.S.A.
American Numismatic Society, New York
Boston Museum of Fine Arts, Boston
United States National Museum,
    Washington D.C.
Carnegie Institute, Pittsburg

FURNITURE
GREAT BRITAIN
Castle Museum, York
Collection of Wooden Bygones, Oxley Wood
    House, Northwood, Mddx
Museum of English Rural Life, University of
    Reading
Townend, Troutbeck, nr Windermere
State Apartments, Hampton Court Palace,
    London
State Apartments, Kensington Palace,
    London
Museum of Welsh Antiquities, Bangor
    (Welsh furniture)
Bowes Museum, Barnard Castle
Holburne of Menstrie Museum, Bath
Cecil Higgins Museum, Bedford
Aston Hall, Birmingham
Art Gallery and Museum, Brighton
Thomas-Stanford Museum, Brighton
Georgian House, Bristol
The Red Lodge, Bristol
Towneley Hall Museum, Burnley
Astley Hall, Chorley
Valence House Museum, Dagenham, Essex
Burrell Collection, Glasgow
West Yorkshire Fold Museum, Halifax
The Old House, Hereford
Wilberforce Museum, Hull
Christchurch Mansion, Ipswich
Broghton House, Kirkcudbright
Temple Newsam House, Leeds
Anne of Cleves House, Southover, Lewes
Victoria and Albert Museum, London
Courtauld Institute of Art, London
Binning Collection, Fenton House, London
Geffrye Museum, Shoreditch, London
St John's Gate, Clerkenwell, London
Wallace Collection, London
City Art Gallery, Manchester
Heaton Hall, Manchester
Wythenshawe Hall, Manchester
The Lady Lever Art Gallery, Port Sunlight
Ford Green Hall, Stoke-on-Trent

Hall's Croft, Old Town, Stratford
Torre Abbey Art Gallery, Torquay
Oak House, West Bromwich
The Priest House, West Hoathly, Sussex

Victorian Furniture
GREAT BRITAIN
Victoria and Albert Museum, London
London Museum, London
William Morris Gallery, Walthamstow,
   London
Shipley Art Gallery, Gateshead

French Furniture
GREAT BRITAIN
Bowes Museum, Barnard Castle
Victoria and Albert Museum, London
Wallace Collection, London

EUROPE
Louvre, Paris
Musée des Arts Décoratifs, Paris
Musée Nissim de Camondo, Paris
Musée Marmottan, Paris
Rijksmuseum, Amsterdam
Residenzmuseum, Munich
Nationalmuseum, Stockholm

U.S.A.
Metropolitan Museum of Art, New York
Frick Collection, New York
Philadelphia Museum of Art
Cleveland Museum of Art, Cleveland, Ohio

American Furniture
U.S.A.
M. H. de Young Memorial Museum, San
   Francisco
Wadsworte Atheneum, Harford, Conn.
Winterthur Museum, Winterthur, Delaware
Colonial Williamsburg, Virginia
Freer Gallery of Art, Washington
Art Institute of Chicago, Chicago
Boston Museum of Fine Arts, Boston,
   Massachusetts
Detroit Institute of Arts, Detroit, Michigan
Brooklyn Museum, Brooklyn, New York
Metropolitan Museum of Art, New York
Cleveland Institute of Art, Cleveland, Ohio
Philadelphia Museum of Art, Philadelphia

Seattle Art Museum, Seattle, Washington
Shelburne Museum, Vermont

Italian Furniture
EUROPE
Palazzo Pitti, Florence
Museo Comunale Stibbert, Florence
Museo Horne, Fondazione Horne, Florence
Civici Instituti di Storia e d'Arte, Milan
Museo Civico, Treviso
Palazzo Rezzonico, Venice
Palazzo Reale, Genoa
Palazzo Reale, Turin
Palazzo Quiranale, Rome
Hofburg, Vienna
Osterreichischcsmuseum für
   Angewandtekunst, Vienna
Palais Czernin, Vienna
Palais Harrach, Vienna
Palais Schonberg, Vienna
Palais Schwarzenberg, Vienna
Osterreichisches Barockmuseum, Vienna
Historichesmuseum der Stadt, Vienna
Niederösterreichisches Landesmuseum,
   Vienna
Bundesmobiliendepot, Vienna

U.S.A.
Ringling Museum, Sarasota, Florida
Frick Collection, New York

GLASS
GREAT BRITAIN
Bowes Museum, Barnard Castle
Holburne of Menstrie Museum, Bath
Cecil Higgins Museum, Bedford
Haworth Art Gallery, Accrington
City Museum and Art Gallery, Birmingham
Public Library Museum, Brierley Hill, Staffs
Museum and Art Gallery, Belfast
Astley Hall, Chorley, Lancs
Museum and Art Gallery, King's Lynn
The Wernher Collection, Luton Hoo
British Museum, London
London Museum, London
Victoria and Albert Museum, London
Art Gallery and Museum, Rawtenstall
Yorkshire Museum, York
Public Library, Museum and Art Gallery,
   Blackburn
Art Gallery and Museum, Brighton

Towneley Hall Art Gallery and Museum,
  Burnley
Library and Museum, Buxton
Public Library and Museum, Castleford
Art Gallery and Museum, Glasgow
Museum of Art, Hove
Bethnal Green Museum, London
Heaton Hall, Manchester
Laing Art Gallery and Museum, Newcastle-
  upon-Tyne
Municipal Art Gallery and Museum,
  Oldham
Harris Museum and Art Gallery, Preston
Saffron Walden Museum, Saffron Walden
Spalding Museum, Spalding
Wollescote Hall, Stourbridge

EUROPE
Rijksmuseum, Amsterdam

U.S.A.
Corning Museum of Glass, New York
Boston Museum of Fine Arts, Boston,
  Massachusetts
Brooklyn Museum, New York
Cincinnati Art Museum, Cincinnati
Cooper Union Museum for the Arts of
  Decoration, New York
Winterthur Museum, Delaware
Metropolitan Museum of Art, New York

JEWELLERY
GREAT BRITAIN
Bowes Museum, Barnard Castle
City Museum and Art Gallery, Birmingham
Tower of London, London
The Waddeston Bequest, British Museum,
  London
The Cheapside Hoard, London Museum,
  London
Victoria and Albert Museum, London
Wallace Collection, London
Peter Jones Collection, Walker Art Gallery,
  Liverpool
Wernher Collection, Luton Hoo
Museum and Art Gallery, Rotherham
Museum and Art Gallery, Worthing

EUROPE
Galleria Nazionale dell'Umbria, Perugia
Musée des Arts Décoratifs, Paris

Museo degli Argenti, Palazzo Pitti, Florence
Museo dell' Opificio delle Pietre Dure,
  Florence

U.S.A.
Maryland Historical Society, Baltimore
The Virginia Museum of Fine Arts,
  Richmond, Virginia
Philadelphia Museum of Art, Philadelphia
National Gallery of Art, Washington D.C.
Currier Gallery of Art, Manchester,
  New Hampshire

METALWORK
GREAT BRITAIN
Bowes Museum, Barnard Castle
The Old Merchants House, Great Yarmouth
Public Museum and Art Gallery, Hastings
John Every Collection, Anne of Cleves
  House, Lewes
Victoria and Albert Museum, London
British Museum, London
Laing Art Gallery and Museum, Newcastle-
  upon-Tyne
City Museum and Art Gallery, Nottingham
Municipal Art Gallery and Museum,
  Wolverhampton

U.S.A.
Henry Ford Museum, Dearborn, Michigan
Old Sturbridge Village, Sturbridge,
  Massachusetts
Old Deerfield, Deerfield, Massachusetts
Colonial Williamsburg, Williamsburg,
  Virginia
Metropolitan Museum of Art, New York
Brooklyn Museum, New York

Firebacks and Dogs
GREAT BRITAIN
John Every Collection, Anne of Cleves House,
  Lewes
Victoria and Albert Museum, London

Pewter
GREAT BRITAIN
Victoria and Albert Museum, London
British Museum, London
London Museum, London
Guildhall, London
Castle Museum, Norwich

City Museum and Art Gallery, Bristol
Fitzwilliam Museum, Cambridge
City Museum and Art Gallery, Birmingham
Yorkshire Museum, York

U.S.A.
Shelburne Museum, Shelburne, Vermont
Old Deerfield, Deerfield, Massachusetts
Henry Ford Museum, Dearborn, Michigan

MIRRORS
GREAT BRITAIN
Victoria and Albert Museum, London
Temple Newsam House, Leeds

U.S.A.
Colonial Williamsburg, Williamsburg,
    Virginia
Henry Ford Museum, Dearborn, Michigan
Winterthur Museum, Delaware
Museum of Fine Arts, Boston

NEEDLEWORK AND
EMBROIDERY
GREAT BRITAIN
Burrell Collection, Art Gallery and Museum,
    Glasgow
Victoria and Albert Museum, London
City Art Gallery, Manchester
Whitworth Art Gallery, Manchester
Galleries of the Regional College of Art,
    Manchester
Thorpe Prebend House and Museum, Ripon
The Priest House, West Hoathly, Sussex
Museum and Muniment Room, Guildford
City Museum and Art Gallery, Hereford
Museum of Art, Hove
Ferens Art Gallery, Hull
Fitzwilliam Museum, Cambridge
Bankfield Museum, Halifax
National Museum of Wales, Cardiff
Gallery of English Costume, Platt Hall,
    Manchester
Hardwick Hall, nr Chesterfield

EUROPE
Herzog Anton Ulrich-Museum, Brunswick
Kestner-Museum, Hanover
Museum für Kunst und Kunstgewerbe,
    Magdeburg

U.S.A.
Boston Museum of Fine Arts, Boston
Cincinnati Art Museum, Cincinnati
Cooper Union Museum for the Arts of
    Decoration, New York
Fine Arts Society of San Diego, San Diego
Colonial Williamsburg, Williamsburg,
    Virginia

PAINTING
GREAT BRITAIN
National Gallery, London
British Museum, London
Victoria and Albert Museum, London
Sir John Soane Museum, London
Wallace Collection, London
National Maritime Museum, London
National Portrait Gallery, London
Dulwich College Gallery, London
The Foundling Hospital, London
Guildhall Art Gallery, London
Ham House, London
Hampton Court, London
Iveagh Bequest, London
Ken Wood, London
South London Art Gallery, London
Leighton House, Holland Park, London
William Morris Gallery, Walthamstow,
    London
Wellington Museum, Apsley House, London
Whitechapel Art Gallery, London
Arts Council Gallery, London
Imperial Institute, London
Royal Academy, London
Art Gallery and Museum, Birmingham
Art Gallery and Museum, Manchester
Art Gallery and Museum, Liverpool
Art Gallery and Museum, York
Art Gallery and Museum, Port Sunlight
Fitzwilliam Museum, Cambridge
Ashmolean Museum, Oxford
Art Gallery and Museum, Norwich
Art Gallery and Museum, Bournemouth
Art Gallery and Museum, Bristol
Art Gallery and Museum, Southampton
Art Gallery and Museum, Plymouth
Art Gallery and Museum, Preston
Art Gallery and Museum, Canterbury
Art Gallery and Museum, Leeds
Art Gallery and Museum, Truro
Art Gallery and Museum, Wakefield

National Museum of Wales, Cardiff
National Gallery of Scotland, Edinburgh
National Portrait Gallery of Scotland,
  Edinburgh
Glasgow Art Gallery, Glasgow
Aberdeen Art Gallery, Aberdeen
Belfast Art Gallery and Museum, Belfast

EIRE
National Gallery of Ireland, Dublin
Gallery of Modern Art, Dublin

FRANCE
Louvre, Paris
Musée de L'Art Moderne, Paris
L'Orangerie, Paris
Petit Palais, Paris
Musée Cognacq, Paris
Collections at:
  Aix, Ajaccio, Amiens, Angers, Avignon,
  Caen, Bordeaux, Dijon, Douai, Grenoble,
  Le Mans, Le Puy, Lille, Lyon, Montauban,
  Monaco, Nice, Nancy, Nantes, Nimes,
  Orléans, Strasbourg, Tours, Toulouse

BELGIUM
Brussels

HOLLAND
The Hague, Amsterdam, Rotterdam

GERMANY
Berlin, Dresden, Munich, Hamburg, Bremen,
Dusseldorf

AUSTRIA
The Albertina, Vienna

SWITZERLAND
Zurich, Basle, Geneva

ITALY *(a selection)*
Accademia, Venice
Palazzo Ducale, Venice
Museo Correro, Venice
Ca' Rezzonico, Venice
Museo Capitolino, Rome
Museo Vaticano, Rome
Galleria Corsini, Rome
Galleria nazionale dell'Arte moderna, Rome

Galleria Borghese, Rome
Bargello, Florence
Biblioteca Laurentiano, Florence
Galleria Riccardiano, Florence
Galleria Uffizi, Florence
Palazzo Pitti, Florence
Galleria dell'Arte Moderna, Florence
Accademia Carraria, Bergamo
Galleria Martinengo, Brescia
Galleria Brera, Milan
Museo Poldi Pezzoli, Milan
Castello Sforzesco, Milan
Galleria Reale, Naples
Museums of:
  San Martino, Padua, Parma, Pisa, Verona,
  Siena, Turin
also Museums of:
  Copenhagen, Stockholm, Budapest, War-
  saw, Madrid, Toledo, Lisbon

U.S.A.
Art Institute of Chicago, Chicago
Baltimore Museum of Art, Baltimore
Boston Museum of Fine Arts, Boston
California Palace of the Legion of Honor,
  San Francisco
Cincinnati Art Museum, Cincinnati
Cleveland Museum of Art, Cleveland
Currier Gallery of Art, Manchester
Detroit Institute of Arts, Detroit
Fine Arts Society of San Diego, San Diego
Fogg Museum of Art, Harvard University
Huntingdon Library, San Marino
Maryland Historical Society, Baltimore
Metropolitan Museum of Art, New York
M. H. De Young Memorial Museum, San
  Francisco
Museum of Modern Art, New York
National Gallery of Art, Washington D.C.
Nelson-Atkins Gallery of Art, Kansas City
Phildelphia Museum of Art, Philadelphia
San Francisco Museum of Art, San
  Francisco
Smith College Museum of Art, Northampton
Solomon R. Guggenheim Museum,
  New York
University of Kansas Museum of Art,
  Lawrence
Virginia Museum of Fine Arts, Richmond
Walters Art Gallery, Baltimore, Maryland
Worcester Art Museum, Worcester

Italian Painting
GREAT BRITAIN
National Gallery, London
Barber Institute, Birmingham University
Fitzwilliam Museum, Cambridge
Ashmolean Museum, Oxford

EUROPE
Louvre, Paris
Uffizi, Florence
Brera, Milan
Accademia, Venice
Museo Vaticano, Rome
Palazzo Pitti, Florence
Prado, Madrid
Kunsthistorischesmuseum, Vienna
*Most of the museums and galleries listed under
Painting above contain collections of Italian
painting.*

Old English Water-colours
GREAT BRITAIN
Haworth Art Gallery, Haworth Park,
    Accrington, Lancs
Cecil Higgins Museum, Bedford
Museum and Art Gallery, Belfast
Victoria Art Gallery, Bath
Museum and Art Gallery, Bolton
City Museum and Art Gallery,
    Birmingham
Art Gallery and Museum, Brighton
Fitzwilliam Museum, Cambridge
Usher Art Gallery, Lincoln
British Museum, London
Victoria and Albert Museum, London
City Art Gallery, Leeds
Fletcher Moss Museum, Manchester
Werneth Park Branch, Oldham, Lancs
Public Museum and Art Gallery,
    Stoke-on-Trent
Literary and Philosophical Society Museum,
    Whitby
Municipal Art Gallery and Museum,
    Wolverhampton

POTTERY AND PORCELAIN
GREAT BRITAIN
Porcelain
Bowes Museum, Bernard Castle
Cecil Higgins Museum, Bedford

Museum and Art Gallery, Derby
Usher Art Gallery, Lincoln
Victoria and Albert Museum, London
British Museum, London
Rapallo House Museum and Art Gallery,
    Llandudno
Public Library, Museum and Art Gallery,
    Blackburn
Royal Museum and Slater Art Gallery,
    Canterbury
Art Gallery and Museum, Cheltenham
Art Gallery and Museum, Glasgow
Bethnal Green Museum, London
Fenton House, London
Fletcher Moss Museum, Manchester
Museum and Art Gallery, Rotherham
    (Rockingham)
Public Library, Museum and Art Gallery,
    Stoke-on-Trent
Bantock House, Wolverhampton

Pottery
Aldbrough Roman Museum, Aldbrough,
    Yorks (Roman)
The Glaisher Collection, Fitzwilliam
    Museum, Cambridge
Willett Collection, Art Gallery and Museum,
    Brighton
City Art Gallery, Leeds
The Schreiber Collection, Victoria and
    Albert Museum, London
Museum and Art Gallery, Nottingham
Williamson Art Gallery, Birkenhead
Public Library, Museum and Art Gallery,
    Blackburn
Museum and Art Gallery, Bootle
Library and Museum, Buxton
Segontium Museum, Caernarvon
Royal Museum and Slater Art Gallery,
    Canterbury
Art Gallery and Museum, Cheltenham
Astley Hall, Chorley
Colchester and Essex Museum, Colchester
Royal Albert Memorial Museum and Art
    Gallery, Exeter
Public Museum and Art Gallery, Hastings
Heaton Hall and Wythenshawe Hall,
    Manchester
Municipal Art Gallery and Museum,
    Oldham
Ypres Tower Museum, Rye

U.S.A.
Pottery and Porcelain
Boston Museum of Fine Arts, Boston
Cincinnati Art Museum, Cincinnati
Cooper Union Museum for the Arts of
   Decoration, New York
Huntingdon Library, San Marino
Frick Collection, New York
Colonial Williamsburg, Williamsburg,
   Virginia
University of Kansas Museum of Art,
   Lawrence
Walker Art Centre, Minneapolis
Carnegie Institute, Pittsburg

Chinese Ceramics
GREAT BRITAIN
Victoria and Albert Museum, London
British Museum, London
Sir Percival David Foundation, London
   University
Museum of Eastern Art, Oxford
Fitzwilliam Museum, Cambridge
City Art Gallery, Bristol
Royal Scottish Museum, Edinburgh
The Burrell Collection, Glasgow
City Art Gallery, Birmingham
City Art Gallery, Manchester
Temple Newsam House, Leeds
Lady Lever Art Gallery, Port Sunlight

EUROPE
Musée Guimet, Paris
Musée des Arts Décoratifs, Paris
Musée Céramique, Sèvres, Paris
Musées Royaux d'Art et d'Histoire, Brussels
Rijksmuseum, Amsterdam
Museum für Ostasiatische Kunst
Museum für Kunst und Gewerbe,
   Hamburg
Kunstindustrimuseum, Copenhagen
National Museum, Copenhagen
National Museum, Stockholm
Ostasiatiska Samlingarna, Stockholm
Hellner Museum, Stockholm

Wedgwood China
GREAT BRITAIN
Stoke-on-Trent Public Museum and Art
   Gallery, Hanley
Victoria and Albert Museum, London

Castle Museum, Nottingham
Lady Lever Art Gallery, Port Sunlight
Wedgwood Collection, Barlaston,
   Stoke-on-Trent and Wigmore Street,
   London

PRINTS AND DRAWINGS
Old English Prints and Drawings
GREAT BRITAIN
Museum and Art Gallery, Birmingham
Victoria and Albert Museum, London
Philpot Museum, Lyme Regis
Harris Museum and Art Gallery, Preston
Thorpe Prebend House and Museum, Ripon
Holburne of Menstrie Museum of Art, Bath
Courtauld Institute of Art, London
Tate Gallery, London

Portrait Miniatures
GREAT BRITAIN
Victoria and Albert Museum, London
Wallace Collection, London
National Portrait Gallery, London
National Maritime Museum, Greenwich
Fitzwilliam Museum, Cambridge
Ashmolean Museum, Oxford
Holburne of Menstrie Museum, Bath
Glynn Vivian Art Gallery, Swansea
Art Gallery, Bristol
Ham House, Ham, Surrey

EUROPE
Nationalmuseum, Stockholm
Rosenborg Castle, Copenhagen

U.S.A.
Metropolitan Museum, New York
Cleveland Museum, Cleveland, Ohio

Silhouettes and Glass Pictures
GREAT BRITAIN
Victoria and Albert Museum, London

Bird Prints
GREAT BRITAIN
Natural History Museum, London

EUROPE
Zoological Museum, Amsterdam
Taylor Museum, Haarlem
University Library, Copenhagen

American Prints
U.S.A.
New York Public Library
New York Historical Society
Mariners' Museum, Newport Mews,
  Virginia
Philadelphia Museum of Art, Philadelphia
Metropolitan Museum of Art, New York
Boston Museum of Fine Arts, Boston
American Antiquarian Society, Worcester,
  Massachusetts
Library of Congress, Washington D.C.
Museum of the City of New York, New York

Japanese Prints
GREAT BRITAIN
British Museum, London
Victoria and Albert Museum, London
Museum of Eastern Art, Oxford
Fitzwilliam Museum, Cambridge
Whitworth Gallery, Manchester
Maidstone Museum, Maidstone

EUROPE
Chester Beatty Library, Dublin, Eire
Bibliothèque Nationale, Paris
Musée Guimet, Paris
Prentenkabinet, Amsterdam
Rijksmuseum, Leiden
Musées Royaux d'Art et d'Histoire, Brussels

SCIENTIFIC INSTRUMENTS
GREAT BRITAIN
Museum of the History of Science, Oxford
National Maritime Museum, Greenwich
Wellcome Historical Medical Museum,
  London
Science Museum, London
Reading Museum and Art Gallery, Reading

EUROPE
Museo Nazionale della Scienza e della
  Tecnica "Leonardo da Vinci", Milan
Musée Astronomique de l'Observatoire
  de Paris, Paris
Musée du Conservatoire National des Arts
  et Metiers, Paris

U.S.A.
Adler Planetarium and Astronomical
  Museum, Chicago

Buffalo Museum of Science, Buffalo
United States National Museum,
  Washington

SCULPTURE AND CARVING
GREAT BRITAIN
British Museum, London
Tate Gallery, London
Victoria and Albert Museum, London
Wallace Collection, London
Ashmolean Museum, Oxford
Bowes Museum, Barnard Castle, Durham
Harris Museum and Art Gallery, Preston
Lady Lever Art Gallery, Port Sunlight
Leeds Art Gallery
Pitt-Rivers Museum, Farnham, Blandford
City Art Gallery and Museum, Wakefield

EUROPE
Acropolis Museum, Athens
National Museum, Athens
Staatlischesmuseum, Berlin
Ny Carlsberg Olyptarek, Copenhagen
Delphi Museum, Delphi
Galleria Uffizi, Florence
The Museum, Istanbul
Hermitage Museum, Leningrad
Prado, Madrid
Glyptothek, Munich
Museo Nationale, Naples
Olympia Museum, Olympia
Louvre, Paris
Villa Albani, Rome
Museo Capitolino, Rome
Museo Conservatori, Rome
Museo Terme, Rome
Museo Vaticano, Rome
Kunsthistorischesmuseum, Vienna
Musée Rodin, Paris

U.S.A.
Art Institute of Chicago, Chicago
Baltimore Museum of Art, Baltimore
Boston Museum of Fine Arts, Boston
Buffalo Fine Arts Academy, Buffalo
Cincinnati Art Museum, Cincinnati
Currier Gallery of Art, Manchester
Fine Arts Society of San Diego, San Diego
Frick Collection, New York
Metropolitan Museum of Art, New York

M. H. De Young Memorial Museum,
San Francisco
Montclair Art Museum, Montclair
Museum of Modern Art, New York
National Gallery of Art, Washington
Nelson-Atkins Gallery of Art, Kansas City
Pennsylvania Academy of the Fine Arts,
Philadelphia
Philadelphia Museum of Art, Philadelphia
Solomon R. Guggenheim Museum,
New York
University of Kansas Museum of Art,
Lawrence
Virginia Museum of Fine Arts, Richmond
Walker Art Centre, Minneapolis
Walters Art Gallery, Baltimore
Worcester Art Museum, Worcester

Antique Bronzes
GREAT BRITAIN
Wallace Collection, London
Victoria and Albert Museum, London
Fitzwilliam Museum, Cambridge
Ashmolean Museum, Oxford

EUROPE
Kunsthistorischesmuseum, Vienna
Staatlischesmuseum, Berlin
Louvre, Paris
Bargello, Florence

U.S.A.
Metropolitan Museum of Art, New York

Antique Statuary and Wax Modelling
GREAT BRITAIN
National Portrait Gallery, London
Victoria and Albert Museum, London
British Museum, London

Carved Wooden Figures
GREAT BRITAIN
Wallace Collection, London
Victoria and Albert Museum, London
British Museum, London
Fitzwilliam Museum, Cambridge

EUROPE
Louvre, Paris
Musée de Dijon
Bayerisches Nationalmuseum, Munich

Stadtische Kunstsammlungen, Augsburg
Nationalmuseum, Nuremberg
Museo di Castello, Milan
Palazza Madama, Turin
Museo Nazionale, Florence
Museo Nazionale, Pisa
Kunsthistorischesmuseum, Vienna
Palazzo Venezia, Rome

Nottingham Alabaster Carving
GREAT BRITAIN
Victoria and Albert Museum, London
Glasgow Museum, Glasgow
British Museum, London
Nottingham City Museum and Art Gallery,
Nottingham
Ashmolean Museum, Oxford
Fitzwilliam Museum, Cambridge
Also isolated plaques in other provincial
museums, and sometimes in churches

Garden Statuary and Furniture
GREAT BRITAIN
Victoria and Albert Museum, London

SILVER
GREAT BRITAIN
Holburne of Menstrie Museum, Bath
Cecil Higgins Museum, Bedford
Museum and Art Gallery, Belfast
British Museum, London
Victoria and Albert Museum, London
Laing Art Gallery and Museum,
Newcastle-upon-Tyne
Ashmolean Museum, Oxford
City Museum and Art Gallery, Birmingham
Thomas-Stanford Museum, Brighton
Art Gallery and Museum, Burrell Collection,
Glasgow
Ormonde Collection, Bankfield Museum,
Halifax
Bethnal Green Museum, London
Heaton Hall, Wythenshawe Hall and
Fletcher Moss Museum, Manchester
Museum and Art Gallery, Sunderland

Continental Silver
GREAT BRITAIN
British Museum, London
Victoria and Albert Museum, London

Wallace Collection, London
Fitzwilliam Museum, Cambridge
Ashmolean Museum, Oxford

EUROPE
Louvre, Paris
Musée Carnavalet, Paris
Museu de Arte Antigua, Lisbon
Bayerisches Nationalmuseum, Munich
Stadtische Kunstsammlungen, Augsburg
Kunsthistorischesmuseum, Vienna
Palazzo Madama, Turin
Palazzo Pitti, Florence
Museo dell' Opera del Duomo, Florence
Museo Nazionale, Messina

American Silver
U.S.A.
Los Angeles County Museum, Los Angeles, California
Wadsworte Atheneum, Hartford, Conn.

Yale University Art Gallery, New Haven, Conn.
Art Institute of Chicago, Chicago, Illinois
Baltimore Museum of Art, Baltimore, Maryland
Museum of Fine Arts, Boston, Mass.
Fogg Museum of Art, Cambridge, Mass.
Detroit Institute of Arts, Detroit, Michigan
Art Museum, Princeton, New Jersey
Metropolitan Museum of Art, New York
Cincinnati Art Museum, Cincinnati, Ohio
Toledo Museum of Art, Toledo Ohio
Philadelphia Museum of Art, Philadelphia, Pennsylvania

Sheffield Plate
GREAT BRITAIN
Sheffield City Museum, Sheffield
City Museum and Art Gallery, Birmingham
Laing Art Gallery and Museum, Newcastle-upon-Tyne

INDEX

Note: the following is a guide to the glossaries and lists in the book. These can be used to supplement the index, which does not contain purely glossarial matter:

N.B. Bold type denotes the plates, and their page
numbers, not plate numbers, are given

D

G

H

K

L

V

U